THE OXFORD ENGLISH-READER'S DICTIONARY

By
A. S. HORNBY
and
E. C. PARNWELL

New Edition

GW00597705

OXFORD UNIVERSITY PRESS
LANGENSCHEIDT

First published 1952
Reprinted (with corrections) 1953, 1954, 1956, 1958
German School Edition 1960
Reprinted 1962, 1963, 1964, 1965, 1967, 1969, 1970,
1971, 1972, 1973, 1974, 1975, 1976, 1977, 1978
Second German School Edition 1979
Reprinted 1980, 1981, 1982, 1983, 1984, 1986, 1987, 1988

© 1979 Oxford University Press
German School Edition: © *1979 Langenscheidt KG, Berlin und München*
Printed by C. H. Beck'sche Buchdruckerei, Nördlingen · Printed in Germany
ISBN 3-468-49003-8

Vorwort

Bewährtes Arbeitsmittel

Das „English-Reader's Dictionary" war eines der ersten einsprachigen Wörterbücher, die im Englischunterricht in Deutschland und Österreich zum Einsatz kamen. Bereits im Jahre 1960 entsprach daher der Langenscheidt-Verlag dem Wunsch vieler Englischlehrer nach einer speziellen Bearbeitung dieses Wörterbuches für die deutschsprachigen Länder. Unter dem Namen „The Oxford English-Reader's Dictionary" gewann es viele Freunde; 20 Auflagen — meist mit kleinen Verbesserungen — wurden in den vergangenen zwei Jahrzehnten gedruckt.

Vollständige Neubearbeitung

Um den hohen Gebrauchswert dieses Wörterbuches auch für die achtziger Jahre zu sichern, entschloß sich der Verlag jetzt zu einer vollständigen Neubearbeitung des „Oxford English-Reader's Dictionary". Dabei wurde der gesamte Inhalt Wort für Wort überprüft; Verbesserungsmöglichkeiten inhaltlicher und formaler Art wurden realisiert. Der Gesamtumfang des Wörterbuches erhöhte sich dabei um 20 %.

Neue Stichwörter

Eine große Anzahl von neuen Wörtern aus allen Lebensbereichen wurden als Stichwörter neu aufgenommen, z. B. *adventure playground, breathalyser, containerize, demo, environmentalist, hang-glider, hatchback, punk*. Auch das Amerikanische Englisch wurde in Wortschatz und Schreibung stärker berücksichtigt. Um dafür Platz zu schaffen, wurde veraltetes und seltenes Wortgut ebenso ausgeschieden wie seltene Schreibvarianten.

Grundwortschatz jetzt definiert

Zum Grundwortschatz gehörende Wörter, die bisher mit ‡ gekennzeichnet und nicht definiert wurden, werden jetzt mit umfangreichen Definitionen und Beispielen dargestellt, z. B. *after, be, go.*

Neue Lautschrift

Die durchgehend neu eingetragene internationale Lautschrift entspricht dem „English Pronouncing Dictionary", 14. Auflage 1977, also dem neuesten Stand des Jones/Gimson.

IV

Mehr Illustrationen und Anwendungsbeispiele

Die Zahl der Illustrationen stieg von 400 auf 500; die Anzahl der Anwendungsbeispiele wurde häufig vermehrt (vgl. z. B. unter *cat* und *business*). Auch die grammatischen Informationen wurden beträchtlich ausgeweitet. Unter den Anhängen findet sich jetzt auch eine Liste der unregelmäßigen Verben und eine Tabelle der Maßeinheiten.

Größere Schrift Größeres Format

Das äußere Erscheinungsbild des neuen „Oxford English-Reader's Dictionary" wurde schülerfreundlicher gestaltet. Es weist jetzt das größere Format und die größere, besser lesbare Schrift der Großen Schulwörterbücher von Langenscheidt auf. Durch stärkere Differenzierung wurden viele Stichwortartikel besser und übersichtlicher gegliedert.

Bewährtes beibehalten

Es versteht sich von selbst, daß Bewährtes beibehalten wurde. Dies gilt vor allem für die einfache sprachliche Einkleidung der Definitionen und die angewandte Erklärungsmethode, die das Abstraktionsvermögen der Lernenden nicht überfordert. Aber auch andere, nicht so zentrale „features", wie z. B. die Angabe der Silbentrennung und die ausführlichen Anhänge mit Abkürzungen und Eigennamen, blieben voll erhalten.

Die Neubearbeitung 1979 des „Oxford English-Reader's Dictionary" wurde von der anglistischen Redaktion des Verlages in enger Zusammenarbeit mit der Oxford University Press durchgeführt. Wir hoffen, daß das Wörterbuch in seiner neuen Gestalt mit jetzt über 23 000 Stichwörtern sich viele neue Freunde erwerben wird. Nach wie vor ist es das umfassendste einsprachige „Learner's Dictionary", das speziell für den Englischunterricht in den deutschsprachigen Ländern geschaffen wurde.

LANGENSCHEIDT

Inhaltsverzeichnis

Hinweise für den Benutzer

Die Benutzung eines Wörterbuches erfordert Sorgfalt und Geduld. Wenn die angeführte Definition nicht gleich verständlich ist, müssen die in der Erläuterung verwandten unbekannten Wörter zunächst nachgeschlagen werden. Durch diese Nachschlagearbeit kann sich der Lernende vergewissern, daß er alle Einzelwörter richtig verstanden hat. Dabei wird er gleichzeitig seinen Wortschatz erweitern.

Bei der Suche nach der Bedeutung zusammengesetzter Wörter empfiehlt es sich, beide Bestandteile nachzuschlagen, da eventuelle Sonderbedeutungen von Zusammensetzungen je nach dem Einzelfall unter dem ersten oder unter dem zweiten Bestandteil, aus Gründen der Platzersparnis aber nicht doppelt, aufgeführt werden.

Alphabetische Anordnung

I. Die **alphabetische Reihenfolge** der halbfetten Stichwörter ist durchweg beachtet worden. Ableitungen und zusammengesetzte Wörter eines Stichwortes erscheinen, ebenfalls in halbfetter Schrift, unter dem Hauptstichwort und nicht als eigene Einträge, sofern keine Besonderheiten vorliegen.

Eigennamen und Abkürzungen sind am Schluß des Buches in einem besonderen Verzeichnis zusammengestellt.

Exponenten

II. 1. Läßt sich ein **Stichwort** in verschiedene Wortarten gliedern, oder hat ein Stichwortartikel größeren Umfang und weist das Stichwort grundsätzlich verschiedene Bedeutungen auf, so erfolgt meist eine Unterteilung durch Exponenten:

> re·cord[1] [rɪˈkɔːd] *v.t.* **1.** ...
> rec·ord[2] [ˈrekɔːd] *n.* **1.** ...

Bedeutungsgliederung

2. Die Definitionen wurden, wenn es erforderlich erschien, durch arabische Ziffern zur Unterscheidung der einzelnen Bedeutungen untergliedert:

> **hand·some** ... **1.** of fine appearance. **2.** (of gifts, etc.) generous.

Anwendungs-beispiele

Anwendungsbeispiele in Auszeichnungsschrift (kursiver Druck) wurden meist unter den zugehörigen Ziffern oder Bedeutungen aufgeführt, bei größerer Anzahl auch unter einer eigenen Ziffer. Eine Definition der Beispiele ist unterblieben, wo die Bedeutung sich von selbst ergibt:

> com·mer·cial ... ‿·ize ... *v.t.* (try to) make money out of: ‿*ize sport.*

Verweiszahl

3. Wenn in einer Definition ein Wort verwandt wird, das mehrere Bedeutungen hat, so ist durch eine Zahl am Ende des Wortes gekennzeichnet, in welchem Sinne es hier benutzt wird. So findet sich unter **pay** ein Eintrag *pay sb. off* = pay him his wages and discharge (4) him. Die Ziffer 4 besagt, daß *discharge* hier im Sinne der vierten Definition (jemand wegschicken) benutzt wird.

Zusammenset-zungen mit Adverb/Präposition

4. Mehrere Zusammensetzungen mit Adverbien und Präpositionen wurden unter einer eigenen arabischen Ziffer zusammengefaßt (siehe Stichwort *come* (8), *go* (17)).

Amerikanische Schreibung

5. Die häufigsten Abweichungen in der amerikanischen Schreibung stehen e i n m a l unmittelbar hinter dem entsprechenden britischen Stichwort und sind als solche stets mit „(U.S.A.)" gekennzeichnet. In den Definitionen erscheint die amerikanische Schreibung aus räumlichen Gründen nicht mehr.

> col·our (U.S.A. **-or**) ...
> fa·vour (U.S.A. **fa·vor**) ...
> trav·el ... *v.i. & t.* (-*ll*-, U.S.A. also -*l*-) ...

Amerikanisches Englisch

6. Haben Wörter des amerikanischen Englisch eine anderslautende Entsprechung im britischen Englisch, so wird von der amerikanischen Form auf die britische verwiesen:

> sta·tion wag·on *n.* (U.S.A.) = estate car

Wird ein Eintrag selten oder gar nicht im amerikanischen Englisch verwendet, so wurde die Abkürzung „(Gt. Brit.)" vor die Definition gesetzt:

> nav·vy ... *n.* (Gt. Brit.) unskilled workman ...

Sprach-gebrauchsebene

7. Bei Stichwörtern, die vom *Standard English* abweichen, wurde vermerkt, auf welcher Sprachgebrauchsebene sie stehen, z. B. durch

> (sl.), (colloq.), (poet.) etc.

Sachgebiete	Der Anwendungsbereich oder das Sachgebiet eines Stichwortes wurde ebenfalls durch Angaben in runden Klammern gegeben, z. B. durch

(fig.), (law), (sport) etc.

Angabe der Wortarten

8. Die Bezeichnung der Wortarten (Substantiv, Verb, Adjektiv, Adverb etc.) wurde vollständig durchgeführt.

Komparativ und Superlativ

Die Steigerungsformen der Adjektive und Adverbien wurden, soweit sie eine Unregelmäßigkeit aufweisen, in runden Klammern und Auszeichnungsschrift gegeben:

am·ple ... *adj.* (*∼r, ∼st*) ...
wit·ty *adj.* (*-ier, -iest*) ...

Unregelmäßige Verben

Die Vergangenheitsformen der unregelmäßigen Verben, sowie deren Zusammensetzungen, wurden ebenfalls in Auszeichnungsschrift hinter den Wortartangaben der betreffenden Verben aufgeführt:

come ... *v.i.* (p.t. *came* ..., p.p. *∼*) ...
over·take ... *v.t.* (p.t. *-took*, p.p. *-taken*) ...

Die unregelmäßigen Grundformen erscheinen noch einmal an ihrer alphabetischen Stelle im Wörterverzeichnis sowie auf der *Liste der unregelmäßigen Verben* im Anhang.

Singular

9. Meist nur im Singular gebrauchte Wörter wurden durch „(no pl.)" gekennzeichnet:

as·phalt ... *n.* (no pl.) ...

Plural

Wird ein Wort im Plural gebraucht, so wurde dieser wie folgt gekennzeichnet:

small arms *n. pl.* ...

Unregelmäßige Pluralbildung und Bildung des Plurals der Substantive auf -o erscheinen in Auszeichnungsschrift hinter den Angaben der Wortart:

bac·te·ri·um ... *n.* (pl. *-ria* [-rɪə]) ...
po·ta·to ... *n.* (*pl. -oes*) ...

Wörter mit Pluralform, die aber meist mit dem Singular konstruiert werden, sind z. B.:

acous·tics ... *n. pl.* (sing. v.) ...

Konsonantenverdoppelung

10. Die Einträge (*-bb-*), (*-dd-*), (*-gg-*), (*-ll-*), (*-mm-*), (*-nn-*), (*-rr-*) und (*-tt-*) weisen darauf hin, daß der Konsonant verdoppelt wird wie bei **beg** *begging*, **rob** *robbed*, **run** *running*, **sit** *sitting*.

X

Silbentrennung

11. Bei mehrsilbigen Stichwörtern wurde die Silbentrennung durch auf Mitte stehenden Punkt oder durch Betonungszeichen angezeigt, z. B.:

'green·fly, 'green|gro·cer

Tilde

III. Die halbfette (~) oder einfache (~) **Tilde** ersetzt das Stichwort; so steht unter **ar·mour** ~ed an Stelle von **ar·moured** und ~ed car an Stelle von *armoured car*.

Auszeichnungsschrift

IV. Wenn innerhalb einer Definition ein oder mehrere Wörter schräg (= **kursiv**) gedruckt werden, so ist das ein Hinweis auf die Wendung, in der das Stichwort gebraucht wird. Unter **come** zeigt z. B. die kursive Schrift die folgenden Wendungen an: *Come here. Come to me. They came at six o'clock*, etc. Unter **adapt** bedeutet der kursive Druck der Präposition *for*, daß das Stichwort häufig mit dieser Präposition konstruiert wird.

Verweise

V. Verweise erfolgen in der Form

cf., see, =

Vergleiche auch den *Zahlenverweis* unter II, 3.

Aussprache

Die Aussprache wird in diesem Wörterbuch in der phonetischen Umschrift der *International Phonetic Association* (*IPA*) in eckigen Klammern beigefügt. Die Übersicht auf Seite XII erläutert die angewandten Zeichen. Für die Lautschrift wurde die vierzehnte Auflage, 1977, des *English Pronouncing Dictionary* von A. C. Gimson und Daniel Jones benutzt. Die verwandte Lautumschrift ist die dort an erster Stelle angegebene.

Um Raum zu sparen, wurden die häufigsten Endungen im Hauptteil des Wörterbuches als eigenes Stichwort mit Lautumschrift gegeben, dann aber im Wörterverzeichnis ohne Umschrift gebracht, sofern keine Akzentverschiebung auftritt. So kann der Benutzer z. B. unter dem Stichwort **adjust** leicht auf die richtige Aussprache der Zusammensetzungen **adjustable** und **adjustment** schließen.

Betonung

Die Betonung ist angegeben durch hochgestellte Betonungszeichen, die der betonten Silbe vorangehen, z. B.:

interest ['ɪntrɪst]   because [bɪ'kɒz]

Wenn neben dem Hauptton in einem längeren Wort ein Nebenton auftritt, wird der letztere durch ein tiefgestelltes Betonungszeichen dargestellt, z. B.:

regulation [ˌregjʊ'leɪʃn]

Wenn zwei Silben im Wort gleich stark betont werden, werden zwei hochgestellte Betonungszeichen gesetzt, unabhängig von einem vielleicht vorhandenen Nebenton, z. B.:

recapitulation ['riːkəˌpɪtjʊ'leɪʃn]

Bei zusammengesetzten Wörtern, deren Bestandteile als selbständige Stichwörter gegeben sind, werden die Betonungszeichen im Stichwort selbst gegeben, z. B. ˌself-de'fence.

Erklärung der Lautumschrift

Lautzeichen	Englisches Beispielwort	Lautumschrift	Lautzeichen	Englisches Beispielwort	Lautumschrift
ɑː	father	'fɑːðə*	n	not	nɒt
æ	bad	bæd	ŋ	long	lɒŋ
aɪ	cry	kraɪ	ŋg	longer	'lɒŋgə*
aʊ	how	haʊ	ɒ	hot	hɒt
b	back	bæk	ɔː	saw	sɔː
d	day	deɪ	ɔɪ	boy	bɔɪ
dʒ	page	peɪdʒ	əʊ	so, sew, sow	səʊ
ð	then	ðen	p	put	pʊt
e	wet	wet	r	red	red
eə	hair	heə*	s	sit, this	sɪt, ðɪs
eɪ	day	deɪ	ʃ	show, wish	ʃəʊ, wɪʃ
ɜː	bird	bɜːd	t	tin, hit	tɪn, hɪt
ə	ago, ladder	ə'gəʊ, 'lædə*	tʃ	church	tʃɜːtʃ
f	full, physics	fʊl, 'fɪzɪks	θ	thin	θɪn
g	get	get	uː	boot	buːt
h	hot	hɒt	ʊ	good, put	gʊd, pʊt
iː	meet	miːt	ʊə	sure	ʃʊə*
ɪ	sit	sɪt	v	very	'verɪ
ɪə	hear	hɪə*	ʌ	cup	kʌp
j	yes	jes	w	wet	wet
k	cold, kill	kəʊld, kɪl	z	zero, his	'zɪərəʊ, hɪz
l	like, fill	laɪk, fɪl	ʒ	pleasure	'pleʒə*
m	make	meɪk			

Ganz vereinzelt werden auch die folgenden französischen Nasallaute gebraucht: [ɑ̃] wie in frz. *blanc*, [ɔ̃] wie in frz. *bonbon* und [ɛ̃] wie in frz. *vin*.

Das Sternchen * zeigt an, daß der r-Laut am Ende nur dann gesprochen wird, wenn das nächste Wort (in der Aussprache) mit einem Vokal beginnt, z. B.: far [fɑː*], far away ['fɑːr ə'weɪ], aber far from here ['fɑː frəm 'hɪə].

Um Raum zu sparen, werden die Endung -ed* und das Plural-s** der englischen Stichwörter an dieser Stelle einmal mit Lautschrift gegeben; sie erscheinen dann aber im Wörterverzeichnis ohne Umschrift, sofern keine Ausnahmen vorliegen:

* [-d] nach Vokalen und stimmhaften Konsonanten;
  [-t] nach stimmlosen Konsonanten;
  [-ɪd] nach auslautendem d und t.
** [-z] nach Vokalen und stimmhaften Konsonanten;
  [-s] nach stimmlosen Konsonanten.

DAS ENGLISCHE ALPHABET

a [eɪ], b [biː], c [siː], d [diː], e [iː], f [ef], g [dʒiː], h [eɪtʃ], i [aɪ], j [dʒeɪ], k [keɪ], l [el], m [em], n [en], o [əʊ], p [piː], q [kjuː], r [ɑː*], s [es], t [tiː], u [juː], v [viː], w ['dʌbljuː], x [eks], y [waɪ], z [zed].

Abkürzungen und Symbole

In einem kurzen Wörterbuch muß Platz gespart werden. Die Anzahl der Stich-wörter konnte erhöht werden durch die Verwendung der nachstehenden Zeichen und Abkürzungen, mit denen sich der Lernende vor Benutzung des Wörterbuchs ebenso vertraut machen sollte wie mit den Zeichen der phonetischen Umschrift.

&, *&*	and	*i.e.*	that is
abbr.	abbreviation	*imper.*	imperative
adj., adjs.	adjective(s)	*impers.*	impersonal
adv., advs.	adverb(s)	*indef. art.*	indefinite article
aer.	aeronautics	*inf.*	infinitive
agr.	agriculture	*int.*	interjection
anat.	anatomy	*interr.*	interrogative
arch.	architecture		
attrib.	attributive(ly)	*lb.*	pound(s) weight
		ling.	linguistics
bibl.	biblical	*lit.*	literal(ly)
biol.	biology	*liter.*	literary style
bot.	botany		
		m.	masculine
cf.	compare	*math.*	mathematics
chem.	chemistry	*mech.*	mechanics
colloq.	colloquial	*med.*	medicine
comm.	commerce	*meteor.*	meteorology
comp.	comparative	*mil.*	military
conj.	conjunction	*mot.*	motoring
contp.	contemptuously	*mus.*	music
def. art.	definite article	*n., ns.*	noun(s)
dem.	demonstrative	*neg.*	negative(ly)
derog.	derogatory		
		opp.	opposite in meaning to
eccl.	ecclesiastical	*opt.*	optics
econ.	economics	*orn.*	ornithology
e.g.	for example		
electr.	electricity	*p.*	page; picture; participle
engin.	engineering	*part.*	participial
esp.	especial(ly)	*pass.*	passive
etc.	et cetera, and others	*pers.*	person
		pers. pron.	personal pronoun
f.	feminine	*phil.*	philosophy
fig.	figurative(ly)	*phot.*	photography
Fr.	French	*phys.*	physics
		physiol.	physiology
geogr.	geography	*pl.*	plural
geol.	geology	*poet.*	poetical style
geom.	geometry	*pol.*	politics
gram.	grammar	*poss.*	possessive
Gt. Brit.	Great Britain	*p.p.*	past participle
		pred.	predicative
hist.	historical; history	*pref.*	prefix
humor.	humorous(ly)		

prep.	preposition(al)	*t.*	tense
pres. p.	present participle	*tech.*	technology
pres. t.	present tense	*tel.*	telegraphy
print.	printing	*teleph.*	telephony
pron., prons.	pronoun(s)	*thea.*	theatre
psych.	psychology		
p.t.	past tense	*U.S.A.*	chiefly American usage; United States of America
refl.	reflexive	*usu.*	usual(ly)
rel.	relative		
rhet.	rhetorical(ly)	*v., vs.*	verb(s)
		v.aux.	auxiliary verb
sb.	somebody	*v.i.*	intransitive verb
scient.	scientific term	*v.refl.*	reflexive verb
Scot.	Scottish	*v.t.*	transitive verb
sing.	singular	*v.t. & i.*	transitive and intransitive verb
sl.	slang		
sth.	something	*vulg.*	vulgar
suff.	suffix		
superl.	superlative	*zool.*	zoology

A

A1 [eɪ'wʌn] *adj.* (colloq.) classified as first-rate; excellent: *an A1 dinner*; *I am A1*, (in excellent health).

a [eɪ, ə], **an** [æn, ən] *indef. art.* **1.** one (cf. *some, any, a few*, with pl. nouns): *I have a pen* (pl. *some pens*). **2.** (with adjs. & prons. of number and quantity): *a great many friends*; *a lot of money*. **3.** that which is called; any; every: *A horse is an animal* (pl. *Horses are animals*). **4.** each; every: *twice a day*; *thirty pence a pound*; *sixty miles an hour*.

A. [eɪ] (Gt. Brit., abbr.) (of films) certified as suitable for adult audiences but not for children.

aback [ə'bæk] *adv. taken* ~, surprised.

ab·a·cus ['æbəkəs] *n.* frame with balls sliding on wires or rods, used for teaching numbers to children, or for calculating (1).

aban·don [ə'bændən] *v.t.* **1.** leave, go away from (not intending to return to). **2.** give up: *Don't* ~ *hope yet.* ~ *oneself to*, give oneself up completely to a passion or impulse. ~**ed** *adj.* given up to bad ways.

abase [ə'beɪs] *v.t.* make lower (in rank, honour, or self-respect).

abashed [ə'bæʃt] *adj.* confused; embarrassed.

abate [ə'beɪt] *v.t. & i.* **1.** make or become less. **2.** (law) put a stop to.

ab·at·toir ['æbətwɑ:*] *n.* place where animals are killed for food; slaughterhouse.

ab·bess ['æbes] *n.* woman at the head of a nunnery or convent; Mother Superior.

ab·bey ['æbɪ] *n.* (pl. ~s) **1.** society of men (called *monks*) or women (called *nuns*) living apart from others in the service of God. **2.** building(s) in which they live(d). **3.** church of an ~.

ab·bot ['æbət] *n.* man at the head of a monastery; Father Superior.

ab·bre·vi·ate [ə'bri:vɪeɪt] *v.t.* make (a word, story, etc.) shorter. **ab·bre·vi·a·tion** [ə,bri:vɪ'eɪʃn] *n.* shortening; short form (esp. of a word), e.g. *Mon.* for *Monday*.

ABC [,eɪbi:'si:] *n.* **1.** the alphabet. **2.** simplest facts of any subject, to be learnt first.

ab·di·cate ['æbdɪkeɪt] *v.t. & i.* give up (a throne, right, position of authority). **ab·di·ca·tion** [,æbdɪ'keɪʃn] *n.*

ab·do·men ['æbdəmən, æb'dəʊmen] *n.* **1.** (also *belly*) lower front part of the body including the stomach and bowels. **2.** last of the three divisions of an insect's body. **ab·dom·i·nal** [æb'dɒmɪnl] *adj.* in or of the ~: *abdominal pains.*

ab·duct [æb'dʌkt] *v.t.* take or lead away (esp. a woman) unlawfully; kidnap (a child). **ab·duc·tion** *n.* unlawful taking away (esp. of a woman).

ab·er·ra·tion [,æbə'reɪʃn] *n.* straying away from the usual, normal, or right; mental lapse (1).

abet [ə'bet] *v.t.* (-*tt*-) *aid and* ~, help and encourage (to do wrong).

abey·ance [ə'beɪəns] *n.* (no pl.) *in* ~, condition of not being in force or in use for a time; suspended.

ab·hor [əb'hɔ:*] *v.t.* (-*rr*-) feel hatred or disgust for. ~**rence** [əb'hɒrəns] *n.* (no pl.) extreme hatred or disgust; sth. for which ~rence is felt. ~**rent** *adj.* causing horror.

abide [ə'baɪd] *v.i. & t.* (p.t. & p.p. *abode* [ə'bəʊd] or ~d) **1.** ~ *by*, be true and faithful to (a promise, etc.). **2.** (old use) live or stay (*at, in*). **3.** put up with; endure: *I can't* ~ *that woman.*

abil·i·ty [ə'bɪlətɪ] *n.* **1.** power (esp. of mind) to do things: *a man of great* (*not much*) ~; *to the best of my* ~. **2.** (pl.) cleverness of mind.

-abil·i·ty [-ə'bɪlətɪ] *suff.* (forming ns.): *availability.*

ab·ject ['æbdʒekt] *adj.* **1.** unreserved; without self-respect: *an* ~ *apology* (*confession*). **2.** deserving contempt: ~ *behaviour.* **3.** (of conditions) wretched: *in* ~ *poverty.*

ab·jure [əb'dʒʊə*] *v.t.* swear or promise publicly and solemnly to give up (a belief, opinion, right, etc.).

ablaze [ə'bleɪz] *adv. & pred. adj.* on fire; bright as if on fire.

able ['eɪbl] *adj.* 1. be ~ *to do sth.*, have the power, time, etc. to do something: *I hope you will be ~ to come tomorrow.* (Cf. *can*[1](1).) 2. (*~r, ~st*) clever; showing skill and knowledge: *an ~ speech (speaker).* **,~-'bod·ied sea·man** *n.* one who has been trained. **ably** *adv.* in an ~ manner.

-able [-əbl] *suff.* (forming adjs.) 1. showing the qualities of: *comfortable; peaceable.* 2. that can be, fit to be: *eatable.*

-ably [-əblɪ] *suff.* (forming advs. from adjs. in -able): *peaceably.*

ab·lu·tion [ə'bluːʃn] *n.* (usu. pl.) washing of the body (esp. as an act of religion).

ab·nor·mal [æb'nɔːml] *adj.* not normal; different from what is ordinary, usual, or expected. **~·i·ty** [ˌæbnɔː-'mælətɪ] *n.* being ~; sth. ~.

aboard [ə'bɔːd] *adv. & prep.* on (to) or in(to) a ship or aircraft, or (U.S.A.) a train or bus.

abode[1] [ə'bəʊd] *n.* (old use) house; dwelling-place.

abode[2], see **abide**.

abol·ish [ə'bɒlɪʃ] *v.t.* stop altogether; put an end to (e.g. war, slavery). **ab·o·li·tion** [ˌæbə'lɪʃn] *n.* (no pl.) act of ~ing; being ~ed.

A-bomb ['eɪbɒm] *n.* atomic bomb.

abom·i·nable [ə'bɒmɪnəbl] *adj.* causing horror and disgust. **abom·i·nate** [ə'bɒmɪneɪt] *v.t.* feel hatred or disgust for. **abom·i·na·tion** [əˌbɒmɪ'neɪʃn] *n.* 1. horror and disgust. 2. object of disgust (*to sb.*).

ab·orig·i·nal [ˌæbə'rɪdʒənl] *adj.* of aborigines; existing (in a place, country) from the earliest times. *n.* sing. form of **ab·orig·i·nes** [ˌæbə'rɪdʒəniːz] *n. pl.* earliest known inhabitants, plants, etc. of a country.

abort [ə'bɔːt] *v.i.* 1. (med.) suffer an abortion (1). 2. (biol.) remain (2) undeveloped. *v.t.* 1. (med.) cause an abortion (1) of. 2. stop (growth, disease, etc.) in the early stages; terminate prematurely: *~ a project.* *v.t. & i.* (aer., space) terminate (a flight) prematurely; stop, abandon, or destroy (a rocket or spacecraft, etc.); fail to complete a flight: *~ a space mission,* cancel it (in space) (e.g. because of mechanical trouble). *n.* (aer., space) 1. unsuccessful flight by a rocket or spacecraft, etc. 2. termination of such a flight.

abor·tion [ə'bɔːʃn] *n.* 1. delivery of a baby before it can live; (esp. deliberate act) bringing this about. 2. creature so produced, usu. misshapen. **~·ist** *n.* person who brings about an ~ (1), esp. illegally. **abor·tive** [ə'bɔːtɪv] *adj.* unsuccessful; imperfect: *an abortive rebellion.*

abound [ə'baʊnd] *v.i.* 1. be plentiful. 2. ~ *in,* ~ *with,* have or exist in great numbers or quantity.

about [ə'baʊt] *prep. & adv.* I. *prep.* 1. (*go, etc.*) in various directions; to various places. 2. (*be, etc.*) in various places in or on: *Men were standing ~ the street corners. He hasn't any money ~ him.* 3. near to: *They live somewhere ~ here.* 4. in connection with; regarding: *We know nothing ~ her. How ~? What ~?* (used at the beginning of a question seeking an opinion, proposing an action, etc.): *How ~ buying ourselves a drink? He's a handsome man, but what ~ his character?* 5. ~ *to,* just going to: *The telephone rang as I was ~ to leave the office.* II. *adv.* 1. a little more or less than; a little before or after: *She's ~ ten years old. It's ~ five o'clock.* 2. (*move, etc.*) to various places, in various directions: *Children usually rush ~.* 3. (*be, sit, lie, etc.*) here and there: *People were sitting ~ on the grass.* 4. *come ~,* happen; *bring ~,* cause (sth.) to happen. 5. facing round; in the opposite direction: *She turned ~.*

above [ə'bʌv] *prep. & adv.* I. *prep.* 1. higher than: *The sun rose ~ the horizon. Your name comes ~ mine on the list.* 2. greater in number, price, weight, etc.: *The temperature has not risen ~ 10° C. all day.* 3. more than: *A good soldier values honour ~ life. ~ all,* more than anything else. 4. too good, great, proud, etc.: *If we want to learn, we should not be ~ asking questions. This book is ~ me* (too difficult for me, beyond my understanding). 5. *He's living ~ his income* (spending more than he receives). II. *adv.* 1. at a higher point; overhead: *Seen from ~, the houses and fields looked quite flat.* 2. earlier (in a book, article, etc.): *I must repeat what I wrote ~.* **~-board** [əˌbʌv'bɔːd] *pred. adj. & adv.* straightforward(ly); hiding nothing.

abra·sive [ə'breɪsɪv] *adj.* that rubs harshly or scrapes. *n.* substance (like emery or sandpaper) used for smoothing a rough surface.

abreast [ə'brest] *adv.* (of persons, ships, etc.) (moving) side by side (in the same direction). ~ *of,* level with: ~ *of the times,* up to date.

abridge [ə'brɪdʒ] *v.t.* make shorter, esp. by using fewer words; cut short (liberties, the time sth. lasts).

abridg(e)·ment *n.* making shorter; sth. (esp. a book or play) made shorter.

abroad [ə'brɔːd] *adv.* **1.** to or in other countries. **2.** everywhere; in all directions.

ab·ro·gate ['æbrəʊgeɪt] *v.t.* put an end to (a law, custom).

abrupt [ə'brʌpt] *adj.* **1.** sudden; unexpected: ~ *turns in a road.* **2.** (of speech, writing, behaviour) sudden; rough. ~**ly adv.**

ab·scess ['æbsɪs] *n.* collection of thick yellowish-white liquid (called *pus*) or other poisonous matter in a hollow place in the body.

ab·scond [əb'skɒnd] *v.i.* go away (*with* sth.) suddenly, secretly, and aware of having done wrong.

ab·sence ['æbsəns] *n.* being away (*from*): *from school through illness.*

ab·sent ['æbsənt] *adj.* not present. [əb'sent] *v.t.* ~ *oneself from,* not be present at. **ab·sen·tee** [,æbsən'tiː] *n.* person who is ~. ~**-mind·ed** [,æbsənt-'maɪndɪd] *adj.* not thinking of what one is doing; not attentive.

ab·so·lute ['æbsəluːt] *adj.* **1.** complete; perfect. **2.** having complete power: *an* ~ *ruler.* ~**ly adv. 1.** completely: *He refused* ~**ly. 2.** unconditionally: *He refused* ~**ly.**

ab·so·lu·tion [,æbsə'luːʃn] *n.* (no pl.) forgiveness (through a religious act) for past wrongdoing.

ab·solve [əb'zɒlv] *v.t.* set or declare free (from blame, guilt, a promise, duty, or the consequences of past sin).

ab·sorb [əb'sɔːb] *v.t.* **1.** take in or up; soak up. **2.** take up or occupy (time, attention): ~*ed in a book.* ~**ent** *adj.* able to ~. ~ *substance that* ~*s moisture.* ~**ing** *adj.* taking up the thoughts, attention, etc. completely. **ab·sorp·tion** [əb'sɔːpʃn] *n.* (no pl.) ~*ing or being* ~*ed*; deep interest (*in*).

ab·stain [əb'steɪn] *v.i.* do without (esp. alcoholic drinks); hold oneself back (*from*). ~**er** *n.* person who ~*s: total* ~*er,* one who ~*s completely from alcoholic drinks.*

ab·ste·mi·ous [əb'stiːmjəs] *adj.* sparing or moderate in the use of enjoyable things (esp. good food, wine).

ab·sten·tion [əb'stenʃn] *n.* abstaining (*from* sth.), esp. not using one's vote at an election; instance of this.

ab·sti·nence ['æbstɪnəns] *n.* (no pl.) abstaining (*from* food, drink, enjoyment): *total* ~, abstaining completely from alcoholic drinks. **ab·sti·nent** *adj.* practising ~.

ab·stract¹ ['æbstrækt] *adj.* opposite to what is material or concrete.

ab·stract² ['æbstrækt] *n.* short account (of the chief ideas of a book, speech, etc.).

ab·stract³ [æb'strækt] *v.t.* ~ (*from*), take away; separate: ~ *metal from ore.* ~**ed** *adj.* not paying attention.

ab·strac·tion [æb'strækʃn] *n.* **1.** state of being abstracted or lost in thought. **2.** idea not concerned with material things, e.g. *truth, whiteness.*

ab·struse [æb'struːs] *adj.* whose meaning or answer is hidden; difficult to understand. ~**ly adv.**

ab·surd [əb'sɜːd] *adj.* foolish; causing laughter; far from what is usual and normal. ~**i·ty** *n.* state of being ~; ~ idea or thing. ~**ly adv.**

abun·dance [ə'bʌndəns] *n.* **1.** great plenty: *food in* ~. **2.** number or quantity that is more than enough: *an* ~ *of good things.* **abun·dant** *adj.* more than enough; plentiful; rich (*in*). **abun·dant·ly adv.**

abuse [ə'bjuːs] *n.* **1.** wrong, rough, or harmful treatment. **2.** angry complaint(s) against sb. or sth.: *a stream of* ~. **3.** wrong or unjust custom, practice, or use: *put an end to* ~*s; an* ~ *of trust.* [ə'bjuːz] *v.t.* make wrong use of; treat badly; say severe and harsh things to or about. **abu·sive** [ə'bjuː-sɪv] *adj.* containing, using, ~. **abu·sive·ly adv.**

abys·mal [ə'bɪzml] *adj.* **1.** (esp. fig., colloq.) very deep: ~ *ignorance.* **2.** (colloq.) very bad; ~ *performance.*

abyss [ə'bɪs] *n.* great hole so deep as to appear bottomless; hell.

ac·a·dem·ic¹ [,ækə'demɪk] *adj.* **1.** of schools, colleges, learning, or teaching. **2.** concerned with theory rather than with practice. **ac·a·dem·i·cal·ly adv.**

ac·a·dem·ic² [,ækə'demɪk] *n.* member of a university; professional (1) scholar (3).

acad·e·my [ə'kædəmɪ] *n.* **1.** school for higher learning, usu. for a special subject or purpose: *a military* ~. **2.** society of learned men: *the Royal A*~.

ac·cede [ək'siːd] *v.i.* **1.** agree (*to* a proposal, etc.). **2.** come or succeed (*to* a position of authority): *When did he* ~ *to the throne?*

ac·cel·er·ate [ək'seləreɪt] *v.t. & i.* increase the speed of; become quicker; make sth. happen sooner. **ac·cel·er·a·tion** [ək,selə'reɪʃn] *n.* (no pl.) increase of speed: *The car has a good accelera-*

tion. **ac·cel·er·a·tor** *n.* device (2) (e.g. the pedal in a motor vehicle) that increases the speed when pressed down.

ac·cent ['æksənt] *n.* **1.** (in speaking) extra force or stress given to one part of a word of more than one syllable, or to certain words in a sentence. **2.** printed mark, usu. above a letter, as *é, ê.* **3.** particular way of speaking or pronouncing a language: *speaking English with a German ~.* [æk'sent] *v.t.* add stress to; mark with a written or printed ~. **ac·cen·tu·ate** [æk'sentjueit] *v.t.* give more force or importance to. **ac·cen·tu·a·tion** [æk,sentju'eɪʃn] *n.*

ac·cept [ək'sept] *v.t.* (agree to) take what is offered. **~able** *adj.* worth ~ing; pleasing and satisfactory. **~ance** *n.* (no pl.) act of ~ing.

ac·cess ['ækses] *n.* (no pl.) **1.** way (in)to a place: *easy of ~,* easy to get at or in; *~ road,* slip-road. **2.** *~ to,* right or opportunity of reaching, using, approaching.

ac·ces·sa·ry [ək'sesəri] *n.* (law) person who helps in any act, esp. a crime.

ac·ces·si·ble [ək'sesəbl] *adj.* easy to reach or approach.

ac·ces·sion [æk'seʃn] *n.* **1.** coming to or reaching power or a position. **2.** (an) addition; (an) increase.

ac·ces·so·ry [æk'sesəri] *n.* **1.** accessary. **2.** sth. extra, helpful and useful, but not an essential (1) part of: *accessories of a bicycle* (e.g. lamps, a pump).

ac·ci·dent ['æksɪdənt] *n.* **1.** chance happening: *by ~,* not on purpose. **2.** unfortunate or disastrous event. **ac·ci·den·tal** [,æksɪ'dentl] *adj.* happening by chance. **ac·ci·den·tal·ly** *adv.*

ac·claim [ə'kleɪm] *v.t.* **1.** welcome (with shouts of approval). **2.** make (sb.) ruler with loud cries: *~ a man king.* **ac·cla·ma·tion** [,æklə'meɪʃn] *n.* loud cries of satisfaction or praise.

ac·cli·ma·tize [ə'klaɪmətaɪz] *v.t.* *~ (to),* get (oneself or an animal or plant) used to a new climate or (fig.) to new conditions, etc.

ac·com·mo·date [ə'kɒmədeɪt] *v.t.* **1.** have or provide room(s) for. **2.** get (plans, etc.) into adjustment or agreement. **ac·com·mo·dat·ing** *adj.* willing to fit in with the wishes of others. **ac·com·mo·da·tion** [ə,kɒmə'deɪʃn] *n.* (U.S.A. usu. pl.) room(s), etc. provided for visitors; lodgings.

ac·com·pa·ni·ment [ə'kʌmpənɪmənt] *n.* sth. that accompanies, esp. (e.g. piano) music to support a voice or solo instrument. **ac·com·pa·ny** [ə'kʌmpənɪ] *v.t.* **1.** go with; happen or do at the same time as. **2.** play music to support a singer or other performer. **ac·com·pa·nist** *n.* person who plays an ~.

ac·com·plice [ə'kʌmplɪs] *n.* helper or companion *in* wrongdoing.

ac·com·plish [ə'kʌmplɪʃ] *v.t.* finish successfully. **~ed** *adj.* skilled (esp. in such social arts as music, painting, talking). **~ment** *n.* **1.** finishing. **2.** sth. done well; sth. one can do well (e.g. playing the piano).

ac·cord [ə'kɔːd] *n.* agreement (e.g. between two countries). *of one's own ~,* without being forced or requested. *v.t. & i.* give (a welcome, etc.); be in harmony (*with*). **~ance** *n.* agreement. **~ing to** *prep.* on the authority of; in a manner that suits or is fitting. **~ing·ly** *adv.* **1.** for that reason. **2.** in agreement with what has been suggested: *I have told you the truth and you must act ~ingly.*

ac·cor·di·on [ə'kɔːdjən] *n.* portable musical instrument with a folding bellows operated (1) by hand, free metal reeds (2), and a keyboard.

an accordion

ac·cost [ə'kɒst] *v.t.* speak to (esp. a stranger in the street).

ac·count [ə'kaʊnt] *v.i. & t.* **1.** *~ for,* explain satisfactorily; give reasons for; keep or give a written statement about (money or goods). **2.** consider: *~ a man innocent.* *n.* **1.** written statement(s) with details (esp. of money received and paid, articles bought and sold, etc.). *on ~,* in part payment. **2.** story or description: *give an ~ of.* **3.** reason; cause: *on no (not on any) ~,* for no reason; *on this ~,* for this reason. **4.** use; profit; importance: *of no ~,* useless; worthless; *take into ~,* consider; *take no ~ of,* pay no attention to; *on one's own ~,* by and for oneself. **~able** *adj.* responsible; expected to give an explanation: *A madman is not ~able for his actions.* **ac·coun·tan·cy** *n.* (no pl.) the work of keeping ~s (1). **ac·coun·tant** *n.* person who keeps ~s(1): *chartered ~ant,* (U.S.A.) *certified public ~ant.*

ac·cred·it [əˈkredɪt] *v.t.* (usu. pass.) send (an ambassador) with an official introduction (*to* a foreign government, etc.).

ac·crue [əˈkruː] *v.i.* come (*to* sb., *from* sth.) as a natural growth or development (esp. of interest on money).

ac·cu·mu·late [əˈkjuːmjuleɪt] *v.i. & t.* come or gather together; become, cause to become, greater in number or amount. **ac·cu·mu·la·tion** [əˈkjuː-mjuˈleɪʃn] *n.* **1.** accumulating or being ⏤d: *the accumulation of money.* **2.** material, etc. ⏤d: *accumulation of papers.* **ac·cu·mu·la·tor** *n.* apparatus (1) for storing electricity.

ac·cu·ra·cy [ˈækjurəsɪ] *n.* (no pl.) state of being **ac·cu·rate** [ˈækjurət] *adj.* careful and exact (in doing things); free from error.

ac·cursed, (old use) **ac·curst** [əˈkɜːst] *adj.* under a curse; hateful.

ac·cu·sa·tion [ˌækjuːˈzeɪʃn] *n.* accusing or being accused.

ac·cu·sa·tive [əˈkjuːzətɪv] *n. & adj.* ⏤ (*case*), (gram.) inflected form of a noun, etc. showing that it is a direct object of a verb or preposition.

ac·cuse [əˈkjuːz] *v.t.* say (sb.) is guilty (*of* sth.). *the* ⏤*d*, the person ⏤*d* in a lawcourt. **ac·cus·er** *n.* **ac·cus·ing·ly** *adv.* in an accusing manner.

ac·cus·tom [əˈkʌstəm] *v.t.* get used (*to*). ⏤*ed adj.* usual.

ace [eɪs] *n.* **1.** playing-card with one mark on it: *the* ⏤ *of spades.* **2.** (colloq.) person who excels at sth., esp. in sports. **3.** *within an* ⏤ *of*, very close to.

ac·e·tate [ˈæsɪteɪt] *n.* salt of acetic acid.

ace·tic [əˈsiːtɪk] *adj.* of vinegar: ⏤ *acid*, the acid contained (1) in vinegar.

acet·y·lene [əˈsetɪliːn] *n.* (no pl.) colourless gas that burns with a bright flame.

ache [eɪk] *n.* continuous pain. *v.i.* have an ⏤.

achieve [əˈtʃiːv] *v.t.* finish; reach; carry out successfully. ⏤**ment** *n.* achieving; sth. ⏤*d*.

ac·id [ˈæsɪd] *n.* **1.** strong, sour liquid. **2.** (chem.) one of a class of substances containing hydrogen, turning blue litmus-paper red. *adj.* with the properties of an ⏤; sour; sharp-tasting: ⏤ *drops*, sweets of boiled sugar with an ⏤ flavour. ⏤ *test*, one that proves the true value of sth.

ac·knowl·edge [əkˈnɒlɪdʒ] *v.t.* **1.** agree, admit (that sth. is true). **2.** send news that one has received sth. **3.** regard (as): *He is* ⏤*d to be an expert on this subject.* **ac·knowl·edg(e)·ment** *n.* **1.**

act of acknowledging. **2.** sth. given or done to ⏤ sth.

ac·me [ˈækmɪ] *n.* highest point: *the* ⏤ *of good behaviour.*

ac·ne [ˈæknɪ] *n.* (no pl.) blackheads and pimples on the face and neck (esp. among young people).

acorn [ˈeɪkɔːn] *n.* seed or fruit of the oak-tree.

acous·tic [əˈkuːstɪk] *adj.* of the sense of hearing. ⏤**s** *n. pl.* (sing. v.) science of sound; (pl. v.) ⏤ properties (of a hall, etc.).

ac·quaint [əˈkweɪnt] *v.t.* make aware; make familiar (*with*): ⏤ *oneself with one's new duties*; *be* ⏤*ed with*, have met personally. ⏤**ance** *n.* **1.** slight personal knowledge: *make sb.'s* ⏤*ance*, *make the* ⏤*ance of sb.*, get to know sb. (e.g. by being introduced (3)). **2.** person whom one has met a few times.

ac·qui·esce [ˌækwɪˈes] *v.i.* agree without protest: *He* ⏤*d in the arrangements.* **ac·qui·es·cence** *n.* **ac·qui·es·cent** *adj.* willing to ⏤.

ac·quire [əˈkwaɪə*] *v.t.* become the owner of; gain for oneself by skill or ability.

ac·qui·si·tion [ˌækwɪˈzɪʃn] *n.* **1.** acquiring. **2.** sth. acquired. **ac·quis·i·tive** [əˈkwɪzɪtɪv] *adj.* eager to acquire; in the habit of acquiring.

ac·quit [əˈkwɪt] *v.t.* (-*tt*-) **1.** say that (sb.) has not done wrong, is not guilty (*of* a crime). **2.** ⏤ *oneself* (*well, etc.*), do one's work or duty (well, etc.). ⏤**tal** *n.*

acre [ˈeɪkə*] *n.* area of 4,840 square yards, or about 4,000 square metres.

ac·rid [ˈækrɪd] *adj.* (of smell or taste) sharp; bitter.

ac·ri·mo·ni·ous [ˌækrɪˈməʊnjəs] *adj.* (of words, temper, etc.) bitter. **ac·ri·mo·ny** [ˈækrɪmənɪ] *n.* (no pl.) bitterness of words, manner, temper.

ac·ro·bat [ˈækrəbæt] *n.* person who can perform gymnastic feats (e.g. on a trapeze or tightrope). ⏤**ic** [ˌækrəʊ-ˈbætɪk] *adj.* ⏤**ics** *n. pl.* (sing. v.) tricks of, or like those of, an ⏤.

across [əˈkrɒs] *prep. & adv.* **I.** *prep.* **1.** from side to side of: *The child ran* ⏤ *the road without looking.* **2.** on the other side of: *There is a garage just* ⏤ *the street.* **3.** so as to cross or to form a cross: *She sat with her arms* ⏤ *her breast.* **II.** *adv.* from one side to the other: *Can you swim* ⏤? *The river is a mile* ⏤ (wide) *at that point.*

act [ækt] *v.i. & t.* **1.** perform actions; do sth.: *If we are to save her life we must* ⏤ *now!* **2.** do what is usual, expected, or required: *The front brake* *on my bicycle won't* ~. **3.** take part in a play on the stage; take the part of (sb.) in a play or film. **4.** pretend: *I know you're not really crying, you're just* ~*ing*. **5.** ~ *as*, do the work or duty of; ~ *upon* (advice, a suggestion), do (what is advised, suggested); ~ (*up*)*on*, have an effect on: *This medicine* ~*s upon the nerves.* **n. 1.** thing done: *a cruel* ~; *little* ~*s of kindness*; *caught in the* ~ *of stealing.* **2.** (*A*~) bill² (3) passed by Parliament. ~**·ing** *adj.* doing the work usu. done by another: *the* ~*ing manager of a business.*

ac·tion ['ækʃn] *n.* **1.** movement; (way of) moving or working (limbs); doing; using energy, influence, etc.: *a time for* ~; *a man of* ~; *out of* ~, not fit to work, to be used, etc. **2.** effect: *the* ~ *of an acid.* **3.** sth. done: *judge a man by his* ~*s.* **4.** fighting; a battle: *killed in* ~; *break off an* ~. **5.** (law) legal process (1): *bring an* ~ (*against*), seek judgement (against) in a lawcourt.

ac·ti·vate ['æktɪveɪt] *v.t.* make active.

ac·tive ['æktɪv] *adj.* **1.** working; at work; in the habit of moving quickly: *an* ~ *brain* (*life*). **2.** practical; effective: *taking an* ~ *part in local affairs*; *on* ~ *service* (of a soldier engaged in fighting). **3.** ~ *voice*, (gram.) the form of the verb which shows that the subject of the verb is doing sth. (Cf. *passive* (2)). ~**·ly** *adv.* **ac·tiv·ist** *n.* person who takes an ~ part (e.g. in a political movement (3)). **ac·tiv·i·ty** [æk'tɪvətɪ] *n.* being ~; purpose about which sb. is ~: *classroom* (*outdoor*) *activities.*

ac·tor ['æktə*] *n.* man who acts on the stage, on television, or in films. **ac·tress** ['æktrɪs] *n.* female ~.

ac·tu·al ['æktʃʊəl] *adj.* real; present; not imagined. ~**·ly** *adv.* really; in truth; for the time being.

acu·men [ə'kjuːmen] *n.* (no pl.) ability to think clearly and shrewdly, esp. in practical matters: *business* ~.

acu·punc·ture ['ækjʊˌpʌŋktʃə*] *n.* (no pl.) (med.) puncturing the skin or tissues with needles to relieve pain and cure disease.

acute [ə'kjuːt] *adj.* **1.** (of pain, etc.) sharp. **2.** (of feelings, senses) keen, delicate. **3.** responding quickly; clever; clear-sighted: *an* ~ *brain* (*observer*). **4.** (of an illness) coming quickly to a turning-point or crisis. **5.** ~ *angle*, less than 90°.

ad [æd] *n.* (colloq., abbr. for) advertisement.

ad- [əd-; 'æd-] *pref.* to, towards: *advance*; *adjoin*.

ad·a·mant ['ædəmənt] *adj.* unyielding: *be* ~, strongly resist persuasion to do sth.

adapt [ə'dæpt] *v.t.* change in order to make suitable (*for* a new purpose). ~**·able** *adj.* able to ~ or be ~ed. **ad·ap·ta·tion** [ˌædæp'teɪʃn] *n.* ~ing; result of ~ing. ~**·er**, ~**·or** *n.* **1.** person who ~s (a play, book, etc.). **2.** device (2) that enables sth. (esp. electrical apparatus) to be used for a new purpose.

add [æd] *v.t. & i.* **1.** put one thing to another: *If you* ~ *5 and 5 you get 10. If the tea is too strong,* ~ *more hot water.* **2.** find the total of: *A* ~ *up these figures.* **3.** make a total of: *These figures* ~ *up to 912.* **4.** say sth. more: *'And now, go away', he* ~*ed.*

ad·den·dum [ə'dendəm] *n.* (pl. -da) thing (omitted) that is to be added.

ad·der ['ædə*] *n.* small poisonous snake.

ad·dict [ə'dɪkt] *v.t.* ~*ed to,* (of a person) in the habit of applying or devoting himself to; given to: ~*ed to drugs* (*alcohol*). ['ædɪkt] *n.* person ~*ed* to (the thing, practice, etc. named): *drug* ~. **ad·dic·tion** [ə'dɪkʃn] *n.* (esp.) condition of taking drug excessively and being unable to cease doing so.

ad·di·tion [ə'dɪʃn] *n.* adding; sth. (to be) added. *in* ~ (*to*), further; besides. ~**·al** *adj.* extra.

ad·di·tive ['ædɪtɪv] *n.* substance added to another in small amounts for a special purpose: *food* ~*s* (e.g. to add colour).

ad·dle ['ædl] *adj.* muddled; confused: ~*-brained,* having confused ideas. *v.i.* (of eggs) become rotten: ~*d eggs.*

ad·dress [ə'dres] *v.t.* **1.** direct (send) a written or spoken message to; deliver a speech to. **2.** ~ *oneself to* (a piece of work), be busy with; give one's attention to. *n.* **1.** particulars of the town, street, etc. where a person may be found or to which his letters, etc. may be sent. **2.** speech to an audience. ~**·ee** [ˌædre'siː] *n.* person to whom a letter is addressed.

-ade [-eɪd] *suff.* (forming ns.): *lemonade*; *arcade.* [(*in, at*).]

ad·ept ['ædept] *n.* expert. *adj.* skilled

ad·e·quate ['ædɪkwət] *adj.* enough; having the qualities needed. **ad·e·qua·cy** *n.* (no pl.).

ad·here [əd'hɪə*] *v.i.* **1.** become or stay stuck fast (*to*) (e.g. with paste or glue). **2.** be faithful (*to*); give support (*to* a religion, party, etc.). **ad·her·ence** *n.* **ad·her·ent** *n.* supporter.

ad·he·sion [əd'hi:ʒn] *n.* (no pl.) being or becoming stuck. **ad·he·sive** [əd-'hi:sɪv] *adj.* sticky: *adhesive tape (plaster)*. *n.* glue; paste (3).

ad·ja·cent [ə'dʒeɪsənt] *adj.* next (*to*) but not necessarily touching.

ad·jec·ti·val [,ædʒek'taɪvl] *adj.* of or like an adjective: *an ~ clause*. **ad·jec·tive** ['ædʒɪktɪv] *n.* word that names a quality, as *large, red, good*.

ad·join [ə'dʒɔɪn] *v.t.* be next or nearest to; be touching: *the ~ing room (field)*.

ad·journ [ə'dʒɜːn] *v.t. & i.* **1.** break off (a meeting, etc.) for a time or to a later date. **2.** (of a group of persons, a meeting) stop doing sth. and separate or go to another place: *We ~ed to the next room*. **~·ment** *n.*

ad·ju·di·cate [ə'dʒuːdɪkeɪt] *v.t. & i.* give a judgement or decision (*upon* sth.) (settling a quarrel, claim, or competition); sit in judgement. **ad·ju·di·ca·tion** [ə,dʒuːdɪ'keɪʃn] *n.*

ad·junct ['ædʒʌŋkt] *n.* **1.** sth. joined to a more important thing. **2.** (gram.) word(s) or phrase added to qualify or define another word in a sentence.

ad·just [ə'dʒʌst] *v.t.* put in order or agreement; make suitable or convenient. **~·able** *adj.* **~·ment** *n.* ~ing or being ~ed; part by which sth. (in a machine) is ~ed.

ad·ju·tant ['ædʒʊtənt] *n.* army officer who does administrative work for a superior officer.

ad lib [,æd'lɪb] *adv.* without restraint. **ad-lib** *attrib. adj.* (colloq.) improvised: *ad-lib comments.* *v.i.* (-bb-) (colloq.) improvise lines or a speech.

ad·man ['ædmæn] *n.* man who composes commercial advertisements.

ad·mass ['ædmæs] *n.* (no pl.) (Gt. Brit.) that part of the public that is easily influenced by advertising, etc.

ad·min·is·ter [əd'mɪnɪstə*] *v.t.* **1.** control, manage, look after (an estate, business affairs, etc.). **2.** put (the law) into operation; give (justice, punishment, etc.). **3.** cause sb. to take: *~ an oath to sb.*; *~ medicine*. **ad·min·is·tra·tion** [əd,mɪnɪs'treɪʃn] *n.* (no pl.) **1.** management (of affairs, business, etc.). **2.** government (of a country). *the Administration*, the Ministry; the Government; (Gt. Brit.) the term (1) or terms of office (3) of the Prime Minister or (U.S.A.) of the President. **3.** giving (of relief, justice, an oath, etc.). **ad·min·is·tra·tive** [əd'mɪnɪs-trətɪv] *adj.* of administration: *administrative work (ability)*. **ad·min-**

is·tra·tor [əd'mɪnɪstreɪtə*] *n.* person who ~s.

ad·mir·able ['ædmərəbl] *adj.* causing admiration; excellent. **ad·mir·ably** *adv.*

ad·mi·ral ['ædmərəl] *n.* naval officer of highest rank; officer who commands a fleet of warships. **~·ty** *n.* branch of government controlling the navy. *the A~ty*, the building in London where ~ty officials work.

ad·mi·ra·tion [,ædmə'reɪʃn] *n.* (no pl.) feeling of pleasure, satisfaction, or respect. **ad·mire** [əd'maɪə*] *v.t.* look at with pleasure; have a high opinion of. **ad·mir·er** *n.* person who admires; man who admires a woman.

ad·mis·si·ble [əd'mɪsəbl] *adj.* that can be allowed or considered. **ad·mis·sion** [əd'mɪʃn] *n.* **1.** admitting or being admitted: *admission free*. **2.** statement admitting (2) sth.: *an unwise admission*; *on his own admission*.

ad·mit [əd'mɪt] *v.t. & i.* (-tt-) **1.** allow to enter: *~ sb. into a house*; *windows to ~ light and air*. **2.** say unwillingly; confess; agree (that sth. is true): *He ~ted having stolen the chicken*. **3.** *~ of*, leave room for: *It ~s of no doubt*. **~·tance** [əd'mɪtəns] *n.* (no pl.) ~ting or being ~ted (to a place): *No ~tance except on business*. **~·ted·ly** [əd'mɪtɪdlɪ] *adv.* as people generally ~ (2).

ad·mon·ish [əd'mɒnɪʃ] *v.t.* advise (sb.) to do right; warn (sb.) against doing what is wrong. **ad·mo·ni·tion** [,ædməʊ'nɪʃn] *n.* advice or warning about behaviour.

ado [ə'duː] *n.* (no pl.) activity, usu. causing excitement.

ad·o·les·cent [,ædəʊ'lesnt] *n. & adj.* (boy or girl) growing up (between the ages of about 13 and 20). **ad·o·les·cence** *n.* (no pl.).

adopt [ə'dɒpt] *v.t.* **1.** take (sb.) into one's own family and treat as one's own child. **2.** follow or use (sb. else's method(s), idea(s), belief(s), etc.). **adop·tion** [ə'dɒpʃn] *n.* act of ~ing.

ador·able *adj.* lovable; delightful. **ad·o·ra·tion** [,ædə'reɪʃn] *n.* (no pl.) worship; deep love and respect.

adore [ə'dɔː*] *v.t.* **1.** worship (God); love deeply and respect highly. **2.** (colloq.) be fond of. **ador·ing** *adj.* showing love and deep respect: *adoring looks*.

adorn [ə'dɔːn] *v.t.* add beauty or ornaments to. **~·ment** *n.* ~ing; sth. used for ~ing.

ad·re·nal [ə'driːnl] *adj.* (anat.) at or

near the kidneys: ~ *glands.* **ad·ren·alin(e)** [əˈdrenəlɪn] *n.* (no pl.) (med.) hormone secreted (2) by the ~ glands.

adrift [əˈdrɪft] *adv. & pred. adj.* (of ships and boats) not under control and driven by wind and water. *turn* ~, send away (from home or employment).

adroit [əˈdrɔɪt] *adj.* ~ (*at, in*), clever; skilful. ~**ly** *adv.*

adult [ˈædʌlt] *n. & adj.* (person or animal) grown to full size and strength; (law) person old enough to vote, marry, etc.: ~ *education.*

adul·ter·ate [əˈdʌltəreɪt] *v.t.* make poorer in quality, make impure, by adding sth. of less value. **adul·ter·a·tion** [ə,dʌltəˈreɪʃn] *n.*

adul·tery [əˈdʌltərɪ] *n.* sexual relationship of a married person with sb. to whom that person is not married. **adul·ter·er** *n.* man guilty of ~. **adul·ter·ess** *n.* woman guilty of ~. **adul·ter·ous** *adj.* of ~.

ad·vance [ədˈvɑːns] *v.i. & t.* **1.** come, go, put, or help forward: *The army* ~*d five miles. The general* ~*d his infantry. Let me* ~ *my opinions.* **2.** (of prices, rates) make or become higher. **3.** pay (money) before it is due; lend (money). *n.* **1.** forward movement: *in* ~ (*of*), in front (of); sooner. **2.** rise in price or value. **3.** sum of money asked for, paid, or given, before it is due. **4.** (pl.) attempts to become a friend or lover. **5.** (attrib.) in ~; ahead of time or need: ~ *booking*; ~ *notice* (1). ~**d** *adj.* far on in time or progress: ~*d studies; the* ~*d level* (abbr. *A level*), (Gt. Brit.) examination that secures (3) the admission to a college or university. ~**ment** *n.* (no pl.) advancing; progress.

ad·van·tage [ədˈvɑːntɪdʒ] *n.* better position; profit; sth. likely to bring success: *have the* ~ *of sb.,* know sb. or sth. that he or she does not know; *take* ~ *of,* make use of (fairly or unfairly); *turn to* ~, use so as to profit from; (*seen*) *to* ~, in a way that shows the good points; *to the* ~ *of,* so as to help or profit. **ad·van·ta·geous** [,ædvənˈteɪdʒəs] *adj.* useful; helpful; profitable.

ad·vent [ˈædvənt] *n.* coming or arrival (usu. of an important person or event); *A~,* the season (with four Sundays) before Christmas; the coming of Christ.

ad·ven·ti·tious [,ædvenˈtɪʃəs] *adj.* coming by chance; accidental.

ad·ven·ture [ədˈventʃə*] *n.* unusual,

exciting, or dangerous journey or activity: ~*s in the jungle; a story of* ~; ~ *playground,* playground with materials that can be used by children for building, climbing on, painting, etc. **ad·ven·tur·er** *n.* **1.** person who seeks ~. **2.** person ready to make a profit for himself by risky and sometimes dishonest means. **ad·ven·tur·ous** *adj.* **1.** fond of, ready for, ~. **2.** full of danger and excitement: *an adventurous voyage.*

ad·verb [ˈædvɜːb] *n.* word that answers questions beginning *how, when, where* and modifies or qualifies (3) another word. **ad·ver·bi·al** [ədˈvɜːbjəl] *adj.* of or like an ~: *an* ~*ial clause.*

ad·ver·sary [ˈædvəsərɪ] *n.* enemy; opponent.

ad·verse [ˈædvɜːs] *adj.* unfavourable; against one's interests: ~ *winds.* **ad·ver·si·ty** [ədˈvɜːsɪtɪ] *n.* trouble.

ad·ver·tise [ˈædvətaɪz] *v.t. & i.* **1.** make known to people by printed notices (in newspapers, magazines, etc.), or by other means (e.g. television), usu. for the purpose of trade: ~ *one's goods.* **2.** ask for by a public notice: ~ *for a servant* (*a lost dog*). ~**ment** [ədˈvɜːtɪsmənt] *n.* **1.** advertising. **2.** public notice (in newspapers, on television, etc.). **ad·ver·tis·er** *n.* person who ~s.

ad·vice [ədˈvaɪs] *n.* **1.** opinion given about what to do, how to act, etc.: *follow the doctor's* ~; *a piece of* ~; *take sb.'s* ~. **2.** (usu. pl.) news, esp. commercial: ~*s from our London branch* (1).

ad·vise [ədˈvaɪz] *v.t.* **1.** give advice to. **2.** (comm.) inform. *ill-*~*d,* unwise; *well-*~*d,* wise. **ad·vis·able** *adj.* wise; to be advised.

ad·vo·cate [ˈædvəkət] *n.* person who speaks (esp. in a lawcourt) in favour of sb. or a cause. [ˈædvəkeɪt] *v.t.* support; speak in favour of (ideas, causes).

aer·ate [ˈeɪəreɪt] *v.t.* let air or put gas into (a substance).

aer·i·al [ˈeərɪəl] *n.* wire(s) or rod(s) for receiving or sending radio waves. *adj.* **1.** of or in the air; moving through the air: ~ *railway* (*ropeway*), system (1) of overhead cables from which cars (3) or containers are suspended (1), usu. driven (2) by electricity. **2.** thin as air; imaginary.

ae·rie [ˈeərɪ] *n.* see *eyrie.*

aero- [ˈeərəʊ-] *pref.* of or relating to aircraft or aeronautics. **~·drome** [ˈeərədrəʊm] *n.* (U.S.A. *airdrome*) airfield. **~·dy·nam·ic** *adj.* of or relating to aerodynamics. **~·dy·nam·i·cist**

[ˌeərəʊdaɪ'næmɪsɪst] *n.* person who specializes in ~. ˌ~·**dy'nam·ics** *n. pl.* (sing. v.) science that deals with the motion of air and with the forces acting (5) on solid (1) bodies moving through air. ~·**naut** ['eərənɔːt] *n.* person who pilots or travels in a balloon or airship. ~·**nau·tics** [ˌeərə-'nɔːtɪks] *n. pl.* (sing. v.) art and science of aviation. ~·**plane** ['eərəpleɪn] *n.* (U.S.A. *airplane*) heavier-than-air flying machine. ~·**sol** ['eərəʊsɒl] *n.* (container of a) substance (e.g. scent, paint, etc.) packed under pressure with a device (2) for releasing (1) it as a fine spray.

aes·thet·ic [iːs'θetɪk] *adj.* concerning beauty in nature, art, literature, music; able to appreciate such beauty; showing good taste (in art, etc.). ~**s** *n. pl.* (sing. v.) science of the laws and principles (1) of beauty.

afar [ə'fɑː*] *adv.* far off.

af·fable ['æfəbl] *adj.* friendly; good-humoured; pleasant and easy to talk to. **af·fably** *adv.* **af·fa·bil·i·ty** [ˌæfə-'bɪlətɪ] *n.*

af·fair [ə'feə*] *n.* **1.** sth. done or thought about; business matter: *That is my* ~, *not yours.* **2.** (pl.) business; events: *a man of* ~*s*, a business man; *mind one's own* ~*s*, not ask questions about, not interfere in, the business of others. *Foreign A*~*s*, relations with foreign countries. **3.** event; happening; thing: *The picnic was a pleasant* ~. ~ *of honour*, duel.

af·fect[1] [ə'fekt] *v.t.* **1.** have a result or effect on: *The climate* ~*ed his health.* **2.** move the feelings of: *deeply* ~*ed by the sad news.* ~·**ing** *adj.* moving the feelings: ~*ing scenes.*

af·fect[2] [ə'fekt] *v.t.* **1.** pretend to have, be, feel, or do: ~ *ignorance.* **2.** show a liking for: ~ *bright colours* (e.g. by wearing brightly coloured clothes). ~·**ed** *adj.* not natural or genuine. **af·fec·ta·tion** [ˌæfek'teɪʃn] *n.* behaviour, show of feeling, that is not natural or genuine.

af·fec·tion [ə'fekʃn] *n.* love; kindly feeling: *win sb.'s* ~(*s*); *in need of* ~. ~·**ate** [ə'fekʃnət] *adj.* loving; showing a feeling of love: *an* ~*ate husband.* ~·**ate·ly** *adv.* *Yours* ~*ately* (used at the close of a letter).

af·fi·da·vit [ˌæfɪ'deɪvɪt] *n.* (law) written statement made on one's oath.

af·fil·i·ate [ə'fɪlɪeɪt] *v.t. & i.* accept as a member or branch of a society; become connected (*to, with*). **af·fil·i·a·tion** [əˌfɪlɪ'eɪʃn] *n.*

af·fin·i·ty [ə'fɪnətɪ] *n.* **1.** close connection (e.g. between animals, plants, languages). **2.** family relation through marriage. **3.** attraction: *the* ~ *of common salt for water.*

af·firm [ə'fɜːm] *v.t.* declare firmly. **af·fir·ma·tion** [ˌæfə'meɪʃn] *n.* ~·**ing**; sth. ~*ed*, esp. (law) a solemn declaration made by sb. not wishing to take an oath. **af·fir·ma·tive** [ə'fɜːmətɪv] *adj. & n.* (answering) 'yes': *an* ~*ative reply*; *answer in the* ~*ative.*

af·fix ['æfɪks] *n.* suffix or prefix. [ə'fɪks] *v.t.* fix or fasten (sth. *to* or *on*); put on (e.g. a postage stamp).

af·flict [ə'flɪkt] *v.t.* cause pain, trouble, or suffering to: ~*ed with*, suffering from. **af·flic·tion** *n.* (cause of) suffering.

af·flu·ence ['æflʊəns] *n.* (no pl.) wealth; abundance: *living in* ~. **af·flu·ent** *adj.* wealthy; abundant: *affluent society*, prosperous society largely concerned with material wealth.

af·ford [ə'fɔːd] *v.t.* **1.** (usu. with *can, could, be able to*) spare or find enough money or time for. **2.** (with *can, could*) risk a disadvantage by doing sth.: *She can't* ~ *to neglect her health.* **3.** (of things) give; provide.

af·fray [ə'freɪ] *n.* fight in a public place, esp. one that disturbs people.

af·front [ə'frʌnt] *v.t.* hurt sb.'s feelings or self-respect, esp. in public. *n.* public insult: *offer an* ~ *to sb.*

afield [ə'fiːld] *adv.* far away from home; to or at a distance.

afire [ə'faɪə*] *pred. adj.* on fire.

aflame [ə'fleɪm] *pred. adj.* on fire; burning: (fig.) ~ *with passion.*

afloat [ə'fləʊt] *adv. & pred. adj.* **1.** floating on the water, etc. **2.** at sea; on board ship. **3.** (of a business) started. **4.** (of rumours, etc.) spreading about.

afoot [ə'fʊt] *pred. adj.* in progress; taking place: *There's mischief* ~. *I wish I knew what's* ~.

afore [ə'fɔː*] *adv.* (in combinations) *aforementioned*, *aforesaid* (i.e. mentioned or named earlier).

afraid [ə'freɪd] *pred. adj.* **1.** frightened; feeling fear: *Are you* ~? *There's nothing to be* ~ *of. I was* ~ *of hurting his feelings* (because I had no wish to do so). *I was* ~ *to offend him* (because he might hit me). **2.** *I'm* ~ ..., polite way of giving information that will not be welcome: *I'm* ~ *your wife has been taken ill. I can't meet you, I'm* ~.

afresh [ə'freʃ] *adv.* again; in a new way.

Af·ri·can ['æfrɪkən] *n. & adj.* (native, esp. dark-skinned, or inhabitant) of Africa.

Af·ro- ['æfrəʊ] *adj.* (of hair style) long and bushy.

Af·ro- ['æfrəʊ-] *pref.* of Africa; African: *Afro-American*, (esp.) American Negro or Negress.

aft [ɑːft] *adv.* at or towards the rear of a ship: *go ~; ~ of the mast.*

af·ter ['ɑːftə*] *prep., adv., & conj.* **I. prep. 1.** following in time; later than: *~ dinner; soon ~ 2 o'clock; ~ that,* then; next; (U.S.A.) *ten minutes ~* (Gt. Brit. past) *nine.* **2.** next in order to; following: *Put the direct object ~ the verb.* **3.** behind (in place): *Shut the door ~ you as you go out.* **4.** because of: *A~ his rudeness to you, he ought to apologize.* **5.** in spite of: *A~ all (his efforts),* he has failed. **6.** *one ~ another, bus ~ bus,* in turn; in succession. **7.** in search of; in pursuit of; making inquiries: *The police are ~ the man who broke into the bank.* **II.** *adv.* later in time: *He fell ill on Monday and died a week ~.* **III.** *conj.* at or during a time later than: *He arrived ~ I had gone home.*

af·ter·math ['ɑːftəmæθ] *n.* (fig.) what follows; the outcome of (an event, etc.): *Misery is often the ~ of war.*

af·ter·noon [,ɑːftə'nuːn] *n.* time between noon and evening.

af·ter·thought ['ɑːftəθɔːt] *n.* thought or explanation that comes to the mind after something has happened.

af·ter·wards ['ɑːftəwədz] *adv.* after; later: *I did not realize what had happened till ~.*

again [ə'gen] *adv.* **1.** once more; a second time: *I did not hear what you said, please say it ~. now and ~,* occasionally; *~ and ~,* time and ~, repeatedly; very often. **2.** as before: *She will soon be well ~.* **3.** *as much ~, as many ~,* twice as much (many). **4.** further; besides: *I did not know him well enough to interfere, and ~, I might have been unwise to do so.*

against [ə'genst] *prep.* **1.** *There were twenty votes ~ the proposal and only fourteen in favour of it.* **2.** *We rowed hard ~ the current, but made little progress.* **3.** *I have hit my head ~ a wall and hurt myself.* **4.** in preparation for: *Save money ~ a time of need.* **5.** *I left the ladder leaning ~ a wall* (which supported it). *The piano stood ~ the wall* (close to it; alongside).

agape [ə'geɪp] *adv. & pred. adj.* with the mouth wide open (in wonder, surprise, or yawning).

age [eɪdʒ] *n.* **1.** length of time a person has lived or a thing has existed: *What's her ~? How old is she? come (be) of ~,* be (over) 18 years old; *under ~,* not yet 18; a minor. **2.** later part of life: *His back was bent with ~.* **3.** great or long period of time: *the ~ we live in; the Stone A~; the Middle A~s* (in Europe, from A.D. 600 to 1450). **4.** (colloq.) a very long time: *We've been waiting for ~s. v.t. & i.* (cause to) grow old; begin to look old: *He's ag(e)ing fast. ~d* **1.** [eɪdʒd] *pred. adj.* of the ~ of: *a boy ~d five.* **2.** ['eɪdʒɪd] *attrib. adj.* having lived long: *an ~d man. ~·less adj.* not growing old; eternal. '*~·long adj.* going on for ~s (4).

-age [-ɪdʒ] *suff.* (forming ns.): *bondage; breakage; postage.*

agen·cy ['eɪdʒənsɪ] *n.* **1.** business, work, or office of an agent (1). **2.** action; operation: *the ~ of water on rocks.* **3.** a means: *through the ~ of friends.*

agen·da [ə'dʒendə] *n.* (list of) things to be done or discussed (e.g. by a committee).

agent ['eɪdʒənt] *n.* **1.** person who acts for, or who manages the business affairs of, another: *house-~,* one who buys, sells, rents, and lets houses for others; *shipping or forwarding ~,* one who sends goods by road, rail, sea, etc. for others. **2.** sth. producing an effect: *Rain and frost are natural ~s which wear away rocks.*

ag·gra·vate ['ægrəveɪt] *v.t.* make (sth.) more serious; (colloq.) annoy. **ag·gra·va·tion** [,ægrə'veɪʃn] *n.*

ag·gre·gate ['ægrɪgɪt] *n. & adj.* total. *in the ~,* taken as a whole.

ag·gres·sion [ə'greʃn] *n.* act of attacking; an attack made without just cause: *a country guilty of ~ against its neighbours.* **ag·gres·sive** [ə'gresɪv] *adj.* fond of attacking; likely to attack without just cause; of or for the purpose of attack: *aggressive weapons.* **ag·gres·sor** *n.* person or country making an aggressive attack.

ag·grieved [ə'griːvd] *adj.* hurt in one's feelings; conscious of unjust treatment.

aghast [ə'gɑːst] *pred. adj.* filled with terror or surprise.

ag·ile ['ædʒaɪl] *adj.* (of living things) quick-moving; active. **agil·i·ty** [ə'dʒɪlətɪ] *n.* (no pl.).

ag·i·tate ['ædʒɪteɪt] *v.t. & i.* **1.** move, shake (liquids). **2.** disturb; cause anxiety to (a person, his feelings). **3.** *~ for,* keep on trying to get (a change

in conditions, etc.): *They ~d for higher wages*. **ag·i·ta·tion** [ˌædʒɪ'teɪʃn] *n*.
ag·i·ta·tor *n*. person who ~s, esp. politically.

aglow [ə'gləʊ] *adv. & pred. adj.* showing warmth from exercise or excitement; giving out light and heat.

ag·nail ['æɡneɪl] *n*. torn skin at the root of a finger-nail.

ag·nos·tic [æɡ'nɒstɪk] *n*. person who believes that nothing can be known about God or of anything except material things. *adj.* of this belief.

ago [ə'ɡəʊ] *adv*. (used with the simple past tense): gone by; past: *The train left ten minutes ~*.

agog [ə'ɡɒɡ] *adv. & pred. adj.* eager; excited; full of interest: *all ~ to know what had happened*.

ag·o·ny ['æɡənɪ] *n*. great pain or suffering (of mind or body). **ag·o·nized** ['æɡənaɪzd] *adj.* expressing ~. **ag·o·niz·ing** ['æɡənaɪzɪŋ] *adj.* causing ~.

agrar·i·an [ə'ɡreərɪən] *adj.* of (esp. farm)land or land ownership: *~ reforms*.

agree [ə'ɡriː] *v.i.* **1.** *~ (to)*, say 'yes'; consent. **2.** be of the same opinion. **3.** get on well with one another. **4.** *~ with*, conform with; be in harmony with; suit the health of; be good for. **~able** [ə'ɡrɪəbl] *adj.* pleasing; ready to ~. **~ably** [ə'ɡrɪəblɪ] *adv*. *~ably surprised*, surprised and pleased. **~ment** *n*. **1.** mutual understanding; having the same opinion(s): *We are in ~ment on that point*. **2.** (law) contract legally binding (4) on the parties (3): *sign an ~ment*.

ag·ri·cul·ture ['æɡrɪkʌltʃə*] *n*. (no pl.) science or practice of farming. **ag·ri·cul·tur·al** [ˌæɡrɪ'kʌltʃərəl] *adj.* of ~.

aground [ə'ɡraʊnd] *adv. & pred. adj.* (of ships) touching the bottom in shallow water: *be (run, go) ~*.

ahead [ə'hed] *adv. & pred. adj.* in front (*of*): *in line ~*, (of ships) sailing one in front of another; *look ~*, think of and prepare for the future; *go ~*, make progress; (colloq.) go on.

ahem [hm] *int.* (usual spelling for) noise made when clearing the throat (uttered to call attention or to give a slight warning).

ahoy [ə'hɔɪ] *int.* greeting or warning cry used by seamen.

aid [eɪd] *v.t. & n.* help; sth. that gives help: *raising funds in ~ of the sick*; *first ~*, treatment given at once to a sick or injured person.

ail [eɪl] *v.t.* trouble; afflict: *What ~s*

him? *v.i.* be ill: *She is always ~ing*. **~ment** *n*. (slight) illness.

aim [eɪm] *v.t. & i.* **1.** point (a gun, etc.) (*at*). **2.** send (a blow, object, etc.) (*at, towards*). **3.** have in view as a purpose or design. *n.* act of ~ing; purpose. **~less** *adj.* without ~ or purpose.

ain't [eɪnt] vulgar form of *am not, is not, are not, has not, have not*.

air [eə*] *n*. **1.** (no pl.) mixture of gases that surrounds the earth and that we breathe. (special uses only): *by ~*, in an aircraft; *on the ~*, through or by means of the radio: *What's on the ~ this evening?* **2.** appearance; way of behaving: *an ~ of importance*; *a triumphant ~*; *put on (give oneself) ~s*, behave unnaturally, trying to appear better or more important than one really is. **3.** tune; melody (2). *v.t.* **1.** put (clothing, bedding, etc.) into the open ~ or into a warm place to dry it. **2.** let ~ come into. **3.** cause others to know (one's opinions, etc.).

air- [eə-*] (compounds and attrib.): '**~borne** *adj.* (of an aircraft) off the ground; (of troops, etc.) transported by air. **~ brake** *n*. brake worked by air pressure. **~ bus** *n*. aircraft that carries passengers on short flights. '**~·con₁di·tioned** *adj.* supplied with pure air at a comfortable temperature. '**~ cor·ri·dor** *n*. route to which aircraft are restricted. '**~craft** *n*. (sing. or pl.) aeroplane(s), etc.; airship(s). '**~craft 'car·ri·er** *n*. ship that carries aeroplanes, with a long, wide deck for taking off and landing. '**~field** *n*. (landing field of an) airport, esp. for military use. **~ force** *n*. branch (2) of armed forces fighting in the air. **~ host·ess** *n*. stewardess in a passenger aircraft. '**~lift** *n*. transport of troops, supplies, etc. by air, esp. in an emergency. '**~line** *n*. air transport system or company. '**~₁lin·er** *n*. aircraft carrying passengers on a regular route. **~ mail** *n*. (no pl.) mail (to be) carried by air. '**~man** *n*. man who flies in an aircraft as a member of the crew, esp. a pilot. **~ pi·rate** *n*. skyjacker. '**~plane** *n*. (U.S.A.) = aeroplane. '**~₁pock·et** *n*. partial vacuum in the air which causes an aircraft suddenly to drop some distance. **~ pol·lu·tion** *n*. pollution of the air. '**~port** *n*. public flying ground for commercial use, with a custom-house, etc. **~ raid** *n*. attack by aircraft: *~raid shelter (warden, warning)*. '**~screw** *n*. propeller of an aircraft. '**~ship** *n*. flying machine lighter than air. '**~space** *n*. the space lying above a certain area of land or water: *violation of the ~ space by military aircraft.* '**~·strip** *n.* strip of ground for the use of aircraft. **~ ter·mi·nal** *n.* place in a town where transport is provided to and from an airport. '**~·tight** *adj.* not allowing air to enter or escape. '**~·,traf·fic con'trol** *n.* (no pl.) system of control that instructs aircraft about which route to follow, at what height to fly, etc. '**~·,traf·fic con'trol·ler** *n.* '**~·way** *n.* **1.** route regularly followed by aircraft. **2.** company that operates a regular service (5) of aircraft.

air·y ['eərɪ] *adj.* (*-ier, -iest*) **1.** with air entering freely. **2.** of or like air; gay; cheerful; not serious. **air·i·ly** *adv.*

aisle [aɪl] *n.* passage between rows of pews or seats.

aitch [eɪtʃ] *n.* letter H.

a·jar [ə'dʒɑː*] *adv. & pred. adj.* (of a door) slightly open.

ajar   akimbo

akim·bo [ə'kɪmbəʊ] *adv.* with arms ~, with the hands on the hips and the elbows bent outwards.

akin [ə'kɪn] *pred. adj.* belonging to the same family. ~ *to*, (fig.) like: *Pity is often ~ to love.*

-al [-əl, -l] *suff.* (forming adjs. and ns.): *central; general; animal; arrival.*

al·a·bas·ter ['æləbɑːstə*] *n.* (no pl.) (name for several kinds of) hard white stone used for making ornaments.

alac·ri·ty [ə'lækrətɪ] *n.* (no pl.) quick and willing eagerness.

alarm [ə'lɑːm] *n.* **1.** sound or signal giving a warning: *give (raise) the ~.* **2.** apparatus used to make such a sound: ~ *(clock)*, one with a bell which rings to wake a sleeping person. **3.** fear or excitement caused by real or imagined danger. *v.t.* give a warning or feeling of danger to. **~ed** *adj.* **~·ing** *adj.*

alas [ə'læs] *int.* cry of sorrow or anxiety.

al·ba·tross ['ælbətrɒs] *n.* very large white sea-bird common in the Pacific and Southern Oceans.

al·bi·no [æl'biːnəʊ] *n.* animal or human being born without natural colouring matter in the skin and hair (which are white) and the eyes (which are usu. pink).

al·bum ['ælbəm] *n.* book in which a collection of photographs, postage stamps, etc. can be kept.

al·bu·men ['ælbjʊmɪn] *n.* (no pl.) (substance as in) white of egg.

al·che·my ['ælkɪmɪ] *n.* (no pl.) early form of chemistry whose chief object was to find how to change other metals into gold. **al·che·mist** *n.*

al·co·hol ['ælkəhɒl] *n.* **1.** (no pl.) (pure, colourless, intoxicating liquid present in) such drinks as beer, wine, whisky. **2.** (chem.) large group of compounds of the same type as the ~ in wine. **~·ic** [,ælkə'hɒlɪk] *adj.* of or containing ~. *n.* person in a diseased condition caused by drinking too much ~.

al·cove ['ælkəʊv] *n.* small space in a room formed by a break in the line of a wall, etc., often occupied by a bed or seat(s).

al·der·man ['ɔːldəmən] *n.* one of the senior members of a city or county council in England.

ale [eɪl] *n.* light-coloured beer; (old use) beer.

alert [ə'lɜːt] *adj.* watchful; fully awake. *n. on the ~*, on the lookout. *v.t.* put (troops, etc.) on the ~.

al·ga ['ælgə] *n.* (pl. *-gae* ['ældʒiː]) (bot.) very simple water plant.

al·ge·bra ['ældʒɪbrə] *n.* branch of mathematics using signs and letters to represent quantities.

alias ['eɪlɪæs] *n.* name that a person uses instead of (usu. to hide) his real name: *The thief had several ~es.*

al·i·bi ['ælɪbaɪ] *n.* the argument or proof that (when an act, esp. a crime, took place) one was in another place.

alien ['eɪljən] *adj.* **1.** of another race, nation, or country; foreign. **2.** ~ *to*, out of harmony with: *Cruelty was quite ~ to his nature. n.* person of another nation or country; foreigner.

alien·ate ['eɪljəneɪt] *v.t.* **1.** lose, turn away, the love or affection of. **2.** transfer (property) to the ownership of another: *Enemy property is usually ~d in time of war.* **alien·ation** [,eɪljə'neɪʃn] *n.*

alight[1] [ə'laɪt] *pred. adj.* burning; lighted up; (fig.) bright-looking and cheerful: *faces ~ with happiness.*

alight[2] [ə'laɪt] *v.i.* **1.** get down (*from* a horse, bus, train, etc.). **2.** come down to rest from the air: *The bird ~ed on a branch.*

align [ə'laɪn] *v.t.* put, bring, three or more things or persons (e.g. soldiers) into a straight line. **~ment** *n.* arrangement in a straight line: *These desks are in (out of)* ~*ment.*

alike [ə'laɪk] *pred. adj.* like one another. *adv.* in the same way.

al·i·men·ta·ry [͵ælɪ'mentərɪ] *adj.* ~ *canal,* series of organs and channels along which food passes through an animal body.

al·i·mo·ny ['ælɪmənɪ] *n.* (no pl.) money (to be) paid by a man to his wife after a legal separation or divorce.

alive [ə'laɪv] *pred. adj.* 1. living. 2. in force; in existence: *keep a claim* ~. 3. ~ *to,* fully aware of: ~ *to the dangers of a situation.*

al·ka·li ['ælkəlaɪ] *n.* (chem.) one of a number of substances (e.g. soda, potash, ammonia) that combine with acids to form salts. **al·ka·line** ['ælkəlaɪn] *adj.*

all [ɔːl] *adj., pron., adv., & n.* **I.** *adj.* (with pl. nouns) the whole number of; (with sing. nouns) the whole extent or amount of: *All horses are animals but not all animals are horses. All five men were killed in the car crash. He has lived all his life in France. All the butter has been eaten.* **II.** *pron.* **1.** everything: *He wants all or nothing.* **2.** everyone; the whole: *All of us want to go. Take all of it. We all want to go. Take it all.* **3.** *All* (= All that) *I want is rest and peace.* **4.** (in prepositional phrases) *above all,* more than anything else: *Above all, I want rest.* **after all,** in spite of our efforts: *After all we missed the train.* **at all:** *If you are at all worried* (worried in any way or in the least degree) *consult a lawyer. I am not at all comfortable* (I am very uncomfortable). *Not at all* (polite answer to an expression of thanks). **once and for all,** for the last or the only time: *I tell you once and for all, you must not do this thing.* **all in all:** *All in all* (considering everything) *they did well. The boy and girl are all in all to each other* (deeply in love). **not ... all that:** *I'm not as ill as all that* (as ill as you seem to think I am). **III.** *adv.* quite; entirely: *They were dressed all in black.* **all along,** (a) for the whole length of: *all along the road;* (b) (colloq.) all the time: *I knew it all along.* **all for,** (colloq.) strongly in favour of: *I'm all for accepting this offer.* **all in,** (a) exhausted: *I'm all in;* (b) all inclusive. **all out:** *We must go all out* (try our hardest) *to win.* **all over,** (a) in every

part of: *He has travelled all over Europe;* (b) at an end: *You've come too late, the party is all over.* **all right,** (a) well; safe: *I'm all right, thank you;* (b) (in answer to a suggestion) yes, I agree. **all together:** *Now, all together* (united, and at the same time), *pull!* **IV.** *n.* *We lost our all* (everything we possessed) *in the flood.* **V.** (in compounds) in the highest degree; without limit: *all-clear,* signal that danger or difficulty is over; *all-purpose,* suitable for several uses; *an all-round sportsman,* good at many games, etc.; *an all-time high (low),* the highest (lowest) speed, etc. ever recorded.

al·lay [ə'leɪ] *v.t.* make (pain, trouble, excitement) less.

al·lege [ə'ledʒ] *v.t.* put forward a statement as a fact; claim sth. to be true: ~ *that sb. is a thief;* ~ *illness as a reason for not going to work.* **al·le·ga·tion** [͵ælɪ'geɪʃn] *n.*

al·le·giance [ə'liːdʒəns] *n.* (no pl.) duty, support, or loyalty that is due (to a ruler, government, or country).

al·le·go·ry ['ælɪgərɪ] *n.* story in which ideas (e.g. Patience, Purity, Truth) appear as living characters. **al·le·gor·i·cal** [͵ælɪ'gɒrɪkl] *adj.*

al·le·lu·ia [͵ælɪ'luːjə] *int.* hallelujah.

al·ler·gic [ə'lɜːdʒɪk] *adj.* ~ *to,* having an allergy to (sth.); (colloq.) having a dislike of (sth. or sb.). **al·ler·gy** ['ælədʒɪ] *n.* (condition of) being unusually sensitive to certain foods, pollen, etc.

al·le·vi·ate [ə'liːvɪeɪt] *v.t.* make (pain or suffering) less or easier to bear. **al·le·vi·a·tion** [ə'liːvɪ'eɪʃn] *n.*

al·ley ['ælɪ] *n.* (pl. ~*s*) narrow passage between buildings: *blind* ~, one with a closed end.

al·li·ance [ə'laɪəns] *n.* union of persons, parties, or states, for a special purpose: *in* ~ *(with),* united (with).

al·lied *adj.* see ally.

al·li·ga·tor ['ælɪgeɪtə*] *n.* reptile like a crocodile, living in lakes and rivers of the tropical parts of America.

al·lit·er·a·tion [ə͵lɪtə'reɪʃn] *n.* (no pl.) succession of words in which the same sound or letter is repeated, as in *safe and sound.*

all-mains [͵ɔːl'meɪnz] *attrib. adj.* (of electrical apparatus) adaptable to current of any voltage.

al·lo·cate ['æləʊkeɪt] *v.t.* decide to put (money, supplies, etc.) to a (given) purpose. **al·lo·ca·tion** [͵æləʊ'keɪʃn] *n.* **1.** allocating. **2.** sth. ~*d* or assigned (*to* sb. or a purpose).

al·lot [ə'lɒt] *v.t.* (*-tt-*) decide a person's share of; make a distribution of. ⁓**ment** *n.* that which is ⁓ted, esp. (in England) a small area of public land rented for growing vegetables, etc.

al·low [ə'laʊ] *v.t. & i.* **1.** permit; let: *Smoking is not ⁓ed.* **2.** agree (that a statement is correct). **3.** agree to give (money, time): ⁓ *sb. one pound a week for pocket money.* **4.** ⁓ *for,* take into account; think about and provide for; leave enough space for. ⁓**ance** *n.* amount (of money, etc.) ⁓ed to sb. regularly. *make ⁓ance(s) for,* not be too severe in judging sb.: *We must make ⁓ance(s) for his youth.*

al·loy ['ælɔɪ] *n.* mixture of two or more metals, esp. of different values. [ə'lɔɪ] *v.t.* mix (metals).

al·lude [ə'lu:d] *v.i.* ⁓ *to,* refer to; speak or write of indirectly; hint at.

al·lure [ə'ljʊə*] *v.t.* attract; tempt.

al·lu·sion [ə'lu:ʒn] *n.* ⁓ (*to*), indirect reference to. **al·lu·sive** [ə'lu:sɪv] *adj.* alluding; hinting.

al·lu·vi·al [ə'lu:vjəl] *adj.* made up of sand, earth, etc. left by rivers or floods: ⁓ *soil.*

al·ly [ə'laɪ] *v.t.* **1.** join, unite (for a special purpose): *countries which were allied during the war.* **2.** *be allied to,* be connected with: *The English language is allied to German.* ['ælaɪ] *n.* person or country allied to another. **al·lied** ['ælaɪd] *attrib. adj.* joined by agreement, common interest, etc.

-al·ly [-(ə)lɪ] *suff.* (forming advs.): *magically.*

al·ma·nac ['ɔːlmənæk] *n.* book or calendar with notes on coming events (e.g. public holidays), information about the sun, moon, tides, etc.

al·mighty [ɔːl'maɪtɪ] *adj.* powerful beyond measure: *A⁓ God. n.* (no pl.) *The A⁓,* God.

al·mond ['ɑːmənd] *n.* nut or seed of a tree allied to the peach and plum; the tree.

al·most ['ɔːlməʊst] *adv.* **1.** nearly: *He slipped and ⁓ fell to the ground. Dinner is ⁓* (will soon be) *ready.* **2.** (with *no, none, nothing, never*): *The speaker said ⁓ nothing* (a few words of little importance).

alms [ɑːmz] *n.* (sing. or pl.) money, clothes, food, etc. given to poor people. '⁓**house** *n.* (old use) house in which poor people, no longer able to earn money, may live without paying rent.

aloft [ə'lɒft] *adv. & pred. adj.* high up; overhead; (in a ship) up the mast(s).

alone [ə'ləʊn] *adv. & pred. adj.* **1.** without anyone else present; without help: *I sat ⁓. I went ⁓. I did the job ⁓.* **2.** with no other(s) near: *The house stood ⁓ on the hillside.* **3.** (following a noun or pronoun) and no other: *Smith ⁓ knows the answer.* **4.** *let sth. or sb. ⁓,* not touch or interfere with it (him).

along [ə'lɒŋ] *prep.* from one end to the other end of; through any part of the length of: *We walked ⁓ the road. There are trees all ⁓ the riverside. adv. Run ⁓, now!* (Go away!) *Come ⁓!* (Hurry up! Come with me!) ⁓**side** [ə'lɒŋsaɪd] *adv. & prep.* against the side of (a ship, pier).

aloof [ə'lu:f] *adv.* apart; *adj.* cool; reserved. ⁓**ness** [ə'lu:fnɪs] *n.*

aloud [ə'laʊd] *adv.* so as to be heard; not in a whisper.

alp [ælp] *n.* high rugged mountain.

al·paca [æl'pækə] *n.* animal of Peru, larger than a goat, with long soft hair; (cloth made from) its wool: *an ⁓ coat.*

al·pha ['ælfə] *n.* the first letter (A) in the Greek alphabet.

al·pha·bet ['ælfəbɪt] *n.* the letters used in writing a language, arranged in order. ⁓**·i·cal** [,ælfə'betɪkl] *adj.* of the ⁓: *in ⁓ical order.*

al·pine ['ælpaɪn] *adj.* of a mountain or mountain side: ⁓ *flowers.* **al·pin·ist** ['ælpɪnɪst] *n.* ⁓ climber.

al·ready [ɔːl'redɪ] *adv.* by this (that) time; before now: *The postman has ⁓ been* (has been ⁓). *Has the postman been ⁓* (so soon)? *I've been there ⁓, so I don't want to go again.*

Al·sa·tian [æl'seɪʃən] *n.* (U.S.A. *German shepherd*) large wolf-like breed of dog, often trained for police work, etc.

al·so ['ɔːlsəʊ] *adv.* too; besides; as well.

al·tar ['ɔːltə*] *n.* **1.** raised place (table or platform) on which offerings are made to a god. **2.** (in a Christian church) Communion table: *lead a woman to the ⁓,* marry her.

al·ter ['ɔːltə*] *v.t. & i.* make or become different; change. ⁓**ation** [,ɔːltə'reɪʃn] *n.* change; act of changing.

al·ter·ca·tion [,ɔːltə'keɪʃn] *n.* quarrelling; quarrel; noisy argument.

al·ter·nate [ɔːl'tɜːnət] *adj.* (of two things or two kinds) first one and then the other: ⁓ *laughter and tears*; (of days, numbers) first and third, second and fourth, etc.: *They met on ⁓ days* (Monday, Wednesday, etc.). ['ɔːltəneɪt] *v.t. & i.* **1.** (of things of two kinds) come, do, put, arrange, by turns; replace (one thing) with (the other): *Wet days ～d with fine days.* ～ *kindness with severity.* **2.** (of two things) keep coming, one after the other. *alternating current,* electric current that travels first one way and then the other along a wire at regular intervals (1). **al·ter·na·tion** [ˌɔːltəˈneɪʃn] *n.*

al·ter·na·tive [ɔːlˈtɜːnətɪv] *adj.* offering the choice between two things: *alternative society,* group of persons with different cultural values than those of the society they live in. *n.* choice between two things; one of more than two possibilities: *I had to go, there was no alternative.*

al·tho [ɔːlˈðəʊ] *conj.* (U.S.A.) = (al)though.

al·though [ɔːlˈðəʊ] *conj.* though.

al·tim·e·ter [ˈæltɪmiːtə*] *n.* instrument for measuring height above sea level. **al·ti·tude** [ˈæltɪtjuːd] *n.* height (esp. height above sea level).

al·to [ˈæltəʊ] *n.* (musical part for or person having a) male singing voice between tenor and treble; lower of two female voices.

al·to·geth·er [ˌɔːltəˈɡeðə*] *adv.* **1.** entirely; wholly: *I don't ～ agree. It's ～ wrong to ill-treat animals.* **2.** on the whole: *The weather was bad and the trains were crowded; ～, we wished we had not gone out.*

al·tru·ism [ˈæltrʊɪzəm] *n.* principle of considering the well-being and happiness of others first. **al·tru·ist** *n.* **al·tru·is·tic** [ˌæltrʊˈɪstɪk] *adj.*

al·u·min·i·um [ˌæljʊˈmɪnjəm], (U.S.A.) **alu·mi·num** [əˈluːmɪnəm]) *ns.* (no pl.) silver-white metal, very light, resisting oxidation.

al·ways [ˈɔːlweɪz] *adv.* **1.** at all times; with no exception: *The sun ～ rises in the east.* **2.** again and again; repeatedly: *Why are you ～ finding fault with me?*

am, see *be.*

amal·gam [əˈmælɡəm] *n.* mixture of mercury and another metal.

amal·ga·mate [əˈmælɡəmeɪt] *v.t. & i.* join together; unite; mix. **amal·ga·ma·tion** [əˌmælɡəˈmeɪʃn] *n.*

amass [əˈmæs] *v.t.* pile up, heap together (esp. riches).

am·a·teur [ˈæmətə*] *n.* person who paints pictures, performs music, plays, etc. for the love of it and not for money; person playing a game, taking part in sports, etc. without being paid for doing so. (Cf. *professional.*) **～ish** [ˌæməˈtɜːrɪʃ] *adj.* not expert.

amaze [əˈmeɪz] *v.t.* fill with great surprise or wonder. **～ment** *n.* (no pl.).

am·bas·sa·dor [æmˈbæsədə*] *n.* minister (2) who represents (4) the government of his country in a foreign country. **am·bas·sa·dress** [æmˈbæsədrɪs] *n.* female ～.

am·ber [ˈæmbə*] *n.* (no pl.) clear, hard, yellowish gum used for making ornaments; its colour.

am·bi·gu·ity [ˌæmbɪˈɡjuːɪtɪ] *n.* **1.** (no pl.) state of being ambiguous. **2.** word, phrase, etc. having more than one possible meaning. **am·big·u·ous** [æmˈbɪɡjʊəs] *adj.* of doubtful meaning or nature. **am·big·u·ous·ly** *adv.*

am·bi·tion [æmˈbɪʃn] *n.* **1.** strong desire (*to* be successful, famous, etc., or *to* do sth.). **2.** that which one desires to do. **am·bi·tious** [æmˈbɪʃəs] *adj.* **1.** full of ～: *an ambitious boy.* **2.** showing ～: *ambitious plans.* **am·bi·tious·ly** *adv.*

am·ble [ˈæmbl] *v.i.* (of a horse) move along without hurrying, lifting the two feet on one side together; (of a person) ride or walk at an easy pace. *n.* slow, easy pace.

am·bu·lance [ˈæmbjʊləns] *n.* closed vehicle for carrying wounded, injured, or sick persons.

am·bush [ˈæmbʊʃ] *n.* (the placing of) men in hiding for making a surprise attack. *v.t. & i.* lie in wait (for); attack from an ～.

ame·lio·rate [əˈmiːljəreɪt] *v.t. & i.* make or become better. **ame·lio·ra·tion** [əˌmiːljəˈreɪʃn] *n.*

amen [ˌɑːˈmen, ˌeɪˈmen] *n. & int.* word used at the end of a prayer or hymn, meaning 'May it be so'.

ame·na·ble [əˈmiːnəbl] *adj.* ～ *to,* (a) (of persons) willing to be guided or persuaded by; (b) (of things) able to be tested by: *The case is not ～ to ordinary rules.*

amend [əˈmend] *v.t.* **1.** improve; correct; make free from faults: *You must ～ your ways.* **2.** make changes in (laws, rules). **～·ment** *n.* alteration to laws, etc.). **～s** *n. pl.* compensation: *make ～s for sth.*

ame·ni·ty [əˈmiːnətɪ] *n.* **1.** pleasantness: *the ～ of the climate.* **2.** sth. that makes life pleasant: *the amenities of town life* (e.g. concerts, public libraries).

Amer·i·can [əˈmerɪkən] *adj.* of or relating to America, esp. the U.S.A.: *～ plan,* (U.S.A., at hotels) system of charges (3) including room, all meals, and service. *n.* native or inhabitant of America; citizen (2) of the U.S.A.

am·e·thyst [ˈæmɪθɪst] *n.* precious stone, purple or violet.

ami·able ['eɪmjəbl] *adj.* lovable; good-tempered; kind-hearted. **ami·a·bil·i·ty** [,eɪmjə'bɪlətɪ] *n.*

amic·able ['æmɪkəbl] *adj.* friendly; peaceful: *settle a question in an ~ way.* **amic·ably** *adv.*

amid(st) [ə'mɪd(st)] *prep.* in the middle of.

amid·ships [ə'mɪdʃɪps] *adv.* in the middle of a ship: *Our cabin is ~.*

amiss [ə'mɪs] *pred. adj. & adv.* wrong(ly); out of order: *There's not much ~ with it. take sth. ~,* feel offended at sth.

am·ity ['æmətɪ] *n.* (no pl.) friendship; friendly behaviour.

am·me·ter ['æmɪtə*] *n.* instrument for measuring electric current in amperes.

am·mo·nia [ə'məʊnjə] *n.* (no pl.) colourless gas with a strong, sharp smell; this gas dissolved in water, used for cleaning.

am·mu·ni·tion [,æmjʊ'nɪʃn] *n.* (no pl.) military stores (esp. shells, bombs, etc.) to be used against the enemy in battle.

am·ne·sia [æm'niːzjə] *n.* (no pl.) partial or total loss of memory.

am·nes·ty ['æmnɪstɪ] *n.* general pardon, esp. for political offence (1).

amoe·ba (U.S.A. **ame·ba**) [ə'miːbə] *n.* (pl. *-bas, -bae* [-biː]) simple form of living matter, always changing shape and too small to be seen except through a microscope.

amok [ə'mɒk] *adv. run ~,* run about wildly with a desire to kill people.

among(st) [ə'mʌŋ(st)] *prep.* 1. surrounded by; in the middle of: *a mother sitting ~ her small children.* (Note the pl. noun. Cf. *between.*) *A~ those present was the Mayor.* 2. (with a superlative) one of: *The Amazon is ~ the longest rivers in the world.* 3. (indicating a sharing of possessions, activity, etc.): *The rich merchant divided his property ~ his four sons. Settle this matter ~ yourselves. There was not a clean face ~ them* (all were dirty).

amor·al [,eɪ'mɒrəl] *adj.* not concerned with morals; non-moral.

am·o·rous ['æmərəs] *adj.* easily moved to love; showing love: *~ looks.* **~·ly** *adv.*

amor·phous [ə'mɔːfəs] *adj.* having no definite shape or form.

amount [ə'maʊnt] *v.i. ~ to,* add up to; be equal to: *What he said ~ed to little* (i.e. was not important, had not much meaning). *n.* 1. the whole; the total. 2. quantity: *large in ~ but poor in quality.*

am·pere ['æmpeə*] *n.* unit for measuring electric current.

am·phet·amine [æm'fetəmɪn] *n.* (no pl.) (med.) drug used medically and by drug addicts.

am·phib·i·an [æm'fɪbɪən] *n.* 1. animal able to live on land and in water (e.g. a frog). 2. aircraft designed to take off from and alight² (2) on water or land. 3. vehicle with a flat bottom that is able to move in water and on land: *~ tank* (2). **am·phib·i·ous** *adj.* adapted for both land and water.

am·phi·the·atre ['æmfɪˌθɪətə*] *n.* 1. round or oval building with rows of seats rising behind and above one another around an open space used for public games and amusements. 2. part of a theatre with rows of seats similarly arranged in a half-circle.

am·ple ['æmpl] *adj.* (*~r, ~st*) 1. roomy; large-sized; with plenty of space. 2. more than enough: *£10 will be ~ for my needs.* **am·ply** *adv.*

am·pli·fy ['æmplɪfaɪ] *v.t.* give fuller information, more details, etc. about; increase the strength of (radio signals, etc.). **am·pli·fi·er** *n.* apparatus (1) for ~ing sound. **am·pli·fi·ca·tion** [,æmplɪfɪ'keɪʃn] *n.*

am·pli·tude ['æmplɪtjuːd] *n.* (no pl.) breadth; abundance.

am·poule (U.S.A. **am·pul(e)**) ['æmpuːl] *n.* (med.) small sealed glass container holding a solution (2) for a hypodermic injection.

am·pu·tate ['æmpjʊteɪt] *v.t.* cut off (e.g. an arm or leg). **am·pu·ta·tion** [,æmpjʊ'teɪʃn] *n.*

amuck [ə'mʌk] *adv.* amok.

am·u·let ['æmjʊlɪt] *n.* sth. worn on the body in the belief or hope that it will protect against harm, disease, or evil powers.

amuse [ə'mjuːz] *v.t.* make time pass happily for; cause smiles or laughter. **~·ment** *n.* being ~d; sth. that ~s: *~ment arcade,* (Gt. Brit.) place for recreation with automatic game-machines, etc. *~ment park* (*grounds*), place with roundabouts (1), shooting galleries, etc. for entertainment. **amus·ing** *adj.* causing ~ment.

an, see *a.*

an- [æn-] *pref.* not; without: *anaesthetic.*

-an [-ən] *suff.* (forming adjs., often used as ns.): *Anglican; American.*

anach·ron·ism [ə'nækrənɪzm] *n.* mistake in dating sth.; sth. out of date now or in a description of past times. **anach·ron·is·tic** [ə,nækrə'nɪstɪk] *adj.*

an·a·con·da [ˌænə'kɒndə] **n.** large South American snake that kills by crushing its prey.

anae·mia (U.S.A. **ane-**) [ə'niːmjə] **n.** (no pl.) lack of enough blood; poor condition of the blood, causing paleness. **anae·mic** (U.S.A. **ane-**) **adj.**

an·aes·the·sia (U.S.A. **an·es-**) [ˌænɪs-'θiːzjə] **n.** (no pl.) the state of being unable to feel (pain, cold, etc.). **an·aes·thet·ic** (U.S.A. **an·es-**) [ˌænɪs-'θetɪk] **n.** substance causing ~. **an·aes·the·tize** (U.S.A. **an·es-**) [æ'niːsθətaɪz] **v.t.** make insensible to pain or pain-.

anal·o·gous [ə'næləgəs] **adj.** that may be compared; similar in use, quality, or relations.

anal·o·gy [ə'nælədʒɪ] **n.** **1.** partial likeness to, or agreement with, another thing or between two things: *the ~ between the heart and a pump.* **2.** process of reasoning from such partial likeness or agreement.

an·a·lyse (U.S.A. **-lyze**) ['ænəlaɪz] **v.t.** examine (sth.) in order to learn what the parts are; separate (sth.) into its parts: *~ a chemical compound (a sentence, the soil).* **anal·y·sis** [ə'næləsɪs] **n.** (pl. **-ses** [-siːz]) process of analysing; statement of the result of this. **an·a·lyst** ['ænəlɪst] **n.** person who is skilled in (esp. chemical) analysis. **an·a·lyt·i·cal** [ˌænə'lɪtɪkl] **adj.**

an·ar·chism ['ænəkɪzəm] **n.** (no pl.) political theory that government and laws are undesirable. **an·ar·chist n.** person who favours ~ or anarchy. **an·ar·chy** ['ænəkɪ] **n.** (no pl.) absence of government or control; disorder.

anat·o·my [ə'nætəmɪ] **n.** (no pl.) science of the structure of the animal body; the study of this structure by the cutting up into parts. **an·a·tom·i·cal** [ˌænə-'tɒmɪkl] **adj.** **anat·o·mist** [ə'nætə-mɪst] **n.**

-ance [-əns] **suff.** (forming ns. of quality or instance of it or action): *arrogance; resemblance; assistance.*

an·ces·tor ['ænsestə*] **n.** any one of those persons from whom one's father or mother is descended. **an·ces·tral** [æn'sestrəl] **adj.** **an·ces·try** ['æn-sestrɪ] **n.** all one's ~s.

an·chor ['æŋkə*] **n.** iron hook lowered to the sea bottom to keep a ship at rest: *come to ~, stop sailing and lower the ~; weigh ~, pull up the ~; lie (be, ride) at ~,* be held fast by an ~. **v.t. & i.** make fast with an ~; lower an ~. **~·age** ['æŋkərɪdʒ] **n.** place where ships ~.

an·cient ['eɪnʃənt] **adj.** **1.** belonging to times long past; not modern: *the ~ Greeks.* **2.** very old: *an ~-looking hat.*

an·cil·lary [æn'sɪlərɪ] **adj.** serving or supporting sth. of greater importance; subordinate (*to*): *~ roads.*

-an·cy [-ənsɪ] **suff.** (forming ns. of quality or state): *constancy; infancy.*

and [ænd, ənd, ən] **conj.** word that joins two or more words, clauses, or sentences.

an·ec·dote ['ænɪkdəʊt] **n.** short, usu. amusing, story about some real person or event.

anew [ə'njuː] **adv.** again; in a new way.

an·gel ['eɪndʒəl] **n.** **1.** (in Christian belief) messenger from God (usu. shown in pictures as a person in white with wings). **2.** person felt to resemble an ~: *She's an ~,* a very kind, good woman. **~·ic** [æn'dʒelɪk] **adj.** of ~s; good, pure, and beautiful.

an·ger ['æŋgə*] **n.** (no pl.) the strong feeling that comes when one has been wronged or treated badly, or when one sees cruelty or injustice; the feeling that makes people want to quarrel or fight. **v.t.** fill with ~; make angry.

an·gle[1] ['æŋgl] **n.** **1.** space between two lines or surfaces that meet. **2.** (fig.) point of view. **'~-park v.t. & i.** park a car at an angle to the roadside. **'~-park·ing n.**

an·gle[2] ['æŋgl] **v.i.** try to catch fish with a rod, line, hook, and bait. *~ for,* (fig.) try by roundabout ways to get sth. *~r n.*

An·gli·can ['æŋglɪkən] **n. & adj.** (member) of the Church of England.

An·gli·cist ['æŋglɪsɪst] **n.** see *Anglist.*

an·gli·cize ['æŋglɪsaɪz] **v.t.** make (a word, etc.) English or similar to English.

An·glist ['æŋglɪst] **n.** student of or scholar in the English language or English literature. **An·glis·tics** [æn-'glɪstɪks] **n. pl.** (sing. v.) study of the English language or of English literature.

An·glo- ['æŋgləʊ-] **pref.** English: *Anglo-American,* of England and America.

an·gry ['æŋgrɪ] **adj.** (**-ier, -iest**) **1.** filled with anger (*with* sb., *about* sth.). **2.** (of the sea, sky) threatening. **3.** (of a wound) red, inflamed. **an·gri·ly adv.**

an·guish ['æŋgwɪʃ] **n.** (no pl.) severe suffering (esp. of mind). **~ed adj.** suffering or expressing ~: *~ed looks.*

an·gu·lar ['æŋgjʊlə*] **adj.** **1.** having angles or sharp corners. **2.** (of a person) thin; with bones showing under the skin.

an·i·line ['ænɪliːn] *n.* oily liquid got from coal tar, used in the manufacture of dyes, drugs, etc.

an·i·mal ['ænɪml] *n.* **1.** living thing that can move about and feel, including men, dogs, birds, insects, fish, snakes. **2.** ~ other than man. **3.** four-footed ~ (e.g. a dog or cat). **4.** (attrib.) of the physical, not spiritual, side of man: ~ *needs* (e.g. food); ~ *spirits*, natural light-heartedness.

an·i·mate ['ænɪmeɪt] *v.t.* make bright and full of life: *A smile ~d her face.* **an·i·mat·ed** *adj.* lively: *an ~d discussion. ~d cartoon*, cinema film made by photographing a series of drawings. **an·i·ma·tion** [,ænɪ'meɪʃn] *n.* **1.** liveliness. **2.** ~d cartoon.

an·i·mos·i·ty [,ænɪ'mɒsətɪ] *n.* active and bitter hate.

an·kle ['æŋkl] *n.* joint (2) and thin part of the human leg just above the foot.

an·nals ['ænlz] *n. pl.* historical records; accounts; year by year, of new knowledge; yearly records of the work of a society.

an·nex[1] ['æneks] *v.t.* add or join to (a larger thing); take possession of (a country or territory). **~·a·tion** [,ænek-'seɪʃn] *n.* (no pl.).

an·nex[2], **an·nexe** ['æneks] *n.* smaller building added to or built close to a larger one: *an ~ to a hotel.*

an·ni·hi·late [ə'naɪəleɪt] *v.t.* destroy completely. **an·ni·hi·la·tion** [ə,naɪə-'leɪʃn] *n.* (no pl.).

an·ni·ver·sa·ry [,ænɪ'vɜːsərɪ] *n.* yearly return of the date on which sth. happened: *celebrate a wedding ~.*

an·no·tate ['ænəʊteɪt] *v.t.* add notes (explaining difficulties, giving opinions, etc.). **an·no·ta·tion** [,ænəʊ'teɪʃn] *n.*

an·nounce [ə'naʊns] *v.t.* make known (news, the name of a guest, speaker, etc.); give or be a sign of. **an·nounc·er** *n.* (esp.) person who ~s radio and television programmes, reads news summaries, etc. **~·ment** *n.*

an·noy [ə'nɔɪ] *v.t.* give trouble to; make rather angry. **~·ance** *n.* **~·ing** *adj.* irritating.

an·nu·al ['ænjʊəl] *adj.* **1.** coming or happening every year. **2.** lasting for one year. **3.** of one year: ~ *income. n.* **1.** plant that lives only for a year. **2.** book, etc. that appears under the same title but with new contents every year. **~·ly** *adv.*

an·nu·i·ty [ə'njuːɪtɪ] *n.* fixed sum of money paid to sb. yearly as income during his lifetime; form of insurance to provide such a regular, annual income.

an·nul [ə'nʌl] *v.t.* (-*ll*-) put an end to (a law, agreement, etc.); (in law) make of no effect.

an·ode ['ænəʊd] *n.* (electr.) positive electrode, from which current enters.

an·o·dyne ['ænəʊdaɪn] *n. & adj.* (medicine, drug) able to lessen pain.

anoint [ə'nɔɪnt] *v.t.* pour or rub oil on (the head or body), esp. at a religious ceremony.

anom·a·lous [ə'nɒmələs] *adj.* not normal or regular. **anom·a·ly** [ə'nɒməlɪ] *n.* ~ thing.

anon·y·mous [ə'nɒnɪməs] *adj.* without a name, or with a name which is not made known: *an ~ gift; an ~ letter* (i.e. unsigned); *by an ~ author. ~·ly adv.*

an·o·rak ['ænəræk] *n.* weatherproof jacket with a hood.

an·oth·er [ə'nʌðə*] *adj. & pron.* a different (one); one more of the same kind. *one ~,* each to each: *Tom and Mary give one ~ presents at Christmas.*

an·swer ['ɑːnsə*] *n.* sth. spoken, written, or done in return to: *give no ~,* say nothing in return. *v.t. & i.* say, write, or do sth. in return (to sth. said, etc.): ~ *a question* (*a letter*). ~ *back,* give an impolite ~, esp. when being corrected; ~ *a purpose,* be suitable or sufficient; ~ *the bell* (*the door*), go to the door when sb. has knocked or rung the bell; ~ *for,* (a) be responsible for: ~ *for a person's honesty;* (b) atone for: ~ *for wrongdoing;* ~ *to,* correspond to: ~ *to a description.* **~·able** ['ɑːnsərəbl] *pred. adj.* responsible (*to* sb. *for* sth.).

ant [ænt] *n.* small, hard-working insect that lives in highly organized societies. **'~·heap, '~·hill** *ns.* pile of earth over ants' nest; nest of termites.

an ant   an antelope

-ant [-ənt] *suff.* (forming adjs. and ns.): *significant; assistant.*

an·tag·o·nism [æn'tægənɪzəm] *n.* hostility; active opposition. **an·tag·o·nist** *n.* opponent; enemy. **an·tag·o·nis·tic** [æn,tægə'nɪstɪk] *adj.* opposed. **an·tag·o·nize** [æn'tægənaɪz] *v.t.* make an enemy of (sb.).

ant·arc·tic [ænt'ɑːktɪk] *adj.* of or near the South Pole. *n.* (no pl.) *the A~,* the area round the South Pole.

an·te- ['æntɪ-] *pref.* before.

an·te·ced·ent [ˌæntɪ'siːdənt] *n.* **1.** (gram.) noun, clause, or sentence to which a following adverb or pronoun refers (*'man'* in *the man who came yesterday*). **2.** (pl.) past history (of a person or persons).

an·te·date [ˌæntɪ'deɪt] *v.t.* **1.** put a date on (e.g. a letter, cheque) earlier than the true one. **2.** come before in time.

an·te·lope ['æntɪləʊp] *n.* deerlike animal.

an·te me·ri·di·em [ˌæntɪ məˈrɪdɪəm] *adj.* (abbr. *a.m.*) between midnight and noon: 9.30 *a.m.*

an·te·na·tal [ˌæntɪ'neɪtl] *adj.* before birth.

an·ten·na [æn'tenə] *n.* (pl. *-ae* [-iː]) **1.** one of the two feelers on the head of an insect, etc. **2.** (pl. usu. *-as*) (esp. U.S.A.) radio or television aerial.

an·te·ri·or [æn'tɪərɪə*] *adj.* coming before in time or position.

an·te·room ['æntɪrʊm] *n.* room leading to a more important one.

an·them ['ænθəm] *n.* piece of sacred music (usu. for choir and organ) sung in churches. *national ~,* the national song or hymn of a country (e.g. 'God Save the Queen').

an·ther ['ænθə*] *n.* (bot.) part of the stamen containing pollen.

an·thol·o·gy [æn'θɒlədʒɪ] *n.* collection of poems or pieces of prose by different writers, or a selection from one writer's works.

an·thro·poid ['ænθrəʊpɔɪd] *adj.* manlike. *n.* manlike animal, esp. an ape (e.g. a chimpanzee).

an·thro·pol·o·gy [ˌænθrəˈpɒlədʒɪ] *n.* (no pl.) science of man, esp. of the beginnings, development, beliefs, and customs of mankind. **an·thro·pol·o·gist** *n.* expert in *~.*

an·ti- ['æntɪ-] *pref.* against; opposite: *anti-aircraft guns.*

an·ti·bi·ot·ic [ˌæntɪbaɪˈɒtɪk] *n.* substance (like penicillin), produced by bacteria, that destroys or prevents the growth of disease germs.

an·tic·i·pate [æn'tɪsɪpeɪt] *v.t.* **1.** do or make use of before the right or natural time: *~ one's next month's pay.* **2.** do sth. before sb. else does it. **3.** see what needs doing and do it in advance: *~ a person's needs.* **4.** look forward to. **5.** expect. **an·tic·i·pa·tion** [ænˌtɪsɪ'peɪʃn] *n.* (no pl.).

an·ti·cli·max [ˌæntɪ'klaɪmæks] *n.* sudden fall or change from sth. noble, serious, or important.

an·tics ['æntɪks] *n. pl.* playful, jumping movements, often amusing; absurd behaviour.

an·ti·cy·clone [ˌæntɪ'saɪkləʊn] *n.* area in which atmospheric pressure is high.

an·ti·dote ['æntɪdəʊt] *n.* medicine to prevent poison or disease from having an effect.

an·ti·freeze ['æntɪfriːz] *n.* (no pl.) substance added to water to lower its freezing-point (e.g. as used in the radiator (2) of a motor car).

an·ti·he·ro ['æntɪˌhɪərəʊ] *n.* hero who is lacking in the traditional characteristics of a hero (e.g. courage).

an·ti·knock [ˌæntɪ'nɒk] *n.* (no pl.) substance added to the fuel in a motor car engine to reduce (1) noise.

an·tip·a·thy [æn'tɪpəθɪ] *n.* fixed, lasting feeling of dislike.

an·tip·o·des [æn'tɪpədiːz] *n. pl.* those parts of the world which are on the opposite side, esp. Australia and New Zealand.

an·ti·quar·i·an [ˌæntɪ'kweərɪən] *adj.* (of the study) of antiquities. *n.* antiquary. **an·ti·quary** ['æntɪkwərɪ] *n.* person who studies, collects, or sells antiquities.

an·ti·quat·ed ['æntɪkweɪtɪd] *adj.* out of date; no longer in use; (of a person) having old-fashioned ways and ideas.

an·tique [æn'tiːk] *adj.* belonging to the distant past; in the style of past times. *n.* furniture, jewellery, etc. of a past period.

an·ti·qui·ty [æn'tɪkwətɪ] *n.* **1.** (no pl.) the distant past; early times in history, esp. the times of the Greeks and Romans: *Athens was a great city of ~.* **2.** (pl.) buildings, ruins, works of art remaining from very early times: *Greek and Roman antiquities.*

an·ti·Sem·ite [ˌæntɪ'siːmaɪt] *n. & adj.* (person) hostile to Jews. **an·ti·Sem·it·ic** [ˌæntɪsɪ'mɪtɪk] *adj.*

an·ti·sep·tic [ˌæntɪ'septɪk] *n. & adj.* (chemical substance for) destroying germs and preventing their growth.

an·ti·so·cial [ˌæntɪ'səʊʃl] *adj.* against the principles on which society is based; not sociable: *~ behaviour.*

an·tith·e·sis [æn'tɪθɪsɪs] *n.* (pl. *-es* [-iːz]) direct opposite; the putting together of opposite ideas.

an·ti·tox·in [ˌæntɪ'tɒksɪn] *n.* substance (usu. a serum) able to counteract a poison.

an·ti·trust [ˌæntɪ'trʌst] *adj.* (U.S.A.)

2*

(of law, etc.) opposed (1) to trusts (5) or other monopolies.

ant·ler ['æntlə*] *n.* branched horn of a stag or other deer; one of the branches.

antlers   an anvil

an·to·nym ['æntəʊnɪm] *n.* word opposite in meaning to another: *Hot is the ~ of cold.* (Cf. *synonym.*)

anus ['eɪnəs] *n.* (anat.) the posterior (2) opening (2) of the alimentary canal.

an·vil ['ænvɪl] *n.* 1. block of iron on which heated metal is hammered into shape. 2. (anat.) bone in the ear.

anx·i·ety [æŋ'zaɪətɪ] *n.* 1. feeling of uncertainty and fear about sth. 2. eager desire: *~ for knowledge.* **anx·ious** ['æŋkʃəs] *adj.* feeling ~; causing ~; strongly wishing (to do or get sth.).

any ['enɪ] *adj., pron., & adv.* I. *adj.* 1. (In neg. and interr. sentences, clauses of condition, etc.; see *some,* I. definition (1).) 2. *We did the work without any difficulty* (easily). *I have hardly any food in the larder* (very little food). *See that you do not do any damage* (do no damage). *Try to prevent any* (even one) *person from entering.* 3. no matter which: *Come any day you like.* 4. in *any case,* whatever happens; *at any rate,* at least. II. *pron.* see *some,* II. III. *adv.* (Cf. *no, none.*) at all; in any degree: *Is your father any better? This pen isn't any use* (i.e. it won't write). **any·body** ['enɪ,bɒdɪ] *n. & pron.* 1. (In neg. and interr., etc. sentences; see *somebody, someone.*) 2. a person (it does not matter who it is): *Anybody who saw the accident is asked to get in touch with the police.* **any·body else,** see *else* (1). 3. person of importance: *Is he anybody, or just a nobody* (unknown person)? **any·how** ['enɪhaʊ] *adv.* 1. by one means or another: *The door was shut and I could not open it anyhow.* 2. carelessly; without order: *The work was done all anyhow. The room was left just anyhow* (untidy). 3. in any case; at any rate: *Anyhow, its too late now.* **any·one** ['enɪwʌn] *n. & pron.* anybody. **any·thing** ['enɪθɪŋ] *n. & pron.* 1. (In neg. and interr.,

etc. sentences; see *something.*) 2. *I don't want anything to eat* (I don't want food) *but I should like something to drink. Has anything* (it does not matter what) *happened since I was last here?* **any·way** ['enɪweɪ] *adv.* anyhow. **any·where** ['enɪweə*] *adv.* 1. (In neg. and interr., etc. sentences; see *somewhere.*) in or to any place: *Do you want to go anywhere special* (to one particular place)? *I don't want to live anywhere* (in a place that is) *damp or cold.* 2. *Put the box down anywhere* (it does not matter where).

aor·ta [eɪ'ɔːtə] *n.* (anat.) great artery (1) that carries blood from the heart to be distributed by branch arteries through the body.

apart [ə'pɑːt] *adv.* 1. distant: *The two houses are a mile ~.* 2. to or on one side: *He took me ~ and whispered the secret. joking ~,* speaking seriously; *set ~,* put on one side; reserve (2) (for). 3. separate(ly): *I can't get these two pieces ~. ~ from,* independently of. 4. to pieces.

apart·heid [ə'pɑːtheɪt] *n.* (no pl.) (S. Africa) (policy of) racial segregation; separate development of Europeans and non-Europeans.

apart·ment [ə'pɑːtmənt] *n.* 1. (pl.) number of rooms, furnished or unfurnished, owned or rented by the week or month: *take ~s at the seaside for the summer holidays.* 2. single room in a house. 3. (U.S.A.) flat¹. *~ house* (U.S.A.), block¹ (3) of flats¹.

ap·a·thy ['æpəθɪ] *n.* (no pl.) lack of feeling, sympathy, or interest. **ap·a·thet·ic** [,æpə'θetɪk] *adj.* showing ~.

ape [eɪp] *n.* large, tailless monkey able to walk on two feet (e.g. a gorilla or chimpanzee). *v.t.* imitate foolishly.

ap·er·ture ['æpə,tjʊə*] *n.* opening (usu. small or narrow), esp. one that admits light (e.g. to the lens of a camera).

aph·o·rism ['æfərɪzəm] *n.* short, wise saying; proverb.

api·ary ['eɪpjərɪ] *n.* place with a number of hives where bees are kept for their honey.

apiece [ə'piːs] *adv.* to, for, or by each one of a group: *They cost a penny ~,* each.

apol·o·get·ic [ə,pɒlə'dʒetɪk] *adj.* offering an apology.

apol·o·gize [ə'pɒlədʒaɪz] *v.i.* make an apology (*to sb. for sth.*).

apol·o·gy [ə'pɒlədʒɪ] *n.* 1. statement of regret for doing wrong, making a mistake, or hurting sb.'s feelings. 2. explanation or defence (of beliefs, etc.).

ap·o·plec·tic [,æpəʊ'plektɪk] *adj.* suffering from apoplexy; easily made angry.

ap·o·plexy ['æpəʊpleksɪ] *n.* (no pl.) loss of power to feel, move, or think, usu. caused by injury to blood-vessels in the brain.

apos·tle [ə'pɒsl] *n.* **1.** one of the twelve men sent out by Jesus to spread his teaching; missionary of the early Christian Church (e.g. St. Paul). **2.** leader or teacher of a faith or movement: *an ~ of temperance.* **ap·os·tol·ic** [,æpə'stɒlɪk] *adj.* **1.** of the ~s (1). **2.** of the pope.

apos·tro·phe [ə'pɒstrəfɪ] *n.* the sign ('), as in *can't, John's,* etc.

apoth·e·cary [ə'pɒθəkərɪ] *n.* (old use) person who prepared and sold medicines and medical goods; chemist (2).

ap·pal (U.S.A. also **-pall**) [ə'pɔːl] *v.t.* (-*ll-*) fill with fear or terror; shock deeply: *They were ~led at the news.* **~l·ing** *adj.*

ap·pa·ra·tus [,æpə'reɪtəs] *n.* **1.** set of tools, instruments, etc., or a machine, assembled for a special purpose. **2.** organs of the body with a special function: *the digestive ~.*

ap·par·el [ə'pærəl] *n.* (no pl.) (old use or liter.) dress; clothing.

ap·par·ent [ə'pærənt] *adj.* **1.** clearly seen or understood: *as will soon become ~,* as you will soon see. **2.** seeming: *The ~ cause, but not the real cause, was ...* **~ly** *adv.*

ap·pa·ri·tion [,æpə'rɪʃn] *n.* the coming into view, esp. of a ghost or spirit (2); ghost.

ap·peal [ə'piːl] *v.i.* **1.** ask earnestly (*for*). **2.** (law, sport) refer (1) a question or decision (*to* a higher court, etc.). **3.** *~ to,* attract, interest, catch the attention of: *Bright colours ~ to small children. n.* **1.** act of ~ing: *an ~ for help; an ~ to a higher court; an ~ to the referee.* **2.** interest; attraction; power of attraction.

ap·pear [ə'pɪə*] *v.i.* **1.** come into view; arrive. **2.** (of an actor, lecturer, etc.) come before the public. **3.** seem. **~·ance** *n.* **1.** act of ~ing: *put in (make) an ~ance,* show oneself; attend. **2.** that which shows or can be seen; what sth. or sb. seems to be: *judge by ~ances,* form an opinion only from the look of things; *keep up ~ances,* keep up an outward show (in order to hide what one does not wish others to see, e.g. that one is poor); *to (by, from) all ~ance(s),* so far as can be seen.

ap·pease [ə'piːz] *v.t.* make calm or quiet: *~ sb.'s anger;* satisfy (usu. by

giving what is wanted): *~ sb.'s hunger (curiosity).* **~·ment** *n.* (no pl.).

ap·pel·la·tion [,æpə'leɪʃn] *n.* name or title; system of names.

ap·pend [ə'pend] *v.t.* add sth. (*to* sth.) at the end, esp. in writing or in print. **~·age** [ə'pendɪdʒ] *n.* sth. added to, fastened to, or forming a natural part of, a larger thing.

ap·pen·di·ci·tis [ə,pendɪ'saɪtɪs] *n.* (no pl.) (med.) inflammation of the vermiform appendix.

ap·pen·dix [ə'pendɪks] *n.* **1.** (pl. *-dices* [-dɪsiːz]) sth. added, esp. at the end of a book. **2.** (pl. also *-dixes*) (anat.) small outgrowth on the surface of a bodily organ, esp. the *vermiform ~,* a worm-shaped appendage of the large intestine.

ap·per·tain [,æpə'teɪn] *v.i. ~ to,* belong to as a right; be appropriate.

ap·pe·tite ['æpɪtaɪt] *n.* desire (esp. for food): *lose one's ~.* **ap·pe·tiz·er** ['æpɪtaɪzə*] *n.* food or drink that stimulates the ~, usu. served before meals. **ap·pe·tiz·ing** ['æpɪtaɪzɪŋ] *adj.* pleasing to, exciting, the ~: *an appetizing smell.*

ap·plaud [ə'plɔːd] *v.t. & i.* **1.** show approval (of) by clapping the hands, cheering, etc. **2.** express approval of. **ap·plause** [ə'plɔːz] *n.* (no pl.) loud approval; handclapping.

ap·ple ['æpl] *n.* (tree having) fruit with firm (1), juicy flesh. *the ~ of one's eye,* sb. or sth. dearly loved. *~ sauce,* sliced ~s stewed.

apples

ap·pli·ance [ə'plaɪəns] *n.* instrument, tool, or apparatus: *an ~ for rescuing sailors from a wrecked ship* (e.g. by firing a rope to them).

ap·pli·cable ['æplɪkəbl] *adj.* fitting; suitable to be applied: *Rule number five is not ~ to this case.*

ap·pli·cant ['æplɪkənt] *n.* person who applies (*for* sth.).

ap·pli·ca·tion [,æplɪ'keɪʃn] *n.* **1.** (making of a) request: *an ~ for a position; on ~ to,* by asking for or writing to; *~ form,* form to be filled in when applying for sth. **2.** applying (2) of one thing to another; substance so applied: *~s of ice to the forehead.* **3.** bringing a rule to bear on a case: *the ~ of the rule to this case.* **4.** putting to practical use: *the ~ of a discovery to industry.* **5.** effort or attention: *show ~ in one's studies, work hard.*

ap·plied, see *apply.*

ap·ply [ə'plaɪ] *v.t. & i.* **1.** ask for: *~ (to sb.) for a position* (5). **2.** put (sth.) into position to serve its purpose: *~ the brake (a bandage).* **3.** put into use: *~ a rule; money to be applied for the benefit of the poor.* **4.** *~ oneself to,* give one's efforts and attention to. **5.** *~ to,* concern; have reference to: *What I have said does not ~ to you. The rule does not ~ to all cases.* **ap·plied** *adj.* put to practical use: *applied art* (e.g. as used in textile designs, etc.); *applied mathematics* (e.g. as used in engineering).

ap·point [ə'pɔɪnt] *v.t.* **1.** fix or decide (a time or place *for*): *The time ~ed for the meeting was 6 p.m.* **2.** choose and name (sb. to fill a position): *~ a secretary. A~ Miss Smith (to be) secretary of the company.* **~·ment** *n.* **1.** *~ing: meet sb. by ~ment,* after fixing a time and place. **2.** arrangement to meet sb.: *make a ~ment with sb.; have an ~ment with one's dentist; keep (break) an ~ment,* meet (fail to meet) sb. as arranged. **3.** position or office: *get a good ~ment in a business firm.*

ap·por·tion [ə'pɔːʃn] *v.t.* divide (*among*); distribute (*among*); give as a share (*to*).

ap·po·si·tion [ˌæpəʊ'zɪʃn] *n.* (no pl.) (gram.) placing of a word or group of words to give additional information. In the sentence: 'Mr Green, our new teacher, has red hair', the words 'our new teacher' are in *~* to 'Mr Green'.

ap·pre·ci·able [ə'priːʃəbl] *adj.* enough to be seen or felt; noticeable: *an ~ difference.*

ap·pre·ci·ate [ə'priːʃɪeɪt] *v.t. & i.* **1.** judge rightly the value of; understand and enjoy: *~ poetry.* **2.** put a high value on; be grateful for: *~ sb.'s help.* **3.** become higher in value: *This land has ~d greatly since 1970.* **ap·pre·ci·a·tion** [əˌpriːʃɪ'eɪʃn] *n.* **1.** judgement; valuation. **2.** proper understanding and recognition: *in ~ of your help.* **ap·pre·cia·tive** [ə'priːʃjətɪv] *adj.*

ap·pre·hend [ˌæprɪ'hend] *v.t.* **1.** (old use) understand. **2.** (formal) fear. **3.** (law) arrest; seize: *~ a thief.* **ap·pre·hen·sion** [ˌæprɪ'henʃn] *n.* **1.** grasping (of ideas); understanding. **2.** fear. **3.** (law) seizure; arrest. **ap·pre·hen·sive** [ˌæprɪ'hensɪv] *adj.* feeling afraid:

apprehensive for sb.'s safety (of danger that sb. will be hurt).

ap·pren·tice [ə'prentɪs] *n.* learner of a trade who has agreed to work for a number of years in return for being taught. *v.t.* bind as an *~*: *The boy was ~d to a carpenter.* **~·ship** [ə'prentɪʃɪp] *n.* (time of) being an *~*: *serve one's ~ship (with sb.).*

ap·proach [ə'prəʊtʃ] *v.t. & i.* **1.** come near or nearer (*to*): *The rainy season is ~ing. He is ~ing manhood.* **2.** go to (sb.) with a request or offer: *~ one's employer for higher pay.* *n.* **1.** act of *~ing.* **2.** way to a place, person, or thing: *The ~es to the palace were all guarded by soldiers.* **3.** thing or state which comes near: *an ~ to comfort and security.*

ap·pro·ba·tion [ˌæprəʊ'beɪʃn] *n.* (no pl.) sanction (2); approval.

ap·pro·pri·ate [ə'prəʊprɪət] *adj.* right or suitable (*for* a purpose, *to* an occasion). [ə'prəʊprɪeɪt] *v.t.* **1.** take and use (as one's own). **2.** put on one side (*for* a special purpose). **~·ly** *adv.* **ap·pro·pri·a·tion** [əˌprəʊprɪ'eɪʃn] *n.*

ap·prov·al [ə'pruːvl] *n.* (no pl.) feeling, showing, or saying, that one is satisfied: *Your plans have my ~. goods on ~,* goods which may be sent back if they are not satisfactory. **ap·prove** [ə'pruːv] *v.t. & i.* give one's *~ (of*); agree to. *approved school,* (Gt. Brit., hist.) see *Borstal (institution).*

ap·prox·i·mate [ə'prɒksɪmət] *adj.* very near (*to*), about right, in quantity, etc. [ə'prɒksɪmeɪt] *v.t. & i.* bring or come near (*to,* esp. in quality, number, etc.). **ap·prox·i·ma·tion** [əˌprɒksɪ'meɪʃn] *n.*

après-ski [ˌæpreɪ'skiː] *attrib. adj. & n.* (of) the evening period after skiing at a resort: *~ clothes.*

apri·cot ['eɪprɪkɒt] *n.* (tree with) round, soft, orange-yellow fruit with a large seed like a stone; (no pl.) colour of this fruit when ripe.

April ['eɪprəl] *n.* fourth month of the year. *~ fool,* person jokingly fooled on 1 April (= *~ Fool's Day*).

apron ['eɪprən] *n.* **1.** loose garment tied over the front of the body to keep clothes clean; any similar covering. **2.** hard-surfaced area on an airfield, used for loading and unloading aircraft.

ap·ro·pos ['æprəpəʊ] *adv. & pred. adj.* **1.** to the purpose; well suited. **2.** *~ of,* concerning. **3.** incidentally; by the way.

apt [æpt] *adj.* **1.** quick at learning:

one of my ⁓*est pupils*; *very* ⁓ *at picking up a new subject* (2). **2.** suitable; to the point: *an* ⁓ *remark*. **3.** ⁓ *to*, having a tendency to; likely to: *a clever boy but* ⁓ *to get into mischief*. ⁓**ly** *adv.* suitably.

ap·ti·tude ['æptɪtjuːd] *n.* natural tendency or talent (*for*).

aq·ua·lung ['ækwəlʌŋ] *n.* portable breathing apparatus (1) with cylinder(s) of compressed air strapped on a diver's back for use in underwater swimming or diving.

an aqualung

aq·ua·naut ['ækwənɔːt] *n.* person trained to live for a long period in an underwater vessel while engaged (3) in underwater exploration and research.

aq·ua·plane ['ækwəpleɪn] *n.* board on which a person stands while being pulled along by a speedboat. *v.i.* **1.** ride on such a board. **2.** (of a vehicle) glide uncontrollably on water covering the road surface.

aquar·i·um [ə'kweərɪəm] *n.* (pl. ⁓*s*, -*ria*) (building with an) artificial pond or tank for keeping and showing living fish and water plants.

aquat·ic [ə'kwætɪk] *adj. & n.* **I.** *adj.* **1.** (of plants, animals, etc.) growing or living in or near water. **2.** (sport, etc.) taking place in or on water. **II.** *n.* **1.** ⁓ plant or animal. **2.** (pl.) (sing. or pl. v.) water sports.

aq·ue·duct ['ækwɪdʌkt] *n.* artificial channel for supplying water, esp. one made of brick or stone and higher than the surrounding land.

aq·ui·line ['ækwɪlaɪn] *adj.* of or like an eagle's : ⁓ *nose*, hooked like an eagle's beak.

Ar·ab ['ærəb] *n. & adj.* (any) of the Arabic-speaking Semitic people of the Arabian Peninsula, now the Middle East generally.

Ara·bi·an [ə'reɪbjən] *n. & adj.* (native or inhabitant) of Arabia.

Ar·a·bic ['ærəbɪk] *adj.* of Arabia or the Arabs: ⁓ *numerals*, the number symbols 0, 1, 2, 3, etc. *n.* language of the Arabs.

ar·able ['ærəbl] *adj.* (of land) ploughed or suitable for ploughing.

ar·bi·ter ['ɑːbɪtə*] *n.* **1.** arbitrator. **2.** person with complete control (*of*).

ar·bi·trary ['ɑːbɪtrərɪ] *adj.* **1.** based on opinion rather than reason: *an* ⁓ *decision*. **2.** overbearing or dictatorial.

ar·bi·trate ['ɑːbɪtreɪt] *v.t. & i.* judge between two parties to a dispute (usu. at the request of the two parties). **ar·bi·tra·tor** *n.* person who ⁓s. **ar·bi·tra·tion** [,ɑːbɪ'treɪʃn] *n.* (no pl.).

ar·bour (U.S.A. **ar·bor**) ['ɑːbə*] *n.* shady place with sides and roof formed mainly by trees or climbing plants.

arc [ɑːk] *n.* part of the circumference of a circle or other curved line.

ar·cade [ɑː'keɪd] *n.* covered passage, usu. with arches, esp. one with shops along one or both sides.

arch[1] [ɑːtʃ] *n.* **1.** curved structure supporting the weight of what is above it: *a bridge with three* ⁓*es*. **2.** curved structure built as an ornament or gateway. **3.** curve like an ⁓ (e.g. the curved underpart of the foot). *v.t. & i.* **1.** form into an ⁓: *The cat* ⁓*ed its back when it saw the dog*. **2.** be like an ⁓: *The trees* ⁓ *over the river*.

an arena   *an arch*[1]

arch[2] [ɑːtʃ] *attrib. adj.* playfully mischievous: *an* ⁓ *smile*.

arch- [ɑːtʃ-] *pref.* **1.** chief. **2.** extreme: *arch-fiend*.

ar·chae·ol·o·gy (U.S.A. **ar·che-**) [,ɑːkɪ'ɒlədʒɪ] *n.* (no pl.) study of (often after digging up) ancient things, esp. of very early times (e.g. ancient cities, buildings, and monuments). **ar·chae·o·log·i·cal** (U.S.A. **ar·che-**) [,ɑːkɪə'lɒdʒɪkl] *adj.* of ⁓. **ar·chae·ol·o·gist** (U.S.A. **ar·che-**) [,ɑːkɪ'ɒlədʒɪst] *n.* expert in ⁓.

ar·cha·ic [ɑː'keɪɪk] *adj.* **1.** of ancient times. **2.** (of language) not now used.

arch·an·gel ['ɑːk,eɪndʒəl] *n.* angel of highest rank. (bishop.)

arch·bish·op [,ɑːtʃ'bɪʃəp] *n.* chief

arch·dea·con [,ɑːtʃ'diːkən] *n.* (in the Church of England) priest next below a bishop.

arch·er ['ɑːtʃə*] *n.* person who shoots with a bow and arrows. ⁓**y** *n.* (no pl.) (art of) shooting with a bow and arrows.

ar·chi·pel·a·go [ˌɑːkɪˈpeləgəʊ] *n.* sea with many islands; group of small islands.

ar·chi·tect [ˈɑːkɪtekt] *n.* person who designs buildings and looks after the work of building. **ar·chi·tec·ture** [ˈɑːkɪtektʃə*] *n.* (no pl.) art and science of building; design or style of building(s). **ar·chi·tec·tur·al** [ˌɑːkɪˈtektʃərəl] *adj.*

ar·chives [ˈɑːkaɪvz] *n. pl.* (place for keeping) government or public records; other historical records.

arch·way [ˈɑːtʃweɪ] *n.* arch¹ (2).

arc·tic [ˈɑːktɪk] *adj.* of or near the region around the North Pole: *the A~ Ocean*; *~ weather*, very cold weather. *n.* (no pl.) *~ regions.*

ar·dent [ˈɑːdənt] *adj.* full of ardour.

ar·dour (U.S.A. **-dor**) [ˈɑːdə*] *n.* enthusiasm; warmth of feeling; earnestness

ar·du·ous [ˈɑːdjʊəs] *adj.* (of work) needing and using up much energy.

are, see *be*.

ar·ea [ˈeərɪə] *n.* 1. surface measure; extent of surface: *an ~ of 20 square metres*; *a field ten acres in ~.* 2. part of the earth's surface; region: *desert ~s of N. Africa.*

are·na [əˈriːnə] *n.* central part, for games and fights, of an amphitheatre; (fig.) any scene of competition or struggle: *the ~ of politics.* (See the picture

aren't, see *be*. [at *arch¹*.)

ar·gue [ˈɑːgjuː] *v.i. & t.* 1. give reasons (for and against plans, opinions, etc.): *~ sb. into (out of) sth.*, persuade sb. to do it (not to do it) by giving reasons. 2. show; be a sign of. 3. maintain one's views in discussion. **ar·gu·ment** [ˈɑːgjʊmənt] *n.* **ar·gu·men·ta·tive** [ˌɑːgjʊˈmentətɪv] *adj.* fond of arguing; full of arguments.

ar·id [ˈærɪd] *adj.* (of soil, land) dry; barren. **arid·i·ty** [əˈrɪdətɪ] *n.* (no pl.).

aright [əˈraɪt] *adv.* rightly.

arise [əˈraɪz] *v.i.* (p.t. *arose* [əˈrəʊz], p.p. *~n* [əˈrɪzn]) 1. come into existence; come to notice: *A new difficulty has ~n.* 2. result (*from*): *conditions arising from (out of) the war.* 3. (old use) get up; stand up.

ar·is·toc·ra·cy [ˌærɪˈstɒkrəsɪ] *n.* 1. (country or state with a) government by persons of the highest social rank. 2. ruling body (5) of nobles; class (1) of nobles. 3. any group of the most distinguished persons: *an ~ of intellect.*

aris·to·crat [ˈærɪstəkræt] *n.* member of the class (1) of nobles; nobleman.

aris·to·crat·ic [ˌærɪstəˈkrætɪk] *adj.*

arith·me·tic [əˈrɪθmətɪk] *n.* (no pl.) science of, working with, numbers. **ar·ith·met·i·cal** [ˌærɪθˈmetɪkl] *adj.* of *~.* **arith·me·ti·cian** [ə,rɪθməˈtɪʃn] *n.* expert in *~.*

ark [ɑːk] *n.* (in the Bible) covered ship in which Noah and his family were saved from the Flood.

arm¹ [ɑːm] *n.* 1. one of the two upper limbs of the human body, from the shoulder to the hand. 2. sleeve. 3. large branch of a tree. 4. sth. resembling an *~*: *an ~ of the sea.* '**~-chair** *n.* chair with supports for the *~s.* '**~-pit** *n.* hollow under the *~* where it joins the shoulder.

arm² [ɑːm] *n.* 1. (usu. pl.) weapon: *in ~s*, having weapons; ready to fight; *bear ~s*, serve in the army; *~s race*, competition among nations on military strength. 2. branch or division of a country's military forces: *the air ~*; *the infantry ~.* 3. (pl.) pictorial design used by a noble family, town, etc.: *coat of ~s*, such a design on a shield, etc. *v.t. & i.* 1. supply with weapons; prepare for war: *the ~ed forces*, the military forces. 2. supply with anything protective or useful: *~ed with patience*; *~ed with answers to all likely questions.*

a suit of armour   a coat of arms

ar·ma·ment [ˈɑːməmənt] *n.* 1. military and naval forces equipped for war. 2. process of preparing for war. 3. (usu. pl.) weapons, esp. guns on a warship, tank, etc.

ar·mi·stice [ˈɑːmɪstɪs] *n.* agreement during a war or battle to stop fighting for a time.

ar·mour (U.S.A. **ar·mor**) [ˈɑːmə*] *n.* (no pl.) 1. defensive metal covering for the body (hist.), for warships, tanks, motor vehicles, etc. 2. motor vehicles, tanks, etc. protected with *~.* **~ed** *adj.* 1. covered or protected with *~*: *~ed car (cruiser).* 2. equipped with *~ed cars, tanks, etc.: *~ed division.*

~·er *n.* 1. maker or repairer of arms² (1) and *~.* 2. man in charge of arms²

(1). '**~-plate** *n.* sheet of metal used as ~.

ar·my ['ɑːmɪ] *n.* **1.** military forces of a country; large body (5) of men trained for fighting on land. **2.** any large body (5) of organized persons: *the Salvation A~; an ~ of officials.*

aro·ma [ə'rəʊmə] *n.* (no pl.) sweet smell. **ar·o·mat·ic** [ˌærəʊ'mætɪk] *adj.* fragrant; spicy.

arose, *see* **arise.**

around [ə'raʊnd] *adv. & prep.* **1.** on every side; in every direction. **2.** about; round; here and there. **3.** (U.S.A.) = approximately.

arouse [ə'raʊz] *v.t.* awaken; stir into activity: *Her jealousy is easily ~d.*

ar·range [ə'reɪndʒ] *v.t. & i.* **1.** put in order. **2.** make plans; give instructions: ~ *a marriage;* ~ *for the car to be there;* ~ *a date for a meeting.* **3.** come to an agreement (*with* sb., *about* sth.). **4.** adapt (a piece of music) for different instruments, etc.; adapt (a play). **5.** settle: ~ *differences.* **~·ment** *n.* **1.** arranging or being ~d. **2.** (pl.) plans; preparations. **3.** agreement; settlement. **4.** result or manner of arranging: *an ~ment (of music) for the piano.*

ar·ray [ə'reɪ] *v.t.* **1.** place (soldiers) in order for battle. **2.** (liter.) dress. *n.* **1.** (liter.) order or arrangement (for fighting): *in battle ~.* **2.** display: *a fine ~ of tools.* **3.** (liter.) dress: *in rich ~.*

ar·rears [ə'rɪəz] *n. pl.* **1.** overdue payments: ~ *of rent (wages).* **2.** work, etc. still waiting to be done: ~ *of correspondence,* letters waiting to be answered; *in ~ (with),* behindhand (with).

ar·rest [ə'rest] *v.t.* **1.** put a stop to (a process, etc.): ~ *the decay of the law.* **2.** catch (sb.'s attention). **3.** make (sb.) a prisoner; seize (a thief, etc.) by the authority of the law. *n.* act of ~ing: *make an ~; under ~,* held as a prisoner. **~·ing** *adj.* likely to catch the attention.

ar·riv·al [ə'raɪvl] *n.* **1.** act of arriving. **2.** sb. or sth. that arrives.

ar·rive [ə'raɪv] *v.i.* **1.** reach the end of a journey; come to a place: ~ *home;* ~ *at a port.* **2.** ~ *at,* agree on; fix; settle: ~ *at a decision (a price).* **3.** (of time) come: *The time for action has ~d.* **4.** establish one's reputation; become well known.

ar·ro·gant ['ærəgənt] *adj.* behaving in or showing a superior, proud manner. **~·ly** *adv.* **ar·ro·gance** *n.* (no pl.).

ar·row ['ærəʊ] *n.* **1.** thin, pointed stick (to be) shot from a bow. **2.** the mark or sign (→). '**~·head** *n.* pointed end of an ~.

arse [ɑːs] *n.* (U.S.A. *ass*²) (vulg.) buttocks.

ar·se·nal ['ɑːsənl] *n.* **1.** government building(s) where weapons and ammunition are made or stored. **2.** (lit. or fig.) store (1) of weapons.

ar·se·nic ['ɑːsənɪk] *n.* (no pl.) (chem.) chemical element; strong poison.

ar·son ['ɑːsn] *n.* (no pl.) act of setting sth. on fire intentionally and unlawfully.

art¹ [ɑːt] *n.* **1.** work of man, not of nature. **2.** study and creation or expression of things which give pleasure to the mind through the senses or feelings; fine skill in such expression: *a work of ~* (e.g. a fine painting or piece of sculpture). *the fine ~s,* those appealing to the mind or to the sense of beauty, as poetry, music, and esp. painting, sculpture, architecture. **3.** activity, esp. branch of learning in which skill and practice are needed as well as knowledge: *Grammar is a science but speaking a language is an ~. the ~s subjects* (e.g. history, literature, etc. contrasted with science subjects); *Bachelor (Master) of A~s,* person who has passed the examination and fulfilled other conditions for the award of a university degree in such branches of learning as history, languages, literature. (Cf. *the sciences.*) **4.** cunning behaviour; tricks.

art² [ɑːt] old pres. t. form of *be,* used with *thou: Thou ~,* you are.

ar·te·ri·al [ɑː'tɪərɪəl] *adj.* of or like an artery: ~ *blood;* ~ *roads,* important main roads.

ar·te·ry ['ɑːtərɪ] *n.* **1.** one of the tubes carrying blood from the heart to all parts of the body (cf. *vein*). **2.** main road or river; channel for supplies: *an ~ of traffic.*

art·ful ['ɑːtfʊl] *adj.* cunning; deceitful.

ar·thri·tis [ɑː'θraɪtɪs] *n.* (no pl.) (med.) inflammation of a joint or joints.

ar·ti·cle ['ɑːtɪkl] *n.* **1.** particular or separate thing: ~*s of clothing;* toilet ~*s.* **2.** piece of writing, complete in itself, in a newspaper or other periodical: *leading ~,* (in a newspaper) ~ expressing the views of the editor(s). **3.** (law) separate clause or item in an agreement. **4.** (gram.) *definite ~,* 'the'; *indefinite ~,* 'a', 'an'. *v.t.* bind (e.g. an apprentice) by ~s.

ar·tic·u·late [ɑː'tɪkjʊlət] *adj.* **1.** (of speech) clear. **2.** (of persons) able to put thoughts and feelings into clear speech. [ɑː'tɪkjʊleɪt] *v.t. & i.* say (words), speak, clearly and distinctly.

ar·tic·u·la·tion [ɑː‚tɪkjʊˈleɪʃn] *n.* (no pl.).

ar·ti·fice [ˈɑːtɪfɪs] *n.* **1.** skill; skilful way of doing sth. **2.** cunning; trick.

ar·ti·fi·cer [ɑːˈtɪfɪsə*] *n.* craftsman.

ar·ti·fi·cial [‚ɑːtɪˈfɪʃl] *adj.* not natural or real; made by man in imitation of a natural object: ~ *flowers* (*teeth, light*); ~ *smiles* (forced; insincere); ~ *respiration*, method of forcing air into and out of the lungs of a person whose breathing has stopped.

ar·til·lery [ɑːˈtɪlərɪ] *n.* (no pl.) big guns, usu. those mounted on wheels; branch of an army that uses these.

ar·ti·san [‚ɑːtɪˈzæn] *n.* skilled workman in industry or trade.

art·ist [ˈɑːtɪst] *n.* **1.** person who practises one of the fine arts, esp. painting. **2.** person of great skill. **ar·tiste** [ɑːˈtiːst] *n.* professional singer, dancer, etc.

ar·tis·tic [ɑːˈtɪstɪk] *adj.* **1.** of art or ~s. **2.** showing, done with, skill and good taste. **3.** fond of, able to appreciate, what is beautiful.

art·less [ˈɑːtlɪs] *adj.* natural; simple; innocent.

arty [ˈɑːtɪ] *adj.* (colloq.) pretending to be artistic.

-ary [-(ə)rɪ] *suff.* (forming adjs. and ns.): *contrary; dictionary*.

as [æz, əz] *adv. & conj.* **I.** *adv.* (followed by *as*, conj.): *I'm as tall as you* (i.e. we are the same height). **II.** *conj.* **1.** when; while: *I saw him as he fell* (*as he was falling*). **2.** (expressing reason) since; seeing that: *As he wasn't ready, we went without him.* **3.** (in comparisons): *It's as easy as ABC. This box is twice as heavy as that one.* **4.** in the way in which: *Do as I do.* **5.** like: *He escaped from prison dressed as a woman.* **6.** in the character of: *We think of Napoleon as a soldier and as a statesman.* **7.** (also *such as*): *I should like to visit the ancient cities of Europe,* (*such*) *as Athens and Rome.* **8.** *Such women as knew Tom* (Those who did know him) *admired him.* **9.** *as if, as though*: *She spoke to me as if* (*as though*) *she knew me, but I had never met her before.* **10.** *so as to*, in order to: *He stood up so as to see better.* **11.** *as* (so) *long as*, (a) on condition that; (b) while. **12.** *as for*, with regard to: *As for you, I never want to see you again.* **13.** *as good as*, the same thing as: *Will he be as good as his word?* Will he do what he promised? *Be as good as dead*, almost dead. **14.** *as much*, so: *I thought as much.*

as·bes·tos [æzˈbestɒs] *n.* (no pl.) soft, fibrous mineral substance that can be woven into a material that will not burn.

as·cend [əˈsend] *v.t. & i.* go or come up (a river, mountain, etc.). ~ *the throne*, become king or queen. **as·cen·dan·cy, as·cen·den·cy** [əˈsendənsɪ] *n.* (no pl.) (position of) having power (over): *gain* (*have*) *the ~ancy over one's rivals.* **as·cen·dant, as·cen·dent** [əˈsendənt] *n.* *in the ~ant*, rising in importance and influence. **as·cen·sion** [əˈsenʃn] *n.* act of ~ing. *the Ascension,* the departure of Jesus from the earth: **as·cent** [əˈsent] *n.* act of ~ing; way up: *the ascent of a mountain.*

as·cer·tain [‚æsəˈteɪn] *v.t.* find out (for certain); get to know.

as·cet·ic [əˈsetɪk] *n. & adj.* (person) leading a severely simple life without ordinary pleasures, often for religious reasons.

ascor·bic ac·id [əˈskɔːbɪk ˈæsɪd] *n.* (no pl.) vitamin C.

as·cribe [əsˈkraɪb] *v.t.* **1.** consider as the cause, origin, reason, or author of: *He ~d his failure to bad luck.* **2.** consider as belonging to: ~ *a wrong meaning to a word.* **as·crip·tion** [əsˈkrɪpʃn] *n.*

asep·tic [əˈseptɪk] *adj.* (of wounds, etc.) free from bacteria.

ash[1] [æʃ] *n.* **1.** (sing. or pl.) powder left after sth. has burnt: *The house was burnt to ~es.* **2.** (pl.) the remains of a human body after cremation.

ash[2] [æʃ] *n.* (wood of a) forest-tree with silver-grey bark.

ashamed [əˈʃeɪmd] *pred. adj.* ~ (of, that, to do sth.), feeling shame: *I feel ~ for you, on your account.*

ash-bin [ˈæʃbɪn] *n.* (U.S.A. *ash can*) dustbin.

ash·en [ˈæʃn] *adj.* of ashes; ash-coloured; pale: *His face turned ~.*

ashore [əˈʃɔː*] *adv.* to, on, on to, the shore: *go ~*; (of a ship) *be driven ~ by the gale.*

ash-tray [ˈæʃtreɪ] *n.* small receptacle for tobacco ash, etc.

Ash Wednes·day [‚æʃ ˈwenzdɪ] *n.* first day of Lent.

ashy [ˈæʃɪ] *adj.* (-*ier*, -*iest*) ashen; covered with ashes.

Asian [ˈeɪʃn] *n. & adj.* (native or inhabitant) of Asia.

aside [əˈsaɪd] *adv.* on or to one side; away: *lay one's book ~; turn ~ from the main road.* *n.* words spoken ~, esp. (on the stage) words spoken which other persons on the stage are not supposed to hear.

ask [ɑːsk] *v.t. & i.* **1.** seek an answer to (a question); make request (*for* help, information). **2.** ~ *after*, make inquiry about the health, etc. of (sb.). **3.** invite: *We have been* ~*ed to dinner with the Joneses tomorrow.* **4.** request (permission): *I must* ~ *to be excused.* **5.** demand (a price): *The owner is* ~*ing £ 50,000 for that house.*

askance [ə'skæns] *adv.* look ~ *at*, look at with suspicion.

askew [ə'skjuː] *adv. & pred. adj.* out of the straight or usual (level) position: *hang a picture* ~; *have one's hat on* ~.

aslant [ə'slɑːnt] *adv. & prep.* in a slanting direction.

asleep [ə'sliːp] *adv. & pred. adj.* sleeping: *He was fast* ~. **2.** (of the arms or legs) without feeling (as when under pressure).

aso·cial [,eɪ'səʊʃl] *adj.* **1.** selfish. **2.** withdrawn from society.

asp [æsp] *n.* small, poisonous snake of N. Africa.

as·par·a·gus [əs'pærəgəs] *n.* (no pl.) plant of which the young shoots are used as a vegetable.

as·pect ['æspekt] *n.* **1.** look or appearance: *a man of fierce* ~. **2.** direction in which a building, etc. faces: *a house with a southern* ~; (fig.) *examine the different* ~*s of a subject* (i.e. from every direction).

as·pen ['æspən] *n.* kind of poplar with leaves that move in the slightest wind.

as·per·i·ty [æs'perətɪ] *n.* roughness; severity (of weather); harshness (of manner).

as·phalt ['æsfælt] *n.* (no pl.) black, sticky, waterproof substance; this substance mixed with gravel or crushed rock to give a smooth surface to roads.

as·phyx·ia [æs'fɪksɪə] *n.* (no pl.) condition caused by lack of enough oxygen in the blood; suffocation. **as·phyx·i·ate** [əs'fɪksɪeɪt] *v.t.* make ill or cause death through lack of oxygen in the blood; suffocate.

as·pic ['æspɪk] *n.* (no pl.) clear meat or fish jelly: *chicken in* ~.

as·pire [əs'paɪə*] *v.i.* desire earnestly (*after, to*): ~ *after knowledge*; ~ *to fame.* **as·pi·ra·tion** [,æspə'reɪʃn] *n.*

as·pi·rin ['æspərɪn] *n.* medicine used for colds and to relieve pain; a tablet of this.

ass[1] [æs] *n.* **1.** (zool.) donkey. **2.** stupid person: *Don't make such an* ~ *of yourself* (i.e. behave so stupidly).

ass[2] [æs] *n.* (U.S.A., vulg.) = arse.

as·sail [ə'seɪl] *v.t.* make an attack upon: *be* ~*ed with doubts and fears.* ~·**ant** *n.* attacker.

as·sas·si·nate [ə'sæsɪneɪt] *v.t.* kill violently and treacherously, esp. for political reasons. **as·sas·sin** [ə'sæsɪn] *n.* person who ~s. **as·sas·si·na·tion** [ə,sæsɪ'neɪʃn] *n.*

as·sault [ə'sɔːlt] *v.t. & n.* (make a) violent and sudden attack (on); rape. *The enemy's positions were taken by* ~.

as·sem·blage [ə'semblɪdʒ] *n.* **1.** collection of persons or things; gathering. **2.** act of assembling; state of being assembled.

as·sem·ble [ə'sembl] *v.t. & i.* **1.** gather together. **2.** put (parts) together: ~ *a car.*

as·sem·bly [ə'semblɪ] *n.* gathering together; number of persons assembled for a special purpose (e.g. a national law-making body). ~ *hall*, one where a school meets for prayers, etc. ~ *line*, (in a factory) line along which parts of machines, motor cars, etc. are put together. ~ *room* (*shop*), place where a machine or its parts are assembled. ~ *rooms*, hall in which meetings, balls, etc. take place.

as·sent [ə'sent] *v.i. & n.* (give one's) agreement (*to*): ~ *to a proposal*; *give one's* ~ (*to* ...).

as·sert [ə'sɜːt] *v.t.* **1.** declare: ~ *one's innocence* (*that one is innocent*). **2.** make a claim to: ~ *one's rights*; ~ *oneself*, insist on one's rights or opinions. **as·ser·tion** [ə'sɜːʃn] *n.* **as·ser·tive** [ə'sɜːtɪv] *adj.* having or showing positive assurance.

as·sess [ə'ses] *v.t.* **1.** fix the amount of (e.g. a tax or fine[3]). **2.** estimate the value of, esp. property for taxation. ~·**ment** *n.* **as·ses·sor** *n.*

as·set ['æset] *n.* **1.** (usu. pl.) anything owned by a person, company, etc. that may be used or sold to pay debts. **2.** valuable or useful quality or skill: *Is your knowledge of English an* ~ *to you?*

as·sid·u·ous [ə'sɪdjuəs] *adj.* diligent; persevering. **as·si·du·ity** [,æsɪ'djuːətɪ] *n.*

as·sign [ə'saɪn] *v.t.* **1.** give (*to* sb.) for use and enjoyment, or as a share or part in a distribution (of work, duty, etc.): *Your teacher* ~*s you work to be done at home.* **2.** name, put forward (as a time, place, reason, purpose, etc.). ~·**ment** *n.* ~*ing*; that which is ~*ed*, esp. (U.S.A.) homework given pupils at school.

as·sim·i·late [ə'sɪmɪleɪt] *v.t. & i.* **1.** (cause food to) become part of the body: *food that* ~*s easily*; ~ *one's food.*

2. (cause people to) become part of another social group or state: *The U.S.A. has ~d people from many European countries.* **3.** (of ideas, etc.) take into the mind. **as·sim·i·la·tion** [əˌsɪmɪˈleɪʃn] *n.* (no pl.).

as·sist [əˈsɪst] *v.t. & i.* help. **~·ance** *n.* (no pl.). **~·ant** *n.* helper: *~ant master* (in a school); *a shop ~ant*, person who serves customers.

as·sizes [əˈsaɪzɪz] *n. pl.* (until 1971) sessions held periodically in every English County to try civil and criminal cases before High Court Judges.

as·so·ci·ate [əˈsəʊʃɪeɪt] *v.t. & i.* **1.** join (persons or things, one *with* another); connect (people, ideas) in one's mind: *~ oneself with others in business*; *~ Egypt with the Nile.* **2.** (*~ with*) be often in the company of. [əˈsəʊʃɪət] *adj.* joined in function or dignity (3). [əˈsəʊʃɪət] *n.* person who ~s with another or others (in work or business). **as·so·ci·a·tion** [əˌsəʊsɪˈeɪʃn] *n.* **1.** associating. **2.** organized body of persons with the same interests (e.g. *the Automobile Association*); *Association football*, (Gt. Brit.) played by two teams of eleven players with a round ball that must not be handled except by the goalkeeper or when throwing in.

as·sort·ed [əˈsɔːtɪd] *adj.* of various sorts; mixed. *ill-(well-)~*, badly (well) suited to one another. **as·sort·ment** [əˈsɔːtmənt] *n.* (esp.) ~ collection of differing examples of one class or several classes.

as·suage [əˈsweɪdʒ] *v.t.* make (pain, suffering, grief, desire) less.

as·sume [əˈsjuːm] *v.t.* **1.** suppose; take as true: *~ the truth of a story (that a story is true).* **2.** take up; undertake: *~ the direction of a business*; *~ office.* **3.** take upon or for oneself: *~ a look of innocence*; *~ a new name.* **as·sum·ing** *adj.* claiming greater importance than one has the right to. **as·sump·tion** [əˈsʌmpʃn] *n.* **1.** act of assuming; sth. ~d. **2.** *the Assumption*, reception of the Virgin Mary bodily into Heaven.

as·sur·ance [əˈʃʊərəns] *n.* **1.** assuring or being assured. **2.** feeling of confidence about oneself, one's abilities, etc.; trust in one's own powers. **3.** (Gt. Brit.) (life) insurance.

as·sure [əˈʃʊə*] *v.t.* **1.** tell with confidence: *I ~ you there is no danger.* **2.** make certain; ensure: *Does hard work always ~ success?* **3.** make (sb.) feel safe or certain of sth.: *Nothing would ~ her that flying was safe. He ~d me of his desire to help.* **4.** (Gt. Brit.)

insure, esp. life. **as·sur·ed·ly** [əˈʃʊərɪdlɪ] *adv.* without doubt.

as·ter·isk [ˈæstərɪsk] *n.* the mark (*).

astern [əˈstɜːn] *adv.* in, at, or towards the stern of a ship or aircraft; backwards: *fall ~ (of)*, get behind (other ships or aircraft); *full speed ~*.

asth·ma [ˈæsmə] *n.* (no pl.) chest disease causing difficulty in breathing. **asth·mat·ic** [æsˈmætɪk] *adj.*

astig·ma·tism [əˈstɪgmətɪzəm] *n.* (no pl.) defect in an eye or lens which prevents a person from seeing clearly.

astir [əˈstɜː*] *adv. & pred. adj.* **1.** in motion; in an excited state: *The whole village was ~.* **2.** up; out of bed: *You're ~ early this morning.*

as·ton·ish [əˈstɒnɪʃ] *v.t.* surprise greatly. **~·ing** *part. adj.* very surprising. **~·ment** *n.* (no pl.) great surprise.

as·tound [əˈstaʊnd] *v.t.* overcome with surprise; shock.

astray [əˈstreɪ] *adv. & pred. adj.* away from, off, the right path, esp. (fig.) into wrongdoing: *lead boys ~.*

astride [əˈstraɪd] *adv. & prep.* with one leg on each side (of): *sitting ~ his father's knee.*

as·trin·gent [əˈstrɪndʒənt] *n.* (kind of) substance that shrinks soft tissues and checks bleeding. *adj.* of or like an ~.

as·trol·o·gy [əˈstrɒlədʒɪ] *n.* (no pl.) art of observing the positions of the stars and telling how they influence human affairs. **as·trol·o·ger** *n.*

as·tro·naut [ˈæstrənɔːt] *n.* space traveller. **as·tro·nau·tics** [ˌæstrəˈnɔːtɪks] *n. pl.* (sing. or pl. v.) science and technology of travel through outer space.

as·tron·o·my [əˈstrɒnəmɪ] *n.* (no pl.) science of the sun, moon, planets, and stars. **as·tron·o·mer** *n.* **as·tro·nom·i·cal** [ˌæstrəˈnɒmɪkl] *adj.*

as·tute [əˈstjuːt] *adj.* **1.** quick at seeing how to gain an advantage. **2.** shrewd. **~·ly** *adv.* **~·ness** *n.*

asun·der [əˈsʌndə*] *adv.* **1.** (of two or more things) apart. **2.** into pieces: *tear (sth.) ~.*

asy·lum [əˈsaɪləm] *n.* **1.** place of rest, peace, and safety. **2.** (formerly) place where mentally ill people were cared for. **3.** protection from persecution, esp. by another country: *ask for political ~.*

at [æt, ət] *prep.* **1.** (place and direction) (a) *She was educated at Oxford* (but *She lives in Spain, New York*). (b) *The child is looking at his mother. Aim at the target. Don't throw stones at the dog.* (c) *Try to guess at the meaning.*

(d) *We saw the elephants at a distance* (far off). **2.** (time and order) (a) *at 2 o'clock*; *at sunset*; (b) *She left school at* (the age of) *15. They couldn't see us at first. They're gone at last!* (c) *At times* (frequently) *she has violent headaches.* **3.** (activity) *He must not be disturbed at work* (at his prayers). *Are you good at games?* **4.** (state) *The country was at war then. Do it at leisure.* **5.** (manner) *The horses went off at a gallop.* **6.** (rate, degree, value, cost) *The ship is steaming at full speed. Tomatoes are selling at 25p per pound* (at a loss). *Tomatoes are at their best this month.* **7.** (cause) *I was surprised at his knowledge of mathematics. They were impatient at the delay.*

ate, see **eat.**

-ate *suff.* **1.** [-ət] (forming adjs.): *passionate.* **2.** [-ət, -eɪt] (forming ns.): *electorate*; *nitrate.* **3.** [-eɪt] (forming vs.): *stimulate.*

athe·ism ['eɪθɪɪzəm] *n.* (no pl.) belief that there is no God. **athe·ist** *n.*

ath·lete ['æθliːt] *n.* person trained for competing in physical exercises and outdoor games.

ath·let·ic [æθ'letɪk] *adj.* **1.** of athletes. **2.** physically strong; large and muscular in build. **ath·let·ics** *n. pl.* (usu. sing. v.) outdoor sports, esp. competitions in running, jumping, etc.

-at·ic [-ætɪk, -ɒtɪk] *suff.* (forming adjs. and ns.): *fanatic*; *lunatic.*

-a·tion [-eɪʃn] *suff.* see *-tion.*

-a·tive [-ətɪv] *suff.* (forming adjs.): *authoritative.*

at·las ['ætləs] *n.* book of maps.

at·mo·sphere ['ætmə‚sfɪə*] *n.* **1.** mixture of gases surrounding the earth. **2.** air in any place. **3.** feeling (of good, evil, etc.) that the mind receives from a place, conditions, etc.: *an ~ of peace and calm.* **at·mo·spher·ic** [‚ætməs-'ferɪk] *adj.* atmospheric conditions (i.e. the weather). **at·mo·spher·ics** *n. pl.* disturbances in radio reception caused by electrical discharges in the ~.

atoll ['ætɒl] *n.* ring-shaped coral reef(s)² enclosing a lagoon.

at·om ['ætəm] *n.* **1.** smallest particle of an element: *Two ~s of hydrogen combine with one ~ of oxygen to form a molecule of water.* **2.** very small bit: *blow to ~s,* destroy completely (by explosion). *There's not an ~ of truth in what he said.*

atom·ic [ə'tɒmɪk] *adj.* of or relating to an atom or atoms. (Cf. *nuclear.*) **~ bomb** *n.* bomb that is exploded by releasing ~ **en·er·gy** *n.* (no pl.) nuclear energy. **~ pile** *n.* nuclear reactor.

~ pow·er *n.* (no pl.) nuclear power. **~ war·fare** *n.* (no pl.) one in which ~ bombs are used.

at·om·ize ['ætəʊmaɪz] *v.t.* reduce to atoms. **at·om·iz·er** *n.* device (2) for producing a fine spray.

atone [ə'təʊn] *v.i.* give satisfaction, make repayment, *for* wrongdoing. **~·ment** *n.* (no pl.).

-a·tor [-eɪtə] *suff.* see *-or.*

atro·cious [ə'trəʊʃəs] *adj.* very wicked; very bad. **atroc·i·ty** [ə'trɒsɪtɪ] *n.* cruel or wicked act.

at·ro·phy ['ætrəfɪ] *n.* (no pl.) wasting away (of a part of the body or a moral quality): *~ of the lungs* (the conscience). *v.t. & i.* suffer or cause ~.

at·tach [ə'tætʃ] *v.t. & i.* **1.** fasten or join (*to*): *~ a document to a letter.* **2.** connect with; consider to have: *Do you ~ much importance to what he says?* **3.** join oneself (*to* a person, company, etc.). **4.** *be ~ed to,* be fond of: *She is deeply ~ed to her young brother.* **5.** be joined (*to*): *No blame ~es to him.* **~·ment** *n.* ~ing or being ~ed; (esp.) sth. ~ed (to a larger thing).

at·ta·ché [ə'tæʃeɪ] *n.* person attached to the staff of an ambassador: *a naval* (military, press) ~.

at·tack [ə'tæk] *n.* **1.** violent attempt to hurt, overcome, or defeat. **2.** adverse criticism in speech or writing. **3.** coming on of disease: *a heart ~; an ~ of fever. v.t. & i.* make an ~ upon. **~·er** *n.* person who ~s.

at·tain [ə'teɪn] *v.t. & i.* **1.** reach; arrive at. **2.** succeed in doing or getting: *~ knowledge* (one's object). **~·able** *adj.* **~·ment** *n.* **1.** act of ~ing: *easy of ~ment,* easy to ~. **2.** (usu. pl.) sth. ~ed, esp. skill in some branch of knowledge: *a man of great ~ments.*

at·tempt [ə'tempt] *n. & v.t.* try.

at·tend [ə'tend] *v.i. & t.* **1.** give thought and care (*to*). **2.** be present at; go to: *~ church* (school); *~ a lecture* (meeting). **3.** wait (*upon* sb.); serve, look after (sb.): *Which doctor is ~ing you?* **4.** accompany: *a method ~ed by great difficulties.* **~·ance** *n.* ~ing or being ~ed upon; number of persons present: *a large ~ance at church.* **~·ant** *n.* **1.** person providing service: *medical ~ant,* one's physician. **2.** one who ~s (a meeting, etc.). *adj.* accompanying: *old age and its ~ant evils* (e.g. deafness).

at·ten·tion [ə'tenʃn] *n.* **1.** act of attending (1) to: *pay ~ to sth. or sb.* **2.** (often pl.) kind or polite act. **3.** drill position in which a man stands straight and still: *come to* (stand at) ~. **at·ten·tive**

[ə'tentɪv] **adj.** giving or paying ~ (to).

at·test [ə'test] **v.t. & i. 1.** be or give a clear sign or proof of: ~ed cattle (milk), (Gt. Brit.) certified free from disease. **2.** declare on oath; put on oath. **3.** bear witness (to).

at·tic ['ætɪk] **n.** room within the roof of a house.

at·tire [ə'taɪə*] **v.t. & n.** (no pl.) (liter. or poet.) dress.

at·ti·tude ['ætɪtjuːd] **n. 1.** manner of placing or holding the body: in a threatening ~. **2.** way of feeling, thinking or behaving: an ~ of hostility; maintain a firm ~.

at·tor·ney [ə'tɜːnɪ] **n.** (pl. ~s) **1.** person with legal authority to act for another in business or law: power of ~. **2.** (U.S.A.) lawyer qualified to act for clients in legal proceedings (2). **3.** A.~-General, chief legal officer of some countries and states.

at·tract [ə'trækt] **v.t. 1.** pull towards (by unseen force): A magnet ~s iron. **2.** arouse interest and pleasure in; get the attention of: Bright colours ~ babies. He shouted to ~ attention. **at·trac·tion** [ə'trækʃən] **n.** (esp.) that which ~s. **at·trac·tive adj.** ~ing or capable of ~ing.

at·tri·bute ['ætrɪbjuːt] **n.** quality, sign, or mark which is characteristic of sth. or sb.: Mercy is an ~ of God. Speech is an ~ of man but not of animals. The crown is an ~ of kingship. **at·trib·ute** [ə'trɪbjuːt] **v.t.** ~ to, consider as belonging to, caused by or owing to (sth. or sb.): ~ one's failure to bad luck; ~ wisdom to one's teachers. **at·trib·ut·able** [ə'trɪbjʊtəbl] **adj.** that can be ~d (to). **at·tri·bu·tion** [ˌætrɪ'bjuːʃən] **n.** **at·trib·u·tive** [ə'trɪbjʊtɪv] **adj.** (gram.) naming an ~. In 'the old man', old is an attributive adjective.

au·burn ['ɔːbən] **adj.** (usu. of hair) reddish-brown.

auc·tion ['ɔːkʃn] **n.** public sale at which goods are sold to the person(s) offering the highest price. **v.t.** sell by ~. **~·eer** [ˌɔːkʃə'nɪə*] **n.** person who conducts an ~.

au·da·cious [ɔː'deɪʃəs] **adj.** daring; bold; impudent. **au·dac·i·ty** [ɔː'dæsə-tɪ] **n.**

au·di·ble ['ɔːdəbl] **adj.** loud enough to be heard. **au·di·bly adv. au·di·bil·i·ty** [ˌɔːdɪ'bɪlətɪ] **n.** capacity for being heard.

au·di·ence ['ɔːdjəns] **n. 1.** whole group of listeners or spectators. **2.** people within hearing (e.g. people all over the

country listening to a radio talk). **3.** formal interview given by a ruler, the Pope, etc.: be granted an ~ by the King. **4.** (of a book) readers.

au·dio- ['ɔːdɪəʊ] **pref.** of hearing: ~-lingual methods, teaching methods that make use of language laboratories, tape recorders, etc. ~ typist, person who types direct from tape recordings. ~-visual aids, teaching aids such as tape recorders, film projectors, television, etc.

au·dit ['ɔːdɪt] **v.t.** examine (business accounts, etc.) to see that they are in order. **n.** examination of this kind.

au·di·tion [ɔː'dɪʃn] **n.** trial hearing, esp. to test a speaker, singer, actor, etc. who is applying (1) for employment.

au·di·to·ri·um [ˌɔːdɪ'tɔːrɪəm] **n.** building, or part of a building, in which an audience sits.

aught [ɔːt] **n.** (liter.) anything.

aug·ment [ɔːg'ment] **v.t. & i.** make or become larger; increase.

au·gur ['ɔːgə*] **n.** (in ancient Rome) religious official who foretold the future by observing (1) the behaviour of birds, etc. **v.t. & i.** foretell; be a sign of. **au·gu·ry** ['ɔːgjʊrɪ] **n.** art or practice of foretelling the future by reading signs; sign or omen.

au·gust [ɔː'gʌst] **adj.** majestic; causing feelings of respect or awe.

Au·gust ['ɔːgəst] **n.** eighth month of the year.

auld lang syne [ˌɔːldlæŋ'saɪn] (Scot., name of a song) the days of long ago.

aunt [ɑːnt] **n.** sister of one's father or mother; wife of one's uncle. **~·ie, ~·y n.** (colloq.) ~.

au pair (girl) [ˌəʊ 'peə ('gɜːl)] **n.** (Gt. Brit.) foreign girl who does light housework for a family in exchange for board and lodging, and the possibility of study.

aus·pic·es ['ɔːspɪsɪz] **n. pl.** under the ~ of, helped and favoured by.

aus·pi·cious [ɔː'spɪʃəs] **adj.** showing signs, giving promise, of future success; favourable.

aus·tere [ɒ'stɪə*] **adj. 1.** (of a person, his behaviour) severely moral and strict. **2.** (of a way of living, of things) simple and plain; without ornament. **aus·ter·i·ty** [ɒ'sterətɪ] **n.**

Aus·tra·lian [ɒ'streɪljən] **n. & adj.** (native or inhabitant) of Australia.

Aus·tri·an ['ɒstrɪən] **n. & adj.** (native or inhabitant) of Austria.

au·then·tic [ɔː'θentɪk] **adj.** genuine; known to be true: ~ news. **au·then·ti·cate** [ɔː'θentɪkeɪt] **v.t.** prove to be ~

au·thor ['ɔːθə*] *n.* **1.** writer of a book, play, etc. **2.** person who begins or creates sth. ~·ess *n.* female ~. ~·ship *n.* (no pl.) **1.** occupation as a writer. **2.** origin of a book, etc.: *a book of unknown* ~*ship.*

au·thor·i·ta·tive [ɔː'θɒrɪtətɪv] *adj.* having or showing authority; commanding.

au·thor·i·ty [ɔː'θɒrətɪ] *n.* **1.** power or right to give orders and make others obey. **2.** person(s) having such power or right. **3.** person with special knowledge; book, etc. supplying information, proof, etc.: *He is an* ~ *on old coins.*

au·tho·rize ['ɔːθəraɪz] *v.t.* give authority to (sb., *to do* sth.). **au·tho·ri·za·tion** [ˌɔːθəraɪ'zeɪʃn] *n.* (no pl.).

au·to ['ɔːtəʊ] *n.* (pl. ~s) (U.S.A., colloq.) automobile.

au·to- ['ɔːtəʊ-] *pref.* **1.** by oneself: *autobiography.* **2.** without help; by itself: *automatic.*

au·to·bahn ['ɔːtəʊbɑːn] *n.* (pl. ~s, ~en) German, Austrian, or Swiss motorway.

au·to·bi·og·ra·phy [ˌɔːtəʊbaɪ'ɒɡrəfɪ] *n.* story of a person's life written by himself.

au·toc·ra·cy [ɔː'tɒkrəsɪ] *n.* (country with a) government by an autocrat.

au·to·crat ['ɔːtəʊkræt] *n.* absolute ruler; dictatorial person. ~·ic [ˌɔːtəʊ-'krætɪk] *adj.*

au·to·graph ['ɔːtəɡrɑːf] *n.* person's own handwriting, esp. his signature.

au·to·mat ['ɔːtəʊmæt] *n.* (U.S.A.) restaurant at which food and drink are obtained from coin-operated closed compartments.

au·to·mat·ic [ˌɔːtə'mætɪk] *adj.* **1.** self-acting; self-moving; (of a machine) able to work or be worked without attention: ~ *pilot*, device (2) that keeps a ship or an aircraft ~ally on its course. **2.** (of acts) done without thought: *Breathing is* ~. **au·to·mat·i·cal·ly** *adv.*

au·to·ma·tion [ˌɔːtə'meɪʃn] *n.* (no pl.) (use of) methods and machines to save mental and manual labour.

au·tom·a·ton [ɔː'tɒmətən] *n.* (pl. ~s, -ata) **1.** self-operating mechanism, esp. a robot. **2.** person who acts in a mechanical way without active intelligence.

au·to·mo·bile ['ɔːtəməʊbiːl] *n.* (esp. U.S.A.) = motor car.

au·ton·o·my [ɔː'tɒnəmɪ] *n.* right of self-government; self-governing group or state. **au·ton·o·mous** [ɔː'tɒnəməs] *adj.*

au·to·pi·lot ['ɔːtəʊˌpaɪlət] *n.* automatic pilot.

au·top·sy ['ɔːtəpsɪ] *n.* (med.) examination of a dead body (by cutting it open) to learn the cause of death.

au·tumn ['ɔːtəm] *n.* (U.S.A. *fall*) third season of the year, between summer and winter. **au·tum·nal** [ɔː'tʌmnəl] *adj.*

aux·il·ia·ry [ɔːɡ'zɪljərɪ] *adj.* supporting; helpful: ~ *troops*; *an* ~ *verb* (e.g. *is* in *He is working* or *has* in *He has gone*). *n.* **1.** (gram.) ~ verb. **2.** sth. or sb. that gives help.

avail [ə'veɪl] *v.t. & i. & n.* (be of) help or use: ~ *oneself of*, make use of; profit by; take advantage of; *of no (little)* ~, useless. ~·**able** *adj.* that may be used or obtained. ~·**abil·i·ty** [əˌveɪlə'bɪlətɪ] *n.* (no pl.).

av·a·lanche ['ævəlɑːnʃ] *n.* loosened mass of snow, ice, and rock, sliding down a mountainside: (fig.) *an* ~ *of letters.*

av·a·rice ['ævərɪs] *n.* (no pl.) greed (for money or possessions). **av·a·ri·cious** [ˌævə'rɪʃəs] *adj.*

avenge [ə'vendʒ] *v.t.* get or take vengeance for: ~ *an insult*; ~ *oneself*; *be* ~*d* (*on* sb., *for* sth.). **aveng·er** *n.* person who ~s.

av·e·nue ['ævənjuː] *n.* **1.** road with trees on each side. **2.** broad street. **3.** (fig.) way of approach: *the best* ~ *to success.*

aver [ə'vɜː*] *v.t.* (-rr-) state (*that* sth. is true).

av·er·age ['ævərɪdʒ] *n.* **1.** result of adding several quantities together and dividing the total by the number of quantities: *The* ~ *of 4, 5, and 9 is 6.* **2.** standard or level usually found: *above (below, up to) the* ~, better than (not so good as, equal to) this level. *adj.* **1.** found by making an ~: *the* ~ *age of the class.* **2.** of the usual or ordinary standard: *men of* ~ *ability.* *v.t.* find the ~ of; amount to as an ~.

averse [ə'vɜːs] *adj.* opposed, disinclined (*to, from*). **aver·sion** [ə'vɜːʃn] *n.* **1.** strong dislike (*from, to, for*). **2.** sth. or sb. that is disliked strongly.

avert [ə'vɜːt] *v.t.* **1.** turn away (one's eyes, etc.) (*from*). **2.** prevent; avoid: ~ *suspicion (an accident).*

avi·ary ['eɪvjərɪ] *n.* place for keeping birds confined (2).

avi·a·tion [ˌeɪvɪ'eɪʃn] *n.* **1.** (art and science of) flying in aircraft. **2.** aircraft manufacture. **avi·a·tor** ['eɪvɪ-eɪtə*] *n.* airman.

av·id ['ævɪd] *adj.* eager; greedy: ~ *for fame.* **avid·i·ty** [ə'vɪdətɪ] *n.* (no pl.).

avoid [ə'vɔɪd] *v.t.* keep or get away

from; escape: ~ *danger*; ~ *being seen.*
~·able *adj.* **~·ance** *n.* (no pl.).
av·oir·du·pois [ˌævədəˈpɔɪz] *n.* system
of weights in which 1 pound = 16
ounces; used for all goods except gold,
silver, jewels, and medicines.
avow [əˈvaʊ] *v.t.* admit; confess; declare openly: ~ *one's faults.* **~·al**
[əˈvaʊəl] *n.* (no pl.) open confession.
~·ed·ly [əˈvaʊɪdlɪ] *adv.* by confession.
await [əˈweɪt] *v.t.* wait for; be in store
for; be waiting for.
awake [əˈweɪk] *v.t. & i.* (p.t. *awoke*
[əˈwəʊk], p.p. *awoke* or ~*d* [əˈweɪkt])
wake. ~ *to*, become aware of; realize.
pred. adj. no longer or not yet asleep:
Is he ~ or asleep? ~ *to*, aware of: *Is he ~
to the danger?* **awak·en** [əˈweɪkən]
v.t. & i. = ~, esp. (fig.): ~*n sb. to*,
make sb. aware of. **awak·en·ing**
n. becoming aware, esp. of sth. unpleasant: *It was a sad ~ning to
find that his friend had deceived him.*
award [əˈwɔːd] *n.* **1.** decision made by
a judge. **2.** sth. given as the result of
such a decision, esp. a prize in a competition. *v.t.* give as an ~: *be ~ed the
first prize.*
aware [əˈweə*] *pred. adj.* having
knowledge or realization (*of* sth.,
that ...). **~·ness** *n.* (no pl.).
awash [əˈwɒʃ] *pred. adj.* washed over,
flooded, by waves: *The ship's deck was
~. rocks ~ at high tide.*
away [əˈweɪ] *adv., adj., & n.* **I.** *adv.*
1. to or at a distance (from the place,
person, or thing in question): *The sea
is two miles ~. Keep the baby ~ from the
fire. Take these books ~, remove them.*
2. continuously; constantly: *The children are working ~ at their lessons.* **3.**
(indicating loss or disappearance):
*The water has all boiled ~. The sound
of music died ~.* **4.** *far and ~*, very much:
*He is far and ~ the best runner. right ~,
straight ~*, at once. **II.** *adj.* (sport)
played on an opponent's ground: *an
~ match* (*win*). **III.** *n.* (sport) ~ match
or win.
awe [ɔː] *n.* (no pl.) respect combined
with fear and reverence. *v.t.* fill with
~. **~·some** *adj.* causing ~. **'~-
ˌstrick·en**, **'~-struck** *adjs.* struck
with ~.
aw·ful [ˈɔːfʊl] *adj.* **1.** dreadful. **2.**
(colloq.) very bad; very great. **~·ly**
[ˈɔːflɪ] *adv.* (chiefly colloq.) very
(much); thanks ~*ly*: ~*ly hot*; thanks ~*ly.*
awhile [əˈwaɪl] *adv.* for a short time:
stay ~.

awk·ward [ˈɔːkwəd] *adj.* **1.** not well
designed for use: *an ~ tool to hold.*
2. (of a person, animal, etc.) clumsy;
having little skill: *Sea-animals are
usually ~ on land.* **3.** causing or experiencing trouble or inconvenience;
embarrassing; embarrassed: *feel ~
about sth.*; *an ~ question*; *an ~ time for
a meeting*; *the ~ age* (i.e. before young
people become self-confident); *an ~
customer* (*situation*) (difficult or dangerous to deal with). **~·ly** *adv.* **~·ness** *n.*
awl [ɔːl] *n.* small, pointed tool for making holes, esp. in leather.

an awl   an axe

aw·ning [ˈɔːnɪŋ] *n.* canvas covering
against sun or rain (e.g. over a ship's
deck or before windows).
awoke, see *awake.*
awry [əˈraɪ] *adv. & pred. adj.* crook-
ed(ly); wrong(ly): *Our plans have
gone ~.*
axe (U.S.A. **ax**) [æks] *n.* (pl. *axes*
[ˈæksɪz]) tool for felling trees or splitting wood.
ax·i·om [ˈæksɪəm] *n.* statement accepted as true without proof or argument. **ax·i·om·at·ic** [ˌæksɪəʊˈmætɪk]
adj.
ax·is [ˈæksɪs] *n.* (pl. *axes* [ˈæksiːz]) **1.**
imaginary line about which a turning
object spins: *The world turns on its ~
once in twenty-four hours.* **2.** line that
divides a regular figure symmetrically
(e.g. the diameter of a circle).
ax·le [ˈæksl] *n.* **1.** rod upon or with
which a wheel turns. **2.** rod passing
through the centres of a pair of wheels.

an axle

ay(e) [aɪ] *adv.* yes. *n.* (pl. *ayes*) affirmative answer or vote: *The ayes have it,*
the persons in favour of a proposal are
in the majority (1).
azure [ˈæʒə*] *adj. & n.* sky-blue.

B

baa [bɑː] *n. & v.i.* (of a sheep or lamb) bleat.

bab·ble ['bæbl] *v.i. & t.* make sounds like a baby; talk foolishly or in a way that is hard to understand; (of streams, etc.) murmur; tell (a secret).

babe [beɪb] *n.* (liter.) baby.

ba·bel ['beɪbl] *n.* noise, esp. of many voices: *What a ~!*

ba·boon [bə'buːn] *n.* large African and Asiatic monkey with a doglike muzzle (1).

ba·by ['beɪbɪ] *n.* **1.** child during the first few years of its life; infant. **2.** (sl.) young woman; sweetheart. **3.** (attrib.) very small of its kind: *a ~ car.* **~·hood** *n.* (no pl.) infancy (1). '**~·sit** *v.i.* (-*tt*-; p.t. & p.p. -*sat*) act as a '**~·sit·ter** *n.* person looking after a ~ while its parents are out of the house for a time. '**~·sit·ting** *n.*

bach·e·lor ['bætʃələ*] *n.* **1.** unmarried man. **2.** (attrib.) of, suitable for, an unmarried person: *~ flats; a ~ girl.* **3.** person who has taken the first university degree: *B~ of Arts.*

ba·cil·lus [bə'sɪləs] *n.* (pl. -*lli* [-laɪ]) rod-shaped bacterium, esp. one that causes disease.

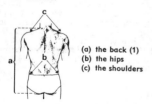

(a) the back (1)
(b) the hips
(c) the shoulders

back [bæk] *n., adv., & v.* **I.** *n.* **1.** rear part of the human body from the neck to the end of the spine (1). **2.** upper surface of an animal's body. **3.** that part of a chair or seat on which a person's ~ rests. **4.** that part of sth. that is farthest from the front, or less used, or less important. **5.** (football) player whose position is behind, near the goal. **II.** *adv.* **1.** to or at the rear:

The policemen held the crowd ~. Sit ~ in your chair and rest comfortably. **2.** in(to) an earlier position or condition: *Put the book ~ on the shelf.* **3.** in return: *If he hits you, don't hit him ~. pay money ~.* **4.** (of time) ago: *some few years ~.* **III.** *v.t. & i.* **1.** go, cause to go, ~: *a car into a garage.* **2.** support: *~ sb. up; ~ a plan (claim).* **3.** ~ *down,* give up a claim, etc.; ~ *out of (a promise or an undertaking),* withdraw from; ~ *a horse,* bet money on its winning a race. '**~·bone** *n.* **1.** line of bones down the middle of the ~. **2.** (fig.) main support. **3.** (fig.) firmness of character. ᵻ**~·date** *v.t.* date ~ to a time in the past. **~·er** *n.* supporter; person who ~s a horse. ᵻ**~·fire** *n.* (noise caused by the) too early explosion of gas in a vehicle engine. *v.i.* produce or make the sound of a ~fire. '**~·ground** *n.* **1.** that part of a view, scene, or description that serves as a setting for the chief objects, persons, etc. **2.** (fig.) person's past experiences, education, environment. **3.** (fig.) obscurity or retirement: *keep (stay) in the ~ground,* stay where one will not be noticed. **4.** information needed to understand a problem or situation. '**~·hand** *n. & adj.* (tennis, etc.) (stroke) played with the ~ of the hand in the direction of the opponent. **~·ing** *n.* (no pl.) **1.** support; group of supporters. **2.** material used to form the ~ of sth. **3.** musical accompaniment to a singer: *vocal ~ing.* '**~·log** *n.* arrears of work to be done, orders to be executed, etc. ~ **num·ber** *n.* old issue of a newspaper, magazine, etc. ~ **seat** *n.* seat at the ~. '**~-seat 'driv·er** *n.* passenger in a motor car who gives unwanted advice to the driver. '**~·slide** *v.i.* (p.t. & p.p. -*slid*) fall away from goodness into bad old ways. '**~·stroke** *n.* swimming stroke used when lying on the ~. **~·ward** ['bæk-wəd] *adj.* **1.** towards the ~ or starting-point: *a ~ward glance.* **2.** having made or making less than the usual or normal progress: *a ~ward child (country).* **3.** shy; reluctant. '**~·ward(s)** *adv.* **1.**

away from one's front; towards the ~:
look ~wards. **2.** with the ~ first: *walk
~wards*. '**~·wash** *n.* (no pl.) movement
of water going away in waves; rush of
water behind a ship. '**~·wa·ter** *n.*
1. part of a river not reached by its
current. **2.** (fig.) place, condition of
mind, untouched by events, progress,
etc. '**~·woods** *n. pl.* wild forest land
far from towns.

ba·con ['beɪkən] *n.* (no pl.) salted or
smoked meat from the sides or back
of a pig.

bac·te·ri·um [bæk'tɪərɪəm] *n.* (pl. *-ria*
[-rɪə]) simplest and smallest form of
plant life existing in air, water, soil,
and in living and dead creatures and
plants, sometimes a cause of disease.
bac·te·ri·ol·o·gist [bæk,tɪərɪ'ɒlədʒɪst]
n. **bac·te·ri·ol·o·gy** [,bæktɪərɪ'ɒlədʒɪ]
n. (no pl.).

bad [bæd] *adj.* (*worse, worst*) **1.** wicked;
evil; immoral: ~ *language*, swear
words. **2.** unpleasant: *What ~ weather
we're having!* **3.** (colloq., of things that
are never good) decided; notable: *a ~
accident (headache, blunder, mistake)*.
4. incorrect; of poor quality: *That is a
~ translation*. **5.** (of food, drink) unfit
for use: *These eggs have gone ~*. **6.** ~ *for*,
hurtful to: *Small print is ~ for the eyes*.
7. painful; diseased: *I've got a ~ leg
(several ~ teeth)*. **8.** too ~, (colloq.)
unfortunate: *It's too ~ that she can't
dance*. **9.** (colloq.) sorry: *feel ~ about
it. n.* (no pl.) **1.** that wich is ~. *go to
the ~*, become completely immoral;
become ruined. **2.** *to the ~*, on the
debit side of the account: *I am £ 500
to the ~*. **~·ly** *adv.* (*worse, worst*) **1.** in
a ~ manner: *~ly dressed (made)*. **2.**
severely; seriously: *~ly wounded*. **3.** by
much: *We were ~ly beaten at tennis*.
4. (with *want, need*) very much. **5.** *~ly
off*, poor. **~·ness** *n.*

bade, see *bid* (v. 2).

badge [bædʒ] *n.* sth. worn (usu. a small
design on cloth or made of metal) to
show rank, position, etc.: *a policeman's ~*.

bad·ger ['bædʒə*] *n.* small, grey animal
living in holes in the earth and going

a badger

about at night. *v.t.* worry (sb.) with
troublesome requests.

bad·min·ton ['bædmɪntən] *n.* (no pl.)
game played with a net, rackets, and
shuttlecocks.

baf·fle ['bæfl] *v.t.* prevent (from doing
sth.); cause to be uncertain; puzzle:
a question that ~d everybody; *a baffling
problem*.

bag [bæg] *n.* container made of paper,
cloth, leather, etc. with an opening at
the top, used for carrying things. ~ *and
baggage*, with all one's belongings. *v.t.
& i.* (*-gg-*) put in a ~; hang loosely
or in folds: *trousers ~ging at the knees.*
~·gy *adj.* (*-ier, -iest*). '**~·pipes** *n. pl.*
wind instrument supplied with air
stored in a ~ held under one arm and
pressed out through pipes.

bags

bag·gage ['bægɪdʒ] *n.* (no pl.) **1.** (esp.
U.S.A.; Gt. Brit. *luggage*) traveller's
belongings: ~ *car* (U.S.A.) = luggage
van. ~ *check* (U.S.A.) = luggage
ticket. ~ *room* (U.S.A.) = cloakroom;
left luggage office. **2.** army equipment
(e.g. tents and bedding): ~ *animals
(for carrying ~)*.

bail[1] [beɪl] *v.t.* ~ (*sb.*) *out*, secure
freedom of (an accused person till
called for trial, by lodging with a lawcourt money which will not be given
back if he does not attend). *n.* (no pl.)
the money so demanded by the court:
go ~ for sb., ~ him out; out on ~, free
after payment of ~.

bail[2] [beɪl] *n.* (cricket) one of the two
cross-pieces of wood placed over the
stumps (3).

bails

bail[3], **bale**[2] [beɪl] *v.t. & i.* **1.** throw
water out of a boat with buckets, etc.:
~ *the boat out*; ~ *water out*. **2.** ~ *out (of)*,
(of an airman) jump with a parachute
from a damaged aircraft.

bai·liff ['beɪlɪf] *n.* **1.** law officer who helps a sheriff. **2.** agent or manager for a landowner.

bait [beɪt] *n.* food, or imitation of food, put on a hook or in a net, trap, etc. to catch fish, birds, or animals. *v.t.* **1.** put ∼ on (a hook, etc.) to catch fish, etc. **2.** worry or annoy in order to make angry.

bake [beɪk] *v.t. & i.* **1.** cook, be cooked, by dry heat in an oven: ∼ *bread* (*cakes*). **2.** make or become hard by heating: *ground* ∼*d hard by the sun.* **3.** be warmed or tanned: *baking in the sun.* **bak·er** *n.* person who ∼s bread, etc. **'bak·er·y** *n.* place where bread is ∼d for many people.

bal·ance ['bæləns] *n.* **1.** apparatus (1) for weighing, with a central pivot, beam (3), and two scales[2]: *in the* ∼, (fig., of a result) still uncertain. **2.** (also ∼*-wheel*) apparatus (1) in a watch or clock that regulates the speed. **3.** condition of being steady; condition that exists when opposing amounts, forces, etc. are equal: *keep* (*lose*) *one's* ∼, remain (fail to remain) upright; ∼ *of power*, condition in which no one country or group of countries is much stronger than another. **4.** difference between two columns of an account (money received and money paid out, etc.): ∼ *sheet*, statement of the details of an account, with the difference between credit and debit; *strike a* ∼, find this difference; ∼ *of trade*, difference between values of exports and imports. **5.** *the* ∼, (colloq.) what is left. *v.t. & i.* **1.** keep, put, be, in a state of ∼: ∼ (*oneself*) *on one foot.* **2.** weigh or compare (two objects, plans, possibilities, etc. against each other). **3.** (accounts) compare debits and credits and record the sum needed to make them equal.

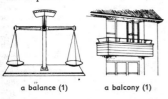

a balance (1)   a balcony (1)

bal·co·ny ['bælkənɪ] *n.* **1.** platform (with a wall or rail) built on an outside wall of a building, reached from an upstairs room. **2.** (in a theatre, hall, etc.) rows of seats above floor level and (usu.) rising one above the other.

bald [bɔːld] *adj.* **1.** having no or not much hair, not many feathers, trees, leaves, etc. **2.** (fig.) plain; without ornament: *a* ∼ *statement of facts.* ∼**·ly** *adv.* ∼**·ness** *n.*

bale[1] [beɪl] *n.* bundle of goods packed (usu. in canvas, etc. and tied with rope or wire) ready for transport. *v.t.* make into, pack in, ∼s: ∼ *hay.*

bale², see *bail³.*

balk, baulk [bɔːk] *v.t. & i.* **1.** prevent; hinder; purposely get in the way of: ∼*ed in one's plans*; ∼ *a person in his purpose.* **2.** ∼ *at*, (e.g. of a horse) refuse to go forward; hesitate. *n.* beam (1).

ball[1] [bɔːl] *n.* **1.** solid or hollow sphere as used in games. ∼*-bearing(s)*, (mech.) bearings in which friction is lessened by the use of small steel ∼s. ∼*-pen*, ∼*-point*, ∼*point-pen*, pen that writes with a tiny ∼ rotating at the end of a narrow tube of ink. **2.** material gathered or wound into a round mass: *a* ∼ *of wool; a snow*∼.

balls   bamboo

ball² [bɔːl] *n.* social gathering for dancing.

bal·lad ['bæləd] *n.* kind of simple song or poem, esp. one that tells a story.

bal·last ['bæləst] *n.* (no pl.) heavy material (e.g. sand, stones) placed in a ship or balloon to keep it steady: *in* ∼, carrying ∼ only. *v.t.* put ∼ in.

bal·let ['bæleɪ] *n.* **1.** musical play, without dialogue or singing, performed by a group of dancers in a theatre. **2.** the dancers. **3.** *the* ∼, this kind of stage dancing as an art.

bal·lis·tic [bə'lɪstɪk] *adj.* of projectiles. ∼ **mis·sile** *n.* missile that is guided only in the ascent but becomes a free-falling object in the descent. ∼**s** *n. pl.* (sing. v.) study or science of projectiles or firearms.

bal·loon [bə'luːn] *n.* bag filled with air or gas lighter than air, esp. one sent up into the sky.

bal·lot ['bælət] *n.* **1.** secret voting. **2.** piece of paper (also ∼*-paper*), ticket, or ball used in secret voting. **3.** votes so recorded. *v.i.* ∼ (*for*), give a secret vote. '**~-box** *n.* box into which ~-papers are dropped by voters.

balm [bɑːm] *n.* (no pl.) **1.** sweet-smelling oil or ointment. **2.** (fig.) that which gives peace of mind. **~y** *adj.* (-*ier*, -*iest*) sweet-smelling; healing; (of air) soft and warm.

bal·sam ['bɔːlsəm] *n.* **1.** balm (1). **2.** flowering plant grown in gardens.

bal·us·ter ['bæləstə*] *n.* upright support for a handrail. **bal·us·trade** [,bælə'streɪd] *n.* row of ~s.

balusters   banisters

bam·boo [bæm'buː] *n.* tall plant with hard, hollow, jointed stems, of the grass family; its wood. (See the picture at *ball¹*.)

ban [bæn] *v.t.* (-*nn*-) order that sth. must not be done, said, etc. *n.* order that ~s sth.: *under a ~.*

ba·nal [bə'nɑːl] *adj.* commonplace; uninteresting: ~ *remarks.*

ba·nana [bə'nɑːnə] *n.* long, finger-shaped, yellow-skinned fruit, growing in bunches; tree on which it grows.

band [bænd] *n.* **1.** flat, thin strip of material, esp. for fastening things together or for placing round an object to strengthen it: *iron ~s round a barrel.* **2.** flat, thin strip of material on an article of clothing: *A shirt has a neck~ and two wrist~s.* **3.** strip or line, different from the rest in colour or design, on sth.: *a white plate with a blue ~ round the rim.* **4.** group of persons acting together under a leader and with a common purpose: *a ~ of robbers;* (esp.) group of persons playing music together: *a brass (jazz) ~; ~master,* conductor (1) of a ~; *~stand,* outdoor stage or platform for a ~ of musicians. *v.t. & i.* (of people) join, bring, or come together: *~ together against a common enemy.*

ban·dage ['bændɪdʒ] *n.* band or strip of material for tying round a wound or injury. *v.t.* tie up with a ~: *a ~d leg.*

ban·dit ['bændɪt] *n.* armed robber; outlaw; gangster.

ban·dy¹ ['bændɪ] *v.t.* pass or send backwards and forwards; exchange (words, blows): *have one's name bandied about,* be a subject for gossip.

ban·dy² ['bændɪ] *adj.* (of the legs) bending outwards at the knees.

bane [beɪn] *n.* (no pl.) cause of ruin, destruction, or trouble.

bang¹ [bæŋ] *n.* violent blow; loud, sudden noise: *a ~ on the head; shut the door with a ~. v.t. & i.* make a ~; give a ~ to: ~ *one's fist on the table; ~ a door. The door ~ed.*

bang² [bæŋ] *v.t.* cut (the front hair) straight across the forehead. *n.* fringe (3) of ~ed hair.

ban·gle ['bæŋgl] *n.* ornamental, rigid band worn round the arm or ankle.

ban·ish ['bænɪʃ] *v.t.* **1.** ~ (*from*), send (sb.) away, esp. out of the country, as a punishment. **2.** (fig.) put away from or out of (the mind): ~ *cares (fear, etc.).* **~ment** *n.* (no pl.).

ban·is·ters ['bænɪstəz] *n. pl.* handrail and upright supports (balusters) at the side of stairs. (See the picture on the left.)

ban·jo ['bændʒəʊ] *n.* (pl. -*os*, -*oes*) musical instrument played by plucking (4) the strings with the fingers.

a banjo

bank¹ [bæŋk] *n.* **1.** sloping land or earth, strip of raised land, often a division between fields: *low ~s of earth between rice-fields.* **2.** bank along each side of a river, canal, etc. **3.** large, usu. flat mass (of sand, snow, clouds, etc.), esp. one formed by wind or water. *v.t. & i.* **1.** make or form into a ~ or ~s: *The snow has ~ed up. ~ up a fire* (i.e. pack coal tightly for slow burning). **2.** (of a car or an aircraft) go with one side higher than the other (e.g. when turning).

bank² [bæŋk] *n.* **1.** establishment for keeping money and valuables safely, for lending and exchanging money, the money being paid out on the customer's order. **2.** place for storing anything for future use: *blood ~,* place where blood or blood plasma is stored for use in hospitals, etc. *v.t.* place, keep (money, etc.) in a ~ (1). '**~-bill** *n.* **1.** bill² (4) drawn by one ~ on another.

2. (U.S.A.) = ⁓note. '⁓-**book** *n.* (also *passbook*) book that contains a record² (1) of a customer's account with a ⁓. ⁓ **card** *n.* credit card issued by a ⁓. ⁓ **clerk** *n.* one who works in a ⁓. ⁓·**er** *n.* person managing the business of a ⁓. ⁓ **hol·i·day** *n.* any weekday on which ⁓s are legally closed, usu. kept as general holiday. '⁓·**note** *n.* piece of paper money issued by a ⁓. ⁓ **rate** *n.* rate at which the central ⁓ will discount bills² (4).

bank·rupt ['bæŋkrʌpt] *n.* person judged by a lawcourt to be unable to pay his debts in full. *adj.* unable to pay debts in full. ⁓ *in* (*of*), completely without: ⁓ *of ideas.* ⁓·**cy** ['bæŋkrəptsɪ] *n.*

ban·ner ['bænə*] *n.* flag or announcement, on one or two poles, carried in demonstrations, etc.

banns [bænz] *n. pl.* public announcement in church that two persons are to be married: *put up* (*publish*) *the* ⁓; *have one's* ⁓ *called.*

ban·quet ['bæŋkwɪt] *n.* feast, esp. official dinner for a special event.

ban·ter ['bæntə*] *v.t. & i.* tease in a playful way (by joking talk). *n.* good-humoured teasing.

bap·tism ['bæptɪzəm] *n.* **1.** ceremony of sprinkling sb. with, or immersing sb. in, water, accepting him as a member of the Christian Church and giving him a Christian name. **2.** (fig.) first experience: ⁓ *of fire,* a soldier's first battle. **bap·tis·mal** [bæp'tɪzml] *adj.* of ⁓. **bap·tize** [bæp'taɪz] *v.t.* give ⁓ to (sb.).

bar [bɑː*] *n.* **1.** long piece of hard, stiff material (e.g. metal, wood, soap, chocolate, etc.): *an iron* ⁓; *a* ⁓ *of chocolate.* **2.** rod or rail across a door, etc. to prevent its being opened or to stop passage: *fasten a gate with a* ⁓; *behind prison* ⁓s. **3.** (fig.) sth. that stops or hinders progress: *Poor health may be a* ⁓ *to success in life.* **4.** bank of mud or sand at the mouth of a river or entrance to a harbour. **5.** narrow band (of colour, light): *a* ⁓ *of silver across the sky.* **6.** place in a lawcourt where the prisoner stands before the judge. **7.** *the B*⁓, the profession of barrister; all those lawyers who are barristers: *called to the B*⁓. **8.** (room in a hotel, an inn, etc. with a) counter where alcoholic drinks are sold and drunk. **9.** counter at which meals, etc. are sold and eaten: *a milk* ⁓; *a snack-*⁓. **10.** specialized department in a large shop: *a heel* ⁓. **11.** (music) upright

line separating divisions equal in time-value; one such division with its notes. *v.t.* (-*rr*-) **1.** put or have a ⁓ or ⁓s across; prevent by means of a ⁓: ⁓ *the doors and windows*; (fig.) ⁓ *the way to success.* **2.** prohibit. **3.** mark with a stripe or stripes: *a sky* ⁓*red with clouds.* *prep.* (also ⁓·**ring**) except. '⁓·**keep**(·**er**) (U.S.A.), '⁓·**maid**, '⁓·**man**, '⁓·**tend·er** *ns.* person serving drinks at a ⁓ (8).

barb [bɑːb] *n.* back-curving point of an arrow, spear, fish-hook, etc. ⁓**ed** *adj.* having ⁓s: ⁓*ed wire.*

barbed wire

bar·bar·ian [bɑː'beərɪən] *adj. & n.* uncivilized (person). **bar·bar·ic** [bɑː'bærɪk] *adj.* in the manner of ⁓s. **bar·ba·rism** ['bɑːbərɪzəm] *n.* state of being uncivilized. **bar·bar·i·ty** [bɑː'bærətɪ] *n.* (esp.) savage cruelty. **bar·ba·rous** ['bɑːbərəs] *adj.* uncivilized; cruel and savage.

bar·be·cue ['bɑːbɪkjuː] *n.* framework for roasting meat, esp. a whole animal; open-air party at which such meat is served (3).

bar·ber ['bɑːbə*] *n.* person whose business is shaving and men's hair-cutting.

bar·bi·tu·rate [bɑː'bɪtjurət] *n.* (chem.) **1.** (kinds of) organic compound with a soporific effect. **2.** pill for settling the nerves or inducing sleep.

bard [bɑːd] *n.* (liter.) poet; singer of old songs.

bare [beə*] *adj.* **1.** not covered, clothed, protected, or decorated; empty: ⁓*headed*; *riding a horse* ⁓*back* (i.e. without a saddle); ⁓ *floors*; ⁓ *shelves.* **2.** mere; minimum: *earn a* ⁓ *living*; *a* ⁓ *possibility.* *v.t.* make ⁓; uncover. ⁓·**ly** *adv.* **1.** in a ⁓ way: *a* ⁓*ly furnished room.* **2.** hardly; scarcely: *We have* ⁓*ly time to catch that train.*

bar·gain ['bɑːgɪn] *n.* **1.** agreement to buy, sell, or exchange sth. **2.** sth. got as the result of a ⁓, *into the* ⁓, in addition. **3.** sth. bought, sold, or offered cheap: *a* ⁓ *sale*; *a* ⁓ *price,* a low price. *v.i.* try to make a ⁓. ⁓ *for,* expect; be ready for: *That's more than I* ⁓*ed for.*

barge [bɑːdʒ] *n.* flat-bottomed boat for carrying goods on rivers, canals, etc. *v.i.* (colloq.) bump heavily (*into*, *against*). ~ *in(to)*, intrude. **bar·gee** [baːˈdʒiː] *n.* man in charge of a ~.

bari·tone [ˈbærɪtəʊn] *n.* male voice between tenor and bass.

bark[1] [baːk] *n.* (no pl.) outer covering or skin on the trunks and branches of trees. *v.t.* take the ~ off.

bark[2] [baːk] *v.i. & n.* (make the) cry of a dog or fox.

bark[3], **barque** [baːk] *n.* **1.** sailing-ship with usu. three masts. **2.** (liter.) any kind of ship.

bar·ley [ˈbaːlɪ] *n.* (no pl.) grass-like plant; its grain, used as food and for making beer and whisky.

barn [baːn] *n.* farm building for storing grain, hay, etc., (U.S.A.) also for the housing of livestock.

bar·na·cle [ˈbaːnəkl] *n.* small sea-animal or shellfish that fastens itself to rocks, the bottoms of ships, etc.

ba·rom·e·ter [bəˈrɒmɪtə*] *n.* instrument for measuring the pressure of the atmosphere, used to get information about the weather, etc.

bar·on [ˈbærən] *n.* **1.** (in Gt. Brit.) nobleman of the lowest rank (called *Lord X*). **2.** (in other countries) nobleman (called *Baron X*). ~**ess** *n.* wife of a ~. **ba·ro·nial** [bəˈrəʊnjəl] *adj.* of a ~. **bar·ony** *n.* rank of a ~.

bar·on·et [ˈbærənɪt] *n.* (in Gt. Brit.) member of the lowest hereditary titled order (9); shortened to *Bart.*, added to the name: *Sir John Williams, Bart.*

ba·roque [bəˈrɒk] *adj. & n.* (of the) florid and highly ornamented style of art and architecture in the 17th-18th century.

bar·rack [ˈbærək] *n.* **1.** (often pl. with sing. v.) large building(s) for soldiers to live in. **2.** any building of plain or ugly appearance.

bar·rage [ˈbærɑːʒ] *n.* **1.** artificial dam across a river. **2.** (mil.) barrier made by heavy, continuous gunfire directed onto a given area.

bar·rel [ˈbærəl] *n.* **1.** round container, made of wooden staves with bands or hoops, or of plastic. **2.** measure of capacity. **3.** metal tube of a gun, revolver, etc. '~-, **or·gan** *n.* instrument

a barrel (1)   a gun-barrel

from which music may be produced by turning a handle that causes a cylinder to revolve.

bar·ren [ˈbærən] *adj.* **1.** (of land) not fertile enough to produce crops. **2.** (of plants, trees) not producing fruit or seeds. **3.** (of women, animals) unable to have young ones. **4.** (fig.) without value, result, or interest: *an attempt ~ of results; a ~ subject.*

bar·ri·cade [ˌbærɪˈkeɪd] *n.* barrier of objects (e.g. carts, barrels) across or in front of sth. as a defence or obstruction. *v.t.* block (a street, etc.) with a ~.

bar·ri·er [ˈbærɪə*] *n.* sth. (e.g. a wall, rail, fence, etc.) that prevents, hinders, or controls progress and movement: *Show your ticket at the ~* (e.g. in a railway station). (fig.) *Poor health may be a ~ to success in life.*

bar·ring *prep.* see *bar* (prep.).

bar·ris·ter [ˈbærɪstə*] *n.* (Gt. Brit.) lawyer who has the right to speak and argue as an advocate in the higher courts.

bar·row[1] [ˈbærəʊ] *n.* small cart with one or two wheels, usu. pushed or pulled by hand.

bar·row[2] [ˈbærəʊ] *n.* bank or heap of earth built in ancient times over a burial place.

bar·ter [ˈbaːtə*] *v.t. & n.* (no pl.) (make an) exchange of goods or property *for* other goods, etc.

base[1] [beɪs] *n.* **1.** lowest part of anything, esp. the part on which sth. rests or is supported: *the ~ of a pillar.* **2.** (geom.) line or surface on which a figure is regarded as standing: *AB is the ~ of the triangle ABC.* **3.** place at which armed forces, expeditions, etc. have their stores, hospitals, etc.: *an air ~; a naval ~.* **4.** (baseball) one of the four stations that must be reached in turn when scoring[1] (3) a run. **5.** substance into which other things are mixed. *v.t.* build or place (*on, upon*). ~**less** *adj.* without cause or foundation.

base[2] [beɪs] *adj.* **1.** (of persons, their behaviour) selfish; dishonourable. **2.** (of thoughts and desires) mean; dishonourable. **3.** (of metals) low in value.

base·ball [ˈbeɪsbɔːl] *n.* (no pl.) American game played with a bat[1] and ball by two teams of nine players on a field with four bases[1] (4). '**base·board** *n.* (U.S.A.) = skirting-board. '**base·ment** *n.* lowest part of a building, partly or wholly below ground level; inhabited room(s) in this part.

ba·ses[1], pl. of *basis*.

batter

bas·es², pl. of **base¹**.
bash [bæʃ] *v.t.* strike violently: ~ *in the lid of a box.*
bash·ful ['bæʃful] *adj.* shy.
ba·sic ['beɪsɪk] *adj.* of, at, or forming a base¹ (1): ~ *principles.*
ba·sin ['beɪsn] *n.* **1.** round, open, wide bowl for holding liquids: *Wash your hands in the* ~. **2.** hollow place (e.g. below a waterfall) where water collects. **3.** deep harbour almost surrounded by land. **4.** area of land from which water is carried away by a river: *the Thames* ~.
ba·sis ['beɪsɪs] *n.* (pl. *-ses* ['beɪsi:z]) **1.** main ingredient. **2.** (usu. fig.) foundation; facts, etc. on which an argument is built up.
bask [bɑːsk] *v.i.* enjoy warmth and light: ~*ing in the sunshine.*
bas·ket ['bɑːskɪt] *n.* container, usu. made of materials that bend and twist easily (e.g. osiers, canes, etc.). '~·**ball** *n.* game in which a ball is thrown through a ~-shaped net that is the goal.
bass [beɪs] *adj.* low in tone; deep-sounding. *n.* singer, instrument, able to give out the lowest notes: *a ~-clarinet.*
bas·soon [bə'su:n] *n.* musical wind instrument made of wood and giving low notes when blown.
bas·tard ['bɑːstəd] *n.* child whose parents were not married at the time it was born.
baste¹ [beɪst] *v.t.* stitch pieces loosely together (as a preparation for regular sewing).
baste² [beɪst] *v.t.* pour melted fat or gravy over (roasting meat, etc.).
bas·tion ['bæstɪən] *n.* (often five-sided) part of a fortification that stands out from the rest.
bat¹ [bæt] *n.* shaped wooden stick used for hitting the ball, esp. in cricket and baseball. *v.i. & t.* (*-tt-*) use a ~; hit (with a ~). '~·**s·man** *n.* (cricket) player who ~s.
bat² [bæt] *n.* small, winged, four-footed, mouse-like animal that flies at night.

a bat²

batch [bætʃ] *n.* **1.** number of loaves, cakes, etc. baked together. **2.** number of persons or things receiving attention as a group: *a* ~ *of recruits for the army (letters to be answered).*
bat·ed ['beɪtɪd] *adj. with* ~ *breath,* with the voice lowered to a whisper (in fear, anxiety, etc.).
bath [bɑːθ] *n.* (pl. ~s [bɑːðz]) **1.** washing of the whole body: *have (take) a* ~; *a shower-*~; *a sun-*~. **2.** water for a ~; liquid in which sth. is washed or dipped: *an oil* ~. **3.** (also ~*-tub*) vessel for bathing in. **4.** (usu. pl.) building for bathing or swimming in: *public swimming-*~*s. v.t. & i.* give a ~ to: ~ *a baby*; take a ~.

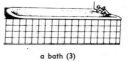

a bath (3)

bathe [beɪð] *v.t. & i.* **1.** go into the sea, a river, lake, etc. for swimming or pleasure. **2.** wash; apply water to (a wound, etc.). **3.** *be* ~*d in,* be made wet or bright all over: ~*d in sweat (sunshine). n.* act of bathing, esp. swimming in the sea, etc.: *Let's go for a* ~. **bath·er** *n.*
bath·ing ['beɪðɪŋ] *n.* act or practice of swimming, etc. '~·,**cos·tume**, '~·**suit** *ns.* garment worn for swimming.
bath·robe ['bɑːθrəʊb] *n.* loose-fitting robe worn before and after taking a bath and sometimes as a dressing-gown. **bath·room** ['bɑːθrʊm] *n.* room in which there is a bath (3) or shower (2), and usu. a wash-hand basin and lavatory.
bat·man ['bætmən] *n.* servant of an army officer.
ba·ton ['bætən] *n.* **1.** policeman's thick stick (used as a weapon). **2.** short, thin stick used by the conductor (1) of a band or an orchestra to beat¹ (4) time.
bat·tal·ion [bə'tæljən] *n.* army unit made up of several companies (6).
bat·ten ['bætn] *n.* long, narrow piece of wood, esp. one used to keep others in place, or to which boards are nailed. *v.t.* make secure with ~s: ~ *down the hatches.*
bat·ter¹ ['bætə*] *v.t. & i.* strike violently and often; beat out of shape: ~ *a door down*; *a ship* ~*ed to pieces by heavy waves*; *a* ~*ed old car (hat).*
bat·ter² ['bætə*] *n.* (baseball) player who bats¹.
bat·ter³ ['bætə*] *n.* (no pl.) beaten

mixture of flour, eggs, milk, etc. for cooking.

bat·tery ['bætərɪ] *n.* **1.** army unit of big guns, with men and vehicles. **2.** group of connected cells from which electric current will flow. **3.** series of cages, etc. in which hens are kept for intensive laying or for fattening: ~ *hens.* (Cf. *free-range.*)

bat·tle ['bætl] *n.* fight between armed forces; (fig.) any struggle. *v.i.* fight or struggle (*with, against*; *for* sth.). '~**field**, '~**ground** *ns.* scene of ~.

bat·tle·ment ['bætlmənt] *n.* (usu. pl.) wall round the flat roof of a tower or castle with open spaces for shooting through.

bau·ble ['bɔːbl] *n.* pretty and pleasing ornament of little value.

baulk, see *balk.*

baux·ite ['bɔːksaɪt] *n.* (no pl.) clay-like substance from which aluminium is obtained.

bawdy ['bɔːdɪ] *adj. & n.* humorously indecent (talk). | *~ out a curse.* |

bawl [bɔːl] *v.t. & i.* shout; cry loudly. |

bay¹ [beɪ] *n.* part of the sea within a deep curve of the coastline: *the B~ of Biscay; Hudson B~.*

bay² [beɪ] *n.* division of a wall between columns or pillars; compartment, recess (2), extension of a room, sometimes with a window (called a ~ *window*), built out beyond the line of an outside wall.

bay³ [beɪ] *n.* kind of laurel with leaves that are used in cooking.

bay⁴ [beɪ] *adj. & n.* reddish-brown (horse).

bay⁵ [beɪ] *v.i. & n.* (give the) bark of large dogs, esp. while hunting. *at* ~, forced to turn and attack; *hold* (*keep*) *at* ~, keep (attackers) off.

bay·o·net ['beɪənɪt] *v.t. & n.* (kill or wound with a) short stabbing blade (1) fixed to the muzzle (3) of a rifle.

ba·zaar [bə'zɑː*] *n.* **1.** shopping centre (in Eastern countries). **2.** shop selling cheap fancy goods. **3.** sale to raise money for charity: *a church* ~.

be [biː, bɪ] *v.i.* (pres.t. *am* [æm, əm], *is* [ɪz], *are* [ɑː*, ə*]; p.t. *was* [wɒz, wəz], *were* [wɜː*, wə*]; p.p. *been* [biːn, bɪn]; (colloq.) contracted forms: *I'm* [aɪm], *he's* [hiːz], *she's* [ʃiːz], *it's* [ɪts], *we're* [wɪə*], *you're* [juə*], *they're* [ðeə*]; neg. *is not,* (colloq.) *isn't* ['ɪznt], *are not,* (colloq.) *aren't* [ɑːnt], *was not,* (colloq.) *wasn't* ['wɒznt], *were not,* (colloq.) *weren't* [wɜːnt]; *am I not is* contracted to *aren't I* [ɑːnt aɪ]; pres. p. *being* [biːɪŋ]) **I.** (full verb) **1.** exist;

occur; live (often with *there*): *God is. There is a God. There were six of us. There is a bus-stop down the road.* For *the time being,* for the present. **2.** (indicating position in space or time). *He is in the garden. The book is on the table. The station is a mile away. Her birthday is on Tuesday. He is ten years old.* **3.** remain; continue: *let it be,* do not disturb it. **4.** (indicating direction, condition, view): *I am off! Are you for London? He is better today. I am for* (against) *capital punishment.* **5.** (esp. with p.p. *been*) (a) go (to a place, etc.): *Have you ever been to London?* (b) (colloq.) called; visited: *I've been to see* (have paid a visit to) *my uncle. Has the postman been* (called) *yet?* **6.** (indicating protest or surprise): *been and ... * (colloq.): *You have been and taken my dictionary!* **II.** (linking verb) **1.** (indicating state or quality): *This is a dictionary. The world is round. I am ill.* **2.** (indicating identity with): *Today is Monday. Who is that? It's I* (colloq. *me*). **3.** (indicating possession, amount, cost, etc.): *The money is John's. Twice two is four. How much is this book?* **4.** signify: *It's nothing to me.* **III.** (linking verb, indicating a change from one quality, place, etc. to another): *What are you going to be* (become) *when you grow up? You can be* (get) *there in five minutes.* **IV.** *v.aux.* **1.** (used with a pres. p. to form the progressive or continuous tenses): *They are* (were) *reading. I shall be seeing him soon. What have you been doing this week?* **2.** (used with a p.p. to form the passive voice): *He was killed in the war. Where were they made? He is to be pitied.* **3.** (used with the infinitive expressing) (a) duty; necessity: *I am to inform you* (I have been told to inform you) *that ...* (b) intention: *They are to be married in May.* (c) possibility: *The book was not to be* (could not be) *found.* (d) supposition or unreal condition: *If I were to tell you ...* (e) destiny: *They were never to meet again.* **...-to-be** *adj.* future ...: *his bride-to-be.*

be- [bɪ-] *pref.* **I.** (forming vs.) **1.** all over: *besmear.* **2.** thoroughly: *begrudge; belabour.* **3.** (*be-* & *v.i.* forming *v.t.*): *bemoan; bewail.* **4.** (from adjs. or ns.) make, cause to be; treat as: *belittle; befool* (make a fool of); *befriend.* **II.** (forming adjs. in *-ed* from ns.) wearing: *bejewelled.*

beach [biːtʃ] *n.* sandy or stony stretch at the edge of the sea covered at high tide. *v.t.* run (a boat) on to a ~.

beat

bea·con ['biːkən] *n.* **1.** warning light at sea, on the coast, on mountains (for aircraft, ships). **2.** (formerly) fire lit on a hilltop as a signal. **3.** (Gt. Brit.) post, bearing a flashing lamp, erected at each end of a street-crossing for pedestrians.

bead [biːd] *n.* **1.** small ball of wood, glass, etc. with a hole through, for threading it on a string or wire. **2.** small drop (of sweat, etc.).

bea·dle ['biːdl] *n.* (hist.) parish officer who helped the priest.

beady ['biːdɪ] *adj.* (-ier, -iest) (of eyes) small and bright.

bea·gle ['biːgl] *n.* small hound used for hunting hares.

beak [biːk] *n.* hard, horny part of a bird's mouth, esp. when hooked.

bea·ker ['biːkə*] *n.* open glass vessel with a lip, esp. as used in chemical laboratories.

beam [biːm] *n.* **1.** long, thick, and usu. squared piece of wood, esp. one used in building (e.g. to support the roof) or in ships (to support decks, etc.). **2.** breadth, side, of a ship: *on her ~-ends*, on her side; *broad in the ~*, (colloq.) having wide hips. **3.** crossbar of a balance (1). **4.** ray of light (e.g. *sun~*); directed electromagnetic waves; radio signal used to direct an aircraft on its course; the exact course so indicated. **5.** (fig.) bright look or smile. *v.t. & i.* send out light and warmth; smile radiantly: *a ~ing face.*

bean [biːn] *n.* plant with seeds growing in pods, used as food; the seed; *~-like* seeds of other plants (e.g. *coffee-~s*).

a bean-pod

a bear²

bear¹ [beə*] *v.t. & i.* (p.t. bore [bɔː*], p.p. borne [bɔːn]) **1.** carry. **2.** produce; give birth to: *trees that ~ fruit*; *~ a child.* (Cf. also *born.*) **3.** carry visibly; show (signs, likeness, love, etc.): *~ marks (traces, etc. of)*; *~ arms*, have weapons; *~ oneself (well, etc.)*, behave. **4.** bring; provide: *~ witness*; *~ sb. company*; *~ a hand*, help. **5.** have in the heart or mind: *~ a grudge*; *~ in mind*, remember. **6.** support; sustain (weight, responsibility, cost). **7.** (usu. with *can*

or *could*, esp. in neg. or interr. sentences) endure: *I cannot ~ her (the pain). She can't ~ being laughed at.* **8.** (in p.p.) carried or transported by: *airborne.* **9.** turn: *~ to the right.* **10.** *~ down*, overcome; defeat: *~ down all resistance*; *~ out*, confirm (sth.); support (sb.): *~ out a statement. He will ~ me out. ~ up*, be brave (*against* misfortune, etc.); *~ (up)on*, be relevant to: *~ upon a problem*; *bring to ~ (up)on*, apply: *bring all one's energies to ~ upon a task*; *bring pressure to ~ on sb.*; *~ with* (sb.), treat patiently or indulgently. **~·able** *adj.* that can be borne or endured.

bear² [beə*] *n.* large, heavy animal with rough hair. (See the picture.) *Great (Little) B~*, two groups of stars in the northern sky.

beard [bɪəd] *n.* growth of hair on the cheeks and chin (not the lip). **~·ed** *adj.* **~·less** *adj.*

bear·er ['beərə*] person who carries or brings sth. (e.g. a coffin, messages, news, a cheque to a bank for payment).

bear·ing ['beərɪŋ] *n.* (in the senses of the verb *bear*, esp.:) **1.** connection, relationship, between one thing and others: *examine a question in all its ~s.* **2.** direction of a place in relation to other places or to the compass (1); (pl.) relative position: *lose one's ~s*, be lost; *get (take) one's ~s*, find one's position by looking round for landmarks (2), etc. **3.** (usu. pl.) part of a machine that supports a moving part and reduces friction: *ball¹-~s.* **4.** way of behaving, walking, etc.: *a soldierly ~.*

beast [biːst] *n.* **1.** four-footed animal. **2.** brutal person. **~·ly** *adj.* (-ier, -iest) like a ~; (colloq.) unpleasant.

beat¹ [biːt] *v.t. & i.* (p.t. ~, p.p. ~en ['biːtn]) **1.** hit or strike repeatedly, esp. with a stick; punish by ~ing; (of the sun, rain, etc.) strike (*on*). **2.** mix thoroughly by using a fork, etc.: *~ eggs (cream).* **3.** win a victory over; do better than. **4.** (of the heart, a bird's wings, etc.) move up and down regularly. *~ time*, make regular movements to show the time in music. **5.** *~ about the bush*, approach a subject (2) without coming to the point (6); *~ up*, *~ (sb.) severely*; *~ it*, (sl.) go away; *dead ~*, exhausted. *n.* **1.** regularly repeated stroke, or sound of this: *the ~ of a drum*; *heart~s.* **2.** unit of time in music; strongly marked rhythm of popular music. **3.**

path or course regularly used or taken; appointed course of a sentinel or policeman: *on (off) his* ~.

beat² [biːt] *attrib. & n.* (of or like a) beatnik: *the* ~ *generation.*

beat·en ['biːtn] *v.* see *beat¹*. *adj.* shaped by beating: ~ *silver; the* ~ *path*, made smooth by use.

beat·er ['biːtə*] *n.* **1.** utensil used for beating (carpets, eggs, etc.). **2.** man employed to rouse and drive game¹ (5) to those waiting with guns to shoot it.

beat·ing ['biːtɪŋ] *n.* defeat; (punishment by) hitting with a stick, etc.

beat·nik ['biːtnɪk] *n.* young person who (often with others) breaks away from convention (e.g. in dress and social behaviour).

beau·ti·cian [bjuː'tɪʃn] *n.* person who runs a beauty parlour; specialist in beauty treatment.

beau·ti·ful ['bjuːtəfʊl] *adj.* giving pleasure or delight to the mind or senses. ~**ly** *adv.* **beau·ti·fy** ['bjuːtɪfaɪ] *v.t.* make ~.

beau·ty ['bjuːtɪ] *n.* **1.** (no pl.) quality that delights the eye, ear or mind: *the* ~ *of a picture (music, a mother's love).* **2.** beautiful person or thing. ~ **par·lour** *n.* establishment (2) in which women receive treatment (of the skin, hair, etc.) to increase their ~. ~ **queen** *n.* girl judged (2) the most beautiful in a ~ contest. ~ **treat·ment** *n.* use of cosmetics, etc. to increase a person's ~.

bea·ver ['biːvə*] *n.* **1.** fur-covered, broad-tailed animal living on land and in water, able to cut down trees with its strong teeth and to build dams across rivers. **2.** (no pl.) its soft brown fur.

be·calmed [bɪ'kɑːmd] *pred. adj.* (of a sailing-ship) stopped because there is no wind.

be·cause [bɪ'kɒz] *conj.* **1.** for the reason that: *I did it* ~ *he told me to do it.* **2.** ~ *of*, by reason of; on account of: *We couldn't go out,* ~ *of the rain.*

beck *n.* beckoning sign: *be at sb.'s* ~ *and call*, be under his orders, compelled to come and go all the time.

beck·on ['bekən] *v.t. & i.* make a sign with the hand or arm (to sb. asking him to come or to follow).

be·come [bɪ'kʌm] *v.i. & t.* (p.t. *became*, p.p. ~) **1.** come, grow, or begin to be: *He became a doctor. He has* ~ *accustomed to the climate. It is becoming expensive to travel.* **2.** ~ *of*, happen to: *Do you know what became of her after she married?* **3.** be suitable

for; look well on: *That hat* ~*s you.* ~ *becoming hat.*

bed¹ [bed] *n.* **1.** piece of furniture etc. on which to sleep: *make the* ~*s* put the sheets, blankets, etc. on them ready for use; *go to* ~; *put to* ~; ~ *and breakfast*, sleeping accommodation and food next morning, as offered by hotels, etc. **2.** mattress: *a feather* ~. **3.** base or foundation on which sth. rests: *a* ~ *of concrete.* **4.** layer (of clay, rock, etc.). **5.** foundation of a road or railway. **6.** ground underneath the sea, a river, or lake: *a dry river-*~. **7.** piece of ground for plants: *flower-*~*(s)* '~**clothes** *n. pl.* sheets, blankets, etc. '~**lin·en** *n.* (no pl.) sheets and pillowcases. '~**rid·den** *adj.* obliged by illness or old age to stay in ~. '~**room** *n.* room for sleeping in. ¡~'**sit·ter** (colloq.), ¡~'**sit·ting-room** *ns.* room used for both living in and sleeping in. '~**spread** *n.* covering spread over a ~ during the day. '~**stead** *n.* framework of a ~. '~**time** *n.* hour for going to ~.

bed² [bed] *v.t.* (-dd-) provide with, put into, a ~; plant: ~ *out plants;* ~ *down a horse with straw;* ~*ded in concrete.* ~**ding** *n.* (no pl.) **1.** mattress, bedclothes, pillows, etc. **2.** straw, etc. for animals to sleep on.

bed·lam ['bedləm] *n.* scene of noisy confusion; (old use) asylum for mad persons.

bed·(o)u·in ['bedʊɪn] *n.* (pl. ~) nomad desert Arab.

be·drag·gled [bɪ'drægld] *adj.* made wet and dirty by bad weather, mud, etc.

bee [biː] *n.* small, flying insect that gathers nectar and pollen from flowers and produces wax and honey. '~**hive** *n.* see *hive* (1). '~, **keep·er**, '~, **mas·ter** *ns.* keeper of ~s. '~**line** *n.* make *a* ~*-line for*, go towards by the shortest way. ~**s·wax** ['biːzwæks] *n.* (no pl.) wax with which ~s make honeycombs.

a bee   a beetle¹

beech [biːtʃ] *n.* forest tree with smooth grey bark, shiny leaves, and triangular nuts which may be eaten; its wood.

beef [biːf] *n.* meat from an ox, cow,

or bull. **~ tea** *n.* (no pl.) stewed juice from ~.

been, see *be.*

beer [bɪə*] *n.* alcoholic drink made from malt and hops.

beet [bi:t] *n.* plant with a large sweet root. red ~, cooked and eaten as a vegetable; white ~, used for making ~ sugar. '**~root** *n.* (Gt. Brit.) root of ~; red ~.

bee·tle[1] ['bi:tl] *n.* insect with hard, shiny wing-covers.

bee·tle[2] ['bi:tl] *v.i.* overhang: *beetling cliffs.* *adj.* projecting; shaggy: ~ *brows.*

be·fall [bɪ'fɔ:l] *v.t. & i.* (p.t. befell, p.p. ~en) happen (to).

be·fit [bɪ'fɪt] *v.t.* (-tt-) be proper for; be right or suitable for.

be·fore [bɪ'fɔ:*] *prep., adv., & conj.* **I. prep. 1.** earlier than. **2.** in front of: *Your name comes ~ mine on the list.* **3.** in the presence of: *He was brought ~ a judge.* **4.** rather than; in preference to: *Death ~ dishonour.* **II. adv. 1.** at an earlier time; already; in the past: *I've seen that film ~.* **2.** (of position) in advance: *The children went on ~.* **III. conj. 1.** previous to the time when: *Do it now ~ you forget.* **2.** rather than: *I'll die ~ I surrender!* **~hand** [bɪ'fɔ:hænd] *adv. & pred. adj.* in readiness; in advance; earlier than necessary.

be·friend [bɪ'frend] *v.t.* act as a friend to; be helpful to.

beg [beg] *v.t. & i.* (-gg-) ask for (money, food, clothes, etc.); ask earnestly (for), or with deep feeling: ~ (*for*) *one's bread*; ~ *a favour of sb.*; ~ (*of*) *sb. to do sth.*; *go ~ing,* (of things) be unwanted; ~ *to differ,* say that one cannot agree; ~ *off,* ask to be excused from sth. *I ~ your pardon,* (a) I am sorry; (b) Please excuse me; (c) Please say that again.

be·gan, see *begin.*

be·get [bɪ'get] *v.t.* (-tt-; p.t. begot [bɪ'gɒt], p.p. begotten [bɪ'gɒtn]) **1.** give existence to (as father). **2.** (liter.) be the cause of: *War ~s misery and ruin.*

beg·gar ['begə*] *n.* person who begs. *v.t.* make poor; ruin. ~ *description,* be so bad (good, etc.) that description is inadequate. **~ly** *adj.* very poor; mean. **~y** *n.* (no pl.) condition of being very poor.

be·gin [bɪ'gɪn] *v.t. & i.* (-nn-; p.t. began [bɪ'gæn], p.p. begun [bɪ'gʌn]) **1.** start: *It's time to ~ work. Sentences ~ with a capital letter and end with a full stop.* **2.** When the sun came out

the snow began to melt. I'm ~ning to understand. **3.** B~ to read (start reading) *at page 96.* (Cf. *start.*) **~ner** *n.* person learning sth. and without much knowledge of it yet. **~ning** *n.* starting-point.

be·gone [bɪ'gɒn] *int. & v.* (imperative only) go away.

be·got(·ten), see *beget.*

be·grudge [bɪ'grʌdʒ] *v.t.* see *grudge.*

be·guile [bɪ'gaɪl] *v.t.* **1.** cause (sb. to do sth.) by guile (deceit, tricks). **2.** cause (time) to pass pleasantly.

be·gun, see *begin.*

be·half [bɪ'hɑ:f] *n.* *on* (U.S.A. *in*) ~ *of,* for, in the interest of; *on* (*in*) *his* (*her, etc.*) ~, for him (her, etc.).

be·have [bɪ'heɪv] *v.i. & refl.* act; conduct oneself; show good manners.

be·hav·iour (U.S.A. *-ior*) [bɪ'heɪvjə*] *n.* (no pl.) way of behaving. **~ism** *n.* (no pl.) (psych.) study of human actions by analysis into stimulus and response. **~ist** *n.*

be·head [bɪ'hed] *v.t.* cut off the head of.

be·hind [bɪ'haɪnd] *prep., adv., & n.* **I. prep. 1.** in, at, or to, the rear of: *The boy was hiding ~ a bush.* **2.** having made less progress than: *John is ~ other boys of the same age.* **3.** remaining after the departure of: *The storm left much damage ~ it.* **4.** later than: ~ *schedule* (*time*), not punctual. **II. adv. 1.** in, at, or to, the rear: *The rest of the runners are a long way ~.* **2.** Stay ~ (*after the others have gone home*) *and help me clean up.* **3.** *You are ~ with* (late in paying) *your rent.* **III. n.** buttocks. **~hand** [bɪ'haɪndhænd] *adv. & pred. adj.* late; after others; ~ *the times:* ~*hand with the rent;* ~*hand in one's work.*

be·hold [bɪ'həʊld] *v.t.* (p.t. & p.p. beheld) (old use, liter.) take notice; see, esp. sth. striking or unusual.

beige [beɪʒ] *n.* (no pl.) colour of sandstone (brown, brownish-grey, or greyish-yellow).

be·in ['bi:'ɪn] *n.* informal gathering of (esp.) young people, usu. in a park or other public place.

be·ing ['bi:ɪŋ] *n.* **1.** (no pl.) state of existing. **2.** human creature. **3.** *the Supreme B~,* God.

be·jew·elled [bɪ'dʒu:əld] *adj.* adorned with jewels.

be·la·bour [bɪ'leɪbə*] *v.t.* beat hard; give hard blows to.

be·lat·ed [bɪ'leɪtɪd] *adj.* coming (too) late; overtaken by darkness.

belch [beltʃ] *v.t. & i.* send out (air,

wind from the stomach, smoke, etc.) with force.

be·lea·guer [bɪ'liːgə*] *v.t.* besiege.

bel·fry ['belfrɪ] *n.* tower, part of a tower, esp. in a church, for bells.

Bel·gian ['beldʒən] *n. & adj.* (native or inhabitant) of Belgium.

be·lie [bɪ'laɪ] *v.t.* **1.** give a false idea of. **2.** fail to justify or fulfil (sth. hoped for or promised).

be·lief [bɪ'liːf] *n.* feeling that sth. is real and true; trust or confidence (*in*): *to the best of my* ∼, so far as my knowledge goes.

be·lieve [bɪ'liːv] *v.t. & i.* **1.** have belief: *I* ∼ *what he says* (i.e. that it is true). **2.** have trust (*in*): *I* ∼ *in that man.* **3.** feel sure of the value of: *He* ∼*s in getting plenty of exercise.* **4.** feel sure of the existence of: ∼ *in God.* **5.** *make* ∼, pretend. **be·liev·er** *n.*

be·lit·tle [bɪ'lɪtl] *v.t.* cause to seem unimportant or of small value.

bell [bel] *n.* **1.** hollow vessel of cast (3) metal that makes a ringing sound when struck. **2.** stroke of a ∼. **'**∼**-bot·tomed** *adj.* (of trousers) made very wide below the knee.

a bell (1)   belts (1)

bel·li·cose ['belɪkəʊs] *adj.* fond of fighting; anxious to fight.

bel·lig·er·ent [bɪ'lɪdʒərənt] *n. & adj.* (nation, party, or person) waging war; pugnacious.

bel·low ['beləʊ] *v.i. & t.* roar (like a bull); shout; utter loudly and usu. angrily. *n.* ∼ing sound.

bel·lows ['beləʊz] *n. pl.* (sing. or pl. v.) apparatus (1) for blowing air into a fire or through the pipes of an organ.

bel·ly ['belɪ] *n.* abdomen (1); stomach. *v.t. & i.* ∼ (*out*), (usu. of sails) swell out.

be·long [bɪ'lɒŋ] *v.i.* **1.** ∼ *to,* be the property of; be a member of. **2.** have as a right or proper place: *Do these books* ∼ *here?* ∼**ings** *n. pl.* personal possessions (not land, a business, etc.).

be·loved [bɪ'lʌvd] *pred. adj.* much loved: *She is* ∼ *by all.* [bɪ'lʌvɪd] *n. & adj.* person (who is) much loved: *flowers for his* ∼; *his* ∼ *wife.*

be·low [bɪ'ləʊ] *prep. & adv.* I. *prep.* **1.** lower than (cf. *under* and *over*): *When the sun sets it sinks* ∼ *the horizon. The temperature is ten degrees* ∼ *zero. The Dead Sea is* ∼ *sea-level.* **2.** downstream from: *ten yards* ∼ *the bridge.* II. *adv.* **1.** at or to a lower level: *The people (in the room)* ∼ *are very noisy. I feel seasick, I must go* ∼ (downstairs to my cabin). **2.** *Sign your name* ∼ (at the bottom of the sheet). *See* ∼ (refer to what is written later).

belt [belt] *n.* **1.** strip of cloth, leather, etc. worn round the waist. **2.** endless (leather, etc.) band used to connect wheels and drive machinery. **3.** any wide strip: *a green* ∼ *round a town* (i.e. area of parks, woods, etc.). *v.t.* fasten on with a ∼; beat with a ∼.

be·moan [bɪ'məʊn] *v.t.* lament

bench [bentʃ] *n.* **1.** long seat of wood or stone. ∼ *seat,* seat across the whole width (2) of a car. **2.** work-table (for a shoemaker, etc.). **3.** judge's seat or office; lawcourt; (collective) judges, magistrates. *be raised to the B*∼, be made a judge or bishop.

bend [bend] *v.t. & i.* (p.t. & p.p. *bent* [bent]) **1.** cause part of sth. straight or upright to be at an angle to the rest, or to curve: *If you* ∼ *that stick too much it will break.* **2.** become curved; bow²; stoop: *Her head was bent over her book. The branches were* ∼*ing down with the weight of the fruit.* **3.** turn; direct; cause (the mind, attention, etc.) to turn (towards): ∼ *one's mind to one's studies. bent on,* having the mind set on; having as a fixed purpose: *bent on mastering English. n.* curve, turn, or angle.

be·neath [bɪ'niːθ] *adv. & prep.* **1.** (old use or liter.) below; under(neath). **2.** not worthy of.

bene·dic·tion [ˌbenɪ'dɪkʃn] *n.* blessing, esp. one given by a priest at the end of a church service.

bene·fac·tion [ˌbenɪ'fækʃn] *n.* good deed (esp. the giving of money for charity; the money so given). **bene·fac·tor** ['benɪfæktə*] *n.* person who has given friendly help; patron (1) of a cause (3) or charitable institution.

be·nef·i·cent [bɪ'nefɪsnt] *adj.* doing good; kind. **be·nef·i·cence** *n.* (no pl.). **ben·e·fi·cial** [ˌbenɪ'fɪʃl] *adj.* having good results. **ben·e·fi·ciary** [ˌbenɪ'fɪʃərɪ] *n.* person who benefits under a will³ (6).

ben·e·fit ['benɪfɪt] *n.* **1.** help; advantage; good done or received. *give sb. the* ∼ *of the doubt,* free him from blame, etc., because there is doubt; ~ *performance*, one of which the profits are used for charity, etc. **2.** financial help in time of sickness, old age, unemployment, etc. provided for under an insurance or social security: *sickness* ~. *v.t. & i.* do good to; receive ~ *(by, from)*.

be·nev·o·lent [bɪ'nevələnt] *adj.* kind and helpful; doing good. **~·ly** *adv.* **be·nev·o·lence** *n.* (no pl.).

be·nign [bɪ'naɪn] *adj.* **1.** (of persons) kind and gentle. **2.** (of diseases) not serious or dangerous. **3.** (of climate, etc.) favourable to growth. **be·nig·nant** [bɪ'nɪgnənt] *adj.* kind; gracious.

bent [bent] *v.* see *bend*. *n.* inclination of the mind; natural skill in and liking *(for)*; aptitude *(for)*: *She has a ~ for sewing* (i.e. is fond of and clever at sewing).

be·numb [bɪ'nʌm] *v.t.* make numb.

ben·zene ['benziːn] *n.* (no pl.) colourless aromatic liquid got from coal tar and petroleum, used as a solvent, motor fuel, etc.

ben·zine ['benziːn] *n.* (no pl.) colourless liquid got from mineral oil, used as a solvent, esp. in dry-cleaning.

ben·zol ['benzɒl], **ben·zole** ['benzəʊl] *n.* (no pl.) benzene.

be·queath [bɪ'kwiːð] *v.t.* arrange (by making a will) to give (property, etc.) at death; hand down to those who come after. **be·quest** [bɪ'kwest] *n.* ~ing; sth. ~ed.

be·reave [bɪ'riːv] *v.t.* **1.** (p.t. & p.p. *bereft* [bɪ'reft]) rob; dispossess: *bereft of*, having lost: *bereft of hope*; *bereft of reason*, insane. **2.** (pret. & p.p. ~d) (of death) leave unhappy by taking away (a relation, etc.): *the ~d husband*. **~·ment** *n.* being ~d; great loss (esp. by death).

be·reft, see *bereave*.

be·ret ['bereɪ] *n.* flat, round felt² or cloth cap without a peak (2).

a beret

·er·ry ['berɪ] *n.* small round fruit containing seed(s): *straw~*; *black~*; *holly berries*.

·erth [bɜːθ] *n.* **1.** sleeping-place in a

train or ship, etc. **2.** place for a ship in a river or harbour. *give a wide ~ to*, keep at a safe distance from. **3.** (colloq.) work; position. *v.t. & i.* get a (ship) into, come into, a ~; provide a ~ (1) for.

be·seech [bɪ'siːtʃ] *v.t.* (p.t. & p.p. *besought* [bɪ'sɔːt]) ask earnestly or urgently: ~ *sb. to help (for help)*.

be·set [bɪ'set] *v.t.* (-*tt*-; p.t. & p.p. ~) attack from all sides; have on all sides: *a problem ~ with difficulties. His ~ting sin* (i.e. the sin of which he is regularly guilty) *is laziness*.

be·side [bɪ'saɪd] *prep.* **1.** at the side of; close to. **2.** compared with: *You're quite tall ~ your sister.* ~ *oneself*, at the end of one's self-control; ~ *the mark (question, point)*, having nothing to do with the question, etc. ~s *prep. & adv.* in addition (to); other than; except; moreover; also; otherwise; else.

be·siege [bɪ'siːdʒ] *v.t.* close in upon, attack, from all sides. ~ *(sb.) with (requests, etc.)*, make a large number of (requests, etc.).

be·smear [bɪ'smɪə*] *v.t.* smear all over (with grease, etc.).

be·sought, see *beseech*.

be·spat·ter [bɪ'spætə*] *v.t.* spatter or sprinkle with mud, dirt.

best [best] *adj., adv., & n.* **I.** *adj.* (superl. of *good*) of the most excellent kind: *That was the ~ dinner I have ever eaten!* ~ *man*, bridegroom's friend attending him at his wedding. *the ~ part of*, most of. ~ *seller*, (author of a) book with large sales. ~ *way*, shortest, surest, easiest, most convenient way. **II.** *adv.* (superl. of *well²*) **1.** in the most excellent way: *He works ~ in the morning. Do as you think ~.* **2.** most. **3.** *had ~* = had better. **III.** *n.* the ~ person(s) or thing(s); the most excellent part, aspect, etc. of sth.: *the ~ of friends*, very close friends. *All the ~!* (Expression of goodwill, used when parting from sb.) *at ~*, taking the most hopeful view; *at its (one's) ~*, in the best condition; *be all for the ~*, be good in the end; *do sth. all for the ~*, act with the ~ of intentions; *do one's ~*, do all one can; *make the ~ of it (things)*, be as contented as possible. *(Sunday) ~*, ~ *clothes*.

bes·tial ['bestjəl] *adj.* of or like a beast; nasty; brutal.

be·stir [bɪ'stɜː*] *v.t.* (-*rr*-) ~ *oneself*, rouse (2) oneself; busy oneself.

be·stow [bɪ'stəʊ] *v.t.* **1.** give: *the advantages ~ed on us by nature.* **2.** put (in a place).

be·stride [bɪ'straɪd] *v.t.* (p.t. *bestrode*,

p.p. *bestridden*) put, sit with, stand with, one leg on each side of: ~ *a horse* (*chair*, *ditch*).

bet [bet] *v.t. & i.* (-*tt*-; p.t. & p.p. ~ or ~*ted*) **1.** risk money, etc. on the result of a race or other event. **2.** (colloq.): *I* ~, I am certain; *you* ~, you may be certain. *n.* act of ~*ting*; the money, etc. offered.

be·take [bɪ'teɪk] *v.t.* (p.t. *betook*, p.p. ~*n*) ~ *oneself to*, go to (a place or person).

be·tray [bɪ'treɪ] *v.t.* **1.** be false or unfaithful to. **2.** give up treacherously (*to* an enemy). **3.** allow (a secret) to become known (by accident or on purpose). **4.** be or give a sign of; show. ~**al** *n.*

be·troth [bɪ'trəʊð] *v.t.* (usu. in p.p.) *be* ~*ed*, promised in marriage. ~**al** *n.* engagement to be married. **be·trothed** *n.* ~ed person.

bet·ter[1] ['betə*] *adj., adv., v., & n.* **I.** *adj.* (comp. of *good*) **1.** *This is good but that is* ~. *He's a* ~ *man than his brother*. *no* ~ *than*, of the same value, merit, etc. as: *He's no* ~ *than a lazy dog* (i.e. a lazy dog would do as much work as he does). *one's* ~ *half*, (colloq.) wife; *the* ~ *part of*, most of. **2.** (of health) (a) less ill: *She's* ~ *today but is still not well enough to get up*. (b) fully recovered: *She's* (*quite*) ~ *now and has gone back to work*. **II.** *adv.* (comp. of *well*[2]) **1.** *You would write* ~ *if you used a good pen. You can do it* ~ *than I* (*can*). *You would like that picture* ~ (*more*) *if you studied it. be* ~ *off*, be richer, more comfortable. **2.** *had* ~, would find it an advantage, wise, etc. to: *I* (*You*) *had* ~ *take a raincoat.* **III.** *v.t.* improve: *The managers should* ~ *the conditions under which the stuff work. He* ~*ed himself* (earned more money, etc.) *by changing his job.* **IV.** *n.* that which is ~: *get the* ~ *of*, defeat; *one's* ~*s*, people who are of higher rank than oneself.

bet·ter[2], **bet·tor** ['betə*] *n.* person who bets.

be·tween [bɪ'twiːn] *prep. & adv.* **I.** *prep.* **1.** (of place): *The letter B comes* ~ *A and C. The Mediterranean Sea is* ~ *Europe and Africa.* **2.** (of rank): *A corporal ranks* ~ *a private soldier and a sergeant.* **3.** (of time): ~ *two and three o'clock*; ~ *Wednesday and Friday*; ~ *the two world wars.* **4.** (of distance, amount, etc.): ~ *five and six miles*; ~ *10p. and 15p.*; ~ *freezing-point and boiling-point.* **5.** ~ *to and from*: *a bus service runs* ~ *the two cities.* **6.** (to show sharing, combining): *Share the money*

~ (*among*) *you. B*~ *the two of them they did much to make the party success.* **7.** (showing relationship, comparison): *We can usually distinguish* ~ *right and wrong. The relations* ~ *teache* *and pupils are excellent.* **II.** *adv.* in(to a place or time that is ~: *I had appoint* *ments in the morning and afternoon an* *no time for lunch* ~. *There are bushes a each side of the garden and flowers in* ~ *The trees are few and far* ~ (few and a wide intervals).

bev·el ['bevl] *n.* sloping surface at a edge.

bev·er·age ['bevərɪdʒ] *n.* kind of drin except water (e.g. tea, coffee, milk wine, beer).

bevy ['bevɪ] *n.* group, company (o women, birds, esp. quail).

be·wail [bɪ'weɪl] *v.t.* wail over; expres sorrow for.

be·ware [bɪ'weə*] *v.t. & i.* (in th imperative and infinitive only) be o guard; be careful (*of*): *B*~ *of the dog You must* ~ (how ...; lest ...; that ... not)

be·wil·der [bɪ'wɪldə*] *v.t.* puzzle confuse greatly. ~**ment** *n.* (no pl.)

be·witch [bɪ'wɪtʃ] *v.t.* **1.** work magi on; put a spell[2] on. **2.** attract or charm ~**ing** *adj. her* ~*ing smile.*

be·yond [bɪ'jɒnd] *prep. & adv.* **prep. 1.** at, on, or to, the farther sid of: *The house is* ~ *the bridge.* **2.** (of time after: *I cannot stay with you* ~ *Thurs day.* **3.** exceeding; out of reach o *Your work is* ~ *all praise*, too good t describe adequately. *He is living* ~ *hi income*, spending more than he earns *This lesson is* ~ *me*, is too difficult fo me to understand. **II.** *adv.* at or to distance; farther on: *I can only se houses from the window—I don't kno what lies* ~.

bi- [baɪ-] *pref.* twice; having two coming once in every two.

bi·an·nu·al [baɪ'ænjʊəl] *adj.* appear ing, etc. twice a year.

bi·as ['baɪəs] *n.* **1.** *have a* ~ *towards* (*against*) *sth.*, be in favour of (opposed to) sth., esp. without full knowledge or examination of all facts. **2.** *cut on the* ~, (dressmaking, etc.) cut in a sloping direction across the material *v.t.* (-*s*- or -*ss*-) give a ~ to; influence esp. unfairly.

bi·ath·lete [baɪ'æθliːt] *n.* athlete who competes in a **bi·ath·lon** [baɪ'æθlɒn] *n.* athletic contest in which each competitor takes part in two different events (cross-country skiing and rifle shooting).

bib [bɪb] *n.* **1.** cloth tied under a child'

billiards

chin for meals. **2.** upper part of an apron or of overalls.

Bi·ble ['baɪbl] *n.* sacred writings of the Jews and the Christian Church. **bib·li·cal** ['bɪblɪkl] *adj.*

bib·li·og·ra·phy [ˌbɪblɪ'ɒɡrəfɪ] *n.* list of books and writings, usu. of one author or on one subject (2). **bib·li·og·ra·pher** *n.*

bi·car·bon·ate [ˌbaɪ'kɑːbənɪt] *n.* (no pl.) salt of carbonic acid, a white powder used in cooking and in medicine.

bi·cen·te·na·ry [ˌbaɪsen'tiːnərɪ] *n.* (celebration of the) 200th anniversary of an event.

bi·cen·ten·ni·al [ˌbaɪsen'tenjəl] *adj.* lasting, happening every, 200 years. *n.* 200th anniversary.

bi·ceps ['baɪseps] *n.* (pl. ~) large muscle on the front of the upper arm.

bick·er ['bɪkə*] *v.i.* quarrel (*with* sb. over, *about* sth. unimportant).

bi·cy·cle ['baɪsɪkl] *n.* (colloq. *bike*) two-wheeled machine for riding on, driven along by the feet. *v.i.* (usu. *cycle*) ride a ~; go (*to*) by ~.

a bicycle

a motor cycle

bid [bɪd] *v.t. & i.* (-dd-) **1.** (p.t. & p.p. ~) make an offer of money (*for*). **2.** (old use, p.t. *bade* [bæd], p.p. ~*den* ['bɪdn]) command; say (goodbye, etc.). *n.* offer to pay a stated sum (*for* sth.). *make a ~ for*, try to obtain. **~·ding** *n.* *do sb.'s ~ding*, obey him.

bide [baɪd] *v.t.* ~ *one's time*, wait for an opportunity.

bi·en·ni·al [baɪ'enɪəl] *adj.* lasting for, happening once in every, two years. *n.* plant that lives two years and has flowers and seed in the second year.

bier [bɪə*] *n.* movable wooden stand for a coffin or a corpse.

bi·fo·cals [ˌbaɪ'fəʊklz] *n. pl.* spectacles with both distant and near vision lenses.

bi·fur·cate ['baɪfəkeɪt] *v.t. & i.* (of rivers, roads, etc.) divide into two branches; fork. **bi·fur·ca·tion** [ˌbaɪfə-'keɪʃn] *n.*

big [bɪɡ] *adj.* (~ger, ~gest) of large size or importance: *John's growing a ~ boy, isn't he? Charles is getting too ~ for his boots*, (sl.) becoming conceited. *They are hunting ~ game* (lions, elephants, tigers, etc.).

big·a·my ['bɪɡəmɪ] *n.* (no pl.) having two wives or two husbands living, a sin and a crime in Christian countries. **big·a·mous** ['bɪɡəməs] *adj.* a bigamous marriage. **big·a·mist** *n.* person guilty of ~.

big·ot·ed ['bɪɡətɪd] *adj.* strict and obstinate beyond reason in holding a belief or opinion. **big·ot** ['bɪɡət] *n.* ~ person. **big·ot·ry** ['bɪɡətrɪ] *n.*

bike [baɪk] *n. & v.i.* (colloq.) bicycle.

bi·ki·ni [bɪ'kiːnɪ] *n.* a woman's small two-piece bathing-suit, worn also for sunbathing.

bi·lat·er·al [ˌbaɪ'lætərəl] *adj.* of, on, with, two sides; (of an agreement, etc.) made between two (persons, governments, etc.).

bile [baɪl] *n.* (no pl.) bitter liquid produced by the liver to help in digesting food; (fig.) bad temper.

bilge [bɪldʒ] *n.* (no pl.) the widest, almost flat part of a ship's bottom; (also ~-*water*) the dirty water that collects there.

bi·lin·gual [baɪ'lɪŋɡwəl] *adj.* speaking two languages (esp. when these are learnt together in childhood); expressed in two languages.

bil·ious ['bɪljəs] *adj.* caused by too much bile: *a ~ attack*; (of a person) subject to sickness owing to trouble in the bile or liver.

bill[1] [bɪl] *n.* horny part of a bird's mouth, beak, esp. when slender or weak.

bill[2] [bɪl] *n.* **1.** note of charges (3) for goods delivered or services rendered. **2.** written or printed notice handed out or stuck on a wall, etc. **3.** proposed law, to be discussed by a parliament (and called an *Act* when passed). **4.** (also ~ *of exchange*) written order to a bank, etc. to pay money to sb. on a certain date. **5.** (U.S.A.) = banknote. '**~·board** *n.* large board for advertisements (at the roadside). '**~·fold** *n.* (U.S.A.) wallet for banknotes. '**~·post·er**, '**~·stick·er** *ns.* person who sticks ~s (2) on walls, etc. (See *fare* (3); *lading*.)

bill[3] [bɪl] *v.t.* **1.** make known by means of bills (2). **2.** submit a bill (1) to.

bil·liards ['bɪljədz] *n. pl.* (sing. v.) indoor game played with balls and long sticks (*cues*[2]) on an oblong, cloth-covered *billiard-table*.

bil·lion ['bɪljən] *n.* one thousand millions; (Gt. Brit. old use) one million millions.

bil·low ['bɪləʊ] *n.* (liter.) great wave; (pl., poet.) the sea. *v.i.* rise or roll like great waves.

bil·ly-goat ['bɪlɪgəʊt] *n.* male goat.

bin [bɪn] *n.* large container or enclosed place, usu. with a lid, for storing coal, grain, etc., or (*dustbin*) for rubbish.

bind [baɪnd] *v.t. & i.* (p.t. & p.p. *bound* [baʊnd]) **1.** tie or fasten together (with rope, etc.); put (one thing) round (another): ~ (*up*) *a wound*; *be bound hand and foot*; ~ *the edge of a carpet.* **2.** fasten together; put (sheets of paper, etc.) into a cover: *a well-bound book.* **3.** become, cause to become, hard, solid, difficult to move: *Frost ~s the soil. The land is frost-bound.* **4.** hold sb. (by legal agreement, promise, or under penalty) to a certain course of action: ~ *oneself to,* promise or guarantee to (do sth.); ~ *sb. over,* ~ *sb. to keep the peace* (under the penalty of appearing before the judge again if he makes further trouble). (See *bound*[4] for special uses of the p.p.) **~·er** *n.* person, thing, machine, that ~s. **~·ing** *n.* **1.** book-cover. **2.** tape (1), braid (2), etc. for protecting an edge of a garment, etc.

bin·go ['bɪŋgəʊ] *n.* (no pl.) gambling game in which numbered squares on cards are covered as the numbers are called at random.

bin·oc·u·lars [bɪ'nɒkjʊləz] *n. pl.* instrument with lenses for both eyes, making distant objects seem nearer.

bio- [baɪəʊ-] *pref.* of life; of living organisms: *biography*; *biology*.

bio·chem·is·try [,baɪəʊ'kemɪstrɪ] *n.* (no pl.) chemistry of living organisms. **bio·chem·ist** *n.*

bi·og·ra·phy [baɪ'ɒgrəfɪ] *n.* person's life-history written by another; branch of literature dealing with persons' lives. **bi·og·ra·pher** *n.* **bio·graph·ic, bio·graph·i·cal** [,baɪəʊ'græfɪk(l)] *adjs.*

bi·ol·o·gy [baɪ'ɒlədʒɪ] *n.* (no pl.) science of life, of animals, and plants. **bi·o·log·i·cal** [,baɪəʊ'lɒdʒɪkl] *adj.* of ~ *biological warfare,* use of germs, etc. against an enemy to spread disease. **bi·ol·o·gist** *n.*

bi·ped ['baɪped] *n.* two-footed animal (e.g. a man or a bird).

bi·plane ['baɪpleɪn] *n.* aircraft with two pairs of wings, one above the other.

birch [bɜːtʃ] *n.* tree with thin, smooth bark; its wood.

bird [bɜːd] *n.* **1.** feathered animal with two legs and two wings. **2.** (sl.) young woman. **3.** (colloq.) person. **~'s-,eye 'view** *n.* general overhead view *of* a town, etc., or (fig.) *of* a subject (2).

birth [bɜːθ] *n.* **1.** (process of) being born: *give* ~ *to,* bring into the world; (fig.) produce. **2.** descent (2): *He's an Englishman by* ~. **~·con·trol** *n.* (no pl.) (methods of) preventing unwanted pregnancies. '**~·day** *n.* day of one's ~ (1); each anniversary of it. '**~·mark** *n.* mark on one's body at or from ~ (1). '**~·place** *n.* place at which one was born. ~ **rate** *n.* number of ~s (1) in one year for every 1,000 persons. '**~·right** *n.* the various rights, privileges, and properties a person is entitled to as a member of his family, a citizen of his country, etc.

bis·cuit ['bɪskɪt] *n.* flat, thin, crisp cake of many kinds, sweetened or unsweetened.

bi·sect [baɪ'sekt] *v.t.* divide into two (usu. equal) parts. **bi·sec·tion** [,baɪ-'sekʃn] *n.* (no pl.).

bish·op ['bɪʃəp] *n.* **1.** clergyman of high rank who organizes the work of the Church in a city or district. **2.** piece in chess. **~·ric** ['bɪʃəprɪk] *n.* office of a ~; district under a ~.

bi·son ['baɪsn] *n.* wild ox; American buffalo.

bit[1] [bɪt] *n.* **1.** very small piece of anything: ~ *by* ~, slowly; gradually; *a* ~ (*better, etc.*), rather, somewhat (*better, etc.*); *not a* ~, not at all; *give sb. a* ~ *of one's mind,* speak severely; show that one is annoyed. **2.** short time or distance: *wait a* ~; *move up a* ~. **3.** small coin.

bit[2] [bɪt] *n.* **1.** steel bar placed in a horse's mouth to control it. **2.** biting or cutting part of certain tools: *a brace and* ~.

bit[3], see *bite* (v.).

bitch [bɪtʃ] *n.* **1.** female dog, wolf, or fox. **2.** (derog.) esp. a spiteful, treacherous, or lewd woman.

bite [baɪt] *v.t. & i.* (p.t. *bit* [bɪt], p.p. *bitten* ['bɪtn]) **1.** cut into with the teeth; (of insects, etc.) sting. **2.** (of acids, etc.) make holes in; damage. **3.** (of wheels, etc.) grip; take hold of. **4.** cause smarting pain to: *frost-bitten fingers and toes. Pepper* ~s *the tongue.* *n.* **1.** act of biting. **2.** piece cut off by biting; food: *have a* ~ *to eat.* **3.** injury caused by the teeth or a sting. **bit·ing** *adj.* sharp; stinging: *a biting wind*; (fig.) *biting words*.

bit·ten, see *bite* (v.).

bit·ter ['bɪtə*] *adj.* **1.** tasting like beer or quinine. **2.** causing sorrow; hard to bear; filled with, showing, caused by, anger, envy, etc.: ~ *quarrels* (*words*). **3.** piercingly cold. *n.* **1.** ~ beer. **2.** (pl.) liquor made from herbs, fruits, etc. used to help digestion or to prepare mixed drinks. **~·ly** *adv.* **~·ness** *n.*

biv·ouac ['bɪvʊæk] *n.* temporary camp without tents or other cover. *v.i.* (p.t. & p.p. *-acked*) make, rest in a ~.

biz [bɪz] *n.* (colloq.) business.

bi·zarre [bɪ'zɑ:*] *adj.* strange; queer.

blackberries

black [blæk] *adj.* (almost) without light (opp. *white*); the colour of this printing-ink: ~ *and blue*, discoloured by bruises; ~ *and white*, written in ~ ink on white paper; (of films) not in colour. *give sb. a* ~ *look, look* ~ *at sb.*, look at with anger; *be in sb.'s* ~ *book(s)*, be quite out of his favour. *n.* **1.** (no pl.) ~ colour. **2.** Negro. ~ *art n.* (no pl.) evil magic. **~·ber·ry** ['blækbərɪ] *n.* small, ~ berry, growing on bushes (called *brambles*). '**~·bird** *n.* European song-bird. '**~·board** *n.* board used in schools, etc. for writing and drawing on with chalk. ~ **cof·fee** *n.* coffee without milk or cream. **~·en** *v.t. & i.* **1.** make or become ~. **2.** speak evil of (sb.'s character). ~ **eye** *n.* discoloured bruise round the eye. **~·guard** ['blægɑːd] *n.* person quite without honour; scoundrel. '**~·head** *n.* pimple with a ~ top, esp. on the face. ~ **hu·mour** *n.* (no pl.) form of humour that presents tragedy, etc. in comic terms (5). '**~·leg** *n.* person who offers to work for employer(s) whose men are on strike. ~ **list** *n.* list of persons who are considered dangerous or who are to be punished. ~ **mag·ic** *n.* (no pl.) witchcraft. '**~·mail** *v.t.* (try to) make (sb.) pay money or do sth. by threatening to tell sth. against him. '**~·mail·er** *n.* ~ **mar·ket** *n.* unlawful buying and selling of goods, currencies, etc. that are officially controlled. '**~·out** *n.* **1.** complete darkening of a place or room when lights are put out or windows, etc. are covered. **2.** sudden attack of blindness; temporary loss of memory or consciousness. ~ **pud·ding** *n.* sausage made of blood, suet, etc. ~ **sheep** *n.* worthless member of a respectable family, group, etc. '**~·smith** *n.* man who forges² iron and makes horseshoes.

blad·der ['blædə*] *n.* **1.** skin bag in the body in which waste liquid collects. **2.** rubber bag in a football.

blade [bleɪd] *n.* **1.** cutting part of a knife, sword, razor, etc. **2.** flat, narrow leaf (e.g. of grass). **3.** flat, wide part of an oar (that goes into the water), a propeller, etc.

blame [bleɪm] *v.t.* find fault with; say that (sb. or sth.) is the cause of what is wrong: *Bad workmen* ~ *their tools. Who is to* ~ *for this disaster?* *n.* (no pl.) blaming; responsibility for failure, etc. **~·less** *adj.*

blanch [blɑːntʃ] *v.t. & i.* (cause to) become white or pale: ~ *celery*.

bland [blænd] *adj.* gentle or polite in manner; mild.

blank [blæŋk] *adj.* **1.** (of paper, etc.) with nothing drawn, written, or printed on it. **2.** (of documents) with spaces left for details, signature, etc. **3.** (of a person's face or look) without interest or expression; puzzled. **3.** ~ *cartridge*, with powder but no bullet. ~ *verse*, without rhyme. ~ *wall*, without doors or windows. *n.* **1.** ~ space (in sth. printed or written): *telegraph* ~, form with ~ spaces for the message, etc. **2.** emptiness: *His mind was a complete* ~. **~·ly** *adv.* **~·ness** *n.*

blan·ket ['blæŋkɪt] *n.* **1.** thick, woollen cloth used as a bedcovering, etc. **2.** thick layer (*of* snow, etc.).

blare [bleə*] *n.* (no pl.) loud sound or noise (of trumpets, horns, etc.). *v.t.* make such sounds.

blas·pheme [blæs'fiːm] *v.t. & i.* speak in an irreverent way of (God or sacred things). **blas·phe·mous** ['blæsfəməs] *adj.* **blas·phe·my** ['blæsfəmɪ] *n.*

blast [blɑːst] *n.* **1.** strong, sudden rush of wind or air: *a* ~ *of hot air from a furnace*; *windows broken by* ~ (e.g. after an explosion). **2.** sound made by a wind instrument, such as a horn or trumpet. *v.t.* **1.** break up or destroy by explosion (e.g. in a quarry or mine): *Danger! B~ing in progress!* **2.**

destroy; bring to nothing: *blossom ~ed by frost; a tree ~ed by lightning.* **3.** ~ *off,* (of a rocket, etc.) take off; *~-off* (n.). '**~-,fur·nace** *n.* furnace for melting iron ore by forcing into it a current of heated air.

bla·tant ['bleɪtənt] *adj.* noisy; trying to attract attention in a vulgar and shameless way.

blaze¹ [bleɪz] *n.* **1.** bright fire, flame, or light; glow of colour: *burst into a ~; put out a big ~* (extinguish a burning house, etc.). **2.** violent outburst of feeling: *in a ~ of anger.* *v.i.* **1.** burn with bright flames; *~ up,* burst into flames. **2.** show bright colours; shine brightly or with warmth: *a garden blazing with colour. The sun ~d down on us.* **3.** burst out with strong feeling: *blazing with indignation.*

blaze² [bleɪz] *v.t.* make a cut or mark on a tree (e.g. to show a path through a forest): *~ a trail,* mark a path by doing this; (fig.) do sth. new and show the way for others to follow.

blaze³ [bleɪz] *v.t.* *~ (sth.) abroad,* make known far and wide.

blaz·er ['bleɪzə*] *n.* coloured or plain light jacket not matching trousers or skirts.

bleach [bliːtʃ] *v.t. & i.* make or become white (by chemical process or by sunlight).

bleak [bliːk] *adj.* (of weather) cold; dismal; (of a place, e.g. a hillside) bare; windy; (of prospects, etc.) dreary; unhopeful.

blear [blɪə*] *adj.* (of eyes or mind) dim; dull; blurred; poorly outlined. **~y** *adj.* (-*ier,* -*iest*). '**~(y)-eyed** *adj.* having ~ eyes or wits.

bleat [bliːt] *v.i. & t. & n.* (make the) cry of a sheep, goat, or calf.

bled, see *bleed.*

bleed [bliːd] *v.i. & t.* (p.t. & p.p. *bled* [bled]) lose blood; cause blood to flow from.

bleep [bliːp] *v.i. & n.* (give out a) high-pitched sound or radio signal.

blem·ish ['blemɪʃ] *n.* mark, etc. that spoils the beauty or perfection of sth. or sb.: *a ~ on the skin* (on *sb.'s character*). *v.t.* spoil the beauty or perfection of.

blend [blend] *v.t. & i.* **1.** (of tea, tobacco, etc.) mix together; mix (so as to make the mixture desired). **2.** (of colours) go well together; have no sharp contrasts: *colours that ~ well. n.* mixture made by ~ing: *an excellent ~ of tea.*

bless [bles] *v.t.* (p.t. & p.p. *~ed, blest* [blest]) **1.** ask God's favour for: *The*

priest ~ed the people (*the crops*). **2** wish good to; make happy: *B~ you, my boy!* **3.** *be ~ed with,* be fortunate in having: *be ~ed with good health; no greatly ~ed with worldly goods* (i.e. no rich). **4.** make sacred or holy: *relic ~ed by the Pope.* **5.** call (God) holy. **6.** (colloq. uses) *B~ me! B~ my soul. Well, I'm blest!* (all showing surprise) **~·ed** ['blesɪd] *adj.* holy; sacred; fortunate; bringing happiness. **~·ing** *n* favour of God; grace (5) (before or after a meal): *ask a ~ing;* sth. that brings happiness; sth. one is glad of

blew, see *blow¹.*

blight [blaɪt] *n.* **1.** plant disease. **2.** evil influence that spoils or interferes with hopes, pleasures, etc.: *a ~ upon my hopes* (*plans, etc.*). *v.t.* be a ~ on: *a lif ~ed by constant illness.*

blind¹ [blaɪnd] *adj.* **1.** unable to see (fig.) unable to judge well: *~ to the faults of her children.* **2.** not controlled by reason or purpose: *in ~ haste; ~ forces.* **3.** having no opening: *a ~ wall* closed at one end: *~ alley;* difficult o impossible to see past: *a ~ turning* (*corner*) (in a road). *v.t.* make ~. **~·ly** *adv.* **~·ness** *n.* **~·fold** ['blaɪndfəʊld *v.t.* cover a person's eyes with a bandage. *adj. & adv.* with the eyes so covered.

blind² [blaɪnd] *n.* (U.S.A. *window shade*) roll of cloth (usu. strong linen fixed on a roller and pulled down to cover a window.

blink [blɪŋk] *v.t. & i.* **1.** shut and open the eyes quickly; *~ the fact,* (fig.) shut the mind to it. **2.** (of lights) come and go; shine in an unsteady way: *the lights of a steamer ~ing on the horizon.*

blip [blɪp] *n.* small image of an object on a radar screen.

bliss [blɪs] *n.* (no pl.) perfect happiness or joy. **~·ful** *adj.*

blis·ter ['blɪstə*] *n.* **1.** small, watery swelling under the skin. **2.** similar swelling, air-filled, under paint, etc. *v.t. & i.* cause, get, ~s on.

blitz [blɪts] *n.* rapid, violent attack, esp. from the air. **~ed** *adj.* damaged or destroyed by such attacks.

bliz·zard ['blɪzəd] *n.* severe snowstorm with violent wind.

bloat·ed ['bləʊtɪd] *adj.* fat to an unhealthy extent; swollen: (fig.) *~ with pride.*

bloat·er ['bləʊtə*] *n.* salted and smoked herring.

bloc [blɒk] *n.* combination of groups, states, etc. wishing to act together (politically or commercially).

block[1] [blɒk] *n.* **1.** large, solid piece of stone, wood, etc.: (*building*) ⁓s, cubes of wood as a child's toy. *the* ⁓*s of stone in the pyramids*; *go to the* ⁓, have one's head cut off (as a punishment). (See *chip* (1).) **2.** number of large buildings joined together, often with streets on all four sides; (esp. U.S.A.) length of one side of such a ⁓: *lived five* ⁓*s away*. **3.** large building: (Gt. Brit.) ⁓ *of flats.* **4.** piece of wood or metal with designs, etc. cut (engraved) on its surface for printing. **5.** obstruction; sth. that stops movement (e.g. a number of cars, buses, held up in a street): *road-*⁓; *traffic* ⁓. **6.** ⁓ *and tackle*, apparatus (pulley in a ⁓ of wood) for lifting and pulling. (See *tackle* (1).) **7.** large quantity of things dealt with as a unit: *a* ⁓ *of shares (seats)*. (See *pad* (3).) '⁓·**head** *n.* stupid person. '⁓·**house** *n.* timber building with loopholes used for military defence; fort. ⁓ **let·ters** *n. pl.* with each letter separate and usu. in capitals.

block[2] [blɒk] *v.t.* **1.** obstruct; make movement difficult or impossible by putting sth., or getting, in the way of: *roads* ⁓*ed by snow*; ⁓ *up the entrance to a cave.* **2.** ⁓ *in* (*out*) draw the general arrangement without details. ⁓·**age** ['blɒkɪdʒ] *n.* state of being ⁓ed; sth. ⁓ing.

block·ade [blɒ'keɪd] *n.* enclosing or surrounding of a place (e.g. by armies or warships) to keep goods and people in or out: *raise a* ⁓, end it; *run a* ⁓, get through it. *v.t.* make a ⁓ of.

bloke [bləʊk] *n.* (Gt. Brit., colloq.) man; fellow.

blond [blɒnd] *n. & adj.* (person) having light-coloured hair and fair complexion. ⁓**e** [blɒnd] *adj. & n.* (of a woman or woman's hair) ⁓.

blood [blʌd] *n.* (no pl.) red liquid flowing throughout the body of man and higher animals in veins and arteries. *in cold* ⁓, not in the heat of anger; deliberately; *make bad* ⁓ (*between*), cause ill-feeling, anger. ⁓ **bank** *n.* see *bank*[2] (2). ⁓ **group** *n.* any one of the classes into which human blood may be divided. '⁓·**hound** *n.* large dog able to trace a person by scent (3). ⁓·**less** *adj.* **1.** without ⁓shed: *a* ⁓*less revolution.* **2.** pale: ⁓*less lips.* '⁓-ˌ**poison·ing** *n.* state[1] (1) that results from the presence of poisonous germs (2) in the ⁓. '⁓·**shed** *n.* killing or wounding; putting to death. '⁓·**shot** *adj.* (of the white of the eyes) red. '⁓·ˌ**thirsty** *adj.* cruel; eager to kill. '⁓-ˌ**ves·sel** *n.*

vein or artery through which ⁓ flows in the body. ⁓**y** *adj.* **1.** (*-ier, -iest*) covered with ⁓. **2.** (*-ier, -iest*) with much ⁓shed: *a* ⁓*y fight.* **3.** (Gt. Brit., sl., expressing praise or contempt, but often with no meaning): *What a* ⁓*y shame! Don't be a* ⁓*y fool!* *adv.* (as in adj. 3): *It's* ⁓*y wonderful! Not* ⁓*y likely!* (often showing anger) Not at all likely.

bloom [bluːm] *n.* flower, esp. of plants admired chiefly for their flowers: *roses in full* ⁓; (fig.) time of greatest beauty or perfection: *in the* ⁓ *of youth.* *v.i.* be in flower.

blos·som ['blɒsəm] *n.* flower, mass of flowers, esp. on fruit-trees and bushes: *The apple-trees are in* ⁓. *v.i.* open into flower(s).

blot [blɒt] *n.* **1.** mark caused by ink spilt on paper. **2.** (fig.) sth. that takes away from the value, beauty, or goodness of; *a* ⁓ *on the landscape* (e.g. an ugly building); *a* ⁓ *on his character.* *v.t.* (*-tt-*) **1.** make a ⁓ or ⁓s on. **2.** dry wet ink-marks by pressing with special paper (called ⁓*ting-paper*). **3.** ⁓ *out*, destroy; hide completely: *words* ⁓*ted out*; *a view* ⁓*ted out by mist.* ⁓·**ter** *n.* piece or pad (3) of blotting-paper.

blotch [blɒtʃ] *n.* large, discoloured mark, usu. irregular in shape (e.g. one on the skin, or a dirty ink-mark). *v.t.* mark with ⁓es.

blouse [blaʊz] *n.* outer garment from neck to waist.

blouses

blow[1] [bləʊ] *v.i. & t.* (p.t. *blew* [bluː], p.p. ⁓*n* [bləʊn]) **1.** (of air or wind) be moving or flowing: *It was* ⁓*ing hard* (i.e. there was a strong wind). **2.** (of things) be moved or carried by the wind or other air current; (of the wind, etc.) cause to move: *My hat blew off. The wind blew my hat off. I was almost* ⁓*n over by the wind.* **3.** force air upon, through, or into: ⁓ (*on*) *one's tea* (to cool it); ⁓ *one's nose* (to clear it); ⁓ (*up*) *the fire* (to make it burn better). **4.** give out, cause to give out, sounds as the result of sending air through: *The whistle blew. I blew* *the whistle.* **5.** breathe hard and quickly. **6.** give shape to (glass) by ⁓ing. **7.** ⁓ *out,* (a) extinguish: ⁓ *out a candle;* ⁓ *out one's brains,* kill oneself by shooting in the head; (b) (of a tyre) burst; (of a fuse) melt because the electric current is too strong: *The fuse blew out.* ⁓-*out* (n.), sudden (violent) escape of air, steam, etc.; (esp.) bursting of a tyre; ⁓ing out of an electric fuse. ⁓ *over,* pass by; (fig.) be forgotten. ⁓ *up,* (a) break or destroy by explosion: *The soldiers blew up the bridge.* (b) fill with air: ⁓ *up a tyre;* (c) (colloq.) enlarge: ⁓ *up a photograph;* (d) exaggerate; (e) explode: *The barrel of gunpowder blew up.* ⁓-*up* (n.), (colloq.) enlarged photograph. ⁓·**er** *n.* **1.** apparatus for forcing air into or through sth. (e.g. a fire). **2.** person who blows or pumps air: *glass-⁓er; organ-⁓er.* '⁓·**pipe** *n.* pipe for sending air or gas into a flame to make it hotter.

blow² [bləʊ] *n.* **1.** hard stroke (given with the hand, etc.): *kill three flies at one ⁓; come to ⁓s,* fight; *strike a ⁓ for,* fight for (freedom, etc.). **2.** shock; misfortune; loss causing unhappiness.

blue¹ [bluː] *adj. & n.* (no pl.) (of the) colour of the sky on a clear day or of the deep sea when the sun is shining; (fig.) sad, depressed. ⁓ *ribbon,* sign of great distinction; the leading position; *a bolt from the ⁓,* sth. sudden, unexpected, and greatly surprising; *Oxford (Cambridge) B⁓,* sportsman who has played (football, etc.) or rowed for his university; ⁓*s,* melancholy song. *the ⁓s,* low spirits (5); melancholy. ⁓ **book** *n.* government report. '⁓·**print** *n.* photographic print, with a white design on a blue background, usu. for building plans. **blu·ish** *adj.* rather ⁓.

blue² [bluː] *v.t.* make blue¹.

bluff¹ [blʌf] *v.t. & i.* deceive (by pretending to be stronger, etc. than one really is). *n.* deception of this kind.

bluff² [blʌf] *n.* headland, cliff, or bank with a broad steep face. *adj.* (of cliffs, etc.) having a broad steep front.

bluff³ [blʌf] *adj.* (of a person, his behaviour, etc.) rough but honest and kind; outspoken but hearty.

blun·der ['blʌndə*] *n.* foolish and careless mistake. *v.t. & i.* make foolish mistakes (in); move about uncertainly, as if unable to see: ⁓ *into a wall.*

blunt [blʌnt] *adj.* **1.** without a point or sharp edge: *a ⁓ instrument.* **2.** (of a person, his speech) not showing polite consideration; plain. *v.t.* make ⁓. ⁓·**ly** *adv.* ⁓·**ness** *n.*

blur [blɜː] *v.t. & i.* (-rr-) make a smear on (sth.); make or become unclear, confused in shape or appearance: *Tears ⁓red her eyes. Mists ⁓red the view. Rain ⁓red the windows. The writing was ⁓red.* *n.* smear of ink; dirty spot or mark; sth. seen only in indistinct outline: *If, when you look at this, the print is only a ⁓, you perhaps need glasses.*

blurt [blɜːt] *v.t.* ⁓ *sth. out,* say or tell sth. (e.g. a secret) suddenly, often without thought.

blush [blʌʃ] *v.i.* become red in the face (from confusion or shame). *n.* redness spreading over the face.

blus·ter ['blʌstə*] *v.i.* be rough or violent. *n.* (no pl.) noise (of stormy weather); noisy threatening talk and behaviour. ⁓·**y** *adj.*

boa ['bəʊə] *n.* large South American snake that kills by crushing its prey.

boar [bɔː*] *n.* **1.** wild male pig. **2.** male domestic pig, not castrated. (Cf. *hog, sow².*)

board [bɔːd] *n.* **1.** long, thin, flat piece of wood with squared edges, used in building walls, floors, boats, ship's decks, etc. **2.** (from the idea of ship's decks) *on ⁓,* aboard; *go by the ⁓* (fig., of plans, hopes, etc.) be given up or abandoned; be lost. **3.** council-table; group of persons controlling a business or government department: *the B⁓ of Governors; the B⁓ of Trade.* **4.** (from the idea of *gambling table* above) *⁓,* openly; without deception; *sweep the ⁓,* win everything; (fig.) be successful. **5.** supply of meals by the week or month (e.g. at a lodging-house) or as payment for services: *B⁓ and lodging, £ 17 weekly. The servant has £ 13 a week and free ⁓.* **6.** flat piece of wood or other material used for a special purpose: *black-⁓; chess-⁓; diving-⁓; notice-⁓; sign⁓.* **7.** thick, stiff paper, sometimes cloth-covered, used for book covers: *bound in cloth ⁓s.* (See *card⁓, paste⁓.*) *v.t. & i.* **1.** make or cover with ⁓s (1): ⁓ *up a window.* **2.** get, supply with, ⁓ (5): *make a living by ⁓ing students;* ⁓ *with a butcher.* **3.** go on ⁓ (a ship, tram, etc.). ⁓·**er** *n.* person who gets ⁓ (5) at sb.'s house; pupil at a ⁓ing-school. '⁓·**ing-card** *n.* card of embarkation, esp. for a ship or an airliner. '⁓·**ing-house** *n.* house that provides ⁓ (5) and lodging. '⁓·**ing-school** *n.* school at which pupils receive ⁓ (5) and lodging as well as lessons. '⁓·**room** *n.* room in which meetings of a ⁓ (3) are held. '⁓·**walk** *n.* (U.S.A.) promenade along a beach.

boast [bəʊst] *n.* **1.** proud words used in praise of oneself, one's acts, belongings, etc. **2.** cause for self-satisfaction. *v.i. & t.* **1.** make ~s. **2.** possess (sth.) with pride: *Our school ~s an excellent library.* ~**er** *n.* ~**ful** *adj.*

boat [bəʊt] *n.* small open vessel for travelling in on water, esp. *rowing-~, sailing-~, fishing-~, motor ~,* or small steamer. *be (all) in the same ~,* have the same dangers, problems, etc., to meet; *burn one's ~s,* do sth. which makes a change of plan impossible. *v.i.* travel by ~, esp. for pleasure. '~·**man** *n.* man who rows or sails a small ~ for pay; man from whom rowing-~s may be hired. ~ **race** *n.* race between rowing-~s. ~**swain** ['bəʊsn] *n.* senior seaman who controls the work of other seamen and is in charge of a ship's rigging, boats, anchors, etc. '~**-train** *n.* train timed to catch or meet a ~.

bob[1] [bɒb] *v.i.* (-bb-) *& n.* (make a) quick, short down-and-up movement (of the body, etc.): *The cork on his fishing-line was ~bing on the water. That question often ~s up* (i.e. is often asked).

bob[2] [bɒb] *v.t.* (-bb-) cut (a woman's or girl's hair) short and allow to hang loose: *have one's hair ~bed. n.* ~bed hair.

bob[3] [bɒb] *n.* (pl. ~) (sl.) shilling (former British coin).

bob·bin ['bɒbɪn] *n.* small roller for thread or yarn, esp. in a machine.

bob·by ['bɒbɪ] *n.* (colloq.) policeman.

bob-sleigh ['bɒbsleɪ], **bob-sled** ['bɒbsled] *ns.* (one of) two short sleighs joined together, used in tobogganing.

bode [bəʊd] *v.t. & i.* tell, show, in advance; be a sign of: *It ~s ill (well) for his future. This ~s you no good.*

bod·ice ['bɒdɪs] *n.* close-fitting upper part of a woman's dress or undergarment.

body ['bɒdɪ] *n.* **1.** whole physical structure of a man or animal. **2.** the same without the head, arms, and legs. **3.** dead ~; corpse. **4.** main part of a structure: *the ~ of a motor car; the ~ of a hall,* the central part where the seats are. **5.** group of persons: *the Governing B~ of the school; in a ~,* all together. **6.** collection (of facts, information, etc.). **7.** piece of matter: *the heavenly bodies,* the sun, stars, etc. **8.** (esp. in compounds) person: *any~; some~; no~.* **bod·i·ly** *adj.* of or in the ~. *adv.* as a whole; completely. '~**-guard** *n.* man, group of men, guarding an important person.

bog [bɒg] *n.* (area of) wet, soft ground. *v.t.* (-gg-) *be (get) ~ged down,* (lit. or fig.) be unable to go forward. ~**gy** *adj.* (-ier, -iest).

bo·gus ['bəʊgəs] *adj.* untrue; not genuine; sham.

bo·he·mi·an [bəʊ'hiːmjən] *n. & adj.* (person) not living in the ways considered normal or conventional.

boil[1] [bɔɪl] *n.* hard (usu. red, often painful) poisoned swelling under the skin which bursts when ripe.

boil[2] [bɔɪl] *v.i. & t.* **1.** (of water, etc. or of a vessel and its contents) reach the temperature at which the change into gas occurs: *The kettle is ~ing.* **2.** cause water, etc. to ~; cook in ~ing water: *~ eggs (vegetables).* **3.** be excited or angry: *~ing with indignation. n.* ~ing-point: *bring sth. to the ~; come to the ~.* ~**er** *n.* metal container for heating or ~ing liquids. '~**-ing-point** *n.* temperature at which water, etc. ~s.

bois·ter·ous ['bɔɪstərəs] *adj.* rough; violent; (of a person, his behaviour) noisy and cheerful.

bold [bəʊld] *adj.* **1.** without fear. **2.** without feelings of shame. **3.** well marked: *~ outlines.* ~**ly** *adv.* ~**ness** *n.*

boll [bəʊl] *n.* seed-vessel of cotton and flax.

bol·lard ['bɒləd] *n.* **1.** (usu. metal) post on a quay or ship round which ropes are fastened. **2.** short post erected to divert traffic away from road repairs, or on a traffic island.

bollards

bol·ster ['bəʊlstə*] *n.* long under-pillow for the head of a bed. *v.t.* (usu. ~ *up*) give greatly needed (often undeserved) support to.

bolt[1] [bəʊlt] *n.* **1.** metal bar used to fasten a door or window. **2.** metal pin for joining parts, usu. with a head at one end and a thread (3) at the other for a nut. (See the picture on page 54.) **3.** thunder~: *a ~ from the blue* (see *blue*[1]). *v.t. & i.* fasten or join with a ~ or ~s.

bolt[2] [bəʊlt] *v.i. & t.* **1.** run away suddenly and unexpectedly: *The horse ~ed. The servant ~ed with all his master's* *money.* **2.** swallow (food) quickly. *n.* *make a ~ for it,* run away.

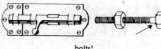

bolts¹

bolt³ [bəʊlt] *adv.* ~ *upright,* quite upright.

bomb [bɒm] *n.* hollow metal ball or shell filled either with explosive for causing destruction on bursting or with smoke, gas, etc. *v.t. & i.* attack with ~s; drop ~s on; throw ~s at. **~er** *n.* aircraft designed (2) for ~ing. '**~shell** *n.* (fig.) great surprise.

bom·bard [bɒm'bɑːd] *v.t.* attack with heavy guns; (fig.) worry (*with* questions, complaints, etc.) **~ment** *n.*

bom·bas·tic [bɒm'bæstɪk] *adj.* (of a person, his talk, behaviour) promising much but not likely to do much; using fine high-sounding words.

bona fide [,bəʊnə'faɪdɪ] *adj. & adv.* (Latin) genuine(ly); sincere(ly).

bond [bɒnd] *n.* **1.** binding (4) written agreement or promise having force in law: *His word is as good as his ~* (i.e. he will keep his spoken promise as faithfully as if it were a legal agreement). **2.** printed paper (e.g. from a government) saying that money has been received and will be paid back with interest: *5% Development B.~s.* **3.** sth. that unites or joins: *the ~s of affection.* **4.** (comm., of goods) *in ~,* in a Customs warehouse (until duties are paid). **5.** (pl.) chains: *in ~s,* in prison or slavery; *burst one's ~s,* get free. **~age** *n.* (no pl.) slavery. **~ed** *adj.* (of goods) placed or held in ~ (4): *~ed warehouse,* one where goods are stored until Customs duties are paid.

bone [bəʊn] *n.* one of the parts that make up the hard framework of an animal's body (the *skeleton*): *a fish has ~s; be only skin and ~,* be very thin; *to the ~,* completely; in a penetrating way: *frozen to the ~. ~ have a ~ to pick with sb.,* have sth. to argue or complain about. *v.t.* take the ~s out of: *~ a chicken.*

bon·fire ['bɒn,faɪə*] *n.* fire made in the open air (e.g. to burn garden rubbish or to celebrate an event).

bon·net ['bɒnɪt] *n.* **1.** small, round head-dress, usu. tied under the chin, worn by women and children. **2.** man's flat, brimless Scotch cap. **3.**

(U.S.A. *hood*) cover of a motor-car engine.

bon·ny, bon·nie ['bɒnɪ] *adj.* healthy-looking: *a ~ baby.*

bo·nus ['bəʊnəs] *n.* (pl. ~es) extra (usu. yearly) payment above the agreed amount.

bony ['bəʊnɪ] *adj.* (-*ier,* -*iest*) (esp.) with little flesh.

boo [buː] *v.t. & i. & n.* (make a) sound showing contempt or disapproval: *The speaker was ~ed by the crowd.*

boo·by ['buːbɪ] *n.* foolish person. **~ prize** *n.* one given to the person who is last in a competition or race. **~ trap** *n.* one to catch an unwary person.

book [bʊk] *n.* **1.** number of sheets of paper, either blank or printed, fastened together in a cover; literary composition written or printed in a ~. **2.** *the B.~,* the Bible. **3.** main division or part of the Bible or of a long poem. **4.** set of stamps, tickets, cheques, matches, etc. fastened together. **5.** *bring sb. to ~,* require him to explain his conduct; *in sb.'s good (black, bad) ~s* having (not having) his favour and approval. *v.t.* **1.** write down (orders, etc.) in a note or list. **2.** give or receive an order for (seats at a theatre, tickets for a journey); engage (sb.) for an occasion (1): *~ seats for the theatre; ~ a singer for a concert.* '**~case** *n.* piece of furniture with shelves for ~s. '**~ing-clerk** *n.* clerk who sells tickets (e.g. at a railway station). '**~ing-office** *n.* office for the sale of tickets. **~ish** *adj.* of ~s or studies; fond of ~s. '**~keeper** *n.* person who keeps (business) accounts. '**~keeping** *n.* (system of) keeping (business) accounts. **~let** ['bʊklɪt] *n.* small ~, usu. in paper covers. '**~maker** *n.* person whose business is the taking of bets (e.g. on horse-races). '**~shop** *n.* shop where ~s are sold. '**~stall** *n.* (U.S.A. *newsstand*) stall where ~s, newspapers, etc. are sold out of doors or in railway stations, etc.

boom¹ [buːm] *n.* **1.** long pole used to keep the bottom of a sail stretched. **2.** pole fastened to the mast of a derrick, used for (un)loading cargo. **3.** heavy chain, mass of logs, etc. across a river or harbour mouth as a defence.

boom² [buːm] *v.i. & t.* (of big guns, thunder, etc.) make (give *out*) with a deep, hollow sound. *n.* deep, hollow sound.

boom³ [buːm] *n.* sudden increase in trade activity, esp. a time when money is being made quickly. *v.i.* have a ~.

boo·mer·ang [ˈbuːməræŋ] *n.* curved throwing-stick of hard wood used in hunting by Australian aborigines — if it fails to hit anything it comes back to the thrower; (fig.) argument that recoils (3).

boon[1] [buːn] *n.* advantage; blessing; request; favour; gift.

boon[2] [buːn] *adj.* ~ *companion*, merry, pleasant companion.

boor [buə*] *n.* rough, ill-mannered person. **~·ish** [ˈbuəriʃ] *adj.*

boost [buːst] *v.t. & n.* (colloq.) (give a) push from below; (give a person, trade, etc.) encouragement or help by means of praise or advertising. **~·er** *n.* thing that ~s; device (2) for increasing force, power, or pressure: ~*er rocket*, rocket that gives initial speed to a missile.

boot [buːt] *n.* 1. outer covering for the foot and lower part of the leg, usu. made of leather or rubber. 2. (U.S.A. *trunk*) compartment for luggage in a car or coach.

boots   a motor-car boot

boo·tee [ˈbuːtiː] *n.* short lined[2] boot for women; infant's knitted woollen boot.

booth [buːð] *n.* 1. shelter (stall) made of boards, canvas, or other light materials, used as a shop. 2. place used for voting, telephoning, etc.: *polling* ~s; *a telephone* ~.

boo·ty [ˈbuːti] *n.* (no pl.) things taken by robbers or captured from the enemy in war.

booze [buːz] *v.i.* drink alcoholic liquor to excess. *n.* alcoholic drink. **booz·er** *n.*

bo·rax [ˈbɔːræks] *n.* (no pl.) white powder used in glass-making and for cleaning.

bor·der [ˈbɔːdə*] *n.* 1. edge; part near an edge. 2. (land near the) line dividing two countries or states. *v.t. & i.* put or be a ~ to; ~ *on* be next to. '**~·land** *n.* district at or near a ~; (fig.) condition between: *the* ~*land between sleeping and waking*.

bore[1] [bɔː*] *v.t. & i.* make a narrow, round, deep hole in sth. by turning a pointed instrument or by digging, etc.: ~ *a tunnel through a mountain*; ~ *for oil*. *n.* 1. hole made by boring. 2. (width of) the hollow within a gun barrel.

bore[2] [bɔː*] *v.t.* make (sb.) tired by dull or uninteresting talk or work: *That man* ~*s me. This is a boring job.* *n.* person or thing that ~s. **~·dom** *n.* (no pl.) state of being ~d.

bore[3], see *bear*[1].

born [bɔːn] a p.p. form of *bear*[1]. *be* ~, come into the world by birth. *adj.* by natural ability: *a* ~ *poet.*

borne, see *bear*[1].

bor·ough [ˈbʌrə] *n.* (in England) town, part of a town, sending one or more members to Parliament.

bor·row [ˈbɒrəʊ] *v.t. & i.* 1. get sth., or the use of sth., after promising to return it. (Cf. *lend*.) 2. use as one's own: ~ *sb.'s ideas.*

Bor·stal [ˈbɔːstl] *n.* ~ *institution*, (Gt. Brit.) place where young offenders receive reformatory training and education.

bo·som [ˈbʊzəm] *n.* 1. centre or inmost part, where one feels joy or sorrow. 2. person's breast.

boss [bɒs] *n.* (colloq.) person who controls or gives orders to workmen; master. *v.t.* be the ~ of; give orders to. **~·y** *adj.* (-ier, -iest) domineering.

bot·a·ny [ˈbɒtəni] *n.* (no pl.) science of the structure of plants. **bo·tan·i·cal** [bəˈtænɪkl] *adj.* of ~: *botanical gardens* (with specimens of plants for study). **bot·a·nist** *n.*

botch [bɒtʃ] *v.t.* repair badly; spoil by poor work. *n.* piece of clumsy, badly done work.

both [bəʊθ] *adj., pron., & adv.* I. *adj.* (of two things, persons, etc.) the two; the one and also the other: *I want* ~ *books* (~ *the books*, ~ *these books*). II. *pron.* the two; not only the one: *B*~ *are good. B*~ *of them are good. We* ~ *want to go. They are* ~ *useful.* III. *adv.* ~ ... *and*, not only ... but also: *He is* ~ *a soldier and a poet.*

both·er [ˈbɒðə*] *v.t. & i.* 1. be or cause trouble to. 2. take trouble. *n.* (no pl.) (cause of) trouble or worry. **~·some** *adj.* causing ~.

bot·tle [ˈbɒtl] *n.* vessel for holding liquids, usu. made of glass or plastic and with a narrow neck but no handle; amount of liquid in a ~. *v.t.* put into, store in, ~s: ~ *fruit*; ~ *up*, hold in (e.g. one's feelings). '**~·neck** *n.* narrow part of a road, between wider parts; that part of a manufacturing process, etc. where production is slowed down (e.g. by shortage of materials).

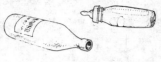

bottles

bot·tom ['bɒtəm] *n.* **1.** lowest part of anything, inside or outside; base. **2.** part farthest from the front or more important part: *at the ~ of my garden.* **3.** surface of land under the sea, a lake, river, etc. **4.** part of the body on which a person sits; buttocks. **5.** seat (of a chair). **6.** basis; source: *get to the ~ of a rumour.* **7.** (attrib.) lowest, last: *the ~ shelf (drawer).* **~·less** *adj.* very deep.

bou·doir ['buːdwɑː*] *n.* woman's private sitting-room or dressing-room.

bough [baʊ] *n.* large branch coming from a tree trunk.

bought, see *buy*.

boul·der ['bəʊldə*] *n.* large piece of rock, large stone, esp. one rounded by weather or water.

bou·le·vard ['buːlvɑː*] *n.* wide street, often with trees on each side.

bounce [baʊns] *v.i. & t.* **1.** (of a ball, etc.) (cause to) spring or jump back when sent against sth. hard. **2.** (cause to) move violently; throw, be thrown, about: *~ into a room; ~ on a bed (out of a chair). The car ~d along the bad road.*

bound¹ [baʊnd] *n.* (usu. pl.) limit: *no ~s to his ambition; out of ~s, (Gt. Brit.)* outside a limited or permitted area. *v.t.* form the ~s of; put ~s to. **~·less** *adj.* without limits.

bound² [baʊnd] *v.i.* jump; move or run in jumps. *n.* jump up or forward: *by leaps and ~s,* very quickly.

bound³ [baʊnd] *adj.* about to start *(for)*; on the way to: *The ship is outward (homeward) ~.*

bound⁴ [baʊnd] *v.* see *bind.* (p.p., special uses only): *~ to,* obliged or compelled to; certain to: *The plan is ~ to succeed. ~ up in,* much interested in; busy with; very fond of.

bound·a·ry ['baʊndərɪ] *n.* line marking a limit: *the ~ between France and Italy.*

boun·ty ['baʊntɪ] *n.* **1.** generosity. **2.** sth. given out of kindness (esp. to the poor). **3.** payment offered (usu. by a government) to encourage an industry

or the destruction of dangerous animals, etc. **boun·te·ous** ['baʊntɪəs] **boun·ti·ful** *adjs.* generous.

bou·quet [bʊˈkeɪ] *n.* bunch of flowers for carrying in the hand.

bout [baʊt] *n.* **1.** period of work, exercise, or other activity: *a wrestling ~, a drinking ~.* **2.** attack (of illness): *a ~ of coughing.*

bou·tique [buːˈtiːk] *n.* small shop or department selling fashionable articles, esp. clothes.

a bow¹ and arrow

bow¹ [bəʊ] *n.* **1.** curved piece of wood with string, used for shooting arrows. **2.** rod of wood with horsehair stretched from end to end, for playing the violin, etc. **3.** curve like a ~ (1) (see *rain~*). **4.** knot with a loop or loops: *a ~-tie; shoe-laces tied in a ~.* **'~-legged** *adj.* with the legs curved outwards at the knees; bandy.

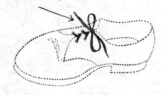

a bow¹ (4)

bow² [baʊ] *v.i. & t.* bend the head or body forward (as a greeting or in respect); bend (the head or body): *he ~ed to her; ~ one's thanks,* express thanks by ~ing. **2.** bend: *~ed with age.* **3.** (fig.) give way *(to)*; yield *(to).* *n.* act of ~ing.

bow³ [baʊ] *n.* (often pl.) front or forward end of a boat or ship.

bow·el ['baʊəl] *n.* **1.** (usu. pl.) the long tube into which food passes from the stomach. **2.** (pl.) innermost part: *in the ~s of the earth* (i.e. deep underground).

bow·er ['baʊə*] *n.* arbour.

bowl¹ [bəʊl] *n.* **1.** deep, round, hollow dish; contents of a ~: *a ~ of rice.* **2.** sth. shaped like a ~: *the ~ of a tobacco-pipe.*

bowl² [bəʊl] *n.* **1.** wooden ball made so that it runs on a curved course. **2.**

(pl., sing. v.) game played with ~s: *have a game of ~s.*

bowl³ [bəʊl] *v.i. & t.* **1.** play bowls² (2) or skittles. **2.** (cricket) send a ball to the batsman; ~ *(out)*, defeat (the batsman) by hitting the wicket with the ball. **2.** move quickly and smoothly (*along* a road) on wheels. **3.** ~ *(sb.) over*, knock down; (fig.) make feel helpless. **~·er** *n.* **1.** person who plays bowls² (2); person who ~s in cricket. **2.** (also ~*er hat*) hard, rounded felt² hat. '**~·ing- ͵al·ley** *n.* long, narrow, covered place for playing skittles, ninepins, and tenpins.

box¹ [bɒks] *n.* **1.** container, usu. with a lid, made of wood, cardboard, metal, etc. for holding solid articles. (See *Christmas-~, letter-~, pillar-~, etc.*) **2.** separate compartment, with seats for several persons, in a theatre, etc., or, in a court of law, for a witness to give his evidence. **B.~ing Day** *n.* (Gt. Brit.) first weekday after Christmas. ~ **num·ber** *n.* **1.** reference number of an advertisement in a newspaper, to be used in addressing replies to be forwarded to the advertiser by the newspaper's staff. **2.** reference number used as part of an address to which letters may be directed at a post office. '**~·͵of·fice** *n.* place where tickets are sold in a theatre, concert hall, etc.: ~*-office success*, (of a play, etc.) great financial success.

box² [bɒks] *v.t. & i.* **1.** ~ *sb.'s ears*, give him a blow there. **2.** fight with the fists, usu. with thick gloves, for sport. **3.** blow with the open hand on the ear(s). **~·er** *n.* **1.** person who ~es (2). **2.** smooth-haired breed of dog of medium size, like a bulldog. **~·ing** *n.* (no pl.) fighting with gloves, practised as a sport: *a ~ing-match.*

boy [bɔɪ] *n.* male child till about 16 years old. '**~-friend** *n.* girl's or young woman's favourite male companion. **~·hood** *n.* (no pl.) period of being a ~. **~·ish** *adj.* of, for, like, a ~. ~ **scout** *n.* see *scout*¹ (2).

boy·cott ['bɔɪkɒt] *v.t.* (join with others and) refuse to have anything to do with, to trade with, etc. *n.* refusal of this kind; ~ing.

bra [brɑ:] *n.* (colloq., abbr. for) bras- sière.

brace¹ [breɪs] *n.* **1.** piece of wood or iron used as a support or to hold things together. **2.** ~ *and bit*, tool which is turned to make holes in wood, etc. **brac·es** ['breɪsɪz] *n. pl.* (U.S.A. *sus- penders*) straps passing over the shoul- ders, used to keep trousers up. *v.t. &*

i. **1.** support; give firmness or strength to: ~ *(up)*, steady oneself: ~ *oneself for a blow. You must ~ up!* **2.** enliven: *a bracing climate.*

brace² [breɪs] *n.* (pl. ~) pair or couple (of dogs, birds): *five ~ of pheasants.*

brace·let ['breɪslɪt] *n.* band or chain (of metal, etc.) worn on the arm or wrist as an ornament.

brack·en ['brækən] *n.* (no pl.) large fern; mass of such ferns.

brack·et ['brækɪt] *n.* **1.** wood or metal support (e.g. for a shelf or lamp on a wall). **2.** one of the pair of marks ( ), [ ], ( ), used in writing and printing. *v.t.* put inside, join with, ~s.

brack·ish ['brækɪʃ] *adj.* (of water) slightly salt.

brag [bræg] *v.i. & t.* (*-gg-*) boast (*of, about*). *n.* boast. **~·gart** ['brægət] *n.* person who ~s.

braid [breɪd] *n.* **1.** band made by twisting together two or more strands² of silk, thread, hair, etc. **2.** such bands used for binding edges of cloth or, if of silver or gold, for decoration, esp. on uniforms. *v.t.* make into ~s; put ~ on; put (hair) into ~s.

braille [breɪl] *n.* (no pl.) system of writing and printing for the blind, to enable them to read by touch.

brain [breɪn] *n.* (often pl.) mass of soft grey matter in the head, centre of the nervous system; centre of thought: *have a good ~; use one's ~s; have sth. on the ~*, be thinking about sth. all the time. (See *blow*¹ (7); *rack*¹ (v. 2).) *v.t.* kill by a hard blow on the head. **~·less** *adj.* stupid. **~s trust** *n.* group of experts invited to answer questions asked by members of an audience. **~ trust** *n.* (U.S.A.) group of experts advising the government. '**~-wash** *v.t.* subject (sb.) to '**~͵wash- ing** *n.* (no pl.) process of forcing sb. (e.g. by persistent examination and instruction) to give up existing ideas or beliefs and accept new ones. '**~- wave** *n.* (colloq.) sudden bright idea. **~y** *adj.* (*-ier, -iest*) clever.

braise [breɪz] *v.t.* cook (meat, etc.) slowly in a covered pan.

brake [breɪk] *n.* apparatus that can be pressed or rubbed against a wheel to reduce the speed (of a motor car, train, etc.). *v.t. & i.* slow down, or stop, by using the ~(s); apply the ~(s).

bram·ble ['bræmbl] *n.* thorn-covered shrub.

bran [bræn] *n.* (no pl.) outer covering of grain (wheat, rye, etc.) separated from flour after grinding.

branch

branch [brɑːntʃ] *n.* **1.** arm-like part of a tree growing out from the trunk or a bough. **2.** anything like a ~, going out from, or managed from, the central part: *a ~ railway (road, office)*; *a ~ of knowledge*. *v.i.* send out, divide into, ~es: *trees ~ing (out) over the river. The main road ~es off to the right.* ~ *out*, become active in a new direction.

brand [brænd] *n.* **1.** piece of burning wood. **2.** red-hot iron used for marking (cattle, etc.); mark or design made in this way. **3.** trade mark printed on boxes or packets of goods; variety of goods of a particular make or trade mark: *the best ~s of coffee*. *v.t.* mark with a ~; (fig.) make a lasting mark on: *~ed on my memory*; *be ~ed as a coward.* **~-new** [ˌbrænd'njuː] *adj.* quite new.

bran·dish ['brændɪʃ] *v.t.* wave about.

bran·dy ['brændɪ] *n.* strong alcoholic drink made from wine.

brass [brɑːs] *n.* **1.** (no pl.) bright yellow alloy made by mixing copper and zinc. **2.** things made of ~: *the ~, ~ musical instruments*; *~ band*, band of musicians with ~ instruments. **3.** (colloq.) impudence. **~y** *adj.* (*-ier, -iest*) **1.** like ~ in colour or sound. **2.** impudent.

bras·sière ['bræsɪə*] *n.* woman's close-fitting support for the breasts.

brat [bræt] *n.* (contemptuous) child.

bra·va·do [brə'vɑːdəʊ] *n.* display of (often foolish) daring or boldness.

brave [breɪv] *adj. & v.t.* (ready to) face danger or pain without fear. **~ly** *adv.* **brav·ery** ['breɪvərɪ] *n.* (no pl.) courage.

bra·vo [ˌbrɑː'vəʊ] *int.* Well done!

brawl [brɔːl] *n.* noisy quarrel. *v.i.* take part in a ~.

brawn [brɔːn] *n.* (no pl.) **1.** strength; muscle. **2.** pig's head, etc. boiled, cut up, and pickled. **~y** *adj.* with strong muscles.

bray [breɪ] *v.i. & n.* (make the) cry of an ass; (make the) sound of a trumpet.

bra·zen ['breɪzn] *adj.* **1.** made of brass; like brass. **2.** shameless. *v.t.* ~ *it out*, behave, in spite of having done wrong, as if one had not.

bra·zier ['breɪzjə*] *n.* open metal framework (like a basket), usu. on legs, for holding burning coals.

breach [briːtʃ] *n.* **1.** act of breaking (a law, duty, promise, etc.): *a ~ of the peace*, unlawful fighting in a public place; *a ~ of contract*; *a ~ of security*. **2.** opening made in a defensive wall, etc., esp. one made by attacking forces: *throw oneself into the ~*, be ready and eager to defend, give support, etc. **3.** gap: *a ~ in the hedge. v.t.* make a ~ (2, 3) in.

bread [bred] *n.* (no pl.) food made by baking flour with water and yeast. (Cf *loaf*¹.)

breadth [bredθ] *n.* **1.** distance or measure from side to side: *five feet in ~*. **2.** ~ *of mind*, quality of not being limited or narrow in one's opinions, views, etc., of being liberal or tolerant.

break [breɪk] *v.t. & i.* (p.t. *broke* [brəʊk], p.p. *broken* ['brəʊkən]) **1.** (cause a whole thing to) divide into two or more pieces (as the result of a blow or other force, not by cutting, etc.): *The window broke. Who broke the window?* **2.** (with advs. & preps.): ~ *away*, (a) become separate; (b) (of members of a group) escape; ~ *down*, (a) (of machines, systems, plans, theories, etc.) fail to work; go wrong; prove to be useless; (b) (of a person, his health) become weak through over-work or strain, etc.; (c) be overcome by emotion; ~ *sth.* (e.g. a door) *down*, use force to get it down; ~ *in(to)*, get in(to) by force; ~ (*a horse, etc.*) *in*, tame; teach discipline to; ~ *in on*, interrupt; ~ *into*, burst suddenly into: ~ *into a laugh.* ~ (*in*)*to pieces*, ~ *in two*, (cause to) come or go into two parts or several pieces; ~ *off*, stop speaking; ~ (*sth.*) *off*, (a) separate: ~ *a branch off*; (b) end: ~ *off an engagement*; ~ *out*, (a) (of fires, war, disease) begin suddenly; (b) (of prisoners) escape; ~ *through*, make a way through (obstacles, etc.); ~ *up*, (a) come or smash to pieces; (b) (of a meeting, school term, relationship, of fine weather, etc.) end; (c) (of a person) lose strength or health; ~ (*sth.*) *up*, (a) ~ *into pieces*; (b) disperse: ~ *up a crowd*; (c) bring to an end: ~ *up a meeting (conversation, etc.*). ~ *with*, end a relationship with: ~ *with a friend.* **3.** (with nouns): ~ *a record*, create a new record; ~ *the back of*, finish the greater or more difficult part of (a piece of work, etc.); ~ *the ice*, (fig.) overcome reserve (6) and get conversation started. (See *habit* (1).) **4.** fail to keep or obey (the law, a promise, etc.). **5.** (cause to) stop for a time; interrupt: ~ *the silence* (*one's journey*). **6.** lessen the force of: *The bushes broke his fall.* ~ *the news*, be the first to give news, esp. of an unwelcome event. **7.** (of the voice) change because of strong feeling or when approaching manhood. *n.* **1.** ~*ing*: ~ *of day*; *day~*.

2. broken place. 3. interval; interruption: *a ~ at school*; *a tea-~*; *a ~ in the conversation*; *without a ~*, continuously.

break·age ['breɪkɪdʒ] *n.* act of breaking; damage by breaking: *In this hotel ~s* (e.g. broken dishes, glasses, etc.) *cost £14 a month.*

break·down ['breɪkdaʊn] *n.* 1. failure (of a machine, system, etc.): *a ~ on the railway.* 2. failure (of body or mind): *a nervous ~.*

break·er ['breɪkə*] *n.* large wave ready to break and fall on the shore or over rocks.

break·fast ['brekfəst] *n.* first meal of the day. *v.i.* have ~.

break·neck ['breɪknek] *adj.* *at (a) ~ speed,* at a speed likely to cause an accident.

break·wa·ter ['breɪkˌwɔːtə*] *n.* wall built (e.g. round a harbour) to break the force of the waves.

breast [brest] *n.* 1. milk-producing part(s) of a woman: *child at the ~,* child having its mother's milk. 2. upper front part of the human body and part of a garment covering this: *a ~ pocket;* corresponding part of an animal's body. 3. feelings; thoughts: *a troubled ~*; *make a clean ~ of,* confess (wrongdoing, etc.). '*~-stroke* *n.* swimming stroke made by extending the arms in front of the head and sweeping them back. '*~-work* *n.* wall (e.g. of earth or sandbags) built ~-high as a defence.

breath [breθ] *n.* air taken into and sent out of the lungs; single act of taking in air and sending it out: *catch (hold) one's ~,* stop taking in ~ for a moment (from excitement, etc.); *lose one's ~,* have difficulty in taking in ~ (e.g. when running); *out of ~,* needing to take in ~ more quickly than usual; *take ~,* pause to get ~; *under one's ~,* in a whisper; *waste one's ~,* talk without result. *~ test,* test with a breathalyser. *~-taking,* exciting; thrilling. *~·less adj.* 1. out of ~. 2. keeping one's ~ back (from excitement, etc.): *with ~less attention.*

breath·a·lys·er (U.S.A. **-lyz·er**) ['breθəlaɪzə*] *n.* device (2) to measure the amount of alcohol in a person's breath.

breathe [briːð] *v.i. & t.* 1. take air into the lungs and send it out. 2. say in a whisper; utter: *Don't ~ a word about it* (i.e. keep it secret).

bred, see *breed* (v.).

breech [briːtʃ] *n.* back part of the barrel of a gun or other firearm, where a cartridge or shell is placed.

breech·es ['brɪtʃɪz] *n. pl.* short trousers fitting closely below the knees: *riding-~* (for wearing on horseback).

breed [briːd] *v.t. & i.* (p.t. & p.p. *bred* [bred]) 1. give birth to young; reproduce. 2. keep (animals, etc.) for the purpose of having young: *~ horses.* 3. train; educate: *an Englishman born and bred; a well-bred boy.* 4. be the cause of: *War ~s misery and want.* *n.* kind or variety of animal, etc.; group of animals, etc. with the same qualities: *a good ~ of cattle.* *~er n.* 1. person who ~s (2) animals. 2. (also *~er reactor*) reactor in which more fissile material is produced than used up. *~·ing n.* (no pl.) (esp.) behaviour: *a man of good ~ing.*

breeze [briːz] *n.* gentle wind. **breezy** *adj.* (*-ier, -iest*) (pleasantly) windy; (fig.) gay and cheerful; lively.

breth·ren ['breðrən] *n. pl.* (old use) brothers.

bre·via·ry ['briːvjərɪ] *n.* book with prayers to be said daily by priests of the Roman Catholic Church.

brev·i·ty ['brevətɪ] *n.* (no pl.) shortness (e.g. in speaking and writing, and of human life).

brew [bruː] *v.t. & i.* 1. prepare (drinks such as tea, beer) by soaking or boiling leaves, grain, etc. in liquid; make tea, beer, etc. 2. (of storm, evil, etc.) be forming. 3. set working (usu. for evil purposes): *They are ~ing mischief.* *n.* result of ~ing; liquid made by ~ing. *~er n.* maker of beer. *~ery* ['bruərɪ] *n.* place where beer is ~ed.

bri·ar ['braɪə*] *n.* 1. hard wood used for making tobacco-pipes. 2. pipe made of this. 3. brier.

bribe [braɪb] *v.t. & n.* (give, offer) money, etc. tempting sb. to do sth. wrong, or sth. he does not want to do, usu. to the advantage of the giver. '**brib·ery** *n.* (no pl.) giving or taking of ~s.

brick [brɪk] *n.* 1. (rectangular block of) clay moulded and baked by fire or sun, used for building houses, etc. 2. child's building block. '**~·lay·er** *n.* workman who builds with ~s.

bricks

bride [braɪd] *n.* woman on her wedding-day; newly-married woman. **~-groom** ['braɪdgrʊm] *n.* man on his wedding-day; newly-married man. **~s·maid** ['braɪdzmeɪd] *n.* girl or young unmarried woman attending a ~. **brid·al** *adj.* of a ~ or wedding.

bridge¹ [brɪdʒ] *n.* **1.** structure of wood, stone, bricks, steel, etc. for carrying a road over a river, railway, etc. **2.** high platform over and across a ship's deck, from which the ship's officers give orders. **3.** upper, bony part of the nose. *v.t.* build a ~ (1) over.

bridge² [brɪdʒ] *n.* (no pl.) card game for four players.

bri·dle ['braɪdl] *n.* headgear with which a horse is controlled, including a headstall, a bit² (1), and reins. *v.t. & i.* **1.** put a ~ on (a horse). **2.** (fig.) control (desires, etc.). **3.** throw back the head in anger: ~ (*up*). **'~-path, '~-road** *ns.* path or road for riders only.

brief¹ [briːf] *adj.* (of time, events, writing, and speaking) short; lasting for only a short time: *be* ~, speak shortly; *in* ~, in a few words. **~ly** *adv.*

brief² [briːf] *n.* **1.** summary of the facts of a case, drawn up for a barrister. **2.** (also ~*ing*) instructions; information. *v.t.* **1.** instruct or employ a barrister. **2.** instruct or inform in advance. **'~-case** *n.* flat case for documents, etc.

briefs [briːfs] *n. pl.* very short pants (1).

bri·er ['braɪə*] *n.* (also *briar*) bush covered with thorns, esp. the wild rose.

brig [brɪg] *n.* ship with two masts and square sails.

bri·gade [brɪ'geɪd] *n.* **1.** army unit of usu. three battalions. **2.** organized and uniformed body of persons with special duties: *the fire* ~. **brig·a·dier** [ˌbrɪgə'dɪə*] *n.* officer commanding a ~.

bright [braɪt] *adj.* **1.** giving out or reflecting strong light; shining. **2.** cheerful and happy. **3.** clever. **~en** *v.t. & i.* make or become ~(er), more cheerful, etc. **~ly** *adv.* **~ness** *n.*

bril·liant ['brɪljənt] *adj.* very bright; clever; splendid. **bril·liance, -lian·cy** *ns.* (no pl.).

brim [brɪm] *n.* **1.** edge of a cup, bowl, etc.: *full to the* ~. **2.** out-turned edge of a hat (giving shade). *v.t. & i.* (-*mm*-) fill or be full to the ~ (1): ~ *over*, overflow. **~-'ful(l)** *adj.* full to the ~ (1): *He's* ~*-full of new ideas.* **~less** *adj.*

brim·stone ['brɪmstən] *n.* (no pl.) (old use) sulphur.

brin·dle(d) ['brɪndl(d)] *adj.* brown with streaks of another colour: *a* ~ *cow* (*cat*).

brine [braɪn] *n.* (no pl.) salt water: *pickled in* ~. **briny** *adj.* (-*ier, -iest*).

bring [brɪŋ] *v.t.* (p.t. & p.p. *brought* [brɔːt]) **1.** cause to come, come, having with one; carry, lead, drive, towards the speaker; cause (sth. or sb.) to be (where the speaker is): *I will* ~ *you the book tomorrow. B~ that chair in from the garden.* **2.** cause; cause to become: ~ *oneself to do sth.*; *Can you* ~ *him to agree to the plan?* ~ *to an end.* **3.** ~ *sth. home to sb.*, cause him to realize it; ~ *to mind*, cause to remember; ~ *to pass*, cause to happen. **4.** (with advs. & preps.): ~ *about*, cause to happen; ~ *back*, (a) return (sth.); (b) cause to remember; call to mind; ~ *down*, (a) shoot down (birds, aircraft, etc.); (b) kill or wound; (c) lower (prices, etc.); ~ *forth*, produce (young, fruit); ~ *forward*, cause to be seen, considered, etc.; ~ *in*, introduce (a fashion, topic, legislation); ~ *off*, cause to be successful; succeed in an attempt; ~ *on*, lead to; help to produce; ~ *out*, (a) cause to appear clearly; (b) publish (a book, etc.); ~ *round*, cause (sb.) to regain consciousness after fainting; ~ *sb. round to* (*one's opinion*), cause, persuade, him to accept it or agree with it; ~ *up*, (a) rear; educate: *well brought up children*; (b) vomit (1); (c) call attention to.

brink [brɪŋk] *n.* **1.** upper end of a steep place. **2.** edge of sth. unknown, dangerous, or exciting: *on the* ~ *of ruin* (*war*).

brisk [brɪsk] *adj.* quick-moving; lively: *a* ~ *walk(er). Trade is* ~.

bris·tle ['brɪsl] *n.* a short, stiff hair. *v.i.* (of hair) stand up on end (with fear, etc.); (of an animal) have the hair on end. ~ *with*, have in large numbers: *a problem bristling with difficulties.* **bris·tly** ['brɪslɪ] *adj.* (-*ier, -iest*) like ~s; full of ~s; (of hair) rough and coarse.

Brit·ish ['brɪtɪʃ] *adj.* of Great Britain, the British Commonwealth, or its inhabitants: *the* ~, the ~ people.

brit·tle ['brɪtl] *adj.* hard but easily broken (e.g. glass, coal).

broach [brəʊtʃ] *v.t.* open (a barrel); tap; (fig.) begin to discuss.

broad [brɔːd] *adj.* **1.** wide; large across: *Rivers get* ~*er as they near the sea. His back is* ~ *enough to carry even that weight.* **2.** in breadth; from side to side: *a table six feet* ~. **3.** (of the mind, ideas, etc.) liberal; not limited; tolerant: *a man of* ~ *views; a* ~*minded man.*

4. full and complete: ~ *daylight*; *in ~ outline*, giving the chief features or ideas without details. **5.** strongly marked: *a ~ hint*; *a ~ accent*. ~**en** *v.t. & i.* make or become ~(er) (1). ~**ly** *adv.* ~*ly speaking*, speaking in a general way, without going into detail.

broad·cast ['brɔːdkɑːst] *v.t. & i.* (p.t. & p.p. *-cast* or ~*ed*) **1.** send out in all directions, esp. by radio or television: ~ *the news*; *a ~ speech*. **2.** speak, sing, play, etc. for ~*ing*. *n.* sth. ~ by radio or television: *the ~ of the Queen's speech*. ~**er** *n.* person ~*ing*.

broad·side ['brɔːdsaɪd] *n.* (firing of) all the guns on one side of a ship. ~ *on* (*to*), with the side turned to.

bro·cade [brəʊ'keɪd] *n.* fine cloth with raised designs (e.g. in silver thread) worked on it.

bro·chure ['brəʊʃə*] *n.* short, usu. descriptive, printed article in a paper cover: *holiday ~s*.

brogue [brəʊg] *n.* **1.** strong, usu. ornamented, shoe for country wear. **2.** countrified way of speaking, esp. the way in which the Irish speak English.

broke [brəʊk] *v.* see *break*. *adj.* (colloq.) without money.

bro·ken ['brəʊkən] *v.* see *break*. *adj.* ~ *English*, imperfect English. *a ~ home*, a home disrupted by change, esp. one in which the parents are divorced or have separated. *a ~ man*, a man crushed by despair or grief. ~**-'heart·ed** *adj.* crushed by grief.

bro·ker ['brəʊkə*] *n.* person who buys and sells for others, shares¹ (3), bonds (2), etc. ~**age** *n.* (no pl.) charge(s) made by a ~.

bro·mide ['brəʊmaɪd] *n.* (no pl.) chemical substance; medicine used to calm nerves and help a person to sleep.

bron·chi·tis [brɒŋ'kaɪtɪs] *n.* (no pl.) illness (with coughing) caused by inflammation of the linings of the two main branches of the windpipe (the *bronchial tubes* ['brɒŋkjəl 'tjuːbz]).

bronze [brɒnz] *n.* **1.** (no pl.) mixture of copper and tin; its colour (reddish brown). **2.** work of art made of ~.

brooch [brəʊtʃ] *n.* ornamental pin for fastening (on) a dress.

brood [bruːd] *n.* all the young birds hatched at one time in a nest. *v.i.* **1.** (of a bird) sit on eggs. **2.** ~ (*on, over*), (fig.) think about (troubles, etc.) for a long time. ~**y** *adj.* (*-ier, -iest*) (of hens) wanting to ~.

brook [brʊk] *n.* small stream.

broom [bruːm] *n.* **1.** brush on a long handle for sweeping floors. **2.** yellow-flowered shrub.

broth [brɒθ] *n.* meat soup.

broth·el ['brɒθəl] *n.* house where prostitutes may be visited.

broth·er ['brʌðə*] *n.* **1.** son of the same parents as sb. speaking or referred to. **2.** man in the same profession, religious society, etc. as another: *a ~ doctor*. ~**hood** *n.* group of men with common interests and aims, esp. a religious society. '~**-in-law** *n.* (pl. ~*s-in-law*) ~ of one's husband or wife; husband of one's sister. ~**ly** *adj.*

brought, see *bring*.

brow [braʊ] *n.* **1.** part of the face above the eyes; forehead. **2.** (also *eye~*) arch of hair above the eye(s): *knit one's ~s*, frown. **3.** top of a slope. '~**·beat** *v.t.* (p.t. *-beat*, p.p. *-beaten*) frighten by shouting or looking stern at.

brown [braʊn] *adj. & n.* (no pl.) colour of chocolate, toasted bread, or coffee mixed with milk.

browse [braʊz] *v.i.* **1.** eat, crop³ (1) (leaves, grass, etc.). **2.** read here and there in a book, newspaper, etc. *n.* (act, period, of) browsing.

bruise [bruːz] *n.* injury to the body or a fruit, etc. so that the skin is discoloured but not broken. *v.t. & i.* cause a ~ or ~s to; get a ~ or ~s: *one's leg*, ~ *easily*.

bru·nette [bruː'net] *n.* woman with brown skin and dark-brown or black hair and eyes.

brunt [brʌnt] *n.* chief force or stress: *bear the ~ of an attack*.

brush [brʌʃ] *n.* **1.** implement of hair, bristles, wire, etc. fastened into a handle, for cleaning, scrubbing, painting, etc. (Cf. *comb*.) **2.** bushy tail of a fox. **3.** short, sharp fight. *v.t. & i.* **1.** use a ~ on. **2.** ~ *up*, get back knowledge or skill which one has lost: ~ *up one's French*; ~ *past* (*against*), touch when passing. '~**·wood** *n.* (no pl.) low bushes; undergrowth.

brusque [brʊsk] *adj.* rough and abrupt (in or of speech, behaviour). ~**ly** *adv.*

bru·tal ['bruːtl] *adj.* savage; cruel. ~**·i·ty** [bruː'tælətɪ] *n.* cruelty. ~**ize** ['bruːtəlaɪz] *v.t.* make ~. ~**ly** *adv.*

brute [bruːt] *n.* **1.** animal (except man). **2.** stupid and cruel person. *adj.* animal-like; cruel; unreasoning: ~ *strength* (i.e. strength without skill).

bub·ble ['bʌbl] *n.* **1.** (in air) floating ball formed of liquid and containing air or gas. **2.** (in liquid) ball of air or gas rising to the surface. *v.i.* send up ~s; rise in ~s; make the sound of ~s.

buc·ca·neer [ˌbʌkə'nɪə*] *n.* pirate; un-scrupulous adventurer.

buck¹ [bʌk] *n.* **1.** male of deer, hare, or rabbit. (Cf. *doe.*) '**ↄ·skin** *n.* (soft leather made from) deerskin, goat-skin, or sheepskin.

buck² [bʌk] *v.i. & t.* (of a horse) jump high with the back arched (in order to throw the rider); throw (a rider) by ↄing.

buck³ [bʌk] *n.* (U.S.A. sl.) dollar.

buck·et ['bʌkɪt] *n.* open vessel of wood, metal, or plastic, for drawing, holding, or carrying liquids.

a bucket   a buckle

buck·le ['bʌkl] *n.* metal fastener for a belt or strap. *v.t. & i.* **1.** ↄ (*on*), fasten with a ↄ. **2.** (of metalwork, etc.) bend, get twisted (from heat or strain).

buck·ler ['bʌklə*] *n.* small round shield.

buck·wheat ['bʌkwiːt] *n.* (no pl.) plant with small, triangular seed (used for feeding horses and hens, also made into flour).

bu·col·ic [bjuː'kɒlɪk] *adj.* of country life and farming; pastoral (2).

bud [bʌd] *n.* leaf, flower, or branch at the beginning of its growth; flower not fully open. *v.i.* (*-dd-*) put out buds; begin to develop: *a ↄding lawyer.*

Bud·dhism ['bʊdɪzəm] *n.* (no pl.) religion founded by Buddha. **Bud·dhist** ['bʊdɪst] *n.* follower of Buddha.

bud·dy ['bʌdɪ] *n.* (colloq.) companion, friend.

budge [bʌdʒ] *v.t. & i.* (usu. neg.) (cause to) move very little: *I can't ↄ it. It won't ↄ.*

bud·get ['bʌdʒɪt] *n.* **1.** estimate of probable future income and payments. **2.** collection of news, letters, etc. *v.i.* ↄ *for*, make a ↄ (1) for: *ↄ for the next year.*

buff [bʌf] *n.* (no pl.) thick, strong, soft leather made of oxhide; its colour, a brownish-yellow.

buf·fa·lo ['bʌfələʊ] *n.* (pl. *-o(s)*, *-oes*) kinds of ox in Asia, Africa, etc.; North American bison.

buff·er ['bʌfə*] *n.* apparatus (usu. with springs) for lessening the effect of a blow, esp. of railway vehicles. ↄ *state*, small country between two larger and more powerful countries.

buf·fet¹ ['bʌfɪt] *n.* blow, esp. one given with the hand. *v.t.* hit; knock about: *ↄed by the waves.*

buf·fet² ['bʌfɪt] *n.* **1.** counter where food and drink may be bought and eaten. **2.** sideboard, table, from which food and drink are served (e.g. in a hotel).

buf·foon [bə'fuːn] *n.* clown.

bug [bʌg] *n.* **1.** small, flat, bad-smelling insect that sucks blood; (U.S.A.) any insect. **2.** (sl.) hidden microphone. *v.t.* (*-gg-*) (sl.) install a hidden microphone in (in order to listen to a conversation).

bug·bear ['bʌgbeə*] *n.* sth. specially feared or disliked, often without good reason.

bug·gy ['bʌgɪ] *n.* **1.** small motor vehicle: *beach ↄ.* **2.** (U.S.A.) = pram.

bu·gle ['bjuːgl] *n.* musical wind instrument of brass or copper, used in the army. **ↄr** *n.*

a bugle

build [bɪld] *v.t. & i.* (p.t. & p.p. *built* [bɪlt]) make (a house, etc.) by putting the materials together: *ↄ in*, make sth. part of the structure: *built-in wardrobes.* ↄ *up*, (a) make bigger or stronger (a business, one's health, etc.); accumulate; (b) become covered with buildings: *built-up areas.* ↄ (*up*)*on*, base (hopes, etc.) on; rely on. *n.* (no pl.) general shape: *a man of powerful ↄ; recognize a man by his ↄ.* **ↄ·er** *n.* (esp.) contractor for ↄing houses. **ↄ·ing** *n.* **1.** constructing houses, etc. **2.** house or other thing that is built for living or working in.

built, see *build* (v.).

bulbs

bulb [bʌlb] *n.* **1.** thick, round part, in the ground, of such plants as onions and lilies, where plant food is stored. **2.** ⁓-shaped object, esp. an electric lamp. **bul·bous** *adj.* ⁓-shaped.

bulge [bʌldʒ] *v.t. & i.* (cause to) swell beyond the usual size; curve outwards: *a sack bulging with cabbages*; *bulging pockets*. *n.* **1.** place where a swelling or curve shows; irregular swelling. **2.** (colloq.) temporary increase in numbers or volume.

bulk [bʌlk] *n.* (no pl.) **1.** quantity or volume, esp. when great. *in* ⁓, loose or in large amounts. **2.** *the* greater part or number (*of*). *v.i.* ⁓ *large*, seem large in respect of size or importance. ⁓**y** *adj.* (-*ier*, -*iest*) taking up much space.

bulk·head [ˈbʌlkhed] *n.* watertight division or dividing wall in a ship, etc.

bull[1] [bʊl] *n.* **1.** uncastrated male of the ox family: *a prize* ⁓; *a* ⁓ *in a china shop*, rough and clumsy person; *take the* ⁓ *by the horns*, attack a problem in a bold and straightforward way. **2.** male of elephant, whale, and some other large animals. '⁓**·dog** *n.* powerful, smooth-haired breed of dog, noted for its great courage. '⁓**'s-eye** *n.* centre of the target (for archers, etc.).

bull[2] [bʊl] *n.* formal order or announcement made by the Pope.

bull[3] [bʊl] *n.* foolish or amusing mistake in language, usu. because there is a contradiction in terms (e.g. 'If you do not get this letter, please write and tell me.').

bull·doz·er [ˈbʊlˌdəʊzə*] *n.* machine for shifting large quantities of earth, levelling land, etc.

bul·let [ˈbʊlɪt] *n.* shaped piece of lead, often coated with another metal, fired from a rifle or revolver. (Cf. *shell* (3), *cartridge* (1).)

bul·le·tin [ˈbʊlɪtɪn] *n.* official statement of news. '⁓**-board** *n.* (U.S.A.) = notice-board.

bul·lion [ˈbʊljən] *n.* (no pl.) gold or silver in bulk or bars, before manufacture.

bul·lock [ˈbʊlək] *n.* castrated bull.

bul·ly [ˈbʊlɪ] *n.* person who uses his strength or power to frighten or hurt those who are weaker. *v.t.* use strength, etc. in this way: ⁓ *sb. into doing sth.*

bul·wark [ˈbʊlwək] *n.* **1.** wall, esp. one built of earth, against attack; (fig.) means of defence. **2.** low wall round (esp. a sailing) ship's deck.

bum [bʌm] *n.* (U.S.A., sl.) = loafer; tramp (3).

bump [bʌmp] *n.* **1.** blow or knock (as when two things come together with force). **2.** swelling of, lump on, the flesh caused by this. **3.** irregularity on a road surface made by traffic. *v.t. & i.* strike or knock (against) with force; move joltingly: ⁓ *one's head against sth.*; ⁓ *along a bad road.* ⁓**y** *adj.* (-*ier*, -*iest*) with many ⁓s.

bump·er [ˈbʌmpə*] *n.* **1.** (attrib., of crops) unusually large. **2.** bar on a motor car to prevent damage from a slight collision.

bump·kin [ˈbʌmpkɪn] *n.* awkward person with unpolished manners, esp. from the country.

bump·tious [ˈbʌmpʃəs] *adj.* self-important; conceited.

bun [bʌn] *n.* **1.** small, round sweet cake, usu. with currants. **2.** *in a* ⁓, (of a woman's hair) twisted into a knot behind and above the neck.

bunch [bʌntʃ] *n.* **1.** number of small, similar things naturally growing together (*a* ⁓ *of grapes*) or gathered together (*a* ⁓ *of flowers, keys*). **2.** (sl.) gang, group. *v.t. & i.* form into a ⁓; come or bring together into a ⁓.

bun·dle [ˈbʌndl] *n.* number of articles wrapped or tied together: *a* ⁓ *of books* (*sticks, old clothes*). *v.t. & i.* **1.** make into a ⁓. **2.** put away without order: ⁓ *everything into a drawer.* **3.** send or go in a hurry: ⁓ *the children off to school.*

bung [bʌŋ] *n.* large (usu. wooden) stopper for closing the hole in a barrel. *v.t.* put a ⁓ into. ⁓*ed up*, closed; stopped up.

bun·ga·low [ˈbʌŋgələʊ] *n.* house with only one storey.

bun·gle [ˈbʌŋgl] *v.t. & i.* do (a piece of work) badly or clumsily. *n.* ⁓d piece of work. ⁓**r** *n.*

bunk [bʌŋk] *n.* sleeping-place fixed on the wall (e.g. in a ship or train); sleeping-berth. '⁓**-bed** *n.* sleeping-place for two people with one bed fixed (1) above the other.

bun·ker [ˈbʌŋkə*] *n.* **1.** part of a ship where fuel is stored. **2.** sandy hollow, made as an obstacle, on a golf-course. **3.** (mil.) fortified underground shelter.

bun·ny [ˈbʌnɪ] *n.* (child's word for) rabbit.

Bun·sen burn·er [ˌbʌnsnˈbɜːnə*] *n.* device (2) for burning gas, for use in a laboratory.

bun·ting [ˈbʌntɪŋ] *n.* (no pl.) (thin cloth used for making) flags and similar decorations.

buoy [bɔɪ] *v.t. & n.* (mark positions on the water with a) floating, fixed object: ~ *a wreck* (*channel*); ~ *up*, prevent from sinking; (fig.) keep up (hopes, etc.). (Cf. *life*~.) **~·ant** ['bɔɪənt] *adj.* able to float or to keep things floating; (fig.) light-hearted. **~·an·cy** ['bɔɪənsɪ] *n.* (no pl.).

a buoy

bur·den ['bɜːdn] *n.* load, esp. a heavy one; sth. difficult to bear: *a ~ of sorrow*; *the ~ of taxation*; *beast of ~*, animal that carries heavy loads. *v.t.* put a ~ on. **~·some** *adj.*

bu·reau ['bjʊərəʊ] *n.* (pl. ~*x*, ~*s*) **1.** (a) government department; (b) office, esp. for public information: *a travel ~*. **2.** (Gt. Brit.) writing-desk with drawers. **3.** (U.S.A.) low chest of drawers with a mirror. **~·crat** ['bjʊərəʊkræt] *n.* government official, esp. one who does not lose his post when another political group comes into power and who follows a narrow, rigid, formal routine. **~·crat·ic** [,bjʊərəʊ'krætɪk] *adj.* **~·cra·cy** [bjʊə'rɒkrəsɪ] *n.* government by ~crats.

bur·glar ['bɜːglə*] *n.* person who breaks into a house, shop, etc. by night to steal. **bur·gla·ry** *n.*

buri·al ['berɪəl] *n.* act of burying (1).

bur·lesque [bɜː'lesk] *v.t. & n.* (make an) amusing imitation (of a book, speech, person's behaviour, etc.).

bur·ly ['bɜːli] *adj.* (of a person) big and strong.

burn [bɜːn] *v.i. & t.* (p.t. & p.p. ~*t* [bɜːnt] or ~*ed*) **1.** use for the purpose of driving, heating, or lighting: *Most large steamships ~ oil.* **2.** destroy by fire; damage or injure by fire, heat, or acid; scorch; be hurt by fire, heat, or acid: *The house was burnt down. The boy was badly burnt about the face.* **3.** make by heat: *~ bricks*; *~ a hole.* **4.** be in flames; be alight; give out heat or light. **5.** (fig.) glow; be filled with strong feeling: *They are ~ing to defeat the enemy.* *n.* injury, mark, made by fire, heat, or acid. **~·er** *n.* that part of a lamp, stove, etc. where the flame is produced. **~·ing** *adj.* **1.** intense. **2.** exciting: *a ~ing question*, one causing heated argument.

bur·nish ['bɜːnɪʃ] *v.t.* polish.

burnt, see *burn* (v.).

bur·row ['bʌrəʊ] *v.t. & i. & n.* (make a) hole in the ground (esp. as dug by rabbits and foxes).

bur·sar ['bɜːsə*] *n.* treasurer, esp. of a college.

burst [bɜːst] *v.t. & i.* (p.t. & p.p. ~) **1.** fly into pieces; (cause to) break open; explode. **2.** make a way (*out, through, into,* etc.): *~ out laughing, ~ into laughter,* begin suddenly to laugh; *~ing with,* overfull of. *n.* **1.** *~ing:* *the ~ of a shell.* **2.** sudden outbreak: *a ~ of flame*; *a ~ of tears* (*laughter*). **3.** short, violent effort: *a ~ of speed* (*energy*).

bury ['berɪ] *v.t.* **1.** put (a dead body) in the ground, in a grave, in the sea, etc. **2.** cover with earth, etc.; hide from view, etc.: *half buried under dead leaves* (*snow,* etc.); *~ oneself in the country,* go and live where one will meet few people; *buried in thought* (*one's books,* etc.), paying no attention to anything else.

bus [bʌs] *n.* (pl. ~*es,* U.S.A. also *-sses* ['bʌsɪz]) large public motor car carrying passengers along a fixed (2) route.

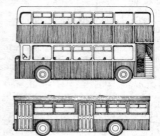

buses

bush [bʊʃ] *n.* **1.** plant with many woody stems coming up from the root. (Cf. *tree,* with a *trunk.*) **2.** (sing. with *the*) wild uncultivated country, esp. in Africa and Australia. **~·y** *adj.* (*-ier, -iest*) **1.** covered with ~es. **2.** growing thickly: *~y eye-brows.*

bush·el ['bʊʃl] *n.* measure for grain and fruit; eight gallons.

busi·ness ['bɪznɪs] *n.* **1.** buying and selling; trade: *on ~,* not for pleasure but for the purpose of doing ~. **2.** shop; commercial firm. **3.** task; duty; concern: *It is the ~ of a teacher to teach. mind your own ~,* confine (1) yourself to your own affairs; *mean ~,* be in earnest; *have no ~ to*, have no right to. **4.** matter; affair: *I'm sick of the whole ~.* **~ hours n. pl.** hours during which regular work is done, shops are open, etc. **'~like adj.** efficient; practical. **'~man n.** man who is engaged in ~ (1).

bust [bʌst] **n. 1.** head and shoulders of a person cut in stone or cast in bronze, etc. **2.** upper front part of a woman's body; measurement of this round the chest and back.

bus·tle ['bʌsl] **v.t. & i.** (cause to) move about quickly and excitedly. **n.** (no pl.) such movement(s).

busy ['bɪzɪ] **adj.** (-*ier*, -*iest*) **1.** working; occupied; having much to do. **2.** full of activity; bustling: *a ~ day.* **3.** (of a telephone line) in use; engaged (3). **v.t.** ~ *oneself* (*with, about*), occupy oneself; keep ~. **'~body n.** person who meddles in sb. else's affairs. **busi·ly adv.**

but [bʌt, bət] **conj., adv., prep., & rel. pron. I. conj.** *Tom was not there ~ his brother was. He's hard-working ~ not clever. Hardly a day passes ~ I think of her* (without my thinking of her). *I cannot ~ admire your courage* (I cannot help admiring, I must admire). *I could not ~ go* (There was nothing else I could do except go). **II. adv.** only (which is the more usual word to use here): *We can ~ try. He's ~ a boy* (not old enough to know better). **III. prep.** except: *They're all wrong ~ me! Who ~ he would do this? Take the next turning ~ one* (take the second turning). *We should have enjoyed the journey ~ for the rain. He would have helped us ~ that he had no money himself* (except that he had ...). **IV. rel. pron.** who or that not: *There is nobody ~ wishes you well* (nobody who does not wish you well).

butch·er ['butʃə*] **n.** person who kills, cuts up, and sells animals for food. **v.t.** kill very violently, esp. with a knife.

but·ler ['bʌtlə*] **n.** head manservant (in charge of the wine-cellar, plate (5), etc.).

butt[1] [bʌt] **n. 1.** thicker (usu. wooden) end of a tool or weapon. **2.** stub of a cigar or cigarette.

butt[2] [bʌt] **n. 1.** mound behind a target. **2.** (pl.) shooting-range. **3.** thing or person as a target for ridicule.

butt[3] [bʌt] **v.t. & i.** strike or hit, esp. with the head, as a goat does. ~ *in*, force oneself into the company or conversation of others; interrupt.

but·ter ['bʌtə*] **n.** (no pl.) fatty food

(usu. yellow or yellowish-white) made from cream. **v.t.** spread ~ on; cook with ~. **'~cup n.** wild plant with yellow flowers. **'~fly n.** insect with feelers and coloured wings. **'~fly stroke n.** swimming stroke executed (1) with both arms lifted at the same time. **'~milk n.** (no pl.) sour milk remaining after ~ has been made.

but·tock ['bʌtək] **n.** either side of that part of the body on which one sits.

but·ton ['bʌtn] **n. 1.** small, usu. round bit of bone, metal, etc. for fastening articles of clothing. **2.** ~-like object, pushed or pressed (e.g. to ring an electric bell). **v.t. & i.** fasten, be fastened, with ~s. **'~hole n. 1.** slit through which a ~ is passed. **2.** flower(s) worn in a ~hole.

but·tress ['bʌtrɪs] **n.** support built against a wall.

bux·om ['bʌksəm] **adj.** (of a woman) healthy-looking, good-looking, and well covered with flesh.

buy [baɪ] **v.t. & i.** (p.t. & p.p. *bought* [bɔːt]) get by paying money or sth. else of value in return. **~er n.** person who ~s.

buzz [bʌz] **n.** sound made by bees when flying, by people talking, by machinery (at a distance). **v.i. & t. 1.** make a ~; be filled with a ~ing sound. **2.** move *about* quickly or busily. **3.** (of an aircraft) fly near (another aircraft) in a threatening way. **~er n.** electric device (2) making a ~ing sound (as a signal or warning).

by [baɪ] **prep. & adv. I. prep. 1.** near; at or to the side of: *Come and sit by me* (*by my side*). *by oneself*, alone: *He did it* (*all*) *by himself* (without help). *stand by sb.*, support him. **2.** (in points of the compass) towards: *East by North* (one point N. of E.). **3.** (showing direction of movement) through; along; across; over: *We came by the shortest route.* **4.** past: *As you go by the station* (pass it), *please get me an evening paper.* **5.** (of time) during: *The sun shines by day and the moon by night.* **6.** (of time) not later than: *Get the work finished by tomorrow.* **7.** (indicating a unit of time, measurements, etc.): *You can rent this house by the month. buy* (*sell*) *cloth by the yard; a room 20 feet by 30 feet.* **8.** through the agency of: *The house is lit by electricity. She was knocked down by a car.* **9.** (manner or method): *Will you travel by sea or by air? Learn this by heart. She took him by the hand. Send the letter by hand* (messenger), *not by post.* **10.** according to: *It's two o'clock by my watch.* **11.** to the extent of: *The car missed me by a few inches.* **II. adv. 1.** near: *When nobody was by, she felt lonely.* **2.** past: *We hurried by, hoping they wouldn't see us.* **3.** aside: *Lay the money by, for use later.* **4.** *by and by,* later on, eventually: *You will understand everything, by and by.*

by(e)- [baɪ-] *pref.* **1.** less important: '**by-road** *n.*; '**by·path** *n.* **2.** made or obtained during the manufacture of sth. else: '**by-,prod·uct** *n.* **3.** (= *by,* adv.) '**by·gone** *adj.* past; '**by,stand-**

er *n.* person standing near and looking on. **4.** '**by-e,lec·tion** *n.* election made necessary by the death or resignation of a member during the life of Parliament. '**by(e)-law** *n.* regulation made by a local authority (e.g. a town or a company. '**by·pass** *n.* road passing round a town or village to avoid through traffic. '**by·word** *n.* person place, etc. regarded and spoken of as a notable example (usu. bad).

bye-bye [,baɪ'baɪ] *int.* (colloq.) good-bye.

byre ['baɪə*] *n.* cow-house.

C

cab [kæb] *n.* **1.** taxi or (hist.) horse carriage that may be hired for short journeys. **2.** part of a railway engine, bus, lorry, etc. reserved for the driver. **'~·man** *n.* ~-driver. **'~-rank, '~-stand** *ns.* place where ~s are allowed to wait for customers.

cab·a·ret [ˈkæbəreɪ] *n.* entertainment (songs and dancing) in a restaurant while guests are at table.

cab·bage [ˈkæbɪdʒ] *n.* plant with a round head of thick, green leaves, used as a vegetable.

a cabbage

a cabinet

cab·by [ˈkæbɪ] *n.* (colloq.) cab-driver.

cab·in [ˈkæbɪn] *n.* **1.** small, roughly-built house (e.g. of logs). **2.** small room in a ship (esp. for sleeping in) or aircraft. **'~-boy** *n.* boy servant in a ship. ~ **class** *n.* (on a ship) grade of accommodation between first class and tourist class.

cab·i·net [ˈkæbɪnɪt] *n.* **1.** piece of furniture with shelves or drawers for storing or displaying things. **2.** *the C~,* group of men (chief ministers) chosen by the head of a government to be responsible for state affairs. **'~-,maker** *n.* skilled workman who makes furniture.

ca·ble [ˈkeɪbl] *n.* **1.** thick, strong rope of hemp, wire, etc. **2.** line containing insulated wires (laid underground or on the ocean bottom) for carrying messages by telegraph or telephone; message so carried. **3.** (as measure) 100 fathoms. *v.t. & i.* send (a message) by ~ (2). **'~-car,** ~ **rail·way** *ns.* one up a steep hillside, worked by a ~ and a stationary engine. **~·gram** [ˈkeɪblgræm] *n.* ~d telegram.

ca·cao [kəˈkɑːəʊ] *n.* (pl. ~s) (tree with a) seed from which cocoa and chocolate are made.

cache [kæʃ] *n.* (hiding-place for) food and stores left (e.g. by explorers) for later use.

cack·le [ˈkækl] *n.* sound made by a hen after laying an egg; loud, shrill talk or laughter. *v.i.* make such a sound.

cac·tus [ˈkæktəs] *n.* (pl. ~es, -ti [ˈkæktaɪ]) plant with thick, fleshy stem(s), (usu.) no leaves, often covered with sharp points.

cad [kæd] *n.* ill-mannered person; person who behaves dishonourably. **~·dish** *adj.* of or like a ~.

ca·dav·er·ous [kəˈdævərəs] *adj.* looking like a corpse; very pale.

cad·die, cad·dy² [ˈkædɪ] *n.* person paid to carry a golfer's clubs for him round the course.

cad·dy¹ [ˈkædɪ] *n.* small box for holding the dried leaves for making tea.

cad·dy², see *caddie.*

ca·dence [ˈkeɪdəns] *n.* rise and fall of music or of the voice in speaking; rhythm.

ca·det [kəˈdet] *n.* student at a military, naval, or air force college. ~ **corps,** organization giving military training to older boys at school.

cadge [kædʒ] *v.t. & i.* (try to) get by begging: *He's always cadging. He ~d a meal.*

ca·fé, ca·fe [ˈkæfeɪ] *n.* small restaurant.

caf·e·te·ria [ˌkæfɪˈtɪərɪə] *n.* self-service restaurant.

cage [keɪdʒ] *n.* **1.** box, place, closed in with wires or bars in which birds or animals are kept. **2.** ~-like part of a lift used for lowering and raising workers, etc. in a mine. *v.t.* put, keep, in a ~: *a ~d bird.*

cairn [keən] *n.* pyramid of rough stones set up as a landmark or memorial.

ca·jole [kəˈdʒəʊl] *v.t.* use flattery or deceit to persuade sb. to do sth. **ca·jol·ery** [kəˈdʒəʊlərɪ] *n.*

cake [keɪk] *n.* **1.** sweet mixture of flour, butter, eggs, etc. baked in an oven. **2.** usu. flat, compressed portion of other kinds of food: *fish ~s; oat~s; pan~s.* **3.** shaped lump of a substance: *a ~ of soap. v.t. & i.* form into a thick, hard mass; coat thickly *with* sth. that dries hard: *shoes ~d with mud.*

cal·a·bash [ˈkæləbæʃ] *n.* (tree with) fruit of which the hard outer skin (or shell) is used for making bottles, bowls, etc.

ca·lam·i·ty [kəˈlæmətɪ] *n.* great and serious misfortune or disaster. **ca·lam·i·tous** [kəˈlæmɪtəs] *adj.*

cal·ci·um [ˈkælsɪəm] *n.* (no pl.) soft white metal forming part of limestone and chalk, present in milk and bones. *~ carbide,* substance used to make acetylene gas.

cal·cu·late [ˈkælkjʊleɪt] *v.t. & i.* **1.** find out by working with numbers: *~ the cost of a journey; calculating-machine.* **2.** plan; arrange; intend: *an advertisement ~d to attract the attention of housewives.* **3.** *~ on,* rely on; be sure of. **cal·cu·lat·ing** *adj.* careful; planning things from selfish motives. **cal·cu·la·tion** [ˌkælkjʊˈleɪʃn] *n.* **cal·cu·la·tor** *n.* person, machine, that ~s.

cal·en·dar [ˈkælɪndə*] *n.* **1.** list of the days, weeks, months, or of events (giving dates and details), of a particular year. **2.** system for fixing the beginning, length, and divisions of a year: *the Muslim ~.*

calf[1] [kɑːf] *n.* (pl. *calves* [kɑːvz]) young of the cow and some other animals. **'~(·skin)** *n.* (no pl.) ~leather.

calf[2] [kɑːf] *n.* (pl. *calves* [kɑːvz]) fleshy part of the back of the leg, below the knee.

cal·i·bre (U.S.A. **-ber**) [ˈkælɪbə*] *n.* **1.** inside measurement across (diameter of) a gun-barrel or any tube, or of a bullet. **2.** quality of mind or character: *a man of good ~.*

cal·i·co [ˈkælɪkəʊ] *n.* (pl. *-oes,* U.S.A. also *-os*) cotton cloth.

call [kɔːl] *v.t. & i.* **1.** name; describe as: *they ~ed him Jack; he ~s himself a doctor*; *~ sb. names,* insult him by giving him bad names. **2.** consider; think: *I ~ that a shame. ~ it a day,* consider that one has done enough work for one day. **3.** (often *~ out*) cry; shout: *Do you hear sb. ~ing? He ~ed (out) for help.* **4.** pay a short visit: *~ on a friend*; (of a ship, etc.) stop *at: ~ at Cape Town. ~ for,* visit a place to get sth. or to go with sb. to another place: *The grocer ~s each week for*

orders. I will ~ for you at six o'clock. **5.** ask for the presence or attention of: *~ a doctor (taxi)*; *~ sb. (up),* telephone to. **6.** (special uses): *~ for,* need; demand: *Your plan will ~ for a lot of money. ~ in,* (a) order the return of (sth.); (b) summon (1) to one's aid; seek advice from; *~ off,* give orders to, decide to, stop sth.: *Please ~ your dog off. The football match was ~ed off. ~ up,* (a) telephone to; (b) summon (1) for military service; *~ up, ~ to mind,* recollect; *~ (sb.) to order,* ask (sb. at a meeting, etc.) to obey the rules; *~ sth. in question,* say that one is doubtful about its truth; *~ a meeting (strike),* announce that there will be one. *n.* **1.** cry; shout: *within ~,* near by; not far away. **2.** message; summons (2): *telephone ~s.* **3.** short visit: *pay a ~ on sb.* **4.** claim (for money, help, etc.): *~s on one's time and purse.* **5.** need: *no ~ for anxiety.* **'~-box** *n.* telephone kiosk. **~er** *n.* person who ~s. **'~-girl** *n.* prostitute who accepts appointments by telephone. **~ing** *n.* (esp.) occupation; profession.

cal·lig·ra·phy [kəˈlɪɡrəfɪ] *n.* (no pl.) handwriting, esp. fine handwriting.

cal·(l)i·pers [ˈkælɪpəz] *n. pl.* instrument for measuring the calibre or diameter of tubes, cylinders, etc.

cal·lous [ˈkæləs] *adj.* **1.** (of the skin) hard; made hard by rough work. **2.** (of a person) disregarding the feelings and sufferings of others.

cal·low [ˈkæləʊ] *adj.* (of a young person) without experience of life.

calm [kɑːm] *adj.* quiet; untroubled. *n.* time when everything is ~. *v.t. & i. ~ (down),* make or become ~. **~·ly** *adv.* **~·ness** *n.*

cal·o·rie [ˈkælərɪ] *n.* unit of heat; unit of energy supplied by food.

cal·um·ny [ˈkæləmnɪ] *n.* untrue and damaging statement about sb. **ca·lum·ni·ate** [kəˈlʌmnɪeɪt] *v.t.* slander.

calve [kɑːv] *v.i.* give birth to a calf.

calves, see *calf*[1,2].

cam·bric [ˈkeɪmbrɪk] *n.* (no pl.) fine, thin cloth of cotton or linen.

came, see *come.*

cam·el [ˈkæml] *n.* long-necked animal, with either one or two humps on its back, much used in desert countries for riding and carrying goods.

cam·eo [ˈkæmɪəʊ] *n.* (pl. *~s*) piece of hard stone, on which is a raised design, often in a different colour, used as a jewel or ornament.

cam·era [ˈkæmərə] *n.* apparatus for taking photographs, moving or tele-

vision pictures: *cine*~, *television* ~.
'~·man *n.* person who operates (1) a ~ in cinema or television.

cam·ou·flage ['kæmʊflɑ:ʒ] *v.t. & n.* (no pl.) (use a) device (2) for hiding or disguising the real appearance of sth.; esp., in war, the use of paint, netting, etc. to deceive the enemy.

camp [kæmp] *n.* place where people (e.g. soldiers, holiday-makers, etc.) live in tents or huts for a time. ~-bed (~-chair, ~-stool, etc.), that can be folded and carried easily. *v.i.* ~ (out), make, live in, a ~: *go ~ing,* spend a holiday living in a tent or tents. '~·site *n.* place for ~ing.

cam·paign [kæm'peɪn] *n.* 1. group of military operations with a set purpose or objective, usu. in one area. 2. series of planned activities to gain a special object: *a political* ~. *v.i.* take part in, go on, a ~. ~·er *n.*

cam·phor ['kæmfə*] *n.* (no pl.) strong-smelling white substance used for medical purposes and to keep away insects. ~·at·ed ['kæmfəreɪtɪd] *adj.* containing ~: ~ated oil.

cam·pus ['kæmpəs] *n.* (pl. ~es) grounds of a college or university.

can¹ [kæn, kən] *v.aux.* (neg. *cannot* ['kænɒt], colloq. *can't* [kɑ:nt], p.t. *could* [kʊd, kəd], neg. *could not,* colloq. *couldn't* ['kʊdnt]) 1. be able to; know how to: *If you shut your eyes, you can't see. C~ you speak English?* 2. (indicating possibility): *That couldn't be true.* 3. (indicating wonder, doubt, etc.): *What can that strange thing be?* 4. (indicating a right): *You can't* (i.e. have no right to) *go into that private garden.* 5. (indicating permission): *The children asked if they could* (if I would let them) *go swimming.* 6. (could indicating inclination): *Could you* (if it were necessary to ask you) *work late to-morrow? I could smack his face* (if I gave way to my feelings, but I don't intend to).

can² [kæn] *n.* 1. metal container for liquids, etc.: *oil-*~; *milk-*~. *carry the* ~, (sl.) take the blame or responsibility. 2. (Gt. Brit. also *tin*) tin-plated container for food, drink, etc., esp. one sealed so as to be airtight; its contents: *a* ~ *of beer. v.t.* (-*nn-*) put into a ~ (2) or ~s and preserve (food, etc.) thus: ~*ned food.* ~·nery *n.* factory where food, etc., is ~ned.

Ca·na·di·an [kə'neɪdjən] *n. & adj.* (native or inhabitant) of Canada.

ca·nal [kə'næl] *n.* 1. channel cut through land for the use of ships (e.g.

the *Suez C*~) or to carry water to irrigate fields. 2. tube in a plant or animal body for food, liquid, etc.: *the alimentary* ~.

ca·nary [kə'neərɪ] *n.* 1. small, yellow song-bird, usu. kept in a cage. 2. (also ~-*yellow*) (no pl.) light yellow.

can·cel ['kænsl] *v.t.* (-*ll*-) 1. cross out; draw a line through (words or figures); make marks on (sth., e.g. postage stamps) to prevent re-use. 2. say that sth. already arranged or decided on will not be done, will not take place, etc.: ~ *an order (a meeting).* ~·la·tion [,kænsə'leɪʃn] *n.*

can·cer ['kænsə*] *n.* diseased growth in the body, often causing death. ~·ous ['kænsərəs] *adj.*

can·did ['kændɪd] *adj.* frank; straight-forward. ~·ly *adv.*

can·di·date ['kændɪdət] *n.* 1. person wishing, or put forward by sb., to take an office or position: *The Socialist* ~ *was elected.* 2. person entered for an examination. **can·di·da·ture** ['kændɪdətʃə*] (Gt. Brit.), **can·di·da·cy** ['kændɪdəsɪ] *ns.* being a ~ (1).

can·dle ['kændl] *n.* slender stick of wax, etc. containing a wick, for giving light. *The game is not worth the* ~, is more trouble (expense, etc.) than it is worth. '~·stick *n.* holder for a candle.

a candle in   a cane
a candlestick   chair

can·dour (U.S.A. **-dor**) ['kændə*] *n.* (no pl.) quality of being candid, saying freely what one thinks; fair-mindedness.

can·dy ['kændɪ] *n.* 1. (also *sugar-*~) sugar made hard by repeated boiling. 2. (U.S.A.) = sweet(s) (2). *v.t.* preserve (e.g. fruit) by boiling in sugar: *candied orange peel.*

cane [keɪn] *n.* 1. long, hollow, jointed stem of grass-like plants and tall reeds, etc. (e.g. bamboo, sugar-~). 2. such stems used for making baskets, furniture, etc.: *a chair with a* ~ *seat.* 3. such a stem used as a walking-stick, as a stick for punishing children with, or to support plants. *v.t.* make or repair with ~(s) (2); punish with a ~ (3). '~-,sug·ar n. (no pl.) sugar made from sugar-~.

ca·nine ['keɪnaɪn] adj. (as) of a dog or dogs.

can·is·ter ['kænɪstə*] n. small (usu. metal) box for tea, tobacco, etc.

can·ker ['kæŋkə*] n. disease that destroys the wood of trees; (fig.) evil influence or tendency causing decay.

canned, can·nery, see can².

can·ni·bal ['kænɪbl] n. person who eats human flesh; animal that eats its own kind.

can·non ['kænən] n. (pl. usu. ~) 1. large gun, fixed to the ground or to a gun-carriage, esp. the old kind firing a solid ball, called a ~-ball. 2. shell-firing gun used in aircraft. ~·ade [,kænə'neɪd] n. continued firing of big guns.

can·not, see can¹.

can·ny ['kænɪ] adj. (-ier, -iest) not prepared to take unknown risks; cautious, esp. about spending money.

ca·noe [kə'nuː] n. light boat moved by one or more paddles. v.i. travel by ~. ~·ist n. person who paddles a ~.

a canoe

can·on ['kænən] n. 1. church law. 2. general standard by which sth. is judged: ~s of conduct (good taste, etc.). 3. body (6) of writings accepted as genuine, esp. those books of the Bible accepted by the Church. 4. priest (with the title The Rev. C~) who is one of a group having duties in a cathedral. 5. list of saints. ca·non·i·cal [kə'nɒnɪkl] adj. according to church laws; belonging to the ~ (3). ~·ize ['kænənaɪz] v.t. place in the ~ (5).

ca·ñon ['kænjən] n. canyon.

can·o·py ['kænəpɪ] n. 1. covering suspended or held over a bed, throne, person, etc.; any similarly placed covering: a ~ of leaves. 2. transparent cover over the cockpit of an aircraft.

cant [kænt] n. (no pl.) 1. insincere talk implying piety; hypocrisy. 2. special talk, words, used by a particular class of people: thieves' ~.

can't, see can¹.

can·tan·ker·ous [kæn'tæŋkərəs] adj. bad-tempered; quarrelsome.

can·ta·ta [kæn'tɑːtə] n. short musical work to be sung by soloists and a choir, usu. a dramatic story but not acted. (Cf. oratorio.)

can·teen [kæn'tiːn] n. 1. place (esp. in factories, barracks, offices) where food, drink, and sometimes other articles are supplied. 2. box or chest of table silver and cutlery. 3. soldier's eating and drinking utensils. 4. water-flask, used esp. by soldiers.

can·ter ['kæntə*] n. easy gallop. v.t. & i. (cause a horse to) go at this pace.

can·ti·le·ver ['kæntɪliːvə*] n. long, large, arm-like bracket extending from a wall or base (e.g. to support a balcony): ~ bridge, bridge of connected ~s.

a cantilever bridge

can·to ['kæntəʊ] n. (pl. ~s) one of the chief divisions of a long poem.

can·ton ['kæntɒn] n. subdivision of a country, esp. Switzerland.

can·vas ['kænvəs] n. strong, coarse cloth used for sails, bags, tents, etc. and by artists for oil-paintings; oil-painting. under ~, (a) sleeping in tents; (b) with sails spread.

can·vass ['kænvəs] v.t. & i. 1. ~ (for), ask (people) for support, orders for goods, votes, etc. 2. examine (a question) thoroughly by asking for opinions.

can·yon ['kænjən] n. deep gorge (usu. with a river flowing through it).

cap [kæp] n. 1. soft head-covering worn by boys and men, by some sailors and soldiers, without a brim but usu. with a peak (2). 2. sth. like a ~ in use or shape (e.g. the ~ of a milk-bottle, of a tube of toothpaste). v.t. (-pp-) put a ~ on. ~ a story, tell a better story; say sth. more amusing (than sb. else has said).

ca·pa·ble ['keɪpəbl] adj. 1. able; gifted. 2. ~ of, (a) (of persons) having the ability, power, or inclination: He's ~ of neglecting his duty. (b) (of things) ready for; admitting of: a situation ~ of improvement. ca·pa·bil·i·ty [,keɪpə'bɪlətɪ] n. power to do things; (pl.) qualities that await development.

ca·pac·i·ty [kə'pæsətɪ] n. ability to

hold, contain, get hold of, learn (things, ideas, knowledge, etc.): *a hall with a large seating* ~; *a mind of great* ~; amount or number that can be held or contained: *filled to* ~ (i.e. quite full). *in the* ~ *of*, acting as; in the position of. **ca·pa·cious** [kə'peɪʃəs] *adj.* able to hold much.

cape[1] [keɪp] *n.* loose outer garment, without sleeves, worn over the shoulders.

cape[2] [keɪp] *n.* high point of land going out into the sea; headland.

ca·per ['keɪpə*] *v.i.* jump about playfully. *n. cut a* ~ or ~*s*, jump about merrily; behave foolishly.

cap·il·lary [kə'pɪlərɪ] *adj. & n.* thin, hairlike (tube) (e.g. joining veins or arteries). ~ *attraction*, force that causes oil to rise through the wick of an oil lamp, or ink to be absorbed by blotting-paper.

cap·i·tal[1] ['kæpɪtl] *n.* top of a column or pillar.

cap·i·tal[2] ['kæpɪtl] *n. & attrib. adj.* **1.** chief town or city of a country, county, etc.: *Paris is the* ~ *of France. London and Paris are* ~ *cities.* **2.** (of letters) not small, e.g. A, P, Z: *write sth. in* ~*s* (in ~ *letters*). **3.** money with which a person, etc. enters into business; wealth (money and property) used for producing more wealth. ~ *goods*, goods (to be) used in producing commodities. (Cf. *consumer goods.*) *adj.* **1.** ~ *punishment* (by death); *a* ~ *crime* (*offence*) (punishable by death). **2.** (colloq.) excellent. **3.** most serious: *a* ~ *error.* ~**ism** ['kæpɪtəlɪzəm] *n.* (no pl.) economic system in which a country's trade and industry are organized and controlled by the owners of ~ (3), the chief elements being competition, profit, supply and demand. (Cf. *socialism.*) ~**ist** ['kæpɪtəlɪst] *n.* (often derog.) person owning and controlling much ~ (3). ~**is·tic** [,kæpɪtə'lɪstɪk] *adj.* ~**ize** ['kæpɪtəlaɪz] *v.t.* change into, use as, ~ (3). ~**iza·tion** [,kæpɪtəlaɪ'zeɪʃn] *n.*

ca·pit·u·late [kə'pɪtjʊleɪt] *v.i.* surrender (on stated conditions). **ca·pit·u·la·tion** [kə,pɪtjʊ'leɪʃn] *n.*

ca·price [kə'priːs] *n.* (tendency towards a) sudden change of mind or behaviour without apparent cause. **ca·pri·cious** [kə'prɪʃəs] *adj.* full of ~; often changing: *a capricious breeze.*

cap·size [kæp'saɪz] *v.t. & i.* (esp. of a boat) overturn.

cap·stan ['kæpstən] *n.* upright, barrel-like object turned by men or by mechanical power, used for winding a cable and raising sails, anchors, etc.

a capstan   a capsule (3)

cap·sule ['kæpsjuːl] *n.* **1.** seed-case on a plant. **2.** tiny soluble container for a dose of medicine. **3.** detachable part of a spacecraft containing (1) scientific instruments and astronauts, etc.

cap·tain ['kæptɪn] *n.* **1.** leader or commander: *the* ~ *of a ship* (*football team*). **2.** army officer below a major and above a lieutenant. **3.** naval officer below a commodore or rear-admiral and above a commander. *v.t.* act as ~ of.

cap·tion ['kæpʃn] *n.* short title or heading of an article in a periodical, etc.; words printed with a picture, photograph, etc.; wording shown on a cinema or television screen.

cap·tious ['kæpʃəs] *adj.* (fond of) finding fault, making protests, esp. about small matters.

cap·ti·vate ['kæptɪveɪt] *v.t.* capture the fancy of; charm.

cap·tive ['kæptɪv] *n. & adj.* (person or animal) taken prisoner: *be taken* ~, be captured. ~ *balloon*, ballon moored to the ground (or a ship). **cap·tiv·i·ty** [kæp'tɪvətɪ] *n.* (no pl.) state of being held ~. **cap·tor** ['kæptə*] *n.* person who takes a ~.

cap·ture ['kæptʃə*] *v.t.* make a prisoner of; take or obtain (2) (by force, skill, trickery, etc.): ~ *a thief* (*sb.'s attention*). *n.* act of capturing; person or thing ~d.

car [kɑː*] *n.* **1.** motor car or tramcar: ~*park*, place where motor ~*s*, etc. may be left for a time. ~*port*, shelter with open sides for a motor vehicle. **2.** (on a railway train) coach (*sleeping-*~, *dining-*~), (U.S.A.) also van[1] (2). **3.** compartment of an airship, a balloon, cable railway, or lift used by passengers. **4.** (poet.) chariot: *the* ~ *of the sun-god.*

car·a·mel ['kærəmel] *n.* **1.** burnt sugar used for colouring and flavouring. **2.** sticky sweet.

car·at ['kærət] *n.* unit of weight for jewels; unit of fineness for gold.

car·a·van ['kærəvæn] *n.* **1.** company of people (e.g. travellers, merchants) making a journey together (usu. across desert or dangerous country). **2.** covered vehicle used for living in (e.g. by holiday-makers, gipsies, etc.), now usu. pulled behind a motor vehicle: ~ *park* (*site*), (Gt. Brit.) place where holiday-makers may park their ~s. (Cf. *trailer* (1).)

car·bide ['kɑːbaɪd] *n.* (no pl.) see *calcium* ~.

car·bo·hy·drate [,kɑːbəʊ'haɪdreɪt] *n.* any of various energy-producing organic compounds of carbon, hydrogen, and oxygen (e.g. sugar, starch).

car·bol·ic ac·id [kɑː'bɒlɪk 'æsɪd] *n.* (no pl.) acid made from coal tar, used as a disinfectant and germkiller.

car·bon ['kɑːbən] *n.* **1.** (no pl.) chemical element, not a metal, present in coal, charcoal, diamonds. **2.** (also ~ *copy*) copy (1) made with ~ paper. ~ *dating*, method of dating the age of organic substances by measuring the amount of radioactive ~ (1) still present in it. ~ *dioxide*, colourless gas formed by the combustion and decomposition of organic substances. ~ *monoxide*, colourless, odourless, very poisonous gas produced by the incomplete combustion of ~ (1), burning with a blue flame, forming ~ dioxide. (also ~ *paper*) thin paper coated with coloured matter, used between sheets of writing-paper for making copies.

car·bon·ic ac·id [kɑː'bɒnɪk 'æsɪd] *n.* (no pl.) acid formed from carbon dioxide dissolved in water.

car·bun·cle ['kɑːbʌŋkl] *n.* **1.** bright-red jewel. **2.** red (usu. painful) swelling under the skin.

car·bu·ret·tor, car·bu·ret·ter (U.S.A. **-ret·or**) ['kɑːbjʊˌretə*] *n.* that part of an engine in which petrol vapour and air are mixed.

car·cass, car·case ['kɑːkəs] *n.* **1.** dead body of an animal, esp. one prepared for cutting up as meat. **2.** (esp. derog.) (dead) human body.

car·cin·o·gen [kɑː'sɪnəʊdʒɪn] *n.* (med.) substance that produces cancer. **car·ci·no·gen·ic** [kɑːˌsɪnəʊ'dʒenɪk] *adj.*

card [kɑːd] *n.* thick, stiff paper (esp. an oblong piece of this) as used for various purposes, e.g. *a post~* (see *post*); *a visiting-~* (giving a person's name, etc.); *Christmas ~s*; *playing-~s* (in sets of 52, used for numerous games); *a ~ index* (list of names, subjects, etc. entered in alphabetical order on separate cards); *put one's ~s on the table*, make one's plans, intentions, etc. known; *play one's ~s well*,

be clever at getting what one wants; *on the ~s*, possible or probable; *have a ~ up one's sleeve*, have a secret plan in reserve. '~**board** *n.* (no pl.) thick ~, used in making boxes, for binding books, etc.

car·di·ac ['kɑːdɪæk] *adj.* (med.) of the heart.

car·di·gan ['kɑːdɪgən] *n.* knitted woollen jacket, with sleeves, that buttons up the front.

car·di·nal ['kɑːdɪnl] *adj.* chief; most important: ~ *numbers*, one, two, three, etc. (Cf. *ordinal numbers*.) ~ *points*, (of the compass) N., S., E., and W. *n.* member of the Sacred College of the Roman Catholic Church which elects Popes.

care [keə*] *n.* **1.** serious attention; watchfulness: *take ~*, be on the watch; pay attention. **2.** protection; charge (5); responsibility: *take ~ of*, look after; see to the safety or welfare of; *in* (*under*) *the ~ of*, looked after by; ~ *of* (usu. written c/o): *John Smith, c/o William Brown, 2 Duke Street, Coventry* (indicating that J. S. is staying at W. B.'s house or that W. B. will forward the letter to J. S.'s address). **3.** troubled state of mind caused by doubt or fear; (cause of) sorrow or anxiety: *free from ~*; *the ~s of a large family. v.i.* **1.** feel interest, anxiety, or sorrow (*for, about*): *We don't ~ (about) what happens.* **2.** ~ *for*, (a) have a liking for; (b) look after; ~ *to* (inf.), be willing to: *Would you ~ to go for a walk?* ~**ful** *adj.* ~**less** *adj.* '~**tak·er** *n.* person taking ~ of a building while its owners are away, etc.

ca·reer [kə'rɪə*] *n.* **1.** progress through life; (a person's) life history: *the ~s of great men.* **2.** way of earning a living; profession or occupation: ~*s open to women.* **3.** quick or violent movement: *in full ~. v.i.* ~ *about* (*along, over, through*) (a place), rush wildly.

ca·ress [kə'res] *v.t. & n.* (give a) loving touch (to); kiss.

car·go ['kɑːgəʊ] *n.* (pl. *-oes*, U.S.A. also *-os*) goods carried in a ship, aircraft, or other vehicle.

car·i·ca·ture ['kærɪkəˌtjʊə*] *n.* picture of sb. or sth., imitation of a person's voice, behaviour, etc. stressing certain features in order to cause amusement or ridicule. *v.t.* make or give a ~ of.

car·ies ['keəriːz] *n.* (pl. ~) (med.) decay (of bones or teeth): *dental ~.* **car·i·ous** ['keərɪəs] *adj.* affected with ~.

car·mine ['kɑːmaɪn] *adj. & n.* (no pl.) deep red.

car·nage ['kɑːnɪdʒ] *n.* (no pl.) the killing of many people.

car·nal ['kɑːnl] *adj.* of the body or flesh; sensual (opp. *spiritual*): ～ *desires.*

car·na·tion [kɑː'neɪʃn] *n.* **1.** garden plant with sweet-smelling flowers; the flower. **2.** (no pl.) rosy-pink colour.

car·ni·val ['kɑːnɪvl] *n.* public merry-making and feasting, esp. in Roman Catholic countries during the week before Lent.

car·niv·o·rous [kɑː'nɪvərəs] *adj.* flesh-eating.

car·ol ['kærəl] *n.* song of joy or praise, esp. a Christmas hymn. *v.i.* (*-ll-*) sing joyfully.

ca·rouse [kə'raʊz] *v.i.* drink heavily and have a merry time. **ca·rous·al** [kə'raʊzl] *n.* merry and noisy drinking-party.

carp¹ [kɑːp] *v.i.* make unnecessary complaints about little things: ～*ing at her husband; a* ～*ing tongue.*

carp² [kɑːp] *n.* (pl. ～) freshwater fish, usu. bred in ponds.

car·pen·ter ['kɑːpəntə*] *n.* workman who makes (esp.) the wooden parts of buildings, etc. (Cf. *joiner, cabinet-maker.*) **car·pen·try** ['kɑːpəntrɪ] *n.* (no pl.) work of a ～.

car·pet ['kɑːpɪt] *n.* large, thick floor-covering of wool, hair, etc. often with designs. *v.t.* cover (as) with a ～.

car·riage ['kærɪdʒ] *n.* **1.** vehicle esp. one with four wheels, pulled by a horse, for carrying people. **2.** railway coach (U.S.A. *car* (2)). **3.** (no pl.) (cost of) carrying goods from place to place: ～ *forward*, cost of ～ to be paid by the receiver; ～ *free*, cost of ～ free to the receiver; ～ *paid*, cost of ～ paid by the sender. **4.** (no pl.) manner of holding the head or body. **5.** moving part of a machine changing the position of other parts: *the* ～ *of a typewriter.* '～**·way** *n.* that part of a road used by vehicles. (See *dual*.)

car·ri·er ['kærɪə*] *n.* **1.** person or company carrying goods or passengers for payment. **2.** support for parcels, boxes, etc. fixed to a bicycle, motor car, etc. **3.** vehicle, ship, etc. built to carry troops, aircraft, etc.: *an aircraft* ～. **4.** person or animal carrying or transmitting a disease, although not himself or itself suffering from it. '～**-bag** *n.* strong paper or plastic bag for shopping.

car·ri·on ['kærɪən] *n.* (no pl.) dead and decaying flesh.

car·rot ['kærət] *n.* (plant with) yellow or orange-red root used as a vegetable.

car·ry ['kærɪ] *v.t. & i.* **1.** hold off the ground and move (sb. or sth.) from one place to another; take from place to place: *The porter was* ～*ing the luggage to the car. He will* ～ *the news to everyone in the village.* **2.** have with one: *He always carries an umbrella.* **3.** support: *pillars that* ～ *the heavy roof.* **4.** keep (the head or body) in a certain way: *He carries himself like a soldier. How well she carries her head!* **5.** win; persuade; overcome (resistance): ～ *one's point* (i.e. get people to agree that it is right); ～ *one's listeners with one* (i.e. have their support); ～ *everything before one* (i.e. succeed in everything); ～ *the enemy's positions* (i.e. capture them). **6.** provide a path for; take along: *pipes* ～*ing water to the town; wires* ～ *electric current.* **7.** make longer; continue: ～ *a fence round a field;* ～ *modesty too far.* **8.** (of sound) be heard: *The sound of the guns carried many miles; a voice that carries well.* **9.** (of guns) send (shells, etc.) a certain distance: *Our guns do not* ～ *far enough.* **10.** ～ *away*, take to another place; (fig.) cause to lose self-control; excite: *He was carried away by his enthusiasm.* ～ *forward*, take (figures) to the top of the next page or add to the next column; ～ *off*, (a) take without permission or by force; (b) win; ～ *on*, proceed; conduct; manage; continue. *C*～ *on!* (i.e. don't stop); ～ *on business* (as), employ oneself (as); ～ *on a conversation with*, talk to; ～ *out*, get done; give effect to: ～ *out orders* (*plans, threats*); ～ *over* = ～ forward; ～ *through*, (a) support (through difficulties); (b) bring to a successful end; ～ *weight*, have influence.

cart [kɑːt] *n.* strong (usu. two-wheeled) vehicle, pulled by an animal, for carrying goods: *a coal-*～; *put the* ～ *before the horse*, do or put things in the wrong order. *v.t.* carry in a ～. ～**age** ['kɑːtɪdʒ] *n.* (no pl.) (cost of) ～ing. ～**·er** *n.* man in charge of a ～.

car·tel [kɑː'tel] *n.* combination of traders, manufacturers, etc. to control output, fix prices, etc. (for their own advantage).

car·ti·lage ['kɑːtɪlɪdʒ] *n.* (structure of) firm elastic substance attached to the joints, in animal bodies; gristle.

car·tog·ra·phy [kɑː'tɒgrəfɪ] *n.* (no pl.) map-drawing.

car·ton ['kɑːtən] *n.* cardboard box for holding goods.

car·toon [kɑː'tuːn] *n.* **1.** drawing dealing with current events (esp. politics) in an amusing way. **2.** cinema film made by photographing a series of drawings: *a Walt Disney (Mickey Mouse)* ~. (See *animated, animation*.) ~**·ist** *n.* person who draws ~s.

car·tridge ['kɑːtrɪdʒ] *n.* **1.** case containing explosive (for blasting), or bullet or shot and explosive (for firearms). **2.** case containing a spool of film or reels of magnetic tape. **3.** small container of ink ready to be inserted in a pen. **4.** removable head of a pickup of a record-player.

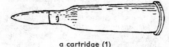

a cartridge (1)

cart·wheel ['kɑːtwiːl] *n.* turn ~s, turn somersaults sideways.

carve [kɑːv] *v.t. & i.* **1.** make (a shape, design, etc.) by cutting: ~ *a statue out of wood*; ~ *one's name on a tree trunk*. **2.** cut up (cooked meat, etc.) into slices or pieces for eating at table: ~ *a chicken*. **carv·er** *n.* person who ~s the meat at table; knife for carving. **carving** *n.* piece of wood shaped by cutting or with a design cut on it.

cas·cade [kæ'skeɪd] *n.* small waterfall; one part of a large broken waterfall.

case¹ [keɪs] *n.* **1.** instance or example of the occurrence of sth.; state or condition: *There have been several accidents here, but only in one ~ was anybody killed. I have often excused you before, but in this ~ you must be punished. in* ~, if; *(just) in* ~, because of a possibility; *in* ~ *of*, in the event of; *in any* ~, whatever may happen; *in no* ~, under no circumstances; *in that* ~, if that is true; if that should happen. **2.** (med.) person suffering from a disease; instance of a diseased condition: *five* ~*s of yellow fever*; *send the worst* ~*s to hospital*. **3.** (law) question to be decided in a lawcourt; the facts, arguments, etc. used on one side: *When will the* ~ *come before the Court? He has a strong* ~. *State your* ~ (i.e. give the facts and arguments in your favour). **4.** (gram.) (change in the) form of a noun, pronoun, or adjective that shows its relation to other words in a sentence.

case² [keɪs] *n.* box or container: *packing-*~; *cigarette-*~; *book*~; *suit*~; cloth covering: *pillow*~.

ca·sein ['keɪsiːɪn] *n.* (no pl.) body-building food present in milk and forming the basis of cheese.

case·ment ['keɪsmənt] *n.* window that opens inwards or outwards like a door. (See the picture at *window*.)

cash [kæʃ] *n.* (no pl.) ready money; money in coin or notes: ~ *down*, ~ *on delivery*, payment on delivery of goods; ~ *and carry*, sale for ~, usu. at reduced prices if the buyer takes the goods away with him. ~ *price*, price for immediate payment. ~ *register*, ~ *box* with a device (2) for visibly recording the amount of each purchase and for storing ~ received. *v.t.* give or get ~ for (a cheque).

cash·ier¹ [kæ'ʃɪə*] *n.* person receiving and paying out cash in a bank, an office, a shop, restaurant, etc.

cash·ier² [kə'ʃɪə*] *v.t.* dismiss (a commissioned officer) with dishonour and disgrace.

cash·mere [kæʃ'mɪə*] *n.* (fabric (1) made from) fine soft wool of Kashmir goats.

cas·ing ['keɪsɪŋ] *n.* covering: *copper wire with a* ~ *of rubber*; *sausage* ~*s*.

ca·si·no [kə'siːnəʊ] *n.* (pl. ~s) public room or building for music, dancing, etc. and in some places for gambling.

cask [kɑːsk] *n.* barrel for liquids.

cas·ket ['kɑːskɪt] *n.* **1.** small box, often ornamented, for jewels, letters, cremated ashes, etc. **2.** (U.S.A.) rectangular coffin.

cas·se·role ['kæsərəʊl] *n.* covered dish in which food is cooked and served at table; food cooked and served in a ~.

cas·sette [kæ'set] *n.* small container of film or reels of magnetic tape that can be inserted into a camera or ~ *tape-recorder* (for automatic play-back or recording). ~ *TV*, ~ *television*, any of various systems in which video tapes in ~s are used in special television receivers (2) so that one can watch any of the taped programmes at any time.

cas·sock ['kæsək] *n.* long close-fitting garment, usu. black, worn by some priests.

cast [kɑːst] *v.t. & i.* (p.t. & p.p. ~) **1.** throw; allow to fall: ~ *a net or line for fish. Snakes* ~ *their skins. The horse* ~ *a shoe* (lost one). ~ *anchor*, lower the anchor; ~ *lots*, choose by lot² (1); let chance decide; ~ *a vote*, give a vote; ~*ing vote*, one given (e.g. by a chairman) to decide a question when votes on each side are equal. ~ *aside*, abandon; *be* ~ *down*, be depressed or unhappy; ~ *off*, abandon; ~*-off clothes*, clothes that their owner does not want to wear again. **2.** send or turn in a particular direction: ~ *a glance at*; ~ *a spell on*, bewitch (1); ~ *a shadow on*; ~ *about for*, look round for. **3.** pour (liquid metal, etc.) into a mould[1]: ~ *iron*; ~ *a bronze statue*. **4.** ~ *up*, add: ~ *up a column of figures*. **5.** give (an actor) a part in a play, film, etc. *n.* **1.** act of throwing (e.g. a net). **2.** sth. made by ~*ing* (3): *His leg was in a plaster* ~. **3.** sth. thrown out or off, shed (e.g. the skin of an insect). **4.** slight twist, esp. of the eye; squint. **5.** (all the) actors in a play, film, etc.: *an all-star* ~. **6.** type or quality: ~ *of features*; ~ *of mind*. '~-**away** *n.* shipwrecked person, esp. one reaching a strange country or lonely island. ~**ing** *n.* sth. made by ~*ing* (3), esp. a metal part for a machine. ~ **iron** *n.* (no pl.) hard brittle mixture of iron, carbon (1), and silicon ~ in a mould[1]. '~-**iron** *adj.*

caste [kɑːst] *n.* one of the fixed social classes among the Hindus; custom of dividing people into such classes; any exclusive social class.

cas·ti·gate ['kæstɪgeɪt] *v.t.* punish severely with blows or by scolding or criticizing. **cas·ti·ga·tion** [ˌkæstɪ-'geɪʃn] *n.*

cas·tle ['kɑːsl] *n.* **1.** large building or group of buildings fortified against attack in olden times. ~*s in the air* (*in Spain*), imagined projects and hopes; day-dreams. **2.** piece in chess.

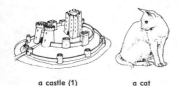

a castle (1)   a cat

cas·tor, cast·er ['kɑːstə*] *n.* **1.** small wheel for the foot of a piece of furniture, to make it easy to move. **2.** small container with one or more holes in the top, for shaking salt, sugar, etc. on to food.

cas·tor oil [ˌkɑːstər'ɔɪl] *n.* (no pl.) thick, yellowish oil, used as a medicine to empty the bowels.

cas·trate [kæ'streɪt] *v.t.* remove the sex organs of (a usu. male animal); take away the power (of a usu. male animal) to breed. **cas·tra·tion** *n.*

ca·su·al ['kæʒjʊəl] *adj.* **1.** happening by chance: *a ~ meeting*. **2.** careless; without special purpose: *a ~ glance*. **3.** (colloq.) unconcerned; informal: ~ clothes. **4.** irregular: ~ *labour*; ~ (*labourer*), one without permanent employment. ~·**ly** *adv.* ~·**ty** ['kæʒjʊəltɪ] *n.* **1.** serious or fatal accident; disaster. **2.** person injured, wounded, or killed (in war, an accident, etc.): ~*ty ward* (*department*), part of a hospital to which persons are taken for urgent treatment (e.g. after a road accident). **3.** sb. or sth. lost or destroyed.

cat [kæt] *n.* **1.** small, furry, domesticated (2) animal kept as a pet[1] (1) or to catch mice. *let the ~ out of the bag*, allow a secret to become known; *like a ~ on hot bricks*, very uneasy or jumpy; *lead a ~-and-dog life*, lead a life full of quarrels; *rain ~s and dogs*, rain very hard; *wait for the ~ to jump, see which way the ~ jumps*, wait to see what others think or do before giving an opinion, etc. **2.** any animal of the ~ family (e.g. a lion or tiger). **3.** (short for) ~-*o'-nine-tails*, whip with many knotted cords, formerly used for punishing wrongdoers. '~'s-**eye** *n.* one of a line of reflector studs on a road; reflector stud on the rear of a vehicle (e.g. a bicycle).

cat·a·clysm ['kætəklɪzəm] *n.* sudden and violent change, esp. in nature (e.g. a cloudburst, earthquake, or flood); political or social upheaval.

cat·a·comb ['kætəkuːm] *n.* (usu. pl.) underground galleries with openings along the sides for burial of the dead, esp. in ancient Rome.

cat·a·logue (U.S.A. also -**log**) ['kætəlɒg] *n.* list (of names, places, books, goods, etc.) in a special order. *v.t.* make a ~ of; put in a ~.

cat·a·lyst ['kætəlɪst] *n.* substance that brings about a chemical change without itself undergoing any change.

cat·a·pult ['kætəpʌlt] *n.* **1.** Y-shaped stick with a piece of elastic, for shooting stones, etc. **2.** apparatus for helping an aircraft to get into the air quickly (e.g. from the deck of a ship). **3.** (olden times) machine for throwing heavy stones in war. *v.t.* launch by or as if by a ~. *v.i.* become ~ed.

cat·a·ract ['kætərækt] *n.* **1.** large, steep waterfall. **2.** eye disease causing partial blindness.

ca·tarrh [kə'tɑː*] *n.* (no pl.) disease of the nose and throat, causing a flow of liquid, as when one has a cold.

ca·tas·tro·phe [kə'tæstrəfɪ] *n.* sudden

happening causing great suffering or destruction (e.g. a flood, earthquake, or big fire). **cat·a·stroph·ic** [ˌkætə-'strɒfɪk] *adj.*

catch [kætʃ] *v.t. & i.* (p.t. & p.p. **caught** [kɔːt]) **1.** stop (sth. moving through the air, etc., e.g. by grasping it, holding out sth. into which it falls, etc.). **2.** capture; seize: ~ *a thief*; ~ *fish* (*mice, etc.*). **3.** be in time for; be able to use, meet, etc.: ~ *a train* (*the bus*), ~ *the post*, post letters before the post-box is emptied. *I caught him as he was leaving the house.* **4.** ~ *sb. up,* ~ *up with sb. or sth.,* draw level with sb. in front; make up for lost time (by working quicker, etc.). **5.** come unexpectedly upon sb. doing sth., esp. sth. wrong: *I caught him stealing vegetables from my garden.* **6.** get; receive (punishment, etc.): ~ *cold* (*an illness*); ~ *sb.'s words* (*his meaning*) (i.e. hear, understand); ~ *sight of* (see for a moment); ~ *sb.'s eye* (attract his attention). *You'll* ~ *it!* (be punished, etc.). **7.** (cause to) become fixed or fastened: ~ *one's fingers in the door. The nail caught her dress. Her dress caught on a nail.* **8.** hit: *He caught him on the nose.* ~ *sb. a blow* (*one*). **9.** ~ *fire,* begin to burn; ~ *one's breath,* take a short, sudden breath (from surprise, etc.); ~ *hold of,* seize; ~ *at,* try to seize; ~ *(sth.) up,* seize quickly. *n.* **1.** act of ~*ing.* **2.** sth. or sb. caught, or that one wants to ~: *a good* ~ *of fish; he* (*she*) *is an excellent* ~, a particularly desirable husband (wife). **3.** device (2) for securing (2) or fastening a door, lock, etc. **4.** sth. intended to trick or deceive: *There's a* ~ *in it somewhere. a* ~ *question in an examination paper.* **5.** song for a number of voices starting one after another. ~**ing** *adj.* **1.** (of a disease, etc.) that can be spread from person to person. **2.** alluring; captivating. '~**word** *n.* **1.** word drawing attention to the subject of a paragraph, speech, etc. **2.** first or last headword of a page in a dictionary, etc., printed at the top of this page. **3.** phrase or slogan in current use. ~**y** *adj.* **1.** (of a tune, etc.) that often returns to the mind. **2.** attractive. **3.** deceptive.

cat·e·chism ['kætɪkɪzəm] *n.* set of questions and answers (esp. in religious teaching for instruction in the elements of the Christian religion). **cat·e·chize** ['kætɪkaɪz] *v.t.* teach or examine by asking a set of questions. **cat·e·go·ry** ['kætɪgərɪ] *n.* one of the divisions or classes in a complete system of grouping. **cat·e·gor·i·cal** [ˌkætɪ'gɒrɪkl] *adj.* (of a statement) unconditional; absolute. **cat·e·gor·i·cal·ly** *adv.*

ca·ter ['keɪtə*] *v.i.* ~ *for,* undertake to provide (food, amusements, etc.). ~**er** *n.* person who provides meals, etc. brought from outside, to clubs, homes, etc.; owner or manager of a hotel or restaurant.

cat·er·pil·lar ['kætəpɪlə*] *n.* moth or butterfly larva.

a caterpillar

ca·the·dral [kə'θiːdrəl] *n.* chief church of a diocese.

cath·ode ['kæθəʊd] *n.* (electr.) negative pole of electric current. (See the diagram at *cell.*)

cath·o·lic ['kæθəlɪk] *adj.* **1.** liberal (2); general; including everything: ~ *tastes and interests.* **2.** (*Roman Catholic*) of the Church of Rome. *n.* member of the Church of Rome. **Ca·thol·i·cism** [kə'θɒlɪsɪzəm] *n.* (no pl.) (*Roman Catholicism*) teaching, beliefs, etc. of the Church of Rome. ~**i·ty** [ˌkæθəʊ'lɪsətɪ] *n.* (no pl.) quality of being ~ (1).

cat·kin ['kætkɪn] *n.* long, soft, downy hanging flower of certain trees (e.g. willow, birch).

cat·tle ['kætl] *n. pl.* oxen (bulls, bullocks, and cows).

caught, see *catch* (v.).

caul·dron, cal·dron ['kɔːldrən] *n.* large, deep pot for boiling.

cau·li·flow·er ['kɒlɪflaʊə*] *n.* (cabbage-like plant with a) large white flower-head, used as a vegetable.

caulk (U.S.A. also **calk**) [kɔːk] *v.t.* make (joints between planks) watertight by filling with a sticky substance, etc.

cause [kɔːz] *n.* **1.** that which produces an effect; person or thing that makes sth. happen: *The* ~ *of the fire was carelessness.* **2.** reason: *no* ~ *for anxiety.* **3.** purpose for which efforts are being made: *work in* (*for*) *a good* ~; *fight in the* ~ *of justice. v.t.* be the ~ of; make happen.

cause·way ['kɔːzweɪ] *n.* raised path or road, esp. across wet land or swamp.

cement

caus·tic ['kɔːstɪk] *adj.* **1.** able to destroy or burn away by chemical action: ~ *soda* **2.** (fig.) biting; sarcastic: ~ *remarks*; *a ~ manner*. **caus·ti·cal·ly** *adv.*

cau·ter·ize ['kɔːtəraɪz] *v.t.* burn (a wound, snake-bite, etc.) with a hot iron or a caustic substance (to destroy infection, etc.).

cau·tion ['kɔːʃn] *n.* **1.** taking care; paying attention (to avoid danger or making mistakes). **2.** warning words. *v.t.* give a ~ (2) to. ~**ary** *adj.* containing, giving, a ~ (2). **cau·tious** ['kɔːʃəs] *adj.* having or showing ~. **cau·tious·ly** *adv.*

cav·al·cade [ˌkævl'keɪd] *n.* company or procession of persons on horseback or in carriages.

cav·a·lier [ˌkævə'lɪə*] *n.* **1.** (old use) horseman or knight. **2.** (in the Civil War, 17th-century England) supporter of Charles I.

cav·al·ry ['kævlrɪ] *n.* (usu. pl. v., collective) soldiers who fight on horseback or move in motor vehicles.

cave [keɪv] *n.* hollow place in the side of a cliff, rock, or hill; large natural hollow under the ground. *v.t. & i.* ~ *in,* (cause to) fall in, give way to pressure. '~·**dwell·er,** '~·**man** *ns.* person living in a ~, esp. in prehistoric times.

cav·ern ['kævən] *n.* (vast) cave. ~·**ous** *adj.* full of caves; shaped, etc. like a cave.

cav·i·are, cav·i·ar ['kævɪɑː*] *n.* (no pl.) pickled roe[1] of the sturgeon or other large fish, served (3) as a delicacy: ~ *to the general,* a choice thing too good to be appreciated by the general public.

cav·il ['kævɪl] *v.i.* (*-ll-,* U.S.A. also *-l-*) ~ *at,* make unnecessary protests against; find fault with.

cav·i·ty ['kævətɪ] *n.* hole; hollow space in a solid body: *a ~ in a tooth*.

cay·enne [keɪ'en] *n.* (no pl.) (also ~ *pepper* ['keɪen 'pepə*]) very pungent red pepper.

cease [siːs] *v.t. & i.* bring or come to an end; stop. ~·'**fire** *n.* (mil.) **1.** order to stop firing. **2.** cessation of active hostilities; truce. ~·**less** *adj.* never ending.

ce·dar ['siːdə*] *n.* (hard, red, sweet-smelling wood of) evergreen tree.

cede [siːd] *v.t.* give up (rights, land, etc.) *to* another (person, state, etc.).

ceil·ing ['siːlɪŋ] *n.* **1.** overhead lining or covering of a room (opp. *floor*). **2.** highest (practicable) level (to be) reached: *price (wage) ~s; an aircraft with a ~ of 20,000 feet*.

cel·e·brate ['selɪbreɪt] *v.t.* **1.** do sth. to show that a day or an event is important, or an occasion for rejoicing: ~ *one's birthday (Christmas, a victory)*. **2.** praise and honour. **cel·e·brat·ed** *adj.* famous. **cel·e·bra·tion** [ˌselɪ'breɪʃn] *n.* **ce·leb·ri·ty** [sɪ'lebrətɪ] *n.* being famous; famous person.

ce·le·ri·ac [sɪ'lerɪæk] *n.* variety of celery with a large edible root.

ce·ler·i·ty [sɪ'lerətɪ] *n.* (no pl.) quickness.

cel·er·y ['selərɪ] *n.* plant whose stems are used as a salad or vegetable.

ce·les·tial [sɪ'lestjəl] *adj.* of the sky; heavenly; perfect.

cel·i·ba·cy [sɪ'lɪbəsɪ] *n.* (no pl.) state of living unmarried. **cel·i·bate** ['selɪbət] *adj. & n.* unmarried (person), esp. (person) who has taken a vow not to marry.

cell [sel] *n.* **1.** small room for one person (esp. in a prison or monastery). **2.** small division of a larger structure: ~*s in a honeycomb*. **3.** unit of living matter: *All animals and plants are made up of ~s*. **4.** unit of an apparatus for producing electric current, part of a battery. **5.** (of a group of persons) centre or nucleus of political (esp. revolutionary) activities: *communist ~s*.

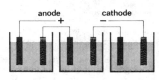

anode   cathode

cells (4)

cel·lar ['selə*] *n.* underground room for storing coal, wine, etc.

cel·lo ['tʃeləʊ] *n.* (pl. ~s), **cel·list** ['tʃelɪst] *n.* see *violoncello, etc.*

cel·lo·phane ['seləʊfeɪn] *n.* (no pl.) transparent sheet used like paper for wrapping food and other goods.

cel·lu·lar ['seljʊlə*] *adj.* formed of cells (2, 3); (of textile material) loosely woven.

cel·lu·loid ['seljʊlɔɪd] *n.* (no pl.) plastic substance made from cellulose.

cel·lu·lose ['seljʊləʊs] *n.* (no pl.) substance forming the chief part of all plants and trees; used for making celluloid, artificial silk, printing-paper, etc.

Cel·si·us ['selsjəs] *adj.* centigrade.

ce·ment [sɪ'ment] *n.* (no pl.) **1.** grey powder (made by burning lime and clay) which after being wetted becomes hard like stone and is used for building. (See *concrete*.) **2.** any similar soft, hard-setting substance, used for filling holes (e.g. in the teeth) or for joining things. *v.t.* put ∼ on or in; join with ∼; (fig.) strengthen; unite.

cem·e·tery ['semɪtrɪ] *n.* area of ground, not a churchyard, for burying the dead.

ceno·taph ['senəʊtɑːf] *n.* monument put up in memory of a person or persons buried elsewhere.

cen·ser ['sensə*] *n.* vessel in which incense is burnt (in churches).

cen·sor ['sensə*] *n.* official with the power to examine letters, books, periodicals, plays, films, etc. and to cut out anything regarded as immoral or in other ways not desirable, or, in time of war, helpful to the enemy. *v.t.* examine, cut (parts) out, as a ∼. **cen·so·ri·ous** [sen'sɔːrɪəs] *adj.* fault-finding. ∼·**ship** *n.* office, duties, etc. of a ∼.

cen·sure ['senʃə*] *v.t. & n.* (express) blame or disapproval (of).

cen·sus ['sensəs] *n.* (pl. ∼*es*) official counting of the population.

cent [sent] *n.* the 100th part of a dollar or other unit of currency; coin of that value. *per* ∼ (%), in, by, or for every 100.

cen·taur ['sentɔː*] *n.* (in Greek mythology) creature, half man and half horse.

cen·te·nar·i·an [ˌsentɪ'neərɪən] *n. & adj.* (person who is) (more than) 100 years old.

cen·te·na·ry [sen'tiːnərɪ] *adj. & n.* (having to do with a) period of 100 years; 100th anniversary. **cen·ten·ni·al** [sen'tenjəl] *adj. & n.* = ∼.

cen·ti·grade ['sentɪɡreɪd] *adj.* in or of the temperature scale that has 100 degrees between the freezing-point and boiling-point of water: *the* ∼ *thermometer*; *100°* ∼ *(100° C).* (Cf. *Fahrenheit.*)

cen·ti·gram(me) ['sentɪɡræm] *n.* the 100th part of a gramme.

cen·time ['sɒntiːm] *n.* the 100th part of a franc.

cen·ti·me·tre (U.S.A. **-ter**) ['sentɪˌmiːtə*] *n.* the 100th part of a metre.

cen·ti·pede ['sentɪpiːd] *n.* small, wingless creature with a long, thin body, having numerous jointed sections, each bearing a pair of feet.

cen·tral ['sentrəl] *adj.* **1.** of, at, in, from, or near the centre: ∼ *heating*, system that heats a building from one source. **2.** chief; most important. *n.* (U.S.A.) = telephone exchange. ∼·**ize**

['sentrəlaɪz] *v.t. & i.* bring to the centre; put, come, under ∼ control. ∼·**iza·tion** [ˌsentrəlaɪ'zeɪʃn] *n.*

cen·tre (U.S.A. **-ter**) ['sentə*] *n.* **1.** middle part or point: *the* ∼ *of London*; *the* ∼ *of a circle.* **2.** place of great activity, esp. one to which people are attracted from surrounding districts or from which they go out: *the shopping* ∼ *of a town*; *a* ∼ *of commerce.* **3.** person or thing that attracts attention, interest, etc. **4.** political party or group with moderate views. *v.t. & i.* place in, bring to, the ∼; have as ∼: ∼ *one's hopes on sth.*; *hopes which* ∼ *on sth.*

cen·trif·u·gal [sen'trɪfjʊɡl] *adj.* moving or tending to move away from the centre: ∼ *force.*

cen·trip·e·tal [sen'trɪpɪtl] *adj.* moving or tending to move towards the centre.

cen·tu·ri·on [sen'tjʊərɪən] *n.* (in ancient Rome) leader of a unit of 100 soldiers.

cen·tu·ry ['sentʃʊrɪ] *n.* **1.** 100 years. **2.** one of the periods of 100 years before or after the birth of Christ: *the 20th* ∼, *1901—2000.* **3.** (cricket) 100 runs.

ce·ram·ic [sɪ'ræmɪk] *adj.* of the art of pottery. ∼**s** *n. pl.* **1.** (sing. v.) art of making pottery. **2.** articles made of pottery.

ce·re·al ['sɪərɪəl] *adj. & n.* (usu. pl.) (of) any kind of grain used for food: *Rice, wheat, and maize are* ∼**s**. *break-fast* ∼**s**.

ce·re·bral ['serɪbrəl] *adj.* of the brain.

cer·e·mo·ny ['serɪmənɪ] *n.* **1.** special act(s), religious service, on an occasion such as a wedding, funeral, the opening of a new public building, etc.: *Master of Ceremonies*, person in charge of ceremonies on some public occasion; *compère.* **2.** behaviour required by social custom, esp. among officials, people of high class, etc.: *stand on* ∼, pay great attention to rules of behaviour. **cer·e·mo·ni·al** [ˌserɪ'məʊnjəl] *n.* special order of ceremony; formality. *adj.* formal; as used for ceremonies: *ceremonial dress.* **cer·e·mo·ni·ous** [ˌserɪ'məʊnjəs] *adj.* fond of, marked by, ∼ (2).

cer·tain ['sɜːtn] *adj.* **1.** (pred.) of which there is no doubt: ∼ *that (of, about, to)*, convinced; having no doubt: *Are you* ∼ *of (about) that? She is* ∼ *to come. for* ∼, without doubt; *make* ∼, inquire in order to be ∼. **2.** sure to come or happen: *face* ∼ *death.* **3.** (attrib.) not named or described although known: *for a* ∼ *reason*; *under* ∼

conditions; *a ~ person.* **4.** (attrib.) some but not much: *There was a ~ coldness in her greeting.* **~·ly** *adv.* **1.** without doubt. **2.** (in answers) yes: *Will you answer the letter? C~ly!* **~·ty** *n.* being ~; sth. that is ~.

cer·tif·i·cate [sə'tɪfɪkət] *n.* written or printed statement that may be used as proof, made by sb. in authority: *a birth (marriage, health) ~.* **cer·tif·i·cat·ed** [sə'tɪfɪkeɪtɪd] *adj.* having the right or authority to do sth. as the result of obtaining a ~.

cer·ti·fy ['sɜːtɪfaɪ] *v.t.* declare (usu. by giving a certificate) that sth. is true, correct, etc.: *certified insane* (by a doctor).

cer·ti·tude ['sɜːtɪtjuːd] *n.* (no pl.) condition of feeling certain.

ces·sa·tion [se'seɪʃn] *n.* (no pl.) ceasing; stop or pause.

ces·sion ['seʃn] *n.* act of ceding or giving up (land, rights, etc.); sth. ceded.

cess·pool ['sespuːl] *n.* underground tank for sewage.

chafe [tʃeɪf] *v.t. & i.* **1.** rub (the skin, etc.) for warmth. **2.** make or become rough or sore by rubbing: *The stiff collar ~d his neck.* **3.** become impatient or irritated: *~ at the delay*; *~ under insults.*

chaff¹ [tʃɑːf] *n.* (no pl.) **1.** outer covering of grain, removed before the grain is used as food. **2.** hay or straw cut up as food for cattle.

chaff² [tʃɑːf] *n.* (no pl.) good-humoured teasing or joking. *v.t.* make good-humoured fun of.

chaf·finch ['tʃæfɪntʃ] *n.* small, common European finch.

cha·grin ['ʃægrɪn] *n.* (no pl.) feeling of shame and annoyance (at having failed, made a mistake, etc.).

chain [tʃeɪn] *n.* **1.** number of (usu. metal) rings or links going through one another to make a line. *in ~s,* kept as a prisoner. **2.** number of connected things, events, etc.: *a ~ of mountains (ideas, reasoning); a ~ of 100 shops (hotels, etc.)* (usu. under a single ownership, management, or control). *~-smoker,* person who smokes continuously. (chem., fig.) *~ reaction.* **3.** measure of length (66 feet). *v.t.* fasten with a ~: *The prisoner was ~ed to the wall. Don't keep your dog ~ed up all day.*

chair [tʃeə*] *n.* **1.** separate movable seat with four legs and a back for one person. **2.** post or position held by a professor at a university: *the C~ of French.* **3.** seat, authority, of sb. who

presides at a meeting: *take the ~,* preside. **'~-lift** *n.* series of chairs on an endless cable for carrying persons up and down mountain slopes, etc. **~·man** ['tʃeəmən] *n.* person presiding at a meeting.

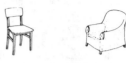

chairs (1)

cha·let ['ʃæleɪ] *n.* summer cottage; hut in a holiday camp, etc. for holiday-makers.

chal·ice ['tʃælɪs] *n.* wine-cup, esp. one used for Holy Communion.

chalk [tʃɔːk] *v.t. & n.* (write or draw with a stick of) soft, white, mineral substance, a kind of limestone.

chal·lenge ['tʃælɪndʒ] *v.t. n.* **1.** invitation or call to play a game, run a race, have a fight, etc. to see who is better, stronger, etc. **2.** order given by a sentry to stop and explain who one is, what one is doing. *v.t.* give, send, be, a ~ to; ask for reasons (to support a statement, etc.).

cham·ber ['tʃeɪmbə*] *n.* **1.** (old use) room, esp. a bedroom. *~ music,* music for a small number of players in a small hall or room. **2.** body (5) of persons making laws; the place where they meet: *the Upper (Lower) C~.* **3.** *C~ of Commerce,* group of persons organized to develop trade, etc. **4.** (pl.) set of rooms in a large building, esp. one occupied by lawyers. **5.** enclosed space in a gun (where a shell or cartridge is laid), or in a machine. **'~-maid** *n.* housemaid at hotels.

cham·ber·lain ['tʃeɪmbəlɪn] *n.* officer who manages the household of a king or queen or great noble.

cha·me·leon [kə'miːljən] *n.* small, long-tongued lizard whose colour changes according to its background.

cham·ois ['ʃæmwɑː] *n.* (pl. ~ ['ʃæmwɑːz]) small, goat-like animal living in the high mountains of Europe and S.W. Asia. *~(-leath·er)* ['ʃæmɪ-(ˌleðə*)] *n.* soft leather from the skin of sheep and goats.

champ¹ [tʃæmp] *v.t. & i.* (of a horse) bite (food or the bit) noisily; (fig.) show impatience.

champ² [tʃæmp] *n.* (sl., abbr. for) champion (2).

cham·pagne [ʃæmˈpeɪn] *n.* (kinds of) white, effervescent wine.

cham·pi·on [ˈtʃæmpjən] *n.* **1.** person who fights on behalf of another or for a cause, etc.: *a ~ of free speech* (*liberty, women's rights, etc.*). **2.** person, team, animal, etc. taking the first place in a competition: *a boxing (swimming) ~; the ~ football team*. *v.t.* support; defend. **~·ship** *n.* **1.** act of ~ing. **2.** position held by a ~. **3.** contest held to determine a ~ (2).

chance [tʃɑːns] *n.* **1.** accident; fortune or luck; happening without known cause or planning: *let ~ decide; take one's ~,* trust to luck, take what comes; *game of ~,* one that luck, not skill, decides; *by ~,* by accident, not from design. **2.** possibility: *on the ~ that,* in view of the possibility that; in the hope that. **3.** opportunity; occasion when success seems certain: *the ~ of a lifetime; have* (*stand*) *a ~* (i.e. of being successful); *take a ~, take ~s,* behave riskily. **4.** (attrib.) coming or happening by ~ (1): *a ~ meeting.* *v.i. & t.* **1.** happen by ~ (1). **2.** *~ (up)on,* find or meet by ~ (1). **3.** (colloq.) take a risk: *~ it.*

chan·cel [ˈtʃɑːnsl] *n.* eastern part of a church, near the altar, used by priests and the choir.

chan·cel·lor [ˈtʃɑːnsələ*] *n.* (in some countries, e.g. Germany and Austria) chief minister of state; (of some universities) head or president; *the C~ of the Exchequer,* chief finance minister in Great Britain; *the Lord (High) C~,* highest judge.

chan·cery [ˈtʃɑːnsərɪ] *n.* (Gt. Brit.) Lord Chancellor's division of the High Court of Justice.

chan·de·lier [ˌʃændəˈlɪə*] *n.* branched support hanging from the ceiling for two or more lights.

chan·dler [ˈtʃɑːndlə*] *n.* (old use) person who makes or sells candles, oil, soap, paint, etc. *ship('s)-~,* dealer in ropes, canvas, and other supplies for ships.

change [tʃeɪndʒ] *v.t. & i.* **1.** take or put one thing in place of another; go from one to another of: *~ one's clothes* (*address*). *It took her a long time to ~* (to put on different clothes). *~ (trains),* get out of one train into another; *~ hands,* pass to another owner. **2.** give sth. and receive sth. else in return; exchange: *~ a £5 note* (i.e. give or get smaller notes, coins, etc. for it); *~ seats* (*places*) *with sb. We ~ed places.* **3.** make or become different: *~ plans. Their plans have ~ed. ~ one's mind,*

come to a different opinion; make different plans. *n.* **1.** changing; making or becoming different; sth. to be exchanged: *Take a ~ of clothes with you* (extra clothes). *a ~ for the better; a ~ of air* (e.g. a holiday away from home); *a ~ in the weather; for a ~,* for the sake of variety. **2.** money in small units or in coin: *~ for a £1 note;* money given for a different currency; money that is the difference between the cost of sth. and any higher amount handed to the seller in payment for it. **~·able** *adj.* likely to ~; able to be ~ed; often changing.

chan·nel [ˈtʃænl] *n.* **1.** stretch of water joining two seas: *the English C~.* **2.** bed of a river; deeper part of a waterway: *The ~ is marked by buoys.* **3.** passage along which a liquid may flow; (fig.) way by which news, ideas, etc. may travel. **4.** band of frequencies (2) for the transmission of radio or television signals.

chant [tʃɑːnt] *n.* often-repeated tune to which, e.g. the psalms, are fitted; several words to one note. (Cf. *hymn.*) *v.i. & t.* sing a ~; use a singing note (e.g. for a prayer in church).

chan·ty [ˈtʃɑːntɪ] *n.* shanty².

cha·os [ˈkeɪɒs] *n.* (no pl.) complete absence of order; confusion. **cha·ot·ic** [keɪˈɒtɪk] *adj.*

chap¹ [tʃæp] *v.t. & i.* (-*pp*-) (of the skin) become rough, sore, cracked; (of the wind, etc.) cause (the skin) to ~.

chap² [tʃæp] *n.* (colloq.) boy; man; fellow.

chap·el [ˈtʃæpl] *n.* **1.** place (not a parish church) used for Christian worship (e.g. in a school, prison, private house, etc.). **2.** small place within a church for private prayer. **3.** service (6) held there.

chap·er·on [ˈʃæpərəʊn] *n.* married or elderly woman in charge of a girl or young unmarried woman on social occasions. *v.t.* act as a ~ to.

chap·lain [ˈtʃæplɪn] *n.* priest or clergyman, esp. in the navy, army, or air force, or in charge of a chapel (1).

chap·ter [ˈtʃæptə*] *n.* **1.** division of a book. **2.** (general meeting of) the whole number of canons of a cathedral church, or members of a monastic order.

char¹ [tʃɑː*] *v.t. & i.* (-*rr*-) make or become black by burning; *~red wood.*

char² [tʃɑː*] *v.i.* (-*rr*-) do the cleaning of offices, houses, etc. with payment by the hour or day. '**~·(ˌwom·an)** *n.* woman who ~s.

char·ac·ter ['kærəktə*] *n.* **1.** (of a person, group of persons, etc.) mental or moral nature; mental and moral qualities that make one person or race different: *a man of weak (fine, etc.)* ~; *the* ~ *of the French.* **2.** moral strength: *a man of* ~. *Should* ~ *building be the chief aim of education?* **3.** person who is well known: *a public* ~; person in a play or book: *the* ~*s in the novels of Dickens*; person who is unusual in his ways: *quite a* ~ (e.g. of an amusing man). **4.** description of a person's qualities and abilities, esp. in a letter by an employer, that may be used when applying for a position. **5.** reputation. **6.** all those special qualities that make a thing, place, etc. what it is and different from other things, places, etc.: *the* ~ *of the desert areas of N. Africa.* **7.** letter, sign, mark, etc. used in a system of writing or printing: *Chinese (Greek, etc.)* ~*s.* ~**·is·tic** [,kærəktə'rɪstɪk] *adj.* forming part of, showing, the ~ of a person, thing, place, etc.: *with his* ~*istic enthusiasm.* *n.* special mark or quality. ~**·is·ti·cal·ly** *adv.* ~**·ize** ['kærəktəraɪz] *v.t.* show the ~ of; be ~istic of.

cha·rade [ʃə'rɑːd] *n.* game in which a word is guessed by the onlookers after the word itself, and each syllable in turn, have been spoken or suggested by acting a little play.

char·coal ['tʃɑːkəʊl] *n.* (no pl.) black substance, used as fuel, as a material for drawing, etc., made by burning wood slowly in an oven.

charge [tʃɑːdʒ] *n.* **1.** accusation; statement that a person has done wrong, esp. that he has broken a law: *bring a* ~ *of murder against sb.* **2.** sudden and violent attack at high speed (by soldiers, animals, etc.): *capture a position after a bayonet* ~. **3.** price asked for goods or services (3, 5, 8): *hotel* ~*s.* **4.** amount of powder, etc. (to be) used in firing a gun or causing an explosion, or of electricity (to be) put into an accumulator, etc. **5.** work given to sb. as a duty; thing or person given to sb. to be taken care of; responsibility: *in* ~ *of*, taking care of; being taken care of by: *Mary was in* ~ *of the baby. The baby was in Mary's* ~. *take* ~ *of*, be responsible for; *give sb. in* ~, give him up to the police. *v.t. & i.* **1.** ~ *sb.* (*with sth.*), bring a ~ (1) against; accuse (of). **2.** make a ~ (2) against: ~ *the enemy.* **3.** ask as a price (*for*); ask in payment. **4.** debit: ~ *it to my account.* **5.** load (a gun); fill; put a ~ (4) into: ~ *an*

accumulator. **6.** ~ *with*, give as a task or duty; ~ *oneself with*, undertake. **7.** give (sb.) orders or instructions: *The judge* ~*d the jury.* ~**·able** ['tʃɑːdʒəbl] *adj.* liable to be ~d (with wrongdoing).

char·gé d'af·faires [,ʃɑːʒeɪdæ'feə*] *n.* (pl. -gés -) person who is in charge of business when an ambassador is absent from his post.

char·i·ot ['tʃærɪət] *n.* two-wheeled car, pulled by a horse, used in ancient times in races and in war. **char·i·o·teer** [,tʃærɪə'tɪə*] *n.* ~-driver.

char·i·ty ['tʃærətɪ] *n.* (kindness in giving) help to the poor; alms; neighbourly love; willingness to judge other persons with kindness. **2.** society or organization for helping poor or suffering people. **char·i·table** ['tʃærətəbl] *adj.* showing, having, for, ~.

char·la·tan ['ʃɑːlətən] *n.* person who pretends to have more skill, knowledge, or ability than he really has, esp. one who pretends to have medical knowledge.

charm [tʃɑːm] *n.* **1.** quality or power of attracting, giving pleasure. **2.** sth. believed to have magic power, good or bad: ~*s against evil spirits; a* ~ *to bring good luck; under a* ~, influenced or affected by magic. *v.t. & i.* **1.** attract; give pleasure to. **2.** use magic on; influence or protect as if by magic: *He bears a* ~*ed life.* ~**·ing** *adj.* full of ~ (1); giving pleasure (e.g. by personal appearance or actions).

chart [tʃɑːt] *n.* **1.** map of the sea, for the use by sailors. **2.** sheet of paper with information, in the form of curves, diagrams, etc. (about such facts as the weather, prices, business conditions, the most popular gramophone records, etc.): *a temperature (weather)* ~. *v.t.* make a ~ of; show on a ~.

char·ter ['tʃɑːtə*] *n.* **1.** (written or printed statement of) rights, permission to do sth., esp. from a ruler or government. **2.** hiring (of a ship, an aircraft, etc.): *a* ~ *flight. v.t.* **1.** give a ~ (1) to; grant a privilege to. **2.** hire or engage (a ship, an aircraft, etc.) for an agreed time, purpose, and payment: *a* ~*ed aircraft.*

chary ['tʃeərɪ] *adj.* (-ier, -iest) ~ *of*, shy, cautious, or careful about.

chase¹ [tʃeɪs] *v.t. & i.* **1.** run after in order to capture, kill, or drive away: ~ *rabbits (a thief, a dog out of a garden).* **2.** hurry; rush. *n.* act of chasing: *the* ~, run after; try to catch. *the* ~, esp. the chasing of animals for sport.

chase² [tʃeɪs] *v.t.* cut patterns or

chasm

designs on (metal or other hard material).

chasm ['kæzəm] *n.* deep opening or crack in the ground; (fig.) wide difference (of feeling or interests, between persons, nations, etc.).

chas·sis ['ʃæsɪ] *n.* (pl. ~ ['ʃæsɪz]) framework of a motor car or carriage on which the body (4) is fastened or built.

chaste [tʃeɪst] *adj.* pure in thought, word, and deed, esp. sexually pure.

chas·ten ['tʃeɪsn] *v.t.* correct (sb.) by giving punishment or pain.

chas·tise [tʃæ'staɪz] *v.t.* punish severely. ~·**ment** ['tʃæstɪzmənt] *n.* (no pl.).

chas·ti·ty ['tʃæstɪtɪ] *n.* (no pl.) being chaste.

chat [tʃæt] *v.i. & n.* (-tt-) (have a) friendly talk about (usu.) unimportant things. ~·**ty** *adj.* (-ier, -iest) fond of ~ting.

cha·teau ['ʃætəʊ] *n.* (pl. ~x ['ʃætəʊz]) castle or large country house in France.

chat·tel ['tʃætl] *n.* piece of movable property (e.g. a chair, motor car, horse): *a person's goods and ~s.*

chat·ter ['tʃætə*] *v.i.* 1. talk quickly or foolishly or without stopping. 2. make quick, indistinct sounds (e.g. like the cries of monkeys or some birds, the noise of typewriter keys or a person's upper and lower teeth striking together from cold or fear). *n.* sounds of the kind noted above. '~·**box** *n.* person who ~s (1), esp. a child.

chauf·feur ['ʃəʊfə*] *n.* man paid to drive a privately-owned motor car.

cheap [tʃiːp] *adj.* 1. low in price or value; costing little money. 2. worth more than the price. 3. easily got. 4. of poor quality. ~·**en** *v.t. & i.* make or become ~. ~·**ly** *adv.* ~·**ness** *n.* (no pl.).

cheat [tʃiːt] *v.t. & i.* try to obtain an advantage or profit by doing sth. dishonest: ~ *in an examination*; ~ *at cards*; ~ *sb. out of sth.*, get sth. from him by ~ing. *n.* person who ~s; dishonest trick.

check¹ [tʃek] *v.t. & i.* 1. examine or compare in order to learn whether sth. or sb. is correct: ~ *a bill (an account, figures, sb.'s statements)*; ~ *sth. up,* ~ *up on sth.*; ~ *up on sb.* 2. hold back; cause to go slow or stop: ~ *sb.'s anger (the enemy's advance).* 3. (chess) threaten the opponent's king. 4. (U.S.A.) leave or accept for safe keeping in exchange for a ~¹ (3). 5. ~ *in,* arrive and register at an airport; ~ *in (out),* arrive and register at (depart

from) a hotel, factory, etc. *n.* 1. ~ing person or thing that ~s or restrains *keep a ~ on, keep sth. in ~,* control 2. examination to make certain that all is correct. 3. receipt (piece of paper bit of wood or metal with a number on it, etc.) showing that a person has a right to sth. (e.g. a hat and coat at a theatre, luggage sent by train or left at a railway station to be collected later). 4. (U.S.A.) = cheque. 5 (U.S.A.) = bill² (1). '~·**list** *n.* list of titles, items, etc. used in ~ing sth. '~·**mate** *v.t.* obstruct or defeat (a person or his plans), as in winning the game of chess. '~·**out** *n.* act of ~ing out; (esp.) pay-desk in a supermarket etc. '~·**point** *n.* place where traffic is halted and documents, vehicles, etc. are ~ed or inspected. '~·**room** *n.* (U.S.A.) = left-luggage office; cloakroom in a hotel or theatre. '~·**up** *n.* careful (esp.) medical examination.

check² [tʃek] *n.* pattern of crossed lines forming squares (often of different shades or colours); cloth with such a pattern.

check·ered, see *chequered.*

cheek [tʃiːk] *n.* 1. each side of the face below the eye. ~*-bone,* bone below the eye. 2. saucy talk or behaviour; impudence. *v.t.* be impudent to. ~·**y** *adj.* impudent; saucy. ~·**i·ly** *adv.*

cheer [tʃɪə*] *v.t. & i.* 1. make sb. feel happy. ~ *sb. (up),* make him happier; comfort him; ~ *up,* become happier; take comfort. 2. give shouts of joy, approval, or encouragement: *The crowds ~ed.* ~ *on,* urge (1) on, esp. by shouts. *n.* 1. (no pl.) state of hope, gladness. 2. shout of joy, encouragement, etc.: *give three ~s for,* shout 'hurrah' three times. 3. (pl., Gt. Brit., colloq.) = cheerio. ~·**ful** *adj.* 1. bringing or suggesting happiness: *a ~ful room (smile).* 2. contented; willing. ~·**i·ly** *adv.* in a ~ful manner. ~·**less** *adj.* without joy or comfort; dull and miserable: *wet and ~less weather.* ~·**y** *adj.* (-ier, -iest) lively; merry: *a ~y smile* (greeting).

cheer·io [,tʃɪərɪ'əʊ] *int.* (Gt. Brit., colloq.) used as a farewell or toast².

cheese [tʃiːz] *n.* solid food made from milk curds; cake (2, 3) of this.

chee·tah ['tʃiːtə] *n.* long-legged, swift-moving, spotted African cat that can be trained to hunt deer and other game.

chef [ʃef] *n.* head male cook in a restaurant, hotel, etc.

chem·i·cal ['kemɪkl] *adj.* of, made by, chemistry: ~ *warfare* (using poison gas and other ~s). *n.* (often pl.) substance used in, obtained by, chemistry.

chem·ist ['kemɪst] *n.* **1.** person with a knowledge of chemistry. **2.** (U.S.A. *druggist*) person who prepares and sells medical goods, toilet articles, etc. **~'s shop** *n.* (U.S.A. *drugstore*) shop selling medical goods, toilet articles, etc. (Cf. *pharmacy* (2).)

chem·is·try ['kemɪstrɪ] *n.* (no pl.) branch of science dealing with the elements (1), how they combine, how they act under different conditions.

cheque (U.S.A. **check**) [tʃek] *n.* written order (usu. on a printed form) to a bank to pay money. '**~-book** *n.* number of blank (2) ~ forms fastened together.

che·quered, check·ered ['tʃekəd] *adj.* having checks²: *a ~ career,* (fig.) one of a great variety, esp. with frequent changes of fortune.

cher·ish ['tʃerɪʃ] *v.t.* care for (sb.) tenderly; keep alive (hope, ambition, etc.) in one's heart.

cher·ry ['tʃerɪ] *n.* (tree with) soft, small, round, red, yellow, or black fruit with a stone-like seed. *adj.* of the colour of ripe red cherries.

cher·ub ['tʃerəb] *n.* small, beautiful, and innocent child.

chess [tʃes] *n.* (no pl.) game for two players with 16 pieces each (called *~-men*), on a board with 64 squares (called a *~-board*).

chest [tʃest] *n.* **1.** large, strong box for storing (e.g. clothes, tools, money, medicine, tea): *a ~ of drawers,* piece of furniture with drawers for clothes. **2.** (anat.) upper front part of the body, enclosed by the ribs, containing the heart and lungs.

chest·nut ['tʃesnʌt] *n.* **1.** (wood of) tree with shiny nuts. **2.** (no pl.) colour of these nuts, reddish-brown. **3.** horse of this colour.

chev·ron ['ʃevrən] *n.* bent stripe (∨ or ∧) worn by soldiers, policemen, etc. on sleeves to show rank.

chew [tʃuː] *v.t. & i.* work (food, etc.) about between the teeth in order to crush it. *n.* act of ~ing; sth. (to be) ~ed. '**~-ing-gum** *n.* sweetened and flavoured gum for ~ing.

chic [ʃiːk] *adj.* (of a woman or her clothes) in the latest fashion; stylish. *n.* (no pl.) superior style.

chi·ca·nery [ʃɪ'keɪnərɪ] *n.* use of unfair arguments or trickery, esp. in law and politics.

chick [tʃɪk] *n.* **1.** newly-hatched chick-

en or other young bird. **2.** (sl.) young woman.

chick·en ['tʃɪkɪn] *n.* **1.** young bird, esp. a young hen. **2.** (no pl.) meat of a ~ as food. '**~-,heart·ed** *adj.* easily frightened. '**~-pox** *n.* (no pl.) disease (esp. of children) causing red spots on the skin.

chic·o·ry ['tʃɪkərɪ] *n.* (no pl.) plant used as a vegetable and for salad; the root is roasted and made into a powder (used with or instead of coffee).

chide [tʃaɪd] *v.t. & i.* (p.t. ~d or *chid* [tʃɪd], p.p. ~d, chid [tʃɪd], or *chidden* ['tʃɪdn]) scold; speak angrily to (because of wrongdoing).

chief [tʃiːf] *n.* leader or ruler; head of a department; highest official. *-in-~,* supreme: *Commander-in-C~.* **attrib. adj.** principal; most important: *the ~ thing to remember; the ~ priest.* **~·ly** *adv.* above all; mainly. **~·tain** ['tʃiːftən] *n.* ~ of a tribe or clan.

chif·fon ['ʃɪfɒn] *n.* (no pl.) thin, transparent, silk material used for dresses, etc.

chil·blain ['tʃɪlbleɪn] *n.* painful swelling, esp. on the hand or foot, occurring in cold weather.

child [tʃaɪld] *n.* (pl. *children* ['tʃɪldrən]) not yet born or newly born human being; young boy or girl; son or daughter (of any age). *be with ~,* be pregnant. '**~-birth** *n.* giving birth to a ~: *She died in ~birth.* **~-hood** *n.* (no pl.) state of being a ~; time during which one is a ~. **~·ish** *adj.* of, behaving like, suitable for, a ~. **~·less** *adj.* having no child(ren). **~·like** *adj.* simple; innocent.

chill [tʃɪl] *n.* **1.** unpleasant cold feeling: *There's a ~ in the air this morning. Take the ~ off the water* (i.e. warm it a little). **2.** illness caused by cold or damp, often with shivering of the body: *catch a ~.* **3.** depressing influence: *cast a ~ over.* **adj.** unpleasantly cold: *a ~ breeze,* (fig.) cold; unemotional: *a ~ greeting.* **v.t. & i.** make or become cold or cool: *be ~ed to the bone; ~ed meat* (preserved at a low temperature to keep it in good condition, but not frozen). **~y** *adj.* (-ier, -iest) rather cold; (fig.) unfriendly.

chime [tʃaɪm] *n.* (series of notes sounded by a) tuned set of (church) bells. **v.i. & t.** (of bells or a clock) make bell or gong sounds; give out bell tones; (of a person) ring ~s on (bells): *The church clock ~d twelve.* ~ *in,* break in on the talk of others (usu. to express agreement); join in.

chim·ney ['tʃɪmnɪ] *n.* **1.** structure through which smoke, etc. is carried away from a fire. **2.** glass tube protecting the flame of an oil-lamp from draughts. '~-pot *n.* tube-shaped pot at the top of a ~ above a roof. '~-stack *n.* brickwork, etc. enclosing a ~ or ~s above a roof. '~-sweep *n.* man who sweeps soot from ~s.

a chimney (1)

chim·pan·zee [,tʃɪmpən'zi:] *n.* African ape, smaller than a gorilla.

chin [tʃɪn] *n.* part of the face below the mouth.

chi·na ['tʃaɪnə] *n.* (no pl.) baked and glazed fine white clay; porcelain; articles (cups, plates, etc.) made of this. **Chi·nese** [,tʃaɪ'ni:z] *n.* (pl. ~) *& adj.* (native, inhabitant, or language) of China.

chink[1] [tʃɪŋk] *n.* narrow crack or opening (through which the wind blows or through which one may peep).

chink[2] [tʃɪŋk] *v.i. & t. & n.* (make or cause to make the) sound of coins, pieces of glass, etc. striking together.

chintz [tʃɪnts] *n.* (no pl.) kind of cotton cloth (usu. glazed) with printed designs in colours; used for curtains, covering furniture, etc.

chip [tʃɪp] *n.* **1.** small piece cut or broken off (from wood, stone, china, etc.): ~ *off the old block*, son very like his father. **2.** thin slice cut from an apple, a potato, etc.: *fish and* ~s, fried fish and potato ~s. **3.** place (e.g. in a cup or plate) from which a ~ has come. **4.** (games) counter[2] (1). *v.t. & i.* (-*pp*-) **1.** cut or knock ~s off or *from*; make into ~s: ~ *the edge of a plate*; ~ *potatoes*. **2.** become ~ped: *things which ~ easily*.

chi·rop·o·dy [kɪ'rɒpədɪ] *n.* (no pl.) expert treatment of troubles of the feet and toe-nails. **chi·rop·o·dist** *n.*

chirp [tʃɜːp] *v.i. & t. & n.* (make) short, sharp sound(s) or note(s) (as) of some birds (e.g. sparrows) and insects (e.g. crickets[1]); utter (a song, etc.) in this way. ~**y** *adj.* (-*ier*, -*iest*) (colloq.) lively.

chir·rup ['tʃɪrəp] *v.i. & n.* (make a) series of chirps.

chis·el ['tʃɪzl] *n.* steel tool with a squared, sharpened end for cutting and shaping wood, stone, or metal. *v.t.* (-*ll*-, U.S.A. also -*l*-) use a ~ on.

chiv·al·ry ['ʃɪvlrɪ] *n.* (no pl.) **1.** laws and customs of knights in the Middle Ages. **2.** the ideal characteristics of a knight (e.g. the qualities of courage, honour, loyalty, readiness to help the weak, devotion to women and children). **3.** (old use) all the knights of a country. **chiv·al·rous** ['ʃɪvlrəs] *adj.* having ~ (2).

chlo·ride ['klɔːraɪd] *n.* compound of chlorine: ~ *of lime* (for bleaching and to disinfect).

chlo·rine ['klɔːriːn] *n.* (no pl.) greenish-yellow, bad-smelling, irritating gas. **chlo·ri·nate** ['klɔːrɪneɪt] *v.t.* treat (e.g. water-supplies) with ~ in order to purify.

chlo·ro·form ['klɒrəfɔːm] *n.* (no pl.) thin, colourless liquid whose vapour is used by doctors to make a person unconscious. *v.t.* make unconscious by giving ~ to.

chlo·ro·phyll ['klɒrəfɪl] *n.* (no pl.) green colouring-matter of plants.

chock [tʃɒk] *n.* block or wedge of wood used to prevent sth. (e.g. a wheel, barrel, door) from moving. '~-'full *adj.* quite full.

choc·o·late ['tʃɒkələt] *n.* **1.** food substance made from crushed seeds of the cacao tree, usu. sweetened and flavoured; drink made by mixing this with hot water or milk. **2.** (no pl.) colour of ~, dark brown. (Cf. *cocoa*.)

choice [tʃɔɪs] *n.* **1.** act of choosing; right or possibility of choosing: *make a wise* ~; *take one's* ~; *for* ~, (a) by preference; (b) if one must choose. **2.** person or thing chosen; number from which to choose: *a large* ~ *of books*. *adj.* specially or carefully chosen; exceptional; rare; uncommonly good.

choir ['kwaɪə*] *n.* company of persons trained to sing together, esp. to lead the singing in church; part of a church for the ~.

choke [tʃəʊk] *v.i. & t.* **1.** be unable to breathe because of sth. in the wind-pipe, or because of emotion: ~ *over one's food*; ~ *with anger*. **2.** stop the breathing of, by pressing the wind-pipe from outside or by filling it: ~ *by smoke*; ~ *the life out of sb*. **3.** (often ~ *up*) fill, partly or completely, a passage, etc. that is usually clear: *a chimney (pipe, etc.)* ~*d up with rubbish*;

a garden ~d with weeds. **n.** valve in a petrol engine that controls the intake of air.

chol·era ['kɒlərə] **n.** (no pl.) infectious (1) disease, common in hot countries, that attacks the bowels and may cause death.

chol·er·ic ['kɒlərɪk] **adj.** easily made angry; angry.

choose [tʃuːz] **v.t. & i.** (p.t. *chose* [tʃəʊz], p.p. *chosen* ['tʃəʊzn]) **1.** pick out from two or more: *~ a wife (one's friends, a new hat).* **2.** decide (between one and another); be determined (to do sth.): *Do whatever you ~.*

chop [tʃɒp] **v.t. & i.** (-pp-) cut by giving blows to, usu. with an axe: *~ wood (into sticks); ~ a tree down; ~ a branch off the tree; ~ up, ~ into small pieces: This meat is already ~ped up for cooking. ~ at sth.,* make a cutting blow at. **n. 1.** ~ping blow. **2.** thick slice of meat (esp. pork or lamb) with a bone in it. **~·per n. 1.** heavy tool with a sharp edge for ~ping meat, wood, etc. **2.** (colloq.) helicopter. **~·py adj.** (-ier, -iest) (of the sea) covered with short, rough waves.

chop·sticks ['tʃɒpstɪks] **n. pl.** sticks used (two in one hand) by the Chinese and Japanese for carrying food from a dish, etc. to the mouth.

chor·al ['kɔːrəl] **adj.** of, for, sung by or together with, a choir: *a ~ service.*

chord [kɔːd] **n. 1.** straight line joining two points on a circle or part of a circle. **2.** (music) combination of usually three or more notes sounded together. **3.** string of a harp, etc. **4.** (also *cord*) (anat.) string-like part (e.g. *vocal ~s; spinal ~*).

chore [tʃɔː*] **n.** small duty or piece of work, esp. an ordinary daily task (in the home or on a farm); unpleasant task.

cho·re·og·ra·phy [ˌkɒrɪ'ɒgrəfɪ] **n.** (no pl.) art of designing ballet or stage-dance. **cho·re·og·ra·pher n.**

cho·ris·ter ['kɒrɪstə*] **n.** member of a choir, esp. a choirboy.

cho·rus ['kɔːrəs] **n. 1.** (music for a) group of singers, esp. on the stage. **2.** (part of a) song for all to sing (after solo verses). **3.** sth. said or cried by many people together: *a ~ of praise; in ~,* all together. **4.** (ancient Greece) group of dancers and singers who take part in religious ceremonies and dramas. **5.** actor who speaks the pro-logue and epilogue in a play.

chose, cho·sen, see *choose.*

chris·ten ['krɪsn] **v.t.** receive (an in-fant) into the Christian church by baptizing; give names to, at baptism; apply a nickname to.

Chris·ten·dom ['krɪsndəm] **n.** (no pl.) all Christian people and Christian countries.

Chris·tian ['krɪstjən] **adj.** of Jesus Christ and his teaching; of the religion, beliefs, church, etc. based on this teaching. *~ name,* first name, given when sb. is christened. **n.** *~ person.*

Chris·tian·i·ty [ˌkrɪstɪ'ænətɪ] **n.** (no pl.) Christian faith or religion.

Christ·mas ['krɪsməs] **n.** yearly cele-bration of the birth of Jesus Christ, 25 Dec. (*~ Day*); *~ Eve,* 24 Dec. **~·box n.** (Gt. Brit.) small present or money given at *~* to delivery boys, the post-man, etc. for their regular services (3) during the year.

chro·mi·um ['krəʊmjəm] **n.** (no pl.) metallic element. **chrome** [krəʊm] **n.** colouring substance obtained from compounds of *~: chrome yellow (orange, etc.); chrome steel,* hard kind contain-ing *~.*

chron·ic ['krɒnɪk] **adj.** (of a disease, pain, etc.) continual, going on for a long time: *a ~ invalid,* person with a *~* illness.

chron·i·cle ['krɒnɪkl] **n.** record of events in the order of their happening. **v.t.** enter or relate in a *~.*

chro·nol·o·gy [krə'nɒlədʒɪ] **n. 1.** (no pl.) science of fixing dates. **2.** arrange-ment of events with dates; list show-ing this. **chro·no·log·i·cal** [ˌkrɒnə-'lɒdʒɪkl] **adj.** *in chronological order,* in order of time.

chro·nom·e·ter [krə'nɒmɪtə*] **n.** kind of watch or clock keeping very exact time, used on a ship in fixing longitude.

chrys·a·lis ['krɪsəlɪs] **n.** (pl. *~es, -lides* [krɪ'sælɪdiːz]) form taken by an insect in the second stage of its life (i.e. be-tween the stage when it creeps or crawls as a larva, caterpillar, etc. and the time when it flies, as a butterfly, moth, etc.); the case covering it during this stage.

chrys·an·the·mum [krɪ'sænθəməm] **n.** (flower of a) garden plant blooming in autumn and early winter.

a chrysanthemum

chub·by ['tʃʌbɪ] *adj.* (-ier, -iest) round-faced; plump.

chuck [tʃʌk] *v.t.* (colloq.) **1.** throw: ~ *away rubbish*; ~ *out*, expel. **2.** ~ *sth. up*, give up: ~ *up one's job.*

chuck·le ['tʃʌkl] *v.i. & n.* (give a) low, quiet laugh with closed mouth (indicating satisfaction or amusement).

chug [tʃʌg] *v.i. & n.* (-gg-) (make the) sound of an engine: *The boat ~ged down the river.*

chum [tʃʌm] *n.* close friend. *v.i.* (-mm-) ~ *up* (*with*), become friendly (with). **~·my** *adj.* (-ier, -iest).

chunk [tʃʌŋk] *n.* thick lump cut off (a loaf, a piece of meat, cheese, etc.).

church [tʃɜːtʃ] *n.* **1.** building for public Christian worship. (Cf. *chapel.*) **2.** (no pl.) service in such a building: *What time does ~ begin?* **3.** *the C~ of Christ*, the whole body (5) of Christians; one of the branches of the Christian religion: *the C~ of England*; *the Methodist C~*; *enter the C~* (become a minister of religion). '~·yard *n.* walled ground round a ~, often used as a burial-place.

churl·ish ['tʃɜːlɪʃ] *adj.* bad tempered; ill bred.

churn [tʃɜːn] *n.* **1.** container in which cream is shaken or beaten to make butter. **2.** (Gt. Brit.) large can for transporting milk. *v.t. & i.* **1.** make (butter), beat and shake (milk or cream) in a ~. **2.** (of the sea, etc.) (cause to) move about violently.

chute [ʃuːt] *n.* **1.** sloping channel along which things (e.g. coal, postal packets, luggage) may slide to a lower level. **2.** smooth, rapid fall of water over a slope. **3.** (colloq.) parachute.

ci·ca·da [sɪ'kɑːdə] *n.* winged insect that makes a loud, shrill noise.

ci·der ['saɪdə*] *n.* (no pl.) fermented drink made from apples.

ci·gar [sɪ'gɑː*] *n.* roll of tobacco-leaves for smoking. **cig·a·rette** (U.S.A. also **-ret**) [ˌsɪgə'ret] *n.* shredded tobacco rolled in thin paper for smoking.

cin·der ['sɪndə*] *n.* small piece of coal or wood partly burned, not yet ash. '~·path, '~·track *ns.* footpath or running-track made with fine ~s.

cine- ['sɪnɪ-] (abbr. for) cinema (used in compounds): '~·cam·era *n.* camera for taking moving pictures. ~ **film** *n.* film used in ~cameras. ~ **pro·jec·tor** *n.* apparatus (1) for showing films on a screen.

cin·e·ma ['sɪnəmə] *n.* **1.** theatre for showing films. **2.** (usu. with *the*) moving pictures as an art or industry.

cin·na·mon ['sɪnəmən] *n.* (no pl.) spice from the inner bark of an E. Indian tree; its colour, yellowish-brown.

ci·pher, cy·pher ['saɪfə*] *n.* **1.** the figure 0, representing nought or zero. **2.** any Arabic numeral. **3.** person or thing of no importance. **4.** (method of, key to) secret writing. *v.t.* **1.** work out by arithmetic. **2.** put (sth.) into secret writing.

cir·ca ['sɜːkə] *prep.* about (with dates) *born ~ 150 B.C.*

cir·cle ['sɜːkl] *n.* **1.** space enclosed by a curved line, every point of which is the same distance from the centre; the line enclosing this space. **2.** sth. round like a ~: *a ~ of trees.* **3.** block of seats in curved rows, one above the other between the highest part (or *gallery*) and the floor of a theatre, cinema, or concert hall. **4.** number of persons bound together by having the same or similar interests, occupations, etc. *He has a large ~ of friends. Business ~ expect prices to fall.* **5.** complete series: *the ~ of the seasons* (i.e. the four seasons in succession). *vicious ~,* series of events following and reacting upon one another. *v.t. & i.* move in a ~, go round: *The aircraft ~d (over) the landing-field.*

cir·clet ['sɜːklɪt] *n.* small round band (1) (e.g. of gold or flowers) worn on the head or arm as an ornament.

cir·cuit ['sɜːkɪt] *n.* **1.** journey round from place to place; (sport) motor racing road; regular journey made by a judge from town to town in England and Wales to try cases; a district visited by such a judge; the judges making the ~. **2.** continuous path of an electric current: *short ~,* faulty shortening of such a path. **3.** regional group of Methodist churches sharing preachers. **cir·cu·i·tous** [sə'kjuːɪtəs] *adj.* indirect; roundabout; going a long way round.

cir·cu·lar ['sɜːkjʊlə*] *adj.* in the shape of a circle; moving round: *a ~ road,* road round a town, for through traffic; *a ~ tour (trip),* journey ending at the starting-point without a place being visited more than once. *n.* printed announcement, letter, etc. sent to a number of people. **~·ize** ['sɜːkjʊləraɪz] *v.t.* send ~s to.

cir·cu·late ['sɜːkjʊleɪt] *v.i. & t.* go round continuously; move or be sent freely from place to place, person to person: *Blood ~s through the body. The news (was) soon ~d.* **cir·cu·la·tion** [ˌsɜːkjʊ'leɪʃn] *n.* **1.** (no pl.) circulation or being ⏝d, esp. of the blood: *He has a good (bad) circulation.* **2.** total number of each issue of a newspaper or other periodical sold to the public.

cir·cum·cise ['sɜːkəmsaɪz] *v.t.* cut off the loose skin covering the end of the male sex organ. **cir·cum·ci·sion** [ˌsɜːkəm'sɪʒn] *n.*

cir·cum·fer·ence [sə'kʌmfərəns] *n.* (geom.) line that marks out a circle or other curved figure; distance round: *the ⏝ of the earth.*

cir·cum·flex ['sɜːkəmfleks] *n.* (also ⏝ *accent*) mark (⌃) placed over a vowel in French, etc. to indicate a certain pronunciation.

cir·cum·lo·cu·tion [ˌsɜːkəmlə'kjuːʃn] *n.* roundabout way of expressing sth.

cir·cum·nav·i·gate [ˌsɜːkəm'nævɪgeɪt] *v.t.* sail round (esp. the world). **cir·cum·nav·i·ga·tion** ['sɜːkəmˌnævɪ-'geɪʃn] *n.*

cir·cum·scribe ['sɜːkəmskraɪb] *v.t.* draw a line round; mark the limit(s) of; narrow down; restrict. **cir·cum·scrip·tion** [ˌsɜːkəm'skrɪpʃn] *n.*

cir·cum·spect ['sɜːkəmspekt] *adj.* paying careful attention to everything before deciding on action; cautious. **cir·cum·spec·tion** [ˌsɜːkəm'spekʃn] *n.* (no pl.).

cir·cum·stance ['sɜːkəmstəns] *n.* **1.** (usu. pl.) conditions, facts, etc. connected with an event or person: *Don't judge the crime until you know the ⏝s.* *in (under) the ⏝s,* the ⏝s being so; such being the state of affairs: *under no ⏝s,* never; not at all; whatever may happen. **2.** fact or detail: *There is one important ⏝ you have not mentioned.* **3.** (pl.) financial condition: *in reduced (straitened) ⏝s,* poor. **cir·cum·stan·tial** [ˌsɜːkəm'stænʃl] *adj.* (of a description) giving full details; (of evidence) based on, consisting of, details that strongly suggest sth. but do not give direct proof.

cir·cum·vent [ˌsɜːkəm'vent] *v.t.* get the better of (sb.); defeat (sb.'s plans).

cir·cus ['sɜːkəs] *n.* (pl. ⏝es) **1.** (round or oval space with seats around it, for a) show of performing animals, clever horse-riding, etc.; persons and animals giving such a show. **2.** place where a number of streets meet: *Piccadilly C⏝.*

cir·rus ['sɪrəs] *n.* (pl. *-ri*) light, feathery cloud, high in the sky. (Cf. *cumulus.*)

cis·tern ['sɪstən] *n.* water-tank, esp. for storing water in a building.

cit·a·del ['sɪtədəl] *n.* fortress for protecting a city.

cite [saɪt] *v.t.* **1.** give as an example, esp. by quoting from a book, in order to support an argument, etc. **2.** summon to appear in a lawcourt. **ci·ta·tion** [saɪ'teɪʃn] *n.* citing; sth. ⏝d.

cit·i·zen ['sɪtɪzn] *n.* **1.** person who lives in a town, not in the country: *the ⏝s of London.* **2.** person having full rights in a State, either by birth or by gaining such rights: *become an American ⏝.* (Cf. *British subject* (1).) **⏝·ship** *n.* being a ⏝ (2); rights and duties of a ⏝.

cit·ric ['sɪtrɪk] *adj.* (chem.) ⏝ *acid,* acid from citrus fruits, esp. lemons and limes.

cit·ron ['sɪtrən] *n.* (tree with) pale-yellow fruit similar to a lemon.

cit·rus ['sɪtrəs] *attrib. adj.* of such fruits as citrons, lemons, limes, oranges, or grapefruit: *⏝ fruit.*

city ['sɪtɪ] *n.* large and important town. *the C⏝,* oldest part of central London, the banking, commercial, and civic centre.

civ·ic ['sɪvɪk] *adj.* of the official life and affairs of a town; of or relating to a citizen: *⏝ duties (virtues); a ⏝ centre* (where the official buildings are situated). *⏝s n. pl.* (sing. v.) study of city government, the rights and duties of citizens, etc.

civ·il ['sɪvl] *adj.* **1.** of human society; of people living together: *⏝ disobedience,* refusal to obey the laws as part of a political campaign; *⏝ engineering* (the design and building of roads, railways, canals, docks, etc.); *⏝ law* (dealing with the private rights of citizens, not with crime); *⏝ marriage* (without a religious ceremony); *⏝ rights,* rights of each citizen (U.S.A. esp. of Negroes) to personal liberty and racial, legal, or social equality; *⏝ war* (between two parties of the same country or State). **2.** not of the armed forces: *the C⏝ Service* (all government departments except the Navy, Army, and Air Force); *⏝ servant,* official in the C⏝ Service. **3.** politely helpful: *give a ⏝ answer.* **ci·vil·i·ty** [sɪ'vɪlətɪ] *n.* **1.** (no pl.) politeness. **2.** (pl.) polite acts. **⏝·ly** *adv.* politely.

ci·vil·ian [sɪ'vɪljən] *n. & adj.* (person) not serving with the armed forces: *get back to ⏝ life* (e.g. after being in the army).

civ·i·li·za·tion [ˌsɪvɪlaɪ'zeɪʃn] *n.* **1.** (no pl.) making, becoming, civilized; state of being civilized. **2.** system, stage, of social development: *the ⏝ of ancient Egypt.* **3.** (no pl.) all civilized States: *an act that horrified ⏝.*

civ·i·lize ['sɪvɪlaɪz] *v.t.* **1.** bring from a savage or ignorant condition to a higher one (by giving teaching in methods of government, morals, art, science, etc.). **2.** refine and educate.

clack [klæk] *v.i. & t. & n.* (make, cause to make, the) sound of objects struck together (e.g. wooden shoes on stone, typewriter keys).

clad [klæd] old p.t. & p.p. of *clothe*: *poorly ~*, poorly dressed.

claim [kleɪm] *v.t.* **1.** demand recognition of the fact that one is, or owns, or has a right to (sth.): *~ the throne. He ~ed to be the owner of the land (that he owned the land)*. **2.** say that sth. is a fact: *He ~ed to have (that he had) done the work without help*. **3.** (of things) need; deserve: *matters ~ing my attention*. *n.* **1.** act of ~ing (1): *lay ~ to sth.*, demand sth. as one's due. **2.** right to ask for: *You have no ~ on my sympathies*. **3.** sth. that is ~ed. **4.** piece of land (e.g. in a gold-bearing region) allotted to a miner. **~·ant** *n.* person who makes a ~.

clair·voy·ant [kleə'vɔɪənt] *n.* person with power to see in his mind what is happening or what exists at a distance; exceptional insight. **clair·voy·ance** *n.* (no pl.) that power.

clam [klæm] *n.* large shellfish used as food.

clam·ber ['klæmbə*] *v.i.* climb with some difficulty, using the hands and feet: *~ over a wall.*

clam·my ['klæmɪ] *adj.* (-ier, -iest) damp, moist, usu. cold and sticky to the touch: *a face ~ with sweat.*

clam·our (U.S.A. **-or**) ['klæmə*] *n.* loud, confused noise, esp. of people complaining angrily or making demands. *v.i.* make a ~: *newspapers ~ing against the high taxes*. **clam·or·ous** ['klæmərəs] *adj.*

clamp [klæmp] *n.* **1.** appliance for holding things together tightly by means of a screw. **2.** iron band for strengthening or making tight. *v.t.* put in a ~ (1); put a ~ (2) or ~s on.

clan [klæn] *n.* large family group, as found in tribal communities. **~·nish** *adj.* showing ~ feeling; in the habit of supporting one another. **~·s·man** ['klænzmən] *n.* member of a ~.

clan·des·tine [klæn'destɪn] *adj.* secret; done secretly.

clang [klæŋ] *v.i. & t. & n.* (make, cause to make, a) loud ringing sound (like that of a large bell or a hammer striking an anvil).

clank [klæŋk] *v.i. & t. & n.* (make,

cause to make, a) ringing sound (like that heard when swords or heavy chains strike together).

clap [klæp] *v.t. & i.* (-*pp*-) **1.** strike the palms of the hands together, esp. to show approval or as a signal, etc.: *~ one's hands. The audience ~ped for five minutes*. **2.** strike or slap lightly with the open hand, usu. in a friendly way: *~ sb. on the back*. **3.** put, place, esp. with haste or energy: *~ sb. in(to) prison; ~ eyes on sb.*, (esp. neg.) catch sight of. *n.* sharp, loud noise: *a ~ of thunder.*

clar·et ['klærət] *n.* kind of red wine; dark-red colour.

clar·i·fy ['klærɪfaɪ] *v.t. & i.* make or become clear; make (a liquid, etc.) free from impurities.

clar·i·net [,klærɪ'net] *n.* musical instrument, wood-wind, with holes and keys.

a clarinet

clar·i·on ['klærɪən] *n.* loud, shrill call; loud sound to rouse and excite; (attrib.) clear and loud: *a ~ call (voice).*

clar·i·ty ['klærɪtɪ] *n.* (no pl.) clearness.

clash [klæʃ] *v.i. & t. & n.* **1.** (make, cause to make, a) loud, broken, confused sound (as when metal objects, e.g. cymbals, pans, strike together). **2.** (be in) disagreement or conflict: *colours that ~; a ~ of colours; ideas (plans, events) that ~; a ~ of views.*

clasp [klɑːsp] *n.* **1.** device (2) with two parts that fasten together, used for keeping together two things or two parts of one thing (e.g. a necklace or belt). **2.** firm hold (with the fingers or arm); handshake; embrace. *v.t. & i.* **1.** fasten with a ~ (1). **2.** hold tightly or closely: *~ sb.'s hand; ~ing a knife; ~ed in each other's arms.* '**~·knife** *n.* folding knife.

class [klɑːs] *n.* **1.** group having common qualities; kind, sort, or division: *A ~ is the highest division of the animal or vegetable kingdom.* (Cf. *family* (4), *order* (12), *species* (1).) There used to be *first-~, second-~, and third-~ carriages on the railways*. **2.** rank or order of society: *Society is divided into upper, middle, and lower ~es. the working ~es.* **3.** group of students taught together;

clear

their time of meeting; their course of teaching; (U.S.A.) group of students who have graduated in the same year from the same institution: *the ~ of 1977.* **4.** year's enrolment of conscripts: *the 1975 ~.* **5.** (Gt. Brit.) grade or merit after examination: *take a first-~ degree.* *v.t.* put in the correct group. **'~-,con·scious** *adj.* realizing one's ~ in society and the differences between social ~es. **'~-,fel·low, '~-mate** *ns.* member of the same ~ in a school or college as another. **'~-room** *n.* place where ~es (3) meet.

clas·sic ['klæsɪk] *adj.* **1.** of the highest quality; excellent; having a value or position recognized and unquestioned. **2.** of the standard of ancient Greek and Latin writers, art, and culture. **3.** with qualities like those of ~ art (i.e. simple, harmonious, and re-strained). **4.** famous because of a long history: *a ~ event* (e.g. a race such as the Marathon or the Oxford and Cambridge boat race). *n.* writer, artist, book, work of art, etc. of the highest class, esp. of ancient Rome and Greece. *the C~s,* works of famous Greek and Latin writers. **clas·si·cal** ['klæsɪkl] *adj.* **1.** in, of, the best (esp. ancient Greek and Roman) art and literature: *~al studies (scholars); a ~al education.* **2.** of the highest class. **3.** of proved value because of having passed the test of time: *~al music* (contrasted with modern music).

clas·si·fy ['klæsɪfaɪ] *v.t.* arrange in classes (1); put into a class or classes (1). **clas·si·fi·ca·tion** [,klæsɪfɪ'keɪʃn] *n.*

clat·ter ['klætə*] *v.i. & t. & n.* **1.** (make, cause to make, a) loud, rattling noise (as of hard things falling or knocking together): *the ~ of machinery* (of plates and dishes on a hard surface); *horses ~ing along a stony road.* **2.** (be full of, echo with) noisy talk: *the ~ of schoolchildren.*

clause [klɔːz] *n.* **1.** (gram.) component part of a sentence, with its own subject and predicate, esp. one doing the work of a noun, adjective, or adverb. **2.** (law) complete paragraph in an agreement, a law, etc.

claw [klɔː] *n.* **1.** one of the long, pointed nails on the feet of some animals and birds; foot with ~s. **2.** instrument like a ~; sth. shaped like a ~ (e.g. on a lobster or crab). *v.t.* get hold of with the ~s or fingers; scratch with the ~s or finger-nails; pull roughly with the ~s.

clay [kleɪ] *n.* (no pl.) stiff, sticky earth that becomes hard when baked; material from which bricks, pots, earthenware, etc. are made. **~·ey** ['kleɪɪ] *adj.* like, containing, ~: *a ~ey soil.*

clean [kliːn] *adj.* **1.** free from dirt or smoke; freshly washed; unused. **2.** not having rough or irregular lines; well formed; of good shape: *a ~ cut* (made by a sharp knife); *~-cut features* (clear and well defined). **3.** pure; innocent. **4.** complete; thorough: *a ~ break* (quick and final); *make a ~ job of,* do sth. thoroughly. (See breast (3).) *adv.* completely: *We ~ forgot you were coming. cut ~ through. v.t. & i.* make or become ~: *~ out,* get dirt, rubbish, unwanted articles, etc. from the inside of: *~ out a desk; ~ up,* make tidy; put in order. *n. ~ing: Give your dirty boots a good ~.* **~·er** *n.* person, machine, etc. that ~s: *(dry-)~ers; window-~er; vacuum ~er.* **~·ly** ['klenlɪ] *adj.* having ~ habits. **~·ly** ['kliːnlɪ] *adv.* exactly; neatly: *catch a ball ~ly.* **~·li·ness** *n.* (no pl.) habit or condition of being ~. **~·ness** *n.* (no pl.).

cleanse [klenz] *v.t.* make thoroughly clean; (esp.) purify of sin. **cleans·er** *n.* cleaning agent (2).

clear [klɪə*] *adj.* **1.** easy to see through: *~ glass;* free from cloud: *a ~ sky;* bright and pure: *a ~ fire;* distinct, easily seen or understood: *a ~ photograph; a line of hills ~ in the morning sky.* **2.** (of sounds) easily heard; pure; distinct: *a ~ voice (note).* **3.** (of and to the mind) easily understood; free from doubt or difficulty: *a ~ thinker (statement); make oneself (one's meaning) ~.* **4.** easy or safe to pass along; free from dangers or obstacles: *The road is ~.* **5.** free: *~ of debt (suspicion).* **6.** free from blame or guilt: *a ~ conscience.* **7.** confident; certain: *be ~ on a point.* **8.** complete: *two ~ days; a ~ profit of £5. adv.* **1.** *~ly;* distinctly: *speak loud and ~.* **2.** completely: *get ~ away.* **3.** apart; without touching: *keep ~ of,* avoid; *stand ~ of the door. n. in the ~,* free of suspicion, guilt, or difficulty. *v.t. & i.* **1.** make or become ~: *~ the streets of snow; ~ a desk* (i.e. put all the papers, books, etc. away); *~ a room,* cause persons to leave it; *~ the table* (esp. take away dishes, etc. after a meal); *~ one's throat* (by coughing). **2.** get past or over without touching: *The horse ~ed the hedge.* **3.** make a profit of. **4.** *~ a ship (its cargo),* do what is necessary (signing papers, etc.) before sailing. **5.** *~ away,* (a) remove; (b) (of clouds, etc.) disappear; ~ out, (a) empty; (b) (colloq.) go away; leave; ~ up, (a) put things in order; (b) make ~; solve (a mystery): ~ up a misunderstanding; (c) become bright: The weather (sky) is ~ing up. **~ance** *n.* **1.** making ~; removal of obstructions, etc. **2.** space left between two things, for moving past. **~-'cut** *adj.* having ~ outlines. **~ing** *n.* (esp.) land made ~ of trees. **~ly** *adv.* **~ness** *n.* (no pl.). **'~way** *n.* (Gt. Brit.) road on which vehicles are not allowed to stop or park.

cleave[1] [kli:v] *v.t. & i.* (p.t. *clove* [kloʊv] or *cleft* [kleft], p.p. *cloven* ['kloʊvn] or *cleft*) cut in two with a blow from a heavy axe, etc.; split; come apart (esp. along the line where there is a natural tendency, e.g. the grain (4) of wood); make by cutting: ~ a path through the jungle. cleft palate, malformation in the roof of the mouth. cloven foot (hoof), divided hoof of cow, ox, the Devil. **cleav·age** ['kli:vɪdʒ] *n.* act of cleaving; state of being cleft; place where cleaving occurs easily or has occurred. **cleav·er** *n.* heavy tool for chopping up carcasses.

cleave[2] [kli:v] *v.i.* (old use) be faithful (to).

clef [klef] *n.* one of three signs used in music to show the pitch (5).

cleft[1], see *cleave*[1].

cleft[2] [kleft] *n.* crack or split (esp. in the ground or in rock).

cle·ma·tis ['klemətɪs] *n.* (kinds of) climbing plant with flowers.

clem·ent ['klemənt] *adj.* (of temper or the weather) mild; (of a person) showing mercy. **'clem·en·cy** *n.* (no pl.).

clench [klentʃ] *v.t.* **1.** (of teeth, fingers, or fist) close, hold, tightly: ~ one's teeth (fist). **2.** grip.

cler·gy ['klɜːdʒɪ] *n.* the ~, (pl. v.) ministers of the Christian Church. **'~·man** *n.* ordained minister.

cler·ic ['klerɪk] *n.* clergyman. **cler·i·cal** ['klerɪkl] *adj.* **1.** of the clergy: ~al dress. **2.** of or made by a clerk or clerks (1): a ~al error (made in writing or copying).

clerk [klɑːk] *n.* **1.** person employed in a bank, office, shop, etc. to copy letters, keep accounts, make entries, etc. **2.** officer in charge of records, etc.: the Town C~; the C~ to the Council, (usu.) a lawyer in charge of official business; ~ of the works, having charge of materials, etc. for building contracts. **3.** (U.S.A.) assistant in a shop or hotel.

clev·er ['klevə*] *adj.* (~er, ~est) (of people) quick in learning and understanding things; skilful; smart[2] (2) (of things) done with skill: a ~ book. **~·ly** *adv.* **~·ness** *n.* (no pl.).

click [klɪk] *v.t. & i. & n.* (strike or move with, make, a) short sharp sound (like that of a lock closing): ~ one's heels. The door ~ed shut.

cli·ent ['klaɪənt] *n.* person who gets help or advice from a lawyer or other professional man; customer (at a shop). **cli·en·tele** [ˌkliːɑ̃n'tel] *n.* customers.

cliff [klɪf] *n.* steep face of rock, esp. at the edge of the sea.

cli·mate ['klaɪmɪt] *n.* **1.** (area with) certain) weather conditions. **2.** (fig.) prevailing (2) condition: the political ~; ~ of opinion, general attitude of people to a policy, etc. **cli·mat·ic** [klaɪ'mætɪk] *adj.*

cli·max ['klaɪmæks] *n.* event, point, of greatest interest, intensity, or importance; culmination.

climb [klaɪm] *v.t. & i.* go up (stairs, a tree, rope, mountain, etc.); go higher. ~ down, get down (with some difficulty or effort) from a tree or other high place; (fig.) admit fault of pride, etc. *n.* act of ~ing; place (to be) ~ed: a difficult ~. **~·er** *n.* **1.** person who ~ mountains. **2.** person who tries to ~ socially. **3.** ~ing plant.

clinch [klɪntʃ] *v.t. & i.* **1.** settle (an argument, a bargain) finally. **2.** (boxing) grapple, with one or both arms round the opponent's body.

cling [klɪŋ] *v.i.* (p.t. & p.p. *clung* [klʌŋ]) hold tight (to); (of clothes) fit close to the skin.

clin·ic ['klɪnɪk] *n.* institution, hospital etc. where medical advice and treatment are given; hospital ward where medical students are taught through observation of cases. **clin·i·cal** *adj.*

clink [klɪŋk] *v.i. & t. & n.* (make or cause to make, the) sound of small bits of metal (e.g. coins or keys), glass, etc. knocking together.

clin·ker ['klɪŋkə*] *n.* **1.** mass of stony material that forms in a coal fire and does not burn. **2.** kind of hard brick made by burning.

clip[1] [klɪp] *n.* wire or metal device (2) for holding papers, etc. together. *v.t.* (-pp-) put or keep together with a ~.

clip[2] [klɪp] *v.t.* (-pp-) cut with scissors, shears, etc.; make short or neat: ~ a hedge (the wool from a sheep's back); ~ his hair close; ~ a ticket, remove small piece of it to show that it has been used; ~ sth. out (of), (U.S.A.) cut sth. from a newspaper, etc. **~·pers** ['klɪpəz] *n. pl.* instrument for ~ping hair. **~·ping**

n. (U.S.A.) sth. ‿ped out (esp. from a newspaper).

clip·per [ˈklɪpəˀ] *n.* fast sailing-ship.

clique [kliːk] *n.* group of persons united by common interests and tastes (e.g. in literature or art), members of which support each other and shut out others from their company.

cloak [kləʊk] *n.* loose outer garment without sleeves; (fig.) anything that hides or covers. *v.t.* (fig.) hide or cover; keep secret. 'ᴗ**·room** *n.* **1.** place where hats, coats, parcels, etc. may be left for a short time. **2.** (Gt. Brit.) lavatory.

clock [klɒk] *n.* instrument (other than a watch²) for showing the time. *v.t. & i.* (colloq.) time (e.g. a race) with a stop-watch; ‿ (up), (colloq.) attain (2) or register (e.g. a certain speed in a race, etc.); ‿ in (out), ‿ on (off), (of workers, etc.) record the time of arrival and departure by means of an automatic recording ‿. 'ᴗ**·wise** *adj. & adv.* moving in a curve in the direction taken by the hands of a ‿. 'ᴗ**·work** *n. & adj.* (machinery) with wheels driven by a spring: *like* ‿*work*, regularly; without trouble.

clod [klɒd] *n.* lump (of earth, clay).

clog¹ [klɒg] *n.* shoe with a heavy wooden sole, or carved out of a block of wood.

clog² [klɒg] *v.t. & i.* (-gg-) be, cause to be, become, blocked with waste matter, dirt, grease, etc. so that movement or the flow of liquid is made difficult: *machinery* ‿*ged (up) with grease*; *pipes* ‿*ged with dirt*.

clois·ter [ˈklɔɪstəˀ] *n.* **1.** covered walk, usu. on the sides of an open square, esp. within a convent, cathedral, or college building. **2.** convent or monastery. *v.t.* put in, live in, a convent or monastery.

close¹ [kləʊz] *v.t. & i.* **1.** shut: ‿ *doors and windows. Many flowers* ‿ *at night. This road is* ‿*d. The shops are* ‿*d on Sundays. closing-time*, time at which shops, etc. stop doing business. **2.** bring or come to an end: ‿ *a discussion.* **3.** (often ‿ *up*) bring or come nearer together; make less space or fewer spaces between: ‿ *the ranks.* **4.** ‿ *down*, (a) (of a business, factory, etc.) ‿ permanently; (b) (Gt. Brit.) (of a broadcasting station) stop transmitting till the next day; ‿ *in (up)on*, come nearer, surround (esp. in order to attack); ‿ *with*, accept (an offer). *n.* (sing. only) end: *towards the* ‿ *of the 19th century*; *draw (bring) to a* ‿.

close² [kləʊs] *adj.* (‿*r*, ‿*st*) **1.** near (in space or time). **2.** near: *a* ‿ *friend*, a very dear friend. **3.** with very little space in between: *in* ‿ *order*; *at* ‿ *quarters.* **4.** severe; strict: *in* ‿ *confinement*; *keep a* ‿ *watch on*, watch carefully. **5.** (of the air, the weather) not fresh; uncomfortably warm; stifling. **6.** receiving care; thorough: ‿ *attention*; *a* ‿ *translation*; with every step clearly shown: *a* ‿ *argument.* **7.** secret; keeping things secret: *keep sth.* ‿, say nothing about it; *be* ‿ *about sth.*, be secretive; *keep (lie)* ‿, hide. **8.** (of vowels) pronounced with only a narrow opening of the lips. **9.** not giving help (esp. money) willingly: *He's very* ‿(-*fisted*). **10.** (of competitions, games, their results) in which two or more competitors are almost equal: *a* ‿ *game (finish).* **11.** ‿ *season*, period of the year when certain wild birds, animals, etc. must not be killed. *a* ‿ *shave*, (fig.) a narrow escape from an accident, etc. ‿-*up*, photograph or film taken with the camera ‿ to the person or object. *adv.* in a ‿ manner; near: *stand or sit* ‿ *to sb.*; ‿ *by (on, to)*, very near to. ‿-*fitting*, (of a dress) fitting ‿ to the body. ‿-*set*, set or placed ‿ together: ‿-*set eyes. n.* **1.** (esp. of a school or cathedral) space with buildings all round. **2.** cul-de-sac. ‿**ly** *adv.* ‿**ness** *n.*

clos·et [ˈklɒzɪt] *n.* **1.** private or small room; cupboard. **2.** (U.S.A.) cupboard or recess (2) for storage, etc. **3.** see *water-*‿. *v.t.* be ‿*d with (together)*, have a private talk with.

clot [klɒt] *n.* half-solid lump formed from liquid, esp. blood. *v.i. & t.* (-*tt-*) form into ‿s.

cloth [klɒθ] *n.* (pl. ‿s) **1.** material made by weaving (cotton, wool, silk, linen, etc.). **2.** piece of ‿ for a special purpose: *a table-*‿.

clothe [kləʊð] *v.t.* (p.t. & p.p. ‿*d*, old form *clad*) **1.** put ‿s on; give ‿s to: ‿ *one's family.* **2.** (fig.) express: ‿ *thoughts in suitable words.*

clothes [kləʊðz] *n. pl.* garments; what one wears on one's body. (Cf. *bed*‿.) 'ᴗ**-line** *n.* rope on which washed ‿ are hung to dry. 'ᴗ**-peg**, 'ᴗ**-pin** *ns.* clip¹ for fastening ‿ to a ‿-line.

cloth·ing [ˈkləʊðɪŋ] *n.* (no pl.) = clothes.

cloud [klaʊd] *n.* **1.** (mass of) visible, condensed water vapour floating in the air, usu. at a considerable height. ‿*burst*, sudden, violent rainstorm. **2.** mass of things (in the air) like a ‿: *a* ‿

of arrows (*mosquitoes*). **3.** (fig.) state of unhappiness or fear: *a ~ of grief*; *the ~s of war*; *under a ~ (of suspicion)*. *v.t. & i.* make or become dark (as) with *~s*: *~ over*, (of the sky) become covered with *~s*. **~·less** *adj.* **~·y** *adj.* (*-ier*, *-iest*) covered with *~s*; not clear.

clouds   a clown

clout [klaʊt] *n.* blow or knock. *v.t.* hit.
clove[1] [kləʊv] *n.* dried, unopened flower-bud of a tropical tree, used to flavour food, etc.

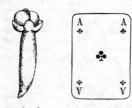

a clove[1]   the ace of clubs[3]

clove[2], **clo·ven**, see *cleave*[1].
clo·ver ['kləʊvə*] *n.* (no pl.) low-growing plant with (usu.) three leaves on each stalk, grown as food for cattle. *in ~*, in great comfort and luxury. '**~-leaf** *n.* highway intersection with flyovers, etc. forming the pattern of four-leaved *~*.
clown [klaʊn] *n.* man (esp. in a circus) who makes a living by performing foolish tricks and antics; person who behaves like a *~*; rude, clumsy man. *v.i.* behave like a *~*. **~·ish** *adj.*
cloy [klɔɪ] *v.t. & i.* make distasteful, become weary of sth. (through excess): *~ed with sweet food (foolish pleasures, etc.)*.
club[1] [klʌb] *n.* heavy stick with a thick end used as a weapon; stick used for hitting the ball in some games (e.g. golf). *v.t.* (*-bb-*) hit with a *~*: *He had been ~bed to death.*
club[2] [klʌb] *n.* society of persons who subscribe money to provide themselves with sport (e.g. football, golf), social entertainment, etc., sometimes in their

own grounds or buildings where meal and bedrooms are available; the room or building(s) used by such a society *v.i.* (*-bb-*) join together for a common cause: *~ together (with others) to rais a sum of money.*
club[3] [klʌb] *n.* playing-card with black designs like a clover-leaf printed on it *the ace of ~s.*
cluck [klʌk] *v.i. & n.* (make the) noise of a hen (e.g. when calling her chickens)
clue [kluː] *n.* fact, idea, etc. that suggests a possible answer to a problem esp. a ·crime, mystery or a crossword puzzle.
clump [klʌmp] *n.* group (*of trees*, shrubs, plants, etc.).
clum·sy ['klʌmzɪ] *adj.* (*-ier*, *-iest*) **1.** heavy and ungraceful in movement or construction; not well designed for a purpose. **2.** lacking tact or skill. **clum·si·ly** *adv.* **clum·si·ness** *n.* (no pl.).
clung, see *cling*.
clus·ter ['klʌstə*] *n.* **1.** number of things of the same kind growing closely together: *a ~ of curls (flowers, berries)*. **2.** number of persons, animals objects, etc. in a small, close group: *a ~ of bees (houses, spectators)*. *v.t. & i.* collect into a *~*; grow, come together, in a *~*.
clutch[1] [klʌtʃ] *v.t. & i.* seize; grasp tightly: *~ (at) a rope.* *n.* **1.** act of *~ing*; strong hold: *in the ~es of*, in the cruel power of. **2.** (mech.) device (2) in a machine for connecting and disconnecting working parts; lever operating such a *~*: *let in (disengage) the ~ of a motor-ear engine.*
clutch[2] [klʌtʃ] *n.* set of eggs put under a hen to hatch at one time; number of young chickens hatched from these.
clut·ter ['klʌtə*] *v.t.* (often *~ up*) make untidy or disordered: *a desk ~ed up with papers.*
co- [kəʊ-] *pref.* together with (another or others): *co-author*; *coeducation* (of boys and girls); *coexist*; *co-operate.*
Co. [kəʊ] (abbr. for) company (4).
coach[1] [kəʊtʃ] *n.* **1.** four-wheeled carriage pulled by four or more horses. **2.** (U.S.A. *car*) railway carriage. **3.** (also *motor ~*) long-distance motor bus: *travel by ~*. '**~·man** *n.* driver of a *~* (1).

a coach[1] (1)

coach² [kəʊtʃ] *n.* teacher, esp. one who gives private lessons to prepare students for public examinations; person who trains athletes for games or contests. *v.t. & i.* teach; train.

co·ag·u·late [kəʊˈægjʊleɪt] *v.t. & i.* (of liquids) change to a more solid state, as blood does in air. **co·ag·u·la·tion** [kəʊˌægjʊˈleɪʃn] *n.* (no pl.).

coal [kəʊl] *n.* **1.** (no pl.) black mineral that is burnt to supply heat, raise steam, generate electricity, make ~ gas, tar, etc. **2.** (Gt. Brit.) piece of this material ready for burning: *carry ~s to Newcastle*, take sth. to a place where it is already plentiful. *v.t. & i.* put ~ into (a ship); take in ~. **'~-field** *n.* region with deposits (n.2) of ~. **'~-mine**, **'~-pit** *ns.* mine where ~ is dug. **~ tar** *n.* (no pl.) thick, black, sticky substance obtained when gas is made from ~.

co·alesce [ˌkəʊəˈles] *v.i.* come together and unite.

co·ali·tion [ˌkəʊəˈlɪʃn] *n.* uniting; union of (esp. political) groups or parties for a special purpose: *a ~ government*.

coarse [kɔːs] *adj.* (*~r*, *~st*) **1.** rough; of poor quality: *~ food*; *clothes made of ~ material*. **2.** not fine and small; rough and lumpy: *~ sand*. **3.** rude (1); uncultured: *~ language (manners)*. **~·ly** *adv.* **~·ness** *n.*

coast [kəʊst] *n.* land near or by the edge of the sea; sea-shore. *v.i. & t.* **1.** go in, sail, a ship along the ~. **2.** go downhill on a bicycle (without working the pedals) or on a sledge. **'~-guard** *n.* officer on police duty on the ~ (to prevent smuggling, report passing ships, etc.). **'~-line** *n.* outline or shape of a ~. **~·al** *adj.* of the ~. **'~-wise** *adj. & adv.* along the ~.

coat [kəʊt] *n.* **1.** outer garment with sleeves, buttoned in front. **2.** animals' covering of hair, etc. **3.** covering of paint, etc.: *put a ~ (3) on*. **~ of arms** *n.* see *arm²* (3). **~·ee** [ˈkəʊtiː] *n.* short ~. **~·ing** *n.* layer or covering: *a ~ing of soot*; material for making ~s (1).

coax [kəʊks] *v.t.* get sb. or sth. to do sth. by kindness or patience: *~ a child to go to bed early*; *~ a fire to burn*.

cob [kɒb] *n.* **1.** strong, short-legged horse for riding. **2.** male swan. **3.** (also *corn-~*) that part of a head of maize on which the grain grows.

co·balt [ˈkəʊbɔːlt] *n.* (no pl.) silver-white metal similar to nickel; deep-blue colouring matter made from it.

cob·ble¹ [ˈkɒbl] *n.* (also *~-stone*) stone worn round and smooth by water (formerly used for paving).

cob·ble² [ˈkɒbl] *v.t.* mend, patch (esp. shoes), or put together roughly. **~r** *n.* mender of shoes.

co·bra [ˈkəʊbrə] *n.* poisonous snake of India or Africa.

cob·web [ˈkɒbweb] *n.* fine network or single thread made by a spider. (See the picture at *web*.)

co·caine [kəʊˈkeɪn] *n.* (no pl.) drug used by doctors to deaden pain; also used as a stimulant.

cock¹ [kɒk] *n.* adult male bird of the domestic (3) fowl; male of any other kind of bird: *pea~*; *turkey~*; *~ sparrow*. (Cf. *hen.*) **'~-crow** *n.* daybreak. **~s-comb** [ˈkɒkskəʊm] *n.* ~'s red crest. **~'sure** *adj.* quite sure (*of*, *about* sth.); too confident.

cock² [kɒk] *n.* **1.** tap and spout for controlling the flow of liquid (from a pipe, barrel, etc.). **2.** lever in a gun: *at half (full) ~*, half-ready (ready) to be fired. *v.t.* **1.** turn upwards (showing attention, defiance, etc.): *~ the ears*; *~ one's eye at*, glance knowingly at (sb.). **2.** raise the ~ (2) of (a gun) ready for firing. **~ed hat** *n.* triangular hat, pointed front and back, worn with some uniforms.

cock³ [kɒk] *n.* small, conical heap of hay, etc. in a field. *v.t.* pile into ~s.

cock·ade [kɒˈkeɪd] *n.* knot of ribbon worn on the hat as a badge.

cock·a·too [ˌkɒkəˈtuː] *n.* crested parrot.

cock·cha·fer [ˈkɒkˌtʃeɪfə*] *n.* large beetle that flies with a whirring sound.

cock·er·el [ˈkɒkərəl] *n.* young cock¹.

cock·ney [ˈkɒknɪ] *adj. & n.* (of a) native of London: *a ~ accent*.

cock·pit [ˈkɒkpɪt] *n.* place where the pilot sits in an aircraft or a spaceship; driver's seat in a racing car.

cock·roach [ˈkɒkrəʊtʃ] *n.* large, dark-brown insect that comes out at night in kitchens and places where food is kept.

cock·tail [ˈkɒkteɪl] *n.* mixed alcoholic drink, usu. taken before meals; mixture of fruits or fruit juices, etc. served in a glass.

co·co [ˈkəʊkəʊ] *n.* tropical palm-tree. **'~-nut** *n.* large, hard, rough, brown nut on the ~(nut palm), filled with milky juice and a hard, white, edible substance. (Cf. *copra*.) **~nut matting** (made from the rough fibre covering the nut).

co·coa [ˈkəʊkəʊ] *n.* powder of crushed cacao seeds; drink made from this with hot water or milk.

co·coon [kə'ku:n] *n.* silky covering made by a caterpillar for protection while it is a chrysalis.

cod [kɒd] *n.* (pl. ~) (also ~*fish*) large sea-fish. ~*-liver oil* (used as a medicine).

cod·dle ['kɒdl] *v.t.* treat very tenderly, or with unnecessary care.

code [kəʊd] *n.* **1.** collection of laws arranged in a system. **2.** system of rules, principles, morals, etc.: *the ~ of honour.* **3.** system of signs, secret writing, etc. **4.** system of sending messages: *the Morse ~; a telegraph ~. v.t.* put into ~ signs. **cod·i·fy** ['kəʊdɪfaɪ] *v.t.* put into the form of a ~ (1).

cod·i·cil ['kɒdɪsɪl] *n.* sth. added to a will.

co·ed [,kəʊ'ed] *n.* (colloq.) female student at a coeducational institution.

co·edu·ca·tion [,kəʊedjuː'keɪʃn] *n.* (no pl.) education of boys and girls together. ~*al adj.*

co·erce [kəʊ'ɜːs] *v.t.* force (sb. *into* doing sth.). **co·er·cion** [kəʊ'ɜːʃn] *n.* (no pl.). **co·er·cive** [kəʊ'ɜːsɪv] *adj.*

co·ex·ist [,kəʊɪg'zɪst] *v.i.* exist at the same time or together (*with*). **co·ex·is·tence** *n.*

cof·fee ['kɒfɪ] *n.* bush or shrub with seeds which, when roasted and ground to powder, are used for making a drink; the seeds; the powder; the drink. ~*-bean*, ~ seed.

cof·fer ['kɒfə*] *n.* large, strong box, esp. for holding money or other valuables.

cof·fin ['kɒfɪn] *n.* box for a dead person to be buried in.

cog [kɒg] *n.* one of a number of teeth on a wheel or rod. '~·wheel *n.* toothed wheel to transfer motion from one part of a machine to another.

cogwheels

co·gent ['kəʊdʒənt] *adj.* (of arguments) powerful. **co·gen·cy** ['kəʊdʒənsɪ] *n.* (no pl.).

cog·i·tate ['kɒdʒɪteɪt] *v.i. & t.* think (over) carefully; meditate. **cog·i·ta·tion** [,kɒdʒɪ'teɪʃn] *n.*

co·gnac ['kɒnjæk] *n.* French brandy.

cog·nate ['kɒgneɪt] *n. & adj.* (word) coming from the same source or starting-point; having much in common: *The English word 'father' is ~ with the Latin 'pater'.*

cog·ni·zance ['kɒgnɪzəns] *n.* (no pl.) being aware; having knowledge (of). **cog·ni·zant** ['kɒgnɪzənt] *adj.*

co·here [kəʊ'hɪə*] *v.i.* stick together; remain united. **co·her·ence**, **co·her·en·cy** *ns.* **co·her·ent** *adj.* cohering; (esp. of speech, thought, ideas) clear; easy to understand. **co·he·sion** [kəʊ'hiːʒn] *n.* cohering. **co·he·sive** [kəʊ'hiːsɪv] *adj.*

coif·fure [kwɑː'fjʊə*] *n.* style of hairdressing.

coil [kɔɪl] *v.t. & i.* wind or twist (rope, etc.) into rings one above the other; curl round and round. *n.* sth. ~ed; a single turn of sth. ~ed: *a ~ of rope;* ~ed wire for electric current.

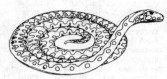

a coiled snake

coin [kɔɪn] *n.* (piece of) metal money. *v.t.* make (metal) into ~s. *be ~ing money*, be making large profits; ~ *a word (phrase)*, invent it. **~·age** ['kɔɪnɪdʒ] *n.* making ~s; ~s so made; system of ~s: *a decimal ~age.*

co·in·cide [,kəʊɪn'saɪd] *v.i.* **1.** (of two or more objects) correspond in area or outline. **2.** (of events) happen at the same time. **3.** (of ideas, etc.) be in agreement (*with*). **co·in·ci·dence** [kəʊ'ɪnsɪdəns] *n.* (esp.) chance coinciding of events, circumstances, etc.

coke[1] [kəʊk] *n.* (no pl.) substance remaining after gas has been taken out of coal by heating in an oven. *v.t.* turn (coal) into ~.

coke[2] [kəʊk] *n.* (no pl.) (sl.) cocaine.

col·an·der ['kʌləndə*] *n.* vessel with many small holes, used to drain off water from vegetables, etc. in cooking.

cold [kəʊld] *adj.* **1.** of low temperature, esp. when compared with that of the human body: ~ *weather*; *feel ~*. **2.** (fig.) not easily excited; unfriendly: *a ~ greeting (manner).* **3.** ~*-blooded*, (fig.) pitiless; ~ *cuts*, sliced, assorted, ~ meats; ~*-hearted*, unfriendly; indifferent; ~ *storage* (see *storage*); ~ *war* (see *war*); *in* ~ *blood* (see *blood*); *throw* ~ *water on* (see *water* (1)); *give sb. the* ~ *shoulder*, treat in an unfriendly way. *n.* **1.** low temperature: *He was shiver-*

ing with ~. **2.** illness with discharge from the nose, sneezing, etc.: catch (a) ~; have a bad ~. **~·ly** adv. **~·ness** n. (no pl.).

col·ic ['kɒlɪk] *n.* severe pain in the stomach and bowels.

col·lab·o·rate [kə'læbəreɪt] *v.i.* **1.** work together with another or others (esp. in writing a book or in art). **2.** co-operate treasonably with the enemy. **col·lab·o·ra·tion** [kə,læbə'reɪʃn] *n.* (no pl.).

col·lapse [kə'læps] *v.i. & t.* **1.** fall down or in; come or break to pieces suddenly; cause to ~. **2.** lose physical strength, courage, mental powers, etc. completely. *n.* complete breakdown, failure, or loss of these kinds. **col·laps·ible** adj. made so as to fold up for packing, storing, or transport: a collapsible boat (chair, table).

col·lar ['kɒlə*] *n.* **1.** part of a garment that fits round the neck. **2.** separate article of clothing (linen, lace, etc.) worn round the neck and fastened to a shirt or blouse. **3.** band of leather, etc. put round the neck of a horse, dog, or other animal. **4.** metal band joining two pipes or rods. *v.t.* seize by the ~; take hold of roughly. **'~-bone** *n.* bone joining the shoulder and the breastbone.

col·late [kɒ'leɪt] *v.t.* make a careful comparison between (two or more books, etc.) to learn the differences between them.

col·league ['kɒliːg] *n.* one of two or more persons working together and (usu.) having similar rank and duties.

col·lect[1] ['kɒlekt] *n.* short prayer of the Church of Rome or the Church of England to be read on certain appointed days.

col·lect[2] [kə'lekt] *v.t. & i.* bring or come together; get from a number of people or places; gather together: ~ money (taxes, stamps, one's thoughts). A crowd soon ~ed. adj. & adv. (U.S.A.) to be paid for by the receiver (1) (of telephone calls, telegrams, parcels, etc.). **~·ed** adj. (esp. of a person) with feelings under control; cool and calm. **col·lec·tion** [kə'lekʃn] *n.* ~ing; number of things that have been ~ed or that have come together; money ~ed at a meeting (e.g. at church). **col·lec·tive** *adj.* of a group or society as a whole: ~ive farms; ~ive ownership. **col·lec·tor** *n.* person who ~s: a stamp-~or; a tax-~or; a ticket-~or (at a railway station).

col·lege ['kɒlɪdʒ] *n.* **1.** school for higher or professional education; body (5) of teachers and students forming part of a university; their building(s). **2.** body (5) of colleagues with common privileges: the C~ of Surgeons; the C~ of Cardinals. **col·le·giate** [kə'liːdʒɪət] adj.

col·lide [kə'laɪd] *v.i.* come together violently; be opposed.

col·lie ['kɒlɪ] *n.* Scottish sheep-dog with long hair and a long, pointed nose.

col·lier ['kɒlɪə*] *n.* coal-miner; ship carrying a cargo of coal. **~y** *n.* coal-mine.

col·li·sion [kə'lɪʒn] *n.* act or instance of colliding: a head-on ~.

col·lo·qui·al [kə'ləʊkwɪəl] adj. (of words, phrases, style) belonging to, suitable for, ordinary conversation; not formal or literary.

col·lo·quy ['kɒləkwɪ] *n.* conversation.

col·lu·sion [kə'luːʒn] *n.* (no pl.) secret agreement or understanding for a wrong purpose.

co·lon[1] ['kəʊlən] *n.* the mark (:) in writing and printing.

co·lon[2] ['kəʊlən] *n.* lower and greater part of the large intestine.

col·o·nel ['kɜːnl] *n.* army officer, above a major, commanding a regiment.

co·lo·nial, col·o·nize, etc. see colony.

col·on·nade [,kɒlə'neɪd] *n.* row of columns (1) with equal spaces between, usu. supporting a roof or row of arches.

col·o·ny ['kɒlənɪ] *n.* **1.** country or territory that has been developed by people from another country and that is still, fully or partly, controlled from the mother country. **2.** group of people from another country, or of people with the same trade or occupation, living together: the American ~ in Paris; a ~ of artists. **co·lo·ni·al** [kə'ləʊnɪəl] *n. & adj.* (native or inhabitant) of a ~ (1). **co·lo·ni·al·ism** [kə'ləʊnɪəlɪzəm] *n.* (no pl.) policy of having and retaining colonies (1). **col·o·nist** ['kɒlənɪst] *n.* person who settles in a new ~ (1). **col·o·nize** ['kɒlənaɪz] *v.t.* form a ~ (1) in; send colonists to. **col·o·ni·za·tion** [,kɒlənaɪ'zeɪʃn] *n.* (no pl.).

co·los·sal [kə'lɒsl] adj. immense.

co·los·sus [kə'lɒsəs] *n.* (pl. -si, -suses) immense statue (esp. of a man, much greater than life-size); gigantic person or personification of sth.

col·our (U.S.A. **-or**) ['kʌlə*] *n.* **1.** The simple (or primary) ~s, red, blue, and yellow, can be mixed together by painters to give all the other ~s. The ~ of blood *is red. Your cheeks are (have) a healthy* ~. *change* ~, grow pale or red; *lose* ~, turn pale. **2.** (pl.) materials used by artists; paint: *oil-*~*s*; *water-*~*s*. **3.** (of events, descriptions) appearance of truth or reality: *give (lend)* ~ *to*, make (sth.) seem reasonable or probable; *local* ~, (in writing) details which make a description more real. **4.** (pl.) flag: *stick to one's* ~*s*, refuse to give up one's beliefs, party, etc.; *lower one's* ~*s*, give up one's demands, etc.; *show one's true* ~*s*, show what one really is; *come off with flying* ~*s*, be very successful. *v.t. & i.* give ~ *to*; put ~ on; misrepresent: ~*ed news*; become ~*ed*: ~ (*up*), blush. ~ **bar** *n.* legal or social discrimination between white and ~*ed* people. '~-**blind** *adj.* unable to see the difference between certain ~*s*, esp. red and green. ~*ed adj.* **1.** having the ~ of: *cream-*~*ed*. **2.** (of persons) other than white-skinned. ~**ing** *n.* (no pl.) (esp.) style in which sth. is ~*ed*, or the way in which an artist uses ~. ~**ful** *adj.* ~**less** *adj.*

colt [kəʊlt] *n.* young male horse (up to 4 or 5 years). (Cf. *filly*.)

col·umn ['kɒləm] *n.* **1.** tall, upright pillar, either supporting or decorating part of a building, or standing alone as a monument. **2.** sth. shaped like a ~: *a* ~ *of smoke*; *the spinal* ~; *add up a* ~ *of figures* (1). **3.** narrow upright division of the printed page of a newspaper or book; part of a newspaper occupied regularly by a special subject. **4.** (mil.) long, deep (2) row (as of soldiers). **col·um·nist** ['kɒləmnist] *n.* journalist who regularly writes a newspaper ~ of various comments on people and events.

a column (1)

a comet

co·ma ['kəʊmə] *n.* unnatural deep sleep.

comb [kəʊm] *n.* **1.** instrument with teeth for making the hair tidy, keeping it in place, etc. **2.** similar instrument in some machines for preparing wool, cotton, etc. for manufacture. **3.** = honeycomb. **4.** red, fleshy crest of fowl, esp. the cock. *v.t.* **1.** use a ~ on

(the hair). **2.** prepare (wool, etc.) with ~*s* for manufacture. **3.** search thoroughly. ~ *out*, take out (unwanted things, persons) from a group.

com·bat ['kɒmbæt] *n. & v.t. & i.* fight; struggle. *single* ~, fight between two persons only. **com·ba·tant** ['kɒmbətənt] *adj. & n.* fighting (man).

com·bi·na·tion [ˌkɒmbɪ'neɪʃn] *n.* **1.** joining or putting together; state of being joined; number of persons or things combined for a purpose. **2.** (pl.) suit of underwear in one piece covering body and legs. **3.** series of numbers etc. used to open a ~ *lock* (used for safes, strong-rooms, etc.).

com·bine [kəm'baɪn] *v.t. & i.* (cause to) join together; possess at the same time. ['kɒmbaɪn] *n.* group of persons or parties, esp. for trade, controlling prices, etc. ~ (*harvester*), ~*d reaping and threshing machine.

com·bus·ti·ble [kəm'bʌstəbl] *n. & adj.* (substance) catching fire and burning easily.

com·bus·tion [kəm'bʌstʃən] *n.* (no pl.) process of burning; destruction by fire.

come [kʌm] *v.i.* (p.t. came [keɪm], p.p. ~) **1.** move nearer to the position of the speaker or a point (in space or time) or a result: *C*~ *here. C*~ *to me. They came at six o'clock. They came towards the house. All his plans came to nothing.* **2.** arrive: *The visitors haven't* ~ *yet.* **3.** occur: *The 2nd May* ~*s on a Friday.* **4.** amount to: *Our expenses came to £ 5.* **5.** prove to be; become: ~ *true*, become real, become a fact: *I hope my dream will* ~ *true.* **6.** become: *My shoe has* ~ *undone. The handle has* ~ *loose.* **7.** happen: *How* ~*s it that ...? How did you* ~ *to hear of it?* **8.** (phrases and special uses with advs. and preps.): ~ *to an agreement*, agree; ~ *to blows* (*with*), begin to fight; ~ *to a decision*, decide; ~ *to an end*, end; ~ *to a halt*, stop; ~ *round*, ~ *to one's senses*, (a) become conscious (after fainting); (b) become sensible (after being foolish); ~ *into a fortune* (*money*), inherit; ~ *into sight* (*view*), appear; ~ *of age*, reach the age of 18; *in years to* ~, in future years; *a coming man*, a man who is likely to become important; ~ *about*, happen; ~ *across*, find or meet by accident; ~ *along*, (colloq., imper.) hurry up; ~ *back*, return; ~ *by sth.*, get possession of sth.; ~ *down*, (a) ~ to a place regarded as lower; (b) collapse; (c) (of rain, etc.) fall; (d) (of prices) fall; ~ *down with*, begin to suffer from a disease: ~ *down* *with measles*; ~ *down in the world*, lose social position; ~ *from*, be the result of; ~ *in*, enter a house or room; ~ *of*, (a) be descended from; (b) be the result of; ~ *off*, (a) (of an expected event) take place; (b) acquit oneself: ~ *off well (badly)*; (c) (of plans, etc.) be successful; ~ *on*, (a) follow; (b) progress; (c) (of rain, night, illness) begin; (d) (used in cajoling or pleading) please! ~ *out*, (a) appear; (b) (of facts) become known; (c) (of books) be published; (d) (of stains) be removed; ~ *out first (last)*, (in an examination) have a certain position; ~ *through*, recover from a serious illness; ~ *to*, recover consciousness; ~ *up*, (a) ~ *to* a place regarded as higher; (b) approach (sb.) for a talk; ~ *up against*, meet (difficulties, opposition); ~ *upon*, ~ *across*. '**~-back** *n.* return to one's earlier powers or status (1). '**~-down** *n.* change for the worse in one's circumstances.

co·me·di·an [kə'miːdjən] *n.* actor in comedies; actor whose aim is to make people laugh.

com·e·dy ['kɒmɪdɪ] *n.* play for the theatre, usu. dealing with everyday life and intended to amuse; this branch of literature; amusing incident in real life.

come·ly ['kʌmlɪ] *adj.* (-ier, -iest) (usu. of a person) pleasant to look at. **come·li·ness** *n.*

com·et ['kɒmɪt] *n.* heavenly body, looking like a star with a tail of light (moving round the sun). (See the picture.)

com·fort ['kʌmfət] *n.* **1.** help or kindness to sb. who is suffering; relief from pain, trouble, or anxiety; person or thing that brings such relief. ~ *station*, (U.S.A.) public lavatory. **2.** state of being free from worry; contentment: *live in* ~. *v.t.* give ~ to; say kind words to (sb. who is sad, in trouble, etc.). **~·able** ['kʌmfətəbl] *adj.* giving ~ to the body: *a ~able chair*; free from pain or trouble: *be (feel) ~able.* **~·ably** *adv.* **~·less** ['kʌmfətlɪs] *adj.* without ~. **~·er** *n.* person who ~s; warm woollen scarf to be worn round the neck; (U.S.A. *pacifier*) dummy teat for babies.

com·fy ['kʌmfɪ] *adj.* (-ier, -iest) (colloq.) comfortable; snug.

com·ic ['kɒmɪk] *adj.* **1.** causing people to laugh; intended to amuse: *a ~ song*; ~ *strips*, narrative sequence of humorous drawings, as in newspapers, etc. **2.** of comedy: ~ *opera*. *n.* **1.** ~ person;

(colloq.) theatre, etc. comedian. **2.** ~ paper; ~ cartoon. **com·i·cal** ['kɒmɪkl] *adj.* amusing.

com·ma ['kɒmə] *n.* the mark (,) used in writing and printing. *inverted ~s*, the marks (" ").

com·mand [kə'mɑːnd] *v.t. & i.* **1.** give an order to; have authority over. **2.** control (the feelings, oneself): ~ *one's temper.* **3.** be in a position to use; have at one's service; deserve to have and get: ~ *great sums of money*; ~ *respect and sympathy.* **4.** (of a place) be in a position that overlooks (and controls): *The fort ~ed the entrance to the valley.* *n.* order; authority; (power to) control; part of an army, etc. under sb.'s ~; mastery; possession: *have a good ~ of the English language*; *have ~ over oneself.* **com·man·dant** [,kɒmən'dænt] *n.* officer in ~ of a fort or other military establishment. **com·man·deer** [,kɒmən'dɪə*] *v.t.* take (horses, stores, buildings, etc.) for military purposes, usu. without asking for the owner's permission. **~·er** *n.* person in ~; (navy) officer above a lieutenant and below a captain. **~·ing** *adj.* that ~s; impressive: ~*ing officer*; *a ~ing view of the valley.* **~·ment** *n.* the *Ten C~ments*, the ten laws given by God to Moses.

com·man·do [kə'mɑːndəʊ] *n.* (pl. -os, -oes) (member of a) specially picked and trained attacking force.

com·mem·o·rate [kə'meməreɪt] *v.t.* keep or honour the memory of (a person or event); (of things) be in memory of. **com·mem·o·ra·tion** [kə,memə-'reɪʃn] *n.* **com·mem·o·ra·tive** [kə-'memərətɪv] *adj.* serving to ~: *commemorative medals (plaque, stamps).*

com·mence [kə'mens] *v.t. & i.* begin; start. **~·ment** *n.* beginning.

com·mend [kə'mend] *v.t.* **1.** praise. **2.** entrust for safe keeping: ~ *one's soul to God.* **~·able** *adj.* deserving praise. **com·men·da·tion** [,kɒmen'deɪʃn] *n.* (no pl.) praise; approval.

com·men·su·rate [kə'menʃərət] *adj.* in the right proportion (*to, with*).

com·ment ['kɒment] *n.* sth. said or written about an event, or in explanation or criticism of sth. *v.i.* make ~s (*on*); give opinions (*on*). **com·men·tary** ['kɒməntərɪ] *n.* **1.** number of ~s (e.g. on a book): *a Bible ~ary.* **2.** continuous ~s on an event: *a broadcast ~ary on a race (football match)*; *running* (i.e. continuous) *~ary.* **com·men·ta·tor** ['kɒmenteɪtə*] *n.*

com·merce ['kɒmɜːs] *n.* (no pl.) trade,

esp. between countries; exchange and distribution of goods.

com·mer·cial [kəˈməːʃl] *adj.* of commerce: ~ *education*; ~ *traveller*, person who travels with samples of goods to obtain orders (6); ~ *television* (*broadcasting*). *n.* **1.** broadcast advertisement. **2.** television or radio programme sponsored by an advertiser. **~·ize** [kəˈməːʃəlaɪz] *v.t.* (try to) make money out of: *~ize sport*.

com·mis·er·ate [kəˈmɪzəreɪt] *v.t. & i.* feel, say that one feels, pity for sb. and his troubles or misfortunes: ~ (*with*) *sb. on his losses*. **com·mis·er·a·tion** [kəˌmɪzəˈreɪʃn] *n.*

com·mis·sar [ˌkɒmɪˈsɑː*] *n.* Soviet state official.

com·mis·sar·i·at [ˌkɒmɪˈseərɪət] *n.* department (esp. in an army) that supplies food, etc.

com·mis·sion [kəˈmɪʃn] *n.* **1.** giving of authority to sb. to act for another; work, business, etc. done. **2.** performance (of wrongdoing): *the ~ of crime*. **3.** payment made to sb. for selling goods, etc., rising in proportion to the results gained: *sell goods on ~* (i.e. draw a percentage of the receipts). **4.** official paper (called a *warrant*) giving a person authority; (esp.) (in Gt. Brit.) royal warrant appointing a naval, air force, or military officer. **5.** body (5) of persons given the duty of making an inquiry and writing a report: *a Royal C~ to report on local government*. **6.** *in ~*, (of a warship) ready to go to sea; with crew and supplies complete. *v.t.* give a ~ to. **~·er** *n.* **1.** member of a ~ (5). **2.** high official in a department of government: *the C~ers of Customs*; *the High C~er for Canada* (e.g. representing the Canadian government in London).

com·mis·sion·aire [kəˌmɪʃəˈneə*] *n.* uniformed door-porter at a cinema, theatre, hotel, etc.

com·mit [kəˈmɪt] *v.t.* (-*tt*-) **1.** perform (a crime, foolish act): ~ *murder* (*suicide*, *an offence*). **2.** entrust, send, hand over to, for safe keeping or treatment: ~ *a prisoner for trial*; ~ *sb. to prison*; ~ *to memory* (learn by heart); ~ *to writing* (put into writing). **3.** ~ *oneself* (*to ...*), make oneself responsible; promise; undertake. **~·ment** *n.* sth. to which one has ~ted oneself; promise or undertaking.

com·mit·tee [kəˈmɪtɪ] *n.* group of persons appointed (usu. by a larger group) to attend to special business: *attend a ~ meeting*; *be* (*sit*) *on a ~*.

com·mo·di·ous [kəˈməʊdjəs] *adj.* having plenty of space for what is needed: *a ~ house* (*cupboard*).

com·mod·i·ty [kəˈmɒdɪtɪ] *n.* useful thing, esp. an article of trade: *household commodities*.

com·mo·dore [ˈkɒmədɔː*] *n.* naval officer having rank above a captain and below a rear-admiral.

com·mon [ˈkɒmən] *adj.* **1.** belonging to, used by, coming from, done by, affecting, (nearly) all members of a group: *a ~ language*; ~ *law* (in England) unwritten law derived from old customs and past decisions made by judges; ~ *knowledge* (what is known to most persons, esp. in a group). **2.** usual and ordinary; happening or found often and in many places: *a ~ flower*; *the ~ man*, the ordinary or average man; ~ *sense*, practical good sense gained by experience of life. **3.** (of persons and their behaviour) vulgar; rude; of inferior quality: ~ *clothes*. *n.* **1.** (usu. in or near a village) area of grassland for all to use. **2.** *House of C~s*, assembly (lower house of Parliament) of those who are elected by the ~ people. **3.** *in ~*, used by all (of a group); *have in ~ with*, share with; *out of the ~*, unusual. (*be on*) *short ~s*, (have) not enough food. **~·er** *n.* one of the ~ (2) people, not a member of the nobility. **~·ly** *adv.* **'~·place** *n. & adj.* (remark, happening, etc. that is) ordinary or usual. **'~-room** *n.* room in a school, college, etc. set aside for the use of teachers, pupils, or students. **'~·wealth** *n.* State; group of States (esp. *the C~wealth of Australia*) associating politically, etc. for their ~ (1) good. *The* (*British*) *C~wealth* (*of Nations*) (consisting of Great Britain and some of the former British dominions, colonies, etc.).

com·mo·tion [kəˈməʊʃn] *n.* noisy confusion; excitement; violent uprising.

com·mu·nal [ˈkɒmjunl] *adj.* **1.** of or for a community: ~ *disturbances*. **2.** for common use: ~ *land* (*kitchens*).

com·mune¹ [kəˈmjuːn] *v.i.* feel at one with; feel in close touch with; talk with in an intimate way: ~ *with nature* (*one's friends*).

com·mune² [ˈkɒmjuːn] *n.* group of persons living together and usu. sharing work, expenses, property, etc. **com·mu·nard** [ˈkɒmjuːnɑːd] *n.* member or inhabitant of a ~.

com·mu·ni·cate [kəˈmjuːnɪkeɪt] *v.t. & i.* **1.** pass on (news, opinions, feelings, heat, motion, a disease, etc.) (*to* sb.).

2. share or exchange (news, etc.) (*with sb.*). **3.** (of rooms, gardens, roads, etc.) be connected (*with*) (by means of doors, gates, etc.). **4.** take Holy Communion. **com·mu·ni·cable** [kə'mju:-nɪkəbl] *adj.* that can be ⁓d (e.g. ideas, disease). **com·mu·ni·ca·tion** [kə-ˌmju:nɪ'keɪʃn] *n.* **1.** act of communicating. **2.** that which is ⁓d (esp. news). **3.** means of communicating; road, railway, telegraph, telephone, etc. that connect places, radio and television: *communications with the north*; *telegraphic communications*. **com·mu·ni·ca·tive** [kə'mju:nɪkətɪv] *adj.* ready and willing to talk and give information. **com·mu·nion** [kə'mju:njən] *n.* **1.** sharing. **2.** group of persons with the same religious beliefs. **3.** exchange of thoughts, feelings, etc. **4.** *Holy C⁓*, (in the Christian Church) celebration of the Lord's Supper.

com·mu·ni·que [kə'mju:nɪkeɪ] *n.* official statement or announcement.

com·mu·nism ['kɒmjʊnɪzəm] *n.* (no pl.) **1.** (belief in the) social system in which property is owned by the community and used for the good of all its members. **2.** (usu. *C⁓*) political system (as in U.S.S.R.) in which all power is held by the highest members of the Communist Party, which controls the land and its resources, the means of production, transport, etc., and directs the activities of the people. **com·mu·nist** ['kɒmjʊnɪst] *n.* believer in, supporter of, ⁓. *adj.* of ⁓.

com·mu·ni·ty [kə'mju:nətɪ] *n.* **1.** *the ⁓*, the people living in one place, district: *work for the good of the ⁓.* **2.** group of persons having the same religion, race, occupation, interests, etc.: *the Jewish ⁓ in London.* **3.** condition of sharing, having things in common, being alike in some way: *⁓ of race (religion, etc.);* *⁓ singing* (in which all those present join).

com·mute [kə'mju:t] *v.t. & i.* **1.** exchange (one thing for another); change (one kind of payment *into, for,* another). **2.** change (one punishment for another, less severe): *⁓ the death penalty* (e.g. by substituting 20 years' imprisonment). **3.** travel daily, esp. by train or car, to and from one's work in a city, etc. **com·mu·ta·tion** [ˌkɒm-ju:'teɪʃn] *n.* commuting. *commutation ticket* (U.S.A.) = season-ticket. **com·mut·er** *n.* person who ⁓s (3).

com·pact¹ ['kɒmpækt] *n.* agreement between parties.

com·pact² [kəm'pækt] *adj.* neatly

fitted; closely packed together. *⁓·ly adv.* *⁓·ness n.* (no pl.).

com·pact³ ['kɒmpækt] *n.* small, flat case for face-powder, carried in a handbag.

com·pan·ion¹ [kəm'pænjən] *n.* **1.** person who goes with, or is often or always with, another: *⁓s on a journey.* **2.** friendly, likeable person, esp. one with similar interests, tastes, etc. **3.** one of two things that go together; one thing that matches another: *the ⁓ to a glove or sock.* **4.** person (usu. a woman) paid to live with an old or sick person. **5.** handbook or reference book: *the Gardener's C⁓.* *⁓·able adj.* friendly; sociable. *⁓·ship n.* (no pl.).

com·pan·ion² [kəm'pænjən] *n.* (usu. *⁓-way*) staircase from the deck to cabins in a ship.

com·pa·ny ['kʌmpənɪ] *n.* **1.** being together with another or others: *have the pleasure of sb.'s ⁓ on a journey; keep (bear) sb. ⁓,* be or go with him; *part ⁓ (with),* separate; *in ⁓ (with),* together (with); *be good (poor, etc.) ⁓,* be entertaining (boring). **2.** number of persons; visitors; guests. **3.** companion(s)¹ (1, 2): *get into bad ⁓.* **4.** number of persons united for business or commerce: *a steamship ⁓; John Smith & Co.* **5.** number of persons working together: *the ship's ⁓,* the crew; *a theatrical ⁓; a ⁓ of actors.* **6.** subdivision of an infantry battalion commanded by a captain or major.

com·par·able ['kɒmpərəbl] *adj.* that can be compared (*to, with*).

com·par·a·tive [kəm'pærətɪv] *adj.* **1.** of comparison or comparing: *the ⁓ method of science (studying, etc.).* **2.** measured by comparing: *living in ⁓ comfort* (i.e. as compared with other persons or with previous times). **3.** (gram.) form of adjectives and adverbs expressing 'more', as in *worse, better, more prettily.* *n.* (gram.) ⁓ degree or form. *⁓·ly adv.*

com·pare [kəm'peə*] *v.t. & i.* **1.** examine, judge, say, how far persons or things are similar or not similar: *⁓ two translations.* **2.** *⁓ to,* point out the likeness or relation between: *⁓ death to sleep. Yours is not to be ⁓d to mine* (i.e. is quite different). **3.** *⁓ with,* bear comparison: *This cannot ⁓ with that* (is far different from that). **4.** (gram.) form the comparative and superlative degrees of adjectives and adverbs (usu. by adding *-er, -est,* or *more, most*). *n.* comparison: chiefly in *beyond (without, past) ⁓.*

com·par·i·son [kəmˈpærɪsn] *n.* **1.** act of comparing; statement which compares: *the ～ of the heart to a pump*; *in ～ with*, when compared with; *by ～*, when compared; *can bear (stand) ～ with*, can be compared favourably with. **2.** *degrees of ～* (for adjectives and adverbs), (gram.) positive, comparative, superlative (e.g. *bad, worse, worst*).

com·part·ment [kəmˈpɑːtmənt] *n.* one of several separate divisions of a structure, esp. of a railway carriage: *the second-class ～s*; *a watertight ～* (in a ship).

com·pass [ˈkʌmpəs] *n.* **1.** instrument with a needle that points north. **2.** (pl.) instrument for drawing circles. **3.** range; extent.

a compass (1)

(a pair of)
compasses (2)

com·pas·sion [kəmˈpæʃn] *n.* (no pl.) pity; feeling for the suffering of others, prompting one to give help: *filled with ～ for*; *take ～ on*. **～·ate** [kəmˈpæʃənət] *adj.* having ～.

com·pat·i·ble [kəmˈpætəbl] *adj.* (of ideas, arguments, etc.) in accord with, suited to, agreeing with, each other: *pleasure ～ with duty*. **com·pat·i·bil·i·ty** [kəmˌpætəˈbɪlətɪ] *n.* (no pl.).

com·pa·tri·ot [kəmˈpætrɪət] *n.* person born in or citizen of the same country as another person; fellow-countryman.

com·pel [kəmˈpel] *v.t.* (-ll-) force (sb. to do sth.); get a result by force.

com·pen·di·ous [kəmˈpendɪəs] *adj.* giving much information briefly.

com·pen·sate [ˈkɒmpenseɪt] *v.t. & i.* make suitable payment to, give sth. to make up (*for* loss, injury, etc.). **com·pen·sa·tion** [ˌkɒmpenˈseɪʃn] *n.* compensating; sth. given to ～.

com·père [ˈkɒmpeə*] *n.* (Gt. Brit.) organizer of a variety show or broadcast entertainment who introduces the performers, etc. *v.t.* act as a ～ to.

com·pete [kəmˈpiːt] *v.i.* take part in a race, an examination, etc.: *～ in a race (for a prize, with or against others).*

com·pe·ti·tion [ˌkɒmpɪˈtɪʃn] *n.* competing; any activity in which persons ～: *trade competition between countries*; *in competition with the world's best athletes*; *swimming competitions*. **com·pet·i·tive** [kəmˈpetɪtɪv] *adj.* in or for which there is competition: *competitive examinations for government posts*. **com·pet·i·tor** [kəmˈpetɪtə*] *n.* person who ～s.

com·pe·tent [ˈkɒmpɪtənt] *adj.* **1.** having power, authority, skill, knowledge, etc. to do what is needed: *The magistrate is ～ to try this case. The teacher is ～ for (in) her work.* **2.** adequate: *a ～ knowledge of English.* **com·pe·tence, -ten·cy** [ˈkɒmpɪtəns(ɪ)] *ns.* **1.** being ～; ability. **2.** income large enough for a person to live on in comfort. **3.** (of a court, etc.) legal power or capacity.

com·pile [kəmˈpaɪl] *v.t.* collect (information) and arrange (in a book, etc.): *～ a guidebook (a dictionary, an index).* **com·pi·la·tion** [ˌkɒmpɪˈleɪʃn] *n.* thing ～d; act of compiling.

com·pla·cent [kəmˈpleɪsnt] *adj.* satisfied with oneself. **com·pla·cence, -cen·cy** [kəmˈpleɪsns(ɪ)] *ns.* self-satisfaction.

com·plain [kəmˈpleɪn] *v.i.* ～ (*to sb. about* or *of sth.*) say that one is not satisfied, that sth. is wrong, that one is suffering in some way: *He ～ed of having (that he had) too much work.* **～·ant** *n.* (law) plaintiff. **～t** [kəmˈpleɪnt] *n.* **1.** ～ing; statement of, grounds for, dissatisfaction: *make (lodge) a ～t against sb.* **2.** illness or disease: *a heart ～t.*

com·plai·sant [kəmˈpleɪzənt] *adj.* ready and willing to do what is pleasing to others; obliging. **com·plai·sance** *n.* (no pl.).

com·ple·ment [ˈkɒmplɪmənt] *n.* **1.** that which makes sth. complete; full number or quantity needed. **2.** (gram.) word(s) completing the predicate. **com·ple·men·ta·ry** [ˌkɒmplɪˈmentərɪ] *adj.* serving to complete: *～ary colours* (giving white when mixed).

com·plete [kəmˈpliːt] *adj.* **1.** having all its parts; whole. **2.** finished; ended. **3.** thorough; in every way: *a ～ surprise*; *a ～ stranger. v.t.* finish; bring to an end; make perfect. **～·ly** *adv.* **com·ple·tion** [kəmˈpliːʃn] *n.* (no pl.) act of completing; state of being ～.

com·plex [ˈkɒmpleks] *adj.* made up of many parts; difficult to explain: *a ～ argument (situation). n.* (pl. *～es*) ～ thing; (psych.) abnormal behaviour or mental state caused by past experiences, repressed ideas, etc. ~·i·ty *n.* [kəm'pleksəti] state of being ~; sth. that is ~.

com·plex·ion [kəm'plekʃn] *n.* **1.** natural colour, appearance, etc. of the skin, esp. of the face. **2.** general character or aspect (of conduct, events, etc.).

com·pli·ance [kəm'plaɪəns] *n.* (no pl.) action of complying: *in ~ with,* complying with. **com·pli·ant** *adj.* ready to comply.

com·pli·cate ['kɒmplɪkeɪt] *v.t.* make complex; make (sth.) difficult to do or understand. **com·pli·cat·ed** *adj.* made up of many parts; complex: *a ~d machine.* **com·pli·ca·tion** [ˌkɒmplɪ-'keɪʃn] *n.* **1.** state of being complex, confused, difficult. **2.** that which makes an illness or other trouble more difficult or serious.

com·plic·i·ty [kəm'plɪsəti] *n.* (no pl.) taking part with another person (in crime or other wrongdoing).

com·pli·ment ['kɒmplɪmənt] *n.* **1.** expression of admiration, approval, etc., either in words or by action (e.g. by asking for sb.'s opinion or advice). **2.** (pl.) greetings: '*My ~s to your husband.*' ['kɒmplɪment] *v.t.* pay a ~ to (sb. *on* sth.). **com·pli·men·ta·ry** [ˌkɒmplɪ'mentərɪ] *adj.* **1.** expressing admiration, praise, etc. **2.** *~ary ticket,* ticket given free.

com·ply [kəm'plaɪ] *v.i.* ~ *with,* act in accordance with (a demand, an order, a rule, etc.).

com·po·nent [kəm'pəʊnənt] *adj.* helping to form (a complete thing). *n.* ~ part.

com·port [kəm'pɔːt] *v.t. & i.* ~ *oneself,* behave; ~ *with,* be in harmony with.

com·pose [kəm'pəʊz] *v.t. & i.* **1.** (usu. in the passive): *be ~d of,* be made up of (parts). **2.** put together (words, ideas, musical notes, etc.) in literary, musical, etc. form: ~ *a letter* (*speech, poem, sentence, song, symphony*). *He also ~s* (writes music). **3.** (printing) set up (type) to form words, paragraphs, pages, etc. **4.** get under control; calm: ~ *oneself* (*one's thoughts, passions*); settle: ~ *a quarrel* (*difference of opinion*).

com·posed *adj.* with feelings under control; calm. **com·pos·ed·ly** [kəm-'pəʊzɪdlɪ] *adv.* **com·pos·er** *n.* (esp.) person who ~s music. **com·pos·i·tor** [kəm'pɒzɪtə*] *n.* person who ~s type for printing.

com·pos·ite ['kɒmpəzɪt] *adj.* made up of different parts or materials.

com·po·si·tion [ˌkɒmpə'zɪʃn] *n.* **1.** act

or art of composing. **2.** that which is composed (e.g. a poem, book, or music); exercise in writing prose; arrangement of objects. **3.** nature of, way of arranging, the parts of which sth. is composed: *the ~ of the soil* (*a picture*). **4.** substance composed of more than one material, esp. an artificial substance.

com·post ['kɒmpɒst] *n.* (no pl.) manure made from decayed vegetable stuff, dead leaves, etc.: ~ *heap* (*pile*). *v.t.* make into ~; treat with ~.

com·po·sure [kəm'pəʊʒə*] *n.* (no pl.) condition of being composed in mind; calmness (of mind or behaviour).

com·pote ['kɒmpɒt] *n.* fruit cooked with sugar in water.

com·pound¹ ['kɒmpaʊnd] *n. & adj.* (sth.) made up of two or more parts. The word *bus-driver* is a ~. *chemical ~,* a combination of elements; ~ *interest,* interest reckoned on the capital and on interest already accumulated. [kəm-'paʊnd] *v.t. & i.* mix together (to make sth. different): ~ *a medicine*; settle (e.g. a debt by part payment); come to terms (*with* sb., *for* sth.).

com·pound² ['kɒmpaʊnd] *n.* (in India, China, etc.) enclosed area with buildings, etc. esp. one used as a trading or commercial centre; large fenced¹ or walled-in area (as for prisoners, cattle, etc.).

com·pre·hend [ˌkɒmprɪ'hend] *v.t.* **1.** understand fully. **2.** include. **com·pre·hen·sible** [ˌkɒmprɪ'hensəbl] *adj.* that can be ~ed. **com·pre·hen·sion** [ˌkɒmprɪ'henʃn] *n.* **1.** act or power of understanding. **2.** exercise testing one's understanding of a language. **com·pre·hen·sive** [ˌkɒmprɪ-'hensɪv] *adj.* that ~s (2) much. *comprehensive* (*school*), large secondary school that provides (1) all types of secondary education.

com·press [kəm'pres] *v.t.* **1.** press together; get into a small(er) space: ~ed *air.* **2.** (of writings, ideas) condense; get into fewer words. ['kɒmpres] *n.* pad of cloth pressed on to a part of the body (to stop bleeding, reduce fever, etc.). **com·pres·sion** [kəm'preʃn] *n.* **com·pres·sor** [kəm'presə*] *n.* machine that ~es gases.

com·prise [kəm'praɪz] *v.t.* include; have as parts.

com·pro·mise ['kɒmprəmaɪz] *n.* settlement of a disagreement by which each side gives up sth. it has asked for and neither side gets all it has asked for. *v.t. & i.* **1.** settle a disagreement, quarrel, etc. by making a ~. **2.** bring (sb.) under suspicion or into danger by unwise behaviour, etc.

comp·trol·ler [kən'trəʊlə*] *n.* controller: ~ *of accounts.*

com·pul·sion [kəm'pʌlʃn] *n.* (no pl.) compelling or being compelled: *under ~, because one is forced or compelled.* **com·pul·sive** [kəm'pʌlsɪv] *adj.* having the power to compel; of, relating to, caused by, psychological ~ or obsession. **com·pul·so·ry** [kəm'pʌlsərɪ] *adj.* that must be done.

com·punc·tion [kəm'pʌŋkʃn] *n.* (no pl.) uneasiness of conscience; feeling of doubt about, or regret for, one's action: *disobey one's superior without the slightest ~.*

com·pute [kəm'pjuːt] *v.t. & i.* reckon; calculate. **com·pu·ta·tion** [ˌkɒmpjuː'teɪʃn] *n.* **com·put·er** [kəm'pjuːtə*] *n.* electronic apparatus (1) that stores information on discs or magnetic tapes, analyses it, and produces information as required from the data (2) on the tapes, etc.: ~*r language.* **com·put·er·ize** [kəm'pjuːtəraɪz] *v.t.* analyse, control, or supply with ~rs.

com·rade ['kɒmreɪd] *n.* **1.** trusted companion; loyal friend. **2.** fellow member of a trade union, etc. **3.** communist; used also as a form of address. **~·ship** *n.*

con¹ [kɒn] *v.t.* (*-nn-*) (often ~ *over*) learn by heart; study: ~ *one's lessons.*

con² [kɒn] *n.* (no pl.) (sl., abbr. for) confidence. ~ *man,* confidence man. *v.t.* (*-nn-*) (sl.) swindle; coax (sb. *into* doing sth.).

con·cave [ˌkɒn'keɪv] *adj.* (of an outline or surface) curved inwards like the inside of a circle or ball. (See diagram at *convex.*) **con·cav·i·ty** [kɒn'kævətɪ] *n.*

con·ceal [kən'siːl] *v.t.* hide; keep secret. ~·ment *n.* act, state of, hiding: *stay in ~ment.*

con·cede [kən'siːd] *v.t.* **1.** admit or allow (a point in an argument, that sth. is true). **2.** allow (a person, country, etc.) to have (a right, privilege, etc.). **con·ces·sion** [kən'seʃn] *n.* conceding; right ~d by an owner of ground (e.g. to take minerals from it); sth. ~d.

con·ceit [kən'siːt] *n.* (no pl.) over-high opinion of, too much pride in, oneself or one's powers, abilities, etc. ~·ed *adj.* full of ~.

con·ceive [kən'siːv] *v.t. & i.* **1.** (of a woman) become pregnant. **2.** form (an idea, plan, etc.) in the mind: *a well-~d scheme.* **con·ceiv·able** *adj.* that can be ~d (2) or believed.

con·cen·trate ['kɒnsəntreɪt] *v.t. & i.* **1.** bring or come together at one point: ~ *soldiers in a town* (*one's attention on one's work*). **2.** increase the strength of (a solution) by reducing its volume (e.g. by boiling). **con·cen·tra·tion** [ˌkɒnsən'treɪʃn] *n.* concentrating or being ~d; power of concentrating; that which is ~d. *concentration camp,* place where civilian political prisoners are confined.

con·cen·tric [kən'sentrɪk] *adj.* having a common centre (*with* another circle, etc.).

con·cept ['kɒnsept] *n.* idea underlying a class of things; general notion. **con·cep·tion** [kən'sepʃn] *n.* **1.** (act of forming an) idea or plan: *have a clear ~ion of what must be done; great powers of ~ion.* **2.** conceiving (1).

con·cern [kən'sɜːn] *v.t.* **1.** have relation to; be about; be of importance to: *Does this ~ me? As* (*So*) *far as I'm ~ed ...* (i.e. so far as the matter affects me, or is important to me); *be ~ed in a crime, etc.,* have some part in it. **2.** ~ *oneself with* (*in, about*), take an interest in; be busy with. **3.** ~*ed about,* made unhappy or troubled: *be ~ed about the future* (*at the news, etc.*). *n.* **1.** relation; connection; reference; sth. in which one is interested or which is important to one: *It's no ~ of yours.* **2.** business or undertaking. **3.** share: *have a ~ in a business.* **4.** anxiety: *filled with ~; ask with deep ~.* ~·ing *prep.* about.

con·cert ['kɒnsət] *n.* **1.** musical entertainment, esp. one given in public by players or singers. **2.** *in ~* (*with*), in agreement or harmony; together. ~·ed [kən'sɜːtɪd] *adj.* planned, designed, performed, by two or more together: ~*ed action; a ~ed attack.*

con·cer·ti·na [ˌkɒnsə'tiːnə] *n.* musical wind instrument consisting of a pair of bellows and with keys at each end.

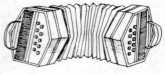

a concertina

con·cer·to [kən'tʃeətəʊ] *n.* (pl. *-tos, -ti*) composition for one or more solo instruments supported by an orchestra: *a piano ~.*

con·ces·sion, see *concede.*

con·cil·i·ate [kən'sɪlɪeɪt] *v.t.* win the support, goodwill, or friendly feelings of; calm sb.'s anger; soothe. **con·cil·i·a·tion** [kən,sɪlɪ'eɪʃn] *n.* (no pl.) **con·cil·ia·to·ry** [kən'sɪlɪətərɪ] *adj.*

con·cise [kən'saɪs] *adj.* (of a person, his speech, or style of writing, etc.) brief; giving much information in few words. ~·**ly** *adv.* ~·**ness** *n.* (no pl.).

con·clave ['kɒnkleɪv] *n.* private or secret meeting: *sitting in* ~.

con·clude [kən'kluːd] *v.t. & i.* **1.** come or bring to an end: ~ *a speech*; ~ *a concert with the National Anthem. The meeting* ~*d at eight o'clock.* **2.** bring about; arrange: ~ *a treaty of peace.* **3.** arrive at the evidence, that ... **con·clu·sion** [kən'kluːʒn] *n.* **1.** end: *in conclusion,* lastly. **2.** belief or opinion that is the result of reasoning: *come to the conclusion that ...* **3.** decision; settling (*of* sth.). **con·clu·sive** [kən'kluːsɪv] *adj.* (of facts, evidence, etc.) ending doubt. **con·clu·sive·ly** *adv.*

con·coct [kən'kɒkt] *v.t.* **1.** prepare by mixing together: ~ *a new kind of soup.* **2.** invent (a story, excuse, etc.). **con·coc·tion** [kən'kɒkʃn] *n.*

con·cord ['kɒŋkɔːd] *n.* agreement or harmony (between persons or things). **con·cor·dance** [kən'kɔːdəns] *n.* **1.** agreement. **2.** arrangement in ABC order of the important words used by an author or in a book: *a Bible (Shakespeare)* ~*ance.* **con·cor·dant** [kən'kɔːdənt] *adj.* agreeing (*with*).

con·course ['kɒŋkɔːs] *n.* coming or moving together of things or persons; crowd of people.

con·crete ['kɒnkriːt] *adj.* of material things; existing in material form. ~ *noun,* (gram.) name of a thing, not of a quality. *n.* (no pl.) building material made by mixing cement with sand, gravel, etc.: ~ *walls (roads, etc.). v.t.* cover with ~.

con·cu·bine ['kɒŋkjʊbaɪn] *n.* woman who lives with a man as his wife although not lawfully married to him; (in some countries, where polygamy is allowed) lesser wife.

con·cur [kən'kɜː*] *v.i.* (-*rr*-) **1.** agree in opinion (*with* sb., *in* sth.). **2.** happen together. ~·**rence** [kən'kʌrəns] *n.* agreement. ~·**rent** [kən'kʌrənt] *adj.* ~·ring.

con·cus·sion [kən'kʌʃn] *n.* violent shaking or shock; (med.) injury (to the brain) caused by a blow, knock, or fall.

con·demn [kən'dem] *v.t.* **1.** say that sb. is, or has done, wrong or that sth.

is faulty or unfit for use. **2.** (law) give judgement against: ~ *a murderer to imprisonment for life.* **3.** doom; send, appoint (to sth. unhappy or painful): ~*ed to suffer a life of pain.* **con·dem·na·tion** [,kɒndem'neɪʃn] *n.* (no pl.).

con·den·sa·tion [,kɒnden'seɪʃn] *n.* condensing; drops of liquid (e.g. dew) formed when vapour condenses.

con·dense [kən'dens] *v.t. & i.* **1.** (cause to) increase in density or strength; (of a gas or vapour) (cause to) become liquid; (of a liquid) (cause to) become thicker: ~*d milk.* **2.** put into fewer words: ~ *a* ~*d account of an event.* **con·dens·er** *n.* apparatus (1) for condensing (e.g. steam into water, or electricity until it has the power needed).

con·de·scend [,kɒndɪ'send] *v.i.* **1.** (genuinely or falsely) behave to sb. of inferior position, ability, etc. as if he were one's equal. **2.** lower oneself to do sth. unworthy. **3.** act in a patronizing (2) manner. **con·de·scen·sion** [,kɒndɪ'senʃn] *n.*

con·di·ment ['kɒndɪmənt] *n.* sth. (e.g. pepper) tasting hot or salty added to food to flavour it.

con·di·tion [kən'dɪʃn] *n.* **1.** sth. needed before sth. else is possible; sth. on which another thing depends: *on* ~ *that,* only if; provided that; *on this (that, no)* ~. **2.** present state of being; nature, character, quality of sth. or sb.: *The* ~ *of my health prevents me from working. Everything arrived in good* ~ (i.e. unbroken, undamaged, fit for use). *in (out of)* ~, in good (bad) ~. **3.** (pl.) circumstances: *under existing* ~*s* (i.e. while things are as they now are); *under favourable* ~*s.* **4.** position in society: *persons of every* ~ (i.e. of all ranks). *v.t.* determine; place ~*s* upon; govern; control: *Your expenditure is* ~*ed by your income.* ~·**al** [kən'dɪʃənl] *adj.* depending *on,* containing, a ~: (gram.) *a* ~*al clause* (beginning with 'if' or 'unless').

con·dole [kən'dəʊl] *v.i.* express sympathy (*with* sb., *on* or *upon* a loss, misfortune, etc.). **con·do·lence** [kən'dəʊləns] *n.* (often pl.) expression of sympathy.

con·done [kən'dəʊn] *v.t.* (of a person) overlook or forgive (an offence); (of an act) make up for, atone for: *a fact that* ~*s his failure to help.*

con·dor ['kɒndɔː*] *n.* large kind of vulture (in S. America).

con·duce [kən'djuːs] *v.i.* ~ *to,* help to produce, contribute to (a result): *Does* *wealth ~ to happiness?* **con·du·cive** [kən'djuːsɪv] *adj.*

con·duct ['kɒndʌkt] *n.* (no pl.) **1.** behaviour (esp. moral): *good and bad ~.* **2.** manner of directing or managing affairs, business, etc. [kən'dʌkt] *v.t. & i.* **1.** lead; guide: *~ visitors round a museum; a ~ed tour.* **2.** control; manage; direct: *~ a meeting; ~ an orchestra* (i.e. guide and control the players). **3.** ~ *oneself,* behave (*well, etc.*). **4.** (of substances) transmit; allow (heat, electric current) to pass along or through. **con·duc·tion** [kən'dʌkʃn] *n.* ~ing (4) of heat, etc. **con·duc·tiv·i·ty** *n.* property (3) of ~ing (4) some form of energy, e.g. electricity. **con·duc·tor** *n.* **1.** person who ~s (1, 2); person on a bus, tram, etc. who collects fares; (U.S.A.) person in charge of a train. **2.** substance that ~s (4) heat or electric current. **con·duc·tress** [kən'dʌktrɪs] *n.* woman ~or, esp. on a bus, etc.

con·duit ['kɒndɪt] *n.* large pipe or waterway; tube covering electric wires, etc.

cone [kəʊn] *n.* **1.** solid figure that narrows to a point from a round, flat base. **2.** sth. of this shape, whether solid or hollow. **3.** fruit of certain evergreen trees (fir, pine, cedar). **con·ic** ['kɒnɪk] *adj.* of a ~ (1). **con·i·cal** ['kɒnɪkl] *adj.* ~-shaped.

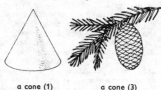

a cone (1)   a cone (3)

con·fec·tion [kən'fekʃn] *n.* mixture of sweet things; sweet cake. **~·er** *n.* person who makes and sells cakes, etc. **~·ery** *n.* cakes, pastries, pies, sweets, etc.; ~er's shop.

con·fed·er·ate [kən'fedərət] *adj.* joined together by an agreement or treaty. *n.* person who joins with another or others (esp. in wrongdoing). **con·fed·er·a·cy** [kən'fedərəsɪ] *n.* group of ~ persons or States; *the Confederacy,* the eleven southern States that separated from the U.S.A. in 1860 and 1861. **con·fed·er·a·tion** [kən,fedə'reɪʃn] *n.* uniting or being united; alliance.

con·fer [kən'fɜː*] *v.t. & i.* (-rr-) **1.** give or grant (a right, title, favour): *~ a*

knighthood on sb. **2.** consult or discuss (*with*): *~ with a lawyer.* **~·ence** ['kɒnfərəns] *n.* (meeting for) discussion, consultation.

con·fess [kən'fes] *v.t. & i.* **1.** acknowledge; admit (that one has done wrong). **2.** tell one's sins or faults to a priest (esp. in the Roman Catholic Church); (of a priest) listen to sb. doing this: *John ~ed to the priest. The priest ~ed John.* **con·fess·ed·ly** [kən'fesɪdlɪ] *adv.* as ~ed. **con·fes·sion** [kən'feʃn] *n.* ~ing; what is ~ed: *a ~ion of guilt; go to ~ion* (i.e. to ~ (2) one's sins); *a ~ion of faith* (a declaration of religious or similar beliefs). **con·fes·sion·al** [kən'feʃənl] *n.* private place in a church where a priest sits to hear ~ions. **con·fes·sor** *n.* priest who hears ~ions.

con·fet·ti [kən'fetɪ] *n. pl.* (sing. v.) small bits of coloured paper showered on people at weddings and carnivals.

con·fi·dant(e) [,kɒnfɪ'dænt] *n.* man (woman) who is trusted with one's private affairs or secrets.

con·fide [kən'faɪd] *v.t. & i.* **1.** tell (a secret *to*); give (sth. or sb. *to* sb.) to be looked after; give (a task or duty *to* sb.) to be carried out. **2.** have trust or faith (*in*): *I feel that I can ~ in that man.* **con·fi·dence** ['kɒnfɪdəns] *n.* **1.** (act of) confiding in or to: *take sb. into one's ~nce; in ~nce* (i.e. as a secret). **2.** secret that is ~d to sb.: *exchange ~nces.* **3.** belief in oneself or others, etc.; belief that one is right: *answer questions with ~nce. adj.* of or relating to swindling by false promises: *~nce trick* (U.S.A. *game*); *~nce man.* **con·fi·dent** ['kɒnfɪdənt] *adj.* feeling or showing ~nce; certain: *be ~nt of success; a ~nt manner.* **con·fi·den·tial** [,kɒnfɪ'denʃl] *adj.* **1.** (to be kept) secret; given in ~nce: *~ntial information.* **2.** having the ~nce of another: *my ~ntial secretary.* **3.** (of persons) inclined to ~.

con·fig·u·ra·tion [kən,fɪgjʊ'reɪʃn] *n.* shape or outline; method of arrangement.

con·fine [kən'faɪn] *v.t.* **1.** restrict within limits: *~ oneself to saying* (say only); *~ one's remarks to* (speak only about). **2.** keep shut up: *be ~d to the house by illness.* **3.** *be ~d,* (passive only) be in bed giving birth to a baby: *She expects to be ~d next month.* ['kɒnfaɪn] *n.* (usu. pl.) limit; boundary. **~d** *adj.* (of space) limited; narrow. **~·ment** [kən'faɪnmənt] *n.* being ~d, esp. in giving birth; imprisonment.

con·firm [kən'fɜːm] *v.t.* **1.** make

(power, ownership, opinions, feelings, rights, etc.) firmer or stronger: ~ sth. **2.** ratify; agree definitely to (a treaty, an appointment, etc.). **3.** admit to full membership of the Christian Church. **~ed** adj. (esp.) unlikely to change or be changed: a ~ed bachelor. **con·fir·ma·tion** [ˌkɒnfəˈmeɪʃn] n. ~ing or being ~ed (all senses).

con·fis·cate [ˈkɒnfɪskeɪt] v.t. (as punishment or in enforcing authority) take possession of the private property of sb. without compensation: houses ~d by the government. **con·fis·ca·tion** [ˌkɒnfɪˈskeɪʃn] n.

con·fla·gra·tion [ˌkɒnfləˈɡreɪʃn] n. great fire, esp. one that destroys buildings, forests, etc.

con·flict [ˈkɒnflɪkt] n. **1.** fight; fighting; struggle; quarrel. **2.** (of opinions, desires, etc.) disagreement; difference: a statement that is in ~ with other evidence. [kənˈflɪkt] v.i. be in opposition or disagreement: wishes that ~ with one's duty; ~ing emotions.

con·flu·ence [ˈkɒnfluəns] n. flowing together; (esp.) place where two rivers unite.

con·form [kənˈfɔːm] v.i. & t. be in agreement (with); comply; make similar (to); adapt (to): ~ to the rules (to the wishes of others). **~·able** [kənˈfɔːməbl] adj. similar; obedient: ~able to your wishes. **con·for·ma·tion** [ˌkɒnfɔːˈmeɪʃn] n. way in which sth. is formed or constructed. **~·i·ty** [kənˈfɔːmətɪ] n. (no pl.) agreement; doing what is asked, required, or expected: in ~ity with your request.

con·found [kənˈfaʊnd] v.t. **1.** fill with, throw into, perplexity or confusion. **2.** mix up; confuse (ideas, etc.). **3.** defeat; overthrow (enemies, plans, etc.). **4.** (mild oath): C~ it! C~ you!

con·front [kənˈfrʌnt] v.t. be, come, bring, face to face (with); be opposite to: be ~ed with evidence of one's wrongdoing. **con·fron·ta·tion** [ˌkɒnfrʌnˈteɪʃn] n. state of hostility (e.g. between two States, esp. when likely to lead to war).

con·fuse [kənˈfjuːz] v.t. put into disorder; mix up in the mind; mistake one thing for another. **con·fu·sion** [kənˈfjuːʒn] n. (no pl.) disorder; being ~d.

con·fute [kənˈfjuːt] v.t. prove (a person) to be wrong; show (an argument, etc.) to be false. **con·fu·ta·tion** [ˌkɒnfjuːˈteɪʃn] n.

con·geal [kənˈdʒiːl] v.t. & i. make or become stiff or solid, esp. as the effect of cold or of the air on blood.

con·ge·nial [kənˈdʒiːnjəl] adj. **1.** (of persons) having the same or a similar nature, common interests, etc. **2.** (of things, occupations, etc.) in agreement with one's nature, tastes, etc.: a ~ climate.

con·gen·i·tal [kənˈdʒenɪtl] adj. (of diseases, etc.) present since birth.

con·gest·ed [kənˈdʒestɪd] adj. **1.** overcrowded; too full: streets ~ with traffic. **2.** (of parts of the body, e.g. the brain, lungs) having too much blood. **con·ges·tion** [kənˈdʒestʃən] n. (no pl.).

con·glom·er·ate [kənˈɡlɒmərət] adj. & n. (made up of a) number of things or parts stuck together in a mass or ball. [kənˈɡlɒməreɪt] v.t. & i. collect into a ball or rounded mass. **con·glom·er·a·tion** [kənˌɡlɒməˈreɪʃn] n. conglomerating; being ~d; mass of ~d things.

con·grat·u·late [kənˈɡrætjʊleɪt] v.t. tell (sb.) that one is pleased about sth. happy or fortunate that has come to (him): ~ sb. on his marriage; ~ oneself, consider oneself fortunate. **con·grat·u·la·tion** [kənˌɡrætjʊˈleɪʃn] n. (often pl.) words that ~ sb.

con·gre·gate [ˈkɒŋɡrɪgeɪt] v.i. & t. come or bring together.

con·gre·ga·tion [ˌkɒŋɡrɪˈgeɪʃn] n. (esp.) body (5) of people (usu. except the minister and choir) taking part in a religious service. **~·al** [ˌkɒŋɡrɪˈgeɪʃənl] adj. of a ~; C~al, of the system in which separate churches manage their own affairs.

con·gress [ˈkɒŋɡres] n. **1.** meeting, series of meetings, of representatives (of societies, etc.) for discussions: a medical ~; the Church C~. **2.** C~, law-making body (5) of U.S.A. and some other republics in America; political party in India. **con·gres·sio·nal** [kɒŋˈɡreʃənl] adj. of a ~: ~ional debates.

con·ic, con·i·cal, see cone.

co·ni·fer [ˈkɒnɪfə*] n. tree of the kind (e.g. pine, fir) that bears cones (3). **co·nif·er·ous** [kəʊˈnɪfərəs] adj. (of trees) bearing cones (3).

con·jec·ture [kənˈdʒektʃə*] v.i. & t. & n. (make a) guess; (put forward an) opinion formed without facts as proof. **con·jec·tur·al** [kənˈdʒektʃərəl] adj.

con·ju·gal [ˈkɒndʒʊɡl] adj. of marriage and of wedded life; of husband and wife: ~ happiness.

con·ju·gate [ˈkɒndʒʊɡeɪt] v.t. (gram.) give the forms of a verb (for number, tense, etc.). **con·ju·ga·tion** [ˌkɒndʒʊˈɡeɪʃn] n. (gram.) scheme or system of verb forms; class of verbs ~d alike.

con·junc·tion [kən'dʒʌŋkʃn] *n.* **1.** (gram.) word that joins other words, clauses, etc. (e.g. *and, but*). **2.** state of being joined: *in ~ with*, together with. **3.** combination of events, etc. **con·junc·tive** [kən'dʒʌŋktɪv] *adj.* **1.** serving to join. **2.** (gram.) being or functioning like a ~.

con·jure ['kʌndʒə*] *v.t. & i.* **1.** do clever tricks that appear magical, esp. by quick movements of the hands: *~ a rabbit out of a hat*. **2.** *~ up*, cause to appear as a picture in the mind: *~ up scenes from one's childhood days*. **con·jur·er, con·ju·ror** ['kʌndʒərə*] *n.* person who ~s (1).

con·nect [kə'nekt] *v.t. & i.* **1.** join, be joined: *towns ~ed by a railway*; *the place where the gas-stove and the gas-pipe ~*; *~ed with a family by marriage. This train ~s with the train from London* (i.e. passengers can continue their journey by the train coming from London). **2.** think of (different things or persons) as being related to each other: *~ Malaya with rubber*. **con·nec·tion** (Gt. Brit. also **con·nex·ion**) [kə-'nekʃn] *n.* **1.** ~ing or being ~ed; part that ~s two things: *a bicycle pump ~ion*; *in this (that) ~ion*, with reference to this (that); *in ~ion with*, with reference to. **2.** train, boat, etc. timed to leave a station, port, etc. soon after the arrival of another, enabling passengers to change from one to the other. **3.** number of persons who are regular customers, patients, clients, etc.: *a shop (dressmaker) with a good ~ion among the well-to-do*. **4.** number of people united in a religious organization: *the Methodist ~ion*. **5.** relative (esp. by marriage). **6.** (sl.) supplier of narcotic drugs. **con·nec·tive** *n. & adj.* (word) that ~s (e.g. a conjunction).

con·ning-tow·er ['kɒnɪŋ,tauə*] *n.* raised structure from which a warship, esp. a submarine, is controlled.

con·nive [kə'naɪv] *v.i. ~ at*, pretend not to know about (what is wrong, what ought to be stopped). **con·niv·ance** [kə'naɪvəns] *n.* (no pl.).

con·nois·seur [,kɒnə'sɜ:*] *n.* person with reliable judgement in matters of taste (5): *a ~ of (in) painting (old porcelain, wine, etc.)*.

con·note [kɒ'nəʊt] *v.t.* (of words) suggest in addition to the fundamental meaning: *The word 'tropics' ~s heat*. **con·no·ta·tion** [,kɒnəʊ'teɪʃn] *n.*

con·quer ['kɒŋkə*] *v.t.* **1.** defeat or overcome (enemies, bad habits, etc.). **2.** take possession of by force, esp. in war. *~ or n.* person who ~s. **con·quest** ['kɒŋkwest] *n.* ~ing; sth. got by ~ing *the Roman conquests in Africa*.

con·san·guin·i·ty [,kɒnsæŋ'gwɪnəti] *n.* (no pl.) relationship by blood or birth.

con·science ['kɒnʃəns] *n.* awareness within oneself of the choice one ought to make between right and wrong: *have a clear (guilty) ~; have sth. on one's ~* (i.e. feel troubled in one's ~ about sth.); *~ money* (paid because one has a troubled ~).

con·sci·en·tious [,kɒnʃɪ'enʃəs] *adj.* **1.** guided by one's sense of duty: *a ~ worker*; *~ objector*, (esp.) person who objects to military service because of his religious beliefs, etc. **2.** done as one's sense of duty directs; done carefully and honestly: *~ work*.

con·scious ['kɒnʃəs] *adj.* **1.** awake; aware; knowing things because one is using the bodily senses and mental powers: *be ~ of one's guilt (that one is guilty). The man was knocked down by a bus and was not ~ when we picked him up. A healthy man is not ~ of his breathing*. **2.** (of actions, feelings, etc.) realized by oneself: *act with ~ superiority* (i.e. knowing that one is superior). **3.** *self-~. ~ly adv. ~ness n.* (no pl.) **1.** being ~. **2.** all the ideas, thoughts, feelings, etc. of a person.

con·script [kən'skrɪpt] *v.t.* compel (sb.) by law to serve in the armed forces; summon (call up for) such service. ['kɒnskrɪpt] *n.* person compelled to serve in this way. **con·scrip·tion** [kən'skrɪpʃn] *n.*

con·se·crate ['kɒnsɪkreɪt] *v.t.* set apart as sacred or for a special purpose (*to*); make sacred. **con·se·cra·tion** [,kɒnsɪ-'kreɪʃn] *n.*

con·sec·u·tive [kən'sekjʊtɪv] *adj.* following continuously; coming one after another in regular order: *on three ~ weeks. ~ly adv.*

con·sen·sus [kən'sensəs] *n.* common agreement (*of* opinion, etc.).

con·sent [kən'sent] *v.i. & n.* (no pl.) (give) agreement or permission: *~ to a proposal*.

con·se·quence ['kɒnsɪkwəns] *n.* **1.** that which follows or is brought about as the result or effect of sth.: *in ~ (of)*, as a result (of). **2.** importance: *It's of no ~* (i.e. it is unimportant). **con·se·quent** ['kɒnsɪkwənt] *adj.* following as a ~ (*on*). **con·se·quen·tial** [,kɒnsɪ'kwenʃl] *adj.* following as a ~ (*on*); (of a person) full of self-importance.

con·ser·va·tion [,kɒnsə'veɪʃn] *n.* (no

pl.) preservation; prevention of loss, waste, damage, etc.

con·ser·va·tism [kən'sɜ:vətɪzəm] *n.* (no pl.) tendency to maintain a state of affairs (esp. in politics) without great or sudden changes.

con·ser·va·tive [kən'sɜ:vətɪv] *adj.* 1. opposed to great or sudden change; *the C~ Party* (British political party). 2. cautious; moderate: *a ~ estimate. n. ~ person; C~,* member of the C~ Party.

con·ser·va·to·ry [kən'sɜ:vətrɪ] *n.* building or part of a building with glass walls and roof in which plants are protected from cold.

con·serve [kən'sɜ:v] *v.t.* keep from change, loss, or destruction. *n.* (usu. pl.) jam.

con·sid·er [kən'sɪdə*] *v.t.* 1. think about. 2. take into account; make allowances for: *~ the feelings of others.* 3. be of the opinion; regard as. *~·able* [kən'sɪdərəbl] *adj.* deserving to be ~ed; great; much. *~·ably adv.* much. *~·ate* [kən'sɪdərət] *adj.* thoughtful (of the needs, etc. of others). *~·ation* [kən,sɪdə'reɪʃn] *n.* 1. quality of being ~ate: *in ~ation of his youth.* 2. act of ~ing: *proposals still under ~ation* (i.e. still being thought about). 3. sth. that must be ~ed: *~ations that influenced him in making his plans.* 4. reward; payment. *~·ing prep.* in view of; having regard to.

con·sign [kən'saɪn] *v.t.* 1. send (goods, etc., by rail, etc. *to* sb.). 2. hand over; give up (*to*). *~·ee* [,kɒnsaɪ'ni:] *n.* person to whom sth. is ~ed. *~·ment n. ~ing;* goods ~ed. *~·or n.* person ~ing goods.

con·sist [kən'sɪst] *v.i.* 1. *~ of,* be made up of. 2. *~ in,* have as the chief (or only) element: *Does happiness ~ in wanting little?* **con·sis·ten·cy, -tence** [kən'sɪstəns(ɪ)] *ns.* 1. (always *~ency*) state of being always the same in thought, behaviour, etc. 2. degree of thickness, firmness, or solidity (esp. of a thick liquid or of sth. made by mixing with a liquid): *mix flour and milk to the right ~ency.* **con·sis·tent** *adj.* 1. (of a person, his behaviour, opinions, etc.) constant to the same principles; regular; conforming to a regular pattern or style. 2. in agreement (*with*): *theories not ~ent with the facts.*

con·sole [kən'səʊl] *v.t.* give comfort or sympathy to (sb. who is unhappy, disappointed, etc.). **con·so·la·tion** [,kɒnsə'leɪʃn] *n.* consoling; sth. that ~s.

con·sol·i·date [kən'sɒlɪdeɪt] *v.t. & i.* 1. make or become solid or strong. 2. unite or combine into one: *~ debts*

(*business companies*). **con·sol·i·da·tion** [kən,sɒlɪ'deɪʃn] *n.*

con·so·nant [ˈkɒnsənənt] *n.* speech sound that is not a vowel sound; letter or symbol representing such a sound.

con·sort[1] [ˈkɒnsɔ:t] *n.* husband or wife, esp. of a ruler. *prince ~,* reigning queen's husband.

con·sort[2] [kən'sɔ:t] *v.i. ~ with,* pass much time in the company of; be in harmony with.

con·spic·u·ous [kən'spɪkjʊəs] *adj.* easily seen; attracting attention; remarkable.

con·spire [kən'spaɪə*] *v.i. & t.* 1. make secret plans (*with* others, esp. to do wrong): *~ against the State.* 2. plot: *~ sb.'s downfall.* 3. combine; unite: *events that ~d to bring about his failure.* **con·spir·a·cy** [kən'spɪrəsɪ] *n.* act of conspiring; plan made by conspiring. **con·spir·a·tor** [kən'spɪrətə*] *n.* person who ~s (1, 2).

con·sta·ble [ˈkʌnstəbl] *n.* (Gt. Brit.) policeman. **con·stab·u·lary** [kən'stæbjʊlərɪ] *n.* police force.

con·stan·cy [ˈkɒnstənsɪ] *n.* (no pl.) quality of being firm or unchanging: *~ of purpose.*

con·stant [ˈkɒnstənt] *adj.* 1. going on all the time; never-ending: *~ complaints.* 2. firm; faithful; unchanging. *~·ly adv.* often; always.

con·stel·la·tion [,kɒnstə'leɪʃn] *n.* group of fixed stars.

con·ster·na·tion [,kɒnstə'neɪʃn] *n.* (no pl.) surprise and fear; dismay.

con·sti·pate [ˈkɒnstɪpeɪt] *v.t.* cause **con·sti·pa·tion** [,kɒnstɪ'peɪʃn] *n.* (no pl.) difficulty in emptying the bowels.

con·stit·u·en·cy [kən'stɪtjʊənsɪ] *n.* (persons living in a) town or district sending a representative to Parliament. **con·stit·u·ent** [kən'stɪtjʊənt] *adj.* 1. having the power to make or alter a political constitution. 2. forming or helping to make a whole: *a ~ part. n.* 1. member of a constituency. 2. component part.

con·sti·tute [ˈkɒnstɪtju:t] *v.t.* 1. give (sb.) authority to hold (a position, etc.); appoint (2). 2. establish; give (a committee, etc.) legal authority. 3. make up (a whole); amount to: *This ~s an infringement of the law.*

con·sti·tu·tion [,kɒnstɪ'tju:ʃn] *n.* 1. system of government; laws and principles according to which a State is governed. 2. general physical structure and condition of a person's body. 3. general structure of a thing. 4. person's mental qualities and nature. *~·al*

[ˌkɒnstɪˈtjuːʃənl] *adj.* of a ~ (1): ~*al government*; *a* ~*al ruler* (i.e. controlled or limited by a ~). **2.** of a person's ~ (2): *a* ~*al weakness*. *n.* regular walk taken for the sake of one's health. ~**·al·ism** [ˌkɒnstɪˈtjuːʃnəlɪzəm] *n.* (belief in) ~al government.

con·strain [kənˈstreɪn] *v.t.* make (sb.) do sth. by using force or strong persuasion; compel. ~**ed** *adj.* (of voice, manner, etc.) forced; unnatural; uneasy. ~**t** [kənˈstreɪnt] *n.* (no pl.) ~ing or being ~ed: *act under* ~*t*.

con·strict [kənˈstrɪkt] *v.t.* make tight or smaller; cause (a vein or muscle) to become tight or narrow. **con·stric·tion** [kənˈstrɪkʃn] *n.*

con·struct [kənˈstrʌkt] *v.t.* build; put or fit together: ~ *a factory* (*an aircraft, a sentence*). **con·struc·tor** *n.* **con·struc·tion** [kənˈstrʌkʃn] *n.* **1.** act or manner of ~ing; being ~ed: *a railway that is under* (*in the course of*) ~*ion.* ~*ion worker*, worker whose occupation is to ~ houses, etc. **2.** sth. ~ed. **3.** meaning; sense in which words, acts, etc. are taken: *put a wrong* ~*ion on what sb. says or does.* **con·struc·tive** *adj.* helping to ~; giving suggestions that help.

con·strue [kənˈstruː] *v.t.* **1.** translate or explain the meaning of (words, sentences, acts). **2.** (gram.) analyse a sentence); combine (words *with* words) grammatically.

con·sul [ˈkɒnsəl] *n.* **1.** State's agent living in a foreign town to help and protect his countrymen there. **2.** (in ancient Rome) one of the two heads of the State before Rome became an empire. **3.** one of the three chief magistrates of the French Republic from 1799 to 1804. ~**·ar** [ˈkɒnsjʊlə*] *adj.* of a ~ or his work. ~**·ate** [ˈkɒnsjʊlət] *n.* ~'s (1) position; ~'s (1) office(s).

con·sult [kənˈsʌlt] *v.t. & i.* **1.** go to (a person, book) for information, advice, opinion, etc.: ~ *one's lawyer* (*a map, etc.*). ~*ing hours*, time during which doctors may be ~ed by their patients. ~*ing room*, room in which doctors examine their patients. **2.** consider; take into account: ~ *sb.'s convenience.* **3.** ~ (*with*), take counsel; confer (2). **con·sul·tant** [kənˈsʌltənt] *n.* expert (e.g. a physician) ~ed for special advice. **con·sul·ta·tion** [ˌkɒnsəlˈteɪʃn] *n.* ~ing; meeting for ~ing.

con·sume [kənˈsjuːm] *v.t. & i.* **1.** eat or drink. **2.** use up; get to the end of. **3.** destroy (by fire, wasting). **4.** *be* ~*d with*, be filled with (desire, envy, grief, etc.). **5.** ~ *away*, waste away. **con·sum·er** *n.* (opp. *producer*) person who uses goods: ~*r goods*, (opp. *capital²* (3) *goods*) commodities such as food and clothing that directly satisfy one's needs.

con·sum·mate [kənˈsʌmɪt] *adj.* complete; perfect: ~ *skill* (*taste*). [ˈkɒnsəmeɪt] *v.t.* make perfect or complete; bring to a perfect finish. **con·sum·ma·tion** [ˌkɒnsəˈmeɪʃn] *n.*

con·sump·tion [kənˈsʌmpʃn] *n.* (no pl.) **1.** using up, consuming (of food, energy, materials, etc.); amount consumed. **2.** disease in which there is a wasting away of part of the body, esp. of the lungs; tuberculosis. **con·sump·tive** [kənˈsʌmptɪv] *adj.* suffering from, having a tendency to, ~ (2). *n.* sufferer from ~ (2).

con·tact [ˈkɒntækt] *n.* (state of) touching or coming together: *be in* ~ *with sb.* (i.e. in communication, exchanging news, views, etc.). ~ *lens*, small lens worn on the eyeball to improve vision. *v.t.* get into touch with: *You ought to* ~ *the police at once.*

con·ta·gion [kənˈteɪdʒən] *n.* the spreading of disease by contact; (fig.) the spreading of evil ideas, false rumours, feelings, etc. **con·ta·gious** [kənˈteɪdʒəs] *adj.* (of disease) spreading by contact; (fig.) spreading easily by example: *contagious laughter* (*gloom*).

con·tain [kənˈteɪn] *v.t.* **1.** have or hold within itself: *The bag* ~*s 14 lb. of potatoes. Whisky* ~*s alcohol.* **2.** keep (feelings, enemy force, etc.) under control, within limits. **3.** (geom.) form the boundary of. ~**·er** *n.* **1.** box, bottle, etc. made to ~ (1) sth. **2.** large, standard (2), metal box, used for transporting goods by road, rail, sea, or air. ~**·er·ize** [kənˈteɪnəraɪz] *v.t.* **1.** pack in and transport by a ~er (2). **2.** equip (a ship, etc.) to carry goods packed in ~ers (2). ~**·er·iza·tion** [kənˌteɪnəraɪˈzeɪʃn] *n.* (no pl.).

con·tam·i·nate [kənˈtæmɪneɪt] *v.t.* make dirty, impure, or diseased. **con·tam·i·na·tion** [kənˌtæmɪˈneɪʃn] *n.*

con·tem·plate [ˈkɒntempleɪt] *v.t. & i.* **1.** look at (with the eyes or in the mind). **2.** have in view as a purpose, intention, or possibility. **3.** muse; meditate. **con·tem·pla·tion** [ˌkɒntemˈpleɪʃn] *n.* (no pl.). **con·tem·pla·tive** [ˈkɒntempleɪtɪv] *adj.* thoughtful; fond of contemplation.

con·tem·po·rary [kənˈtempərərɪ] *adj.* of the time or period to which reference is being made; belonging to the same time: *a* ~ *record of events* (i.e. one made by persons then living). **n.** person ~ with another: *John and I were contemporaries at college.* **con·tem·po·ra·ne·ous** [kən͵tempə'reɪnjəs] *adj.* existing, happening, at the same time (*with*).

con·tempt [kən'tempt] *n.* (no pl.) **1.** condition of being looked down upon or despised: *fall into ~ by foolish or bad behaviour.* **2.** mental attitude of despising; disregard; disrespect: *feel ~ for a liar; show one's ~ of danger or death in battle.* **3.** ~ *of court,* act disobeying an order made by a court of law; disrespect shown to a judge. **~·ible** *adj.* rightly deserving ~. **con·temp·tu·ous** [kən'temptjʊəs] *adj.* showing ~. **con·temp·tu·ous·ly** *adv.*

con·tend [kən'tend] *v.i. & t.* **1.** struggle, be in rivalry or competition (*with* sb. or sth., *for* a purpose). **2.** argue (*that*).

con·tent[1] [kən'tent] *pred. adj.* **1.** not wanting more; satisfied with what one has. **2.** ~ *to,* willing or ready to. **n.** condition of being ~ (1). *v.t.* make ~ (1); satisfy: ~ *oneself with,* be satisfied with. **~·ed** *adj.* satisfied; showing or feeling ~. **~·ment** *n.* (no pl.) state of being ~.

con·tent[2] ['kɒntent] *n.* **1.** (pl.) that which is contained in sth.: *the ~s of a room (book, etc.).* **2.** amount that a vessel will contain: *the ~(s) of a cask.* **3.** subject matter (of a book, speech, etc.).

con·ten·tion [kən'tenʃn] *n.* contending; argument used in contending. *bone of ~,* subject (2) of dispute. **con·ten·tious** [kən'tenʃəs] *adj.* fond of contending; likely to cause contention.

con·test [kən'test] *v.t. & i.* **1.** take part in a struggle or competition (*for*). **2.** argue against: ~ *a statement.* ['kɒntest] *n.* struggle; fight; competition. **con·tes·tant** [kən'testənt] *n.* person taking part in a ~.

con·text ['kɒntekst] *n.* what comes before and after (a word, phrase, statement, etc.), helping to fix the meaning. **con·tex·tu·al** [kɒn'tekstjʊəl] *adj.*

con·tig·u·ous [kən'tɪgjʊəs] *adj.* ~ *to,* touching; neighbouring; next; **con·ti·gu·ity** [͵kɒntɪ'gjuːətɪ] *n.* (no pl.) being ~.

con·ti·nent[1] ['kɒntɪnənt] *adj.* self-controlled; having control of one's feelings and desires. **con·ti·nence** ['kɒntɪnəns] *n.* (no pl.).

con·ti·nent[2] ['kɒntɪnənt] *n.* one of the main land masses (Europe, Asia, Africa, etc.): *the C~,* (usu.) Europe without the British Isles. **con·ti·nen·tal** [͵kɒntɪ'nentl] *adj.* belonging to, typical of, a ~; (esp.) of the mainland of Europe.

con·tin·gent [kən'tɪndʒənt] *adj.* **1.** uncertain; accidental. **2.** dependent (on sth. that may or may not happen). **n.** body (5) of troops, number of ships, sent to form part of a larger force; group of persons forming part of a larger one. **con·tin·gen·cy** [kən'tɪndʒənsɪ] *n.* ~ event.

con·tin·ue [kən'tɪnjuː] *v.i. & t.* **1.** go further; go on (being); go on (doing); go on (to do); stay (*in, at*); remain (*in, at*). **2.** start again after stopping. **con·tin·u·al** [kən'tɪnjʊəl] *adj.* going on all the time without stopping or with only short breaks. **con·tin·u·ance** [kən'tɪnjʊəns] *n.* (no pl.) (esp.) time for which sth. ~s: *during the continuance of the war.* **con·tin·u·a·tion** [kən͵tɪnjʊ'eɪʃn] *n.* continuing; part, etc. by which sth. is ~d: *The continuation of the story is on page 17.* **con·ti·nu·ity** [͵kɒntɪ'njuːətɪ] *n.* (no pl.) **1.** state of being continuous. **2.** arrangement of the parts of a film or television story. **3.** connecting comments, etc. between the parts of a broadcast. **con·tin·u·ous** [kən'tɪnjʊəs] *adj.* going on without a break.

con·tort [kən'tɔːt] *v.t.* force or twist out of the usual shape or appearance. **con·tor·tion** [kən'tɔːʃn] *n.* **con·tor·tion·ist** *n.* acrobat clever at ~ing his body.

con·tour ['kɒn͵tʊə*] *n.* outline (of a coast, mountain, etc.); (on a map, design, etc.) line separating differently coloured parts. ~ *line,* line (on a map) joining all points at the same height above sea-level. ~ *map,* map with ~ lines at fixed intervals (e.g. of 100 metres).

contra- ['kɒntrə-] *pref.* against.

con·tra·band ['kɒntrəbænd] *n.* (no pl.) bringing into or taking out of a country goods contrary to the law; (trade in) goods so brought in or taken out.

con·tra·cep·tive [͵kɒntrə'septɪv] *n.* means to prevent conception (2). *adj.* preventing conception (2): ~ *pills.*

con·tract[1] ['kɒntrækt] *n.* agreement (between persons, groups, States); business agreement to supply goods, do work, etc. at a fixed price. [kən'trækt] *v.t. & i.* **1.** make a ~: ~ *to build a railway;* ~ *a marriage.* **2.** become liable for: ~ *debts.* **3.** catch; form; acquire: ~ *a disease (bad habits, a friendship).* **con·trac·tor** *n.* (esp.) person that ~s to erect buildings: *a building ~or*.

con·tract² [kən'trækt] *v.t. & i.* **1.** make or become smaller or shorter: *~ 'I will' to 'I'll'. Metals ~ when they become cool.* **2.** make or become tighter or narrower: *~ a muscle; a valley that ~s as one goes up it*. **con·trac·tion** [kən'trækʃn] *n.* ~ing² or being ~ed²; sth. ~ed².

con·tra·dict [ˌkɒntrə'dɪkt] *v.t.* **1.** say (that sth. said or written) is not true. **2.** (of facts, statements, etc.) be contrary to. **con·tra·dic·tion** [ˌkɒntrə'dɪkʃn] *n.* **con·tra·dic·to·ry** [ˌkɒntrə'dɪktərɪ] *adj.*

con·tral·to [kən'træltəʊ] *n.* (*pl.* ~s) lowest female voice; woman with such a voice; musical part to be sung by her.

con·trap·tion [kən'træpʃn] *n.* (colloq.) strange-looking apparatus (1) or device (2).

con·trary ['kɒntrərɪ] *adj.* **1.** opposite in nature or tendency (*to*). **2.** (of the wind) unfavourable (for sailing). **3.** ([kən-'treərɪ], colloq.) obstinate; self-willed. *adv.* in opposition *to*; against: *act ~ to one's interests. n. the ~*, the opposite (of sth.). *on the ~* (used to make a denial or contradiction more emphatic): *'Have you nearly done it?' 'On the ~, I have only just begun.' to the ~*, to the opposite effect. **con·trar·i·ly** *adv.* **con·trar·i·ness** *n.* (no pl.) being ~ (3).

con·trast [kən'trɑːst] *v.t. & i.* **1.** compare (one thing *with* another) so that their difference is made clear. **2.** show a difference when compared: *actions that ~ with his promises*. ['kɒntrɑːst] *n.* **1.** act of ~ing. **2.** difference that is clearly seen when unlike things or persons are put together; sth. or sb. showing such a difference (*to*).

con·tra·vene [ˌkɒntrə'viːn] *v.t.* **1.** act in opposition to; go against (a law, custom). **2.** dispute (a statement, etc.). **3.** (of things) be out of harmony with. **con·tra·ven·tion** [ˌkɒntrə'venʃn] *n.*

con·trib·ute [kən'trɪbjuːt] *v.t. & i.* **1.** join with others in giving (help, money, etc. to a common cause); give (ideas, suggestions, etc.). **2.** have a share in; help to bring about: *His hard work ~d to the success of the exhibition*. **3.** write (articles, etc.) and send in (*to* a newspaper). **con·tri·bu·tion** [ˌkɒntrɪ-'bjuːʃn] *n.* act of contributing; sth. ~d. **con·trib·u·tor** [kən'trɪbjʊtə] *n.*

con·trite ['kɒntraɪt] *adj.* filled with, showing, deep sorrow for wrongdoing. **con·tri·tion** [kən'trɪʃn] *n.* (no pl.).

con·trive [kən'traɪv] *v.t. & i.* invent; design; find a way of doing (sth.), of causing (sth. to happen): *~ an escape from prison; ~ to live on one's income*. **con·triv·ance** [kən'traɪvns] *n.* sth. ~d, esp. an invention or apparatus (1).

con·trol [kən'trəʊl] *n.* **1.** power or authority to rule, order, or direct: *have ~ over one's children; lose (get) ~ over (of) one's horse; get flood waters under ~*. **2.** means of regulating, directing, or keeping in order; ~ *of traffic (foreign exchange); government ~s on trade and industry*. **3.** (usu. pl.) means by which machines are operated: *at the ~s of an aircraft; a dual-~ car; the ~ tower of an aiport* (from which air traffic is ~led). *v.t.* (-*ll*-) have ~ of: *~ one's temper (a horse, oneself*); regulate (prices, etc.); check. ~**ler** *n.* person who ~s: *the Food C~ler*.

con·tro·ver·sy ['kɒntrəvɜːsɪ] *n.* prolonged argument, esp. over social, moral, or political matters. **con·tro·ver·sial** [ˌkɒntrə'vɜːʃl] *adj.* likely to cause ~; (of a person) fond of ~.

con·tu·sion [kən'tjuːʒn] *n.* bruise.

co·nun·drum [kə'nʌndrəm] *n.* puzzling question, esp. one asked for fun; riddle.

con·va·lesce [ˌkɒnvə'les] *v.i.* recover health and strength after an illness. **con·va·les·cent** [ˌkɒnvə'lesnt] *n. & adj.* (person who is) recovering from illness. **con·va·les·cence** *n.* (no pl.).

con·vene [kən'viːn] *v.t. & i.* call (persons) to come together (for a meeting, etc.); come together (for a meeting, council, etc.).

con·ve·nience [kən'viːnjəns] *n.* **1.** quality of being convenient: *at your ~, whenever you wish*. **2.** sth. that is convenient; useful appliance: *a house with all modern ~s* (e.g. hot water supply, central heating, etc.); *public ~s*, lavatories; *make a ~ of sb.*, use his services unreasonably. **con·ve·nient** *adj.* suitable; not causing trouble or difficulty: *a convenient time and place for a meeting*.

con·vent ['kɒnvənt] *n.* **1.** society of women (called *nuns*) living apart from others in the service of God. **2.** building(s) in which they live.

con·ven·tion [kən'venʃn] *n.* **1.** general conference of members of societies, political parties, etc. devoted to a special object. **2.** agreement between States, etc. (less formal than a treaty). **3.** general consent (esp. about forms of behaviour); practice or custom based on such general consent. ~**al** [kən-'venʃənl] *adj.* **1.** based on ~ (3): *~al remarks (greetings)*. **2.** using ~s (3); traditional: *~al art (weapons)*.

con·verge [kən'vɜːdʒ] *v.i. & t.* (of lines, moving objects, opinions) come, cause to come, towards each other and meet at a point; tend to do this. **con·ver·gent** *adj.*

con·ver·sant [kən'vɜːsənt] *adj.* ~ *with*, having a knowledge of.

con·ver·sa·tion [ˌkɒnvə'seɪʃn] *n.* talk (-ing). **~·al** [ˌkɒnvə'seɪʃənl] *adj.* fond of ~; (of words, etc.) used in ~.

con·verse[1] [kən'vɜːs] *v.i.* talk (*with* sb., *about, on*, sth.).

con·verse[2] ['kɒnvɜːs] *n. & adj.* (idea, statement that is) opposite (to another): '*Hot*' *is the* ~ *of* '*cold*'. **~·ly** *adv.*

con·ver·sion [kən'vɜːʃən] *n.* converting or being converted.

con·vert [kən'vɜːt] *v.t.* **1.** change (from one form, use, etc. *into* another): ~ *rags into paper* (*cream into butter*). **2.** cause (a person) to change beliefs, etc.: ~ *a man to Christianity*. ['kɒnvɜːt] *n.* person ~ed, esp. to a religious belief. **~·ed** *adj.* that has been ~ed (1). **con·vert·ible** [kən'vɜːtəbl] *adj.* that can be ~ed (1): *These banknotes are not* ~*ible into gold. n.* motor car with a detachable or folding top.

con·vex ['kɒnveks] *adj.* with the surface curved like the outside of a ball. (Cf. *concave*.)

concave   convex

con·vey [kən'veɪ] *v.t.* **1.** carry, take, from one place to another. **2.** make known (ideas, news, feelings, etc.) to another person. **3.** (law) give (*to* sb.) full legal rights (in property). **~·ance** [kən'veɪəns] *n.* **1.** ~ing; sth. that ~s; carriage or other vehicle. **2.** (law) form of agreement ~ing property. **~·er**, **~·or** *n.* person or thing that ~s, esp. (~*er* or ~*or belt*) an endless belt for moving goods, etc.

con·vict [kən'vɪkt] *v.t.* make (sb.) feel sure that he has done wrong: ~ *sb. of his errors*; (of a jury or judge) declare in a lawcourt that (sb.) is guilty (*of* crime). ['kɒnvɪkt] *n.* person ~ed of crime and undergoing punishment. **con·vic·tion**[1] [kən'vɪkʃn] *n.* the ~ing of a person of crime.

con·vic·tion[2] [kən'vɪkʃn] *n.* **1.** act of convincing: *carry* ~, be convincing. **2.** firm belief.

con·vince [kən'vɪns] *v.t.* make (sb.)

feel certain (*of* sth., *that* ...); cause (sb.) to realize. **con·vinc·ing** *adj.*

con·viv·ial [kən'vɪvɪəl] *adj.* **1.** gay; fond of drinking and merry-making: ~ *companions.* **2.** marked by drinking and merry-making: *a* ~ *evening.*

con·vo·ca·tion [ˌkɒnvəʊ'keɪʃn] *n.* convoking; meeting or assembly, esp. to discuss affairs of the Church or of a University.

con·voke [kən'vəʊk] *v.t.* call together; summon (a meeting).

con·voy ['kɒnvɔɪ] *v.t.* (esp. of a warship) go with (other ships) to protect (them). *n.* ~ing; protecting force (of ships, etc.); number of ships sailing together for self-protection or accompanied by warship(s); number of vehicles travelling thus together.

con·vulse [kən'vʌls] *v.t.* cause violent movements or disturbances: ~*d by an earthquake* (*civil war*); ~*d with laughter.* **con·vul·sion** [kən'vʌlʃn] *n.* **con·vul·sive** [kən'vʌlsɪv] *adj.*

coo [kuː] *v.i. & n.* (make a) soft, murmuring sound (as of doves). *v.t.* say in a soft murmur.

cook [kʊk] *v.t. & i.* prepare (raw food) for use, by heating (e.g. boiling, baking, frying); undergo ~ing. *n.* person who ~s food. **~·er** *n.* sth., esp. a stove, for ~ing food: *a gas-*~*er.* **~·ery** ['kʊkərɪ] *n.* (no pl.) art or practice of ~ing: ~*ery book*, book containing recipes.

cool [kuːl] *adj.* **1.** between warm and cold; enabling a person to feel thus: *a* ~ *day* (*room*). **2.** calm; unexcited: *be* ~ *in the face of danger.* **3.** impudent in a calm way; without shame. **4.** (of behaviour) not showing interest or enthusiasm. *v.t. & i.* ~ (*down, off*), make or become ~. **~·ly** *adv.*

coo·lie, **coo·ly** ['kuːlɪ] *n.* unskilled workman or porter (in the East).

coop [kuːp] *n.* small cage, esp. for hens with small chickens. *v.t.* put or keep in a ~: ~ *up* (*in*), keep in a small room or space.

co-op ['kəʊɒp] *n.* (colloq.) co-operative society or store.

coop·er ['kuːpə*] *n.* maker of tubs, casks, barrels, etc.

co-op·er·ate [kəʊ'ɒpəreɪt] *v.i.* work or act together to bring about a result. **co-op·er·a·tion** [kəʊˌɒpə'reɪʃn] *n.* (no pl.). **co-op·er·a·tive** [kəʊ'ɒpərətɪv] *adj.* of co-operation; willing to ~: *co-operative society*, group of persons who ~ (e.g. to buy machines and services for all members to share, or to produce, buy, and sell goods amongst themselves for mutual benefit, or to save and lend money); *co-operative shop* (*store*) (belonging to a co-operative society). *n.* (shop of a) co-operative society.

co-opt [kəʊ'ɒpt] *v.t.* (of a committee) add (a person) as a member by the votes of those who are already members.

co-or-di-nate [kəʊ'ɔ:dnət] *adj.* equal in importance. *n.* ~ thing. [kəʊ'ɔ:dɪneɪt] *v.t.* make ~; bring or put into proper relation. **co-or-di-na-tion** [kəʊ,ɔ:dɪ'neɪʃn] *n.* act of co-ordinating; state of being ~.

cop [kɒp] *n.* (sl.) policeman.

cope[1] [kəʊp] *n.* long, loose cloak worn by the clergy on some special occasions.

cope[2] [kəʊp] *v.i.* ~ with, manage successfully; be equal to: ~ with difficulties.

co-pi-lot ['kəʊ,paɪlət] *n.* assistant pilot in an aircraft.

cop-ing ['kəʊpɪŋ] *n.* line of (sometimes overhanging) stonework or brickwork on top of a wall.

co-pi-ous ['kəʊpjəs] *adj.* plentiful; (of a writer) writing much. ~ly *adv.*

cop-per[1] ['kɒpə*] *n.* 1. (no pl.) common reddish-brown metal. 2. coin made of ~ or bronze. 3. large vessel made of metal, used for boiling clothes, etc. *v.t.* cover with a coating of ~.

cop-per[2] ['kɒpə*] *n.* (sl.) policeman.

cop-pice ['kɒpɪs] *n.* small area of small trees and undergrowth.

co-pra ['kɒprə] *n.* (no pl.) dried kernel of coconut, used in soap-making.

copse [kɒps] *n.* coppice.

copy ['kɒpɪ] *n.* 1. thing made to be like another; reproduction of a letter, picture, etc.: *rough* ~, imperfect draft (1) of sth. written; *fair* ~, final form of sth. written. 2. one example of a book, newspaper, etc. of which many have been made. 3. handwritten or typed matter (to be) sent to a printer. *v.t. & i.* 1. make a ~ of: ~ *sth. down from the blackboard.* 2. do, try to do, the same as; imitate. '~-book *n.* exercise book that contains models for learners to imitate. '~-right *n.* (no pl.) legal right, held for a certain period of years only, by the author or composer of a work or by someone allowed by him, to print, publish, sell, broadcast, perform, film, or record his work or any part of it. *adj.* protected by ~right. *v.t.* secure ~right for (a book, etc.).

cor-al ['kɒrəl] *n.* hard, red, pink, or white substance built on the sea-bed by small sea-creatures (till it reaches the surface, forming reefs and islands). *adj.* pink or red like ~.

cord [kɔ:d] *n.* 1. (length of) twisted threads, thicker than string, thinner than rope. 2. part of the body like a ~: *the spinal* ~; *the vocal* ~s. *v.t.* put a ~ or ~s (1) round. ~age ['kɔ:dɪdʒ] *n.* (no pl.) ~s, ropes, etc., esp. the rigging of a ship.

cor-dial ['kɔ:djəl] *adj.* warm and sincere (in feeling, behaviour): *a* ~ *welcome.* *n.* drink that gives a feeling of warmth; sweetened and concentrated fruit juice. ~ly *adv.* ~i-ty [,kɔ:dɪ'ælə-tɪ] *n.*

cord-ite ['kɔ:daɪt] *n.* (no pl.) smokeless explosive.

cor-don ['kɔ:dn] *n.* line, ring, of police, etc. acting as guards. *v.t.* ~ off, enclose (a crowd, an area) with a ~.

cor-du-roy ['kɔ:dərɔɪ] *n.* thick, coarse, strong, cotton cloth with raised lines on it; (pl.) trousers made of this cloth.

core [kɔ:*] *n.* 1. hard, middle part, with seeds, of such fruits as the apple and pear. 2. central or most important part of anything: *the* ~ *of a subject*; *true to the* ~ (i.e. thoroughly faithful). *v.t.* take out the ~ (1) of.

cork [kɔ:k] *n.* 1. (no pl.) light, tough material forming the thick outer bark of the tree called ~-oak. 2. round piece of this used as a stopper for a bottle. *v.t.* put a ~ in. '~-screw *n.* tool for pulling out ~s from bottles.

corn[1] [kɔ:n] *n.* 1. (no pl.) (collective sing.) seed of various cereal plants, chiefly wheat, barley, oats, rye, and (in U.S.A.) maize; such plants while growing. 2. single grain (of wheat, pepper, etc.). '~-flour *n.* (no pl.) flour made from maize, rice, or other grain.

corn[2] [kɔ:n] *n.* small area of hardened skin on a toe, etc.

corn[3] [kɔ:n] *v.t.* preserve (meat) in salt: ~ed beef.

cor-ner ['kɔ:nə*] *n.* 1. place where two lines, sides, edges, or surfaces meet; angle enclosed by two walls, sides, etc. that meet. *turn the* ~, (fig.) pass safely from a crisis (e.g. in a serious illness); *a tight* ~, a difficult situation. 2. (comm.) *make a* ~ *in* (e.g. wheat), buy up all available supplies in order to control the price. 3. (football) (also called ~-kick) free kick from the ~ of the field. *v.t.* 1. drive into a ~; put in a difficult position. 2. make a ~ (2) in (goods, etc.). '~-stone *n.* (fig.) foundation; that on which sth. is based: *Hard work was the* ~-stone *of his success.*

cor-net ['kɔ:nɪt] *n.* 1. small musical

instrument of brass, like a trumpet. **2.** (Gt. Brit.) cone-shaped wafer filled with ice cream.

cor·ol·la·ry [kə'rɒlərɪ] *n.* natural consequence or outcome of sth.

co·ro·na [kə'rəʊnə] *n.* (pl. ~s, -nae) ring of light seen round the sun or moon, esp. during an eclipse.

cor·o·na·tion [ˌkɒrə'neɪʃn] *n.* ceremony of crowning a king, queen, or other sovereign ruler.

cor·o·ner ['kɒrənə*] *n.* official who inquires into the cause of any violent or unnatural death: ~'s inquest, such an inquiry (held with a jury).

cor·o·net ['kɒrənɪt] *n.* small crown worn by a noble; ornament designed like a ~.

cor·po·ral[1] ['kɔːpərəl] *adj.* of the body: ~ punishment (whipping, beating).

cor·po·ral[2] [kɔ:pərəl] *n.* (army) non-commissioned officer (below a sergeant).

cor·po·ra·tion [ˌkɔːpə'reɪʃn] *n.* **1.** group of persons elected to govern a town: *the mayor and ~.* **2.** group of persons allowed by law to act, for business purposes, as one person. **3.** (colloq.) large belly. **cor·po·rate** ['kɔːpərət] *adj.* **1.** of a ~: *corporate property.* **2.** of or belonging to a body (5): *corporate responsibility.*

corps [kɔ:*] *n.* (pl. ~ [kɔ:z]) **1.** one of the technical branches of an army: *the Royal Army Medical Corps.* **2.** military force made up of two or more divisions.

corpse [kɔ:ps] *n.* dead body (usu. of a human being). (Cf. *carcass.*)

cor·pu·lent ['kɔ:pjʊlənt] *adj.* (of a person's body) fat and heavy. **cor·pu·lence, -len·cy** ['kɔ:pjʊləns(ɪ)] *ns.* (no pl.).

cor·pus·cle ['kɔːpʌsl] *n.* one of the red or white cells in the blood.

cor·ral [kɒˈrɑːl] *n.* enclosure for horses and cattle or the capture of wild animals.

cor·rect [kə'rekt] *adj.* true; right; proper: *a ~ answer.* *v.t.* make ~; take out mistakes from; point out faults; punish. **cor·rec·tion** [kə'rekʃn] *n.* ~ing; sth. ~ put in place of an error: *a schoolboy's essay covered with ~ions.*

cor·rec·tive [kə'rektɪv] *n. & adj.* (sth.) serving to ~.

cor·re·late ['kɒrəleɪt] *v.t. & i.* bring (one thing) into mutual relation (*with* another); have a mutual relation (*with, to*). **cor·re·la·tion** [ˌkɒrə'leɪʃn] *n.*

cor·re·spond [ˌkɒrɪ'spɒnd] *v.i.* **1.** be in harmony (*with*). **2.** be equal (*to*); be similar (*to*). **3.** exchange letters (*with*

sb.). **cor·re·spon·dence** *n.* **1.** agreement; similarity. **2.** (no pl.) letter-writing; letters. ~ence course, course in which students are taught by ~ence.

cor·re·spon·dent *n.* **1.** person with whom one exchanges letters. **2.** *newspaper ~ent,* person regularly contributing local news or special articles to a newspaper.

cor·ri·dor ['kɒrɪdɔ:*] *n.* long, narrow passage from which doors open into rooms or compartments.

cor·rob·o·rate [kə'rɒbəreɪt] *v.t.* give support or certainty to (a statement, theory, etc.). **cor·rob·o·ra·tion** [kə-ˌrɒbə'reɪʃn] *n.* (no pl.).

cor·rode [kə'rəʊd] *v.t. & i.* wear away, destroy slowly by chemical action or disease; be worn away thus. **cor·ro·sion** [kə'rəʊʒn] *n.*(no pl.). **cor·ro·sive** [kə'rəʊsɪv] *n. & adj.* (substance) corroding.

cor·ru·gated ['kɒrʊgeɪtɪd] *part. adj.* shaped into narrow folds or wave-like furrows: ~ *iron (cardboard);* ~ *roads in tropical countries.*

corrugated

cor·rupt [kə'rʌpt] *adj.* **1.** (of persons, their actions) bad; dishonest (esp. through taking bribes). **2.** impure: ~ *air.* *v.t. & i.* make or become ~. ~**ible** [kə'rʌptəbl] *adj.* (esp.) that can be ~ed by bribes. **cor·rup·tion** [kə'rʌpʃn] *n.* (no pl.) ~ing; being ~.

cor·set ['kɔ:sɪt] *n.* tight-fitting undergarment confining the waist and hips.

cosh [kɒʃ] *v.t. & n.* (Gt. Brit., sl.) (strike with a) weighted weapon, like a lead pipe, etc.

cos·met·ic [kɒz'metɪk] *n. & adj.* preparation, substance) designed to make the skin or hair beautiful. **cos·me·ti·cian** [ˌkɒzmə'tɪʃn] *n.* expert in the use of ~s.

cos·mo·naut ['kɒzmənɔ:t] *n.* (esp. Russian) astronaut.

cos·mo·pol·i·tan [ˌkɒzmə'pɒlɪtən] *adj.* of or from all, or many different, parts of the world; free from national prejudices because of wide experience of the world: *a ~ outlook.* *n.* ~ person.

cos·mos ['kɒzmɒs] *n.* (no pl.) the universe, all space, considered as a well-ordered system (contrasted with *chaos*).

cos·mic ['kɒzmɪk] *adj.* of the ~.

cost [kɒst] *v.i. & t.* (p.t. & p.p. ~)
1. be obtainable at the price of; require the payment of; result in the loss
or disadvantage of. **2.** (p.t. & p.p. ~ed
['kɒstɪd]) (comm.) estimate the price to
be charged for an article based on the
expense of producing it. *n.* **1.** price (to
be) paid; that which is needed in order
to obtain. **2.** (pl., law) expenses of having sth. decided in a law court. **3.** *at all
~s*, however much expense, trouble,
etc., may be needed; *at the ~ of*, at the
loss or expense of; *count the ~*, consider the risks before doing sth.; *to
one's ~*, to one's loss or disadvantage.
~·ly *adj.* (-ier, -iest) of great value;
~ing much.

cos·ter, cos·ter·mon·ger ['kɒstə-
(ˌmʌŋgə*)] *n.* (Gt. Brit.) person selling
fruit, vegetables, etc. from a barrow in
the street.

cos·tume ['kɒstjuːm] *n.* **1.** (no pl.) style
of dress: *actors wearing historical ~* (i.e.
clothes in the fashion of a period of
past time); *a ~ piece* (*play*) (in which
the actors wear historical ~); *~ jewellery*, artificial jewellery worn as an
adornment. **2.** woman's suit (short
coat and skirt of the same material).

co·sy (U.S.A. **co·zy**) ['kəʊzɪ] *adj.* (-ier,
-iest) warm and comfortable. *n.* padded covering for a teapot or a boiled
egg to keep the heat. **co·si·ly** (U.S.A.
co·zi·ly) *adv.*

cot [kɒt] *n.* easily moved bed, esp. for a
small child (with tall sides, U.S.A. =
crib). [birds: *dove~*.]

cote [kəʊt] *n.* shelter for animals or
cot·tage ['kɒtɪdʒ] *n.* small house, esp.
in the country: *farm-labourers' ~s*;
small house designed for use during
the summer holidays.

cot·ton ['kɒtn] *n.* (no pl.) **1.** soft, white,
fibrous substance round the seeds of
the *~-plant*, used for making thread,
cloth, etc. **2.** thread spun from ~ yarn,
used for sewing, etc. **3.** cloth made of
~. *~ wool*, cleaned raw or natural ~ as
used for padding, bandaging.

a cotton-plant   a reel of
                        cotton (2)

couch [kaʊtʃ] *n.* **1.** (liter.) bed. **2.** long,
bed-like seat for sitting or lying on
during the day. *v.t. & i.* **1.** put (a
thought, etc. *in* words). **2.** (of animals)
lie flat (either to hide or in readiness
for a jump forward).

cou·chette [kuːˈʃet] *n.* (berth in a) railway carriage with seats convertible
into sleeping-berths.

cou·gar ['kuːgə*] *n.* (U.S.A.) = puma.

cough [kɒf] *v.i. & t.* send out air from
the lungs violently and noisily. *~ sth.
up* (*out*), get sth. out of the throat by
~ing. *n.* **1.** act or sound of ~ing. **2.** condition, illness, causing a person to ~
often: *have a bad ~*.

could, see *can*[1].

coun·cil ['kaʊnsl] *n.* group of persons
appointed or chosen to give advice,
make rules, carry out plans, manage
affairs, etc., esp. of government: *a
county ~*. *~lor* (U.S.A. also *~or*) *n.*
member of a ~.

coun·sel ['kaʊnsl] *n.* **1.** advice; opinions; suggestions: *keep one's own ~*,
keep one's views, plans, etc. secret;
hold (*take*) *~ with* (*sb.*), consult in order
to get suggestions, etc. **2.** (pl. ~) barrister(s) giving advice, etc. in a law
case. *Queen's* (*King's*) *Counsel*, barrister appointed to act for the British
Government, higher in authority than
other barristers. *v.t.* (-ll-, U.S.A. also
-l-) give ~ to. *~lor* (U.S.A. also *~or*)
n. adviser.

count[1] [kaʊnt] *v.t. & i.* **1.** say or name
(the numerals) in order. **2.** include;
take into account; be included: *fifty
people, not ~ing the children. That
doesn't ~* (i.e. need not be taken into
account or considered). **3.** consider;
look upon (as): *~ oneself fortunate; ~ sb.
as lost.* **4.** *~ against*, consider to the disadvantage of; *~ down, ~ backwards*
(e.g. 10, 9, 8, etc.) in preparing to
launch a space rocket; *~-down* (n.); *~
for much* (*little, nothing*), be of much
(little, no) importance; *~ in*, include;
~ on (*upon*), rely upon; consider as
certain: *You mustn't ~ upon any help
from me. ~ out*, (a) *~* things one by one;
(b) not include; (c) *be ~ed out*, (of a
boxer) fail to rise to his feet before the
~ing of ten seconds after being knocked
down; *~ up*, find the total of. *n.* **1.** act
of ~ing; number got by ~ing. *take the
~*, (boxing) be ~ed out (see above). **2.**
account; notice: *take no ~ of what
people say.* **3.** (law) one of several
things of which a person has been accused: *guilty on all ~s*. *~·ing-house n.*
building or room for bookkeeping (e.g.

in a bank). **~·less** *adj.* too many to be ~ed.

count² [kaʊnt] *n.* title of nobility in some countries (but not Gt. Brit.). **~·ess** ['kaʊntɪs] *n.* wife or widow of an earl or a count; woman with rank equal to that of an earl or a count.

coun·te·nance ['kaʊntənəns] *n.* **1.** face, including its appearance and expression: *a fierce* ~; *keep one's* ~, control one's expression, esp. in hiding amusement; *put. sb. out of* ~, cause him to feel troubled or at fault. **2.** support; approval: *give* ~ *to a proposal.* *v.t.* give ~ (2) to.

coun·ter¹ ['kaʊntə*] *n.* table on which goods are shown, customers are served, in a shop or bank.

coun·ter² ['kaʊntə*] *n.* **1.** small, round, flat piece of metal, plastic, etc. used for keeping count in games, etc. **2.** (tech.) device (2) for keeping count.

coun·ter³ ['kaʊntə*] *adv.* against; in the opposite direction: *acting* ~ *to my wishes.* *v.t. & i.* act ~ to; oppose.

coun·ter- ['kaʊntə*] *pref.* **1.** opposite in direction: ~*march*; ~*attraction.* **2.** made in answer to: ~*attack*; ~*claim.* **3.** corresponding: ~*part.*

coun·ter·act [ˌkaʊntə'rækt] *v.t.* act against and make (action, force) of less or no effect: ~ *a poison.* **coun·ter·ac·tion** [ˌkaʊntə'rækʃn] *n.*

coun·ter·bal·ance ['kaʊntəˌbæləns] *n.* weight, force, etc. equal to another and balancing it. [ˌkaʊntə'bæləns] *v.t.* act as a ~ to.

coun·ter-clock·wise [ˌkaʊntə'klɒkwaɪz] *adv.* moving in the direction opposite to that taken by the hands of a clock.

coun·ter-es·pi·o·nage [ˌkaʊntər'espjənɑːʒ] *n.* (no pl.) action directed against an enemy's espionage.

coun·ter·feit ['kaʊntəfiːt] *v.t. & adj.* (sth.) false; (sth.) made in imitation of another thing in order to deceive: ~ *money.* *v.t.* copy or imitate (coin, handwriting) in order to deceive.

coun·ter·foil ['kaʊntəfɔɪl] *n.* (U.S.A. *stub*) section of a cheque, receipt, etc. kept by the sender as a record.

coun·ter-in·tel·li·gence [ˌkaʊntərɪnˌtelɪdʒəns] *n.* (no pl.) counter-espionage.

coun·ter·mand [ˌkaʊntə'mɑːnd] *v.t.* take back, cancel, a command already given. [spread.]

coun·ter·pane ['kaʊntəpeɪn] *n.* bed-f

coun·ter·part ['kaʊntəpɑːt] *n.* person or thing exactly like, or corresponding closely to, another.

coun·ter·sign ['kaʊntəsaɪn] *n.* password; secret word to be given, on demand, to a sentry to prove that one is not an enemy: '*Advance and give the* ~.' *v.t.* add another signature to a document to give it more authority.

coun·try ['kʌntrɪ] *n.* **1.** land occupied by a nation. **2.** land in which a person was born, etc. **3.** the people of a ~ (1); the nation as a whole. **4.** region of open spaces, of land used for farming: *Do you like living in the* ~? *We passed through miles of densely wooded* ~. (Cf. *town.*) **coun·tri·fied** ['kʌntrɪfaɪd] *adj.* with the ways and habits of the ~ (4), not of towns. **~·man** ['kʌntrɪmən] *n.* man of the ~ (4), not of a town; (also *fellow* ~*man*) man of the same nation as another. '**~·side** *n.* (no pl.) district in the ~ (4).

coun·ty ['kaʊntɪ] *n.* **1.** division of Great Britain, the largest unit of local government: ~ *town,* chief town in a ~. **2.** (U.S.A.) subdivision of a State.

coup [kuː] *n.* sudden action taken to get power, obtain a desired result, etc.

cou·ple ['kʌpl] *n.* **1.** two persons or things, seen or associated together: *a* ~ *of,* (approximately) two; a few. **2.** two persons (to be) married to one another; pair of partners in a dance. *v.t.* **1.** join (two things) together. **2.** associate (two things) in thought. **~t** ['kʌplɪt] *n.* two successive lines of verse, equal in length and with a rhyme. **cou·pling** ['kʌplɪŋ] *n.* (esp.) link, etc. that joins two parts of a machine, two railway coaches or other vehicles.

cou·pon ['kuːpɒn] *n.* ticket, part of a document, paper, bond, etc. that gives the holder the right to receive sth. or do sth.

cour·age ['kʌrɪdʒ] *n.* (no pl.) bravery; quality that enables a person to control fear in face of danger or pain. **cou·ra·geous** [kə'reɪdʒəs] *adj.* brave.

cou·ri·er ['kʊrɪə*] *n.* **1.** person who is paid to conduct parties of tourists, esp. abroad. **2.** messenger carrying news or important government papers.

course¹ [kɔːs] *n.* **1.** forward movement in space or time: *the* ~ *of events*; *in* ~ *of,* in process of: *a railway in* ~ *of construction* (i.e. being built); *in the* ~ *of,* during; *in due* ~, in the proper or natural order. **2.** direction taken by sth.; line along which sth. moves; line of action: *The ship is on her right* ~. *The disease ran its* ~ (i.e. developed in the usual way). *the* ~*s open to us* (i.e. the ways in which we may proceed to act); (*as*) *a matter of* ~, that which one would expect (to do, happen, etc.); of ~, naturally; certainly. **3.** ground for golf: *a golf-~*; place for races: *a race~*. **4.** series (of talks, treatments, etc.): *a ~ of lectures (mud baths)*. **5.** continuous layer (1) of stone or brick in a wall. **6.** one of the separate parts of a meal (e.g. soup, meat, dessert).

course² [kɔːs] *v.t. & i.* **1.** chase (esp. hares) with dogs. **2.** move quickly; (esp. of liquids) run. **cours·ing** *n.* (no pl.) sport of chasing hares.

court [kɔːt] *n.* **1.** place where law cases are heard; those persons (judges and other officers) who hear law cases: *~ of law, law~*. **2.** (residence of a) great ruler (king, emperor, etc.), his family and officials, councillors, etc.; State gathering or reception given by a ruler. **3.** space marked out for certain games: *a tennis-~*. **4.** (also *~yard*) space with walls or buildings round it; the houses round such a space. **5.** (no pl.) special service or politeness offered in order to please sb.: *pay ~ to a woman*, try to win her affections. *v.t.* **1.** pay one's ~ (5) to; try to win or obtain (support, approval, etc.). **2.** take action that may lead to (defeat, danger). **cour·te·ous** [ˈkɜːtjəs] *adj.* having, showing, good manners; polite and kind. **cour·te·sy** [ˈkɜːtɪsɪ] *n.* ~eous behaviour; ~eous act. **~ier** [ˈkɔːtjə*] *n.* person belonging to the ~ (2) of a ruler. **~ly** [ˈkɔːtlɪ] *adj.* polite and dignified. **~ mar·tial** [ˌkɔːtˈmɑːʃl] *n.* (pl. *~s martial*) ~ (1) for trying offences against military law. **~-'mar·tial** *v.t.* (-*ll*-, U.S.A. also -*l*-) try (sb.) by this ~. **~·ship** *n.* (no pl.) (time of) paying ~ (5) to a woman. **~·yard** [ˈkɔːtjɑːd] *n.* court (4).

cous·in [ˈkʌzn] *n.* (*first ~*) child of one's uncle or aunt; (*second ~*) child of one's parent's first ~.

cove [kəʊv] *n.* small bay¹.

cov·e·nant [ˈkʌvənənt] *v.i. & t. & n.* (make a) solemn agreement.

cov·er [ˈkʌvə*] *v.t.* **1.** place (one substance or thing) over or in front of (another); hide or protect (sth.) in this way; lie or extend over; occupy the surface of. **2.** travel (a distance): *~ ten miles in an hour*. **3.** aim at (with a gun or pistol). **4.** protect; provide with an insurance (*against*): *have one's property ~ed (by insurance) against loss.* **5.** (of money) be enough for: *£5 will ~ my needs for the journey*. *n.* **1.** thing that ~s, hides, protects, or encloses. **2.** binding of a book, magazine, etc.; either board (7) of this: *read a book from ~ to ~* (from beginning to end).

3. place giving shelter: *take ~ from the enemy's fire*; *get under ~* (e.g. when it rains). **4.** place laid for each person at table for a meal. **~·age** [ˈkʌvərɪdʒ] *n.* (no pl.) reporting of events, etc.: *television ~age of the Olympic Games*. **~·ing** *n.* sth. that ~s. **~·let** [ˈkʌvəlɪt] *n.* bedspread.

co·vert¹ [ˈkʌvət] *adj.* (of glances, threats, etc.) half-hidden; disguised. **~·ly** *adv.*

co·vert² [ˈkʌvə*] *n.* area of thick undergrowth in which animals hide.

cov·et [ˈkʌvɪt] *v.t.* desire eagerly (usu. sth. belonging to sb. else). **~·ous** [ˈkʌvɪtəs] *adj.*

cow¹ [kaʊ] *n.* female of any animal of the ox family, esp. the domestic species. **'~·boy** *n.* man looking after cattle on a ranch, etc. **'~·herd** *n.* person looking after cows at pasture. **'~·hide** *n.* leather from the skin of cows. **~·poke** [ˈkaʊpəʊk], **~·punch·er** [ˈkaʊˌpʌntʃə*] *ns.* (U.S.A.) = ~boy.

a cow¹   *a cowboy*

cow² [kaʊ] *v.t.* frighten (sb.) into submission.

cow·ard [ˈkaʊəd] *n.* person unable to control his fear; person who runs away from danger. **~·ice** [ˈkaʊədɪs] *n.* (no pl.) feeling, way of behaving, of a ~. **~·ly** *adj.* not brave; contemptible: *a ~ly act (lie)*.

cow·er [ˈkaʊə*] *v.i.* lower the body as when frightened; crouch; droop; shrink (from cold, misery, fear, or shame).

cowl [kaʊl] *n.* **1.** long, loose gown with a hood that can be pulled up over the head. **2.** the hood alone. **3.** metal cap for a chimney, etc.

cow·rie, **cow·ry** [ˈkaʊrɪ] *n.* small shell formerly used as money in parts of Africa and Asia.

cow·slip [ˈkaʊslɪp] *n.* yellow flower growing wild in temperate countries.

cox [kɒks] *n.* (colloq., abbr. of) **coxswain** [ˈkɒkswein, ˈkɒksn] *n.* person who steers a rowing-boat; person in charge of a ship's boat and crew.

cox·comb [ˈkɒkskəʊm] *n.* vain, foolish

person, esp. one who pays too much attention to his clothes.

coy [kɔɪ] *adj.* (esp. of a girl) shy; (pretending to be) modest. ~·**ly** *adv.* ~·**ness** *n.* (no pl.).

coy·ote ['kɔɪəʊt] *n.* North American prairie wolf.

crab¹ [kræb] *n.* shellfish with five pairs of legs; its meat as food.

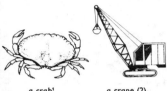

a crab¹   a crane (2)

crab² [kræb] *n.* (also ~-*apple*) wild apple-tree; its hard, sour fruit.

crab·bed ['kræbɪd] *adj.* bad-tempered; (of handwriting) difficult to read.

crack [kræk] *n.* **1.** line of division where sth. is broken, but not into separate parts: ~s *in a cup*; ~s *in the ground during dry weather.* **2.** sudden, sharp noise (of a gun, whip, etc.). **3.** sharp blow which can be heard: *a* ~ *on the head.* **4.** good player, good horse, etc. *v.t. & i.* **1.** get or make a ~ or ~s (1) in. **2.** (cause to) make a ~ or ~s (2). **3.** (of the voice) become harsh; undergo a change (esp. of a boy's voice when he is reaching manhood). **4.** ~ *up*, (colloq.) lose strength (e.g. in old age); ~ *sth. up*, (colloq.) praise highly; ~ *a joke*, make a joke. *attrib. adj.* first-rate; very clever: *a* ~ *polo-player; a* ~ *shot*¹ (5). ~·**er** *n.* **1.** thin, hard, dry biscuit. **2.** firework that makes a ~ or ~s (2) when set off or pulled apart. **3.** (pl., also *nut·*~ers) instrument for ~ing nuts. ~·**le** ['krækl] *v.i. & n.* (no pl.) (make) small ~ing sounds: *the* ~*le of machine-gun fire.*

cra·dle ['kreɪdl] *n.* small bed or cot, mounted on rockers, for a baby; (fig.) place where sth. is born or begins. *v.t.* place, hold, in or as in a ~.

craft [krɑːft] *n.* **1.** occupation, esp. one in which skill in the use of the hands is needed: *the* ~ *of the wood-carver; a school for arts and* ~s. **2.** cunning; trickery; skill in deceiving. **3.** (pl. ~) boat(s); ship(s): *a harbour full of all kinds of* ~. ~s·**man** ['krɑːftsmən] skilled workman. ~**y** *adj.* (-*ier*, -*iest*) cunning; full of ~ (2). ~·**i·ly** *adv.* ~·**i·ness** *n.*

crag [kræg] *n.* high, sharp rock. ~·**gy** *adj.* (-*ier*, -*iest*) with many ~s.

cram [kræm] *v.t. & i.* (-*mm-*) **1.** make too full; put, push, force too much *into* (*in, down*). **2.** fill the head with facts in preparation (*for* an examination). ~·**mer** *n.* person who ~s (2) pupils for examinations by special lessons.

cramp [kræmp] *n.* painful tightening of muscles, usu. caused by cold or overwork, making movement difficult: *a swimmer seized with* ~. *v.t.* **1.** affect¹ (1) with ~. **2.** (lit., fig.) keep in a narrow space; hinder or prevent movement or growth. ~**ed** *part. adj.* (of space) ~ing; (of handwriting) with small letters close together and for this reason difficult to read.

cran·ber·ry ['krænbərɪ] *n.* small, red, acid berry, used for making jam and sauce.

crane [kreɪn] *n.* **1.** large water-bird with long legs and neck. **2.** machine for lifting heavy loads. (See the picture.) *v.t. & i.* stretch out (the neck) to see: ~ *one's neck.*

cra·ni·um ['kreɪnjəm] *n.* (pl. -*nia*, ~s) bony part of the head enclosing the brain.

crank¹ [kræŋk] *n.* person with fixed (often strange) ideas, esp. on one matter (e.g. a man who refuses to sleep indoors). ~**y** *adj.* (-*ier*, -*iest*) (of people) odd; rather mad; (of buildings, etc.) unsteady; shaky.

crank² [kræŋk] *n.* L-shaped arm and handle used to turn a machine. *v.t.* (cause to) move by turning a ~-handle: ~ *up an engine* (to make it start.)

cran·ny ['krænɪ] *n.* small crack or hole (e.g. in a wall).

crape [kreɪp] *n.* (no pl.) black silk or cotton material with a wrinkled surface.

crash [kræʃ] *v.i. & t.* **1.** fall or strike suddenly, violently, and noisily (esp. of things that break): *The bus* ~*ed into a house. The aircraft* ~*ed.* **2.** (of a business, government, etc.) come to ruin; meet disaster. **3.** (colloq.) enter without permission. **4.** cause to ~. *n.* **1.** (noise made by a) violent fall, blow, or breaking. **2.** ruin, downfall (of a government, business). ~ **bar·ri·er** *n.* rail, etc. designed to prevent cars from leaving the road, etc. '~-,**hel·met** *n.* helmet worn by a motor-cyclist to protect his head in a ~.

crass [kræs] *adj.* (of a quality such as ignorance, stupidity) complete; very great.

crate [kreɪt] *n.* large framework of light

boards or basketwork for goods in transport. *v.t.* put in a ~.

cra·ter ['kreɪtə*] *n.* mouth of a volcano; hole in the ground made by a bomb or shell, etc.

cra·vat [krə'væt] *n.* old-fashioned kind of necktie.

crave [kreɪv] *v.t. & i.* ask earnestly for; have a strong desire for. **crav·ing** *n.* desire.

crawl [krɔ:l] *v.i.* 1. move (on hands and knees) with the body close to the ground. 2. go very slowly. 3. be full of ~ing things: *a garden ~ing with ants.* 4. (of the flesh) feel as if covered with ~ing things. *n.* 1. ~ing movement: *go at a ~* (i.e. slowly). 2. *the ~,* fast swimming stroke.

cray·fish ['kreɪfɪʃ] *n.* lobster-like shell-fish living in rivers.

cray·on ['kreɪən] *n.* stick or pencil of soft coloured chalk or other material for drawing, etc.

craze [kreɪz] *v.t.* make crazy (1). *n.* 1. strong enthusiasm, esp. for sth. which is popular for a short time: *a boyish ~ for stamp-collecting.* 2. object of such enthusiasm.

cra·zy ['kreɪzɪ] *adj.* (-ier, -iest) 1. mad. 2. distraught; excited: *~ with pain; ~ on the cinema.* 3. foolish: *a ~ idea.* 4. (of buildings, etc.) unsafe; likely to collapse. **cra·zi·ly** *adv.* **cra·zi·ness** *n.*

creak [kri:k] *v.i. & n.* (make a) sound like that of new leather boots, a dry or rusty door-hinge, or badly fitting floorboards when trodden on. **~y** *adj.* (-ier, -iest) ~y stairs.

cream [kri:m] *n.* 1. fatty or oily part of milk that rises to the surface and can be made into butter. 2. substance containing ~ or like ~ in appearance; ~like paste, etc.: *~ cheese; face ~.* 3. best part of anything: *the ~ of society* (the 'best' people). 4. (no pl.) colour of ~. **~·ery** ['kri:mərɪ] *n.* place where ~, milk, butter, etc. are sold. **~y** *adj.* (-ier, -iest)

crease [kri:s] *n.* 1. line made (on cloth, paper, etc.) by crushing, folding, or pressing. 2. (cricket) chalk line on the ground marking certain players' positions by the wicket. *v.t. & i.* make, get, ~s in.

cre·ate [kri:'eɪt] *v.t.* cause sth. to exist; make (sth. new or original); produce. **cre·ation** [kri:'eɪʃn] *n.* act of creating; sth. ~d. *the Creation,* the world or universe as ~d by God. **cre·ative** [kri:'eɪtɪv] *adj.* having power to ~; of creation. **cre·ator** [kri:'eɪtə*] *n.* one who ~s. *the Creator,* God.

crea·ture ['kri:tʃə*] *n.* 1. living being; (of persons): *a lovely (poor, sickly) ~;* (of animals): *dumb ~s.* 2. person who is merely a tool of another person, carrying out his orders without question. 3. *~ comforts,* material or physical comforts (as food and drink).

crèche [kreɪʃ] *n.* public nursery where babies are looked after while their mothers are at work.

cre·dence ['kri:dəns] *n.* (no pl.) *give ~ to,* believe (what is said, etc.).

cre·den·tials [krɪ'denʃlz] *n. pl.* letters or papers showing that a person is what he claims to be.

cred·i·ble ['kredəbl] *adj.* that can be believed. **cred·i·bly** *adv.* **cred·i·bil·i·ty** [ˌkredɪ'bɪlətɪ] *n.*

cred·it ['kredɪt] *n.* 1. belief; trust. 2. good name; reputation. 3. honour; approval; favourable notice or regard: *The work does you ~. He is cleverer than I gave him ~ for.* 4. person, thing, act, etc. that adds to the reputation or good name of someone responsible for him (it): *pupils who are a ~ to their teacher.* 5. belief of others that a person, etc. can pay his debts or will keep a promise to pay: *His ~ is good only for £10. No ~ given at this shop* (i.e. all goods must be paid for in cash). *~ account,* account with a shop, etc. that enables a customer (1) to pay for goods, etc. at a later date. *~ card,* card that authorizes the holder to obtain goods on ~. *letter of ~* (from one bank to another giving authority for a stated payment). 6. money shown as owned by a person, etc. in his account with a bank. 7. (bookkeeping) record of money, etc. possessed by, or due to (sb., a business) (opp. *debit*). *v.t.* 1. believe; put trust in: *~ sb. with,* believe that he has. 2. enter on the ~ (7) side of an account. **~·able** ['kredɪtəbl] *adj.* bringing ~ (2, 3). **cred·i·tor** *n.* person to whom one owes money.

cred·u·lous ['kredjʊləs] *adj.* (too) ready to believe things. **cre·du·li·ty** [krɪ'dju:lətɪ] *n.*

creed [kri:d] *n.* (system of) beliefs or opinions. *the C~,* summary of the essential Christian beliefs.

creek [kri:k] *n.* 1. (Gt. Brit.) narrow inlet of water on the sea-shore or in a river-bank. 2. (U.S.A.) small river or tributary of a river.

creel [kri:l] *n.* wicker basket for carrying fish.

creep [kri:p] *v.i.* (p.t. & p.p. *crept* [krept]) move along with the body close to the ground or floor; move slowly, quietly, or secretly. *make sb.'s flesh* ~, frighten. *n. pl. the* ~s, (colloq.) feeling of horror or disgust as if insects were ~ing over one's flesh: *give sb. the* ~. *n.* insect, bird, etc. that ~s; (esp.) plant that ~s along the ground, over walls, etc. ~**y** *adj.* (-*ier*, -*iest*) having or causing the ~s.

cre·mate [krɪ'meɪt] *v.t.* burn (a dead body) to ashes. **cre·ma·tion** [krɪ'meɪʃn] *n.* **crem·a·to·ri·um** [ˌkreməˈtɔːrɪəm] *n.* (pl. -*ria*, ~s) furnace, place, for cremation.

cre·o·sote [ˈkrɪəsəʊt] *n.* (no pl.) oily liquid made from wood tar.

crêpe [kreɪp] *n.* (no pl.) name for crape-like materials, usu. white or coloured. ~ *rubber*, raw rubber with a wrinkled surface used for soles of shoes. ~ *paper*, paper with a wavy or wrinkled surface.

crept, see *creep*.

cre·scen·do [krɪˈʃendəʊ] *n.* (pl. ~s), *adj. & adv.* (passage of music to be played, sth. heard) with, of, increasing loudness.

cres·cent [ˈkresnt] *n.* (sth. shaped like the) curve of the moon in the first or last quarter. *adj.* (of the moon) increasing; growing.

cress [kres] *n.* (no pl.) name of various green plants with small, hot-tasting leaves, used in salads.

crest [krest] *n.* **1.** tuft of feathers on a bird's head or of hair on an animal's head; cock's comb. **2.** ~-like decoration formerly worn on the top of a helmet. **3.** design over the shield of a coat of arms, or used on notepaper, etc. **4.** top of a slope, hill, etc.; white top of a large wave. *v.t.* supply with, decorate with, a ~; get to the top of: ~ *a wave.* '~**fall·en** *adj.* dejected; disappointed (at failure, etc.).

cre·tonne [ˈkretɒn] *n.* (no pl.) cotton cloth with printed designs, used for curtains, etc.

cre·vasse [krɪˈvæs] *n.* deep, open crack, esp. in ice on a glacier.

crev·ice [ˈkrevɪs] *n.* narrow opening or crack (in a rock, etc.).

crew[1] [kruː] *n.* **1.** all the persons working a ship, aircraft, rowing a boat, etc. **2.** all these persons but the officers: *officers and* ~.

crew[2], see *crow*[2] (v.).

crib[1] [krɪb] *n.* **1.** baby's or child's bed with sides of rails or bars. **2.** rack (framework) from which animals eat hay, etc. *v.t.* (-*bb*-) shut up in a small space.

crib[2] [krɪb] *n.* sth. copied dishonestly

from the work of sb. else; translation of a foreign text used (esp. illegitimately) by students while taking exams, etc. *v.t. & i.* (-*bb*-) copy (another's written work) dishonestly; use a ~; cheat.

crick [krɪk] *n.* (no pl.) stiff condition of neck or back muscles causing sharp, sudden pain.

crick·et[1] [ˈkrɪkɪt] *n.* small, brown, jumping insect that makes a shrill noise by rubbing its front wings together.

crick·et[2] [ˈkrɪkɪt] *n.* (no pl.) ball game played on a grass field with bats and wickets by two teams of eleven players each. *not* ~, (colloq.) unfair; unsportsmanlike. ~**·er** *n.*

cried, **cri·er**, see *cry*.

crime [kraɪm] *n.* **1.** offence(s) for which there is severe punishment by law; serious law-breaking: *commit a* ~. **2.** (in the army) serious breaking of rules, not necessarily an offence against the civil law. **3.** foolish or wrong act (not necessarily an offence against the law). **crim·i·nal** [ˈkrɪmɪnl] *adj.* of ~; guilty of ~. *n.* person who commits a ~ or ~s. **crim·i·nol·o·gy** [ˌkrɪmɪˈnɒlədʒɪ] *n.* (no pl.) science of ~; study of ~ and criminals.

crimp [krɪmp] *v.t.* make (e.g. hair) wavy or curly (as with a hot iron).

crim·son [ˈkrɪmzn] *adj. & n.* (no pl.) deep red. *v.t. & i.* make or become ~.

cringe [krɪndʒ] *v.i.* **1.** move (the body) back or down in fear. **2.** behave (towards a superior) in a way that shows lack of self-respect; be too humble.

crin·kle [ˈkrɪŋkl] *n.* small, narrow wave or fold (in material such as cloth or paper). *v.t. & i.* make or get a ~ or ~s in.

crin·o·line [ˈkrɪnəliːn] *n.* light framework covered with stiff material, formerly worn to make a skirt swell out; skirt with this.

crip·ple [ˈkrɪpl] *n.* person unable to walk or move properly, through injury or disease in the spine or limbs. *v.t.* make a ~ of; (fig.) damage or weaken seriously.

cri·sis [ˈkraɪsɪs] *n.* (pl. -*ses* [ˈkraɪsiːz]) turning-point (in illness, life, history, etc.); time of danger, difficulty, or anxiety about the future.

crisp [krɪsp] *adj.* **1.** hard, dry, and easily broken (esp. of food). **2.** (of the weather, air) frosty; cold. **3.** with small tight curls or wrinkles: ~ *hair*. **4.** (of style, manners) quick, precise, and decided. *n.* (usu. pl.) (Gt. Brit.) thin slice cut from a potato, fried and dried

(usu. sold in packets): *potato ~s.* **~·ly**
adv. **~·ness** *n.* (no pl.).

cri·te·ri·on [kraɪ'tɪərɪən] *n.* (pl. *-ria*
[-rɪə], *~s*) standard of judgement;
principle by which sth. is measured
for value.

crit·ic ['krɪtɪk] *n.* **1.** person who judges
and writes about literature, art, music,
etc. **2.** person who finds fault, points
out mistakes, etc.

crit·i·cal ['krɪtɪkl] *adj.* **1.** of or at a
crisis: *a ~ moment in our history*; *a
patient who is in a ~ condition.* **2.** of the
work of a critic: *~ opinions on literature.*
3. fault-finding: *~ remarks.* **~·ly** *adv.*

crit·i·cism ['krɪtɪsɪzəm] *n.* **1.** work of a
critic; judgement(s) given by a critic. **2.**
fault-finding. **crit·i·cize** ['krɪtɪsaɪz]
v.t. form and give a judgement of; find
fault with.

croak [krəʊk] *n.* hoarse sound (as)
made by frogs and ravens. *v.i. & t.* **1.**
make this sound; speak or say in a ~ing
voice. **2.** express dismal views about
the future; foretell (evil).

cro·chet ['krəʊʃeɪ] *v.t. & i.* make
(needlework) with threads looped over
others with the help of a small *~-hook.*
n. (no pl.) needlework of this kind.

crock¹ [krɒk] *n.* pot or jar made of
baked earth (e.g. for containing water);
broken piece of such a pot. **~·ery**
['krɒkərɪ] *n.* (no pl.) pots, plates, cups,
and other dishes made of baked clay.

crock² [krɒk] *n.* (colloq.) broken-down
animal (esp. horse); person who cannot work well because of bad health,
lameness, etc. *v.t. & i. ~ up,* (colloq.)
(cause to) collapse.

croc·o·dile ['krɒkədaɪl] *n.* river reptile
with a long body and tail, covered
with hard skin. *~ tears,* insincere sorrow.

a crocodile

cro·cus ['krəʊkəs] *n.* (pl. *~es*) early
spring flower growing from a bulb.

cro·ny ['krəʊnɪ] *n.* close friend.

crook [krʊk] *n.* **1.** stick with a rounded
hook at one end, esp. such a stick used
by a shepherd. **2.** bend or curve. **3.**
(colloq.) person who makes a living by
dishonest or criminal means. *v.t. & i.*
bend, curve, like a ~. **~·ed** ['krʊkɪd]
adj. bent; not straight; (of a person,

his actions) dishonest; not straightforward.

croon [kruːn] *v.t. & i.* hum or sing
gently in a narrow range of notes: *~ t*
oneself; ~ a lullaby. **~·er** *n.* kind of
entertainer singing sentimental songs
in a smooth voice.

crop¹ [krɒp] *n.* **1.** yearly (or season's)
produce of grain, grass, fruit, etc.: *the*
potato ~; a good ~ of wheat; (pl.) agri-
cultural plants in the fields: *get the ~*
in. **2.** group of persons or things
amount of anything, appearing on
produced together: *a ~ of questions pu*
to the Minister of Defence.

crop² [krɒp] *n.* **1.** bag-like part in
bird's throat where food is broken up
for digestion before going into the
stomach. **2.** handle of a whip. **3.** ver
short haircut.

crop³ [krɒp] *v.t. & i.* (*-pp-*) **1.** (of ani
mals) bite off the tops of (grass, plants
etc.). **2.** cut short (hair, a horse's tai
or ears). **3.** *~ up,* appear or arise unex
pectedly: *difficulties that ~ped up; ~ u*
(out), (of rock, minerals) show abov
the surface of the earth.

crop·per ['krɒpə*] *n. come a ~,* (colloq
have a bad fall; meet with failure (e.g
in an examination).

cro·quet ['krəʊkeɪ] *n.* (no pl.) gam
played on short grass with woode
balls which are knocked with woode
mallets through hoops.

cro·sier, cro·zier ['krəʊʒə*] *n.* bishop
staff, usu. shaped like a shepherd
crook.

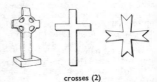

crosses (2)

cross [krɒs] *n.* **1.** the mark (X): *at t*
place marked with a X. **2.** post wi
another piece of wood across it. *the C*
structure on which Jesus was crucifie
(fig.) *sb.'s ~,* his burden of sorrow; *be*
one's ~. **3.** *~-shaped badge or deco*
tion. **4.** offspring of two animals
plants of different breeds or sorts:
mule is a ~ between a horse and an a
adj. **1.** (colloq.) bad-tempered; irri
ble. **2.** passing or lying across; *~*
winds) contrary. **3.** *be at ~ purposes,*
two persons) be talking of differe
things, having different purposes, e

v.t. & i. **1.** pass from one side to the other of; go across: ~ *the road*; ~ *from Dover to Calais*; ~ *one's mind*, (of an idea) occur to, come into, the mind. **2.** place ~wise: ~ *one's legs (arms)*; *keep one's fingers* ~*ed* (to bring good luck). **3.** draw a line across: ~ *out (off)*, cancel (sth. written); ~ *a cheque*, draw two lines across it so that payment can be made only through a bank. **4.** make the sign of the C~ on or over as a religious act: ~ *oneself*; ~ *one's heart* (as a sign of one's sincerity). **5.** produce a ~ (4) by mixing breeds, etc. **6.** oppose; obstruct (sb. or his plans or wishes). **7.** meet and pass. '~·**bar** *n.* horizontal bar (e.g. of a football goal or bicycle). ~·**bow** ['krɒsbəʊ] *n.* old kind of bow placed across a grooved wooden support. ‚~·'**coun·try** *adj. & adv.* across fields, etc.: ~*-country skiing*. ‚~·**ex·'am·ine** *v.t.* question closely, esp. to test answers already given in answer to sb. else. '~·**ex‚am·i'na·tion** *n.* '~·**eyed** *adj.* with one or both eyes turned towards the nose. ‚~·'**head·ing** *n.* (in a book, newspaper, etc.) short announcement printed across the column to point out the contents of what is beneath. ~·**ing** *n.* (*level* or U.S.A. *grade* ~*ing*) place where a road and a railway ~; (*street* ~*ing*) place marked for a street. ~·**ly** *adv.* irritably. ‚~·'**ref·er·ence** *n.* reference from one part of a book to another part of the same book. '~·**roads** *n. pl.* (sing. v.) place where two or more roads ~; (fig.) time when one must make an important choice (of action, etc.). ‚~·'**sec·tion** *n.* (drawing of) what is seen when sth. is cut through vertically; (fig.) typical selection (of people or things). ~·**wise** *adv.* across; diagonally. '~·**word** ('**puz·zle**) *n.* square with spaces in which letters forming words (indicated by clues) are to be written across and downwards. **crotch·et** ['krɒtʃɪt] *n.* **1.** black-headed note (♩) in music. **2.** strange, unreasonable idea. ~**y** *adj.* full of ~s (2).

crouch [krautʃ] *v.i.* stoop with the limbs together (in fear, or to hide, or, of animals, ready to jump). *n.* ~*ing* position.

crow[1] [krəʊ] *n.* large, black bird with a harsh cry. *as the* ~ *flies*, in a straight line.

crow[2] [krəʊ] *v.i.* (p.t. ~*ed* or (only of birds) **crew** [kruː], p.p. ~*ed*) **1.** (of a cock) cry. **2.** (of a baby) make sounds showing happiness. **3.** (of persons) express triumph at having succeeded: ~ *over a defeated enemy. n.* ~*ing* sound.

crow·bar ['krəʊbɑː*] *n.* long, iron bar or rod useful as a lever for moving heavy objects.

crowd [kraud] *n.* large number of people in one place, esp. out of doors: *A* ~ *(C*~*s) of people watched the procession. v.i. & t.* form, come together in, a ~; (cause to) fill a space: ~ *a hall with people*; ~*ing into the buses.*

a crown (1)

crown [kraun] *n.* **1.** ornamental head-dress of gold, jewels, etc. worn by a king or queen on special occasions. **2.** symbol, sign, of royal power or victory: *the C*~, royal authority; *officer of the C*~, State official; *C*~ *Court*, court (1) of criminal jurisdiction in England and Wales. **3.** top of the head or of a hat; part of a tooth that shows. **4.** *half-crown*, (formerly) British coin, value 2s. 6d. (= 12$\frac{1}{2}$p). *v.t.* **1.** put a ~ (1) on (a king, etc.); reward as with a ~ (2). **2.** be or have at the top of: *hill* ~*ed with a wood.*

cro·zier, see *crosier*.

cru·cial ['kruːʃl] *adj.* critical (1).

cru·ci·ble ['kruːsɪbl] *n.* pot in which metals are melted.

cru·ci·fix ['kruːsɪfɪks] *n.* small model of the Cross with the figure of Jesus on it. ~·**ion** [‚kruːsɪ'fɪkʃn] *n.* crucifying. *the C*~*ion,* that of Jesus. **cru·ci·fy** ['kruːsɪfaɪ] *v.t.* put to death by nailing or binding to a cross.

crude [kruːd] *adj.* **1.** (of materials) in a natural state; not refined or manufactured: ~ *oil (sugar).* **2.** (of persons, their behaviour) rough; not polite or refined. **3.** of unskilled workmanship: *a* ~ *hut.* ~·**ly** *adv.* ~·**ness** *n.* **cru·di·ty** ['kruːdətɪ] *n.*

cru·el [kruəl] *adj.* (~*er,* ~*est*; also *-ll-*) taking pleasure in, causing or ready to cause, pain or suffering. ~·**ly** *adv.* ~·**ty** *n.*

cru·et ['kruːɪt] *n.* container(s) for condiment(s) to be used at table.

cruise [kruːz] *v.i.* sail about, either for pleasure, or (in war) looking for enemy ships. *n.* cruising voyage. **cruis·er** *n.* large warship; *cabin* ~*r,* motor boat with a cabin, for pleasure ~s.

crumb [krʌm] *n.* very small piece of

dry food, esp. a bit of bread or cake rubbed off or dropped from a large piece; (fig.) small amount: *a few ~s of comfort (information)*.

crum·ble ['krʌmbl] *v.t. & i.* break, rub, or fall into crumbs or small pieces: *crumbling cliffs*.

crum·ple ['krʌmpl] *v.t. & i.* press or crush into folds or creases; become full of folds or creases. *~ up*, (lit., fig.) crush; collapse.

crunch [krʌntʃ] *v.t. & i.* crush noisily with the teeth when eating; crush noisily under foot, under wheels, etc. *n.* noise made by ~ing.

cru·sade [kru:'seɪd] *n.* 1. any one of the wars made by the Christian rulers and people of Europe during the Middle Ages to get the Holy Land back from the Muslims. 2. any struggle or movement in support of sth. believed to be good or against sth. believed to be bad. *v.i.* take part in a ~. **cru·sad·er** *n.*

crush [krʌʃ] *v.t. & i.* 1. press, be pressed, so that there is breaking or harming: *~ sth. to powder*. 2. subdue; overwhelm. *n.* crowd of people pressed together. *~-barrier*, (temporary) barrier to keep back a crowd. *~ing adj.* overwhelming.

crust [krʌst] *n.* hard outer part of bread; piece of this; hard outer covering of a pie; hard surface: *a ~ of ice*; *the earth's ~. v.t. & i.* cover with, form into, a ~; become covered with a ~. *~y adj.* (*-ier, -iest*) 1. having much ~; hard like a ~. 2. (of persons) easily made cross (1).

crus·ta·cean [krʌˈsteɪʃjən] *n.* any of numerous water animals with a hard, outer covering (e.g. crabs, lobsters, etc.).

crutch [krʌtʃ] *n.* support put under the arm to help a lame person to walk: *a pair of ~es*.

crux [krʌks] *n.* (pl. *~es, cruces*) part of a problem that is the most difficult to solve.

cry [kraɪ] *v.i. & t.* (p.t. & p.p. *cried* [kraɪd]) 1. make (loud) sounds of pain, grief, fear; weep; shed tears. 2. shout; announce; advertise. *~ sth. down*, suggest that it is worth little. *n.* 1. loud sound made in ~ing. 2. fit of weeping. 3. *in full ~*, (of a pack of dogs) barking together as they hunt or pursue (an animal). *~ing adj.* demanding attention: *a ~ing evil (need)*. **cri·er** ['kraɪə*] *n.* (esp. *town crier*) person making public announcements.

crypt [krɪpt] *n.* underground room, esp. of a church, used for burials.

cryp·tic ['krɪptɪk] *adj.* secret; with hidden meaning or a meaning no easily seen.

crys·tal ['krɪstl] *n.* 1. clear, natural sub stance like quartz; piece of this cut a an ornament. 2. glassware of bes quality, made into bowls, vessels, etc 3. (science) one of the fragments, reg ular and clearly defined in shape, int which certain minerals separate natu rally: *sugar and salt ~s*. *~-gaz·ing n* (no pl.) looking into a ~ ball in an at tempt to see future events picture there. *~line* ['krɪstəlaɪn] *adj.* of or lik ~; very clear. *~lize* ['krɪstəlaɪz] *v.t. & i.* (cause to) form into ~s; cover (fruit sweets, etc.) with sugar ~s; (fig. o ideas, plans) become, cause to be clear and definite.

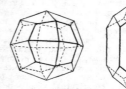

crystals (1, 3)

cub [kʌb] *n.* young lion, bear, fox, tiger badly-behaved young man.

cube [kju:b] *n.* 1. solid body having six equal square sides; block of sth. s shaped: *a flash ~*. 2. (math.) product o a number multiplied by itself twice **cu·bic** ['kju:bɪk] *adj.* ~-shaped; of a ~ *cubic metre*, volume of a ~ whose edge is one metre; *cubic content*, volume ex pressed in cubic metres, feet, etc.

cu·bi·cle ['kju:bɪkl] *n.* small division o a larger room, walled or curtained t make a separate compartment (e.g. fo sleeping in, dressing, etc.).

cuck·oo ['kuku:] *n.* bird whose call sounds like its name; it lays its eggs in the nests of other birds.

cu·cum·ber ['kju:kʌmbə*] *n.* plant with long, green fleshy fruit used fo salads, etc.

cud [kʌd] *n.* (no pl.) food that oxen and some other animals bring back from the first stomach and chew again.

cud·dle ['kʌdl] *v.t. & i.* hold close and lovingly in one's arms; lie close and snug; nestle together: *~ a doll*.

cud·gel ['kʌdʒəl] *v.t. & n.* (*-ll-*, U.S.A also *-l-*) (beat with a) short, thick stick

cue¹ [kju:] *n.* sth. (e.g. the last words of an actor's speech) that shows sb. else is to do or say sth.

cue² [kju:] *n.* billiard-player's long stick.

cuff¹ [kʌf] *n.* end of a shirt or coat sleeve at the wrist.

cuff² [kʌf] *v.t. & n.* (give sb. a) light blow with the fist or open hand.

cul-de-sac [ˌkʊldə'sæk] *n.* street with an opening at one end only.

cu·li·nary ['kʌlɪnərɪ] *adj.* of cooking or a kitchen.

cul·mi·nate ['kʌlmɪneɪt] *v.i.* (of a career, of efforts, hopes, etc.) reach the highest point (*in*). **cul·mi·na·tion** [ˌkʌlmɪ'neɪʃn] *n.*

cul·pa·ble ['kʌlpəbl] *adj.* blameworthy; deserving punishment.

cul·prit ['kʌlprɪt] *n.* person who has done wrong; offender.

cult [kʌlt] *n.* system of religious belief and worship; devotion to a person, thing, or practice: *the ~ of archery.*

cul·ti·vate ['kʌltɪveɪt] *v.t.* **1.** prepare (land) for crops by ploughing, etc.; help (crops) to grow. **2.** give care, thought, time, etc. in order to develop sth.: *~ the mind (one's manners, sb.'s friendship).* **cul·ti·vat·ed** *adj.* (of a person) having good manners and education. **cul·ti·va·tion** [ˌkʌltɪ'veɪʃn] *n.* (no pl.). **cul·ti·va·tor** ['kʌltɪveɪtə*] *n.* (esp.) machine for breaking up ground, destroying weeds, etc.

cul·tur·al ['kʌltʃərəl] *adj.* of or relating to culture: *a ~ institute.*

cul·ture ['kʌltʃə*] *n.* **1.** advanced development of the human powers; development of the body, mind, and spirit by training and experience. **2.** evidence of intellectual development (of arts, science, etc.) in human society or of a particular nation: *Greek ~.* **3.** cultivating; the rearing of bees, silkworms, etc. **4.** growth of bacteria. **~d** *adj.* (of a person) having ~ of the mind; (of interests, etc.) refined.

cul·vert ['kʌlvət] *n.* channel built to carry water or electric cables under the ground.

cum·ber·some ['kʌmbəsəm], **cum·brous** ['kʌmbrəs] *adjs.* burdensome; heavy and awkward to move or carry.

cu·mu·la·tive ['kju:mjʊlətɪv] *adj.* increasing in amount by one addition after another.

cu·mu·lus ['kju:mjʊləs] *n.* (pl. *-li* [-laɪ]) rounded masses of cloud, flat on the under side. (Cf. *cirrus.*)

cu·nei·form ['kju:nɪɪfɔ:m] *adj.* wedge-shaped: *~ characters* (as used in Assyrian writing).

cun·ning ['kʌnɪŋ] *adj.* (often *~er, ~est*) **1.** clever at deceiving; showing such cleverness; *a ~ old fox; a ~ trick.* **2.** (old use) skilful. *n.* (no pl.) quality of being ~. *~·ly adv.*

cup [kʌp] *n.* **1.** drinking-vessel, usu. with a handle and used with a saucer: *a tea~ (coffee-~);* contents of a ~: *a ~ of tea (coffee).* **2.** vessel (usu. gold or silver) given as a prize in competitions. **3.** sth. shaped like a ~. *v.t.* (*-pp-*) put into the shape of a ~: *~ one's hands;* place (as if) in a ~: *~ping his chin in his hand.* *~·ful n.*

a cup (1)
and saucer

a cupola

cup·board ['kʌbəd] *n.* set of shelves enclosed by a door or doors, either a separate piece of furniture or built into a room, used for stores (3), dishes, clothes, etc.

cu·pid·i·ty [kju:'pɪdətɪ] *n.* (no pl.) greed, esp. for money or property.

cu·po·la ['kju:pələ] *n.* small dome.

cur [kɜ:*] *n.* bad-tempered or worthless dog; cowardly or badly-behaved man.

cur·able, cu·ra·tive, see **cure.**

cu·rate ['kjʊərət] *n.* clergyman who helps a rector or vicar. **cu·ra·cy** ['kjʊərəsɪ] *n.* ~'s office (3) and work.

cu·ra·tor [ˌkjʊə'reɪtə*] *n.* official in charge, esp. of a museum.

curb¹ [kɜ:b] *n.* chain or leather strap under a horse's lower jaw, used to control it; (fig.) sth. that restrains: *keep a ~ on one's temper.* *v.t.* control (a horse) by means of a ~; keep (feelings, etc.) under control.

curb² [kɜ:b] see **kerb.**

curd [kɜ:d] *n.* thick, soft substance formed when milk turns sour, used to make cheese; substance resembling ~: *lemon-~.* **cur·dle** ['kɜ:dl] *v.t. & i.* (cause to) form into ~s; become ~-like.

cure [kjʊə*] *v.t. & i.* **1.** bring back to health; make well again. **2.** take away, get rid of, sth. wrong or evil: *~ poverty.* **3.** treat (meat, fish, skins, tobacco, etc.) in order to keep it in good condition by salting, drying, etc. **4.** effect a ~. *n.*

curing or being ~d (1); substance or treatment that ~s (1). **cu·rable** [ˈkjʊərəbl] *adj.* that can be ~d. **cu·ra·tive** [ˈkjʊərətɪv] *adj.* helping to, able to, ~ ill health.

cur·few [ˈkɜːfjuː] *n.* **1.** (old use) ringing of a bell as a signal for lights to be put out and fires covered; bell for this; hour at which the bell was rung. **2.** time or signal (under martial law) for people to remain indoors.

cu·rio [ˈkjʊərɪəʊ] *n.* (pl. ~s) work of art of a strange or unusual character and therefore valued.

cu·ri·ous [ˈkjʊərɪəs] *adj.* **1.** eager to learn or know. **2.** having or showing too much interest in the affairs of others: ~ *neighbours.* **3.** strange; unusual; difficult to understand. **cu·ri·os·i·ty** [ˌkjʊərɪˈɒsətɪ] *n.* **1.** (no pl.) being ~ (1, 2). **2.** ~ (3) thing; strange or rare object. **~·ly** *adv.*

curl [kɜːl] *n.* sth. shaped like or twisted into a shape like the thread of a screw: ~*s of hair falling over a girl's shoulders; keep one's hair in ~ with pins; a ~ of smoke.* *v.t. & i.* make into ~s; grow or be in ~s: ~ *one's hair; hair that ~s naturally; ~ up in a big chair; smoke ~ing upwards.* **~·y** *adj.* (-ier, -iest) full of ~s; arranged in ~s: ~*y hair.*

a curl

cur·rant [ˈkʌrənt] *n.* **1.** small, sweet, dried, seedless grape used in cooking. **2.** (bush with) small black, white, or red juicy fruit growing in clusters: *black (white, red) ~.*

cur·ren·cy [ˈkʌrənsɪ] *n.* being current (1): *words in common ~.* **2.** money at present in use in a country: *foreign currencies.*

cur·rent¹ [ˈkʌrənt] *adj.* **1.** in common or general use: ~ *words (coin).* ~ *account,* account with a bank from which money may be drawn without notice. **2.** now passing; of the present time: *the ~ year,* this year; *the ~ issue of a magazine.*

cur·rent² [ˈkʌrənt] *n.* **1.** stream of water, air, or gas, esp. one flowing through slower-moving or still water, etc. **2.** flow of electricity through sth.

or along a wire, etc. **3.** course or movement (of events, thought, opinions life).

cur·ric·u·lum [kəˈrɪkjʊləm] *n.* (pl. *-la* ~s) course of study in a school, college etc. ~ *vitae,* short, written account of one's career and qualifications (1) used when applying (1) for a position

cur·ry¹ [ˈkʌrɪ] *n.* dish of food (meat eggs, fish, etc.) cooked with ~*-powder* (made from hot-tasting spices). *v.t.* prepare (food) with ~-powder.

cur·ry² [ˈkʌrɪ] *v.t.* rub down or clean (a horse) with a special comb. ~ *favour with,* try to win the favour or approval of (by using flattery, etc.).

curse [kɜːs] *n.* **1.** words or phrases calling for the punishment, injury, or destruction of sb. or sth. **2.** word or words used in violent language expressing anger. **3.** cause of misfortune, ruin, etc.: *Gambling is often a ~.* *v.t. & i.* **1.** use a ~ against; utter ~s (*at*). **2.** *be ~d with,* suffer misfortune, trouble, etc. because of: *be ~d with idle daughters* ~**d** [ˈkɜːsɪd] *adj.* hateful; deserving to be ~d: *This work is a ~d nuisance.*

cur·so·ry [ˈkɜːsərɪ] *adj.* (of work, reading, etc.) quick; hurried; done without attention to details: *a ~ glance (inspection).*

curt [kɜːt] *adj.* (of a speaker or what he says) short-spoken; hardly polite. ~**·ly** *adv.*

cur·tail [kɜːˈteɪl] *v.t.* make shorter than was at first planned: ~ *a speech (one's holidays).* ~**·ment** *n.*

cur·tain [ˈkɜːtn] *n.* **1.** piece of cloth or lace hung in front of a window, door, etc. **2.** sheet of heavy material separating the stage of a theatre from the part where the audience sits. **3.** sth. that hides or covers like a ~. *v.t.* furnish, cover, shut *off*, with a ~ or ~s.

curt·sey, curt·sy [ˈkɜːtsɪ] *n.* (pl. *-seys, -sies*) movement of respect (bending the knees) made by women and girls (e.g. to a queen): *make (drop) a ~.* *v.i.* make a ~ (*to*).

curve [kɜːv] *n.* line of which no part is straight. *v.t. & i.* (cause to) have the form of a ~. **cur·va·ture** [ˈkɜːvətjə*] *n.* curving; state of being ~d: *the curvature of the earth's surface.*

cush·ion [ˈkʊʃn] *n.* small bag filled with feathers, etc. (to make a seat more comfortable, etc.); sth. like a ~. *v.t.* supply or protect with ~s.

cus·tard [ˈkʌstəd] *n.* mixture of eggs and milk, sweetened and flavoured, baked or boiled.

cus·to·dy [ˈkʌstədɪ] *n.* (no pl.) **1.** (duty of) keeping safe, under one's control, caring for. **2.** imprisonment. **cus·to·di·an** [kʌˈstəʊdjən] *n.* person who has ～ of sb. or sth.; caretaker of a public building.

cus·tom [ˈkʌstəm] *n.* **1.** generally accepted behaviour among members of a social group. (Cf. *habit* (1) for sth. done regularly by an individual.) **2.** regular support given to a tradesman by those who buy his goods: *take away one's ～ from a shop because prices are too high.* **3.** (pl.) taxes due to the government on goods imported into a country; import duties: *the C～s, department of government collecting such taxes.* (Cf. *excise*[1].) **～·ary** [ˈkʌstəmərɪ] *adj.* in agreement with, according to, ～ (1). **～·er** *n.* **1.** person who gives his ～ (2) to a tradesman; person buying things in a shop. **2.** (colloq.) person or fellow, esp.: *a queer (an awkward) ～er.* **～(s)-house** [ˈkʌstəm(z)haʊs] *n.* office at a port or station where ～s (3) are collected.

cut [kʌt] *v.t. & i.* (*-tt-*; p.t. & p.p. ～) **1.** divide or separate into two, etc.; make an opening, tear, or wound in (using a knife, razor, pair of scissors, etc.); detach or sever by ～ting; shorten (hair, nails, etc.); reduce (wages, prices, etc.); shape or fashion by ～ting. **2.** (with advs., preps., or adjs.): ～ *at sth.,* aim a sharp blow at (e.g. with a stick); ～ *sth. away,* remove by ～ting; ～ *sth. back,* (a) prune; (b) reduce (expenditure, etc.); ～ *sth. down,* (a) bring down by ～ting; (b) make smaller in size or amount; ～ *in,* (mot.) return to one's own side of the road too soon after having overtaken another vehicle; ～ *in(to),* interrupt; ～ *sth. (sb.) off,* (a) remove by ～ting; (b) stop, separate, or interrupt: ～ *off the enemy's retreat; be ～ off while telephoning;* ～ *sth. out,* remove, make, or shape by ～ting: ～ *out a picture from a magazine;* ～ *out a dress (from cloth); be ～ out for,* be suited to; have the necessary qualities for: *He's not ～ out for that sort of work.* ～ *sth. up,* cut to pieces; destroy; be ～ *up by,* be made very unhappy by; ～ *sth. short,* make short(er): ～ *a long story short.* **3.** pass (a person) and pretend not to know (him): ～ *a man (dead) in the street.* **4.** stay away from (a class or lecture at school, etc.). **5.** ～ *a tooth,* have a new tooth showing through the gums; ～ *cards,* (in card games) divide the pack into two parts to select the dealer, etc.; ～ *both ways,* (of an argument, etc.) have advantages and disadvantages; ～ *a loss,* ～ *one's losses,* accept financial losses and make a fresh start in good time; ～ *and dried,* (of opinions, plans, etc.) all decided and ready. *n.* **1.** act of ～ting; stroke, blow, with a knife, razor, sword, or whip; wound made by ～ting. **2.** reduction in size or amount: *a ～ in prices (wages); a power (3) ～.* **3.** ～ting out; part that is ～ out (e.g. in a film, book, etc.). **4.** sth. obtained by ～ting: *a nice ～ of beef; cold ～s* (see *cold* (3)). **5.** style in. which clothes, etc. are made by ～ting: *the ～ of a coat.* **6.** (cricket, tennis, etc.) sharp, quick stroke: *a ～ to the boundary.* **7.** *a short ～,* (see *short* (2)). (See *wood～.*) **～·ter** *n.* **1.** person or thing that ～s: *a tailor's ～ter; wire-～ters.* **2.** sailing-vessel with one mast. **3.** warship's boat for rowing or sailing to or from it. **'～·throat** *n.* murderer. *adj.* (fig.) deadly: ～*throat competition.* **～·ting** *n.* **1.** unroofed passage dug through the ground (for a road, railway, canal, etc.). **2.** (U.S.A. *clipping*) sth. cut from a newspaper, etc. **3.** short piece of stem, etc. cut from a plant, to be used for growing a new plant. *adj.* (of words, etc.) unkind; wounding the feelings.

cute [kjuːt] *adj.* (～*r,* ～*st*) (colloq.) sharp-witted; quick-thinking; (U.S.A.) attractive.

cu·ti·cle [ˈkjuːtɪkl] *n.* outer layer of skin (esp. at the base of the fingernails or toe-nails).

cut·lass [ˈkʌtləs] *n.* (sailor's) short sword; cacao-grower's or copra-grower's cutting tool.

cut·ler [ˈkʌtlə*] *n.* man who makes or repairs knives and other cutting instruments. **～·y** *n.* (no pl.) cutting instruments; (esp.) knives, forks, and spoons.

cut·let [ˈkʌtlɪt] *n.* thick slice of meat or fish cut off before frying: *a veal ～.*

cy·ber·net·ics [ˌsaɪbəˈnetɪks] *n. pl.* (sing. v.) comparative study of the systems of control and communications in animals and machines. **cy·ber·net·ic** *adj.*

cy·cle [ˈsaɪkl] *n.* **1.** series of events taking place in a regularly repeated order: *the ～ of the seasons;* complete set or series: *a song-～.* **2.** (short for) bicycle or motor ～. *v.i.* ride a ～ (2). **cy·clist** [ˈsaɪklɪst] *n.* person who rides a ～ (2).

cy·clone [ˈsaɪkləʊn] *n.* violent wind moving round a calm central area.

cy·clo·pae·dia [ˌsaɪkləʊˈpiːdjə] *n.* = encyclopaedia.

cyl·in·der [ˈsɪlɪndə*] *n.* **1.** long, round, solid or hollow body. **2.** ~-shaped chamber (in an engine) in which gas or steam works a piston: *a six-~ motor car.* **cy·lin·dri·cal** [sɪˈlɪndrɪkl] *adj.*

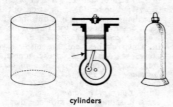

cylinders

cym·bal [ˈsɪmbl] *n.* one of a pair of round metal plates struck together to make clanging sounds.

cyn·ic [ˈsɪnɪk] *n.* person who finds pleasure in detecting and sneering at human weaknesses. **cyn·i·cal** [ˈsɪnɪkl] *adj.* of or like a ~; contemptuous. **cyn·i·cism** [ˈsɪnɪsɪzəm] *n.*

cy·no·sure [ˈsɪnəˌzjʊə*] *n.* sth. or sb. that draws everyone's attention.

cy·pher, see *cipher.*

cy·press [ˈsaɪprəs] *n.* evergreen tree with dark leaves and hard wood.

cyst [sɪst] *n.* (biol.) small, bag-like structure in the body, usu. containing liquid matter.

Czech·o·slo·vak [ˌtʃekəʊˈsləʊvæk], **Czech·o·slo·va·ki·an** [ˌtʃekəʊsləʊˈvækɪən] *n. & adj.* (native or inhabitant) of Czechoslovakia.

D

dab [dæb] *v.t. & i.* (*-bb-*) touch, put on, lightly and gently. *n.* quick, light touch; small quantity (of paint, etc.) dabbed on sth.

dab·ble ['dæbl] *v.t. & i.* **1.** splash (the hands, feet, etc.) about in water. **2.** ~ *in* or *at* (*politics, art, etc.*), take an interest in, study, but not professionally.

dachs·hund ['dækshʊnd] *n.* small breed of dog with a long body, short legs, and drooping ears.

dad(·dy) ['dæd(ɪ)] *n.* child's word for 'father'. **dad·dy-long-legs** [ˌdædɪˈlɒŋlegz] *n.* long-legged flying insect.

daf·fo·dil ['dæfədɪl] *n.* yellow flower with long narrow leaves growing from a bulb.

daft [dɑːft] *adj.* foolish; reckless; crazy.

dag·ger ['dægə*] *n.* short, pointed, two-edged knife used as a weapon.

dahl·ia ['deɪljə] *n.* garden plant with bright-coloured flowers.

dai·ly ['deɪlɪ] *adj. & adv.* happening, done, appearing, every day (or every weekday). *n.* newspaper published every weekday; (Gt. Brit., colloq.) female domestic employee coming daily.

dain·ty ['deɪntɪ] *adj.* (*-ier, -iest*) **1.** delicate (1, 2) in appearance or to the taste: ~ *china* (*food*). **2.** (of a person) having delicate (5) tastes; difficult to please. *n.* choice and delicate (7) food. **dain·ti·ly** *adv.* **dain·ti·ness** *n.* (no pl.).

dairy ['deərɪ] *n.* **1.** building or part of a building where milk is kept and butter made. **2.** shop selling milk, butter, eggs, etc.; ~ *farm*, farm producing milk, etc.; ~*maid*, girl or woman working in a ~ farm.

da·is ['deɪɪs] *n.* low platform for a lecturer, a throne, etc. facing an audience.

dai·sy ['deɪzɪ] *n.* small, white flower with a yellow centre, commonly growing wild; similar garden flower.

dale [deɪl] *n.* valley.

dal·li·ance ['dælɪəns] *n.* (no pl.) trifling behaviour; love-making for amusement.

dal·ly ['dælɪ] *v.i.* **1.** waste time. **2.** ~ *with*, trifle with; think idly about.

dam[1] [dæm] *n.* wall to hold back water. *v.t.* (*-mm-*) make a ~ across; hold back by means of a ~.

dam[2] [dæm] *n.* mother (of an animal).

dam·age ['dæmɪdʒ] *n.* **1.** (no pl.) harm, injury, causing loss of value. **2.** (pl.) (law) money asked from or paid by a person causing loss or injury. *v.t.* cause ~ (1) to.

dam·ask ['dæməsk] *n.* (no pl.) silk or linen material with designs shown by reflection of light.

dame [deɪm] *n.* **1.** (old use), woman, esp. a married woman. **2.** (title of a) woman who has received an honour corresponding to that of knighthood: *D~ of the Order of the British Empire*.

damn [dæm] *v.t.* **1.** condemn to everlasting punishment. **2.** say that sth. is worthless, bad, etc.: *a book ~ed by the critics*. **3.** (esp. as int.) used to express anger, annoyance, etc.: *I'll be ~ed if I'll ...*, *I refuse to ... n. I don't care* (*give*) *a ~*, I don't care at all. *Not worth a ~*, worthless. **dam·nable** ['dæmnəbl] *adj.* deserving ~ation; hateful. **dam·nably** *adv.* **dam·na·tion** [dæmˈneɪʃn] *n.* (no pl.) being ~ed; ruin. **~ed** *adj.* ~able: *a ~ed fool*. *adv.* extremely: *~ed funny*.

damp [dæmp] *adj.* not quite dry; having some moisture (in or on): ~ *clothes*; *wipe a window with a ~ cloth*. *n.* (no pl.) **1.** state of being ~; moisture in the air or on the surface of sth. **2.** (also *fire-~*) dangerous gas that may collect in coal-mines. *v.t.* **1.** make ~. **2.** (also ~*en*) make sad or dull. **3.** ~ *down*, cause (a fire) to burn slowly. **~·er** *n.* **1.** metal plate that regulates the flow of air through a fire in a stove or furnace. **2.** person or thing that ~s (1, 2). **~·ness** *n.* (no pl.).

dam·sel ['dæmzl] *n.* (old use) girl; young unmarried woman.

dam·son ['dæmzən] *n.* (tree producing) small dark, purple plum.

dance [dɑːns] *v.i. & t.* move with rhythmical steps, usu. to music; per-

dancing

form as a ~r: ~ *a waltz. She loves to* ~. **n.** act or instance of dancing.
danc·er **n.**

dan·de·li·on ['dændılaıən] **n.** common wild plant with bright yellow flowers.

a dandelion

dan·dle ['dændl] **v.t.** move (e.g. a child) up and down on one's knee(s) or in one's arms.

dan·druff ['dændrʌf] **n.** (no pl.) dead skin that forms on the scalp and comes off in small scales³ (2).

dan·dy ['dændı] **n.** person who pays great attention to his clothes and personal appearance.

Dane [deın] **n.** native or inhabitant of Denmark. (*Great*) ~, very large breed of dog.

dan·ger ['deındʒə*] **n.** chance of suffering, receiving injury, or being killed; sth. or sb. that causes ~. **~ous** ['deındʒərəs] **adj.** likely to be a ~ or cause ~ **~·ly** **adv.**

dan·gle ['dæŋgl] **v.i. & t. 1.** hang or swing loosely; hang or carry (sth.) so that it swings loosely. **2.** ~ *round* (*about, after,* sb.), stay near (sb.) as a follower, lover, etc.

Dan·ish ['deınıʃ] **n. & adj.** (language) of Denmark or the Danes.

dank [dæŋk] **adj. 1.** wet: ~ *undergrowth in a forest.* **2.** unpleasantly damp: ~ *weather* (*climate, air*).

dap·per ['dæpə*] **adj.** well and smartly dressed; neat.

dapple ['dæpl] **v.t. & i.** mark, become marked, with patches of different colours or shades of colour, esp. of an animal, of sunlight and shadow.

dare [deə*] **v.t.** (p.t. ~*d* or, less often,

durst [dɜːst]) **1.** be brave enough to; be bold or impudent enough to: *How ~ you say that I am a liar? I ~ say,* I think it likely, it seems to me probable: *He's not here yet, but I ~ say he will come later.* **2.** attempt; face the risks of (sth.): ~ *any danger*; ~ *sb.'s anger.* **3.** suggest that a person is unwilling to do sth.; challenge: ~ *sb. to jump across a stream.* '~,**dev·il adj. & n.** foolishly bold (person). **dar·ing n.** (no pl.) **& adj.** (quality of being) bold and adventurous.

dark [dɑːk] **adj. 1.** with no or very little light. **2.** (of colour) near black. **3.** (of the skin) not fair. **4.** *keep sth.* ~, keep it secret; *look on the ~ side of things,* see only what is sad or cheerless. **n.** absence of light: *We came home in the ~. keep sb. in the ~,* keep things secret from him; *be in the ~ about,* have no knowledge of. **~·en v.t. & i.** make or become ~. **~·ly adv. ~·ness n.** (no pl.).

dar·ling ['dɑːlıŋ] **n. & attrib. adj.** (person or object) much loved.

darn [dɑːn] **v.t.** mend (esp. a hole in sth. knitted, e.g. a sock) by passing thread in and out and across in two directions. **n.** place mended by ~ing. **~·ing n.** (esp.) things needing to be ~ed.

dart [dɑːt] **v.t. & i.** (cause to) move forward suddenly and quickly: ~ *an angry look at sb.;* ~ *out of a shop; a snake ~ing out its tongue.* **n. 1.** small, sharp-pointed object, esp. one thrown at a ~*board* in the indoor game called ~s. **2.** quick, sudden, forward movement.

dash [dæʃ] **v.t. & i. 1.** send or throw violently; move, be moved, quickly and violently. **2.** (fig.) destroy; discourage: ~ *a person's hopes.* **3.** splash (with water, mud, etc.). **n. 1.** sudden and violent forward movement: *make a ~ for shelter* (*freedom*). **2.** sound made by water, etc. when striking sth. or when being struck: *the ~ of the waves* (*of oars on the water*). **3.** small amount of sth. added or mixed: *a ~ of pepper in the soup.* **4.** stroke of the pen or a mark (—) used in printing. **5.** (no pl.) (capacity for) vigorous action; energy: *a soldier with plenty of ~.* '~**·board n.** board beneath the windscreen of a motor car, etc. that contains the instruments and controls (3). **~·ing** ['dæʃıŋ] **adj.** showing energy; full of life (8) and gallantry (1): *a ~ing young officer.*

das·tard ['dæstəd] **n.** brutal coward. **~·ly adj.**

deal

da·ta ['deɪtə] *n. pl.* **1.** facts; things certainly known (from which conclusions may be drawn). **2.** (usu. sing. v.) information prepared for and operated (1) on by a computer or computers. **~ bank** *n.* centre where information for computers is stored in large amounts. **~ pro·cess·ing** *n.* (no pl.) automatic processing of information by computers.

date[1] [deɪt] *n.* **1.** statement of the time, day, month, year, when something happened or is due to happen: *~ of birth*; *out of ~*, no longer used; old-fashioned; *out-of-~* (attrib. adj.); *up to ~*, in line with, according to, what is now known, used, etc.: *up-to-~ ideas* (*methods, etc.*). **2.** (colloq.) meeting fixed with sb. at a certain time and place. *v.t. & i.* **1.** have, put, (a ~ (1) on; give a ~ (1) to: *~ from*, *~ back to*, have existed since: *a house dating from the 17th century.* **2.** (colloq.) make a ~ (2) with.

date[2] [deɪt] *n.* small, brown, sweet fruit of the *~-palm*, common in N. Africa and W. Asia.

da·tive ['deɪtɪv] *n. & adj.* ~ (*case*), (gram.) form of a word (in Latin and other languages, but not English) showing that it is an indirect object of the verb.

daub [dɔ:b] *v.t. & i.* **1.** put (paint, clay, plaster, etc.) roughly on a surface. **2.** make dirty marks on. **3.** paint (pictures) without skill. *n.* material used for ~ing (e.g. clay); badly painted picture. **~·er** *n.*

daugh·ter ['dɔ:tə*] *n.* one's female child. **'~-in-law** *n.* (pl. *~s-in-law*) one's son's wife.

daunt [dɔ:nt] *v.t.* discourage. **~·less** ['dɔ:ntlɪs] *adj.* not ~ed; persevering.

dav·it ['dævɪt] *n.* one of a pair of metal arms supporting a ship's boat. (See the picture at *derrick*.)

daw·dle ['dɔ:dl] *v.i.* be slow; waste time. **~r** *n.*

dawn [dɔ:n] *n.* first light of day; (fig.) beginning: *the ~ of intelligence.* *v.i.* begin to grow light; (fig.) begin to appear: *~ on sb.*, grow clear to his mind.

day [deɪ] *n.* **1.** time between sunrise and sunset; period of twenty-four hours, from midnight: *pass the time of ~ (with sb.)*, exchange greetings, etc. (with); *the other ~*, a few ~s ago; *one ~*, on a ~ (past or future); *some ~*, on some ~ in the future; *have one's ~*, have a period of power, success, etc. **2.** event; contest. *The ~ is ours. We've won the ~*

(i.e. we have won). **'~·break** *n.* dawn. **'~·dream** *v.i. & n.* (have) idle, pleasant thoughts. **'~·light** *n.* (no pl.) light of ~, from dawn to darkness. **'~·light 'sav·ing 'time** *n.* system of having the time usu. one hour later than natural time, so as to make better use of daylight hours in the summer. **'~·time** *n.* (no pl.) day (1): *in the ~time.*

daze [deɪz] *v.t.* make (sb.) feel stupid or unable to think clearly. *n.* (no pl.) *in a ~*, in a ~d state.

daz·zle ['dæzl] *v.t.* make (sb.) unable to see clearly or act naturally because of too much light, brilliance, splendour, etc.: *~d by bright lights*; *dazzling sunshine* (*diamonds, beauty*).

de- [,di:-, dɪ-] *pref.* the negative, reverse, or opposite of: *defrost*; *depopulate*; *devalue.*

dea·con ['di:kən] *n.* minister or officer who has various duties in certain Christian churches. **~·ess** *n.*

dead [ded] *adj.* **1.** (of plants, animals, persons) no longer living: *~ leaves*; *the ~* (all who have ever died); (of matter) never having had life. **2.** without movement or activity: *the ~ hours of the night.* **3.** complete: *in ~ earnest*; *come to a ~ stop.* **4.** used up; not working: *a ~ match*, match that has already been used. *The telephone is ~. ~ letter*, rule, law, etc. to which attention is no longer paid; letter kept by the post office because the person to whom it is addressed cannot be found. **5.** exact: *~ heat*, race, etc. in which two or more persons, horses, etc. reach the winning-post together; *~ shot*, shot going to the exact point aimed at; person who hits the target without fail; *in the ~ centre*, exactly in the centre. *adv.* absolutely: *~ beat* (*tired*) (i.e. tired out, exhausted). *n.* (no pl.) *the ~ of night* (*winter*) (the most inactive and quietest part). **~·en** ['dedn] *v.t.* take away force or feeling: *drugs to ~en pain.* **'~·line** *n.* fixed limit of time for completion, etc. **'~·lock** *n.* complete failure to settle a grievance or quarrel or reach an agreement. **~·ly** *adj.* (-*ier*, -*iest*) causing, likely to cause, death. *adv.* as if ~.

deaf [def] *adj.* unable to hear; (fig.) unwilling to listen. **~·en** ['defn] *v.t.* make so much noise that hearing is difficult or impossible: *~ening cheers.* **~·ness** *n.* (no pl.)

deal[1] [di:l] *n.* (board of) fir or pine-wood: *a ~ table.*

deal[2] [di:l] *n.* (no pl.) *a good* (*great*) *~ (of)*, (very) much, a lot (of). *adv. a good ~ better*, very much better.

deal

deal³ [di:l] *v.t. & i.* (p.t. & p.p. ~t [delt]) **1.** give out to several persons: ~ out money; ~ cards. **2.** ~ a blow (at), hit; strike. **3.** stock; sell; do business; buy from: shops that ~ in goods of all kinds; ~ with Smith, the butcher; ~ at a small shop. **4.** ~ with, (a) be about: a book ~ing with E. Africa; (b) behave towards; have relations with: ~ fairly with one's neighbours; people who are difficult to ~ with; (c) attend to; manage: a difficult problem to ~ with. *n.* **1.** (in games, etc.) act of ~ing cards. a new ~, a new plan or system, esp. one that is thought to be just or fair; a square ~, fair treatment. **2.** business agreement, esp. (colloq.) a bargain: It's a ~ (i.e. I agree to the terms proposed). **~er** *n.* **1.** trader. **2.** person who ~s cards. **~ings** *n. pl.* business relations: have no ~ings with a dishonest man.

dealt, see **deal³** (v.).

dean [di:n] *n.* **1.** church officer at the head of a cathedral chapter. **2.** (in some universities) person with authority to maintain discipline; head of a department of studies. **~ery** *n.* position or house of a ~ (1).

dear [dɪə*] *adj.* **1.** loved; lovable. **2.** polite form of address: D~ Sir (Madam); D~ Miss Smith; My ~ Jack. **3.** high-priced in relation to value: Potatoes are ~ this week. **4.** precious: Her house and garden are very ~ to her. *adv.* He got rich by buying cheap and selling ~. *n.* lovable person: She is a ~. Yes, ~(est). *int.* (often with some other word: Oh ~! D~ me!) to express surprise, impatience, wonder, dismay, etc. **~ly** *adv.* **1.** very much: He would ~ly love to see his mother again. He loved his mother ~ly. **2.** at great cost: Victory was ~ly won (at the cost of many lives).

dearth [dɜ:θ] *n.* (no pl.) scarcity; small supply, esp. of food.

death [deθ] *n.* ending of life; dying; killing or being killed: The murderer was put to ~, executed. ~ du·ties *n. pl.* (Gt. Brit.) (U.S.A. ~ tax) taxes to be paid on the property of a person who has died. **~less** *adj.* never dying: ~less glory (fame). **~ly** *adj.* like ~. ~ rate *n.* average number of persons who die each year among every 1,000 people. '~-trap *n.* dangerous place, esp. on a road.

de·bar [dɪ'bɑ:*] *v.t.* (-rr-) shut out (from); prevent (sb.) by a regulation (from doing or having sth.).

de·base [dɪ'beɪs] *v.t.* make lower in value, poorer in quality, character, etc. **~ment** *n.*

de·bate [dɪ'beɪt] *n.* discussion (esp. at a public meeting or in Parliament). *v.t. & i.* have a ~ about: take part in a ~; think over in order to decide. **de·bat·er** *n.* **de·bat·able** *adj.* that can be ~d; open to question.

de·bauch [dɪ'bɔ:tʃ] (liter.) *v.t.* cause sb. to lose virtue, to turn away from good taste or judgement, or to act immorally. *n.* occasion of over-drinking immoral behaviour, usu. in company.

de·ben·ture [dɪ'bentʃə*] *n.* certificate given by a business corporation, etc. a receipt for money lent at a fixed rate of interest till the loan is repaid.

de·bil·i·tate [dɪ'bɪlɪteɪt] *v.t.* make (a person, his constitution) feeble. **de·bil·i·ty** [dɪ'bɪlətɪ] *n.* (no pl.) weakness (of health, purpose).

deb·it ['debɪt] *n.* (bookkeeping) entry (in an account) of a sum owing; left hand side of an account, on which such entries are made. (Cf. credit (7).) *v.t.* put on the ~ side of an account.

deb·o·nair [,debə'neə*] *adj.* cheerful bright and light-hearted.

de·bris ['deɪbri:] *n.* (no pl.) scattered broken pieces.

debt [det] *n.* payment that must be but has not yet been, made to sb obligation: in (out of) ~, owing (not owing) money. National D~, money owed by the State to those who have lent it money. **~or** *n.* person in ~ to another.

dé·but (U.S.A. **de·but**) ['deɪbu:] *n.* (esp. of a young woman) first appearance at adult parties and other social events; (of an actor, musician, etc.) first appearance on a public stage. **déb·u·tante** (U.S.A. **deb-**) ['debjutɑ:nt] *n.* young woman making her

dec·ade ['dekeɪd] *n.* period of ten years.

de·ca·dent ['dekədənt] *adj.* (of a person, art, literature, community, society) becoming less worthy, honourable or moral (2). **de·ca·dence** *n.* (no pl.)

Deca·logue ['dekəlog] *n.* (no pl.) the Ten Commandments of Moses.

de·camp [dɪ'kæmp] *v.i.* leave suddenly and often secretly.

de·cant [dɪ'kænt] *v.t.* pour (wine) from a bottle into another vessel slowly and carefully so as not to disturb any sediment. **~er** *n.* vessel into which wine is ~ed before being brought to the table.

de·cap·i·tate [dɪ'kæpɪteɪt] *v.t.* cut off the head of.

de·car·bon·ize [ˌdiː'kɑːbənaɪz] *v.t.* remove carbon from (esp. the engine of a motor car, etc.).

de·cath·lete [dɪ'kæθliːt] *n.* athlete who competes in a **de·cath·lon** [dɪ'kæθlɒn] *n.* athletic contest in which each competitor takes part in ten different events.

de·cay [dɪ'keɪ] *v.i.* go bad; lose power, health: ~*ing teeth* (*fruit, empires*). *n.* (no pl.) ~*ing.*

de·cease [dɪ'siːs] *n.* (esp. law) (a person's) death. *v.i.* (law) die. *the* ~*d,* (law) person(s) who has (have) recently died.

de·ceit [dɪ'siːt] *n.* deceiving; dishonest trick. ~**ful** *adj.* in the habit of deceiving; intended to deceive. ~**ful·ly** *adv.* ~**ful·ness** *n.*

de·ceive [dɪ'siːv] *v.t.* cause (sb.) to believe sth. false; play a trick on; mislead, esp. on purpose. **de·ceiv·er** *n.* person who ~s. **de·cep·tion** [dɪ'sepʃn] *n.* deceiving; being ~d; trick intended to ~ sb. **de·cep·tive** [dɪ'septɪv] *adj.* deceiving; easily causing a person to be ~d. **de·cep·tive·ly** *adv.*

de·cel·er·ate [ˌdiː'seləreɪt] *v.t. & i.* (cause to) slow down.

De·cem·ber [dɪ'sembə*] *n.* twelfth month of the year.

de·cent ['diːsnt] *adj.* **1.** right and suitable; respectable. **2.** modest; not likely to cause shame or shock to others: ~ *language and behaviour.* **3.** (colloq.) good; satisfactory: ~ *weather*; *a* ~ *meal.* ~**ly** *adv.* **de·cen·cy** *n.* being ~; general opinion as to what is ~: *an offence against decency.*

de·cen·tral·ize [ˌdiː'sentrəlaɪz] *v.t.* give greater powers (for self-government, etc.) to (places, branches, etc. away from the centre). **de·cen·tral·iza·tion** [diːˌsentrəlaɪ'zeɪʃn] *n.*

de·cep·tion, de·cep·tive(·ly), see *de-ceive.*

deci- ['desɪ-] *pref.* one-tenth: *decilitre; decimetre.*

de·cide [dɪ'saɪd] *v.t. & i.* **1.** settle (a question, doubt); give judgement (*be-tween, for, in favour of, against*). **2.** think about and come to a conclusion; resolve. **3.** cause to ~ (2). **de·cid·ed** *adj.* clear; definite; (of a person) having definite opinions. **de·cid·ed·ly** *adv.*

de·cid·u·ous [dɪ'sɪdjuəs] *adj.* (of trees) losing their leaves annually, esp. in autumn.

dec·i·mal ['desɪml] *adj.* of tens or one-tenths: *the* ~ *system* (for money, weights, and measures); *the* ~ *point*

(e.g. the point in 15.61); *go* ~, adopt the ~ system of coins.

dec·i·mate ['desɪmeɪt] *v.t.* kill or destroy at least one-tenth of: *a population* ~*d by disease.*

de·ci·pher [dɪ'saɪfə*] *v.t.* find the meaning of (sth. written in cipher, bad handwriting, sth. puzzling, or difficult to understand).

de·ci·sion [dɪ'sɪʒn] *n.* **1.** deciding; making up one's mind; result of this; settlement of (a question): *come to a* ~. **2.** ability to decide and act accordingly: *a man of* ~.

de·ci·sive [dɪ'saɪsɪv] *adj.* **1.** causing the result of sth. to be decided or certain: *a* ~ *battle.* **2.** showing decision (2); decided; definite. ~**ly** *adv.*

deck¹ [dek] *n.* floor in a ship, usu. of wooden planks, in or above the hull, or any similar surface: *clear the* ~*s,* make ready for a fight; (fig.) make ready for activity of any kind. ~**chair,** folding chair of wood or metal and canvas.

a deck-chair

deck² [dek] *v.t.* decorate (1).

de·claim [dɪ'kleɪm] *v.i. & t.* speak with strong feeling (*against*); speak in the manner of addressing an audience or reciting a poem; recite (a poem). **dec·la·ma·tion** [ˌdeklə'meɪʃn] *n.*

de·clare [dɪ'kleə*] *v.t. & i.* **1.** make known publicly and clearly: ~ *war* (*the result of an election*). **2.** say solemnly or to show that one has no doubt or hesitation: *The accused man* ~*d that he was not guilty.* ~ *for* (*against*), say that one is in favour of (against) (sth.). **3.** make a statement (to customs officials) of dutiable goods brought into a country, or (to a tax inspector) of one's income. **4.** (int.) *Well, I* ~*!* (expressing surprise). **dec·la·ra·tion** [ˌdeklə'reɪʃn] *n.* declaring; that which is ~d: *a declaration of war; the Declaration of Inde-pendence; a declaration of income.*

de·cline [dɪ'klaɪn] *v.t. & i.* **1.** say 'no' to; refuse (sth. offered, sth. one is asked to do). **2.** (of the sun) go down. **3.** continue to become smaller, weaker, lower: *a declining birth rate*; *prices beginning to ～*; *an empire that has ～d*; *a man's declining years* (when, because of age, he is losing strength). **4.** (gram.) give the cases[1] (4) of. *n.* declining; gradual and continued loss of strength: *a ～ in prices*; *fall into a ～*, lose strength; (esp. old use) suffer from tuberculosis.

de·cliv·i·ty [dɪ'klɪvətɪ] *n.* downward slope.

de·clutch [ˌdiː'klʌtʃ] *v.i.* disconnect the clutch (of a motor car, etc.) so as to be ready to change gear.

de·code [ˌdiː'kəʊd] *v.t.* put in plain language (sth. written in code).

de·col·o·nize [ˌdiː'kɒlənaɪz] *v.t.* give a colony an independent status (2). **de·col·o·ni·za·tion** *n.* (no pl.).

de·com·pose [ˌdiːkəm'pəʊz] *v.t. & i.* **1.** separate (a substance, light, etc.) into its parts. **2.** (cause to) become bad or rotten; decay. **de·com·po·si·tion** [ˌdiːkɒmpə'zɪʃn] *n.* (no pl.).

de·con·tam·i·nate [ˌdiːkən'tæmɪneɪt] *v.t.* remove that which poisons or spreads disease.

dec·o·rate ['dekəreɪt] *v.t.* **1.** put ornaments on; make more beautiful by placing adornments on or in: *～ streets with flags* (*a church with flowers*). **2.** paint (a house); put new paper, etc. on (walls of rooms). **3.** give (sb.) a mark of distinction or honour (e.g. a rank, medal, etc.): *～d for bravery in battle*. **dec·o·ra·tion** [ˌdekə'reɪʃn] *n.* decorating; sth. used for decorating; medal, ribbon, etc. given and worn as an honour or reward. **dec·o·ra·tive** ['dekərətɪv] *adj.* suitable for decorating (1); ornamental. **dec·o·ra·tor** ['dekəreɪtə*] *n.* (esp.) workman who ～s (2) houses.

de·co·rum [dɪ'kɔːrəm] *n.* right and proper behaviour, as required by good manners. **de·co·rous** ['dekərəs] *adj.*

de·coy [dɪ'kɔɪ] *n.* (real or imitation) bird or animal used to attract others so that they may be caught; person or thing used to tempt sb. into a position of danger. *v.t.* trick into a place of danger by means of a ～.

de·crease [diː'kriːs] *v.t. & i.* (cause to) become shorter, smaller, less. ['diːkriːs] *n.* decreasing; amount by which sth. ～s: *Is crime on the ～?*

de·cree [dɪ'kriː] *n.* **1.** order given by a ruler or authority and having the force of a law. **2.** judgement or decision by

some law courts. *v.t. & i.* make a ～ (*that*).

de·crep·it [dɪ'krepɪt] *adj.* made weak by old age. **de·crep·i·tude** [dɪ'krepɪtjuːd] *n.* (no pl.) being ～.

de·cry [dɪ'kraɪ] *v.t.* try, by speaking against sth., to make it seem less valuable or useful.

ded·i·cate ['dedɪkeɪt] *v.t.* **1.** give up (*to a noble cause or purpose*): *～ one's life to missionary work*. **2.** devote with solemn ceremonies (*to God, to* a sacred use): *～ a new church building*. **3.** (of an author) write (or print) a person's name at the beginning of a book (to show gratitude or friendship). **ded·i·ca·tion** [ˌdedɪ'keɪʃn] *n.* dedicating; (esp.) words used in dedicating a book.

de·duce [dɪ'djuːs] *v.t.* arrive at (knowledge, a theory, etc.) by reasoning (*from* facts); reach a conclusion (*from*).

de·duct [dɪ'dʌkt] *v.t.* take away (an amount or a part). (Cf. *subtract* for numbers.)

de·duc·tion [dɪ'dʌkʃn] *n.* **1.** act of deducting; amount deducted. **2.** deducing; conclusion reached by reasoning from general laws to a particular case. **de·duc·tive** [dɪ'dʌktɪv] *adj.* of, reasoning by, ～ (3).

deed [diːd] *n.* **1.** sth. done; act: *be rewarded for one's good ～s*. **2.** (law) written (or printed) and signed agreement, esp. about ownership or rights.

deem [diːm] *v.t.* believe; consider.

deep [diːp] *adj.* **1.** going or lying far down from the surface or top. *～ sea*; *～ space*, space beyond the solar system or the earth's atmosphere. **2.** going far in from the front, edge, or surface: *a ～ shelf* (*wound*). **3.** (of colour) dark; strong (cf. *pale*). **4.** (of sounds) low. **5.** (of persons) inclined to secrecy; having ways of thinking and behaving that are difficult to understand. **6.** (of feelings) keen, intense: *～ sorrow*. **7.** *～ in* (*thought, study, etc.*) having all one's attention centred on. *adv.* far down or in. *n. the ～*, (poet.) the sea. **～·en** ['diːpən] *v.t. & i.* make or become ～(er). **ˌ～-'freeze** *v.t.* freeze (food) quickly in order to keep it for long periods at a very low temperature. **～·ly** *adv.*

deer [dɪə*] *n.* (pl. ～) graceful, quick-running animal, the male of which has horns.

de·es·ca·late [ˌdiː'eskəleɪt] *v.t. & i.* reduce in scale[1] (6) or size.

de·face [dɪ'feɪs] *v.t.* spoil the appearance of (by marking, damaging, the surface of).

de·fame [dɪ'feɪm] *v.t.* attack the good

defuse

reputation of; say evil things about.
def·a·ma·tion [ˌdefəˈmeɪʃn] *n.* (no pl.). **de·fam·a·to·ry** [dɪˈfæmətərɪ] *adj.* intended to ~.

de·fault [dɪˈfɔːlt] *v.i.* fail to perform a duty, or to appear (e.g. in a court of law) when required to do so, or to pay a debt. *n.* (no pl.) act of ~ing: *by ~*, because the other person (or side) did not appear: *win a case (game) by ~*; *in ~ of*, in the absence of; if (sth.) is not to be obtained, does not take place, etc. **~·er** *n.* person (esp. a soldier) who fails to perform a duty.

de·feat [dɪˈfiːt] *v.t.* 1. overcome; beat; win a victory over; 2. bring to nothing; make useless: *Our hopes were ~ed. n.* 1. (no pl.) ~ing or being ~ed. 2. instance of this. **~·ism** [dɪˈfiːtɪzəm] *n.* (no pl.) attitude, argument, conduct, based on expectation of ~.

de·fect [ˈdiːfekt] *n.* fault; imperfection; shortcoming; sth. lacking in completeness or perfection: *~s in a system of education.* [dɪˈfekt] *v.i.* desert¹ (2), esp. to another country. **de·fec·tion** [dɪˈfekʃn] *n.* (instance of) falling away from loyalty to a cause (3), leader, etc. **de·fec·tive** [dɪˈfektɪv] *adj.* having a ~ or ~s: *mentally ~ive*, not quite sane.

de·fence (U.S.A. **de·fense**) [dɪˈfens] *n.* (no pl.) defending from attack; fighting against attack. 2. sth. that protects or guards against attack. 3. (law) argument(s) used in favour of an accused person; the lawyer(s) acting for such a person. **~·less** *adj.* having no ~; unable to defend oneself.

de·fend [dɪˈfend] *v.t.* 1. guard, protect, make safe (*against, from*). 2. speak or write in support of (an accused person, etc.). **de·fen·dant** [dɪˈfendənt] *n.* person against whom a legal action is brought. **~·er** *n.* person who ~s; (football) player who guards the goal area. **de·fen·si·ble** [dɪˈfensɪbl] *adj.* able to be ~ed. **de·fen·sive** [dɪˈfensɪv] *adj.* used for, intended for, ~ing. *n. on the defensive*, ready to ~; resisting, expecting, attack.

de·fer¹ [dɪˈfɜː*] *v.t.* (-*rr*) put off to a later time; postpone: *a ~red telegram* (sent later at a cheaper rate). **~·ment** *n.*
de·fer² [dɪˈfɜː*] *v.t. & i.* (-*rr*) ~ to, give way to; yield to (often to show respect): *~ to one's elders (to sb.'s opinions).* **def·er·ence** [ˈdefərəns] *n.* (no pl.) ~ring; respect: *in ~ence to the opinion of the court.* **def·er·en·tial** [ˌdefəˈrenʃl] *adj.* showing great respect.

de·fi·ance, de·fi·ant, see *defy*.
de·fi·cient [dɪˈfɪʃnt] *adj.* wanting (*in*);

not having enough of: *~ in courage*; *mentally ~*, weak-minded; half-witted. **de·fi·cien·cy** [dɪˈfɪʃnsɪ] *n.* being ~; amount by which sth. is ~.

def·i·cit [ˈdefɪsɪt] *n.* amount by which sth., esp. a sum of money, is too small; amount by which payments exceed receipts. (Cf. *surplus.*)

de·file¹ [dɪˈfaɪl] *v.t.* make unclean or impure. **~·ment** *n.*
de·file² [ˈdiːfaɪl] *n.* narrow way, gorge, between mountains.

de·fine [dɪˈfaɪn] *v.t.* 1. explain the meaning of (e.g. words). 2. state or show clearly: *~ sb.'s duties (powers)*; *hills clearly ~d* (= outlined) *against the sky.* 3. lay down, decide the shape, outlines, or limits of sth.: *~ a country's boundaries.* **def·i·nite** [ˈdefɪnɪt] *adj.* clear; not doubtful or uncertain. *definite article*, the word 'the'. **def·i·nite·ly** *adv.* **def·i·ni·tion** [ˌdefɪˈnɪʃn] *n.* 1. defining; statement that ~s. 2. clearness of outline; making or being distinct in outline. **de·fin·i·tive** [dɪˈfɪnɪtɪv] *adj.* final; to be looked upon as decisive and without the need for, or possibility of, change or addition.

de·flate [dɪˈfleɪt] *v.t.* 1. make (a tyre, balloon, etc.) smaller by letting out air or gas. 2. take action to reduce the amount of money in circulation, in order to lower prices of salable goods. (Cf. *inflate* (2).) **de·fla·tion** [dɪˈfleɪʃn] *n.* (no pl.).

de·flect [dɪˈflekt] *v.t. & i.* (cause to) turn aside (*from*). **de·flec·tion** [dɪˈflekʃn] *n.*

de·form [dɪˈfɔːm] *v.t.* spoil the form or appearance of; put out of shape. **~ed** *adj.* (esp. of the body, or part of the body; fig., of the mind) badly shaped; unnaturally formed. **de·for·mi·ty** [dɪˈfɔːmɪtɪ] *n.* being ~ed; ~ed part of the body.

de·fraud [dɪˈfrɔːd] *v.t.* trick (sb.) out of what is rightly his: *~ an author of his royalties by ignoring copyright.*

de·fray [dɪˈfreɪ] *v.t.* supply the money needed for sth.; pay (the cost or expenses of sth.).

de·frost [ˌdiːˈfrɒst] *v.t.* remove ice or frost (from a refrigerator, the windscreen of a motor car, etc.).

deft [deft] *adj.* quick and clever (esp. at doing things with the fingers); (of work) showing such skill. **~·ly** *adv.* **~·ness** *n.*

de·funct [dɪˈfʌŋkt] *adj.* dead; no longer existing or in use.

de·fuse [ˌdiːˈfjuːz] *v.t.* 1. remove the fuse from (an explosive). 2. (fig.) remove the likelihood of trouble arising from (an explosive situation, etc.).

de·fy [dɪ'faɪ] *v.t.* **1.** resist openly; say that one is ready to fight. **2.** refuse to obey or show respect to: ~ *the law* (*one's superiors*). **3.** ~ *sb. to do sth.*, call on sb. to do sth. one believes he cannot or will not do. **4.** offer difficulties that cannot be overcome. **de·fi·ance** [dɪ'faɪəns] *n.* (no pl.) ~ing; refusal to obey, to show respect to: *act in defiance of orders*; *set the law at defiance*. **de·fi·ant** [dɪ'faɪənt] *adj.* showing defiance; openly disobedient.

de·gen·er·ate [dɪ'dʒenəreɪt] *v.i.* pass from a state of goodness to a lower state by losing qualities that are considered normal and desirable. [dɪ'dʒenərət] *adj.* having ~d. *n.* ~ person or animal. **de·gen·er·a·tion** [dɪ,dʒenə'reɪʃn] *n.* (no pl.) degenerating; being ~.

de·grade [dɪ'greɪd] *v.t.* **1.** reduce (e.g. a soldier) to a lower rank or position, usu. as a punishment. **2.** cause (sb.) to be less moral or less deserving of respect: ~ *oneself by cheating* (*living an idle life*). **deg·ra·da·tion** [,degrə'deɪʃn] *n.* (no pl.).

de·gree [dɪ'griː] *n.* **1.** unit of measurement for angles: *an angle of ninety ~s* (90°). **2.** unit of measurement for temperature: *Water freezes at 32 ~s Fahrenheit* (32° F.) *or zero Centigrade* (0° C.). **3.** step or stage in a scale or process showing extent, quantity, or progress: *various ~s of skill*; *a high ~ of excellence*; *by ~s*, gradually; step by step; slowly; *to a high* (*to the last*) ~, intensely; exceedingly; *to what ~*, to what extent. **4.** position in society: *people of high ~.* **5.** rank or grade given by a university to one who has passed an examination: *the ~ of Master of Arts*; *study for a ~.* **6.** (gram.) one of the three forms of comparison of an adjective or adverb: '*Good*', '*better*', and '*best*' *are the positive, comparative, and superlative ~s of 'good'.*

de·hy·drate [,diː'haɪdreɪt] *v.t. & i.* deprive (a substance) of water or moisture; lose water: ~d *vegetables*.

de·ice [,diː'aɪs] *v.t.* remove ice (e.g. from the wings of an aeroplane) or prevent its formation.

de·ify ['diːɪfaɪ] *v.t.* make a god of; worship as a god.

deign [deɪn] *v.i.* condescend; be kind and gracious enough (*to do sth.*).

de·ity ['diːɪtɪ] *n.* **1.** (no pl.) divine quality or nature; state of being a god(dess). **2.** god(dess): *the Greek deities. the D~,* God.

de·ject·ed [dɪ'dʒektɪd] *adj.* sad; gloomy; in low spirits; hopeless. **de·jec·tion** [dɪ'dʒekʃn] *n.* (no pl.) ~ state.

de·lay [dɪ'leɪ] *v.t. & i.* **1.** make or be slow or late: *be ~ed by the traffic*. **2.** put off until later: ~ *a journey*. *n.* **1.** (no pl.) ~ing or being ~ed: *start without ~.* **2.** instance of this: *after a ~ of several hours.*

de·lec·table [dɪ'lektəbl] *adj.* (ironical) pleasant; delightful.

del·e·gate ['delɪgeɪt] *v.t.* **1.** appoint and send as a representative to a meeting. **2.** entrust (duties, rights, etc.) *to sb.* ['delɪgət] *n.* person to whom sth. is ~d. **del·e·ga·tion** [,delɪ'geɪʃn] *n.* delegating; group of persons to whom sth. is ~d.

de·lete [dɪ'liːt] *v.t.* strike or take out (sth. written or printed). **de·le·tion** [dɪ'liːʃn] *n.* deleting; sth. ~d.

de·lib·er·ate [dɪ'lɪbəreɪt] *v.t. & i.* consider, talk about, carefully. [dɪ'lɪbərət] *adj.* **1.** done on purpose; intentional: *a ~ insult*. **2.** slow and cautious (in action, speech, etc.). ~ly *adv.* **de·lib·er·a·tion** [dɪ,lɪbə'reɪʃn] *n.* deliberating; discussion, esp. with arguments for and against; being ~ (2).

del·i·ca·cy ['delɪkəsɪ] *n.* **1.** (no pl.) quality of being delicate. **2.** delicate (7) kind of food.

del·i·cate ['delɪkət] *adj.* **1.** soft; tender; exquisite; of fine or thin material: *as ~ as silk*. **2.** easily injured; becoming ill easily; needing great care: ~ *china* (*plants*); *a ~-looking child.* **3.** requiring careful treatment or skilful handling: *a ~ surgical operation*; *a ~ international situation*. **4.** (of colours) soft; not strong. **5.** (of the senses, instruments) able to appreciate or indicate very small changes or differences: *a ~ sense of smell*; *the ~ instruments used by scientists* (e.g. in weighing things, measuring, etc.). **6.** taking or showing care not to be immodest or to hurt the feelings of others. **7.** (of food) pleasing to the taste: *fish with a ~ flavour.* ~ly *adv.*

del·i·ca·tes·sen [,delɪkə'tesn] *n.* (shop selling) delicacies (2) (e.g. prepared salads, cooked meats).

de·li·cious [dɪ'lɪʃəs] *adj.* giving delight, esp. to the senses of taste and smell, and to the sense of humour.

de·light [dɪ'laɪt] *v.t. & i.* **1.** give great pleasure to. **2.** find great pleasure (*in sth., in doing sth., to do sth.*). *n.* great pleasure; sth. that causes great pleasure. ~ed *adj.* filled with ~. ~ful *adj.* giving great ~; charming.

de·lin·eate [dɪ'lɪnɪeɪt] *v.t.* show by drawing or describing.

de·lin·quent [dɪ'lɪŋkwənt] *n. & adj.* (person) doing wrong, failing to perform a duty. **de·lin·quen·cy** [dɪ'lɪŋkwənsɪ] *n.* wrongdoing; failure to perform a duty.

de·lir·i·um [dɪ'lɪrɪəm] *n.* (no pl.) violent mental disturbance, esp. during a feverish illness, often accompanied by wild talk; great excitement. **de·lir·i·ous** [dɪ'lɪrɪəs] *adj.* suffering from ~; wild (*with* excitement, etc.).

de·liv·er [dɪ'lɪvə*] *v.t.* **1.** take (letters, parcels, goods, etc.) to houses, to the person(s) to whom they are addressed, to the buyer(s). **2.** rescue, save, set free (*from* danger, temptation, etc.). **3.** give or recite (a speech, sermon, course of lectures). **4.** aim, send against: ~ *a blow in the cause of freedom*. **5.** ~ *up* or *over* (*to*), give up; hand over. **6.** *be ~ed of* (a child), give birth to. **~·ance** [dɪ'lɪvərəns] *n.* (no pl.) rescue; being set free. **~y** *n.* ~ing (1); manner of making a speech, sermon, etc.; childbirth.

dell [del] *n.* small valley with trees.

del·ta ['deltə] *n.* Greek letter *d* (Δ, δ); land in the shape of a capital ~ (Δ) at the mouth of a river between two or more branches (e.g. the Niger D~).

de·lude [dɪ'luːd] *v.t.* deceive; mislead (on purpose). **de·lu·sion** [dɪ'luːʒn] *n.* deluding or being ~d; false opinion or belief, esp. as a form of madness. **de·lu·sive** [dɪ'luːsɪv] *adj.* deceptive.

del·uge ['deljuːdʒ] *n.* **1.** great flood; heavy rush of water or violent rainfall: *the D~*, Noah's flood. **2.** anything coming in a heavy rush: *a ~ of words* (*questions*). *v.t.* flood; come down on (sb. or sth.) like a ~.

de luxe [də'lʊks] *adj.* of very high quality; luxurious.

delve [delv] *v.t. & i.* (old use) dig; ~ *into*, (fig.) make researches into (e.g. old books or manuscripts).

dem·a·gogue ['deməgɒg] *n.* political leader who tries, by speeches appealing to the feelings instead of the reason, to stir up the people. **dem·a·gogy** ['deməgɒgɪ] *n.* (no pl.). **dem·a·gog·ic** ['deməgɒgɪk] *adj.*

de·mand [dɪ'mɑːnd] *v.t.* **1.** ask for (sth.) as if ordering, or as if one has a right. **2.** require; need. *n.* **1.** act of ~ing (1); sth. ~ed (1): *on ~*, when ~ed; when asked for. **2.** desire, by people ready to buy, employ, etc. (*for* goods, services, etc.): *a great ~ for good typists*; *goods in great ~*.

de·mar·cate ['diːmɑːkeɪt] *v.t.* mark or fix the limits of. **de·mar·ca·tion** [‚diːmɑː'keɪʃn] *n.* (no pl.).

de·mean [dɪ'miːn] *v.t.* ~ *oneself*, lower oneself in dignity. **de·mea·nour** (U.S.A. **-nor**) [dɪ'miːnə*] *n.* (no pl.) behaviour; manner.

de·ment·ed [dɪ'mentɪd] *adj.* mad; (colloq.) wild with worry. **~·ly** *adv.*

demi- ['demɪ-] *pref.* half.

de·mil·i·ta·rize [‚diː'mɪlɪtəraɪz] *v.t.* remove military forces or installation from (a country or part of it).

de·mise [dɪ'maɪz] *n.* (law) death.

de·mist [‚diː'mɪst] *v.t.* wipe condensation from (the windscreen of a motor car, etc.).

demo ['deməʊ] *n.* (pl. ~s) (colloq., abbr. for) demonstration (2).

de·mob [‚diː'mɒb] *v.t.* (*-bb-*) *& n.* (Gt. Brit., colloq., abbr. for) demobilize, demobilization.

de·mo·bi·lize [diː'məʊbɪlaɪz] *v.t.* release after military service. **de·mo·bi·li·za·tion** ['diː‚məʊbɪlaɪ'zeɪʃn] *n.*

de·moc·ra·cy [dɪ'mɒkrəsɪ] *n.* **1.** (country with the principle of) government in which all adult citizens share through their elected representatives. **2.** (country with a) government that encourages and allows free discussion of policy, majority rule, accompanied by respect for the rights of minorities, freedom of religion, opinion, speech, and association. **3.** society in which citizens treat each other as equals. **dem·o·crat** ['deməkræt] *n.* person who favours or supports ~. *Democrat*, (U.S.A.) member of the Democratic Party. **dem·o·crat·ic** [‚demə'krætɪk] *adj.* of, like, supporting, ~; (esp.) paying no attention to class divisions based on birth or wealth. *Democratic Party*, (U.S.A.) one of the two main political parties. (Cf. *Republican*.)

de·mol·ish [dɪ'mɒlɪʃ] *v.t.* pull down; destroy; overthrow. **de·mo·li·tion** [‚demə'lɪʃn] *n.*

de·mon ['diːmən] *n.* evil, wicked, or cruel supernatural being or spirit.

dem·on·strate ['demənstreɪt] *v.t. & i.* **1.** show clearly by giving proof(s) or example(s). **2.** make known (one's feelings, sympathies). **3.** (of workmen, students, etc.) support, protest, by means of processions, public meetings, etc. **dem·on·stra·tion** [‚demən'streɪʃn] *n.* **1.** demonstrating (1, 2). **2.** public display of opinion on political or other questions; demonstrating (3). **de·mon·stra·tive** [dɪ'mɒnstrətɪv] *adj.* **1.** showing the feelings. **2.** (gram.)

pointing out: '*This*', '*that*', '*these*', and '*those*' are demonstrative pronouns.

dem·on·stra·tor ['demənstreɪtə*] *n.*
1. person who ~s (3) at a public meeting. **2.** person who teaches or explains by demonstrating (1).

de·mor·al·ize [dɪ'mɒrəlaɪz] *v.t.* **1.** hurt or weaken the morals of. **2.** weaken the courage, confidence, self-discipline, etc. of (e.g. an army). **de·mor·al·iza·tion** [dɪˌmɒrəlaɪ'zeɪʃn] *n.* (no pl.).

de·mur [dɪ'mɜ:*] *v.i.* (-rr-) raise an objection *to* (*at*); protest or hesitate about: ~ *at working on Sundays.* *n.* hesitation or protest: *obey without* ~.

de·mure [dɪ'mjʊə*] *adj.* quiet and serious; pretending to be shy.

den [den] *n.* **1.** animal's hidden lying-place (e.g. a cave). **2.** secret place for ill-doers: *an opium* ~. **3.** (colloq.) room in which a person works or studies without being disturbed.

de·na·tion·al·ize [ˌdi:'næʃnəlaɪz] *v.t.* transfer to private ownership (an industry acquired by the State).

de·ni·al, see **deny**.

den·im ['denɪm] *n.* **1.** (no pl.) twilled cotton cloth, used for overalls, etc. **2.** (pl.) overalls or trousers made of usu. blue ~.

den·i·zen ['denɪzn] *n.* person, kind of animal or plant, having a permanent home in the district mentioned.

de·nom·i·na·tion [dɪˌnɒmɪ'neɪʃn] *n.* **1.** name, esp. one given to a class or religious group. **2.** class of units (of weight, length, money, etc.).

de·nom·i·na·tor [dɪ'nɒmɪneɪtə*] *n.* number below the line in a fraction (e.g. 4 in $^3/_4$).

de·note [dɪ'nəʊt] *v.t.* be the sign of; stand as, be, a name for.

de·nounce [dɪ'naʊns] *v.t.* speak publicly against; betray; give notice that one intends to end (a treaty or agreement).

dense [dens] *adj.* (~*r*, ~*st*) **1.** (of liquids, vapour) thick, not easily seen through: *a* ~ *fog.* **2.** (of things, people) packed close together and in great numbers: *a* ~ *forest; a* ~ *crowd.* **3.** (of a person) stupid. **~·ly** *adv.* **den·si·ty** ['densətɪ] *n.* **1.** (no pl.) being ~ (1, 2). **2.** (phys.) relation of weight to volume.

dent [dent] *n.* hollow in a hard surface made by a blow or by pressure. *v.t.* make a ~ in.

den·tal ['dentl] *adj.* of or for the teeth.

den·tist ['dentɪst] *n.* person who fills or removes decayed teeth and fits artificial ones. **den·tist·ry** *n.* (no pl.) work of a dentist. **den·ture** ['dentʃə*] *n.* plate (6) of artificial teeth.

de·nude [dɪ'nju:d] *v.t.* make bare; take away clothing, covering, posses[sions]: *hillsides* ~*d of trees.*

de·nun·ci·a·tion [dɪˌnʌnsɪ'eɪʃn] *n.* de[nouncing].

de·ny [dɪ'naɪ] *v.t.* **1.** say that (sth.) i[s] not true. **2.** say 'no' to (a request)[;] refuse to give (sth. asked for or needed)[.] **3.** say that one knows nothing about[:] *He denied the signature* (said that [it] was not his). **de·ni·al** [dɪ'naɪəl] *n.* ~*ing*[.]

de·odor·ant [di:'əʊdərənt] *n.* prepara[-]tion that destroys or conceals unpleas[ant] odours. **de·odor·ize** [di:'əʊdəraɪ[z] *v.t.* remove a (bad) smell from.

de·part [dɪ'pɑ:t] *v.i.* go away (*from*[);] leave; do or be sth. different: ~ *fro[m]* *old customs.* **de·par·ture** [dɪ'pɑ:tʃə[*]* *n.* ~*ing.*

de·part·ment [dɪ'pɑ:tmənt] *n.* one [of] several divisions of a governmen[t,] business, shop, university, etc. ~ *sto[re]* large shop selling all kinds of goods [in] different ~s.

de·pend [dɪ'pend] *v.i.* **1.** ~ (*up*)*on*, nee[d,] rely on (the support, etc. of) in ord[er] to exist or to be true or to succee[d:] *The old woman still* ~*s on her own ear[n-]ings* (i.e. she has no one else to provi[de] for her). *Good health* ~*s on good foo[d,]* *sleep, and exercise. That* ~*s. It all* (i.e. the result ~*s* on something els[e).]* **2.** ~ (*up*)*on*, trust; be certain abou[t:] *You can always* ~ *on John to be the[re] when needed. Depend upon it!* (i.e. y[ou] can be quite certain about the resu[lt])[.] **~·able** [dɪ'pendəbl] *adj.* that can [be] ~*ed* (2) upon. **de·pen·dant, -dent** sb. who ~*s* (1) upon another for [a] home, food, etc.; servant. **de·pe[n-]dence** *n.* (no pl.) state of ~*ing* (1, [2),] on sb. or sth. **de·pen·den·cy** *n.* country governed by another count[ry.] **de·pen·dent** *adj.* ~*ing* (1, 2) (*on, upo[n*)] *n.* = ~*ant.*

de·pict [dɪ'pɪkt] *v.t.* represent by [a] picture; describe in words.

de·plete [dɪ'pli:t] *v.t.* use up, em[pty] out until little or none remains. [**de·**]**ple·tion** [dɪ'pli:ʃn] *n.*

de·plore [dɪ'plɔ:*] *v.t.* show that (on[e]) is filled with sorrow or regret [for.] **de·plor·able** [dɪ'plɔ:rəbl] *adj.* that [is] or should be ~*d.*

de·ploy [dɪ'plɔɪ] *v.t. & i.* (of troo[ps,] warships) spread out in line of bat[tle;] (fig., of resources) put to practical [use.]

de·pop·u·late [ˌdi:'pɒpjʊleɪt] *v.t.* les[sen] the number of people living in (a co[un-]try): *a country* ~*d by war.* **de·pop[·u·]la·tion** [di:ˌpɒpjʊ'leɪʃn] *n.* (no pl.)[.]

de·port[1] [dɪ'pɔ:t] *v.t.* send (an [...]

wanted person) out of the country.
de·por·ta·tion [ˌdiːpɔː'teɪʃn] *n.* ~ing
or being ~ed.

de·port² [dɪ'pɔːt] *v.t.* ~ oneself, behave:
~ oneself with dignity. ~ment *n.* (no
pl.) behaviour; way of bearing oneself.

de·pose [dɪ'pəʊz] *v.t. & i.* 1. remove
(sb., esp. a ruler such as a king) from
a position of authority; dethrone. 2.
give evidence (esp. on oath in a law
court). **de·po·si·tion** [ˌdepə'zɪʃn] *n.*
deposing or being ~d (1); evidence
given on oath.

de·pos·it [dɪ'pɒzɪt] *v.t.* 1. put (e.g.
money, valuables) in a place, or in
sb.'s care, for safe keeping: ~ money
in a bank. 2. (esp. of a liquid, a river)
leave a layer of matter on: rivers that
~ mud and sand on the fields during a
flood. 3. make part payment of money
that is or will be owed. *n.* 1. money
that is ~ed (1, 3); valuables ~ed (1): ~
account, account with a bank from
which money may not be drawn without notice, and on which interest (7)
is payable. (Cf. current¹ (1) account.)
2. layer of matter ~ed (2): a ~ of gravel
(tin, volcanic ash). **de·pos·i·tor** *n.*
person who makes a ~ (1) in a bank.
de·pos·i·to·ry [dɪ'pɒzɪtərɪ] *n.* place
where goods are ~ed; storehouse.

de·pot ['depəʊ] *n.* 1. storehouse, esp.
for military supplies; warehouse. 2.
bus or (U.S.A.) railway station.

de·praved [dɪ'preɪvd] *adj.* morally
bad; (of tastes, habits) corrupt; evil;
low. **de·prav·i·ty** [dɪ'prævətɪ] *n.* (no
pl.) ~ state.

dep·re·cate ['deprɪkeɪt] *v.t.* feel and
express disapproval of.

de·pre·ci·ate [dɪ'priːʃɪeɪt] *v.t. & i.*
make or become less in value; say sth.
has little value. **de·pre·ci·a·tion** [dɪ-
ˌpriːʃɪ'eɪʃn] *n.* (no pl.) lessening of
value.

dep·re·da·tion [ˌdeprɪ'deɪʃn] *n.* (usu.
pl.) destruction or robbery of property.

de·press [dɪ'pres] *v.t.* 1. press, push,
or pull down: ~ a lever (the keys of a
piano). 2. make sad. 3. make less active;
cause (prices) to be lower. ~ing *adj.*
making sad or unhappy: ~ing news
(weather). **de·pres·sion** [dɪ'preʃn] *n.*
1. (no pl.) being ~ed (2). 2. hollow
place in the surface of the ground. 3.
time when business is ~ed (3). 4. lowering of atmospheric pressure; (esp.)
centre where this pressure is lowest.

de·prive [dɪ'praɪv] *v.t.* ~ sb. or sth. of,
take away from; prevent from using
or enjoying: trees that ~ a house of
light and air.

depth [depθ] *n.* 1. being deep: the ~ of
the ocean. 2. measure from top to
bottom, or from front to back: snow
three feet in ~; out of one's ~, (a) in
water too deep to stand in; (b) (fig.)
considering sth. beyond one's understanding. 3. middle of a time: in the ~
of winter.

de·pute [dɪ'pjuːt] *v.t.* give (one's work,
authority, etc.) to a substitute; give
(another person) authority (to do sth.)
as one's representative. **dep·u·ty**
['depjʊtɪ] *n.* person to whom work,
authority, is ~d; parliamentary representative. **dep·u·ta·tion** [ˌdepjʊ-
'teɪʃn] *n.* group of representatives.
dep·u·tize ['depjʊtaɪz] *v.i.* act as
deputy (for).

de·rail [dɪ'reɪl] *v.t.* (usu. passive)
cause (a train, tram) to go off the rails.
~ment *n.*

de·range [dɪ'reɪndʒ] *v.t.* put into confusion or out of working order: mentally ~d, mad. ~ment *n.* (no pl.).

der·e·lict ['derɪlɪkt] *adj.* (esp. of a ship
at sea) deserted (usu. because dangerous or useless); abandoned; ownerless.

de·ride [dɪ'raɪd] *v.t.* laugh scornfully
at; mock. **de·ri·sion** [dɪ'rɪʒn] *n.* (no
pl.) **de·ri·sive** [dɪ'raɪsɪv] *adj.* showing
or deserving scorn: derisive laughter;
a derisive offer. **de·ri·so·ry** [dɪ'raɪsərɪ]
adj. not to be taken seriously.

de·rive [dɪ'raɪv] *v.t. & i.* 1. get: ~ great
pleasure from one's studies. 2. have as a
starting-point or origin: English words
~d from Latin. **der·i·va·tion** [ˌderɪ-
'veɪʃn] *n.* (esp.) first form and meaning
of a word; statement of how a word
was formed and how it changed. **de·**
riv·a·tive [dɪ'rɪvətɪv] *n. & adj.*
(thing, word, substance) ~d from another; sth. not original.

de·rog·a·to·ry [dɪ'rɒgətərɪ] *adj.* tending to damage one's credit, etc.:
remarks ~ to one's reputation.

der·rick ['derɪk] *n.* machine for moving or lifting heavy weights, esp. a
ship's cargo; framework over an oil-
well or a borehole.

der·vish ['dɜːvɪʃ] *n.* Muslim monk
who has vowed to live a life of poverty.

a derrick   davits

de·scend [dɪ'send] *v.i. & t.* **1.** come or go down. **2.** be ~ed *from*, have as ancestors. **3.** (of property, qualities, rights) pass (from father to son) by inheritance; come from earlier times. **4.** ~ *upon*, attack suddenly. **5.** ~ *to*, lower oneself to: ~ *to cheating*. **de·scen·dant** *n.* person ~ed from person(s) named. **de·scent** [dɪ'sent] *n.* **1.** ~ing (1); downward slope. **2.** (no pl.) ancestry: *of French descent*. **3.** sudden attack.

de·scribe [dɪ'skraɪb] *v.t.* **1.** say what a person or thing is like; give a picture of in words. **2.** ~ *as*, say that (sb. or sth.) has certain characteristics; call. **3.** draw (a geometrical figure). **de·scrip·tion** [dɪ'skrɪpʃn] *n.* **1.** describing; picture in words. **2.** *of any (every) description*, of any kind at all (of all kinds). **de·scrip·tive** [dɪ'skrɪptɪv] *adj.*

de·scry [dɪ'skraɪ] *v.t.* catch sight of; see (esp. sth. a long way off).

des·e·crate ['desɪkreɪt] *v.t.* use (a sacred place or thing) in an unworthy or wicked way. **des·e·cra·tion** [,desɪ'kreɪʃn] *n.* (no pl.).

de·seg·re·gate [,diː'segrɪgeɪt] *v.t. & i.* abolish racial segregation in (schools, etc.); bring about **de·seg·re·ga·tion** [,diːsegrɪ'geɪʃn] *n.* (no pl.).

de·sert[1] [dɪ'zɜːt] *v.t. & i.* **1.** go away from; leave without help or support, esp. in a wrong or cruel way. **2.** run away from; leave (esp. service in a ship, the armed forces) without authority or permission: *soldiers who* ~. **3.** fail: *His courage* ~*ed him.* ~**er** *n.* person, esp. a soldier or sailor, who ~s (2). **de·ser·tion** *n.* [dɪ'zɜːʃn] (instance of) ~ing or being ~ed.

des·ert[2] ['dezət] *n.* large area of dry, waste land, esp. sand-covered. *adj.* barren; uninhabited: *a* ~ *island*.

de·sert[3] [dɪ'zɜːt] *n.* (usu. pl.) what sb. deserves: *get one's* ~*s.*

de·serve [dɪ'zɜːv] *v.t.* be worthy of (reward, etc.) because of one's qualities, actions: ~ *praise* (*punishment*) *for good* (*careless*) *work.* **de·serv·ed·ly** [dɪ'zɜːvɪdlɪ] *adv.* justly; as ~*d.* **de·serv·ing** *adj.* worthy (*of*).

des·ic·cate ['desɪkeɪt] *v.t.* dry out all the moisture from (esp. solid food): ~*d apples.*

de·sign [dɪ'zaɪn] *n.* **1.** drawing or outline from which sth. may be made: ~*s for a dress* (*garden*). **2.** general arrangement or plan (of a picture, book, building, machine, etc.). **3.** pattern, arrangement of lines, shapes, details, as ornament (e.g. on a bowl or carpet).

4. purpose; intention: *have* ~*s on* (*against*), intend to harm, take, or steal. *v.t. & i.* **1.** make ~s (1) for: ~ *wallpaper* (*carpets*). **2.** intend; plan; have in mind: *a room* ~*ed for a workshop.* **3.** be a ~er. ~**ed·ly** [dɪ'zaɪnɪdlɪ] *adv.* on purpose. ~**er** *n.* person who ~s. ~**ing** *adj.* (esp.) cunning; having ~s (4) on sth. or sb.

des·ig·nate ['dezɪgneɪt] *v.t.* **1.** point out or mark: ~ *boundaries*. **2.** serve as a distinguishing name or mark for. **3.** appoint (sb.) to a position: *He* ~*d Smith as* (*for*) *his successor. adj.* (after a noun) appointed but not yet in office. **des·ig·na·tion** [,dezɪg'neɪʃn] *n.*

de·sire [dɪ'zaɪə*] *n.* **1.** strong wish or longing (*for*). **2.** (no pl.) request: *at the* ~ *of the manager.* **3.** thing that is wished for: *get one's* ~. *v.t.* **1.** have a ~ (1) for. **2.** (old use) request. **de·sir·able** [dɪ'zaɪərəbl] *adj.* to be ~*d* (1), causing ~ (1). **de·sir·abil·i·ty** [dɪ,zaɪərə'bɪlətɪ] *n.* **de·sir·ous** [dɪ'zaɪərəs] *pred. adj.* feeling ~ (1): *desirous of success.*

de·sist [dɪ'zɪst] *v.i.* ~ *from*, (liter.) cease.

desk [desk] *n.* piece of furniture with a flat or sloping top for reading, writing, or office work.

des·o·late ['desələt] *adj.* **1.** (of a place) in a ruined, neglected condition; (of land, a house, a country) unoccupied; unfit to live in. **2.** friendless; wretched; hopeless. ['desəleɪt] *v.t.* make ~. **des·o·la·tion** [,desə'leɪʃn] *n.* (no pl.) making or being ~.

de·spair [dɪ'speə*] *v.i. & n.* (no pl.) (be in the) state of having lost all hope. ~**ing** *adj.* feeling or showing ~.

des·patch, see *dispatch*.

des·per·a·do [,despə'rɑːdəʊ] *n.* (pl. -oes, U.S.A. also -os) person ready to do any dangerous or criminal act.

des·per·ate ['despərət] *adj.* **1.** (of a person) filled with despair and ready to do anything, regardless of danger. **2.** lawless; violent: ~ *criminals.* **3.** extremely serious or dangerous: *a* ~ *state of affairs.* **4.** done as a last attempt: ~ *remedies.* ~**ly** *adv.* **des·per·a·tion** [,despə'reɪʃn] *n.* (no pl.).

de·spise [dɪ'spaɪz] *v.t.* feel contempt for; consider worthless. **de·spic·able** ['despɪkəbl] *adj.* deserving to be ~*d.*

de·spite [dɪ'spaɪt] *prep.* in spite of. *n.* (*in*) ~ *of*, in spite of.

de·spoil [dɪ'spɔɪl] *v.t.* (liter.) rob, plunder (*of*).

de·spond [dɪ'spɒnd] *v.i.* lose hope. **de·spon·den·cy** *n.* (no pl.). **de·spon-**

dent *adj.* having or showing loss of hope.

des·pot ['despɒt] *n.* ruler with unlimited powers, esp. one using these powers wrongly or cruelly. **~·ic** [de'spɒtɪk] *adj.* of or like a ~. **des·po·tism** ['despətɪzəm] *n.* rule of a ~; ~ic government or State.

des·sert [dɪ'zɜːt] *n.* **1.** (Gt. Brit.) course of fresh fruit, etc. at the end of dinner. **2.** sweet course (e.g. pie, pudding) at the end of a meal.

des·ti·na·tion [,destɪ'neɪʃn] *n.* place to which a person or thing is going or is being sent.

des·tined ['destɪnd] *adj.* intended, designed (by God, fate, or a person) *to* be or do sth., or *for* sth. **des·ti·ny** ['destɪnɪ] *n.* **1.** (no pl.) power believed to control events. **2.** that which happens to sb., thought of as determined in advance by that power.

des·ti·tute ['destɪtjuːt] *adj.* **1.** without food, clothes, and other things necessary for life. **2.** ~ *of*, lacking; without: *entirely ~ of sympathy*. **des·ti·tu·tion** [,destɪ'tjuːʃn] *n.* (no pl.).

de·stroy [dɪ'strɔɪ] *v.t.* break to pieces; make useless; put an end to. **~·er** *n.* (esp.) small, fast warship armed with missiles. **de·struc·ti·ble** [dɪ'strʌktəbl] *adj.* that can be ~ed. **de·struc·tion** [dɪ'strʌkʃn] *n.* (no pl.) ~ing or being ~ed; cause of ruin. **de·struc·tive** [dɪ'strʌktɪv] *adj.* causing destruction; fond of, in the habit of, ~ing.

des·ul·to·ry ['desəltərɪ] *adj.* without system, purpose, or regularity: ~ *reading*.

de·tach [dɪ'tætʃ] *v.t.* **1.** unfasten and take apart (*from*); separate. **2.** (armed forces) send (a party) away from the main body. **~ed** *adj.* (of the mind, opinions, etc.) not influenced by others; impartial; (of a house) not joined to another on either side. **~·able** *adj.* that can be ~ed. **~·ment** *n.* **1.** (no pl.) ~ing or being ~ed. **2.** (no pl.) ~ed state of mind; being uninfluenced by surroundings, the opinions of others. **3.** (armed forces) party of men, number of ships, etc. acting separately.

de·tail ['diːteɪl] *n.* **1.** small, particular fact or item. **2.** collection of such small facts: *go into ~s, explain sth. in ~* (i.e. give all the small points of fact separately). **3.** (armed forces) small detachment (3). *v.t.* **1.** give full ~s of; describe fully. **2.** appoint for special duty: *Three soldiers were ~ed to guard the bridge.*

de·tain [dɪ'teɪn] *v.t.* keep waiting;

keep back; prevent from leaving: *be ~ed at the office; be ~ed by the police for questioning.* **de·ten·tion** [dɪ'tenʃn] *n.* (no pl.) ~ing or being ~ed.

de·tect [dɪ'tekt] *v.t.* discover (the existence or presence of sb. or sth., the identity of sb. guilty of wrongdoing). **de·tec·tion** [dɪ'tekʃn] *n.* (no pl.) ~ing: *the ~ion of crime.* **de·tec·tive** *n.* person whose business is to ~ criminals: *~ive story (novel),* one that describes crime and the ~ion of a criminal or criminals.

de·ter [dɪ'tɜː*] *v.t.* (-rr-) discourage, hinder (sb. *from doing* sth.): *Let nothing ~ you from trying to succeed in life.* **~·rent** [dɪ'terənt] *n. & adj.* (thing) tending to, intended to, ~ or discourage.

de·ter·gent [dɪ'tɜːdʒənt] *adj.* cleansing. *n.* substance used for removing dirt, esp. from the surface of things.

de·te·ri·o·rate [dɪ'tɪərɪəreɪt] *v.t. & i.* make or become worse or of less value. **de·te·ri·o·ra·tion** [dɪ,tɪərɪə'reɪʃn] *n.*

de·ter·mine [dɪ'tɜːmɪn] *v.t. & i.* **1.** be the fact that decides (sth.): *The size of your feet ~s the size of your shoes.* **2.** decide (sb.'s future); make up one's mind (*to do* sth.); settle. **3.** cause to decide. **4.** learn, find out, exactly: ~ *the meaning of a word.* **~d** *adj.* strong-willed; of fixed purpose. **de·ter·mi·na·tion** [dɪ,tɜːmɪ'neɪʃn] *n.* determining; firmness of purpose. **de·ter·mi·nate** [dɪ'tɜːmɪnət] *adj.* limited; definite.

de·ter·rent, see *deter*.

de·test [dɪ'test] *v.t.* hate. **~·able** *adj.* deserving to be hated; hateful. **de·tes·ta·tion** [,diːte'steɪʃn] *n.* hatred; sth. ~ed.

de·throne [dɪ'θrəʊn] *v.t.* remove (a ruler) from his position of authority.

det·o·nate ['detəneɪt] *v.t. & i.* (cause to) explode with a loud noise. **det·o·na·tor** *n.* (esp.) part of a bomb, shell, etc. that sets off the explosion. **det·o·na·tion** [,detə'neɪʃn] *n.*

de·tour ['diː,tʊə*] *n.* turning aside; roundabout way: *make a ~.*

de·tract [dɪ'trækt] *v.i.* ~ *from*, take away from (the credit or value of). **de·trac·tion** [dɪ'trækʃn] *n.* **de·trac·tor** *n.* person who says things to lessen sb.'s credit or reputation.

det·ri·ment ['detrɪmənt] *n.* (no pl.) damage; harm: *A child cannot smoke without ~ to its health.* **det·ri·men·tal** [,detrɪ'mentl] *adj.*

de·val·ue [,diː'væljuː] *v.t.* reduce the value of (esp. a currency, relative to that of gold or other currencies). **de·val·u·a·tion** [,diːvæljʊ'eɪʃn] *n.*

dev·as·tate ['devəsteɪt] *v.t.* ruin; make desolate. **dev·as·ta·tion** [,devə'steɪʃn] *n.*

de·vel·op [dɪ'veləp] *v.t. & i.* **1.** (cause to) grow larger, fuller, or mature; (cause to) unfold: ⁓*ing country*, country that is ⁓ing better economic and social positions. **2.** (of sth. not at first active or visible) come or bring it into a form in which it is active or can be seen: ⁓ *a cold.* **3.** treat (an exposed film, etc.) with chemicals so that the picture shows. **4.** use (land) for buildings, etc., thereby increasing its value. **⁓·er** *n.* substance used to ⁓ photographic material. **⁓·ment** *n.* **1.** (no pl.) ⁓ing or being ⁓ed; growth: ⁓*ment area*, (Gt. Brit.) area where new industries are encouraged by the government as a means of reducing heavy unemployment there. **2.** new stage that is the result of ⁓ing: *the latest ⁓ments in foreign affairs.*

de·vi·ate ['diːvɪeɪt] *v.i.* turn away (*from* the right or usual way, a rule, custom, etc.). **de·vi·a·tion** [,diːvɪ'eɪʃn] *n.*

de·vice [dɪ'vaɪs] *n.* **1.** plan; scheme; trick. *leave sb. to his own ⁓s*, let him do as he wishes, without help or advice. **2.** sth. thought out, invented, or adapted for a special purpose. **3.** sign, symbol, or crest (3).

dev·il ['devl] *n.* **1.** spirit of evil; wicked spirit; cruel or mischievous person. *the D⁓*, Satan. **2.** (usu. *poor ⁓*) wretched or luckless person. **3.** (in exclamations) *How the ⁓ ...*, How ever; *the ⁓ of a time*, a time of difficulty, excitement, etc. (according to context); *like the ⁓*, with great energy, etc. **⁓·ish** ['devlɪʃ] *adj.* wicked; cruel.

de·vi·ous ['diːvjəs] *adj.* winding; not straightforward; roundabout.

de·vise [dɪ'vaɪz] *v.t.* plan; invent.

de·vi·tal·ize [,diː'vaɪtəlaɪz] *v.t.* take away strength and vigour from.

de·void [dɪ'vɔɪd] *adj.* ⁓ *of*, empty of; without: ⁓ *of sense.*

de·volve [dɪ'vɒlv] *v.i. & t.* ⁓ (*up*)*on*, (of work, duties) be passed on to (another person, a deputy); pass (work, duties) (*to* or *upon* sb.): *When Smith is ill, his work ⁓s upon me.*

de·vote [dɪ'vəʊt] *v.t.* give up (oneself, one's time, energy, etc.) (*to* sth. or sb.): ⁓ *all one's spare time to sport.* **de·vot·ed** *adj.* very loving or loyal. **dev·o·tee** [,devəʊ'tiː] *n.* person ⁓d to (e.g. some form of religion). **de·vo·tion** [dɪ'vəʊʃn] *n.* being ⁓d (*to*); strong, deep love; (pl.) prayers.

de·vour [dɪ'vaʊə*] *v.t.* **1.** eat (fig. look at, hear) hungrily (and anxiously); (of flames) destroy. **2.** ⁓*ed by* (fig., anxiety, etc.), having one's whole attention taken up by.

de·vout [dɪ'vaʊt] *adj.* paying serious attention to religious duties; (of prayers, wishes) deep-felt; sincere. **⁓·ly** *adv.*

dew [djuː] *n.* (no pl.) tiny drops of moisture formed between evening and morning on cool surfaces from water vapour in the air. **⁓·y** *adj.* (-*ier*, -*iest*) wet with ⁓.

dex·ter·ous ['dekstərəs], **dex·trous** ['dekstrəs] *adj.* clever and quick, esp. in using the hands. **dex·ter·i·ty** [dek-'sterətɪ] *n.* (no pl.).

dhow [daʊ] *n.* single-masted ship as used by Arab sailors.

di·a·bol·ic, **di·a·bol·i·cal** [,daɪə'bɒl-ɪk(l)] *adjs.* of or like the Devil; very wicked or cruel.

di·ag·nose ['daɪəgnəʊz] *v.t.* determine (4) the nature of (esp. a disease) from symptoms (1). **di·ag·no·sis** [,daɪəg-'nəʊsɪs] *n.* (pl. *-ses* [-siːz]) diagnosing; statement about this.

di·ag·o·nal [daɪ'ægənl] *n. & adj.* (straight line) going across a straight-sided figure (e.g. an oblong) from corner to corner. **⁓·ly** *adv.* in the slanting direction of a ⁓.

a diagonal

di·a·gram ['daɪəgræm] *n.* drawing, design, or plan to explain or illustrate sth. **⁓·mat·ic** [,daɪəgrə'mætɪk] *adj.*

di·al ['daɪəl] *n.* **1.** face (of a clock or watch). **2.** marked face or flat plate with a pointer for measuring (weight, pressure, etc.). **3.** plate, etc. on a radio receiver or television set with names or numbers for selecting broadcasting stations. **4.** part of an automatic telephone used when calling a number. *v.t. & i.* (-*ll*-, U.S.A. also -*l*-) call by means of a telephone ⁓: ⁓ *6652*; ⁓ *the hospital.*

di·a·lect ['daɪəlekt] *n.* form of a spoken language, way of speaking, used in part of a country or by a class of people: *the Yorkshire ⁓*; *the Negro ⁓, America*; ⁓ *words* (*pronunciations*).

dials

square sides marked with spots, used in games of chance, etc. *the die is cast* (i.e. the course is determined, there is no turning back now). *v.i. & t.* **1.** play ~. **2.** cut (food, e.g. carrots) into pieces shaped like ~.

dice

di·a·logue (U.S.A. also **-log**) ['daɪəlɒg] *n.* (writing in the form of a) conversation or talk; talk between two persons.

di·am·e·ter [daɪ'æmɪtə*] *n.* (length of a) straight line passing from side to side of a circle or sphere through the centre; measurement across any other geometrical figure; width; thickness. **di·a·met·ri·cal·ly** [ˌdaɪə'metrɪkəlɪ] *adv.* completely; directly.

di·a·mond ['daɪəmənd] *n.* **1.** brilliant precious stone or jewel, the hardest substance known. ~ *wedding*, sixtieth anniversary of a wedding. **2.** figure with four equal sides whose angles are not right angles; this figure printed in red on some playing-cards: *the ace of ~s.*

the ace of diamonds (2)

a diamond (1, 2)

di·a·per ['daɪəpə*] *n.* (U.S.A.) = napkin (2); nappy.

di·aph·a·nous [daɪ'æfənəs] *adj.* (of dress materials) transparent.

di·a·phragm ['daɪəfræm] *n.* **1.** wall of muscle between chest and abdomen. **2.** thin, round plate in some instruments (e.g. a microphone).

di·ar·rhoea (U.S.A. **-rhea**) [ˌdaɪə'rɪə] *n.* (no pl.) too frequent emptying of the bowels.

di·a·ry ['daɪərɪ] *n.* daily record of events, thoughts; book for this: *keep a ~*.

di·a·tribe ['daɪətraɪb] *n.* angry or violent attack in words.

dice [daɪs] *n. pl.* (sing. *die* [daɪ]) small pieces of wood, bone, etc. with six

dic·tate [dɪk'teɪt] *v.t. & i.* **1.** say (words) for another person to write down: ~ *a letter.* **2.** ~ *to*, give authoritative orders to. ~**s** ['dɪkteɪts] *n. pl.* directions or orders (given by one's reason, conscience, common sense). **dic·ta·tion** [dɪk'teɪʃn] *n.* dictating; sth. ~d. **dic·ta·tor** [dɪk'teɪtə*] *n.* ruler with absolute power, esp. one who has obtained such power by force or in an irregular way. **dic·ta·tor·ship** *n.* (country with a) government by a dictator. **dic·ta·to·ri·al** [ˌdɪktə'tɔːrɪəl] *adj.* of or like a dictator; fond of giving orders.

dic·tion ['dɪkʃn] *n.* (no pl.) choice and use of words; style or manner of speaking and writing.

dic·tio·nary ['dɪkʃənrɪ] *n.* book dealing with the words of a language or of some special subject (e.g. the Bible, architecture), and arranged in ABC order.

did, didn't, see *do.*

di·dac·tic [dɪ'dæktɪk] *adj.* **1.** intended to teach: ~ *poetry.* **2.** having the manner of a teacher.

die¹ [daɪ] *v.i.* (p.t. & p.p. *died* [daɪd], pres. p. *dying* ['daɪɪŋ]) come to the end of life; cease to live: ~ *of cold;* ~ *by violence;* ~ *from a wound;* be dying (*for sth., to do sth.*), have a strong wish.

die², see *dice.*

die³ [daɪ] *n.* metal block with a design, etc. cut in it, used for shaping coins, medals, etc., or stamping (2) (words, etc.) on paper, leather, etc.

die·sel ['diːzl] *n.* (also ~ *engine*) engine burning heavy oil (not motor spirit).

di·et¹ ['daɪət] *n.* **1.** sort of food a person usually eats. **2.** sort of food to which a person is limited (e.g. for medical reasons): *The doctor put her on a ~. v.t. & i.* restrict oneself, be restricted, to a ~ (2). **di·eti·tian, -cian** [ˌdaɪə'tɪʃn] *n.* trained person who plans ~s (2) (e.g. in a hospital).

di·et² ['daɪət] *n.* series of meetings for

discussion of national, international, or church affairs; any of various national or provincial legislatures.

dif·fer ['dɪfə*] *v.i.* be unlike. ~ *from*, disagree; be of another opinion. ~·**ence** ['dɪfrəns] *n.* 1. state of being unlike. 2. amount, degree, etc. in which things are unlike. 3. disagreement. ~·**ent** ['dɪfrənt] *adj.* not the same; various. ~·**en·ti·ate** [,dɪfə'renʃɪeɪt] *v.t. & i.* see or be the ~·ence between; (cause to) become ~·ent.

dif·fi·cult ['dɪfɪkəlt] *adj.* requiring much effort, skill, thought, etc.; not easy. **dif·fi·cul·ty** ['dɪfɪkəltɪ] *n.* state or quality of being ~; sth. ~.

dif·fi·dent ['dɪfɪdənt] *adj.* not having, not showing, much belief in one's own abilities. **dif·fi·dence** *n.* (no pl.).

dif·fract [dɪ'frækt] *v.t.* break up a beam of light) into dark and light bands or the spectrum.

dif·fuse [dɪ'fju:z] *v.t. & i.* 1. (cause to) spread, in every direction. 2. (of gases, fluids) mix slowly with one another. [dɪ'fju:s] *adj.* 1. using too many words. 2. spread about; scattered. **dif·fu·sion** [dɪ'fju:ʒn] *n.* (no pl.).

dig [dɪg] *v.t. & i.* (-gg-; p.t. & p.p. dug [dʌg]) 1. use a spade, etc. to break up and move (earth); make (a hole, way, etc.) by doing this; get (potatoes, etc.) from the ground in this way. 2. push (a pointed thing into): ~ *a person in the ribs* (with one's fingers). 3. get by searching (e.g. information *out* of a book). *n.* 1. push or poke with sth. pointed. 2. (pl.) (Gt. Brit., colloq.) lodgings. ~·**ger** *n.* person who ~s. ~·**gings** ['dɪgɪŋz] *n. pl.* gold-field; (Gt. Brit., colloq.) lodgings.

di·gest [dɪ'dʒest] *v.t. & i.* 1. (of food) change, be changed, in the stomach and bowels so that it can be used in the body. 2. take into the mind; reduce (a mass of facts, etc.) to order. ['daɪdʒest] *n.* short, condensed account; summary: *a ~ of the week's news*. ~·**ible** [dɪ'dʒestəbl] *adj.* that can be ~ed (1) easily. (esp.) **di·ges·tion** [dɪ'dʒestʃən] *n.* (no pl.) (esp.) person's power of ~ing food. **di·ges·tive** [dɪ'dʒestɪv] *adj.* of ~ion.

dig·it ['dɪdʒɪt] *n.* 1. any one of the numbers 0 to 9. 2. finger or toe. **dig·i·tal** ['dɪdʒɪtl] *adj.* of ~s: ~al clock (watch), one that shows time not by hands (4) but by displayed ~s.

dig·ni·fy ['dɪgnɪfaɪ] *v.t.* give dignity to; make worthy or honourable. **dig·ni·fied** *adj.* having, showing, dignity.

dig·ni·tary ['dɪgnɪtərɪ] *n.* person hold-

ing a high position, esp. in the church (e.g. a bishop).

dig·ni·ty ['dɪgnətɪ] *n.* 1. (no pl.) true worth; quality that wins or deserves respect. 2. (no pl.) calm and serious behaviour: *lose one's ~* (e.g. by making a foolish mistake); *beneath one's ~*, not worthy of a person's position or powers. 3. high or honourable rank, post, or title.

di·gress [daɪ'gres] *v.i.* (esp. in speaking or writing) turn aside (*from* the main subject). **di·gres·sion** [daɪ'greʃn] *n.*

digs [dɪgz] *n. pl.* (Gt. Brit., colloq.) lodgings.

dike, dyke [daɪk] *n.* 1. ditch (for carrying away water from land). 2. long wall of earth, etc. (to keep back water and prevent flooding).

di·lap·i·dat·ed [dɪ'læpɪdeɪtɪd] *adj.* (of buildings, furniture, etc.) falling to pieces; in a state of disrepair. **di·lap·i·da·tion** [dɪ,læpɪ'deɪʃn] *n.* (no pl.) being or becoming ~.

di·late [daɪ'leɪt] *v.t. & i.* 1. (cause to) become wider, larger, further open: *with ~d eyes (nostrils)*. 2. ~ *upon*, speak or write at great length about.

dil·a·to·ry ['dɪlətərɪ] *adj.* slow in doing things; causing delay.

di·lem·ma [dɪ'lemə] *n.* situation in which one has to choose between two things, courses of action, etc. that are either unfavourable or undesirable.

dil·et·tante [,dɪlɪ'tæntɪ] *n.* (pl. -ti [-ti:], ~s) lover of the fine arts; person who studies the arts but not seriously and not with real understanding.

dil·i·gent ['dɪlɪdʒənt] *adj.* hard-working; showing care and effort. **dil·i·gence** *n.* (no pl.).

dil·ly-dal·ly ['dɪlɪdælɪ] *v.i.* (colloq.) waste time (by not making up one's mind); dawdle.

di·lute [daɪ'lju:t] *v.t.* make (a liquid or colour) weaker or thinner (by adding water or other liquid); (fig.) weaken the force of (by mixing). *adj.* thus weakened. **di·lu·tion** [daɪ'lu:ʃn] *n.*

dim [dɪm] *adj.* (-mm-) not bright; not clearly to be seen; (of the eyes) not able to see clearly: *eyes ~ with tears*. *v.t. & i.* (-mm-) make or become ~. ~·**ly** *adv.* [ten cents.]

dime [daɪm] *n.* (U.S.A.) coin worth ten cents.

di·men·sion [dɪ'menʃn] *n.* measurement of any sort (breadth, length, thickness, area, etc.); (pl.) size: *of great ~s*.

di·min·ish [dɪ'mɪnɪʃ] *v.t. & i.* make or become less. **dim·i·nu·tion** [,dɪmɪ'nju:ʃn] *n.*

di·min·u·tive [dɪˈmɪnjʊtɪv] *adj.* very small. *n.* word that indicates a small size of sth., often a word with a suffix such as *-let*: *Streamlet is a ~ of stream.*

dim·ple [ˈdɪmpl] *n.* small hollow that appears in the chin or in the cheeks when sb. smiles. *v.t. & i.* make or form ~s.

din [dɪn] *n.* (no pl.) loud, confused noise that continues. *v.i. & t.* (*-nn-*) **1.** make a ~. **2.** ~ *sth. into sb.*, tell him again and again.

dine [daɪn] *v.i. & t.* have dinner; give a dinner for. **din·er** [ˈdaɪnə*] *n.* dining-car on a train. **'din·ing-car** *n.* railway coach in which meals are served (3). **'din·ing-room** *n.* room in which meals are eaten.

ding-dong [ˈdɪŋˈdɒŋ] *adv. & n.* (with the) sound of two bells striking alternately.

din·ghy [ˈdɪŋgɪ] *n.* small, open boat.

din·gy [ˈdɪndʒɪ] *adj.* dirty-looking.

din·ner [ˈdɪnə*] *n.* main meal of the day: *Have you had ~ yet? We enjoyed the ~ they served.*

dint [dɪnt] *n.* **1.** dent. **2.** *by ~ of*, by force or means of.

di·o·cese [ˈdaɪəsɪs] *n.* bishop's district. **di·oc·e·san** [daɪˈɒsɪsn] *adj.* of a ~.

di·ox·ide [daɪˈɒksaɪd] *n.* (chem.) oxide with two atoms of oxygen in the molecule: *carbon ~.*

dip [dɪp] *v.t. & i.* (*-pp-*) **1.** put, lower, (sth.) into a liquid and take it out again: *~ one's pen in the ink.* **2.** put (one's hand, a spoon, etc. *into* sth.) and take out (liquid, grain, etc.); get (liquid, grain, etc.) by doing this: *~ a bucket into a lake*; *~ up a bucket of water.* **3.** go below a surface or level; (of land) slope downwards: *The sun ~ped below the horizon. The birds rose and ~ped in their flight.* **4.** (cause to) go down and up again: *~ a flag* (as a salute); *~ the headlights of a car.* **5.** ~ *into* (a book, subject), examine or study but not thoroughly. *n.* **1.** act of ~ping; (colloq.) short swim or bathe. **2.** cleansing liquid in which sheep are ~ped. **3.** downward slope: *a ~ in the road.*

liph·the·ria [dɪfˈθɪərɪə] *n.* (no pl.) serious infectious disease of the throat.

liph·thong [ˈdɪfθɒŋ] *n.* union of two vowel sounds or vowel letters (e.g. the sounds [aɪ] in *pipe* [paɪp], the letters *ou* in *doubt*).

li·plo·ma [dɪˈpləʊmə] *n.* educational certificate of proficiency.

li·plo·ma·cy [dɪˈpləʊməsɪ] *n.* (no pl.) **1.** management of international relations (4); skill in this. **2.** art of, skill in,

dealing with people so that business is done smoothly. **di·plo·mat** [ˈdɪpləmæt], **di·plo·ma·tist** [dɪˈpləʊmətɪst] *ns.* **1.** person engaged in ~ for his government (e.g. an ambassador). **2.** person clever in dealing with people. **dip·lo·mat·ic** [ˌdɪpləˈmætɪk] *adj.* **1.** of ~: *the diplomatic service.* **2.** tactful.

dip·per [ˈdɪpə*] *n.* cup-shaped vessel on a long handle for dipping out liquids.

dire [daɪə*] *adj.* (*~r, ~st*) dreadful; terrible.

di·rect [dɪˈrekt] *adj. & adv.* **1.** (going) straight; not curved or crooked; not turned aside: *in a ~ line with*; *a ~ hit.* **2.** with nothing or no one in between; in an unbroken line. **3.** straightforward; going straight to the point: *a ~ answer*; *a ~ way of speaking* (*doing things*). **4.** exact: *~ opposite.* **5.** ~ *action*, use of strike action by workers to get their demands. ~ *current*, electric current flowing in one ~ion only (cf. *alternating current*). ~ *speech*, speaker's actual words. *v.t. & i.* **1.** tell or show (sb.) how to do sth., how to get somewhere; manage; control: *~ sb. to the post office*; *~ workmen.* **2.** address (a letter, etc. *to*); speak or write (remarks, etc. *to*). **3.** guide (*to*); cause to turn (the eyes, one's attention) straight (*to* sth.): *~ one's attention to what is being done.* **4.** act as ~or. **di·rec·tion** [dɪˈrekʃn] *n.* **1.** course taken by a moving person or thing; point towards which a person or thing looks, moves, etc.: *people running in every ~ion.* **2.** (often pl.) information about what to do, where to go, how to do sth., etc.; command. **3.** (usu. pl.) address on a letter, parcel, etc. **4.** act of ~ing, managing, giving orders: *work under the ~ion of an expert.* **di·rec·tion·al** [dɪˈrekʃənl] *adj.* relating to or indicating ~ion (in space). **di·rec·tive** [dɪˈrektɪv] *n.* detailed instructions as given to staff (3) to guide them in their work. **~·ly** *adv.* **1.** in a ~ manner. **2.** at once; now. *conj.* (colloq.) as soon as. **~·ness** *n.* **di·rec·tor** *n.* **1.** person who ~s, esp. one of a group (called *the Board of D~ors*) ~ing the affairs of a business company. **2.** person who supervises the acting, etc. of a film, play, etc. **di·rec·tor·ate** [dɪˈrektərət] *n.* board of ~ors. **di·rec·to·ry** [dɪˈrektərɪ] *n.* list of names (and usu. addresses) in ABC order: *a telephone ~ory.*

dirge [dɜːdʒ] *n.* song sung at a burial or for a dead person.

dirk [dɜːk] *n.* kind of dagger.

dirt [dɜːt] *n.* (no pl.) unclean matter (e.g. dust, mud), esp. where not wanted (e.g. on the body, clothing, buildings); (fig.) unclean thought or talk. **~y** *adj.* (*-ier*, *-iest*) **1.** not clean; covered with ~. **2.** (of the weather) rough; stormy; rainy. **3.** obscene. **4.** mean: *play a ~y trick on sb.* *v.t. & i.* make or become ~y. **~·i·ly** *adv.* **~·i·ness** *n.*

dis- [dɪs-] *pref.* (indicating the opposite of) not (to): **~·ad'van·tage**, **~·ad·van'ta·geous**, **~·ap·pro'ba·tion**, **~·ap'prove**, **~·ap'prov·al**, **~·ar'range**, **~·be'lieve**, **~·be'lief**, **~'cour·te·ous**, **~'cour·te·sy**, **~·em'bark**, **~·(·en·)·'fran·chise**, **~·en'gaged**, **~·en'tan·gle**, **~·es'tab·lish**, **~'fa·vour**, **~'heart·en**, **~'mount**, **~·o'bey**, **~·o'be·di·ence**, **~·o'be·di·ent**, **~'please**, **~'plea·sure**, **~·re'spect**, **~'sat·is·fy**, **~'sim·i·lar**.

dis·able [dɪs'eɪbl] *v.t.* make unable to do sth., esp. take away the power of using the limbs: *soldiers ~d in the war* (i.e. crippled). **dis·abil·i·ty** [ˌdɪsə'bɪlətɪ] *n.* being ~d; sth. that ~s.

dis·abuse [ˌdɪsə'bjuːz] *v.t.* free (sb., his mind) from false ideas; put (a person) right (in his ideas).

dis·af·fect·ed [ˌdɪsə'fektɪd] *adj.* unfriendly; discontented; disloyal. **dis·af·fec·tion** [ˌdɪsə'fekʃn] *n.* (no pl.).

dis·agree [ˌdɪsə'griː] *v.i.* **1.** take a different view; not agree (*with* sb.). **2.** ~ *with*, (of food, climate, etc.) be unsuited to; have bad effects on. **~·able** [ˌdɪsə'grɪəbl] *adj.* unpleasant; bad-tempered. **~·ment** *n.*

dis·al·low [ˌdɪsə'laʊ] *v.t.* refuse to allow or accept as correct.

dis·ap·pear [ˌdɪsə'pɪə*] *v.i.* go out of sight; be seen no more. **~·ance** *n.* (no pl.).

dis·ap·point [ˌdɪsə'pɔɪnt] *v.t.* fail to do or be equal to what is hoped for or expected; prevent (a plan, hope, etc.) from being realized. **~·ed** *a~̣.* sad at not getting what was hoped for, etc. **~·ment** *n.* being ~ed; person or thing that ~s.

dis·arm [dɪs'ɑːm] *v.t. & i.* **1.** take away weapons, etc. from. **2.** (of a country) reduce the size of, give up the use of, armed forces. **3.** make it hard for sb. to feel anger, suspicion, doubt. **dis·ar·ma·ment** [dɪs'ɑːməmənt] *n.* (no pl.) **~·ing** or being ~ed (2).

di·sas·ter [dɪ'zɑːstə*] *n.* great or sudden misfortune. **di·sas·trous** [dɪ'zɑːstrəs] *adj.* causing ~.

dis·avow [ˌdɪsə'vaʊ] *v.t.* say that one

does not know; refuse to approve of. **~·al** [ˌdɪsə'vaʊəl] *n.* (no pl.).

dis·band [dɪs'bænd] *v.t. & i.* (of a force of soldiers, etc.) break up (as an organized body (5)).

dis·burse [dɪs'bɜːs] *v.t. & i.* pay out (money). **~·ment** *n.*

disc, disk [dɪsk] *n.* **1.** thin, flat, round plate (e.g. a coin, record[2] (4)); round surface appearing to be flat: *the sun's ~;* ~ *jockey*, (colloq.) compère of broadcast programmes of records[2] (4) (esp.) of popular music. **2.** layer of cartilage between vertebrae: *a slipped* ~, a slightly dislocated (1) ~.

dis·card [dɪs'kɑːd] *v.t.* throw out or away, put aside, give up (sth. useless, sth. not wanted).

dis·cern [dɪ'sɜːn] *v.t.* see clearly (with the senses or with the mind); (esp.) see with an effort. **~·ing** *adj.* able to understand and judge well. **~·ment** *n.*

dis·charge [dɪs'tʃɑːdʒ] *v.t. & i.* **1.** unload (cargo from a ship). **2.** fire (a gun); shoot (an arrow, etc.). **3.** give or send out (liquid, gas, electric current, etc. that is inside sth.): *chimneys discharging smoke; rivers that ~ (themselves) into the ocean.* **4.** (of persons) send away (from); allow to leave: *men ~d from prison; patients ~d from hospital; a servant ~d for laziness* (i.e. dismissed). **5.** pay (a debt); perform (a duty). *n.* discharging or being ~d; sth., esp. a liquid, that is ~d: *the ~ of water from a reservoir.*

dis·ci·ple [dɪ'saɪpl] *n.* follower of any leader of religious thought, art, learning, etc.; one of the twelve personal followers of Jesus Christ.

dis·ci·pline ['dɪsɪplɪn] *n.* **1.** training, esp. of the mind and character, to produce self-control, habits of obedience, etc. **2.** result of such training; order kept (e.g. among schoolchildren, soldiers). **3.** set of rules for conduct. **4.** branch of knowledge; subject of instruction. *v.t.* apply ~ (1) to. **dis·ci·pli·nar·i·an** [ˌdɪsɪplɪ'neərɪən] *n.* person good at maintaining ~ (2). **dis·ci·plin·ary** ['dɪsɪplɪnərɪ] *adj.* of ~: *disciplinary measures* (intended to maintain ~ (2)).

dis·claim [dɪs'kleɪm] *v.t.* say that one does not own, that one has not said or done, that one has no connection with.

dis·close [dɪs'kləʊz] *v.t.* uncover; allow to be seen; make known. **dis·clo·sure** [dɪs'kləʊʒə*] *n.* disclosing; sth. ~d.

dis·co ['dɪskəʊ] *n.* (pl. ~s) (colloq., abbr. for) discothèque.

dis·col·our (U.S.A. **-or**) [dɪs'kʌlə*]

v.t. & i. change, spoil, the colour of; become changed or spoilt in colour.

dis·col·o(u)r·a·tion [dɪsˌkʌləˈreɪʃn] *n.*

dis·com·fit [dɪsˈkʌmfɪt] *v.t.* upset the plans of; embarrass. **dis·com·fi·ture** [dɪsˈkʌmfɪtʃə*] *n.* (no pl.).

dis·com·fort [dɪsˈkʌmfət] *n.* uneasiness; absence of comfort; sth. that causes uneasiness; hardship.

dis·com·pose [ˌdɪskəmˈpəʊz] *v.t.* disturb the composure or calmness of. **dis·com·po·sure** [ˌdɪskəmˈpəʊʒə*] *n.* (no pl.).

dis·con·cert [ˌdɪskənˈsɜːt] *v.t.* spoil or upset (sb.'s plans, etc.); upset the calmness or self-possession of.

dis·con·nect [ˌdɪskəˈnekt] *v.t.* detach from; take (two things) apart. **~ed** *adj.* (of talk or writing) having the ideas, etc. badly connected.

dis·con·so·late [dɪsˈkɒnsələt] *adj.* unhappy; without hope or comfort.

dis·con·tent [ˌdɪskənˈtent] *n.* cause of, feeling of, dissatisfaction or restlessness. **~ed** *adj.* dissatisfied; not contented. **~ed·ly** *adv.*

dis·con·tin·ue [ˌdɪskənˈtɪnjuː] *v.t. & i.* put an end to; give up; come to an end. **dis·con·tin·u·ous** [ˌdɪskənˈtɪnjʊəs] *adj.* not continuous.

dis·cord [ˈdɪskɔːd] *n.* **1.** disagreement; quarrelling. **2.** lack of harmony; chord (2) that jars[1]. **dis·cor·dant** [dɪs-ˈkɔːdənt] *adj.* not in agreement or harmony; unpleasing to the ear.

dis·co·thèque, dis·co·theque [ˈdɪskəʊtek] *n.* club or other place of entertainment where people dance to recorded popular music.

dis·count [ˈdɪskaʊnt] *n.* amount of money that may be taken off the full price, e.g. of (a) goods bought by shopkeepers for resale, (b) an account if paid promptly, (c) a bill of exchange not yet due for payment. *at a ~,* (of goods) not in demand; easily obtained. [ˈdɪskaʊnt, dɪˈskaʊnt] *v.t.* **1.** give or receive the present value of a bill of exchange not yet due. **2.** refuse complete belief in (a story, piece of news, etc.).

dis·cour·age [dɪˈskʌrɪdʒ] *v.t.* **1.** lessen, take away, the courage or confidence of. **2.** *~ from,* try to persuade (sb.) not to do sth. **~·ment** *n.*

dis·course [ˈdɪskɔːs] *n.* speech; lecture; sermon; treatise. [dɪˈskɔːs] *v.i.* lecture; speak or write at length (*on* sth.).

dis·cov·er [dɪˈskʌvə*] *v.t.* find out, bring to view (sth. existing but not yet known); realize (sth. new or unexpected). **~er** [dɪˈskʌvərə*] *n.* **~y** [dɪˈskʌvərɪ] *n.* **~ing;** sth. **~ed.**

dis·cred·it [dɪsˈkredɪt] *v.t.* refuse to believe; cause the truth, value, or credit of sth. or sb. to seem doubtful. *n.* (no pl.) loss of credit or reputation; person, thing, causing such loss; doubt; disbelief. **~·able** [dɪsˈkredɪtəbl] *adj.* bringing *~*.

dis·creet [dɪˈskriːt] *adj.* careful, tactful, in what one does and says; prudent. **dis·cre·tion** [dɪˈskreʃn] *n.* (no pl.) **1.** being *~*; prudence. **2.** freedom to act according to one's own judgement, to do what seems best.

dis·crep·an·cy [dɪˈskrepənsɪ] *n.* (in statements, accounts) difference; absence of agreement.

dis·crim·i·nate [dɪˈskrɪmɪneɪt] *v.t. & i.* **1.** see, make, a difference between: *good books from bad (between good and bad books)*. **2.** make distinctions; treat differently: *laws that do not ~ against anyone.* **dis·crim·i·nat·ing** *adj.* able to see or make small differences; giving special or different treatment: *discriminating duties (tariffs)*. **dis·crim·i·na·tion** [dɪˌskrɪmɪˈneɪʃn] *n.* (no pl.).

dis·cur·sive [dɪˈskɜːsɪv] *adj.* (of a person, what he says or writes) wandering from one point or subject to another.

dis·cus [ˈdɪskəs] *n.* heavy disc thrown in ancient and modern athletic contests: *the ~ throw* (this contest); *~ thrower*.

dis·cuss [dɪˈskʌs] *v.t.* examine and argue about (a subject). **dis·cus·sion** [dɪˈskʌʃn] *n.*

dis·dain [dɪsˈdeɪn] *v.t.* look at with contempt; be too proud (to do sth.). *n.* contempt; scorn. **~·ful** *adj.*

dis·ease [dɪˈziːz] *n.* illness of the body, mind, a plant; particular sort of such disorder with its own name. **~d** *adj.* suffering from, injured by, *~*.

dis·em·bod·ied [ˌdɪsɪmˈbɒdɪd] *adj.* (of the soul, spirit) apart from the body.

dis·en·chant [ˌdɪsɪnˈtʃɑːnt] *v.t.* free from enchantment or illusion.

dis·fig·ure [dɪsˈfɪɡə*] *v.t.* spoil the appearance or shape of. **~·ment** *n.* disfiguring or being *~d*; sth. that *~s*.

dis·gorge [dɪsˈɡɔːdʒ] *v.t.* throw up and out from, or as from, the throat; (fig.) give up (esp. sth. taken wrongfully).

dis·grace [dɪsˈɡreɪs] *n.* (no pl.) **1.** loss of respect, favour, reputation; fall from an honourable position; public shame. **2.** person or thing causing *~*. *v.t.* bring *~* upon; be a *~* to; remove (sb.) from his position with *~*. **~·ful** *adj.*

dis·grun·tled [dɪsˈɡrʌntld] *adj.* discontented; in a bad temper (*with* sb., *at* sth.).

dis·guise [dɪs'gaɪz] *v.t.* change the appearance of, in order to deceive or hide the identity of: *He ~d his looks but could not ~ his voice.* *n.* disguising; ~d condition; dress, actions, manner, etc. used to ~.

dis·gust [dɪs'gʌst] *n.* (no pl.) strong feeling of distaste; violent turning away: *~ at (for) sth. dirty (bad-smelling, etc.).* *v.t.* cause ~ in: *~ed at his laziness.* **~ing** *adj.*

dish [dɪʃ] *n.* (often oval) plate, bowl, etc. from which food is served at table; food brought to table in or on a ~: *wash up the ~es,* clean them after a meal; *~washer,* machine for washing ~es, etc. *v.t.* put into or on a ~ or ~es: *~ up the dinner.*

dis·har·mo·ny [ˌdɪs'hɑːmənɪ] *n.* (no pl.) lack of harmony. **dis·har·mo·ni·ous** [ˌdɪshɑː'məʊnjəs] *adj.*

di·shev·elled (U.S.A. also **-eled**) [dɪ-'ʃevld] *adj.* with the hair uncombed; (of the hair and clothes) in disorder; untidy.

dis·hon·est [dɪs'ɒnɪst] *adj.* not honest; insincere. **dis·hon·es·ty** *n.*

dis·hon·our (U.S.A. **-or**) [dɪs'ɒnə*] *n.* (no pl.) **1.** disgrace or shame; loss, absence of, honour and self-respect. **2.** person or thing bringing ~. *v.t.* bring shame, disgrace, loss of honour, on. *~ a cheque,* (of a bank) refuse to make payment. **~able** [dɪs'ɒnərəbl] *adj.*

dis·il·lu·sion [ˌdɪsɪ'luːʒn] *v.t.* set (sb.) free from mistaken beliefs. *n.* state of being ~ed. **~ment** *n.*

dis·in·cline [ˌdɪsɪn'klaɪn] *v.t.* be ~d for (sth., *to do* sth.), be unready or unwilling to. **dis·in·cli·na·tion** [ˌdɪsɪn-klɪ'neɪʃn] *n.* unwillingness: *a disinclination to work (for hard work).*

dis·in·fect [ˌdɪsɪn'fekt] *v.t.* make free from infection by disease germs. **dis·in·fec·tant** *adj. & n.* **~ing** (substance).

dis·in·gen·u·ous [ˌdɪsɪn'dʒenjʊəs] *adj.* insincere.

dis·in·her·it [ˌdɪsɪn'herɪt] *v.t.* take away the right (of sb.) to inherit. **dis·in·her·i·tance** *n.* (no pl.).

dis·in·te·grate [dɪs'ɪntɪgreɪt] *v.t. & i.* (cause to) break up into small pieces: *rocks ~d by frost and rain.* **dis·in·te·gra·tion** [dɪsˌɪntɪ'greɪʃn] *n.* (no pl.).

dis·in·ter·est·ed [dɪs'ɪntrəstɪd] *adj.* not influenced by personal feelings or interests.

dis·joint·ed [dɪs'dʒɔɪntɪd] *adj.* (of speech and writing) not connected;\
disk, see disc. [broken.]\
dis·like [dɪs'laɪk] *v.t.* not like. *n.* feeling of not liking: *have a ~ of (for) sth.*

dis·lo·cate ['dɪsləʊkeɪt] *v.t.* **1.** put (esp. a bone in the body) out of position: *~ one's shoulder.* **2.** put (traffic, machinery, etc.) out of order. **dis·lo·ca·tion** [ˌdɪsləʊ'keɪʃn] *n.*

dis·lodge [dɪs'lɒdʒ] *v.t.* force (sb. or sth.) from the place occupied.

dis·mal ['dɪzməl] *adj.* gloomy; sad; miserable; comfortless.

dis·man·tle [dɪs'mæntl] *v.t.* **1.** take away fittings, furnishings, etc. from: *~ an old warship (a fort).* **2.** take to pieces: *~ a machine.*

dis·may [dɪs'meɪ] *n.* (no pl.) feeling of fear and discouragement. *v.t.* fill with ~.

dis·mem·ber [dɪs'membə*] *v.t.* tear or cut the limbs from; divide up (a country, etc.). **~ment** *n.* the *~ment of the old Austrian Empire.*

dis·miss [dɪs'mɪs] *v.t.* **1.** send away (esp. from one's employment, from service): *~ workmen.* **2.** put away from the mind: *~ thoughts of revenge.* **~al** [dɪs'mɪsl] *n.*

dis·oblige [ˌdɪsə'blaɪdʒ] *v.t.* refuse to be helpful or to think about another person's wishes or needs.

dis·or·der [dɪs'ɔːdə*] *n.* **1.** absence of order; confusion. **2.** political trouble marked by angry outbursts or rioting. **3.** disturbance of the normal working of the body or mind; disease: *a digestive ~; ~s of the mind.* *v.t.* put into ~. **~ly** *adj.* in ~; lawless: *~ly behaviour; ~ly crowds.*

dis·or·ga·nize [dɪs'ɔːgənaɪz] *v.t.* throw into confusion; upset the system or order of. **dis·or·ga·ni·za·tion** [dɪsˌɔː-gənaɪ'zeɪʃn] *n.* (no pl.).

dis·own [ˌdɪs'əʊn] *v.t.* say that one does not know (sb. or sth.), that one has not, or no longer wishes to have, any connection with (sb. or sth.).

dis·par·age [dɪ'spærɪdʒ] *v.t.* say things to suggest that (sb. or sth.) is of small value or importance. **~ment** *n.* **dis·par·ag·ing·ly** *adv.*

dis·par·i·ty [dɪ'spærətɪ] *n.* inequality; difference: *~ in age (intelligence).*

dis·pas·sion·ate [dɪ'spæʃnət] *adj.* free from passion; not taking sides, not showing favour (in a quarrel, etc. between others).

dis·patch, des·patch [dɪ'spætʃ] *v.t.* **1** send off (to a destination, on a journey for a special purpose): *~ letters (telegrams, messengers).* **2.** finish, get through (business, a meal) quickly. **3** kill: *~ a murderer.* *n.* **1.** *~ing* or being *~ed.* **2.** sth. *~ed (1),* esp. a government military, or newspaper message o report. **3.** promptness; speed: *act with* ~.

dis·pel [dɪ'spel] *v.t.* (-ll-) drive away; scatter (clouds, fears, doubts).

dis·pen·sa·ry [dɪ'spensərɪ] *n.* place where medicines are dispensed (2) (e.g. in a hospital). **dis·pen·sa·tion** [ˌdɪspen'seɪʃn] *n.* **1.** act of dispensing (1); sth. looked upon as dispensed (1) or ordered by God. **2.** authority given by the Church to do sth. usually forbidden, or not to do sth. that must usually be done. **dis·pense** [dɪ'spens] *v.t. & i.* **1.** distribute; administer: *dispense justice.* **2.** mix, prepare, give out (medicine). **3.** *dispense with*, do without: *dispense with the cook's services.* **dis·pens·er** *n.* **1.** person who makes up medicines from a doctor's prescriptions. **2.** container (1) that dispenses (1) a certain quantity of sth. at a time: *a dispenser for liquid soap* (*paper cups*).

dis·perse [dɪ'spɜːs] *v.t. & i.* (cause to) go in different directions; scatter; send out, space out, go out (esp. troops under attack), to separate positions. **dis·per·sal** [dɪ'spɜːsl] *n.*

dis·pir·it·ed [dɪ'spɪrɪtɪd] *adj.* discouraged; depressed.

dis·place [dɪs'pleɪs] *v.t.* put out of the right or usual position; take the place of; put sb. or sth. in the place of: ~d *person*, stateless refugee in exile. ~·ment, *n.* (no pl.) (esp.) amount of water ~d by a solid body in it, or floating in it: *a ship of 10,000 tons* ~ment.

dis·play [dɪ'spleɪ] *v.t.* **1.** show; place or arrange so that things may be seen easily: ~ *goods in windows.* **2.** allow to be seen: ~ *one's ignorance.* *n.* ~ing; sth. ~ed: *a fashion* ~; *a* ~ *of one's knowledge.*

dis·port [dɪ'spɔːt] *v.t.* ~ *oneself*, (liter.) enjoy or amuse oneself (e.g. in the sea or in the sunshine).

dis·pos·a·ble [dɪ'spəʊzəbl] *adj.* **1.** made so that it may be easily disposed of after (one) use: ~ *nappies* (*bottle*). **2.** at one's disposal. *n.* article that is ~ (1).

dis·pos·al [dɪ'spəʊzl] *n.* (no pl.) act of disposing (1, 2): *the* ~ *of property* (*business affairs, troops*); *at one's* ~, *to be used as one wishes: place one's time,* etc. *at sb. else's* ~.

dis·pose [dɪ'spəʊz] *v.i. & t.* **1.** ~ *of*, finish with; get rid of; deal with: ~ *of rubbish* (*business, sb.'s arguments*). **2.** place (persons, objects) in good order or in suitable positions. **3.** *be* (*feel*) ~d, be willing or ready: *feel* ~d *for a*

10*

walk; *be not at all* ~d *to help*; *well-*~d (i.e. friendly and helpful) *toward*.

dis·po·si·tion [ˌdɪspə'zɪʃn] *n.* **1.** arrangement; disposing (2). **2.** person's natural qualities of mind and character: *a man with a cheerful* ~; *a woman with a* ~ *to jealousy.*

dis·pos·sess [ˌdɪspə'zes] *v.t.* ~ (*sb.*) *of*, take away (property, esp. land) from; compel (sb.) to give up (the house he occupies). **dis·pos·ses·sion** [ˌdɪspə-'zeʃn] *n.*

dis·pro·por·tion [ˌdɪsprə'pɔːʃn] *n.* (no pl.) state of being out of proportion. ~·ate [ˌdɪsprə'pɔːʃnət] *adj.* relatively too large or small; being out of proportion.

dis·pute [dɪ'spjuːt] *v.i. & t.* **1.** argue, quarrel (*with* or *against* sb.; *on* or *about* sth.); question the truth or justice of (sth.). **2.** try to prevent; oppose: ~ *the enemy's advance*; try to win (a victory, possession, etc.). *n.* disputing; argument. *beyond* (*past*) ~, undoubtedly. **dis·put·a·ble** [dɪ'spjuːtəbl] *adj.* that may be ~d; questionable. **dis·pu·tant** [dɪ'spjuːtənt] *n.* person taking part in a ~.

dis·qual·i·fy [dɪs'kwɒlɪfaɪ] *v.t.* make unfit or unable (*for* sth., *from doing* sth.).

dis·qui·et [dɪs'kwaɪət] *v.t.* make troubled, anxious, uneasy. *n.* anxiety; troubled condition. ~ude [dɪs'kwaɪə-tjuːd] *n.* (no pl.) state of ~.

dis·qui·si·tion [ˌdɪskwɪ'zɪʃn] *n.* long, elaborate speech or piece of writing on a subject.

dis·re·gard [ˌdɪsrɪ'gɑːd] *v.t.* pay no attention to; show no respect for. *n.* (no pl.) inattention; indifference; neglect.

dis·re·pair [ˌdɪsrɪ'peə*] *n.* (no pl.) state of needing repair: *old buildings in* ~.

dis·rep·u·ta·ble [dɪs'repjʊtəbl] *adj.* having a bad reputation; not respectable in appearance or character. **dis·re·pute** [ˌdɪsrɪ'pjuːt] *n.* (no pl.) discredit; condition of being ~: *fall into disrepute.*

dis·robe [ˌdɪs'rəʊb] *v.i. & t.* (esp.) take off official or ceremonial robes.

dis·rupt [dɪs'rʌpt] *v.t.* break up, separate by force (a State, communications, other non-physical things). **dis·rup·tion** [dɪs'rʌpʃn] *n.* (no pl.). **dis·rup·tive** [dɪs'rʌptɪv] *adj.*

dis·sect [dɪ'sekt] *v.t.* cut up (parts of an animal, a plant, etc.) in order to study its structure; (fig.) examine (a theory, an argument, etc.) part by part

to judge its value. **dis·sec·tion** [dɪ-
'sekʃn] *n.*

dis·sem·ble [dɪ'sembl] *v.t. & i.* speak,
behave, so as to hide one's real feelings,
thoughts, plans, etc., or give a wrong
idea of them. **~r** *n.*

dis·sem·i·nate [dɪ'semɪneɪt] *v.t.* distribute or spread widely (ideas, doctrines, etc.). **dis·sem·i·na·tion** [dɪ-
ˌsemɪ'neɪʃn] *n.*

dis·sent [dɪ'sent] *v.i.* 1. ~ *from*, have
a different opinion from; refuse to
assent to. 2. (esp.) refuse to accept the
religious doctrine of the Church of
England. *n.* **~ing. dis·sen·sion** [dɪ-
'senʃn] *n.* angry disagreement; quar-
rel(ling). **~er** *n.* (often *D~er*) Protestant Nonconformist.

dis·ser·ta·tion [ˌdɪsə'teɪʃn] *n.* long
spoken or written account *on* a subject,
esp. as submitted (2) for a higher
university degree.

dis·ser·vice [dɪs'sɜːvɪs] *n.* (no pl.)
harmful or unhelpful action; ill turn.

dis·si·dent ['dɪsɪdənt] *n. & adj.* (person) disagreeing, esp. with an established government.

dis·sim·u·late [dɪ'sɪmjʊleɪt] *v.t. & i.*
dissemble. **dis·sim·u·la·tion** [dɪ-
ˌsɪmjʊ'leɪʃn] *n.*

dis·si·pate ['dɪsɪpeɪt] *v.t. & i.* 1. drive
away (clouds, fear, ignorance, etc.);
disperse. 2. waste (time, money, etc.)
foolishly. **dis·si·pat·ed** *adj.* given up
to foolish and often harmful pleasures.
dis·si·pa·tion [ˌdɪsɪ'peɪʃn] *n.* (esp.)
foolish wasting of energy, money, etc.
on harmful pleasures.

dis·so·ci·ate [dɪ'səʊʃɪeɪt] *v.t.* separate
(in thought, feeling) (*from*); not associate.

dis·so·lute ['dɪsəluːt] *adj.* given up to
immoral conduct; immoral.

dis·so·lu·tion [ˌdɪsə'luːʃn] *n.* breaking
up; undoing or ending (*of* a marriage,
partnership, etc.); (esp.) ending of
Parliament before a general election.

dis·solve [dɪ'zɒlv] *v.t. & i.* 1. (of a
liquid) soak into a solid so that the
solid itself becomes liquid: *Water ~s
salt.* 2. (of a solid) become liquid as the
result of being taken into a liquid:
Salt ~s in water. 3. cause (a solid) to ~:
He ~d the salt in water. 4. (cause to)
disappear or vanish: *The view ~d in
mist.* 5. bring to, come to, an end: ~ *a
marriage* (*Parliament*).

dis·so·nant ['dɪsənənt] *adj.* discor-
dant; not harmonious. **dis·so·nance**
n. discord.

dis·suade [dɪ'sweɪd] *v.t.* advise
against; (try to) turn (sb.) away (*from*

sth., *from* doing sth.): ~ *a friend fron
marrying a fool.* **dis·sua·sion** [dɪ
'sweɪʒn] *n.* (no pl.).

dis·taff ['dɪstɑːf] *n.* stick round which
wool, flax, etc. is wound for spinnin
by hand. *the ~ side*, the mother's side
of the family.

dis·tance ['dɪstəns] *n.* 1. measure o
space between two points, places, etc.
being far off; that part of a view, etc
that is a long way off: *to* (*from*) *a ~
in the ~,* far away. 2. space of time
look back over a ~ of fifty years. **dis
tant** ['dɪstənt] *adj.* 1. far away i
space or time; far off in family rela
tionship: *a distant cousin.* 2. (of behav
iour) reserved; cool.

dis·taste [dɪs'teɪst] *n.* dislike: *a ~ fc
hard work.* **~ful** *adj.* disagreeable
causing ~.

dis·tem·per¹ [dɪs'tempə*] *n.* (no pl
contagious dog-disease marked b
fever, catarrh, and weakness.

dis·tem·per² [dɪs'tempə*] *n.* (no pl
(method of painting with) colourir
matter (to be) mixed with water an
brushed on ceilings, etc. *v.t.* put ~ on

dis·tend [dɪs'tend] *v.t. & i.* (cause t
swell out (by pressure from inside):
~ed stomach.

dis·til (U.S.A. **-till**) [dɪs'tɪl] *v.t. &
(*-ll-*) 1. turn (a liquid) to vapour b
heating, cool the vapour and collect th
drops of liquid that condense from th
vapour; purify (a liquid) thus; drive o
or *out* impurities thus; make (whisk
essences) thus. 2. (let) fall in drop
~la·tion [ˌdɪstɪ'leɪʃn] *n.* ~ling or bei
~led. **~l·ery** *n.* place where spir
such as whisky and gin are ~led.

dis·tinct [dɪs'tɪŋkt] *adj.* 1. easily hea
seen, understood; plain; clear
marked: *a ~ pronunciation.* 2. differe
in kind; separate. **~ly** *adv.* in a
manner: *speak ~ly.* **dis·tinc·tive** *ac
serving to make or mark a ~ (1) diffe
ence. **~ness** *n.* (no pl.).

dis·tinc·tion [dɪs'tɪŋkʃn] *n.* 1. bein
keeping things, different or distinct (2
distinguishing, being distinguished,
different. 2. that which makes o
thing different from another. 3. quali
of being superior, excellent, disti
guished: *a writer* (*novel*) *of ~.* 4. de
oration; reward; mark of honour; et
etc.

dis·tin·guish [dɪs'tɪŋgwɪʃ] *v.t. & i.
see, hear, recognize, understand we
the difference (*between* two things) o
one thing *from* another). 2. make o
by listening, looking, etc. 3. be a ma
of character, difference. 4. make (o

self) well known; do credit to: ~ one-self in an examination. **~ed** adj. famous; remarkable; showing distinction (3).

dis·tort [dɪˈstɔːt] v.t. **1.** pull, twist, out of the usual shape: a face ~ed by pain. **2.** give a false account of; twist away from the truth: ~ed accounts of what happened. **dis·tor·tion** [dɪˈstɔːʃn] n.

dis·tract [dɪˈstrækt] v.t. draw away (a person's attention from sth.): have one's mind ~ed from one's work. **~ed** adj. with the mind confused or bewildered; with the attention drawn in different directions: ~ed between love and duty. **dis·trac·tion** [dɪˈstrækʃn] n. ~ing or being ~ed; sth. (either a pleasure, an amusement or annoyance) that ~s: to ~ion, almost to a state of madness.

dis·traught [dɪˈstrɔːt] adj. distracted; violently upset in mind.

dis·tress [dɪˈstres] n. (no pl.) **1.** (cause of) great pain, sorrow, or discomfort; (suffering caused by) want of money or other necessary things. **2.** serious danger or difficulty: a ship in ~. v.t. cause ~ (1) to.

dis·trib·ute [dɪˈstrɪbjuːt] v.t. **1.** give or send out (to or among a number of persons or places). **2.** spread out (over a larger area). **3.** put into groups or classes. **dis·tri·bu·tion** [ˌdɪstrɪˈbjuːʃn] n. **dis·trib·u·tive** [dɪˈstrɪbjʊtɪv] adj. of distribution: the distributive trades (e.g. shipping, shopkeeping). **dis·trib·u·tor** [dɪˈstrɪbjʊtə*] n. person or thing (e.g. in a petrol engine) that ~s.

dis·trict [ˈdɪstrɪkt] n. part of a country: mountainous ~s of Scotland; part of a country or town marked out for a special purpose: postal ~s of London; ~ heating, supply of heat or hot water from a central source to a district or community (1), or a group of buildings.

dis·trust [dɪsˈtrʌst] v.t. & n. (no pl.) (have) doubt or suspicion (about): ~ what one reads in a newspaper; look at sb. with ~. **~ful** adj. **~ful·ly** adv.

dis·turb [dɪsˈtɜːb] v.t. break the quiet, calm, peace, or order of; put out of the right or usual position: ~ sb.'s sleep (papers, desk, plans). **dis·tur·bance** n. ~ing or being ~ed; (esp.) social or political disorder.

dis·use [ˌdɪsˈjuːs] n. (no pl.) state of being no longer used: rusty from ~. **~d** [ˌdɪsˈjuːzd] adj. no longer used.

ditch [dɪtʃ] n. narrow channel dug in or between fields, etc. to hold or carry off water.

dit·to [ˈdɪtəʊ] n. (pl. ~s) (abbr. do.) the same. (Used in lists to avoid writing words again.)

dit·ty [ˈdɪtɪ] n. short, simple song.

di·van [dɪˈvæn] n. long, low, soft, backless seat, used also as a bed.

dive [daɪv] v.i. (U.S.A. also p.t. & p.p. dove [dəʊv]) **1.** go head first into water; go under water. diving-board, flexible, elevated board from which to ~. **2.** go quickly to a lower level; move the hand (into sth.) quickly and suddenly: ~ into one's pocket. n. act of diving. **div·er** n. (esp.) person who works under water in a special dress (called a diving-suit).

di·verge [daɪˈvɜːdʒ] v.i. (of paths, opinions, etc.) get farther apart from each other or from a point as they progress; turn or branch away (from). **di·ver·gence, -gen·cy** ns. **di·ver·gent** adj.

di·vers [ˈdaɪvɜːz] adj. (old use) several; more than one.

di·verse [daɪˈvɜːs] adj. quite unlike in quality or character; of different kinds. **di·ver·si·fy** [daɪˈvɜːsɪfaɪ] v.t. make ~. **di·ver·si·ty** [daɪˈvɜːsətɪ] n.

di·ver·sion [daɪˈvɜːʃn] n. diverting; (esp.) sth. that turns the attention from serious things; sth. giving rest or amusement. traffic ~, (Gt. Brit.) (instance of) directing traffic away from a road (e.g. when under repair or blocked by an accident). create (make) a ~, manœuvre to divert the attention from sth.

di·vert [daɪˈvɜːt] v.t. **1.** turn in another direction: ~ the course of a river. **2.** turn the attention away (from sth.); amuse; entertain: an easily ~ed child. **~ing** adj. amusing.

di·vest [daɪˈvest] v.t. **1.** take off (clothes): ~ a king of his robes. **2.** take away from: ~ a man of his rank and honours. **3.** ~ oneself of, give up; get rid of.

di·vide [dɪˈvaɪd] v.t. & i. **1.** separate, be separated (into); split or break up. **2.** find out how often one number is contained in another: ~ 20 by 5. **3.** cause disagreement: opinions are ~d. n. watershed. **div·i·dend** [ˈdɪvɪdend] n. **1.** (math.) number to be ~d by another. **2.** periodical payment of a share of a business company's profits to shareholders: pay a 10%/o ~nd. **di·vid·ers** [dɪˈvaɪdəz] n. pl. pair of measuring-compasses. (See the picture on p. 150.) **di·vis·i·ble** [dɪˈvɪzəbl] adj. that can be ~d. **di·vi·sion** [dɪˈvɪʒn] n. **1.** dividing or being ~d; the effect of dividing; line that ~s; ~d part. **2.**

(army) unit of two or more brigades. **3.** disagreement. **di·vi·sor** [dɪ'vaɪzə*] *n.* (math.) number by which another number is ~d.

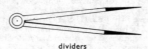

dividers

di·vine¹ [dɪ'vaɪn] *adj.* (~*r*, ~*st*) **1.** of, from, or like God or a god: *D~ Service,* public worship of God. **2.** (colloq.) excellent; very beautiful: *~ weather.* ~**er.** *n.* priest trained in theology. **di·vin·i·ty** [dɪ'vɪnətɪ] *n.* **1.** quality of being ~: *the divinity of Christ;* ~ being. **2.** (study of) theology: *a doctor of divinity* (abbr. *D.D.*).

di·vine² [dɪ'vaɪn] *v.t. & i.* discover or learn (sth.) about future events, hidden things, etc. by means not based on reason: *~ sb.'s intentions.* **di·vin·er.** *n.* person who ~s, esp. one who claims to have the power to find out where water, metals, etc. lie under the earth by using a Y-shaped stick (called a *divining-rod*). **div·i·na·tion** [ˌdɪvɪ-'neɪʃn] *n.*

di·vis·i·ble, di·vi·sion, di·vi·sor, see *divide.*

di·vorce [dɪ'vɔːs] *n.* **1.** legal ending of a marriage. **2.** ending of a connection or relationship between two things. *v.t.* **1.** put an end to a marriage by law. **2.** separate (things usually together).

di·vulge [daɪ'vʌldʒ] *v.t.* make known (sth. secret).

diz·zy ['dɪzɪ] *adj.* (*-ier, -iest*) (of a person) feeling as if everything were turning round, as if unable to balance; (of places, conditions) causing such a feeling: *a ~ height (speed).* **diz·zi·ly** *adv.* **diz·zi·ness** *n.* (no pl.).

do [duː, dʊ] *v.* pres. t. *do,* 3rd person sing. *does* [dʌz, dəz]; p.t. *did* [dɪd], p.p. *done* [dʌn]; neg. *do not,* (colloq.) *don't* [dəʊnt], *does not,* (colloq.) *doesn't* ['dʌznt], *did not,* (colloq.) *didn't* ['dɪdnt]; pres. p. *doing* ['duːɪŋ]. **I.** *v. aux.* **1.** (used to form the expanded present and past tenses): (a) *Does (Did) he want it?* (b) *He did not go. Do not go yet.* **2.** (used for emphasis): *'Do stop that noise! I 'do want you to know how sorry I am.* **II.** *verb substitute* (in a question phrase, answer, or comment, replacing the verb in a preceding statement): *He lives in London, doesn't he? You don't blame me, do you? Who broke the window? — I did.* **III.** *v.t. & i.* **1.**

perform, carry out (an action); busy oneself with: *When are you going to do the housework? I've nothing to do.* do it yourself, (esp.) do house decorating, upkeep, etc. oneself instead of by one specially trained; *do-it-yourself* (attrib. adj.); *do-it-yourselfer* (n.), person who makes and repairs things himself at home. **2.** work at: *do one's lessons (homework).* **3.** make tidy; clean: *do one's hair;* have one's hair done; *do the bedrooms.* **4.** serve, be convenient, suitable, or satisfactory (*for*); be good enough: *These shoes won't do for mountain-climbing.* **5.** cook to the right degree: *The meat isn't done yet.* **6.** (sl.) cheat; get the better of: *do sb. out of sth.,* get sth. from him by trickery. **7.** (sl.) ruin; spoil; kill. **8.** (colloq.) visit; see the sights of: *do London in a day.* **9.** *do for,* (colloq.) (a) ruin; destroy; kill: *be done for,* be ruined, made worthless, etc.; (b) look after (a person's) rooms, etc.; cook and clean for. *do in,* (a) (sl.) ruin; kill; (b) (colloq.) tire out: *be done in. do sth. up,* (a) make like new again; restore; repair: *The houses need to be done up.* (b) tie up (into a parcel); (c) fasten up (clothing, etc.). **10.** *(can, could)* do with, be ready for; welcome; need; be satisfied with: *I could do with a drink. He could do with a new hat. do without,* manage without; deny oneself: *do without tobacco in prison. do away with,* put an end to. *have to do with,* result from; be concerned with; contribute to. *have (something, nothing, etc.) to do with,* have relations, business, etc. with. *have done with,* make an end of; finish with: *Let's be quick and have done with it.*

do. ['dɪtəʊ] (abbr. for) ditto.

doc·ile ['dəʊsaɪl] *adj.* easily trained or controlled. **do·cil·i·ty** [dəʊ'sɪlətɪ] *n.* (no pl.).

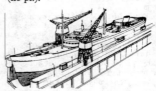

a dry dock

dock¹ [dɒk] *n.* **1.** place in a harbour or river, with gates through which water may be let in and out, where ships are (un)loaded or repaired. *dry ~,* one from which water may be pumped out.

2. (pl.) (also ~*yard*) row of ~s with wharves, sheds, offices, etc. ~s with *v.i. & t.* (of ships) come, go, bring, into a ~; (of a spacecraft) connect with another orbiting spacecraft; connect (orbiting spacecraft). ~**er** *n.* ~yard labourer. ~**ing** *n.* joining of orbiting spacecraft: ~*ing in orbit is difficult.* (attrib.) *the* ~*ing collar of a spacecraft.*

dock² [dɒk] *n.* place in a criminal court where the prisoner stands.

dock³ [dɒk] *v.t.* cut short (an animal's tail); make (wages, allowances, supplies) less.

doc·tor ['dɒktə*] *n.* **1.** person who has received the highest university degree in any faculty: *D~ of Laws.* **2.** person who has been trained in medical science. *v.t.* (colloq.) **1.** give medical treatment to or for. **2.** make (esp. food and drink) inferior by adding sth.; add drugs to. **3.** make false: ~ *accounts* (*evidence*). ~**ate** ['dɒktərɪt] *n.* ~'s degree.

doc·trine ['dɒktrɪn] *n.* body (6) of teaching; beliefs and teachings (of a church, political party, school of scientists, etc.).

doc·u·ment ['dɒkjʊmənt] *n.* sth. written or printed, to be used as a record or in evidence. **doc·u·men·ta·ry** [,dɒkjʊ'mentərɪ] *adj.* consisting of ~s: ~*ary proof.* *n.* (also ~*ary film*) factual film (e.g. on a scientific or historical subject).

dodge [dɒdʒ] *v.t. & i.* move quickly to one side, change position or direction, in order to escape or avoid sth.; get round (difficulties, etc.) by cunning or trickery. *n.* act of dodging; trick; clever expedient.

doe [dəʊ] *n.* female deer, hare, or rabbit.

does, doesn't, see *do.*

dog [dɒg] *n.* common domestic animal, of many breeds. *v.t.* (-gg-) keep close behind, in the footsteps of. '~-,eared *adj.* (of books) with the corners of the pages turned down with use. ,~-'tired *adj.* very tired.

a dog   a dome

dog·ged ['dɒgɪd] *adj.* obstinate.

dog·ger·el ['dɒgərəl] *n.* irregular, inexpert verse.

dog·gie, dog·gy ['dɒgɪ] *n.* small dog; (child's pet name for a) dog.

dog·ma ['dɒgmə] *n.* belief, system of beliefs, put forward by some authority, esp. the Church, to be accepted as true without question. ~**t·ic** [dɒg'mætɪk] *adj.* put forward as ~s; (of a person) making purely personal statements as if they were ~s. ~**tize** ['dɒgmətaɪz] *v.i.* make ~tic statements.

dol·drums ['dɒldrəmz] *n. pl.* *in the* ~, (fig.) in low spirits.

dole [dəʊl] *v.t.* ~ *out*, give out (food, money, etc.) in small amounts (e.g. to poor people). *n.* **1.** sth. ~d out. **2.** *the* ~, (Gt. Brit., colloq.) weekly payment made by the State to the unemployed: *be* (*go*) *on the* ~, receive such payments.

dole·ful ['dəʊlfʊl] *adj.* sad; mournful; dismal. ~**ly** *adv.*

doll [dɒl] *n.* model of a baby or person, usu. for a child to play with. *v.t. & i.* (colloq.) dress *up* smartly: *be all* ~*ed up for a party.*

dol·lar ['dɒlə*] *n.* (symbol $) unit of money in the U.S.A., Canada, etc.

do·lor·ous ['dɒlərəs] *adj.* sorrowful; distressed; distressing.

dol·phin ['dɒlfɪn] *n.* sea animal like a porpoise. ~**ar·i·um** [,dɒlfɪ'neərɪəm] *n.* aquarium for ~s.

dolt [dəʊlt] *n.* stupid person.

-dom [-dəm] *suff.* (forming ns.) **1.** state of being: *freedom.* **2.** rank, position, lands of: *kingdom; dukedom.*

do·main [dəʊ'meɪn] *n.* lands under the rule of a king, government, etc.; (fig.) field or province of thought, knowledge, activity.

dome [dəʊm] *n.* rounded roof with a circular base; sth. of this shape: *the blue* ~ *of the sky.*

do·mes·tic [dəʊ'mestɪk] *adj.* **1.** of the home, family, household: ~ *servants.* **2.** not foreign; native; of one's own country: ~ *news* (*loans*). **3.** (of animals) kept by, living with, man: *Cows and sheep are* ~ *animals.* (Cf. *wild* (1).) **do·mes·ti·cate** [dəʊ'mestɪkeɪt] *v.t.* **1.** (chiefly in p.p., ~*ated*) make fond of, interested in, household work: *be not at all* ~*ated*, be not fond of housekeeping, cooking, etc. **2.** tame (animals). ~**i·ty** [,dəʊme'stɪsətɪ] *n.* (no pl.) home or family life.

do·mi·cile ['dɒmɪsaɪl], **dom·i·cil** ['dɒmɪsɪl] *n.* dwelling-place; (law) place where a person lives permanently.

dom·i·nate ['dɒmɪneɪt] *v.t. & i.* have

control, authority, commanding influence, over; (of a place, esp. a height) overlook. **dom·i·nance** *n.* state of being dominant; control. **dom·i·nant** ['dɒmɪnənt] *adj.* dominating. **dom·i·na·tion** [,dɒmɪ'neɪʃn] *n.* (no pl.) dominating or being ⁓d. **dom·i·neer** [,dɒmɪ'nɪə*] *v.i.* act, speak, in a dominating manner.

do·min·ion [də'mɪnjən] *n.* **1.** authority to rule. **2.** (often pl.) territory of a sovereign (1) or government; used formerly to describe certain self-governing territories of the British Commonwealth of Nations.

dom·i·noes ['dɒmɪnəʊz] *n. pl.* (sing. v.) table game played with 28 small, flat, oblong pieces of wood, etc., marked with spots.

don [dɒn] *n.* **1.** (esp. at Oxford or Cambridge) head (10), tutor (2), or fellow (4) of a college. **2.** Spanish gentleman; Spanish title (used before a man's name): *Don Juan.*

do·nate [dəʊ'neɪt] *v.t.* give (money, etc. to a cause, charity). **do·na·tion** [dəʊ'neɪʃn] *n.* giving; sth. given.

done, see *do.*

don·key ['dɒŋkɪ] *n.* (pl. ⁓s) horse-like animal with long ears; ass[1] (1). **⁓ en·gine** *n.* small auxiliary engine. **'⁓work** *n.* (no pl.) drudgery.

a donkey   a door

do·nor ['dəʊnə*] *n.* giver: *blood* ⁓, person who gives his own blood for transfusion.

don't, see *do.*

doom [du:m] *n.* **1.** ruin; death; sth. evil that is to come. **2.** (also ⁓*sday*) the Day of Judgement. **⁓ed** *p.p.* condemned (*to* sth., *to do* sth.); facing certain death.

door [dɔ:*] *n.* that which closes or opens the entrance to a building, room, cupboard, etc.: *next* ⁓, (in, to) the next house; *out of* ⁓s, outside; in the open air; *within* ⁓s, inside; in the house. **'⁓way** *n.* opening into which a ⁓ is fitted[1] (4).

dope [dəʊp] *n.* (no pl.) **1.** thick, heavy liquid used as varnish. **2.** (sl.) harmful

drug (e.g. opium); narcotic: *a* ⁓*fiend*, a drug addict. **3.** (sl.) information about a subject not generally known. *v.t.* give ⁓ (2) to; make unconscious with ⁓ (2); stimulate with a drug. **dop·ey** ['dəʊpɪ] *adj.* (-*pier*, -*piest*) (sl.) (as if) drugged.

dor·mant ['dɔ:mənt] *adj.* in a state of inactivity but awaiting development or activity: *a* ⁓ *volcano*; ⁓ *faculties*; *plants that are* ⁓ *during the winter.*

dor·mer ['dɔ:mə*] *n.* (also ⁓ *window*) upright window in a sloping roof.

dor·mi·to·ry ['dɔ:mɪtrɪ] *n.* sleeping-room with several or many beds, esp. in a boarding-school.

dor·mouse ['dɔ:maʊs] *n.* (pl. -*mice* [-maɪs]) small animal (like a mouse) that sleeps through the winter.

dor·sal ['dɔ:sl] *adj.* (anat.) of, on, near, the back: *the* ⁓ *fin.*

dose [dəʊs] *n.* amount (of medicine) to be taken at one time. *v.t.* give a ⁓ or ⁓s to.

dos·si·er ['dɒsɪeɪ] *n.* set of papers giving information about a person or an event, esp. a person's record.

dot [dɒt] *n.* small, round (pen) mark (as over the letter i). *v.t.* (-*tt*-) mark with a ⁓; make with, cover with, ⁓s: ⁓ *one's i's*; *a* ⁓*ted line*; ⁓*ted about*, scattered here and there.

dot·age ['dəʊtɪdʒ] *n.* (no pl.) weakness of mind caused by old age: *in his* ⁓.

dote [dəʊt] *v.i.* ⁓ *on*, show much, or too much, fondness for.

dou·ble ['dʌbl] *adj.* **1.** twice as much (large, good, etc.): ⁓ *width*; *a* ⁓ *share*. **2.** having two like things or parts: *a gun with a* ⁓ *barrel*; ⁓ *doors*. **3.** made for two persons or things: *a* ⁓ *bed*. **4.** combining two qualities or qualities: *serve a* ⁓ *purpose*. **5.** (of flowers) having more than one set or circle of petals. *adv.* **1.** twice (as much): *cost* ⁓. **2.** *see* ⁓, see two things when there is only one. *n.* **1.** quantity. **2.** person or thing very or exactly like another. **3.** *at the* ⁓, at slow run. **4.** (pl.) (tennis) game between two pairs of players. **5.** sharp turn or twist. *v.t. & i.* **1.** make or become twice as great. **2.** bend or fold in two. ⁓ *up*, (a) fold up; (b) (of a person) bend the body with pain or in laughter. **3.** run at ⁓ the speed. **4.** ⁓ *back*, turn sharply back to avoid capture, etc. ⁓'**deal·er** *n.* person who deceives esp. in business. ⁓'**deck·er** [,dʌb'dekə*] *n.* bus (ship, etc.) with two decks[1]. ⁓'**en·try** *n.* system of book-keeping in which everything is written in two places. ⁓'**park** *v.t. & i.* par (a car) beside a row of cars already parked parallel to the kerb.

dou·blet ['dʌblɪt] *n.* close-fitting garment for the upper part of the body, worn by men (about A.D. 1400–1600).

doubt [daʊt] *n.* uncertainty of mind; feeling of uncertainty: *in ⁓*, uncertain; *without* (a) ⁓, certainly; *no ⁓*, very probably. *v.t. & i.* feel ⁓ (about). ⁓**·ful** *adj.* feeling, full of, ⁓; causing ⁓. ⁓**·ful·ly** *adv.* ⁓**·less** *adv.* certainly; very probably.

dough [dəʊ] *n.* (no pl.) **1.** mixture of flour, water, etc. in a paste (for making bread, etc.). **2.** (sl.) money.

dough·ty ['daʊtɪ] *adj.* (old use) brave; strong; valiant.

dour [dʊə*] *adj.* (Scot.) stern; severe; obstinate.

dove¹ [dʌv] *n.* **1.** kind of pigeon. **2.** symbol of peace. **3.** (pol.) person opposed to war or the use of force in a conflict (opp. *hawk*¹ (2)). ⁓**·-col·our(ed)** *adj.* soft grey. ⁓**·tail** [*v.t. & i.*] join together, interlock (pieces of wood; fig., plans, etc.). *n.* interlocking joint for two pieces of wood.

dove², see *dive*.

dow·a·ger ['daʊədʒə*] *n.* woman with title or property from her late husband: *the queen ⁓; the ⁓ duchess.*

dow·dy ['daʊdɪ] *adj.* (-ier, -iest) (of clothes, etc.) shabby or unfashionable; (of a person) dressed in ⁓ clothes. **dow·di·ly** *adv.*

down¹ [daʊn] *adv.* **1.** from a high(er) to a low(er) level: *The sun went ⁓.* **2.** from an upright to a lying position: *She was knocked ⁓ by a bus.* **3.** to or in a less erect attitude or less important place or position: *Sit ⁓. He has gone ⁓ three places in class. They have gone ⁓ to the country for a holiday.* **4.** to a lower degree, etc.: *The temperature has gone ⁓. The wind died ⁓. The clock has run ⁓* (needs to be wound up). **5.** firmly; permanently; on paper: *Put your name ⁓ for a ticket. She put her foot ⁓* (insisted). **6.** from an earlier to a later time: *the history of Europe ⁓ to 1914.* **7.** *walk up and ⁓*, backwards and forwards; *be ⁓ and out*, exhausted; beaten. *adj.* directed ⁓wards. ⁓ *train*, train that comes or goes from a more important place (e.g. a capital) or a place regarded as higher. ⁓ *platform*, platform at which ⁓ trains stop. **prep. 1.** from a high(er) to a low(er) level: *run ⁓ a hill.* **2.** at a lower part of: *They live ⁓ the road.* **3.** along: *Pass ⁓ the bus and make room for more passengers.* **4.** from an earlier to a more recent time: *Has*

mankind improved ⁓ the centuries? v.t. put ⁓: ⁓ *tools* (refuse to work); ⁓ *an enemy*, (colloq.) knock him ⁓. ⁓**·cast** ['daʊnkɑ:st] *adj.* (of a person) sad; (of eyes) looking ⁓wards. ⁓**·fall** ['daʊnfɔ:l] *n.* heavy fall (e.g. of rain); (fig.) ruin; sudden fall from fortune or power. ⁓**·heart·ed** [,daʊn'hɑ:tɪd] *adj.* sad; dejected. ⁓**·hill** [,daʊn'hɪl] *adj.* sloping ⁓. *adv.* towards the bottom of a hill. *n.* **1.** ⁓ward slope. **2.** ⁓ race in skiing. ⁓**·pour** ['daʊnpɔ:*] *n.* heavy fall (esp. of rain). ⁓**·right** ['daʊnraɪt] *adj.* honest; straightforward; thorough. *adv.* thoroughly; completely. ⁓**·stairs** [,daʊn'steəz] *adv.* to, at, or on a lower floor. ⁓**·stream** [,daʊn'stri:m] *adv. & adj.* in the direction in which a stream or river flows. ⁓**·town** [,daʊn'taʊn] *adv.* (U.S.A.) to or in the main or business part of a town. ⁓**·trod·den** ['daʊn-,trɒdn] *adj.* oppressed; kept ⁓ and treated badly. ⁓**·ward** ['daʊnwəd] *adj.* moving, leading, pointing, to what is lower. ⁓**·wards** ['daʊnwədz] *adv.* towards what is lower.

down² [daʊn] *n.* stretch of bare, open, high land.

down³ [daʊn] *n.* soft hair or feather(s), esp. the first, soft under-feathers of young birds. ⁓**y** *adj.* (-ier, -iest) made of, covered with, ⁓; soft like ⁓.

dow·ry ['daʊərɪ] *n.* property or money brought by a bride to her husband.

dox·ol·o·gy [dɒk'sɒlədʒɪ] *n.* words of praise to God, used in church services (e.g. 'Glory be to God ...').

doz. (abbr. for) dozen.

doze [dəʊz] *v.i.* sleep lightly; be half asleep: ⁓ *off*, fall lightly asleep. *n.* short, light sleep.

doz·en ['dʌzn] *n.* (pl. ⁓s, ⁓) twelve. ⁓*s of*, (colloq.) a large number of.

drab [dræb] *adj.* **1.** (also *n.*) muddy brown. **2.** (fig.) dull; uninteresting; monotonous.

draft [drɑ:ft] *n.* **1.** outline (in the form of rough notes) of sth. to be done: *a ⁓ for a speech (a letter);* rough sketch or plan: *a ⁓ for a machine.* **2.** written order for payment of money by a bank; drawing of money by means of such an order. **3.** party of men chosen from a larger group for a special purpose; (U.S.A., mil.) conscription. **4.** (U.S.A.) = draught. *v.t.* make a ⁓ (1) of; choose men for a ⁓ (3); (U.S.A.) conscript. ⁓**s-man** *n.* **1.** man who ⁓s (1) documents. **2.** draughtsman (2).

drag [dræg] *v.t. & i.* (-gg-) **1.** pull along, esp. with effort and difficulty: ⁓ *a box out of a cupboard.* **2.** (allow to) move slowly and with effort: *walk with ~ging feet*. **3.** (of time, work, an entertainment) go on slowly in a dull manner. **4.** use nets, etc. to search the bottom of a river, lake, etc. (usu. for something lost or missing). *n.* **1.** sth. that is ~ged, e.g. a net (~*-net*) pulled over the bottom of a river to catch fish. **2.** (fig.) sth. or sb. that slows down progress; bore[2]: *Driving back and forth every day is a ~*.

drag·gled ['drægld] *adj.* wet, dirty, or muddy (as if dragged through mud, etc.).

drag·o·man ['drægəʊmən] *n.* (pl. ~s, -men) guide and interpreter, esp. for travellers in countries speaking Arabic, Turkish, or Persian.

drag·on ['drægən] *n.* (in old stories) reptile-like creature with wings and claws, often breathing fire. '~*-fly n.* insect with a stick-like body and two pairs of wings.

a dragon-fly

dra·goon [drə'gu:n] *n.* horse-soldier; cavalryman. *v.t.* force (sb. *into doing* sth.).

drain [dreɪn] *n.* **1.** pipe, channel, trench, etc. for carrying away water and other unwanted liquids. **2.** sth. that continually uses up force, time, wealth, etc.: *a ~ on sb.'s resources (strength)*. *v.t. & i.* **1.** lead off (liquid) by means of ~s (1); ~ *swamps*; (of liquid) flow away. **2.** (cause to) lose (strength, wealth, etc.) by degrees: *a country ~ed of its manpower and wealth by war*. **3.** drink; empty (a cup, etc.). **~·age** ['dreɪnɪdʒ] *n.* ~ing or being ~ed; system of ~s (1).

drake [dreɪk] *n.* male duck.

dram [dræm] *n.* ¹/₁₆ ounce (avoirdupois) (= 1.77 grams); ¹/₈ ounce for medical substances (= 3.54 grams).

dra·ma ['drɑːmə] *n.* **1.** play for the theatre; art of writing and performing plays. **2.** series of exciting events. **~·t·ic** [drə'mætɪk] *adj.* of ~; sudden or exciting, like an event in a ~. **~·t·i·cal·ly** *adv.* **~·t·ics** *n. pl.* (usu. sing. v.) ~tic performances or behaviour. **~·tist** ['dræmətɪst] *n.* writer of plays. **~·tize** ['dræmətaɪz] *v.t.* make (a story, etc.) into a ~.

drank, see *drink* (v.).

drape [dreɪp] *v.t.* **1.** hang (curtains, cloth, clothes, etc.) in folds round or over sth.: *~ curtains over a window* (a *cloak round one's shoulders*). **2.** cover or decorate with cloth, etc.: *walls ~d with flags*. **drap·er** *n.* (Gt. Brit.) dealer in cloth, linen, articles of clothing, esp. a shopkeeper selling such things. **drap·ery** *n.* **1.** (Gt. Brit.) goods sold by a ~r. **2.** (Gt. Brit.) ~r's trade. **3.** clothing, curtains, etc. arranged in folds.

dras·tic ['dræstɪk] *adj.* (of actions, methods, medicines) having a strong or violent effect. **dras·ti·cal·ly** *adv.*

draught [drɑːft] *n.* (U.S.A. *draft*) **1.** current of air in a room, chimney, or other shut-in place. **2.** pulling in of a net for fish; fish caught in it. **3.** depth of water needed to float a ship. **4.** drawing of liquid from a container (1) (e.g. a barrel): *beer on ~; ~ beer*. **5.** (amount drunk during) one continuous act of swallowing: *a long ~ of water. He swallowed the beer at a (one) ~*. **6.** (of animals) used for pulling: *a ~horse*. **7.** (pl., sing. v.) board game for two players using 24 flat, round pieces (called *~smen*). **8.** draft (1). **~s·man** *n.* **1.** ['drɑːftsmæn] see ~ (7). **2.** ['drɑːftsmən] man who makes drawings, plans, or sketches. **3.** ['drɑːftsmən] draftsman (1). **~·y** *adj.* (U.S.A. *drafty*) (-ier, -iest) with ~s (1) blowing through.

draw [drɔː] *v.t. & i.* (p.t. *drew* [dru:], p.p. *~n* [drɔːn]) **1.** move by pulling: *~ a boat up out of the water; ~ sb. aside*. **2.** cause to move either or behind by pulling: *a train ~n by two engines*. **3.** take or get out by pulling: *~ a cork from a bottle; have a tooth ~n*. **4.** obtain from a source: *~ water from a well; ~ rations from a store; ~ money from a bank*. **5.** take in: *~ a deep breath*; (of a chimney) allow air to flow through: *The chimney ~s well*. **6.** make longer by pulling; become longer: *~ wire*; (fig.) *long-~n-out discussions*. **7.** cause to come or be directed towards; attract: *a film that drew large audiences*. **8.** (of a ship) need (a certain depth of water) in order to float. **9.** cause (a person) to say what he knows, to show his feelings, etc.: *~ sb. out; ~ information from a witness; ~ tears from sb.* **10.** move or come (towards, near, forward, away from, level with, to an end, etc.): *The two ships drew level. The day drew to its close.* **11.** (of two teams, etc.) end (a game, competition, etc.) without a result, neither side winning: *a ~n game; ~*

2—2. **12.** make (lines, designs, pictures, etc.) with a pen, pencil, chalk, etc.; use a pencil, etc. for doing this: ~ a tree; ~ a pen through a word; ~ the line at, refuse to go as far as. **13.** write out (a cheque, etc.); compose; put into writing: ~ up a document (agreement, etc.). **14.** (of tea) infuse (2): let the tea ~. **15.** (with advs.): ~ in, (of days) get shorter (as in autumn); ~ out, (of days) get longer (as in spring); ~ oneself up, stand up straight; ~ up, (of a carriage, etc.) stop; (of troops, etc.) get into formation or order. **n.** act of ~ing; (esp.) sb. or sth. that ~s attention or attracts; ~ing of lots (see lot² (1)); game or competition that is ~n (11). '**~·back** **n.** disadvantage; sth. that lessens one's satisfaction. '**~·bridge** **n.** bridge that can be pulled up at the end(s) by chains. **~·er** **n.** **1.** [drɔ:*] container (1) that slides in and out of a piece of furniture, etc., used for clothes, etc. **2.** ['drɔ:ə*] person who ~s. **~·ers** [drɔ:z] **n. pl.** two-legged undergarment fastened at the waist. **~·ing** **n.** art of ~ing (12); sth. ~n (12) with a pencil or crayon. '**~·ing-board** **n.** flat board for spreading paper on for ~ing. '**~·ing-pin** **n.** (U.S.A. thumbtack) pin with a flat head, used e.g. for fastening papers to a notice-board, etc. '**~·ing-room** **n.** room in which guests are received. **~n** **v.** see ~. **adj.** (of the face, eyes) distorted with pain, fear, or worry.

drawl [drɔ:l] **v.i. & t.** speak so that the sounds of the vowels are longer than usual. **n.** slow way of speaking.

dray [dreɪ] **n.** low, flat, four-wheeled cart for heavy loads.

dread [dred] **n.** (no pl.) great fear and anxiety. **v.t.** feel great fear of. **~·ful** **adj.** causing ~; (colloq.) unpleasant. **~·ful·ly** **adv.**

dream [dri:m] **n.** **1.** sth. that one seems to see or experience during sleep. **2.** state of mind in which what is happening seems like a ~ (1). **3.** mental picture(s) of the future: have ~s of wealth and happiness. **4.** beautiful or pleasing person or thing. **v.t. & i.** (p.t. & p.p. ~ed or ~t [dremt]) have ~s; see, etc. in a ~; imagine; think possible. **~y** **adj.** (-ier, -iest) (of a person) with thoughts far away from his surroundings; (of things) vague; unreal. **~·i·ly** **adv.**

drea·ry ['drɪərɪ] **adj.** (-ier, -iest) dull; gloomy; causing low spirits: ~ weather (work, surroundings). **drea·ri·ly** **adv.**

dredge¹ [dredʒ] **n.** apparatus for bringing up mud, etc. from the bed of the sea, rivers, etc. **v.t. & i.** bring up with a ~; clean, make a channel, etc., with a ~. **dredg·er** **n.** boat carrying a ~.

dredge² [dredʒ] **v.t.** scatter (flour, sugar, etc.) on.

dregs [dregz] **n. pl.** **1.** bits of worthless matter that sink to the bottom of a glass, bottle, barrel, etc. of liquid. **2.** (fig.) worst and useless part (e.g. of society). (Cf. scum (2).)

drench [drentʃ] **v.t.** make wet all over, right through.

dress [dres] **n.** **1.** long, outer garment worn by a woman or girl; frock. **2.** clothing: pay too much attention to ~; full ~, clothes for special occasions (esp. uniform); evening ~, clothes for formal social occasions (e.g. dinner-parties, dances); ~ suit, evening ~ for a man. **v.t. & i.** **1.** put on (clothes). **2.** (in passive): be ~ed in, be wearing. **3.** make ready for use; prepare: ~ leather (make it smooth); ~ a salad (add ~ing to). **4.** clean and bandage (a wound, etc.). **5.** brush and comb (one's hair). **6.** adorn; make attractive: ~ a ship (street) with flags; ~ a shop-window (with attractive goods). **7.** ~ sb. down, (fig.) scold or thrash him; a ~ing-down, a severe reproof. **~·er** **n.** **1.** (esp.) person employed to help a doctor to ~ wounds. **2.** piece of furniture with shelves for dishes, etc. **~·ing** **n.** (esp.) **1.** covering used in ~ing (4) wounds. **2.** mixture of oil and other things as a sauce for salads, etc. '**~·ing-gown** **n.** loose gown worn over night-clothes.

drew, see draw (v.).

drib·ble ['drɪbl] **v.i. & t. 1.** (of liquids) fall, allow to fall, drop by drop (esp. a trickling flow from the side of the mouth). **2.** (football) take (the ball) forward between the feet. **drib·let** ['drɪblɪt] **n.** small amount: in (by) driblets.

drier, see dry.

drift [drɪft] **v.i. & t.** be carried along by, or as by, a current of air or water; (fig., of persons) go through life without aim, purpose, or self-control, cause to ~. **n.** ~ing movement: the ~ of the tide; sth. caused by ~ing: ~s of snow; (fig.) general tendency or meaning; way in which events, etc. tend to move. **~·er** **n.** kind of fishing-boat. '**~·wood** **n.** (no pl.) wood carried and left on beaches by tides.

drill¹ [drɪl] **n.** pointed instrument for making holes in or through hard substances. **v.t. & i.** make (a hole) with a ~; use a ~.

drill² [drɪl] **n.** army training or exercises in the handling of weapons, marching, etc.; physical training (in groups); training (e.g. in grammar) by practical exercises. *v.t. & i.* train, be trained, by means of ~s: ~ *troops on the parade ground.*

drill³ [drɪl] *n.* furrow (long channel where seeds are to be sown); machine for sowing seeds in a ~; row of seeds sown in this way.

drill⁴ [drɪl] *n.* (no pl.) heavy, strong, linen or cotton cloth.

drink [drɪŋk] *v.t. & i.* (p.t. *drank* [dræŋk], p.p. *drunk* [drʌŋk]) **1.** take (liquid) into the mouth and swallow. **2.** take alcoholic liquors (beer, wine, etc.), esp. in excess. **3.** ~ *sth. in*, take into the mind eagerly or with pleasure. *n.* **1.** (kind of) liquid for ~ing: *soft* ~s (without alcohol). **2.** alcoholic liquors: *He's too fond of* ~. ~**able** *adj.* suitable or fit for ~ing.

drip [drɪp] *v.i. & t.* (-pp-) (of a liquid) fall, allow to fall, in drops: *a* ~*ping tap*; *sweat* ~*ping from his face. n.* drop-by-drop fall of a liquid. ₁~'**dry** *adj.* that will dry when hung up to ~ (without previous wringing): ~-*dry shirts.* ~**ping** *n.* fat melted out of roasting meat.

drive [draɪv] *v.t. & i.* (p.t. *drove* [drəʊv], p.p. ~*n* ['drɪvn]) **1.** operate, cause to work or move (an engine, tram, motor car, etc.) as required; cause to move in a certain direction: ~ *cattle to market* (*the enemy away*); *a ship* ~*n on the rocks by a gale*; ~ *a car*; *driving licence*, licence that allows a person to ~ a motor vehicle after having passed a *driving test* first. **2.** (usu. passive) be the power to operate: ~*n by steam* (*water-power*, *etc.*). **3.** go, take, be taken, in a carriage, motor car, etc.: ~ (*a friend*) *to the station*; ~-*in*, bank, cinema, restaurant, etc. at which customers get service while remaining in their motor cars: *a* ~-*in cinema.* **4.** force: ~*n by hunger to steal.* **5.** ~ *at*, mean: *What's he driving at?* (i.e. What's the purpose behind what he is saying?) **6.** ~ *a bargain*, make one. **7.** (of clouds, rain) be carried along violently by the wind: *clouds driving across the sky*; *rain driving into our faces.* **8.** force (a post, nail, screw, etc.) (*into* sth.); strike (a ball, e.g. in golf) hard; *let* ~ *at*, aim a blow at. *n.* **1.** driving or being ~*n* in a car, etc.: *go for a* ~. **2.** private road through a garden or park to a house. **3.** (mech.) transmission of power to machinery, the wheels of a motor vehicle, etc.: *belt* ~;

front-wheel ~; position of the steering-wheel and other controls (3) of a motor vehicle: *left-hand* (*right-hand*) ~. **4.** stroke (given to a ball); force with which a ball is struck; (fig.) energy; capacity to get things done. **driv·er** *n.* **1.** person who ~s (animals, a car, etc.): ~*r's license* (U.S.A.), driving licence. **2.** tool for driving (8): *screw* ~.

driv·el ['drɪvl] *v.i. & n.* (-ll-, U.S.A. also -l-) (talk) nonsense. ~**ler** (U.S.A. also ~**er**) *n.*

driz·zle ['drɪzl] *v.i. & n.* (no pl.) rain (in very small, fine drops).

droll [drəʊl] *adj.* causing amusement (because strange or peculiar).

drom·e·dary ['drɒmədərɪ] *n.* fast, one-humped riding-camel.

drone [drəʊn] *n.* **1.** male bee. **2.** person who does no work and lives on others. **3.** (no pl.) low, humming sound (as) made by bees. *v.i. & t.* make a ~ (3); talk or sing in a low, monotonous tone: ~ *out a song or poem.*

droop [druːp] *v.i. & t.* bend or hang down (through tiredness or weakness): ~*ing flowers*; ~*ing spirits.*

drop [drɒp] *n.* **1.** tiny ball of liquid: *rain* ~s. **2.** (pl.) liquid medicine taken in ~s: *eye* (*nose*) ~s. **3.** sth. like a ~ in shape or appearance: *acid* ~s. **4.** movement from a higher to a lower level, esp. the distance of a fall: *a* ~ *in temperature* (*in prices*). *v.i. & t.* (-pp-) **1.** fall, allow to fall: ~ *anchor* (lower it). *Don't* ~ *the baby.* **2.** (allow to) become weaker or lower: *The wind* (*temperature*) *has* ~*ped. He* ~*ped his voice to a whisper.* **3.** give up: ~ *a bad habit.* **4.** utter or send casually: ~ *sb. a hint*, give him a hint or warning; ~ *sb. a few lines.* **5.** stop talking about: ~ *a subject.* **6.** omit in speech: ~ *the letter h.* **7.** ~ *sb. at*, allow him to get out of a car, etc.: *D* ~ *me at the post office.* ~ *behind*, fail to keep up (with); ~ *in* (*on sb.*), pay a casual visit (to); ~ *off*, (a) become fewer or less: *His friends* (*customers*) *are* ~*ping off.* (b) fall asleep; ~ *out*, (a) cease to compete (in a contest); (b) cease to appear or take part (e.g. in a course of study); (c) reject or withdraw from conventional society. '~-**out** *n.* **1.** person who ~s out. **2.** person who withdraws from established society. ~**pings** *n. pl.* (esp.) dung of animals or birds.

dross [drɒs] *n.* (no pl.) waste material rising to the surface of melted metals; (fig.) anything considered worthless, mixed with something else.

drought [draʊt] *n.* continuous dry weather causing distress.

drove[1], see *drive* (v.).

drove[2] [drəʊv] *n.* large number of animals driven together. **drov·er** *n.* man who drives cattle, sheep, etc. to market; cattle-dealer.

drown [draʊn] *v.t. & i.* **1.** (cause sb. to) die in water because unable to breathe: *a ⁓ing man*; *be ⁓ed*. **2.** (of sound) be strong enough to prevent another sound from being heard. **3.** *be ⁓ed out*, be forced to leave a place by floods, etc.

drowse [draʊz] *v.i. & t.* be half asleep; make drowsy; pass *away* (time) half asleep. **drowsy** *adj.* (*-ier, -iest*) feeling sleepy; making one feel sleepy. **drows·i·ness** *n.*

drudge [drʌdʒ] *n. & v.i.* (person who must) work hard and long at unpleasant tasks. **drudg·ery** *n.* (no pl.) laborious, dull, or distasteful work.

drug [drʌg] *n.* **1.** substance used for a medical purpose, either alone or in a mixture; (esp.) narcotic: *a ⁓ addict*. **2.** unsalable article: (usu.) *a ⁓ on the market*. *v.t.* (*-gg-*) **1.** add a harmful ⁓, esp. narcotic or poison, to (food or drink). **2.** give ⁓s, esp. narcotics, to. **⁓·gist** *n.* **1.** (Gt. Brit.) tradesman in ⁓s. **2.** (U.S.A.) person who owns or manages a '⁓·store *n.* (U.S.A.) chemist's shop, also selling a wide variety of articles, light refreshments, etc.

drum [drʌm] *n.* **1.** musical instrument made of a hollow cylinder with a tight skin stretched over each opening, and struck by hand or with a stick. **2.** sth. shaped like a ⁓ (e.g. a container for oil, a cylinder on which thick wire is wound). *v.i. & t.* (*-mm-*) **1.** play the ⁓; make ⁓-like sounds: *⁓ on the table with one's fingers*. **2.** ⁓ *sth. into sb.* (*into sb.'s head*), make him remember sth. by repeating it to him many times. **⁓·mer** *n.* **⁓**-player.

drums

drunk [drʌŋk] *v.* see *drink*. *pred. adj. be ⁓*, be overcome by drinking alcoholic drinks; *get ⁓*, become intoxicated (1). *n.* person who is ⁓. **⁓·ard** ['drʌŋkəd] *n.*

person who is often ⁓. **⁓·en** *adj.* associated with, showing the effect of, drinking too much: *⁓en revels*. **⁓·en·ness** *n.* (no pl.).

dry [draɪ] *adj.* **1.** (*-ier, -iest*) free from moisture. **2.** ⁓ *bread*, without butter; ⁓ *goods*, corn; (U.S.A.) cloth, textiles, etc.; ⁓ *wines*, etc., not sweet; ⁓ *humour*, presented in a serious way; ⁓ *books* (*subjects*, *etc.*), uninteresting. *v.t. & i.* make or become ⁓. ₁⁓·'clean *v.t.* clean (clothes, etc.) not with water but with organic solvents (e.g. petrol). ₁⁓·'clean·ers *n.* ₁⁓·'clean·ing *n.* **dri·er, ⁓·er** *n.* apparatus (1) for ⁓ing wet clothing, hair, etc. **dri·ly, ⁓·ly** *adv.* **⁓·ness** *n.* (no pl.).

dry·ad ['draɪæd] *n.* (in Greek mythology) tree nymph.

du·al ['djuːəl] *adj.* of two; double; divided in two: *⁓-control car*, car controlled by the instructor as well as by the learner; ⁓ *carriageway*, road divided along the centre so that the two streams (2) of traffic are separated.

dub [dʌb] *v.t.* (*-bb-*) **1.** give a nickname to. **2.** make (sb.) a knight by touching him on the shoulder with a sword. **3.** provide (a film) with a new sound-track, esp. in a different language; add (sound effects) to a film, etc.

du·bi·ous ['djuːbjəs] *adj.* doubtful; causing doubt.

du·cal ['djuːkl] *adj.* of a duke.

duch·ess ['dʌtʃɪs] *n.* wife or widow of a duke. **duchy** ['dʌtʃɪ] *n.* land ruled by a royal duke or ⁓.

duck[1] [dʌk] *n.* (pl. ⁓s, collective ⁓) common water-bird; female of this; its flesh as food. *make a ⁓*, score 0 at cricket.

a duck[1]

duck[2] [dʌk] *v.i. & t.* move quickly down or to one side (to avoid being seen or hit); go, push sb., quickly under water. *n.* quick, downward or sideways movement of the head or body. **⁓·ing** *n.* thorough wetting.

duct [dʌkt] *n.* tube for carrying liquid, esp. in the body: *tear-⁓s. air-⁓*, channel through which air is forced for ventilating or warming (rooms, cabins, etc.).

dud [dʌd] *n. & adj.* (colloq.) (thing or person) of no use.

dud·geon ['dʌdʒən] *n.* in high ~, feeling very indignant.

due [djuː] *adj.* **1.** owing; to be paid. **2.** suitable; right: *after ~ consideration.* **3.** (to be) expected: *When is the train ~ (in)?* **4.** ~ *to*, caused by. *adv.* ~ (*north, east, etc.*), exactly; directly. *n.* **1.** (sing.) that which sb. deserves. **2.** (pl.) sums of money to be paid (e.g. for use of a harbour, membership of a club).

du·el ['djuːəl] *n.* unlawful fight between two persons who have quarrelled, usu. with swords or pistols, at a meeting arranged and conducted according to rules; any two-sided contest. *v.i.* (-*ll*-, U.S.A. also -*l*-) fight a ~ or ~s. ~·**list** (U.S.A. also ~·**ist**) *n.*

du·et [djuː'et] *n.* piece of music for two voices or instruments.

duf·fle, duf·fel ['dʌfl] *n.* (no pl.) coarse, woollen cloth with a thick nap²: *a ~-coat.*

a duffle-coat   dungarees

dug, see *dig* (v.).

dug·out ['dʌgaʊt] *n.* **1.** rough, covered shelter made by digging, esp. by soldiers for protection in war. **2.** canoe made by hollowing a tree trunk.

duke [djuːk] *n.* nobleman of high rank (next below a prince). ~·**dom** *n.* position and duties, rank, land, of a ~.

dull [dʌl] *adj.* **1.** opposite of clear or bright. **2.** slow in understanding. **3.** (of trade) inactive. **4.** monotonous: *a ~ book (speech).* **5.** (of pain) not acute. **6.** not sharp: *a ~ knife. v.t. & i.* make or become ~. **dul·ly** *adv.* ~·**ness** *n.* ~·**ard** ['dʌləd] *n.* person with a ~ mind.

du·ly ['djuːlɪ] *adv.* in a right or suitable manner; at the right time.

dumb [dʌm] *adj.* **1.** unable to speak. **2.** not saying anything. ~ *show*, giving ideas by actions without words. **3.** stupid. **dum(b)·found** [dʌm'faʊnd] *v.t.* make ~ with surprise.

dum·my ['dʌmɪ] *n.* object made to look like and serve the purpose of the real person or thing: *a tailor's ~ (for clothes); a baby's ~ (for sucking);* (attrib.) *a ~ gun* (to deceive the enemy).

a baby's dummy

dump [dʌmp] *n.* **1.** place where rubbish, etc. may be unloaded and left. **2.** place for the temporary storage of military supplies. *v.t.* **1.** put on a ~ (1); put or throw down carelessly. **2.** (comm.) sell abroad at low prices goods that are unwanted in the home country.

dump·ling ['dʌmplɪŋ] *n.* small, round mass of dough cooked by boiling or steaming, sometimes enclosing an apple or other fruit.

dun [dʌn] *adj.* dull greyish-brown.

dunce [dʌns] *n.* slow learner.

dune [djuːn] *n.* low ridge of loose, dry sand formed by the wind, esp. near the sea-shore.

dung [dʌŋ] *n.* (no pl.) waste matter dropped by domestic animals; manure.

dun·ga·rees [ˌdʌŋɡə'riːz] *n. pl.* worker's overalls (trousers and blouse, combined).

dun·geon ['dʌndʒən] *n.* dark underground room used as a prison.

dupe [djuːp] *v.t.* cheat; deceive. *n.* person who is ~d.

du·plex ['djuːpleks] *adj.* double: *a ~ apartment* (U.S.A.), a two-storey flat. *n.* two-family house.

du·pli·cate ['djuːplɪkeɪt] *v.t. & [-kət] n.* (make an) exact copy (of a letter, etc.); (make a) thing exactly like another: *in ~,* (of documents, etc.) with a ~; make double: *~ one's efforts.* ['djuːplɪkət] *adj.* exactly like. **du·pli·ca·tor** *n.* machine that ~s sth. written or typed.

du·plic·i·ty [djuː'plɪsətɪ] *n.* (no pl.) deceit.

du·rable ['djʊərəbl] *adj.* likely to last for a long time. **du·ra·bil·i·ty** [ˌdjʊərə-'bɪlətɪ] *n.* (no pl.).

du·ra·tion [djʊə'reɪʃn] *n.* (no pl.) time during which sth. lasts or exists.

du·ress [djʊə'res] *n. under ~,* compelled (by use of force).

dur·ing ['djʊərɪŋ] *prep.* **1.** for as long as sth. lasts; throughout: *The band played ~ the afternoon.* **2.** at a moment within a period of time: *He called to see me ~ my stay in hospital.*

durst, see *dare.*

dusk [dʌsk] *n.* (no pl.) time just before it gets quite dark.

dust [dʌst] *n.* (no pl.) dried earth, etc. in the form of powder that settles on a surface or is blown about by the wind. *throw ~ in sb.'s eyes,* mislead him; keep him from seeing the truth; *shake the ~ off one's feet,* go away in anger or scorn. *v.t. & i.* **1.** remove ~ from (e.g. books, furniture). **2.** cover with powder: ~ *a cake with sugar.* '**~·bin** *n.* (U.S.A. *ash can, garbage can*) container for household waste and rubbish. '**~-,cov·er** *n.* paper jacket of a book. *~·er n.* cloth for taking ~ off things. '**~-,jack·et** *n. ~-*cover of a book. '**~·man** *n.* (Gt. Brit.) man who empties ~bins and takes rubbish, etc. away. '**~·pan** *n.* pan into which ~, etc. is swept from the floor. *~y adj.* (*-ier, -iest*) covered with ~; like ~.

Dutch [dʌtʃ] *adj.* of or from the Netherlands. *n.* **1.** *the ~,* (pl.) the people of the Netherlands. **2.** their language. *double ~,* unintelligible language.

du·ty ['dju:tɪ] *n.* **1.** what one is obliged to do (by morality, law, conscience, etc.); inner force urging one to behave in a certain way: *one's ~ to one's parents; a postman's duties; be on (off) ~,* be actually engaged (not engaged) in one's usual work; *do ~ for,* be used instead of. **2.** payment demanded by the government on certain goods imported or exported (*customs duties*), or manufactured in the country (*excise*[1] *duties*), or when property, etc. is transferred to a new owner by sale or death (*stamp ~, death ~*). ,**~-'free** *adj.* (of goods) allowed to enter without payment of customs duties: *~-free shop,* shop that sells ~-free goods (e.g. at an airport). **du·ti·able** ['dju:tjəbl] *adj.* on which customs duties must be paid.

du·ti·ful ['dju:tɪfʊl] *adj.* doing one's ~ (1) well; showing respect and obedience.

dwarf [dwɔ:f] *n.* (pl. ~s, *dwarves* [dwɔ:vz]) person, animal, or plant much below the usual size; (attrib.) undersized. *v.t.* prevent from growing to full size; cause to appear small by contrast or distance.

dwell [dwel] *v.i.* (p.t. & p.p. *dwelt* [dwelt] or *~ed*) **1.** live (*in, at, etc.*). **2.** ~ (*up)on,* think, speak, or write at length about. *~·ing n.* (also *~ing-place*) house, etc. to live in.

dwin·dle ['dwɪndl] *v.i.* become less or smaller by degrees.

dye [daɪ] *v.t. & i.* (3rd pers. sing. pres.t. *dyes* [daɪz], p.t. & p.p. *dyed,* pres. p. *dyeing* ['daɪɪŋ]) **1.** colour, usu. by dipping in a liquid: ~ *a white dress blue.* **2.** take colour from ~ing: *cloth that ~s well. n.* substance used for ~ing cloth; colour given by ~ing. **dy·er** *n.* tradesman who ~s clothes.

dy·ing, see *die*[1].

dyke, see *dike.*

dy·nam·ic [daɪ'næmɪk] *adj.* of physical power and forces producing motion; (of a person) having energy, force of character. *~s n. pl.* (sing. v.) branch of physics dealing with matter in motion.

dy·na·mite ['daɪnəmaɪt] *n.* (no pl.) powerful explosive (used in mining and quarrying). *v.t.* blow up with ~.

dy·na·mo ['daɪnəməʊ] *n.* (pl. ~s) machine for changing steam-power, water-power, etc. into electrical energy.

dy·nas·ty ['dɪnəstɪ] *n.* succession of rulers belonging to one family. **dy·nas·tic** [dɪ'næstɪk] *adj.*

dys·en·tery ['dɪsntrɪ] *n.* (no pl.) painful disease of the bowels.

dys·pep·sia [dɪs'pepsɪə] *n.* (no pl.) indigestion. **dys·pep·tic** [dɪs'peptɪk] *adj.* of ~. *n.* person suffering from ~.

E

each [iːtʃ] *adj. & pron.* **I.** *adj.* (of two or more) every one (thing, group, person, etc.) taken separately or individually. **II.** *pron.* **1.** ~ thing, person, group, etc.: *They gave ~ of their four sons a watch. The four boys ~ received a watch.* **2.** ~ other (cf. *one another*): *We see ~ other* (i.e. each of us sees the other) *every day.*

ea·ger ['iːgə*] *adj.* full of, showing, strong desire (*for* sth., *to do* sth.). ~**·ly** *adv.* ~**·ness** *n.*

ea·gle ['iːgl] *n.* large, strong bird of prey with keen sight.

an eagle

ear¹ [ɪə*] *n.* **1.** organ of hearing. **2.** ability to distinguish between sounds: *have a good ~ for music; play by ~,* play sth. from memory, without having read the printed music; *be all ~s,* be listening attentively. '~**-drum** *n.* thin membrane of the middle ~. '~**-mark** *v.t.* mark (sheep, etc.) on the ~ with a sign of ownership; (fig.) put (money, etc.) aside *for* a special purpose. '~**-phone** *n.* device (2) worn over or inserted into the ~ to listen to radio, telephone, etc. communications. '~**-shot** *n. within (out of) ~shot,* near enough (too far away) to be heard.

earphones

an earwig

ear² [ɪə*] *n.* part of a grain plant on which the seeds appear.

earl [ɜːl] *n.* title of a British nobleman of high rank. ~**·dom** *n.* rank, lands, of an ~.

ear·ly ['ɜːlɪ] *adj. & adv.* (*-ier, -iest*) near to the beginning of a period of time; sooner than usual; sooner than others.

earn [ɜːn] *v.t.* get in return for work or as a reward for one's qualities. ~**·ings** *n. pl.* money ~ed.

ear·nest¹ ['ɜːnɪst] *adj.* serious; determined. *n.* seriousness: *in ~,* serious(ly); in a determined, not in a joking, manner. ~**·ly** *adv.* ~**·ness** *n.* (no pl.).

ear·nest² ['ɜːnɪst] *n.* part payment made as a pledge that full payment will follow; sth. coming in advance as a sign of what is to come after.

earth [ɜːθ] *n.* **1.** land and sea; (often *E~*) planet on which we live. *why (where, what, who) on ~?,* why (etc.) ever? (used for emphasis). **2.** dry land. **3.** soil: *fill a hole with ~.* **4.** ground: *it fell to ~.* **5.** hole of a fox or badger: *run to ~,* chase (a fox) to its hole; (fig.) find sth. hidden. **6.** (electr.) ~connection as the completion of a circuit. ~**·en** ['ɜːθn] *adj.* made of ~ or baked clay. ~**·en·ware** ['ɜːθnweə*] *n.* (no pl.) dishes, pots, etc. made of baked clay. '~**·ly** *adj.* **1.** of this world, not of heaven: *~ly joys (possessions).* **2.** (colloq.) possible: *not an ~ly chance,* no chance at all. ~**·quake** ['ɜːθkweɪk] *n.* sudden, violent shaking of the ~'s surface. '~**·work** *n.* bank or wall of ~ built for defence.

ear·wig ['ɪəwɪg] *n.* small insect with large forceps at the end of the body.

ease [iːz] *n.* (no pl.) freedom from work, discomfort, trouble, anxiety: *a life of ~; stand at ~,* (mil.) with the legs apart in a restful position; *ill at ~,* uncomfortable, feeling anxious or embarrassed; *with ~,* without difficulty. *v.t. & i.* **1.** give ~ to (the body or mind). **2.** make looser, less tight; lessen (speed, efforts): *~ off,* (cause to) become less intense.

ea·sel ['iːzl] *n.* wooden frame to support a picture or blackboard.

east [i:st] *adv.*, *adj.*, *& n.* (no pl.) (towards, at, near, the) point of the horizon where the sun rises: ∼ *wind,* wind blowing from the ∼. *the E∼,* (a) the Orient; (b) the north-eastern region of the U.S.A.; (c) the Communist States of eastern Europe; *the Far E∼,* China, Japan, etc.; *the Middle E∼,* countries from Egypt to Iran; *the Near E∼,* (a) the Middle E∼; (b) (old use) Turkey, etc. ∼·**er·ly** ['i:stəlɪ] *adj. & adv.* in an ∼ern position or direction; (of the wind) blowing from the ∼. ∼·**ern** ['i:stən] *adj.* lying towards the ∼; of, from, or in, the ∼. '∼·**wards** *adv.*
Eas·ter ['i:stə*] *n.* anniversary of the Resurrection: ∼ *Day (Sunday);* ∼ *week* (beginning on ∼ Sunday).
easy ['i:zɪ] *adj.* (*-ier, -iest*) **1.** within one's strength, ability, etc.; not requiring much effort: *Everybody can do this exercise, it is quite* ∼. **2.** free from pain or anxiety: *feel* ∼ *about one's future.* **3.** comfortable in or for body or mind: ∼ *chair,* soft, restful one. *adv.* go ∼, *take things* ∼, not work hard; go slowly. '∼·**go·ing** *adj.* (of a person) fond of comfort; not taking trouble; careless; lazy. **eas·i·ly** *adv.*
eat [i:t] *v.t. & i.* (p.t. **ate** [et], p.p. ∼**en** ['i:tn]) **1.** take (solid food, also soup) into the mouth and swallow (it). **2.** destroy as if by ∼ing: ∼*en into by acids.* ∼·**able** *adj.* fit to be ∼en. *n. pl.* food.
eaves [i:vz] *n. pl.* overhanging edges of a roof. '∼·**drop** *v.i.* (*-pp-*) listen secretly to private conversation.

(a) eaves
(b) a gable roof

ebb [eb] *v.i.* (of the tide) flow back from the land; (fig.) grow less; become weak or faint. *n.* flowing out of the tide: *the* ∼ *and flow of the sea;* (fig.) low state; decay. '∼·**tide** *n.* ∼ing of the sea.
eb·on·y ['ebənɪ] *n.* (no pl.) hard, black wood. *adj.* black like ∼; made of ∼.
ec·cen·tric [ɪk'sentrɪk] *adj.* **1.** (of circles) not concentric; (of orbits) not circular. **2.** (of a person, his behaviour) peculiar; not normal. *n.* ∼ (2) person. ∼·**i·ty** [,eksen'trɪsətɪ] *n.* strangeness of

behaviour; strange or unusual act or habit.
ec·cle·si·as·tic [ɪ,kli:zɪ'æstɪk] *n.* clergyman. **ec·cle·si·as·ti·cal** *adj.* of the Christian Church; of clergymen.
echo ['ekəʊ] *n.* (pl. ∼**es**) **1.** sound reflected or sent back (e.g. from a wall of rock): *an* ∼*-sounder,* an apparatus (1) for showing the depth of the sea beneath a ship. **2.** (fig.) person who, statement, thing, etc. that, is a copy or repetition of another. *v.i. & t.* send back an ∼; be sent back as an ∼; be an ∼ of; repeat the words, etc. of.
eclipse [ɪ'klɪps] *n.* total or partial cutting off of the light of the sun (when the moon is between it and the earth), or of the reflected light of the moon (when the earth's shadow falls on it); (fig.) loss of brilliance, power, reputation, etc. *v.t.* (of a planet, etc.) cause an ∼; cut off the light from; (fig.) make (sth. or sb.) appear dull by comparison; outshine.
ecol·o·gy [i:'kɒlədʒɪ] *n.* (no pl.) branch of biology dealing with the balanced relationship between organisms and their environment. **eco·log·i·cal** [,i:kə-'lɒdʒɪkl] *adj.* of ∼. **ecol·o·gist** [i:'kɒl-ədʒɪst] *n.*
econ·o·my [ɪ'kɒnəmɪ] *n.* **1.** (instance of) avoidance of waste of money, strength, or anything else of value. **2.** control and management of the money, goods, and other resources of a community, society, or household. **eco·nom·ic** [,i:kə'nɒmɪk] *adj.* of economics; designed to give a profit. **eco·nom·ics** *n. pl.* (sing. v.) science of production and distribution of money and goods. **eco·nom·i·cal** *adj.* careful in the spending of money, time, etc., and in the use of goods; not wasteful. **econ·o·mist** [ɪ'kɒnəmɪst] *n.* **1.** expert in economics. **2.** person who is economical. **econ·o·mize** [ɪ'kɒnəmaɪz] *v.t. & i.* be economical; use or spend less than before: *economize on,* use sparingly.
ec·sta·sy ['ekstəsɪ] *n.* feeling of great joy and spiritual uplift: *in an* ∼ *of delight.* **ec·stat·ic** [ɪk'stætɪk] *adj.* of, in, causing, ∼.
ec·u·men·i·cal [,i:kju'menɪkl] *adj.* of or representing the whole Christian world: *the* ∼ *movement* (seeking worldwide Christian unity).
ec·ze·ma ['eksɪmə] *n.* (no pl.) itching skin disease.
-ed (also **-d**) [-ɪd, -d, -t] *suff.* **1.** (forming p.t. & p.p. of verbs): *acted; forced.* **2.** (forming adjs. from ns.) having the

characteristics of: *diseased*; *talented*; *wooded*.

ed·dy ['edɪ] *n.* circular or spiral movement (of wind, smoke, fog, dust, water). *v.i.* move in small circles; move in eddies.

Eden ['iːdn] *n.* (Bible) garden where Adam and Eve lived; place of delight.

edge [edʒ] *n.* 1. sharp, cutting part of a knife, sword, or other tool or weapon. *take the ~ off sth.*, make blunt or dull; (of the appetite) satisfy partly; make less troublesome or painful; *put an ~ on*, sharpen; *on ~*, (fig.) with the nerves upset or jarred. 2. (line marking the) outer limit or boundary of a (flat) surface: *sit on the ~ of a table*; *the ~ of a lake*. *v.t. & i.* (cause to) move slowly forward or along: *~ oneself (one's way) through a crowd*; *~ along a cliff*. **~ways** ['edʒweɪz], **~·wise** ['edʒwaɪz] *advs.* with the ~ outwards or forwards. *be unable to get a word in ~ways*, be unable to speak because others never stop talking. **edg·ing** *n.* narrow border.

ed·i·ble ['edɪbl] *n.* (usu. pl.) *& adj.* (thing that) is fit to be eaten.

edict ['iːdɪkt] *n.* order issued by authority (e.g. the Pope).

ed·i·fice ['edɪfɪs] *n.* (esp. large) building.

ed·i·fy ['edɪfaɪ] *v.t.* improve in morals or mind. **ed·i·fi·ca·tion** [,edɪfɪ'keɪʃn] *n.* (no pl.).

ed·it ['edɪt] *v.t.* 1. prepare (another person's writing) for publication, esp. in a newspaper or other periodical. 2. plan and direct the publication of a newspaper, magazine, book, etc. 3. put together the various sections of a film, tape-recording, etc. in suitable order. **edi·tion** [ɪ'dɪʃn] *n.* form in which a book is published; total number of copies of a book, newspaper, etc. printed from the same types. **ed·i·tor** *n.* person who ~s: *the financial (sports) ~or of a newspaper*. **ed·i·to·ri·al** [,edɪ'tɔːrɪəl] *adj.* of an ~or. *n.* special article or discussion of news in a newspaper, etc., usu. written by the ~or.

ed·u·cate ['edju:keɪt] *v.t.* give intellectual and moral training to. **ed·u·ca·tion** [,edju:'keɪʃn] *n.* (no pl.) systematic instruction; development of character or mental powers. **ed·u·ca·tion·al** [,edju:'keɪʃənl] *adj.* of, connected with, education: *educational broadcasting (film, television)*. **e·du·ca·tion·ist** [,edju:'keɪʃnɪst], **e·du·ca·tion·al·ist** [,edju:'keɪʃnəlɪst] *ns.* expert in education. **ed·u·ca·tor** ['edju:-keɪtə*] *n.* person who ~s.

eel [iːl] *n.* long, snake-like fish.

ee·rie, ee·ry ['ɪərɪ] *adj.* causing a feeling of fear or mystery.

ef·face [ɪ'feɪs] *v.t.* rub or wipe out. *~ oneself*, keep oneself in the background in order to escape notice.

ef·fect [ɪ'fekt] *n.* 1. result; outcome: *of no ~*, useless; *take ~*, produce the result expected or required; come into force; *give ~ to*, cause to become active or to have a result; *bring (carry) into ~*, cause to operate. 2. impression made on the mind; general appearance: *cloud (sound) ~s*; *talk for ~*; *calculated for ~* (i.e. to impress people); *to the ~ that* (i.e. with the general meaning of). 3. (pl.) goods; property: *personal ~s*. *v.t.* bring about; accomplish; cause to happen. **ef·fec·tive** *adj.* having an ~; making a striking impression; (mil.) ready for service. **ef·fec·tu·al** [ɪ'fek-tʃʊəl] *adj.* bringing about the result required.

ef·fem·i·nate [ɪ'femɪnət] *adj.* womanish; unmanly. **ef·fem·i·na·cy** [ɪ'femɪ-nəsɪ] *n.* (no pl.).

ef·fer·vesce [,efə'ves] *v.i.* give off bubbles of gas. **ef·fer·ves·cence** *n.* (no pl.) **ef·fer·ves·cent** *adj.*

ef·fete [ɪ'fiːt] *adj.* exhausted; weak and worn out.

ef·fi·ca·cious [,efɪ'keɪʃəs] *adj.* (of things) producing the desired result. **ef·fi·ca·cy** ['efɪkəsɪ] *n.* (no pl.).

ef·fi·cient [ɪ'fɪʃənt] *adj.* producing an effect; (of persons) capable; able to perform duties well. **ef·fi·cien·cy** *n.* (no pl.).

ef·fi·gy ['efɪdʒɪ] *n.* person's portrait or image (in wood, stone, etc.).

ef·fort ['efət] *n.* trying hard; use of mental powers or bodily strength.

ef·fron·tery [ɪ'frʌntərɪ] *n.* shameless boldness; impudence.

ef·fu·sion [ɪ'fju:ʒn] *n.* sending or pouring out (of liquid, e.g. blood); outpouring of thoughts or feeling. **ef·fu·sive** [ɪ'fju:sɪv] *adj.* (of the feelings, signs of pleasure, gratitude) pouring out too freely.

egg[1] [eg] *n.* female oval or round reproducing cell, containing the germ of a new individual: *The hen has laid an ~*. *Have chickens hatched (out) from those ~s yet? Have those ~s hatched?* '*~head* *n.* (colloq.) intellectual person.

egg[2] [eg] *v.t.* ~ *sb. on*, urge (to do sth.).

ego·ism ['egəʊɪzəm] *n.* (no pl.) continual selfishness. **ego·ist** *n.* selfish person. **ego·is·tic** [,egəʊ'ɪstɪk], **ego·is·ti·cal** *adjs.*

ego·tism ['egəʊtɪzəm] *n.* (no pl.) practice of talking about oneself.

egress ['iːgres] *n.* (right of) going out; way out.

ei·der ['aɪdə*] *n.* 1. (also ~ *duck*) large, wild duck. 2. (also ~-*down*) small, soft feathers from its breast. **'~·down** *n.* bed-covering filled with ~ (2).

eight [eɪt] *n. & adj.* 8. **eighth** [eɪtθ] *n. & adj.* 8th; ¹/₈. **eigh·teen** [,eɪ'tiːn] *n. & adj.* 18. **eigh·teenth** [,eɪ'tiːnθ] *n. & adj.* 18th; ¹/₁₈. **~·ty** ['eɪtɪ] *n. & adj.* 80. **~·i·eth** ['eɪtɪɪθ] *n. & adj.* 80th; ¹/₈₀.

ei·ther ['aɪðə*] I. *adj. & pron.* 1. one or the other of two. (Cf. *any*, for numbers greater than two). 2. (Cf. *both, each*.) *There was a chair on ~ side of the fireplace.* II. *adv. & conj.* 1. after *not*: *I don't like this one, and I don't like that one,* ~ (i.e. I dislike both of them). (Cf. *neither*.) 2. used to introduce the first of two alternatives: *He must be ~ mad or drunk. We must ~ go now or stay till the end.* (Cf. *neither ... nor*.)

ejac·u·late [ɪ'dʒækjʊleɪt] *v.t.* 1. say suddenly. 2. eject (fluid, e.g. se-men) from the body. **ejac·u·la·tion** [ɪ,dʒækjʊ'leɪʃn] *n.*

eject [ɪ'dʒekt] *v.t.* expel (sb. *from* a place, a pilot *from* an aircraft, esp. in an emergency); send out (liquid, lava, etc.). **ejec·tion** [ɪ'dʒekʃn] *n.* **ejec·tor** *n.* sth. that ~s. **~·or seat** (for ~ing the pilot).

eke [iːk] *v.t.* ~ *out*, make (small supplies of sth.) enough for one's needs by adding sth. extra; make (a living) by doing this.

elab·o·rate [ɪ'læbərət] *adj.* worked out with much care and in detail. [ɪ'læbə-reɪt] *v.t.* work out, describe, in (greater) detail. **elab·o·ra·tion** [ɪ,læbə-'reɪʃn] *n.*

elapse [ɪ'læps] *v.i.* (of time) pass.

elas·tic [ɪ'læstɪk] *adj.* 1. having the tendency to go back to the normal size or shape after being pulled or pressed. 2. (fig.) not firm or fixed; able to be adapted. *n.* (no pl.) cord or material made ~ by weaving rubber into it.

elate [ɪ'leɪt] *v.t.* *be ~d*, be in high spirits (because of success). **ela·tion** [ɪ'leɪʃn] *n.*

el·bow ['elbəʊ] *n.* 1. (outer part of) joint between the two parts of the arm. *out at ~s*, (of dress) worn-out; (of sb.) in worn-out clothes. 2. sharp bend or angle in a pipe, etc. *v.t.* push or force (one's way through, forward, etc.).

el·der ['eldə*] *adj.* (of two persons,

esp. relations) older. *n.* 1. (pl.) persons deserving respect, possessing author-ity, because of age. 2. official in some Christian churches. **~·ly** *adj.* rather old. **el·dest** *adj.* (of persons) oldest; first-born.

elect [ɪ'lekt] *v.t.* 1. choose (sb.) by vote. 2. choose (sth., *to do* sth.). *adj.* 1. chosen: *the bishop ~* (chosen, but not yet in office). 2. *the ~*, those persons specially chosen or considered to be the best. **elec·tion** [ɪ'lekʃn] *n.* choosing or selection (by vote) of candidates for an office, for Parliament, etc. **elec·tion·eer·ing** [ɪ,lekʃə'nɪərɪŋ] *n.* (no pl.) working in an ~ion. **elec·tor** *n.* person having the right to ~ by voting. **elec·tor·al** [ɪ'lektərəl] *adj.* of an ~ion: ~oral campaign. **elec·tor·ate** [ɪ'lektərət] *n.* whole body (5) of ~ors.

elec·tric·i·ty [,ɪlek'trɪsətɪ] *n.* (no pl.) property or condition developed in and around substances by rubbing, chemical change, etc. that can be used to produce heat, light, etc. and to drive machines; science of this; supply of electric current. **elec·tric** [ɪ'lektrɪk] *adj.* of, producing, worked by, ~. **elec·tri·cal** *adj.* having to do with ~: *electrical engineering.* **elec·tri·cian** [,ɪlek'trɪʃn] *n.* expert in setting up and servicing electrical apparatus (1). **elec·tri·fy** [ɪ'lektrɪfaɪ] *v.t.* 1. fill (sth.) with ~; alter (railway, etc.) for working by ~. 2. excite, shock (sb.), as by ~: *electrify an audience.* **elec·tri·fi·ca·tion** [ɪ,lektrɪfɪ'keɪʃn] *n.*

elec·tro·cute [ɪ'lektrəkjuːt] *v.t.* put to death, kill accidentally, by means of an electric current. **elec·tro·cu·tion** [ɪ,lektrə'kjuːʃn] *n.*

elec·trode [ɪ'lektrəʊd] *n.* either pole (*anode, cathode*) of an electric battery.

elec·trol·y·sis [,ɪlek'trɒlɪsɪs] *n.* (no pl.) separation of a substance into its chemical parts by electric current.

elec·tron [ɪ'lektrɒn] *n.* negative elec-tric charge forming part of an atom. **~·ic** [,ɪlek'trɒnɪk] *adj.* **~·ics** *n. pl.* (sing. v.) science and technology of the phenomena of ~s (as in transistors, television tubes, computers, etc.).

elec·tro·plate [ɪ'lektrəʊpleɪt] *v.t.* coat (dishes, spoons, etc.) with silver, chromium, etc. by electrolysis. *n.* (no pl.) articles plated (2) in this way.

el·e·gant ['elɪgənt] *adj.* showing, hav-ing, good taste; beautiful; graceful. **el·e·gance** *n.* (no pl.).

el·e·gy ['elɪdʒɪ] *n.* poem or song of sorrow, esp. for the dead. **ele·gi·ac** [,elɪ'dʒaɪək] *adj.*

el·e·ment ['elɪmənt] *n.* **1.** (science) substance which has not so far been separated into simpler substances. **2.** one of the parts of which something is composed; necessary feature or part: *the ~s of geometry*, the simplest parts which are learnt first. **3.** *the ~s*, the weather; storms, etc. *in (out of) one's ~*, in (not in) one's natural or satisfying surroundings. **4.** suggestion, indication; trace: *an ~ of doubt, etc.* **el·e·men·tal** [,elɪ'mentl] *adj.* of the forces of nature; uncontrolled. **el·e·men·ta·ry** [,elɪ'mentərɪ] *adj.* of or in the beginning stages; not developed; simple: *~ary school*, school in which *~ary* subjects are taught to young children.

el·e·phant ['elɪfənt] *n.* largest four-footed animal on earth, with tusks and a trunk. *white ~*, costly or troublesome possession useless to its owner.

el·e·vate ['elɪveɪt] *v.t.* lift up; make (the mind, morals) higher and better. **el·e·va·tion** [,elɪ'veɪʃn] *n.* **1.** elevating or being *~d*. **2.** height (esp. above sea level); hill or high place. **3.** flat drawing of one side of a building. **el·e·va·tor** *n.* **1.** (U.S.A.) = lift (2). **2.** machine for hoisting hay, etc.

elev·en [ɪ'levn] *n. & adj.* 11. **~th** [ɪ'levnθ] *n. & adj.* 11th; ¹/₁₁.

elf [elf] *n.* (*pl. elves* [elvz]) small fairy. **~in** ['elfɪn] *adj.* of elves.

elic·it [ɪ'lɪsɪt] *v.t.* draw out (a quality *from* sb.); get (an answer, the truth, applause) (*from* sb.).

elide [ɪ'laɪd] *v.t.* drop (a vowel or syllable from a word) in speech. **eli·sion** [ɪ'lɪʒn] *n.*

el·i·gi·ble ['elɪdʒəbl] *adj.* fit, suitable, to be chosen (*for*). **el·i·gi·bil·i·ty** [,elɪdʒə'brlɪtɪ] *n.* (no pl.).

elim·i·nate [ɪ'lɪmɪneɪt] *v.t.* remove; take or put away (*from*); get rid of (because unwanted).

elix·ir [ɪ'lɪksə*] *n.* preparation by means of which medieval scientists hoped to change metals into gold and to lengthen life for ever.

elk [elk] *n.* (*pl. ~s*, ~) large kind of deer in N. Europe and Asia; moose.

el·lipse [ɪ'lɪps] *n.* regular oval. **el·lip·ti·cal** [ɪ'lɪptɪkl] *adj.* shaped like an ~.

elm [elm] *n.* common European tree; its hard, heavy wood.

el·o·cu·tion [,elə'kju:ʃn] *n.* (no pl.) art or style of speaking well, esp. in public.

elon·gate ['i:lɒŋgeɪt] *v.t.* make longer. **elon·ga·tion** [,i:lɒŋ'geɪʃn] *n.*

elope [ɪ'ləup] *v.i.* (of a woman) run away (from home) (*with* a lover). **~ment** *n.*

el·o·quence ['eləkwəns] *n.* (no pl.) skilful use of language to persuade or to appeal to the feelings; fluent speaking. **el·o·quent** *adj.*

else [els] *adv.* **1.** besides; in addition: *anybody (someone) ~*, any (some) other person(s). *What ~ have you to do?* **2.** or *~*, otherwise; if not: *Run, or ~ you will miss the bus.* **~where** [,els'weə*] *adv.* in, at, to, some other place.

elu·ci·date [ɪ'lu:sɪdeɪt] *v.t.* explain; make clear.

elude [ɪ'lu:d] *v.t.* escape from (esp. by means of a trick); avoid. **elu·sive** [ɪ'lu:sɪv] *adj.* tending to ~; not easy to remember: *an elusive word.*

elves, see *elf*.

ema·ci·at·ed [ɪ'meɪʃɪeɪtɪd] *adj.* lean; wasted away; skinny. **ema·ci·a·tion** [ɪ,meɪʃɪ'eɪʃn] *n.* (no pl.).

em·a·nate ['eməneɪt] *v.i.* come out (*from* a source). **em·a·na·tion** [,emə'neɪʃn] *n.* sth. coming from a source.

eman·ci·pate [ɪ'mænsɪpeɪt] *v.t.* set free (esp. from legal, political, or moral restraint): *an ~d woman*. **eman·ci·pa·tion** [ɪ,mænsɪ'peɪʃn] *n.* (no pl.).

emas·cu·late [ɪ'mæskjuleɪt] *v.t.* make weak or effeminate.

em·balm [ɪm'bɑ:m] *v.t.* prevent (a dead body) from decaying by using spices or chemicals.

em·bank·ment [ɪm'bæŋkmənt] *n.* wall of earth, stone, etc. to hold back water or support a raised road or railway.

em·bar·go [em'bɑ:gəu] *n.* (*pl. -goes*) order forbidding trade, movement of ships, etc.: *lay an ~ on*; *be under an ~*.

em·bark [ɪm'bɑ:k] *v.i. & t.* **1.** go, put, take, on board a ship. **2.** ~ (*up*)*on*, start; take part in. **em·bar·ka·tion** [,embɑ:'keɪʃn] *n.* (no pl.).

em·bar·rass [ɪm'bærəs] *v.t.* **1.** cause perplexity, mental discomfort or anxiety to: *~ing questions*. **2.** hinder the movement of. **~ment** *n.*

em·bas·sy ['embəsɪ] *n.* duty, mission, residence, of an ambassador; ambassador and his staff.

em·bel·lish [ɪm'belɪʃ] *v.t.* make beautiful; add ornaments to; (fig.) add fictitious details to. **~ment** *n.*

em·ber ['embə*] *n.* (usu. *pl.*) small piece of burning coal or wood in a dying fire.

em·bez·zle [ɪm'bezl] *v.t.* use (money placed in one's care) in a wrong way for one's own benefit. **~ment** *n.*

em·bit·ter [ɪm'bɪtə*] *v.t.* arouse bitter feelings in.

em·blem ['embləm] *n.* symbol; device (3) representing sth. **~at·ic** [ˌembli-'mætik] *adj.* serving as an ~ (*of* sth.).

em·body [ɪm'bɒdɪ] *v.t.* give form to (ideas, feelings); include; comprise. **em·bod·i·ment** [ɪm'bɒdɪmənt] *n.* (esp.) that which gives form to sth.

em·bold·en [ɪm'bəʊldən] *v.t.* give courage or confidence to (sb., *to do* sth.).

em·bo·lism ['embəlɪzəm] *n.* (med.) sudden obstruction of a blood-vessel by a clot of blood, etc.

em·brace [ɪm'breɪs] *v.t.* **1.** put one's arms round (lovingly). **2.** accept (an offer, belief, etc.). **3.** (of things) include. *n.* act of embracing (1).

em·bra·sure [ɪm'breɪʒə*] *n.* opening in a (castle) wall suitably shaped for shooting through.

em·bro·ca·tion [ˌembrəʊ'keɪʃn] *n.* liquid rubbed into a bruised or aching part of the body.

em·broi·der [ɪm'brɔɪdə*] *v.t.* ornament (cloth) with needlework; (fig.) add fictitious details to (a story). **~y** *n.* ornamental needlework.

em·broil [ɪm'brɔɪl] *v.t.* cause (sb., oneself) to be mixed up (*in* a quarrel, etc.).

em·bryo ['embrɪəʊ] *n.* (pl. ~s) offspring of an animal before birth or of a bird, etc. before coming out of the egg; thing in an early stage of development. **em·bry·on·ic** [ˌembrɪ'ɒnɪk] *adj.*

emend [iː'mend] *v.t.* take out errors from. **emen·da·tion** [ˌiːmen'deɪʃn] *n.* improvement by ~ing.

em·er·ald ['emərəld] *n.* bright green precious stone.

emerge [ɪ'mɜːdʒ] *v.i.* **1.** come into view; (esp.) come out (*from* water, etc.). **2.** (of facts, ideas) appear; become known. **emer·gen·cy** [ɪ'mɜː-dʒənsɪ] *n.* sudden, serious happening that makes quick action necessary: ~ncy exit, for use in an emergency; ~ncy landing (2).

em·ery ['emərɪ] *n.* (no pl.) hard metal used (esp. in powdered form) for polishing metal, etc.

emet·ic [ɪ'metɪk] *n.* medicine causing a person to throw up food from the stomach.

em·i·grate ['emɪgreɪt] *v.i.* go away *from* one's country *to* another to settle there. **em·i·grant** *n.* person who ~s. **em·i·gra·tion** [ˌemɪ'greɪʃn] *n.*

em·i·nent ['emɪnənt] *adj.* (of a person) distinguished; (of qualities) remarkable in degree. **~ly** *adv.* in an unusually high degree. **em·i·nence** ['em-

inəns] *n.* **1.** being ~. **2.** high or rising ground. **3.** *His (Your) Eminence,* title used of, to, a cardinal.

emir [e'mɪə*] *n.* Arab prince or governor.

em·is·sary ['emɪsərɪ] *n.* person sent on (usu. an unpleasant) errand.

emit [ɪ'mɪt] *v.t.* (-*tt*-) give or send out (light, liquid, sound, etc.). **emis·sion** [ɪ'mɪʃn] *n.* ~ting; sth. ~ted.

emol·u·ment [ɪ'mɒljʊmənt] *n.* profit from employment or office; fee; salary.

emo·tion [ɪ'məʊʃn] *n.* stirring-up, excitement, of the mind or the feelings; excited state of mind or the feelings. **~al** [ɪ'məʊʃənl] *adj.* **1.** of the ~s. **2.** having ~s easily roused; capable of expressing ~s.

em·per·or ['empərə*] *n.* ruler of an empire.

em·pha·sis ['emfəsɪs] *n.* (pl. *-ses*) force or stress laid on word(s) in order to show their importance; placing of special value or importance on sth. **em·pha·size** ['emfəsaɪz] *v.t.* give ~ to. **em·phat·ic** [ɪm'fætɪk] *adj.* having, showing, using, ~. **em·phat·i·cal·ly** *adv.*

em·pire ['empaɪə*] *n.* **1.** group of countries under one ruler, called *emperor.* **2.** supreme and wide political power.

em·pir·i·cal [em'pɪrɪkl], **em·pir·ic** [em'pɪrɪk] *adjs.* based on observation and experiment, not on theory.

em·place·ment [ɪm'pleɪsmənt] *n.* prepared position for artillery.

em·ploy [ɪm'plɔɪ] *v.t.* **1.** give work to, usu. for payment. **2.** make use of. *n. in the ~ of,* working for. **~ee** (U.S.A. also **em·ploye**) [ˌemplɔɪ'iː] *n.* person ~ed for salary or wages. **~er** *n.* person who ~s (1). **~ment** *n.* (no pl.) being ~ed; one's regular work or profession: *be in (out of) ~ment,* have (have not) a job.

em·pow·er [ɪm'paʊə*] *v.t.* give power or authority (*to do* sth.).

em·press ['emprɪs] *n.* wife of an emperor; woman governing an empire.

emp·ty ['emptɪ] *adj.* (*-ier, -iest*) having nothing inside; containing nothing. *v.t. & i.* make or become ~; remove what is inside (sth.). **emp·ti·ness** *n.* (no pl.).

em·u·late ['emjʊleɪt] *v.t.* try to do as well as or better than. **em·u·la·tion** [ˌemjʊ'leɪʃn] *n.* (no pl.).

emul·sion [ɪ'mʌlʃn] *n.* creamy liquid holding oil or fat.

en- [ɪn-] *pref.* **1.** put into or on: *encase; endanger; engulf.* **2.** make into, cause to be: *enlarge; enrich; enslave.*

-en [-ən] *suff.* (forming vs.) **1.** from

adjs.: *deepen*; *harden*; *shorten*. **2.** from
ns.: *heighten*; *lengthen*.

-(e)n¹ [-(ə)n] *suff.* (forming p.p. of
strong vs.): *spoken*; *sworn*.

-(e)n² [-(ə)n] *suff.* (forming adjs.) **1.**
denoting material: *wooden*; *woollen*.
2. showing resemblance to: *golden*;
silken.

en·able [ɪ'neɪbl] *v.t.* make able, give
authority or means (*to do* sth.).

en·act [ɪ'nækt] *v.t.* **1.** make (a law);
ordain (1); decree. **2.** play (a scene
or part in a play or in real life). **⁓·ment**
n. ⁓ing or being ⁓ed; a law.

enam·el [ɪ'næml] *n.* (no pl.) **1.** glass-
like coating on metal, etc. **2.** (⁓ *paint*)
paint that hardens to make such a coating. **3.** hard outer covering of teeth.
v.t. (*-ll-*, U.S.A. also *-l-*) cover, decorate, with ⁓.

en·am·oured (U.S.A. **-ored**) [ɪ'næm-
əd] *adj.* ⁓ *of*, in love with; delighted
with.

en·camp·ment [ɪn'kæmpmənt] *n.*
camp (esp. military).

en·case [ɪn'keɪs] *v.t.* put into a case;
cover as with a case.

-ence [-əns] *suff.* see *-ance*: *absence*.

en·chant [ɪn'tʃɑːnt] *v.t.* **1.** charm;
delight. **2.** work magic on. **⁓·er**, **⁓·ress**
ns. man, woman, who ⁓s. **⁓·ment** *n.*
being ⁓ed; thing which ⁓s; charm;
delight.

en·cir·cle [ɪn'sɜːkl] *v.t.* surround.

en·clave ['enkleɪv] *n.* territory surrounded by that of another country.

en·close [ɪn'kləʊz] *v.t.* **1.** put a wall,
fence, etc. round; shut in on all sides.
2. put (sth.) in (an envelope, parcel,
etc.), esp. with a letter. **en·clo·sure**
[ɪn'kləʊʒə*] *n.* enclosing; sth. ⁓d (e.g.
a fenced playground); article sent (in
the same envelope) with a letter.

en·core [ɒŋ'kɔː*] *int.* Repeat! Again!
v.t. & n. (call for a) repetition (of a
song, etc.) or further performance by
the same person(s).

en·coun·ter [ɪn'kaʊntə*] *v.t. & n.*
(have a) sudden or unexpected meeting
(e.g. with a friend, or with danger).

en·cour·age [ɪn'kʌrɪdʒ] *v.t.* give hope,
courage, or confidence to; urge (sb.
to do sth.). **⁓·ment** *n.* encouraging;
sth. that ⁓s.

en·croach [ɪn'krəʊtʃ] *v.i.* go beyond
what is right or natural (*on* or *upon*
what belongs to sb. else). **⁓·ment** *n.*

en·crust·ed [ɪn'krʌstɪd] *adj.* covered
as with a crust: *a crown ⁓ with jewels*.

en·cum·ber [ɪn'kʌmbə*] *v.t.* get in the
way of; be a burden to; weigh down.
en·cum·brance [ɪn'kʌmbrəns] *n.*

-en·cy [-ənsɪ] *suff.* see *-ancy*: *despon-
dency*.

en·cy·clo·p(a)e·dia [en,saɪkləʊ'piːdjə*
n. book, or set of books, giving information about every branch o
knowledge, or on one subject, wit
articles in ABC order. **en·cy·clo
p(a)e·dic** [en,saɪkləʊ'piːdɪk] *adj.*

end [end] *n.* **1.** farthest or last part
the ⁓ of a journey; *on ⁓*, (of a barre[
etc.) upright; *for* (*five, etc.*) *hour*
(*days, etc.*) *on ⁓*, consecutively; withou
an interval; *make both ⁓s meet*, manag
to earn as much as one needs to spend
put an ⁓ to, *make an ⁓ of*, destroy
abolish; stop. **2.** small piece that re
mains: *a candle ⁓*. **3.** finish; conclu
sion: *I've come to the ⁓ of my book*
4. death: *He's nearing his ⁓* (is dying)
5. purpose; aim: *I hope she will gai*
(*achieve*) *her ⁓*(*s*). *v.t. & i.* (cause to
come to an ⁓; reach an ⁓: *⁓ up*, finish
⁓·ing *n.* end of a story; end of a word
⁓·less(·ly) *adj. & adv.* infinite(ly)
without ⁓; incessant(ly). **⁓·way[**
['endweɪz], **⁓·wise** ['endwaɪz] *advs*
with the end towards the spectator o
forward or up; end to end.

en·dan·ger [ɪn'deɪndʒə*] *v.t.* put i[
danger; cause danger to.

en·dear [ɪn'dɪə*] *v.t.* make dear o
precious. **⁓·ment** *n.* (act, word, expression, of) affection.

en·deav·our (U.S.A. **-or**) [ɪn'devə*
n. & v.i. attempt.

en·dem·ic [en'demɪk] *n. & adj*
(disease) regularly present in a country
or among a class of people.

en·dive ['endɪv] *n.* **1.** salad plant. **2**
(U.S.A.) crown of chicory, used a[
salad.

en·dorse [ɪn'dɔːs] *v.t.* **1.** write one'[
name or comments on (a document)
2. approve, support (a claim, statement, etc.). **⁓·ment** *n.*

en·dow [ɪn'daʊ] *v.t.* **1.** give (money
property, etc.) to provide a regula[
income for (e.g. a college). **2.** *be ⁓e[*
with, possess naturally; be born wit[
(a quality). **⁓·ment** *n.*

en·dure [ɪn'djʊə*] *v.t. & i.* suffer
undergo (pain, hardship, etc.). **2.** bear
put up with: *She can't ⁓ seeing animal[*
cruelly treated. **3.** last; continue in existence. **en·dur·able** [ɪn'djʊərəbl] *adj*
that can be ⁓d. **en·dur·ance** *n.* **1**
ability to ⁓: *past* (*beyond*) *endurance*
to an extent that cannot be ⁓d. **2.** act
instance of, enduring.

en·e·my ['enəmɪ] *n.* **1.** one who hates
wishes to harm, or attacks, another
anything that harms or injures. **2**

enrage

(collective pl.) *the* armed forces of a country with which one's own country is at war: *the ~ were forced to retreat.*

en·er·gy ['enədʒɪ] *n.* **1.** force; vigour; (pl.) (person's) powers available for or used in working. **2.** (no pl.) (phys.) capacity for, power of, doing work: *electrical ~.* **en·er·get·ic** [,enə'dʒetɪk] *adj.* full of, done with, ~ (1).

en·er·vate ['enə:veɪt] *v.t.* cause to lose (physical, moral) strength.

en·fee·ble [ɪn'fiːbl] *v.t.* make (sb. or his efforts) feeble.

en·fold [ɪn'fəʊld] *v.t.* put one's arms round; cover or wrap up.

en·force [ɪn'fɔːs] *v.t.* **1.** compel obedience to (a law, etc.). **2.** get (sb.) by force (to do sth.). **3.** give force or strength to (an argument, demand). **~·ment** *n.* (no pl.).

en·fran·chise [ɪn'fræntʃaɪz] *v.t.* **1.** give political rights to (esp. the right to vote at parliamentary elections). **2.** set free (slaves). **~·ment** [ɪn'fræntʃɪzmənt] *n.*

en·gage [ɪn'geɪdʒ] *v.t. & i.* **1.** get the right to occupy (a seat, taxi, etc.) or to employ (e.g. a workman, guide). **2.** promise; undertake. **3.** *be ~d,* (of a telephone line or number) someone else is using it; *be ~d in,* be occupied with; have one's time or attention taken up with: *~d in conversation.* **4.** begin fighting (*with* the enemy); attack. **5.** (of parts of a machine) lock together; (cause to) fit into. **~d** *adj.* (esp.) having given a promise of marriage (*to*). **~·ment** *n.* **1.** promise or undertaking, esp. (a) to marry or (b) to go or be somewhere, meet sb., at a fixed time. **2.** battle. **en·gag·ing** *adj.* attractive; pleasing; charming.

en·gen·der [ɪn'dʒendə*] *v.t.* be the cause of (a situation or condition).

en·gine ['endʒɪn] *n.* machine producing power or motion: *the ~ of a motor car; a fire-~; a steam-~.* '**~·driv·er** *n.* man who drives a railway-~. **en·gi·neer** [,endʒɪ'nɪə*] *n.* **1.** person who designs machines, bridges, railways, ships, docks, etc. **2.** person in control of a ship's ~s. *v.t.* construct as an ~er; (colloq.) arrange or bring about, esp. artfully: *~er a scheme.*

Eng·lish ['ɪŋglɪʃ] *adj.* of England; of, written or spoken in, the ~ language. *n.* the language of the ~ people. *the ~,* (pl.) the people of England. '**~·man** *n.* '**~·wom·an** *n.*

en·graft [ɪn'grɑːft] *v.t.* insert (a shoot of one tree) (*into* or *upon* another).

en·grave [ɪn'greɪv] *v.t.* cut (lines, words, designs, etc.) (*on, upon* a hard

surface). **en·grav·er** *n.* **en·grav·ing** *n.* picture, etc. printed from an ~d plate.

en·gross [ɪn'grəʊs] *v.t.* **1.** take up all the time or attention of: *~ed in one's work; an ~ing story.* **2.** write (a legal document) in large letters.

en·gulf [ɪn'gʌlf] *v.t.* swallow up.

en·hance [ɪn'hɑːns] *v.t.* add to (the value, attraction).

enig·ma [ɪ'nɪgmə] *n.* question, person, thing, circumstance, that is puzzling. **~·tic** [,enɪg'mætɪk] *adj.* puzzling. **~·t·i·cal·ly** *adv.*

en·join [ɪn'dʒɔɪn] *v.t.* give an order for (silence, action); command.

en·joy [ɪn'dʒɔɪ] *v.t.* **1.** get pleasure from; take delight in: *~ a good meal.* **2.** have: *~ good health (a good income).* **3.** *~ oneself,* experience pleasure. **~·able** *adj.* **~·ment** *n.*

en·kin·dle [ɪn'kɪndl] *v.t.* cause (flame, passions, war, etc.) to flare up; (fig.) inflame with passion.

en·large [ɪn'lɑːdʒ] *v.t. & i.* make or become larger. **~** (*up*)*on,* say or write more about. **~·ment** *n.* sth. ~d, esp. a photograph; sth. added to.

en·light·en [ɪn'laɪtn] *v.t.* give more knowledge to; free from ignorance, misunderstanding or false beliefs. **~·ment** *n.* (no pl.).

en·list [ɪn'lɪst] *v.t. & i.* **1.** obtain (sb.'s help, support, etc.). **2.** take into, enter, the armed forces: *~ed men,* (U.S.A.) soldiers or sailors below the rank of officer. **~·ment** *n.*

en·liv·en [ɪn'laɪvn] *v.t.* make lively.

en·mesh [ɪn'meʃ] *v.t.* take (as) in a net.

en·mi·ty ['enmətɪ] *n.* hatred.

en·no·ble [ɪ'nəʊbl] *v.t.* **1.** make (sb.) a noble. **2.** make morally noble; make dignified.

en·nui [ɑː'nwiː] *n.* (no pl.) weariness of mind caused by lack of interesting occupation.

enor·mi·ty [ɪ'nɔːmətɪ] *n.* **1.** great wickedness. **2.** serious crime. **3.** immense size: *the ~ of a problem.*

enor·mous [ɪ'nɔːməs] *adj.* very great; immense. **~·ly** *adv.*

enough [ɪ'nʌf] *n. & adj.* (quantity or number) as great as is needed; as much or as many as necessary. *adv.* **1.** sufficiently: *Are you warm ~? you know well ~ ...* (quite well). **2.** *oddly (curiously, etc.) ~,* sufficiently odd, etc. to be mentioned.

en·quire, en·qui·ry, see *inquire, inquiry.*

en·rage [ɪn'reɪdʒ] *v.t.* fill with rage: *be ~d at (by, with)* sb.'s stupidity.

en·rap·ture [ɪnˈræptʃə*] *v.t.* fill with great delight or joy.

en·rich [ɪnˈrɪtʃ] *v.t.* make rich; improve (the mind, the soil) by adding sth.: *soil ~ed with manure.*

en·rol(l) [ɪnˈrəʊl] *v.t. & i.* (*-ll-*) put (sb.'s name) on a list or register; enter one's name on a list, etc.

en route [ɑ̃:nˈru:t] (Fr.) *adv.* on the way (*to, for*).

en·sign [ˈensaɪn] (in the navy [ˈensn]) *n.* 1. flag, esp. as used on ships: *white ~* (used by the Royal Navy); *red ~* (used by British merchant ships). 2. [ˈensaɪn] (U.S.A.) lowest commissioned officer in the navy.

an ensign (1)

en·slave [ɪnˈsleɪv] *v.t.* make a slave of.

en·sue [ɪnˈsju:] *v.i.* happen later; take place as a result (*from*).

en·sure [ɪnˈʃʊə*] *v.t.* make certain; make safe (*against* risks, etc.).

-ent [-ənt] *suff.* see *-ant*: *persistent; student.*

en·tail [ɪnˈteɪl] *v.t.* make necessary.

en·tan·gle [ɪnˈtæŋɡl] *v.t.* catch in a net or among obstacles; (fig.) cause (sb.) to be in difficulty: *~d with money-lenders.* *~·ment n.*

en·ter [ˈentə*] *v.t. & i.* 1. come or go into; become a member of. 2. put (notes, names, records, etc.) down in writing: *~ for an examination; ~ figures in an account.* 3. *~ into*, take part in; begin to deal with or talk about; *~ upon*, make a start upon (new work, duties, etc.).

en·ter·prise [ˈentəpraɪz] *n.* 1. undertaking, esp. one that offers difficulty: *free (private) ~.* 2. courage, eagerness, to start new *~s.* **en·ter·pris·ing** *adj.* having, showing, *~* (2).

en·ter·tain [ˌentəˈteɪn] *v.t. & i.* 1. receive (people) as guests; give food or drink to. 2. amuse; interest. 3. be ready to consider: *~ a proposal;* have in the mind: *~ ideas (feelings).* *~·er n.* person who *~s* (2) professionally. *~·ing adj.* amusing. *~·ment n.* hospitality; amusement; public performance or show.

en·thral(l) [ɪnˈθrɔ:l] *v.t.* (*-ll-*) take the whole attention of (usu. fig.); please greatly.

en·throne [ɪnˈθrəʊn] *v.t.* place (e.g. a bishop) on a throne. *~·ment n.*

en·thuse [ɪnˈθju:z] *v.t. & i.* (colloq.) fill with, show, enthusiasm.

en·thu·si·asm [ɪnˈθju:zɪæzəm] *n.* (no pl.) strong feeling of, interest in, admiration for. **en·thu·si·ast** [ɪnˈθju:zɪæst] *n.* person filled with *~.* **en·thu·si·as·tic** [ɪnˌθju:zɪˈæstɪk] *adj.* showing, having, *~.* **en·thu·si·as·ti·cal·ly** *adv.*

en·tice [ɪnˈtaɪs] *v.t.* tempt or persuade (a person, etc.) (*away from* sth., *to do* or *into doing* sth.). *~·ment n.*

en·tire [ɪnˈtaɪə*] *adj.* whole; complete; not broken. *~·ly adv. ~·ty* [ɪnˈtaɪətɪ] *n.* being *~: in its ~ty,* as a whole.

en·ti·tle [ɪnˈtaɪtl] *v.t.* give a title to (a book, etc.); (of conditions, qualities, etc.) give (sb.) a right (*to*).

en·ti·ty [ˈentətɪ] *n.* 1. something that has real existence. 2. being; existence.

en·to·mol·o·gy [ˌentəʊˈmɒlədʒɪ] *n.* (no pl.) study of insects. **en·to·mol·o·gist** *n.*

en·trails [ˈentreɪlz] *n. pl.* bowels; intestines.

en·trance[1] [ˈentrəns] *n.* 1. opening; gate; door; way into. 2. act of coming or going in, of entering (*into* or *upon* an office or position). 3. right of entering: *~ fees (examinations).*

en·trance[2] [ɪnˈtrɑ:ns] *v.t.* (usu. passive) overcome, carry away as in a dream, with pleasure.

en·trant [ˈentrənt] *n.* person entering (a profession, *for* a competition, etc.).

en·treat [ɪnˈtri:t] *v.t.* beg (sb.) earnestly (*to do* sth.). *~·y n.* earnest request.

en·trench [ɪnˈtrentʃ] *v.t.* 1. surround with trenches: *~ oneself,* dig oneself into the ground. 2. (fig., of legal clauses, customs) establish firmly. *~·ment n.*

en·trust [ɪnˈtrʌst] *v.t.* give (sth. *to* sb.) as a responsibility, task, or duty; trust (sb. *with* a task).

en·try [ˈentrɪ] *n.* 1. (act of) entering. 2. (place of) entrance. 3. item noted in an account book, etc. 4. list, number, of persons, etc. entering for a competition, etc.

en·twine [ɪnˈtwaɪn] *v.t.* make by twining; curl (one thing) (*with* or *round* another).

enu·mer·ate [ɪˈnju:məreɪt] *v.t.* count; go through (a list of articles) naming them one by one. **enu·mer·a·tion** [ɪˌnju:məˈreɪʃn] *n.*

enun·ci·ate [ɪ'nʌnsɪeɪt] *v.t. & i.* **1.** say, pronounce (words). **2.** express (a theory, etc.) clearly or definitely. **enun·ci·a·tion** [ɪ,nʌnsɪ'eɪʃn] *n.*

en·vel·op [ɪn'veləp] *v.t.* wrap up, cover, on all sides: ⁓*ed in mist (a shawl).*

en·ve·lope ['envələup] *n.* wrapper or covering, esp. one made of paper for a letter.

an envelope   an epaulette

en·vi·able, en·vi·ous, see *envy.*

en·vi·ron·ment [ɪn'vaɪərənmənt] *n.* surroundings, conditions, and circumstances that influence the life of an individual or society. **en·vi·ron·men·tal** [ɪn,vaɪərən'mentl] *adj.* of, relating to, ⁓: ⁓*al pollution,* uncontrolled pollution of man's ⁓. **en·vi·ron·men·tal·ist** *n.*

en·vi·rons [ɪn'vaɪərəns] *n. pl.* districts surrounding a town, etc.

en·vis·age [ɪn'vɪzɪdʒ] *v.t.* face (danger, facts); picture in the mind.

en·voy ['envɔɪ] *n.* messenger, esp. one sent on a special mission by one government to another.

en·vy ['envɪ] *n.* (no pl.) **1.** ⁓ *at* (sth.), ⁓ *of* (sb.), feeling of disappointment or ill will (at another's better fortune). **2.** object of such feeling. *v.t.* feel ⁓ of. **en·vi·able** ['envɪəbl] *adj.* causing ⁓; likely to be envied. **en·vi·ous** ['envɪəs] *adj.* having, feeling, or showing ⁓.

ep·au·lette (U.S.A. also **-let**) ['epɔʊlet] *n.* shoulder ornament on a naval or military officer's uniform. (See the picture.)

ephem·er·al [ɪ'femərəl] *adj.* living, lasting, for a very short time.

ep·ic ['epɪk] *n. & adj.* (poetic account) of the deeds of one or more great heroes or of a nation's past history.

ep·i·cure ['epɪ,kjʊə*] *n.* person who understands the pleasures to be had from delicate (7) eating and drinking.

ep·i·dem·ic [,epɪ'demɪk] *n. & adj.* (disease) widespread among many people in the same place for a time. (Cf. *endemic.*)

ep·i·gram ['epɪgræm] *n.* short saying that expresses an idea in a clever and amusing way. **⁓·mat·ic** [,epɪgrə'mæt-ɪk] *adj.*

ep·i·lep·sy ['epɪlepsɪ] *n.* (no pl.) nervous disease causing a person to fall unconscious (often with violent, involuntary movements). **ep·i·lep·tic** [,epɪ'leptɪk] *adj.* of ⁓. *n.* person suffering from ⁓.

ep·i·logue (U.S.A. also **-log**) ['epɪlɒg] *n.* last part of a literary work, esp. a poem spoken at the end of a play.

epis·co·pal [ɪ'pɪskəpl] *adj.* of, governed by, bishops. **epis·co·pa·lian** [ɪ,pɪskəʊ'peɪljən] *n. & adj.* (member) of an ⁓ church.

ep·i·sode ['epɪsəʊd] *n.* (description of) one event in a chain of events.

epis·tle [ɪ'pɪsl] *n.* (old word for) letter. *the E⁓s,* (Bible) the letters written by the apostles. **e·pis·to·lary** [ɪ'pɪstələrɪ] *adj.* of ⁓s.

ep·i·taph ['epɪtɑːf] *n.* words (e.g. on a tombstone) describing a dead person. (Cf. *obituary.*)

ep·i·thet ['epɪθet] *n.* adjective expressing a quality; word added to a name, as in 'Alfred the *Great*'.

epit·o·me [ɪ'pɪtəmɪ] *n.* short summary of a book, speech, etc.; sth. which shows, on a small scale, the characteristics of sth. much larger.

ep·och ['iːpɒk] *n.* (beginning of a) period of time (in history, life, etc.) marked by special events or characteristics: ⁓*-making,* marking the beginning of a new era: *an ⁓-making discovery.*

equable ['ekwəbl] *adj.* steady; regular; not changing much: *an ⁓ climate* (*temper*).

equal ['iːkwəl] *adj.* the same in size, amount, number, degree, etc. ⁓ *to* (a task, etc.), strong enough for, capable of. *n.* person or thing ⁓ to another. *v.t.* (**-ll-,** U.S.A. also **-l-**) be ⁓ to. **⁓·ly** *adv.* **⁓·i·ty** [iː'kwɒlətɪ] *n.* (no pl.) state of being ⁓. **⁓·ize** ['iːkwəlaɪz] *v.t. & i.* make or become ⁓. **⁓·i·za·tion** [,iːkwə-laɪ'zeɪʃn] *n.* **⁓·iz·er** ['iːkwəlaɪzə*] *n.*

equa·nim·i·ty [,iːkwə'nɪmətɪ] *n.* (no pl.) calmness of mind or temper.

equate [ɪ'kweɪt] *v.t.* consider, treat, one thing as being equal (*to* or *with* another). **equa·tion** [ɪ'kweɪʒn] *n.* making or being equal; (maths.) expression of equality between two quantities by the sign (=).

equa·tor [ɪ'kweɪtə*] *n.* imaginary line round the earth, real line drawn on maps, to represent points at an equal distance from the north and south poles. **equa·to·ri·al** [,ekwə'tɔːrɪəl] *adj.* of or near the ⁓.

eques·tri·an [ɪ'kwestrɪən] *adj.* **1.** on

horseback: *an ~ statue*. **2.** of horse-riding: *~ skill*. *n.* rider or performer on horseback.

equi·dis·tant [ˌiːkwɪˈdɪstənt] *adj.* separated by equal distance(s).

equi·lat·er·al [ˌiːkwɪˈlætərəl] *adj.* having all sides equal.

equi·lib·ri·um [ˌiːkwɪˈlɪbrɪəm] *n.* (no pl.) state of being balanced.

equine [ˈiːkwaɪn] *adj.* of, like, a horse.

equi·nox [ˈiːkwɪnɒks] *n.* time of the year at which the sun crosses the equator and when day and night are of equal length. **equi·noc·tial** [ˌiːkwɪˈnɒkʃl] *adj.* of, at, near, the ~.

equip [ɪˈkwɪp] *v.t.* (-pp-) supply (a person, oneself, a ship, etc.) (*with* what is needed, *for* a purpose). **~·ment** *n.* ~ping or being ~ped; things needed for a purpose.

eq·ui·ty [ˈekwətɪ] *n.* (no pl.) fairness; right judgement; (esp., English law) principles of justice used to correct laws when these would apply unfairly in special circumstances. **eq·ui·ta·ble** [ˈekwɪtəbl] *adj.* fair; just; reasonable.

equiv·a·lent [ɪˈkwɪvələnt] *n. & adj.* (sth.) equal in value, amount, meaning (*to*). **equiv·a·lence** *n.*

equiv·o·cal [ɪˈkwɪvəkl] *adj.* having a double or doubtful meaning; open to doubt.

-(e)r [-ə*] *suff.* (forming the comparative): *smaller; stronger; wider*.

-er [-ə*] *suff.* (forming ns.) **1.** person or thing that does sth.: *learner; tin-opener*. **2.** person who lives in: *villager; Londoner; New Yorker*.

era [ˈɪərə] *n.* period in history, starting from a particular time or event: *the Christian ~*.

erad·i·cate [ɪˈrædɪkeɪt] *v.t.* pull up by the roots; destroy or put an end to: *~ crime*.

erase [ɪˈreɪz] *v.t.* rub out. **eras·er** *n.* sth. with which to ~: *a pencil ~r*. **era·sure** [ɪˈreɪʒə*] *n.* rubbing out; thing rubbed out.

ere [eə*] *conj. & prep.* (poet.) before.

erect [ɪˈrekt] *adj.* upright; standing on end. *v.t.* **1.** set ~: *a pole*. **2.** build; establish; set up: *~ a new school* (*flag-staff*). **erec·tion** [ɪˈrekʃn] *n.*

er·mine [ˈɜːmɪn] *n.* small animal with (in winter) white fur and black-pointed tail; (garment made of) its fur.

erode [ɪˈrəʊd] *v.t.* (of acids, rain, currents, etc.) wear away; eat into. **ero·sion** [ɪˈrəʊʒn] *n.* (no pl.) eroding; being ~d: *soil erosion* (by wind and rain). **ero·sive** [ɪˈrəʊsɪv] *adj.*

erot·ic [ɪˈrɒtɪk] *adj.* of sexual love.

err [ɜː*] *v.i.* make a mistake or mistakes; do or be wrong.

er·rand [ˈerənd] *n.* **1.** short journey to take or get sth. (e.g. a message, goods from a shop): *go on ~s; run ~s*. **2.** object or purpose of such a journey. **'~·boy** *n.* boy paid to run ~s.

er·rat·ic [ɪˈrætɪk] *adj.* (of a person) irregular in behaviour or opinion; (of a clock, etc.) irregular; uncertain in movement.

er·ra·tum [eˈrɑːtəm] *n.* (pl. *-ta* [-tə]) mistake in printing or writing.

er·ro·ne·ous [ɪˈrəʊnjəs] *adj.* incorrect; mistaken.

er·ror [ˈerə*] *n.* **1.** sth. done wrong; mistake: *spelling ~s; an ~ of judgement*. **2.** condition of being wrong in belief or conduct: *lead sb. into ~*.

er·u·dite [ˈeruːdaɪt] *adj.* having, showing, great learning; scholarly. **er·u·di·tion** [ˌeruːˈdɪʃn] *n.* (no pl.).

erupt [ɪˈrʌpt] *v.i.* (esp. of a volcano) burst out. **erup·tion** [ɪˈrʌpʃn] *n.* outbreak (of a volcano; fig., of war, disease, etc.).

-(e)ry [-ərɪ] *suff.* (forming ns.) **1.** place of work, cultivation, etc.: (*oil, sugar*) *refinery*; (*fish*) *cannery*. **2.** state or condition of being: *slavery*. **3.** occupation: *archery; embroidery*. **4.** class of goods or things: *drapery; machinery*.

es·ca·late [ˈeskəleɪt] *v.t. & i.* increase by stages; (of warfare) (cause to) become more violent and extensive. **es·ca·la·tion** [ˌeskəˈleɪʃn] *n.*

es·ca·la·tor [ˈeskəleɪtə*] *n.* moving stairs carrying people up or down.

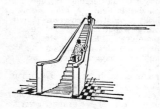

an escalator

es·ca·pade [ˌeskəˈpeɪd] *n.* daring, mischievous, or adventurous act, often one causing gossip or trouble.

es·cape [ɪˈskeɪp] *v.i. & t.* **1.** get free (*from*); get away (*from*); **2.** (of gas, liquid) flow out. **3.** avoid. **4.** be forgotten or unnoticed by: *his name ~s me*. *n.* escaping; means of escaping: *a fire-~*.

es·cape·ment [ɪˈskeɪpmənt] *n.* device

in a clock or watch to regulate the movement.

es·chew [ɪs'tʃuː] *v.t.* avoid; keep oneself away from (bad conduct).

es·cort ['eskɔːt] *n.* person(s), ship(s), going with another or others to give protection as a sign of honour: *under police ~.* [ɪ'skɔːt] *v.t.* go with as an ~: *a convoy ~ed by destroyers*; *~ the king to the palace.*

es·cutch·eon [ɪ'skʌtʃən] *n.* shield with a coat of arms on it. *a blot on one's ~*, a stain on one's reputation.

-ese [-iːz] *suff.* (forming adjs. and ns., used with names of some countries and towns): *Japanese; Milanese.*

es·pe·cial [ɪ'speʃl] *adj.* particular; exceptional. *~ly adv.* to an exceptional degree; in particular.

es·pi·o·nage [ˌespɪə'nɑːʒ] *n.* (no pl.) spying (1).

es·pouse [ɪ'spauz] *v.t.* **1.** give one's support to (a cause, theory, etc.). **2.** (old use of a man) marry.

es·prit de corps [ˌespriːdə'kɔː*] (Fr.) *n.* (no pl.) spirit of loyalty and devotion that unites the members of a group or society.

es·py [ɪ'spaɪ] *v.t.* catch sight of.

es·quire [ɪ'skwaɪə*] *n.* title (written as *Esq.*), used (esp. in an address on a letter) *after* a man's name instead of Mr *before* it.

-ess[1] [-es, -ɪs] *suff.* (forming ns. denoting females): *actress; hostess; lioness.*

-ess[2] [-es] *suff.* (forming abstract ns. from adjs.): *duress.*

es·say[1] ['eseɪ] *n.* piece of writing (not poetry), usu. short, on any one subject. *~ist n.*

es·say[2] [e'seɪ] *v.t.* try; attempt.

es·sence ['esns] *n.* **1.** (no pl.) that which makes a thing what it is; the inner nature or most important quality of a thing: *the ~ of her character.* **2.** extract (1) (usu. a liquid, obtained from a substance by removing, e.g. by boiling away, everything except the most important or valuable part): *meat ~; ~ of peppermint.*

es·sen·tial [ɪ'senʃl] *adj.* **1.** necessary; most important; indispensable: *conditions ~ to good health.* **2.** of an essence (2): *~ oils.* *n.* (esp. pl.) fundamental element or thing: *~s of English grammar.* *~ly adv.*

-(e)st [-ɪst] *suff.* (forming the superlative): *smallest; strongest; widest.*

es·tab·lish [ɪ'stæblɪʃ] **1.** set up, put on a firm foundation (e.g. a state, business, etc.). **2.** settle, place (a person, oneself) in a position, office, place: *~*

sb. as governor. **3.** cause people to accept (a belief, claim, custom, etc.). **4.** make (a church) national by law. *~ment n.* **1.** *~ing* or being *~ed.* **2.** that which is *~ed*, e.g. a large organized body (5) of persons (in the army or navy, a civil service, a business firm, a household and the servants in it). **3.** *the E~ment,* the ruling groups or institutions of a country exercising authority or influence, and generally resisting changes. **4.** conventional society.

es·tate [ɪ'steɪt] *n.* **1.** piece of property in the form of land, esp. in the country: *~ agent,* (Gt. Brit.) person managing an *~*; person who buys and sells buildings and land for others. (Cf. U.S.A. *realtor.*) *~ car,* (Gt. Brit.) light saloon motor car that carries both passengers and goods in one compartment, usu. with rear doors (U.S.A. *station wagon*). **2.** all a person's property: *real ~,* land and buildings; *personal ~,* money and other kinds of property. **3.** (old use) condition: *reach man's ~; the holy ~ of matrimony.*

es·teem [ɪ'stiːm] *v.t.* **1.** have a high opinion of; respect greatly. **2.** consider: *I shall ~ it a favour if ... n.* (no pl.) high regard. **es·ti·mable** ['estɪməbl] *adj.* worthy of *~*.

es·ti·mate ['estɪmeɪt] *v.t.* form a judgement about; calculate (the cost, value, size, etc. of sth.). ['estɪmət] *n.* judgement; approximate calculation (about the cost, value, size, etc. of sth.).

es·ti·ma·tion [ˌestɪ'meɪʃn] *n.* (no pl.) judgement; regard: *in the ~ of his friends; be held in high ~.*

es·trange [ɪ'streɪndʒ] *v.t.* bring about a separation in feeling and sympathy; *foolish behaviour that ~d his friends.* *~ment n.*

es·tu·ary ['estjʊərɪ] *n.* river mouth into which the tide flows.

et·cet·era [ɪt'setərə] (usu. shortened to *etc.*) and other things; and so on.

etch [etʃ] *v.t. & i.* (by the use of acids) engrave (a picture, etc.) on a metal plate from which copies may be printed. *~ing n.* print made in this way; art of making pictures in this way. *~er n.*

eter·nal [iː'tɜːnl] *adj.* **1.** without beginning or end; lasting for ever. *the E~,* God. **2.** (colloq.) unceasing: *~ arguments.* **eter·ni·ty** [iː'tɜːnətɪ] *n.* time without end; future life; (colloq.) very long time.

ether[1] ['iːθə*] *n.* (no pl.) colourless liquid made from alcohol, used as an anaesthetic.

ether[2] ['i:θə*] *n.* (no pl.) **1.** *the* ~, elastic fluid once thought to fill all space providing a means for waves of light, etc. to pass across. **2.** (poet.) pure, upper air above the clouds. **ethe·re·al** [i:'θɪərɪəl] *adj.* **1.** of or like the ~[2] (1). **2.** of supernatural delicacy; seeming too light or spiritual for this world: ~*eal beauty* (*music*).

eth·ic ['eθɪk] *n.* system of moral principles. ~**s** *n. pl.* (sing. or pl. v.) science of morals; rules of conduct. **eth·i·cal** ['eθɪkl] *adj.* of morals or moral questions; moral.

eth·nog·ra·phy [eθ'nɒgrəfɪ] *n.* (no pl.) description of the world's peoples. **eth·nog·ra·pher** [eθ'nɒgrəfə*] *n.* **eth·no·graph·ic** [,eθnəʊ'græfɪk] *adj.*

eth·nol·o·gy [eθ'nɒlədʒɪ] *n.* (no pl.) science of the races of mankind, their relations to one another, etc. **eth·nol·o·gist** *n.* **eth·no·log·i·cal** [,eθnəʊ-'lɒdʒɪkl] *adj.*

et·i·quette ['etɪket] *n.* (no pl.) rules of behaviour among polite people, a class of society, or members of a profession.

et·y·mol·o·gy [,etɪ'mɒlədʒɪ] *n.* **1.** (no pl.) science of the origin and history of words. **2.** account of the origin and history of a word. **et·y·mo·log·i·cal** [,etɪmə'lɒdʒɪkl] *adj.*

eu·ca·lyp·tus [,ju:kə'lɪptəs] *n.* sorts of evergreen tree from which an oil, used for colds, is obtained.

Eu·cha·rist ['ju:kərɪst] *n.* *the E*~, Holy Communion; the bread and wine taken at the ~.

eu·gen·ics [ju:'dʒenɪks] *n. p*[1]. (sing. v.) science of producing healthy offspring and thus improving the human race.

eu·lo·gy ['ju:lədʒɪ] *n.* (speech or writing full of) high praise. **eu·lo·gize** ['ju:-lədʒaɪz] *v.t.* praise highly in speech or writing.

eu·phe·mism ['ju:fɪmɪzəm] *n.* (example of) use of other, usu. more pleasing or less exact, words or phrases in place of words required by truth or accuracy: *'Pass away' is a* ~ *for 'die'*. **eu·phe·mis·tic** [,ju:fɪ'mɪstɪk] *adj.*

eu·pho·ny ['ju:fənɪ] *n.* pleasantness of sound; pleasing sound.

Eu·ro- ['jʊərəʊ-] *pref.* Europe; European: '~**cheque** *n.* credit (5) card used for obtaining goods and services in various European countries. '~**dol·lar** *n.* U.S.A. dollars deposited in European banks and used in the European money market. '~**vi·sion** *n.* European television network.

Eu·ro·pe·an [,jʊərə'pi:ən] *n. & adj.* (native or inhabitant) of Europe.

evac·u·ate [ɪ'vækjʊeɪt] *v.t.* **1.** (esp. of soldiers) withdraw from; leave empty: ~ *a fort.* **2.** remove (people) from a place or district (e.g. during a war). **evac·u·a·tion** [ɪ,vækjʊ'eɪʃn] *n.* **evac·u·ee** [ɪ,vækjʊ'i:] *n.* person who is ~d (2).

evade [ɪ'veɪd] *v.t.* **1.** get, keep, out of the way of: ~ *one's enemies* (*a blow*). **2.** find a way of not doing sth.: ~ *paying one's debts.* **eva·sion** [ɪ'veɪʒn] *n.* evading; statement, excuse, etc. made to ~ sth. **eva·sive** [ɪ'veɪsɪv] *adj.* trying to, intended to, ~: *an evasive answer.*

eval·u·ate [ɪ'væljʊeɪt] *v.t.* find out, decide, the amount or value of.

ev·a·nes·cent [,i:və'nesnt] *adj.* quickly fading; soon going from the memory.

evan·gel·i·cal [,i:væn'dʒelɪkl] *adj.* **1.** of, according to, the teachings of the Gospel. **2.** of the beliefs and teachings of those who maintain that the soul can be saved only by faith in the atoning death of Jesus Christ. **evan·ge·list** [ɪ'vændʒəlɪst] *n.* **1.** writer of one of the four Gospels. **2.** journeying preacher of the Gospel.

evap·o·rate [ɪ'væpəreɪt] *v.t. & i.* **1.** (cause to) change into vapour. **2.** remove water or other liquid from (a substance, e.g. by heating): ~*d milk.* **3.** (fig.) disappear; come to nothing: *hopes that* ~*d.* **evap·o·ra·tion** [ɪ,væpə-'reɪʃn] *n.*

eva·sion, eva·sive, see *evade.*

eve [i:v] *n.* **1.** day or evening before a special day: *New Year's E*~, 31 Dec. **2.** *on the* ~ *of* (*great events*), at the time just before.

even[1] ['i:vn] *n.* (poet.) evening. '~**song** *n.* evening prayer in the Church of England. '~**tide** *n.* (old use) evening.

even[2] ['i:vn] *adj.* **1.** level; smooth. **2.** regular; steady: ~ *breathing*; *at an* ~ *pace.* **3.** having the same quality throughout; uniform: ~ *work* (*writing*). **4.** (of amounts, distances, values) equal. *be* (*get*) ~ *with* (*sb.*), have revenge on. **5.** (of numbers) that can be divided by two with no remainder. (Cf. *odd* (1). *v.t.* ~ (*up*), make ~ or equal. ~**ly** *adv.* in an ~ manner; ~*ly divided.*

even[3] ['i:vn] *adv.* **1.** *It is warm there,* ~ *in winter* (and so you can be sure it will be very warm there in summer). *E*~ *a child can understand the book* (therefore you can be sure it is a simple one). *I* ~ *puzzled* ~ *the experts* (and so it was a very difficult problem). **2.** ~ *if,* ~ *though: I'll go,* ~ *if* (*though*) *you forbid me to.* **3.** still, yet: *You know* ~ *less than I do about it* (suggesting that I now only a little about it). **4.** ~ *so*, in pite of that: *The book is expensive, but* ~ *so you ought to buy it.*

e·ning ['i:nɪŋ] *n.* that part of the day between about 6 p.m. and bedtime.

ent [ɪ'vent] *n.* **1.** happening, usu. an important one: *the chief* ~*s of last year*; *t all* ~*s*, whatever happens; *in that* ~, *f that is the case.* **2.** one of the races, tc. in a sports programme. ~**ful** *adj.* full of important ~s. **e·ven·tu·al** [ɪ'ventʃʊəl] *adj.* likely to happen under certain circumstances; coming at last (as result). **e·ven·tu·al·ly** *adv.* in the end. **e·ven·tu·al·i·ty** [ɪ,ventʃʊ'ælətɪ] *n.* possible event.

·er ['evə*] *adv.* **1.** at any time: *Do* ou ~ *wish you were rich?* **2.** at any time up to the present: *Have you* ~ *seen a ceberg?* **3.** at all times: *He has been unappy* ~ *since he left home. I will love you for* ~ *(and* ~*). E*~ *Yours, Yours* ~ (ending a letter to an intimate friend). (after comparison): *It is raining arder than* ~ *the best thing I* ~ *heard.* ~**green** *n. & adj.* (tree) having green eaves throughout the year; (sth.) always green or fresh. ~**last·ing** *adj.* oing on for ~. *the Everlasting*, God. ~**more** *adv.* for ~.

~**ery** ['evrɪ] *adj.* **1.** all or each one of group, without exception: *I've read* ~ ook *on that shelf. E*~ *boy in the class assed the test. He enjoyed* ~ *minute of is holiday.* **2.** used to indicate regular ntervals of space or time: *Buses run* ~ en minutes (i.e. six per hour). *Plant rees* ~ *twenty yards.* ~ *other line*, each lternate line; ~ *now and then*, occaionally. ~**body**, ~**one** *prons.* ~ erson. ~**day** *adj.* happening or used very day. ~**thing** *pron.* **1.** all things. thing of the greatest importance: *Money is* ~*thing to him.* ~**where** *adv.* n, at, to, ~ place.

ict [ɪ'vɪkt] *v.t.* turn (sb.) out from, ispossess (sb.) of, house or land, by uthority of the law: ~*ed for not paying* ent. **evic·tion** [ɪ'vɪkʃn] *n.*

·i·dence ['evɪdəns] *n.* anything that ives reason for believing sth.; facts, tatements, etc. giving support for or roof of a belief: *give* ~ *in a lawcourt*; *ear* ~ *of* (i.e. show signs of); *in* ~, cleary or easily seen. *v.t.* prove by ~; be ~ f. **ev·i·dent** *adj.* plain and clear (to he eyes or the mind); obvious. **evi·i·ent·ly** *adv.*

il ['i:vl] *adj.* wicked; sinful. *the E*~ *ne*, Satan. *n.* **1.** (no pl.) wickedness, n. **2.** ~ thing; disaster.

evince [ɪ'vɪns] *v.t.* show that one has (a feeling or quality).

evoke [ɪ'vəʊk] *v.t.* call up, bring out (memories, admiration, feelings).

evo·lu·tion [,i:və'lu:ʃn] *n.* **1.** (no pl.) process of opening out or developing: *the* ~ *of a plant from a seed.* **2.** (no pl.) *Theory of E*~, theory that living things have been developed from earlier, simpler forms and are not each the result of special creation. **3.** movement according to plan (of dancers, soldiers, warships, etc.). ~**ary** [,i:və'lu:ʃnərɪ] *adj.*

evolve [ɪ'vɒlv] *v.t. & i.* (cause to) unfold; develop, be developed, naturally and gradually: ~ *a new theory.*

ewe [ju:] *n.* female sheep.

ew·er ['ju:ə*] *n.* large, wide-mouthed jug for holding water.

ex- [eks] *pref.* **1.** out, out of, from: *extract.* **2.** former(ly): *ex-king*; *ex-president*; *ex-Prime-Minister.*

ex·act[1] [ɪg'zækt] *adj.* correct in every detail; free from error. ~**ly** *adv.* ~**ness, ex·ac·ti·tude** [ɪg'zæktɪtju:d] *ns.* (no pl.) (quality of) being ~.

ex·act[2] [ɪg'zækt] *v.t.* demand and get by force: ~ *payment from a debtor*; insist on: ~ *respect* (*obedience*). ~**ing** *adj.* making great demands; severe: *an* ~*ing master.* **ex·ac·tion** [ɪg'zækʃn] *n.* ~ing (of money, etc.); sth. ~ed, esp. a tax which is considered too high.

ex·ag·ger·ate [ɪg'zædʒəreɪt] *v.t. & i.* stretch (description) beyond the truth; make sth. seem larger, better, worse, etc. than it really is. **ex·ag·ger·a·tion** [ɪg,zædʒə'reɪʃn] *n.*

ex·alt [ɪg'zɔ:lt] *v.t.* **1.** make high(er) in rank, great(er) in power or dignity. **2.** praise highly. ~**ed** *adj.* dignified; of high rank. **ex·al·ta·tion** [,egzɔ:l-'teɪʃn] *n.* (no pl.) (esp.) state of spiritual delight or elation.   [examination.

ex·am [ɪg'zæm] *n.* (colloq., abbr. for)

ex·am·ine [ɪg'zæmɪn] *v.t.* **1.** look at carefully in order to learn about or from. **2.** put questions to in order to test knowledge or to get information. **ex·am·i·na·tion** [ɪg,zæmɪ'neɪʃn] *n.* examining or being ~d; instance of this: *examination-paper* (*questions*) (testing knowledge or ability). **ex·am·in·ee** [ɪg,zæmɪ'ni:] *n.* person who is ~d. **ex·am·in·er** *n.* person who ~s.

ex·am·ple [ɪg'zɑ:mpl] *n.* **1.** fact, thing, etc. that illustrates or represents a general rule: *for* ~, by way of illustration. **2.** specimen showing the quality of others in the same group or of the same kind: *a good* ~ *of his work.* **3.** person's conduct to be copied or imitated:

follow sb.'s ~; *set sb. a good* ~. **4.** warning: *Let this be an* ~ *to you.* make an ~ of *sb.*, punish him as a warning to others.

ex·as·per·ate [ɪgˈzɑːspəreɪt] *v.t.* irritate; make angry; make (ill feeling, anger, etc.) worse. **ex·as·per·a·tion** [ɪgˌzɑːspəˈreɪʃn] *n.* (no pl.).

ex·ca·vate [ˈekskəveɪt] *v.t.* make by digging: ~ *a trench*; uncover by digging: ~ *a buried city*. **ex·ca·va·tor** *n.* person engaged in, machine used for, **ex·ca·va·tion** [ˌekskəˈveɪʃn] *n.*

ex·ceed [ɪkˈsiːd] *v.t.* **1.** be greater than. **2.** go beyond what is necessary or allowed: ~ *the speed limit.* ~**ing·ly** *adv.* extremely.

ex·cel [ɪkˈsel] *v.t. & i.* (-*ll*-) do better than; be very good (*at* sth.).

ex·cel·lent [ˈeksələnt] *adj.* very good; of high quality. ~**ly** *adv.* **ex·cel·lence** *n.* **Your (His) Ex·cel·len·cy** *n.* title used when speaking to, of, an ambassador or governor.

ex·cept [ɪkˈsept] *prep.* **1.** not including; but not: *They were all tired* ~ *John.* **2.** *That was a good essay,* ~ *for* (apart from) *a few spelling mistakes.* **3.** *She knows nothing about him* ~ *that* (apart from the fact that) *he is handsome and well dressed. v.t.* set apart (e.g. not include sth. in a list, statement, etc.). **ex·cep·tion** [ɪkˈsepʃn] *n.* **1.** sth. or sb. ~ed; sth. not following or covered by a general rule. **2.** objection: *take* ~*ion to,* object to; disagree with; protest against. **ex·cep·tion·al** [ɪkˈsepʃənl] *adj.* uncommon; out of the ordinary. **ex·cep·tion·al·ly** *adv.* unusually.

ex·cerpt [ˈeksɜːpt] *n.* passage, extract (2), from a book, speech, etc.

ex·cess [ɪkˈses] *n.* **1.** fact of being, amount by which sth. is, more than sth. else or more than is expected or proper. *in* ~ *of,* more than; *to* ~, to an extreme degree. **2.** (pl.) personal acts which go beyond the limits of good behaviour, morality, or humanity. **3.** (attrib.): ~ *luggage,* weight above what is carried free; ~ *postage,* fee charged when a letter, etc. has been understamped. **ex·ces·sive** [ɪkˈsesɪv] *adj.* too much; too great; extreme.

ex·change [ɪksˈtʃeɪndʒ] *v.t.* give (one thing) and receive (another) for it: ~ *blows,* fight; ~ *words,* quarrel. *n.* **1.** act of exchanging: *an* ~ *of views*; *give English lessons in* ~ *for German lessons.* **2.** giving and receiving of the money of one country for that of another; relation in value between kinds of money used in different countries. **3.** place where merchants or financiers meet for

business: *the Cotton E*~; *the Stock E*. **4.** *employment* ~, *labour* ~ (colloq. hist.), (Gt. Brit.) office where employers and unemployed workme may be brought together. *telephone* central office where lines are con nected.

ex·che·quer [ɪksˈtʃekə*] *n.* **1.** *the E* (Gt. Brit.) government department charge of public money: *Chancellor* the *E*~, minister at the head of th department. **2.** supply of money (pub lic or private).

ex·cise[1] [ˈeksaɪs] *n.* (no pl.) governmen tax on certain goods manufacture sold, or used within a country: *the* (*duty*) *on beer.* (Cf. *customs.*)

ex·cise[2] [ekˈsaɪz] *v.t.* cut out (a part o the body, a passage from a book, etc. **ex·ci·sion** [ekˈsɪʒən] *n.* excising being ~d; sth. ~d.

ex·cite [ɪkˈsaɪt] *v.t.* **1.** stir up the feel ings of; cause (sb.) to feel strongly **2.** set (a feeling) in motion; rouse: envy (affection) in sb.* **3.** cause (a bodi organ) to be active: ~ *the nerves.* **ex cit·able** [ɪkˈsaɪtəbl] *adj.* easily ~ **ex·cit·abil·i·ty** [ɪkˌsaɪtəˈbɪlətɪ] *n.* (n pl.). ~**ment** [ɪkˈsaɪtmənt] *n.* state o being ~d; exciting thing, event, etc.

ex·claim [ɪkˈskleɪm] *v.t. & i.* cry ou say, suddenly and loudly (from pai anger, surprise, etc.). **ex·cla·ma·tio** [ˌekskləˈmeɪʃn] *n.* sudden short cr expressing pain, surprise, etc. *exclama tion mark,* the mark (!). **ex·clam·a·to ry** [ɪkˈsklæmətərɪ] *adj.* containing o consisting of an exclamation.

ex·clude [ɪkˈskluːd] *v.t.* **1.** prevent (sb *from* getting in somewhere): ~ *sb. from membership of a club.* **2.** prevent (th chance of doubt, etc. arising). **ex·clu sion** [ɪkˈskluːʒn] *n.* (no pl.) excludin or being ~d. *to the exclusion of,* so a to ~. **ex·clu·sive** [ɪkˈskluːsɪv] *adj.* **1** (of a person) not willing to mix wit others, esp. those considered to b inferior. **2.** (of a group or society) no readily admitting new members. **3.** (o a shop, things sold in it, etc.) abov the ordinary sort; superior. **4.** reserve to the person(s) concerned: *exclusiv rights* (*privileges*) (i.e. not shared wit others). **5.** *exclusive of,* not including

ex·com·mu·ni·cate [ˌekskəˈmjuːnɪkeɪt *v.t.* exclude (as a punishment) from the privileges of a member of th Christian Church (e.g. Christian buri al, Holy Communion). **ex·com·mu ni·ca·tion** [ˈekskəˌmjuːnɪˈkeɪʃn] *n.*

ex·cre·ment [ˈekskrɪmənt] *n.* solid waste matter discharged from the body

ex·cres·cence [ɪk'skresns] *n.* unnatural (usu. ugly and useless) outgrowth on an animal or vegetable body.

ex·crete [ek'skriːt] *v.t.* (of an animal or plant) discharge from the system (e.g. waste matter, sweat). **ex·cre·tion** [ek'skriːʃn] *n.* excreting; sth. ~d.

ex·cru·ci·a·ting [ɪk'skruːʃɪeɪtɪŋ] *adj.* (of pain) very severe.

ex·cul·pate ['ekskʌlpeɪt] *v.t.* free from blame; say that (sb.) is not guilty of wrongdoing.

ex·cur·sion [ɪk'skɜːʃn] *n.* short journey, esp. one made by a party for pleasure.

ex·cuse [ɪk'skjuːz] *v.t.* 1. give reasons showing, or intended to show, that a person or his action is not to be blamed; overlook (a fault, etc.): ~ *sb.'s rudeness*; ~ *sb. for being late*; ~ *me* (used as an apology). 2. set (sb.) free *from* a duty or punishment. 3. ~ *one-self (from* a duty, etc.), ask (take) leave to be set free from. [ɪk'skjuːs] *n.* reason (true or invented) given to explain or defend one's conduct. **ex·cus·able** [ɪk'skjuːzəbl] *adj.* that may be ~d.

ex·e·crable ['eksɪkrəbl] *adj.* very bad; deserving hate. **ex·e·crate** ['eksɪkreɪt] *v.t.* express or feel hatred for.

ex·e·cute ['eksɪkjuːt] *v.t.* 1. carry out; do: ~ *a plan (sb.'s commands).* 2. give effect to: ~ *a will.* 3. make legally binding: ~ *a legal document* (by having it signed, witnessed, sealed, and delivered). 4. carry out punishment by death on (sb.): ~ *a murderer.* 5. perform (on the stage, at a concert, etc.). **ex·ec·u·tant** [ɪg'zekjutənt] *n.* person who ~s (1) a design, etc., or who performs music, etc. **ex·e·cu·tion** [,eksɪ'kjuːʃn] *n.* 1. carrying out or performance (of a piece of work, design, etc.). 2. skill in performing music. 3. putting to death as a legal penalty. **ex·e·cu·tion·er** *n.* public official who ~s (4) criminals. **ex·ec·u·tive** [ɪg'zekjutɪv] *adj.* 1. having to do with managing or executing (1): *executive duties*; *executive ability.* 2. having authority to carry out laws and decisions: *the executive branch of a government. n.* 1. *the executive*, the executive branch of a government. 2. person who manages a business, etc. **ex·ec·u·tor** [ɪg'zekjutə*] *n.* person who is chosen to carry out the terms of a will. **ex·ec·u·trix** [ɪg'zekjutrɪks] *n.* woman executor.

x·em·pla·ry [ɪg'zemplərɪ] *adj.* serving as an example or warning: ~ *conduct (punishment).*

x·em·pli·fy [ɪg'zemplɪfaɪ] *v.t.* illustrate by example; be or serve as an example.

ex·empt [ɪg'zempt] *vt. & adj.* (set) free *(from* taxes, work, etc.). **ex·emp·tion** [ɪg'zempʃn] *n.*

ex·er·cise ['eksəsaɪz] *n.* 1. use, practice (of mental or physical powers, rights): *the ~ of patience.* 2. training (of mind or body); activity, drill, etc. designed for this purpose: *vocal (gymnastic)* ~s; ~s *in grammar.* 3. (pl.) series of movements for training troops, crews of warships, etc.: *military* ~s. *v.t. & i.* 1. take ~; give ~ to. 2. employ (2): ~ *patience (one's rights).* 3. trouble (the mind): *be* ~d *about one's shortcomings.*

ex·ert [ɪg'zɜːt] *v.t.* 1. put forth; bring into use; use (one's strength, influence, etc. to do sth.). 2. ~ *oneself*, make an effort; use one's powers. **ex·er·tion** [ɪg'zɜːʃn] *n.*

ex·e·unt ['eksɪʌnt] *v.i.* (Latin) (stage direction in plays) 'they go out' (i.e. off the stage). (Cf. *exit.*)

ex·hale [eks'heɪl] *v.t. & i.* breathe out; give off (gas, vapour); be given off (as gas or vapour). **ex·ha·la·tion** [,ekshə-'leɪʃn] *n.* act of exhaling; sth. ~d.

ex·haust [ɪg'zɔːst] *v.t.* 1. use up completely: ~ *one's strength (patience); feel* ~ed, feel tired out. 2. make empty. 3. say, find out, all there is to say about (sth.). *n.* (outlet, in an engine or machine, for) steam, vapour, etc. that has done its work: (attrib.) ~*-pipe.* **ex·haus·tion** [ɪg'zɔːstʃən] *n.* (no pl.) ~ing or being ~ed; total loss of strength. **ex·haus·tive** [ɪg'zɔːstɪv] *adj.* (of writing, discussion) thorough; complete.

ex·hib·it [ɪg'zɪbɪt] *v.t.* 1. show publicly (for sale, in a competition, etc.): ~ *paintings in an art gallery.* 2. give clear evidence of (a quality). *n.* 1. sth. ~ed: *an* ~ *in a museum.* 2. document or object produced in a lawcourt for use as evidence. **ex·hi·bi·tion** [,eksɪ'bɪʃn] *n.* 1. collection of things ~ed publicly (e.g. in a museum). 2. display of goods, etc. for commercial advertisement. 3. act of ~ing (a quality, etc.): *an* ~*ion of bad temper*; *make an* ~*ion of oneself*, behave in public so that one suffers contempt. 4. (Gt. Brit.) money allowance to a student from school or college funds. **ex·hib·i·tor** [ɪg'zɪbɪtə*] *n.* person who ~s (as in an ~*ion* (2)).

ex·hil·a·rate [ɪg'zɪləreɪt] *v.t.* make glad; fill with high spirits. **ex·hil·ara·tion** [ɪg,zɪlə'reɪʃn] *n.*

ex·hort [ɪg'zɔːt] *v.t.* urge, advise, earnestly (to do good, to give up bad ways, etc.). **ex·hor·ta·tion** [,egzɔː'teɪʃn] *n.*

ex·hume [eks'hju:m] *v.t.* take out (a dead body) from the earth (for examination). **ex·hu·ma·tion** [ˌɛkshju:'meɪʃn] *n.*

ex·i·gence ['eksɪdʒəns], **ex·i·gen·cy** ['eksɪdʒənsɪ, ɪg'zɪdʒənsɪ] *ns.* condition of great need.

ex·ile ['eksaɪl] *v.t.* send (sb.) away from his country as a punishment. *n.* (condition of) being ⁓d; person who is ⁓d.

ex·ist [ɪg'zɪst] *v.i.* be; have being; live; continue living. **ex·is·tence** *n.* ⁓ing; everything that ⁓s; way of living: *lead a happy ⁓ence.*

ex·it ['eksɪt] *n.* **1.** passage, etc. for going out; way out. **2.** departure of an actor from the stage. *v.i.* (Latin) (stage direction in plays) 'he (she) goes out' (i.e. off the stage). (Cf. *exeunt*.)

ex·o·dus ['eksədəs] *n.* (no pl.) going out or away of many people.

ex·on·er·ate [ɪg'zɒnəreɪt] *v.t.* free (sb. *from* blame or responsibility); set free *from* obligation.

ex·or·bi·tant [ɪg'zɔːbɪtənt] *adj.* (of a price, charge, or demand) much too high or great.

ex·or·cize ['eksɔːsaɪz] *v.t.* drive out (an evil spirit *from* sb. or *from* a place) by prayers or magic.

ex·ot·ic [ɪg'zɒtɪk] *adj.* (of plants, fashions, words, etc.) introduced from another country; strikingly strange or unusual.

ex·pand [ɪk'spænd] *v.t. & i.* **1.** make or become larger or wider. **2.** unfold or spread out. **3.** (of a person) become good-humoured or genial. **ex·panse** [ɪk'spæns] *n.* wide area: *the broad ⁓ of the sky.* **ex·pan·sion** [ɪk'spænʃn] *n.* (no pl.) ⁓ing or being ⁓ed. **ex·pan·sive** [ɪk'spænsɪv] *adj.* **1.** able to ⁓; covering a large area. **2.** (of a person) ⁓ing (3) in company.

ex·pa·ti·ate [ek'speɪʃɪeɪt] *v.i.* ⁓ (*up*)*on*, write or speak at great length, in detail, about.

ex·pa·tri·ate [eks'pætrɪət] *n. & adj.* (person) living away from his own country.

ex·pect [ɪk'spekt] *v.t.* regard as likely; think that sth. or sb. will come, that sth. will happen; wish for and feel confident that one will receive. **ex·pec·tan·cy** [ɪk'spektənsɪ] *n.* (no pl.) state of ⁓ing. **ex·pec·tant** *adj.* expecting: ⁓*ant mother*, pregnant woman. **ex·pec·ta·tion** [ˌekspek'teɪʃn] *n.* **1.** ⁓ing; probability: ⁓*ation of life* (i.e. years a person is ⁓ed to live). **2.** (pl.) prospects of inheritance.

ex·pe·di·ent [ɪk'spiːdjənt] *n. & adj.* (plan, action, device) likely to be helpful or useful for a purpose.

ex·pe·dite ['ekspɪdaɪt] *v.t.* help the progress of; speed up (business, etc.). **ex·pe·di·tious** [ˌekspɪ'dɪʃəs] *adj.* acting, done, quickly.

ex·pe·di·tion [ˌekspɪ'dɪʃn] *n.* **1.** (men, ships, etc., making a) journey or voyage with a definite purpose: *hunting (exploring) ⁓s.* **2.** warlike enterprise. **3.** (no pl.) promptness.

ex·pel [ɪk'spel] *v.t.* (*-ll-*) send out or away by force: ⁓ *the enemy from a town*; send away (from a place) as a punishment. **ex·pul·sion** [ɪk'spʌlʃn] *n.*

ex·pend [ɪk'spend] *v.t.* spend. **ex·pen·di·ture** [ɪk'spendɪtʃə*] *n.* ⁓ing; money ⁓ed.

ex·pense [ɪk'spens] *n.* **1.** (no pl.) spending (of money, energy, time, etc.): *at the ⁓ of*, at the cost of (so as to cause loss, damage, or discredit to). **2.** (usu. pl.) money used or needed for sth.: *travelling ⁓s.* **ex·pen·sive** *adj.* causing ⁓; high priced.

ex·pe·ri·ence [ɪk'spɪərɪəns] *n.* **1.** (no pl.) process of gaining knowledge or skill by doing and seeing things; knowledge or skill so gained. **2.** event, activity, that has given one ⁓. *v.t.* have ⁓ of; find by ⁓. ⁓**d** *adj.* having ⁓; having knowledge or skill as the result of ⁓.

ex·per·i·ment [ɪk'sperɪmənt] *n.* test or trial carried out carefully in order to study what happens and gain new knowledge. [ɪk'sperɪment] *v.i.* make ⁓s (*on, with*). **ex·per·i·men·tal** [ekˌsperɪ'mentl] *adj.* **ex·per·i·men·tal·ly** *adv.*

ex·pert ['ekspɜːt] *n.* person with special knowledge, skill, or training. *adj.* (also [eks'pɜːt] when pred.) skilful; trained by practice. ⁓**ly** *adv.* ⁓**ness** *n.* (no pl.).

ex·pi·ate ['ekspɪeɪt] *v.t.* make amends, submit to punishment (for wrongdoing). **ex·pi·a·tion** [ˌekspɪ'eɪʃn] *n.* (no pl.).

ex·pire [ɪk'spaɪə*] *v.i. & t.* **1.** (of a period of time) come to an end. **2.** (liter.) die. **3.** breathe out. **ex·pi·ra·tion** [ˌekspɪ'reɪʃn] *n.* **1.** breathing out. **2.** ending (*of* a period of time). **ex·pi·ry** [ɪk'spaɪərɪ] *n.* ending (*of* a period of time).

ex·plain [ɪk'spleɪn] *v.t.* **1.** make clear and understood; show the meaning of. **2.** account for: *Can you ⁓ your absence from work yesterday?* ⁓ *oneself*, make one's meaning clear; give reasons for one's conduct; ⁓ *sth. away*, show why one should not be blamed for a fault mistake, etc. **ex·pla·na·tion** [ˌeksplə-'neɪʃn] *n.* **ex·plan·a·tory** [ɪk'splæn-ətərɪ] *adj.* serving or intended to ~: *explanatory notes.*

ex·plic·it [ɪk'splɪsɪt] *adj.* (of a statement, etc.) clearly and fully expressed. ~·**ly** *adv.*

ex·plode [ɪk'spləʊd] *v.t. & i.* **1.** (cause to) burst with a loud noise. **2.** (of feelings) burst out; (of a person) show violent emotion: *His anger ~d. He ~d with rage.* **3.** show that (an idea, theory, etc.) is false. **ex·plo·sion** [ɪk'spləʊʒn] *n.* **ex·plo·sive** [ɪk'spləʊsɪv] *n. & adj.* (substance) tending to explode or likely to ~.

ex·ploit[1] [ɪk'splɔɪt] *v.t.* **1.** use, work, or develop (mines, waterpower, and other natural resources). **2.** use selfishly or for one's own profit. **ex·ploi·ta·tion** [ˌeksplɔɪ'teɪʃn] *n.* (no pl.).

ex·ploit[2] ['eksplɔɪt] *n.* bold or adventurous act.

ex·plore [ɪk'splɔ:*] *v.t.* **1.** travel into or through (a country, etc.) for the purpose of discovery. **2.** examine thoroughly (problems, etc.) in order to test, learn about. **ex·plor·er** *n.* traveller in unknown lands. **ex·plo·ra·tion** [ˌeksplə'reɪʃn] *n.* **ex·plor·a·to·ry** [ek-'splɔrətərɪ] *adj.*

ex·plo·sion, ex·plo·sive, see *explode.*

ex·po·nent [ek'spəʊnənt] *n.* **1.** person explaining or interpreting (a theory, etc.). **2.** (math.) symbol that indicates what power of a factor (1) is to be taken (e.g. in 4², the figure 2 is the ~).

ex·port [ek'spɔ:t] *v.t.* send (goods) to another country. ['ekspɔ:t] *n.* (business of) ~ing; sth. ~ed. **ex·por·ta·tion** [ˌekspɔ:'teɪʃn] *n.* ~ing of goods; goods ~ed. ~·**er** [ek'spɔ:tə*] *n.* trader who ~s goods.

ex·pose [ɪk'spəʊz] *v.t.* **1.** uncover; leave unprotected; ~ *soldiers to the enemy's fire;* ~*d to the weather.* **2.** display (e.g. goods for sale). **3.** show up (sb. or his wrongdoing). **4.** allow light to reach (camera film, etc.). **ex·po·sure** [ɪk-'spəʊʒə*] *n.* (instance of) exposing or being ~d.

ex·po·si·tion [ˌekspəʊ'zɪʃn] *n.* **1.** expounding or explaining. **2.** exhibition (2).   [make a friendly protest.}

ex·pos·tu·late [ɪk'spɒstjʊleɪt] *v.i.}

ex·po·sure, see *expose.*

ex·pound [ɪk'spaʊnd] *v.t.* explain, make clear, by giving details: ~ *the Scriptures (a theory).*

ex·press [ɪk'spres] *v.t.* **1.** make known, show (by words, looks, actions); ~ *one's feelings (meaning);* ~ *oneself,* say what one means. **2.** send (a letter, goods)

fast by special delivery. *adj.* **1.** clearly said or indicated: *an ~ wish (command).* **2.** going, sent, quickly; designed for high speed: *an ~ train (messenger, letter);* *an ~way,* an urban motorway. *n.* ~ train. *adv.* by special delivery; by ~ train. **ex·pres·sion** [ɪk'spreʃn] *n.* **1.** (no pl.) process of ~ing (one's meaning, feeling, etc.): *give ~ion to one's gratitude.* **2.** word or phrase: *a polite ~ion.* **3.** look (2) on sb.'s face ~ing his feelings. **ex·pres·sive** [ɪk'spresɪv] *adj.* serving to ~ the feelings: *looks that were ~ive of despair.*

ex·pul·sion, see *expel.*

ex·punge [ek'spʌndʒ] *v.t.* wipe or rub out, omit (words, etc. *from*).

ex·pur·gate ['ekspɜ:geɪt] *v.t.* take out (what are considered) improper passages (6): *an ~d edition.*

ex·qui·site ['ekskwɪzɪt] *adj.* **1.** of great excellence; brought to a high state of perfection. **2.** (of pain, pleasure, etc.) keenly felt. **3.** (of power to feel) keen; delicate. ~·**ly** *adv.* ~·**ness** *n.*

ex·ser·vice·man [ˌeks'sɜ:vɪsmən] *n.* (U.S.A. *veteran*) man who formerly served in the armed forces.

ex·tant [ek'stænt] *adj.* still in existence.

ex·tem·po·re [ek'stempɔri] *adv. & adj.* (spoken or done) without preparation or previous thought: *speak ~* (without notes).

ex·tend [ɪk'stend] *v.t. & i.* **1.** make longer (in space or time): ~ *a wall;* ~ *a visit.* **2.** stretch out (one's arms, legs) to full length: ~ *one's hand to sb.* **3.** offer: ~ *an invitation to sb.* **4.** (of space, land, etc.) reach; stretch: *land ~ing for hundreds of miles.* **ex·ten·sion** [ɪk'stenʃn] *n.* **1.** (no pl.) ~ing or being ~ed. **2.** sth. ~ed; sth. added: *an extension to a hotel.* **3.** additional telephone connected to the principal line. **ex·ten·sive** [ɪk'stensɪv] *adj.* far-reaching; ~ing far.

ex·tent [ɪk'stent] *n.* (no pl.) **1.** length; area; range. **2.** degree: *to a certain ~* (i.e. partly).

ex·ten·u·ate [ek'stenjʊeɪt] *v.t.* make (wrongdoing) seem less serious (by finding an excuse). **ex·ten·u·a·tion** [ek,stenjʊ'eɪʃn] *n.*

ex·te·ri·or [ek'stɪərɪə*] *adj.* outer; situated on or coming from the outside. *n.* outside; outward aspect or appearance.

ex·ter·mi·nate [ɪk'stɜ:mɪneɪt] *v.t.* make an end of (disease, ideas, beliefs); destroy completely. **ex·ter·mi·na·tion** [ɪk,stɜ:mɪ'neɪʃn] *n.*

ex·ter·nal [ek'stɜ:nl] *adj.* outside;

situated outside; for use on the outside of the body. ~·ly *adv.*

ex·tinct [ɪk'stɪŋkt] *adj.* **1.** no longer burning; no longer active: *an ~ volcano.* **2.** no longer in existence; having died out: *an ~ species.* **ex·tinc·tion** [ɪk'stɪŋkʃn] *n.* (no pl.).

ex·tin·guish [ɪk'stɪŋgwɪʃ] *v.t.* **1.** put out (a light, fire). **2.** destroy; end the existence of (hope, love, etc.). ~·er *n.* device (2) for ~ing fire, etc.: *a fire ~er.*

ex·tir·pate ['ekstɜːpeɪt] *v.t.* pull up by the roots; destroy.

ex·tol [ɪk'stəʊl] *v.t.* (-ll-) praise highly.

ex·tort [ɪk'stɔːt] *v.t.* obtain (money, promises, etc.) by threats, violence, etc. (*from* sb.). **ex·tor·tion** [ɪk'stɔːʃn] *n.* **ex·tor·tion·ate** [ɪk'stɔːʃnət] *adj.* (of a demand, price) too high.

ex·tra ['ekstrə] *adj.* additional; beyond what is usual, expected, or arranged for. *n.* ~ thing; sth. for which an ~ charge is made.

ex·tract [ɪk'strækt] *v.t.* **1.** take, pull, or get out (usu. with effort); get (money, information, etc. *from* sb. unwilling to give it). **2.** obtain (juices, etc.) by crushing, boiling, etc.: *~ oil from cotton seed.* **3.** select and copy out words, examples, passages, etc. (*from* a book). ['ekstrækt] *n.* **1.** liquid ~ed (2): *beef ~.* **2.** passage ~ed (3) *from* a book, etc. **ex·trac·tion** [ɪk'strækʃn] *n.* (no pl.) **1.** ~ing or being ~ed (1): *the ~ion of a tooth.* **2.** (of persons) descent or origin: *of French ~ion.*

ex·tra·dite ['ekstrədaɪt] *v.t.* give up, hand over (a person) from the territory of one State to that of another where he is (alleged to be) guilty of wrongdoing. **ex·tra·di·tion** [ˌekstrə'dɪʃn] *n.*

ex·tra·mar·i·tal [ˌekstrə'mærɪtl] *adj.* adulterous.

ex·tra·mu·ral [ˌekstrə'mjʊərəl] *adj.* **1.** outside the walls or boundaries (of a town or city). **2.** (of lectures, etc., esp. for non-resident students) from outside a university: *~ studies.* (Cf. *intramural.*)

ex·tra·neous [ek'streɪnjəs] *adj.* not related (*to* the object to which it is attached); not belonging (*to* what is being dealt with).

ex·traor·di·nary [ɪk'strɔːdnrɪ] *adj.* unusual; remarkable.

ex·trav·a·gant [ɪk'strævəgənt] *adj.* **1.** wasteful; (in the habit of) wasting money: *an ~ man; ~ habits.* **2.** (of ideas, speech, behaviour) going beyond what is reasonable; uncontrolled. **ex·trav·a·gance** *n.*

ex·treme [ɪk'striːm] *adj.* **1.** situated at the end(s); farthest from the centre. **2.** reaching the highest degree: ~ *patience* (*danger*); *in ~ pain.* **3.** (of persons, their ideas, etc.) far from moderate: *hold ~ opinions; ~ measures.* *n.* **1.** ~ part or degree. **2.** (pl.) qualities, etc. that are as wide apart as possible: *the ~s of heat and cold; go to ~s, take ~ measures.* **ex·trem·ist** *n.* person with ~ (3) views. **ex·trem·i·ty** [ɪk'stremətɪ] *n.* **1.** ~ point, end, or limit; (pl.) hands and feet. **2.** ~ degree (of joy, misery, esp. of misfortune): *help friends in extremity.* **3.** (pl.) ~ measures (e.g. for punishing wrongdoers).

ex·tri·cate ['ekstrɪkeɪt] *v.t.* ~ *from*, set free, get (sb., oneself) free, from (difficulties, etc.).

ex·trin·sic [ek'strɪnsɪk] *adj.* (of qualities, values, etc.) not a part of the real character; operating from the outside. (Cf. *intrinsic.*)

ex·tro·vert ['ekstrəʊvɜːt] *adj. & n.* ~·ed ['ekstrəʊvɜːtɪd] *adj.* sociable or unreserved (person) (opp. *introvert(ed)*).

ex·u·ber·ant [ɪg'zjuːbərənt] *adj.* **1.** growing luxuriantly. **2.** full of life and vigour; high-spirited. **ex·u·ber·ance** *n.* (no pl.).

ex·ude [ɪg'zjuːd] *v.i. & t.* (of drops of liquid) come or pass out slowly; give off: *Sweat ~s through the pores.*

ex·ult [ɪg'zʌlt] *v.i.* rejoice greatly (*at* or *in* sth., to learn that ...); triumph (*over* sb.). **ex·ul·tant** *adj.* ~ing; triumphant. **ex·ul·ta·tion** [ˌegzʌl'teɪʃn] *n.* (no pl.) great joy (*at*); triumph (*over*).

eye [aɪ] *n.* **1.** organ of sight. *see ~ to ~* (*with* sb.), have the same opinion; *have an* (*a good*) *~ for*, be a good judge of; be able to see quickly; *with an ~ to*, hoping for; *keep an ~ on*, watch carefully; *make ~s at*, look lovingly at. **2.** thing like an eye, esp. the hole in a needle. *v.t.* look at. '~·brow *n.* see *brow* (2). '~·glass·es *n. pl.* spectacles (4). '~·lash *n.* one of the hairs on the edge of the eyelids. ~·let ['aɪlɪt] *n.* (metal ring round a) small hole made in leather, etc. for a shoe-lace, etc. to go through. '~·lid *n.* one of two movable fleshy coverings of the eye. '~·sight *n.* (no pl.) power or faculty of seeing: *have good* (*poor*) *~sight.* '~·sore *n.* ugly thing. ~·'wit·ness *n.* person who can describe an event because he saw it. [*blue-~; one-~.*]

-eyed [-aɪd] *adj.* (in compounds):

ey·rie ['aɪərɪ] *n.* nest of birds of prey, esp. an eagle's nest, or of other bird that build high up.

F

a·ble ['feɪbl] *n.* **1.** short tale, not based
on fact, esp. one with animals in it
e.g. *Aesop's ~s*) and intended to give
moral teaching. **2.** lie; false account.

ab·ric ['fæbrɪk] *n.* **1.** material, esp.
woven material. **2.** framework or
structure. **fab·ri·cate** ['fæbrɪkeɪt] *v.t.*
1. construct; manufacture. **2.** make up
(sth. false); forge (documents). **fab·
ri·ca·tion** *n.* sth. ~ated.

ab·u·lous ['fæbjʊləs] *adj.* **1.** celebrated in fables (1). **2.** incredible: ~
wealth. **3.** (colloq.) marvellous.

a·çade [fə'sɑːd] *n.* front of a building.

ace [feɪs] *n.* **1.** front part of the head
(forehead, eyes, nose, mouth, cheeks,
and chin): ~ *to* ~ *with,* confronting;
make (pull) a ~ (at), pull the ~ out of
shape (e.g. as a sign of disgust); *set
one's ~ against,* oppose; *save (lose)
one's ~,* escape (suffer) loss of honour
or reputation; *put a good ~ on (sth.),*
make it seem less bad than it is; ~ *it
boldly; keep a straight ~,* hide one's
amusement. **2.** surface of one side, esp.
the front, of a many-sided object: *the ~
of a clock;* ~ *value,* value marked on a
coin, banknote, etc.; (fig.) apparent
value: *take sth. at ~ value.* **3.** outward
appearance of a situation: *on the ~ of
it,* from its appearance; from what it
appears to be. *v.t. & i.* **1.** have or turn
the ~ to or in a certain direction; be
opposite to. **2.** meet confidently or
defiantly: ~ *dangers;* ~ *the music,* show
no fear at a time of danger or trial; ~
it out, refuse to give way; ~ *the facts,*
recognize their existence. **3.** cover
with a layer of different material: *a
wall ~d with concrete; a coat ~d with
silk* (lined near the edges with silk).
fa·cial ['feɪʃl] *adj.* of or for the ~.

ac·et ['fæsɪt] *n.* one of the many sides
of a cut stone or jewel.

a·ce·tious [fə'siːʃəs] *adj.* (intended to
be) humorous; fun-making.

ac·ile ['fæsaɪl] *adj.* **1.** easily done or
obtained. **2.** (of a person) able to do
things easily; (of speech, writing) done
easily but without enough attention to
quality. **fa·cil·i·tate** [fə'sɪlɪteɪt] *v.t.*

make easy; lessen the difficulty of. **fa·
cil·i·ty** [fə'sɪlətɪ] *n.* **1.** (no pl.) quality
that makes learning and doing things
easy or simple. **2.** (pl.) things, circumstances, that facilitate (work, travel,
etc.).

fac·sim·i·le [fæk'sɪmɪlɪ] *n.* exact copy
(of writing, etc.).

fact [fækt] *n.* sth. that has happened or
been done; sth. known to be true or
accepted as true: *in (point of) ~,* the
truth is that ...; really; *as a matter of ~,*
really.

fac·tion ['fækʃn] *n.* **1.** discontented,
usu. selfish and troublesome group of
persons within a party (esp. political).
2. quarrelling of ~s. **fac·tious** ['fækʃəs]
adj.

fac·tor ['fæktə*] *n.* **1.** whole number
(except 1) by which a larger number
can be divided exactly: *The ~s of 12
are 2, 3, 4, 6.* **2.** fact, circumstance, etc.
helping to bring about a result.

fac·to·ry ['fæktərɪ] *n.* building(s) where
goods are made, esp. by machinery.

fac·tu·al ['fæktʃʊəl] *adj.* concerned
with fact.

fac·ul·ty ['fækltɪ] *n.* **1.** power of mind;
power of doing things. **2.** sense (e.g.
hearing, sight). **3.** branch of learning,
esp. as studied in a university: *the F~
of Law;* all the teachers in one of these;
(U.S.A.) the whole teaching staff of a
university or college.

fad [fæd] *n.* fanciful fashion, interest,
preference, enthusiasm, unlikely to
last. **~·dish** *adj.* having ~s; having odd
likes and dislikes (e.g. about food).

fade [feɪd] *v.t. & i.* **1.** (cause to) lose
colour or freshness. **2.** go slowly out of
view, hearing, or the memory, etc.

fag [fæg] *v.i. & t.* (-*gg*-) do very tiring
work; (of work) make very tired. *n.*
(no pl.) (Gt. Brit.) hard work.

fag·got (U.S.A. also **fag·ot**) ['fægət] *n.*
bundle of sticks for burning as fuel.

Fahr·en·heit ['færənhaɪt] *n.* name of a
thermometer scale with freezing-point
at 32° and boiling-point at 212°. (Cf.
centigrade.)

fail [feɪl] *v.i. & t.* **1.** be unsuccessful

(in doing sth. one tries to do): ~ *to pass an examination*; ~ *in an attempt*. **2.** (of examiners) decide that (a candidate) has ~ed. **3.** be too little or insufficient; come to an end while still needed: *crops (water-supplies) that ~ed because of the hot summer*. **4.** (of health, eyesight, etc.) become weak. **5.** neglect (to do sth.). **6.** become bankrupt. **n.** (only in) *without* ~, certainly. **~·ing** *n.* weakness or fault (of character). **~·ure** ['feɪljə*] *n.* **1.** (instance of) ~ing; person, thing, or attempt that ~s: *~ure in an examination*; *be a ~ure as a teacher*; *heart ~ure*. **2.** bankruptcy.

faint [feɪnt] **adj. 1.** weak; indistinct; not clear. **2.** *feel (look)* ~ (as if about to lose consciousness). **3.** (fig.) weak; vague; timid. **v.i.** become unconscious (because of loss of blood, the heat, etc.). **n.** act, state, of ~ing (2). **~·ly** *adv.* **,~-'heart·ed** *adj.* having little courage.

fair¹ [feə*] **adj. 1.** just; acting in a just and honourable manner; in accordance with justice or the rules (of a game, etc.): *a ~ share*; *~ play*; *~-minded*, just. **2.** average; quite good: *a ~ chance of success*. **3.** (of the weather) good; dry and fine; (of winds) favourable. **4.** (of the skin, hair) pale; light in colour: *~-haired*; *a ~ complexion*. **5.** (old use) beautiful: *the ~ sex*, women. **6.** *~ copy*, clear and clean copy of a draft (1); *~ name*, good reputation. **adv.** in a ~ (1) manner: *play ~*. **~·ly** *adv.* **1.** justly. **2.** moderately: *speak English ~ly well*. **~·ness** *n.* (no pl.).

fair² [feə*] **n. 1.** market (esp. for farm products, cattle, etc.), often with entertainments, held regularly in a particular place. **2.** large-scale exhibition (2): *a book (world) ~*.

fairy ['feərɪ] **n.** small imaginary being with magic powers, able to help people. **'~-tale** *n.* **1.** tale about fairies. **2.** untrue story.

faith [feɪθ] **n. 1.** trust; strong belief; unquestioning confidence: *have (put one's) ~ in God*. **2.** system of religious belief: *the Christian ~*; belief in religious doctrines. **3.** promise: *keep (break) ~ (with sb.)*. **4.** *in good (bad) ~*, with (without) sincerity. **~·ful** *adj.* **1.** keeping ~; loyal and true (*to* sb., *to* a cause). **2.** true to the facts; exact: *a ~ful copy (description)*. **~·ful·ly** *adv.* in a ~ful manner. *yours ~fully* (used before the signature at the end of a business or formal letter). **~·less** *adj.* false; disloyal.

fake [feɪk] **v.t. & n.** (make up a) story,

work of art, etc. that looks genuine b‿ is not.

fal·con ['fɔːlkən] **n.** small bird of pr‿ trained to hunt and kill other bir‿ and small animals.

fall [fɔːl] **v.i.** (p.t. **fell** [fel], p.p. ~ ['fɔːlən]) **1.** come or go downwards ‿ to the ground by force of weight, lo‿ of balance or support, etc.: *~ flat ‿ one's face*. **2.** (of a fort, town, etc.) b‿ captured in war. **3.** give way to tempt‿ tion. **4.** drop down, wounded or kille‿ *~ in battle*. **5.** become; occur: *Chris‿ mas Day ~s on a Saturday this year. ‿ in love (with)*, become filled with lo‿ (for); *~ asleep*, begin to sleep; *~ sho‿ (of)*, be not enough; be unequal ‿ (what is wanted). **6.** (with advs. an‿ preps.): *~ back*, move or turn back; ‿ *back on*, make use of (when sth. els‿ has failed); turn to for support; *~ b‿ hind*, fail to keep level with; *~ in*, (‿ of a building, etc.) collapse; (b) (mil‿ take place(s) in the ranks; *~ in wit‿ agree to (sb.'s plans, etc.)*; *~ off*, (esp‿ become fewer or smaller; *~ on* (th‿ enemy), attack; *~ out*, quarrel (*with*). ‿ *fell out that*, it happened that. *~ through*, come to nothing; *~ to*, beg‿ to eat, fight, etc.; **n. 1.** act of ~ing: *a ~ from a chair*; *a ~ in prices*; *a ~ in th‿ temperature*. **2.** (U.S.A.) = autumn‿ **3.** (often pl.) place where a river ~ suddenly to a lower level: *the Niagar‿ F~s*. **4.** amount (of rain, snow) that ~s‿ extent to which sth. (a river, tempera‿ ture) ~s.

fal·la·cy ['fæləsɪ] **n.** mistaken belief‿ false reasoning or argument. **fal·la‿ cious** [fə'leɪʃəs] **adj.**

fal·li·ble ['fæləbl] **adj.** liable to error‿ **fal·li·bil·i·ty** [,fælə'bɪlətɪ] **n.** (no pl.).

fall-out ['fɔːlaʊt] **n.** (no pl.) radioactiv‿ dust in the atmosphere from a nuclea‿ explosion.

fal·low ['fæləʊ] **n.** (no pl.) **& adj‿** (land) ploughed but not sown o‿ planted.

false [fɔːls] **adj.** not true or genuine: ~‿ *ideas (alarms, teeth)*. **adv.** *play sb. ~*, b‿ ~ to him, betray him. **~·ly** *adv.* **~‿ hood** *n.* untrue statement; lie; telling‿ lies. **fal·si·fy** ['fɔːlsɪfaɪ] **v.t. 1.** make‿ (records, etc.) ~; tell (a story, etc.) ~ly‿ **2.** disappoint (fears, hopes, etc.). **fal‿ si·fi·ca·tion** [,fɔːlsɪfɪ'keɪʃn] **n.**

fal·set·to [fɔːl'setəʊ] **n.** (pl. ~s) mal‿ voice forced to an unnaturally hig‿ pitch.

fal·ter ['fɔːltə*] **v.i. & t.** move, walk‿ act, speak, in an uncertain or hesitating‿ manner.

ame [feɪm] **n.** (no pl.) (condition of) being known or talked about by all; what people say about sb. (esp. good). **∼d** [feɪmd] **adj.** famous: ∼d for their courage.

a·mil·iar [fə'mɪljə*] **adj. 1.** ∼ with, having a good knowledge of. **2.** ∼ to, well known to. **3.** common; often seen, heard, etc.: ∼ scenes (voices). **4.** close; intimate: ∼ friends; too ∼ with a stranger. **5.** sexually intimate (with). **fa·mil·iar·i·ty** [fə,mɪlɪ'ærətɪ] **n. 1.** (no pl.) being ∼. **2.** (pl.) (instance of) ∼ behaviour. **fa·mil·iar·ize** [fə'mɪljəraɪz] **v.t.** make (oneself, sb.) well acquainted (with); make (sth.) well known.

am·i·ly ['fæməlɪ] **n. 1.** parents and children. **2.** all descendants of a man and wife. **3.** all persons related by blood. **4.** group of living things (plants, animals, etc.) or of languages, with common characteristics and having a common source. **5.** (attrib.) ∼ name, surname. ∼ planning, regulation or limitation of the size of a ∼ by birth control.

am·ine ['fæmɪn] **n.** extreme scarcity (esp. of food) in a region.

am·ish ['fæmɪʃ] **v.i.** be ∼ed, be suffering from extreme hunger.

a·mous ['feɪməs] **adj.** known widely; having fame.

an¹ [fæn] **n.** object (waved in the hand or operated by electricity) for making a current of air. **v.t. & i.** (-nn-) send a current of air on to: ∼ oneself (a fire); (of a breeze) blow gently on; spread out in ∼ shape.

a fan¹

an² [fæn] **n.** fanatical supporter or admirer: film ∼s.

a·nat·ic [fə'nætɪk] **n. & adj.** (person) having a too passionate enthusiasm for sth., esp. religion. **fa·nat·i·cal adj.** = ∼. **fa·nat·i·cism** [fə'nætɪsɪzəm] **n.** (instance of) violent, unreasonable enthusiasm.

an·cy ['fænsɪ] **n. 1.** (power of creating a) mental picture; sth. imagined. **2.** idea, belief, without foundation. **3.**

fondness; liking; desire (for): take a ∼ to sb., begin to like him. **adj. 1.** (esp. of small things) decorated; brightly coloured; made to please the eye: ∼ cakes (goods). **2.** not plain or ordinary: ∼ dress, dress of a fantastic or unusual kind, as worn at a ∼-dress ball. ∼ price, unusually high price. **v.t. 1.** picture in the mind; imagine. **2.** have a ∼ (3) for (sth.). **3.** have a ∼ (2) (that sth. will happen). **4.** (as an exclamation of surprise): Just ∼! How surprising! **5.** ∼ oneself, have a high opinion of oneself. **fan·ci·ful adj.** full of fancies (2); unreal; curiously designed. '∼-work **n.** (no pl.) ornamental needlework.

fang [fæŋ] **n.** long, sharp tooth, esp. of a dog or wolf; snake's poison-tooth.

fan·tas·tic [fæn'tæstɪk] **adj. 1.** wild and strange: ∼ dreams. **2.** (of ideas, plans) impossible to carry out; absurd. **3.** (colloq.) marvellous. **fan·tas·ti·cal·ly adv.**

fan·ta·sy ['fæntəsɪ] **n. 1.** fancy (1). **2.** sth. highly imaginative and dreamlike.

far [faː*] **adv.** (farther ['faːðə*] or further ['fɜːðə*], farthest ['faːðɪst] or furthest ['fɜːðɪst]) **1.** indicating distance in space or time: Did you walk ∼? They talked ∼ into the night. **2.** in so ∼ as, as ∼ as, to the degree to which: in so ∼ as I am concerned; ∼ and away, very much (better, etc.). **adj.** (farther or further, farthest or furthest) a long way off; distant: the F∼ East. be a ∼ cry, be a long way; more distant: at the ∼ end of the street. ∼-**away adj.** distant; (of a person's look) as if fixed on sth. far away in space or time. ∼-'fetched **adj.** (of a comparison, etc.) forced; unnatural. ∼-off [,faːr'ɒf] **adj.** far-away. ∼-'reach·ing **adj.** having wide effects. ∼-'see·ing **adj.** (fig.) wise; having good judgement of future needs, etc. ∼-'sight·ed **adj. 1.** able to see to a great distance. **2.** (fig.) ∼-seeing.

farce [faːs] **n. 1.** play for the theatre, full of ridiculous situations designed to make people laugh; this style of drama. **2.** series of actual events like a ∼. **far·ci·cal** ['faːsɪkl] **adj.**

fare [feə*] **n. 1.** money charged for a journey (by ship, taxi, etc.). **2.** passenger in a hired vehicle. **3.** (no pl.) food and drink. bill of ∼, menu. **v.i. 1.** get on; progress: How did you ∼? What happened to you? He ∼d well (was successful). **2.** (poet.) travel.

fare·well [,feə'wel] **int.** good-bye. **n.** leave-taking.

farm [fɑːm] *n.* **1.** area of land, with barns, etc. for growing crops, raising animals, etc. **2.** (also ~*house*) farmer's house on a ~. *v.t. & i.* **1.** use (land) for growing crops, raising animals, etc. **2.** ~ *out*, send (work) out to be done by others. ~**er** *n.* man who manages a ~. '~**-hand** *n.* person who works on a farm. '~**-yard** *n.* space enclosed by ~ buildings (sheds, barns, etc.).

far·ther, far·thest, see *far.*

fas·ci·nate ['fæsɪneɪt] *v.t.* **1.** charm or attract greatly. **2.** take away the power of movement by a fixed look, as a snake does. **fas·ci·nat·ing** *adj.* very interesting or charming; captivating. **fas·ci·na·tion** [ˌfæsɪ'neɪʃn] *n.* fascinating or being ~d; power to ~; thing that ~s.

fash·ion ['fæʃn] *n.* **1.** (of clothes, behaviour, thought, speech, etc.) that which is considered best and most to be admired and imitated during a period or at a place: *the Paris* ~s; *changes of* ~; *styles which are in (out of)* ~; *be all the* ~, (esp. of dress and behaviour) be very popular; *set the* ~, give the example by adopting new ~s. ~ *designer*, person who designs dresses. **2.** manner of doing or making sth.: *behave in a strange* ~; *in some* ~, *after a* ~, somehow or other, but not well. *v.t.* form or shape: ~ *a canoe from a tree-trunk.* ~**able** *adj.* following the ~ (1); used by, visited by, many people, esp. of the upper classes: *a* ~*able tailor (hotel).* ~**ably** *adv.*

fast¹ [fɑːst] *adj.* **1.** firmly fixed: *be* ~ *in the ground.* **2.** (of friends) close; loyal. **3.** (of colours) unfading. *adv.* strongly; firmly; *hold* ~ (*to sth.*); ~ *asleep*, in a deep sleep; *play* ~ *and loose with*, repeatedly change one's attitude towards.

fast² [fɑːst] *adj.* **1.** quick; rapid: *a* ~ *train.* **2.** (of a person, his way of living) immodest; intent on worldly pleasures: *a* ~ *life (woman).* **3.** *This clock is ten minutes* ~ (at 2 o'clock, for example, the hands point to 2.10). *adv.* quickly: *speak* ~; *raining* ~ (i.e. heavily).

fast³ [fɑːst] *v.i.* go without (certain kinds of) food, esp. as a religious duty. *n.* act of, period of, ~ing.

fas·ten ['fɑːsn] *v.t. & i.* **1.** make fast; fix firmly; tie or join together: ~ *doors and windows (two things together).* **2.** become ~ed: *Most jackets* ~ *with buttons.* **3.** ~ *upon*, take hold of ~. ~**er,** ~**ing** *ns.* sth. that ~s things together.

fas·tid·i·ous [fə'stɪdɪəs] *adj.* not easily pleased; particular (3).

fat [fæt] *n.* **1.** oily substance in animal bodies; this substance purified for cooking purposes. **2.** oily substance obtained from certain seeds: *vegetable cooking* ~s; *live on the* ~ *of the land*, have the best of everything to eat. *adj.* (-*tt*-) **1.** covered with, having, much fat (1): ~ *men (meat).* **2.** thick; well filled: *a* ~ *pocket-book.* **3.** profitable, fertile: *a* ~ *job;* ~ *lands. v.t. & i.* (-*tt*-) fatten: ~*ted cattle.* '~**-head** *n.* stupid person.

fa·tal ['feɪtl] *adj.* causing, ending in death or disaster (*to*): *a* ~ *accident.* ~**ly** *adv.* ~*ly wounded.* ~**ism** ['feɪtəlɪzəm] *n.* (no pl.) belief that events are determined by fate (1). ~**ist** *n.* person who has this belief. ~**is·tic** [ˌfeɪtə'lɪstɪk] *adj.* of ~ism. ~**i·ty** [fə'tælətɪ] *n.* (instance of) death in an accident, in war etc.: *bathing* ~*ities.*

fate [feɪt] *n.* **1.** (no pl.) power looked upon as controlling all events. **2.** future fixed by ~ for sb. or sth. **3.** (no pl.) death; ruin; destruction: *meet (go to) one's* ~. **fat·ed** ['feɪtɪd] *adj.* fixed by ~. ~**ful** *adj.* deciding the future.

fa·ther ['fɑːðə*] *n.* **1.** male parent. **2.** founder or first leader: *the F.s of the Church.* **3.** priest, esp. in the Roman Catholic Church. *v.t.* **1.** be the originator of (an idea, plan, etc.). **2.** ~ *sth on sb.*, cause him to seem responsible for. ~**hood** *n.* (no pl.) state of being a ~. ~**-in-law** ['fɑːðərɪnlɔː] *n.* (pl. ~s *in-law*) ~ of one's wife or husband. ~**ly** *adj.* of or like a ~.

fath·om ['fæðəm] *n.* (pl. ~s or often ~ when used with numbers) measure (= six feet) of depth of water. *v.t.* **1.** measure (the depth of water) with a sounding-line. **2.** (fig.) understand; get to the bottom of. ~**less** *adj.* too deep to ~.

fa·tigue [fə'tiːg] *n.* **1.** (no pl.) condition of being very tired. **2.** tiring task; (mil.) non-military task such as cleaning cooking, etc. ~s, garments worn for this task. *v.t.* cause ~ (1) to.

fat·ten ['fætn] *v.t. & i.* make or become fat: ~ *cattle.*

fat·u·ous ['fætjʊəs] *adj.* foolish; showing foolish self-satisfaction.

fau·cet ['fɔːsɪt] *n.* (U.S.A.) = tap¹.

fault [fɔːlt] *n.* **1.** sth. making a thing or person imperfect; defect: *find* ~ *with*, point out ~s in; complain about; *at* ~, in the wrong; at a loss; *to a* ~, excessively. **2.** responsibility for being wrong: *It's your own* ~ *if you've hurt yourself.* **3.** offence; mistake; (in a racket game) ball wrongly served. **4.**

place where a layer of rock, etc. is broken. ~·less *adj.* without ~. ~·less·ly *adv.* ~y *adj.* (-*ier,* -*iest*) imperfect. ~·i·ly *adv.*

faun [fɔ:n] *n.* (ancient Rome) god of the woods and fields, with goat's horns and legs.

fau·na ['fɔ:nə] *n.* all the animals of an area or epoch: *the ~ of E. Africa.*

fa·vour (U.S.A. **fa·vor**) ['feɪvə*] *n.* **1.** friendly regard; willingness to help; aid; support: *in ~ of,* (a) in sympathy with; willing to help; (b) on behalf of; *in sb.'s ~,* to the advantage of; *out of ~ (with),* not popular or liked. **2.** sth. done from kindness: *do sb. a ~, do a ~ for sb.,* do sth. to help sb.; *ask a ~ of sb.* (i.e. ask him for help). **3.** partiality; too generous treatment. *v.t.* **1.** show ~ to; support; approve. **2.** show more ~ to (one person) than to others; treat with partiality: *He should not ~ one of his pupils.* **3.** be like (sb.) in appearance. ~·able ['feɪvərəbl] *adj.* giving or showing approval; helpful. ~·ably *adv.* ~·ite ['feɪvərɪt] *n. & adj.* (person or thing) specially ~ed. ~·it·ism *n.* (no pl.) practice of ~ing (2).

fawn[1] [fɔ:n] *n.* **1.** young deer. **2.** (no pl.) light yellowish brown.

fawn[2] [fɔ:n] *v.i.* **1.** (of dogs) show pleasure and affection by jumping up, tail-wagging, etc. (*on* sb.). **2.** (fig.) try to win sb.'s favour by flattery: *~ on a rich relative.*

fear [fɪə*] *n.* **1.** being afraid; uncomfortable feeling caused by danger, evil, threats; alarm: *for ~ of, for ~ that (lest),* to avoid the risk of. **2.** risk; likelihood. **3.** reverence and dread; awe: *the ~ of God. v.i. & t.* have ~; feel ~ of; be anxious. ~·ful *adj.* causing ~; terrible; (colloq.) annoying; very great. ~·ful·ly *adv.* ~·less *adj.* without ~.

fea·si·ble ['fi:zəbl] *adj.* that can be done. **fea·si·bil·i·ty** [,fi:zə'bɪlətɪ] *n.* (no pl.).

feast [fi:st] *n.* **1.** day kept (2) in memory of an important event. **2.** meal (esp. a public one) with many good things to eat and drink. *v.t. & i.* give a ~ to; take part in a ~.

feat [fi:t] *n.* difficult action done well, esp. sth. showing daring, skill, or strength.

feath·er ['feðə*] *n.* one of the light coverings that grow on a bird's body. *birds of a ~,* people of the same sort; *show the white ~,* show fear; *in high ~,* in high spirits. *~ bed,* mattress stuffed with ~s. *~weight,* very light thing or person, esp. a boxer. *v.t.* put ~s on (e.g. an arrow). *~ one's nest,* make things comfortable for oneself.

feathers

fea·ture ['fi:tʃə*] *n.* **1.** one of the named parts of the face; (pl.) the face as a whole. **2.** characteristic or striking part: *geographical ~s of a district* (e.g. mountains, lakes); *unusual ~s* (points) *in a speech.* **3.** prominent article or subject in a newspaper or magazine. **4.** (also ~ *film*) principal film in a cinema programme. *v.t. & i.* be a ~ (2) of; make (sb. or sth.) a ~ (2) of; have a prominent part for (e.g. an actor in a film); play a significant part (*in*). ~·less *adj.* without ~s (2).

Feb·ru·ary ['februərɪ] *n.* second month of the year.

fed, see *feed* (v.). *be ~ up (with),* (sl.) have had too much of; be bored (*with*); be discontented (*with*).

fed·er·al ['fedərəl] *adj.* of, based upon, federation. ~·ism ['fedərəlɪzəm] *n.* (no pl.) principle of, belief in, ~ government. **fed·er·ate** ['fedəreɪt] *v.t. & i.* (of states, societies) organize, combine, as a ~ group. **fed·er·a·tion** [,fedə'reɪʃn] *n.* **1.** political system (5) in the U.S.A.) in which States govern themselves but leave foreign affairs, defence, etc. to the central (federal) government. **2.** such a union of States; similar union of societies, trade unions, etc. **3.** act of federating.

fee [fi:] *n.* **1.** charge or payment for professional advice or services (e.g. instruction at schools, examiners, doctors, lawyers, surveyors). **2.** entrance money for an examination, a society (5), etc. **3.** money paid for the transfer of a footballer, etc.

fee·ble ['fi:bl] *adj.* (~r, ~st) weak. **fee·bly** *adv.*

feed [fi:d] *v.t. & i.* (p.t. & p.p. *fed* [fed]) **1.** give food to; supply (one's family, etc.) with food: *~ing-bottle* (for hand-fed infants). (See also *fed.*) **2.** (chiefly of animals or colloq.) eat: *cows ~ing in the meadows*; *~ on,* take as food; consume: *Cows ~ on grass.* **3.** supply (a machine) with material; supply (material) (*in*)*to* (a machine). *n*. **1.** food for animals. **2.** (of animals and babies or colloq.) meal. **3.** ⁀ing of a machine; material supplied. ⁀·**er** *n*. **1.** (of animals, plants, persons) one that ⁀s: *a good ⁀er*. **2.** child's ⁀ing-bottle; (Gt. Brit.) bib. **3.** ⁀ing apparatus (1) in a machine. **4.** (often attrib.) branch (2) transportation line¹ (7, 8) (e.g. a road, railway line, airline, canal, etc.) that links outlying areas with the main communications (3) system.

feel [fiːl] *v.t. & i.* (p.t. & p.p. *felt* [felt]) **1.** touch with the hand; be aware of by touching; learn about by touching: ⁀ *one's way*, (a) find it by groping; (b) (fig.) proceed carefully. **2.** search (*about*) with the hand(s), etc. (*after*, *for*). **3.** be aware through the senses; know that one is (cold, hungry, happy, etc.). ⁀ *like* (*doing sth.*), have a wish to do sth.); ⁀ *equal to*, ⁀ *up to*, be ready to face (sth.). **4.** seem, appear (smooth, rough, etc.) to the senses: *A baby's hand ⁀s smooth. Her skin ⁀s like silk.* **5.** have a vague idea (*that*). **6.** be moved by; be sensitive to: ⁀ *sorrow for sb.*; ⁀ *the heat* (i.e. suffer from it). *n*. (no pl.) *by the* ⁀, by ⁀ing. ⁀·**er** *n*. **1.** organ of touch in some insects. **2.** suggestion put forward to discover what others think. ⁀·**ing** *n*. **1.** power to ⁀; awareness: *a ⁀ing of discomfort*. **2.** sth. felt in the mind: ⁀*ings of joy*. **3.** (pl.) non-intellectual part of the character: *rouse the ⁀ings* (i.e. make excited, angry, etc.); *hurt sb.'s ⁀ings* (i.e. offend him). **4.** sympathy; understanding. **5.** ⁀*ing for* (art, beauty, etc.), appreciation, awareness, of. *adj*. having, showing, ⁀ing (2) or sympathy.

feet, see *foot*.

feign [feɪn] *v.t.* pretend.

fe·lic·i·tate [fəˈlɪsɪteɪt] *v.t.* congratulate (on).

fe·lic·i·tous [fəˈlɪsɪtəs] *adj*. (of words, remarks) well chosen.

fe·lic·i·ty [fəˈlɪsətɪ] *n*. (no pl.) great happiness or contentment.

fe·line [ˈfiːlaɪn] *adj*. of or like a cat.

fell¹, see *fall* (v.).

fell² [fel] *v.t.* cause to fall; knock (sb.) down; cut (a tree) down.

fel·low [ˈfeləʊ] *n*. **1.** (colloq.) man; boy. **2.** (pl.) companions; those sharing experiences: ⁀s *in misfortune*. **3.** (attrib.) of the same class, kind, etc.: ⁀*citizens*; ⁀*passengers*; ⁀*countryman* (from the same country or nation). **4.** member of a learned society (*F⁀ of the British Academy*) or of the governing body (5) of some university colleges. ⁀·ˈ**feel-**

ing *n*. sympathy; feeling that is shared. ⁀·**ship** *n*. **1.** (no pl.) friendly association; companionship. **2.** (membership of a) group or society. **3.** position of a college ⁀.

fel·on [ˈfelən] *n*. person who has committed a serious crime. **fel·o·ny** *n*. serious crime (e.g. murder).

felt¹, see *feel* (v.).

felt² [felt] *n*. (no pl.) wool, hair, etc. pressed and rolled flat: ⁀ *hats* (*slippers*); ⁀(-*tipped*) *pen*, pen with the point (1) made of ⁀.

fe·male [ˈfiːmeɪl] *adj*. **1.** of the sex able to produce offspring or lay eggs; (of plants) producing fruit. **2.** of women. *n*. ⁀ animal or person.

fem·i·nine [ˈfemɪnɪn] *adj*. **1.** of, like, suitable for, women: ⁀ *hobbies* (e.g. needlework). **2.** of female gender: '*Actress*' *is a* ⁀ *noun*. (Cf. *masculine*.)

fem·i·nism [ˈfemɪnɪzəm] *n*. (no pl.) movement for giving women the same rights as men. **fem·i·nist** [ˈfemɪnɪst] *n*. person who advocates feminism.

fen [fen] *n*. area of low, wet land.

fence¹ [fens] *v.t. & n*. (surround, divide, with a) barrier made of wooden stakes, wire, etc. **fenc·ing¹** *n*. (no pl.) material for ⁀s.

a fence¹

fence² [fens] *v.i.* **1.** (sport) practise the art of fighting with swords. **2.** (fig.) avoid giving a direct answer to (a question). **fenc·er** *n*. (sport) person who ⁀s (1). **fenc·ing²** *n*. (no pl.) (sport) art of fighting with swords.

fence³ [fens] *n*. receiver (1) of stolen goods.

fend [fend] *v.t. & i.* **1.** ⁀ *off* (*a blow*), defend oneself from. **2.** ⁀ *for* (*oneself*, *young ones*), provide (food, etc.) for; care for.

fend·er [ˈfendə*] *n*. **1.** metal frame bordering an open fireplace. **2.** (on the sides of a ship, on machinery, on the front of a tramcar, etc.) part or appliance which lessens shock or damage in a collison. **3.** (U.S.A.) bumper (2) or mudguard of a motor car, etc.

fer·ment [fəˈment] *v.t. & i.* **1.** (cause to) undergo chemical change through the action of organic bodies (esp.

yeast). **2.** (fig.) (cause to) become excited. ['fɜːment] *n.* **1.** substance (e.g. yeast) causing others to ~. **2.** *in a* ~, (fig.) in a state of (e.g. social, political) excitement. **fer·men·ta·tion** [ˌfɜː-menˈteɪʃn] *n.* (no pl.) **1.** ~ing or being ~ed. **2.** (fig.) excitement; agitation.

a fender (1, 2)   fern(s)

fern [fɜːn] *n.* sorts of feathery, green-leaved, flowerless plant.

fe·ro·cious [fəˈrəʊʃəs] *adj.* fierce; cruel; savage. **~·ly** *adv.* **fe·roc·i·ty** [fəˈrɒsətɪ] *n.* fierceness; savage cruelty; ~ act.

fer·ret ['ferɪt] *n.* small animal clever at killing rats and forcing rabbits from their burrows. *v.t. & i.* **1.** hunt (rabbits, etc.) with ~s. **2.** ~ (*sth.* or *sb.*) *out*, discover after a careful search.

fer·ro·con·crete [ˌferəʊˈkɒŋkriːt] *n.* (no pl.) concrete with an iron or steel framework inside it.

fer·rous ['ferəs] *adj.* of, relating to, containing, iron.

fer·ry ['ferɪ] *n.* (place where there is a) boat (called also ~-*boat*) or aircraft that carries people and goods across a river, channel, etc. *v.t. & i.* take, go, across in a ~.

fer·tile ['fɜːtaɪl] *adj.* **1.** (of land, plants, etc.) producing much; (of a person, his mind, etc.) full of ideas, plans, etc. **2.** (opp. *sterile*) able to produce fruit, young; capable of developing: ~ *seeds* (*eggs*). **fer·til·i·ty** [fəˈtɪlətɪ] *n.* (no pl.) being ~. **fer·til·ize** ['fɜːtɪlaɪz] *v.t.* make ~. **fer·til·iza·tion** [ˌfɜːtɪlaɪˈzeɪʃn] *n.* (no pl.). **fer·til·iz·er** ['fɜːtɪlaɪzə*] *n.* substance for making land òr soil ~; artificial manure.

fer·vent ['fɜːvənt] *adj.* **1.** hot; glowing. **2.** (fig.) passionate; feeling deeply: ~ *love*; *a* ~ *lover*. **fer·vour** (U.S.A. **-vor**) ['fɜːvə*] *n.* (no pl.) deep feeling. **fer·vid** ['fɜːvɪd] *adj.* ~ (2).

fes·ter ['festə*] *v.i.* **1.** (of a wound) fill with poisonous matter. **2.** (fig.) cause bitterness; act like poison on the mind.

fes·ti·val ['festəvl] *n.* **1.** (day or season for) merry-making; public celebra-tions. **2.** periodic performance(s) of cultural events or entertainment: *the Salzburg F~.* **fes·tive** ['festɪv] *adj.* of a feast or ~: *festive scenes.* **fes·tiv·i·ty**

[feˈstɪvətɪ] *n.* **1.** (no pl.) ~ (1). **2.** (pl.) joyful events: *wedding festivities.*

fes·toon [feˈstuːn] *n.* chain of flowers, leaves, etc. hanging between two points, as a decoration. *v.t.* make into, decorate with, ~s.

a festoon

fetch [fetʃ] *v.t. & i.* **1.** go for and bring back (sb. or sth.). **2.** cause (a sigh, blood, tears) to come out. **3.** (of goods) bring in; sell for (a price). **4.** deal (a blow): ~ *sb. a box*[2] *on the ears.*

fête [feɪt] *n.* (usu. outdoor) festival.

fet·id ['fetɪd] *adj.* bad-smelling.

fe·tish, fe·tich ['fiːtɪʃ] *n.* object wor-shipped by pagan people because they believe a spirit lives in it; anything to which foolishly excessive respect is paid.

fet·ter ['fetə*] *n.* chain for the ankles of a prisoner or the leg of a horse; (fig., usu. pl.) anything that hinders prog-ress. *v.t.* put in ~s; hinder.

fet·tle ['fetl] *n.* *in fine* (*good*) ~, in good health (spirits).

feud [fjuːd] *n.* bitter quarrel between two persons, families, or groups, over a long period of time.

feu·dal ['fjuːdl] *adj.* of the method of holding land (by giving services to the owner) during the Middle Ages in Europe. **~·ism** ['fjuːdəlɪzəm] *n.* (no pl.) ~ system.

fe·ver ['fiːvə*] *n.* **1.** (no pl.) condition of the body with temperature higher than normal, esp. as a sign of illness. **2.** (no pl.) one of a number of diseases in which there is high ~: *scarlet* ~. **3.** excited state: *in a* ~ *of impatience.* **~·ish** *adj.* of, having, caused by, ~: ~*ish dreams.*

few [fjuː] *adj. & n.* **1.** not many: *F~ people live to be ninety, even ~er live to be 100. Who made the ~est* (smallest number of) *mistakes? no ~er than*, as many as. **2.** *a* ~, a small number (of): *Would you like to have a* ~ *friends to supper?*

fez [fez] *n.* red felt[2] head-dress worn by some Muslim men.

fi·an·cé(e) [fɪˈɑ̃ːŋseɪ] *n.* man (woman) to whom one is engaged to be married.

fi·as·co [fɪˈæskəʊ] *n.* (pl. ~s, U.S.A. -coes) complete failure, breakdown, in sth. attempted.

fi·at [ˈfaɪæt] *n.* order made by a ruler; decree.

fib [fɪb] *n.* untrue statement (esp. about sth. unimportant). *v.i.* (-bb-) tell a ~.

fi·bre (U.S.A. **fi·ber**) [ˈfaɪbə*] *n.* **1.** one of the slender threads of which many animal and vegetable growths are formed (e.g. cotton, wood, nerves). **2.** substance formed of a mass of ~s (e.g. cotton ~) for manufacture into cloth, etc. **fi·brous** [ˈfaɪbrəs] *adj.* made of, like, ~s.

fick·le [ˈfɪkl] *adj.* (of moods, weather, etc.) often changing.

fic·tion [ˈfɪkʃn] *n.* **1.** sth. invented or imagined (contrasted with truth). **2.** (no pl.) (branch of literature concerned with) stories, novels, and romances: *works of ~.* **fic·ti·tious** [fɪkˈtɪʃəs] *adj.* not real; imagined or invented.

fid·dle [ˈfɪdl] *n.* violin; any instrument of the violin family. *fit as a ~,* very well; in good health; *play second ~ to,* take a less important place than. *v.t. & i.* **1.** play (a tune, etc. on) the ~. **2.** play aimlessly (*with* sth. in one's fingers). ~**r** *n.* person who plays the ~. '~**sticks** *int.* nonsense!

a fiddle

fi·del·i·ty [fɪˈdelətɪ] *n.* (no pl.) **1.** loyalty; faithfulness (*to* sb. or sth.). **2.** accuracy; exactness. (Cf. *high ~; hi-fi.*)

fid·get [ˈfɪdʒɪt] *v.t. & i.* (cause sb. to) move the body (or part of it) about restlessly; make (sb.) nervous. *n.* **1.** (pl.) ~ing movements. **2.** person who ~s. ~**y** *adj.*

field [fiːld] *n.* **1.** area of land (usu. enclosed by a fence or hedge) for pasture or growing crops. **2.** (usu. in compounds) land from which minerals, etc. are obtained: *gold-~; coal~; oil~.* **3.** (usu. in compounds) expanse; open space: *ice-~; air~; flying ~; football ~.* **4.** branch of study; range of activity or use: *the ~ of politics (science, medical research); the ~ of a telescope; ~ of vision.* **5.** area in which forces can be felt: *a magnetic ~.* **6.** place, area, where a battle or war is fought; battle~: *take the ~,* begin a war. *~ artillery (gun, etc.)* (light and mobile, for use in battle); *~ hospital,* temporary hospital near a battle~. *v.i. & t.* (stand on the cricket or baseball ~ ready to) catch or stop (the ball). *~ events n. pl.* certain athletic contests (e.g. jumping, javelin-throwing, etc.) contrasted with *track events.* '~-,**glass·es** *n. pl.* long-distance glasses for outdoor use with both eyes. **F~ Mar·shal** *n.* (Gt. Brit.) army officer of highest rank. *~ sports n. pl.* hunting, shooting, and fishing. '~-**work** *n.* (no pl.) outdoor scientific, technical, or social investigation made by surveyors, geologists, etc. '~-,**work·er** *n.*

fiend [fiːnd] *n.* **1.** *The* Devil; demon. **2.** very wicked or cruel person. **3.** person devoted or addicted to sth.: *a fresh-air ~; a dope (drug) ~.* ~**ish** *adj.* savage and cruel.

fierce [fɪəs] *adj.* (~r, ~st) **1.** violent; cruel; angry: *~ dogs (looks, winds).* **2.** (of heat, desire, etc.) intense. ~**ly** *adv.* ~**ness** *n.*

fi·ery [ˈfaɪərɪ] *adj.* flaming; looking like, hot as, fire; (of a person) quickly or easily made angry; passionate.

fife [faɪf] *n.* small musical wind instrument.

fif·teen [ˌfɪfˈtiːn] *n. & adj.* 15. ~**th** [ˌfɪfˈtiːnθ] *n. & adj.* 15th; ¹/₁₅. **fifth** [fɪfθ] *n. & adj.* 5th; ¹/₅. **fif·ty** [ˈfɪftɪ] *n. & adj.* 50. **fif·ti·eth** [ˈfɪftɪɪθ] *n. & adj.* 50th; ¹/₅₀.

fig [fɪg] *n.* (tree having) soft, sweet fruit full of small seeds.

fight [faɪt] *v.t. & i.* (p.t. & p.p. *fought* [fɔːt]) **1.** struggle (with hands, weapons) against (sb. or sth.). **2.** engage in (a battle *against* or *with*): *~ shy of,* keep away from; *~ off,* struggle against; *repel; ~ it out,* settle by ~ing. *n.* struggle; battle. ~**er** *n.* person or thing that ~s, esp. a fast aircraft.

fig·ment [ˈfɪgmənt] *n.* sth. unreal and imagined.

fig·u·ra·tive [ˈfɪgjʊrətɪv] *adj.* (of words) used not in the literal sense but in an imaginative way (as when *fiery* is used of a man who is easily made very angry). ~**ly** *adv.*

fig·ure [ˈfɪgə*] *n.* **1.** sign for a number, esp. 0 to 9. **2.** (pl.) arithmetical calculations: *be good at ~s.* **3.** price: *buy sth. at a low ~.* **4.** human form, esp. the appearance and what it suggests: *a fine ~ of a man; a ~ of distress.* **5.** person, esp. his influence: *Churchill, the greatest ~ of his time.* **6.** person's ~ drawn or painted, cut in stone, etc.; drawing, painting, image, of the body of a bird, animal, etc.; diagram or illustration. **7.** movement, series of movements, in a dance, etc. **8.** ~ *of speech*, word(s) used figuratively. *v.t. & i.* **1.** have a part; appear: ~ *(as sb., in a play; in* history). **2.** ~ *sth. out*, reach a result, esp. by using ~s (1); think about until one understands. **3.** represent (in art); form a mental picture of. **~d** [ˈfɪɡəd] *adj.* marked with designs or patterns. **'~-head** *n.* **1.** carved ~ (6) at the prow of a ship. **2.** person with high position but no power. ~ **skat·ing** *n.* (no pl.) skating in which the skater executes (1, 5) prescribed ~s (7).

fil·a·ment [ˈfɪləmənt] *n.* slender thread, esp. a conducting wire in an electric lamp bulb.   [value).\

filch [fɪltʃ] *v.t.* steal (things of small/ **file**[1] [faɪl] *n.* holder, folder, case, etc. for keeping papers, etc. together and in order; (set of) letters, documents, newspapers, etc. kept together on or in a ~. *v.t.* put on or in a ~.

file[2] [faɪl] *n.* metal tool with a rough face for cutting or smoothing hard surfaces. *v.t.* use a ~ on. **fil·ings** *n. pl.* bits ~d off.

file[3] [faɪl] *n. in (single) ~, (of persons)* in one line, one behind the other. *v.i.* ~ *in (out)*, go in (out) in ~(s).

fil·ial [ˈfɪljəl] *adj.* of a son or daughter: ~ *duty.*

fil·i·gree [ˈfɪlɪɡriː] *n.* ornamental lacelike work of gold or silver wire.

fill [fɪl] *v.t. & i.* **1.** make or become full; occupy all the space in. **2.** ~ *in,* (esp.) write what is needed to complete (a form, etc.); ~ *out,* (a) make or become larger, rounder, or fatter; (b) (U.S.A.) ~ *in;* ~ *up,* make or become full: ~ *up the tank of a motor car.* **3.** execute (an order for goods, a prescription). *n. eat (drink, have) one's ~* (as much as one wants or can take). **~·ing** *n.* sth. put in to ~ (a hole in) sth. **~·ing sta·tion** *n.* place where petrol, etc. is sold to motorists.

fil·let [ˈfɪlɪt] *n.* **1.** band worn to keep the hair in place. **2.** slice of fish or meat without bones. *v.t.* cut (fish, meat) into ~s.

fil·ly [ˈfɪlɪ] *n.* young female horse (up to 4 years). (Cf. *colt.*)

film [fɪlm] *n.* **1.** thin coating or covering: *a ~ of dust (mist).* **2.** roll or sheet of thin flexible material prepared for use in photography. **3.** cinema picture: *travel ~s; ~ actors; ~ star. v.t. & i.* **1.** cover, become covered, with a ~ (1). **2.** make a ~ (3) of. **'~-strip** *n.* strip of ~ with a number of photographs, diagrams, etc. to be projected (2) as a teaching aid. **~y** *adj.* (-*ier, -iest*) like a ~ (1): ~*y clouds.*

fil·ter [ˈfɪltə*] *n.* **1.** apparatus (1) (containing, e.g., sand, charcoal, paper, or cloth) for holding back solid substances in impure liquid poured through it. **2.** coloured glass to put on a camera lens (as used in photography). *v.t. & i.* (cause to) flow through a ~; (fig., of a crowd, news, etc.) make its way (*out, through, etc.*). **'~-tip** *n.* **1.** cigarette end designed to act as a ~ to purify the smoke. **2.** cigarette with such a ~ at the mouth end. **'~-tipped** *adj.*

filth [fɪlθ] *n.* (no pl.) disgusting dirt. **~y** *adj.* (-*ier, -iest*). **~·i·ly** *adv.*

fin [fɪn] *n.* **1.** one of the winglike parts of a fish used in swimming. **2.** sth. resembling a ~ in appearance and function (e.g. the tail-~ of an air-craft).

fi·nal [ˈfaɪnl] *adj.* **1.** at the end. **2.** putting an end to doubt or argument: ~ *judgements. n.* (often pl.) ~ examinations or contests: *take one's ~s; the Cup F.~, the last football match in a series to decide a competition for the cup (2).* **fi·na·le** [fɪˈnɑːlɪ] *n.* ~ part of a piece of music; closing scene of an opera or play; end. **~·ly** *adv.* lastly.

fi·nance [faˈnæns] *n.* **1.** (no pl.) (science of the) management of (esp. public) money. **2.** (pl.) money (esp. of a government or business company). *v.t.* provide money for (a scheme, etc.). **fi·nan·cial** [faˈnænʃl] *adj.* **fi·nan·cier** [faˈnænsɪə*] *n.* person skilled in ~.

finch [fɪntʃ] *n.* kinds of small songbird: *gold~, chaf~.*

find [faɪnd] *v.t.* (p.t. & p.p. *found* [faʊnd]) **1.** look for and get back (sth. or sb. lost, etc.); discover (sth. or sb. not lost) as a result of searching; discover by chance. **2.** ~ *one's feet,* discover one's powers and begin to do well. **3.** learn by experience: ~ *that one is mistaken.* **4.** (often ~ *out*) learn by inquiry; discover: ~ *(out) when the train starts (how to do sth., etc.)*; ~ *sb. out,* learn that he has done sth. wrong, is at fault, etc. **5.** *You don't ~ much vegetation here* (i.e. There isn't ...). *I ~ some sense in it* (i.e.

There is ...). **6.** get, supply (money, other needs): ~ *one's daughter in clothes.* ~ *favour with,* win the favour or approval of. **7.** (law) reach a decision: ~ *a prisoner guilty.* **n.** sth. found, esp. sth. valuable or pleasing. **~·er** *n.* person who ~s sth. (lost). **~·ing** *n.* (often pl.) legal decision(s); sth. discovered after inquiries.

fine¹ [faɪn] *adj.* (~r, ~st) **1.** (of weather) bright; not raining. **2.** enjoyable; pleasing; splendid: *a ~ view;* ~ *clothes; have a ~ time.* **3.** delicate: ~ *workmanship.* **4.** of very small particles: ~ *dust.* **5.** very thin; sharp: ~ *thread; a ~ point.* **6.** (of metals) refined; pure. **7.** in good health: *I am ~.* **fin·ery** ['faɪnərɪ] *n.* (no pl.) splendid clothes, ornaments, etc.

fine² [faɪn] *adv.* ~ly; (colloq.) very well: *That will suit me ~. cut (run) it ~,* leave oneself hardly enough time, etc.

fine³ [faɪn] *n.* sum of money (to be) paid as a penalty for breaking a law or rule. **v.t.** make (sb.) pay a ~: *He ~d him £ 20.*

fine⁴ ['faɪnɪ] *n. in ~,* in short; finally.

fi·nesse [fɪ'nes] *n.* (no pl.) artful or delicate way of dealing with a situation.

fin·ger ['fɪŋgə*] *n.* one of the five terminal parts of the hand. **v.t.** touch with the ~s. **'~·post** *n.* signpost at a crossroads. **'~·print** *n.* mark made by the ~tip(s), esp. as used to detect criminals. **'~·tip** *n.* end of a ~.

the fingers   a fingerprint

fin·i·cal ['fɪnɪkl], **fin·ick·ing** ['fɪnɪkɪŋ], **fin·icky** ['fɪnɪkɪ] *adjs.* too fussy or fastidious (about food, details).

fin·ish ['fɪnɪʃ] *v.t. & i.* **1.** bring or come to an end. **2.** make complete or perfect; polish. *n.* (no pl.) **1.** last part. **2.** ~ed (2) state.

fi·nite ['faɪnaɪt] *adj.* **1.** limited. **2.** (gram.) limited by number and person: *'Am' is a ~ form of 'be'.*

fiord, fjord [fjɔːd] *n.* (as in Norway) narrow arm of the sea, between high cliffs.

fir [fɜː*] *n.* (wood of) evergreen tree with needle-like leaves.

fire ['faɪə*] *n.* **1.** (condition of) burning: *set the house on ~;* instance of burn-

ing: *light a ~ in the sitting-room; a forest ~.* **2.** shooting (from guns): *open (cease) ~,* start (stop) shooting; *under~,* being shot at. **3.** angry or excited feeling. **v.t. & i. 1.** cause to begin burning: ~ *a haystack.* **2.** harden in an oven: ~ *bricks.* **3.** supply (a furnace, etc.) with fuel. **4.** shoot (5) with, pull the trigger of, discharge (2) (a rifle, etc.); send (a bullet, shell) from a gun; (of a gun) go off. **5.** excite (the imagination, etc.): ~ *up,* become excited or angry. **6.** (colloq.) dismiss (an employee). **'~·a,larm** *n.* bell, etc. that is sounded as a signal of an outbreak of ~. **'~·arm** *n.* (usu. pl.) rifle, gun, revolver, etc. **'~·brand** *n.* person who stirs up social or political discontent. ~ **bri·gade** *n.* company of men who put out ~s. **'~·,crack·er** *n.* ~work that explodes with a cracking sound. **'~·damp** *n.* (no pl.) explosive gas in coal-mines. **'~·,en·gine** *n.* vehicle, manned by ~men, that carries the equipment used to extinguish ~s or to pump water from flooded buildings, etc. **~·es·cape** ['faɪərɪ,skeɪp] *n.* kind of extending ladder, or outside stairs, for escaping from a burning building. **'~·fly** *n.* flying insect giving out light in the dark. **'~·guard** *n.* wire protection round a ~ in a room. **'~·,irons** *n. pl.* poker, tongs, etc. for keeping a ~ burning in a ~place. **'~·man** *n.* member of a ~ brigade; stoker on a steam-engine; man who looks after the ~ in a furnace. **'~·place** *n.* place where a ~ may be made in a room. **'~·proof** *adj.* that does not burn; that does not break if heated. **'~·side** *n.* part of a room round the ~place. **'~·work** *n.* device (2) containing gunpowder, etc., used for display or signals.

firm¹ [fɜːm] *adj.* **1.** solid; hard. **2.** not easily changed or influenced; having or showing strength of character, etc. *adv.* ~ly: *stand ~.* **~·ly** *adv.* **~·ness** *n.* (no pl.).

firm² [fɜːm] *n.* (two or more) persons carrying on a business.

fir·ma·ment ['fɜːməmənt] *n.* sky.

first [fɜːst] *adv.* **1.** before anyone or anything else. **2.** for the ~ time. **3.** before some other time: *I must finish my homework ~.* **4.** in preference: *She said she would starve ~* (rather than steal, for example). *adj.* coming before all others in time, order, importance, merit, etc. ~ **aid** *n.* (no pl.) see *aid.* ~ **class** *adj.* of the best quality. ~ **floor** *n.* see *floor* (2). **'~·hand** *adj. & adv.* obtained through practice, observation of facts, etc., not from books, etc. **~ly** *adv.* in the ~ place. **~ name** *n.* Christian name. '**~-rate** *adj.* excellent.

irth [fɜ:θ] *n.* narrow arm of the sea; (esp. in Scotland) river estuary.

is·cal ['fɪskl] *adj.* of public money.

ish [fɪʃ] *v.i. & t. & n.* (pl. ~es, collective pl. ~) (try to catch a) cold-blooded animal living wholly in water, breathing through gills and having fins and tail for swimming. *~ for* (*information, compliments*), try to get (by indirect methods); *~ sth. up* (*out of* ...), pull up (e.g. from one's pocket). *~ing-rod, ~ing-line* (for catching ~). '**~-er·man** *n.* man who catches ~, esp. for a living. (Cf. *angler.*). **~·mon·ger** ['fɪʃ-,mʌŋgə*] *n.* (Gt. Brit.) person who sells ~. **~y** *adj.* (-ier, -iest) (colloq.) causing a feeling of doubt: *a ~y story.*

is·sile ['fɪsaɪl] *adj.* capable of being split (in a nuclear reactor): *~ material.*

is·sion ['fɪʃn] *n.* splitting, e.g. (biol.) of one cell into new cells; (phys.) splitting of the nucleus of an atom.

is·sure ['fɪʃə*] *n.* deep crack (in rocks, etc.).

ist [fɪst] *n.* hand when tightly closed (as in fighting).

it¹ [fɪt] *adj.* (-tt-) **1.** suitable, right (*for*), good enough (*for sth., to do, to be* ...). **2.** right or proper: *think* (*see*) *~ to*, decide or choose to. **3.** in good health or condition: *feel quite ~; not ~ to travel.* *v.t. & i.* (-tt-) **1.** be the right size and shape: *shoes that ~ well; a badly ~ting door.* **2.** put on (esp. clothing) to see that it is the right size, shape, etc.: *have a new coat ~ted* (*on*). **3.** make (a person) ~ (1) (*for, to do, to be*): *~ oneself for new duties.* **4.** put into place: *~ a new tap.* **5.** *~ in* (*with*), (cause to) be in harmony (with); *~ sth. or sb. in,* find the right or a suitable place or time for; *~ sb. or sth. out* (*up*), equip: *~ out a ship* (*a boy for school*). *n.* way sth. ~s; result of ~ting: *a good* (*bad, exact*) ~. **~·ness** *n.* (no pl.) **1.** propriety. **2.** state of being physically ~. **~·ter** *n.* person whose work is ~ting clothing; mechanic who ~s parts of machinery, etc. together. **~·ting** *adj.* suitable; right (for the purpose). *n.* (pl.) things fixed in a building: *electric light ~tings.*

it² [fɪt] *n.* **1.** sudden attack of illness: *a ~ of coughing;* esp. one with violent movements or unconsciousness; *fall down in a ~.* **2.** sudden outburst (of laughter, anger, etc.). *by ~s and starts,* in efforts that start and stop irregularly. **~·ful** *adj.* irregular.

five [faɪv] *n. & adj.* 5.

fix [fɪks] *v.t. & i.* **1.** make (sth.) fast so that it cannot be moved: *~ a post in the ground.* **2.** determine or decide: *~ prices* (*a date for a meeting*). **3.** direct (the eyes, one's attention) steadily (*on*). **4.** treat (photographic films, colour used in dyeing, etc.) so that light does not affect them. **5.** (often *~ up*) arrange or provide for: *~ sb. up with a job; ~ up a friend for the night* (i.e. give him a bed); *~ up a quarrel* (i.e. settle it). **6.** repair; mend: *~ a motor car.* **7.** (sl.) inject *oneself* with a drug; take such an injection. *n.* **1.** dilemma: *in a ~,* in a difficult or awkward state of affairs. **2.** (sl.) injection of a narcotic drug. **~ed** [fɪkst] *adj.* immovable; fast¹ (1); unchanging. **~·ed·ly** ['fɪksɪdlɪ] *adv.* look *~edly at,* look at with a ~ed stare. **~·ture** ['fɪkstʃə*] *n.* **1.** sth. ~ed in place, esp. (pl.) built-in cupboards, firegrates, electric light fittings, etc. that are bought with a building. **2.** (day ~ed (2) for a) sporting event.

fizz [fɪz] *v.i. & n.* (no pl.) (make a) hissing sound (as when gas escapes from a liquid).

fiz·zle ['fɪzl] *v.i.* make a slight fizzing sound. *~ out,* end feebly; end in failure.

fjord, see *fiord.*

flab·ber·gast ['flæbəgɑ:st] *v.t.* overcome with amazement.

flab·by ['flæbɪ] *adj.* (-ier, -iest) **1.** (of the muscles, flesh) soft; not firm. **2.** (fig.) weak; without moral force. **flab·bi·ness** *n.* (no pl.).

flac·cid ['flæksɪd] *adj.* flabby.

flag¹ [flæg] *n.* piece of coloured cloth, used as the distinctive symbol of a country or as a signal. *v.t.* (-gg-) make signals with a ~ or ~s; decorate with ~s. '**~·ship** *n.* admiral's ship. '**~·staff** *n.* pole from which a ~ is flown.

a flag¹   flagons

flag² [flæg] *n.* (also *~stone*) flat, square, or oblong piece of stone for a floor, path, or pavement.

flag³ [flæg] *v.i.* (-gg-) **1.** (of plants, etc.) droop. **2.** (fig.) become tired or weak.

flag·on ['flægən] *n.* large, rounded container for wine.

fla·grant ['fleɪgrənt] *adj.* (of crime)

openly and obviously wicked: ~ *offences*.

flail [fleɪl] *n.* strong stick hinged on a long handle, used to beat corn, etc. in order to separate grain from straw.

flair [fleə*] *n.* natural ability (to see or do what is best, most advantageous, etc.): *have a ~ for languages*.

flake [fleɪk] *n.* small, light, leaf-like piece: *snow~s*; *~s of rust*; *corn~s*, toasted flavoured maize *~s. v.i.* fall (*off*) in *~s.* **flaky** *adj.* (*-ier*, *-iest*) made up of *~s.*

flam·boy·ant [flæm'bɔɪənt] *adj.* brightly coloured or decorated; (fig.) showy.

flame [fleɪm] *n.* **1.** burning gas: *in ~s*, burning; on fire. **2.** blaze of colour. *v.i.* **1.** send out *~s*; be like *~s* in colour. **2.** (fig.) blaze with anger.

fla·min·go [flə'mɪŋgəʊ] *n.* (pl. *-gos*, *-goes*) water-bird with long legs and light-red wing feathers.

flange [flændʒ] *n.* projecting edge or rim of an object, such as an engine wheel, to keep it in position.

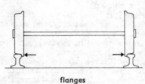

flanges

flank [flæŋk] *n.* **1.** side of a human being or animal, between ribs and hip. **2.** side of a mountain, building, or (esp.) an army or fleet: *attack the left ~*; *a ~ attack. v.t.* **1.** be at or on the *~ of.* **2.** (mil.) go round the *~* of (the enemy).

flan·nel ['flænl] *n.* **1.** (no pl.) soft, smooth, woollen material: *~ trousers*. **2.** (Gt. Brit.) piece of *~* for cleaning the floor or washing the face and hands, etc.: *a face-~.* **3.** (pl.) esp. *~* trousers for sports wear in summer. **~·ette** [ˌflænl-'et] *n.* (no pl.) cotton material made to look like *~* (1).

flap [flæp] *v.t. & i.* (*-pp-*) **1.** (of wings, flags, other soft and flat things) (cause to) move up and down or from side to side. **2.** hit lightly, with sth. soft and wide. **3.** (colloq.) get into a *~* (3). *n.* **1.** (sound of a) flapping blow or movement. **2.** bit of material that hangs down or covers an opening, attached by one side only: *the ~ of an envelope* (*a pocket*). **3.** (colloq.) *be in* (*get into*) *a ~*, be(come) nervous or confused.

flare[1] [fleə*] *v.i.* burn with a bright unsteady flame; burst into bright flame. *~ up*, (fig.) burst into anger. *n.* flaring flame; device (2) for giving such a light used as a signal.

flare[2] [fleə*] *v.i. & t.* (of a skirt) become, make, wider at the bottom.

flash [flæʃ] *n.* **1.** sudden burst of flame or light: *a ~ of lightning*; *~es of gun-fire*. **2.** *~light* (3). **3.** (also *news·*) brief item of news received by radio, telegraph etc. **4.** (fig.) *a ~ of hope*; *in a ~*, in an instant. *v.t. & i.* **1.** send, give, out a *~* or *~es.* **2.** come suddenly (into view or into the mind). **3.** send instantly: *~ news across the world.* **~ bulb** *n.* bulb that gives a momentary bright light for a *~light* photograph. **~ cube** *n.* small plastic cube that contains a bulb on each of four sides, used for *~light* photographs. **~·er** *n.* device (2) for switching lights (e.g. the headlights of a motor car) rapidly on and off. '**~·light** *n.* **1.** light that *~es* (e.g. in a lighthouse). **2.** small electric torch. **3.** brilliant light used for taking photographs indoors etc. **~y** *adj.* (*-ier*, *-iest*) looking smart and brilliant but not in good taste.

flask [flɑːsk] *n.* **1.** narrow-necked bottle used in laboratories, or for oil, wine etc. **2.** flat bottle for carrying drink in the pocket.

flat[1] [flæt] *n.* (U.S.A. *apartment*) set of rooms (living-room, bedroom, kitchen etc.) on one floor as a residence. (See *block*[1] (3) of *~s*, U.S.A. *apartment* (3) *house*.)

flat[2] [flæt] *adj.* (*~ter*, *~test*) **1.** smooth, level; spread out on the ground; with a broad level surface: *a ~ dish.* **2.** dull, uninteresting; (of beer, etc.) tasteless because the gas has gone. **3.** (mus.) below the true pitch: *B ~*, note half a tone lower than B. **4.** absolute; downright: *a ~ denial.* **5.** *~ rate*, common price paid for each of different things or services bought in quantity. *adv.* in a *~* manner: *sing ~. n.* **1.** *~* part of sth. (e.g. a sword). **2.** stretch of *~* land esp. near water: *river ~s*; *a mud ~.* **3.** *~* tyre (e.g. after a puncture). **4.** (mus.) *~* note; the sign (♭). **~·ly** *adv.* (deny) in a *~* (4) manner. **~·ten** ['flætn] *v.t. & i.* make, become, *~*.

flat·ter ['flætə*] *v.t.* **1.** praise too much; praise insincerely. **2.** give a feeling of pleasure to: *be ~ed by an invitation to address a meeting.* **3.** (of a picture, artist, etc.) show (sb.) as better-looking than he is. **4.** *~ oneself* (*that*), be pleased with one's belief (that). **~·er** *n.* **~y** *n.*

flirtatious

flat·u·lence ['flætjʊləns] *n.* (no pl.) (having) gas in the stomach or bowels.

flaunt [flɔːnt] *v.t. & i.* display proudly, esp. by waving about; shamelessly try to attract attention to: ~ *one's riches*.

flau·tist ['flɔːtɪst] *n.* flute-player.

fla·vour (U.S.A. **-vor**) ['fleɪvə*] *n.* sensation of taste and smell; aroma: *food with little* ~; *a* ~ *of onion. v.t.* give a ~ to. ~**ing** *n.* sth. used to give ~.

flaw [flɔː] *n.* crack; sth. that lessens the value, beauty, or perfection of a thing. ~**less** *adj.* perfect.

flax [flæks] *n.* (no pl.) plant cultivated for the fibres obtained from its stems; ~ *fibres* (for making linen). ~**en** *adj.* (of hair) pale yellow.

flay [fleɪ] *v.t.* take the skin or hide off (an animal); (fig.) criticize severely.

flea [fliː] *n.* small jumping insect that feeds on blood.

fleck [flek] *n.* **1.** small spot or patch: ~*s of colour on a bird's breast.* **2.** particle (of dust, etc.). *v.t.* mark with ~*s*.

fled, see **flee**.

fledged [fledʒd] *adj.* (of birds) with fully grown wing feathers; able to fly. **fledg(e)·ling** ['fledʒlɪŋ] *n.* young bird just able to fly; (fig.) inexperienced person.

flee [fliː] *v.i. & t.* (p.t. & p.p. **fled** [fled]) run or hurry away (from).

fleece [fliːs] *n.* sheep's woolly coat; ~-like mass or covering. *v.t.* rob (sb.) of money, property, etc. by trickery. **fleecy** *adj.* (-ier, -iest) looking like ~: *fleecy clouds.*

fleet¹ [fliːt] *n.* **1.** number of warships under one commander; all the warships of a country. **2.** number of ships, aircraft, buses, etc. moving or working under one command or ownership.

fleet² [fliːt] *adj.* (poet. or liter.) quick-moving; swift. ~**ing** *adj.* (of a visit, thoughts) passing quickly.

flesh [fleʃ] *n.* (no pl.) **1.** soft substance, esp. muscle, between the skin and bones of animal bodies. **2.** body (1) 'as contrasted with mind or soul: *one's own* ~ *and blood*, one's near relations; *in the* ~, in bodily form. **3.** physical or bodily desires: *the sins of the* ~. **4.** pulpy part of fruits and plants. **5.** plumpness; fat: *lose* (*put on*) ~, grow thinner (fatter). ~**y** *adj.* (-ier, -iest) of ~; plump; fat; (of fruits, etc.) \}

flew, see **fly¹**. [pulpy.\}

flex¹ [fleks] *n.* (Gt. Brit.) (length of) flexible insulated wire for electric current.

flex² [fleks] *v.t.* (anat.) bend (a joint, limb); move (one's muscles).

flex·i·ble ['fleksəbl] *adj.* easily bent without breaking; (fig.) easily changed to suit new conditions, etc.; adaptable: ~ *working hours.* **flex·i·bil·i·ty** [ˌfleksə'bɪlɪtɪ] *n.* (no pl.).

flick [flɪk] *v.t. & n.* (give a) quick tap or light blow to (e.g. with a whip or the end of one's finger).

flick·er ['flɪkə*] *v.i.* **1.** (of a light; fig. of hopes, etc.) burn or shine unsteadily; flash and die away by turns. **2.** move back and forth: ~*ing shadows. n.* ~*ing light or movement.*

fli·er, see **fly¹**; **flyer**.

flight¹ [flaɪt] *n.* **1.** (no pl.) flying; movement and path through the air. **2.** journey made by flying. **3.** number of birds or objects in ~: *a* ~ *of swallows* (*arrows*). **4.** group of aircraft as a unit: *the Queen's* ~; *F~ Commander of the Royal Air Force.* **5.** set of stairs between two landings. ~**y** *adj.* (-ier, -iest) fickle; frivolous.

flight² [flaɪt] *n.* (act of) fleeing or running away (from danger, etc.): *put* (*the enemy*) *to* ~, cause (them) to run away.

flim·sy ['flɪmzɪ] *adj.* (-sier, -siest) (of material) light and thin; (of objects, etc.) easily injured or destroyed.

flinch [flɪntʃ] *v.i.* start (3) back or away (*from*) (in fear or pain).

fling [flɪŋ] *v.t. & i.* (p.t. & p.p. **flung** [flʌŋ]) **1.** throw violently: ~ *a stone at sb. or sth.* **2.** put (*out*) or move (hands, etc. *about*) violently; move (oneself) hurriedly and carelessly or angrily: ~ *oneself into a chair;* ~ *up one's hands.* **1.** act of ~*ing;* ~*ing movement. have a* ~ *at*, make an attempt at; *have one's* ~, have a time of unrestricted pleasure. **2.** kind of dance with quick movements.

flint [flɪnt] *n.* very hard stone, esp. a chip of this struck against steel to produce sparks.

flip [flɪp] *v.t. & i.* (-pp-) **1.** put (sth.) in motion with a flick; throw with a jerk. **2.** strike lightly. **3.** ~ (*out*), (sl.) lose one's mind; go crazy. *n.* quick, light blow. ~ *side*, reverse (2) side of a record² (4).

flip·pant ['flɪpənt] *adj.* not showing due respect. **flip·pan·cy** *n.*

flip·per ['flɪpə*] *n.* **1.** broad, flat limb used to swim with: *Penguins, seals, and turtles have* ~*s*. **2.** flat rubber shoe for underwater swimming.

flirt [flɜːt] *v.i.* **1.** make love without serious intentions: ~*ing with the girls.* **2.** ~ *with*, consider (a scheme, etc.) but not seriously. *n.* person who ~*s* (1). **flir·ta·tion** [flɜː'teɪʃn] *n.* **flir·ta·tious**

flit

[flɜː'teɪʃəs] *adj.* fond of, given to, ~ing.

flit [flɪt] *v.i* (*-tt-*) fly or move lightly and quickly (from place to place).

float [fləʊt] *v.i. & t.* **1.** be held up in air, gas, or (esp.) on the surface of liquid: *dust ~ing in the air*; *boats ~ing down the river*. **2.** cause to ~; keep ~ing. **3.** get financial support in order to start (sth.): *~ a business company.* **4.** allow the foreign exchange value (of a currency) to vary: *~ the pound (dollar).* *n.* **1.** piece of cork, etc. used to keep a net, etc. from sinking. **2.** cart with a low floor: *a milk ~.* **~ing** *adj.* fluctuating.

flock[1] [flɒk] *n.* **1.** number of birds or animals (usu. sheep, goats) of one kind, either kept together or feeding and travelling together: *a ~ of wild geese.* **2.** (of people) in ~s, in great numbers. **3.** Christian congregation; large family of children. *v.i.* gather, come, or go together, in great numbers.

flock[2] [flɒk] *n.* tuft of wool; (pl.) wool waste for mattresses, etc.

floe [fləʊ] *n.* sheet of floating ice.

flog [flɒg] *v.t.* (*-gg-*) beat with a rod or whip. **~·ging** *n.* beating or whipping.

flood [flʌd] *n.* **1.** (coming of a) great quantity of water in a place usually dry: *in ~,* (of a river) overflowing its banks. **2.** outburst (of rain, anger, words, tears, etc.). *v.t. & i.* **1.** cover with water; fill with water. **2.** come, send, in large numbers or amounts: *be ~ed with requests for help.* '**~·light** *n.* (usu. pl.) strong lamp(s) for lighting up the outside of buildings. *v.t.* (p.t. & p.p. *~lit*) light up with such lamps. '**~·tide** *n.* incoming tide.

floor [flɔː*] *n.* **1.** lower surface of a room; part of a building on which one walks (opp. *ceiling*). (Cf. *ground*[1](1).) **2.** rooms on one level of a building: *ground ~* (level with the street); *first ~* (above the ground ~); U.S.A. = *ground ~*). **3.** *take* (*have*) *the ~,* take (have) one's turn in speaking during a public debate. *v.t.* **1.** put a ~ in a

U.S.A.

second floor	third floor
first floor	second floor
ground floor	first floor

building. **2.** knock down; (of a problem, arguments, etc.) defeat; puzzle. '**~·cloth** *n.* piece of cloth for washing ~s. **~· ~·ing** *n.* (no pl.) material for ~s. '**~·walk·er** *n.* (U.S.A.) = shopwalker.

flop [flɒp] *v.i. & t.* (*-pp-*) **1.** move, fall, clumsily or helplessly. **2.** put or throw down clumsily or roughly. **3.** (sl.) (of a book, play, etc.) fail. *n.* **1.** act or sound of ~ping. **2.** (sl.) (of a book, play, etc.) failure. *adv.* with a ~: *fall ~ into the water.* **~·py** *adj.* (*-ier, -iest*) hanging down loosely; not stiff: *a ~py hat.*

flo·ra ['flɔːrə] *n.* (pl. *~e* [-iː], *~s*) all the plants of a particular area or period.

flo·ral ['flɔːrəl] *adj.* of flowers: *a ~ design.*

flor·id ['flɒrɪd] *adj.* **1.** (of the face) naturally red. **2.** very much ornamented; too rich in ornament and colour.

flor·in ['flɒrɪn] *n.* (formerly) British coin, value 2s. (= 10p.).

flor·ist ['flɒrɪst] *n.* shopkeeper selling or growing flowers.

floss [flɒs] *n.* (no pl.) rough silk threads on a silkworm's cocoon; silk spun from these for needlework.

flo·til·la [fləʊ'tɪlə] *n.* fleet of small warships (e.g. destroyers).

flot·sam ['flɒtsəm] *n.* (no pl.) parts of a wrecked ship or its cargo floating in the sea. (Cf. *jetsam*.)

flounce[1] [flaʊns] *n.* strip of cloth or lace sewn by the upper edge to a woman's skirt as an ornament.

flounce[2] [flaʊns] *v.i. & n.* (move, go with a) quick, angry or impatient movement of the body: *~ out of a room.*

floun·der[1] ['flaʊndə*] *v.i.* **1.** make violent and usu. vain efforts (as when trying to get out of deep snow or mud, or when one is in deep water and unable to swim). **2.** (fig.) hesitate, make mistakes, when trying to do sth. (e.g. make a speech in a foreign language).

floun·der[2] ['flaʊndə*] *n.* small, edible, flat sea-fish.

flour ['flaʊə*] *n.* (no pl.) fine meal[2], powder, made from grain, used for bread, cakes, etc. *v.t.* sprinkle or cover with ~.

flour·ish ['flʌrɪʃ] *v.i. & t.* **1.** grow in a healthy manner; be well and active; prosper. **2.** wave about and show: *~ a sword.* *n.* *~ing* movement; curve or decoration in handwriting; loud, exciting passage of music, esp. for trumpets.

flout [flaʊt] *v.t.* oppose; treat with contempt: *~ sb.'s advice.*

flow [fləʊ] *v.i.* **1.** move along or over as a river does; move smoothly. **2.** (of hair, articles of dress, etc.) hang down loosely. **3.** (of the tide) come in; rise. *n.* (no pl.) ~ing movement; quantity that ~s: *a good ~ of water; a ~ of angry words.*

flow·er ['flaʊə*] *n.* **1.** (usu. colourful) part of a plant from which fruit or seed is later developed: *in ~,* with the ~s open. **2.** (fig.) finest part: *the ~ of the nation's youth.* **3.** ~s of speech, ornamented phrases. *v.i.* produce ~s. ~y *adj.* (fig.) full of ~s of speech.

flown, see *fly¹.*

flu [fluː] *n.* (no pl.) (colloq.) influenza.

fluc·tu·ate ['flʌktjʊeɪt] *v.i.* (of prices, levels, etc.) move up and down; be irregular. **fluc·tu·a·tion** [ˌflʌktjʊ'eɪʃn] *n.*

flue [fluː] *n.* pipe in a chimney, etc. for carrying away smoke; passage for taking hot air through a boiler, round an oven, etc.

flu·ent ['fluːənt] *adj.* (of a person) able to speak smoothly and readily; (of speech) coming easily: *speak ~ English.* ~·ly *adv.* **flu·en·cy** *n.* (no pl.).

fluff [flʌf] *n.* (no pl.) soft feathery stuff that comes from blankets or other soft woolly material; soft woolly fur, feathers, hair, etc. *v.t.* make like ~ by shaking, spreading out: *~ out a pillow.* ~y *adj.* (*-ier, -iest*) like ~; covered with ~.

flu·id ['fluːɪd] *n. & adj.* (substance) able to flow (as gases and liquids do); (of ideas, etc.) not fixed. ~·i·ty [fluː'ɪdətɪ] *n.* (no pl.).

fluke [fluːk] *n.* sth. resulting from a fortunate accident; lucky stroke: *win by a ~* (e.g. a game¹ (1)).

flung, see *fling* (v.).

flun·k(e)y ['flʌŋkɪ] *n.* (usu. derog.) manservant in uniform; footman.

flu·o·res·cent [ˌfluːə'resnt] *adj.* (esp.) ~ *lighting,* type of electric lighting with a lamp giving violet, etc. light.

flu·o·rine ['flʊəriːn] *n.* (no pl.) pale-yellow gas.

flur·ry ['flʌrɪ] *n.* **1.** short, sudden rush of wind or fall of rain or snow. **2.** (fig.) nervous hurry. *v.t.* cause (sb.) to be in a ~ (2).

flush¹ [flʌʃ] *v.i. & t.* **1.** (of a person, his face) become red through a rush of blood to the skin. **2.** (of health, heat, emotions, etc.) cause the face to become red in this way: *~ed with happiness* (*wine, etc.*); (of blood) make (the skin) red. **3.** clear or wash (e.g. drains, a lavatory) with a flood of water; (of water) rush out in a flood.

n. **1.** sudden rush of water; cleansing of drains, a lavatory, etc. by ~ing. **2.** ~ing (1) of the face. **3.** rush of strong feeling (e.g. pleasure); high point (of growth, powers, etc.).

flush² [flʌʃ] *adj.* **1.** level; in a line: *a door ~ with the wall.* **2.** well supplied (*with* money).

flus·ter ['flʌstə*] *v.t.* make nervous or confused. *n.* (no pl.) ~ed condition.

flute [fluːt] *n.* (musical wind instrument) long wooden pipe with holes to be stopped by the fingers. *v.i.* play the ~. **flut·ist** *n.* (U.S.A.) = flautist.

a flute   a housefly

flut·ter ['flʌtə*] *v.t. & i.* **1.** (of birds) cause (the wings) to move or move the wings hurriedly and irregularly but without flying, or in short flights only. **2.** (cause to) move about in a quick, irregular way; (of the heart) beat irregularly. *n.* ~ing movement; nervous condition; excitement: *in a ~; cause a ~.*

flux [flʌks] *n.* (no pl.) constant change of movement or conditions: *in a state of ~.*

fly¹ [flaɪ] *v.i. & t.* (p.t. *flew* [fluː], p.p. *flown* [fləʊn]) **1.** move through the air as a bird does, or in an aircraft; direct or control the flight of (aircraft); transport (passengers, goods) in aircraft. **2.** (of flags, kites, etc.) float in the air; cause to do this. **3.** go or run quickly; move quickly: *~ to the rescue; a ~ing visit* (i.e. a short one); *~ open* (*to bits, into pieces*), come open (break to bits, etc.) suddenly; *let ~ at,* shoot at; attack angrily; *~ into a rage,* become angry suddenly. **fli·er, ~·er** ['flaɪə*] *n.* airman. '~·leaf *n.* blank (1) leaf at the beginning or end of a book. '~·over *n.* (U.S.A. *overpass*) bridge carrying a road, railway, etc. over another at an intersection. '~·wheel *n.* heavy wheel in a machine to keep its speed regular.

fly² [flaɪ] *n.* **1.** flap (2) on a garment (esp. trousers) to contain or cover the fastening. **2.** flap (2) of canvas at the entrance of a tent.

fly³ [flaɪ] *n.* two-winged insect, esp.

the common *housefly*. (See the picture at *flute*.) '**~-blown** *adj.* (of meat, etc.) (going bad because) containing flies' eggs.

fly·ing ['flaɪɪŋ] *adj.* (in compounds): **~ field** *n.* airfield. **~ ma·chine** *n.* (heavier-than-air) machine able to fly in the air. **~ sau·cer** *n.* unidentified, saucer-shaped, ~ object (thought to have been) seen moving across the sky.

foal [fəʊl] *n.* young horse or ass. *in* (*with*) ~, (of a mare) going to give birth to a ~. *v.i.* give birth to a ~.

foam [fəʊm] *n.* (no pl.) **1.** white mass of small air bubbles formed in or on liquid by motion, or on an animal's lips (e.g. after exertion). **2.** (also ~ *rubber*) spongy rubber used as filling for mattresses, cushions, etc. *v.i.* form ~; break into ~; send out ~: *~ing beer*; (fig.) *~ with rage*.

fob [fɒb] *v.t.* (-*bb*-) ~ *sth. off on sb.*, ~ *sb. off with sth.*, get a person to accept sth. of little or no value by deceit or trickery.

fo'·c's'le ['fəʊksl] *n.* forecastle.

fo·cus ['fəʊkəs] *n.* (pl. *foci* [-saɪ], ~*es*) **1.** meeting-point of rays of light (heat, etc.); point, distance, at which the sharpest outline is given (to the eye, through a telescope, on a camera plate, etc.): *in* (*out of*) ~. **2.** point at which interests, tendencies, etc. meet. *v.t. & i.* (cause to) come together at a ~; adjust (an instrument, etc.) so that it is in ~: ~ *a lens on sth.*; (fig.) ~ *one's attention on sth.* **fo·cal** ['fəʊkl] *adj.* of or at a ~.

fod·der ['fɒdə*] *n.* (no pl.) dried food, hay, etc. for cattle, horses, etc.

foe [fəʊ] *n.* (poet. or rhet.) enemy.

fog [fɒg] *n.* thick mist (on land or sea surface). *v.t.* (-*gg*-) cover as with a ~. '**~-horn** *n.* horn used to warn ships during ~. **~gy** *adj.* (-*gier*, -*giest*).

fo·g(e)y ['fəʊgɪ] *n.* (usu. *old* ~) person with old-fashioned ideas which he is unwilling to change.

foi·ble ['fɔɪbl] *n.* certain slight peculiarity of character, often one of which a person is wrongly proud.

foil[1] [fɔɪl] *n.* **1.** (no pl.) metal rolled or hammered very thin like paper: *aluminium* ~. **2.** person or thing that contrasts with, and thus shows up, the qualities of another.

foil[2] [fɔɪl] *n.* light sword without a sharp point or edge, for fencing.

foil[3] [fɔɪl] *v.t.* baffle; prevent (sb.) from carrying out a plan; make (purposes) ineffective.

foist [fɔɪst] *v.t.* ~ *sth.* (*off*) *on sb.*, trick him into accepting a useless or valueless article.

fold[1] [fəʊld] *v.t. & i.* **1.** bend one part of a thing over on itself; become ~ed or be able to be ~ed. **2.** ~ *one's arms*, cross them over the chest; ~ (*a child*) *in one's arms*, hold to one's breast. *n.* part that is ~ed; line made by ~ing. **~·er** *n.* **1.** ~ing holder for loose papers. **2.** ~ing card with advertisements, railway time-tables, etc. on it.

fold[2] [fəʊld] *n.* **1.** enclosure for sheep. **2.** (fig.) body (5) of religious believers. *v.t.* put (sheep) in a ~.

-fold [-fəʊld] *suff.* (forming adjs.,advs., and ns.): *a twofold increase*; *repay sb. tenfold*; *a hundredfold*.

fo·liage ['fəʊlɪɪdʒ] *n.* (no pl.) leaves (on trees and plants).

folk [fəʊk] *n.* (pl. ~, ~s) a people; nation; race. **2.** (pl.) people in general. **3.** *one's* ~s, (pl.) (colloq.) one's relations. '**~-dance** (**-song**) *ns.* old-time dance (song) handed down, esp. among country ~. '**~-lore** *n.* (no pl.) (study of) old beliefs, tales, customs, etc. of a people.

fol·low ['fɒləʊ] *v.t. & i.* **1.** come, go, have a place, after (in space, time, or order). **2.** go along, keep to (a road, etc.); understand (an argument, sth. said, studied, etc.). **3.** engage in (as a business, trade, etc.): ~ *the sea* (*the plough*, *the law*, *the trade of a hatter*). **4.** take or accept (as a guide, example, etc.): ~ *sb.'s advice* (*the fashion*). **5.** be necessarily true: *It ~s from what you say that ... That does not ~ at all.* ~ *sth. up*, pursue, work at, further; *as ~s*, as now to be given. **~·er** *n.* supporter. **~·ing** *n.* body (5) of supporters or ~ers.

fol·ly ['fɒlɪ] *n.* foolishness; foolish act, etc.

fo·ment [fəʊ'ment] *v.t.* put warm water or cloths, lotions, etc. on (a part of the body, to lessen pain, etc.); (fig.) cause or increase (trouble, ill feeling, discontent). **fo·men·ta·tion** [,fəʊmen-'teɪʃn] *n.* ~ing; sth. used for ~ing.

fond [fɒnd] *adj.* **1.** *be ~ of*, like; enjoy. **2.** loving and kind. **3.** foolishly loving: *a young wife with a ~ old husband*. **4.** (of hopes, ambitions) held but unlikely to be realized. **~·ly** *adv.* **1.** lovingly. **2.** in a ~ (3) manner.

fon·dle ['fɒndl] *v.t.* touch lovingly.

font[1] [fɒnt] *n.* basin to hold water for baptism, in a church.

font[2] [fɒnt] *n.* see *fount* (2).

food [fuːd] *n.* substance(s) that can be eaten by people or animals or used by

plants to nourish them. **~·less** *adj.*
without ~. '**~·stuff** *n.* material used
as ~.

fool [fu:l] *n.* **1.** person without much
sense; stupid or rash person: *make
a* ~ *of*, trick; cause to seem like a ~.
~'s errand, one that in the end is seen
to be useless. *~'s paradise*, unthinking
happiness that is unlikely to last. **2.**
(in the Middle Ages) person employed by a ruler to make jokes, etc.;
jester: *play the* ~, make silly jokes;
act like a ~. *v.i. & t.* **1.** behave like a
~: *stop ~ing about!* **2.** trick (sb.) so
that he looks silly. **3.** ~ *away* (*one's time,
money, etc.*), waste it. **~·ery** *n.* ~ing;
~ish act. '**~·har·dy** *adj.* ~ishly bold.
~·ish *adj.* silly; without sense. **~·ish·ly**
adv. '**~·proof** *adj.* so simple or easy
that even a ~ cannot make a mistake.
~·scap ['fu:lskæp] *n.* size of writing
paper (17″ × 13¹⁄₂″ unfolded).

foot [fut] *n.* (pl. *feet* [fi:t]) **1.** bottom
part of the leg, below the ankle, on
which one walks; corresponding part
of an animal's leg (cf. *paw*): *on* ~,
walking; *set sth. on* ~, set it going;
set (sb.) on his feet, (esp.) make him
able to support himself (in trade, etc.);
put one's ~ *down*, (a) accelerate a motor
vehicle; (b) object; protest; be firm;
sweep (carry) sb. off his feet, fill him
with enthusiasm; *put one's* ~ *in it*,
say or do sth. unsuitable; blunder.
2. step; tread: *a light* ~; *swift of* ~.
3. bottom: *the* ~ *of a page* (mountain).
4. lower end of a bed or grave (opp.
head (9)). **5.** measure of length, 12
inches (= 30.48 centimetres): *a pole
ten feet long*; *a ten-* ~ *pole.* **6.** division
or unit of verse, each with one strong
stress and one or more weak stresses.
v.t. & i. **1.** make a ~ for (e.g. a sock).
2. ~ *the bill*, (agree to) pay it. '**~·ball**
n. (inflated leather ball kicked in the)
field-game. '**~·ball·er** *n.* person who
plays ~ball or soccer. '**~·brake** *n.*
brake on a vehicle operated (1) by ~
pressure. '**~·fall** *n.* sound of a ~step.
'**~·hills** *n. pl.* low hills at the ~ of a
mountain range. '**~·hold** *n.* safe place
for the ~ (when climbing rocks, etc.).
~·ing *n.* **1.** ~hold. **2.** position (e.g. in
society); relationships (with people).
'**~·lights** *n. pl.* lights along the front
of the stage in a theatre. '**~·man** *n.*
manservant who admits visitors, waits
at table, etc. '**~·note** *n.* note at the ~
of a printed page. '**~·path** *n.* narrow
path, esp. across fields or open
country, or at the side of a country
road. '**~·print** *n.* mark left by a ~ on

13*

the ground. '**~·sore** *adj.* having sore
feet, esp. from walking. '**~·step** *n.*
tread. '**~·wear** *n.* (no pl.) boots, shoes,
etc.

fop [fɔp] *n.* man who pays too much
attention to his clothes.

for [fɔ:*, fə*] *prep. & conj.* **I.** *prep.*
1. (indicating destination): *sailing* ~
home; *the train* ~ *London.* **2.** (indicating progress): *The time is getting on* ~
two o'clock (advancing towards two
o'clock). **3.** (indicating what is intended): *Reserve a seat* ~ *me. He is
studying* ~ *the law.* **4.** (indicating preparation): *Buy some coal* ~ *the winter.*
5. (indicating purpose): *Let us go* ~
a walk. What is this tool ~ *? They chose
him* ~ *their leader.* **6.** (indicating liking,
suitability, skill, etc.): *have a liking* ~
sb.; *have a good ear* ~ *music*; *bad* ~ *the
health.* **7.** (with *too*): *She is too good* ~
such a man (to be his wife). (with
enough): *This coat is good enough* ~
gardening. **8.** in view of: *That's good
work* ~ (in view of the fact that it
was done by) *a beginner.* **9.** instead of;
representing: *Please act* ~ *me in this
matter. Who is the Member of Parliament* ~ *Oxford?* **10.** in favour of: *Are
you* ~ *or against the proposal?* **11.** with
regard to: *We are anxious* ~ *news.* **12.**
because of: *I went* ~ *her sake* (~ *a
good reason*). **13.** as the result of: *My
shoes are the worse* ~ *wear.* **14.** in spite
of: *F* ~ *all the care I took, I lost my
way.* **15.** as penalty, reward, or in
exchange: *suffer* ~ *one's sins*; *payment
~ work done*; *a medal* ~ *bravery*; *pay
75p* ~ *a book.* **16.** (indicating extent in
time or space): *go away* ~ *a week*;
walk ~ *miles without seeing a house.*
II. *conj.* because; for this reason.

for·age ['fɔrɪdʒ] *n.* (no pl.) food for
horses and cattle. *v.i.* search (for
food).

for·ay ['fɔreɪ] *v.i. & n.* (make a)
sudden attack (esp. to get food, etc.).

for·bear¹ [fɔ:'beə*] *v.t. & i.* (p.t. *-bore*
[fɔ:'bɔ:*], p.p. *-borne* [fɔ:'bɔ:n]) refrain (from); keep oneself back (from
doing sth. one wishes to do): ~ *to ask
(from asking) questions*; *beg sb. to* ~.
~·ance [fɔ:'beərəns] *n.* (no pl.) patience.

for·bear² ['fɔ:beə*] *n.* (usu pl.) ancestor.

for·bid [fə'bɪd] *v.t.* (p.t. *-bade* [fə'bæd],
p.p. *-bidden* [fə'bɪdn]) order (sb.) not
to do sth.; order that sth. must not
be done: ~ *a girl to marry*; ~ *a marriage.* **~·ding** *adj.* stern; threatening.

force [fɔ:s] *n.* **1.** (no pl.) strength;

power of body or mind; physical power: *the ~ of a blow (an explosion, an argument)*; *the ~s of nature* (e.g. storms). **2.** sth. tending to cause change (e.g. in society): *Fascism and Communism have been powerful ~s in world affairs.* **3.** (intensity of, measurement of) pressure or influence exerted at a point, tending to cause movement: *the law of ~s.* **4.** body (5) of armed men: *the Air F~; join the F~s* (Navy, Army, Air F~); *in ~,* in great numbers. **5.** (no pl.) (law) authority; power of binding (4): *put (a law) into ~,* make it binding. *v.t.* **1.** use ~ to get or do sth., to make sb. do sth.; break open by using ~: *~ a person's hand,* make him do sth. *~d landing,* landing that an aircraft is compelled to make because of engine trouble, etc. *~d march,* rapid one made by soldiers, requiring special effort. **2.** cause (plants, etc.) to mature earlier than usual (e.g. by giving warmth in winter). **~·ful** *adj.* (of a person, his character, of an argument, etc.) full of ~. **for·ci·ble** ['fɔ:sǝbl] *adj.* done by the use of ~; showing ~; ~ful. **for·ci·bly** *adv.*

for·ceps ['fɔ:seps] *n.* (pl. ~) instrument used by doctors and dentists for gripping things.

ford [fɔ:d] *n.* shallow place in a river where it is possible to walk across. *v.t.* cross (a river) at a ~. **~·able** *adj.* that can be ~ed.

fore [fɔ:*] *n.* (no pl.) front part. *come to the ~,* become prominent. *adj.* situated in the front.

fore- [fɔ:*-] *pref.* **1.** front: '**~·foot** *n.* '**~·leg** *n.* '**~·mast** *n.* '**~·part** *n.* **2.** in advance; before in time: **~·'see** *v.t.* '**~·taste** *n.* **~·'warn** *v.t.*

fore·arm ['fɔ:rɑ:m] *n.* arm from elbow to wrist or fingertips.

fore·bode [fɔ:'bǝud] *v.t.* be a warning of (*trouble*); have a feeling *that* (trouble is coming). **fore·bod·ing** *n.* feeling that trouble is coming.

fore·cast [fɔ:'kɑ:st] *v.t.* (p.t. & p.p. *-cast* or *~ed*) say in advance what is likely to happen. ['fɔ:kɑ:st] *n. the weather ~.*

fore·cas·tle ['fǝuksl] *n.* (in some ships) part in the bows where sailors eat and sleep.

fore·fa·thers ['fɔ:ˌfɑ:ðǝz] *n. pl.* ancestors.

fore·fin·ger ['fɔ:ˌfiŋgǝ*] *n.* first finger, next to the thumb.

fore·front ['fɔ:frʌnt] *n.* (no pl.) most forward part; centre of activity: *in the ~ of the battle.*

fore·go·ing [fɔ:'gǝuiŋ] *adj.* preceding; which goes before (in time, etc.).

fore·gone ['fɔ:gɒn] *adj.* *~ conclusion,* (a) predetermined conclusion; (b) ending that can be seen or could have been seen from the start.

fore·ground ['fɔ:graund] *n.* **1.** part of a view (esp. in a picture) nearest to the observer. **2.** (fig.) most conspicuous position: *keep oneself in the ~.*

fore·hand ['fɔ:hænd] *n. & adj.* (tennis, etc.) (stroke) played with the palm of the hand in the direction of the opponent.

fore·head ['fɒrid] *n.* part of the face above the eyes.

for·eign ['fɒrin] *adj.* **1.** of or from another country, not one's own: *~ worker,* (esp. in West Germany) worker who has come from another country to supplement the labour (3) shortage. **2.** of relations with other countries: *F~ Minister,* ~ secretary in other countries than the United Kingdom. *the F~ Office,* (Gt. Brit.) the department of state dealing with ~ affairs. *F~ Secretary,* (Gt. Brit.) head (10) of the F~ Office. **3.** *~ to,* not natural to; unconnected with. **4.** coming from outside: *a ~ body in the eye* (a bit of dirt, etc.). **~·er** *n.* person born in or from a ~ country.

fore·man ['fɔ:mǝn] *n.* workman in authority over others; chief member and spokesman of a jury.

fore·most ['fɔ:mǝust] *adj.* first; most important. *adv.* first in position: *first and ~,* in the first place.

fore·name ['fɔ:neim] *n.* first or Christian name.

fore·noon ['fɔ:nu:n] *n.* part of the day between sunrise and noon.

fore·run·ner ['fɔ:ˌrʌnǝ*] *n.* sign of what is to follow; person who foretells and prepares for the coming of another in history.

fore·see [fɔ:'si:] *v.t.* (p.t. *-saw* [fɔ:'sɔ:], p.p. *-seen* [fɔ:'si:n]) see in advance: *~ trouble; ~ what will happen.*

fore·shad·ow [fɔ:'ʃædǝu] *v.t.* be a sign or warning of (sth. to come).

fore·shore ['fɔ:ʃɔ:*] *n.* part of the shore between the sea and land that is cultivated, built on, etc.

fore·short·en [fɔ:'ʃɔ:tn] *v.t.* (in drawing pictures) show (an object) with shortening of lines (to give perspective).

fore·sight ['fɔ:sait] *n.* (no pl.) ability to see future needs; care in preparing for these.

or·est ['fɒrɪst] *n.* large area of tree-covered land. **~·er** *n.* man in charge of a ~. **~·ry** *n.* (no pl.) (science of) planting and caring for ~s.

ore·stall [fɔː'stɔːl] *v.t.* do sth. before sb. else and so prevent him from doing it; anticipate (the action of another or an event): ~ *a rival.*

ore·tell [fɔː'tel] *v.t.* (p.t. & p.p. *-told* [fɔː'təʊld]) forecast.

ore·thought ['fɔːθɔːt] *n.* (no pl.) careful thought or planning for the future.

or·ev·er [fə'revə*] *adv.* (U.S.A.) = for ever. (See *ever* (3).)

ore·word ['fɔːwɜːd] *n.* introductory comments on a book, printed in it, esp. by someone not the author. (Cf. *preface.*)

or·feit ['fɔːfɪt] *v.t.* (have to) suffer the loss of sth. as a punishment or consequence or because of rules. *n.* sth. (to be) ~ed. *adj.* (to be) ~ed. **for·fei·ture** ['fɔːfɪtʃə*] *n.* (no pl.) ~ing.

or·gath·er [fɔː'gæðə*] *v.i.* come together; meet (*with*).

orge¹ [fɔːdʒ] *v.i.* ~ *ahead,* go forward, get in front, through hard work, by making efforts.

orge² [fɔːdʒ] *n.* workshop with fire and anvil where metal is heated and shaped, esp. one used by a smith for making shoes for horses, repairing farm machinery, etc. *v.t.* shape (metal) by heating, hammering, etc.

orge³ [fɔːdʒ] *v.t. & i.* make a copy of sth. (e.g. a signature, banknote) in order to deceive; commit ~ry. **forg·er** *n.* person who does this. **forg·ery** *n.* forging; sth. ~d, esp. a person's signature.

or·get [fə'get] *v.t. & i.* (p.t. *-got* [fə'gɒt], p.p. *-gotten* [fə'gɒtn]) ~ (*about*), fail to remember or recall; ~ *oneself,* (a) behave thoughtlessly in a way not suited to one's dignity, or to the circumstances; (b) act unselfishly. **~·ful** *adj.* in the habit of ~ting.

or·give [fə'gɪv] *v.t. & i.* (p.t. *-gave* [fə'geɪv], p.p. *-given* [fə'gɪvn]) pardon (wrongdoing, a person); show mercy to (sb.); (say that one does) not wish to punish (sb. *for* wrongdoing); give up hard feelings towards (sb.); grant ~ness. **~·ness** *n.* (no pl.) forgiving; willingness to ~; being ~n.

or·go [fɔː'gəʊ] *v.t.* (p.t. *-went* [fɔː'went], p.p. *-gone* [fɔː'gɒn]) do without; give up.

ork [fɔːk] *n.* **1.** handle with two or more points (*prongs*), used for lifting food. **2.** farm tool for breaking up ground, lifting hay, straw, etc. ~*-lift,*

~*-lift truck,* vehicle for hoisting heavy objects by means of steel fingers inserted under the load. **3.** place where a road, tree trunk, etc. divides into branches. *v.t. & i.* **1.** lift, move, carry, with a ~ (2). **2.** (of a road, etc.) divide in two directions.

for·lorn [fə'lɔːn] *adj.* unhappy; uncared for; forsaken.

form [fɔːm] *n.* **1.** shape or outward appearance. **2.** general arrangement or structure; sort or variety: ~*s of government.* **3.** (gram.) shape taken by a word (in sound or spelling) to show its use, etc.: *The past tense ~ of 'run' is 'ran'.* **4.** fixed order: ~*s of worship*; manner of behaving or speaking: *good* (*bad*) ~, behaviour according to (not according to) custom or etiquette. **5.** printed paper with spaces to be filled in: *income-tax* (*telegraph*) ~*s.* **6.** physical condition (esp. of horses, athletes): *in good* ~; *out of* ~. **7.** long wooden bench, usu. without a back, for several persons to sit on. **8.** class in schools: *a* ~ *room. v.t. & i.* **1.** give ~ or shape to; make: ~ *words and sentences.* **2.** (of ideas, etc.) give shape to; take shape. **3.** be; become; come into existence: *Ice began to* ~. **4.** (cause to) move into a particular order: ~ (*a regiment*) *into columns.* **for·mal** ['fɔːml] *adj.* **1.** in accordance with rules and customs. **2.** of the outward shape (not the reality or substance): *a* ~*al resemblance.* **3.** regular or geometric in design: ~*al gardens.* **4.** (of behaviour) stiff or ceremonious: *a* ~*al bow.* **for·mal·i·ty** [fɔː'mælətɪ] *n.* ~*al* behaviour; observance required by custom or rules: *legal* ~*alities.* **for·ma·tion** [fɔː'meɪʃn] *n.* ~ing; sth. ~ed; (esp.) structure or arrangement. **for·ma·tive** ['fɔːmətɪv] *adj.* **1.** tending to give ~: *a* ~*ative influence* (e.g. on the character of a child). **2.** pliable: *the* ~*ative years in the life of a child* (during which its character is ~ed). **~·less** *adj.* without ~.

for·mer ['fɔːmə*] *adj.* **1.** of an earlier period: *her* ~ *husband.* **2.** *the* ~, the first-named of the two. (Cf. *the latter.*) ~*·ly adv.* in ~ times.

for·mi·da·ble ['fɔːmɪdəbl] *adj.* **1.** causing fear. **2.** requiring great effort to deal with or overcome: ~ *opposition* (*enemies*).

for·mu·la ['fɔːmjʊlə] *n.* (pl. ~*e* [-liː], ~*s*) **1.** form of words used regularly (e.g. 'How d'you do?'). **2.** statement of a rule, fact, etc. esp. one in symbols and figures, as in chemistry, mathematics,

19

etc. **3.** set of directions (usu. in symbols) for a medical preparation. **4.** (sport) classification of a racing car: *a ~-I car (race).* **~te** ['fɔːmjʊleɪt] *v.t.* express clearly and exactly.

for·ni·ca·tion [ˌfɔːnɪˈkeɪʃn] *n.* (no pl.) voluntary sexual intercourse between persons not married to one another, esp. between unmarried persons. **for·ni·cate** ['fɔːnɪkeɪt] *v.i.* commit ~.

for·sake [fəˈseɪk] *v.t.* (p.t. *-sook* [fəˈsʊk], p.p. *-saken* [fəˈseɪkən]) go away from; give up; desert.

for·swear [fɔːˈsweə*] *v.t.* (p.t. *-swore* [fɔːˈswɔː*], p.p. *-sworn* [fɔːˈswɔːn]) **1.** give up doing or using (s.th.). **2.** ~ *oneself,* after taking an oath to tell the truth, say sth. that is untrue; perjure oneself.

fort [fɔːt] *n.* building(s) specially erected or strengthened for military defence.

forth [fɔːθ] *adv.* **1.** out. **2.** onwards; forwards: *from this day ~; back and ~,* to and fro; *and so ~,* and so on. **ˌ~ˈcom·ing** *adj.* **1.** about to come out: *~coming books.* **2.** *be ~coming,* (of help, money, etc.) be ready when needed. **3.** (of a person) informative; responsive. **'~ˈright** *adj.* outspoken; straightforward. **ˌ~ˈwith** *adv.* at once; without losing time.

for·ti·eth, see *forty.*

for·ti·fy ['fɔːtɪfaɪ] *v.t.* strengthen (a place) against attack (with walls, trenches, guns, etc.); support or strengthen (oneself, one's courage, etc.). **for·ti·fi·ca·tion** [ˌfɔːtɪfɪˈkeɪʃn] *n.* ~ing; fort.

for·ti·tude ['fɔːtɪtjuːd] *n.* (no pl.) calm courage, self-control, in the face of pain, danger, or difficulty.

fort·night ['fɔːtnaɪt] *n.* period of two weeks. **~ly** *adj. & adv.* occurring every ~.

for·tress ['fɔːtrɪs] *n.* fortified town; fort.

for·tu·itous [fɔːˈtjuːɪtəs] *adj.* happening by chance.

for·tune ['fɔːtʃuːn] *n.* **1.** chance; chance looked upon as a power deciding or influencing the future of sb. or sth.; fate; (good or bad) luck coming to a person or undertaking: *have ~ on one's side; tell sb. his ~,* say (e.g. by means of cards) what will happen to him. *a ~-teller,* one who claims to be able to tell ~s. **2.** prosperity; success. **3.** great sum of money; wealth: *a small ~,* a lot of money. **for·tu·nate** ['fɔːtʃnət] *adj.* having, bringing, brought by, good ~.

for·ty ['fɔːtɪ] *n. & adj.* 40. **for·ti·eth** ['fɔːtɪɪθ] *n. & adj.* 40th; ¹/₄₀.

fo·rum ['fɔːrəm] *n.* (ancient Rome) public place for meetings, etc.; any place for public discussion.

for·ward ['fɔːwəd] *adj.* **1.** directed towards the front; situated in front; moving on; advancing. **2.** well advanced or early. **3.** ready and willing (to help, etc.). **4.** too eager; presumptuous. **5.** (of opinions, etc.) advanced or extreme. *n.* front-line, attacking, player (in football, etc.). *v.t.* help or serve ~; send (letters, etc.) after a person to a new address. *adv.* (also ~s) to or towards what is before or in front: *bring sth. ~; come ~; look ~ to,* think usu. with pleasure, about sth. coming in the future; *carriage ~* (see *carriage* (3)); *carry ~* (see *carry* (10)).

fos·sil ['fɒsl] *n.* **1.** recognizable (part of a) prehistoric animal or plant once buried in earth, now hardened like rock. **2.** person who is out of date and unable to accept new ideas. **3.** (attrib.) of or like a ~: *~ shells.* **~ize** ['fɒsɪlaɪz] *v.t. & i.* (cause to) become a ~.

fos·ter ['fɒstə*] *v.t.* care for; help the growth or development of; (fig.) encourage. **'~-ˌbroth·er (-ˌsis·ter)** *ns.* boy (girl) adopted by one's parent(s) and brought up as a member of the family. **'~-child** *n.* child brought up by ~-parents. **'~-ˌpar·ent (-ˌmoth·er, -ˌfa·ther)** *ns.* one who acts as parent in place of a real parent.

fought, see *fight* (v.).

foul [faʊl] *adj.* **1.** causing disgust; having a bad smell or taste; filthy. **2.** wicked; (of language) full of oaths; (of the weather) stormy; rough. **3.** *play,* (a) (sport) sth. contrary to the rules; (b) violent crime, esp. murder. *n.* (sport) action contrary to the rules. *adv. fall (run) ~ of,* (of ships) collide with; become entangled with; (fig.) get into trouble with. *v.t. & i.* **1.** make or become dirty. **2.** (of ships) collide with; (of anchors, chains, nets, etc.) (cause to) become entangled with. **3.** (sport) commit a ~ against (a player).

found¹, see *find* (v.).

found² [faʊnd] *v.t.* **1.** begin the building of; lay the base¹ (1) of: *~ a new city.* **2.** get sth. started (by providing money, etc.): *~ a new school.* **3.** *~ (up)on,* base¹ on: *arguments ~ed on facts.*

foun·da·tion [faʊnˈdeɪʃn] *n.* **1.** founding; sth. founded, esp. an organization or institution such as a school or hospital; fund of money to be used for such an organization, etc. **2.** (often pl.) **strong** base¹ (1) of a building, usu. below ground level, on which it is built up. **3.** ~ (*cream*), base¹ (5) for the application (2) of cosmetics. **4.** ~ (*garment*), woman's corset.

found·er¹ ['faʊndə*] *n.* person who founds² (2) a school, etc.

foun·der² ['faʊndə*] *v.t. & i.* **1.** (of a ship) (cause to) fill with water and sink. **2.** (of a horse) fall; stumble (esp. in mud); cause (a horse) to break down from overwork.

found·ling ['faʊndlɪŋ] *n.* deserted child of unknown parents.

found·ry ['faʊndrɪ] *n.* place where metal or glass is melted and moulded.

fount [faʊnt] *n.* **1.** (poet.) spring of water. **2.** (U.S.A. *font²*) set of printer's type of the same size and style.

foun·tain ['faʊntɪn] *n.* spring of water; water forced through small holes in a pipe for ornamental purposes, or to provide drinking-water in a public place. '~-pen *n.* pen with a supply of ink in the holder.

four [fɔː*] *n. & adj.* **4.** *on all* ~s, on the hands and knees. ~'post·er *n.* old-fashioned bed with four posts supporting curtains. ~'score *adj.* 80. ~·teen [‚fɔː'tiːn] *n. & adj.* **14.** ~·teenth [‚fɔː'tiːnθ] *n. & adj.* **14th;** ¹/₁₄. ~·th [fɔːθ] *n. & adj.* **4th;** ¹/₄.

fowl [faʊl] *n.* (pl. ~s, ~) **1.** (old use) any bird. **2.** domestic cock or hen.

fox [fɒks] *n.* (female *vixen*) wild animal of the dog family, with (usu.) red fur and a bushy tail. '~-hound *n.* dog used in fox-hunting.

frac·tion ['frækʃn] *n.* **1.** small part or bit. **2.** number that is not a whole number (e.g. ¹/₃, ⁵/₈, 0.76).

frac·tious ['frækʃəs] *adj.* irritable; peevish.

frac·ture ['fræktʃə*] *n.* (esp. of a bone) breaking; breakage. *v.t. & i.* break; crack.

frag·ile ['frædʒaɪl] *adj.* easily injured, broken, or destroyed. **fra·gil·i·ty** [frə'dʒɪlətɪ] *n.* (no pl.).

frag·ment ['frægmənt] *n.* part broken off; (of a book, conversation, etc.) incomplete part. **frag·men·ta·ry** ['frægməntərɪ] *adj.* incomplete.

fra·grant ['freɪɡrənt] *adj.* sweet-smelling. **fra·grance** *n.* (no pl.).

frail [freɪl] *adj.* physically or morally weak; fragile. ~·ty *n.* tendency to do wrong; weakness.

frame [freɪm] *n.* **1.** skeleton or main structure (e.g. steel girders, brick

walls, wooden struts²) of a ship, a building, an aircraft, etc. that makes its shape. **2.** human or animal body. **3.** border of wood, etc. round a picture, window, or door; part of spectacles (4) that holds the lenses. **4.** structure of wood and glass for protecting plants from cold. **5.** ~ *of mind*, state or condition of mind. *v.t.* **1.** put together; build up: ~ *a plan* (*a theory, a sentence*). **2.** put a ~ (3) on or round. '~·work *n.* part of a structure giving shape and support: *a bridge with a steel* ~*work*; *the* ~*work of a government* (*novel*).

fran·chise ['fræntʃaɪz] *n.* full rights of citizenship given by a country or town, esp. the right to vote at elections; special right given by public authorities to a person or company.

frank [fræŋk] *adj.* showing clearly the thoughts, etc.; open: *be quite* ~ *with sb.; a* ~ *confession.* ~·ness *n.* (no pl.).

fran·tic ['fræntɪk] *adj.* wildly excited (with pain, anxiety, etc.): *drive sb.* ~. **fran·ti·cal·ly** *adv.*

fra·ter·nal [frə'tɜːnl] *adj.* brotherly. **fra·ter·ni·ty** [frə'tɜːnətɪ] *n.* **1.** (no pl.) brotherly feeling. **2.** society of men (e.g. monks) who treat each other as brothers; men with the same interests: *the fraternity of the press*¹ (5), newspaper writers. **frat·er·nize** ['frætənaɪz] *v.i.* make friends (*with*).

fraud [frɔːd] *n.* **1.** criminal (act of) deception. **2.** person or thing that deceives. ~·u·lent ['frɔːdjʊlənt] *adj.*

fraught [frɔːt] *adj.* (only in) ~ *with*, filled with, having (meaning); involving, threatening (unpleasant consequences): ~ *with risks.*

fray¹ [freɪ] *n.* fight; contest.

fray² [freɪ] *v.t. & i.* (of cloth, rope, etc.) make or become worn by rubbing so that there are loose threads: ~*ed cuffs* (*ropes*).

freak [friːk] *n.* **1.** absurd or most unusual idea, act, or occurrence. **2.** (also ~ *of nature*) person, animal, or plant that is abnormal in form (e.g. a five-legged sheep). **3.** (sl.) (a) person who has broken away from conventional society; (b) drug addict; (c) (U.S.A.) enthusiast. *v.t. & i.* ~ (*out*), (sl.) (cause to) have narcotic hallucinations or an intense emotional experience. ~·ish *adj.* abnormal: ~*ish behaviour.* ~·out *n.* (sl.) **1.** person who is under the influence of a hallucinogenic drug. **2.** action or conduct of a ~·out. ~·y *adj.* (-*ier, -iest*) ~·ish; (sl.) of or relating to ~s (3) or ~-outs.

freck·le ['frekl] *n.* one of the small,

light-brown spots sometimes caused by sunlight on a fair skin. *v.t. & i.* (cause to) become covered with ~s.

free [fri:] *adj.* (*freer* ['fri:ə*], *freest* ['fri:ɪst] **1.** (of a country) self-governing; having a system of government that allows private rights. **2.** (of a person) not a slave; not in prison; not prevented from doing what one wants to do: *have* (*give sb.*) *a ~ hand* (permission to do what seems best without consulting others). **3.** (of things) not fixed, controlled, or held back: *the F~ Churches,* the nonconformists. **4.** without payment; not subject to tax, duty, trade-restrictions, or fees: *~ admission; ~ trade,* the admission of goods into a country without payment of import duties. **5.** (of place or time) not occupied or engaged; (of a person) not having time occupied. **6.** (of a translation) not word for word but giving the general meaning. **7.** *be ~ with* (*of*) (one's money, etc.), use readily; *make ~ with,* use (another person's things) as if they were one's own; *be ~ from* (*error, etc.*), be without. *v.t.* (p.t. & p.p. *freed* [fri:d]) make ~. **~·dom** *n.* condition of being ~ (all senses). **~ en·ter·prise** *n.* (no pl.) ~dom of private business from government control. **~ fight** *n.* fight in which anyone may join. '**~-hand** *adj.* (of drawing) done without the help of a ruler, compasses, etc. ,**~-'hand·ed** *adj.* generous; giving readily. '**~·hold** *n. & adj.* (land) (to be) held as absolute property. **~ kick** *n.* (football) kick allowed to be taken for a minor penalty without opposition from the opponents. **~ lance** *n.* person, esp. an independent journalist or writer, who works for no fixed employer or company. '**~-lance** *v.i.* work in this way. **~·ly** *adv.* in a ~ manner; readily. **~·man** ['fri:mæn] *n.* **1.** person not a slave. **2.** ['fri:mən] person given all the privileges of a city. '**F~,ma·son** *n.* member of a secret society that has branches throughout the world. ,**~-'range** *adj.* (of hens, etc.) allowed to range (2) freely in seeking food. (Cf. *battery* (3).) **~ speech** *n.* (no pl.) right to express facts and opinions of any kind without interference from the authorities. '**~-style** *n.* (no pl.) **1.** (swimming) race in which any stroke may be used. **2.** wrestling with few or no restrictions. **~ think·er** *n.* person not accepting traditional religious teaching but basing his ideas on reason. (Hence ~ *thought.*) '**~·way**

n. expressway; (U.S.A.) toll-free highway. ,**~-'wheel** *v.i.* ride a bicycle without working the pedals; coast (2). **~ will** *n.* (no pl.) power of guiding one's actions without being controlled by events or necessity.

freeze [fri:z] *v.i. & t.* (p.t. *froze* [frəʊz], p.p. *frozen* ['frəʊzn]) **1.** *it is freezing,* it is so cold that water becomes ice. **2.** (of water) become ice; (of other substances) become hard or stiff from cold. **3.** make cold; make hard: *frozen roads; ~ one's blood,* fill with terror. **freez·er** *n.* compartment or room for keeping food frozen at a very low temperature or for freezing food rapidly. '**freez·ing-point** *n.* temperature at which a liquid, esp. water, ~s.

freight [freɪt] *n.* (money charged for the) carriage of goods from place to place in containers or by water, (U.S.A.) also by land; goods carried: *~liner,* (Gt. Brit.) train that carries goods in containers; *~ train* (U.S.A.), goods (6) train. *v.t.* load (a ship) with cargo. **~·er** *n.* cargo ship; aircraft that carries mainly ~.

French [frentʃ] *adj.* of France; of, written or spoken in, the ~ language: *~ fries* (U.S.A.), potato chips; *~ window,* one that serves as both window and door. *take ~ leave,* go away, do sth., without asking permission. *n.* the language of the ~ people. *the ~, (pl.)* the people of France. '**~·man** *n.* '**~,wom·an** *n.*

fre·net·ic [frə'netɪk] *adj.* frantic; frenzied.

fren·zy ['frenzɪ] *n.* (no pl.) violent excitement. **fren·zied** *adj.* filled with, showing, ~.

fre·quent ['fri:kwənt] *adj.* often happening; numerous; common; habitual. [fri'kwent] *v.t.* go ~ly to, be often found in or at. **~·ly** *adv.* often. **fre·quen·cy** ['fri:kwənsɪ] *n.* **1.** being ~. **2.** rate of occurrence.

fres·co ['freskəʊ] *n.* (pl. *-os, -oes*) (method of) painting on moist plaster (of walls or ceilings).

fresh [freʃ] *adj.* **1.** newly made, produced, gathered, grown, arrived, etc. **2.** new or different. **3.** (of food) not frozen, salted, or tinned; (of water) not salt: *~water,* of ~ water, not of the sea: *~water fish.* **4.** (of a person's complexion) healthy-looking. **5.** (of weather, the wind) cool; refreshing: *in the ~ air,* out of doors. **~·en** [freʃn] *v.t. & i.* make or become ~. **~·ly** *adv.* **~·ness** *n.* (no pl.).

fret¹ [fret] *v.i. & t.* (*-tt-*) **1.** worry; (cause to) be discontented or bad-tempered. **2.** wear away by rubbing or biting at. **~ful** *adj.* discontented; irritable.

fret² [fret] *v.t.* (*-tt-*) ornament (wood, etc.) with designs made by cutting. **'~saw** *n.* narrow saw for cutting (designs in) thin wood. **'~work** *n.* (no pl.) wood cut in this way.

fri·ar ['fraɪə*] *n.* man who is a member of one of certain religious orders, esp. one who has vowed to live in poverty.

fric·tion ['frɪkʃn] *n.* **1.** rubbing of one thing against another, esp. when this wastes energy. **2.** difference of opinion leading to arguments, etc.

Fri·day ['fraɪdɪ] *n.* fifth day of the week. *Good ~s* before Easter.

fridge [frɪdʒ] *n.* (Gt. Brit., colloq., abbr. for) refrigerator.

friend [frend] *n.* **1.** person, other than a relative, whom one likes and knows well; helpful person or thing: *make ~s with*, become the ~(s) of. **2.** *F~*, member of the *Society of F~s*; Quaker. **~ly** *adj.* (*-ier, -iest*) acting, ready to act, as a ~. **~li·ness** *n.* (no pl.) ~ly feeling or behaviour. **~ship** *n.* being ~s; relationship or feeling between ~s.

frieze [friːz] *n.* ornamental band or strip along a wall (usu. at the top).

frig·ate ['frɪgɪt] *n.* fast sailing-ship formerly used in war; (modern use) fast escort vessel.

fright [fraɪt] *n.* **1.** great and sudden fear: *filled with ~*; *give sb. a ~*. **2.** ridiculous-looking person or thing. **~en** ['fraɪtn] *v.t.* fill with ~; give a ~ to. **~ful** *adj.* **1.** causing fear; horrible. **2.** unpleasant; unsatisfactory. **~ful·ly** *adv.* (colloq.) very.

frig·id ['frɪdʒɪd] *adj.* **1.** cold: *the ~ zones* (within the polar circles). **2.** unfriendly; without warmth of feeling. **fri·gid·i·ty** [frɪ'dʒɪdətɪ] *n.* (no pl.).

frill [frɪl] *n.* **1.** ornamental edging. **2.** (usu. pl.) unnecessary adornment (e.g. of speech or writing). **~ed** *adj.* having ~s.

fringe [frɪndʒ] *n.* **1.** ornamental border of loose threads (e.g. on a shawl or rug). **2.** edge (of a crowd, forest, etc.). **3.** part of (usu. woman's) hair allowed to cover the forehead. *v.t.* put a ~ on; serve as a ~ to: *~ed with trees.*

frisk [frɪsk] *v.i. & t.* **1.** jump and run about playfully. **2.** feel over and search (sb.) for concealed weapons, etc. (usu. rapidly). **~y** *adj.* (*-ier, -iest*) ready to ~; lively: *a ~y kitten.*

frit·ter¹ ['frɪtə*] *v.t.* ~ *away*, waste (time, energy, etc.) bit by bit.

frit·ter² ['frɪtə*] *n.* batter² fried in fat, usu. with a slice of apple or other fruit in it.

friv·o·lous ['frɪvələs] *adj.* not serious or important; (of persons) lacking in seriousness. **fri·vol·i·ty** [frɪ'vɒlətɪ] *n.*

friz·zle ['frɪzl] *v.i. & t.* fry, grill, etc. with a sputtering noise.

fro [frəʊ] *adv.* *to and ~*, backwards and forwards.

frock [frɒk] *n.* **1.** woman's dress (1) or gown; child's dress. **2.** long robe worn by a monk.

frog [frɒg] *n.* small, cold-blooded, tailless, jumping animal living in water and on land. **'~man** *n.* person skilled in swimming under water equipped with a rubber suit, flippers (2), and an aqualung.

a frog

frol·ic ['frɒlɪk] *v.i.* (p.t. & p.p. *-icked*) play about in a gay, lively way. *n.* happy, lively play; outburst of merry-making. **~some** *adj.*

from [frɒm, frəm] *prep.* (indicating) **1.** starting-point in space: *travelling ~ London to Rome.* **2.** beginning of a period: *~ the first of May to the third of June*; *~ time to time*, occasionally. **3.** place concerned with distance, absence, etc.: *ten miles ~ the coast*; *stay away ~ school*; *be away ~ home.* **4.** giver, sender, etc.: *I've received a letter (a present) ~ my brother.* **5.** source; origin: *a passage ~ Shake-speare*; *a painting ~ nature* (sth. which the artist was looking at). *Wine is made ~ grapes.* **6.** escape; separation; release: *flee ~ the enemy*; *released ~ prison. Take the knife away ~ the baby.* **7.** cause; motive: *collapse ~ weakness*; *do sth. ~ a sense of duty.* **8.** distinction; difference: *You can't distinguish the one ~ the other. This is different ~ that.* **9.** advs. or adverbial phrases of place, time, or prepositions: *~ long ago*; *~ above*; *~ abroad*; *~ under the table*; *~ behind her spectacles.*

frond [frɒnd] *n.* leaf-like part of a fern or a palm-tree.

front [frʌnt] *n.* **1.** foremost or most

important side: *Visitors go to the ~ door. a ~ seat at the theatre*, in the first few rows nearest the stage. **2.** (mil.) part where fighting is taking place. **3.** road bordering part of a town facing the sea; road or path bordering a lake. **4.** *put on (show) a bold ~,* show, pretend to have, no fear. **in ~** *adv.* **go in ~. in ~ of** *prep.* directly before: *The car stood in ~ of the house.* *v.t. & i.* be opposite; have the ~ facing: *hotels ~ing the sea.* **~age** ['frʌntɪdʒ] *n.* extent of land or building along its ~, esp. bordering a road or river. **fron‧tal** ['frʌntl] *adj.* of, on, or to, the ~.

fron‧tier ['frʌn‚tɪə*] *n.* part of a country bordering on another country; boundary. **~s‧man** *n.* man who lives on a ~, on or beyond the borders of civilization.

fron‧tis‧piece ['frʌntɪspiːs] *n.* picture coming before the title-page or text of a book.

frost [frɒst] *n.* **1.** (no pl.) weather condition with temperature below the freezing-point of water. **2.** (no pl.) white powder-like coating of frozen vapour on ground, roofs, plants, etc. **3.** (sl.) event that fails to come up to expectations; failure. *v.t.* **1.** cover with ~ (2). **2.** kill or damage by ~ (1): *~ed plants.* **3.** *~ed glass* (made opaque). **'~‧bite** *n.* (no pl.) injury to a part of the body from ~. **'~‧bit‧ten** *adj.* having ~‧bite. **~‧ing** *n.* (no pl.) icing (1). **~y** *adj.* (*-ier, -iest*) cold with ~ (1); covered with ~ (2); (fig.) without warmth of feeling.

froth [frɒθ] *n.* (no pl.) **1.** creamy mass of small bubbles; foam. **2.** light, worthless talk or ideas. *v.i.* give off ~. **~y** *adj.* (*-ier, -iest*) of, like, covered with, ~ (1, 2).

frown [fraʊn] *v.i.* (in anger, puzzlement) draw the eyebrows together causing lines on the forehead: *~ on,* show disapproval of. *n.* ~ing look.

frow‧zy ['fraʊzɪ] *adj.* (*-ier, -iest*) **1.** dirty; untidy. **2.** ill-smelling; close² (5).

froze, fro‧zen, see *freeze.*

fru‧gal ['fruːgl] *adj.* **1.** economical (esp. of food). **2.** costing little. **~ly** *adv.* **~‧i‧ty** [fruːˈgælətɪ] *n.*

fruit [fruːt] *n.* **1.** part of a plant containing the seed(s). **2.** (usu. pl.) vegetable products fit for food: *~s of the earth.* **3.** (collective pl. ~) sweet ~ that can be used as food (e.g. apples, bananas): *eat much ~.* **4.** (fig.) profit, result or outcome of industry, labour, study, etc. *v.i.* (of trees and plants) bear ~. **~‧er‧er** ['fruːtərə*] *n.* person

who sells ~. **~‧ful** *adj.* producing ~ or (fig.) good results. **fru‧ition** [fruːˈɪʃn] *n.* (no pl.) realization of hopes; getting what was wanted: *aims brought to fruition.* **~‧less** *adj.* without ~ or (fig.) success. **~y** *adj.* (*-ier, -iest*) of or like ~ in taste or smell.

frus‧trate [frʌˈstreɪt] *v.t.* prevent (sb.) from doing sth.; prevent (sb.'s plans, etc.) from being carried out; disappoint. **frus‧trat‧ed** *adj.* discontented through the inability to achieve one's desires. **frus‧tra‧tion** [frʌˈstreɪʃn] *n.* state or instance of being ~d; defeat; disappointment.

fry¹ [fraɪ] *v.t. & i.* cook, be cooked, in boiling fat.

fry² [fraɪ] *n.* (pl. ~) newly hatched fishes. *small f~,* unimportant persons, children, etc.

fud‧dle ['fʌdl] *v.t.* make stupid, esp. with alcoholic drink.

fu‧el [fjʊəl] *n.* material for burning (e.g. wood, coal, oil, petrol). *v.t. & i.* (*-ll-,* U.S.A. also *-l-*) supply with ~; take in ~.

fu‧gi‧tive ['fjuːdʒɪtɪv] *n.* person running away *from* justice, danger, etc. *adj.* **1.** running away (from justice, danger, etc.). **2.** not lasting very long.

-ful [-fʊl] *suff.* **1.** (forming adjs. from vs.): *forgetful.* **2.** (forming adjs. from abstract ns.) full of; having the quality of: *graceful; hopeful; masterful.* **3.** (forming ns. from concrete ns.) amount that fills: *cupful; handful.*

ful‧crum ['fʌlkrəm] *n.* (pl. ~s, *-cra*) point on which a lever turns or is supported.

ful‧fil (U.S.A. also **-fill**) [fʊlˈfɪl] *v.t.* (*-ll-*) perform or carry out (a task, duty, promise, etc.); complete (an undertaking, etc.); do what is required (by conditions, etc.). **~‧ment** *n.* (no pl.).

full [fʊl] *adj.* **1.** holding as much or as many as possible; filled completely. **2.** *~ of,* having or holding plenty of; crowded: *a dictionary ~ of examples; a train ~ of passengers.* **3.** complete: *drive at ~ (top) speed. Write it in ~,* with all particulars. *a ~ stop,* punctuation mark ending a sentence. **4.** completely occupied with: *He was ~ of his own importance.* **5.** (of clothing) allowing plenty of room for the body or limbs; (of people) plump: *be rather ~ in the face.* **6.** *~ back,* (football, etc.) player behind the half-backs; defender. *~ dress,* ceremonial uniform. *~ face* (portrait), looking directly at the camera. *~‧time,* occupying all one's working time: *a ~‧time job; working*

~-time. adv. completely: ~-grown; ~-blown, (of flowers) quite open. **ful·ly** adv. ~·ness n. (no pl.).

-ful·ly [-fʊlɪ] suff. forming advs. corresponding to the adjs. in -ful.

ful·mi·nate ['fʌlmɪneɪt] v.i. protest loudly and bitterly (against).

ful·some ['fʊlsəm] adj. (of praise, flattery, etc.) excessive and insincere; sickening.

fum·ble ['fʌmbl] v.i. & t. feel about uncertainly with the hands; use the hands awkwardly.

fume [fjuːm] n. 1. (usu. pl.) strong-smelling smoke, gas, or vapour. 2. (fig.) fit of anger: in a ~. v.i. & t. 1. give off ~s. 2. show signs of anger or discontent. 3. darken the surface of wood with ~s. **fu·mi·gate** ['fjuːmɪgeɪt] v.t. disinfect by means of ~s. **fu·mi·ga·tion** [ˌfjuːmɪˈgeɪʃn] n.

fun [fʌn] n. (no pl.) amusement; playfulness; sport (4): in ~, not seriously; make ~ of, poke ~ at, tease; cause others to laugh at. ~-fair, (Gt. Brit.) amusement park.

func·tion ['fʌŋkʃn] n. 1. special activity or purpose of a person or thing: the ~s of a judge (of the nerves, of education). 2. public ceremony or event. v.i. fulfil a ~ (1); operate: ~ as, do the duty of. ~·al ['fʌŋkʃənl] adj. ~·ary n. person with official ~s; official.

fund [fʌnd] n. 1. store or supply (of non-material things): a ~ of common sense (funny stories). 2. (also pl.) sum of money available for a purpose: a relief ~ (to help in a disaster, etc.); in ~s, having money to spend.

fun·da·men·tal [ˌfʌndəˈmentl] adj. of or forming a foundation; of great importance. n. (usu. pl.) ~ rule or principle; essential part. ~·ly adv.

fu·ner·al ['fjuːnərəl] n. burial or burning of a dead person with religious ceremonies. **fu·ne·re·al** [fjuːˈnɪərɪəl] adj. of or like a ~; dark, sad, or gloomy.

fun·gus ['fʌŋgəs] n. (pl. -gi ['fʌŋgaɪ], ~es) plant (e.g. mushroom) without green leaves that usu. grows on other plants or on decaying matter (e.g. old wood).

fu·nic·u·lar [fjuːˈnɪkjʊlə*] adj. ~ railway, cable railway in which an ascending car counterbalances a descending car (3). n. ~ railway.

funk [fʌŋk] n. (sl.) 1. great fear: in a ~. 2. coward. v.i. & t. show fear; (try to) escape (doing sth.).

fun·nel ['fʌnl] n. 1. tube or pipe, wide at the top and narrowing at the bottom, for pouring liquids or powder into small openings. 2. outlet for smoke from a steamer, railway engine, etc.

funnels

fun·ny ['fʌnɪ] adj. (-ier, -iest) 1. causing fun or amusement. 2. strange; surprising; difficult to understand. ~-bone n. sensitive part of the elbow. **fun·ni·ly** adv.

fur [fɜː*] n. 1. (no pl.) soft thick hair covering certain animals (e.g. cats, rabbits). 2. animal skin with the ~ on it, used as clothing: a fox ~; a ~ coat. 3. (no pl.) rough coating on a person's tongue when ill, or on the inside of a kettle or boiler when water is chalky. ~·red adj. covered with ~ (3). ~·ry adj. (-ier, -iest) of or like ~; covered with ~.

fur·bish ['fɜːbɪʃ] v.t. ~ (sth.) up, make like new; polish up.

fu·ri·ous ['fjʊərɪəs] adj. violent; uncontrolled; full of fury.

furl [fɜːl] v.t. & i. (of sails, flags, umbrellas) roll up.

fur·long ['fɜːlɒŋ] n. 220 yards (= 201.17 metres).

fur·lough ['fɜːləʊ] n. (permission for) absence from duty (esp. missionaries, civil officials, members of the armed forces, living abroad): going home on ~; six months' ~.

fur·nace ['fɜːnɪs] n. 1. shut-in fireplace for heating water to warm buildings, etc. by hot pipes. 2. enclosed space for heating metals, making glass, etc.

fur·nish ['fɜːnɪʃ] v.t. supply or provide (with); put furniture in. **fur·ni·ture** ['fɜːnɪtʃə*] n. (no pl.) such things as tables, chairs, beds, etc. needed for a room, house, or office.

fur·row ['fʌrəʊ] n. long, deep cut made in the ground by a plough; line on the forehead. v.t. make ~s in.

fur·ther ['fɜːðə*] adv. 1. at a greater distance in time or space. (See far.) 2. besides; in addition; moreover. adj. beyond what exists; additional. v.t. help forward, promote (2) (plans, undertakings, etc.). **fur·thest** adj. & adv. see far. ~'more adv. in addition; moreover. '~·most adj. farthest.

fur·tive [ˈfɜːtɪv] *adj.* (of actions) done secretly or without wishing to attract attention; (of a person) having a wish to escape notice.

fu·ry [ˈfjʊərɪ] *n.* **1.** violent excitement, esp. anger; outburst of wild feeling. **2.** violently furious woman.

furze [fɜːz] *n.* (no pl.) shrub with thorns and yellow flowers; gorse.

fuse [fjuːz] *v.t. & i.* melt with great heat; (of an electric circuit) be broken through melting of the ∼; join or become one whole as the result of fusing. *n.* **1.** (in an electric circuit) short piece of wire that melts and breaks the circuit if a fault develops. **2.** device (2) for carrying a spark to explode powder, etc. **3.** (U.S.A. usu. *fuze*) mechanical or electrical device (2) designed to detonate the explosive charge of a bomb, projectile, etc.

fu·se·lage [ˈfjuːzɪlɑːʒ] *n.* body (4) of an aircraft.

fu·sion [ˈfjuːʒn] *n.* mixing or blending of different things into one: *the ∼ of copper and tin*; *a ∼ of races*.

fuss [fʌs] *n.* (no pl.) unnecessary excitement, esp. about unimportant things. *v.i. & t.* get into a ∼; make nervous or excited. **∼y** *adj.* (*-ier, -iest*) full of, showing, nervous excitement; worrying about little things.

fus·ty [ˈfʌstɪ] *adj.* (*-ier, -iest*) smelling of dust and mould; stale.

fu·tile [ˈfjuːtaɪl] *adj.* of no use; unlikely to do much. **fu·til·i·ty** [fjuːˈtɪlətɪ] *n.*

fu·ture [ˈfjuːtʃə*] *n.* (no pl.) *& adj.* (time, events) coming after the present: *for the ∼, in ∼*, from this time onwards. *n.* (no pl.) (gram.) ∼ tense of a language; verb form in the ∼ tense. **fu·tu·ri·ty** [fjuːˈtjʊərətɪ] *n.* ∼ time; ∼ event.

fu·tur·ol·o·gy [ˌfjuːtʃəˈrɒlədʒɪ] *n.* (no pl.) systematic forecasts about future developments in science and technology and their effect upon society. **fu·tur·ol·o·gist** *n.*

fuze [fjuːz] see *fuse* (3).

fuzzy [ˈfʌzɪ] *adj.* (*-ier, -iest*) blurred, indistinct (in shape or outline).

G

ab·ble ['gæbl] *v.t. & i.* say things quickly and indistinctly. *n.* (no pl.) ast, indistinct talk.

·ble ['geɪbl] *n.* three-cornered part f an outside wall between sloping oofs. (Cf. *eaves*.)

ad [gæd] *v.i.* (-dd-) ~ *about,* go from lace to place looking for excitement or leasure.

ad·fly ['gædflaɪ] *n.* fly that bites livetock.

ad·get ['gædʒɪt] *n.* small convenient ontrivance or apparatus (1).

aff [gæf] *n.* hook for landing fish aught with rod and line.

ag [gæg] *n.* **1.** sth. put into a person's nouth to keep it open, or into or over t to keep him quiet. **2.** words or actions dded to his part by an actor; stage oke. *v.t. & i.* (-gg-) **1.** put a ~ (1) nto or over the mouth of. **2.** (of an ctor) use ~s (2).

age¹ [geɪdʒ] *n.* sth. given as security r guarantee. **2.** gauntlet¹ (1).

age², see *gauge.*

ai·ety, gai·ly, see *gay.*

ain [geɪn] *v.t. & i.* **1.** obtain (sth. vanted or needed): ~ *experience;* ~ *trength* (after an illness); ~ *time* (i.e. mprove one's chances by postponing th., etc.). **2.** make progress; be improved: ~ *in weight.* **3.** (of a watch, lock) become fast² (3): *My watch* ~s *even minutes a day.* **4.** ~ (*up*)*on,* (a) get nearer to (other runners who are ahead n a race); (b) get further ahead of others who are behind). *n.* sth. ~ed; profit: *a* ~ *in health; the love of* ~. ~**ul** *adj.* yielding profit or pay: ~*ful ccupations.*

ain·say [,geɪn'seɪ] *v.t.* (p.t. & p.p. ~*said*) deny; contradict: *There is no* ~*ing is honesty.*

ait [geɪt] *n.* manner of walking.

ai·ter ['geɪtə*] *n.* cloth or leather covering for the leg from knee to ankle or or the ankle.

a·la ['gɑːlə] *n.* occasion of public nerry-making; (attrib.) ~ *night,* event with special features (e.g. at a theatre).

gal·axy ['gæləksɪ] *n.* **1.** irregular band of stars not seen separately but making the sky bright. **2.** group (of brilliant, famous, etc. persons).

gale [geɪl] *n.* strong wind.

gall¹ [gɔːl] *n.* (no pl.) **1.** bitter liquid (bile) produced by the liver. **2.** (fig.) bitter feeling.

gall² [gɔːl] *n.* painful swelling on an animal (esp. a horse) caused by rubbing; place rubbed bare. *v.t. & i.* **1.** rub sore; become sore by rubbing. **2.** (fig.) hurt the feelings of (sb.); vex.

gal·lant ['gælənt] *adj.* **1.** brave. **2.** fine; beautiful; stately: *a* ~ *ship.* **3.** very attentive to women; amorous. *n.* young man of fashion, esp. one fond of and attentive to women. ~**ry** ['gæləntrɪ] *n.* **1.** (no pl.) bravery. **2.** polite words, acts, etc. of a ~. **3.** (no pl.) devotion, polite attention, to women.

gal·le·on ['gælɪən] *n.* Spanish sailingship (15th to 17th centuries).

gal·lery ['gælərɪ] *n.* **1.** room or building for the display of works of art. **2.** (people in the) highest and cheapest seats in a theatre: *play to the* ~, try to win approval by appealing to popular taste. **3.** raised floor or platform extending from an inner wall of a hall, church, etc. **4.** covered walk or corridor, partly open at one side. **5.** horizontal underground passage in a mine. (Cf. *shaft* (4).) **6.** long, narrow room; passage: *a shooting-*~.

gal·ley ['gælɪ] *n.* **1.** (hist.) low flat ship with one deck, rowed by slaves or criminals; ancient Greek or Roman warship. **2.** ship's kitchen.

gal·li·vant [,gælɪ'vænt] *v.i.* (colloq.) gad about.

gal·lon ['gælən] *n.* measure of capacity for liquids; four quarts (= 4.54 litres, U.S.A. 3.78 litres).

gal·lop ['gæləp] *n.* (of a horse, etc.) fastest pace with all four feet off the ground at each stride; a ride at this pace. *v.t. & i.* (cause to) go at a ~; (fig.) hurry (*through* work, etc.).

gal·lows ['gæləʊz] *n. pl.* (usu. sing. v.) wooden framework for putting criminals to death by hanging. **'~-bird** *n.* person who deserves hanging.

ga·lore [gə'lɔː*] *adv.* in plenty: *gin and whisky ~.*

ga·losh, go·losh [gə'lɒʃ] *n.* rubber overshoe: *a pair of ~es.*

gal·van·ic [gæl'vænɪk] *adj.* of, produced by, galvanism. **gal·va·nism** ['gælvənɪzəm] *n.* (no pl.) (science of, medical use of) electricity produced by chemical action. **gal·van·ize** ['gælvənaɪz] *v.t.* **1.** coat (sheet iron, etc.) with metal (e.g. zinc) by galvanism. **2.** (fig.) shock or rouse (a person into doing sth.).

gam·bit ['gæmbɪt] *n.* opening move in chess.

gam·ble ['gæmbl] *v.i. & t.* play games of chance for money; take great risks on the chance of making a profit or winning sth. *n.* undertaking or attempt with risk of loss and chance of profit or advantage. **~r** *n.* person who ~s. **gam·bling** *n.* (no pl.) playing games to win money; taking serious risks in business, etc.

gam·bol ['gæmbl] *v.i.* (-*ll-*, U.S.A. also -*l*-) *& n.* (usu. pl.) (make) quick, playful, jumping or skipping movements.

game¹ [geɪm] *n.* **1.** form of play, esp. with rules (e.g. tennis, football, cards): *play the ~,* keep the rules; (fig.) be honest. *~s-master* (*mistress*), teacher in charge of athletics or sports at a school. **2.** (pl.) athletic contests: *the Olympic G.~s.* **3.** single round in some contests (e.g. tennis); points, score, needed by a player to win. **4.** scheme, plan, or undertaking; dodge or trick: *having a ~ with them,* playing a trick on them; *making ~ of me,* ridiculing me. *The ~ is up,* everything has failed. **5.** (no pl.) (collective) (flesh of) animals and birds hunted for sport and food: *big ~,* elephants, lions, tigers, etc. **~ acts, ~ laws** *ns. pl.* laws on the killing and preservation of ~ (5). **'~-keep·er** *n.* man employed to breed and protect ~ (5). **'~-,war·den** *n.* official supervising ~ (5) and hunting.

game² [geɪm] *adj.* **1.** brave; ready to go on fighting. **2.** having the spirit or energy (*for* sth., *to do* sth.).

game³ [geɪm] *adj.* (of a leg, arm, etc.) crippled; that cannot be used.

gam·ut ['gæmət] *n.* whole range of musical notes, (fig.) of feeling, etc.

gan·der ['gændə*] *n.* male goose.

gang [gæŋ] *n.* number of labourers, slaves, prisoners, criminals, working together; (colloq.) group of persons

going about together, usu. causing d: approval. **~ster** *n.* member of a ~ criminals.

gang·plank ['gæŋplæŋk] *n.* movab plank placed between a ship a land.

gan·grene ['gæŋgriːn] *n.* (no pl.) dec of a part of the body, usu. because t supply of blood has been stopped.

gang·way ['gæŋweɪ] *n.* **1.** opening in ship's side; movable bridge from th to the land. **2.** passage between rows seats or persons.

gan·try ['gæntrɪ] *n.* structure suppor ing a travelling crane, railway signal etc.

gaol, jail [dʒeɪl] *n.* (U.S.A. usu. *ja* public prison. **'~-bird** person often in ~. **~·er, jail·er, jail·** *n.* person in charge of a ~ or the priso ers in it.

gap [gæp] *n.* **1.** break or opening (in wall, hedge, etc.). **2.** unfilled spac interval; wide separation (of idea etc.): *~s in one's education* (what o failed to learn while at school, etc.).

gape [geɪp] *v.i.* open the mouth wid yawn; stare with open mouth and surprise (*at* sth.). *n.* yawn.

ga·rage ['gærɑːdʒ] *n.* building or she in which to keep motor cars; roadsi petrol and service station.

garb [gɑːb] *n.* (no pl.) (style of) dres esp. as worn by a particular kind person: *in clerical ~. v.t.* (usu. passiv dress (*in* or as): *~ed as a sailor.*

gar·bage ['gɑːbɪdʒ] *n.* (no pl.) **1.** was food put out as worthless, or for pig etc. **2.** (U.S.A.) refuse², rubbish (any kind): *~ can,* dustbin.

gar·ble ['gɑːbl] *v.t.* make an unfa selection from (statements, facts, etc in order to give false ideas.

gar·den ['gɑːdn] *n.* **1.** (piece of) groun used for growing flowers, vegetable lawns, etc.: *~ city (suburb),* one laid o with spacious and ~-like surroundin **2.** (often pl.) public park. *v.i.* cultivat work in, a ~. **~·er** *n.* person who ~ **~·ing** *n.* (no pl.) cultivating of ~ (attrib.) *~ing tools.*

gar·gle ['gɑːgl] *v.t. & i.* wash th throat with liquid kept in motion by stream of breath. *n.* liquid used f this purpose.

gar·goyle ['gɑːgɔɪl] *n.* stone or met spout, usu. in the form of a grotesqu human or animal creature, to carry o rain-water from the roof of a buildin (esp. a church).

gar·ish ['geərɪʃ] *adj.* too bright; over coloured or over-decorated.

gar·land ['gɑːlənd] *n.* circle of flowers or leaves as ornament or decoration.

gar·lic ['gɑːlɪk] *n.* (no pl.) onion-like plant with a strong taste and smell, used in cooking.

gar·ment ['gɑːmənt] *n.* article of clothing.

gar·ner ['gɑːnə*] *v.t.* store; collect.

gar·nish ['gɑːnɪʃ] *v.t.* decorate, esp. a dish of food.

gar·ret ['gærɪt] *n.* room on the top floor, esp. in the roof.

gar·ri·son ['gærɪsn] *n.* military force stationed in a town or fort. *v.t.* supply with a ⁓.

gar·ru·lous ['gærʊləs] *adj.* talkative. **gar·ru·li·ty** [gæ'ruːlətɪ] *n.* (no pl.).

gar·ter ['gɑːtə*] *n.* (elastic) band worn round the leg to keep a stocking in place.

gas [gæs] *n.* (pl. ⁓es ['gæsɪz]) **1.** any air-like substance that is not solid or liquid at ordinary temperatures. **2.** (no pl.) the kinds of ⁓, natural or manufactured from coal, used for heating, etc. **3.** (no pl.) (U.S.A., colloq.) = gasoline (petrol): *step on the* ⁓, increase speed by pressing down the accelerator pedal with the foot. *v.t. & i.* (-ss-) **1.** poison or overcome by ⁓. **2.** (colloq.) talk for a long time without saying much that is useful. '⁓·bag *n.* (derog.) person who talks too much. ⁓·e·ous ['gæsjəs] *adj.* of or like ⁓. ⁓·hold·er ['gæs- ˌhəʊldə*], gas·om·e·ter [gæ'sɒmɪtə*] *ns.* large, round tank in which ⁓ is stored for distribution. ⁓ ring *n.* ring pierced with small holes for gas (2), used for cooking. ⁓ sta·tion *n.* (U.S.A.) = petrol station.

gash [gæʃ] *n.* long deep cut or wound. *v.t.* make a ⁓ in.

gas·ket ['gæskɪt] *n.* (tech.) strip of hemp or flat piece of other material (as rubber), used to pack (3) joints, etc. to prevent steam, water, etc. from escaping.

gas·o·line, gas·o·lene ['gæsəʊliːn] *n.* (no pl.) (U.S.A.) = petrol.

gasp [gɑːsp] *v.i. & t.* take short, quick breaths as a fish does out of water; struggle for breath. *n.* catching of the breath through pain, surprise, etc: *at one's last* ⁓, exhausted; at the point of death.

gas·tric ['gæstrɪk] *adj.* of the stomach: ⁓ *ulcer*.

gate [geɪt] *n.* **1.** opening in a wall, fence, etc. that can be closed by a barrier; barrier, usu. on hinges, that closes such an opening; means of entrance or exit; numbered place of access to an aircraft at an airport. **2.** (total sum, also called ⁓-*money*, paid by a) number of people attending a football match, etc. '⁓·crash *v.t.* enter (e.g. a building), attend (e.g. a party), etc. without a ticket or an invitation. '⁓- ˌcrash·er *n.* person doing this. '⁓·way *n.* way in or out, closed by a ⁓ or ⁓s.

gath·er ['gæðə*] *v.t. & i.* **1.** get, come, or bring together. **2.** pick (flowers, etc.); collect (one's papers, books, etc.). **3.** obtain (2) gradually: ⁓ *experience (information)*. **4.** understand; conclude: *I* ⁓ *he was in a hurry. What did you* ⁓ *from his statement?* **5.** draw (cloth, the brows) together into small folds. **6.** (of an abscess) fester; form pus and swell. ⁓·ing *n.* **1.** coming together of people; meeting. **2.** swelling with pus in it.

gaud·y ['gɔːdɪ] *adj.* (-ier, -iest) too bright and showy: ⁓ *decorations*. **gaud·i·ly** *adv.*

gauge (U.S.A. also **gage**) [geɪdʒ] *n.* **1.** standard measure; size or extent: *take the* ⁓ *of sb.'s character*, estimate it. **2.** distance between rails or a pair of wheels; thickness of wire or sheet metal; diameter of a bullet, etc. **3.** instrument for measuring (e.g. rainfall, the strength of wind, the size of tools, the thickness of wire, etc.). *v.t.* measure accurately; (fig.) form an opinion or estimate of.

gaunt [gɔːnt] *adj.* lean; thin; (of a place) desolate; grim.

gaunt·let[1] ['gɔːntlɪt] *n.* **1.** glove with metal plates formerly worn by soldiers: *fling* or *throw down (pick* or *take up) the* ⁓, give (accept) a challenge to fight. **2.** strong glove covering the wrist.

gaunt·let[2] ['gɔːntlɪt] *n.* *run the* ⁓, run between two rows of men who strike the runner with sticks, etc. as a punishment.

gauze [gɔːz] *n.* (no pl.) thin, transparent net-like material of silk, cotton, etc., or of wire (for screening windows, etc.).

gave, see *give* (v.).

gay [geɪ] *adj.* light-hearted; cheerful; full of fun; (colloq.) homosexual. *n.* (colloq.) homosexual. **gai·ly** ['geɪlɪ] *adv.* **gai·e·ty** ['geɪətɪ] *n.* cheerfulness; merry-making.

gaze [geɪz] *v.i. & n.* (no pl.) (take a) long and steady look (*at* sth. or sb.).

ga·zelle [gə'zel] *n.* small antelope.

ga·zette [gə'zet] *n.* (government) periodical with news (of appointments, promotions, etc. of officers and officials).

gaz·et·teer [ˌgæzəˈtɪə*] *n.* index (2) of geographical names.

gear [gɪə*] *n.* **1.** equipment or apparatus (1) for a special purpose: *hunting-~; steering-~; the landing ~ of an aircraft.* **2.** (modern use, colloq.) clothes, esp. for young people. **3.** set of toothed wheels working together in a machine, esp. such a set to connect a motor-car engine with the road wheels: *in (out of) ~,* with the ~wheels connected with (disconnected from) the engine; *high (low) ~,* ~ *that causes high (low) speed; change ~; ~-lever,* (U.S.A.) ~*shift,* lever used to engage or change ~. *v.t. & i.* put in ~: ~ *up (down),* put into high (low) ~.

gearwheels

geese, see *goose.*

Gei·ger count·er [ˈgaɪgə* ˌkaʊntə*] *n.* device (2) for detecting and counting charged particles sent out by radioactive substances.

gel [dʒel] *n.* semi-solid solution or jelly.

gel·a·tin(e) [ˌdʒeləˈtiːn] *n.* (no pl.) clear, tasteless substance, made by boiling bones and waste parts of animals, dissolved in water to make jelly.

geld [geld] *v.t.* castrate. **~ing** [ˈgeldɪŋ] *n.* castrated animal, esp. a male horse.

gem [dʒem] *n.* **1.** precious stone or jewel, esp. when cut and polished. **2.** sth. or sb. valued because of great beauty or usefulness.

gen·der [ˈdʒendə*] *n.* any of the three classes, *masculine, feminine,* and *neuter,* used of nouns and pronouns.

gene [dʒiːn] *n.* (biol.) one of the factors that control heredity.

ge·ne·al·o·gy [ˌdʒiːnɪˈælədʒɪ] *n.* **1.** (no pl.) science of development f plants and animals from earlier forms. **2.** descent of persons from ancestors; diagram (called a *family tree*) illustrating this. **ge·ne·al·o·gist** *n.* **ge·ne·a·log·i·cal** [ˌdʒiːnɪəˈlɒdʒɪkl] *adj.*

gen·er·a, see *genus.*

gen·er·al [ˈdʒenərəl] *adj.* **1.** of, affecting, all or nearly all; not special or particular: *a matter of ~ interest; a ~ election,* one for parliamentary representatives over the whole country; ~ *knowledge* (of a variety of subjects); *a ~ practitioner,* a doctor who is not a specialist; *as a ~ rule, in ~,* usually. **2.**

not in detail: *a ~ outline of a scheme.* **3.** (after an official title) chief: *inspector-~.* *n.* army officer with highest rank below Field Marshal; (old use) *the public* (cf. *caviare*). **gen·er·a·lis·si·mo** [ˌdʒenərəˈlɪsɪməʊ] *n.* (pl. *-os*) supreme commander of land, sea, and air forces or of combined armies. **~·i·ty** [ˌdʒenəˈrælətɪ] *n.* **1.** ~ rule or statement. **2.** (no pl.) quality of being ~ (1). **3.** majority (*of*). **~·ize** [ˈdʒenərəlaɪz] *v.i. & t.* **1.** draw a ~ conclusion (*from*); make a ~ statement. **2.** bring into ~ use. **~·iza·tion** [ˌdʒenərəlaɪˈzeɪʃn] *n.* **~·ly** [ˈdʒenərəlɪ] *adv.* usually; widely; in a ~ sense.

gen·er·ate [ˈdʒenəreɪt] *v.t.* cause to exist or occur; produce: ~ *heat (electricity, bitter feelings).* **gen·er·a·tion** [ˌdʒenəˈreɪʃn] *n.* **1.** (no pl.) generating. **2.** single stage or step in family descent: *three generations* (children, parents, grandparents). **3.** all persons born about the same time: *the rising generation.* **4.** average period (regarded as 30 years) in which children grow up, marry, and have children: *generation gap,* differences of opinion between the younger and older generations. **gen·er·a·tor** [ˈdʒenəreɪtə*] *n.* machine, apparatus (1), for generating steam, electric current, etc.

ge·ner·ic [dʒɪˈnerɪk] *adj.* of a genus; common to a whole group or class; not special.

gen·er·ous [ˈdʒenərəs] *adj.* **1.** ready to give freely; given freely; noble-minded. **2.** plentiful: *a ~ harvest.* **gen·er·os·i·ty** [ˌdʒenəˈrɒsətɪ] *n.*

gen·e·sis [ˈdʒenɪsɪs] *n.* beginning; starting-point.

ge·net·ics [dʒɪˈnetɪks] *n. pl.* (sing. v.) science (branch of biology) dealing with breeding, principles of heredity.

ge·nial [ˈdʒiːnjəl] *adj.* **1.** kindly; sympathetic; sociable. **2.** (of climate, etc.) warm; mild; favourable to growth. **~·ly** *adv.* **~·i·ty** [ˌdʒiːnɪˈælətɪ] *n.* (no pl.) quality of being ~.

gen·i·tal [ˈdʒenɪtl] *adj.* of animal reproduction. **~s** *n. pl.* external sex organs.

gen·i·tive [ˈdʒenɪtɪv] *n. & adj.* ~ (*case*), (gram.) case of nouns, etc. showing source or possession.

ge·nius [ˈdʒiːnjəs] *n.* (pl. *~es, genii* [-ɪaɪ]) **1.** (person with) unusually great powers of mind or imagination. **2.** special character or spirit of a nation, period, institution, language, etc. **3.** (*sb.'s*) *good (evil) ~,* other person or spirit with good (evil) influence upon him.

en·teel [dʒen'tiːl] *adj.* **1.** (formerly) polite and well-bred. **2.** (modern use, usu. ironical) imitating the speech, ways of living, of the upper classes. **gen·til·i·ty** [dʒen'tɪlətɪ] *n.* (no pl.). **en·tile** ['dʒentaɪl] *n. & adj.* (person) not of the Jewish race; heathen. **en·tle** ['dʒentl] *adj.* (~r, ~st) **1.** kind; friendly; not rough or violent. **2.** (of a slope) not steep. **3.** (of a family) with good social position. **'~·folk(s)** *n. pl.* persons of good social position. **'~·man** *n.* **1.** man of honourable and kindly behaviour: *~man's agreement*, agreement that is binding in honour, but cannot be enforced at law. **2.** (polite name for) man. **3.** (formerly) man who did not have to earn his living. **4.** (pl.) polite form of address: *Ladies and Gentlemen!* **'~·man·ly** *adj.* well-behaved. **'~·wom·an** *n.* lady. **gen·tly** *adv.* in a ~ manner.

en·try ['dʒentrɪ] *n. pl.* persons of good social position but without titles of nobility.

en·u·ine ['dʒenjʊɪn] *adj.* true; really what it is said to be. **~·ly** *adv.* **~·ness** *n.* (no pl.).

e·nus ['dʒiːnəs] *n.* (pl. *genera* ['dʒenərə]). **1.** (science) division of animals or plants within a family: ~ *Homo*, mankind. **2.** sort; class.

·og·ra·phy [dʒɪ'ɒgrəfɪ] *n.* (no pl.) science of the earth's surface, climate, vegetation, products, population, etc. **ge·og·ra·pher** *n.* expert in ~. **geo·graph·i·cal** [dʒɪə'græfɪkl] *adj.*

·ol·o·gy [dʒɪ'ɒlədʒɪ] *n.* (no pl.) science of the earth's history as shown by its crust, rocks, etc. **ge·ol·o·gist** *n.* expert in ~. **geo·log·i·cal** [,dʒɪəʊ'lɒdʒɪkl] *adj.*

·om·e·try [dʒɪ'ɒmətrɪ] *n.* (no pl.) science of the properties and relations of lines, angles, surfaces, and solids. **geo·met·ric, geo·met·ri·cal** [,dʒɪəʊ'metrɪk(l)] *adjs.*

·ra·nium [dʒɪ'reɪnjəm] *n.* kind of garden plant with red, pink, or white flowers.

·rm [dʒɜːm] *n.* **1.** portion of living organism capable of becoming a new organism; (fig.) beginning or starting-point (of an idea, etc.). **2.** microbe or bacillus, esp. one causing disease.

er·man ['dʒɜːmən] *adj.* of Germany, its people or language: ~ *shepherd (dog)* (U.S.A.), Alsatian. *n.* native or inhabitant of Germany; the language of Germany.

r·mi·cide ['dʒɜːmisaɪd] *n.* germ-destroying substance.

ger·mi·nate ['dʒɜːmɪneɪt] *v.t. & i.* (of seeds) (cause to) start growth. **ger·mi·na·tion** [,dʒɜːmɪ'neɪʃn] *n.* (no pl.).

ger·und ['dʒerənd] *n.* (gram.) the *-ing* form of an English verb when used as a noun (as in 'fond of *swimming*').

ges·tic·u·late [dʒe'stɪkjʊleɪt] *v.i.* make movements of the hands, arms, or head while, or instead of, speaking. **ges·tic·u·la·tion** [dʒe,stɪkjʊ'leɪʃn] *n.*

ges·ture ['dʒestʃə*] *n.* movement of the hand or head to indicate or illustrate an idea, feeling, etc.; sth. done to convey an attitude.

get [get] *v.t. & i.* (-tt-; p.t. *got* [gɒt], p.p. *got*, old use or U.S.A. *gotten* ['gɒtn]) **1.** obtain; buy; earn; win; fetch; be given; receive; (colloq.) understand or see (the point or meaning of sth. said or written). **2.** (cause to) become: ~ *tired*; ~ *a door open*; ~ *sb. elected*. **3.** (cause to) arrive, come, or go, somewhere: ~ *home*; ~ *the children to bed*. **4.** catch (a disease); suffer; experience: ~ *a shock*. **5.** cause sth. to be done: ~ *one's hair cut*. **6.** engage, persuade, (sb.) to do sth.: ~ *the doctor to call tomorrow*. **7.** ~ *well (better)*, recover from an illness. **8.** (with advs. & preps.): ~ *about*, (of news, etc.) spread; (of people) travel; ~ *sth. across*, (colloq.) cause people to understand or accept it: ~ *a joke (a new idea) across*; ~ *along*, make progress; manage; live sociably (*with sb.*); ~ *at*, reach; find out; (colloq.) bribe; (colloq.) imply: *What are you ~ting at?* ~ *away (with)*, leave; escape; avoid the penalty of: ~ *away with murder*; ~ *back*, come home, etc.; recover (sth. lost); ~ *by heart*, learn by heart; ~ *down*, (colloq.) depress (sb.); swallow (sth.); write (sth.) down; ~ *down to*, begin work on; ~ *in*, arrive; be elected; ~ *(sth.) in*, collect (e.g. debts, crops); (colloq.) start; escape (punishment); alight² from a bus, etc.; ~ *on*, make progress; advance; proceed (*with* sth.); ~ *on with sb.*, be friendly together; ~ *ting on for*, approaching: *It's ~ting on for tea-time.* ~ *out of*, escape (doing sth.); give up (a habit); ~ *over*, overcome (difficulties); recover from (an illness, etc.); finish (a task); ~ *round* (*a rule, etc.*), evade it; ~ *round sb.*, persuade him to do what is desired: *A pretty young wife easily ~s round an old husband.* ~ *through*, pass (an examination); reach the end of (work, money, etc.); ~ *(down) to* (*work, business, etc.*), start; ~ *to know* (*like, etc.*), reach the stage of knowing (liking, etc.); ~ *together*, come or meet together; ~ *up*, stand; ~ out of bed; (of wind) become strong; ~ up to, reach; overtake; ~ up to mischief, engage in it; ~ (sth.) up, arrange the appearance of (hair, oneself, the binding and print of a book); prepare (clothes, goods, etc.) for use or display; organize (an entertainment); ~ up steam, produce steam; (fig.) collect one's energy; become excited or angry. **9.** (in the perfect tenses, colloq.): have got = have; have got to = must; have not got to = need not. **~-at-able** [get-'ætəbl] adj. able to be reached. **'~-up** n. style in which sth. appears; costume: Mrs S. appeared in a new ~-up.

gey·ser n. **1.** ['gaɪzə*] natural spring sending up at intervals a column of hot water or steam. **2.** ['gi:zə*] (Gt. Brit.) apparatus (1) for heating water (e.g. by gas) in a kitchen, bathroom, etc.

ghast·ly ['ga:stlɪ] adj. (usu. -ier, -iest) **1.** death-like; pale and ill: looking ~. **2.** causing horror or fear: a ~ accident. **3.** (of a smile, etc.) painfully forced. adv. ~ pale.

gher·kin ['gɜ:kɪn] n. small, green cucumber used for pickling.

ghet·to ['getəʊ] n. (pl. -os, U.S.A. also -oes) **1.** (hist.) (in some countries) Jewish quarter of a town. **2.** part of a town, esp. a slum area, where members of a minority (3) group live.

ghost [gəʊst] n. **1.** spirit of a dead person appearing to sb. living. **2.** (old use) spirit of life; give up the ~, die. Holy G~, third Being of the Trinity. **3.** sth. shadowy: not the ~ of a chance, not even a small chance. **~·ly** adj. (-ier, -iest) like, suggesting, a ~.

gi·ant ['dʒaɪənt] n. **1.** (in fairy-tales) man of very great height and size. **2.** man, animal, or plant much larger than normal. **3.** (attrib.) of great size.

gib·ber ['dʒɪbə*] v.i. talk fast or make meaningless sounds. **~·ish** ['dʒɪbərɪʃ] n. (no pl.) meaningless talk or sounds.

gib·bet ['dʒɪbɪt] n. wooden post on which corpses of criminals were formerly exposed as a warning.

gibe, jibe [dʒaɪb] v.i. jeer or mock (at); make fun of. n. mocking word(s).

gib·lets ['dʒɪblɪts] n. pl. heart, liver, etc. of a hen, goose, etc. taken out before it is cooked.

gid·dy ['gɪdɪ] adj. (-ier, -iest) **1.** causing, having, the feeling that everything is turning round: a ~ height; feeling ~. **2.** too fond of pleasure; not serious. **gid·di·ly** adv. **gid·di·ness** n. (no pl.).

gift [gɪft] n. **1.** sth. given or received without payment. **2.** natural ability or talent: a boy with a ~ for languages.

3. (no pl.) (law) right or power to give. **~·ed** ['gɪftɪd] adj. having great natural ability.

gig [gɪg] n. **1.** small, light, two-wheele[d] carriage pulled by one horse. **2.** ship[']s small boat.

gi·gan·tic [dʒaɪ'gæntɪk] adj. of im[-] mense size.

gig·gle ['gɪgl] v.i. & t. & n. (give, ex[-] press with, a) silly, often nervous[,] laugh.

gild¹ [gɪld] v.t. cover with gold leaf o[r] gold-coloured paint; make bright: ~ the pill, make sth. unpleasant seem at[-] tractive. **~·ing** n. (no pl.) material wit[h] which things are ~ed. **gilt** [gɪlt] adj[.] ~ed: gilt-edged paper; gilt-edged securi[-] ties (3), (fig.) investments considere[d] to be very safe. n. (no pl.) ~ing.

gild², see **guild**.

gill¹ [gɪl] n. (usu. pl.) organ with whic[h] a fish breathes.

gill² [dʒɪl] n. one-quarter of a pint liq[-] uid measure.

gilt, see **gild¹**.

gim·crack ['dʒɪmkræk] adj. chea[p,] badly-made (ornament, etc.).

gim·let ['gɪmlɪt] n. tool for making [a] small hole in wood.

gim·mick ['gɪmɪk] n. (sl.) ingeniou[s] method of attracting attention or get[-] ting publicity.

gin¹ [dʒɪn] n. (no pl.) colourless al[-] coholic drink made from grain.

gin² [dʒɪn] n. machine for separating[,] cotton from its seeds. v.t. (-nn-) trea[t] (cotton) in a ~.

gin³ [dʒɪn] n. trap for catching animals[.]

gin·ger ['dʒɪndʒə*] n. (no pl.) **1.** (plan[t] with a) hot-tasting root used in cook[-] ing and as a flavouring. **2.** light red[-] dish-yellow; (as adj.) ~ hair. **3.** spirit[,] liveliness. v.t. ~ up, make more vigor[-] ous. **'~·bread** n. cake or biscuit mad[e] with treacle and flavoured with ~.

gin·ger·ly ['dʒɪndʒəlɪ] adj. & adv[.] cautious(ly).

gip·sy, gyp·sy ['dʒɪpsɪ] n. member o[f] an Asiatic race, wandering in parts o[f] Europe, making a living by hors[e] dealing, fortune-telling, basket-mak[-] ing, etc.

gi·raffe [dʒɪ'ra:f] n. African anima[l] with dark spots on yellow skin, and [a] very long neck and long legs.

gird [gɜ:d] v.t. (p.t. & p.p. ~ed o[r] **girt** [gɜ:t]) (liter.) put (on): ~ on one[']s sword (fasten with a belt, etc.).

gir·der ['gɜ:də*] n. wood, iron or stee[l] beam to support the joists of a floo[r,] bridge, etc.

gir·dle ['gɜ:dl] n. **1.** cord or belt fas[-]

tened round the waist. **2.** sth. that
encircles: *a ~ of green fields round a
town. v.t.* encircle.
girl [gɜ:l] *n.* female child; daughter;
unmarried woman; girl or woman
working in a shop, office, etc. '~·
friend *n.* female friend, esp. a boy's or
man's favourite female companion. **G~
Guide,** (U.S.A.) **G~ Scout** *ns.* see
guide (5), *scout*[1] (2). **~·hood** *n.* (no pl.)
period of being a ~. **~·ish** *adj.* of, for,
like, a ~.
gi·ro ['dʒaɪrəu] *n.* (pl. ~s) (comm.) system of credit transfer between banks[2]
(1), post offices, etc.
girt, see *gird.*
girth [gɜ:θ] *n.* **1.** band fastened round
the belly of a horse to keep a saddle in
place. **2.** measurement round sth. (e.g.
a tree): *30 ft. (= 9 metres) in ~.*
gist [dʒɪst] *n.* (no pl.) *the ~ of (sb.'s
remarks, etc.),* the substance or general
sense; the main points.
give [gɪv] *v.t. & i.* (p.t. *gave* [geɪv],
p.p. ~*n* ['gɪvn]) **1.** hand over as a
present; cause (sb.) to have without
payment; cause (sb.) to have in exchange for sth. else or for payment;
hand over to sb. to use or keep; furnish; supply; provide. **2.** ~ *sb. to understand that* ..., assure him, cause him to
think, that ... **3.** (be able to) to be forced
out of the natural or usual shape; be
elastic: *The foundations are giving. The
branch gave but didn't break. The
marshy ground gave under our feet.* **4.**
(with advs. & preps., special senses
only): ~ *(sth.) away,* allow (a secret) to
become known; ~ *sb. away,* betray, be
false to; him; ~ *(the bride) away,* hand
her over to the bridegroom; ~ *in,* stop
struggling, trying to do or get sth.; ~ *on
(to)* or *upon,* (of doors, windows) open
on to; overlook; ~ *out,* (of supplies,
etc.) come to an end; be used up; ~
(sth.) out, distribute; announce; ~ *over,*
stop (*doing* sth.); ~ *up,* stop (*doing* sth.);
discontinue (a habit); surrender: ~ *up
one's seat to sb.* **5.** (with nouns): ~ *a
laugh* (*groan, etc.*), laugh (groan, etc.);
~ *a hand,* help; ~ *evidence of,* show
that one has; ~ *ground,* (of an army)
retire; ~ *rise to,* cause; produce; ~ *way,*
(of a rope, structure, of ice) break; (of an
army) be forced back; surrender oneself (to despair, etc.); ~ *place* (to). *n.*
(no pl.) quality of being elastic or yielding to pressure: *A stone floor has no ~
in it.* ~ *and take,* willingness to compromise. **giv·en** ['gɪvn] *p.p.* (special
uses) **1.** agreed upon: *at a ~n time and
place.* **2.** ~*n to,* addicted to (a habit, e.g.

boasting). **3.** ~*n name,* name given to a
child in addition to the family name.
giv·er *n.*
giz·zard ['gɪzəd] *n.* bird's second
stomach, for grinding food.
gla·cial ['gleɪsjəl] *adj.* of ice: *the ~ era
(epoch),* the time when the northern
hemisphere was mostly covered with
ice.
gla·cier ['glæsjə*] *n.* mass of ice,
formed by snow on mountains, moving
slowly along a valley.
glad [glæd] *adj.* (-*dd*-) pleased; joyful.
~·ly *adv.* **~·ness** *n.* (no pl.). **~·den**
['glædn] *v.t.* make ~.
glade [gleɪd] *n.* clear, open space in a
forest.
glad·i·a·tor ['glædɪeɪtə*] *n.* (in ancient
Rome) man trained to fight with weapons at public entertainments.
glam·our (U.S.A. also **-or**) ['glæmə*]
n. (no pl.) charm or enchantment;
power of beauty or romance to move
the feelings; alluring beauty or charm,
often with sex appeal: *a ~ girl.* **glam-
or·ous** ['glæmərəs] *adj.* full of ~.
glance [glɑ:ns] *v.i. & t.* **1.** take a quick
look (*at, over, through, etc.*). **2.** (of
bright objects, light) flash. **3.** (of a
weapon or blow) slip or slide (*off*). *n.*
quick look.
gland [glænd] *n.* organ in an animal
body that secretes (2) substances that
are to be used by or expelled from the
body: *a snake's poison ~; sweat ~s.*
glan·du·lar ['glændjʊlə*] *adj.* of or
like a ~.
glare [gleə*] *v.i. & n.* (shine with a)
strong, bright light; (give an) angry or
fierce look (*at*). **glar·ing** *adj.* dazzling;
(esp. of errors) easily seen.
glass [glɑ:s] *n.* **1.** (no pl.) hard, easily
broken substance of which window-
panes are made. **2.** ~ drinking-vessel;
its contents: *have a ~ of milk.* **3.** look-
ing-~; ~ mirror. **4.** telescope; (pl.) binoculars. **5.** barometer. **6.** (pl.) eye~es;
spectacles (4). **7.** (no pl.) vessels made
of ~ (bowls, dishes, wine~es, etc.):
plenty of ~ and china. '~·**blow·er** *n.*
workman who blows molten ~ to shape
it into bottles, etc. '~·**house** *n.* build-

glasses

ing with ~ sides and a ~ roof (for growing plants, etc.). **~y** *adj.* (*-ier, -iest*) like ~; (of the eyes, a look) dull; fixed.

glaze [gleɪz] *v.t. & i.* **1.** fit glass into: ~ *a window*. **2.** cover (pots, etc.) with a glass-like coating. **3.** (of eyes) become lifeless in appearance. *n.* (substance used for, surface obtained by giving, a) thin, glassy coating on pots, etc. **glazier** ['gleɪzjə*] *n.* workman who ~s windows.

gleam [gliːm] *v.i. & n.* (give or send out a) ray of soft light, esp. one that comes and goes; (fig.) brief show of hope, humour, etc.

glean [gliːn] *v.t. & i.* pick up grain left in a harvest field by the workers; (fig.) gather in small quantities (news, facts, etc.). **~ings** *n. pl.* what is ~ed.

glee [gliː] *n.* **1.** (no pl.) delight given by triumph, etc. **2.** song for three or four voices singing different parts in harmony. **~ful** *adj.* **~ful·ly** *adv.*

glen [glen] *n.* narrow valley.

glib [glɪb] *adj.* (*-bb-*) (of a person, what he says) ready and smooth, but not sincere: *a ~ talker* (*excuse*); *have a ~ tongue.*

glide [glaɪd] *v.i.* move along smoothly and continuously. *n.* such a movement. **glid·er** *n.* kind of aircraft without an engine. (Cf. *hang-~.*) **glid·ing** *n.* (no pl.) sport of flying in ~rs.

glim·mer ['glɪmə*] *v.i. & n.* (send out a) weak, uncertain light: *a ~ of light*; *not a ~ of hope*, (fig.) no hope at all.

glimpse [glɪmps] *v.t. & n.* (catch a) short, imperfect view (of sb. or sth.).

glint [glɪnt] *v.i. & n.* gleam; glitter.

glis·ten ['glɪsn] *v.i.* (esp. of wet or polished surfaces, tear-filled eyes) shine: *~ing raindrops*; *pavements ~ing in the rain.*

glit·ter ['glɪtə*] *v.i. & n.* (no pl.) (shine brightly with) flashes of light: *clothes ~ing with jewels*; *the ~ of stars on a moonless night.*

gloam·ing ['gləʊmɪŋ] *n.* (no pl.) evening twilight.

gloat [gləʊt] *v.i.* ~ *over*, look at (one's possessions, successes, the ruin of a rival) with selfish delight.

glob·al ['gləʊbl] *adj.* **1.** world-wide: ~ *economic problems.* **2.** comprehensive; total.

globe [gləʊb] *n.* object shaped like a ball, esp. one with a map of the earth on it; ~-shaped glass lamp-shade, etc. **'~-·trot·ter** *n.* sight-seeing traveller visiting many countries. **glob·u·lar** ['glɒbjʊlə*] *adj.* ~-shaped; made of

globules. **glob·ule** ['glɒbjuːl] *n.* tiny ~, esp. of liquid; drop.

a globe

a goblet

gloom [gluːm] *n.* (no pl.) **1.** semi-darkness; obscurity. **2.** feeling of sadness and hopelessness. **~y** *adj.* (*-ier, -iest*). **~·i·ly** *adv.*

glo·ri·fy, see *glory.*

glo·ry ['glɔːrɪ] *n.* (no pl.) **1.** high fame and honour won by great achievements. **2.** adoration and thanksgiving offered to God. **3.** (sometimes pl.) reason for pride; subject for boasting; sth. deserving respect and honour. **4.** quality of being beautiful or magnificent: *the ~ of a sunset. v.i.* ~ *in*, rejoice in; take great pride in. **glo·ri·fy** ['glɔːrɪfaɪ] *v.t.* give ~ (2, 3) to; worship. **glo·ri·ous** ['glɔːrɪəs] *adj.* having or causing ~; enjoyable.

gloss[1] [glɒs] *n.* (no pl.) smooth, bright surface. *v.t.* ~ *over*, give a ~ to; cover up or explain away (an error, etc.). **~y** *adj.* (*-ier, -iest*) shiny.

gloss[2] [glɒs] *n.* explanation (in a footnote or list in a book) of a difficult word or term. *v.t. & i.* add a ~ or ~es to; write a ~ or ~es. **glos·sa·ry** *n.* list of ~es.

glove [glʌv] *n.* covering of leather, wool, etc. for the hand, usu. with separated fingers: *be hand in ~ with*, be very intimate with.

glow [gləʊ] *v.i. & n.* (no pl.) **1.** (send out) brightness and warmth without flame. **2.** (have a) warm or flushed look or feeling (as after exercise or when excited): *~ing with pride*; *in a ~ of enthusiasm.* **'~-worm** *n.* insect of which the wingless female gives out a green light at its tail.

glow·er ['glaʊə*] *v.i.* look in an angry or threatening way (*at*).

glu·cose ['gluːkəʊs] *n.* (no pl.) grape-sugar.

glue [gluː] *n.* (no pl.) sticky substance used for joining (esp. wooden) things. *v.t.* stick, make fast, with ~. **glu·ey**

['gluːɪ] *adj.* (gluier, gluiest) sticky, like ~.

lum [glʌm] *adj.* (-mm-) gloomy.

lut [glʌt] *v.t.* (-tt-) **1.** supply too much to: ~ *the market.* **2.** overeat: ~ *oneself.* *n.* (no pl.) supply in excess of demand.

lu·ti·nous ['gluːtɪnəs] *adj.* sticky.

lut·ton ['glʌtn] *n.* person who eats too much; (fig.) *a ~ for work.* **~ous** *adj.* very greedy (for food). **~y** *n.* (no pl.)

lyc·er·ine (U.S.A. also **-in**) ['glɪsəriːn, U.S.A. -ɪn] *n.* (no pl.) thick, sweet, colourless liquid made from fats and oils, used in medical and toilet preparations and explosives.

narled [naːld] *adj.* (of tree trunks) twisted and rough; covered with knobs.

nash [næʃ] *v.i. & t.* (of teeth) strike together (e.g. in rage); (of a person) cause (the teeth) to do this.

nat [næt] *n.* small, two-winged, blood-sucking fly. *strain at a ~,* hesitate about a trifle.

naw [nɔː] *v.t. & i.* **1.** bite steadily at (something hard): *a dog ~ing (at) a bone.* **2.** (of pain, anxiety, etc.) trouble or torment (sb.) steadily.

nome [nəʊm] *n.* (in tales) small goblin living under the ground.

o [gəʊ] *v.i.* (pres. t. ~, 3rd person sing. ~*es*; p.t. *went*, p.p. *gone* [gɒn]) **1.** start, move, pass, continue moving, from one point to another, etc.; proceed. **2.** lie, point, in a certain direction; extend; stretch: *How far does this road ~?* **3.** make one's way *to (towards, into)*: *This road ~es to London.* ~ *to school (a university)*; ~ *to market.* **4.** journey; travel: ~ *by car*; ~ *for a walk*; ~ *on a journey*; ~ *slow,* (esp.) work at a deliberately slow pace; ~-*slow* (n.), such action as a protest against sth. or to draw attention to demands. **5.** (of time) pass: *a fortnight to ~ before Christmas.* **6.** (of events) turn out well, etc.: *How are things ~ing?* **7.** pass into a specified condition; become: ~ *blind*; ~ *mad*; ~ *bad* (e.g. food); ~ *to sleep.* **8.** (of machines, etc.) work; be in working order: *Is your clock ~ing? It ~es by electricity.* **9.** be or live, esp. as a habit: ~ *armed (naked)*; ~ *in fear of one's life.* **10.** be usually or normally kept or placed: *These books ~ on the top shelf.* **11.** give way; break (down): *The masts went in the storm.* **12.** *let oneself ~,* relax; give way to one's feelings, an impulse, etc. **13.** (of money) be spent (*in* or *on* sth.). **14.** be sold: ~ *for only £5*; ~ *cheap.* **15.**

be given up, lost: *the car must ~*; *my headache has gone.* **16.** (of verse, tune, etc.) have a certain wording or tune. **17.** (with advs. and preps.): ~ *about sth.,* set to work at it: *We're not ~ing about it in the right way.* ~ *after,* try to obtain or overtake; ~ *ahead,* (a) start; make progress; (b) proceed without hesitation; ~-*ahead* (n.), permission to proceed: *give sb. the ~-ahead*; ~ *away,* leave (home); move to a distance; ~ *back (up)on,* withdraw from (a promise, etc.); ~ *by,* pass; be guided by: *a good rule to ~ by*; ~ *by the name of,* be called; ~ *down,* (of a ship) sink; (of the sea, wind, etc.) become calm; (of the sun) set; (of a story, play, etc.) find acceptance *with*; ~ *for,* (a) attack; (b) go to fetch; (c) be considered of no value: *All his work went for nothing.* ~ *in for,* take part in (a competition, examination); take up (as a hobby, pursuit, etc.): ~ *in for golf (stamp-collecting)*; ~ *into,* enter: ~ *into business (society)*; examine: ~ *into the evidence*; occupy oneself with: ~ *into details*; (of a number) be capable of being contained in another exactly: *3 ~es into 9*; *9 into 5 won't ~*; ~ *off,* (of a gun, explosives, etc.) be fired with a loud noise; (of food, etc.) lose quality: *This milk has gone off* (i.e. is bad). *The goods in this shop have gone off* (i.e. are now inferior). ~ *off well (badly),* (of an entertainment, plan, etc.) have (fail to have) the result hoped for; ~ *on,* (a) continue; happen; (b) (of time) pass; (c) behave, esp. in a wrong way; *be ~ing on for,* be getting near to; ~ *out,* (of a fire or light) stop burning; ~ *over (through),* examine or study thoroughly; ~ *round,* be enough for everyone: *not enough food to ~ round*; ~ *through,* suffer; undergo (hardships, etc.); ~ *through with,* complete (an undertaking, etc.); ~ *together,* be satisfactory when together; (of a young couple) be courting; ~ *with,* (of colours) be in harmony with; ~ *without,* endure the lack of. **18.** ~ *to sea,* become a sailor; ~ *halves,* divide equally; ~ *shares,* share equally; ~ *to law,* start legal action (against sb.); ~ *to pieces,* break up (physically or in intellect); ~ *to seed,* (fig.) become careless of one's appearance, etc.; *to ~,* (U.S.A., of food, etc.) for taking away from the place of supply before consumption. *adj.* (colloq.) functioning properly; (aer.) ready for launching; progressive. *n.* **1.** energy; enthusiasm: *full of ~.* **2.** have a ~ (*at* sth.), attempt; *on the ~,* busy; active; *all the ~,* in fashion. '**~·be,tween** *n.* intermediary; negotiator. **~·ing** *n.* (no pl.) condition of a road, etc. for travelling; method or speed of working or travelling. '**~·ings-'on** *n. pl.* (colloq.) strange or surprising behaviour or happenings.

goad [gəʊd] *n.* pointed stick for urging cattle on; sth. urging a person to action. *v.t.* urge (to do sth.): ~ed by hunger to steal.

goal [gəʊl] *n.* **1.** point marking the end of a race; (football, etc.) posts between which the ball is to be driven; point(s) made by doing this: score a ~. **2.** (fig.) object of efforts; destination: one's ~ in life. '**~·keep·er**, (colloq.) **~·ie** ['gəʊlɪ] *ns.* player whose duty is to keep the ball out of the ~.

goat [gəʊt] *n.* small, horned animal kept for its flesh and hair, and for the milk of the female. '**~·herd** *n.* person looking after a flock of ~s.

gob·ble ['gɒbl] *v.t. & i.* eat fast, noisily, and greedily.

gob·let ['gɒblɪt] *n.* drinking-glass with a stem and base. (See the picture at globe.) [demon.\
gob·lin ['gɒblɪn] *n.* mischievous, ugly /

god [gɒd] *n.* **1.** any being regarded as, worshipped as, having power over nature and control over human affairs (e.g. Jupiter, Neptune); image in wood, stone, etc. to represent such a being. **2.** (no pl.) G~, creator and ruler of the universe. '**~·child**, '**~·daugh·ter**, '**~·son** *ns.* person for whom a ~parent acts as sponsor (1) at baptism. **~·dess** ['gɒdɪs] *n.* female ~. '**~·fa·ther**, '**~·moth·er**, '**~·par·ent** *ns.* sponsor (1) at baptism. '**~·fear·ing** *adj.* reverent; living a good life. '**~·for,sak·en** *adj.* (of places) wretched. **~·less** *adj.* wicked; not having belief in G~. **~·ly** *adj.* (-ier, -iest) loving and obeying G~; deeply religious. '**~·send** *n.* piece of good fortune coming unexpectedly; sth. welcome because it is a great help.

gog·gle ['gɒgl] *v.i. & t.* roll the eyes about, or at sth.; (of the eyes) open widely; roll. '**~·box** *n.* (sl.) television set. **~s** *n. pl.* large glasses with side shields to protect the eyes from the wind, dust, etc.

go·ing, see go.

go-kart ['gəʊkɑːt] *n.* small, open, low racing car with a skeleton (3) body (4).

gold [gəʊld] *n.* (no pl.) **1.** precious, yellow metal used for making jewellery, prize medals, coins, etc. **2.** coins made of ~; money in large sums; wealth. **3.** (fig.) precious, beautiful, or brilliant quality: a heart (voice) of ~.

4. colour of the metal. **~ leaf** *n.* (no pl.) sheet of ~ beaten extremely thin for use in gilding, in stamping titles on book covers, etc. '**~·smith** *n.* person who makes articles of ~. **~·en** ['gəʊldən] *adj.* of ~ or like ~ in value or colour: ~en hair; the ~en age, (in Greek stories) earliest and happiest period in history; period in a nation's history when art and literature were most flourishing; ~en mean, moderation; ~en wedding, 50th anniversary of the wedding-day.

golf [gɒlf] *n.* (no pl.) game played by two or four persons with a small, hard ball, driven with ~clubs into a series of 9 or 18 holes over a stretch of land called a ~course or ~links. **~·er** *n.* person who plays ~.

go·losh, see galosh.

gon·do·la ['gɒndələ] *n.* long, light, flat-bottomed boat as used on canals in Venice. **gon·do·lier** [,gɒndə'lɪə*] *n.* man who propels a ~.

gone, see go (v.).

gon·er ['gɒnə*] *n.* (sl.) person or thing that is doomed.

gong [gɒŋ] *n.* round metal plate struck with a stick as a signal (e.g. for meals).

good [gʊd] *adj.* (better, best) **1.** having the right qualities; giving satisfaction; pleasing; agreeable; amusing; beneficial; wholesome; kind; able to do well what is required; complete; strong: ~ for, having a ~ effect upon: ~ for the health. **2.** thorough: Give him a ~ beating. **3.** rather more than: He took a ~ half of the cake. It's a ~ five miles. **4.** considerable in number or quantity: a ~ many, a ~ few, a considerable number; a ~ way, quite a long way. **5.** (esp. of a child) well-behaved: be a ~ girl. **6.** as ~ as, practically: The battle was as ~ as lost. **7.** in ~ time (for), early enough (for); all in ~ time, when the right time comes. **8.** eatable; untainted. **9.** be ~ for, have the necessary energy, money, etc. for; be in a condition to undertake, pay, etc.: ~ for a ten-mile walk; ~ for £50. **10.** make sth. ~, replace, restore, pay for (sth. lost or damaged); carry out (a promise); accomplish (a purpose). *n.* (no pl.) **1.** that which is ~. **2.** advantage; benefit: do sb. ~, make him healthier, happier, etc. **3.** use (3): It's no ~ trying. **4.** for ~ (and all), for ever. **5.** ten pounds to the ~, as a balance on the right side. **6.** (pl.) property; things bought and sold; things carried by road and rail: a ~s train. (Cf. cargo.) **~·bye** (U.S.A. also **-by**) [,gʊd'baɪ] *int. & n.* (saying of) farewell.

~-for·noth·ing [ˈɡʊdfə,nʌθrɪŋ] **n. & adj.** (person who is) useless. **¡~-ˈhu·moured adj.** cheerful; ~-natured; **¡~-ˈlook·ing adj.** handsome. **~·ly adj.** (-ier, -iest) pleasant-looking; of considerable size. **¡~-ˈna·tured adj.** having, showing, kindness, willingness to help. **~·ness n.** (no pl.) **1.** quality of being ~. **2.** strength or essence: *meat with the ~ness boiled out.* **int.** (used for) God: *Thank ~ness! For ~ness' sake!* **¡~-ˈwill n.** (no pl.) **1.** friendly feeling. **2.** privilege of trading as the successor to a well-established business.

goose [ɡuːs] **n.** (pl. *geese* [ɡiːs]) **1.** waterbird larger than a duck; female of this (cf. *gander*); its flesh as food. **2.** silly person.

goose·ber·ry [ˈɡʊzbərɪ] **n.** (bush with) green, hairy, smooth berry (used for jam, tarts, etc.).

go·pher [ˈɡəʊfə*] **n.** burrowing rodent in N. America.

gore¹ [ɡɔː*] **n.** (no pl.) thickened blood from a cut or wound. **gory** [ˈɡɔːrɪ] **adj.** (-ier, -iest).

gore² [ɡɔː*] **v.t.** (of horned animals) pierce with the horns.

gorge [ɡɔːdʒ] **n. 1.** contents of the stomach: *make one's ~ rise*, cause a feeling of disgust. **2.** narrow opening between hills or mountains. **v.t. & i.** eat greedily; fill oneself: ~ (oneself) on (with) sth.

gor·geous [ˈɡɔːdʒəs] **adj.** richly coloured; magnificent; (colloq.) very pleasant: *a ~ meal; had a ~ time.*

go·ril·la [ɡəˈrɪlə] **n.** man-sized, tree-climbing African ape.

gorse [ɡɔːs] **n.** (no pl.) furze.

gos·ling [ˈɡɒzlɪŋ] **n.** young goose.

gos·pel [ˈɡɒspl] **n. 1.** *G~,* (life and teaching of) Jesus Christ as recorded in the) first four books of the New Testament; any one of these four books. ~ *truth,* sth. absolutely true. **2.** form of Negro religious music combining elements of the spiritual, the blues, and jazz: (attrib.) ~ *music (song).*

gos·sa·mer [ˈɡɒsəmə*] **n. 1.** (thread of) fine silky substance of webs made by small spiders, floating in calm air or spread on grass, etc. **2.** (no pl.) soft, light, delicate material.

gos·sip [ˈɡɒsɪp] **n.** (person fond of) idle talk about the affairs of other people: *She's an old ~. ~ column (columnist, writer)* (in a magazine, newspaper, etc.). **v.i.** talk ~.

got(·ten), see *get.*

Goth·ic [ˈɡɒθɪk] **adj. 1.** of the style of architecture common in Western Europe in the 12th to 16th century that is characterized by pointed arches and vaults¹ (1), etc. **2.** in the literary style popular in the 18th and 19th centuries, with horrifying or supernatural events: *a ~ novel.*

gouge [ɡaʊdʒ] **n.** tool with sharp semicircular edge for cutting grooves in wood. **v.t.** cut with a ~: ~ *sth. out,* shape with a ~; force out with, or as with, a ~.

gourd [ɡʊəd] **n.** (hard-skinned, fleshy fruit of) kinds of climbing or trailing plant; bottle or bowl consisting of the dried skin of this fruit.

gourds

gour·mand [ˈɡʊəmənd] **n.** lover of food; glutton.

gour·met [ˈɡʊəmeɪ] **n.** person who enjoys, and is expert in judging, food and wine.

gout [ɡaʊt] **n.** (no pl.) disease causing painful swellings in joints, esp. of fingers, toes, and knees. **~y adj.** (-ier, -iest).

gov·ern [ˈɡʌvn] **v.t. & i. 1.** rule (a country, city, etc.). **2.** control (e.g. one's temper). **3.** influence; determine: *be ~ed by the opinions of others.* **~·ment n.** (system of) ~ing; ministry (2); body (5) of persons who ~ a State; body (5) of Ministers of State. **gov·er·nor n. 1.** person who ~s a province or colony or (U.S.A.) a State. **2.** member of the ~ing body (5) of an institution (e.g. a college). **3.** regulator. **4.** (sl.) employer; father.

gov·ern·ess [ˈɡʌvnɪs] **n.** woman who is paid to teach children at home.

gown [ɡaʊn] **n. 1.** woman's dress. **2.** loose, flowing robe worn by members of a university, judges, etc.

grab [ɡræb] **v.t. & i.** (-bb-) take roughly or selfishly; snatch (at). **n.** ~bing; a sudden snatch.

grace [ɡreɪs] **n. 1.** (no pl.) quality of being pleasing, attractive, or beautiful, esp. in structure or movement. **2.** (usu. pl.) pleasing accomplishment; elegance of manner. **3.** favour; approval; goodwill: *an act of ~,* sth. freely given, not taken as a right; *days of ~,* time allowed after the day on which a payment is due; *be in sb.'s good* ~s, enjoy his favour and approval. **4.** (no pl.) (do sth.) *with a good (bad)* ~, willingly (unwillingly). **5.** short prayer of thanks before or after a meal: *say (a)* ~. **6.** (no pl.) God's mercy and favour towards mankind; influence and result of this: *in the year of* ~ *1975*, A. D. 1975, after the birth of Jesus. **7.** *His (Her, Your) G~* (used in speaking of or to a duke, duchess, or an archbishop). *v.t.* add ~ to; confer honour or dignity on; be an ornament to. **~ful** *adj.* having or showing ~ of looks or movement. **~ful·ly** *adv.* **~less** *adj.* without a sense of what is right and proper.

gra·cious ['greɪʃəs] *adj.* **1.** pleasant; kind; agreeable. **2.** (of God) merciful. **3.** (in exclamations expressing indignation or surprise): *Good* ~! **~ly** *adv.*

gra·da·tion [grə'deɪʃn] *n.* **1.** gradual change from one state or quality to another: ~*s in shades of colour.* **2.** (step or stage in) development.

grade [greɪd] *n.* **1.** step or degree (in rank, quality, value, etc.); number or class of things of the same ~. **2.** (U.S.A.) class or form in a school: ~ *school*, elementary school. **3.** mark (5) given to a pupil for his work in school. **4.** slope; gradient: *on the up (down)* ~, rising (falling); ~ *crossing* (U.S.A.), level crossing. *v.t.* **1.** arrange in order of ~s. **2.** make (land, esp. for roads) more nearly level by reducing the slope.

gra·di·ent ['greɪdjənt] *n.* degree of slope: *a* ~ *of one in twenty; a steep* ~.

grad·u·al ['grædʒuəl] *adj.* **1.** taking place by degrees. **2.** (of a slope) not steep. **~ly** *adv.*

grad·u·ate ['grædjʊeɪt] *v.t. & i.* **1.** mark with degrees for measuring: *a ruler* ~*d in both inches and centimetres.* **2.** arrange according to grade. **3.** (U.S.A.) move up to the next school grade; give an academic degree, diploma, or certificate to. **4.** take a university degree: ~ *from Oxford (Cambridge)*; ~ *in law*; (U.S.A. also) receive a diploma of other institutions. ['grædʒʊət] *n.* **1.** person who has taken a university degree. **2.** (U.S.A.) person who has completed a school course: *a high school* ~; ~ *nurse*, trained nurse. **grad·u·a·tion** [ˌgrædjʊ'eɪʃn] *n.*

graft[1] [grɑːft] *n.* **1.** shoot from a branch of a living tree, fixed in a cut made in another tree, to form a new growth. **2.** (surgery) piece of skin, bone, etc.

from a living person or animal, applied to another body or another part of the same body to become part of it. *v.t. & i.* put a ~ *(in, on, into).*

graft[2] [grɑːft] *n.* profit-making, getting business advantages, etc. by dishonest methods, esp. using political influence. *v.i.* practise ~.

grain [greɪn] *n.* **1.** (no pl.) (collective sing.) seed of food plants such as wheat and rice. **2.** single seed of such a plant. **3.** tiny, hard bit (of sand, salt, gold, etc.); (fig.) *without a* ~ *of sense.* **4.** smallest unit of weight, 1/7000 of 1 pound (avoirdupois) (= 0.065 grams). **5.** (no pl.) natural arrangement of lines of fibre in wood, etc.: *against the* ~, (fig.) contrary to one's wishes or inclination.

gram, gramme [græm] *n.* metric unit of weight; weight of 1 cubic centimetre of water at maximum density.

gram·mar ['græmə*] *n.* (no pl.) study or science of, rules for, the words and structure of a language. ~ *school*, (a) (Gt. Brit.) secondary school in which Latin was once the chief subject, now one that teaches languages, history, science, etc.; (b) (U.S.A.) school intermediate between a primary school and high school. **~i·an** [grə'meərɪən] *n.* expert in ~. **gram·mat·i·cal** [grə'mætɪkl] *adj.* of, conforming to the rules of, ~. **gram·mat·i·cal·ly** *adv.*

gra·na·ry ['grænərɪ] *n.* storehouse for grain.

a grand piano

grand [grænd] *adj.* **1.** chief; most important. **2.** complete: *the* ~ *total.* **3.** splendid; magnificent-looking: *a* ~ *view*; *living in* ~ *style.* **4.** self-important. **5.** (colloq.) very fine or enjoyable: *have a* ~ *time.* **6.** ~ *piano*, large one with horizontal strings; ~*stand*, roofed rows of seats for spectators at races, sports-meetings, etc. **gran·deur** ['grændʒə*] *n.* (no pl.) greatness; magnificence.

grand- [grænd-] *pref.*: '~**child** ['græn-], '~**daugh·ter** ['grɑːn-], '~**son** ['græn-] *ns.* daughter or son of one's son or daughter. '~**par·ent**

a grandstand

['græn-], '‿ֽfa·ther ['grænd-], '‿-
ֽmoth·er ['græn-] *ns.* father or mother of one's father or mother. '‿ֽfa-
ther('s) clock *n.* clock in a tall,
wooden case.

gran·dil·o·quent [græn'dɪləkwənt]
adj. using, full of, pompous words.
gran·dil·o·quence *n.* (no pl.).

gran·di·ose ['grændɪəʊs] *adj.* planned
on a large scale; imposing.

grange [greɪndʒ] *n.* country house with
farm buildings.

gran·ite ['grænɪt] *n.* (no pl.) hard, usu.
grey, stone used for building.

gran·ny, gran·nie ['grænɪ] *n.* (colloq.
or child's name for) grandmother.

grant [grɑːnt] *v.t.* 1. consent to give or
allow (what is asked for). 2. agree (that
sth. is true): *take (sth.) for ‿ed*, regard
it as true or as certain to happen. *n.*
sth. ‿ed (e.g. money or land by a government).

gran·u·lat·ed ['grænjʊleɪtɪd] *adj.* in
the form of grains. gran·ule ['græn-
juːl] *n.* tiny grain.

grape [greɪp] *n.* green or purple berry
growing in clusters on vines, used for
making wine. '‿ֽfruit *n.* large, round,
yellow fruit with an acid taste. '‿-ֽsug-
ar *n.* (no pl.) form of sugar made from
ripe ‿s; glucose.

graph [græf] *n.* diagram consisting of
a line or lines showing the variation of
two quantities (e.g. the temperature at
each hour).

graph·ic ['græfɪk] *adj.* 1. of writing,
drawing, and painting: *the ‿ arts.* 2.
(of descriptions) causing one to have
a clear picture in the mind. *n.* product
of ‿ arts. graph·i·cal·ly *adv.*

graph·ite ['græfaɪt] *n.* (no pl.) form of
carbon used as a lubricant and in making lead pencils.

grap·nel ['græpnl] *n.* 1. anchor with
more than two hooks. 2. instrument
like this formerly used in sea battles
for grappling with enemy ships.

grap·ple ['græpl] *v.t. & i.* seize firmly;
struggle (*with*) at close quarters; (fig.)
try to deal (*with* a problem). *n.* (also
grappling-iron) grapnel (2).

grasp [grɑːsp] *v.t. & i.* 1. seize firmly
with the hand(s) or arm(s); understand
with the mind. 2. ‿ *at*, try to seize;
accept eagerly. *n.* (usu. no pl.) (power
of) ‿ing: *in the ‿ of one's enemies; have
a thorough ‿ of a problem.* ‿ing *adj.*
greedy (for money, etc.).

grass [grɑːs] *n.* kinds of wild (usu. low-
growing) plant, also sown to make
lawns and pastures, grazed by animals
and cut and dried to make hay. ‿y *adj.*
(-ier, -iest). '‿ֽhop·per *n.* jumping insect that makes a shrill noise with its
wings.

grate¹ [greɪt] *v.t. & i.* 1. rub into
small pieces, usu. against a rough surface; rub small bits off; make a harsh
noise by rubbing. 2. have an irritating
effect (on a person, his nerves). grat·er
n. device (2) with a rough surface for
grating (food, etc.).

grate² [greɪt] *n.* metal frame for holding coal, etc. in a fireplace.

a grate²

grate·ful ['greɪtfʊl] *adj.* 1. feeling or
showing thanks (*to* sb., *for* help, kindness, etc.). 2. agreeable; comforting.

grat·i·fy ['grætɪfaɪ] *v.t.* give pleasure
or satisfaction to: ‿ *sb.'s desire* (*thirst
for knowledge*), pleasing;
satisfying. grat·i·fi·ca·tion [ˌgrætɪfɪ-
'keɪʃn] *n.*

grat·ing ['greɪtɪŋ] *n.* framework of
bars placed across an opening.

gra·tis ['greɪtɪs] *adv. & adj.* free of
charge.

grat·i·tude ['grætɪtjuːd] *n.* (no pl.)
thankfulness; being grateful (*to* sb.,
for sth.).

gra·tu·i·tous [grə'tjuːɪtəs] *adj.* 1. given,
obtained, or done, without payment.
2. unjustifiable: *a ‿ insult.* ‿ly *adv.*

gra·tu·i·ty [grə'tjuːətɪ] *n.* 1. gift of
money) to an employee, etc. for
services. 2. (Gt. Brit.) money given to
soldiers at the end of their period of
service. 3. tip (for service).

grave¹ [greɪv] *n.* hole dug in the ground
for a dead person. '‿ֽstone *n.* stone
over a ‿, with particulars of the dead
person. '‿ֽyard *n.* burial ground.

grave² [greɪv] *adj.* (‿r, ‿st) serious;
requiring careful consideration. ‿ly
adv.

grav·el ['grævl] *n.* (no pl.) small stones with coarse sand, as used for roads and paths. *v.t.* (-*ll*-, U.S.A. also -*l*-) cover with ~: ~*led paths.*

grav·i·tate ['græviteit] *v.i.* move or be attracted (*to, towards*). **grav·i·ta·tion** [,grævi'teiʃn] *n.* (no pl.).

grav·i·ty ['grævəti] *n.* (no pl.) **1.** degree of attraction between any two objects, esp. that force which attracts objects towards the centre of the earth. **2.** seriousness; serious or solemn appearance. **3.** weight: *specific* ~, relative weights of any kind of matter and the same volume of water or air.

gra·vy ['greivi] *n.* juice that comes from meat while cooking; sauce made [from this.]

gray, see **grey.**

graze[1] [greiz] *v.i. & t.* **1.** (of animals) eat growing grass. **2.** put (cattle, etc.) in fields to ~.

graze[2] [greiz] *v.t.* touch or scrape lightly in passing; scrape the skin from: *The bullet ~d his cheek.* *n.* place where skin is ~d.

grease [gri:s] *n.* (no pl.) **1.** animal fat melted soft. **2.** any thick, semi-solid, oily substance. [gri:z] *v.t.* put or rub ~ on or in (esp. parts of a machine). ~ *sb.'s palm,* bribe him. **greasy** ['gri:zi] *adj.* (-*ier,* -*iest*) covered with ~; slippery.

great [greit] *adj.* **1.** above the average in size, quantity, or degree. **2.** important; noted. **3.** of great ability: ~ *poets and painters.* **4.** (colloq.) very satisfactory. **5.** *a ~ many,* very many; *a ~ deal,* (a) a large amount; (b) very much. '~·**coat** *n.* heavy overcoat. ~·**ly** *adv.* much. ~·**ness** *n.* (no pl.).

great- [greit-] *pref.*: ~-'**grand**,**fa·ther** *n.* one's father's or mother's grandfather. ~-'**grand·son** *n.* grandson of one's son or daughter.

greed [gri:d] *n.* (no pl.) strong desire for more (food, wealth, etc.), esp. for more than is right. ~·**y** *adj.* (-*ier,* -*iest*). ~·**i·ly** *adv.* ~·**i·ness** *n.* (no pl.) quality or state of being ~·y.

Greek [gri:k] *n. & adj.* (native, inhabitant, or language) of Greece.

green [gri:n] *adj.* **1.** colour of growing grass. **2.** (of fruit) not yet ripe; (of wood) not yet dry enough for use. **3.** (of a person) inexperienced or untrained. *n.* **1.** ~ colour; what is ~. **2.** (pl.) ~ leaf vegetables (e.g. cabbage). **3.** area of grass-covered land, esp. one for public use in a village or for a special purpose: *village* ~; *bowling-*~; *putting-*~. ~ **card** *n.* ~-coloured international insurance document covering

(4) motorists against accidents in foreign countries. ~·**ery** ['gri:nəri] *n.* (no pl.) ~ plants, leaves, etc. '~·**fly** *n. pl.* (Gt. Brit.) small, ~ insects that attack plants. '~·**gro·cer** *n.* (Gt. Brit.) shopkeeper selling fresh vegetables and fruit. '~·**horn** *n.* inexperienced person easily tricked. '~·**house** *n.* glass house for growing plants that need protection from weather.

greet [gri:t] *v.t.* **1.** say words of welcome to; express one's feelings on receiving (news, etc.); write (in a letter) words expressing respect, friendship, etc.: *a friend with a smile; ~ed with loud applause.* **2.** (of sights and sounds) meet the eyes (ears): *the view that ~ed us at the hilltop.* ~·**ing** *n.* first words used on seeing sb. or in writing to sb. (e.g. 'Good morning' or 'Dear Sir').

gre·gar·i·ous [gri'geəriəs] *adj.* living in groups or societies; liking the company of others.

gre·nade [gri'neid] *n.* small bomb thrown by hand or fired from a rifle.

grew, see **grow.**

grey (U.S.A. **gray**) [grei] *adj. & n.* (no pl.) between black and white, coloured like ashes or the sky on a cloudy day.

grey·hound ['greihaund] *n.* slender, long-legged dog, able to run fast.

grid [grid] *n.* **1.** system of overhead cables for distributing electric current over a large area. **2.** system of squares on maps, numbered for reference. **3.** grating so placed (e.g. at a gate) as to prevent cattle from straying on to a road, etc.: *a cattle* ~. '~·**iron** *n.* framework of metal bars used for grilling, etc.

grief [gri:f] *n.* **1.** deep or violent sorrow; sth. causing this. **2.** *bring (come) to* ~, (cause to) be injured or ruined or come to a bad end. **grieve** [gri:v] *v.t. & i.* cause ~ to; feel ~. **griev·ance** ['gri:vns] *n.* real or imagined cause for complaint or protest. **griev·ous** ['gri:vəs] *adj.* causing ~; painful; severe.

grif·fin ['grifin], **grif·fon** ['grifn], **gryph·on** ['grifn] *n.* fabulous creature with the head and wings of an eagle and a lion's body.

grill [gril] *n.* **1.** grating; grille; gridiron. **2.** (dish of) ~ed food: *a mixed* ~, steak, bacon, etc. **3.** (also ~-*room*) (part of a) restaurant, room in a hotel, where ~s (2) are served. *v.t. & i.* cook, be cooked, on a gridiron or under a fire or other direct heat.

grille, grill [gril] *n.* **1.** grating; latticed screen across an opening (e.g. a window) or over a counter (e.g. in a bank or post office). **2.** metal grid to protect the radiator of a motor vehicle.

grim [grɪm] *adj.* (-mm-) stern; severe; merciless; cruel; of forbidding aspect. **~·ly** *adv.*

gri·mace [grɪˈmeɪs] *n.* ugly, twisted expression (on the face), expressing pain, disgust, etc. or intended to cause laughter. *v.i.* make ~s.

grime [graɪm] *n.* (no pl.) dirt, esp. a thick coating on the surface of sth. or on the body. **grimy** *adj.* (-ier, -iest) covered with ~.

grin [grɪn] *v.i.* (-nn-) & *n.* (give a) broad smile.

grind [graɪnd] *v.t.* & *i.* (p.t. & p.p. **ground** [graʊnd]) **1.** crush to grains or powder: ~ *wheat*. **2.** produce in this way: ~ *flour*. **3.** (fig.) crush or oppress: *ground down by taxation (cruel rulers)*. **4.** polish or sharpen by rubbing on or with a rough, hard surface: ~ *a knife*. **5.** rub together, esp. with a circular motion: ~ *one's teeth; a ship ~ing on the rocks.* **6.** work by turning: ~ *a coffee-mill (barrel-organ).* **7.** work hard: ~ *away at one's studies. n.* (no pl.) (colloq.) long, monotonous work. **'~·stone** *n.* stone, esp. one shaped like a wheel and used for sharpening and polishing tools, etc. *keep sb.'s nose to the ~stone*, force him to work hard without rest.

grip [grɪp] *v.t.* & *i.* (-pp-) take and keep a firm hold (of): ~ *sb.'s hand; brakes that fail to ~; (fig.) ~ the attention of an audience. n.* **1.** (power, manner, act of) ~*ping*: *let go one's ~ of sth.; have a good ~ (i.e. understanding) of a problem; be at (come or get to) ~s with,* attack in earnest; *get a ~ on oneself*, get control, mastery, over oneself. **2.** (U.S.A. ~*sack*) travelling-bag; suit-case. **3.** part of a machine that ~s or is to be ~ped.   [horror.\

gris·ly [ˈgrɪzlɪ] *adj.* (-ier, -iest) causing/

grist [grɪst] *n.* (no pl.) grain to be ground. *all ~ to the mill*, yields a profit.

gris·tle [ˈgrɪsl] *n.* (no pl.) tough, elastic substance in animal bodies, esp. in meat for cooking.

grit [grɪt] *n.* (no pl.) **1.** grains of stone, sand, etc.: *get a bit of ~ in one's eye (shoe).* **2.** (colloq.) quality of courage and endurance. *v.t.* (-tt-) ~ *the teeth*, keep the jaws tight together. **~·ty** *adj.* (-ier, -iest) **1.** like, containing, ~ (1): *The sandstorm made the food ~ty.* **2.** (colloq.) having ~ (2); plucky.

grits [grɪts] *n. pl.* husked, unground oats; coarse oatmeal.

griz·zled [ˈgrɪzld] *adj.* grey-haired.

griz·zly [ˈgrɪzlɪ] *n.* (also ~ *bear*) large, fierce, N. American bear.

groan [grəʊn] *v.i.* & *t.* & *n.* **1.** (make) deep sound(s) forced out by pain or expressing despair, etc. **2.** (fig.) be weighted down: *tables ~ing with food.*

gro·cer [ˈgrəʊsə*] *n.* person who sells tea, sugar, butter, tinned and bottled food, etc. **~·y** [ˈgrəʊsərɪ] *n.* ~'s trade; (pl.) goods sold by a ~.

grog [grɒg] *n.* drink of rum (or whisky, etc.) mixed with water.

grog·gy [ˈgrɒgɪ] *adj.* (-ier, -iest) **1.** un-steady and likely to collapse: *a table with ~ legs.* **2.** weak and unsteady as the result of illness, shock, etc.: *feel ~.*

groin [grɔɪn] *n.* curved part where the thighs and belly join.

groom [gruːm] *n.* **1.** servant in charge of horses. **2.** bride~. *v.t.* **1.** ~ (horses) well brushed, etc. **2.** *be well ~ed*, (of a person) be neatly dressed, with the hair well brushed.

groove [gruːv] *n.* **1.** long, hollow cut in the surface of wood, etc., esp. one made to guide the motion of sth. that slides into it; spiral cut in a record² (4) for the needle or stylus. **2.** way of living that has become a habit. **3.** (sl.) sth. very enjoyable, satisfying, or excellent. *v.t.* make ~s in. **groovy** [ˈgruːvɪ] *adj.* (-ier, -iest) (sl.) in the latest fashion: *groovy clothes (people); a groovy restaurant.*

a groove (1)

grope [grəʊp] *v.i.* & *t.* feel about (*for* or *after* sth.) as one does in the dark; search (*for*); find (*one's way*) by groping.

gross [grəʊs] *adj.* **1.** vulgar; not re-fined: ~ *jokes (manners).* **2.** (of error, injustice, etc.) obviously bad. **3.** (of a person) too fat; (of the senses) dull; heavy; (of food) coarse. **4.** (opp. *net²*) total; whole: *the ~ income* (i.e. before any deductions are made). *n.* (pl. ~) 12 dozen (= 144). **~·ly** *adv.* obviously (*unfair, etc.*).

gro·tesque [grəʊˈtesk] *adj.* absurd; fantastic; comically extravagant (2): ~ *manners (mistakes).*

ground¹ [graʊnd] *n.* **1.** solid surface of the earth: *The runner fell to the ~, ex-hausted. above ~*, alive; *below ~*, dead and buried; *from the ~ up*, (colloq.)

completely. *Our plans fell to the ~* (failed). *hold one's ~*, (fig.) stand firm; *shift one's ~*, change one's arguments; *suit sb. down to the ~*, please him in every respect; *cover much ~*, (a) travel far; (b) (of a report, etc.) be far-reaching. **2.** sea bottom: *touch ~*. **3.** piece of land for a special purpose: *cricket* (*football*) *~*; *play~*; *fishing-~s*, parts of the sea regularly fished. **4.** (pl.) land, gardens, round a building, usu. enclosed with walls, fences, or hedges. **5.** (pl.) particles of solid matter that sink to the bottom of a liquid, esp. *coffee-~s*. **6.** reason(s) for saying, doing, or believing sth.: *excused on the ~ of* (because of) *his youth*. **7.** surface on which a design is painted, printed, cut, etc.; undecorated part. *v.t. & i.* **1.** (of a ship) (cause to) touch the sea bottom; (of aircraft) compel to stay on the ~ (e.g. because of bad weather). **2.** base (a belief, etc. *on*): *arguments ~ed on experience*. **3.** give (sb.) teaching or training (*in* a subject, etc.). **~ con·trol** *n.* (no pl.) directing of the landing of an aircraft from the ~. **~ crew** *n.* ~ **staff**. **~·ing** *n.* thorough teaching of the elements of a subject. **~·less** *adj.* without good reason: *~less fears.* **'~·nut** *n.* (nut of a) plant whose seed-pods bend to the ~ and develop and ripen in the soil; the

ground-nuts

seeds are used as food and for making oil. **~·'plan** *n.* plan of a building at ~ level. **'~·rent** *n.* rent paid to the owner of land used for building on. **~·s·man** ['graʊndzmən] *n.* man in charge of a sports ~. ~ **staff** *n.* mechanics who service aircraft on the ~; non-flying members of the airfield staff. **~ swell** *n.* heavy, slow-moving waves caused by a distant or recent storm. **'~·work** *n.* (usu. fig.) basis; foundation.

ground², see **grind** (v.).

group [gruːp] *n.* number of persons or things gathered or placed together or naturally associated: *a ~ of trees*; *people standing about in a ~*. *v.t. & i.* form into, gather in, a ~. **~·ie** ['gruːpɪ] *n.* (sl.) girl who is a fan² of pop ~s and follows them where they perform.

grouse¹ [graʊs] *n.* (pl. ~) (sorts of) bird with feathered feet, shot for sport and food.

grouse² [graʊs] *v.i. & n.* (sl.) grumble; (make a) complaint. [wood.]

grove [grəʊv] *n.* group of trees; small}

grov·el ['grɒvl] *v.i.* (-ll-, U.S.A. also -l-) lie down on one's face in front of sb. whom one fears, (as if) begging for mercy; humble oneself.

grow [grəʊ] *v.t. & i.* (p.t. **grew** [gruː], p.p. **~n** [grəʊn]) **1.** develop; increase in size, height, length, etc.: *~ out of*, become too big for (e.g. one's clothes) or too old for (e.g. childish habits); *~ up*, (of persons, animals) reach the stage of full development; become adult. **2.** cause or allow to ~: *~ vegetables* (*a beard*). **3.** become: *~ older, ~ smaller.* **4.** *~* (*up*)*on*, (a) become more deeply rooted: *a habit that ~s upon one*; (b) win the liking of: *a book* (*piece of music*) *that ~s upon one*, of which one gradually becomes fonder. **~·er** *n.* **1.** (in compounds) person who ~s things: *a fruit-~er.* **2.** plant that ~s in a certain way: *a rapid ~er.* **~·n·'up** *adj.* adult. **'~·n-up** *n.* adult person. **~·th** [grəʊθ] *n.* **1.** process of ~ing: *a period of quick ~th.* **2.** increase. **3.** sth. that ~s or has ~n: *a week's ~th of beard.* **4.** diseased formation in the body (e.g. cancer).

growl [graʊl] *v.i. & n.* (esp. of dogs) (make a) low threatening sound.

grub¹ [grʌb] *v.t. & i.* (-bb-) turn over the soil, esp. to get sth. up: *~ up weeds.* **~·by** *adj.* (-ier, -iest) dirty.

grub² [grʌb] *n.* larva of an insect.

grub³ [grʌb] *n.* (no pl.) (sl.) food.

grudge [grʌdʒ] *v.t.* be unwilling to give or allow. *n.* feeling of ill will or resentment: *have a ~ against sb.*; *bear* (*owe*) *sb. a ~*, feel ill will against him. **grudg·ing·ly** *adv.* unwillingly.

gru·el [grʊəl] *n.* (no pl.) liquid food of oatmeal boiled in milk or water. **~·ling** (U.S.A. **~·ing**) *adj.* tiring; strenuous: *a ~ling race.*

grue·some ['gruːsəm] *adj.* filling one with horror and fear; frightful.

gruff [grʌf] *adj.* (of a person, his voice, behaviour) rough; surly.

grum·ble ['grʌmbl] *n.* (bad-tempered) complaint or protest; noise like distant thunder. *v.i. & t.* utter ~s; say with ~s. **~r** *n.* [bad-tempered.]

grumpy ['grʌmpɪ] *adj.* (-ier, -iest)}

grunt [grʌnt] *v.i. & t. & n.* (esp. of pigs) (make a) low, rough sound.

gua·no ['gwɑːnəʊ] *n.* (no pl.) waste matter dropped by sea-birds, used as a fertilizer.

guar·an·tee [ˌgærən'tiː] *n.* **1.** (in law *guaranty*) promise or undertaking (usu. in writing or print) that certain conditions agreed to in a transaction will be fulfilled: *a clock with a year's ~*. **2.** (in law *guaranty*) undertaking given by one person to another that he will be responsible for sth. to be done (e.g. payment of a debt) by a third person. **3.** (in law *guarantor*) person who gives such an undertaking: *be ~ for a friend's good behaviour. If I try to borrow money from the bank, he will be my ~*. **4.** (in law *guaranty*) sth. offered (e.g. the deeds of a house) as security for the fulfilling of conditions in a ~ (1, 2). **5.** (colloq.) sth. that seems to make an occurrence likely: *Blue skies are not always a ~ of good weather*. *v.t.* **1.** give a ~ (1, 2) for sth. or sb. **2.** (colloq.) promise. **guar·an·tor** [ˌgærənˈtɔː*] *n.* (legal word for) ~ (3). **guar·an·ty** [ˈgærəntɪ] *n.* (legal word for) ~ (1, 2, 4).

guard [gɑːd] *n.* **1.** (no pl.) state of watchfulness against attack, danger, or surprise: *be on ~; keep ~*. **2.** (no pl.) attitude of readiness (to defend oneself): *on (off) one's ~*. **3.** soldier(s) keeping ~; sentry. **4.** (U.S.A. *conductor* (1)) man in charge of a railway train. **5.** (U.S.A.) prison warder. **6.** (esp. in compounds) (part of an) apparatus (1) designed to prevent injury or loss: *fire-~* (in front of a fireplace); *mud~* (over the wheel of a bicycle, etc.). *v.t. & i.* **1.** protect; keep from danger; control (an exit). **2.** ~ *against*, use care and caution to prevent: *~ against misunderstandings*. **~·ed** *adj.* (esp. of statements) cautious; not promising or telling too much. **'~-room** *n.* room for soldiers on ~ or for soldiers under arrest.

guard·ian [ˈgɑːdjən] *n.* (official or private) person who guards, esp. (law) one who is responsible for the care of a young or incapable person and his property. **~·ship** *n.*

guer·ril·la, gue·ril·la [gəˈrɪlə] *n.* **1.** (usu. ~ *war*) war carried on by fighters who are not members of a regular army. **2.** person engaged in such a war.

guess [ges] *v.t. & i. & n.* (form an) opinion, (give an) answer, (make a) statement, based on supposition, not on careful thought, calculation, or definite knowledge.

guest [gest] *n.* **1.** person staying at or paying a visit to another's house, or being entertained at a meal. **2.** person staying at a hotel or having a meal at a restaurant. **'~-room** *n.* bedroom for ~s. **~ work·er** *n.* foreign (1) worker.

guf·faw [gʌˈfɔː] *v.i. & n.* (give a) noisy laugh.

guide [gaɪd] *n.* **1.** person who shows others the way; person paid to point out interesting sights on a journey or visit. **2.** sth. that directs or influences (conduct, etc.): *Instinct is not always a good ~*. **3.** (also *~book*) book of information for travellers, tourists, etc. **4.** book with information about a subject; manual. **5.** *G~*, (Gt. Brit.) member of an organization for girls, like the Scouts' Association for boys: *Girl G~*. *v.t.* act as ~ to. *~d missile*, rocket whose course may be altered during flight by electronic devices (2). *~d tour*, tour accompanied by a ~ (1). **guid·ance** [ˈgaɪdns] *n.* (no pl.) guiding; being ~d.

guild (old spelling **gild²**) [gɪld] *n.* society of persons for helping one another, forwarding common interests (e.g. trade, social welfare).

guile [gaɪl] *n.* (no pl.) deceit; cunning. **~·less** *adj.* without ~; frank.

guilt [gɪlt] *n.* (no pl.) **1.** condition of having done wrong; responsibility for wrongdoing. **2.** feeling of deserving punishment. **~·y** *adj.* (-ier, -iest) having done wrong; showing or feeling ~: *a ~y look (conscience)*.

guin·ea [ˈgɪnɪ] *n.* formerly the sum of 21s. (now £1.05); former British gold coin.

guin·ea-pig [ˈgɪnɪpɪg] *n.* short-eared animal like a big rat, often used in experiments; sb. allowing himself to be used in medical or other experiments.

a guinea-pig

guise [gaɪz] *n.* dress; outward appearance: *in the ~ of a monk; under the ~ of*, under pretence of being.

gui·tar [gɪˈtɑː*] *n.* six-stringed musical instrument plucked with the fingers or a small piece of hard material.

gulf [gʌlf] *n.* **1.** part of the sea almost surrounded by land. **2.** deep hollow; chasm; abyss; (fig.) dividing line, division (*between* opinions, etc.).

a gull¹

gull

gull¹ [gʌl] *n.* large sea-bird. (See the picture on page 221.)

gull² [gʌl] *v.t.* cheat; trick. *n.* person who is easily ⌣ed. **⌣·ible** *adj.* easily ⌣ed.

gul·let ['gʌlɪt] *n.* food passage from mouth to stomach; throat.

gul·ly ['gʌlɪ] *n.* narrow channel cut or formed by rain-water or made for carrying away water from a building.

gulp [gʌlp] *v.t. & i.* **1.** swallow (*down*) food or drink quickly or greedily: ⌣ *back* (*down*), suppress (tears, sobs). **2.** make a swallowing motion; gasp. *n.* act of ⌣ing; amount ⌣ed.

gum¹ [gʌm] *n.* (usu. pl.) firm, pink flesh round the teeth. **'⌣·boil** *n.* abscess on the ⌣.

gum² [gʌm] *n.* (no pl.) **1.** sticky substance obtained from some trees, used for sticking things together. **2.** chewing-⌣. *v.t.* (*-mm-*) put ⌣ on; fasten (*down, together*) with ⌣. **'⌣·boot** *n.* high rubber boot. **⌣·my** *adj.* (*-ier, -iest*) sticky.

gun [gʌn] *n.* general name for any kind of firearm that sends shot¹ (3), bullets, or shells from a metal tube. *stick to one's ⌣s*, defend one's opinions against attack. *v.t.* (*-nn-*) shoot at; shoot (*down*). **'⌣·boat** *n.* small warship with heavy ⌣s. **'⌣-¡car·riage** *n.* wheeled support for a heavy ⌣. **'⌣-¡cot·ton** *n.* (no pl.) explosive of acid-soaked cotton. **'⌣·man** *n.* man who uses a ⌣, esp. as a professional killer. **'⌣-¡met·al** *n.* alloy of copper and tin or zinc. **⌣·ner** *n.* man operating large ⌣s. **'⌣·pow·der** *n.* explosive powder used in fireworks and blasting. **'⌣-¡run·ner** *n.* person engaged (3) in the illegal introduction of firearms into a country. **'⌣-¡run·ning** *n.* **'⌣·shot** *n.* range of a ⌣: *within ⌣shot*. **'⌣·smith** *n.* maker of small firearms.

gun·wale ['gʌnl] *n.* upper edge of a ship's or boat's side.

gur·gle ['gɜːgl] *v.i. & n.* (make a) bubbling sound as of water flowing from a narrow-necked bottle.

gu·ru ['guru:] *n.* **1.** Hindu religious teacher and spiritual guide. **2.** leading figure in some field (4). **3.** expert; authority.

gush [gʌʃ] *v.i. & n.* **1.** (come out with a) rushing outflow: *oil ⌣ing from a new well.* **2.** (talk with) excessive enthusiasm: *girls ⌣ing over film actors.* **⌣·er** *n.* oil-well from which oil ⌣es.

gust [gʌst] *n.* sudden, violent rush of wind; burst of rain, fire, etc.; (fig.) outburst (of strong feeling). **⌣·y** *adj.* (*-ier, -iest*).

gus·to ['gʌstəʊ] *n.* (no pl.) enjoyment in doing sth.

gut [gʌt] *n.* **1.** (usu. pl.) intestines; bowels; (fig.) courage and determination. **2.** strong cord made from intestines of animals, used for the strings of a violin, etc. *v.t.* (*-tt-*) **1.** take the ⌣s (1) out of (fish, etc.). **2.** destroy the inside or contents of: *a building ⌣ted by fire.*

gut·ter ['gʌtə*] *n.* channel fixed under the edge of a roof, channel at the side of a road, to carry off rain-water. *v.i.* (of a candle) burn unsteadily so that the wax flows down the sides.

gut·tur·al ['gʌtərəl] *n. & adj.* (sound) produced in the throat.

guy¹ [gaɪ] *n.* rope or chain used to keep sth. steady or secure.

guy² [gaɪ] *n.* **1.** (Gt. Brit.) figure in the form of a man, dressed in old clothes. **2.** (Gt. Brit.) person dressed in a strange or queer-looking way. **3.** (U.S.A.; Gt. Brit. = sl.) man; fellow.

guz·zle ['gʌzl] *v.i. & t.* eat or drink greedily. **⌣r** *n.*

gym [dʒɪm] *n.* (colloq., abbr. for) gymnasium, gymnastics.

gym·kha·na [dʒɪm'kɑːnə] *n.* display of athletics; sports events.

gym·na·si·um [dʒɪm'neɪzjəm] *n.* (pl. ⌣s, *-sia*) room with apparatus (1) for physical training.

gym·nas·tic [dʒɪm'næstɪk] *adj.* of bodily training. **gym'nas·tics** *n. pl.* (often sing. v.) (forms of) exercises for physical training. **'gym·nast** *n.* person skilled in ⌣s.

gy·nae·col·o·gy (U.S.A. **gy·ne-**) [ˌgaɪnɪ'kɒlədʒɪ] *n.* (no pl.) science of the physiological functions and diseases of women. **ˌgy·nae·'col·o·gist** (U.S.A. **gy·ne-**) *n.* specialist in ⌣.

gyp·sy, see **gipsy**.

gy·rate [ˌdʒaɪə'reɪt] *v.i.* move round in circles or spirals. **gy·ra·tion** *n.*

a gyroscope

gy·ro·scope ['dʒaɪərəskəʊp] *n.* heavy wheel that, when turning fast, keeps steady the object in which it is fixed. **gy·ro·scop·ic** [ˌdʒaɪərə'skɒpɪk] *adj.*

H

hab·er·dash·er ['hæbədæʃə*] *n.* shop-keeper selling small articles of dress, pins, cotton, thread, etc. **~y** *n.* (no pl.) **~'s** goods or business.

hab·it ['hæbɪt] *n.* **1.** person's settled practice, esp. sth. that cannot easily be given up: *the ~ of smoking*; *~-forming drugs*; *be in (fall into) the ~ of*, have (acquire) the ~ of: *be in the ~ of getting up late*; *break sb. (oneself) of a ~*, succeed in getting him (oneself) to give it up; *break with old ~s*, give them up; *get out of a ~*, abandon it. **2.** usual behaviour: *do sth. from force of ~*. **3.** dress (esp. one worn by members of a religious order): *a nun's ~*; *riding-~*, woman's coat and skirt for horse-riding. **ha·bit·u·al** [hə'bɪtjʊəl] *adj.* regular; usual; from ~. **ha·bit·u·al·ly** *adv.* as a usual practice. **ha·bit·u·ate** [hə'bɪtjʊeɪt] *v.t.* accustom; get (sb., oneself) used to.

hab·it·a·ble ['hæbɪtəbl] *adj.* fit to be lived in. **hab·i·tat** ['hæbɪtæt] *n.* (of plants, animals) natural place of growth or home. **hab·i·ta·tion** [,hæbɪ'teɪʃn] *n.* **1.** living in: *not fit for habitation.* **2.** place of abode.

ha·bit·u·al(·ly), ha·bit·u·ate, see *hab-it.*

hack¹ [hæk] *v.t. & i.* cut roughly; chop: *~ sth. to pieces*; *~ at a branch*; *a ~ing cough*, one that seems to tear the chest. **'~-saw** *n.* saw for cutting metal.

hack² [hæk] *n.* **1.** horse that may be hired. **2.** person paid to do undistinguished literary work.

hack·neyed ['hæknɪd] *adj.* (esp. of sayings) too common; repeated too often.

had, see *have.*

had·dock ['hædək] *n.* (pl. ~, ~s) sea-fish much used for food, esp. when smoked.

haem·or·rhage (U.S.A. **hem-**) ['hem-ərɪdʒ] *n.* escape of blood from blood-vessels; bleeding.

haft [hɑːft] *n.* handle of a knife, dagger, etc.

hag [hæg] *n.* ugly, old woman; witch.

hag·gard ['hægəd] *adj.* (of the face) looking tired and lined, esp. from worry, lack of sleep.

hag·gle ['hægl] *v.i.* argue, dispute (*about* or *over* the price of sth.).

hail¹ [heɪl] *n.* frozen raindrops falling from the sky; sth. coming in great numbers and force: *a ~ of blows (curses).* *v.i. & t.* **1.** *It's ~ing*, ~ *is falling.* **2.** (fig., of blows, etc.) come down like ~. **'~·stone** *n.* small ball of ice.

hail² [heɪl] *v.t. & i.* **1.** greet; give a welcoming cry to; call out to (to attract attention): *be ~ed by a friend*; *~ a taxi.* **2.** *~ from*, have come from. *n. within ~*, near enough to be ~ed; *be ~-fellow-well-met with (sb.)*, be very informal with.

hair [heə*] *n.* **1.** fine, thread-like growth on the skin of a person or animal. **2.** (no pl.) (collective sing.) mass of such growths, esp. that which covers the human head: (describe sth.) *to a ~*, exactly; *not turn a ~*, give no sign of being troubled; *make one's ~ stand on end*, fill one with terror. **'~·brush** *n.* brush for smoothing the ~. **'~·cut** *n.* act or style of cutting the ~. **'~-do** *n.* (colloq.) style of ~dressing. **'~·dress·er** *n.* person who dresses (5) and cuts ~, esp. of women. **'~·pin** *n.* pin for keeping the ~ in place. **,~·pin 'bend** *n.* sharp bend in a road, esp. on a hillside. **'~-,split·ting** *adj.* making or showing differences too small to be important. **'~·spring** *n.* very delicate spring in a watch. **'~-style** *n.* particular way of dressing (5) the ~. **~·less** *adj.* bald. **~y** *adj.* (*-ier, -iest*) of or like ~; covered with ~.

hal·cy·on ['hælsɪən] *adj.* *~ days*, *~ weather*, calm and peaceful.

hale¹ [heɪl] *adj.* (usu. of old persons): *~ and hearty*, strong and healthy.

hale² [heɪl] *v.t.* take, drag, by force (*away, off, to prison, etc.*).

half [hɑːf] *n.* (pl. *halves* [hɑːvz]) one of two equal or corresponding parts into which a thing can be divided; *½.* *go halves (with sb., in sth.)*, share equally; *do sth. by halves*, do it incompletely or badly; *too clever by ~*, far too clever; *one's better ~*, (colloq.) one's wife. **adj.** forming a ~: ~ *moon*; *a ~ share*; ~ *the time*. **adv.** to the extent of a ~: *the meat is only ~ cooked*; ~ *dead*; *not ~*, not nearly; (colloq.) not at all: *not ~ bad*; (sl.) to the greatest possible extent. ,~-'**back** *n.* (football, hockey) (position of the) player immediately behind the forwards. '~-**blood** *n.* (relationship of) persons having the same father or mother but not both. '~-**breed**, '~-**caste** *ns.* **1.** person with parents of different races, esp. differently coloured races. **2.** offspring of two animals or plants of different species. ,~-'**broth·er** *n.* brother by one parent only. ,~-'**crown** *n.* ~ a crown, (formerly) British coin, value 2s. 6d. (= $12^1/_2$p.). ,~-'**heart·ed** *adj.* done with, showing, little interest or enthusiasm. ~ **hol·i·day** *n.* day of which half (usu. the afternoon) is free from work or duty. ,~-'**mast** *n. at ~mast*, position, near the middle of a mast, of a flag flown to indicate mourning. ~**pen·ny** ['heɪpnɪ] *n.* British coin worth ~ a penny (= $^1/_2$p.). ~**pen·ny·worth** ['heɪpnɪwɜːθ, 'heɪpəθ] *n.* '~-,**sis·ter** *n.* sister by one parent only. ,~-'**term** *n.* (Gt. Brit.) period about ~-way through a school term. ,~-'**time** *n.* **1.** time at which ~ a game or contest is completed; interval between the two halves of a game. **2.** work and pay for ~ the usual time: *be on ~-time*. ,~-'**way** *adj. & adv.* midway between two points; (fig.) compromise. ,~-'**wit** *n.* ~-witted person. ,~-'**wit·ted** *adj.* weak-minded.

hal·i·but ['hælɪbət] *n.* (pl. ~, ~s) large, flat sea-fish used for food.

hall [hɔːl] *n.* **1.** (building with a) large room for meetings, concerts, public business, etc.: *city ~*; *music-~*. **2.** large room for meals (in colleges of some universities): *dine in ~*. **3.** space into which the main entrance of a building opens.

hal·le·lu·jah [,hælɪ'luːjə] *n. & int.* (song of, cry of) praise to God.

hall·mark ['hɔːlmɑːk] *n.* mark stamped on gold or silver articles as a guarantee of quality. *v.t.* stamp the ~ on.

hal·lo [hə'ləʊ] *int.* cry to attract attention; greeting.

hal·low ['hæləʊ] *v.t.* make holy; regard as holy: *~ed ground*.

hal·lu·ci·na·tion [hə,luːsɪ'neɪʃn] *n.* seeming to see sth. not present; sth. so imagined. **hal·lu·ci·na·to·ry** [hə'luː-sɪnətərɪ], **hal·lu·ci·no·gen·ic** [hə,luː-sɪnəʊ'dʒenɪk] *adjs.* (of drugs, etc.) inducing (2) ~.

ha·lo ['heɪləʊ] *n.* (pl. -oes, -os) circle of light round the sun or moon or (in paintings, etc.) shown above the head of a sacred figure (5).

halt[1] [hɔːlt] *n.* **1.** (esp. of soldiers) short stop on a march or journey. **2.** stop; pause. **3.** (Gt. Brit.) minor stopping-place for a railway train. *v.i. & t.* stop marching; come, bring, to a stop.

halt[2] [hɔːlt] *v.i.* walk in a hesitating way; hesitate: ~ *between two opinions*. ~**ing·ly** *adv.*

hal·ter ['hɔːltə*] *n.* rope or leather strap put round a horse's head; rope used for hanging (2) a person.

halve [hɑːv] *v.t.* divide into two equal parts; lessen by one half.

hal·yard ['hæljəd] *n.* rope for raising or lowering a sail or flag.

ham [hæm] *n.* (salted and smoked) upper part of a pig's leg.

ham·burg·er ['hæmbɜːgə*] *n.* ground or chopped beef made into round, flat cakes and fried, served hot between the two halves of a bread roll.

ham·let ['hæmlɪt] *n.* group of houses in the countryside.

ham·mer ['hæmə*] *n.* **1.** tool with a heavy metal head, used for breaking things, driving in nails, etc. *go at it ~ and tongs*, fight, argue, with great energy and noise; *come under the ~*, be sold by auction. **2.** (anat.) bone in the ear. *v.t. & i.* strike with, or as with, a ~: ~ *a nail in*; ~ *sth. flat*; ~ *at a door*. **2.** (fig.) produce by hard work: ~ *out a scheme*; work hard: ~ *away at sth.*

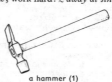

a hammer (1)

ham·mock ['hæmək] *n.* hanging bed of canvas or rope network.

ham·per[1] ['hæmpə*] *v.t.* hinder; prevent free movement or activity.

ham·per[2] ['hæmpə*] *n.* basket with a lid, esp. one for food (usu. given as a present): *a Christmas ~*.

ham·string ['hæmstrɪŋ] *v.t.* (p.t. & p.p. -*strung* or ~*ed*) cripple (a person or animal) by cutting the tendons.

hand [hænd] *n.* **1.** part of the human arm beyond the wrist: *at ~*, within reach; present; *live from ~ to mouth*, spend money as soon as it is earned, saving nothing; *give a (helping) ~ to sb.*,

a hammock   a hand

help him; *in* ~, (a) held in reserve, available, for use; (b) receiving attention; *on* ~, available; *out of* ~, (a) out of control; (b) at once; without preparation; *win* ~*s down*, win easily; *keep one's* ~ *in*, keep one's skill by practice; *with a heavy* ~, cruelly; severely; *with a high* ~, arrogantly. **2.** (pl.) care; keeping; possession: *The matter is in your* ~*s. change* ~*s*, pass to another owner. **3.** worker in a factory, dockyard, etc.; member of a ship's crew. **4.** pointer on a watch or clock: *the hour- (minute-)*~. **5.** source of information: *hear sth. at first (second)* ~, directly (indirectly, by hearsay). **6.** side; direction: *on all* ~*s*, to or from all sides; *on the one* ~, ... *on the other* ~ (contrasting two sides of a question). **7.** ~writing; signature: *set one's* ~ *to an agreement*. **8.** (a) cards dealt to, held by, a player; (b) player at cards; (c) one round in a game of cards. **9.** unit of measurement, four inches (= 10.16 centimetres), used for the height of a horse. **10.** (colloq.) applause: *He got a big* ~. **11.** (attrib.) (a) operated by ~: ~*-brake*; (b) done by ~, not by a machine: ~*-knitted*; (c) held or carried in the ~: ~*bag*. *v.t.* give; pass; help with the ~(s): ~ *sb. a book*; ~ *in an essay*, ~*ed down from one generation to another*; ~ *on the news*, tell it to others; ~ *sb. out of a carriage, etc.* '~**·bag** *n.* (U.S.A. also *purse*) woman's bag for carrying money, handkerchief, etc. '~**·bill** *n.* printed advertisement distributed by ~. '~**·book** *n.* small guidebook or book of information on a subject. '~**·brake** *n.* brake in a motor vehicle, operated by ~. '~**·cart** *n.* cart pushed or pulled by ~. '~**·cuff** *n.* one of a pair of metal rings joined by a short chain, placed round a prisoner's wrists. *v.t.* put ~cuffs on. ~**·ful** *n.* (a) as much as a ~ holds; (b) a small number; (c) (colloq.) person or animal difficult to control. '~**·writ·ing** *n.* (person's style of) writing with a pen or pencil. ~**y** *adj.* (-*ier*, -*iest*) **1.** clever with the ~. **2.** available for use; not far away. **3.** (of tools, etc.) easily used; useful. ~**·i·ly** *adv.*

hand·i·cap [ˈhændɪkæp] *n.* **1.** sth. that hinders or lessens one's chance of success. **2.** race, etc. in which the strongest competitors are ~ped, so that everyone may have a fair chance of winning. *v.t.* (-*pp-*) give or be a ~ to: ~ped *by ill health*.

hand·i·craft [ˈhændɪkrɑːft] *n.* art or craft needing skill with the hands (e.g. pottery).

hand·i·work [ˈhændɪwɜːk] *n.* sth. done or made by the hands or by a named person.

hand·ker·chief [ˈhæŋkətʃɪf] *n.* square piece of cotton, silk, linen, etc. carried in the pocket for blowing the nose on, wiping the face, or worn for ornament.

han·dle [ˈhændl] *n.* part of a tool, cup, door, etc. by which it may be held in the hand. *fly off the* ~, (colloq.) lose self-control. *v.t.* **1.** touch with, take in, the hands. **2.** manage, control (thing, person). '~**·bar** *n.* bar for steering a bicycle.

hand·some [ˈhænsəm] *adj.* (~*r*, ~*st*) **1.** of fine appearance. **2.** (of gifts, etc.) generous.

hang [hæŋ] *v.t. & i.* (p.t. & p.p. *hung* [hʌŋ]) **1.** support, be supported, from above so that the lower end is free: ~ *a lamp from the ceiling; curtains* ~*ing over the window.* **2.** (p.t. & p.p. ~*ed*) put, be put, to death by ~*ing* with a rope round the neck. **3.** ~ *a door*, attach it with hinges to a frame; ~ *the head*, let it fall forward (when ashamed); ~ *fire*, (a) (of a gun) be slow in going off; (b) (of events) be slow in developing. **4.** (with advs. and preps.): ~ *about (around)*, be or remain near, waiting or idling; ~ *back*, hesitate; show unwillingness to act; ~ *on to*, hold tightly; refuse to give up; ~ *together*, (of persons) support one another; (of a story, its parts) fit together well; ~ *up*, (a) place on a hook, etc.; (b) end a telephone conversation by replacing the receiver; (c) *be hung up*, be delayed. *n.* (no pl.) **1.** way in which sth. (esp. a garment) ~s. **2.** *get the* ~ *of sth.*, understand how to do or use sth.; *not care a* ~, (colloq.) care not at all. '~**·dog** *adj.* (of sb.'s look) sly and ashamed. ~**·er** *n.* (esp.) wooden bar on which to ~ dresses, coats, etc.: *dress- (clothes-, coat-)*~*er.* ,~**·er-'on** *n.* (pl. ~*ers-on*) person forcing his company on others in the hope of profit or advantage. '~**-,glid·er** *n.* flying apparatus consisting of a light frame, usu. in the form of a triangle, with cloth, etc. stretched over it, controlled and stabilized by the movements of the operator sitting or hanging in it. **~·ings** *n. pl.* curtains. '**~·man** *n.* executioner by ~ing (2). '**~·over** *n.* (sl.) unpleasant after-effects of (esp.) excessive drinking.

han·gar ['hæŋə*] *n.* shed for aircraft.

hank [hæŋk] *n.* coil or twist of wool, silk, etc. thread.

hank·er ['hæŋkə*] *v.i.* ~ *after* (*for*), be continually wishing for.

han·som ['hænsəm] *n.* (also ~ *cab*) (no longer used) two-wheeled horse-cab for two passengers, with the driver's seat high at the back.

hap·haz·ard [,hæp'hæzəd] *adj.*, *adv.* **& n.** (by) mere chance; (by) accident.

ha'p'orth, see *halfpennyworth*.

hap·pen ['hæpən] *v.i.* **1.** take place; come about. **2.** ~ *on*, find or meet by chance. **~·ing** *n.* **1.** (usu. pl.) event. **2.** spontaneous or improvised public performance, display, spectacle, etc., often involving the audience or spectators.

hap·py ['hæpɪ] *adj.* (*-ier*, *-iest*) **1.** feeling or expressing pleasure; pleased; lucky. **2.** (of words, ideas, suggestions) well suited to the situation. **~·go-'lucky** *adj.* taking what fortune brings; carefree. **hap·pi·ly** *adv.* **hap·pi·ness** *n.* (no pl.).

ha·rangue [hə'ræŋ] *n.* long, loud (often scolding) speech or talk. *v.i.* **& t.** make a ~ (to).

har·ass ['hærəs] *v.t.* trouble; worry; make repeated attacks on.

har·bin·ger ['hɑːbɪndʒə*] *n.* sb. or sth. that foretells the coming of sb. or sth.

har·bour (U.S.A. **-bor**) ['hɑːbə*] *n.* place of shelter for ships; (fig.) place of safety. *v.t.* **1.** give shelter to; hide: ~ *a criminal*. **2.** hold (ill feeling, etc.) in the mind.

hard[1] [hɑːd] *adj.* **1.** firm; solid; not easily cut or dented; severe; harsh: ~ *of hearing*, rather deaf; ~ *and fast* (rules, etc.), that cannot be altered to fit special cases; ~ *luck*, ~ *lines*, worse fortune than is deserved; ~ *times*, times of money shortage, unemployment, etc. '**~·back** *n.* **& adj.** (book) bound in ~ covers (opp. *paperback*). ~ **cash** *n.* (no pl.) coins, notes, not a cheque or promise to pay. ~ **cov·er** *n.* stiff, durable binding of a book. ~ **drink**, ~ **li·quor** *ns.* drink or liquor with high alcoholic content. ~ **drugs** *n. pl.* drugs likely to lead to addiction. ~·**en** *v.t.* **& i.** make or become ~. ~ **hat** *n.* **1.** bowler hat. **2.** protective headgear worn on building-sites, etc. **3.** reactionary person. '**~·hat** *n.* (U.S.A.) = construction worker. ,**~·'head·ed** *adj.* unsentimental; shrewd; astute. ,**~·'heart·ed** *adj.* pitiless; unfeeling. ~ **la·bour** *n.* (no pl.) imprisonment with ~ physical labour. ~ **line** *n.* (no pl.) rigid adherence to a firm policy. '**~·line** *adj.* following a ~ line; inflexible. '**~·lin·er** *n.* ~·**ship** *n.* severe suffering; painful condition. '**~·top** *n.* motor car with a metal roof, not a sliding roof. '**~·ware** *n.* (no pl.) **1.** metal goods such as pans, locks, nails. **2.** physical components of a computer, rocket, missile, etc. (opp. *software*).

hard[2] [hɑːd] *adv.* with great energy; with all one's force; severely; heavily; with difficulty: ~ *up*, short of money; *be ~ put to it*, *be ~ pressed*, be in difficult circumstances; ~ *by*, near; ~ *upon*, not far behind.

hard·ly ['hɑːdlɪ] *adv.* **1.** with difficulty; severely. **2.** scarcely; only just: ~ *any*, very few; very little.

har·dy ['hɑːdɪ] *adj.* (*-ier*, *-iest*) **1.** strong; able to endure suffering or hardship. **2.** bold. **3.** (of plants) not damaged by frost. **har·di·hood** *n.* (no pl.) boldness. **har·di·ly** *adv.* **har·di·ness** *n.* (no pl.).

hare [heə*] *n.* field animal with a divided upper lip, like, but larger than, a rabbit. '**~·brained** *adj.* rash; wild.

har·em ['hɑːriːm] *n.* women's part of a Muslim household; its occupants.

har·i·cot ['hærɪkəʊ] *n.* (also ~ *bean*) ripe, white seed of any of several beans; kidney bean; French bean.

hark [hɑːk] *v.i.* (chiefly imperative) listen (*to*, *at*): ~ *at him!*

har·le·quin ['hɑːlɪkwɪn] *n.* comic character in pantomime.

har·lot ['hɑːlət] *n.* (old use) prostitute.

harm [hɑːm] *v.t.* **& n.** (no pl.) (cause) damage or injury (to). ~·**ful** *adj.* causing ~. ~·**less** *adj.* causing no ~.

har·mo·nium [hɑː'məʊnjəm] *n.* musical instrument like a small organ, but with reeds (2) instead of pipes.

har·mo·ny ['hɑːmənɪ] *n.* **1.** (no pl.) agreement (of feeling, interests, opinions, etc.): *in ~ with*. **2.** (music) pleasing combination of notes sounded together; pleasing association of colours seen together. **har·mo·ni·ous** [hɑː'məʊnjəs] *adj.* in agreement; pleasingly combined or arranged; sweet-sounding; tuneful. **har·mo·nize** ['hɑːmənaɪz] *v.t.* **& i.** bring into, be in, ~ (with); (music) add notes (to a melody) to make chords.

har·ness ['hɑːnɪs] *n.* (no pl.) (collective sing.) all the leatherwork and metalwork by which a horse is controlled and fastened to whatever it pulls or carries: *in* ~, (fig.) doing one's regular work. *v.t.* **1.** put a ~ on (a horse). **2.** use (a river, waterfall) to produce (esp. electric) power.

harp [hɑːp] *n.* stringed musical instrument played with the fingers. *v.i.* play the ~: ~ *on*, (fig.) talk repeatedly or tiringly about (e.g. one's misfortunes). **~·er, ~·ist** *ns.* player on the ~.

a harp

har·poon [hɑːˈpuːn] *n.* spear attached to a rope, thrown by hand or fired from a gun (e.g. for catching whales). *v.t.* strike or capture with a ~.

harp·si·chord [ˈhɑːpsɪkɔːd] *n.* piano-like instrument dating from the 16th century.

har·py [ˈhɑːpɪ] *n.* (in classical mythology) cruel creature with a woman's face and bird's wings and claws.

har·ri·er [ˈhærɪə*] *n.* hound used for hunting hares.

har·row [ˈhærəʊ] *n.* heavy frame with metal teeth or discs for breaking up ground after ploughing. *v.t.* pull a ~ over; (fig.) distress (the feelings).

har·ry [ˈhærɪ] *v.t.* lay waste and plunder; attack frequently; worry.

harsh [hɑːʃ] *adj.* **1.** rough and disagreeable, esp. to the senses. **2.** stern; cruel; severe. **~·ly** *adv.* **~·ness** *n.* (no pl.).

har·um-scar·um [ˌheərəmˈskeərəm] *n.* reckless, impulsive person.

har·vest [ˈhɑːvɪst] *n.* **1.** (season for) cutting and gathering in of grain and other food crops; quantity obtained. **2.** consequence(s) of action or behaviour. *v.t.* cut, gather, dig up (a crop): ~ *rice* (*potatoes*). **~·er** *n.* reaper; reaping-machine, esp. one that also binds grain into sheaves.

has, see *have.*

hash¹ [hæʃ] *v.t.* ~ (*up*), cut up (meat) into small pieces. *n.* (no pl.) dish of cooked meat, ~ed and re-cooked: *make a* ~ *of sth.*, (fig.) do it badly.

hash² [hæʃ] *n.* (no pl.) (colloq.) hashish.

hash·ish [ˈhæʃiːʃ] *n.* (no pl.) dried hemp leaves made into a drug for smoking or chewing.

hasp [hɑːsp] *n.* metal fastening for a door, etc., used with a staple.

a hasp and staple

has·sock [ˈhæsək] *n.* cushion for kneeling on (e.g. in church).

haste [heɪst] *n.* (no pl.) quickness of movement; hurry: *make* ~, hurry; *in* (*great*) ~, in a hurry; hastily. **has·ten** [ˈheɪsn] *v.i.* & *t.* **1.** move or act with speed. **2.** cause (sb.) to hurry; cause (sth.) to be done or to happen quickly or earlier. **hasty** *adj.* (*-ier, -iest*) **1.** said, made or done (too) quickly. **2.** quick-tempered. **hast·i·ly** *adv.* **hast·i·ness** *n.* (no pl.).

hat [hæt] *n.* covering for the head, usu. with a brim, worn out of doors. (Cf. *cap* (1), *bonnet* (1, 2), without a brim.) *talk through one's* ~, (sl.) talk foolishly.

hatch¹ [hætʃ] *n.* (movable covering over an) opening in a wall or floor, esp. (~*way*) one in a ship's deck: *under* ~*es*, below deck; opening or door in an aircraft or a spacecraft. '~·back *n.* car with a door at the back that opens upwards.

hatch² [hætʃ] *v.t.* & *i.* **1.** (cause to) break out (of an egg): ~ *chickens* (*eggs*). **2.** think out and develop (a plot). **~·ery** *n.* place for ~ing (esp. fish).

hatch·et [ˈhætʃɪt] *n.* axe with a short handle. *bury the* ~, stop quarrelling.

hate [heɪt] *v.t.* & *n.* (no pl.) (have a) violent dislike (of). **~·ful** *adj.* showing, causing, ~. **hat·red** [ˈheɪtrɪd] *n.* (no pl.) hate.

haugh·ty [ˈhɔːtɪ] *adj.* (*-ier, -iest*) arrogant. **haugh·ti·ly** *adv.* **haugh·ti·ness** *n.* (no pl.) arrogance.

haul [hɔːl] *v.t.* & *i.* pull (with effort or force): *elephants* ~*ing logs*; ~ *at a rope*; ~ (*sb.*) *over the coals*, find fault with; scold. *n.* act of ~ing; amount gained as the result of effort, esp. of fish ~ed up in a net. **~·age** [ˈhɔːlɪdʒ] *n.* (no pl.) transport (of goods). **~·ier** [ˈhɔːljə*], (U.S.A.) **~·er** *ns.* firm or person engaged in the transport of goods by road.

haunch [hɔːntʃ] *n.* (in man and animals) part of the body round the hips, or between the ribs and thighs.

haunt [hɔ:nt] *v.t.* visit, be with, habitually or repeatedly: *idle students who* ~ *discothèques; wrongdoers* ~*ed by fear of discovery.* *n.* place frequently visited by the person(s) named: *the* ~ *of criminals.* ~**ed** *adj.* (of a place) frequently visited by ghosts.

have [hæv, həv] *v.t. & aux.* (pres. t. *have*, colloq. *'ve* [v], 3rd person sing. *has* [hæz, həz], colloq. *'s* [z, s]; p.t. & p.p. *had* [hæd, həd], colloq. *'d* [d]; neg. *have not*, colloq. *haven't* ['hævnt], *has not*, colloq. *hasn't* ['hæznt], *had not*, colloq. *hadn't* ['hædnt]; pres. p. *having* ['hævɪŋ]; colloq. *have got* = *have*) **I.** *v.aux.* used to form the perfect tenses and the perfect infinitive. **II.** *v.t.* **1.** (in sentences where *be* is possible): *I* ~ *no doubt that ...* (There is no doubt ...). *Has June thirty-one days?* **2.** possess: *He has* (colloq. *has got*) *a lot of books. Has she* (colloq. *Has she got*) *blue eyes or brown?* **3.** experience in the mind: *I've no doubt about it. What reason* ~ *you for thinking so?* **4.** allow: *I won't* ~ *such behaviour in my house.* **5.** expressing obligation: ~ *to*, (colloq.) ~ *got to*, must: *When* ~ *you to go to the dentist? We shall have to go soon.* **6.** suffer from: *Do you often* ~ *pain?* **7.** give birth to: *The cat has just had kittens.* **8.** receive; obtain: *What presents did you* ~ *at Christmas?* **9.** take; choose; accept: *What shall we* ~ *for dinner? Will you* ~ *me for a partner?* **10.** wish; expect: *What would you* ~ *me do in that case?* **11.** ~ *sth. done*, cause (sb.) to do sth.: ~ *one's hair cut.* **12.** ~ *to do with*, be concerned with: *What has she to do with that?* (How is she concerned?) ~ *something* (*nothing*) *to do with*, be connected (be unconnected) with; ~ *something out with sb.*, discuss and settle (a matter under dispute).

ha·ven ['heɪvn] *n.* harbour; (fig.) place of safety or rest.

hav·er·sack ['hævəsæk] *n.* canvas bag, esp. as used by soldiers, for carrying food, etc.

hav·oc ['hævək] *n.* (no pl.) widespread damage; destruction.

haw [hɔ:] *n.* fruit (a red berry) of the hawthorn bush.

hawk[1] [hɔ:k] *n.* **1.** strong, swift, keensighted bird of prey. **2.** (pol.) person who favours war or the use of (military) force in a conflict (opp. *dove*[1] (3)).

hawk[2] [hɔ:k] *v.t.* go from street to street, house to house, with goods for sale. ~**er** *n.*

haw·ser ['hɔ:zə*] *n.* thick, heavy rope; thin steel cable (used on ships).

haw·thorn ['hɔ:θɔ:n] *n.* thorny shrub with white or red blossom and red berries called *haws.*

hay [heɪ] *n.* (no pl.) grass cut and dried for use as animal food. ~ *fever*, disease affecting the nose and throat, caused by pollen (the dust) from various plants. '~**rick**, '~**stack** *ns.* mass of ~ firmly piled in a field till needed.

haz·ard ['hæzəd] *n.* risk; danger: *exposed to the* ~*s of a life at sea.* *v.t.* **1.** take the risk of; expose to danger. **2.** venture to make (a guess, remark). ~**ous** *adj.* risky.

haze [heɪz] *n.* (no pl.) thin mist; (fig.) vagueness of mind or mental perception. **hazy** *adj.* (-ier, -iest) misty; (fig.) vague; not clear.

ha·zel ['heɪzl] *n.* **1.** small nut-tree. **2.** (no pl.) (esp. of eyes) reddish-brown colour.

H-bomb ['eɪtʃbɒm] *n.* hydrogen bomb.

he [hi:, hɪ] *pron.* male person, animal, etc. previously referred to. *attrib. adj.* male: *a* ~*goat;* ~*man*, masterful or virile man. *n.* male; man: *This cat is a* ~*, not a she.*

head [hed] *n.* **1.** that part of the body that contains the brain, the mouth, etc. **2.** life: *lose one's* ~*. It cost him his* ~*.* **3.** sth. like a ~ in form or position, e.g. the striking part of a hammer, the flat end of a nail, the top of a mast, foam on beer, a mass of leaves (e.g. *a* ~ *of lettuce*) or flowers at the top of a stem, etc., a device (2) for recording, reading, or erasing material on a magnetic tape: *tape-recorder* ~*s.* **4.** brain; imagination; power to reason: *make sth. up out of one's* ~*; lose* (*keep*) *one's* ~*,* become overexcited (remain calm) in the face of difficulty, danger, etc.; *off one's* ~*,* mad; *take it into one's* ~ *that,* come to believe that; (*talk*) *above their* ~*s,* beyond their power to understand; ~ *over heels,* upside-down; deeply and completely: *be* ~ *over heels in love.* **5.** picture or image of a ~, esp. on coins: ~*s or tails; be unable to make* ~ *or tail of sth.,* be completely puzzled by it. **6.** one person: *50p. a* ~*, 50p. for each person; crowned* ~*s,* kings; queens. **7.** (pl. ~) unit of a flock or herd: *40* ~ *of cattle.* **8.** front (part); chief position: *at the* ~ *of the list.* **9.** upper end (opp. *foot* (4)): *the* ~ *of a valley* (*lake, bed*). **10.** ruler; chief; master: *the* ~ *of the school; the* ~ *waiter.* **11.** main division in a speech or essay. **12.** point rising from a boil[1], etc., esp. when about to burst: *come to a* ~*,* (fig.) reach a crisis or climax. *v.t. & i.* **1.** be at the ~ of (e.g. a procession). **2.**

move in the direction indicated: ⁓*ing south*; ⁓ *for home*; ⁓ *sb. off*, get in front in order to turn him back. **3.** strike with the ⁓: (football) ⁓ *the ball*. '⁓**·ache** *n.* continuous pain in the ⁓: *have a bad* ⁓*ache*. '⁓**·dress** *n.* (esp. ornamental) ⁓*-covering*. ⁓**·er** *n.* **1.** (colloq.) fall or dive ⁓ first. **2.** (football) act of striking the ball with the ⁓. '⁓**·gear** *n.* hat; cap; ⁓*-dress*; ⁓**·ing** *n.* word(s) at the top of a section of printed matter. '⁓**·land** *n.* promontory; cape². '⁓**·light** *n.* large lamp on the front of a motor car, etc. '⁓**·line** *n.* newspaper ⁓*ing*, usu. in large type. '⁓**·long** *adj. & adv.* with the ⁓ first; (fig.) thoughtless(ly) and hurried(ly). ⁓**·man** ['hedmæn] *n.* chief of a tribe or village. ¡⁓**'mas·ter**, ¡⁓**'mis·tress** *ns.* principal master, mistress, of a school. ¡⁓**·'on** *adj. & adv.* (of vehicles) (colliding) directly, front to front: *a* ⁓*-on collision*. '⁓**·phones** *n. pl.* radio, telephone, etc. receivers (2) held over the ears by a band worn over the ⁓; earphones. ¡⁓**'quar·ters** *n. pl.* (sing. or pl. v.) place from which (e.g. police, army) activities are controlled. '⁓**·room** *n.* over⁓ space. '⁓**·square** *n.* scarf for the ⁓. '⁓**·stall** *n.* part of a bridle or halter that fits round a horse's ⁓. '⁓**·strong** *adj.* self-willed; obstinate. '⁓**·way** *n.* (no pl.) progress. '⁓**·word** *n.* word used as a ⁓*ing*, esp. the first word, in heavy type, of a dictionary entry.

heal [hi:l] *v.t. & i.* make or become well: ⁓ *a wound*; *wounds that* ⁓ *slowly*; ⁓ *a quarrel*, (fig.) end it.

health [helθ] *n.* **1.** (no pl.) condition of the body or the mind; *good (poor)* ⁓. **2.** (no pl.) state of being free from illness. **3.** (no pl.) (as a social custom) raise one's glass and wish good ⁓ to. ⁓**·y** *adj.* (-ier, -iest) having, showing, producing, good ⁓: ⁓*y exercise*.

heap [hi:p] *n.* **1.** number of things, mass of material, piled up like a small hill: *a* ⁓ *of books (sand)*. **2.** (pl.) (colloq.) a large number; plenty: *have* ⁓*s of books (time)*. *v.t.* **1.** put in a ⁓; make into a ⁓: ⁓ *(up) stones*. **2.** fill; load: ⁓ *a plate with food*; *a* ⁓*ed spoonful*; ⁓ *favours upon a friend*.

hear [hɪə*] *v.t. & i.* (p.t. & p.p. ⁓*d* [hɜ:d]) **1.** become aware of (sound) through the ears: ⁓ *from*, receive news, a message, from; ⁓ *of*, have news, knowledge, about. **2.** (of a judge) try (a case); judge. **3.** *H⁓! H⁓!* cry expressing approval or agreement. ⁓**·ing** *n.* **1.** (no pl.) ability to ⁓; distance within which one can ⁓: *within (out*

of) ⁓*ing*, near enough (too far off) to be heard. **2.** trial. **3.** opportunity of being heard, esp. in self-defence. '⁓**·say** *n.* (no pl.) what one ⁓s said, whether true or not.

hear·ken ['hɑ:kən] *v.i.* (old use or liter.) listen.

hearse [hɜ:s] *n.* carriage, car, for carrying a coffin.

heart [hɑ:t] *n.* **1.** that part of the body that pumps the blood through it. **2.** centre of the affection or emotions, esp. of love: *not have the* ⁓ *to (disappoint sb.)*, be too sympathetic to (do so); *lose* ⁓, feel discouraged; *take* ⁓, be confident; *take sth. to* ⁓, be much affected by it; *a change of* ⁓, change making one a better person; *after one's own* ⁓, of the sort most liked or approved. **3.** centre: *in the* ⁓ *of the forest*. **4.** playing-card marked with red ⁓s. '⁓**·ache** *n.* deep sorrow. '⁓**·beat** *n.* one movement of the ⁓'s regular motion. '⁓**·,break·ing** *adj.* causing great sorrow. '⁓**·,brok·en** *adj.* suffering from deep sorrow. '⁓**·burn** *n.* burning feeling below the ⁓, caused by indigestion. '⁓**·,burn·ing** *n.* envy; discontent. ⁓**·en** *v.t.* give courage to: ⁓*ening news*. ⁓ **fail·ure** *n.* failure of the ⁓ to function normally, esp. if fatal. '⁓**·felt** *adj.* (of feelings, esp. sympathy) sincere; deeply felt. ⁓**·less** *adj.* unkind; without pity. '⁓**·,rend·ing** *adj.* causing deep grief. '⁓**·strings** *n. pl.* deepest feelings. '⁓**·whole** *adj.* not yet in love. ⁓**·y** *adj.* (-ier, -iest) **1.** sincere: *my* ⁓*y approval*; *a* ⁓*y welcome*. **2.** strong; healthy: *still hale and* ⁓*y at 95*. **3.** (of meals, appetites) big: *a* ⁓*y meal (eater, appetite)*. ⁓**·i·ly** *adv.*

hearth [hɑ:θ] *n.* floor of a fire-place; (fig.) home. (See the picture at *grate*².) '⁓**·rug** *n.* rug spread in front of a ⁓.

heat [hi:t] *n.* **1.** (no pl.) hotness. **2.** (no pl.) intense feeling: *in the* ⁓ *of the argument*. **3.** trial race, etc. the winners of which take part in (the further races, etc. leading to) the finals. **4.** (no pl.) (of female mammals) sexual excitement during the breeding season. *v.t. & i.* make or become warm or hot. ⁓**·ed·ly** *adv.* angrily. ⁓**·er** *n.* apparatus (1) for warming a room, motor car, etc. or for ⁓*ing* water. ⁓ **shield** *n.* device (2) that gives protection against excessive ⁓, esp. on a spacecraft during re-entry. ⁓ **wave** *n.* period of unusually hot weather.

heath [hi:θ] *n.* **1.** area of flat waste land. **2.** (sorts of) low-growing bush or shrub growing on ⁓s, hillsides, etc.

hea·then ['hi:ðən] *n. & adj.* (person)

of a religion neither Christian, Muslim, Jewish, nor Buddhist; (fig.) savage.

heath·er ['heðə*] *n.* (no pl.) kind of heath (2) with small, light-purple flowers.

heave [hiːv] *v.t. & i.* (p.t. & p.p. ~d or (nautical use) *hove* [həʊv]) **1.** raise, lift up (sth. heavy); pull (*at, on,* a rope). **2.** (colloq.) lift and throw: ~ *one's luggage into a taxi.* **3.** utter: ~ *a groan* (*sigh*). **4.** rise and fall: *heaving waves; a heaving bosom.* **5.** (of a ship) ~ *in sight,* come into view; come to a stop: *The ship hove to. n.* act of heaving.

heav·en ['hevn] *n.* **1.** home of God and the Saints. **2.** (usu. *H*~) God; Providence: *It is the will of H*~. *Good H*~*s!* (in exclamations). **3.** place, condition, of great happiness. **4.** (often pl.) the sky. ~**ly** *adj.* **1.** of, from, like, ~: *the* ~*ly bodies* (see *body* (7)). **2.** (colloq.) very beautiful or pleasing.

heavy ['hevɪ] *adj.* (-ier, -iest) **1.** having great weight; difficult to lift or move. **2.** of more than usual size, amount, force, etc.: ~ *crops* (*rain, work, blows*); ~ *roads* (e.g. because of mud); ~ *going* (of conditions that make progress difficult). **3.** (of persons, writing, etc.) dull; tedious. *adv.* heavily: *time hanging* ~ *on his hands* (passing slowly). '~**weight** *n.* boxer weighing 175 pounds (= 79.3 kilograms) or more. **heav·i·ly** *adv.* **heav·i·ness** *n.*

He·brew ['hiːbruː] *n.* **1.** Jew; Israelite. **2.** language of the ancient Jews or the modern form as spoken in Israel. *adj.* of the ~ language or people.

heck·le ['hekl] *v.t.* ask many troublesome questions at a public meeting. ~**r** *n.*

hec·tic ['hektɪk] *adj.* **1.** unnaturally red: ~ *cheeks* (*colouring*) (as of a person suffering from tuberculosis). **2.** full of excitement and without rest: *a* ~ *life; having a* ~ *time.*

hec·to- ['hektəʊ-] *pref.* hundred: ~*gram(me); ~litre.*

hedge [hedʒ] *n.* row of bushes, tall plants, etc. usu. trimmed, forming a boundary (for a field, garden, etc.). *v.t. & i.* **1.** put a ~ or (fig.) barrier round: ~*d in with regulations,* unable to act freely. **2.** avoid giving a direct answer to a question. '~**hog** *n.* small, spine-covered animal that rolls itself into a ball when attacked. ~**row** ['hedʒrəʊ] *n.* hedge.

heed [hiːd] *v.t.* pay attention to: ~ *a warning. n.* (no pl.) attention: *take no* ~ *of what people say.* ~**ful** *adj.* attentive. ~**less** *adj.* inattentive.

heel¹ [hiːl] *n.* back part of the human foot; part of a sock, etc. covering this; part of a shoe supporting this. *take to one's* ~*s, show a clean pair of* ~*s,* run away; *cool* (*kick*) *one's* ~*s,* be kept waiting; *come to* ~, (of a dog) walk at its master's ~*s*; (fig.) submit to control; *down at* ~, (of shoes) worn down at the ~*s*; (fig.) poorly dressed. *v.t.* put new ~*s* on (shoes, etc.).

heel² [hiːl] *v.t. & i.* (of a ship) (cause to) lean (*over*).

hefty ['heftɪ] *adj.* (-ier, -iest) big and strong.

heif·er ['hefə*] *n.* young cow that has not yet had a calf.

height [haɪt] *n.* **1.** distance from bottom to top; distance to the top of sth. from a level, esp. sea-level: *the* ~ *of a mountain.* **2.** high place. **3.** utmost degree: *the* ~ *of his ambition; at its* ~. ~**en** *v.t. & i.* make or become high(er); make or become greater in degree: ~*en the effect.*

hein·ous ['heɪnəs] *adj.* (of crime) very wicked; atrocious.

heir [eə*] *n.* person with the legal right to receive a title, property, etc. when the owner dies. ~**ess** ['eərɪs] *n.* female ~. '~**loom** *n.* sth. handed down in a family for several generations.

held, see *hold*¹ (v.).

he·li·cop·ter ['helɪkɒptə*] *n.* kind of aircraft with horizontal, revolving blades (3) or rotors that requires only a small landing-space.

rotor

a helicopter

he·li·port ['helɪpɔːt] *n.* place for helicopters to take off and land.

he·li·um ['hiːljəm] *n.* (no pl.) light, colourless gas that does not burn.

hell [hel] *n.* **1.** (in some religions) place of punishment after death. **2.** place, condition, of great suffering or misery. **3.** (colloq., as int. expressing anger or disgust): *Go to* ~*! What a* ~ *of a noise!*

hel·lo, see *hallo, hullo.*

helm [helm] *n.* handle (also called *tiller*) or wheel for moving the rudder of a boat or ship. ~**s·man** ['helmzmən] *n.* man at the ~; steersman.

hel·met ['helmɪt] *n.* protective head-covering worn by soldiers, firemen, divers, motor-cyclists, some workers, some policemen, etc.

help [help] *v.t. & i.* **1.** do sth. that eases another person's work or benefits him in some way; assist. **2.** escape; avoid: *I can't ~ doing it. It can't be ~ed.* **3.** serve with the housework: *mother's ~ self to the beer.* *n.* **1.** act of ~ing; person or thing that ~s. **2.** girl or woman who ~s with the housework: *mother's ~,* (Gt. Brit.) person who ~s in a house with the children. **3.** escape; avoidance: *There's no ~ for it,* one cannot escape from it or avoid it. **~·er** *n.* person who ~s. **~·ful** *adj.* giving ~; useful. **~·ing** *n.* portion of food served on a person's plate. **~·less** *adj.* without ~; unable to look after oneself. '**~·mate** *n.* friend who ~s; (esp.) one's husband or wife.

hel·ter-skel·ter [,heltə'skeltə*] *adv.* in disorderly haste.

hem [hem] *n.* border or edge of cloth, esp. when turned and sewn down. *v.t.* (*-mm-*) **1.** make a ~ on. **2.** ~ *about* (*in*), confine; surround. '**~·line** *n.* lower edge of a skirt or dress: *lower* (*raise*) *the ~-line,* make a skirt, etc. longer (shorter). '**~·stitch** *n.* ornamental stitching. *v.t.* decorate cloth with this.

hemi- ['hemi-] *pref.* half.

hemi·sphere ['hemisfiə*] *n.* half a sphere; half the earth: *the Northern and Southern ~s.*

hemp [hemp] *n.* (no pl.) plant and its fibre, used in rope-making.

hen [hen] *n.* adult female bird, esp. of the domestic (3) fowl. (Cf. *cock*[1].) '**~-pecked** *adj.* (of a man) ruled by his wife.

hence [hens] *adv.* **1.** from here; from now: *a week ~,* in a week's time. **2.** for this reason. **~·forth** [,hens'fɔ:θ], **~-for·ward** [,hens'fɔ:wəd] *advs.* from this time on.

hench·man ['hentʃmən] *n.* faithful, unquestioning (esp. political) supporter.

her [hɜ:*, hə*] *pron.* object form of *she: She's in the garden; I can see ~.* **poss. pron. attrib.** *This is ~ book.* **~s** [hɜ:z] *poss. pron.* *This book is ~s* (belongs to ~).

her·ald ['herəld] *n.* **1.** (historical) person making public announcements for, carrying messages from, a ruler. **2.** person or thing foretelling the coming of sb. or sth.: *In England the cuckoo is a ~ of spring.* *v.t.* make known the coming of. **~·ry** *n.* (no pl.) science dealing with coats of arms, descent, and history of old families. **her·al·dic** [he'rældɪk] *adj.* of ~ry.

herb [hɜ:b] *n.* low, soft-stemmed plant that dies down after flowering, esp. one whose leaves are used in medicine or for flavouring food. **~·age** ['hɜ:bɪdʒ] *n.* (no pl.) ~s collectively; grass and other field plants. **~·al·ist** ['hɜ:bəlɪst] *n.* person who grows or sells ~s for medical use.

her·ba·ceous [hɜ:'beɪʃəs] *adj.* ~ border, bed with plants that come up and flower year after year.

her·cu·le·an [,hɜ:kjʊ'li:ən] *adj.* having, needing, great powers of body or mind.

herd [hɜ:d] *n.* number of cattle, etc. feeding or going about together. *the common* (*vulgar*) *~,* (derog.) the mass of ordinary people. **~s·man** ['hɜ:dzmən] *n.* man who looks after ~.

here [hɪə*] *adv.* in, at, to, this point or place: *~ and there,* in various places; *neither ~ nor there,* not important; not to the point. **~·abouts** [,hɪərə,baʊts] *adv.* near or about ~. **~·af·ter** [,hɪər-'ɑ:ftə*] *adv. & n.* (in) the future; (in) the world to come. **~·upon** [,hɪərə-'pɒn] *adv.* at this point. **~·with** [,hɪə-'wɪð] *adv.* with this.

he·red·i·tary [hɪ'redɪtərɪ] *adj.* (having a position) passed on from parent to child, from one generation to following generations: *~ rulers* (*beliefs, disease*).

he·red·i·ty [hɪ'redətɪ] *n.* (no pl.) tendency of living things to pass their characteristics on to offspring.

her·e·sy ['herəsɪ] *n.* (holding of a) belief or opinion contrary to what is generally accepted, esp. in religion. **her·e·tic** ['herətɪk] *n.* person supporting a ~. **he·ret·i·cal** [hɪ'retɪkl] *adj.* of ~ or heretics.

her·i·tage ['herɪtɪdʒ] *n.* that which has been or may be inherited.

her·met·ic [hɜ:'metɪk] *adj.* air-tight. **her·met·i·cal·ly** *adv.* ~ally *sealed,* sealed so as to keep air in or out.

her·mit ['hɜ:mɪt] *n.* person (esp. man in early Christian times) living quite alone.

he·ro ['hɪərəʊ] *n.* (pl. *-oes*) **1.** boy or man respected for bravery or noble qualities. **2.** chief man in a poem, story, or play. **~·ic** [hɪ'rəʊɪk] *adj.* of, like, fit for, a ~. **her·o·ine** ['herəʊɪn] *n.* female ~. **her·o·ism** ['herəʊɪzəm] *n.* (no pl.) great courage; ~ic qualities and acts.

her·o·in ['herəʊɪn] *n.* (no pl.) narcotic drug prepared from and acting like morphine.

her·on ['herən] *n.* long-legged bird living in marshy places.

her·ring ['herɪŋ] *n.* (pl. ~, ~s) sea-fish much used for food.

hers, see *her.*

her·self [hɜː'self, hə-] **pron. 1.** refl. form: *She has hurt ∼.* **2.** *She ∼ did it* (nobody else). **3.** *She sat by ∼* (alone). *She did it by ∼* (without help). **4.** in her normal state of health or mind: *She is quite ∼ again.*

hes·i·tate ['hezɪteɪt] **v.i.** show signs of uncertainty or unwillingness in speech or action. **hes·i·tant** ['hezɪtənt] **adj.** inclined to ∼. **hes·i·tat·ing·ly, hes·i·tant·ly advs.** in a hesitating manner. **hes·i·ta·tion** [,hezɪ'teɪʃn] **n.**

hes·si·an ['hesɪən] **n.** (no pl.) strong, coarse cloth of hemp or jute; sackcloth.

het·er·o·dox ['hetərəʊdɒks] **adj.** not orthodox. **∼y n.** opp. of orthodoxy.

het·er·o·ge·neous [,hetərəʊ'dʒiːnjəs] **adj.** different; unlike; made up of different kinds.

het·ero·sex·u·al [,hetərəʊ'seksjʊəl] **n. & adj.** (person) characterized by the normal attraction to the opposite sex.

hew [hjuː] **v.t.** (p.t. **∼ed** [hjuːd], p.p. **∼n** [hjuːn]) cut (by striking or chopping); shape by chopping: *∼ down a tree*; *∼n timber.*

hexa·gon ['heksəgən] **n.** straight-sided figure with six (usu. equal) angles.

a hexagon

hex·am·e·ter [hek'sæmɪtə*] **n.** line of verse (esp. Greek or Latin) with six feet.

hey [heɪ] **int.** word used to attract attention or express surprise.

hey·day ['heɪdeɪ] **n.** (no pl.) time of greatest prosperity or power.

hi [haɪ] **int.** hey; (U.S.A.) = hallo.

hi·a·tus [haɪ'eɪtəs] **n.** space or gap in a series, making it incomplete.

hi·ber·nate ['haɪbəneɪt] **v.i.** (of some animals) pass the winter in a state like sleep. **hi·ber·na·tion** [,haɪbə'neɪʃn] **n.** (no pl.).

hic·cup, hic·cough ['hɪkʌp] **v.i. & n.** (have a) sudden stopping of the breath with a cough-like sound: *have the ∼s.*

hid(·den), see *hide¹.*

hide¹ [haɪd] **v.t. & i.** (p.t. hid [hɪd], p.p. hidden ['hɪdn]) put or keep out of sight; prevent from being seen, found, or known; conceal oneself. **hid·ing n.** (no pl.) (of a person) *go into hiding, ∼*

oneself; *be in hiding,* be hidden. **'hid ing-place n.** place where sb. or sth. i or could be hidden.

hide² [haɪd] **n.** animal's skin, esp. as a article of commerce and manufacture (humor.) human skin. **'∼-bound adj** narrow-minded. **hid·ing n.** (colloq beating or whipping: *give sb. a goo hiding.*

hid·eous ['hɪdɪəs] **adj.** very ugly frightful.

hi·er·ar·chy ['haɪərɑːkɪ] **n.** organiza tion (e.g. the Church) with grades o authority.

hi·ero·glyph ['haɪərəʊglɪf] **n.** pictur of an object representing a word, syl lable, or sound, as used in the ancien writing of the Egyptians and Mexican ∼ic [,haɪərəʊ'glɪfɪk] **adj. ∼ics n.pl. ∼**

hi-fi [,haɪ'faɪ] **adj.** (colloq., abbr. for high fidelity. **n.** equipment for high fidelity reproduction of sound.

hig·gle·dy-pig·gle·dy [,hɪgldɪ'pɪgldɪ **adj. & adv.** mixed up; without order

high [haɪ] **adj. 1.** extending far up wards; measuring (the given distance from bottom to top (cf. *tall* for men) chief; important; extreme; intense noble; worthy; (of sounds) at or nea the top of the scale; shrill. *the ∼ seas* the open ocean, away from the land; *∼ sea,* one with big waves; *a man of ∼* (worthy) *principles.* **2.** (of time) far ad vanced: *∼ summer. It's ∼ time yo started,* you should start at once. **3.** (o food) beginning to go bad. **4.** (colloq. intoxicated or under the influence o hallucinogenic drugs. **5.** in an exalte state: *be ∼ on,* be excited about; b especially fond of. **adv.** in or to a degree: *play ∼,* play cards, etc. fo large sums of money; *run ∼,* (of the sea be rough; (fig., of the feelings) b roused or excited. **n.** ∼ level or figure *from on ∼,* from heaven or a ∼ place; '**∼ born adj.** born of a noble family. '**∼ brow n. & adj.** (person) with taste and interests considered superior t those of most people. **H∼ Court n** (Gt. Brit.) supreme court of justice **∼·er ed·u·ca·tion n.** (no pl.) (at a uni versity, etc.). **∼ fi·del·i·ty n.** (no pl. reproduction of sound with a ∼ degre of faithfulness to the original. **,∼-fi 'del·i·ty adj.** (of radios, tapes, etc. giving such a ∼-quality sound repro duction. '**∼-flown adj.** (of speech writing, etc.) sounding important bu often not very sensible. **,∼-'hand·ed adj.** overbearing. **∼ jump n.** athletic contest of jumping as ∼ as possible over an adjustable horizontal bar. '**∼·**

lands *n. pl.* mountainous country, esp. the ~lands of N.W. Scotland. '~**land·er** *n.* native of these ~lands. '~**lights** *n. pl.* parts of a picture, photograph, etc. reflecting most light; (fig.) outstanding features (2). ~**ly** *adv.* in or to a ~ degree: *a ~ly paid man*; *think ~ly of sb.* ,~-'**mind·ed** *adj.* of morally ~ character. ~**ness** *n.* **1.** (no pl.) **2.** *His (Her, Your) H~ness*, title used when speaking of or to princes(ses). ~ **priest** *n.* chief priest, esp. of Jews. ~ **road** *n.* main road. ~ **school** *n.* secondary school giving education more advanced than that of an elementary school. ~ **street** *n.* principal street of a town with shops, etc. ,~(·**ly**)-'**strung** *adj.* sensitive; with nerves easily upset. ~ **tea** *n.* (Gt. Brit.) early evening meal. ~ **tide** *n.* tide when the water is at its ~est level. ~ **wa·ter** *n.* ~ tide; time when the tide is at the full. ,~-'**wa·ter mark** *n.* mark showing the level reached at ~ water. '~**way** *n.* public road; main route. '~**way·man** *n.* (hist.) man, usu. on horseback, who robbed travellers on ~ways.

hi·jack ['haɪdʒæk] *v.t.* **1.** steal (goods) in transit. **2.** seize control of (a vehicle, e.g. a lorry with goods, or esp. an aircraft in flight) by the use of violence or the threat of violence in order to achieve certain aims or to force an aircraft, etc. *to* a new destination. (Cf. *skyjack*.) *n.* ~**ing**. ~**er** *n.*

hike [haɪk] *v.i. & n.* (go for a) long country walk. **hik·er** *n.*

hi·lar·i·ous [hɪ'leərɪəs] *adj.* noisily merry. **hi·lar·i·ty** [hɪ'lærɪtɪ] *n.* (no pl.)

hill [hɪl] *n.* small mountain; slope (on a road, etc.). ~**y** *adj.* (-*ier*, -*iest*) having many ~s. ~**ock** ['hɪlək] *n.* small ~. ,~'**side** *n.* slope of a ~. ,~'**top** *n.* summit of a ~.

hilt [hɪlt] *n.* handle of a sword or dagger. *up to the ~*, completely.

him [hɪm] *pron.* object form of *he*: *He loves my sister; and she loves ~*. ~**self** [hɪm'self] *pron.* **1.** refl. form: *He cut ~self.* **2.** *He said so ~self* (nobody else). **3.** *He did it by ~self* (without help). *He sat by ~self* (alone). **4.** in his normal state of health or mind: *He is quite ~self again.*

hind[1] [haɪnd] *n.* female of (esp. the red) deer.

hind[2] [haɪnd] *adj.* (esp. opp. *fore*) situated at the back: *the ~ legs of a horse*; *the ~ wheels of a wagon.* '~**most** *adj.* farthest back.

hin·der ['hɪndə*] *v.t.* obstruct; delay;

prevent. **hin·drance** ['hɪndrəns] *n.* sth. that ~s.

Hin·du [,hɪn'du:] *n.* person whose religion is ~**ism** ['hɪnduːɪzəm] *n.* (no pl.) a religion, philosophy, and culture of India.

hinge [hɪndʒ] *n.* joint on which a lid, door, or gate opens and shuts. *v.t. & i.* **1.** attach with a ~. **2.** ~ (*up*)*on*, (fig.) turn or depend upon.

hinges

hin·ny ['hɪnɪ] *n.* offspring of a she-ass and a stallion. (Cf. *mule.*)

hint [hɪnt] *n.* slight suggestion or indication. *v.t. & i.* give a ~: *I ~ed that he ought to work harder. I ~ed at his laziness.*

hin·ter·land ['hɪntəlænd] *n.* parts of a country behind the coast or a river's banks.

hip[1] [hɪp] *n.* bony part of each side of the body just above the leg. (See the picture at *back.*)

hip[2] [hɪp] *n.* fruit of the wild rose.

hip[3] [hɪp] *int. H~, ~, hurrah!* cry, cheer, of approval.

hip·pie, hip·py ['hɪpɪ] *n.* person who rejects established social conventions and institutions and expresses his personality by unusual styles of dress, living habits, etc., and maintaining a philosophy of love and fellowship. He often lives in a commune[2] and prefers the use of drugs to alcohol.

hip·po·pot·a·mus [,hɪpə'pɒtəməs] *n.* (pl. ~**es**, -**mi** [-maɪ]) large, thick-skinned African river animal.

a hippopotamus

hire ['haɪə*] *v.t.* obtain or allow the use or services of in return for fixed payment: *~ a horse (a concert-hall); ~*

out boats. (Cf. *rent*[3] for buildings occupied for a long period.) *n.* (no pl.) (money paid for) hiring: *pay for the ~ of a hall*; *bicycles* (*cars*) *on ~*; *~car*, car available for *~.* **~·ling** ['haɪəlɪŋ] *n.* (usu. derog.) hiring: person whose services may be *~d.* **,~'pur·chase** *n.* (no pl.) (Gt. Brit.) system by which sth. *~d* becomes the property of the *~r* after a number of agreed payments have been made. **hir·er** *n.*

hir·sute ['hɜːsjuːt] *adj.* hairy; shaggy.

his [hɪz] *poss. pron.* belonging to him: *This is ~ book. This book is ~.*

hiss [hɪs] *v.i. & t.* (make the) sound of *s*, or that made by a snake; (make) such sounds to show disapproval: *~ an actor off the stage*; (make the) sound of water on a very hot surface.

his·to·ry ['hɪstərɪ] *n.* (orderly description of) past events; branch of knowledge dealing with past events, political, social, economic, of a country or of the world. **his·to·ri·an** [hɪ'stɔːrɪən] *n.* writer of *~*. **his·tor·ic** [hɪ'stɒrɪk] *adj.* famous in *~*; associated with past times. **his·tor·i·cal** [hɪ'stɒrɪkl] *adj.* **1.** of *~* (esp. as contrasted with legend and fiction): *historical events* (not imaginary). **2.** based on *~*: *historical novels and plays.*

his·tri·on·ic [,hɪstrɪ'ɒnɪk] *adj.* of drama, the theatre, acting: *~ ability.* **~s** *n. pl.* theatrical performances; speech and behaviour designed for effect, like that of an actor.

hit [hɪt] *v.t. & i.* (-tt-; p.t. & p.p. *~*) **1.** come against (sth.) with force; strike; give a stroke[1] (1) to: *~ it off with sb.*, agree with; get on well with; *be hard ~* (by sth.), be much troubled; be severely affected. **2.** *~* (*up*)*on* (a plan, etc.), discover by chance. *n.* **1.** blow[2] (1); stroke[1] (1). **2.** *a lucky ~*, a successful attempt; *make a ~*, win general approval. **3.** popular success in public entertainment: *~ songs*; *~ parade*, programme of top selling popular records. **,~-and-'run** *attrib. adj.* (of a road accident) in which a pedestrian or vehicle is *~* by a vehicle whose driver does not stop: *a ~-and-run driver.*

hitch [hɪtʃ] *v.t. & i.* **1.** pull (*up*) with a quick movement: *~ up one's trousers.* **2.** fasten, become fastened, on or to a hook, etc., or with a loop of rope, etc. *n.* **1.** sudden pull. **2.** kind of knot used by sailors. **3.** sth. that stops progress: *Everything went off without a ~* (i.e. smoothly).

hitch-hike ['hɪtʃhaɪk] *v.i.* travel by asking drivers of cars or lorries for free rides. **'hitch-,hik·er** *n.*

hith·er ['hɪðə*] *adv.* (old use) here. *~-to* [,hɪðə'tuː] *adv.* up to now.

hive [haɪv] *n.* **1.** box (of wood, straw, etc.) made for bees to live in; colony of bees. **2.** place full of busy people.

hoard [hɔːd] *n.* carefully saved and guarded store of money, food, or other treasured objects; mass of facts. *v.t. & i.* save and store (*up*).

hoard·ing ['hɔːdɪŋ] *n.* **1.** wooden fence round waste land, building work, etc., often covered with advertisements. **2.** (U.S.A. *billboard*) structure designed to carry outdoor advertising.

hoar-frost [,hɔː'frɒst] *n.* white frost; frozen moisture on the surface of leaves, roofs, etc.

hoarse [hɔːs] *adj.* (*~r*, *~st*) (of the voice) rough and harsh; (of a person) having a *~* voice. **~·ly** *adv.*

hoary ['hɔːrɪ] *adj.* (-ier, -iest) grey or white with age; very old.

hoax [həʊks] *n.* mischievous trick played on sb. for a joke. *v.t.* deceive in this way.

hob [hɒb] *n.* flat metal shelf at the side of a fireplace where pans, etc. can be kept warm.

hob·ble ['hɒbl] *v.i. & t.* **1.** walk as when lame, as when the feet or legs are hurting. **2.** tie a horse's legs to keep it from going far away. *n.* limping way of walking.

hob·by ['hɒbɪ] *n.* interesting occupation, not one's regular business, for one's leisure time. **'~-horse** *n.* wooden horse for children; (fig.) sb.'s favourite subject of conversation.

a hobby-horse   a hod

hob·gob·lin ['hɒbgɒblɪn] *n.* mischievous imp.

hob·nail ['hɒbneɪl] *n.* short nail with a heavy head used for boot-soles.

hob·nob ['hɒbnɒb] *v.i.* (-bb-) have a friendly talk, drink (*with* sb.).

hock[1] [hɒk] *n.* middle joint of an animal's hind leg.

hock[2] [hɒk] *n.* (no pl.) (Gt. Brit.) German white wine.

homage

hock·ey ['hɒkɪ] *n.* (no pl.) game played on a field (also called *field* ~) or on ice (also called *ice* ~) by two teams of eleven or six players respectively with curved ~ *sticks*.

ho·cus-po·cus [,həʊkəs'pəʊkəs] *n.* (no pl.) talk, behaviour, designed to draw away one's attention from sth.

hod [hɒd] *n.* light, open box with a long handle used by workmen for carrying bricks, mortar, etc. on the shoulder. (See the picture.)

hoe [həʊ] *n.* tool for loosening soil, cutting up weeds among growing crops. *v.t. & i.* work with a ~.

hog [hɒg] *n.* castrated male pig; (fig.) dirty, greedy person. *go the whole* ~, do sth. thoroughly.

hoist [hɔɪst] *v.t. & n.* (lift up with an) apparatus (1) of ropes and pulleys, or kind of elevator (esp. on a warship): *ammunition* ~s.

hold¹ [həʊld] *v.t. & i.* (p.t. & p.p. held [held]) **1.** have and keep fast in or with the hand(s) or some other part of the body, or with a tool, etc.; keep or support (oneself or a part of the body) in a certain position or manner. **2.** (be able to) contain: *a trunk* ~*ing all my clothes*. **3.** have or keep in mind; consider: ~ *strange opinions*; ~ (*the view*) *that the soul is immortal.* **4.** restrain; keep back: ~ *one's breath*; ~ *one's hand*; ~ *one's tongue* (*one's peace*), be silent. **5.** be the owner or tenant of: ~ *shares* (*land*); occupy (a place or office): ~ *office*, be in a position of authority. **6.** have (a meeting, debate, conversation, examination). **7.** remain the same; keep or stay in the same position, etc.: *How long will the fine weather* ~? ~ *good*, be still in force; be valid. *H*~ *hard!* Don't go on doing that! ~ *one's own* (*one's ground*), not give way; keep one's position. **8.** (with advs. & preps.): ~ *back*, show unwillingness to do sth.; ~ *sth. back*, keep it secret; ~ (*sb., oneself*) *back*, restrain; deter; ~ *by* (*to*), keep to (a purpose, etc.); ~ *forth*, (usu. derog.) preach; talk at length; ~ *in*, check; restrain; ~ *off*, keep at a distance; ~ *on*, (a) keep one's grasp on sth.: ~ *on to one's hat*; (b) (colloq., imper.) stop: *H*~ *on a minute!* (c) (esp. on the telephone) wait; ~ *out*, (a) keep one's position or strength; (b) (of supplies, etc.) last; ~ *out sth.* (e.g. hopes), offer; ~ *sth. over*, postpone it; ~ *together*, (cause to) remain united; ~ *sb. or sth. up*, (a) delay; (b) stop by force for the purpose of robbery; ~ *with*, approve of. *n.* **1.** act,

manner, or power, of ~*ing*: *catch* (*get, have, keep, lose*) ~ *of sth.* **2.** part or place that may be used for ~*ing*. (Cf. *foot*~.) '~*all n.* portable bag or case for carrying clothes, etc. when travelling. ~*er n.* person who ~s (5) sth.: *office*~*ers*; (sport) *title*~*er*; thing that ~s sth.: *pen*~*er*. ~*ing n.* sth. held, esp. land (*small*-~*ings*) or shares in a business. '~*up n.* act of ~*ing up* (see *hold* (8) *up*): *a traffic* ~*up*; *a bank* ~*up*.

hold² [həʊld] *n.* part of ship below decks where cargo is stored.

hole [həʊl] *n.* opening or hollow place in a solid body; animal's burrow; hollow place in the surface of the ground made by digging, etc. *pick* ~ *in*, find fault with; *in a* ~, (colloq.) in an awkward situation; ~-*and-corner* (methods, etc.), secret; not open and straightforward. *v.t.* make ~s in; put into a ~.

hol·i·day ['hɒlədɪ] *n.* day of rest from work; (usu. pl.) period of this (U.S.A. = *vacation*): *the school* ~s; *make* (*take*) *a* ~; *on* ~, having a ~; *bank* ~, week-day on which all the banks² (1) are closed by law, usu. a general ~.

ho·li·ness, see *holy.*

hol·low ['hɒləʊ] *adj.* **1.** not solid; with a hole or empty space inside: *a* ~ *tree*. **2.** (of sounds) as if coming from sth. ~. **3.** (fig.) unreal; false; insincere: ~ *words* (*sympathy*). **4.** sunken: ~ *cheeks*; ~-*eyed. adv. beat sb.* ~ (completely). *n.* ~ *place*; hole; valley. *v.t.* make a ~ in: *river banks* ~*ed out by water.*

hol·ly ['hɒlɪ] *n.* evergreen shrub with hard, dark-green, sharp-pointed leaves and red berries.

hol·ly·hock ['hɒlɪhɒk] *n.* tall garden plant with brightly coloured flowers.

ho·lo·caust ['hɒləkɔːst] *n.* large-scale destruction, esp. of human lives by fire, etc.

hol·ster ['həʊlstə*] *n.* leather case for a pistol or revolver.

ho·ly ['həʊlɪ] *adj.* (-*ier,* -*iest*) **1.** of God; associated with God or with religion: *the H*~ *Bible*; *the H*~ *Land* (where Jesus lived); *H*~ *Week* (before Easter). **2.** devoted to religion: *a* ~ *man*; *living a* ~ *life.* **ho·li·ness** *n.* **1.** (no pl.) being ~ or sacred. **2.** *His* (*Your*) *Holiness*, title used of or to the pope.

ho·ly·stone ['həʊlɪstəʊn] *v.t. & n.* (no pl.) (clean with) soft sandstone (formerly) used for scrubbing the wooden decks of ships.

hom·age ['hɒmɪdʒ] *n.* **1.** (no pl.) expression of respect, tribute paid (*to* sb., his merits): *paying* ~ *to* (*the genius* *of*) *Shakespeare*. **2.** (in feudal times) acknowledgement of loyalty to a lord or ruler.

home [həʊm] **n. 1.** place where one lives, esp. with one's family; land of one's birth: *at* ~, in the house; *at* ~ (*to*), expecting and ready to receive (visitors, etc.); (*be, feel, make oneself*) *at* ~, as if in one's own ~; not feeling strange. **2.** institution or place (for the care of children, old or sick people). **3.** (sport) ~ match or win. **4.** (attrib.) of the ~: ~ *life*; of or inside the country in question: ~ *industries*; *the H~ Office*, department of *the H~ Secretary* or Secretary of State for H~ Affairs, controlling local government, police, etc. in England and Wales. **adv.** to, at, in, one's ~ or country. *bring sth.* ~ *to sb.*, make him fully conscious of it. **~·less** **adj. '~·like** *adj*. **'~·made** *adj*. made at ~. **'~·sick** *adj*. sad because away from ~. **'~·sick·ness** *n*. **'~·spun** *n. & adj.* (cloth) made at ~. **'~·stead** *n*. farmhouse with land and outbuildings. **'~·ward** *adj. & adv.*, **'~·wards** *adv.* (going) towards ~. **'~·work** *n*. (no pl.) work that a pupil is required to do at ~.

home·ly ['həʊmlɪ] *adj*. (-ier, -iest) **1.** simple and plain, of the sort used every day. **2.** causing one to think of home or to feel at home: *a* ~ *atmosphere* (*boarding-house*). **3.** (U.S.A., of persons) plain-faced.

ho·mi·cide ['hɒmɪsaɪd] *n*. killing, killer, of a human being. **ho·mi·ci·dal** [,hɒmɪ'saɪdl] *adj*.

ho·mo·ge·neous [,hɒməʊ'dʒiːnjəs] *adj*. (formed of parts) of the same sort.

hom·o·nym ['hɒməʊnɪm] *n*. word with the same form or sound as another but different in meaning, e.g. *pail*, *pale*.

ho·mo·sex·u·al [,hɒməʊ'seksjʊəl] *n. & adj.* (person) characterized by being sexually attracted only by members of the same sex.

hon·est ['ɒnɪst] *adj*. not telling lies; not cheating or stealing; straightforward. **~·ly** *adv*. **hon·es·ty** *n*. (no pl.).

hon·ey ['hʌnɪ] *n*. (no pl.) sweet, sticky, yellowish liquid made by bees from nectar. **'~·comb** *n*. structure of six-sided cells made by bees for ~ and eggs. *v.t.* fill with holes, tunnels, etc. **~·ed, hon·ied** ['hʌnɪd] *adj*. (of words, etc.) sweet. **'~·moon** *n*. holiday taken by a newly married couple. **'~·suck·le** *n*. (no pl.) sweet-scented climbing plant.

honk [hɒŋk] *v.i. & n*. (make the) sound of a motor horn.

hon·o·ra·ri·um [,ɒnə'reərɪəm] *n*. (pl.

~s, -ria) fee offered (not claimed) fo professional services.

hon·or·ary ['ɒnərərɪ] *adj*. **1.** (of position) unpaid: *the* ~ *secretary*. **2.** (o a degree, rank, etc.) given as an hon our, without the usual requirements *an* ~ *vice-president*.

hon·our (U.S.A. **-or**) ['ɒnə*] *n*. **1** (no pl.) high public regard; great re spect: *win* ~ *in war*; *do* ~ *to the King*; *guard of* ~; *a ceremony in* ~ *of sb*. **2.** (n pl.) good personal character; reputa tion for good behaviour: *on my* ~, ac cording to my reputation for tellin the truth; *bound in* ~ (but not by law *to do sth.*; *word of* ~, solemn promise **3.** (as a polite formula): *May I hav the* ~ *of your company at dinner?* **4.** (pl. civilities to guests, visitors, etc.: *d the* ~s (*of the table, the town, etc.*), ac as host, guide, etc. **5.** *Your* (*His*) *H~* form of address used to or of som judges. **6.** person or thing bringin credit: *an* ~ *to the school*. **7.** (pl.) mark of respect, distinction, titles, etc.: *th* ~s *list* (of titles, etc. conferred by th reigning Sovereign). **8.** (pl.) (in uni versities) special distinction for extr proficiency: *take an* ~s *degree*; *pas with* ~s. *v.t.* **1.** feel ~ for; show ~ to confer ~ on. **2.** accept and pay (cheque, etc.) when due. ~ *a promise* keep it. **~·able** ['ɒnərəbl] *adj*. **1** worthy of, bringing, consistent with, (1, 2): ~*able conduct* (*peace, burial*). **2** (shortened to *Hon*.) title of judges an other high officials, of members of th House of Commons (when referred t during a debate), and of children o some peers.

hood [hʊd] *n*. **1.** bag-like covering fo the head and neck, often fastened to cloak so that it can hang down at th back when not in use. **2.** folding roof o a carriage or motor car. **3.** (U.S.A. bonnet of a motor car. **4.** any ~-shape or ~-like thing. **~·ed** ['hʊdɪd] *adj*. hav ing, wearing, a ~.

-hood [-hʊd] *suff*. (forming ns.) **1** time or condition of being: *boyhood manhood*. **2.** group or society of *brotherhood*; *priesthood*. **3.** quality *falsehood*.

hood·lum ['huːdləm] *n*. young ruffian thug.

hood·wink ['hʊdwɪŋk] *v.t.* deceive trick; mislead.

hoof [huːf] *n*. (pl. ~s [huːfs] or *hoove* [huːvz]) horny part of the foot of horse, etc.

hook [hʊk] *n*. **1.** curved or bent piece o metal, etc. for catching hold of sth. o for hanging sth. on. **2.** curved tool for cutting (grain, etc.) or chopping (branches, etc.). *by ~ or by crook*, by one means or another. *v.t. & i.* fasten, be fastened, catch, with a ~ or ~s: *a dress that ~s (is ~ed) at the back; ~ a fish.* **~ed** [hŏkt] *adj.* made with, having, ~s; ~-shaped: *the ~ed beak of a bird of prey.* '**~·worm** *n.* worm that ~s itself to the intestine and causes disease.

a hook (1)

hooky, hookey ['hŏkɪ] *n. play ~* (U.S.A.), play truant.

hoo·li·gan ['huːlɪɡən] *n.* disorderly man (usu. one of a gang) making disturbances in the streets or other public places. **~ism** *n.* (no pl.)

hoop [huːp] *n.* band of wood or metal (put round a barrel); similar band bowled along the ground as a plaything.

hoot [huːt] *n.* **1.** cry of an owl. **2.** sound made by a motor horn, steam whistle, etc. **3.** shout or cry expressing disapproval or scorn. *v.i. & t.* make a ~ or ~s (*at*); drive away by ~s: *~ an actor off the stage.* **~er** *n.* siren (3) (e.g. in a factory); (Gt. Brit.) motor horn.

hooves, see *hoof*.

hop¹ [hŏp] *n.* tall climbing plant with flowers growing in clusters; (pl.) these flowers, dried and used in beer-making.

hop² [hŏp] *v.i. & t.* (*-pp-*) **1.** (of persons) jump with one foot; (of birds) jump forward on both feet. **2.** cross (*over*), go (*across*), by ~ping. *n.* action of ~ping; short jump; stage of journey by plane.

hope [həʊp] *n.* **1.** feeling of expectation and desire; feeling of trust or confidence. **2.** cause for ~; person, circumstance, etc. on which ~ is based. *v.t. & i.* expect and desire: ~ (*for sth., that ..., to have, etc.*). **~ful** *adj.* having or giving ~. **~ful·ly** *adv.* **~less** *adj.* having no ~; giving or promising no ~; (of persons) incurable: *a ~less invalid.* **~less·ness** *n.* (no pl.).

hop·per ['hŏpə*] *n.* **1.** structure like an inverted cone or pyramid through which grain passes to a mill, coal to a furnace, etc. **2.** flea or young locust.

horde [hɔːd] *n.* **1.** wandering tribe: ~s *of Tartars.* **2.** (usu. derog.) large crowd.

ho·ri·zon [hə'raɪzn] *n.* line at which earth or sea and sky seem to meet. **hor·i·zon·tal** [ˌhɒrɪ'zɒntl] *adj.* parallel to the ~; flat or level. **hor·i·zon·tal·ly** *adv.*

hor·mone ['hɔːməʊn] *n.* (biol.) substance, formed by internal secretion, that passes into the blood and stimulates the bodily organs to action; synthetic substance that acts like a ~.

horn [hɔːn] *n.* **1.** one of the hard, pointed, usu. curved, outgrowths on the heads of cattle, deer, and some other animals; substance of these. **2.** ~-like part (e.g. on the head of a snail). *draw in one's ~s*, show less willingness to do sth.; draw back. **3.** (sorts of) wind instrument: *a huntsman's ~; French ~* (made of brass); instrument for making warning sounds: *a fog-~; a motor ~.* **~ed** *adj.* having ~ (1): *~ed cattle.* '**~·pipe** *n.* (music for) sailor's lively dance. **~y** *adj.* (*-ier, -iest*) of, like, ~: *hands ~y from hard work.*

hor·net ['hɔːnɪt] *n.* large insect of the wasp family with a powerful sting.

hor·o·scope ['hɒrəskəʊp] *n.* diagram of, observation of, the position of stars at a certain time (e.g. a person's birth) for the purpose of forecasting a person's future; such a forecast.

hor·ror ['hɒrə*] *n.* (sth. causing) feeling of extreme fear or dislike. '**~·struck, '~·strick·en** *adjs.* overcome with ~. **hor·ri·ble** ['hɒrəbl] *adj.* **hor·rid** ['hɒrɪd] *adj.* causing ~; (colloq.) disagreeable; annoying. **hor·ri·fy** ['hɒrɪfaɪ] *v.t.* fill with ~; shock.

hors-d'œuvre [ɔː'dɜːvrə] *n.* tasty dish served before the main meal.

horse [hɔːs] *n.* **1.** four-legged, solid-hoofed animal with flowing mane and tail, used to carry loads, etc., and for riding on. (Cf. *stallion, mare.*) **2.** (collective sing.) soldiers mounted on ~s: *~ and foot*, cavalry and infantry. **3.** wooden framework with legs (for jumping over in physical training). '**~·back** *n. on ~ back*, (riding) on a ~. '**~·man** *n.* man skilled in riding and managing ~s. '**~·man·ship** *n.* (no pl.) skill in riding ~s. '**~·play** *n.* rough, noisy fun. '**~·pow·er** *n.* (shortened to *h.p.*) unit of power (of engines, etc.). '**~·race** *n.* race between ~s with riders. '**~·rac·ing** *n.* (no pl.) sport or profession of running ~s in races. '**~·rad·ish** *n.* plant with hot-tasting root used for meat sauces. **~ sense** *n.* ordinary wisdom. **~·shoe** ['hɔː∫uː] *n.* ∩-shaped

horsewhip

metal shoe for a ～. '～·whip n. & v.t. (-pp-) (thrash with a) whip for ～s. '～·‚wom·an n. woman who rides on ～-back. hor·sy adj. (-ier, -iest) of ～s and ～-racing; (esp. of a person) showing by dress, speech, etc. a fondness for, familiarity with, ～s.

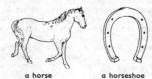

a horse   a horseshoe

hor·ti·cul·ture ['hɔːtɪkʌltʃə*] n. (no pl.) (art of) growing flowers, fruit, and vegetables. hor·ti·cul·tur·al [‚hɔːtɪ'kʌltʃərəl] adj.

hose¹ [həuz] n. rubber or canvas tube for directing water on to gardens, fires, etc. v.t. water (a garden, etc.) with a ～; wash (a motor car, etc.) by using a ～.

hose² [həuz] n. 1. (collective as pl.) (trade name for) stockings. 2. close-fitting outer garment from the waist to the knees or feet, worn by men in former times: doublet and ～. ho·sier ['həuzɪə*] n. shop-keeper who sells men's socks, collars, underwear, etc. ho·siery ['həuzɪərɪ] n. (no pl.) such goods.

hos·pice ['hɒspɪs] n. house of rest for travellers, esp. one kept by a religious order (e.g. in the Swiss mountains).

hos·pit·able ['hɒspɪtəbl] adj. giving, liking to give, hospitality.

hos·pi·tal ['hɒspɪtl] n. place where people are treated for, nursed through, their sickness or injuries: go to ～, (U.S.A.) go to the ～; in ～, (U.S.A.) in the ～. ～·ize v.t. place in ～ as a patient. ～·iza·tion [‚hɒspɪtəlaɪˈzeɪʃn] n.

hos·pi·tal·i·ty [‚hɒspɪ'tælətɪ] n. (no pl.) friendly and generous reception and entertainment of guests, esp. in one's own home.

host¹ [həust] n. 1. person who entertains guests. 2. innkeeper; hotel-keeper. ～·ess ['həustɪs] n. 1. woman who acts as ～¹. 2. see air ～ess.

host² [həust] n. 1. great number: ～s of friends; a ～ of difficulties. 2. (old use) army.

host³ [həust] n. the ～, bread eaten at Holy Communion.

hos·tage ['hɒstɪdʒ] n. person (less often, thing) given or seized as a pledge that demands will be satisfied: take sb. ～.

hos·tel ['hɒstl] n. building in whi board and lodging are provided (wi the support of authorities concerne for students and others under the care: youth ～, one for young people o walking-tours, etc. ～·ry n. (old us inn.

host·ess, see host¹.

hos·tile ['hɒstaɪl] adj. of an enemy: a army; feeling or showing enmity (to); looks; ～ to reform. ～·ly adv. hos·til·i·t [hɒ'stɪlɪtɪ] n. enmity; (pl.) (acts o war.

hot [hɒt] adj. (-tt-) 1. having great he or high temperature (cf. feverish producing a burning sensation on th tongue: Pepper is ～. get into ～ wate (colloq.) get into trouble (for foolis acts); ～ air, (sl.) boastful or foolis talk. 2. (of a scent in hunting) stron and fresh: ～ on the trail, near to what being pursued. 3. (of jazz) strong emotional and rhythmical. 4. (as adv eagerly; hotly. blow ～ and cold, (fig be favourable and unfavourable b turns. '～·bed n. bed of earth heated b rotting manure to quicken growth (fig.) place, conditions, favourable t growth (of crime, etc.). ～ dog n (colloq.) hot sausage served betwee the two halves of a bread roll. '～·hea n. impetuous person. ‚～·'head·ed ad impetuous. '～·house n. heated buil ing, usu. of glass, for growing delica plants. ～ line n. direct telephone o teleprinter line open for instant com munication between leaders of differ ent governments in case of an eme gency. ～ pants n. pl. close-fittin brief shorts worn by girls and wome in place of a skirt. '～·pot n. dish o meat, potatoes, etc. cooked in a tigh lidded pot. ～·ly adv. (fig.) eagerly passionately: ～ly pursued by the enem ～·ness n.

hotch·potch ['hɒtʃpɒtʃ] n. jumble.

ho·tel [həuˈtel] n. building where mea and rooms are provided for trave lers.

hound [haund] n. 1. (kinds of) dog use for hunting and racing: blood～; fox～ grey～. 2. contemptible man. v.t. chas or hunt with, or as with, ～s: ～ed b one's creditors.

hour ['auə*] n. 1. 60 minutes: at th eleventh ～, when almost too late; th small ～s, the three or four ～s after mid night. 2. point of time by the clock: clock that strikes the ～s. 3. (pl.) fixe periods of time, esp. for work: offic ～s, 9.30 a.m. to 5.30 p.m.; keep earl (late, etc.) ～s, get up and go to be early (late, etc.). **4.** a particular, or the present, point in time: *in the ~ of danger*; *questions of the ~* (i.e. now being discussed). **~ly** *adj. & adv.* (done, occurring) every ~.

house [haʊs] *n.* (pl. ~s ['haʊzɪz]) **1.** building, esp. one constructed as a home for a family: *keep ~, manage the affairs of a ~hold.* **2.** (usu. with a pref.) building made or used for some particular purpose or occupation: *a ware~; the custom-~.* **3.** *H~s of Parliament*, buildings used by the British Parliament. **4.** (spectators, audience, in a) theatre: *a full ~* (i.e. all seats filled); *bring down the ~*, (of an actor) win very loud applause. **5.** family line: *the H~ of Windsor* (the present British Royal Family). **6.** business firm. [haʊz] *v.t.* **1.** provide ~s for: *the housing problem*; *a housing estate*, large group of dwelling-~s planned and built by one organization. **2.** store in a ~ or room: *Where to ~ all my books is a problem.* '~-,**agent** *n.* (U.S.A. *realtor*) person who sells or lets ~s for others. '~·**boat** *n.* boat fitted up for living in on a river, etc. '~-,**break·er** *n.* **1.** (U.S.A. *~wrecker*) workman who pulls down old buildings. **2.** man who forces his way into a ~ by day (cf. *burglar* by night) to steal. '~-,**bro·ken** *adj.* ~-trained. '~·**hold** *n.* all persons (family and servants) living in a ~. '~,**hold·er** *n.* person leasing or owning and occupying a ~ (not one living in a hotel, in lodgings, etc.). '~,**keep·er** *n.* woman employed to manage the affairs of a ~hold. '~,**keep·ing** *n.* (no pl.) management of ~hold affairs. '~·**maid** *n.* woman servant in a ~, esp. one who cleans rooms and bedrooms. '~-,**mas·ter**, '~,**mis·tress** *ns.* teacher in charge of a school boarding-~. '~-**trained** *adj.* (Gt. Brit., of domestic animals) trained to be clean and behave well in the ~. '~,**warm·ing** *n.* party to celebrate the taking possession of a new home. '~·**wife** *n.* **1.** woman who does the cleaning, cooking, shopping, etc., for her family. (Cf. ~*keeper*.) **2.** ['hʌzɪf] small folding case of needles, thread, etc. '~·**work** *n.* (no pl.) work done in a ~ (cleaning, cooking, etc.).

~ove, see *heave* (v.).

~ov·el ['hɒvl] *n.* small miserable dwelling.

~ov·er ['hɒvə*] *v.i.* (of birds) remain in the air over one place; (of persons) wait about. '~·**craft** *n.* craft (3) that travels above ground or water on a cushion of air produced by jet engines.

a hovercraft

how [haʊ] *adv.* **1.** in what way or manner; by what means; in what degree; to what extent. **2.** in what state of health: *H~ are you? H~ do you do?* (used as a merely formal greeting). **3.** introducing an indirect statement: *He told me ~* (= that) *he had seen it in the newspaper.* **4.** introducing a question asking for an opinion, decision, etc.: *H~ about going for a walk* (shall we go or not)? *H~'s that for a beginner?* (expecting the answer, 'Very good'). **~·ev·er** [haʊ'evə*] *adv.* in whatever way or degree. *conj.* nevertheless; but yet.

howl [haʊl] *n.* long, loud cry (e.g. of a wolf); long cry of a person in pain or of sb. expressing scorn, amusement, etc. *v.i. & t.* utter such cries; make sounds suggesting these: *the wind ~ing through the trees*; *~ing with pain (laughter)*; *~ a speaker down.* **~·er** *n.* (colloq.) stupid and laughable mistake.

hub [hʌb] *n.* central part of a wheel; (fig.) centre of activity.

hub·bub ['hʌbʌb] *n.* (no pl.) confused noise (e.g. of many voices); uproar.

huck·le·ber·ry ['hʌklbərɪ] *n.* (dark-blue to black berry of a) low shrub from N. America.

hud·dle ['hʌdl] *v.i. & t.* **1.** crowd or press together in disorder or distress: *sheep huddling together for warmth.* **2.** ~ (oneself) *up*, draw the knees up to the body for warmth.

hue[1] [hjuː] *n.* (shade of) colour.

hue[2] [hjuː] *n.* ~ *and cry*, general outcry of alarm (as when a criminal is being pursued, or when there is opposition to sth.).

huff [hʌf] *n.* *in a ~*, ill-tempered. **~·ish**, **~·y** *adjs.* (-*ier*, -*iest*) (easily made) ill-tempered.

hug [hʌg] *v.t.* (-*gg-*) **1.** put the arms round tightly, esp. to show love. **2.** show fondness for (e.g. beliefs); (of a ship) keep close to (the shore). *n.* act of ~ging.

huge [hjuːdʒ] *adj.* very great.

hulk [hʌlk] *n.* **1.** body of an old ship no longer used at sea and left in disrepair. **2.** big clumsy person. **~·ing** *adj.* clumsy; big and awkward.

hull[1] [hʌl] *v.t. & n.* (remove) outer covering (of beans, peas).

hull[2] [hʌl] *n.* body or frame of a ship.

hul·la·ba·loo [ˌhʌləbəˈluː] *n.* (no pl.) uproar; outcry; disturbance: *What a ~!*

hul·lo [həˈləʊ] *int.* cry expressing surprise, or to get attention; informal greeting.

hum [hʌm] *v.t. & i.* (-*mm*-) make a continuous sound like that made by bees; sing with closed lips: *~ (a song) to oneself; a factory ~ming with activity*; *make things ~*, (colloq.) bring about a state of lively activity. *n.* ~ming sound: *the distant ~ of traffic.* [hmm] *int.* used to express doubt. '**~·ming-bird** *n.* bird whose rapidly moving wings make a ~ming sound.

hu·man [ˈhjuːmən] *adj.* 1. of man or mankind: *a ~ being*, a person. 2. having or showing the (esp. better) qualities that distinguish man. **~·ly** *adv.* (esp.) by ~ means: *all that was ~ly possible.*

hu·mane [hjuːˈmeɪn] *adj.* 1. tender; kind-hearted. 2. *~ learning, ~ studies* (other than science). **~·ly** *adv.* in a ~ (1) manner.

hu·man·ism [ˈhjuːmənɪzəm] *n.* (no pl.) 1. devotion to human interests; system concerned with ethical (not religious) standards and with the study of mankind. 2. literary culture, esp. that of the humanists. **hu·man·ist** *n.* 1. student of human nature or human affairs. 2. student (esp. in the 14th—16th centuries) of Greek and Roman literature and antiquities. **hu·man·is·tic** [ˌhjuːmənˈɪstɪk] *adj.*

hu·man·i·tar·i·an [hjuːˌmænɪˈteərɪən] *adj. & n.* (of, holding the views of, a) person working for the welfare of all human beings (by reducing suffering, reforming laws about punishment, etc.). **~·ism** *n.* (no pl.).

hu·man·i·ty [hjuːˈmænɪtɪ] *n.* 1. (no pl.) the human race; mankind. 2. (no pl.) human nature. 3. (no pl.) quality of being humane (1). 4. *the humanities*, branches of learning concerned with Greek and Latin culture; literature, history, and philosophy.

hu·man·ize [ˈhjuːmənaɪz] *v.t.* make human or humane (1).

hum·ble [ˈhʌmbl] *adj.* (~*r*, ~*st*) 1. having or showing a modest opinion of oneself, one's powers, position, etc. 2. poor; mean (1); low in rank, etc.: *men of ~ birth; ~ occupations* (e.g. street-cleaning). *v.t.* make ~; make lower in rank or self-opinion. **hum·bly** *adv.*

hum·bug [ˈhʌmbʌg] *n.* dishonest and

deceiving act, behaviour, talk, person, etc.; nonsense. *v.t.* (-*gg*-) deceive or trick (*sb. into, out of*).

hum·drum [ˈhʌmdrʌm] *adj.* dull; commonplace; monotonous.

hu·mid [ˈhjuːmɪd] *adj.* (esp. of air, climate) damp. **~·i·ty** [hjuːˈmɪdətɪ] *n.* (no pl.) (degree of) dampness (of the atmosphere).

hu·mil·i·ate [hjuːˈmɪlɪeɪt] *v.t.* cause to feel ashamed or humble. **hu·mil·i·a·tion** [hjuːˌmɪlɪˈeɪʃn] *n.*

hu·mil·i·ty [hjuːˈmɪlətɪ] *n.* (no pl.) humble condition or state of mind.

hum·mock [ˈhʌmək] *n.* hillock.

hu·mour (U.S.A. **hu·mor**) [ˈhjuːmə*] *n.* (no pl.) 1. (capacity to cause or feel) amusement: *a story full of ~; have a good sense of ~.* 2. person's state of mind (esp. at a particular time); temper: *in a good (bad) ~; not in the ~ for work*, not feeling inclined to work. *v.t.* give way to, gratify (a person, his desires). **hu·mor·ist** [ˈhjuːmərɪst] *n.* humorous talker or writer. **hu·mor·ous** [ˈhjuːmərəs] *adj.* having or showing a sense of ~; causing amusement: *humorous remarks.*

hump [hʌmp] *n.* fleshy lump, e.g. on a camel's back or (as a deformity) on a person's back. '**~·back** *n.* (person having a) back with a ~. '**~·backed** *adj.* having such a back.

humph [mm] *int.* used to show doubt or dissatisfaction.

hu·mus [ˈhjuːməs] *n.* (no pl.) earth formed by decay of vegetable matter (dead leaves, plants, etc.).

hunch [hʌntʃ] *n.* 1. hump. 2. thick piece (of bread, etc.). 3. *have a ~ that ...*, have an idea or a feeling that ... *v.t.* bend (*out, up*) to form a hump: *~ the shoulders.* '**~·back** *n.*, '**~·backed** *adj.* humpback(ed).

hun·dred [ˈhʌndrəd] *n. & adj.* 100. **~·th** [ˈhʌndrədθ] *n. & adj.* 100th; 1/100. '**~·weight** *n.* (written *cwt.*) 1/20 of a ton (= 50.8 kilograms).

hung, see *hang* (v.).

Hun·gar·i·an [hʌŋˈgeərɪən] *n. & adj.* (native, inhabitant, or language) of Hungary.

hun·ger [ˈhʌŋgə*] *n.* (no pl.) 1. need, desire, for food: *die of ~; satisfy one's ~.* 2. (fig.) any strong desire: *a ~ for adventure. v.i.* feel, suffer from, ~ (fig.) have a strong desire (*for, after*). '**~·strike** *n.* refusal to eat food in order to get release from prison, improvement of conditions, etc. **hun·gry** [ˈhʌŋgrɪ] *adj.* (-*ier, -iest*) feeling, showing signs of, ~. **hun·gri·ly** *adv.*

unk [hʌŋk] *n.* hunch (2).

unt [hʌnt] *v.t. & i.* **1.** go after (wild animals) for food or sport. **2.** look for; ry to find: ~ *for a lost book*; ~ *sb. or sth. down*, look for, pursue, and find; ~ *sth. up*, search for (e.g. records, bits of information). *n.* (no pl.) act of ~ing. *~er n.* **1.** person who ~s. **2.** horse for ~ing. **~ing** *n.* (no pl.) act of ~ing. **~ress** ['hʌntrɪs] *n.* female ~er. **~s·man** *n.* **1.** ~er (1). **2.** man who looks after the hounds.

ur·dle ['hɜːdl] *n.* **1.** movable oblong frame of wood, etc. used for making temporary fences (e.g. for sheep-pens). **2.** light frame to be jumped over in a ~-race (for running and jumping). *~r n.* runner in a ~-race.

url [hɜːl] *v.t.* throw violently.

ur·ly-bur·ly ['hɜːlɪ₁bɜːlɪ] *n.* (no pl.) noisy commotion; uproar.

ur·rah [hʊ'rɑː], **hur·ray** [hʊ'reɪ] *int.* cry of welcome, joy, triumph.

ur·ri·cane ['hʌrɪkən] *n.* violent wind-storm.

ur·ry ['hʌrɪ] *n.* (no pl.) haste; wish to get sth. done quickly; eager haste; (with neg. or in the interr.) need for haste: *There's no* ~. *What's the* ~? *in a* ~, acting, anxious to act, quickly. *v.t. & i.* (cause to) move or do sth. quickly or too quickly: *H~ up! Be quick!* ~ *away*, go off quickly; ~ (*over*) *one's work*. **hur·ried** *adj.* done in a ~. **hur·ried·ly** *adv.*

urt [hɜːt] *v.t. & i.* (p.t. & p.p. ~) cause injury or pain to; come to harm. *n.* harm; injury. **~ful** *adj.* causing suffering to.

urtle ['hɜːtl] *v.t. & i.* (cause to) rush or fly violently.

us·band ['hʌzbənd] *n.* man to whom a woman is married. *v.t.* use sparingly: ~ *one's strength.* '**~·man** *n.* (old use) farmer. '**~·ry** *n.* (no pl.) farming; careful) management.

ush [hʌʃ] *v.t. & i.* make or become silent: *H~! Be silent!* ~ *sth. up*, prevent t from becoming public knowledge. *n.* (no pl.) silence; quiet.

usk [hʌsk] *n.* dry outer covering of seeds, esp. of grain. *v.t.* remove the ~s from. **~y** *adj.* (-*ier*, -*iest*) **1.** (dry) like ~s. **2.** (of the voice) hoarse. **~·i·ly** *adv.* **~·i·ness** *n.* (no pl.).

us·sar [hʊ'zɑː] *n.* soldier of a light cavalry regiment.

us·sy ['hʌsɪ] *n.* worthless woman; ill-mannered girl.

us·tle ['hʌsl] *v.t. & i.* push roughly; make sb.) act quickly and with energy. *n.* (no pl.) quick and energetic activity.

hut [hʌt] *n.* small, roughly made house or shelter.

hutch [hʌtʃ] *n.* box with a front of wire-netting, esp. one for rabbits.

hy·a·cinth ['haɪəsɪnθ] *n.* kind of plant growing from a bulb; its sweet-smell-ing flowers.

hy·ae·na, see *hyena*.

hy·brid ['haɪbrɪd] *n. & adj.* (animal, plant, etc.) from parents of different sorts: *A mule is a* ~ (*animal*).

hy·dra ['haɪdrə] *n.* (in Greek mytholo-gy) great sea serpent with many heads that grow again if cut off.

hy·drant ['haɪdrənt] *n.* pipe, esp. in a street, to which water hoses can be attached for street-cleaning, putting out fires, etc.

hy·drate ['haɪdreɪt] *v.t.* cause to take up or combine with water.

hy·drau·lic [haɪ'drɔːlɪk] *adj.* of water or other liquid moving through pipes, etc.; worked by the pressure of a liq-uid: ~ *brakes*; *a* ~ *lift.* **~s** *n. pl.* (usu. sing. v.) science of using water or other liquid to produce power.

hy·dro- ['haɪdrəʊ-] *pref.* **1.** of water. **2.** of ~gen. '**~'car·bon** *n.* organic compound of ~gen and carbon. **~·e'lec·tric** *adj.* of electricity produced by water-power. '**~·foil** *n.* boat with metal plates or fins (2) that lift the hull[2] out of the water as speed is in-creased. **~gen** ['haɪdrədʒən] *n.* (no pl.) gas without colour, taste, or smell, that combines with oxygen to form water. **~gen bomb**, bomb whose im-mense explosive power is due to the sudden release of atomic energy achieved by converting ~gen nuclei into helium nuclei. ₁~'**pho·bia** *n.* (no pl.) rabies. '**~·plane** *n.* speedboat with a flat bottom designed to skim (2) over the surface; seaplane.

hy·e·na, **hy·ae·na** [haɪ'iːnə] *n.* flesh-eating wild animal, like a wolf, with a laugh-like cry.

hy·giene ['haɪdʒiːn] *n.* (no pl.) science of, rules for, healthy living. **hy·gien·ic** [haɪ'dʒiːnɪk] *adj.* of ~; likely to pro-mote health; free from disease germs. **hy·gien·i·cal·ly** *adv.*

hymn [hɪm] *n.* song of praise to God, esp. one for use in a religious service. **~·al** ['hɪmnəl] *n.* book of ~s.

hy·per- ['haɪpə*] *pref.* too: ~*critical*; ~*sensitive.*

hy·per·bo·le [haɪ'pɜːbəlɪ] *n.* exagger-ated statement made for effect.

hy·per·mar·ket ['haɪpə₁mɑːkɪt] *n.* very large self-service store occupying an extensive area, usu. outside a town, selling all varieties of goods.

hy·phen ['haɪfn] *n.* the mark (-) used to join two words together (as in *Anglo-French*), or to join separated syllables of words broken at the end of a line, etc.

hyp·no·sis [hɪp'nəʊsɪs] *n.* (pl. *-ses* [-siːz]) state like deep sleep in which a person's acts may be controlled by another person. **hyp·not·ic** [hɪp'nɒtɪk] *adj.* of ~. **hyp·no·tism** ['hɪpnətɪzəm] *n.* (no pl.) production of ~. **hyp·no·tize** ['hɪpnətaɪz] *v.t.* produce ~ in (sb.).

hy·poc·ri·sy [hɪ'pɒkrəsɪ] *n.* (making a) pretence of virtue or goodness. **hyp·o·crite** ['hɪpəkrɪt] *n.* person guilty of ~. **hyp·o·crit·i·cal** [ˌhɪpəʊ'krɪtɪkl] *adj.* of ~ or a hypocrite. **hyp·o·crit·i·cal·ly** *adv.*

hy·po·der·mic [ˌhaɪpəʊ'dɜːmɪk] *adj.* (med., of drugs, etc.) injected beneath the skin: ~ *needle* (*syringe*), used for giving ~ *injections* (of drugs).

hy·pot·e·nuse [haɪ'pɒtənjuːz] *n.* side of a right-angled triangle opposite the right angle.

hy·poth·e·sis [haɪ'pɒθɪsɪs] *n.* (pl. *-ses* [-siːz]) idea, suggestion, put forward as a starting-point for reasoning or explanation. **hy·po·thet·i·cal** [ˌhaɪpəʊ'θetɪkl] *adj.* of, based on, a ~, not of certain knowledge.

hys·te·ria [hɪ'stɪərɪə] *n.* (no pl.) **1.** disturbance of the nervous system, with outbursts of emotion, often uncontrollable. **2.** senseless, uncontrolled excitement. **hys·ter·i·cal** [hɪ'sterɪkl] *adj.* caused by, suffering from, ~. **hys·ter·ics** [hɪ'sterɪks] *n. pl.* (usu. sing. v) attack(s) of ~: *go into hysterics.*

I

I [aɪ] *pron.* used by a speaker or writer in referring to himself.

-ial [-ɪəl] *suff.* (forming adjs.): *dictatorial*; *trivial*.

-ian [-ɪən, -jən] *suff.* (forming adjs. and ns.) of; having to do with: *Austrian*; *Christian*.

-ibil·i·ty [-ə'bɪlətɪ] *suff.* (forming ns. from adjs. in *-ible*): *possibility*.

-ible [-əbl] *suff.* see *-able*: *possible*; *terrible*.

-i·bly [-əblɪ] *suff.* (forming advs. from adjs. in *-ible*): *possibly*; *terribly*.

-ic, -i·cal [-ɪk(l)] *suffs.* (forming adjs. and ns.) having the properties or nature of: *alcoholic*; *artistic*; *sulphuric*; *alphabetic(al)*; *geometric(al)*; *critic*; *music*.

-i·cal·ly [-ɪkəlɪ] *suff.* (forming advs. from adjs. in *-ic* or *-ical*): *comically*; *musically*.

ice [aɪs] *n.* **1.** (no pl.) frozen water. *break the* ~, get (people) on friendly terms; get well started on sth. **2.** frozen sweet, esp. ~ cream or water-~. *v.t. & i.* **1.** make (food, etc.) very cold: ~*d water*. **2.** cover, become covered (*over*, *up*), with a coating of ~. **3.** cover (a cake) with icing.

an iceberg

~·berg ['aɪsbɜːg] *n.* mass of ~ (broken off a glacier) floating in the sea. '**~-bound** ('~-**free**) *adj.* (of harbours, etc.) obstructed by (free from) ~. ~ **cream** *n.* frozen, flavoured cream or custard. '**~-field** *n.* expanse of ice, esp. in the polar regions. ~ **hock·ey**, see *hockey*. '**~-pack** *n.* wide

area of ~ covering the sea. **ici·cle** ['aɪsɪkl] *n.* hanging piece of ~ formed by the freezing of dripping water. **ic·ing** *n.* (no pl.) **1.** sugary coating for or on a cake. **2.** formation of ice on the wings of an aircraft. **icy** *adj.* (*-ier*, *-iest*) very cold; covered with ~; (fig.) unfriendly in manner. **ic·i·ly** *adv.*

icon ['aɪkɒn] *n.* (Eastern Church) painting of a sacred person.

-ics [-ɪks] *suff.* (forming ns. with sing. or pl. v.) indicating science or a specific activity: *mathematics*; *politics*; *athletics*.

ide·a [aɪ'dɪə] *n.* **1.** thought; picture in the mind. **2.** plan; scheme: *He's full of new* ~*s*.

ide·al [aɪ'dɪəl] *adj.* **1.** satisfying one's highest ideas; perfect: ~ *weather*. **2.** existing only as an idea; not likely to be achieved (opp. *real*). *n.* idea, example, looked upon as perfect: *the high* ~*s of the Christian religion*. ~·**ism** *n.* (no pl.) **1.** living according to, being guided by, one's ~*s*. **2.** (in art) imaginative treatment so that things are pictured in perfect form (opp. *realism*). ~·**ist** *n.* ~·**ize** *v.t.* make, think of, as ~. ~·**ly** *adv.*

iden·ti·cal [aɪ'dentɪkl] *adj.* the same: ~ *with*, like in every way. **iden·ti·fy** [aɪ'dentɪfaɪ] *v.t.* **1.** say, show, prove, who or what sb. or sth. is. **2.** *identify oneself with*, give support to, associate oneself with. **iden·ti·fi·ca·tion** [aɪˌdentɪfɪ'keɪʃn] *n.* (no pl.).

iden·ti·ty [aɪ'dentətɪ] *n.* **1.** (no pl.) state of being identical. **2.** who sb. is; what sth. is.

ide·ol·o·gy [ˌaɪdɪ'ɒlədʒɪ] *n.* system of ideas, esp. for an economic or political system.

id·i·om ['ɪdɪəm] *n.* **1.** (special form of a) language peculiar to a class of people, a part of a country, etc. **2.** (gram.) word-group (e.g. *in order to*) whose meaning must be learnt as a whole. ~·**at·ic** [ˌɪdɪə'mætɪk] *adj.*

id·io·syn·cra·sy [ˌɪdɪə'sɪŋkrəsɪ] *n.* kind of behaviour, view, peculiar to sb.

id·i·ot ['ɪdɪət] *n.* person of feeble mind; (colloq.) stupid person. **id·i·o·cy** ['ɪdɪəsɪ] *n.* (no pl.) extreme stupidity. **~ic** [ˌɪdɪ'ɒtɪk] *adj.* stupid. **~i·cal·ly** *adv.*

idle ['aɪdl] *adj.* (*~r*, *~st*) 1. not being worked; not being used: *~ machinery.* 2. (of persons) not working: *~ because of trade disputes.* 3. lazy; not working hard: *an ~, worthless boy.* 4. useless; worthless: *~ gossip. v.i. & t.* 1. be *~*; do nothing: *~ away one's time,* pass one's time doing nothing. 2. (of a car engine) run slowly in neutral gear: *the engine is idling. ~r n.* person who *~s.* **idly** *adv.* **~ness** *n.* (no pl.)

idol ['aɪdl] *n.* 1. image (in wood, stone, etc.) of a god. 2. sb. or sth. greatly loved or admired. **~a·ter** [aɪ'dɒlətə*] *n.* person who worships *~s.* **~a·trous** [aɪ'dɒlətrəs] *adj.* of *~* worship. **~a·try** *n.* worship of *~s.* **~ize** ['aɪdəlaɪz] *v.t.* love or admire too much.

idyl(l) ['ɪdɪl] *n.* short description, usu. in verse, of a simple scene or event; scene, etc. suitable for this. **idyl·lic** [ɪ'dɪlɪk] *adj.*

if [ɪf] *conj.* 1. on condition that; supposing that: *If you want to go there I will take you. If it rains, we shall not go.* 2. when; whenever: *If I do not wear my spectacles I get a headache.* 3. although: *I will do it, (even) if it takes me all day.* 4. whether: *Do you know if Mr Smith is at home?* 5. *as if,* as it would be if: *She spoke to me as if she knew me.* 6. (in exclamations of wish, surprise, etc.): *If only I had known that* (emphasizing one's regret that one did not know it).

-i·fy [-ɪfaɪ] *suff.* (forming vs.) make or become: *simplify; solidify; glorify.*

ig·loo ['ɪglu:] *n.* (pl. *~s*) Eskimo's hut made of blocks of hard snow.

ig·ne·ous ['ɪgnɪəs] *adj.* (of rocks) formed by heat of volcanic action.

ig·nite [ɪg'naɪt] *v.t. & i.* set on fire; take fire. **ig·ni·tion** [ɪg'nɪʃn] *n.* igniting or being *~d;* process or means of igniting a fuel mixture (e.g. in a petrol engine or a rocket engine): *switch on the ignition.*

ig·no·ble [ɪg'nəʊbl] *adj.* dishonourable; of low repute.

ig·no·min·i·ous [ˌɪgnəʊ'mɪnɪəs] *adj.* bringing contempt, disgrace, shame; dishonourable. **ig·no·mi·ny** ['ɪgnə-mɪnɪ] *n.* public dishonour or shame; dishonourable act or behaviour.

ig·no·rant ['ɪgnərənt] *adj.* having, showing, little or no knowledge; not aware (*of* sth.). **ig·no·rance** *n.* (n pl.) state of being *~.* **ig·no·ra·mu** [ˌɪgnə'reɪməs] *n.* *~* person.

ig·nore [ɪg'nɔ:*] *v.t.* take no notice of refuse to take notice of.

il- [ɪ-] *pref.* opposite of: not: **il'le·ga** **il'leg·i·ble**, **ˌil·le'git·i·mate**, **il'lib** **er·al**, **il'log·i·cal** *adjs.*

-il [-(ɪ)l], **-ile** [-aɪl] *suffs.* (formin adjs. or ns.) denoting relation o capability: *civil; utensil; fragile; ver satile.*

ill [ɪl] *adj.* 1. (usu. pred.) in ba health: *fall ~; be taken ~.* 2. (attrib bad: *~ breeding. n.* 1. (no pl.) evil: *do ~.* 2. misfortune; trouble: *th many ~s of life. adv.* badly; imper fectly; unfavourably: *~ at ease, un* comfortable; embarrassed. *I can afford it,* I can hardly afford the mone for it. **ˌ~'bred** *adj.* badly brought up rough in behaviour. **ˌ~'fat·ed** *adj* destined to misfortune. **ˌ~'favoure** *adj.* (of a person) of unattractive ap pearance. **ˌ~'got·ten** *adj.* gained b wrong or unlawful methods. **ˌ~'na** tured *adj.* bad-tempered. **~ness** *n* 1. (no pl.) being *~.* 2. disease. *~* **'treat**, **ˌ~'use** *v.t.* treat badly o cruelly.

il·lic·it [ɪ'lɪsɪt] *adj.* unlawful.

il·lit·er·ate [ɪ'lɪtərət] *n. & adj.* (per son) with little or no education, un able to read or write. **il·lit·er·a·cy** *n*

il·lu·mi·nate [ɪ'lju:mɪneɪt] *v.t.* 1. giv light to; throw light on. 2. decorat (streets, etc.) with bright lights (as sign of rejoicing, etc.). **il·lu·mi·na tion** [ɪˌlju:mɪ'neɪʃn] *n.* 1. (no pl.) lighting. 2. (usu. pl.) lights, etc. use to *~* (2) a town. **il·lu·mine** [ɪ'lju:mɪn *v.t.* (liter.) give light to or on.

il·lu·sion [ɪ'lu:ʒn] *n.* (seeing of sth. that does not really exist or o sth. as different from the reality; fals idea or belief. **il·lu·sive** [ɪ'lu:sɪv] **il·lu·so·ry** [ɪ'lu:sərɪ] *adjs.* unreal caused by *~.*

il·lus·trate ['ɪləstreɪt] *v.t.* explain b examples, pictures, etc.; provide (book, etc.) with pictures, diagrams etc. **il·lus·tra·tor** *n.* person makin illustrations for a book, etc. **il·lus·tra tion** [ɪlə'streɪʃn] *n.* 1. (no pl.) il lustrating or being *~d.* 2. sth. that *~s* picture, etc.

il·lus·tri·ous [ɪ'lʌstrɪəs] *adj.* cele brated; greatly distinguished.

im- [ɪm-, ɪ-] *pref.* opposite of; not **ˌim·ma'ture**, **im'mea·sur·able**, **im 'mo·bile**, **im'mod·er·ate**, **im'mu table**, **im'pen·i·tent**, **ˌim·per'cep**

ti·ble, im'per·fect, im'prob·able, im'pru·dent, im'pure *adjs.*

im·age ['ɪmɪdʒ] *n.* **1.** likeness or copy of the shape of sb. or sth., esp. one made in wood, stone, or metal. **2.** mental picture. **3.** simile; metaphor: *speak in* ~*s*. **4.** *be the (very)* ~ *of (sb.)*, be exactly like. **im·ag·ery** ['ɪmɪdʒərɪ] *n.* (no pl.) ~s (1); use of ~s (3) in writing.

imag·ine [ɪ'mædʒɪn] *v.t.* **1.** form a picture in the mind. **2.** think of (sth.) as probable; take (an idea, etc.) into one's head. **imag·in·able** [ɪ'mædʒɪnəbl] *adj.* that can be ~d. **imag·i·nary** [ɪ'mædʒɪnərɪ] *adj.* unreal; existing only in the mind. **imag·i·na·tion** [ɪ,mædʒɪ'neɪʃn] *n.* power of the mind to ~; sth. ~d. **imag·i·na·tive** [ɪ'mædʒɪnətɪv] *adj.* of, having, using, showing, imagination.

imam [ɪ'mɑːm] *n.* title of various Muslim leaders.

im·be·cile ['ɪmbɪsiːl] *adj.* weak-minded; stupid. *n.* ~ person. **im·be·cil·i·ty** [,ɪmbɪ'sɪlətɪ] *n.* **1.** (no pl.) stupidity. **2.** stupid act, remark, etc.

im·bed [ɪm'bed], see *embed*.

im·bibe [ɪm'baɪb] *v.t.* drink; take in (ideas).

im·bue [ɪm'bjuː] *v.t.* ~*d with*, filled with (patriotism, hatred, etc.).

im·i·tate ['ɪmɪteɪt] *v.t.* **1.** copy the behaviour of; take as an example. **2.** be like; make a likeness of. **im·i·ta·tion** [ɪmɪ'teɪʃn] *n.* **1.** (no pl.) imitating. **2.** sth. that ~s; copy; (attrib.) not real: *imitation jewellery*. **im·i·ta·tive** ['ɪmɪtətɪv] *adj.* following the model or example of: *the imitative arts*, painting and sculpture. **im·i·ta·tor** *n.* person who ~s.

im·mac·u·late [ɪ'mækjʊlət] *adj.* faultless; pure; correct in every detail.

im·ma·nent ['ɪmənənt] *adj.* (of qualities) present, inherent (*in*).

im·ma·te·ri·al [,ɪmə'tɪərɪəl] *adj.* **1.** unimportant. **2.** not having physical substance.

im·me·di·ate [ɪ'miːdjət] *adj.* **1.** without others coming between; nearest: *my* ~ *neighbours*. **2.** occurring at once: *an* ~ *answer*. ~**ly** *adv.* (esp.) at once; without delay.

im·me·mo·ri·al [,ɪmɪ'mɔːrɪəl] *adj.* going back beyond the reach of memory: *from time* ~.

im·mense [ɪ'mens] *adj.* very large. ~**ly** *adv.* **im·men·si·ty**, ~**ness** *ns.* (no pl.) great size.

im·merse [ɪ'mɜːs] *v.t.* **1.** put under the surface of (water or other liquid). **2.** *be* ~*d in*, be deep in (debt, difficulties, thought, a book). **im·mer·sion** [ɪ'mɜːʃn] *n.* immersing or being ~d. *immersion heater*, electrical apparatus (1) ~d in (a tank of) water for heating it.

im·mi·grate ['ɪmɪɡreɪt] *v.i.* come (*into* a country) as a settler (i.e. to live there). **im·mi·grant** ['ɪmɪɡrənt] *n.* person who ~s. **im·mi·gra·tion** [,ɪmɪ'ɡreɪʃn] *n.*

im·mi·nent ['ɪmɪnənt] *adj.* (esp. of danger) likely to come or happen soon. **im·mi·nence** *n.* (no pl.) nearness (of an event, etc.).

im·mor·tal [ɪ'mɔːtl] *adj.* living for ever; never forgotten. *n.* ~ being: *the* ~*s*, the gods of ancient Greece and Rome. ~**ize** [ɪ'mɔːtəlaɪz] *v.t.* give endless life or fame to. ~**i·ty** [,ɪmɔː'tælətɪ] *n.* (no pl.) endless life or fame.

im·mov·able [ɪ'muːvəbl] *adj.* **1.** that cannot be moved: ~ *property* (e.g. buildings, land). **2.** fixed (in purpose, etc.). **im·mov·ably** *adv.*

im·mune [ɪ'mjuːn] *adj.* free, secure (*from* or *against* the possibility of catching a disease, etc.). **im·mu·ni·ty** *n.* (no pl.) safety, security (*from* disease, etc.); exemption (*from* taxation, etc.). **im·mu·nize** ['ɪmjuːnaɪz] *v.t.* make ~ (*against*).

imp [ɪmp] *n.* child of the devil; little devil; (playfully) mischievous child.

im·pact ['ɪmpækt] *n.* collision; striking (*on, against*, sth.) with force.

im·pair [ɪm'peə*] *v.t.* weaken; damage.

im·pale [ɪm'peɪl] *v.t.* pierce through, pin down, with a sharp-pointed stake, spear, etc.

im·part [ɪm'pɑːt] *v.t.* give, pass on (a share of sth., a secret, news, etc. *to* sb.).

im·par·tial [ɪm'pɑːʃl] *adj.* fair (in giving judgements, etc.). ~**ly** *adv.* ~**i·ty** ['ɪm,pɑːʃɪ'ælətɪ] *n.* (no pl.).

im·pass·able [ɪm'pɑːsəbl] *adj.* (of roads, etc.) that cannot be travelled on or through.

im·passe [æm'pɑːs] *n.* place, position, from which there is no way out; deadlock.

im·pas·sioned [ɪm'pæʃnd] *adj.* full of, showing, deep feeling.

im·pas·sive [ɪm'pæsɪv] *adj.* showing no sign of feeling; unmoved.

im·pa·tient [ɪm'peɪʃnt] *adj.* not patient. **im·pa·tience** *n.* (no pl.).

im·peach [ɪm'piːtʃ] *v.t.* **1.** question, raise doubts about (sb.'s character, etc.). **2.** accuse (sb. *of* or *with* wrong-doing); (esp.) accuse (sb.) of a crime against the State. **~·ment** *n.*

im·pec·ca·ble [ɪm'pekəbl] *adj.* fault-less; incapable of doing wrong.

im·pe·cu·ni·ous [ˌɪmpɪ'kjuːnjəs] *adj.* having little or no money.

im·pede [ɪm'piːd] *v.t.* get in the way of; hinder. **im·ped·i·ment** [ɪm'pedɪmənt] *n.* (esp.) defect in speech (e.g. a stammer).

im·pel [ɪm'pel] *v.t.* (-ll-) drive forward; force (sb. *to do* sth., *to* an action).

im·pend·ing [ɪm'pendɪŋ] *adj.* about to happen; imminent: *the ~ storm.*

im·pen·e·tra·ble [ɪm'penɪtrəbl] *adj.* that cannot be penetrated.

im·per·a·tive [ɪm'perətɪv] *adj.* **1.** urgent; needing immediate attention. **2.** not to be disobeyed; done, given, with authority: *~ orders (looks, gestures).* **3.** (gram., of mood) form of verb expressing commands. *n.* (gram.) *~ mood.*

im·pe·ri·al [ɪm'pɪərɪəl] *adj.* **1.** of an empire or its ruler: *~ trade.* **2.** (of weights and measures) used by law in the U.K. **3.** majestic; magnificent. **~·ism** *n.* (no pl.) belief in the value of colonies; policy of extending a country's empire and influence. **~·ist** *n.* supporter of, believer in, ~·ism.

im·per·il [ɪm'perəl] *v.t.* (-ll-), U.S.A. also -l-) put in, bring into, danger.

im·pe·ri·ous [ɪm'pɪərɪəs] *adj.* commanding; displaying authority.

im·per·me·able [ɪm'pɜːmjəbl] *adj.* ~ (*to*), that cannot be permeated (esp. by fluids); impervious (1).

im·per·son·al [ɪm'pɜːsnl] *adj.* **1.** not influenced by personal feeling. **2.** not referring to a particular person: *~ remarks.* **3.** (gram., of verbs) used after *it*, as in *It is raining.*

im·per·son·ate [ɪm'pɜːsəneɪt] *v.t.* **1.** act the part of (in a play); pretend to be (another person). **2.** personify.

im·per·ti·nent [ɪm'pɜːtɪnənt] *adj.* **1.** not showing proper respect. **2.** not pertaining to the matter in hand. **im·per·ti·nence** *n.*

im·per·turb·able [ˌɪmpə'tɜːbəbl] *adj.* not easily moved or troubled; calm.

im·per·vi·ous [ɪm'pɜːvjəs] *adj.* **1.** (of materials) not allowing (water, etc.) to pass through: *These boots are ~ to water.* **2.** ~ *to*, not moved or influenced by: *~ to argument.*

im·pet·u·ous [ɪm'petjuəs] *adj.* moving quickly or violently; acting, inclined to act, energetically but with insuffi-

cient thought or care; done or sai hastily. **im·pet·u·os·i·ty** [ɪmˌpetjʊ'ɒsətɪ] *n.*

im·pe·tus ['ɪmpɪtəs] *n.* force wit which a body moves; (fig.) impulse driving force.

im·pinge [ɪm'pɪndʒ] *v.i.* fall or strik forcibly (*on, against*).

im·pi·ous ['ɪmpjəs] *adj.* not pious wicked.

im·pla·ca·ble [ɪm'plækəbl] *adj.* tha cannot be appeased; relentless: *hatred.*

im·plant [ɪm'plɑːnt] *v.t.* fix or pu (ideas, feelings, etc., *in* the mind).

im·ple·ment ['ɪmplɪmənt] *n.* tool o instrument: *farm ~s.* ['ɪmplɪment *v.t.* carry (an undertaking, agreement promise) into effect.

im·pli·cate ['ɪmplɪkeɪt] *v.t.* show tha (sb.) has a share (*in* a crime, etc. **im·pli·ca·tion** [ˌɪmplɪ'keɪʃn] *n.* **1** (no pl.) implicating or being ~·d. **2** implying; sth. implied.

im·plic·it [ɪm'plɪsɪt] *adj.* **1.** implied ~ *threats.* **2.** unquestioning (belief obedience, etc.).

im·plore [ɪm'plɔː*] *v.t.* request ear nestly. **im·plor·ing·ly** *adv.*

im·ply [ɪm'plaɪ] *v.t.* give or make suggestion; convey (2) the truth (beyond what is definitely stated) *an implied rebuke. Silence sometime implies consent* (i.e. failure to say 'no may be thought to mean 'yes').

im·pon·der·able [ɪm'pɒndərəbl] *adj* (fig.) of which the effect cannot be estimated.

im·port [ɪm'pɔːt] *v.t.* **1.** bring (esp foreign goods) into (a country). **2** mean; signify. ['ɪmpɔːt] *n.* **1.** (usu pl.) goods ~·ed (1). **2.** (no pl.) act o ~·ing (1) goods. **3.** (no pl.) meaning. **~·er** *n.* sb. who ~s (1).

im·por·tant [ɪm'pɔːtənt] *adj.* **1.** of great influence; to be treated seriously; having a great effect. **2.** (of a person) having a position of authority. **~·ly** *adv.* **im·por·tance** *n.* (no pl.).

im·por·tu·nate [ɪm'pɔːtjʊnət] *adj.* **1.** (of persons) making repeated and inconvenient requests. **2.** (of affairs, etc.) urgent. **im·por·tu·ni·ty** [ˌɪm-pɔː'tjuːnətɪ] *n.*

im·pose [ɪm'pəʊz] *v.t. & i.* **1.** lay or place (a duty, tax, etc. *on* or *upon* sb. or sth.). **2.** ~ (*up*)*on*, take advantage of (sb., his good nature); deceive. **im·pos·ing** *adj.* important-looking; causing admiration. **im·po·si·tion** [ˌɪmpə'zɪʃn] *n.* **1.** (no pl.) act of imposing (taxes, etc.). **2.** sth. ~·d; tax, etc.; (Gt.

Brit.) work set as punishment at school. **3.** fraud; overcharge.

im·pos·si·ble [ɪmˈpɒsəbl] *adj.* **1.** not possible. **2.** that cannot be endured: *It's an ~ situation!* **im·pos·si·bil·i·ty** [ɪmˌpɒsəˈbɪlətɪ] *n.*

im·pos·tor [ɪmˈpɒstə*] *n.* person pretending to be what he is not. **im·pos·ture** [ɪmˈpɒstʃə*] *n.* act of deception by an ~.

im·po·tent [ˈɪmpətənt] *adj.* lacking sufficient strength (to do sth.); unable to act; (usu. of males) wholly lacking in sexual power. **im·po·tence** *n.* (no pl.).

im·pound [ɪmˈpaʊnd] *v.t.* take possession of by law or authority.

im·pov·er·ish [ɪmˈpɒvərɪʃ] *v.t.* cause to become poor; take away good qualities: *~ed soil.*

im·prac·ti·ca·ble [ɪmˈpræktɪkəbl] *adj.* **1.** that cannot be done or effected; impossible. **2.** (of routes) that cannot be used; impassable.

im·pre·ca·tion [ˌɪmprɪˈkeɪʃn] *n.* curse.

im·preg·na·ble [ɪmˈpregnəbl] *adj.* that cannot be overcome or taken by force.

im·preg·nate [ˈɪmpregneɪt] *v.t.* make pregnant; fertilize; saturate; fill (*with* feelings, etc.).

im·press [ɪmˈpres] *v.t.* **1.** press (one thing *on* or *with* another); make a mark, etc. by doing this. **2.** have a strong influence on; fix deeply (on the mind, memory): *I was not much ~ed,* I did not form a favourable opinion. **im·pres·sion** [ɪmˈpreʃn] *n.* **1.** mark made by pressing (e.g. of a seal on wax). **2.** print (of an engraving, etc.). **3.** (printing of) number of copies forming one issue (4) of a book or newspaper. **4.** effect produced on the mind or feelings. **5.** (vague or uncertain) idea or belief: *be under the ~ion that,* have the idea that. **im·pres·sion·able** *adj.* easily influenced. **im·pres·sive** *adj.* ~ing (2) the mind or feelings.

im·print [ɪmˈprɪnt] *v.t.* print; stamp: *ideas ~ed on the mind.* [ˈɪmprɪnt] *n.* sth. (e.g. a fingerprint) ~ed or impressed.

im·pris·on [ɪmˈprɪzn] *v.t.* put or keep in prison. **~ment** *n.* (no pl.).

im·promp·tu [ɪmˈprɒmptjuː] *adv. & adj.* without preparation.

im·prop·er [ɪmˈprɒpə*] *adj.* not suited to the occasion; indecent; incorrect. **im·pro·pri·ety** [ˌɪmprəˈpraɪətɪ] *n.*

im·prove [ɪmˈpruːv] *v.t. & i.* make or become better: *~ (up)on,* do (sth.) better than (what is mentioned). **~ment** *n.*

im·prov·i·dent [ɪmˈprɒvɪdənt] *adj.* wasteful; not looking to future needs. **~ly** *adj.*

im·pro·vise [ˈɪmprəvaɪz] *v.t. & i.* **1.** compose music while playing, verse while reciting, etc. **2.** provide, make, or do sth. quickly, in time of need, using whatever happens to be available.

im·pu·dent [ˈɪmpjʊdənt] *adj.* shamelessly rude. **im·pu·dence** *n.* (no pl.).

im·pulse [ˈɪmpʌls] *n.* **1.** push or thrust; impetus: *an ~ to trade.* **2.** sudden inclination to act without thought: *seized with an ~ to do sth.; a man who acts on ~.* **3.** brief electric signal. **im·pul·sive** [ɪmˈpʌlsɪv] *adj.* acting on, resulting from, ~ (2).

im·pu·ni·ty [ɪmˈpjuːnətɪ] *n.* (no pl.) *with ~,* without risk of punishment or injury.

im·pute [ɪmˈpjuːt] *v.t. ~ sth. to,* consider as the act, quality, or outcome of: *innocent of the crime ~d to him; ~ a boy's failure to stupidity.* **im·pu·ta·tion** [ˌɪmpjuːˈteɪʃn] *n.* accusation or suggestion of wrongdoing.

in¹ [ɪn] *prep., adv., & adj.* **I.** *prep.* **1.** (of place; cf. *at*): *the highest mountain in the world; in Africa; in London; in school; children playing in the street; standing in the corner of the room* (cf. *the house at the corner); a holiday in the country* (cf. *at the seaside); lying in bed* (cf. *sitting on the bed); sitting in an armchair* (cf. *on a chair without arms); read about sth. in the newspapers.* **2.** (of direction): *in this (that) direction; in all directions.* **3.** (indicating direction of motion or activity) into: *put it in your pocket. He dipped his pen in the ink. Cut (break) it in two. They fell in love.* **4.** (of time when): *in the 20th century; in 1980; in spring; in my absence; in his youth; in old age; in these (those) days; in the morning (afternoon, evening)* (cf. *on Monday morning); at nine o'clock in the night* (cf. *at* night). **5.** (of time) in the course of; within the space of: *I shall be back in a short time (in a few days, in a week's time, etc.).* **6.** (indicating inclusion): *seven days in a week.* **7.** (indicating ratio): *a slope (gradient) of one in five. Not one in ten of the boys could spell well.* **8.** (of dress, etc.): *dressed (clothed) in rags; the woman in white,* wearing white clothes. **9.** (indicating physical surroundings, circumstances, etc.): *go out in the rain; sitting in the sun; a temperature of 68° F. (= 20° C.) in the shade.* **10.** (indicating state or condition): *in a troubled state*; *in good order*; *in poor health*. **11.** (indicating form, shape, arrangement): *standing about in groups*; *in alphabetical order*; *a novel in three parts*. **12.** (indicating the method of expression, the means, material, etc.): *speaking (writing) in English*; *written in ink (pencil)*; *in a loud voice*. **13.** (indicating degree or extent): *in large (small) quantities*; *in great numbers*. **in all**, as the total: *We were fifteen in all*. **14.** (indicating identity): *You will always have a good friend in me*, I shall always be a friend to you. **15.** (indicating relation, reference, respect): *in some (all) respects*; *in every way*; *a country rich in minerals*. **16.** (indicating occupation, activity, etc.): *He's in the army (in insurance)*: *He is in politics* (is a politician). *How much time do you spend in reading?* **17.** (used in numerous prepositional phrases; see the noun entries, e.g.): *in defence of*; *in exchange for*; *in justice to*; *in memory of*; *in touch with*. **18.** *in so far as, in as far as,* in such measure as; to the extent that: *He is a Russian in so far as he was born in Russia*, *but became a French citizen in 1920*. *in itself*, in its own nature; considered apart from its surroundings, other things, etc.: *Card playing is not in itself a bad thing*. **II.** *adv.* (contrasted with *out*) **1.** used with many verbs, as *come in* (= enter) and *give in* (= surrender); see the verb entries for these. **2.** (used with verbs indicating enclosure): *fenced (locked, walled) in*. **3.** (used with the verb *be*) (a) at home: *Is there anyone in?* (b) arrive: *Is the steamer (train) in yet?* (Has it arrived?) (c) (of crops) harvested; brought in from the fields: *The wheat crop (The harvest) is safely in*. (d) in season; obtainable: *Strawberries are in now*. (e) in fashion: *Long skirts are in again*. (f) elected; in power; in office: *The Democrats are in. The Liberal candidate is in* (has been elected). (g) burning: *Is the fire still in?* (h) (cricket, baseball) batting: *Which side is in?* **4.** *in for*, (a) likely to experience (usu. sth. unpleasant): *I'm afraid we're in for a storm*. (b) committed to; having agreed to take part in: *I'm in for the competition*, I shall be a competitor. *be in on*, (colloq.) participate in; share in: *be in on a scheme*. *in and out*, now in and then out: *He's always in and out of hospital. He is frequently ill and in hospital*. *day in, day out*, day

after day. **III.** *adj.* (preceding a noun) **1.** internal; living, etc. inside: *an in patient* (*in-patient*), one who lives in a hospital while receiving treatment (contrasted with *out-patient*); *the in train*, the incoming train. **2.** most up to date or exclusive (of its kind); fashionable: *in-crowd*; *in-language*; *in-thing*.

in² [ɪn] *n.* (only) *the ins and the outs*, the different parts; the details: *know all the ins and outs of a problem*.

in- [ɪn-, ɪ-] *pref.* not; the opposite of: **in'ac·cu·rate**, **in'ca·pable**, ˌin·co·'her·ent, **in**ˌcom·pre'hen·si·ble, **in**con'sid·er·ate, **in**·ef'fi·cient, **in**·of·'fen·sive, **in**·or'gan·ic, **in**·sig'nif·i·cant, **in**·sin'cere, **in**·suf'fi·cient, **in'vari·able**, **in'vis·i·ble**, **in'vul·ner·able** *adjs.*

-in [-ɪn] *suff.* usu. added to a verb to indicate participation in any kind of public demonstration or group activity: *sit-in*; *teach-in*.

in·abil·i·ty [ˌɪnəˈbɪlətɪ] *n.* (no pl.) being unable; lack of power or means.

in·ad·ver·tent [ˌɪnədˈvɜːtənt] *adj.* not paying or showing proper attention; (of actions) done thoughtlessly or not on purpose. **~·ly** *adv.* **in·ad·ver·tence** *n.*

in·alien·able [ɪnˈeɪljənəbl] *adj.* (of rights, etc.) that cannot be given away or taken away.

inane [ɪˈneɪn] *adj.* foolish. **~·ly** *adv.* **inan·i·ty** [ɪˈnænɪtɪ] *n.* foolish or purposeless behaviour, act, etc.

in·an·i·mate [ɪnˈænɪmət] *adj.* **1.** lifeless. **2.** without animal life: *~ nature* (outside the animal world). **3.** spiritless; dull: *~ conversation*.

in·a·ni·tion [ˌɪnəˈnɪʃn] *n.* (no pl.) emptiness; extreme weakness from want of food.

in·apt [ɪnˈæpt] *adj.* unskilful; not bearing on the subject: *~ remarks*.

in·as·much [ˌɪnəzˈmʌtʃ] *adv.* *~ as*, since; because.

in·au·gu·rate [ɪˈnɔːɡjʊreɪt] *v.t.* **1.** introduce (a new official, esp. the President of the U.S., a professor, etc.) at a special ceremony. **2.** enter, with public formalities, upon (an undertaking, etc.); open (an exhibition, a public building) with formalities. **3.** begin, introduce, a start or opening of. **in·au·gu·ral** [ɪˈnɔːɡjʊrəl] *adj.* of or for an inauguration: *an inaugural lecture*. **in·au·gu·ra·tion** [ɪˌnɔːɡjʊ-ˈreɪʃn] *n.*

in·born [ˌɪnˈbɔːn, attrib. also ˈɪnbɔːn]

incompetent

adj. (of a quality) possessed (by a person or animal) at birth: *an ~ love of mischief.*

n·bred [ˌɪn'bred, attrib. also 'ɪnbred] **adj.** inborn.

n·breed·ing [ˌɪn'briːdɪŋ] **n.** (no pl.) breeding from closely related individuals or animals.

n·can·des·cent [ˌɪnkæn'desnt] **adj.** giving out, able to give out, light when heated: *~ lamp.* **in·can·des·cence n.** (no pl.).

n·can·ta·tion [ˌɪnkæn'teɪʃn] **n.** (form of) words used in magic.

n·ca·pac·i·tate [ˌɪnkə'pæsɪteɪt] **v.t.** make incapable or unfit (*for* work, etc.; *for* or *from doing* sth.). **in·ca·pac·i·ty** [ˌɪnkə'pæsəti] **n.** (no pl.) inability, powerlessness (*for* sth.; *for doing* sth.; *to do* sth.).

n·car·cer·ate [ɪn'kɑːsəreɪt] **v.t.** imprison.

n·car·nate [ɪn'kɑːneɪt] **adj.** having (esp. a human) body: *a devil ~.* ['ɪnkɑːneɪt] **v.t. 1.** make ~. **2.** put (an idea, etc.) into a real or material form. **3.** (be) a living form of (a quality): *a wife who ~s all the virtues.* **in·car·na·tion** [ˌɪnkɑː'neɪʃn] **n. 1.** (esp.) *the Incarnation,* the taking of bodily form by Jesus Christ. **2.** person looked upon as a type of a quality: *She's the incarnation of health.*

n·cen·di·ary [ɪn'sendjərɪ] **n. & adj. 1.** (person) setting fire to property unlawfully and with an evil purpose; (person) tending to stir up violence. **2.** (bomb) causing fire.

n·cense¹ [ɪn'sens] **v.t.** make angry.

n·cense² [ɪn'sens] **n.** (no pl.) (smoke of) a substance producing a sweet smell when burning.

n·cen·tive [ɪn'sentɪv] **n.** motive; that which encourages sb. to do sth.

n·cep·tion [ɪn'sepʃn] **n.** start.

n·ces·sant [ɪn'sesnt] **adj.** continual; often repeated: *a week of ~ rain.*

in·cest ['ɪnsest] **n.** (no pl.) sexual intercourse between near blood relations (e.g. brother and sister).

nch [ɪntʃ] **n.** measure of length, one-twelfth of a foot (= 2.54 centimetres): *by ~es,* bit by bit; *every ~ (a soldier),* completely; in every way.

in·ci·dence ['ɪnsɪdəns] **n.** *the ~ of a disease,* the range or extent of its effect; *the ~ of a tax,* the way it falls to certain people to pay it.

in·ci·dent ['ɪnsɪdənt] **n.** event, esp. one of less importance than others; happening that attracts general attention; public event causing trouble, etc. **in-**

ci·den·tal [ˌɪnsɪ'dentl] **adj. 1.** accompanying, but not forming a necessary part: *~al music to a play.* **2.** small and unimportant; additional to the main expenses. **3.** *~al to,* likely to occur in connection with. **in·ci·den·tal·ly adv. 1.** by chance; casually. **2.** in passing; by the way.

in·cin·er·ate [ɪn'sɪnəreɪt] **v.t.** burn to ashes. **in·cin·er·a·tor n.** enclosed fireplace for burning rubbish, etc.

in·cip·i·ent [ɪn'sɪpɪənt] **adj.** beginning; in an early stage.

in·ci·sion [ɪn'sɪʒn] **n.** cutting; cut (esp. one made in a surgical operation).

in·ci·sive [ɪn'saɪsɪv] **adj.** sharp; (fig.), of a person's mind, remarks) acute; clear-cut. **in·ci·sor** [ɪn'saɪzə*] **n.** sharp-edged front cutting-tooth.

in·cite [ɪn'saɪt] **v.t.** stir up, rouse (sb. *to do* sth., *to* anger, etc.). **~ment n.**

in·clem·ent [ɪn'klemənt] **adj.** (of weather) severe; cold and stormy. **in·clem·en·cy n.** (no pl.).

in·cli·na·tion [ˌɪnklɪ'neɪʃn] **n. 1.** leaning (of the mind or heart, *to* sth.); liking or desire (*for* one thing rather than another, *to* sth.). **2.** slope or slant.

in·cline [ɪn'klaɪn] **v.t. & i. 1.** (cause to) slope or slant. **2.** direct the mind in a certain direction; cause (sb.) to have a tendency or wish: *The news ~s me (I am ~d) to start at once.* ['ɪnklaɪn] **n.** upward or downward path.

in·close, in·clo·sure, see *enclose, enclosure.*

in·clude [ɪn'kluːd] **v.t.** bring in, reckon, as part of the whole: *Price £4.75, postage ~d.* **in·clu·sion** [ɪn'kluːʒn] **n.** (no pl.). **in·clu·sive** [ɪn'kluːsɪv] **adj.** including everything between named points: *from October to May inclusive; inclusive terms,* (e.g. at a hotel) charge (3) for a bedroom and all meals, etc. during one's stay.

in·cog·ni·to [ɪn'kɒgnɪtəʊ] **adv.** with one's name kept secret: *travel ~.*

in·come ['ɪŋkʌm] **n.** money received during a given period (as salary, receipts from trade, interest from investments, etc.). *~ tax* **n.** tax levied on *~.*

in·com·ing ['ɪn,kʌmɪŋ] **adj.** coming in: *the ~ tide (tenant).*

in·com·mode [ˌɪnkə'məʊd] **v.t.** cause trouble or inconvenience to.

in·com·pa·rable [ɪn'kɒmpərəbl] **adj.** that cannot be compared (*to, with*); matchless; without equal.

in·com·pe·tent [ɪn'kɒmpɪtənt] **adj.** not qualified or able (*to do* sth.).

in·con·gru·ous [ɪn'kɒŋgruəs] *adj.* not in harmony or agreement (*with*); out of place. **in·con·gru·ity** [,ɪnkɒŋ-'gru:ətɪ] *n.*

in·con·se·quent [ɪn'kɒnsɪkwənt] *adj.* not following naturally what has been said or done before; (of a person) saying ~ things. **in·con·se·quen·tial** [,ɪnkɒnsɪ'kwenʃl] *adj.* ~; unimportant.

in·con·ve·nience [,ɪnkən'vi:njəns] *n.* (cause of) discomfort. *v.t.* cause ~ to (sb.). **in·con·ve·nient** *adj.* causing discomfort, trouble, or annoyance.

in·cor·po·rate [ɪn'kɔ:pəreɪt] *v.t. & i.* make, become, united in one body or group; (law) form into, become, a corporation (2). [ɪn'kɔ:pərət] *adj.* formed into a corporation (2). **in·cor·po·ra·tion** [ɪn,kɔ:pə'reɪʃn] *n.*

in·cor·ri·gi·ble [ɪn'kɒrɪdʒəbl] *adj.* (of a person, his bad ways) that cannot be cured or corrected.

in·crease [ɪn'kri:s] *v.t. & i.* make or become greater in size, number, degree, etc. ['ɪnkri:s] *n.* ~ (*in*), increasing; growth; amount by which sth. ~s.

in·cred·i·ble [ɪn'kredəbl] *adj.* that cannot be believed; (colloq.) hard to believe; surprising.

in·cred·u·lous [ɪn'kredjʊləs] *adj.* sceptical; expressing disbelief: *an* ~ *smile.*

in·cre·ment ['ɪnkrɪmənt] *n.* profit; increase; amount of increase.

in·crim·i·nate [ɪn'krɪmɪneɪt] *v.t.* say, be a sign, that (sb.) is guilty of wrongdoing.

in·cu·bate ['ɪnkjʊbeɪt] *v.t. & i.* hatch (eggs) by sitting on them or by artificial warmth; sit on eggs. **in·cu·ba·tor** *n.* apparatus (1) for hatching eggs by artificial warmth or for rearing babies born prematurely.

in·cul·cate ['ɪnkʌlkeɪt] *v.t.* fix (ideas, etc.) well by repetition (*upon* or *in* sb. or his mind).

in·cum·bent [ɪn'kʌmbənt] *adj.* ~ *upon sb.*, resting upon him as a duty (*to do* sth.). *n.* rector; vicar.

in·cur [ɪn'kɜ:*] *v.t.* (-*rr*-) bring (debt, danger, hatred, etc.) upon oneself.

in·cur·sion [ɪn'kɜ:ʃn] *n.* sudden attack or invasion.

in·debt·ed [ɪn'detɪd] *adj.* in debt, under an obligation (*to*).

in·de·cent [ɪn'di:snt] *adj.* 1. morally offensive. 2. unbecoming; unsuitable: ~ *haste.*

in·de·ci·sion [,ɪndɪ'sɪʒn] *n.* state of being unable to decide; hesitation. **in·de·ci·sive** [,ɪndɪ'saɪsɪv] *adj.* not decisive; hesitating.

in·deed [ɪn'di:d] *adv.* really; truly. *int.* expressing surprise, interes irony, etc.

in·de·fat·i·ga·ble [,ɪndɪ'fætɪgəbl] *ad,* untiring; that cannot be tired out.

in·def·i·nite [ɪn'defɪnət] *adj.* vagu *the* ~ *article,* (gram.) the word *a* or *ar*

in·del·i·ble [ɪn'deləbl] *adj.* that cann be rubbed or wiped out.

in·del·i·cate [ɪn'delɪkət] *adj.* (of person, his behaviour, speech, etc not refined; immodest. **in·del·i·ca cy** *n.*

in·dem·ni·fy [ɪn'demnɪfaɪ] *v.t.* 1 make (sb.) safe (*from*, *against* harm loss, punishment, etc.). 2. pay bac (sb. *for* loss, expenses, etc.). **in·dem ni·fi·ca·tion** [ɪn,demnɪfɪ'keɪʃn] *n.* ~ing or being indemnified. **in·dem ni·ty** [ɪn'demnətɪ] *n.* being indem nified; payment to compensate fo loss.

in·dent [ɪn'dent] *v.t. & i.* 1. brea into the edge or surface of (as wit teeth): *an* ~*ed* (i.e. very irregula *coastline.* 2. start (a line of print o writing) further from the margin tha the others. 3. make an order (*on o upon* sb. *for* goods, etc.); order good by means of an ~. ['ɪndent] *n.* trad order (placed esp. in the United King dom) for goods to be exported; (G Brit.) official requisition for stores.

in·den·ture [ɪn'dentʃə*] *n.* agreeme (of which two copies are made), es (usu. pl.) one binding an apprentic to his master.

in·de·pen·dent [,ɪndɪ'pendənt] *adj 1.* not dependent on or controlled b (other persons or things); not relyin on others; not needing to work for living. 2. self-governing. 3. acting o thinking along one's own lines: *an* *thinker. n.* (esp.) Member of Parlia ment, candidate, etc. who does no belong to a political party. ~*ly adv **in·de·pen·dence** *n.* (no pl.) state o being ~.

in·de·ter·mi·nate [,ɪndɪ'tɜ:mɪnət] *adj not fixed; vague; indefinite.

in·dex ['ɪndeks] *n.* (pl. ~*es*, esp. tech *indices* ['ɪndɪsi:z]) 1. sth. that point to or indicates; pointer (on an in strument): *the* ~ (*finger*), the fore finger, used for pointing. 2. list o names, references, etc. in ABC orde at the end of a book, or on cards, et *v.t.* make an ~ for (a book, etc.); pu (words, etc.) in an ~.

In·dia ['ɪndjə] *n.* ~ *paper*, very thin printing-paper (e.g. for airmail edi tions of newspapers). ~ *rubber*, i.*rub* *ber*, piece of rubber for rubbing out pencil or ink marks.

In·dian ['ɪndjən] *n. & adj.* **1.** (native or inhabitant) of India. **2.** (*American*, *Red*) $\sim$, (one) of the aboriginal inhabitants of America. **3.** *West* $\sim$, (native or inhabitant) of the West Indies. **4.** $\sim$ *corn*, maize; *in* $\sim$ *file*, in single file (see *file³*); $\sim$ *summer*, period of calm, dry, hazy weather in late autumn.

in·di·cate ['ɪndɪkeɪt] *v.t.* point to; point out; make known; be a sign of. **in·di·ca·tion** [ɪndɪ'keɪʃn] *n.* that which $\sim$s or is $\sim$d. **in·dic·a·tive** [ɪn'dɪkətɪv] *adj.* **1.** *indicative mood*, (gram.) form of a verb used in stating or asking for facts. **2.** *indicative of*, giving indications of. *n.* (gram.) indicative mood. **in·di·ca·tor** ['ɪndɪ-keɪtə*] *n.* (esp.) pointer, recording apparatus (1), on a machine or vehicle (to show speed, pressure, direction): *traffic indicator*, device (2) on a vehicle to indicate the intended change of direction.

in·di·ces, see *index*.

in·dict [ɪn'daɪt] *v.t.* (law) accuse (sb. *for* riot, *as* a rioter, *on* a charge of rioting, etc.). $\sim$**·able** *adj.* liable to be $\sim$ed; for which sb. may be $\sim$ed: $\sim$*able offences*. $\sim$**·ment** *n.* written statement $\sim$ing sb.

in·dif·fer·ent [ɪn'dɪfrənt] *adj.* **1.** $\sim$ *to*, not interested in; neither for nor against. **2.** commonplace; not of good quality or ability: *an* $\sim$ *book* (*footballer*). **in·dif·fer·ence** *n.* (no pl.) absence of interest or feeling; unimportance.

in·dig·e·nous [ɪn'dɪdʒɪnəs] *adj.* native (*to*); belonging naturally (*to* a country, etc.).

in·di·gent ['ɪndɪdʒənt] *adj.* poor; without money. **in·di·gence** *n.* (no pl.).

in·di·ges·tion [ɪndɪ'dʒestʃən] *n.* (no pl.) (pain from) difficulty in digesting food.

in·dig·nant [ɪn'dɪgnənt] *adj.* angry and scornful, esp. at injustice or because of undeserved blame, etc.: $\sim$ *with sb. at a false accusation*; $\sim$ *looks*. $\sim$**·ly** *adv.* **in·dig·na·tion** [ɪndɪg'neɪʃn] *n.* (no pl.).

in·dig·ni·ty [ɪn'dɪgnətɪ] *n.* unworthy treatment causing shame or loss of respect: *subjected to numerous indignities by the rough soldiers*.

in·di·go ['ɪndɪgəʊ] *n.* (no pl.) deep blue (dye).

in·di·rect [ɪndɪ'rekt] *adj.* not straight or direct: $\sim$ *speech*, (gram.) reported speech.

in·dis·creet [ɪndɪ'skriːt] *adj.* not careful or wary. **in·dis·cre·tion** [ɪndɪ-'skreʃn] *n.* (esp.) indiscreet remark, act, behaviour.

in·dis·crim·i·nate [ɪndɪ'skrɪmɪnət] *adj.* acting, given, without enough care or taste: $\sim$ *praise*; $\sim$ *in making friends*.

in·dis·pens·able [ɪndɪ'spensəbl] *adj.* necessary; that one cannot do without.

in·dis·posed [ɪndɪ'spəʊzd] *adj.* **1.** unwell. **2.** not inclined (*for* sth., *to do* sth.). **in·dis·po·si·tion** [ɪndɪspə'zɪʃn] *n.* (esp.) slight illness.

in·di·vid·u·al [ɪndɪ'vɪdjʊəl] *adj.* **1.** (opposite of *general*) specially for one person or thing. **2.** characteristic of a single person or thing: *an* $\sim$ *style of speaking*. **3.** considered or taken by itself: *in this* $\sim$ *case. n.* any one human being (contrasted with *society* (1)). $\sim$**·ly** *adv.* separately; one by one. $\sim$**·i·ty** ['ɪndɪvɪdjʊ'ælətɪ] *n.* $\sim$ character (esp. those features of it which are strongly marked); (pl.) $\sim$ *tastes*, etc.

in·doc·tri·nate [ɪn'dɒktrɪneɪt] *v.t.* fill the mind (*with* particular ideas or beliefs).

in·do·lent ['ɪndələnt] *adj.* lazy; inactive. **in·do·lence** *n.* (no pl.).

in·dom·i·table [ɪn'dɒmɪtəbl] *adj.* unconquerable; unyielding.

in·door ['ɪndɔː*] *adj.* situated, carried on, inside a building. $\sim$**s** [ɪn'dɔːz] *adv.* in(to) a house, etc.

in·dorse, in·dorse·ment, see *endorse*, *endorsement*.

in·du·bi·table [ɪn'djuːbɪtəbl] *adj.* that cannot be doubted.

in·duce [ɪn'djuːs] *v.t.* **1.** persuade (sb. *to do* sth.). **2.** bring about: *illness* $\sim$*d by overwork*. $\sim$**·ment** *n.* sth. that $\sim$s (1).

in·duc·tion [ɪn'dʌkʃn] *n.* method of reasoning that obtains or discovers general laws from particular facts or examples; production (of facts) to prove a general statement. **in·duc·tive** *adj.* (of reasoning) based on $\sim$.

in·dulge [ɪn'dʌldʒ] *v.t. & i.* gratify; give way to and satisfy (desires, etc.): $\sim$ *a sick child*; $\sim$ *in a holiday.* **in·dul·gence** [ɪn'dʌldʒəns] *n.* **1.** sth. in which a person $\sim$s (e.g. a cigar, a visit to the theatre). **2.** (R.C. Church) granting of freedom from punishment still due for sin. **in·dul·gent** *adj.* inclined to $\sim$: $\sim$*nt parents*.

in·dus·try ['ɪndəstrɪ] *n.* **1.** (no pl.) quality of being hard working; constant employment in useful work. **2.** (branch of) trade or manufacture (often contrasted with *distribution* and *commerce*). **in·dus·tri·al** [ːn'dʌstrɪəl] *adj.* of industries (2): *industrial area* (city). **in·dus·tri·al·ize** [ɪn'dʌstrɪəlaɪz] *v.t. & i.* make or become industrial. **in·dus·tri·ous** [ɪn'dʌstrɪəs] *adj.* hard-working; showing ~ (1).

ine·bri·ate [ɪ'niːbrɪeɪt] *v.t.* intoxicate. [ɪ'niːbrɪət] *n. & adj.* (person who is habitually) intoxicated.

in·ef·fable [ɪn'efəbl] *adj.* too great to be described in words: ~ *beauty*.

in·ept [ɪ'nept] *adj.* absurd; said, done, at the wrong time. **in·ep·ti·tude** [ɪ'neptɪtjuːd] *n.* (esp.) ~ *action*, etc.

in·ert [ɪ'nɜːt] *adj.* **1.** without power to move or act: ~ *matter*. **2.** (of a person) slow; dull. **3.** having no power to act chemically: ~ *gases*. **in·er·tia** [ɪ'nɜːʃjə] *n.* (no pl.).

in·es·ti·mable [ɪn'estɪməbl] *adj.* too great to be estimated or given a value.

in·ev·i·table [ɪn'evɪtəbl] *adj.* that cannot be avoided; sure to happen.

in·ex·o·rable [ɪn'eksərəbl] *adj.* relentless; unyielding.

in·ex·pe·ri·ence [ˌɪnɪk'spɪərɪəns] *n.* (no pl.) lack or want of experience. ~**d** *adj.* lacking experience.

in·ex·press·ible [ˌɪnɪk'spresəbl] *adj.* that cannot be expressed in words.

in·ex·tri·cable [ɪn'ekstrɪkəbl] *adj.* that cannot be escaped from, solved, reduced to order or untied.

in·fa·mous [ˈɪnfəməs] *adj.* wicked; shameful. **in·fa·my** [ˈɪnfəmɪ] *n.* being ~; ~ *act*; ~ *behaviour*.

in·fant [ˈɪnfənt] *n.* baby; very young child: ~ *school*, (Gt. Brit.) school for young children, usu. under 7 years of age. **in·fan·cy** [ˈɪnfənsɪ] *n.* (no pl.) **1.** state of being, period when one is, an ~. **2.** early stage of development: *Space research is no longer in its infancy.* **in·fan·ti·cide** [ɪn'fæntɪsaɪd] *n.* (no pl.) crime of killing an ~. **in·fan·tile** [ˈɪnfəntaɪl] *adj.* of, or as of, ~s: ~*ile diseases*.

in·fan·try [ˈɪnfəntrɪ] *n.* (collective sing.) part of an army that fights on foot.

in·farct [ˈɪnfɑːkt], **in·farc·tion** [ɪn-'fɑːkʃn] *ns.* (med.) area of dead tissue (as of the heart) caused by the blocking of the blood-circulation: *cardiac* ~.

in·fat·u·ate [ɪn'fætjʊeɪt] *v.t.* be ~**d** (*with*), be foolishly in love (with); be affected foolishly (by). **in·fat·u·a·tion** [ɪnˌfætjʊ'eɪʃn] *n.*

in·fect [ɪn'fekt] *v.t.* affect (a person, his body, mind) (*with* disease); give disease germs (fig. feelings, ideas) to:

a pupil whose high spirits ~*ed the whole class.* **in·fec·tion** [ɪn'fekʃn] *n.* (esp.) disease that ~s. **in·fec·tious** [ɪn'fekʃəs] *adj.* **1.** ~ing with disease; (of disease) that can be spread by germs carried in air or water. (Cf. *contagious*.) **2.** (fig.) quickly influencing others: ~*ious laughter* (*yawns*).

in·fer [ɪn'fɜː*] *v.t.* (-*rr*-) conclude (3); reach an opinion (from facts, reasoning). ~**ence** [ˈɪnfərəns] *n.* **1.** (no pl.) process of ~ring: *by* ~*ence*. **2.** sth. ~red; conclusion.

in·fe·ri·or [ɪn'fɪərɪə*] *adj.* low(er) in rank, social position, importance, quality, etc.: *goods* ~ *to samples*. *n.* person who is ~ (in rank, etc.). ~**·i·ty** [ɪnˌfɪərɪ'ɒrətɪ] *n.* (no pl.) state of being ~: ~*ity complex*, state of mind in which a feeling of being ~ to others causes a person to try to win importance for himself (e.g. by being aggressive or by boasting).

in·fer·nal [ɪn'fɜːnl] *adj.* of hell; devilish; abominable: ~ *cruelty*. **in·fer·no** [ɪn'fɜːnəʊ] *n.* (pl. ~s) hell.

in·fer·tile [ɪn'fɜːtaɪl] *adj.* not fertile.

in·fest [ɪn'fest] *v.t.* (of rats, insects, brigands, etc.) be present in large numbers: *warehouses* ~*ed with rats*.

in·fi·del [ˈɪnfɪdəl] *n.* person with no belief in (what is considered to be) the true or accepted religion.

in·fi·del·i·ty [ˌɪnfɪ'delətɪ] *n.* (act of) disloyalty or unfaithfulness (esp. to a wife or husband).

in·fil·trate [ˈɪnfɪltreɪt] *v.t. & i.* (cause to) pass through or into by filtering; (of troops) pass through defences without attracting notice; (of ideas) pass into people's minds. **in·fil·tra·tion** [ˌɪnfɪl'treɪʃn] *n.*

in·fi·nite [ˈɪnfɪnət] *adj.* endless; without limits: *the* ~, ~ *space; the I.*~), God. ~**·ly** *adv.* **in·fin·i·tes·i·mal** [ˌɪnfɪnɪ'tesɪml] *adj.* too small to be measured. **in·fin·i·tive** [ɪn'fɪnɪtɪv] *adj. & n.* (gram.) (of) the form of the verb not changed for person, number, or time, used with or without *to* (e.g. let him *go*; allow him *to go*). **in·fin·i·ty** [ɪn'fɪnɪtɪ] *n.* (no pl.) (math.) infinite number, quantity, measure, or distance.

in·firm [ɪn'fɜːm] *adj.* **1.** physically weak, esp. from age. **2.** mentally or morally weak: ~ *of purpose*. **in·fir·ma·ry** [ɪn'fɜːmərɪ] *n.* hospital; (in a school, etc.) room used for people who are ill or injured. **in·fir·mi·ty** [ɪn'fɜːmətɪ] *n.* weakness.

in·flame [ɪn'fleɪm] *v.t. & i.* (cause to)

become red, angry, overheated: ‿d *eyes*; ‿ *popular feeling*. **in·flam·mable** [ɪnˈflæməbl] *adj.* easily set on fire; (fig.) easily excited. **in·flam·ma·tion** [ˌɪnfləˈmeɪʃn] *n.* ‿d condition (esp. of part of the body). **in·flam·ma·to·ry** [ɪnˈflæmətərɪ] *adj.* **1.** of inflammation of the body. **2.** (of speeches, etc.) likely to ‿ (angry) feelings.

in·flate [ɪnˈfleɪt] *v.t.* **1.** fill (a tyre, balloon, etc.) with air or gas; cause to swell: (fig.) ‿d *with pride.* **2.** take action to increase the amount of money in circulation so that prices rise. (Cf. *deflate* (2).) **in·flat·able** *adj.* capable of being ‿d. **in·fla·tion** [ɪnˈfleɪʃn] *n.* **in·fla·tion·a·ry** [ɪnˈfleɪʃnərɪ] *adj.* of, caused by, inflation: *the inflationary spiral* (i.e. prices and wages rise in turn as the supply of money is increased).

in·flect [ɪnˈflekt] *v.t.* **1.** (gram.) change the ending or form of (a word) to show its relationship to other words in a sentence. **2.** modulate (the voice). **in·flec·tion,** (esp. Gt. Brit.) **in·flex·ion** [ɪnˈflekʃn] *n.* **1.** ‿ing; an ending (e.g. -*ed*) used for ‿ing. **2.** rise or fall of the voice in speaking.

in·flict [ɪnˈflɪkt] *v.t.* ‿ *sth. on sb.*, cause him to suffer by means of (a blow, wound, penalty, punishment, etc.): ‿ *oneself* (*one's company*) (*up*)*on sb.*, force one's company on him. **in·flic·tion** [ɪnˈflɪkʃn] *n.*

in·flow [ˈɪnfləʊ] *n.* flowing in; that which flows in: *an ‿ of capital.*

in·flu·ence [ˈɪnflʊəns] *n.* **1.** (no pl.) action of natural forces (*on*): *the ‿ of the moon* (on the tides), *of climate* (on vegetation). **2.** power to affect sb.'s character, beliefs, or actions (through example, fear, admiration, etc.); person or fact that exercises such power; the exercise of such power (*on* or *upon* sb. or sth.): *be under the ‿ of drink or drugs.* **3.** (no pl.) power due to wealth, position, etc.: *use one's ‿ to get a job for a friend. v.t.* have, use, ‿ upon. **in·flu·en·tial** [ˌɪnflʊˈenʃl] *adj.* having ‿.

in·flu·en·za [ˌɪnflʊˈenzə] *n.* (no pl.) infectious disease with fever and catarrh.

in·flux [ˈɪnflʌks] *n.* flowing in (e.g. of visitors *into* a place).

in·form [ɪnˈfɔːm] *v.t. & i.* **1.** give knowledge to: ‿ *sb. that,* ‿ *sb. of sth.* **2.** ‿ *against sb.*, bring an accusation against him to the police. ‿·ant *n.* person giving **in·for·ma·tion** [ˌɪnfə-ˈmeɪʃn] *n.* sth. told; news or knowledge given: *a useful piece of ‿ation.*

in·for·ma·tive [ɪnˈfɔːmətɪv] *adj.* instructive; giving ‿ation. ‿·er *n.* (esp.) sb. who ‿s the authorities of offences against the law.

in·for·mal [ɪnˈfɔːml] *adj.* not formal. ‿·ly *adv.* ‿·i·ty [ˌɪnfɔːˈmælətɪ] *n.*

in·frac·tion [ɪnˈfrækʃn] *n.* breaking (of a rule, law, etc.).

in·fra·struc·ture [ˈɪnfrəˌstrʌktʃə*] *n.* underlying foundation or basic framework (of an organization or a system); (esp.) permanent installations required for military purposes.

in·fringe [ɪnˈfrɪndʒ] *v.t. & i.* **1.** break (a rule, etc.). **2.** ‿ (*up*)*on* (sb.'s rights), trespass upon. ‿·ment *n.*

in·fu·ri·ate [ɪnˈfjʊərɪeɪt] *v.t.* fill with fury; make very angry.

in·fuse [ɪnˈfjuːz] *v.t. & i.* **1.** put, pour (a quality, etc. into): ‿ *courage* (*new life*) *into soldiers.* **2.** pour (hot) liquid on leaves, herbs, etc. to flavour it or to extract its component parts; undergo infusion: *let the tea ‿ for three minutes.* **in·fu·sion** [ɪnˈfjuːʒn] *n.* infusing or being ‿d; sth. (e.g. tea) made by infusing.

-ing [-ɪŋ] *suff.* (added to the roots of verbs to form) **1.** the present participle and the participial adj.: *amusing*; *interesting.* **2.** the gerund: *swimming.* **3.** thing produced: the *binding* of a book; iron *filings*; floor *sweepings.* **4.** collective ns.: *bedding*; *shipping*; *washing.*

in·ge·nious [ɪnˈdʒiːnjəs] *adj.* **1.** (of a person) clever and skilful (at making or inventing). **2.** (of things) skilfully made. **in·ge·nu·ity** [ˌɪndʒɪˈnjuːətɪ] *n.*

in·gen·u·ous [ɪnˈdʒenjʊəs] *adj.* frank; innocent; natural.

in·glo·ri·ous [ɪnˈɡlɔːrɪəs] *adj.* **1.** shameful; dishonourable. **2.** obscure (2).

in·got [ˈɪŋɡət] *n.* (usu. brick-shaped) lump of metal (esp. gold or silver).

in·graft, see *engraft.*

in·grained [ˌɪnˈɡreɪnd] *adj.* (of habits, stains, etc.) deeply fixed; difficult to get rid of.

in·gra·ti·ate [ɪnˈɡreɪʃɪeɪt] *v.t.* bring (oneself) into favour (*with* sb.), esp. in order to win an advantage.

in·gre·di·ent [ɪnˈɡriːdjənt] *n.* one of the parts of a mixture.

in·hab·it [ɪnˈhæbɪt] *v.t.* live in. ‿·able *adj.* that can be lived in. **in·hab·i·tant** *n.* person living in a place.

in·hale [ɪnˈheɪl] *v.t. & i.* take or draw (air, gas, smoke) into the lungs.

in·her·ent [ɪnˈhɪərənt] *adj.* existing (*in*) as a natural and permanent part or quality of.

in·her·it [ɪnˈherɪt] *v.t.* **1.** receive (property, a title, etc.) as heir. **2.** derive (qualities, etc.) from ancestors. **in·her·i·tance** [ɪnˈherɪtəns] *n.* ~ing; sth. ~ed.

in·hib·it [ɪnˈhɪbɪt] *v.t.* hinder; restrain: ~ed, unable or unwilling to express one's feelings. **in·hi·bi·tion** [ˌɪnhɪˈbɪʃn] *n.* impulse or desire that is ~ed.

in·hu·man [ɪnˈhjuːmən] *adj.* unfeeling; cruel. ~·i·ty [ˌɪnhjuːˈmænətɪ] *n.*

in·im·i·cal [ɪˈnɪmɪkl] *adj.* unfriendly or harmful (*to*).

in·im·i·table [ɪˈnɪmɪtəbl] *adj.* too good, clever, etc. to be imitated.

in·iq·ui·tous [ɪˈnɪkwɪtəs] *adj.* very wicked or unjust. **in·iq·ui·ty** [ɪˈnɪkwətɪ] *n.*

ini·tial [ɪˈnɪʃl] *adj.* of or at the beginning. *n.* (pl.) first letters of a person's names (e.g. T.S. for Tom Smith). *v.t.* (-*ll*-, U.S.A. -*l*-) mark or sign (sth.) with one's ~s. ~·ly *adv.* at the start.

ini·ti·ate [ɪˈnɪʃɪeɪt] *v.t.* **1.** begin; set (a scheme, etc.) working. **2.** admit or introduce (sb. *into* a society, etc.); give (sb.) instruction (*in* or *into* mysteries, etc.). [ɪˈnɪʃɪət] *n. & adj.* (person) who has been ~d (2). **ini·ti·a·tion** [ɪˌnɪʃɪˈeɪʃn] *n.* **ini·tia·tive** [ɪˈnɪʃɪətɪv] *n.* **1.** first step: *take the initiative*, make the first move; *on one's own initiative*, without an order or suggestion from others. **2.** capacity or right to ~ (1); enterprise: *have (the) initiative*. **ini·ti·a·tor** [ɪˈnɪʃɪeɪtə*] *n.*

in·ject [ɪnˈdʒekt] *v.t.* drive or force (a liquid, drug, etc. *into* sth.) with or as with a syringe; fill (sth. *with* a liquid, etc.) by ~ing. **in·jec·tion** *n.* **1.** ~ing; instance of this. **2.** liquid or solution (2) ~ed. **3.** (aer.) insertion (3).

in·junc·tion [ɪnˈdʒʌŋkʃn] *n.* order, esp. written order from a lawcourt demanding that sth. shall or shall not be done.

in·jure [ˈɪndʒə*] *v.t.* hurt; damage. ~d *adj.* hurt; wronged; offended: *in an ~d voice*; *the ~d*, people hurt in an accident, etc. **in·ju·ry** *n.* damage; wounding; wounded place; wrong. **in·ju·ri·ous** [ɪnˈdʒʊərɪəs] *adj.* causing, likely to cause, injury.

in·jus·tice [ɪnˈdʒʌstɪs] *n.* **1.** (no pl.) lack of justice. **2.** unjust act: *do sb. an* ~, judge him unfairly.

ink [ɪŋk] *n.* coloured liquid used for writing and printing. *v.t.* mark, make dirty, with ~. ~·y *adj.* (-*ier*, -*iest*).

in·kling [ˈɪŋklɪŋ] *n.* slight suggestion or idea (*of*).

in·land [ˈɪnlənd] *adj.* **1.** in the interior of a country. **2.** carried on, obtained within the limits of a country: ~ (= domestic (2)) *trade*; ~ *revenue* (Gt Brit., consisting of taxes and ~ duties). [ɪnˈlænd] *adv.* away from the coast

in·lay [ˌɪnˈleɪ] *v.t.* (p.t. & p.p. *inlaid* [ˌɪnˈleɪd]) set pieces of (designs in wood, metal, etc. in the surface of another kind of wood, metal, etc. so that the resulting surface is smooth and even: *ivory inlaid with gold*. [ˈɪnleɪ] *n.* inlaid work; filling for a cavity in a tooth.

in·let [ˈɪnlet] *n.* strip of water extending into the land from a larger body of water, or between islands.

in·mate [ˈɪnmeɪt] *n.* one of a number of persons living together (esp. in a prison, hospital, or other institution).

in·most [ˈɪnməʊst] *adj.* most inward; farthest from the surface.

inn [ɪn] *n.* **1.** public house where lodging, drink, and meals may be had: ~keeper, person who keeps (4) an ~. **2.** *I.~s of Court*, (buildings of) four London law societies.

in·nate [ˌɪˈneɪt] *adj.* (of a quality, etc.) in one's nature; possessed from birth.

in·ner [ˈɪnə*] *adj.* (of the) inside. ~most *adj.* inmost.

in·nings [ˈɪnɪŋz] *n. pl.* time during which a player or team (cricket, etc.) is batting; (fig.) period of power or opportunity to show one's ability.

in·no·cent [ˈɪnəsnt] *adj.* **1.** not guilty (*of* wrongdoing). **2.** harmless: ~ *pastimes*. **in·no·cence** *n.* (no pl.).

in·noc·u·ous [ɪˈnɒkjʊəs] *adj.* causing no harm.

in·no·vate [ˈɪnəʊveɪt] *v.i.* make changes (*in* old customs, etc.); bring in sth. new. **in·no·va·tion** [ˌɪnəʊˈveɪʃn] *n.*

in·nu·en·do [ˌɪnjuːˈendəʊ] *n.* (pl. -*oes*, ~s) indirect reference (usu. sth. unfavourable to a person's reputation).

in·nu·mer·able [ɪˈnjuːmərəbl] *adj.* too many to be counted.

in·oc·u·late [ɪˈnɒkjʊleɪt] *v.t.* introduce disease germs into (a person or animal) so that a mild form of the disease may keep him safe (*against* severe attacks). **in·oc·u·la·tion** [ɪˌnɒkjʊˈleɪʃn] *n.*

in·op·er·a·ble [ɪnˈɒpərəbl] *adj.* (of a tumour, etc.) that cannot be cured by operation (4).

in pa·tient, in-pa·tient [ˈɪnˌpeɪʃnt] *n.* person lodged at a hospital during treatment. (Cf. *out-patient*.)

in·put [ˈɪnpʊt] *v.t.* (-*tt*-; p.t. & p.p. ~ or ~ted) supply (data (2), etc. *to* a computer). **n. 1.** what is put in or supplied, e.g. power or energy put into a machine, data (2) fed (3) into a computer. **2.** place where energy, data (2), etc. enters a system.

in·quest ['ɪnkwest] **n.** official inquiry to learn facts, esp. concerning a death that may be the result of crime or other unnatural causes: *coroner's* ~.

in·quire [ɪn'kwaɪə*] **v.t. & i. 1.** ask to be told: ~ *sb.'s name (how to get somewhere,* etc.). **2.** ~ *into,* try to learn the facts about; ~ *after,* ask about (sb.'s health or welfare); ~ *for (sb.),* ask to see (him). **in·quir·er n.** person who ~s. **in·qui·ry** [ɪn'kwaɪərɪ] **n. 1.** (no pl.) asking; inquiring. **2.** question; investigation: *hold an inquiry into sth.*

in·qui·si·tion [ˌɪnkwɪ'zɪʃn] **n.** thorough investigation, esp. one made officially. **in·quis·i·tive** [ɪn'kwɪzətɪv] **adj.** fond of, showing a fondness for, inquiring into other people's affairs.

in·road ['ɪnrəʊd] **n. 1.** sudden attack (*into* a country, etc.). **2.** *make* ~s *on,* (fig.) use up (one's) leisure time, savings, etc.).

in·rush ['ɪnrʌʃ] **n.** rushing in (of water, etc.).

in·sane [ɪn'seɪn] **adj.** mad; foolish. **in·san·i·ty** [ɪn'sænətɪ] **n.** (no pl.) madness; extreme folly.

in·san·i·tary [ɪn'sænɪtərɪ] **adj.** not sanitary: ~ *conditions.*

in·sa·tiable [ɪn'seɪʃjəbl] **adj.** that cannot be satisfied; very greedy.

in·scribe [ɪn'skraɪb] **v.t.** write (words, one's name, etc., *in* or *on*); mark (sth. *with* words, etc.). **in·scrip·tion** [ɪn'skrɪpʃn] **n.** sth. ~d (e.g. words on a coin).

in·scru·table [ɪn'skruːtəbl] **adj.** mysterious; that cannot be known.

in·sect ['ɪnsekt] **n.** sorts of small animal having six legs and no backbone (e.g. ant, fly, wasp); (incorrectly) any similar creeping or flying creature (e.g. a spider). **in·sec·ti·cide** [ɪn-'sektɪsaɪd] **n.** substance for killing ~s.

in·sen·sate [ɪn'senseɪt] **adj.** unfeeling; stupid: ~ *rocks (cruelty).*

in·sen·si·ble [ɪn'sensəbl] **adj. 1.** unconscious (as the result of injury, illness, etc.). **2.** unaware (*of* danger, etc.). **3.** unfeeling; unsympathetic. **4.** (of changes) too small or gradual to be observed. **in·sen·si·bly adv.** without being observed. **in·sen·si·bil·i·ty** [ɪn-ˌsensə'bɪlətɪ] **n.** (no pl.).

in·sen·si·tive [ɪn'sensətɪv] **adj.** not sensitive (*to* touch, light, the feelings of other people).

in·sert [ɪn'sɜːt] **v.t.** put (sth. *in, into, between*): ~ *a key in a lock (an advertisement in a newspaper,* etc.). **in·ser·tion** [ɪn'sɜːʃn] **n. 1.** (no pl.) ~ing. **2.** sth. ~ed (e.g. a piece of lace ~ed in a dress, an advertisement in a newspaper). **3.** (also called *injection*) (aer.) process of putting a spacecraft into a desired orbit.

in·set ['ɪnset] **n.** extra pages inserted in a book, etc.; small diagram, map, etc. within the border of a printed page or larger map.

in·side [ˌɪn'saɪd] **n., adj., adv., & prep. I n. 1.** inner side or surface; part(s) within: ~ *out,* with the inner side out. **2.** part of a road, etc. on the inner side of a curve; part of a pavement or footpath farthest from the roadway. **3.** (colloq.) stomach and bowels. **II. adj.** situated on or in, coming from the inner part or inner edge. **III. adv.** on or in the ~. **IV. prep.** on the inner side of. **in·sid·er n.** person who is in a position of power or has access to confidential information. (Cf. *outsider*.) ~ **left (right) ns.** (football, etc.) inside forward on the left (right) side.

in·sid·i·ous [ɪn'sɪdɪəs] **adj.** doing harm secretly, unseen.

in·sight ['ɪnsaɪt] **n.** power of seeing with the mind (*into* a problem, etc.); deep understanding.

in·sig·nia [ɪn'sɪgnɪə] **n. pl.** symbols *of* office (e.g. a king's crown); (mil.) badges.

in·sin·u·ate [ɪn'sɪnjʊeɪt] **v.t. 1.** make a way for (oneself or sth.) gently and craftily (*into* sth.). **2.** suggest unpleasantly and indirectly (*that*). **in·sin·u·a·tion** [ɪnˌsɪnjʊ'eɪʃn] **n.**

in·sip·id [ɪn'sɪpɪd] **adj.** tasteless; uninteresting; dull.

in·sist [ɪn'sɪst] **v.i. & t. 1.** urge with emphasis, against opposition or disbelief (*on* sth.); declare emphatically: ~ *on one's innocence (that one is innocent).* **2.** declare that a purpose cannot be changed: *He* ~s *on being present.* **in·sis·tent adj.** (esp.) demanding attention: ~*ent requests.* **in·sis·tence n.** (no pl.).

in·so·lent ['ɪnsələnt] **adj.** insulting; offensive; contemptuous. **in·so·lence n.** (no pl.).

in·som·ni·a [ɪn'sɒmnɪə] **n.** (no pl.) inability to sleep.

in·so·much [ˌɪnsəʊ'mʌtʃ] **adv.** to such a degree or extent (*that*).

in·spect [ɪn'spekt] **v.t.** examine carefully; visit officially to see that rules, etc. are obeyed. **in·spec·tion** [ɪn-ˈspekʃn] *n.* **in·spec·tor** *n.* **1.** official who ~s (e.g. schools, factories, mines): ~or of taxes, (Gt. Brit.) official who assesses the income tax to be paid. **2.** (Gt. Brit.) police-officer below a superintendent and above a sergeant.

in·spire [ɪnˈspaɪə*] *v.t.* **1.** put uplifting thoughts, feelings, or aims into: ~ sb. with hope. **2.** fill with creative power: *an ~d poet.* **in·spi·ra·tion** [ˌɪnspəˈreɪʃn] *n.* **1.** (no pl.) influence(s) causing the creation of works of art, music, etc. **2.** person or thing that ~s. **3.** good thought or idea that comes to the mind suddenly.

in·sta·bil·i·ty [ˌɪnstəˈbɪlətɪ] *n.* (no pl.) lack of stability (usu. of character).

in·stall (U.S.A. also **in·stal**) [ɪnˈstɔːl] *v.t.* **1.** place (sb.) in his new position of authority with the usual ceremony. **2.** put (a heating system, telephone, etc.) into a building, ready for use. **3.** settle (oneself) in a place. **in·stal·la·tion** [ˌɪnstəˈleɪʃn] *n.* ceremony of ~ing (1); sth. ~ed (2).

in·stal·ment (U.S.A. also **in·stall·ment**) [ɪnˈstɔːlmənt] *n.* **1.** any one of the parts in which sth. is supplied over a period of time. **2.** any of the parts of a payment spread over a period of time: *paying for a radio by monthly ~s; installment plan* (U.S.A.), hire-purchase.

in·stance [ˈɪnstəns] *n.* **1.** example; fact, etc. supporting a general truth: *in the first ~,* firstly; *for ~,* as an example. **2.** *at the ~ of,* at the request of. *v.t.* give as an ~ (1).

in·stant [ˈɪnstənt] *adj.* **1.** coming or happening at once. **2.** (trade correspondence) of this month: *your letter of the 9th inst(ant).* **3.** (of coffee powder, etc.) quickly and easily made ready for use. **4.** urgent: *in ~ need of help. n.* **1.** point of time; moment. **2.** *this ~,* now; *the ~ (that),* as soon as. **~·ly** *adv.* at once. **in·stan·ta·neous** [ˌɪnstənˈteɪnjəs] *adj.* happening, done, in an ~.

in·stead [ɪnˈsted] *adv.* in place (*of*).

in·step [ˈɪnstep] *n.* upper surface of a foot or shoe between the toes and the ankle.

in·sti·gate [ˈɪnstɪgeɪt] *v.t.* excite and urge (sb. to do sth.); cause (sth.) by doing this: *~ a strike.*

in·stil (U.S.A. also **in·still**) [ɪnˈstɪl] *v.t.* (-*ll*-) introduce (ideas, etc., *into* sb.'s mind) gradually.

in·stinct [ˈɪnstɪŋkt] *n.* natural tendency to behave in a certain way without reasoning. **in·stinc·tive** [ɪnˈstɪŋktɪv] *adj.* based on ~: *an ~ive dread of fire.*

in·sti·tute [ˈɪnstɪtjuːt] *n.* society or organization for a special (usu. social or educational) purpose. *v.t.* establish, get started (an inquiry, rule, custom, etc.). **in·sti·tu·tion** [ˌɪnstɪˈtjuːʃn] *n.* **1.** (no pl.) instituting or being ~d. **2.** long-established law, custom, or practice. **3.** (building of an) organization with a charitable purpose or for social welfare (e.g. an orphanage).

in·struct [ɪnˈstrʌkt] *v.t.* **1.** teach. **2.** give orders to. **in·struc·tion** [ɪnˈstrʌkʃn] *n.* **1.** (no pl.) teaching. **2.** (pl.) orders; directions. **in·struc·tion·al** [ɪnˈstrʌkʃənl] *adj.* educational: *~ional films* (*television*). **in·struc·tive** *adj.* giving knowledge. **in·struc·tor** *n.* person who ~s; teacher.

in·stru·ment [ˈɪnstrʊmənt] *n.* **1.** simple apparatus (1) used in performing an action, esp. for delicate or scientific work: *optical ~s* (e.g. a microscope). (Cf. *tool, utensil.*) **2.** apparatus (1) for producing musical sounds. **3.** person used by another for his own purposes. **in·stru·men·tal** [ˌɪnstrʊˈmentl] *adj.* **1.** (of music) played on ~s. **2.** serving as a means: *~al in (doing) sth.* **in·stru·men·tal·ist** [ˌɪnstrʊˈmentəlɪst] *n.* player of an ~ (2).

in·sub·or·di·nate [ˌɪnsəˈbɔːdɪnət] *adj.* disobedient; reckless. **in·sub·or·di·na·tion** [ˈɪnsəˌbɔːdɪˈneɪʃn] *n.*

in·suf·fer·able [ɪnˈsʌfərəbl] *adj.* over-proud; unbearably conceited.

in·su·lar [ˈɪnsjʊlə*] *adj.* of an island; of or like islanders; narrow-minded. **~·i·ty** [ˌɪnsjʊˈlærətɪ] *n.* (no pl.).

in·su·late [ˈɪnsjʊleɪt] *v.t.* **1.** cover or separate (sth.) with non-conducting material to prevent loss of heat, electricity, etc. **2.** separate (sb. or sth.) *from* surroundings; isolate. **in·su·la·tion** [ˌɪnsjʊˈleɪʃn] *n.* being ~d; act of insulating; insulating material. **in·su·la·tor** *n.* (esp.) substance, device (2), for insulating electric wire.

an insulator

in·sult ['ɪnsʌlt] *n.* sth. said or done intended to hurt, or actually hurting, a person's feelings or dignity. [ɪn'sʌlt] *v.t.* treat (sb.) with ~s.

in·su·per·able [ɪn'sju:pərəbl] *adj.* (of difficulties, etc.) that cannot be overcome.

in·sup·port·able [ˌɪnsə'pɔ:təbl] *adj.* that cannot be endured.

in·sur·ance [ɪn'ʃuərəns] *n.* (no pl.) 1. (undertaking, by a company, society, or the State, to provide) safeguard against loss, provision against sickness, death, etc. in return for regular payments. 2. payment made to or by such a company, etc. ~ **pol·i·cy** *n.* agreement covering ~. **in·sure** [ɪn'ʃuə*] *v.t.* make an agreement about ~: *insure one's house against fire (one's life for £ 30,000). the insured,* the person to whom payment (of a sum of money) will be made.

in·sur·gent [ɪn'sɜ:dʒənt] *adj.* rebellious. *n.* rebel soldier.

in·sur·mount·able [ˌɪnsə'mauntəbl] *adj.* that cannot be climbed or overcome.

in·sur·rec·tion [ˌɪnsə'rekʃn] *n.* rising against the government.

in·tact [ɪn'tækt] *adj.* undamaged; untouched; complete.

in·take ['ɪnteɪk] *n.* 1. place where water, gas, etc. is taken into a pipe, channel, etc. 2. quantity, number, entering (during a given period).

in·tan·gi·ble [ɪn'tændʒəbl] *adj.* (esp.) that cannot be grasped by the mind.

in·te·ger ['ɪntɪdʒə*] *n.* whole number (contrasted with a *fraction*); thing complete in itself. **in·te·gral** ['ɪntɪgrəl] *adj.* 1. necessary for completeness. 2. whole. 3. (math.) of, denoted by, an ~; made up of ~s.

in·te·grate ['ɪntɪgreɪt] *v.t. & i.* 1. make complete; combine (parts) into a whole. 2. join with other social groups, esp. without regard to race, colour, or religion; desegregate: ~ *school districts.* 3. become ~d (2). **in·te·gra·tion** [ˌɪntɪ'greɪʃn] *n.* (no pl.) integrating or being ~d: *the integration of immigrants into the local community (of Negro children into the Southern school system).*

in·teg·ri·ty [ɪn'tegrətɪ] *n.* (no pl.) 1. quality of being honest and upright in character: *commercial ~.* 2. condition of being complete.

in·tel·lect ['ɪntəlekt] *n.* (no pl.) power of the mind to reason (contrasted with *feeling* and *instinct*). **in·tel·lec·tu·al** [ˌɪntə'lektjuəl] *adj.* 1. of the ~. 2.

having or showing good reasoning power: *an ~ual man (face). n.* ~ual person.

in·tel·li·gence [ɪn'telɪdʒəns] *n.* (no pl.) 1. (power of) understanding and learning. 2. news; information. **in·tel·li·gent** *adj.* having, showing, ~. **in·tel·li·gen·tsia** [ɪn,telɪ'dʒentsɪə] *n.* that part of a nation that can be regarded as capable of serious independent thinking.

in·tel·li·gi·ble [ɪn'telɪdʒəbl] *adj.* clear to the mind; easily understood. **in·tel·li·gi·bil·i·ty** [ɪn,telɪdʒə'bɪlətɪ] *n.* (no pl.).

in·tend [ɪn'tend] *v.t.* have in mind as a purpose or plan.

in·tense [ɪn'tens] *adj.* 1. (of qualities) high in degree: ~ *heat.* 2. (of feelings, etc.) strong; violent. ~**ly** *adv.* **in·ten·si·fy** [ɪn'tensɪfaɪ] *v.t. & i.* make, become, ~. **in·ten·si·fi·ca·tion** [ɪn,tensɪfɪ'keɪʃn] *n.* **in·ten·si·ty** [ɪn'tensətɪ] *n.* (no pl.) being ~; strength (of feeling, etc.). **in·ten·sive** *adj.* deep and thorough; concentrated: *intensive study; intensive care,* medical treatment with constant observation of the patient.

in·tent [ɪn'tent] *adj.* 1. (of looks) eager; earnest. 2. (of persons) ~ *on,* with the attention or desires directed towards. *n.* purpose: *shooting with ~ to kill; to all ~s and purposes,* in all essential points.

in·ten·tion [ɪn'tenʃn] *n.* purpose; intending. ~**al** *adj.* said or done on purpose. ~**al·ly** *adv.*

in·ter [ɪn'tɜ:*] *v.t.* (*-rr-*) bury.

in·ter- ['ɪntə*-] *pref.* between; among; one with or on another: *intercontinental; international.*

in·ter·cede [ˌɪntə'si:d] *v.i.* plead (*with* sb. *for* or *on behalf of* sb. else). **in·ter·ces·sion** [ˌɪntə'seʃn] *n.*

in·ter·cept [ˌɪntə'sept] *v.t.* stop, catch, seize (sb. or sth.) between the starting-point and the destination: ~ *a letter.*

in·ter·change [ˌɪntə'tʃeɪndʒ] *v.t.* 1. make an exchange of (views, etc.). 2. put (each of two things) in the other's place. ~**able** *adj.* that can be ~d.

in·ter·com ['ɪntəkɒm] *n.* (colloq.) two-way intercommunication system with microphone and loudspeaker at each station for communication (e.g. between offices in the same building or in aircraft).

in·ter·com·mu·ni·cate [ˌɪntəkə-'mju:nɪkeɪt] *v.i.* communicate with one another. **in·ter·com·mu·ni·ca·tion** ['ɪntəkə,mju:nɪ'keɪʃn] *n.*

in·ter·con·ti·nen·tal [ˈɪntəˌkɒntɪˈnentl] *adj.* **1.** carried on between continents. **2.** capable of travelling between continents: ~ *ballistic missile*.

in·ter·course [ˈɪntəkɔːs] *n.* (no pl.) **1.** social dealings or communication; exchange (of trade, ideas, etc. between persons, societies, nations, etc.). **2.** sexual ~.

in·ter·est [ˈɪntrɪst] *n.* **1.** (no pl.) condition of wanting to know or learn about sth.: *taking a great ~ in sport.* **2.** (no pl.) quality that excites curiosity. **3.** sth. with which one concerns oneself: *His chief ~s are horse-racing and football.* **4.** (no pl.) importance: *a matter of considerable ~.* **5.** (what is to sb.'s) advantage or profit: *look after one's own ~s.* **6.** legal right to a share in sth., esp. in its profits. **7.** (no pl.) money charged or paid for the loan of capital: *a loan at 6 per cent ~.* [ˈɪntərest] *v.t.* cause (sb.) to give his attention to: *Can I ~ you in this question?* **~ed** *adj.* having an ~ (6, 7) in; showing ~ (1); taking an ~ (1) *in.* **~ing** *adj.* holding the attention.

in·ter·fere [ˌɪntəˈfɪə*] *v.i.* **1.** (of persons) ~ *in,* break in upon (other persons' affairs) without right or invitation. **2.** ~ *with,* (a) come into opposition with: *allowing pleasure to ~ with duty;* (b) (of person) meddle with. **in·ter·fer·ence** [ˌɪntəˈfɪərəns] *n.* (no pl.).

in·ter·im [ˈɪntərɪm] *n.* **1.** *in the ~,* meanwhile; between these two events. **2.** (attrib.) as an instalment; for the meantime.

in·te·ri·or [ɪnˈtɪərɪə*] *adj.* **1.** situated inside; of the inside parts. **2.** inland. **3.** domestic (not foreign). *n.* **1.** inside (parts of sth.); (attrib.) ~ *decorator,* workman who decorates the inside of a building or room (with paint or wallpaper). **2.** inland areas. **3.** (department dealing with the) home affairs of a country: *Minister of the I.~; Department of the I.~* (U.S.A.), Home Office.

in·ter·ject [ˌɪntəˈdʒekt] *v.t.* put in suddenly (a remark, etc.) between statements, etc. made by another. **in·ter·jec·tion** *n.* word(s) used as exclamation (e.g. *Oh! Good! Indeed!*).

in·ter·lock [ˌɪntəˈlɒk] *v.t. & i.* lock or join together; clasp firmly together.

in·ter·lop·er [ˈɪntələʊpə*] *n.* person who, esp. for profit, pushes himself in where he has no right.

in·ter·lude [ˈɪntəluːd] *n.* **1.** interval between two events or two periods of time of different character, esp. the interval between two acts of a play. **2.** music played during an interval.

in·ter·me·di·ary [ˌɪntəˈmiːdjərɪ] *n. & adj.* (sb. or sth.) acting between (persons, groups).

in·ter·me·di·ate [ˌɪntəˈmiːdjət] *adj.* situated or coming between (in time, space, degree, etc.): ~ *courses* between elementary and advanced).

in·ter·mi·na·ble [ɪnˈtɜːmɪnəbl] *adj.* endless; tedious because too long.

in·ter·mis·sion [ˌɪntəˈmɪʃn] *n.* pause; interval.

in·ter·mit·tent [ˌɪntəˈmɪtənt] *adj.* with some intervals: ~ *fever,* fever that keeps coming and going.

in·tern[1] [ɪnˈtɜːn] *v.t.* compel (persons, esp. aliens during a war) to live inside certain fixed limits or in a special camp. **~ment** *n.* (no pl.).

in·tern[2], **in·terne** [ˈɪntɜːn] *n.* (U.S.A.) **1.** advanced student or recent graduate in medicine residing in a hospital to gain supervised practical experience. **2.** teacher undergoing practical training.

in·ter·nal [ɪnˈtɜːnl] *adj.* **1.** of or in the inside. ~ *combustion engine,* engine in which motive power is produced by the explosion of gases or vapours inside a cylinder. **2.** of the home or domestic affairs of a country. **3.** derived from within the thing itself: ~ *evidence* (e.g. of when a book was written). **~ly** *adv.*

in·ter·na·tion·al [ˌɪntəˈnæʃənl] *adj.* existing, carried on, between nations.

in·ter·play [ˈɪntəpleɪ] *n.* (no pl.) operation of two things on each other.

in·ter·po·late [ɪnˈtɜːpəʊleɪt] *v.t.* make (usu. misleading) additions to a book, manuscript, etc. **in·ter·po·la·tion** [ɪnˌtɜːpəʊˈleɪʃn] *n.*

in·ter·pose [ˌɪntəˈpəʊz] *v.t. & i.* **1.** put forward (an objection, a veto, etc.) as an interference. **2.** say (sth.) as an interruption. **3.** come in (between others); mediate (*in* a dispute).

in·ter·pret [ɪnˈtɜːprɪt] *v.t. & i.* **1.** show, make clear, the meaning of (either in words or by artistic performance of music, etc.). **2.** consider to be the meaning of. **3.** act as **~er** *n.* person who gives an immediate oral translation of words spoken in another language. **in·ter·pre·ta·tion** [ɪnˌtɜːprɪˈteɪʃn] *n.*

in·ter·ro·gate [ɪnˈterəʊgeɪt] *v.t.* put questions to, esp. closely or formally: ~ *a prisoner.* **in·ter·ro·ga·tion** [ɪn-

ˌterəʊˈgeɪʃn] *n.* interrogating; question: *note* (*mark, point*) *of* interrogation, question mark (?). **in·ter·rog·a·tive** [ˌɪntəˈrɒgətɪv] *adj.* of or for questions.

in·ter·rupt [ˌɪntəˈrʌpt] *v.t. & i.* **1.** break the continuity of: *traffic ~ed by floods.* **2.** speak to sb. while he is saying sth.: *Don't ~* (*me*) *while I'm speaking. a bad habit of ~ing.* **in·ter·rup·tion** *n.* ~ing or being ~ed; sth. that ~s.

in·ter·sect [ˌɪntəˈsekt] *v.t. & i.* **1.** divide by cutting, passing, or lying across. **2.** (of lines) cut or cross each other. **in·ter·sec·tion** *n.* (esp.) point where two lines, etc. ~; place where two roads ~.

in·ter·sperse [ˌɪntəˈspɜːs] *v.t.* place here and there (*between, among*).

in·ter·val [ˈɪntəvl] *n.* **1.** time (between two events or two parts of an action); (esp.) time between two acts of a play, two parts of a concert, etc. **2.** space between (two objects or points): *at ~s,* with ~s between.

in·ter·vene [ˌɪntəˈviːn] *v.i.* **1.** (of circumstances, events) come between (others) in time. **2.** (of persons) interfere so as to prevent sth. or change the result. **3.** (of time) come or be between: *intervening years.* **in·ter·ven·tion** [ˌɪntəˈvenʃn] *n.* intervening (2).

in·ter·view [ˈɪntəvjuː] *n.* meeting with sb. for discussion or conference (e.g. between an employer and an applicant for a post¹ (4), etc.); meeting (of a reporter, etc.) with sb. whose views are requested. *v.t.* conduct an ~ with.

in·tes·tate [ɪnˈtesteɪt] *adj.* not having made a will before death occurs.

in·tes·tine [ɪnˈtestɪn] *n.* (usu. pl.) lower part of the food canal below the stomach.

intestines

in·ti·mate¹ [ˈɪntɪmət] *adj.* **1.** close and familiar: *~ friends*; *on ~ terms.* **2.** innermost; private and personal: *~ details of one's life.* **~·ly** *adv.* **in·ti·ma·cy** [ˈɪntɪməsɪ] *n.* **1.** (no pl.) being ~. **2.** (pl.) ~ actions (e.g. caresses).

in·ti·mate² [ˈɪntɪmeɪt] *v.t.* make known; show clearly: *~ one's approval.* **in·ti·ma·tion** [ˌɪntɪˈmeɪʃn] *n.* (esp.) sth. ~d; suggestion.

in·tim·i·date [ɪnˈtɪmɪdeɪt] *v.t.* frighten, esp. in order to force (sb.) *into* doing sth. **in·tim·i·da·tion** [ɪnˌtɪmɪˈdeɪʃn] *n.* (no pl.).

in·to [ˈɪntʊ, ˈɪntə] *prep.* **1.** (indicating movement towards a point within): *Let us go ~ the garden.* (of a spacecraft, etc.) *ten minutes ~ the flight* (*mission*). **2.** (indicating a change of condition or a result from action): *Water turns ~ ice when it is very cold. He got himself ~ serious trouble.*

in·tol·er·able [ɪnˈtɒlərəbl] *adj.* that cannot be endured: *~ pain* (*insolence*). **in·tol·er·ably** *adv.*

in·tol·er·ant [ɪnˈtɒlərənt] *adj.* not tolerant (*of*). **~·ly** *adv.* **in·tol·er·ance** *n.*

in·tone [ɪnˈtəʊn] *v.t.* recite (a prayer, etc.) in a singing voice; speak with a particular tone. **in·to·na·tion** [ˌɪntəʊˈneɪʃn] *n.* (no pl.) (esp.) the rise and fall of the voice in speaking.

in·tox·i·cate [ɪnˈtɒksɪkeɪt] *v.t.* **1.** make stupid with, cause to lose self-control as the result of taking, alcoholic drink. **2.** excite greatly, beyond self-control: *~d with* (*by*) *success.* **in·tox·i·cant** *adj. & n.* intoxicating (drink). **in·tox·i·ca·tion** [ɪnˌtɒksɪˈkeɪʃn] *n.* (no pl.).

in·tra·mu·ral [ˌɪntrəˈmjʊərəl] *adj.* **1.** within the walls or boundaries (of a town, etc.). **2.** intended for full-time residential students. (Cf. *extramural.*)

in·tran·si·tive [ɪnˈtrænsɪtɪv] *adj.* (gram.) characterized by not having or containing a direct object: *an ~ verb.*

in·trep·id [ɪnˈtrepɪd] *adj.* fearless.

in·tri·cate [ˈɪntrɪkət] *adj.* complicated; puzzling. **in·tri·ca·cy** [ˈɪntrɪkəsɪ] *n.*

in·trigue [ɪnˈtriːg] *n.* secret plotting; plot; (old use) secret love affair. *v.i.* engage in ~: *~ with A against B.*

in·trin·sic [ɪnˈtrɪnsɪk] *adj.* (of value, quality) belonging naturally; existing within, not coming from outside. (Cf. *extrinsic.*)

in·tro·duce [ˌɪntrəˈdjuːs] *v.t.* **1.** bring in or forward: *~ a bill before Parliament.* **2.** bring (sth.) into use or into operation for the first time; cause (sb.) to be acquainted with (sth.). **3.** make (persons) known by name *to* one another, esp. in the usual formal way. **4.** insert (*into*). **in·tro·duc·tion** [ˌɪntrəˈdʌkʃn] *n.* introducing or being ~d; sth. ~d or that ~s; (esp.) explanatory article at or before the beginning of a book. **in·tro·duc·to·ry** [ˌɪntrə-'dʌktərɪ] *adj.* serving to ~ sb. or sth.

in·tro·spec·tion [ˌɪntrəʊ'spekʃn] *n.* (no pl.) examination by oneself of one's thoughts and feelings. **in·tro·spec·tive** *adj.*

in·tro·vert ['ɪntrəʊvɜːt] *adj. & n.*, ~ed [ˌɪntrəʊ'vɜːtɪd] *adj.* unsociable or reserved (person) (opp. *extrovert* (-ed)).

in·trude [ɪn'truːd] *v.t. & i.* force (oneself *into* a place, *on* or *upon* sb.); enter without invitation. **in·tru·der** *n.* **in·tru·sion** [ɪn'truːʒn] *n.*

in·tu·ition [ˌɪntjuː'ɪʃn] *n.* (power of) immediate understanding of sth. without reasoning. **in·tu·itive** [ɪn'tjuːɪtɪv] *adj.* of, possessing, perceiving by, ~.

in·un·date ['ɪnʌndeɪt] *v.t.* flood: ~d *fields*; (fig.) overwhelmed: ~d *with requests*. **in·un·da·tion** [ˌɪnʌn'deɪʃn] *n.*

in·ure [ɪ'njʊə*] *v.t.* accustom (sb. *to* sth.).

in·vade [ɪn'veɪd] *v.t.* 1. enter (a country) with armed forces in order to attack; swarm into. 2. (fig., of feelings, diseases, etc.) attack. 3. violate, interfere with: ~ *sb.'s rights.* **in·vad·er** *n.* **in·va·sion** [ɪn'veɪʒn] *n.*

in·va·lid¹ ['ɪnvəlɪd] *n. & adj.* (person who is) weak or disabled through illness or injury; suitable for such a person: *an* ~ *chair (diet).* ['ɪnvəliːd] *v.t.* (esp. of a member of the armed forces) remove from active service as an ~; send *home*, etc. as an ~: *He was* ~*ed home.*

in·val·id² [ɪn'vælɪd] *adj.* not valid.

in·val·u·a·ble [ɪn'væljʊəbl] *adj.* having a value too great to be measured.

in·va·sion, see *invade.*

in·vec·tive [ɪn'vektɪv] *n.* abusive language.

in·veigh [ɪn'veɪ] *v.i.* ~ *against,* attack violently in words.

in·vei·gle [ɪn'veɪgl] *v.t.* lure (sb. *into* a place, *into doing* sth.) by using flattery, etc.

in·vent [ɪn'vent] *v.t.* 1. create or design (sth. not existing before). 2. make up (a story, excuse, etc.). **in·ven·tion** [ɪn'venʃn] *n.* ~ing; capacity to ~; sth. ~ed. **in·ven·tive** *adj.* able to ~: *an* ~*ive mind.* **in·ven·tor** *n.*

in·ven·to·ry ['ɪnvəntrɪ] *n.* detailed list (of household goods, stocks, etc.).

in·verse [ˌɪn'vɜːs] *adj.* inverted: *in* ~ *proportion (ratio),* that between two quantities one of which decreases in the same proportion that the other increases.

in·vert [ɪn'vɜːt] *v.t.* put upside down or in the opposite order, position, o relation: ~*ed commas* (Gt. Brit.) quotation marks (" " or ' '). **in·ver·sion** [ɪn'vɜːʃn] *n.* ~ing or being ~ed sth. ~ed.

in·vest [ɪn'vest] *v.t. & i.* 1. put (mone) *in* a business, *in* stocks and shares etc.). 2. ~ *in,* (colloq.) buy (sth. considered useful). 3. clothe (sb. *in* o *with*); clothe, endow (*with* insignia o office, rank, authority, qualities, etc.) 4. surround (e.g. a town) with armed forces. **in·ves·ti·ture** [ɪn'vestɪtʃə*] *n* ceremony of ~ing (3) sb. with a rank etc. ~·ment *n.* ~ing of money; sum of money ~ed; business undertaking etc. in which money is ~ed: *a good* (*bad*) ~*ment.* ~·or *n.* person who ~ money.

in·ves·ti·gate [ɪn'vestɪgeɪt] *v.t.* examine; inquire into: ~ *a crime (the cause of an accident).* **in·ves·ti·ga·tion** [ɪn-ˌvestɪ'geɪʃn] *n.*

in·vet·er·ate [ɪn'vetərət] *adj.* (esp. o habits, prejudices) deep-rooted; long-established.

in·vid·i·ous [ɪn'vɪdɪəs] *adj.* likely t cause ill feeling (because of real o apparent injustice): ~ *distinctions.*

in·vig·o·rate [ɪn'vɪgəreɪt] *v.t.* make vigorous; make strong or confident.

in·vin·ci·ble [ɪn'vɪnsəbl] *adj.* too strong to be overcome or conquered

in·vi·o·la·ble [ɪn'vaɪələbl] *adj.* not to be disturbed, disobeyed, or treated disrespectfully: *an* ~ *law (oath).*

in·vi·o·late [ɪn'vaɪələt] *adj.* unbroken untouched; held in respect: *keep an oath (a rule)* ~; *remain* ~.

in·vite [ɪn'vaɪt] *v.t.* 1. ask (sb. to accept hospitality, do sth., come somewhere, etc.). 2. ask for (suggestions etc.). 3. encourage; attract. **in·vit·ing** *adj.* attractive. **in·vi·ta·tion** [ˌɪnvɪ-'teɪʃn] *n.* inviting or being ~ed; request to come or go somewhere, do sth.

in·vo·ca·tion, see *invoke.*

in·voice ['ɪnvɔɪs] *v.t. & n.* (make a) list of goods sold with the price(s) charged: ~ *sb. for sth.*

in·voke [ɪn'vəʊk] *v.t.* 1. call upon (God, the power of the law, etc.) for help or protection. 2. request earnestly. 3. summon (by magic). **in·vo·ca·tion** [ˌɪnvəʊ'keɪʃn] *n.* (prayer used for) invoking.

in·vol·un·ta·ry [ɪn'vɒləntərɪ] *adj.* done without intention; done unconsciously.

in·volve [ɪn'vɒlv] *v.t.* 1. cause (sb. or sth.) to be caught or mixed up (*in* trouble, etc.); get (sb. or sth.) into a complicated or difficult condition: ~d in debt (crime). **2.** have as a necessary consequence: plans that ~ further expenditure. **~d** adj. complicated in thought or form: an ~d sentence.

in·ward ['ɪnwəd] adj. **1.** situated within; inner. **2.** turned towards the inside. **~·ly** adv. (esp.) in mind or spirit. **~(s)** adv. towards the inside; into or towards the mind or soul.

io·dine ['aɪəʊdiːn] n. (no pl.) chemical substance used as an antiseptic and in dyeing and photography.

ion ['aɪən] n. electrically charged particle formed when a neutral atom loses or gains one or more electrons.

io·ta [aɪ'əʊtə] n. Greek letter i: not an ~ of truth, no truth at all.

IOU [,aɪəʊ'juː] n. (= I owe you) signed paper acknowledging that one owes the sum of money stated.

-iour (U.S.A. **-ior**) [-jə*] suff. (forming ns.): saviour.

-ious [-ɪəs, -əs] suff. (forming adjs.) characterized by; full of: curious; envious; religious; spacious.

ir- [ɪ-] pref. not: ir'ra·tio·nal, ir-'reg·u·lar, ir,reg·u'lar·i·ty, ir'rel·e·vant, ir'rel·e·vance, ir're·le·van·cy, ir'rep·ar·able, ,ir·re'place·able, ir-'res·o·lute, ir'rev·er·ent, ir're·vo·cable, etc.

iras·ci·ble [ɪ'ræsəbl] adj. easily made angry.

irate [aɪ'reɪt] adj. angry. **ire** ['aɪə*] n. (no pl.) (rhet. or poet.) anger.

iris ['aɪərɪs] n. **1.** coloured part round the pupil of the eye. **2.** flowering plant with sword-shaped leaves.

an iris (2)

Irish ['aɪərɪʃ] adj. of Ireland. n. the language of Ireland. the ~, (pl.) natives or inhabitants of Ireland or their descendants.

irk [ɜːk] v.t. trouble; annoy: It ~s me to ... **~·some** adj. tiresome.

iron ['aɪən] n. **1.** (no pl.) commonest and most important metal, from which steel is made. strike while the ~ is hot, act while circumstances are favourable; rule with an ~ hand (a rod of ~), rule with great severity; a man of ~, an unfeeling, merciless man. **2.** tool, etc. made of ~, esp. tool heated and used for smoothing clothes, etc. (also

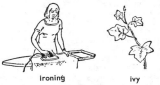

ironing   ivy

called flat-~). too many ~s in the fire, too many plans, etc. needing attention at the same time. **3.** (pl.) ~ chains for a prisoner's hands or feet: put a man in ~s. v.t. smooth (clothes, etc.) with an ~ (a flat-~). **'~·mon·ger** n. (Gt. Brit.) dealer in goods made of metal. **'~·mon·gery** n. (no pl.) (Gt. Brit.) business of an ~monger; his goods. **'~-mould** n. spot caused by ~-rust or ink.

iro·ny ['aɪərənɪ] n. **1.** (no pl.) expression of one's meaning by saying sth. that is the direct opposite of one's thoughts, in order to make one's remarks forceful. **2.** event, situation, that is itself desirable, but that, because of the circumstances, is of no value: the ~ of fate; one of life's ironies. **iron·i·cal** [aɪ'rɒnɪkl] adj. of, using, showing, ~.

ir·re·proach·able [,ɪrɪ'prəʊtʃəbl] adj. free from blame.

ir·re·sis·ti·ble [,ɪrɪ'zɪstəbl] adj. that cannot be resisted; very attractive.

ir·re·spec·tive [,ɪrɪ'spektɪv] adj. ~ of, not paying consideration to.

ir·re·spon·si·ble [,ɪrɪ'spɒnsəbl] adj. **1.** (esp. of behaviour) done without proper care. **2.** not responsible; not to be blamed.

ir·ri·gate ['ɪrɪgeɪt] v.t. **1.** supply (land, crops) with water (by means of rivers, water-channels, etc.). **2.** construct reservoirs, canals, ditches, etc. for distribution of water (for crops). **ir·ri·ga·tion** [,ɪrɪ'geɪʃn] n. (no pl.).

ir·ri·tate ['ɪrɪteɪt] v.t. **1.** make angry or annoyed. **2.** cause discomfort to (part of the body); make sore or inflamed. **ir·ri·table** ['ɪrɪtəbl] adj. easily ~d. **ir·ri·tant** ['ɪrɪtənt] n. & adj. (thing) causing **ir·ri·ta·tion** [,ɪrɪ-'teɪʃn] n.

is, see be.

-ish [-ɪʃ] *suff.* (forming adjs.) **1.** of nationality: *British*; *Spanish*. **2.** of the nature of; like: *childish*; *foolish*. **3.** somewhat; near to: *greenish*; *oldish*.

Is·lam ['ɪzlɑ:m] *n.* (no pl.) faith, religion, taught by the prophet Muhammad; all Muslims; all the Muslim world. **~·ic** [ɪz'læmɪk] *adj.*

is·land ['aɪlənd] *n.* piece of land surrounded by water; thing considered to be like an ~ because it is surrounded by sth. different: *a traffic* ~. **~·er** *n.* person born on or living on an ~.

isle [aɪl] *n.* (poet. except in proper names) island.

-ism [-ɪzəm] *suff.* (forming abstract ns.) **1.** from vs. in *-ize*: *baptism*; *criticism*. **2.** quality, state, characteristic: *barbarism*; *heroism*; *realism*. **3.** peculiarity in language: *Americanism*. **4.** system or doctrine: *communism*; *socialism*; *conservatism*.

i·so·bar ['aɪsəʊbɑ:*] *n.* line on a map joining places with the same atmospheric pressure at a particular time.

i·so·late ['aɪsəleɪt] *v.t.* separate, put or keep away, from others. **i·so·la·tion** [,aɪsə'leɪʃn] *n.* (no pl.).

Is·rae·li [ɪz'reɪlɪ] *n. & adj.* (native or inhabitant) of Israel.

is·sue ['ɪʃu:] *v.i. & t.* **1.** come, go, flow, out: *smoke issuing from chimneys*. **2.** give or send out; publish (journals, etc.); distribute: ~ *commands* (*banknotes, stamps, orders*). *n.* **1.** outgoing: *the point of* ~. **2.** result, outcome, or consequence: *a problem with important* ~s. **3.** question that arises for discussion: *debating an* ~; *the point* (*matter*) *at* ~, the point being discussed; *join* (*take*) ~ *with sb.* (*on* sth.), proceed to argue with him (about it). **4.** publication, edition (of newspapers, etc.); sending out (*of* new coins, postage stamps, etc.); that which is sent out, etc.: *new* ~s *of banknotes*. **5.** (no pl.) (law) offspring: *die without* ~ (i.e. childless).

-ist [-ɪst] *suff.* (forming ns.) **1.** from verbs in *-ize*: *antagonist*; *dramatist*. **2.** follower of a creed, etc. in *-ism*: *atheist*; *nonconformist*. **3.** person concerned with any subject: *motorist*; *tobacconist*; *violinist*.

isth·mus ['ɪsməs] *n.* neck of land joining two larger bodies of land.

it [ɪt] *pron.* (pl. *they, them*) **1.** (used in referring to lifeless things, animals, infants): *Where's my book? Have you seen it?* **2.** (used to refer to a phrase or clause that follows): *Is it difficult to learn Chinese?* **3.** (used as a subject for the verb *be*, etc. balancing the complement): *It's raining. It's six o'clock. It's a cold day.* **4.** (used to emphasize one part of a sentence): *It was John I gave the book to, not Harry*. **its** *poss. pron.* of it: *The dog wagged its tail*. **it·self** [ɪt'self] *pron.* **1.** refl. form: *The dog got up and stretched itself*. **2.** *by itself*, (a) automatically; (b) apart from its surroundings; alone. *in itself* (see *in*[1] (18)).

Ital·ian [ɪ'tæljən] *n. & adj.* (native, inhabitant, or language) of Italy.

ital·ic [ɪ'tælɪk] *adj.* (of letters) sloping: *This is* ~ *type.* ~s *n. pl.* ~ *letters*. **ital·i·cize** [ɪ'tælɪsaɪz] *v.t.* print in ~s.

itch [ɪtʃ] *v.i. & n.* **1.** (have a) feeling of irritation on the skin, causing one to want to scratch. **2.** (have a) restless longing (*for* sth., *to do* sth.). ~**y** *adj.* (*-ier, -iest*).

item ['aɪtəm] *n.* **1.** single article or unit in a list, etc. **2.** detail or paragraph (of news). ~**ize** ['aɪtəmaɪz] *v.t.* give, write, every ~ of: *an* ~*ized account*.

itin·er·ant [ɪ'tɪnərənt] *adj.* going from place to place: ~ *musicians*.

itin·er·ary [aɪ'tɪnərərɪ] *n.* (plan for, details or records of, a) journey; route.

-i·tion [-ɪʃn] *suff.* (forming ns.): *position*; *recognition*.

-i·tious [-ɪʃəs] *suff.* (forming adjs.) of, relating to, having the characteristics of: *ambitious*.

-i·tis [-aɪtɪs] *suff.* (forming ns., esp. names of inflammatory diseases): *appendicitis*; *bronchitis*.

-i·tive [-ətɪv] *suff.* (forming adjs.): *positive*; *transitive*.

its, it·self, see *it*.

-ity [-ətɪ] *suff.* (forming ns.) **1.** denoting quality or condition: *authority*; *humility*. **2.** denoting instance or degree of this: *monstrosity*; *humidity*.

-ive [-ɪv] *suff.* **1.** (forming adjs.) tending to, having a quality of: *active*; *constructive*. **2.** (forming ns.): *adjective*.

ivo·ry ['aɪvərɪ] *n.* (no pl.) white, bone-like substance forming the tusks of elephants, etc., used for ornaments, piano-keys, etc.

ivy ['aɪvɪ] *n.* (no pl.) climbing, clinging, evergreen plant with dark, shiny (often five-pointed) leaves. (See the picture at *iron*.)

-ize [-aɪz] *suff.* (forming vs.) **1.** make like; change into: *dramatize*; *harmonize*; *legalize*. **2.** act with the qualities of: *criticize*.

J

jab [dʒæb] *v.t.* (*-bb-*) force (a pointed weapon, the elbow, etc.) suddenly and roughly (*into* sb. or sth.); aim a blow (*at* sb. or sth.). *n.* blow of this sort.

jab·ber ['dʒæbə*] *v.i. & t.* talk excitedly; utter (words, sounds) fast and indistinctly. *n.* (no pl.) chatter; rapid, confused talk.

a jack (1)

jack [dʒæk] *n.* **1.** device (2) for raising heavy objects (e.g. cars, engines) off the ground, in order to remove wheels, etc. **2.** ship's flag to show nationality, esp. *the Union J~* (of the United Kingdom). *v.t.* ~ (*up*) raise with a ~ (1). **~·ass** ['dʒækæs] *n.* male ass; foolish person. **'~-knife** *n.* large clasp-knife for the pocket. ~ **of all trades** *n.* person knowing something of many trades. **'~·pot** *n.* hit the ~*pot*, be very lucky. **jack·al** ['dʒækɔːl] *n.* wild, dog-like animal.

jack·et ['dʒækɪt] *n.* **1.** short, sleeved coat. **2.** outer covering round a boiler, pipe, etc. **3.** skin (of a potato), etc.: *potatoes cooked in their ~s.* **4.** (also *dust-~*) loose paper wrapper to protect a book.

jade [dʒeɪd] *n.* (no pl.) hard, usu. green, stone, carved into ornaments. **jad·ed** ['dʒeɪdɪd] *adj.* tired out; wearied by excess: *a ~ appetite.*

jag [dʒæg] *n.* sharp, rough point of rock. **~·ged** ['dʒægɪd] *adj.* with rough, uneven edges: *~ged rocks.*

jag·uar ['dʒægjuə*] *n.* large, fierce, spotted, cat-like animal, of Central and S. America.

jail [dʒeɪl] *n.* (chiefly U.S.A.) = gaol.

jam[1] [dʒæm] *v.t. & i.* (*-mm-*) **1.** crush, be crushed, between two surfaces or things: *a ship ~med in the ice; logs that ~ in a river* (i.e. become tightly packed). **2.** (of parts of a machine, etc.) (cause to) become fixed so that movement or action is prevented: *~ on the brakes of a car. The brakes ~med.* **3.** push (things) together (into a mass or into sth.): *~ clothes into a drawer; a corridor ~med by people.* **4.** ~ *a broadcast*, interfere with the reception of a broadcast from another station. *n.* **1.** number of things or people crowded together so that movement is difficult: *a traffic ~.* **2.** (colloq.) awkward position; dilemma: *be in a ~.*

jam[2] [dʒæm] *n.* fruit boiled with sugar and preserved in jars, etc.

jamb [dʒæm] *n.* side post of a doorway or window.

jam·bo·ree [ˌdʒæmbə'riː] *n.* merry meeting; rally, esp. of Scouts.

jan·gle ['dʒæŋgl] *v.i. & t. & n.* (no pl.) (give out, cause to give out a) harsh, metallic noise.

jan·i·tor ['dʒænɪtə*] *n.* doorkeeper; caretaker of a building.

Jan·u·ary ['dʒænjuərɪ] *n.* first month of the year.

Jap·a·nese [ˌdʒæpə'niːz] *n.* (pl. ~) *& adj.* (native, inhabitant, or language) of Japan.

jar[1] [dʒɑː*] *v.i. & t.* (*-rr-*) **1.** strike (*on* or *against* sth.) with a harsh, unpleasant sound. **2.** have an unpleasant effect (*on* sb., his ears or nerves): *sounds that ~ on the ear.* **3.** ~ *with*, be out of harmony with: *a ~ring note. n.* **1.** ~*ring* sound. **2.** bodily or mental shock. **3.** disagreement or quarrel.

jar[2] [dʒɑː*] *n.* tall vessel, usu. round, with a wide mouth, of glass, stone, or earthenware; its contents.

a jam jar   a javelin

jar·gon ['dʒɑːgən] *n.* **1.** language difficult to understand, because it is either a bad form or spoken badly. **2.** language full of technical or special words: *the ~ of radio technicians.*

jas·min(e) ['dʒæsmɪn] *n.* (kinds of) shrub with sweet-smelling, white or yellow flowers.

jaun·dice ['dʒɔːndɪs] *n.* (no pl.) disease, caused by stoppage of bile, marked by yellow skin; (fig.) mental outlook marked by spite, envy, and jealousy. **~d** *adj.* jealous and spiteful.

jaunt [dʒɔːnt] *v.i. & n.* (take a) short journey for pleasure.

jaun·ty ['dʒɔːntɪ] *adj.* (-ier, -iest) feeling or showing self-confidence and self-satisfaction. **jaun·ti·ly** *adv.* **jaun·ti·ness** *n.* (no pl.).

jave·lin ['dʒævlɪn] *n.* light spear thrown by hand: *throwing the ~, ~ throw* (in athletic contests). (See the picture at *jar*.)

jaw [dʒɔː] *n.* **1.** *lower (upper)* ~, one or other of the bone structures containing the teeth. **2.** (pl.) the mouth, its bones and teeth; mouth of a valley, etc.; (esp.) entrance to a dangerous place. **3.** gripping part (e.g. of a vice²). **4.** (colloq.) talkativeness: *hold your ~,* stop talking. **5.** tedious moral lecture. *v.i. & t.* (sl.) talk, esp. at tedious length; rebuke (sb.). [bird.]

jay [dʒeɪ] *n.* noisy, bright-coloured

jazz [dʒæz] *n.* (no pl.) rhythmical music and dancing of American Negro origin. *adj.* (also ~y) (e.g. of patterns) of strongly contrasted colours and shapes; flashy; showy. *v.i. & t.* play or dance ~; arrange as ~.

jeal·ous ['dʒeləs] *adj.* **1.** feeling or showing fear or ill will because of possible or actual loss of rights or love: *a ~ husband*; *~ looks.* **2.** feeling or showing unhappiness because of the better fortune, etc. of others: *~ of sb. else's success.* **3.** taking watchful care *(of* one's reputation, etc.). **~ly** *adv.* **jeal·ou·sy** *n.* being ~; instance of this.

jean [dʒiːn] *n.* (no pl.) strong cotton cloth. **~s** *n. pl.* workman's overalls; tight-fitting informal trousers.

jeer [dʒɪə*] *v.i. & t.* ~ *(at sb.),* mock, laugh rudely (at sb.). *n.* ~ing remark.

jel·ly ['dʒelɪ] *n.* soft, semi-transparent food substance made from gelatin; similar substance made with fruit juice. *v.t. & i.* (cause to) become like ~. **'~·fish** *n.* ~-like sea animal. **jel·lied** *adj.* set in ~; like ~: *jellied eels.*

jem·my ['dʒemɪ] *n.* (U.S.A. *jimmy*) short iron bar used (by burglars) for forcing windows, doors, drawers, etc open.

a jellyfish

jeop·ar·dy ['dʒepədɪ] *n.* (no pl.) *in ~,* in danger. **jeop·ar·dize** ['dʒepədaɪz] *v.t.* put in danger.

jerk [dʒɜːk] *v.t. & i. & n.* **1.** (give a sudden pull or twist: *The train stopped with a ~ (~ed to a stop). The old bus ~ed along.* **2.** (give a) sudden twitch of the muscles. **3.** *physical ~s,* physical exercises. **~y** *adj.* (-ier, -iest) with sudden stops and starts. **~i·ly** *adv.*

jer·kin ['dʒɜːkɪn] *n.* short, sleeveless close-fitting jacket, usu. of leather.

jer·ry-built ['dʒerɪbɪlt] *adj.* (of buildings) badly made of bad materials.

jer·sey ['dʒɜːzɪ] *n.* close-fitting, knitted woollen garment with sleeves.

a jersey

jest [dʒest] *n.* sth. said or done to cause amusement; joke: *in ~,* not in earnest. *v.i.* make ~s; act or speak lightly. **~·er** *n.* (esp.) man kept in former times by a king or noble to provide amusement by his ~s. **~·ing·ly** *adv.*

jet¹ [dʒet] *n.* **1.** strong stream of gas, liquid, steam, or flame, forced out of a small opening: *~ aircraft (engined plane),* one driven forward by ~s of gas directed backwards from it. **2.** (colloq.) ~ engine or plane: *~ set,* wealthy social set² (3) that gathers in fashionable places in many parts of the world, often travelling by ~ planes.

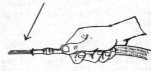

a jet¹ (1)

3. narrow opening from which a ~ comes out. *v.i. & t.* (*-tt-*) **1.** come, send out, in a ~ or ~s. **2.** (colloq.) travel by ~ plane.

jet² [dʒet] *n.* (no pl.) hard, black mineral taking a brilliant polish and used for buttons, ornaments, etc. *adj.* black.

jet·sam ['dʒetsəm] *n.* (no pl.) goods thrown overboard from a ship at sea to lighten it (e.g. in a storm); such goods washed to the sea-shore. (Cf. *flotsam.*)

jet·ti·son ['dʒetɪsn] *v.t.* throw (goods) overboard in order to lighten a ship (e.g. during a storm).

jet·ty ['dʒetɪ] *n.* structure built as a breakwater or as a landing-place for boats or ships.

Jew [dʒuː] *n.* person of the Hebrew race; person whose religion is Judaism. **~·ess** ['dʒuːɪs] *n.* female ~. **~·ish** ['dʒuːɪʃ] *adj.* of the ~s.

jew·el ['dʒuːəl] *n.* **1.** precious stone (e.g. a diamond or ruby); ornament with ~s set in it. **2.** sth. or sb. highly valued. *v.t.* (*-ll-*, U.S.A. also *-l-*) adorn with ~s. **~·ler**, (U.S.A.) **~·er** *n.* trader in ~s; person who sets ~s. **~·ry**, **~·lery** ['dʒuːəlrɪ] *n.* (no pl.) ~s.

jib¹ [dʒɪb] *n.* small, triangular sail.

jib² [dʒɪb] *v.i.* (*-bb-*) **1.** (of a horse, etc.) stop suddenly; refuse to go forward; (fig.) refuse to proceed with sth. **2.** ~ *at*, show unwillingness or dislike: *He ~bed at working overtime.*

jibe, see *gibe.*

jif·fy ['dʒɪfɪ] *n.* (colloq.) *in a ~*, in a moment; very soon.

jig [dʒɪg] *n.* (music for a) quick, lively dance. *v.i. & t.* (*-gg-*) dance a ~; move up and down in a quick, jerky way. **'~·saw** *n.* machine fretsaw. **'~·saw (·puz·zle)** *n.* picture, map, etc. pasted on thin board and cut in irregularly shaped pieces which are to be fitted together again.

jilt [dʒɪlt] *v.t.* (usu. of a woman) give up, send away, a lover after giving him encouragement or a promise to marry. *n.* woman who does this.

jim·my ['dʒɪmɪ] see *jemmy.*

jin·gle ['dʒɪŋgl] *v.i. & t. & n.* (make a) light, ringing sound (as of coins or keys striking together, or small bells); succession of words having similar sounds.

jinks [dʒɪŋks] *n. pl.* high ~, noisy merry-making; uncontrolled fun.

jit·ters ['dʒɪtəz] *n. pl.* (colloq.) extreme nervousness. **jit·tery** *adj.* nervous; jumpy.

job [dʒɒb] *n.* **1.** complete(d) piece of work: *make a good ~ of it*, do it well; *odd ~s*, bits of work not connected with each other. **2.** *That's a good (bad) ~*, that is (un)fortunate. **3.** regular employment: *out of a ~*, unemployed; *looking for a ~. v.t. & i.* (*-bb-*) **1.** do odd ~s (usu. present participle): *a ~bing gardener* (not working for one employer only). **2.** do business for others (as a broker on the Stock Exchange, in markets, etc.).

jock·ey ['dʒɒkɪ] *n.* person (esp. a professional) who rides horses in races. *v.t. & i.* trick (sb.) (*out of* sth., *into* doing sth.).

jo·cose [dʒəʊ'kəʊs] *adj.* humorous; playful. **~·ly** *adv.*

joc·u·lar ['dʒɒkjʊlə*] *adj.* humorous; given to joking. **~·i·ty** [,dʒɒkjʊ'lærətɪ] *n.* **~·ly** *adv.*

jo·cund ['dʒɒkənd] *adj.* merry; cheerful.

jog [dʒɒg] *v.t. & i.* (*-gg-*) *& n.* **1.** (give a) slight knock or push: ~ *sb.'s elbow*; ~ *sb.'s memory*, (fig.) cause him to remember sth. **2.** (run, move, at a) pace causing an unsteady, shaking motion: *The old bus ~ged us up and down. We ~ged along the bad roads.* **3.** ~ *on* (*along*), (fig.) make slow, uneventful progress. **'~·trot** *n.* slow, regular trot.

join [dʒɔɪn] *v.t. & i.* **1.** put or come together; unite or be united; connect (two points, things) with a line, rope, bridge, etc. **2.** become a member of (a society, the armed forces, etc.). **3.** come into the company of; associate with (sb. *in* sth.): *I'll soon ~ you. Will you ~ us in a game of cards?* *n.* point (1).

join·er ['dʒɔɪnə*] *n.* skilled workman who makes furniture, house fittings, and other woodwork, lighter than a carpenter's. **~·y** *n.* (no pl.) work of a ~.

joint [dʒɔɪnt] *n.* **1.** place at which two things are joined. **2.** structure by which two things (e.g. two pipes, two bones) are joined: *finger-~s.* **3.** limb or other division of a sheep, ox, etc. that a butcher serves to his customers. **4.** (sl.) shabby or disreputable place of meeting. **5.** (sl.) marijuana cigarette. *adj.* held or done by, belonging to,

finger-joints

a joint of meat

two or more persons together: ~ *ownership*; ~ *stock*, capital² (3) contributed by a number of persons. *v.t.* **1.** fit together by means of ~s (2): *a ~ed fishing-rod.* **2.** divide at a ~ (2) or into ~s (3).

joist [dʒɔɪst] *n.* one of the parallel pieces of timber (from wall to wall) to which floor boards are nailed.

joists

joke [dʒəʊk] *n.* sth. said or done to cause amusement; circumstance that causes amusement: *practical ~*, trick played on sb. to make him seem ridiculous. *It's no ~*, it's a serious matter. *v.i.* make ~s. **jok·er** *n.* **jok·ing·ly** *adv.*

jol·ly [dʒɒlɪ] *adj.* (-*ier*, -*iest*) **1.** joyful; gay; merry. **2.** (colloq.) delightful. *adv.* (colloq.) very. **jol·li·fi·ca·tion** [ˌdʒɒlɪfɪ'keɪʃn] *n.* merry-making; festivity. **jol·li·ty** *n.* (no pl.) ~ condition; fun.

jolt [dʒəʊlt] *v.t. & i. & n.* **1.** (give sb. or sth. a) jerk or sudden shake. **2.** (of a cart, etc.) move with ~s: *The old bus ~ed along (~ed its passengers badly).*

jos·tle [dʒɒsl] *v.t. & i.* push roughly (against); hustle; push (sb. *away* or *from*).

jot¹ [dʒɒt] *v.t.* (-*tt*-) ~ *sth. down*, make a quick written note of it. **~·tings** *n. pl.* brief notes ~ted down.

jot² [dʒɒt] *n.* very small amount: *not a ~*, not a bit; not at all.

joule [dʒuːl] *n.* unit of energy or work.

jour·nal ['dʒɜːnl] *n.* **1.** daily newspaper; other periodical. **2.** daily record of news, events, business accounts, etc. **~·ese** [ˌdʒɜːnə'liːz] *n.* (no pl.) style of English composition common in second-rate ~s. **~·ism** ['dʒɜːnəlɪzəm] *n.* (no pl.) work of writing for, editing, or publishing, newspapers. **~·ist** *n.* person engaged in ~ism.

jour·ney ['dʒɜːnɪ] *n.* (distance travelled in) going to a place, esp. a distant place (usu. by land; cf. *voyage*): *a three days' ~*; *go on (make) a ~ (from ... to ...). v.i.* make a ~. **·man** ['dʒɜːnɪmən] *n.* workman who has learned a trade and works for a master (contrasted with an *apprentice*).

joust [dʒaʊst] *v.i. & n.* (engage in a fight on horseback with lances (as between knights in the Middle Ages).

jo·vial ['dʒəʊvjəl] *adj.* full of fun and good humour. **~·ly** *adv.* **jo·vi·al·i·ty** [ˌdʒəʊvɪ'æləti] *n.*

jowl [dʒaʊl] *n.* jaw; lower part of the face. *cheek by ~*, close together.

joy [dʒɔɪ] *n.* (sth. that gives) deep pleasure. **~·ful** *adj.* filled with, showing, causing. **~·ful·ly** *adv.* **~·less** *adj.* sad. **~·less·ly** *adv.* **~·ous** ['dʒɔɪəs] *adj.* full of ~.

ju·bi·lant ['dʒuːbɪlənt] *adj.* triumphant; showing joy. **ju·bi·la·tion** [ˌdʒuːbɪ'leɪʃn] *n.*

ju·bi·lee ['dʒuːbɪliː] *n.* (celebration of an) anniversary of some event: *silver ~*, 25th, *golden ~*, 50th, *diamond ~*, 60th anniversary.

Ju·da·ism ['dʒuːdeɪɪzəm] *n.* (no pl.) religion of the Jews.

judge [dʒʌdʒ] *n.* **1.** public officer with authority to hear and decide cases¹ (3) in a court of justice. **2.** person who decides a contest, competition, dispute, etc. **3.** person qualified and able to give opinions on merits or values: *a good ~ of horses. v.t. & i.* **1.** act as a ~ (1) in a court of justice; state what punishment is to be given. **2.** give a decision (in a competition, etc.). **3.** estimate; consider; form an opinion about: *~ it better to postpone a meeting*; *~ a man by his actions.* **judg(e)·ment** ['dʒʌdʒmənt] *n.* **1.** judging or being ~d; decision of a ~ (1) or court. **2.** power, ability, to ~ (2, 3); good sense: *a man of ~ment.* **3.** misfortune considered as a punishment by God. **4.** *J~ment Day*, day of ~ment, day when God will ~ all men.

ju·di·ca·ture ['dʒuːdɪkətʃə*] *n.* administration of justice; body (5) of judges.

ju·di·cial [dʒuː'dɪʃl] *adj.* **1.** of or by a court of justice or a judge. **2.** critical; impartial.

ju·di·cious [dʒuː'dɪʃəs] *adj.* showing or having good sense; prudent. **~·ly** *adv.* **~·ness** *n.* (no pl.).

ju·do ['dʒuːdəʊ] *n.* (no pl.) Japanese style of wrestling and self-defence; refined form of ju-jitsu. **~·ka** ['dʒuːdəʊkɑː] *n.* (pl. ~) student of or expert in ~.

jug [dʒʌg] *n.* deep vessel for liquids, with a handle and lip; its contents: *a ~ of milk.*

jug·ger·naut ['dʒʌgənɔːt] *n.* (fig.) cause or belief to which persons are sacrificed or to which they sacrifice themselves: *the ~ of war.*

a jug

jug·gle ['dʒʌgl] *v.i. & t.* **1.** perform (*with* objects, e.g. by throwing many balls up into the air and catching them). **2.** play tricks (*with* objects, facts, figures, etc.) in order to deceive. **3.** play tricks with; deceive. **~r** *n.*

jug·u·lar ['dʒʌgjʊlə*] *adj.* ~ *veins*, those in the neck returning blood from the head to the heart.

juice [dʒuːs] *n.* liquid part of fruits, vegetables, meat; fluid in animal organs: *digestive ~s.* **juicy** *adj.* (*-ier, -iest*) full of ~.

ju·jit·su [dʒuː'dʒɪtsuː] *n.* (no pl.) Japanese art of self-defence in which an opponent's own strength and weight are used against him.

juke-box ['dʒuːkbɒks] *n.* cabinet containing a record-player that automatically plays selected records when a coin is inserted in a slot.

Ju·ly [dʒuː'laɪ] *n.* seventh month of the year.

jum·ble ['dʒʌmbl] *v.t. & i.* mix, be mixed, in a confused way. *n.* confused mixture. **~ sale** *n.* (Gt. Brit.) sale of a mixed collection of second-hand articles, usu. for charity.

jum·bo ['dʒʌmbəʊ] *n.* (pl. *~s*) **1.** very large specimen of its kind. **2.** (attrib.) very large: *~ jet; ~-sized.* **3.** = **~ jet** *n.* large jet plane that is able to carry several hundred passengers.

jump [dʒʌmp] *v.i. & t.* **1.** move quickly, rise suddenly (*up*), by sudden use of the muscles. **2.** make a sudden movement (e.g. from fear). **3.** ~ *at* (an offer, etc.), accept eagerly; ~ (*up*)*on* (sb.), scold; punish; ~ *to conclusions*, come to conclusions over-hastily. **4.** (cause to) pass over by ~*ing*: ~ (*a horse over*) *a fence.* **n. 1.** act of ~*ing*: *the long* (*high*) ~ (in athletic contests). **2.** sudden movement caused by fear. **3.** sudden rise (e.g. in prices). **~y** *adj.* (*-ier, -iest*) nervous.

jump·er ['dʒʌmpə*] *n.* outer garment pulled on over the head and coming down to the hips.

junc·tion ['dʒʌŋkʃn] *n.* (place of) joining, esp. railway station where lines join or roads. **junc·ture** ['dʒʌŋktʃə*] *n.* **1.** joining. **2.** *at this ~*, now, with affairs as they are.

June [dʒuːn] *n.* sixth month of the year.

jun·gle ['dʒʌŋgl] *n.* (land covered with) thickly growing trees and undergrowth, esp. in the tropics.

ju·nior ['dʒuːnjə*] *adj.* **1.** younger in years; lower in rank, authority, etc. **2.** (after a person's name) indicating the younger person with the same name: *Tom Brown, J~* (abbr. *Jun., Jnr.,* or *Jr.*). *n.* **1.** ~ *person*: *She is my ~ by three years.* **2.** (U.S.A.) student in his or her third year at high school or college.

ju·ni·per ['dʒuːnɪpə*] *n.* evergreen shrub with berries from which an oil is obtained.

junk[1] [dʒʌŋk] *n.* (no pl.) **1.** old things of little or no value. **2.** (sl.) narcotic drug, esp. heroin. **~·ie, ~y** ['dʒʌŋkɪ] *n.* (sl.) drug (esp. heroin) addict.

junk[2] [dʒʌŋk] *n.* flat-bottomed, Chinese sailing-vessel.

a junk[2]

jun·ket ['dʒʌŋkɪt] *n.* (dish of) milk curdled by the addition of acid, often sweetened and flavoured; feast. **~·ing** *n.* feasting; merry-making.

jun·ta ['dʒʌntə] *n.* group of persons (esp. military officers) controlling a government after having seized power by a revolution, etc.

ju·ris·dic·tion [,dʒʊərɪs'dɪkʃn] *n.* (no pl.) administration of justice; legal authority; extent of this.

ju·ris·pru·dence [,dʒʊərɪs'pruːdəns] *n.* (no pl.) science of human law.

ju·rist ['dʒʊərɪst] *n.* expert in law.

ju·ry ['dʒʊərɪ] *n.* **1.** body (5) of persons who swear to give a true decision (a *verdict*) on a case[1] (3) in a court of justice. **2.** body (5) of persons chosen to award prizes in a competition. **ju·ror, '~·man, '~·wom·an** *ns.* member of a ~.

just[1] [dʒʌst] *adv.* **1.** (used with a verb

to indicate the immediate past): *They have ~ gone* (i.e. they went a very short time ago). **2.** exactly: *It's ~ two o'clock. This is ~ as good as that.* **3.** at this (that) very time: *We're (We were) ~ going.* **4.** *only ~*, almost not: *We only ~ caught the train.* **5.** *~ now*, at this moment: *I'm busy ~ now*; a short time ago: *Tom was here ~ now.* **6.** only; merely: *He's ~ an ordinary man.* **7.** (colloq.) absolutely: *Did you enjoy the party? Yes, it was ~ lovely.*

just² [dʒʌst] *adj.* **1.** fair; in accordance with what is right: *a ~ sentence.* **2.** well-deserved: *a ~ reward.* **~·ly** *adv.*

jus·tice ['dʒʌstɪs] *n.* **1.** (no pl.) just conduct; quality of being right and fair: *treat all men with ~*; *do ~ to*, treat fairly; show that one has a just opinion of or knows the value of. **2.** (no pl.) the law and its administration: *bring a man to ~*; *a court of ~*. **3.** judge of the Supreme Court. **4.** *J~ of the Peace*, lay⁴ (2) magistrate. *Department of J~*

(U.S.A., headed by the Attorney-General).

jus·ti·fy ['dʒʌstɪfaɪ] *v.t.* **1.** show that (a person, statement, act, etc.) is right, reasonable, or proper. **2.** be a good reason for (doing sth.). **jus·ti·fi·able** *adj.* that can be justified. **jus·ti·fi·ca·tion** [,dʒʌstɪfɪ'keɪʃn] *n.* (no pl.) (esp.) sth. that justifies.

jut [dʒʌt] *v.i.* (-tt-) *~ out*, stand out (*from* a line or edge on either side, or *over* sth. underneath).

jute [dʒuːt] *n.* (no pl.) fibre from the outer skin of certain plants, used for making canvas, rope.

ju·ve·nile ['dʒuːvənaɪl] *n.* young person. *adj.* of, characteristic of, suitable for, *~s*: *~ books*; *~ court* (where children are tried); *~ delinquency*, violation of the law committed by *~s*; *~ delinquent*, young offender.

jux·ta·pose ['dʒʌkstəpəʊz] *v.t.* place side by side. **jux·ta·po·si·tion** [,dʒʌks-təpə'zɪʃn] *n.* (no pl.).

K

ka·lei·do·scope [kə'laɪdəskəʊp] **n.** (fig.) constantly changing pattern of bright scenes.

kan·ga·roo [,kæŋgə'ru:] **n.** Australian animal that jumps along on its hind legs.

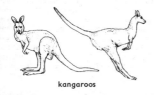

kangaroos

ka·pok ['keɪpɒk] **n.** (no pl.) soft, cotton-like material (from seeds of a tropical tree) used for filling cushions, etc.

ka·ra·te [kə'rɑːtɪ] **n.** (no pl.) Japanese method of self-defence without a weapon. ~ **chop n.** sharp, slanting stroke with the hand, used in ~.

keel [kiːl] **n.** timber or steel structure on which the framework of a ship is built up: *on an even* ~, (fig.) steady. **v.t. & i.** ~ *over*, (cause to) turn over; overturn.

keen [kiːn] **adj. 1.** (of points and edges) sharp; (fig.) cutting: *a* ~ *wind.* **2.** (of interest, the feelings) strong; deep. **3.** (of the mind, the senses) active; sensitive; sharp: ~ *sight*; *a* ~ *intelligence.* **4.** (of persons, their character, etc.) eager; anxious to do things: *a* ~ *sportsman*; ~ *to help*; ~ *on*, (colloq.) interested in; fond of. ~**ly adv.** ~**ness n.** (no pl.).

keep [kiːp] **v.t. & i.** (p.t. & p.p. **kept** [kept]) **1.** continue to have; have and not give away; not lose: *May I* ~ *this? He always* ~*s old letters. K~ hold of it*, don't let go. ~ *a firm (tight) hold on sth.*, not let it go; ~ *sth. in mind*, remember it; ~ *one's temper*, remain calm; ~ *one's seat on a horse*, not fall off. **2.** pay proper regard to; celebrate (a ceremony, Christmas, the Sabbath); observe (the law); be faithful to (a promise, treaty, etc.). **3.** provide what is needed for; support: *earning enough* to ~ *oneself (one's family)*; ~ *one's family in clothes (in comfort).* **4.** own and look after, esp. for profit: ~ *bees (pigs)*; ~ *a shop (an inn).* (Cf. *shopkeeper, innkeeper.*) **5.** ~ *house*, be responsible for cleaning, cooking, shopping, etc. (Cf. *housekeeper, housekeeping.*) **6.** make entries in or records of (business, etc.): ~ *a diary*; ~ *accounts (books).* (Cf. *bookkeeping, bookkeeper.*) **7.** not let people know: ~ *secrets*; ~ *(back) nothing from a friend.* **8.** (cause to) continue in a certain place, direction, relation, condition, etc.: ~ *the children quiet*; ~ *quiet*; *straight on*; *kept indoors by bad weather*; ~ *fit*, do physical exercises to remain in good health. *Traffic in England* ~*s to the left* (i.e. runs on the left side of the road). **9.** guard; protect: ~ *goal.* (Cf. *goalkeeper.*) **10.** (of food) not go bad: *Meat does not* ~ *in hot weather.* (fig.) *news that will* ~ (i.e. may be told later). **11.** continue doing (sth.); do (sth.) frequently or repeatedly: *Why does she* ~ *giggling? My shoe-lace* ~*s coming undone.* ~ *smiling*; ~ *going*, not stop; not give up. **12.** ~ *(sb. or sth.) from (doing sth.)*, prevent or hold back: *What kept you from joining me?* **13.** (with advs. & preps.): ~ *at*, (cause to) work persistently at; ~ *away*, avoid going, prevent (sb.) from going, to or near; ~ *back*, stay at a distance (*from*); hold back; prevent progress of; restrain; ~ *down*, hold under; make (expenses, etc.) low; ~ *from*, abstain from, prevent, or restrain (sb. or sth.) from (doing sth.); ~ *in*, (of a fire) continue burning; restrain (one's feelings, etc.); see that (a fire) continues burning; confine (a boy) after school hours; ~ *in with (sb.)*, remain on good terms with; ~ *one's hand (eye) in*, practise in order to retain one's skill; ~ *off*, (cause to) stay at a distance; say nothing about (a question, etc.); ~ *on*, continue (to have, do, use, wear, etc.): ~ *on although one is tired*; ~ *one's hat on*; ~ *an old servant on*; ~ *on doing sth.*, do sth. repeatedly (used of actions, not states): *Don't ~ on asking silly questions*. *~ out*, prevent from entering; stay outside: *Danger! K~ out! ~ under*, control; hold down; *~ up*, prevent (one's courage, spirits) from sinking; observe (e.g. old customs); prevent or hinder (sb.) from going to bed; carry on (a correspondence *with* sb.); *~ up with*, go forward at the same pace or rate as; *~ it up*, go on without slackening; *~ up appearances*, behave as usual, in spite of a change in circumstances. **14.** *~ (oneself) to oneself*, avoid the society of others; *~ sth. to oneself*, refuse to share it; *~ early (good)* or *late (bad) hours*, finish work, go to bed, early (or late); *~ pace with*, go at the same rate as; *~ track of*, keep in touch with the progress of; *~ watch*, be on watch (*for* sth.); *~ one's feet (balance)*, not fall. *n.* **1.** (no pl.) (food needed for) support: *earn one's ~.* **2.** (hist.) strong tower. **3.** *for ~s*, (colloq.) permanently. **~·er** *n.* **1.** guard (e.g. in a zoo, museum). **2.** (chiefly in compounds: see *shopkeeper*, *goalkeeper*, etc.): (esp.) *gamekeeper* (see *game*[1] (5)). **~·ing** *n.* (no pl.) **1.** care; *in safe ~ing*. **2.** *in (out of) ~ing with*, in (not in) harmony or agreement with. **'~·sake** *n.* sth. kept in memory of the giver.

keg [keg] *n.* small cask or barrel.

ken [ken] *n.* (no pl.) range of knowledge: *beyond (outside) my ~.*

ken·nel ['kenl] *n.* **1.** hut for a dog. **2.** (usu pl.) establishment for the breeding or boarding of dogs.

kept, see *keep* (v.).

kerb [kɜːb] *n.* (U.S.A. *curb*[2]) stone edging of a raised path. **'~·stone** *n.* one of the stones in such an edging.

ker·chief ['kɜːtʃɪf] *n.* piece of cloth or lace used as a head-covering.

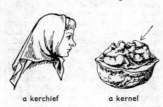

a kerchief   a kernel

ker·nel ['kɜːnl] *n.* inner part (seed) of a nut or fruit-stone; (fig.) important part of a subject, problem, etc.

ker·o·sene, ker·o·sine ['kerəsiːn] *n.* (no pl.) paraffin oil.

kes·trel ['kestrəl] *n.* small hawk.

ketch·up ['ketʃəp] *n.* (no pl.) sauce made from the juice of tomatoes, mushrooms, etc.

ket·tle ['ketl] *n.* metal vessel with a lid, spout, and handle, for boiling water. *a pretty ~ of fish*, an awkward state of affairs. **'~·drum** *n.* metal drum, shaped like a hemisphere, with parchment stretched across.

key [kiː] *n.* **1.** metal instrument for moving the bolt of a lock; instrument for winding a watch or clock by tightening the spring. **2.** (fig.) sth. that provides an answer to a problem or mystery. **3.** set of answers to exercises or problems; translation from a foreign language. **4.** (also attrib.) place that, from its position, gives control of a route or area: *the ~ to the Mediterranean*; *a ~ position*. **5.** (attrib.) *~ industries*, those (e.g. coal-mining) essential to the carrying on of others. **6.** operating part of a piano, organ, typewriter, etc. pressed down by

a keyboard

finger: *~board*, row of *~s* (6). **7.** (music) scale of notes definitely related to each other and based on a particular note called the *~note*; (fig. of thought, feelings, talk) general tone or style: *all in the same ~* (i.e. monotonously). *v.t. ~ up*, tune (the strings of a musical instrument by tightening or loosening); (fig.) stimulate or raise the standard of (a person, his activity, etc.). **'~·stone** *n.* middle stone of an arch locking the whole together; (fig.) controlling or central principle.

kha·ki ['kɑːkɪ] *n. & adj.* (cloth, military uniform, of a) dull yellowish-brown.

kick [kɪk] *v.t. & i.* strike with the foot; make movements as if doing this; drive, move, (sth.) by doing this: *The baby was ~ing and screaming*. *~ football*; *~ one's slippers off*; *~ one's heels*, be kept waiting (wasting time); *~ against*, protest; show annoyance; *~ off*, (football) start the game; *~-off* (n.) start of the game by *~ing the ball*; *~-off at 3.30*; *~ up a row*, (colloq.) cause a disturbance (by protesting). *n.* **1.** act of *~ing*; blow resulting from *~ing*. **2.** (esp. in football) sudden propelling of the ball with a blow of the foot. **3.** (colloq.) pleasure and excitement; thrill: *get a ~ out of sth.* **4.** recoil of a gun when fired. **5.** (fig.) power to react: *with no ~ left in him* (i.e. no power to resist further).

kid[1] [kɪd] *n.* **1.** young goat. **2.** (no pl.) leather made from its skin: *~ gloves.* **3.** (sl.) child; (U.S.A., sl.) young person. **~·dy**, **~·die** ['kɪdɪ] *n.* (sl.) small child.

kid[2] [kɪd] *v.t. & i.* (-dd-) (sl.) deceive; tease; joke: *Don't ~ yourself. You're ~ding (me)!*

kid·nap ['kɪdnæp] *v.t.* (-pp-, U.S.A. also -p-) steal (a child); carry away (sb.) by force and unlawfully, esp. to obtain a ransom. **~·per** (U.S.A. **~·er**) *n.* person who ~s.

kid·ney ['kɪdnɪ] *n.* one of a pair of organs in the abdomen separating waste liquid from the blood; *~ of* sheep, cattle, etc. as food.

the kidneys

kill [kɪl] *v.t. & i.* put to death; cause the death of; destroy; put an end to; spoil the effect of. *~ time*, do sth. to interest oneself while waiting. *n.* (no pl.) act of ~ing (esp. by a sportsman); animal(s) ~ed in hunting. **~·er** *n.* person who ~s, thing that, ~s.

kiln [kɪln] *n.* large furnace or oven for burning (*lime-~*), baking (*brick-~*), or drying (*hop-~*). [kilogram(me).\
ki·lo ['ki:ləʊ] *n.* (pl. ~s) (abbr. for)∫
ki·lo- ['ki:ləʊ-] *pref.* 1,000, esp. in *~cycle, ~gram(me), ~metre, ~watt.*
kilt [kɪlt] *n.* short, pleated skirt, esp. as worn by men in the Scottish High-

a kilt

lands; similar skirt worn by women and children.

ki·mo·no [kɪ'məʊnəʊ] *n.* (pl. ~s) long, loose, Japanese robe; loose garment worn as a dressing-gown.

kin [kɪn] *n.* (collectively) family; relations: *next of ~,* nearest relation(s).

kind[1] [kaɪnd] *n.* **1.** race, natural group, of plants, animals: *man~; the four-legged ~.* **2.** sort, class, or variety: *something of the ~,* something like the thing mentioned; *nothing of the ~,* not at all like it; *of a ~,* (a) of the same ~; (b) scarcely deserving the name: *coffee of a ~.* **3.** *pay in ~,* pay in goods instead of in money; *repay sb. in ~,* treat him as he has treated you.

kind[2] [kaɪnd] *adj.* having, showing, thoughtfulness, sympathy, or love for others: *Will you be ~ enough to ...,* will you, please ...? *It was ~ of you to ...,* you were ~ to ... *Give my ~ regards to Y,* tell Y that I have ~ thoughts of him. **~·ly** *adv. Will you ~ly tell me,* will you, please, tell me? **~·ly** *adj.* (-ier, -iest) behaving with, showing, ~ behaviour; *~ act.* **~·ness** *n.* ~ behaviour.

kin·der·gar·ten ['kɪndə,gɑ:tn] *n.* school for very young children; nursery school.

kin·dle ['kɪndl] *v.t. & i.* **1.** (cause to) catch fire or burst into flame. **2.** (fig.) rouse, be roused, to a state of strong feeling, interest, etc. **'kin·dling** *n.* (no pl.) material (e.g. dry sticks) for start-\
kind·ly, see *kind*[2].   [ing a fire.∫
kin·dred ['kɪndrɪd] *n.* (no pl.) **1.** relationship by birth between persons: *claim ~ with sb.* **2.** (pl. v.) all one's relations. *adj.* **1.** related; having a common source. **2.** similar.

ki·net·ic [kaɪ'netɪk] *adj.* of, due to, motion. **~s** *n. pl.* (sing. v.) science that deals with the effect of forces upon the motions of material bodies.

king [kɪŋ] *n.* **1.** male (usu. hereditary) supreme ruler of an independent state. **2.** person of great influence (e.g. in industry): *an oil ~.* **3.** piece in chess; playing-card with the picture of a ~: *~ of hearts (spades).* **~·dom** *n.* **1.** country ruled by a ~ or queen. **2.** any one of the three divisions of the natural world: *the animal, vegetable, and mineral ~doms.* '**~·fish·er** *n.* small, brightly-coloured bird feeding on fish in rivers, etc. **~·ly** *adj.* (-ier, -iest) royal; like, suitable for, a ~. '**~-size(d)** *adj.* extra large.

kink [kɪŋk] *n.* **1.** irregular or back twist in wire, pipe, cord, etc. **2.** abnormal way of thinking. *v.t. & i.* make a ~

kinky

in; form a ~. **~y adj.** (*-ier, -iest*) odd; queer; eccentric; perverted (esp. sexually).

kins·folk ['kɪnzfəʊk] **n. pl.** relations. **kin·ship n.** (no pl.) relationship. **kinsman** ['kɪnzmən], **kins·wom·an** ['kɪnz-ˌwʊmən] **ns.** male, female, relation.

ki·osk ['kiːɒsk] **n.** small, enclosed stall, etc. for a public telephone or the sale of newspapers, etc.

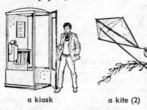

a kiosk   a kite (2)

kip·per ['kɪpə*] **n.** salted herring, dried or smoked.

kirk [kɜːk] **n.** (Scot.) church.

kiss [kɪs] **v.t. & i.** touch with the lips to show affection or as a greeting. **n.** touch given with the lips.

kit [kɪt] **n. 1.** all the equipment (esp. clothing) of a soldier, sailor, or other person who travels. **2.** equipment needed by a workman for his trade: *a plumber's ~; a do-it-yourself ~,* set of parts to be assembled or from which things may be made, etc. by the purchaser. **3.** equipment needed for a special activity: *skiing ~.* '**~·bag n.** bag for ~ (1).

kitch·en ['kɪtʃɪn] **n.** room used for cooking. **~·ette** [ˌkɪtʃɪ'net] **n.** small room or alcove used as a ~. ~ **gar·den n.** garden where vegetables, etc. are grown. '**~·maid n.** servant who helps the cook.

kite [kaɪt] **n. 1.** bird of prey of the hawk family. **2.** framework of wood, etc. covered with paper or cloth, made to fly at the end o. a long string or wire. (See the picture.)

kith [kɪθ] **n.** (only in) ~ *and kin,* friends and relations.

kitsch [kɪtʃ] **n.** (no pl.) artistic or literary material of low quality. **~y adj.** (*-ier, -iest*).

kit·ten ['kɪtn] **n.** young cat.

knack [næk] **n.** cleverness (acquired through practice or intuitive) enabling one to do sth. skilfully: *There's a ~ in it. have (get) the ~ of sth.*

knap·sack ['næpsæk] **n.** canvas or leather bag carried on the back by soldiers, travellers, etc.

knave [neɪv] **n.** dishonest man; ma without honour. **knav·ery** ['neɪvərɪ] **n.** dishonesty; dishonest act. **knav·ish** ['neɪvɪʃ] **adj.** deceitful.

knead [niːd] **v.t. 1.** make (flour an water, wet clay, etc.) into a firm past by working with the hands; mak (bread, pots) in this way. **2.** massag (muscles).

knee [niː] **n. 1.** joint between the thigh and the lower part of the leg; uppe surface of the thigh of a sitting person *hold a child on one's ~.* **2.** part of garment covering the ~(s). '**~·cap n** flat bone forming the front part o the ~. '**~·joint n.** joint (2) of the ~

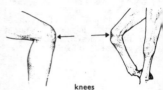

knees

kneel [niːl] **v.i.** (p.t. & p.p. **knelt** [nelt] U.S.A. also ~ed) go down on one's knee(s); rest on one's knee(s).

knell [nel] **n.** (no pl.) slow sounding of a bell, esp. for a death or at a funeral (fig.) sign of death or the coming end of sth.

knew, see *know* (v.).

knick·er·bock·ers ['nɪkəbɒkəz] **n. pl** loose, wide breeches gathered in below the knees.

knick·ers ['nɪkəz] **n. pl.** (Gt. Brit.) woman's or girl's undergarment similar to *pants* (2).

knick-knack ['nɪknæk] **n.** small, unimportant ornament, piece of jewellery, article of dress, piece of furniture, etc.

knife [naɪf] **n.** (pl. **knives** [naɪvz]) sharp steel blade with a handle, used to cut or stab. *get one's ~ into sb.,* have the wish to harm him. **v.t.** wound with a ~.

knight [naɪt] **n. 1.** (in the Middle Ages) man, usu. of noble birth, raised to honourable military rank. **2.** (modern use) man on whom a title of honour (*Sir* before Christian name and surname) has been conferred, as a reward for services to his country. **3.** piece in chess, usu. made with a horse's head. **v.t.** make (sb.) a ~ (2). **~·hood n.** rank of a ~. **~·ly adj.** chivalrous; brave and generous; like a ~ (1).

knit [nɪt] **v.t. & i.** (*-tt-*; p.t. & p.p. ~ted or, esp. fig., ~) **1.** make (an article of clothing, etc.) by looping wool, silk, etc. yarn on long needles. **2.** unite firmly or closely: ~ *broken bones*; *a closely-~ argument* (of which the parts hold together firmly). **3.** ~ *the brows*, frown. **~·ter** *n.* person who ~s. **~·ting** *n.* action of one who ~s; material being ~ted. '**~·ting-,nee·dle** *n.* one of two or more slender rods of steel, wood, or plastic, used in ~ting. **~·wear** *n.* ~ted garments.

knitting

nives, see *knife.*

nob [nɒb] *n.* **1.** rounded end of a door- or drawer-handle, of a walking-stick, etc.; attachment of this shape for pulling, turning, etc. **2.** rounded swelling on, or rounded part standing out from, a surface (e.g. a tree trunk). **3.** small lump (e.g. of coal). **~·bly** *adj.* (-*ier*, -*iest*) having ~s (2).

nock [nɒk] *v.t. & i.* **1.** hit; strike; get *(down, in, etc.)* by hitting: ~ *the bottom of a box out*; ~ *a man down*; ~ *at a door (on a window)* (to call attention); ~ *(sb. or sth.) about*, treat roughly; ~ *about the world*, make many long journeys; ~ *sb. out*, (in boxing) send him to the floor with a blow so that he cannot continue; (fig.) overwhelm (with surprise, etc.). **2.** ~ *off* (*work*), stop working; ~ *off*, deduct (sum *from a* price, bill, etc.); ~ *sb. up*, (Gt. Brit.) wake him by ~ing (at his door); ~ *sth. up*, make, put together, roughly and quickly; *be ~ed up*, (Gt. Brit.) be tired out. **3.** (of a petrol engine) make a ~ing sound. *n.* (short, sharp sound of a) blow. '**~-about** *adj.* (of a comic performance in a theatre) rough and noisy. **~·er** *n.* (esp.) hinged metal device (2) for striking against a metal plate on a door to call attention. '**~-out** *n.* blow that ~s sb. out (see (1) above).

noll [nəʊl] *n.* small hill.

not [nɒt] *n.* **1.** parts of one or more pieces of string, rope, etc. twisted together to make a fastening; (fig.) sth. that ties together. **2.** piece of ribbon, etc. twisted and tied as an ornament. **3.** difficulty; hard problem: *tie oneself in ~s*, (colloq.) get badly confused about sth. **4.** hard lump in timber

where a branch grew out from a bough or trunk: ~*-hole* (in a board where such a ~ has fallen out). **5.** group (of persons): *people standing about in ~s.* **6.** measure of speed for ships: *a vessel of 20 ~s* (i.e. able to sail 20 nautical miles an hour). *v.t. & i.* (-*tt*-) make a ~ or ~s in; tie (sth.) with ~s; form ~s. **~·ty** *adj.* (-*ier*, -*iest*) full of ~s; (fig.) puzzling: *a ~ty problem.*

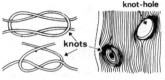

knot-hole

knots

knots

know [nəʊ] *v.t. & i.* (p.t. *knew* [njuː], p.p. ~*n* [nəʊn]) have news or information about; have in one's mind by learning or by experience; be acquainted with (sb.); be able to recognize or distinguish. *You ought to ~ better than to do that*, you ought to ~ that it is wrong, foolish, etc.; ~ *one's own mind*, be purposeful, know one's own purpose, ideas, etc.; ~ *what's what*, ~ *one's own business*, have common sense, good judgement, practical experience; ~ *how*, ~ *the way to do sth.*; ~*-how* (n.), faculty of ~ing how to do sth. smoothly and efficiently; practical ~ledge. *n.* (only) *in the* ~, (colloq.) having information not shared by all. **~·ing** *adj.* having, showing that one has, intelligence, sharp wits, etc.: *a ~ing child*; ~*ing looks.* **~·ing·ly** *adv.* **1.** consciously. **2.** in a ~ing manner. **~l·edge** ['nɒlɪdʒ] *n.* (no pl.) **1.** ~ing; understanding. **2.** all that is ~n; what a person ~s: *to (the best of) my ~ledge*, as far as I ~. **~l·edge·able** ['nɒlɪdʒəbl] *adj.* (colloq.) well-informed; having much ~ledge.

knuck·le ['nʌkl] *n.* bone at a finger-joint; (in animals) knee-joint or part joining leg to foot (esp. as food). *v.i.* ~ *down to*, apply oneself earnestly to (a task, etc.); ~ *under*, submit, yield (*to*).

kook [kuːk] *n.* (U.S.A., sl.) odd, crazy, or eccentric (person). **~y** *adj.* (-*ier*, -*iest*) (sl.) odd; crazy; eccentric.

kosh·er ['kəʊʃə*] *n. & adj.* (food, foodshop) fulfilling requirements of Jewish rites.

kung fu [kʊn'fuː] *n.* (no pl.) Chinese form of karate.

L

lab [læb] *n.* (colloq., abbr. for) laboratory.

la·bel ['leɪbl] *v.t.* (-*ll*-, U.S.A. also -*l*-) & *n.* (stick, tie, or pin on sth. a) piece of paper, metal, etc. for describing sth., where it is to go, etc.

la·bi·al ['leɪbjəl] *adj.* of the lip(s).

la·bor·a·to·ry [lə'bɒrətərɪ] *n.* place for scientific experiments, esp. in chemistry.

la·bour (U.S.A. **la·bor**) ['leɪbə*] *n.* **1.** (no pl.) work. **2.** task; piece of work: *a ~ of love*, work undertaken for the pleasure of doing it or for the good of sb. one loves. **3.** (no pl.) workers as a class (contrasted with *capitalists*): *the L~ Party*, political party representing the interests of this class; *labor union* (U.S.A.), trade union. **4.** (collectively) ~ers. **5.** (no pl.) pains or process of childbirth: *a woman in ~. v.i. & t.* **1.** work hard, esp. with the hands. **2.** try hard (*for* sth., *to do* sth.). **3.** move, breathe, slowly and with difficulty. **4.** ~ *under*, be the victim of (a disadvantage, delusion, etc.). **5.** work out in detail: *~ the point*, treat it at too great length. ~**ed** *adj.* ~*ed breathing*, slow and troublesome; *a ~ed style*, not easy and natural. ~**·er** *n.* man who does unskilled, physical work. **la·bo·ri·ous** [lə'bɔːrɪəs] *adj.* **1.** hard-working; needing great effort. **2.** showing signs of great effort. **la·bo·ri·ous·ly** *adv.*

lab·y·rinth ['læbərɪnθ] *n.* network of winding paths, roads, etc. through which it is difficult to find one's way without help.

lace [leɪs] *n.* **1.** (no pl.) delicate, ornamental open-work fabric of threads: *gold* (*silver*) ~, braid for trimming uniforms. **2.** string or cord put through small holes in shoes, etc. to draw the sides together: *a pair of shoe-~s. v.t. & i.* **1.** fasten, tighten, with ~s (2) ~ *one's shoes* (*up*). **2.** flavour, strengthen (a liquid) *with* a dash (3) of spirits: *a cup of coffee ~d with whisky.*

lac·er·ate ['læsəreɪt] *v.t.* tear (the flesh; fig. the feelings). **lac·er·a·tion** [ˌlæsə'reɪʃn] *n.*

lack [læk] *v.t. & i.* **1.** be without, have less than enough of: *~ words*, be ~*ing in courage*; *~ for*, have none or not sufficient of. **2.** *be ~ing*, be wanting: *Money for this plan wa~ ~ing. n.* (no pl.) need; shortage: *no ~ of*, plenty of; *for ~ of*, because of the absence of.

lack·a·dai·si·cal [ˌlækə'deɪzɪkl] *adj.* appearing tired, uninterested, unenthusiastic.

lack·ey ['lækɪ] *n.* manservant (usu. in livery); slavish person; servile follower.

la·con·ic [lə'kɒnɪk] *adj.* using, expressed in, few words. **la·con·i·cal·ly** *adv.*

lac·quer ['lækə*] *n.* (sorts of) varnish used to give a hard, bright coating for metal, etc. *v.t.* put ~ on.

lac·tic ['læktɪk] *adj.* of milk: *~ acid* (in sour milk).

lacy ['leɪsɪ] *adj.* (-*ier*, -*iest*) of or like lace (1).

lad(·die) ['læd(ɪ)] *n.* boy.

lad·der ['lædə*] *n.* **1.** two lengths of wood, metal, or rope, with cross-

a ladder (1)

pieces (called *rungs*), used in climbing up and down walls, a ship's side, etc.

lace (1)

2. (U.S.A. *run*[2] (12)) fault in a stocking caused by broken thread. *v.i. & t.* (Gt. Brit., of stockings) develop a ~; make a ~.

lad·en ['leɪdn] *adj.* ~ *with*, weighted or burdened with.

lad·ing ['leɪdɪŋ] *n.* (no pl.) *bill of* ~, list of a ship's cargo.

la·dle ['leɪdl] *n.* large, deep, cup-shaped spoon for dipping out liquids. *v.t.* (often ~ *out*) serve with or as from a ~.

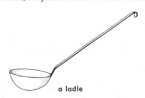

a ladle

la·dy ['leɪdɪ] *n.* **1.** woman belonging to the upper classes; woman of good manners; polite term for any woman. **2.** (pl.) polite form of address: *Ladies and Gentlemen.* **3.** (attrib., usu. courteous or formal) female: *a ~ doctor.* **4.** *L*~, title (in Gt. Brit.) used of and to the wives and daughters of some nobles and the wife of a knight. ~*-in-waiting*, ~ in attendance on a queen or princess. **5.** *Our L*~, Mary, Mother of Jesus. '~**·bird**, (U.S.A.) '~**·bug** *ns.* small, flying insect, usu. reddish-brown or yellow with black spots. '~**·like** *adj.* behaving as a ~ (1). ~**·ship** *n.* (no pl.) *Your* (*Her*) *L*~*ship* (used in speaking to or of a titled ~).

a ladybird

lag [læg] *v.i.* (-*gg*-) (often ~ *behind*) move too slowly. *n. time* ~, period of time by which sth. is slower or later. ~**·gard** ['lægəd] *n.* person who ~s.

la·ger ['lɑːgə*] *n.* sort of light beer; bottle or glass of this.

la·goon [lə'guːn] *n.* salt-water lake separated from the sea by a sandbank or coral reef[2].

laid, see *lay*[1].

lain, see *lie*[2] (v.).

lair [leə*] *n.* wild animal's resting-place or den.

laird [leəd] *n.* landowner in Scotland.

lais·sez-faire [ˌleɪseɪ'feə*] (Fr.) *n.* (no pl.) policy of allowing individual activities, esp. in commerce, to be conducted without government control.

la·ity ['leɪətɪ] *n. the* ~, (pl. v.) laymen.

lake [leɪk] *n.* large area of water surrounded by land.

lam [læm] *v.t. & i.* (-*mm*-) (sl.) thrash; hit (*into* sb.).

lamb [læm] *n.* young sheep; its flesh as food.

lame [leɪm] *adj.* **1.** not able to walk normally because of an injury or defect. **2.** (of an argument, etc.) unconvincing. *v.t.* make ~. ~**·ly** *adv.* ~**·ness** *n.* (no pl.).

la·ment [lə'ment] *v.t. & i.* ~ (*for*, *over*), show, feel, express, great sorrow or regret. *n.* expression of grief; song or poem expressing grief. **la·men·table** ['læməntəbl] *adj.* regrettable; to be ~ed. **lam·en·ta·tion** [ˌlæmen-'teɪʃn] *n.*

lamp [læmp] *n.* container for oil and wick, used to give light; other device (2) for giving light: *gas and electric* ~s. '~**·post** *n.* post for a street ~.

lam·poon [læm'puːn] *n.* piece of writing attacking and ridiculing sb. *v.t.* write a ~ against.

lance[1] [lɑːns] *n.* long spear used by soldiers on horseback. **lanc·er** *n.* soldier armed with a ~. ~**-'cor·po·ral** *n.* lowest grade of non-commissioned officer in the army.

lance[2] [lɑːns] *v.t.* cut into, cut open, with a lancet.

lan·cet ['lɑːnsɪt] *n.* pointed, two-edged knife used by surgeons.

land [lænd] *n.* **1.** (no pl.) solid part of the earth's surface (contrasted with *sea, water*). **2.** (no pl.) ground, earth, used for farming, etc.: *working on the* ~; ~*-workers.* **3.** (no pl.) ground owned. **4.** (pl.) estates. **5.** country: *one's native* ~. *v.t. & i.* **1.** put, go, come, on ~ (from a ship, aircraft, etc.); bring (a fish, aircraft) to ~. **2.** bring to, reach, a position or situation: ~ *oneself in difficulties*; ~ *on one's feet like a cat.* ~**ed** *adj.* owning ~. ~**·er** *n.* space satellite or vehicle designed (2) for ~ing instead of orbiting. '~**·hold·er** *n.* owner or tenant of ~. ~**·ing** *n.* **1.** platform at the top of a flight of stairs on to which doors open; platform between two flights of stairs. **2.** act of ~ing: *make a safe* (*soft*) ~*ing*; *make an emergency* ~*ing* (see *forced* ~*ing*); *make a crash* ~*ing*, (of aircraft or airman) ~*ing with a* crash, with the aircraft partly or wholly out of control. **3.** (usu. ~**ing-place**, ~**ing-stage**) platform onto which passengers ~ from a ship. '~**ing-field (-strip)** *ns.* field (3), strip of ground, where aircraft ~ or take off. ~**ing ve·hi·cle** *n.* ~**er.** ~**la·dy** ['læn,leɪdɪ] *n.* woman keeping an inn or boarding-house, or letting rooms to tenants. '~**-locked** *adj.* (of a harbour, etc.) almost enclosed by ~. ~**lord** ['lænlɔːd] *n.* person from whom another rents ~ or a building; person keeping an inn, a hotel, a boarding-house. '~**lub·ber** *n.* (sailor's name for a) person not accustomed to the sea. '~**mark** *n.* **1.** sth. marking the boundary of a piece of ~. **2.** object, etc. easily seen from a distance and helpful to travellers, etc. **3.** (fig.) event, etc. marking a stage or turning-point (e.g. in a nation's history). '~**own·er** *n.* owner of ~. ~**scape** ['lænskeɪp] *n.* (picture of) in~ scenery; branch of art dealing with this. '~**slide** *n.* **1.** sliding down of a mass of earth, rock, etc. from the side of a cliff, etc. **2.** (fig.) great majority of votes, overwhelming victory, for one side, esp. in an election. '~**slip** *n.* ~slide (1).

lane [leɪn] *n.* **1.** narrow country road. **2.** narrow side-street. **3.** way made or left to allow people to move freely. **4.** regular or prescribed route of ships or aircraft. **5.** strip of road for a single line of vehicles: *three-~ traffic.* **6.** strip of track (6) or water for a runner, rower, or swimmer in a race.

lan·guage ['læŋgwɪdʒ] *n.* **1.** (no pl.) words and their use. **2.** form of ~ used by a nation or race: ~ *laboratory*, room(s) equipped with tape-recorders, etc. for learning foreign ~s. **3.** (no pl.) manner of using words; words, phrases, etc. used by a profession: *legal* ~; *the* ~ *of diplomacy.* **4.** *bad (strong)* ~; ~ full of oaths (violent words). **5.** signs used as ~: *finger* ~ (to the deaf or by the dumb).

lan·guid ['læŋgwɪd] *adj.* lacking in energy; slow-moving. **lan·guish** ['læŋgwɪʃ] *v.i.* become ~; lose health and strength; be unhappy because of a desire (*for* sth.): *languishing looks* (showing desire for sympathy or love). **lan·guor** ['læŋgə*] *n.* weakness; lack of energy; stillness.

lank [læŋk] *adj.* (of hair) long and lying limp or flat; tall and lean. ~**y** *adj.* (-*ier,* -*iest*) (of a person) tall and lean; (of arms or legs) long and thin.

lan·tern ['læntən] *n.* case (usu. metal and glass) protecting a light from wind, etc. outdoors. ~ *jaws*, long, thin jaws.

a lantern

lan·yard ['lænjəd] *n.* cord worn (by sailors and soldiers) for a whistle or knife; short rope used on a ship for fastening or moving sth.

lap[1] [læp] *n.* resting-place formed by the legs when a person is seated: *sitting with her baby on (her hands in) her* ~. '~**-dog** *n.* small pet dog.

lap[2] [læp] *v.t. & i.* (-*pp*-) **1.** fold (cloth, etc.) *round* or *in*: (fig.) ~*ped in luxury.* **2.** (cause to) over~. *n.* **1.** amount by which one thing ~s over. **2.** one circuit round a race-track: *on the last* ~.

lap[3] [læp] *v.t. & i.* (-*pp*-) **1.** drink by taking *up* (water, etc.) with the tongue, as a cat does. **2.** (of waves, etc.) move (*against* sth.) with a ~ping sound. *n.* act or sound of ~ping.

la·pel [lə'pel] *n.* part of the breast of a coat folded back (forming a continuation of the collar).

lapels

lapse [læps] *n.* **1.** slight error in speech or behaviour; slip of memory. **2.** falling away from what is right: *a* ~ *from virtue; a* ~ *into heresy.* **3.** (of time) passing away; interval. **4.** (law) ending of a right, etc. (e.g. from failure to use it). *v.i.* **1.** fail to keep one's position; fall *from* good ways *into* bad ways: ~ *from virtue into vice.* **2.** (law, of rights, etc.) be lost because not claimed or used.

lar·ce·ny ['lɑːsənɪ] *n.* (law) crime of theft; instance of this.

larch [lɑːtʃ] *n.* tree with small cones and light-green leaves.

latent

lard [lɑːd] *n.* (no pl.) pork fat prepared for use in cooking. *v.t.* put ~ on.

lard·er ['lɑːdə*] *n.* room or cupboard where meat and other kinds of food are stored.

large [lɑːdʒ] *adj., n. & adv.* **I. adj.** (~r, ~st) **1.** of considerable size; taking up much space; able to contain much. **2.** liberal; generous: *a ~-hearted man.* **3.** with a wide range; unrestricted: *a man with ~ ideas.* **II. n.** *at ~,* free; not in prison; *people (the world) at ~,* people in general. **III. adv.** *by and ~,* taking everything into consideration. **~·ly** *adv.* to a great extent.

lar·i·at ['læriət] *n.* rope used to picket grazing animals, esp. horses; lasso.

lark¹ [lɑːk] *n.* (sorts of) small songbird, esp. the *sky~.*

lark² [lɑːk] *n.* bit of fun; sth. amusing. *v.i.* play (*about*).

lar·va ['lɑːvə] *n.* (pl. *-vae* ['lɑːviː]) insect in the first stage of its life history, after coming out of the egg.

lar·ynx ['læriŋks] *n.* (pl. ~es) upper part of the windpipe where the vocal cords are. **lar·yn·gi·tis** [,lærin-'dʒaitis] *n.* (no pl.) inflammation of the ~.

the larynx

las·civ·i·ous [lə'siviəs] *adj.* lustful. **~·ly** *adv.*

la·ser ['leizə*] *n.* device (2) that amplifies an input of light, producing an extremely narrow, intense, and highly directional beam: (attrib.) *~ beams.*

lash [læʃ] *v.t. & i.* **1.** beat or strike violently (as) with a whip: *rain ~ing (against) the windows.* **2.** make violent movements; move up and down: *The horse ~ed out at me* (tried to kick me). *The wounded animal ~ed its tail.* **3.** scold angrily; rouse or excite to anger: *~ oneself (one's audience) into a fury.* **4.** fasten tightly with rope, etc. *n.* **1.** part of a whip with which strokes are given; stroke given with a whip. **2.** eye*~.* **~·ing** *n.* **1.** whipping. **2.** cord or thin rope.

lass [læs], **las·sie** ['læsi] *ns.* girl.

las·si·tude ['læsitjuːd] *n.* (no pl.) tiredness; state of being uninterested.

las·so [læ'suː] *n.* (pl. *-os, -oes*) long rope looped with a slip-knot for catching horses and cattle. *v.t.* catch with a ~.

last¹ [lɑːst] *adj., adv. & n.* **I. adj.** **1.** coming after all others in time or order: *December is the ~ month of the year. ~ name,* surname. **2.** coming immediately before the present: *~ night.* **3.** only remaining (one): *I've spent my ~ shilling.* **4.** least suitable, etc.: *He's the ~ person to trust with money.* **5.** final: *I've said my ~ word on this subject.* **II. adv.** **1.** after all others. **2.** on the ~ (2) occasion before the present. **III. n.** that which comes at the end: *at ~,* in the end, after long delay; *to (till) the ~,* till the end; *till death.* **~·ly** *adv.*

last² [lɑːst] *v.i.* go on; be enough (for): *enough food to ~ (us) three days.* **~·ing** *adj.* continuing (for a long time): *a ~ing peace.*

last³ [lɑːst] *n.* wooden model of the foot for making shoes on. *stick to one's ~,* not try to do things one cannot do well.

latch [lætʃ] *n.* **1.** simple fastening for a door, gate, or window: *on the ~,* fastened with a ~ but not locked. **2.** small spring lock for a house door opened from outside with a *~key: ~key child,* child given a key to enter his home on his return from school, etc. because both parents are away at work all day. *v.t. & i.* fasten with a ~.

a latch (1)

late [leit] *adj.* **1.** (~r, ~st) after the right or usual time; far on in the day or some other period. **2.** no longer living: *her ~ husband.* **3.** who or that was until recently: *the ~ prime minister; the ~ political troubles.* **4.** *of ~,* recently: *of ~ years,* in the last few years; *at (the) ~st,* before or not ~r than. *adv.* **1.** after the usual, expected, or proper time. **2.** recently: *I saw him as ~ as yesterday* (i.e. very recently). **3.** *~r on,* at a ~r time; afterwards; *sooner or ~r,* at some future time. **~·ly** *adv.* a short time ago; recently. **lat·est** *adj.* most recent; newest (fashions, etc.). **lat·ish** *adj.* rather ~.

la·tent ['leitənt] *adj.* (of qualities, etc.)

lateral

present but not active and not seen: ~ *energy*.

lat·er·al ['lætərəl] *adj.* of, at, from, to, the side(s): ~ *buds*.

lath [lɑːθ] *n.* (pl. ~s [lɑːðz, lɑːðz]) long, thin strip of wood, esp. as used for plaster walls and ceilings.

lathe [leɪð] *n.* machine for holding and turning pieces of wood or metal while they are being shaped, etc.

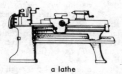

a lathe

lath·er ['lɑːðə*] *n.* (no pl.) **1.** soft mass of white froth from soap and water (as made on a man's face before shaving). **2.** frothy sweat on a horse. *v.t. & i.* **1.** make ~ on. **2.** form ~.

Lat·in ['lætɪn] *n.* language of ancient Rome. *adj.* of the ~ language; of peoples speaking languages based on ~.

lat·i·tude ['lætɪtjuːd] *n.* **1.** (no pl.) distance north or south of the equator measured in degrees. **2.** (pl.) *high (low)* ~s, places a long way from (near to) the equator. **3.** (no pl.) (measure of) freedom in action or opinion: *allow people great ~ in political belief.*

la·trine [lə'triːn] *n.* (in places where there are no sewers, e.g. army camps) pit or trench to receive waste matter from the human body.

lat·ter ['lætə*] *adj.* **1.** recent; belonging to the end (of a period). **2.** *the ~,* the second of two already named. (Cf. *the former.*) ~·ly *adv.* nowadays; recently.

lat·tice ['lætɪs] *n.* framework of crossed laths or metal strips as a screen, or for climbing plants to grow over, etc.: ~ *window,* one with small, square- or diamond-shaped pieces of glass in a framework of lead.

a lattice window

a laughing face

laud [lɔːd] *v.t.* (esp. in hymns) praise ~·able *adj.* deserving praise. ~·abl *adv.*

laugh [lɑːf] *v.i. & t.* make sounds an movements of the face and body showing pleasure, amusement, scorn etc.: ~ *at,* (a) be amused by: ~ *at funny clown;* (b) smile at; (c) mak fun of; ridicule; ~ *in (up) one's sleeve* be secretly amused. *n.* sound or ac of ~ing: *have (get) the ~ of (on) sb* reverse a situation so that you ma laugh at him; outwit him; *raise a ~* cause amusement. '~·ing-stock *n* person or thing causing general ridi cule. ~·able *adj.* causing ~ter. ~·te *n.* (no pl.) ~ing.

launch[1] [lɔːntʃ] *v.t. & i.* **1.** set a ship (esp. one newly built) afloat; send (missile, spacecraft) into outer space **2.** send (a blow, a spear, etc. *at o against*). **3.** get started: ~ *an attack (a enterprise).* **4.** ~ *out (into),* make a star on sth. new. *n.* act of ~ing. ~·ing pa *n.* platform from which rockets ar ~ed. ~·ing site *n.* place for ~ing pads ~ pad *n.* ~ing pad.

launch[2] [lɔːntʃ] *n.* passenger-carrying motor boat (on rivers, in harbours etc.).

laun·der ['lɔːndə*] *v.t. & i.* wash an press (clothes). ~·ette [ˌlɔːndə'ret] *n* self-service laundry. **laun·dress** ['lɔːn drɪs] *n.* woman who ~s as an occupa tion. **laun·dry** ['lɔːndrɪ] *n.* establish ment for ~ing linen, etc.; clothes (t be) ~ed.

lau·re·ate ['lɔːrɪət] *adj. & n.* (*Poet L~,* poet appointed by the King o Queen of Great Britain to write poem on national occasions.

lau·rel ['lɒrəl] *n.* evergreen shrub with glossy leaves; (pl.) victory, honour (i war, art, writing, etc.): *gain (win one's ~s.*

la·va ['lɑːvə] *n.* (no pl.) molten matte flowing from a volcano; this sub stance when it has cooled and hard ened.

lav·a·to·ry ['lævətərɪ] *n.* room fo washing the hands and face in; water closet; toilet (4).

lav·en·der ['lævəndə*] *n.* plant with pale purple, sweet-scented flowers.

lav·ish ['lævɪʃ] *v.t.* give abundantly and generously: ~*ing care on an onl child. adj.* giving, producing, gener ously; given generously or abundantly ~·ly *adv.*

law [lɔː] *n.* **1.** rule made by authority for the proper regulation of a com munity or society or for correct con duct in life. **2.** (no pl.) *the* ~, the body (6) of ~s. **3.** (no pl.) such a body (6) of rules as a subject of study and as a profession: *a* ~ *student; go to* ~, appeal to the ~courts. **4.** (no pl.) controlling influence of the ~s: *maintain* ~ *and order*, see that the ~s are respected; ~-*and-order* (adj.), supporting or advocating strict measures to suppress violence and crime, including rioting and other forms of violent demonstrations: *a* ~-*and-order campaign.* **5.** correct statement of what always happens (in nature, in science) in certain circumstances; regularity in nature (e.g. the order of the seasons): *the* ~*s of nature; Newton's* ~. '~-a‚bid·ing *adj.* obeying the ~. '~-court *n.* court of justice. ~·ful *adj.* allowed by, according to, the ~. ~·ful·ly *adv.* ~·less *adj.* not obeying the ~; contrary to the ~; *claim made in a* ~*court*. ~·yer ['lɔːjə*] *n.* person who has studied ~ and advises others in matters of ~.

lawn¹ [lɔːn] *n.* area of grass kept closely cut and smooth. '~-‚mow·er *n.* machine for cutting grass on ~s.

a lawn-mower

lawn² [lɔːn] *n.* (no pl.) kind of fine linen.

lax [læks] *adj.* **1.** negligent; inattentive. **2.** not strict or severe: ~ *morals.* **3.** relaxed. ~·ity ['læksəti] *n.*

lax·a·tive ['læksətiv] *n. & adj.* (substance, drug) causing the bowels to empty easily.

lay¹ [lei] *v.t. & i.* (p.t. & p.p. *laid* [leid]) **1.** put on to a surface; put down in a certain position or place: ~ *linoleum on the floor;* ~ *a submarine cable.* **2.** (of birds and insects) produce (eggs). **3.** (with various objects) put down; cause to be down or settle: *sprinkle the road to* ~ *the dust; crops laid* (i.e. flattened) *by rain-storms.* **4.** make ready; prepare: ~ *a snare* (*trap, an ambush*); ~ *a fire;* set plates, etc. on the table for a meal: ~ *the table;* ~ *supper.* **5.** (special phrases): ~ *about one*, strike out in all directions; ~ *sth. aside*, (a) save for future needs; (b) put down (e.g. a book); (c) give up

(e.g. old habits); ~ *bare*, reveal; ~ *sth. by*, save for future use; ~ *claim to*, claim as one's own; ~ *down one's life*, sacrifice it; ~ *down the law*, speak, give opinions, (as if) with authority; ~ *it down* (*that*), declare firmly; ~ (*one's*) *hands on*, (a) seize; (b) do violence to; (c) find: *can't* ~ *my hands on it*, can't find it; ~ *hold of* (*on*), get hold of; ~ *in*, provide a store of; ~ (*sb.*) *low*, overcome; overthrow; ~ *on*, (a) impose (taxes); (b) apply (blows, etc.) with violence; (c) supply (gas, water) through pipes into a building; ~ *out*, (a) spread out on view or in readiness; (b) prepare (a corpse) for burial; (c) make a plan for (a garden, a printed page, the spending of money, etc.); ~ *oneself out to*, take pains to; ~ *up*, save; store; *be laid up*, be forced to stay in bed by illness, etc. '~-by *n.* (pl. ~-bys) (Gt. Brit.) space beside a main road where vehicles may stop for a short time without hindering traffic.

lay², see *lie²* (v.).

lay³ [lei] *n.* song; poem intended for singing.

lay⁴ [lei] *attrib. adj.* **1.** of, for, done by, persons who are not priests: *a* ~ *brother*, a member, but not a priest, of a religious order. **2.** of, for, done by, persons outside a class of persons with expert knowledge; non-professional (esp. in law and medicine). '~-man *n.* ~ person.

lay·er ['leiə*] *n.* **1.** thickness of material (esp. one of several) laid or lying on or spread over a surface or forming one horizontal division: *a* ~ *of clay;* ~ *cake*, cake made in ~s with a filling of cream, jam, etc. between. **2.** *a good* (*bad*) ~, a hen that lays eggs in large (small) numbers. **3.** shoot of a plant fastened down to take root while still growing from the parent plant.

lay·ette [lei'et] *n.* clothing, etc. needed for a new-born child.

lay·out ['leiaut] *n.* arrangement; general design of a printed page, a book, an advertisement, etc.

la·zy ['leizi] *adj.* (-*ier*, -*iest*) unwilling to work; doing little work. **laze** [leiz] *v.i.* be ~; do nothing. '~-bones *n.* person. **la·zi·ly** *adv.* **la·zi·ness** *n.* (no pl.).

L-driv·er ['el‚draivə*] *n.* (Gt. Brit.) learner(-driver).

lea [liː] *n.* (poet.) stretch (2) of grassland.

lead¹ [led] *n.* **1.** (no pl.) heavy, soft, grey metal. **2.** lump of this, tied to a line, for measuring the depth of the sea. **3.** (no pl.) (also *black~*) (stick of) graphite as used in a ~ pencil. **~en** *adj.* **1.** of ~: a ~en coffin. **2.** heavy as ~: ~en limbs; ~en sleep. **3.** ~-coloured; suggesting ~: ~en clouds.

lead² [li:d] *v.t. & i.* (p.t. & p.p. led [led]) **1.** go in front, take, guide, towards some place. **2.** conduct (sb.) by the hand, by touching him, or (an animal) by a rope, etc.: ~ *a horse*; ~ *sb. astray*, tempt him to sin; ~ *sb. by the nose*, make him do everything one wishes him to do; ~ *sb. up the garden path*, (colloq.) mislead him. **3.** direct by example or persuasion; direct the movements of: ~ *an army* (*expedition*); ~ *the singing* (*the choir*). **4.** have the first place in; go first: ~*s the world in the production of steel. His horse is* ~*ing* (e.g. in a race). **5.** (cause sb. to) pass, go through, spend (life, etc.): ~ *a good life*; ~ *sb. a dog's life* (i.e. make his life wretched). **6.** ~ *to*, (of a road, etc.) go to; (of acts, etc.) have as a result: *extravagance that led to his bankruptcy*; ~ *up to*, be a preparation for or an introduction to (a subject); direct the conversation towards (a subject). **7.** guide the actions or opinions of; influence; persuade: *What led you to this conclusion?* ~ *sb. to think* (*believe*), cause him to do so. *n.* **1.** (no pl.) action of ~ing or guiding: *take the* ~; *follow sb.'s* ~ (example). **2.** ~ing position; distance by which one ~s: *have a* ~ *of five yards*. **3.** strap, etc. for ~ing a dog. **4.** (actor or actress taking the) chief part in a play. **5.** (in card games) act or right of playing first. **~·er** *n.* person who ~s; (Gt. Brit.) ~ing article. **~·er·ship** *n.* (no pl.). **~·ing** *adj.* chief; most important: ~*ing lady*, chief actress in a play; ~*ing article*, (Gt. Brit., in a newspaper) one giving editorial opinions on events, policies, etc.; ~*ing question*, one that suggests the answer that is hoped for.

leaf [li:f] *n.* (pl. *leaves* [li:vz]) **1.** one of the parts (usu. green and flat) growing from the stem, etc. of a plant: *trees in* ~ (*coming into* ~). **2.** single sheet of paper forming two pages of a book: *turn over a new* ~, (fig.) make a new and better start. **3.** hinged or loose part of an extending table. **4.** (no pl.) *gold* ~, gold hammered into very thin sheets. *v.i.* ~ *through*, turn over the leaves or pages of (a book, etc.). **~·less** *adj.* without leaves. **~·let** *n.* **1.** young ~. **2.** printed sheet (unbound but sometimes folded) with announcements,

etc. ~y *adj.* (-ier, -iest) of or like, shaded by, leaves.

league¹ [li:g] *n.* **1.** agreement between persons, groups, or nations for their common welfare. **2.** group of sport clubs playing matches among themselves: ~ *football*. *v.t. & i.* form into, become, a ~.

league² [li:g] *n.* (old) measure of distance (about three miles = 4.8 kilometres).

leak [li:k] *n.* hole, crack, etc. through which liquid, gas, etc. may wrongly get in or out. *v.t. & i.* **1.** let liquid (of liquid) pass, through a ~. **2.** (fig.) of news, a secret) (cause to) become known: ~ *secret information to the press*, supply it purposely. *The news has* ~*ed out.* **~·age** ['li:kɪdʒ] *n.* ~ing; sth. that ~s out or in. **~·y** *adj.* (-ier, -iest) having a ~.

lean¹ [li:n] *adj.* **1.** (of persons, animals, meat) having less fat than usual. **2.** not productive: ~ *harvests* (*years*). *n.* (no pl.) meat without fat. **~·ness** *n.* (no pl.).

lean² [li:n] *v.i. & t.* (p.t. & p.p. ~ed or Gt. Brit. ~t [lent]) **1.** be or put in a sloping position: ~ *backwards*; ~ *out of a window*. **2.** rest, cause to rest, in a sloping position for support: ~ *upon one's elbows*; ~ *on sb.'s arm*; ~ *a ladder against a wall* (*one's elbows on a table*). **3.** have a tendency (*towards*). **4.** ~ (*up*)*on*, (fig.) depend (up)on (*for* sth.). **~·ing** *n.* tendency (of mind, *toward* sth.). **~·to** ['li:ntu:] *n.* building (e.g. a shed) whose roof is supported against the wall of another building.

leap [li:p] *v.i. & t.* (p.t. & p.p. ~ed or ~t [lept]) jump. *n.* jump: *by* ~*s and bounds*, very rapidly. '**~·frog** *n.* (no pl.) game in which one player bends down and another ~s over him with parted legs. ~ *year n.* year in which February has 29 days.

leap-frog

learn [lɜːn] *v.t. & i.* (p.t. & p.p. ~ed or ~t [lɜːnt]) **1.** gain knowledge of or skill in, by study, practice, or being taught: ~ *by heart*, commit to memory; ~ *a foreign language*. **2.** be told or in-

left

formed (*that, how, whether*). **⁓ed**
['lɜ:nɪd] *adj.* having or showing much
knowledge: *a ⁓ed man; the ⁓ed pro-
fessions,* those needing much knowledge. **⁓ed·ly** *adv.* in the way sth.
is ⁓ing; beginner. '**⁓er(-,driv·er)** *n.*
(Gt. Brit.) person who is learning to
drive a motor vehicle. **⁓ing** *n.* (no
pl.) advanced knowledge gained by
careful study.

lease [li:s] *n.* legal agreement by which
the owner of land or a building (called
the lessor) agrees to let another (called
the lessee) have the use of it for a
certain time for a regular payment
(called *rent*): *take land by (on) ⁓; a new
⁓ of* (U.S.A. *on*) *life,* a better chance
of living longer or of being happier,
more active. *v.t.* give, take possession
of (land, industrial plants, etc.), by ⁓.
'**⁓hold** *n. & adj.* (land) (to be) held
for a term of years on ⁓ (cf. *freehold*).
'**⁓hold·er** *n.* person who holds a ⁓.

leash [li:ʃ] *n.* dog's lead² (3): *hold in ⁓,*
(fig.) control. *v.t.* tie together, hold,
with a ⁓.

least [li:st] *adj. & n.* smallest (quantity,
degree, etc.): *at ⁓,* at any rate; *not
less, even if more is impossible; (not)
in the ⁓,* (not) at all. *adv.* in the ⁓
degree.

leath·er ['leðə*] *n.* (no pl.) material
made by curing (3) animal skins.

leave¹ [li:v] *v.t. & i.* (p.t. & p.p. **left**
[left]) **1.** go away from: *⁓ for,* go away
to. **2.** neglect or forget to take, bring,
or do sth.: *one's umbrella in the train;
⁓ half one's work until the next day;
⁓ the door open; ⁓ (sb. or sth.) alone,*
not touch, trouble, interfere with. **3.**
cease to attend (school), reside at (a
place), serve (an employer), etc.:
When did you ⁓ school? **4.** hand over;
entrust; deposit: *⁓ word (with sb., for
sb.),* give a message, etc. *left luggage,*
(Gt. Brit.) luggage deposited (1) at a
railway office, etc. **5.** *⁓ hold of,* stop
holding; *⁓ off,* stop; give up; *⁓ out,*
omit; neglect to think about. **6.** give
(money, etc.) by will to sb., at one's
death; *⁓ behind* at one's death. **7.** pass
(a place, etc.) so that it is in a certain
relation or direction: *L⁓ the church
on your left and go straight on.* **8.** be
left, remain: *There's nothing left for
you.* **leav·ings** *n. pl.* what is left, esp.
sth. unwanted or worthless.

leave² [li:v] *n.* **1.** (no pl.) permission,
consent, authority (to do sth., esp. to
be absent from duty in the armed
forces or government service): *ask for
⁓ go home on) ⁓; by your ⁓,* with your

permission. **2.** period of such absence:
six months' ⁓; two ⁓s in six years. **3.**
(no pl.) departure: *take one's ⁓, take
⁓ of sb.,* go away; say farewell; *take ⁓
of one's senses,* behave as if mad.

leav·en ['levn] *n.* (no pl.) substance
(e.g. yeast) used to make dough rise
before it is baked; (fig.) quality or
influence spreading in and changing
sth. *v.t.* add ⁓ to; act like ⁓ upon.

leaves, see *leaf.*

lech·er·ous ['letʃərəs] *adj.* lustful.

lec·tern ['lektɜ:n] *n.* sloping reading-
desk as for a Bible in church.

lec·ture ['lektʃə*] *v.i. & t. & n.* **1.**
(give a) talk (to an audience or class)
for the purpose of teaching. **2.** (give
sb. a) scolding or reproof. **lec·tur·er**
n. **⁓ship** *n.* post as ⁓r at a university,
etc.

led, see *lead²* (v.).

ledge [ledʒ] *n.* narrow shelf coming
out from a wall, cliff, or other upright
surface: *a window ⁓.*

led·ger ['ledʒə*] *n.* book in which a
business firm's accounts are kept.

lee [li:] *n.* (place giving) protection
against wind; (attrib.) of or on the
side sheltered from the wind: *the ⁓
side of a ship; a ⁓ shore* (towards which
the wind is blowing). **⁓ward** ['li:wəd]
adj. & adv. on or to the sheltered
side (opp. *windward*). '**⁓way** *n.* (no
pl.) sideways drift (of a ship) in the
direction towards which the wind is
blowing: *make up ⁓way,* (fig.) make up
for lost time; get back into position.

leech [li:tʃ] *n.* small, blood-sucking
worm living in wet places: *stick like
a ⁓,* (fig.) be difficult to get rid of.

leek [li:k] *n.* onion-like vegetable with
a long, white bulb.

 leek   lemons

leer [lɪə*] *n.* unpleasant look that suggests evil desire or ill will. *v.i. ⁓ at,*
look at in this way.

lees [li:z] *n. pl.* dregs (1).

left¹, see *leave¹.* **⁓overs** ['left,əʊvəz]
n. pl. (esp.) food not consumed at an
earlier meal.

left² [left] *adj. & n. & adv.* (opp.
right¹) **I.** *adj. & n.* (of, in, on, the)

side of the body that is towards the west when one faces the north: *Few people write with the ~ hand. Turn to the ~ at the corner. the L~,* the more radical political group(s), party or parties (e.g. socialists, communists). **II.** *adv.* on or to the ~ side: *Turn ~ at the corner.* ,~-'**hand·ed** *adj.* using the ~ hand more often or more easily than the right. **L~·ist** *n.* supporter of the doctrines of the L~.

leg [leg] *n.* **1.** one of the limbs of a person's or animal's body used in walking, running, and jumping. *give sb. a ~ up*, help him in time of need; *pull sb.'s ~*, try, for a joke, to make him believe sth. that is untrue; *not have a ~ to stand on*, have nothing to support one's opinion, defence, etc.; *on its last ~s*, almost useless or at an end. **2.** that part of a garment that covers (part of) the ~. **3.** more or less ~-shaped support of a chair, table, etc.: *the four ~s of a bed.* **4.** (of a long-distance flight or journey) part that lies between two turning points; stage (4). **~·gings** ['legɪŋz] *n. pl.* leather coverings for the lower part of the ~s. **~·less** *adj.* having no ~s.

leg·a·cy ['legəsɪ] *n.* money, etc. (to be) received by a person under the will of and at the death of another person.

le·gal ['liːgl] *adj.* connected with, in accordance with, authorized or required by, the law: *~ action* (5); *~ offence*, offence against the law; *~ tender*, form of money that must be accepted if offered in payment. **~·ly** *adv.* **~·i·ty** [liːˈgælətɪ] *n.* (no pl.) being ~. **~·ize** ['liːgəlaɪz] *v.t.* make ~. **~·iza·tion** [,liːgəlaɪˈzeɪʃn] *n.*

leg·ate ['legɪt] *n.* pope's ambassador to a country.

le·ga·tion [lɪˈgeɪʃn] *n.* (house, offices, etc., of a) diplomatic minister below the rank of ambassador, with those under him, representing his government in a foreign country.

leg·end ['ledʒənd] *n.* **1.** old story handed down from the past, esp. one of doubtful truth; literature of such stories: *famous in ~.* **2.** inscription on a coin or medal; explanatory words on a map, picture, etc. **leg·en·da·ry** ['ledʒəndərɪ] *adj.* famous, known only, in ~s.

legged [legd] *adj.* (in compounds) having legs: *long-~.*

leg·i·ble ['ledʒəbl] *adj.* (of handwriting, print) that can be read easily. **leg·i·bly** *adv.* **leg·i·bil·i·ty** [,ledʒɪˈbɪlətɪ] *n.* (no pl.).

le·gion ['liːdʒən] *n.* **1.** division several thousand men in an old Roma army. **2.** very great number.

leg·is·late ['ledʒɪsleɪt] *v.i.* make law **leg·is·la·tion** [,ledʒɪsˈleɪʃn] *n.* (no pl making laws; the laws made. **leg·is la·tive** ['ledʒɪslətɪv] *adj.* law-making *legislative assemblies (councils).* **leg·is la·tor** ['ledʒɪsleɪtə*] *n.* member of law-making body (5). **leg·is·la·tur** ['ledʒɪsleɪtʃə*] *n.* law-making body ((e.g. Parliament in U.K.).

le·git·i·mate [lɪˈdʒɪtɪmət] *adj.* **1.** law ful; regular: *the ~ king*; *~ purpose* **2.** reasonable; that can be justified *~ absence from school.* **3.** born of pe sons married to one another. **le·git·i ma·cy** *n.* (no pl.) quality or state being ~. **le·git·i·ma·tize** [lɪˈdʒɪtɪma taɪz] *v.t.* make lawful or legal.

lei·sure ['leʒə*] *n.* (no pl.) **1.** spar time; time free from work: *at ~, n* occupied; *when there is ~; at one's ~* when one has free time. **2.** (attrib.) *clothes* (suitable for ~); *~ hours (time* **~d** *adj.* having plenty of ~. **~·ly** *ad & adv.* unhurried(ly).

lem·on ['lemən] *n.* (tree with a) pale yellow fruit with acid juice used fo drinks and flavouring. (See the pictur at *leek.*) **~·ade** [,lemə'neɪd] *n.* drin made from ~s.

lend [lend] *v.t.* (p.t. & p.p. *lent* [lent] **1.** give (sb.) the use of (sth.) for period of time, after which it is to b returned: *~ing library*, library fror which books may be borrowed. **2.** *a (helping) hand*, help; *~ oneself t* give one's support to; *~ itself to*, b useful or helpful to a purpose. **3.** con tribute: *facts that ~ probability to* *theory.*

length [leŋθ] *n.* **1.** measurement fror end to end (space or time): *at ~, a* last; *for a long time; at full ~,* wit the body stretched out and flat; *kee sb. at arm's ~,* avoid being friendly *go to all ~s (any ~),* do anythin necessary to get what one wants. **2** piece of cloth, etc. long enough for purpose: *a dress ~.* **~·en** ['leŋθən] *v.t & i.* make or become longer. '**~·way** *adv.,* '**~·wise** *adv. & adj.* in th direction of ~. **~·y** *adj.* (-*ier*, -*iest* (of speech, writing) very long; to long.

le·nient ['liːnjənt] *adj.* not severe: *~ punishment*; *~ towards wrongdoer* **~·ly** *adv.* **le·nience** ['liːnjəns], **le nien·cy** *ns.* (no pl.).

lens [lenz] *n.* piece of glass or glass like substance with one or both side curved, for use in eyeglasses, cameras, telescopes.

lent, see *lend*.

Lent [lent] *n.* (in the Christian Church) period of forty days before Easter.

len·til ['lentɪl] *n.* kind of bean plant; seed of this: ~ *soup*.

leop·ard ['lepəd] *n.* large, flesh-eating animal with yellowish coat and dark spots.

a leopard

lep·er ['lepə*] *n.* person with **lep·ro·sy** ['leprəsɪ] *n.* (no pl.) skin disease that slowly eats into the body, resulting in deformities and mutilations. **lep·rous** ['leprəs] *adj.* of, having, leprosy.

les·bi·an ['lezbɪən] *n.* homosexual woman.

less [les] *adj., n., adv. & prep.* (cf. *little, least, few*) **I.** *adj.* **1.** not so much (in amount); a smaller quantity or degree of. **2.** (followed by *than*): *I have ~ money than* (not so much money as) *you.* **II.** *n.* smaller amount, time, quantity, etc.: *I want ~ of this and more of that.* **III.** *adv.* **1.** to a smaller extent; not so much: *He was ~ hurt than frightened.* **2.** not so: *Tom is ~ clever than his brother.* **IV.** *prep.* minus; with (what is stated) taken away: *£10 ~ £3 for taxes.* **~·en** ['lesn] *v.t. & i.* make or become ~. **~·er** *adj.* not so great as the other.

-less [-lɪs] *suff.* (forming adjs. from ns.) **1.** without: *childless; homeless; treeless.* **2.** that does not: *ceaseless; endless.*

les·see [le'si:] *n.* person who holds land, a building, etc. on a lease.

les·son ['lesn] *n.* **1.** sth. to be learnt or taught; period of time given to teaching or learning: *a ~ in English.* **2.** (pl.) systematic instruction in a subject: *give (take) ~s in English.* **3.** sth. experienced, esp. sth. serving as an example or warning: *Let this be a ~ to you!* **3.** reading from the Bible during a church service.

les·sor [le'sɔ:*] *n.* person who grants a lease.

lest [lest] *conj.* for fear that; in order that ... not; (after *fear, be afraid*) that.

let [let] *v.t. & i.* (-tt-; p.t. & p.p. ~) **1.** allow to: *~ sb. do sth.; ~ the fire go out* (on purpose or not). **2.** (with advs. & preps.): *~ sth. down*, cause it to be down; make (a dress, etc.) longer by unstitching the hem; *~ sb. down*, fail to help him in time of need; *~ oneself (sb.) in for*, cause oneself (sb.) to be responsible for (esp. sth. troublesome); *~ sb. into a secret, ~ a secret out* (share it); *~ off*, fire or discharge (a gun, firework, etc.); allow (sb.) to go unpunished or with slight punishment; *~ out*, (a) make (a garment) wider or looser by undoing stitches; (b) hire out (see 4); (c) open a door for the exit of; allow to depart or escape; *~·out* (n.), way out; means of escape. **3.** (other special phrases): *~ (sth. or sb.) alone*, leave undisturbed; not touch or trouble; *~ alone*, (as prep.) not to mention; far less (more) than; *~ fly (at)*, throw (sth.) violently (at); say angry words (to); *~ go (of)*, stop holding; *~ oneself go* (see go (12)). **4.** allow the use of a building in return for rent: *~ a house; houses to ~; (often ~ out)* hire out: *~ out horses by the day.* **5.** (with first and third persons only, used to make suggestions or give orders): *L~'s start at once! L~ every man do his duty!* **6.** (with third person only, used to indicate a challenge): *L~ him do his worst! L~ them try to trespass on my land again! n. ~ting (4);* lease.

-let [-lɪt] *suff.* (forming ns., usu. diminutive) **1.** *booklet; coverlet; streamlet.* **2.** in names of articles of attire: *wristlet.*

le·thal ['li:θl] *adj.* causing, designed to cause, death: *~ weapons*, guns, etc.

leth·ar·gy ['leθədʒɪ] *n.* (no pl.) (state of) being tired, uninterested; want of energy. **le·thar·gic** [le'θɑ:dʒɪk] *adj.*

let·ter ['letə*] *n.* **1.** character or sign representing a sound: *capital ~,* A, etc.; *small ~,* a, etc.; *keep the ~ of the law (an agreement),* carry out its stated conditions without regard to its spirit or true purpose. **2.** written message, etc. sent by one person to another: *~·box* (U.S.A. *mailbox*), box into which ~s are delivered or posted; *pillar-box.* **3.** (pl.) literature; books: *a man of ~s.*

let·tuce ['letɪs] *n.* garden plant with green leaves used in salads.

leu·kae·mia (U.S.A. **leu·ke-**) [lju:-'ki:mɪə] *n.* disease in which there is an excess of white corpuscles in the tissues (2) and usu. in the blood.

lev·el ['levl] *n.* **1.** surface parallel with the horizon; such a surface with reference to its height: *at* (*above*) *sea-~*; *on a ~ with*, at the same height as; (fig.) equal with. **2.** instrument for testing whether a surface is *~*: *a spirit-~*. **3.** (no pl.) (group of persons having) equal rank or authority: *consultations at Cabinet ~*. **adj. 1.** having a horizontal surface: *~ ground*; *~ crossing* (U.S.A. *grade crossing*), place where a railway crosses a road on the same *~*. **2.** *have a ~ head*, *be ~-headed*, be steady and well balanced; be able to judge well; *do one's ~ best*, (colloq.) do all that one can do. **3.** on an equality (*with*): *a ~ race*; *draw ~ with the other runners*. **v.t. & i.** (*-ll-*, U.S.A. also *-l-*) **1.** make or become *~*; make equal by removing distinctions: *Death ~s all men.* **2.** *~ up* (*down*), raise (lower) to a certain *~*. **3.** pull or knock down: *~ a building to the ground.* **4.** aim (a gun, an accusation *at* or *against*).

le·ver ['li:və*] **n.** bar or other tool turned on a pivot to lift sth. or to force sth. open. **v.t.** move (sth. *up*, *along*, *into position*, *etc.*) with a *~*. **~·age** ['li:vərɪdʒ] **n.** (no pl.) action of, power gained by using, a *~*.

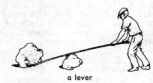

a lever

le·vi·a·than [lɪ'vaɪəθən] **n. 1.** sea monster. **2.** anything of very great size and power.

lev·i·ty ['levətɪ] **n.** tendency to treat serious matters without respect; lack of seriousness; instance of this.

levy ['levɪ] **v.t. 1.** impose, collect by authority or force (taxes, a ransom); raise (an army) by using compulsion. **2.** *~ war* (*upon*, *against*), declare and make war (on). **n.** act of *~ing*; amount of money, number of men, so obtained: *capital ~*, seizure of part of the private wealth of persons in a community or union.

lewd [lu:d] **adj.** indecent; lustful.

lex·i·cog·ra·phy [ˌleksɪ'kɒɡrəfɪ] **n.** (no pl.) dictionary-compiling. **lex·i·cog·ra·pher n.** person who compiles a dictionary.

lex·i·con ['leksɪkən] **n.** dictionary, esp. of Greek or Hebrew.

li·able ['laɪəbl] **adj. 1.** *~ for*, responsible according to law: *He is ~ for his wife's*

debts. **2.** *be ~ to*, (a) have a tendency (make mistakes, etc.); be likely (suffer, experience sth. undesirab (b) be subject to (tax, punishm etc.). **li·a·bil·i·ty** [ˌlaɪə'bɪlətɪ] **n.** (no pl.) being *~*: *liability for mili service.* **2.** (pl.) debts or other pers responsibilities.

li·ai·son [lɪ'eɪzən] **n.** (no pl.) (n connection; link: *~ officer*, off keeping two military units, esp. different nationalities, in touch v each other.

li·ar ['laɪə*] **n.** person who tells truths or who has told an untruth.

Lib, lib [lɪb] **n.** (colloq., abbr. liberation. (See *woman* (1).)

li·bel ['laɪbl] **n. 1.** (publishing of) w ten or printed statement about that damages his reputation. **2.** a thing that does not do justice or br discredit (*on*). **v.t.** (*-ll-*, U.S.A. *-l-*) publish a *~* against; fail to do justice to. **~·lous** (U.S.A. also *~·o* ['laɪbləs] **adj.**

lib·er·al ['lɪbərəl] **adj. 1.** giving given freely; generous. **2.** op minded; having, showing, (of edu tion) directed towards, a broad m free from prejudice. **3.** (pol.) mod ately progressive; of the L*~* (a Brit political) Party. **n.** member of the Party; person favouring equality opportunity for all and opposing much government control. **~·i** ['lɪbərəlɪzəm] **n.** (no pl.) *~* vie opinions, and principles. **~·i·ty** [ˌlɪ 'rælətɪ] **n.** generosity; broadmind ness; instance of this.

lib·er·ate ['lɪbəreɪt] **v.t.** set free. **l er·a·tor n. lib·er·a·tion** [ˌlɪbə'reɪ **n.** (no pl.).

lib·er·tine ['lɪbəti:n] **n.** man v gives himself up to immoral pleasu

lib·er·ty ['lɪbətɪ] **n. 1.** (no pl.) state being free: *~ of conscience*, freedom have one's own (esp. religious) bel without interference. **2.** (no pl.) ri or power to decide for oneself wha do, how to live, etc.: *You are at ~ leave whenever you wish.* **3.** *take liber with*, behave without proper resp for.

li·brary ['laɪbrərɪ] **n.** (building, roo for a) collection of books. **li·brar·i** [laɪ'breərɪən] **n.** person in charge a *~*.

li·bret·to [lɪ'bretəʊ] **n.** (pl. *-tos*, [-tɪ]) book of words of an opera musical play.

lice, see *louse*.

li·cence (U.S.A. **li·cense**) ['laɪsəns]

1. (written or printed statement giving) permission from someone in authority for sb. to do sth.: *a ～ to drive a car, a driving ～,* (U.S.A.) *a driver's license; marry by ～; license plate* (U.S.A.), number-plate. **2.** (no pl.) wrong use of freedom; disregard of laws, customs, etc.

li·cense, li·cence ['laɪsəns] *v.t.* give a licence to: *shops ～d to sell tobacco; ～d premises,* hotels, restaurants, where the sale of alcoholic drinks is allowed.

li·cens·ee [,laɪsən'siː] *n.* (esp.) person who holds a licence to sell alcoholic liquor.

li·cen·tious [laɪ'senʃəs] *adj.* immoral, esp. in sexual relationships.

lich·en ['laɪkən] *n.* (sorts of) small, dry-looking plant without flowers growing like a crust on stones, tree-trunks, etc.

lick [lɪk] *v.t. & i.* **1.** pass the tongue over: *～ one's lips; ～ sth. up (off),* get it by *～ing; ～ a plate clean; ～ recruits into shape,* (fig.) train them. **2.** (of flames, waves) move gently over. **3.** (sl.) beat; whip. *n.* **1.** act of *～ing* with the tongue. **2.** (also *salt-～*) place to which animals go for salt. **～ing** *n.* (sl.) beating; whipping; defeat.

lic·o·rice, see *liquorice*.

lid [lɪd] *n.* **1.** movable cover of a container: *the ～ of a box (kettle).* **2.** eye*～*.

lie¹ [laɪ] *v.i.* (p.t. & p.p. *～d* [laɪd], pres. p. *lying* ['laɪɪŋ]) *& n.* (make a) statement that one knows to be untrue: *in the habit of lying; tell ～s; give a person the ～,* accuse him of lying.

lie² [laɪ] *v.i.* (p.t. *lay* [leɪ], p.p. *lain* [leɪn], pres. p. *lying* ['laɪɪŋ]) **1.** be, put oneself, flat on a horizontal surface: *～ in bed.* **2.** be resting flat on sth.: *a book lying open on the table.* **3.** be kept, remain, in a certain position or state: *ships lying at anchor; money lying idle in the bank; men who lay (= were) in prison for years; a town lying in ruins.* **4.** be spread out to view: *The valley lay before us.* **5.** be present; exist: *The blame ～s at your door,* you are responsible. *The trouble ～s in the engine.* **6.** (with advs., etc.): *～ down under* (an insult, etc.), fail to protest, resist, etc.; *～ in,* (a) (Gt. Brit., colloq.) stay in bed after one's usual time; *～in* (n.): *have a ～in;* (b) remain in bed to give birth to a child; *～ low,* keep out of the way to avoid being seen; *～ up,* stay in bed or in one's room (through illness, etc.). *n.* (no pl.) way in which sth. *～s: the ～ of the land,* its natural features; (fig.) the state of affairs.

lien [lɪən] *n.* (law) legal claim *upon* property till the owner has repaid a loan or debt connected with it.

lieu [ljuː] *n. in ～ of,* instead of.

lieu·ten·ant [lef'tenənt, U.S.A. luː-] *n.* **1.** army commissioned officer below a captain; junior officer in the navy. **2.** (in compounds) officer with the highest rank under: *～-colonel, ～-general* (army); *～-commander* (navy). **3.** deputy or substitute who acts for a superior.

a lifebelt   a life-jacket

life [laɪf] *n.* (pl. *lives* [laɪvz]) **1.** (no pl.) condition that distinguishes animals and plants from earth, rock, etc.: *How did ～ begin?* **2.** (no pl.) living things in general; all living things: *Is there any ～ on the planet Mars?* **3.** (no pl.) state of existence as a human being: *with great loss of ～,* many were killed. **4.** state of existence as an individual living being: *How many lives were lost? take sb.'s ～,* kill him; *save sb.'s ～.* **5.** period between birth and death, between one's birth and now. **6.** way of living: *country ～ and town ～.* **7.** written account of sb.'s *～.* **8.** (no pl.) activity; liveliness; interest: *children who are full of ～* (i.e. active and cheerful); *put more ～ into one's work.* **9.** period during which sth. is active and useful: *the ～ of a steamship. ～ as·sur·ance* *n.* (esp. Gt. Brit.) = *～ insurance.* '**～·belt** *n.* belt of cork or other buoyant material to keep a person afloat in the water. '**～·boat** *n.* boat for saving lives of those in danger at sea or along the coast. '**～·buoy** *n.* ring of buoyant material to support a person in the water. '**～·guard** *n.* expert swimmer on duty at places where people swim. **L～ Guards** *n. pl.* cavalry regiment in the British army. *～ his·to·ry* *n.* (biol.) series of developments of an organism from the primary stage (3) to its natural death. *～ in·sur·ance* *n.* insurance providing payment on death of the insured person. '**～·jack·et** *n.* jacket of cork or other buoyant material or that can be inflated, worn to keep a person afloat in the water. *～·less adj.*

1. dead. **2.** not lively. '~-like *adj.* resembling real ~. '~-long *adj.* lasting throughout ~. ~ **pre·serv·er** *n.* (U.S.A.) device (2) (as a ~belt, ~jacket) to save a person from drowning by buoying up the body while in the water. ,~-'size(d) *adj.* of the same size as the original. '~-sup,port 'sys-tem *n.* any mechanical device (2) that enables man to live, and usually work, in an environment in which he could not otherwise survive (e.g. in a space-craft or submarine). '~-time *n.* dura-tion of an individual's existence: *the chance of a ~time,* an opportunity that occurs only once in a person's ~. ~ **vest *n.** (U.S.A.) = ~-jacket. ,~-'work *n.* entire or principal work of one's ~time; work extending over a ~time.

lift [lɪft] *v.t. & i.* **1.** raise to a higher level or position, hoist (*up, off, out*): ~ (*up*) *a table;* ~ *sth. out;* ~ *up one's voice,* cry out. **2.** (of clouds, mist) pass away; rise. **3.** dig up (root crops as potatoes, etc.). **4.** steal. *n.* **1.** act of ~ing. *give sb. a ~ (get a ~),* offer sb. (be offered) a ride in a car or other vehicle. **2.** (U.S.A. *elevator*) apparatus (1) for taking persons or goods up or down to another floor. ~-off [ˈlɪftɒf] *n.* vertical take-off of a rocket or spacecraft.

lig·a·ment [ˈlɪgəmənt] *n.* band of strong tissue holding bones together in the body.

lig·a·ture [ˈlɪgəˌtʃʊə*] *n.* bandage, piece of thread, etc. for binding or tying.

light[1] [laɪt] *n.* **1.** (no pl.) (opp. *dark-ness*) that which enables things to be seen: *the ~ of the sun; reading by the ~ of a lamp; come to ~, be brought to ~,* become known as the result of in-quiry, etc. **2.** source of ~; sth. (e.g. a candle, lamp) that gives ~: *traffic-~(s). Turn (switch) the ~s on (off). strike a ~,* strike a match. **3.** (no pl.) new knowledge helping to understand or explain sth.: *discoveries that throw new ~ on the problem.* **4.** aspect in which sth. is viewed: *place in a good ~,* represent favourably. *adj.* (opp. *dark*) that is well provided with ~; pale-coloured: *a ~ complexion; ~ eyes. v.t. & i.* (p.t. & p.p. *lit* [lɪt] or ~*ed*) **1.** cause to burn or shine. **2.** ~ *up,* (a) make or become bright; (b) switch on (electric) ~s. **3.** give ~ to: ~ *sb. on his way.* ~**en** [ˈlaɪtn] *v.t. & i.* make or become ~(er). **2.** send out ~ning: *It's thundering and ~ening.* ~**er** *n.* device (2) for producing flame: *a cigarette-~er; a*

fire-~er. '~-**house** *n.* tower or building (on a cliff, rock, etc.) with a strong ~ to guide and warn ships. ~**ning** [ˈlaɪtnɪŋ] *n.* (no pl.) flash of bright ~ produced by natural electricity in the sky, with thunder. '~**ning-con,duc-tor,** (U.S.A.) '~**ning-rod** *ns.* metal rod fixed on the top of high buildings, etc. and connected with the earth, to prevent damage by ~ning. '~**ship** *n.* moored ship with the same purpose as a ~house.

a lighthouse

light[2] [laɪt] *adj.* **1.** of little weight, esp. for its size. **2.** not made to support anything heavy: *a ~ bridge (railway).* **3.** gentle; delicate: *a ~ wind; with ~ footsteps; give sb. a ~ touch on the shoulder.* **4.** (of books, plays, etc.) for entertainment: ~ *comedy;* (of food) easily digested; (of meals) small in quantity: *a ~ supper; a ~ eater;* (of sleepers) easily waked; (of beer, wines) not very strong; (of punishment, etc.) not severe; (of work) easily done. **5.** not important: *make ~ of,* treat as of no importance: *make ~ of one's illness.* **6.** free from sorrow; cheerful: *a ~ heart. adv.* in a ~ manner: *sleep ~; travel ~* (with little luggage). ~**en** [ˈlaɪtn] *v.t. & i.* make or become ~(er): ~*en a ship.* '~-'fin·gered *adj.* skilful in using the hands, esp. for stealing things from people's pockets. ,~-'head·ed *adj.* dizzy. ,~-'heart·ed *adj.* gay; free from care. ~**ly** *adv.* ~**ness** *n.* (no pl.). '~**weight** *n. & adj.* (esp. boxing) (boxer) weighing be-tween 126 and 135 lb. (= 57 to 61 kilograms).

light[3] [laɪt] *v.i.* (p.t. & p.p. *lit* [lɪt] or ~*ed*) ~ (*up*)*on,* find, come upon, by chance

light·er [ˈlaɪtə*] *n.* **1.** boat for carrying goods to and from ships in harbour. **2.** see *light*[1].

like[1] [laɪk] *adj., prep., adv., conj., & n.* **I.** *adj.* **1.** similar; having the same qualities; such as; resembling; characteristic of; (after *feel*) in the mood for; ready for; likely to. *nothing ~ as* (*good, etc.*), not nearly so (good, etc.). **II. prep.** in the manner of; to the same degree as: *Don't talk ~ that*. **III. adv.** (old use or colloq.) ~ly. **IV. conj.** (colloq.) as (which is considered to be more correct). **V. n.** ~ person or thing; that which is equal or similar: *We have never seen the ~* (e.g. such bad weather). *He doesn't play chess and the ~* (indoor games). **~ly adj.** (*-ier, -iest; more or most ~ly*). **1.** probable. **2.** that seems suitable, reasonable: *a ~ly excuse* (reason for his absence). **3.** (as adv.) probably: *I shall very ~ly be away tomorrow*. **~li·hood** ['laıklıhʊd] **n.** (no pl.) degree to which sth. is ~ly: *not much ~lihood of finding him at home*. **lik·en** ['laıkn] **v.t.** point out the ~ness of one thing (*to another*): *~n the heart to a pump*. **~ness n.** quality of being ~; resemblance: *The painting is a good ~ness of you*. '**~wise adv.** in the same way; also.

like² [laık] **v.t. 1.** be fond of; find satisfactory or agreeable; have a taste (4) for. **2.** (in negative sentences with inf.) be unwilling: *I didn't ~ to trouble him*. **3.** (with *would, should*) expressing a wish: *They would ~ to come*. **n.** (pl. only) things one ~s: *~s and dis~s*. **~·able, lik·able adj.** pleasing; of a kind that is ~d. **lik·ing n.** (no pl.) *have a liking for*, be fond of; have a taste for; *to one's liking*, as one ~s it; satisfactory.

-like [-laık] **suff.** (forming adjs. from ns.) resembling; similar to: *childlike; godlike; ladylike*.

li·lac ['laılək] **n.** shrub with white or purple flowers growing in clusters; pale purple or pinkish-purple.

lilt [lılt] **n.** (lively song or tune with a) well-marked rhythm; **v.t. & i.** sing with a ~.

lily ['lılı] **n.** (sorts of) plant growing from a bulb whose flowers are of many shapes, sizes, and colours.

limb [lım] **n. 1.** leg, arm, or wing. **2.** bough of a tree.

lim·bo ['lımbəʊ] **n.** (pl. ~s) condition of being forgotten and unwanted; place for forgotten and unwanted things.

lime¹ [laım] **n.** (no pl.) white substance obtained by burning ~stone, used in making cement and mortar: *quick-~, dry ~; slaked ~, ~ after being acted upon by water*. **v.t.** put ~ on (fields, etc.). '**~·light n.** (no pl.) intense, white light formerly used for lighting the stage in theatres: *in the ~light*, (fig.) receiving great publicity. '**~·stone n.** (no pl.) stone containing much ~.

lime² [laım] **n.** round, juicy fruit like, but more acid than, a lemon.

lime³ [laım] **n.** (also *~-tree, linden* ['lındən]) tree with smooth, heart-shaped leaves and sweet-smelling, yellow blossoms.

lim·er·ick ['lımərık] **n.** humorous or nonsense poem of five lines.

lim·it ['lımıt] **n.** line or point that may not or cannot be passed; greatest or smallest amount, degree, etc. of what is possible, to be allowed, etc.: *set a ~ to one's expenses; off ~s* (U.S.A.), out of bounds¹. *That's the ~!* (sl.) that's the most that can be accepted, endured, etc. **v.t.** put a ~ or ~s to; be the ~ of: *~ one's expenses* (to £10). **~ed adj.** (of quantity) small; (of views, etc.) restricted; narrow. *~ed liability company*, business company whose members are liable for its debts only to the extent of the capital sum they have provided. **~·less adj.** without ~s. **lim·i·ta·tion** [,lımı'teıʃn] **n.** ~ing; condition that ~s; disability: *He knows his ~ations* (what qualities, abilities, etc. he lacks).

limp¹ [lımp] **adj.** not stiff or firm; (fig.) tired. **~ly adv.**

limp² [lımp] **v.i.** walk lamely or unevenly as when one leg or foot is hurt or stiff. **n.** lame walk: *walk with a bad ~*. **~·ing·ly adv.**

lim·pet ['lımpıt] **n.** small shellfish that fastens itself tightly to rocks.

lim·pid ['lımpıd] **adj.** (of liquids, the atmosphere, the eyes, liter.) clear. **~ly adv.**

linch·pin ['lıntʃpın] **n.** pin passed through the end of an axle.

lin·den, see *lime³*.

line¹ [laın] **n. 1.** mark made by drawing the point of a pen, etc. along a surface. **2.** length of thread, string, rope, or wire for various purposes: *clothes-~; fishing-~s; telephone ~s. The ~ is engaged* (U.S.A. busy), the telephone ~ is already in use. *hold the ~*, maintain the telephone connection. **3.** (no pl.) use of ~s (1) in drawing, etc.: *a ~ drawing* (done with pen or pencil). **4.** (games) mark made to limit a court or ground or special parts of them: *The ball crossed the ~*. **5.** mark like a ~ (1) on the skin; furrow or wrinkle: *~s of care on sb.'s face*. **6.** row: *a ~ of trees; boys standing in (a) ~; in ~ with*, (fig.) in agreement with. **7.** railway;

single track of rails: *the main (a branch)* *~; cross the ~ by the bridge.* **8.** organized system of transport: *a steamship ~; an air ~.* **9.** row of words on a page of writing or in print: *~ 17 on page 65; read between the ~s,* (fig.) find more meaning than the words express. **10.** short letter: *Send me a ~ to say you have arrived.* (colloq.) *drop sb. a ~.* **11.** series of connected military defence posts, trenches, etc.: *the front ~; behind the ~s; successful all along the ~* (at every point). **12.** family, esp. several generations: *a long ~ of great kings.* **13.** direction; course; way of behaving, dealing with a situation, etc.: *be studying a subject on sound ~s (on the wrong ~s)* (i.e. by good (bad) methods); *taking one's own ~,* being independent. **14.** edge, boundary, that divides; (esp.) the equator: *cross the L~.* **15.** kind of business or commercial activity: *He's in the drapery ~. That's not much in my ~,* is sth. I know little about. **16.** class of commercial goods: *several good ~s in cheap underwear.* **17.** one's lot or fate: *Hard ~s! Bad luck!* *v.t. & i.* mark or cover (sth.) with ~s; form a ~ or ~s: *roads ~d with trees; ~ up soldiers; soldiers who ~ up smartly.* **lin·eage** ['lɪnɪɪdʒ] *n.* (no pl.) family ~; ~ of descent. **lin·eal** ['lɪnɪəl] *adj.* in the direct ~ of descent (from father to son, etc.). **lin·ear** ['lɪnɪə*] *adj.* of or in ~s: *~ar designs; ~ar measure* (of length only). **lin·er** *n.* ship, aircraft, of a ~ (8) of ships or aircraft. **'~s·man** *n.* (sport) man who helps the referee (e.g. by signalling when the ball has crossed one of the ~s (4). **'~-up** *n.* way in which persons, States, etc. are allied: *a new ~-up of European powers.* **line²** [laɪn] *v.t.* add a layer of (usu. different) material to the inside of (bags, boxes, articles of clothing): *fur-~d gloves.* **lin·ing** *n.* **1.** layer of material added to the inside of a garment, etc.: *a coat with a removable lining.* **2.** (no pl.) kind of material so used. **lin·ea·ment** ['lɪnɪəmənt] *n.* (usu. pl.) line, detail, etc. that mark the character, esp. of a face. **lin·en** ['lɪnɪn] *n.* (no pl.) *& adj.* (cloth) made of flax; articles made of ~, esp. shirts and collars, bedsheets, tablecloths. **lin·ger** ['lɪŋgə*] *v.i.* be late or slow in going away; stay long(er than others) at a place. **~·ing** *adj.* (of an illness) lasting a long time.

lin·ger·ie ['læ:nʒərɪ] *n.* (no pl.) women's underclothing. **lin·go** ['lɪŋgəʊ] *n.* (pl. *-oes*) (humor. or derog.) language, esp. one that one does not know. **lin·gual** ['lɪŋgwəl] *adj.* of the tongue; of speech or languages. (See *audio-*. **lin·guist** ['lɪŋgwɪst] *n.* person skilled in foreign languages. **lin·guis·tic** [lɪŋ'gwɪstɪk] *adj.* of (the study of) languages. **lin·guis·tics** *n. pl.* (sing v.) science of language(s), esp. as regards nature and structure. **lin·i·ment** ['lɪnɪmənt] *n.* liquid for rubbing on stiff or aching parts of the body. **lin·ing,** see *line²*. **link** [lɪŋk] *n.* **1.** one ring or loop of a chain. **2.** one of a pair of ~ed buttons for fastening the cuffs of a shirt: *cuff-~s, sleeve-~s.* **3.** person or thing that unites or connects two others *v.t. & i.* join, be joined, with, or as with, a ~ or ~s *(together, to* or *with* sth.). **links** [lɪŋks] *n. pl.* **1.** (Scot.) sand-hills, dunes, esp. near the sea-shore. **2.** (sing. or pl. v.) golf-course: *a ~.* **li·no·leum** [lɪ'nəʊljəm] *n.* (no pl.) strong floor-covering of canvas treated with powdered cork and oil. **lin·seed** ['lɪnsi:d] *n.* (no pl.) seed of flax. **lint** [lɪnt] *n.* (no pl.) linen, with one side scraped fluffy, used for dressing wounds. **lin·tel** ['lɪntl] *n.* horizontal piece of wood or stone forming the top of a doorway or window-frame. **li·on** ['laɪən] *n.* large, flesh-eating animal of the cat family found in Africa and S. Asia and having a tawny body with a tufted tail and a shaggy mane in the male. *the ~'s share,* the largest part. **~·ess** *n.* female ~. **~·ize** ['laɪənaɪz] *v.t.* treat (sb.) as a celebrated person.

a lion

lip [lɪp] *n.* **1.** one of the two fleshy edges of the opening of the mouth. **2.** edge of a cup, etc.; part like a lip.

¹⁓‚ser·vice *n.* approval, respect, etc. given in words but not sincere. '⁓‚stick *n.* (stick of) colouring material for the lips.

liq·ue·fy ['lɪkwɪfaɪ] *v.t. & i.* make or become liquid. **liq·ue·fac·tion** [,lɪkwɪ-'fækʃn] *n.*

li·queur [lɪ'kjʊə*] *n.* (kinds of) strong-flavoured alcoholic drink, usu. sipped after a meal.

liq·uid ['lɪkwɪd] *n.* substance like water or oil that flows freely and is neither a solid nor a gas. *adj.* **1.** in the form of a ⁓: ⁓ *food;* ⁓ *measure,* (unit for the) measurement of the volume of ⁓s. **2.** bright and moist-looking: ⁓ *eyes.* **3.** (of sounds) clear; soft: ⁓ *notes.* **4.** not fixed; easily changed: ⁓ *opinions.* **5.** ⁓ *assets,* property that can easily be changed into cash.

liq·ui·date ['lɪkwɪdeɪt] *v.t. & i.* **1.** pay (a debt). **2.** bring (esp. an unsuccessful business company) to an end by dividing up its property to pay debts. **3.** (of a company) go through this process. **4.** get rid of (an enemy) by violence; kill. **liq·ui·da·tion** [,lɪkwɪ-'deɪʃn] *n.* **go into liquidation**, become bankrupt.

liq·uor ['lɪkə*] *n.* **1.** (kind of) alcoholic drink. **2.** liquid produced by boiling or fermenting a food substance.

li·quo·rice, lic·o·rice ['lɪkərɪs] *n.* (plant from whose dried root is obtained a) black substance used in medicine and in confectionery.

lisp [lɪsp] *v.i. & t.* fail to use the sounds [s] and [z] correctly (e.g. by saying [,θɪkθ'ti:n] for *sixteen*). *n.* (no pl.) a ⁓ing way of speaking: *speak with a bad* ⁓.

lis·som, lis·some ['lɪsəm] *adj.* quick and graceful in movement; lithe.

list¹ [lɪst] *n.* number of names (of persons, items, things, etc.) written or printed: *a shopping* ⁓; *put sb.'s name on the* ⁓; ⁓ *price,* (comm.) price as shown in a published ⁓. *v.t.* make a ⁓ of; put on a ⁓.

list² [lɪst] *v.i.* (esp. of a ship) lean over to one side (e.g. because of cargo that has shifted). *n.* ⁓ing of a ship: *a* ⁓ *to starboard.*

list³ [lɪst] *v.i. & t.* (old use) listen (*to*).

lis·ten ['lɪsn] *v.i.* try to hear; pay attention (*to*): ⁓ *in,* (a) ⁓ *to* a radio programme; (b) tap¹ (2) telephone lines. ⁓*er n.* person who ⁓s.

list·less ['lɪstlɪs] *adj.* too tired to show interest or do anything.

lists [lɪsts] *n. pl.* (in former times) enclosure for fights between men on horseback: *enter the* ⁓s, (fig.) send out, accept, a challenge to a contest.

lit, see **light**¹ (v.).

lit·a·ny ['lɪtənɪ] *n.* form of prayer for use in church services, recited by a priest with responses from the congregation.

lit·er·a·cy ['lɪtərəsɪ] *n.* (no pl.) ability to read and write.

lit·er·al ['lɪtərəl] *adj.* **1.** connected with, expressed in, letters of an alphabet. **2.** corresponding exactly to the original: *a* ⁓ *copy (translation).* **3.** taking words in their usual and obvious sense. ⁓**ly** *adv.* giving, taking, words in their ordinary meaning, not figuratively; word for word.

lit·er·ary ['lɪtərərɪ] *adj.* of literature or authors: ⁓ *style* (contrasted with colloquial, etc. styles).

lit·er·ate ['lɪtərət] *n. & adj.* (person) able to read and write.

lit·er·a·ture ['lɪtərətʃə*] *n.* (no pl.) **1.** (the writing or study of) books, etc. valued as works of art (drama, fiction, essays, poetry, biography, etc., contrasted with technical books and journalism). **2.** all the writings of a country or period; books dealing with a special subject: *travel* ⁓; *English* ⁓; *18th century* ⁓.

lithe [laɪð] *adj.* (of a person, body) bending, twisting, or turning easily.

li·thog·ra·phy [lɪ'θɒgrəfɪ] *n.* (no pl.) process of printing from parts of a flat stone or metal surface that have been prepared to receive ink.

lit·i·gate ['lɪtɪgeɪt] *v.i. & t.* go to law; contest (sth.) at a court of law. **lit·i·gant** *n.* person engaged in a lawsuit. **lit·i·ga·tion** [,lɪtɪ'geɪʃn] *n.* (no pl.).

li·ti·gious [lɪ'tɪdʒəs] *adj.* fond of going to law.

lit·mus ['lɪtməs] *n.* (no pl.) blue colouring-matter that is turned red by an acid and restored to blue by an alkali. ⁓*paper* (stained with ⁓ and used as a test for acids or alkalis).

li·tre (U.S.A. **li·ter**) ['li:tə*] *n.* unit of capacity in the metric system. 1 ⁓ = about 1³/₄ pints.

lit·ter¹ ['lɪtə*] *n.* **1.** couch or bed (usu. with a covering and curtains) arranged for carrying a person about. **2.** sort of stretcher for carrying a sick or injured person.

lit·ter² ['lɪtə*] *n.* **1.** (no pl.) various articles, scraps of paper, etc. left lying about untidily. ⁓*basket,* ⁓*bin* (for waste paper, etc.). **2.** (no pl.) straw, etc. used as bedding for animals. **3.** newly-born young ones of an animal:

a ~ of puppies (pigs). v.t. & i. **1.** put, leave, ~ (1) about: *a room ~ed with books and papers.* **2.** ~ *(down),* supply (a horse, etc.) with ~ (2) as a bed; put ~ (2) down (for animals). **3.** (of animals) give birth to a ~ (3).

lit·tle ['lɪtl] *adj.* **1.** small; young(er): *a ~ boy; her ~ brother; the ~ ones,* the children. **2.** of the smaller or smallest size: *the ~ finger (toe).* **3.** short in stature, distance, or time: *a ~ man. Come a ~ way with me. stay for a ~ while.* **4.** unimportant: *every ~ difficulty.* **5.** *(less, least)* not much: *a ~,* a small quantity or amount. **6.** arousing a feeling of tenderness, sympathy, or amusement: *that dear ~ man. Poor ~ girl! a ~ rascal. n.* small amount; not much: *after (for) a ~,* after (for) a short time or distance; *~ by ~,* gradually. *adv.* not much; hardly at all: *a ~,* rather: *He's a ~ better this morning.*

lit·tor·al ['lɪtərəl] *n. & adj.* (that part of a country that is) along the coast.

lit·ur·gy ['lɪtədʒɪ] *n.* fixed form of public worship used in a church.

live [lɪv] *v.i. & t.* **1.** be alive; have existence as an animal or plant; continue to be alive; remain alive: *~ on,* continue to ~; *~ and let ~,* be tolerant. **2.** conduct, direct, or pass one's life: *~ happily (honestly).* **3.** spend; pass; experience: *~ a double life; ~ a happy life.* **4.** *~ sth. down, ~* in such a way that (earlier wrongdoing, mistake, etc.) is forgotten; *~ in (at),* reside: *~ abroad; ~ in (out),* (not) ~ in the place where one is employed; *~ on* (a) have as food or diet: *~ on fruit;* (b) get what one needs for support from: *~ on one's income (friends); ~ up to* (one's principles, faith, etc.), reach the standard which has been set; *~ with sth.,* accept and endure ~: *learn to ~ with an illness.* [laɪv] *attrib. adj.* (cf. *alive*) **1.** having life; full of energy, activity, interest, etc.: *~ coals* (burning); *~ shells* (not yet exploded); *make the question a ~ issue.* **2.** (of a broadcast) not recorded, but heard or seen during the occurrence of an event. **~·li·hood** ['laɪvlɪhʊd] *n.* means of living: *earn one's ~lihood by farming.* **~·long** ['lɪvlɒŋ] *adj.* (only in) *the ~long day,* etc., the whole length of the day, etc. **~·ly** ['laɪvlɪ] *adj.* *(-ier, -iest)* full of life and gaiety; cheerful; quick-moving. **~·li·ness** *n.* (no pl.) state of being ~ly. **liv·en** ['laɪvn] *v.t. & i. ~n (up),* (colloq.) make or become ~ly. **~·stock** ['laɪvstɒk] *n.* (no pl.) animals kept for use or profit. **liv·ing** ['lɪvɪŋ] *adj.* **1.** alive; now existent:

living creatures (languages); the living (pl.) those now alive. **2.** (of a picture etc.) true to life. *n.* **1.** ~lihood: *make a ~ living as a shopkeeper.* **2.** (no pl.) manner of life: *plain living; high standards of living; living-room, room* for general use by day; *living wage,* wage that is enough to ~ on.

liv·er ['lɪvə*] *n.* **1.** reddish-brown organ in the body purifying the blood. **2.** (no pl.) animal's ~ as food. **~·ish** (colloq.) **~y** *adjs.* ill because the ~ is out of order.

a lizard

liv·ery ['lɪvərɪ] *n.* **1.** special dress worn by menservants in a great household. **2.** *~ stable,* stable where horses are kept for owners; stable from which horses may be hired.

lives, see *life.*

liv·id ['lɪvɪd] *adj.* of the colour of lead: *~ marks on the body* (e.g. because of bruises); *~ with cold (anger).*

liv·ing, see *live.*

liz·ard ['lɪzəd] *n.* small, creeping, long-tailed, four-legged reptile.

lla·ma ['lɑːmə] *n.* S. American animal related to the camel but smaller and without a hump, used as a beast of burden and a source of wool.

a llama

load [ləʊd] *n.* **1.** that which is (to be) carried or supported; (fig.) weight of care, responsibility, etc. **2.** amount that a cart, etc. can take: *a cart-~ of hay. v.t. & i.* **1.** put a ~ (1) on or in; put (goods) into or on: *~ a donkey; ~ coal on to carts.* **2.** put a cartridge, shell, etc. into (a gun); insert a length of film into (a camera). **3.** *~ (up),* (of a ship, aircraft, vehicle, or person) take a ~ aboard. *~ line n.* line painted on a ship's side to mark the highest safe water-level.

load·stone, see *lodestone*.

loaf[1] [ləʊf] *n.* (pl. **loaves** [ləʊvz]) mass of bread baked as a separate quantity.

a loaf[1]

loaf[2] [ləʊf] *v.i. & t.* waste time; wait about idly: *~ing at street corners*; *~ about*; *~ away one's time.* **~er** *n.* person who *~s.*

loam [ləʊm] *n.* (no pl.) rich soil with much decayed vegetable matter. **~y** *adj.* (*-ier, -iest*).

loan [ləʊn] *n.* **1.** sth. lent, esp. a sum of money: *government ~s*, capital lent to the government. **2.** (no pl.) lending or being lent: *books on ~*; *ask for the ~ of.* *v.t.* lend.

loath, loth [ləʊθ] *pred. adj.* unwilling (*to do* sth.): *nothing ~*, quite glad (to).

loathe [ləʊð] *v.t.* dislike greatly; feel disgust for. **loath·ing** *n.* (no pl.) disgust. **loath·some** *adj.* disgusting.

loaves, see *loaf*[1].

lob·by ['lɒbɪ] *n.* entrance-hall; corridor: *in the hotel ~.*

lobe [ləʊb] *n.* **1.** lower, rounded end of the outer ear. **2.** subdivision of the lungs, the liver, or the brain: *~ of the lungs.*

lob·ster ['lɒbstə*] *n.* shellfish with eight legs and two claws, bluish-black before and scarlet after being boiled; its flesh as food.

a lobster   a lock[1] of hair

lo·cal ['ləʊkl] *adj.* **1.** of, peculiar to, a place or district: *~ news*; *the ~ doctor*; *~ government*; *~ time*, time at any place in the world as calculated (1) from the position of the sun. **2.** of a part, not of the whole: *a ~ pain.* **~ly** *adv.* **~i·ty** [ləʊ'kælətɪ] *n.* **1.** thing's position; place; district; place where an event occurs. **2.** (no pl.) faculty of

remembering and recognizing places, finding one's way, etc.: *a good sense of ~ity.* **~ize** ['ləʊkəlaɪz] *v.t.* make *~*, not general.

lo·cate [ləʊ'keɪt] *v.t.* **1.** discover, show, the position of: *~ a town on a map.* **2.** *be ~d*, be situated. **3.** establish in a place: *~ a school in a new suburb.* **lo·ca·tion** [ləʊ'keɪʃn] *n.* **1.** (no pl.) locating or being *~d.* **2.** position or place of or on. **3.** (S. Africa) suburb for non-Europeans. **4.** place outside a film studio where a film or part of it is made: *on location*, shooting a film in this way.

loch [lɒx] *n.* (Scot.) **1.** long, narrow arm of the sea. **2.** lake.

lock[1] [lɒk] *n.* portion of hair that naturally clings together. (See the picture.)

lock[2] [lɒk] *n.* **1.** mechanism, worked by turning a key, for sliding a bolt to fasten a door, gate, lid, etc.: *under ~ and key*, (safely) *~ed up.* **2.** mechanism by which a gun is fired. *~, stock, and barrel*, the whole of a thing; completely. **3.** section of a canal or other water-way, closed at each end by gates fitted with sluices, in which boats are raised or lowered to another water-level. **4.** *air~*, stoppage of a pump, etc. because of an air-bubble. *v.t. & i.* **1.** fasten (a door, box, etc.) by turning the key of a *~*: *~ (sb.) in (out)*, keep in (out) by *~ing the door (gate, etc.)*; *~ sth. up*, put in a *~ed place*; *~ the doors, etc. of a building.* **2.** (cause to) become fixed and unable to move: *jaws tightly ~ed*; *~ed wheels.* **~er** *n.* small cupboard with a *~.* **'~-jaw** *n.* (no pl.) disease in which the jaws become tightly fixed. **'~-out** *n.* refusal of employers to allow workers to enter their place of work until they accept certain conditions. **'~-smith** *n.* maker and repairer of *~s* for doors, etc. **'~-up** *n.* (place used as a) prison. *attrib. adj.* that can be *~ed*: *a ~-up garage* (e.g. at a hotel).

a canal lock[2] (3)

lock·et ['lɒkɪt] *n.* small (often gold or silver) case for a portrait, lock of hair, etc. worn hung from the neck.

lo·co·mo·tion [ˌləʊkə'məʊʃn] *n.* (no pl.) (power of) going from one place to another. **lo·co·mo·tive** ['ləʊkə-ˌməʊtɪv] *adj.* of, having, causing, ~. *n.* railway engine.

lo·cust ['ləʊkəst] *n.* winged insect that flies in great swarms and destroys crops and vegetation.

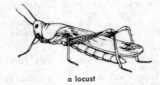

a locust

lo·cu·tion [ləʊ'kjuːʃn] *n.* style of using words; phrase or idiom.

lode [ləʊd] *n.* vein of metal ore. **'~-star** *n.* star by which a ship may be steered, esp. the pole-star. **~-stone, load-stone** ['ləʊdstəʊn] *n.* kind of iron ore that is magnetic.

lodge [lɒdʒ] *n.* **1.** small house, at the gateway to a large, private estate. **2.** country house used in the hunting or shooting season: *a hunting-~ in the Scottish Highlands.* *v.t. & i.* **1.** supply (sb.) with room(s) for living in. **2.** live (*at, with*) as a ~r. **3.** enter and become fixed (*in*); cause to do this: *The bullet ~d in his jaw.* **4.** put (money, etc.) for safety (*with* sb., *in* a place); place (a statement, complaint, etc.) *with* the proper authorities (*against* sb.). **lodg-er** *n.* person paying for rooms, etc. in sb.'s house: *make a living by taking in ~rs.* **lodg·ing** *n.* (usu pl.) place where one ~s (2); room(s) occupied by a ~r. **'lodg·ing-house** *n.* house in which lodgings are let.

loft [lɒft] *n.* room, place, used for storing things, in the highest part of a house, under the roof.

lofty ['lɒftɪ] *adj.* (-ier, -iest) **1.** (not of persons) very high: *a ~ tower.* **2.** (of thoughts, aims, feelings) noble; distinguished. **3.** (of manner) proud. **loft-i·ly** *adv.*

log¹ [lɒg] *n.* rough length of a tree-trunk that has been cut down; short piece of this for fuel: *~ cabin,* hut built of ~s.

log² [lɒg] *n.* **1.** apparatus (1) for measuring a ship's speed. **2.** (also *~-book*) daily record of a ship's or aircraft's rate of progress, events of a voyage, etc. *~-book,* (Gt. Brit.) registration book of a motor vehicle.

log·a·rithm ['lɒgərɪðəm] *n.* one of a series of numbers set out in tables that make it possible to work out problems in multiplication and division easily by adding and subtracting.

log·ger·head ['lɒgəhed] *n. at ~s,* on bad terms, in disagreement (*with* sb.).

log·ic ['lɒdʒɪk] *n.* (no pl.) science, method, of reasoning; ability to argue and convince. **log·i·cal** *adj.* in accordance with the laws of ~; able to reason rightly. **log·i·cal·ly** *adv.*

-l·o·gist [-lədʒɪst] *suff.* (forming ns.) expert in; student of: *biologist; geologist.*

-logue (U.S.A. **-log**) [-lɒg] *suff.* (forming ns.) **1.** sth. spoken: *dialogue; monologue.* **2.** compilation: *catalogue.*

-l·o·gy [-lədʒɪ] *suff.* (forming ns.) names of doctrines or sciences: *biology; geology; etymology; theology.*

loin [lɔɪn] *n.* **1.** (pl.) lower part of the body between the hip-bones and the ribs. **2.** joint of meat from this part of an animal: *~ of mutton.*

loi·ter ['lɔɪtə*] *v.i. & t.* go slowly and stop frequently on the way somewhere; stand about; pass (time) thus: *~ the hours away.* **~·er** *n.*

loll [lɒl] *v.i. & t.* rest, sit, or stand (*about*) in a lazy way; (of the tongue) hang (*out*); let (the tongue) hang (*out*).

lol·li·pop ['lɒlɪpɒp] *n.* lump of boiled sweet on the end of a small stick. *~ man* (*woman*), (Gt. Brit., colloq.) one who carries a circular sign on a stick to stop traffic so that children may cross a busy road (e.g. outside a school).

lol·ly ['lɒlɪ] *n.* (colloq.) lollipop: *iced lollies,* frozen fruit juice on a stick.

lone [ləʊn] *attrib. adj.* (chiefly liter.; *alone* and *lonely* are more usual) without companions; unfrequented. **~·ly** *adj.* (-ier, -iest) **1.** without companions. **2.** (of places) without many people; not often visited; far from inhabited places or towns: *a ~ly village.* **3.** *feeling ~ly,* feeling sad because alone. **~·li·ness** *n.* (no pl.) state of being ~ly. **~·some** *adj.* ~ly.

long¹ [lɒŋ] *adj.* **1.** (opp. *short*) measuring much from end to end in space or time. **2.** (various uses): *a ~ dozen,* thirteen; *a ~ face,* a sad, dismal look; *in the ~ run,* in the end; as the final result; *two inches* (*six weeks*) *~* (having the length indicated); *all day ~,* throughout the day. *n.* (no pl.) *~ time* or interval: *before ~,* before a ~ time has passed; *the ~ and the short of it,* all that can or need be said; the general effect or outcome of it all. *adv.* for a ~ time: *as (so) ~ as*, for as ~ a time as; on condition that; *~-drawn(-out)*, taking an unnecessarily ~ time. '**~·bow** *n.* bow bent by hand. *draw the ~bow*, tell untrue or exaggerated stories. **,~-'dis·tance** *attrib. adj.* covering a ~ distance: (sport) *a ~-distance runner*; *a ~-distance telephone call*. ~ **drink** *n.* large quantity (e.g. of beer) served in a tall glass. **lon·gev·i·ty** [lɒn'dʒevətɪ] *n.* (no pl.) ~ life. '**~·hand** *n.* (no pl.) ordinary writing (not *shorthand*). ~ **jump** *n.* (Gt. Brit.; U.S.A. = *broad jump*) athletic contest of jumping as far as possible. **,~-'play·ing** *adj.* (abbr. *L.P.*, of a record² (4)) playing for a ~ time on each side. **,~-'range** *attrib. adj.* of ~ distances or ~ periods of future time: *~-range missiles*; *~-range weather forecast*. '**~·shore·man** *n.* man who loads ships. **,~-'suf·fer·ing** *adj. & n.* patient and uncomplaining (behaviour). '**~·ways**, '**~·wise** *advs.* lengthways. **~·wind·ed** [,lɒŋ-'wɪndɪd] *adj.* (of talk, writing) tediously long.

long² [lɒŋ] *v.i.* desire earnestly (*for, to do*, sth.). **~·ing** *n.* strong desire. *adj.* showing, having, strong desire. **~·ing·ly** *adv.*

lon·gi·tude ['lɒndʒɪtjuːd] *n.* distance east or west (measured in degrees) from a meridian, esp. that of Greenwich, in London.

look [lʊk] *v.i. & t.* **1.** try to see; turn one's eyes towards: *L~ at him! They were ~ing at some books* (inspected, examined, them). **2.** (with advs. and preps.): ~ *after* (*sb. or sth.*), take care of; watch over; attend to; ~ *down on*, regard with contempt; have a low opinion of; ~ *for*, try to find; be on the watch for; ~ *forward to*, expect, wait for (usu. with pleasure); ~ *in on* (*sb.*), visit while passing; ~ *into*, examine; investigate; ~ *on*, be a spectator; not taking part; ~ (*up*)*on* (*sb. or sth.*) *as*, consider as; ~ *out*, be on one's guard, watch (*for* sth.); ~ *sth. over*, inspect it; ~ *sth. through*, glance at it; read it; ~ *to*, attend to; take care of; ~ *up*, (a) raise the eyes (b) improve in price or prosperity: *business is ~ing up*; ~ *sb. up*, (colloq.) go to visit him; ~ (*sth.*) *up*, find (e.g. a word in a dictionary); ~ *up to*, respect. **3.** ~ *like*, seem to be; seem likely: *It ~s like rain*, rain seems likely; ~ *alive* (*sharp*), be quick; hurry. *n.* **1.** act of ~ing: *Have a ~ at this*, ~ at it. **2.** appearance; what sth. suggests when

seen: *angry ~s*; *a ~ of pleasure*. **3.** (pl.) person's appearance: *good ~s*, beauty. **~·er** *n.* person having an appearance of a specified kind: *a good-~er*. **,~-er-'on** *n.* (pl. *~ers-on*) spectator. '**~-in** *n.* not have a ~*in*, not have a chance to win. '**~·ing-glass** *n.* mirror made of glass. '**~-out** *n.* **1.** (place for) keeping watch; person who keeps watch. **2.** (no pl.) state of being watchful: *be on the ~-out for or to do*; *keep a good ~-out*. **3.** (no pl.) prospect; future: *It's a poor ~-out for this generation* (i.e. their future seems dismal). *That's his (your, etc.) ~-out*, that's (a risk, etc.) for him (you) only.

loom¹ [luːm] *n.* machine for weaving cloth.

a loom¹

loom² [luːm] *v.i.* appear indistinctly and in a threatening way.

loo·ny ['luːnɪ] *n. & adj.* (sl.) lunatic. '**~-bin** *n.* (sl.) mental home or hospital.

loop [luːp] *n.* (shape produced by a) curve crossing itself; part of a length of string, wire, ribbon, etc. in such a shape, esp. as a knot or fastening. *v.t. & i.* **1.** form or bend into a ~ or ~s. **2.** ~ *sth. up* (*back*), keep or fasten sth. up (back) in the form of, or with, a ~. '**~·hole** *n.* narrow opening in a wall; (fig.) way of escape from control, esp. one provided by careless or inexact wording of a rule: *find a ~hole in the law*.

loops

loose [luːs] *adj.* (*~r, ~st*) **1.** free; not held together, packed, or contained in sth.; not fastened or tied up: *small change in one's pocket* (i.e. not in a purse); *break ~*, (of an animal) escape confinement. **2.** not tight or close-fitting: *a ~ collar*. **3.** moving more freely than is right or usual: *a ~ tooth (window-frame)*; *~ bowels*, tendency to diarrhoea; _come_ ~, (of fastenings, etc.) come unfastened or insecure; _have a screw_ ~, (colloq.) be slightly mad; _have a_ ~ _tongue_, talk too freely. **4.** (of talk, behaviour, etc.) not sufficiently controlled: ~ (i.e. immoral) _conduct_; _living a_ ~ _life_; ~ (i.e. inexact or careless) _thinking_; _a_ ~ (i.e. badly connected) _argument_. **5.** not compact; not tightly packed, etc.: _a_ ~ _soil_. **6.** _at a_ ~ _end_, with nothing to do. _v.t._ make ~. ~**ly** _adv._ **loos·en** ['luːsn] _v.t. & i._ make or become ~(r); make less tight: _Wine_ ~_ned his tongue._

loot [luːt] _v.t. & i._ take (goods, esp. private property) unlawfully and by force, esp. in time of war: _soldiers_ ~_ing the town._ _n._ (no pl.) property so taken.

lop¹ [lɒp] _v.t._ (-_pp-_) cut (branches, etc.) _off_ (from a tree, etc.); cut _off_ or _away_ with one blow.

lop² [lɒp] _v.i._ (-_pp-_) hang down loosely. ~**-eared** _adj._ with drooping ears. ~**-'sid·ed** _adj._ with one side lower than the other.

lope [loʊp] _v.i._ move with long, easy steps or strides (as a hare does).

lo·qua·cious [loʊˈkweɪʃəs] _adj._ talkative. **lo·quac·i·ty** [loʊˈkwæsətɪ] _n._ (no pl.).

lord [lɔːd] _n._ **1.** supreme ruler: _our sovereign_ ~ _the King._ **2.** (_the_) L~, God; _the L~'s Prayer_; _the L~'s Supper_; _the L~'s Day_, Sunday. **3.** peer; nobleman: _the House of L~s_, (Gt. Brit.) the upper division of Parliament. **4.** (person with) position of authority; official position: _the L~s of the Admiralty_; _the L~ Mayor of London._ _v.t._ ~ _it over_, rule over like a ~. ~**ly** _adj._ like, suitable for, a ~. **Lord·ship** _n._ _His_ (_Your_) L~_ship_, (used when speaking of or to a ~).

lore [lɔː*] _n._ (no pl.) learning or knowledge, esp. handed down from past times (e.g. _folk_~, _gipsy_ ~) or of a special subject (e.g. _bird_ ~).

lor·ry ['lɒrɪ] _n._ (U.S.A. _truck_) large motor vehicle for transporting heavy goods.

lose [luːz] _v.t. & i._ (p.t. & p.p. _lost_ [lɒst]) **1.** have no longer; have taken away from one (by accident, carelessness, death, etc.). **2.** be unable to find: ~ _one's way_, ~ _oneself_, _be lost_, not know where one is; be unable to find the right road, etc.; ~ _track of_, not know what has happened to (sb. or sth.). **3.** fail to be in time for; miss; fail to see, hear, etc.: ~ _one's train_ (_the post_); ~ (i.e. not hear) _the end of a sentence._ **4.** fail to keep: ~ _one's hair_; ~ _courage_,

become less brave; ~ (_one's_) _patience_, become impatient (_with_); ~ _one's temper_, get angry; ~ _one's reason_, become insane; ~ _one's head_, become confused or excited; ~ _face_, fail to keep one's dignity; be made to look small. **5.** spend (time, opportunities, efforts) to no purpose; waste: ~ _no time_ (_in doing sth._), do it at once; _be lost_ (_up_)_on sb._, fail to influence him or attract his attention. **6.** fail to win; be defeated: ~ _a game_ (_lawsuit_). **7.** _be lost to_ (all sense of shame, etc.), be no longer affected by; ~ _oneself in_, _be lost in_ (wonder, etc.), be filled with; be wholly given up to. **8.** (of a watch or clock) go too slowly: _losing five minutes a day._ **los·er** _n._ person who ~s.

loss [lɒs] _n._ losing; sth. lost; waste; disadvantage caused by losing sth.: _at a_ ~, perplexed; uncertain what to do or say: _at a_ ~ _for words._

lost, see _lose._

lot¹ [lɒt] _n._ _the_ ~, _the whole_ ~, all; everything; _a_ ~ (_of_), ~_s_ (_of_), (colloq.) a great number or amount (of): _spend a_ ~ _of money on books_; _have_ ~_s of friends_; _a_ ~ (_better, etc._), much.

lot² [lɒt] _n._ **1.** (one of a set of objects used in the) making of a selection or decision by methods depending on chance: _draw_ (_cast_) ~_s_; _decide sth. by_ ~. **2.** that which comes to a person by luck or destiny: _His_ ~ _has been a hard one._ _cast_ (_throw_) _in one's_ ~ _with_, decide to share the fortunes of. **3.** number of various objects offered for sale together, esp. by auction. **4.** _bad_ ~, (colloq.) bad person. **5.** small piece of land, (esp. U.S.A.) for a specific purpose: _a parking_ ~.

loth, see _loath._

lo·tion ['loʊʃn] _n._ liquid preparation for cosmetic and medicinal use on the skin.

lot·tery ['lɒtərɪ] _n._ arrangement to give prizes to holders of numbered tickets previously bought by them and drawn by lot² (1).

lo·tus ['loʊtəs] _n._ kinds of water-lily.

loud [laʊd] _adj._ **1.** easily heard; noisy; not quiet or soft. **2.** (of a colour, behaviour, etc.) of the kind that forces itself on the attention. ~**'speak·er** _n._ apparatus (1) that changes electric waves into sound waves loud enough to be heard without earphones. ~**ly** _adv._

lounge [laʊndʒ] _v.i._ sit, stand about (leaning against sth.), in a lazy way. _n._ room (e.g. in a hotel) with comfortable chairs for lounging: _the hotel_

~. ~ **suit** *n.* (Gt. Brit.) man's suit of jacket and trousers (and waistcoat) for informal day wear.

louse [laʊs] *n.* (pl. *lice* [laɪs]) sorts of small insect living on the bodies of human beings and animals existing under dirty conditions; similar insect living on plants. **lousy** [ˈlaʊzɪ] *adj.* (*-ier, -iest*) **1.** having lice. **2.** (sl.) disgusting.

lout [laʊt] *n.* clumsy, ill-mannered man. **~·ish** *adj.* of or like a ~: ~*ish behaviour.*

love [lʌv] *n.* warm and tender feeling as between parents and children, husband and wife, and close friends; fondness; affection: *be in ~ (with),* have ~ and desire (for); *fall in ~ (with),* begin to be in ~ (with); *make ~ (to),* show that one is in ~ (with); have or seek sexual intercourse (with). *v.t. & i.* **1.** have strong affection and tender feeling for; be in ~. **2.** find pleasure in; be very fond of; like: ~ *comfort (mountain climbing);* ~ *to do sth.,* ~ *doing sth.,* be (habitually) inclined to do it; (colloq.) like, be delighted, to do it. **lov·able** *adj.* deserving ~; having qualities that cause ~. **~·less** *adj.* not feeling, showing, having, ~: *a ~less marriage.* **lov·er** *n.* **1.** person who ~s sth.: *a ~r of good food.* **2.** man who is in ~. **3.** (pl.) man and woman in ~. **lov·ing** *adj.* feeling or showing ~. **lov·ing·ly** *adv.* **~·sick** *adj.* unhappy through feelings of unsatisfied ~.

love·ly [ˈlʌvlɪ] *adj.* (*-ier, -iest*) **1.** beautiful; pleasant; attractive. **2.** (colloq.) delightful; amusing. **love·li·ness** *n.* (no pl.).

low[1] [ləʊ] *adj.* **1.** (contrasted with *high, tall*) not reaching far upwards. **2.** below the usual level: ~ *pressure* (see *pressure*); ~ *tide (water),* state of tide when the water is at its ~est level; ~*-water mark,* mark showing the level reached at ~ water. **3.** not loud or shrill: *a ~ voice.* **4.** not highly developed: ~ *forms of life.* **5.** feeble: *in a ~ state of health; in ~ spirits,* sad; ~*-spirited* (adj.). **6.** vulgar; common: ~ *manners;* ~ *tastes.* **7.** of or in humble rank or position: *of ~ birth; high and ~;* ~*er deck* (in the Navy) ratings (2); those who are not officers. **8.** of small amount as measured by a scale or by degrees: ~ *prices; a ~ temperature.* *adv.* in or to a ~ position; in a ~ manner: *bring ~,* make ~ in health, wealth, or position: *brought ~ by misfortune; feel ~,* be sad; *lay ~,* overthrow; humble; *be laid ~,* be forced to stay in bed through injury, illness, etc.; *be running ~,* (of supplies,

etc.) be getting near the end; *speak ~,* speak in a ~ voice (softly). '~·brow *n. & adj.* (person) having or showing little taste for intellectual things, esp. art, music, and literature. '~·down *adj.* (of behaviour, etc.) dishonourable; mean. **L~·er House** *n.* House of Commons. '~·lands *n. pl.* ~ country, esp. the southern parts of Scotland.

low[2] [ləʊ] *v.i.* make the usu. deep sound characteristic of cows and other cattle. *n.* this characteristic sound.

low·er [ˈləʊə*] *v.t. & i.* **1.** let down (a flag, sail, etc.). **2.** make or become less high: ~ *one's voice;* ~ *prices.*

low·ly [ˈləʊlɪ] *adj.* (*-ier, -iest*) humble; simple; modest.

loy·al [ˈlɔɪəl] *adj.* true, faithful (to one's country, friends, etc.). **~·ly** *adv.* **~·ist** *n.* ~ subject, esp. during a revolt. **~·ty** *n.*

loz·enge [ˈlɒzɪndʒ] *n.* **1.** four-sided, diamond-shaped figure. **2.** small sweet, esp. one containing medicine: *cough ~s.*

L-plate [ˈelˌpleɪt] *n.* (Gt. Brit.) plate marked with a large letter L, fixed to the front and back of a motor vehicle to show that the driver is a learner who has not passed his driving test.

£.s.d. [ˈelesˈdiː] (abbr.) (in former British currency) pounds, shillings, and pence; money.

lu·bri·cate [ˈluːbrɪkeɪt] *v.t.* put oil or grease into (machine parts) to make (them) work smoothly. **lu·bri·cant** [ˈluːbrɪkənt] *n.* substance used for this purpose. **lu·bri·ca·tion** [ˌluːbrɪˈkeɪʃn] *n.* (no pl.).

lu·cerne, lu·cern [luːˈsɜːn] *n.* (Gt. Brit.) clover-like plant used for feeding animals.

lu·cid [ˈluːsɪd] *adj.* **1.** clear; easy to understand: *a ~ explanation.* **2.** ~ *intervals,* periods of sanity between periods of insanity. **~·i·ty** [luːˈsɪdətɪ] *n.* (no pl.).

luck [lʌk] *n.* (no pl.) **1.** good or bad fortune; chance; sth. that comes by chance: *in (out of) ~,* having (not having) good ~; *for ~,* to bring good ~. **2.** good fortune; the help of chance: *as ~ would have it ...; try one's ~.* **~·less** *adj.* unfortunate. **~·y** *adj.* (*-ier, -iest*) having, bringing, resulting from, good ~. **~·i·ly** *adv.*

lu·cra·tive [ˈluːkrətɪv] *adj.* profitable.

lu·di·crous [ˈluːdɪkrəs] *adj.* ridiculous.

lug [lʌg] *v.t. & i.* (*-gg-*) pull or drag roughly and with much effort (*at*).

lug·gage [ˈlʌgɪdʒ] *n.* (no pl.) (U.S.A. *baggage*) bags, trunks, etc. and their

luggage-van

contents taken on a journey. '**~-van** *n.* railway carriage for the passengers' ~.

lug·ger ['lʌgə*] *n.* small ship with one or more four-cornered sails.

lu·gu·bri·ous [luːˈguːbrɪəs] *adj.* dismal; mournful; gloomy.

luke·warm ['luːkwɔːm] *adj.* neither hot nor cold; (fig.) not eager in either supporting or opposing.

lull [lʌl] *v.t. & i.* make or become quiet or less active: ~ *a baby to sleep*; ~ *sb.'s suspicions. The wind ~ed.* *n.* interval of quiet; period of lessened activity, etc.: *a ~ in the conversation*; *a ~ in the storm*; (fig.) *the ~ before the coming storm.*

lul·la·by ['lʌləbaɪ] *n.* song for lulling a baby to sleep.

lum·ba·go [lʌmˈbeɪgəʊ] *n.* (no pl.) muscular pain in the lower part of the back.

lum·ber ['lʌmbə*] *n.* (no pl.) **1.** (esp. U.S.A.) roughly prepared timber (e.g. planks, boards): ~*jack*, ~*man*, man who fells, saws, or conveys (1) ~. **2.** useless or unwanted articles stored away (in a ~*-room*) or taking up space. *v.i. & t.* **1.** ~ *along* (*by, past*), move in a heavy, slow, and noisy way. **2.** ~ *up*, fill space inconveniently: *a room ~ed up with useless things.*

lu·mi·nary ['luːmɪnərɪ] *n.* star; the sun or moon; (fig.) moral or intellectual leader.

lu·mi·nous ['luːmɪnəs] *adj.* giving out light; bright. **lu·mi·nos·i·ty** [ˌluːmɪˈnɒsətɪ] *n.* (no pl.).

lump [lʌmp] *n.* **1.** mass without regular shape: ~*s of clay*; *a ~ of sugar*; *broken into ~s.* **2.** *a ~ sum*, one payment for a number of separate purchases. **3.** swelling or bump. *v.i. & t.* **1.** form into ~s. **2.** put or group (*together*) in a mass; treat (things) as if they were the same. **3.** *If you don't like it you can ~ it*, this must be endured, whether you like it or not. ~*ish adj.* (of a person) clumsy; stupid. ~*y adj.* (*-ier, -iest*) full of, covered with, ~s.

lu·nar ['luːnə*] *adj.* of the moon: *a ~ month*, the interval between successive new moons, about 29¹/₂ days; *~ module*, manned spacecraft carried by a larger spacecraft and detached while in orbit round the moon so that it may land on the surface of the moon and take off again.

lu·na·tic ['luːnətɪk] *adj. & n.* insane (person); mad(man). **lu·na·cy** ['luːnəsɪ] *n.* madness.

lunch [lʌntʃ] *n.* meal taken in the middle of the day: ~*-hour*; ~*-time.* *v.i.*

& *t.* eat ~; provide ~ for. **lun·cheon** ['lʌntʃən] *n.* (formal word for) ~.

lung [lʌŋ] *n.* either of the two breathing organs in the chest of man and other animals.

the lungs

lunge [lʌndʒ] *n.* sudden forward push (e.g. with a sword) or forward movement of the body (when striking a blow). *v.i.* make a ~.

lurch¹ [lɜːtʃ] *n.* (only in) *leave sb. in the ~*, leave him when he is in difficulties and needing help.

lurch² [lɜːtʃ] *n.* sudden change of weight to one side; sudden roll. *v.i.* move along with a ~ or ~es.

lure [ljʊə*] *n.* sth. that attracts; attraction or interest that sth. has: *the ~ of the sea for adventurous boys.* *v.t.* attract, tempt (to do sth., go somewhere): ~*d away from one's work.*

lu·rid ['ljʊərɪd] *adj.* **1.** highly coloured, esp. suggesting flame and smoke: *a ~ sunset.* **2.** sensational; violent and shocking: *a ~ description*; ~ *details of an aircraft crash.* ~*ly adv.*

lurk [lɜːk] *v.i.* be, keep, out of view, lying in wait or ready to attack.

lus·cious ['lʌʃəs] *adj.* rich and sweet in taste or smell; (of writing, music, art) too rich in ornament.

lush [lʌʃ] *adj.* (of grass, vegetation) luxuriant.

lust [lʌst] *n.* intense desire, esp. strong sexual desire (*for*); passionate enjoyment (*of*): *a ~ for power (gold)*; *the ~ of the flesh*, bodily desires. *v.i.* ~ *after* (*for*), have ~ for. ~*ful adj.* full of ~.

lus·tre (U.S.A. **-ter**) ['lʌstə*] *n.* (no pl.) **1.** quality of being bright, esp. of a polished or smooth surface: *the ~ of pearls.* **2.** (fig.) glory. **lus·trous** ['lʌstrəs] *adj.*

lusty ['lʌstɪ] *adj.* (*-ier, -iest*) healthy and strong. **lust·i·ly** *adv.* in a manner: *shout (work) lustily.*

lute [luːt] *n.* stringed musical instrument dating from the 14th century.

lux·u·ri·ant [lʌgˈzjʊərɪənt] *adj.* strong in growth; abundant: ~ *vegetation.* **lux·u·ri·ance** *n.* (no pl.) ~ growth. **lux·u·ri·ate** [lʌgˈzjʊərɪeɪt] *v.i.* take great delight (*in* sth.).

lux·u·ry [ˈlʌkʃərɪ] *n.* **1.** (no pl.) state of life in which one has and uses things that please the senses (good food, clothes, comfort, beautiful surroundings): *live in* ~; *a life of* ~. **2.** sth. pleasing to have but not essential. **3.** (attrib.) relating to luxuries: *a* ~ *flat* (*hotel*). **lux·u·ri·ous** [lʌgˈzjʊərɪəs] *adj.* loving ~; having ~: *luxurious hotels* (*food*).

-ly [-lɪ] *suff.* **1.** (forming adjs. from ns.) having the qualities of: *brotherly*; *ghostly*; *manly*. **2.** (forming adjs. or advs. from ns.) regular occurrence: *daily*; *hourly*; *weekly*. **3.** (forming advs. from adjs.): *gloomily*; *quickly*; *recently*.

ly·ing, see *lie*[1,2].

lymph [lɪmf] *n.* (no pl.) colourless liquid in the body, like blood but without colouring matter.

lynch [lɪntʃ] *v.t.* put to death without a lawful trial (sb. believed guilty of a crime).

lynx [lɪŋks] *n.* (pl. ~, ~*es*) short-tailed wild animal of the cat family, noted for its keen sight: ~-*eyed*.

lyre [ˈlaɪə*] *n.* kind of harp with strings vertically fixed in a U-shaped frame, used by the ancient Greeks.

lyr·ic [ˈlɪrɪk] *adj.* of, composed for, singing. *n.* ~ poem; (pl.) ~ verses. **lyr·i·cal** *adj.* **1.** = ~. **2.** (colloq.) full of emotion; enthusiastic (*over*).

M

ma [mɑː] *n.* (colloq., abbr. for) mamma.
ma'am [mæm, mɑːm] *n.* madam.
ma·ca·bre [məˈkɑːbrə] *adj.* gruesome;
grim; suggesting death.
mac·ad·am [məˈkædəm] *n.* (no pl.) ~
road, road with a surface of crushed
rock or stone. **~ize** [məˈkædəmaɪz]
v.t. make or cover with such a surface:
~*ized road*.
mac·a·ro·ni [ˌmækəˈrəʊnɪ] *n.* (pl. *-nis*,
-nies) flour paste formed into long
tubes, cooked for food.
mace [meɪs] *n.* rod or staff carried as a
sign of office or authority.

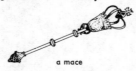

a mace

mach·i·na·tion [ˌmækɪˈneɪʃn] *n.* evil
plot(ting) or scheme.
ma·chine [məˈʃiːn] *n.* **1.** apparatus (1)
or appliance with parts working together to apply power, often steam or
electric power (*printing-*~), but sometimes human power (*bicycle, sewing-*~).
2. persons organized to control a political group; controlling system: *party*
(*propaganda, war*) ~. *v.t.* make or operate on (sth.) with a ~ (esp. of sewing
and printing). **~-gun** [məˈʃiːŋgʌn] *n.*
gun firing continuously while the trigger is pressed. **~-read·able** [məˈʃiːn-
ˌriːdəbl] *adj.* in a form that a computer can directly respond to. **~ry**
[məˈʃiːnərɪ] *n.* **1.** parts or works of a ~;
~s collectively. **2.** methods, organization (e.g. of government). **ma·chin·ist**
n. worker who makes or controls ~s; ~
(e.g. a sewing-~) worker.
mack·er·el [ˈmækrəl] *n.* (pl. ~s, collective pl. ~) small striped sea-fish
used as food.
mack·in·tosh [ˈmækɪntɒʃ] *n.* (Gt.
Brit., colloq. abbr. *mac, mack*) rain-
proof coat made of cloth treated with
rubber.
mac·ro- [ˈmækrəʊ-] *pref.* large; large-

scale; great; long: *macrocosm*, (a) the
great world or universe; (b) any great
whole.
mad [mæd] *adj.* (*-dd-*) **1.** having, resulting from, a diseased mind. **2.** very
foolish: *be* (*go*) ~; *like* ~, wildly or
furiously: *They ran like* ~. **3.** much
excited; filled with enthusiasm: *She
is* ~ *about pop music.* **4.** (colloq.)
angry: ~ *at missing the train.* **~·den**
[ˈmædn] *v.t. & i.* make or become ~;
irritate; annoy. **'~·cap** *n.* person acting
recklessly or on impulse. **'~·man**, **'~-
ˌwom·an** *ns.* ~ person. **~·ly** *adv.* **~·
ness** *n.* (no pl.) state of being ~; extreme folly.
mad·am [ˈmædəm] *n.* respectful form
of address to a woman, used in speaking and writing: *Good morning,* ~. *Dear
M*~, ... (Cf. *sir.*)
made, see *make* (v.).
mad·ri·gal [ˈmædrɪgl] *n.* short love
song or poem; (esp.) song, usu. of five
or six parts, for voice only.
mael·strom [ˈmeɪlstrɒm] *n.* violent
whirlpool; (fig.) violent or destructive
force; whirl of events: *the* ~ *of war.*
mag·a·zine [ˌmægəˈziːn] *n.* **1.** store for
arms, ammunition, explosives, etc. **2.**
chamber holding cartridges fed (3)
automatically into the breech of a rifle
or gun; similar device (2) in a camera,
slide-projector, etc. **3.** paper-covered
(usu. weekly or monthly) periodical,
with stories, articles, etc. by various
writers.
ma·gen·ta [məˈdʒentə] *adj. & n.* (no
pl.) bright crimson (substance used as
a dye).
mag·got [ˈmægət] *n.* larva, grub, esp.
as found in bad meat.
mag·ic [ˈmædʒɪk] *n.* (no pl.) **1.** art of
controlling events by the pretended
use of supernatural forces: *black*
(*white*) ~, ~ done with (without) the
help of devils. **2.** identification of a
symbol with the thing it stands for (as
when the wearing of a lion's skin is
thought to give the wearer a lion's
courage). **3.** art of obtaining mysterious
results by stage tricks. **4.** mysterious

quality or charm: *the ~ of poetry.* **adj.** done by, or as by, ~; possessing ~; used in ~. ~ *lantern*, simple form of a modern *slide-projector.* **mag·i·cal** ['mædʒɪ-kl] **adj.** = ~. **mag·i·cal·ly** **adv.** **ma·gi·cian** [mə'dʒɪʃn] **n.** person skilled in ~ (1, 3).

mag·is·te·ri·al [,mædʒɪ'stɪərɪəl] **adj.** of a magistrate; having, showing, authority: *a ~ manner.*

mag·is·trate ['mædʒɪstreɪt] **n.** civil officer acting as judge in the lowest courts; Justice of the Peace.

mag·nan·i·mous [mæg'nænɪməs] **adj.** having, showing, generosity. **mag·na·nim·i·ty** [,mægnə'nɪmətɪ] **n.**

mag·nate ['mægneɪt] **n.** wealthy, leading man of business or industry.

mag·ne·sia [mæg'niːʃə] **n.** (no pl.) white, tasteless powder, carbonate of magnesium, used in medicine.

mag·ne·sium [mæg'niːzɪəm] **n.** (no pl.) silver-white metal that burns brightly.

mag·net ['mægnɪt] **n.** piece of iron able to attract iron: *bar ~; horseshoe ~.* **~·ic** [mæg'netɪk] **adj.** of, like, produced by, a ~: *a ~ic needle; ~ic tape* (see *tape* (3)); (fig.) exercising attraction: *a ~ic smile.* **mag·ne·tism** **n.** (no pl.) (science of) ~ic properties and phenomena. **mag·ne·tize** **v.t.** give properties of a ~ to; (fig.) attract like a ~.

mag·ne·to [mæg'niːtəʊ] **n.** (pl. ~s) electrical apparatus (1) for producing sparks for the ignition in an internal combustion engine.

mag·nif·i·cent [mæg'nɪfɪsnt] **adj.** splendid; remarkable; important-looking. **mag·nif·i·cence** **n.** (no pl.).

mag·ni·fy ['mægnɪfaɪ] **v.t. 1.** make (sth.) appear larger (as with a lens or microscope): *a ~ing glass*, a lens that magnifies objects seen through it. **2.** exaggerate; intensify.

mag·nil·o·quent [mæg'nɪləʊkwənt] **adj.** (of words, speech, etc.) pompous; (of a person) using pompous words.

mag·ni·tude ['mægnɪtjuːd] **n.** size; (degree of) importance.

mag·pie ['mægpaɪ] **n.** noisy black-and-white bird noted for thieving.

ma·hog·a·ny [mə'hɒgənɪ] **n.** (tropical tree with) red-brown wood much used for furniture.

maid [meɪd] **n. 1.** (liter.) girl. **2.** (old use) young, unmarried woman: *old ~*, elderly woman now unlikely to marry; *~ of honour*, unmarried woman attending a queen or princess. **3.** *~(servant)*, female servant.

maid·en ['meɪdn] **n.** (liter.) girl; young, unmarried woman. **attrib. adj.** ~

name, woman's family name before marriage; *~ speech*, (sb.'s) first speech made in public or in Parliament; *~ voyage*, ship's first voyage.

mail¹ [meɪl] **n.** body armour of metal rings or plates. **~ed adj.** *the ~ed fist*, armed force.

mail² [meɪl] **n. 1.** letters, parcels, etc. sent or delivered by post; letters, etc. sent, collected, or delivered at one time. **2.** (no pl.) system of carrying and delivering letters, etc.; post²: *by air ~.* **v.t.** send (a letter, etc.) by post. **'~·box n.** (U.S.A.) = letter-box. **~ car·ri·er, '~·man ns.** (U.S.A.) = postman. **~ or·der n.** order for goods to be delivered by post: *~order firm*, (U.S.A.) *~order house*, establishment whose business is conducted by post.

maim [meɪm] **v.t.** wound so that some part of the body is useless.

main [meɪn] **attrib. adj.** chief; most important: *have an eye to the ~ chance*, look after one's own interests. **n. 1.** *the ~s*, the principal pipes bringing water or gas, the principal wires transmitting electric current, from the source of supply into a building (contrasted with pipes from a cistern in a building, etc.): *a ~s set*, a radio set to be connected to the ~s, not a battery set. **2.** (only in) *with might and ~*, with all one's physical strength. **3.** *in the ~*, for the most part. **4.** (poet.) sea. **~·land** ['meɪn-lənd] **n.** country or continent without its islands. **~·ly adv.** chiefly; for the most part. **'~·spring n. 1.** chief spring in a watch or clock. **2.** (fig.) driving force or motive. **'~·stay n.** (fig.) chief support.

main·tain [meɪn'teɪn] **v.t. 1.** keep in working order; keep up (e.g. friendship). **2.** support. **3.** ~ *an opinion, that ...*, claim as true. **main·te·nance** ['meɪntənəns] **n.** (no pl.) (esp.) what is needed to support life.

mai·son·(n)ette [,meɪzə'net] **n.** small house; part of a house used separately, usu. of two storeys.

maize [meɪz] **n.** (no pl.) (also called *Indian corn*) sort of grain plant.

a maize-cob

maj·es·ty ['mædʒəstɪ] **n.** kingly or queenly appearance, conduct, speech,

causing respect; stateliness; royal power. *His (Her, Your) M~,* form used when speaking of or to a king or queen.
ma·jes·tic [mə'dʒestɪk] *adj.* having, showing, ~.

ma·jor¹ ['meɪdʒə*] *adj.* **1.** greater or more important: ~ *road.* **2.** (in schools) elder of two brothers: *Smith* ~. **3.** ~ *scale,* (music) scale having two full tones between the keynote and the third note. *n.* **1.** person of full legal age. **2.** (U.S.A.) student's special subject or course: *take English literature as one's* ~. **3.** (U.S.A.) student who specializes in a subject: *a history* ~. *v.i.* (U.S.A.) pursue (2) an academic ~: ~*ing in history.* **~·i·ty** [mə'dʒɒrətɪ] *n.* **1.** greater number or part (of); number by which votes for one side exceed those for the other side: *The bill was passed by a large ~ity. He was elected by a ~ity of 503.* **2.** legal age of reaching manhood or womanhood: *reach one's ~ity.*

ma·jor² ['meɪdʒə*] *n.* army officer between a captain and a colonel. **~·'gen·er·al** *n.* army officer next above a brigadier and under a lieutenant-general.

make [meɪk] *v.t. & i.* (p.t. & p.p. *made* [meɪd]) **1.** create; bring into existence; construct; produce; prepare: ~ *cloth (machines, clothes);* ~ *a hole in sth.;* ~ *a noise; made of wood;* ~ *money (a profit, one's fortune);* ~ (i.e. prepare) *tea (the beds);* ~ *fun (game, sport) of (sb.),* ridicule; laugh at; ~ *light of (sth.),* treat as not serious or not difficult; ~ *the most of sth.,* use to the greatest advantage. **2.** compel; force: ~ *sb. do sth.; be made to do sth.;* persuade: ~ *sb. believe sth.* **3.** cause to be, become, do, sth.; cause to take place: ~ *sb. happy;* ~ *sth. stronger;* ~ *a man president;* ~ *the fire burn up.* **4.** earn; win; gain: ~ *£3000 a year;* ~ *a fortune.* **5.** bring about the prosperity of: *The cotton trade made Manchester.* **6.** reach; accomplish: (of a ship) ~ *port; making only nine knots;* ~ *a journey in three hours.* **7.** reckon; consider to be: *What do you ~ the time (the total)?* **8.** (with advs. and preps. and in phrases): ~ *for,* go towards; rush violently at; ~ *off,* go or run away (esp. after doing sth. wrong); ~ *off (away) with sth.,* steal it; take it without permission; ~ *out,* (a) write out (e.g. a cheque, a bill); (b) succeed in seeing, reading, understanding; (c) give the idea (that); ~ *sth. over (to sb.),* transfer the possession of sth. (esp. by a formal agreement); ~ *up* (a) invent (a story); (b) supply (what is needed for completion); (c) prepare (medicine, etc.); (d) put together (things into parcels, bundles, etc.); (e) settle (a dispute); become friendly again (after a quarrel); (f) prepare (an actor for the stage); (g) put cosmetics on (the face); ~ *up one's mind (to),* determine (to); ~ *believe,* pretend. *n.* way a thing is made; structure: *cars of all* ~*s; of our own* ~, *made by us.* **'~·be·lieve** *n.* pretending; pretence; **mak·er** *n.* **1.** person or thing that ~s: *a dress ~r.* **2.** *the (our) M~r,* God. **'~·shift** *n.* sth. used until sth. better can be obtained. **'~·up** *n.* **1.** arrangement; composition. **2.** face-powder, rouge, etc. **'~·weight** *n.* small quantity added to ~ the weight right. **'mak·ing** *n.* be the making of, cause the well-being of; *have the makings of,* have the necessary qualities for becoming.

mal- [mæl-] *pref.* **1.** bad(ly): *maladministration; malfunction.* **2.** not: *maladroit.*

mal·ad·just·ed [,mælə'dʒʌstɪd] *adj.* **1.** badly adjusted. **2.** (psych., of a person) unable to adjust oneself properly to one's environment and conditions of life. **mal·ad·just·ment** *n.*

mal·a·dy ['mælədɪ] *n.* disease; illness.

ma·lar·i·a [mə'leərɪə] *n.* (no pl.) fever spread by a certain kind of mosquito. **ma·lar·i·al** *adj.* ~*l regions.*

mal·con·tent ['mælkən,tent] *n. & adj.* (person who is) discontented and inclined to rebel.

male [meɪl] *adj.* of the sex that can beget offspring. (Cf. *female.*) *n.* ~ person or animal.

male·dic·tion [,mælɪ'dɪkʃn] *n.* curse. **male·fac·tor** ['mælɪfæktə*] *n.* wrong-doer; criminal.

ma·lev·o·lent [mə'levələnt] *adj.* wishing evil to others; spiteful. **ma·lev·o·lence** *n.* (no pl.).

mal·for·ma·tion [,mælfɔ:'meɪʃn] *n.* state of being badly formed or shaped; badly formed part. **mal'formed** *adj.* badly formed.

mal·ice ['mælɪs] *n.* (no pl.) active ill will; desire to harm others: *bear sb. no* ~. **ma·li·cious** [mə'lɪʃəs] *adj.* feeling, showing, ~. **ma·li·cious·ly** *adv.*

ma·lign [mə'laɪn] *v.t.* speak ill of (sb.); tell lies about. *adj.* (of things) injurious: *a ~ influence.* **ma·lig·nant** [mə'lɪgnənt] *adj.* **1.** (of persons, their actions) filled with, showing, desire to hurt. **2.** (of diseases) harmful to life: ~*ant tumour.* **ma·lig·nan·cy** [mə'lɪgnənsɪ] *n.* (no pl.). **ma·lig·ni·ty** [mə'lɪgnətɪ] *n.*

ma·lin·ger [məˈlɪŋgə*] *v.i.* pretend to be ill (esp. in order to escape one's duty). ~**er** *n.* person who ~s.

mal·le·able [ˈmælɪəbl] *adj.* **1.** (of metals) that can be hammered or pressed into new shapes. **2.** (fig., e.g. of character) easily trained or adapted.

mal·let [ˈmælɪt] *n.* wooden-headed hammer.

a mallet

mal·nu·tri·tion [ˌmælnjuːˈtrɪʃn] *n.* (no pl.) condition caused by not getting enough food or the right sort of food.

mal·odor·ous [mælˈəʊdərəs] *adj.* ill-smelling.

mal·prac·tice [ˌmælˈpræktɪs] *n.* (law) wrongdoing; neglect of duty; instance of this.

malt [mɔːlt] *n.* (no pl.) grain (usu. barley) prepared for use in beer-making. *v.t.* make (grain) into ~; prepare with ~.

mal·treat [ˌmælˈtriːt] *v.t.* treat roughly or cruelly. ~**ment** *n.* (no pl.).

ma(m)·ma [məˈmɑː] *n.* (child's word for) mother.

mam·mal [ˈmæml] *n.* any of the class of animals that feed their young with milk from the breast.

mam·mo·gram [ˈmæməʊgræm], **mam·mo·graph** [ˈmæməʊgrɑːf] *ns.* X-ray picture of the female breast.

mam·mog·ra·phy [məˈmɒgrəfɪ] *n.* (no pl.) X-ray examination of the female breast to detect cancer.

mam·mon [ˈmæmən] *n.* (no pl.) wealth (when looked upon as an evil influence).

mam·moth [ˈmæməθ] *n.* large kind of elephant now extinct; (attrib.) immense: *a ~ project.*

man [mæn, as a suff. often -mən] *n.* (pl. **men** [men, as a suff. often -mən]) **1.** adult male human being (i.e. not a woman, boy, or girl); human being, without regard to sex or age: *All men must die. the ~ in the street,* person looked upon as representing the interests and opinions of ordinary people; *~ of the world,* one with wide experience of business and society; *~ of letters,* writer and scholar. **2.** (no pl.) the human race; all mankind: *M~ is mortal.* **3.** male person under the authority of another: *masters and men (=*

employees); *officers and men. v.t.* (*-nn-*) supply (ships, a fort, etc.) with the men needed: *a ~ned spacecraft.* ~**ful** *adj.* fearless; determined; resolute. ~**ful·ly** *adv.* '~**han·dle** *v.t.* move by physical strength; (sl.) handle roughly. '~**hole** *n.* opening through which a ~ may enter (a boiler, tank, underground sewer, etc.). ~**hood** *n.* (no pl.) **1.** state of being a ~: *reach ~hood.* **2.** ~**ly** qualities. '~**hour** *n.* work done by one ~ in one hour. ~**kind** *n.* (no pl.) the human race; all men. '~**like** *adj.* having the qualities (good or bad) of a ~. ~**ly** *adj.* (*-ier, -iest*) having the qualities expected of a ~. ~**nish** *adj.* (of a woman) ~like; more suitable for a ~ than for a woman. ~**-of-war** [ˌmænəvˈwɔː*] *n.* (old use) warship. '~**pow·er** *n.* **1.** power supplied by the physical (3) effort of ~. **2.** number of men available for military or other service. '~**ser·vant** *n.* (pl. *menservants*) male servant. '~**slaugh·ter** *n.* (no pl.) act of killing a person unlawfully but not wilfully.

man·a·cle [ˈmænəkl] *n.* (usu. pl.) fetter or chain for the hands or feet; (fig.) restraint. *v.t.* put ~s on; (fig.) restrain.

man·age [ˈmænɪdʒ] *v.t. & i.* **1.** control: *~ a business.* **2.** succeed; be able (to do sth.): *I can't ~ without help. He ~d to keep* (succeeded in keeping) *his temper.* ~**able** *adj.* that can be ~d or controlled. ~**ment** *n.* **1.** managing or being ~d: *failure caused by bad ~ment.* **2.** *the ~ment,* persons who ~ a business. **man·ag·er** *n.* person who controls a business, hotel, etc. **man·ag·er·ess** [ˌmænɪdʒəˈres] *n.* female ~. **man·a·ge·ri·al** [ˌmænəˈdʒɪərɪəl] *adj.* of ~rs.

man·da·rin[1] [ˈmændərɪn] *n.* (old use) name for a high Chinese government official; form of Chinese used by educated classes and for official purposes.

man·da·rin[2], **man·da·rine** [ˈmændərɪn] *n.* ~ (*orange*), tangerine (1).

man·date [ˈmændeɪt] *n.* **1.** order from a superior; command given with authority. **2.** control over certain territories authorized by the League of Nations after the First World War. **3.** authority given to representatives by voters, members of a trade union, etc. **man·dat·ed** [ˈmændeɪtɪd] *adj.* under a ~ (2). **man·da·ta·ry** [ˈmændətərɪ] *n.* person or (hist.) state to whom a ~ has been given. **man·da·to·ry** [ˈmændətərɪ] *adj.* of, conveying, a command; compulsory. *n.* mandatary.

mandolin

man·do·lin ['mændəlɪn] *n.* musical instrument with 6 or 8 metal strings stretched in pairs on a rounded body.

a mandolin

mane [meɪn] *n.* long hair on the neck of some animals (esp. horse, lion, etc.).

ma·neu·ver, etc. (U.S.A.) = manœuvre, etc.

man·ga·nese ['mæŋgəniːz] *n.* (no pl.) hard, brittle, light-grey metal.

mange [meɪndʒ] *n.* (no pl.) skin disease, esp. of dogs and cats. **mangy** *adj.* (-ier, -iest) suffering from ~; dirty; neglected.

man·ger ['meɪndʒə*] *n.* long open box or trough for horses or cattle to feed from.

man·gle[1] ['mæŋgl] *v.t. & n.* (put through a) machine (also called *wringer*) with rollers for pressing out water from and smoothing laundry, etc.

a mangle[1]

man·gle[2] ['mæŋgl] *v.t.* cut up, tear, damage, badly.

man·go ['mæŋgəʊ] *n.* (pl. *-oes, -os*) tropical tree having pear-shaped fruit with yellow flesh.

man·grove ['mæŋgrəʊv] *n.* tropical tree growing in salt-water swamps and sending down new roots from its branches.

ma·nia ['meɪnjə] *n.* 1. (no pl.) violent madness. 2. great enthusiasm (*for* sth.). **ma·ni·ac** ['meɪnɪæk] *n.* raving madman. **ma·ni·a·cal** [mə'naɪəkl] *adj.*

mani·cure ['mænɪˌkjʊə*] *n.* 1. (no pl.) care of the hands and finger-nails. 2. manicurist. *v.t.* give ~ treatment to. **mani·cur·ist** ['mænɪˌkjʊərɪst] *n.* person who gives ~ treatment.

man·i·fest ['mænɪfest] *adj.* clear and obvious. *v.t.* 1. show clearly; give signs of. 2. (of a thing) reveal *itself*; appear.

n. list of a ship's cargo. **man·i·fes·ta·tion** [ˌmænɪfe'steɪʃn] *n.* **man·i·fes·to** [ˌmænɪ'festəʊ] *n.* (pl. *-os, -oes*) public declaration of principles, purposes, etc. by a ruler, group of persons, etc.

man·i·fold ['mænɪfəʊld] *adj.* having or providing for many uses, copies, etc.; many and various.

Ma·nila, Ma·nil·la [mə'nɪlə] *n.* ~ (*hemp*), plant fibre used for making rope, mats, etc.

ma·nip·u·late [mə'nɪpjʊleɪt] *v.t.* operate, handle, use with skill (instruments, etc.); manage or control (sb. or sth.) cleverly, esp. by using one's influence. **ma·nip·u·la·tion** [məˌnɪpjʊ-'leɪʃn] *n.*

man·ne·quin ['mænɪkɪn] *n.* person (now usu. called a *model*) employed to display new clothes for sale by wearing them.

man·ner ['mænə*] *n.* 1. way a thing is done or happens. 2. (no pl.) person's way of behaving towards others: *an awkward* ~. 3. (pl.) habits and customs. 4. (pl.) social behaviour: *good (bad)* ~s. *He has no* ~s (i.e. does not behave well). 5. sort: *all* ~ *of*, every kind of; *by no* ~ *of means*, in no circumstances; *in a* ~, to some extent. **~ed** *adj.* behaving in a specified way: *ill- (well-)~ed*, having bad (good) ~s. **~ism** *n.* peculiarity of behaviour, esp. one that is habitual. **~ly** *adj.* well-bred; having good ~s.

ma·nœu·vre (U.S.A. **ma·neu·ver**) [mə'nuːvə*] *n.* planned movement (of military forces); movement or plan, made to deceive or to escape from sb., to win or do sth. *v.t. & i.* (cause to) perform ~s; force (sb. or sth.) (*into* doing sth., *into* or *out of* a position) by clever handling. **ma·nœuvr·able** [mə'nuːvrəbl] (U.S.A. **ma·neu·ver·able** [mə'nuːvərəbl]) *adj.* that can be ~d.

a mangrove swamp

man·or ['mænə*] *n.* unit of land under the feudal system; (modern use) piece of land over which the lord (or lady) of the ~ has or had certain rights: *~-house*, mansion of the lord of the ~. **ma·no·ri·al** [mə'nɔːrɪəl] *adj.* of a ~.

marine

man·sion ['mænʃn] *n.* **1.** large and stately house. **2.** (pl.) (Gt. Brit., in proper names) block of flats.

man·tel ['mæntl] *n.* (usu. ~piece) shelf above a fireplace.

man·tis ['mæntɪs] *n.* long-legged insect that holds up its forelegs as if praying.

a mantis

man·tle ['mæntl] *n.* loose, sleeveless cloak; (fig.) overall covering: *a ~ of snow.*

man·u·al ['mænjʊəl] *adj.* of, done with, the hands: ~ *work*; ~ *labourers.* *n.* **1.** textbook; handbook. **2.** keyboard of an organ. ~·ly *adv.*

man·u·fac·ture [,mænjʊ'fæktʃə*] *v.t.* make, produce (goods, etc.), esp. on a large scale by machinery; (fig.) invent (evidence, a story). *n.* making of goods; (pl.) ~d goods. **man·u·fac·tur·er** *n.*

ma·nure [mə'njʊə*] *n.* (no pl.) animal waste or other material, natural or artificial, used for making soil fertile; fertilizer. *v.t.* put ~ on (land).

manu·script ['mænjʊskrɪpt] *n.* book, etc. as first written by hand: *poems still in ~.*

many ['menɪ] *adj. & n.* (contrasted with *few*; cf. *more, most*) **1.** (used with pl. nouns; cf. *much*, used with sing. nouns) a large number (of), a lot (of): *Were there ~ people at the meeting? There were a great ~* (a very large number). **2.** ~ *a* (with sing. noun): *M~ a man, ~ men. be one too ~ for,* be cleverer than; outwit. ~'sid·ed *adj.* (fig.) having ~ abilities, capabilities, aspects, etc.

Mao·ism ['maʊɪzəm] *n.* (no pl.) political theories and practice developed chiefly by the Chinese communist leader Mao Tse-tung [,maʊtse'tʊŋ]. **Mao·ist** ['maʊɪst] *n.* believer in, supporter of, ~. *adj.* of ~.

map [mæp] *n.* representation, usu. on a flat surface, of the whole or a part of the surface of the earth, etc., or of the sky, showing position of the stars, etc. *v.t.* (-pp-) **1.** make a ~ of; show on a ~. **2.** ~ *out*, plan; arrange.

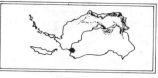

a map

ma·ple ['meɪpl] *n.* (wood of) sorts of tree: ~ *sugar* (*syrup*), sugar (syrup) got from the sap of one kind of ~.

mar [mɑ:*] *v.t.* (-rr-) injure; spoil.

mar·a·thon ['mærəθən] *n.* long-distance road race on foot.

ma·raud·er [mə'rɔ:də*] *n.* person who makes raids in search of plunder.

mar·ble ['mɑ:bl] *n.* **1.** (no pl.) sorts of hard limestone used, when cut and polished, for building and sculpture. **2.** (pl.) works of art in ~. **3.** small ball of stone or glass used in children's games: *playing ~s.*

March [mɑ:tʃ] *n.* third month of the year.

march [mɑ:tʃ] *v.i. & t.* walk as soldiers do, with regular and measured steps; cause to do this: *The soldiers ~ed into the town. n.* **1.** act, instance, of ~ing: *a ~ of 10 miles.* **2.** music for ~ing to: *a dead ~* (in slow time for a funeral). **3.** (no pl., with def. art.) (fig.) progress; onward movement: *the ~ of events* (*time*).

mar·chio·ness ['mɑ:ʃənɪs] *n.* wife or widow of a marquis.

mare [meə*] *n.* female horse. ~'s *nest,* discovery that turns out to be false or worthless.

mar·ga·rine [,mɑ:dʒə'ri:n] *n.* (no pl.) butter substitute made from animal or vegetable fat. **marge** [mɑ:dʒ] *n.* (no pl.) (colloq., abbr. for) ~.

mar·gin ['mɑ:dʒɪn] *n.* **1.** blank space round the printed or written matter on a page. **2.** edge or border (e.g. of a lake). **3.** amount (of time, money, etc.) above what is estimated as necessary. ~·al ['mɑ:dʒɪnl] *adj.* of or in a ~ (1): ~al *notes.*

mar·i·jua·na, -hua·na [,mærɪ'hwɑ:nə] *n.* (no pl.) dried leaves and flowering tops of the hemp plant, used as a hallucinogenic drug and smoked esp. in cigarettes (called *reefers* or *joints*).

ma·rine [mə'ri:n] *adj.* **1.** of, by, found in, produced by, the sea: ~ *products.* **2.** of ships, etc.: ~ *insurance* (of ships and cargo). *n.* **1.** *merchant ~,* all the merchant ships of a country. **2.** soldier serving on a warship and trained for fighting at sea or on land. **mar·i·ner** ['mærɪnə*] *n.* (liter. or official) sailor.

mar·i·o·nette [,mærɪə'net] *n.* doll or puppet moved by strings on a small stage.

mar·i·tal ['mærɪtl] *adj.* of a husband; of or between husband and wife; of marriage.

mar·i·time ['mærɪtaɪm] *adj.* of the sea: ~ *law*; near the sea: ~ *provinces*.

mark [mɑːk] *n.* **1.** line, scratch, cut, stain, etc. that spoils the appearance of sth. **2.** noticeable spot on the body: *a white ~ on a horse's head; a birth-~.* **3.** natural sign or indication (of quality, character, intelligence). **4.** figure, design, line, etc. made as a sign or indication: *punctuation ~s; price-~s; trade ~s.* **5.** unit for measuring quality or result (e.g. of school work): *full ~s for science; 95 ~s out of 100 for English.* **6.** sth. aimed at; target: *beside the ~,* not to the point; irrelevant; *wide of the ~,* inaccurate. **7.** normal level: *up to (below) the ~,* as good as (not so good as) the normal. **8.** *make one's ~,* attain distinction; become famous. *v.t.* **1.** put or be a ~ (4) on or against: ~ *prices on goods;* ~ *a pupil absent.* **2.** give ~s (5) to: ~ *examination papers.* **3.** pay attention to: *M~ how it is done.* **4.** ~ *time,* raise the feet as when marching but without moving forward; (fig.) act in a listless or unproductive manner; wait for an opportunity to advance or progress. **5.** (Gt. Brit., sport) keep close to (a member of an opposing team) so as to hamper. **6.** ~ *sth. down (up),* put a lower (higher) price on it; ~ *sth. off,* separate by a limit; ~ *sth. out,* make lines to show the limits of (e.g. a tennis-court); ~ *sb. out for* (e.g. promotion), decide in advance (that he will be promoted later). **~ed** [mɑːkt] *adj.* clear; readily seen: *a ~ed difference; a ~ed man,* one who is watched with suspicion and who is to be attacked or punished. **~ed·ly** ['mɑːkɪdlɪ] *ad~.* **~er** *n.* (esp.) person who ~s the score at games; sth. that ~s or indicates. **~ing** *n.* (esp.) different colours of feathers, fur, etc. **~s·man** ['mɑːksmən] *n.* person skilled in shooting. **~s·man·ship** *n.* skill in shooting.

mar·ket ['mɑːkɪt] *n.* **1.** public place (open space or building) where people meet to buy and sell goods: *going to (the) ~ to sell eggs; ~-day,* day fixed by law for holding a ~; ~ *town,* (esp.) one where there is a cattle-~. **2.** trade in a certain class of goods: *the coffee ~;* state of trade as shown by prices, etc.:

a lively ~. The ~ rose (i.e. prices advanced). **3.** (no pl.) buying and selling *come into, be on, the ~,* be offered for sale. **4.** area, country, in which good may be sold: *finding new ~s for manu factures. v.i. & t.* buy or sell in a ~; take or send to ~: *go ~ing;* ~ *one's goods.* **~·able** *adj.* that can be sold. **~ gar·den** *n.* (Gt. Brit.) garden where vegetables etc. are grown for ~s.

mar·ma·lade ['mɑːməleɪd] *n.* orange jam.

mar·mot ['mɑːmət] *n.* small, burrow ing rodent with coarse fur, a short bushy tail, and very small ears, tha hibernates in winter.

ma·roon[1] [mə'ruːn] *adj. & n.* (no pl. brownish-crimson (colour).

ma·roon[2] [mə'ruːn] *n.* firework, esp the kind used as a warning signal.

ma·roon[3] [mə'ruːn] *v.t.* put (sb.) on a desert island, uninhabited coast, etc and leave him there.

mar·quee [mɑː'kiː] *n.* large tent.

mar·quis, mar·quess ['mɑːkwɪs] *n* nobleman next in rank below a duke (Cf. *marchioness.*)

mar·riage, mar·riage·able, mar ried, see **marry.**

mar·row ['mærəʊ] *n.* **1.** (no pl.) soft fatty substance that fills the hollow parts of bones. **2.** (often *vegetable ~*) vege table of the gourd family, used as food

mar·ry ['mærɪ] *v.t. & i.* **1.** take (sb. as one's husband or wife; take a hus band or wife. **2.** (of a priest, etc.) joi as husband and wife. **3.** give (e.g. one's daughter) in marriage: ~ *off,* find a wife or husband for (one's son or daughter). **4.** obtain by ~ing: ~ *a for tune.* **mar·ried** *adj.* **1.** united in mar riage: *the married couple.* **2.** of persons so united: *married life.* **mar·riage** ['mærɪdʒ] *n.* union of a man and wom an as husband and wife; state of being married; wedding ceremony. **mar riage·able** *adj.* (of a young person) old enough or fit for marriage: *be of marriageable age.*

marsh [mɑːʃ] *n.* area of low-lying wet land. **~y** *adj.* (-*ier,* -*iest*).

mar·shal ['mɑːʃl] *n.* **1.** officer of high est rank: (Gt. Brit.) *Field M~* (Army) *Air M~* (Air Force). **2.** official respon sible for important public events. **3** (U.S.A.) official with the functions of a sheriff; head of a city police depart ment or fire department. *v.t.* (-*ll-* U.S.A. also -*l-*) **1.** arrange (military forces, railway waggons, facts, etc.) in the right order. **2.** guide or lead (sb.) with ceremony.

master

mar·su·pi·al [mɑːˈsjuːpjəl] *n. & adj.* (one) of the class of animals (e.g. the kangaroo) having a pouch in which to carry their young which are born before developing completely.

mar·ten [ˈmɑːtɪn] *n.* small animal of the weasel family; its fur.

mar·tial [ˈmɑːʃl] *adj.* of, associated with, warfare: ~ *music*; ~ *law*, military government replacing the operation of ordinary law for a time.

mar·tin [ˈmɑːtɪn] *n.* kind of swallow².

mar·ti·net [ˌmɑːtɪˈnet] *n.* person who expects and enforces very strict discipline.

mar·tyr [ˈmɑːtə*] *n.* 1. person put to death or caused to suffer for his religious beliefs or for the sake of a great cause. 2. *be a* ~ *to* (e.g. rheumatism), suffer great pain because of. *v.t.* put to death, cause to suffer, as a ~. **~dom** *n.* ~'s suffering or death; (fig.) torment: *a lifelong* ~*dom*.

mar·vel [ˈmɑːvl] *n.* 1. sth. causing great surprise, pleased astonishment: *the* ~*s of modern science*. 2. sb. or sth. showing a good quality in a surprising way: *She's a* ~ *of patience. v.i.* (*-ll-*, U.S.A. also *-l-*) be much surprised: ~ *at sth.*; ~ *that* (*how, etc.*). **~lous** (U.S.A. also **~ous**) [ˈmɑːvələs] *adj.* wonderful; causing pleased surprise.

mas·ca·ra [mæˈskɑːrə] *n.* (no pl.) cosmetic for darkening the eyelashes and eyebrows. *v.t.* apply ~ to: ~*ed eyelashes*.

mas·cot [ˈmæskət] *n.* person, animal, or object considered likely to bring good fortune.

mas·cu·line [ˈmæskjʊlɪn] *adj.* 1. of, like, the male sex. 2. of male gender: '*Actor*' *is a* ~ *noun.* (Cf. *feminine*.)

ma·ser [ˈmeɪzə*] *n.* device (2) for producing or amplifying microwaves.

mash [mæʃ] *n.* (no pl.) 1. grain, bran, etc. cooked in water for horses, etc. 2. any substance softened and crushed. *v.t.* beat or crush into a ~: ~*ed potatoes*.

mask [mɑːsk] *n.* 1. covering for the face or part of the face. 2. (also *gas* ~) covering for the head worn as a protection against gas (e.g. in mines). 3. false face

a mask (1)

a megaphone

worn by an actor. *v.t.* cover with a ~; keep (sth.) from view; conceal.

ma·son [ˈmeɪsn] *n.* 1. stone-cutter; worker who builds with stone. 2. *M*~, freemason. **~ic** [məˈsɒnɪk] *adj.* of freemasons. **~ry** *n.* stonework.

masque [mɑːsk] *n.* drama in verse, usu. with music, dancing and fine dresses, common in the 16th and 17th centuries.

mas·quer·ade [ˌmæskəˈreɪd] *n.* ball² at which masks and other disguises are worn. *v.i.* appear, be, in disguise: *a prince who* ~*d as a shepherd*.

mass [mæs] *n.* 1. lump, quantity of matter, without regular shape; large number, quantity or heap (of): ~*es of dark clouds*; *the* ~*es*, the great body of ordinary working people; ~ *media*, means of communication (as newspapers, radio, television, etc.) designed to reach large numbers of people; ~ *meeting*, large meeting, esp. of people wanting to express their views; ~-*produce* (v.t.), produce large numbers of (identical articles), usu. by machinery; ~ *production*, manufacture of large numbers of identical articles. 2. (no pl.) (science) quantity of matter in a body. *v.t. & i.* form or collect into a ~: *troops* ~*ing on the frontiers*.

Mass [mæs] *n.* celebration (esp. Roman Catholic) of Holy Communion.

mas·sa·cre [ˈmæsəkə*] *n.* cruel killing of large numbers of (esp. defenceless) people. *v.t.* make a ~ of.

mas·sage [ˈmæsɑːʒ] *n.* rubbing and pressing of the body to lessen pain, stiffness, etc. *v.t.* apply ~ to. **mas·seur** [mæˈsɜː*], **mas·seuse** [mæˈsɜːz] *ns.* man, woman, trained in ~.

mas·sif [ˈmæsiːf] *n.* compact group of mountain heights.

mas·sive [ˈmæsɪv] *adj.* 1. heavy and solid; heavy-looking. 2. (fig.) substantial.

mast [mɑːst] *n.* upright support (of wood or metal) for a ship's sails; tall staff (2) (for a flag); tall steel structure for aerials of a radio or television transmitter.

mas·ter [ˈmɑːstə*] *n.* 1. man who has others working for or under him; male owner of a dog, horse, etc.; captain of a merchant ship; male head of a household; male teacher. 2. *M*~ *of Arts* (*Science, etc.*), holder of this university degree. 3. skilled workman, self-employed: *a* ~ *builder*. 4. *the old* ~*s*, great painters, esp. those of 1200—1700, and the pictures they painted. 5. person who has control (*of*): *be* ~ *of one's fate*;

masterful

make oneself ~ *of a subject,* learn it thoroughly. **6.** (with a boy's name) young Mr: *M*~ *Tom; M*~ *T. Smith.* **v.t.** become the ~ of; overcome: ~ *one's temper,* control it. **adj.** commanding; superior: *a* ~ *mind.* ~**ful adj.** fond of controlling others; imperious. '~**key n.** key that will open many different locks. ~**ly adj.** skilful; expert. '~**piece n.** sth. made or done with great skill. ~**y n.** (no pl.) complete control or knowledge (*of*).

mas·ti·cate ['mæstɪkeɪt] **v.t.** soften, grind up, (food) with the teeth; chew.

mas·tiff ['mæstɪf] **n.** large, strong dog, used as a watch-dog.

mat¹ [mæt] **n.** piece of material used for a floor covering or (*a door*~) to wipe dirty shoes on; piece of material placed on a table, etc. to prevent damage (e.g. from hot dishes). ~**ted** ['mætɪd] **adj.** (of hair, etc.) tangled; knotted.

mat², **matt** [mæt] **adj.** (of a surface) dull (1), not glossy or polished.

mat·a·dor ['mætədɔ:*] **n.** man whose task it is to kill the bull in the sport of bullfighting.

match¹ [mætʃ] **n.** short piece of wood or other material tipped with a mixture that bursts into flame when rubbed on a rough or specially prepared surface. '~**book n.** small book (4) containing rows of ~es. '~**box n.** small box for holding ~es. '~**wood n.** small broken bits of wood.

a box of matches¹

match² [mætʃ] **n. 1.** contest; game: *a football* (*cricket*) ~. **2.** person able to meet another as his equal in strength, skill, etc.: *find* (*meet*) *one's* ~. **3.** marriage: *They decided to make a* ~ *of it* (to marry). **4.** prospective partner in marriage: *be a good* ~, be considered satisfactory or desirable as a possible partner, esp. in regard to rank or fortune. **5.** person or thing exactly like, corresponding to, or combining well with, another: *colours* (*materials*) *that are a good* ~. **v.t. & i. 1.** put in competition (*with* or *against*). **2.** be equal to or corresponding (with) (in quality, colour, etc.): *curtains that* ~ *the carpet; a*

brown dress with a hat to ~. **3.** be, obtain, a ~ (2) for: *a well-*~*ed pair* (e.g. boxers about equal in skill, or a husband and wife fitted to live together happily). ~**less adj.** unequalled. '~·**mak·er n.** person fond of bringing about marriages.

mate [meɪt] **n. 1.** fellow worker. **2.** ship's officer below the captain: *firs (second, etc.)* ~. **3.** one of a pair of birds or animals living together: *the lioness and her* ~. **v.t. & i.** (cause to) unite (to produce young): *the mating season.*

ma·te·ri·al [mə'tɪərɪəl] **n.** that of which sth. is or can be made or with which sth. is done: *raw* ~s, not yet used in manufacture; *dress* ~, cloth; *writing* ~s, pen, paper, etc. **adj. 1.** made of, connected with, matter or substance (contrasted with *spiritual*): *the* ~ *world.* **2.** of the body; of physical needs: ~ *comforts and pleasures; a* ~ *point of view.* **3.** important, essential (*to*): (law) ~ *evidence* (*facts*). ~**ism n.** (no pl.) **1.** theory, belief, that only physical things exist. **2.** interest in, attention to, things (money, bodily comfort, and pleasures) only. ~**ist n.** believer in ~ism; person who ignores religion, art, music, etc. ~**is·tic** [mə,tɪərɪə'lɪstɪk] **adj.** of ~ism or ~ists. ~**is·ti·cal·ly adv.** ~**ize v.t. & i.** (cause to) take a ~ form; (cause to) become fact: *His plans didn't* ~*ize.*

ma·ter·nal [mə'tɜ:nl] **adj. 1.** of or like a mother; motherly. **2.** related through the mother: ~ *aunt,* aunt on the mother's side of the family. ~**ly adv.** **ma·ter·ni·ty** [mə'tɜ:nətɪ] **n.** (no pl.) **1.** motherhood; motherliness. **2.** (attrib.) for women during and just after childbirth: *maternity hospital* (*ward*); for pregnant women: *maternity dress* (*wear*).

math·e·mat·ics [,mæθə'mætɪks] **n. pl.** (usu. sing. v.) science of space and number. **math·e·mat·i·cal adj.** of ~. **math·e·ma·ti·cian** [,mæθəmə'tɪʃn] **n.** expert in ~.

maths [mæθs] (U.S.A. **math** [mæθ]) **n.** (colloq., abbr. for) mathematics.

mat·i·née (U.S.A. **-nee**) ['mætɪneɪ] **n.** afternoon performance at a cinema or theatre.

mat·ins ['mætɪnz] **n. pl.** morning prayer (Church of England); prayers at daybreak (Roman Catholic Church).

ma·tri·arch ['meɪtrɪɑ:k] **n.** female head of a family or tribe.

mat·ri·cide ['meɪtrɪsaɪd] **n. 1.** killing of one's mother. **2.** person guilty of this.

ma·tric·u·late [mə'trɪkjʊleɪt] *v.t. & i.* (allow to) enter a university as a student, usu. after passing an examination. **ma·tric·u·la·tion** [mə,trɪkjʊ'leɪʃn] *n.* matriculating; special examination for this.

mat·ri·mo·ny ['mætrɪmənɪ] *n.* (no pl.) state of being married. **mat·ri·mo·nial** [,mætrɪ'məʊnjəl] *adj.*

ma·trix ['meɪtrɪks] *n.* (pl. *matrices* ['meɪtrɪsiːz], ~*es*) mould into which hot metal, etc. is poured to be shaped; rock-mass in which gems, metals, etc. are found embedded.

ma·tron ['meɪtrən] *n.* **1.** woman housekeeper in a school or other institution. **2.** woman controlling nursing staff in a hospital. **3.** married woman or widow (usu. marked by dignified maturity or social distinction). ~**ly** *adj.* of or like a ~; dignified.

matt, see *mat²*.

mat·ter ['mætə*] *n.* **1.** (no pl.) physical substance (in contrast with *mind* and *spirit*): *organic* ~. **2.** (no pl.) *printed* ~, anything printed; *reading* ~, books, etc. **3.** subject; sth. to which thought or attention is given: *money* ~*s*; *a* ~ *I know little about*; *as a* ~ *of fact*, in reality; although you might not think so; *a* ~ *of course*, sth. naturally to be expected; *for that* ~*, for the* ~ *of that*, so far as that is concerned. **4.** what is said in (contrasted with *style*, etc. of) a book, speech, etc. **5.** (no pl.) (physiol.) substance in or from the body; pus. **6.** *be the* ~ *(with)*, be wrong (with); *no* ~ *what*, whatever; *no* ~ *when (where, who, how)*, it is unimportant when, etc. *v.i.* be important (*to* sb.): *It doesn't* ~ *to me how you do it.* ~**-of-fact** [,mætərəv'fækt] *adj.* keeping to facts; unimaginative; ordinary.

mat·ting ['mætɪŋ] *n.* (no pl.) woven material for floor coverings, packing goods, etc.

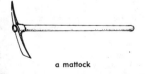

a mattock

mat·tock ['mætək] *n.* tool resembling a pick¹ in shape, used for breaking up hard ground, etc.

mat·tress ['mætrɪs] *n.* long, thick, flat, oblong pad of wool, hair, feathers, foam rubber, straw, etc., sometimes containing springs, on which to sleep:

spring ~, framework of springs and wires as part of a bed or divan.

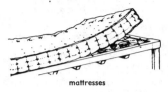

mattresses

ma·ture [mə'tjʊə*] *v.t. & i.* bring or come to full development or to a state ready for use. *adj.* (~*r*, ~*st*) ripe; fully grown or developed; carefully thought out; perfected; (comm., of bills) due for payment. **ma·tu·ri·ty** [mə'tjʊərɪtɪ] *n.* (no pl.).

maud·lin ['mɔːdlɪn] *adj.* sentimental in a silly or tearful way.

maul [mɔːl] *v.t.* injure by rough or brutal handling.

Maun·dy Thurs·day ['mɔːndɪ 'θɜːzdɪ] *n.* Thursday before Easter.

mau·so·le·um [,mɔːsə'liːəm] *n.* magnificent tomb.

mauve [məʊv] *adj. & n.* (no pl.) pale purple.

maw [mɔː] *n.* animal's stomach.

mawk·ish ['mɔːkɪʃ] *adj.* foolishly sentimental; sweet and sickly.

max·i ['mæksɪ] *n. & adj.* (colloq.) (woman's skirt, dress, coat, etc.) reaching to the ankle or just above it: *a* ~*-coat*; *a* ~*-skirt.*

max·i- ['mæksɪ-] *pref.* very large or long.

max·im ['mæksɪm] *n.* widely accepted general truth or rule of conduct expressed in few words.

max·i·mum ['mæksɪməm] *n.* (pl. *-ma* [-mə], ~*s*) *& adj.* (opp. *minimum*) greatest possible or recorded degree, quantity, etc.: ~ *price (speed, temperature).*

May [meɪ] *n.* **1.** fifth month of the year. **2.** *m*~, hawthorn (blossom). ~ **Day** *n.* 1st of ~ as a country festival or Labour Day. '**m**~**-pole** *n.* flower-decorated pole danced round on ~ Day.

may [meɪ] *v.aux.* (pres.t. ~; p.t. *might* [maɪt]; neg. ~ *not*, (colloq.) ~*n't* [meɪnt], *might not*, (colloq.) *mightn't* ['maɪtnt]) **1.** (used to indicate possibility or probability): *That* ~ *or* ~ *not be true. That might be true one day* (i.e. in the future). **2.** (used to indicate (a request for) permission): *M*~ *I come in? Yes, you* ~. **3.** (used to express a wish): *M*~ *you live to be a* *hundred!* **4.** (used in clauses after *wish,* *fear,* etc. or to express purpose): *I fear you ~ blame me for this. Write to him today, so that he ~ know when to expect you.* '~·**be** *adv.* perhaps; possibly.

may·on·naise [ˌmeɪə'neɪz] *n.* (no pl.) thick dressing of eggs, oil, and vinegar, used on cold food, esp. salads.

may·or [meə*] *n.* head of a town corporation. **~·al·ty** ['meərəltɪ] *n.* ~'s (period of) office. **~·ess** ['meərɪs] *n.* ~'s wife or female relative helping in social duties; female ~.

maze [meɪz] *n.* network of paths, lines, etc.; number of confusing facts, etc.: *in a ~,* bewildered; puzzled.

me [miː, mɪ] *pron.* object form of the pronoun *I.*

mead [miːd] *n.* (poet.) meadow.

mead·ow ['medəʊ] *n.* piece of grassland, esp. one used for hay.

mea·gre (U.S.A. **-ger**) ['miːgə*] *adj.* **1.** (of a person) thin. **2.** not enough: *a ~ meal; a ~ attendance at a meeting.*

meal¹ [miːl] *n.* occasion of eating (e.g. breakfast); food for a ~.

meal² [miːl] *n.* (no pl.) grain (e.g. wheat) coarsely ground: *oat~.* **~y** *adj.* (*-ier, -iest*) powdery, like ~.

mean¹ [miːn] *v.t. & i.* (p.t. & p.p. ~t [ment]) **1.** convey to the mind (through the eyes, the ears, etc.) sth. that can be understood; intend to convey (a sense) or indicate (an object): *By running round after you he ~s to show sympathy. No, I don't ~ you, I am pointing to him.* **2.** design; have in mind: *I ~ to go to America one of these days. This medicine is not ~t for children.* **3.** have as a purpose or plan: *He ~s mischief* (has an evil plan in his mind). *~ business,* be ready to act, not merely to talk; *~ sb. no harm,* have no intention to harm him. **4.** be a sign of: *Does this incident ~ war?* **5.** ~ *much* (*a great deal, little,* etc.) *to,* be of much, little, importance to. **~·ing** *n.* **1.** that which is meant. **2.** purpose. *adj. a ~ing look,* a look that shows a purpose; a look full of ~ing. **~·ing·ful** *adj.* **~·ing·less** *adj.* **~·ing·ly** *adv.*

mean² [miːn] *adj.* **1.** poor in appearance: *a ~ house in a ~ street.* **2.** selfish; ungenerous. **3.** (of behaviour) unworthy; discreditable. **4.** (of intelligence, etc.) low in quality. **~·ly** *adv.* **~·ness** *n.*

mean³ [miːn] *n. & adj.* **1.** (condition, quality, number) equally distant from two opposites or extremes: *the happy* (*golden*) *~,* a moderate course of action; *the ~ annual temperature.* ˌ~'**time** *adv.*

& n. (in) the time between. ˌ~'**whil**
adv. & n. ~**time.**

mean⁴ [miːn] *n.* **1.** (usu. pl., often wit indef. art. and sing. v.) method, pro cess, way, by which a result may be ob tained: *by ~s of,* through; with the hel of; *by all ~s,* certainly; at all costs; *b no ~s,* not at all; *by some ~s* (*or other somehow* (or other). **2.** (pl.) money property; resources: *a man of ~s,* a ric man; *live within one's ~s,* not spen more than one's income.

me·an·der [mɪ'ændə*] *v.i.* wande here and there; (of a stream) win about.

meant, see *mean¹.*

mea·sles ['miːzlz] *n. pl.* (sing. or p v.) infectious disease causing fever an red spots on the body.

mea·sly ['miːzlɪ] *adj.* (*-ier, -iest*) (sl.) o poor quality; of small value or amoun

mea·sure ['meʒə*] *n.* **1.** (no pl.) syste for calculating size, quantity, degree etc.: *give full ~,* give the full amount (*clothes*) *made to ~,* specially mad for sb. after taking his ~ments. unit, standard, or system used i stating size, quantity, or degree: *A inch is a ~ of length. liquid* (*dry*) *~; capacity.* **3.** sth. with which to test size quantity, etc.: *a tape-~; a pint ~.* **4.** ex tent: *in some ~,* to some extent or de gree; *in a great ~,* largely; *beyond ~ very great*(ly). **5.** (proposed) law. proceeding; step: *take ~s agains wrongdoers,* do sth. to stop or punis them. **7.** (no pl.) verse-rhythm; time i music. *v.t. & i.* **1.** find the size amount, etc. of (sth. or sb.). **2.** ~ *ou give a ~d quantity of; mark out. **3.** b (a certain length, etc.). **~d** *adj.* **1.** (esp of language) carefully considered. **2.** i slow and regular rhythm. **mea·sur able** ['meʒərəbl] *adj.* that can be ~d **mea·sur·ably** *adv.* **~·ment** *n.* (esp pl.) detailed figures about length breadth, height, etc.

meat [miːt] *n.* **1.** (no pl.) flesh of ani mals used as food, usu. excluding fis and poultry. **2.** (old use) food of an kind.

me·chan·ic [mɪ'kænɪk] *n.* skilled work man, esp. one who makes or work machines: *a motor ~.* **~s** *n. pl.* (sing. o pl. v.) science of motion and force science of machinery. **me·chan·i·ca 1.** of, connected with, produced by machines: *~al transport.* **2.** (of person or actions) like a machine; automatic *~al movements.* **me·chan·i·cal·ly** *adv* **mech·a·nism** ['mekənɪzəm] *n.* work ing parts of a machine; structure o arrangement of parts working together; way in which sth. works. **mech·a·nize** ['mekənaız] *v.t.* use machines in or for: *mechanized forces* (e.g. in the army, using motor transport). **mech·a·ni·za·tion** [,mekənar'zeıʃn] *n.*

med·al ['medl] *n.* flat piece of metal, usu. shaped like a coin, with words and a design stamped on it, given as an award or made to commemorate an event. **me·dal·lion** [mɪ'dæljən] *n.* large ~; large flat circular ornamental design (e.g. on a carpet). **~list** (U.S.A. also **~ist**) *n.* person rewarded with a ~ after a competition.

med·dle ['medl] *v.i.* busy oneself with sth. without being invited; interfere *in* sb. else's affairs). **~some** *adj.* in the habit of meddling.

me·dia, see *medium*.

me·di·ate ['miːdɪeɪt] *v.i. & t.* 1. act as go-between or peacemaker: ~ *between employers and workers.* 2. bring about by mediating: ~ *a peace.* **me·di·a·tion** [,miːdɪ'eɪʃn] *n.* (no pl.). mediating. **me·di·a·tor** *n.* person who ~s.

med·i·cal ['medɪkl] *adj.* of the art of medicine: ~ *students; the ~ ward of a hospital* (cf. *surgical*). **~ly** *adv.* **me·di·ca·ment** [me'dɪkəmənt] *n.* substance used in ~ treatment, internally or externally. **med·i·cat·ed** ['medɪkeɪtɪd] *adj.* (of a liquid, cloth, etc.) containing a substance used ~ly: *medicated gauze.*

me·dic·i·nal [me'dɪsɪnl] *adj.* having ~ properties: *medicinal preparations.*

med·i·cine ['medsɪn] *n.* 1. (no pl.) art and science of the prevention and cure of disease. 2. substance (esp. one taken through the mouth) used in medicine. **med·i·cine-man** *n.* witch-doctor.

me·di·eval, me·di·ae·val [,medɪ'iːvl] *adj.* of the Middle Ages.

me·di·o·cre [,miːdɪ'əʊkə*] *adj.* not very good; second-rate. **me·di·oc·ri·ty** [,miːdɪ'ɒkrətɪ] *n.* 1. (no pl.) quality of being ~. 2. ~ person.

med·i·tate ['medɪteɪt] *v.t. & i.* 1. think about; consider: ~ *revenge.* 2. give oneself up to serious thought: ~ *upon one's past life.* **med·i·ta·tion** [,medɪ'teɪʃn] *n.*

Med·i·ter·ra·nean [,medɪtə'reɪnjən] *adj.* of, relating to, the ~ Sea or the countries bordering this sea.

me·di·um ['miːdjəm] *n.* (pl. *-dia* [-djə], *-s*) 1. that by which or through which sth. is done: *Newspapers are a ~ for advertising.* 2. middle quality or degree *(between* extremes): *the happy ~.* 3. substance within which sth. exists or through which sth. (e.g. sound) moves.

4. person acting as a go-between (esp. in spiritualism, as between living people and the spirits of the dead). *adj.* coming half-way between; not extreme: *of ~ height; ~ wave* (in radio).

med·ley ['medlɪ] *n.* (pl. ~*s*) mixture of different things, colours, sounds, etc.: ~ *relay,* (sport) relay race between teams in which each member uses a different swimming-stroke or runs a different distance.

meek [miːk] *adj.* mild and patient; unprotesting. **~ly** *adv.* **~ness** *n.* (no pl.).

meet [miːt] *v.t. & i.* (p.t. & p.p. *met* [met]) 1. come face to face with (sb. or sth. coming from the opposite or a different direction); come together from anywhere. 2. ~ *with,* experience: ~ *with misfortune.* 3. go to a place and wait for the arrival of sb. or sth.: ~ *a train; ~ a friend at the airport.* 4. be introduced to; make the acquaintance of: (as a form of introduction) *I'd like you to ~ my brother. M~ my sister. Pleased to ~ you.* 5. satisfy; come into agreement with (sb., his wishes): *Will this ~ the case* (be satisfactory)? *n.* gathering of persons and hounds for a hunt. **~ing** *n.* coming together of persons for some purpose, esp. discussion.

mega·phone ['megəfəʊn] *n.* horn for speaking through, to carry one's voice to a distance. (See the picture at *mask.*)

mega·ton ['megətʌn] *n.* explosive force equivalent to that of a million tons of T.N.T.

mel·an·choly ['melənkəlɪ] *n.* (no pl.) *& adj.* (being) sad, in low spirits.

mê·lée (U.S.A. **me·lee**) ['meleɪ] (Fr.) *n.* confused struggle; confused crowd of people.

mel·lif·lu·ous [me'lɪflʊəs] *adj.* (of words, voices, music) smooth-flowing and sweet-sounding.

mel·low ['meləʊ] *adj.* 1. (of fruit) soft and sweet in taste; (of wine) well-matured; soft, pure, and rich in colour or sound. 2. made sympathetic and wise by experience: *a ~ judg(e)ment. v.t. & i.* make or become ~.

melo·dra·ma ['meləʊ,drɑːmə] *n.* exciting and emotional drama, usu. with a happy ending. **~t·ic** [,meləʊdrə'mæt-ɪk] *adj.* (esp. of a person, his behaviour) theatrical; in the manner of an actor of ~.

mel·o·dy ['melədɪ] *n.* 1. (no pl.) sweet music; tunefulness. 2. song or tune; principal line or part in harmonized music. **me·lo·di·ous** [mɪ'ləʊdjəs] *adj.* sweet-sounding.

mel·on ['melən] *n.* large, juicy, round fruit growing on a plant that trails along the ground.

melt [melt] *v.t. & i.* **1.** (cause to) become liquid through heating: ~ing snow. **2.** soften; be softened: *a heart* ~ing with pity. **3.** fade; go slowly (away): *The mists ~ed away. In the rainbow one colour ~s into another.* **mol·ten** ['məʊltən] (old p.p. now used only of minerals) ~ed: *molten steel* (lava).

mem·ber ['membə*] *n.* **1.** person belonging to a group, society, etc. **2.** (old use) part of the body (e.g. an arm, the tongue). ~**ship** *n.* state of being a ~ (of a society, etc.); number of ~s (in a society).

mem·brane ['membreɪn] *n.* soft, thin, skin-like substance covering or connecting inside parts of an animal or plant.

me·men·to [mɪ'mentəʊ] *n.* (pl. -oes, -os) sth. that serves to remind one of a person or event.

memo ['meməʊ] *n.* (pl. ~s) (colloq.) memorandum (cf. *memory, etc.*).

mem·oir ['memwɑ:*] *n.* **1.** short life history, esp. one by someone with first-hand knowledge. **2.** (pl.) person's own written account of his life or experiences.

mem·o·ry ['memərɪ] *n.* **1.** power of remembering: *have a good* (bad) ~; *commit sth. to* ~, learn it by heart; *speaking from* ~ (i.e. without reference to books, notes, etc.); *to the best of my* ~, as far as I can remember. **2.** (no pl.) period over which the ~ can go back: *within living* ~, in the time that can be remembered by people now alive. **3.** remembrance: *in* ~ *of*, to keep (sb. or sth.) in the ~. **4.** sth. that is remembered; sth. from the past stored in the ~: *memories of childhood.* **5.** (in a computer) store (3). **mem·o·rable** ['memərəbl] *adj.* deserving to be remembered. **mem·o·ran·dum** [,memə'rændəm] *n.* (pl. -da [-də], ~s) **1.** note or record for future use. **2.** informal business communication, usu. without a personal signature. **mem·o·rize** ['meməraɪz] *v.t.* learn by heart; commit to ~. **me·mo·ri·al** [mɪ'mɔ:rɪəl] *n. & adj.* **1.** (sth.) made or done to remind people of an event or person: *a war memorial*, a monument with the names of men killed in wars; *a memorial service.* **2.** written statement sent to authorities making a request or protest. **me·mo·ri·al·ize** [mɪ'mɔ:rɪəlaɪz] *v.t.* present a memorial (2) to.

men, see **man**. ~**folk** ['menfəʊk] *n. pl.*

men, esp. the male members of family.

men·ace ['menɪs] *n.* threat; dange *v.t. & i.* threaten. **men·ac·ing·ly** *adv* in a threatening manner.

me·nag·er·ie [mɪ'nædʒərɪ] *n.* collec tion of wild animals in cages, etc., esp for a travelling show. (Cf. *zoo.*)

mend [mend] *v.t. & i.* **1.** remake, re pair, or set right sth. broken, worn ou or torn; restore to good condition o working order. **2.** amend (1): ~ *one* ways. **3.** regain health. *n.* **1.** hole damaged part, etc. that has been ~e **2.** *on the* ~, improving (in health, etc.

men·da·cious [men'deɪʃəs] *adj.* un truthful. **men·dac·i·ty** [men'dæsət *n.*

men·di·cant ['mendɪkənt] *n. & adj* (person) getting a living by begging o asking for alms: ~ *friars.*

me·nial ['mi:njəl] *adj.* (of service degrading; (usu. derog., of a servant domestic (1). *n.* (usu. derog.) ~ servant

men·su·ra·tion [,mensjʊə'reɪʃn] *n* mathematical rules for finding length area, volume.

-ment [-mənt] *suff.* (forming ns. result or means of an action: *enjoy ment; government; management.*

men·tal ['mentl] *adj.* of or in th mind: ~ *arithmetic*, done in the head not on paper; ~ *patient*, person suffer ing from a diseased mind; ~ *home* (hos pital), place where ~ patients are care for. ~**ly** *adv.* ~**i·ty** [men'tælətɪ] *n* **1.** (no pl.) ~ power or capacity. **2.** mod or way of thought; ~ disposition: *a wa* ~*ity.*

men·tion ['menʃn] *v.t.* speak or writ sth. about; refer to; say the name of *Don't* ~ *it* (phrase used to indicate tha thanks or an apology are not necessary *n.* ~ing.

men·tor ['mentɔ:*] *n.* adviser an helper (of an inexperienced person).

menu ['menju:] *n.* list of food dishes t be served at a meal.

mer·can·tile ['mɜ:kəntaɪl] *adj.* of trad and merchants: ~ *marine*, country merchant ships and seamen.

mer·ce·nary ['mɜ:sɪnərɪ] *adj.* workin only for money or other reward: ~ *politicians*; based on love of money: ~ *motives. n.* hired soldier in foreig service.

mer·chan·dise ['mɜ:tʃəndaɪz] *n.* (n pl.) goods bought and sold; trad goods.

mer·chant ['mɜ:tʃənt] *n.* (usu. whole sale) trader, esp. one doing busines with foreign countries: ~ *service*, ship

metaphor

and seamen engaged in carrying goods and passengers. '**∼·man** *n.* ∼ ship.

mer·cu·ry ['mɜːkjʊrɪ] *n.* (no pl.) heavy, silver-coloured metal (usu. liquid, as in thermometers). **mer·cu·ri·al** [mɜː-'kjʊərɪəl] *adj.* (also fig.): *a mercurial* (i.e. lively) *temperament*; *a mercurial* (i.e. inconstant) *person*.

mer·cy ['mɜːsɪ] *n.* **1.** (no pl.) (capacity for) holding oneself back from punishing, from causing suffering to, sb. whom one has the right to punish or power to hurt; compassion; forbearance: *show ∼ to a defeated enemy*; *have ∼ on* (*sb.*), treat him kindly; (*be) at the ∼ of*, (be) in the power of; *be left to the tender mercies of*, be exposed to the probable unkind or cruel treatment of. **2.** sth. to be thankful for; piece of good fortune: *that's a ∼*, a blessing. **mer·ci·ful** *adj.* having, showing, ∼. **mer·ci·less** *adj.* without ∼; cruel.

mere [mɪə*] *adj.* (∼r, ∼st) not more than; only: *a ∼* (*the ∼st*) *trifle*. **∼·ly** *adv.* only.

mer·e·tri·cious [ˌmerɪ'trɪʃəs] *adj.* attractive on the surface but of little value.

merge [mɜːdʒ] *v.t. & i.* **1.** (cause to) become part of or absorbed into sth. greater; (esp. of business companies) (cause to) become one. **2.** ∼ *into*, become absorbed in, swallowed up in. **merg·er** *n.* (esp.) act of merging business companies into one company.

me·rid·i·an [mə'rɪdɪən] *n.* **1.** half-circle round the globe, passing through a given place and the north and south poles: *the ∼ of Greenwich*. **2.** highest point reached by the sun or other star as viewed from a point on the earth's surface. **3.** (fig.) point of greatest success, power, fame.

me·ringue [mə'ræŋ] *n.* cake made of white of egg and sugar.

me·ri·no [mə'riːnəʊ] *n.* (pl. ∼s) **1.** ∼ (*sheep*), kind of sheep. **2.** (no pl.) yarn or cloth made from its long, fine wool or from wool and cotton.

mer·it ['merɪt] *n.* **1.** (no pl.) praiseworthy quality. **2.** (pl.) sth. that deserves reward (or, less often, punishment). *v.t.* deserve; be worthy of.

mer·i·toc·ra·cy [ˌmerɪ'tɒkrəsɪ] *n.* (government by) persons selected according to merit in competition; society thus governed.

mer·i·to·ri·ous [ˌmerɪ'tɔːrɪəs] *adj.* praiseworthy.

mer·maid ['mɜːmeɪd], **mer·man** ['mɜːmæn] *ns.* (in stories) woman, man, with a fish's tail in place of legs.

mer·ry ['merɪ] *adj.* (-*ier*, -*iest*) happy; cheerful; bright: *make ∼*, be gay and cheerful; *hold a ∼ party*. **mer·ri·ly** *adv.* **mer·ri·ment** *n.* '**∼·**ˌ**mak·ing** *n.* (no pl.) being joyful and gay; festivity. '**∼·go·**ˌ**round** *n.* revolving machine with wooden horses, cars, etc. at a funfair.

a merry-go-round

mesh [meʃ] *n.* one of the spaces in netting; (pl.) network; (fig.) snares: *the ∼es of political intrigue*. *v.t. & i.* **1.** catch in a net. **2.** (of toothed wheels) interlock.

mess¹ [mes] *n.* (usu. sing. with indef. art.) state of confusion, disorder, or dirt: *make a ∼ of sth.*; *get into a ∼*. *v.t. & i.* make a ∼ of: ∼ *sth. up*, spoil it; ∼ *about*, be busy with odd jobs but without getting much done. **∼·y** *adj.* (-*ier*, -*iest*) dirty; untidy.

mess² [mes] *n.* group of persons taking meals together (esp. in the armed forces); these meals; room in which they are eaten. *v.i.* eat meals in a ∼-*room*: ∼*ing allowance*, money for that purpose.

mes·sage ['mesɪdʒ] *n.* spoken or written request or piece of news sent to sb.: *take a ∼ to sb. Got the ∼?* (colloq.) Have you understood? **mes·sen·ger** ['mesɪndʒə*] *n.* person carrying a ∼.

Mes·si·ah [mɪ'saɪə] *n.* person expected by the Jews to come and set them free; the Saviour, Jesus Christ.

Messrs. ['mesəz] title used before names of business firms: *Messrs. Smith, Brown & Co.*, and as plural of *Mr.*: *Messrs. John and Charles Smith*.

met, see *meet* (v.).

met·al ['metl] *n.* **1.** any one of a class of mineral substances such as tin, iron, gold, and copper. **2.** *road-∼*, broken stone used for road-making. **3.** (pl.) (Gt. Brit.) railway-lines. **me·tal·lic** [mɪ'tælɪk] *adj.* of or like ∼. **me·tal·lur·gy** [me'tælədʒɪ] *n.* (no pl.) art of separating ∼ from ore and of working ∼.

meta·mor·pho·sis [ˌmetə'mɔːfəsɪs] *n.* (pl. -*ses* [-siːz]) change of form or character.

met·a·phor ['metəfə*] *n.* (example of the) use of words to indicate sth. different from the literal meaning, as in: 'I'll make him *eat his words*'; 'He has a *heart of stone*'. **~·i·cal** [ˌmetəˈfɒrɪkl] *adj.*

meta·phys·ics [ˌmetəˈfɪzɪks] *n. pl.* (sing v.) branch of philosophy dealing with the nature of existence, truth, and knowledge; (popular use) mere theory. **meta·phys·i·cal** *adj.*

mete [miːt] *v.t.* (liter., old use) ~ out, give (rewards, punishments).

me·te·or [ˈmiːtjə*] *n.* small body rushing from outer space into the earth's atmosphere and becoming bright. **~·ic** [ˌmiːtɪˈɒrɪk] *adj.* bright and swift like a ~. **~·ite** [ˈmiːtjəraɪt] *n.* ~ that has fallen to earth.

me·te·o·rol·o·gy [ˌmiːtjəˈrɒlədʒɪ] *n.* (no pl.) science of the weather. **me·te·o·ro·log·i·cal** [ˌmiːtjərəˈlɒdʒɪkl] *adj.* of the weather or the atmosphere.

me·ter [ˈmiːtə*] *n.* apparatus (1) that measures, or indicates, esp. one that records[1] the amount of whatever passes through it (e.g. gas, water), or the distance travelled, fare (1) payable, etc.: ~ *maid*, woman employed to report offences against parking-meter regulations.

a meter

meth·od [ˈmeθəd] *n.* **1.** way of doing sth. **2.** (no pl.) system; orderliness. **me·thod·i·cal** [mɪˈθɒdɪkl] *adj.* following, done with, a ~; orderly. **me·thod·i·cal·ly** *adv.*

Meth·od·ism [ˈmeθədɪzəm] *n.* (no pl.) teaching and organization of Christian Churches started by John Wesley. **Meth·od·ist** *adj. & n.*

meth·yl·at·ed spir·it [ˈmeθɪleɪtɪd ˈspɪrɪt] *n.* (no pl.) form of alcohol used for lighting and heating.

me·tic·u·lous [mɪˈtɪkjʊləs] *adj.* giving, showing, great attention to details. **~·ly** *adv.*

me·tre (U.S.A. **me·ter**) [ˈmiːtə*] *n.* **1.** unit of length (39.37 inches) in the metric system. **2.** (particular form of) verse-rhythm. **met·ric** [ˈmetrɪk] *adj.* of the ~: *metric system*, decimal measuring system based on the ~ as the unit of length; *go metric*, adopt the

metric system of measurement. **met·ri·cal** [ˈmetrɪkl] *adj.* **1.** of or in verse rhythm. **2.** of measurement. **met·ri·cal·ly** *adv.*

me·trop·o·lis [mɪˈtrɒpəlɪs] *n.* chief city of a country. **met·ro·pol·i·tan** [ˌmetrəˈpɒlɪtən] *adj.* of a ~.

met·tle [ˈmetl] *n.* (no pl.) quality (of a person, horse) of endurance and courage: *be on one's* ~, *put sb. on his* ~ (in a position that tests this quality and moves a person to do his best). **~·some** *adj.* high-spirited.

mews [mjuːz] *n. pl.* (sing v.) (Gt. Brit.) street or square of stables, buildings for coaches.

mi·ca [ˈmaɪkə] *n.* (no pl.) transparent mineral substance easily divided into thin layers.

mice, see *mouse.*

mi·cro- [ˈmaɪkrəʊ-] *pref.* small: *microfilm; microwave.*

mi·crobe [ˈmaɪkrəʊb] *n.* tiny living creature, esp. kind of bacteria causing diseases and fermentation.

mi·cro·cosm [ˈmaɪkrəʊkɒzəm] *n.* **1.** man considered (esp. by the ancient philosophers) as representing mankind or the universe. **2.** miniature representation (*of*).

mi·cro·film [ˈmaɪkrəʊfɪlm] *n.* film bearing a photographic record on a reduced scale[1] (5) of printed or other graphic matter. *v.t. & i.* photograph on ~; take ~s.

mi·crom·e·ter [maɪˈkrɒmɪtə*] *n.* instrument for measuring very small distances, etc.

mi·cro·phone [ˈmaɪkrəfəʊn] *n.* instrument for changing sound waves into electrical waves, as used in telephones, radio, etc.

a microphone   a microscope

mi·cro·scope [ˈmaɪkrəskəʊp] *n.* instrument with lenses for magnifying objects too small to be seen without it. **mi·cro·scop·ic** [ˌmaɪkrəˈskɒpɪk] *adj.* too small to be seen except with a ~.

mi·cro·wave [ˈmaɪkrəweɪv] *n.* very short wave (as used in radio, etc.).

mid[1] [mɪd] *adj.* in the middle of; mid-

mill

dle: in ~-Atlantic; in ~-June; in ~-air, high above the ground. '~-day **n.** noon. **the M~lands** ['mɪdləndz] **n. pl.** the central counties of England. '~most **adj.** in the exact middle. '~-night **n.** **1.** 12 o'clock at night. **2.** (often attrib.) of, during, the middle of the night: ~-night hours (studies). '~summer **n.** (no pl.) M~summer Day, 24 June. ,~-'way **adv.** halfway. ,~'win·ter **n.** (no pl.) period about 22 December.

mid[2] [mɪd] **prep.** (poet.) amid; among.

mid·den ['mɪdn] **n.** heap of dung or rubbish.

mid·dle ['mɪdl] **n. & attrib. adj.** (point, position, or part, that is) at an equal distance from two or more points, etc., or between beginning and end. ~ age, period of life midway between youth and old age; ~-aged, of ~ age; the M~ Ages, time (in European history) from about A.D. 500 to about 1500; the ~ class(es), those between the highest and lowest classes of society; ~ name, name between the first name and surname; ~ watch, (on ships) period from midnight to 4 a.m.; ~weight, (esp.) boxer weighing about 165 lb. (= 75 kilograms). '~-man **n.** any trader through whose hands goods pass between producer and consumer. '**mid·dling adj.** of ~ or medium size, quality, etc.; moderately good. **adv.** moderately; fairly well.

mid·dy ['mɪdɪ] **n.** (colloq. abbr. for) midshipman.

midge [mɪdʒ] **n.** small, winged insect like a gnat.

mid·get ['mɪdʒɪt] **n.** extremely small person or thing.

mid·i ['mɪdɪ] **n. & adj.** (colloq.) (woman's skirt, dress, or other garment) usu. reaching to the mid-calf: a ~-coat; a ~-skirt.

mid·i- ['mɪdɪ-] **pref.** reaching to the mid-calf: midi-coat.

mid·ship·man ['mɪdʃɪpmən] **n.** boy training to become a junior naval officer.

midst [mɪdst] **n.** in the ~ of, in the middle of; while occupied with; in our ~, among us. **prep.** (poet.) amidst; in the middle of.

mid·wife ['mɪdwaɪf] **n.** (pl. -wives) woman trained to help women in childbirth. ~ry ['mɪdwɪfərɪ] **n.** (no pl.) profession and work of a ~.

mien [miːn] **n.** (liter.) person's bearing, appearance (showing a mood, etc.).

might[1], see **may**.

might[2] [maɪt] **n.** (no pl.) great power or strength. ~y **adj.** (-ier, -iest) of great

power or size; (colloq.) great: high and ~y, arrogant. **adv.** (colloq.) very: ~y proud.

mi·grate [maɪ'greɪt] **v.i.** **1.** move from one place to another (to live there). **2.** (of birds) come and go regularly with the seasons. **mi·grant** ['maɪgrənt] **n. & adj.** (esp.) (bird) that ~s. **mi·gra·tion** [maɪ'greɪʃn] **n.** **mi·gra·to·ry** ['maɪgrətərɪ] **adj.** migrating: migratory birds.

mike [maɪk] **n.** (colloq.) microphone.

milch [mɪltʃ] **adj.** giving milk: ~ cow.

mild [maɪld] **adj.** **1.** soft; gentle; not severe: ~ weather (punishment). **2.** (of food, drink, tobacco) not sharp or strong in taste: ~ ale. ~ly **adv.** ~ness **n.** (no pl.).

mil·dew ['mɪldjuː] **n.** (no pl.) (usu. destructive) growth of tiny fungi forming on plants, leather, food, etc. in warm, wet weather.

mile [maɪl] **n.** measure of distance, 1,760 yards (= 1.6093 kilometres). **mil(e)·age** ['maɪlɪdʒ] **n.** distance travelled, measured in ~s; travelling expenses (per mile). '~stone **n.** roadside stone marking distance in ~s; (fig.) important stage or event in life or history.

mil·i·tant ['mɪlɪtənt] **adj.** actively engaged in (esp. spiritual) warfare.

mil·i·tary ['mɪlɪtərɪ] **adj.** of or for soldiers, an army, war on land: in ~ uniform; ~ training. **n.** (pl. ~, -taries) the ~, soldiers; the army. **mil·i·ta·rism n.** (no pl.) belief in, reliance upon, ~ strength and virtues.

mil·i·tate ['mɪlɪteɪt] **v.i.** ~ against, (of facts, evidence) act, operate, have force, against.

mi·li·tia [mɪ'lɪʃə] **n.** force of civilians trained as soldiers but not part of the regular army.

milk [mɪlk] **n.** (no pl.) **1.** white liquid produced by female mammals as food for their young, esp. that of cows which is drunk by human beings and made into butter and cheese. **2.** ~-like juice of some plants and trees (e.g. in the coconut). **v.t.** draw the ~ from (a cow, etc.). '~maid **n.** woman who ~s cows and makes butter, etc. '~man **n.** man who delivers ~ to the houses of his customers. '~sop **n.** unmanly youth or man. '~-tooth **n.** one of the first set of teeth. ~y **adj.** (-ier, -iest) of or like ~. the M~y Way, galaxy.

mill [mɪl] **n.1.** (building with) machinery (driven e.g. by water-power) for grinding grain into flour. **2.** building, factory, workshop for industry: paper-

millstone

(cotton-, steel-, saw-)~s. **3.** small machine for grinding: *a coffee-~.* **v.t. & i. 1.** put through a machine for grinding; produce by doing this: *~ grain (flour).* **2.** produce regular markings on the edge of (a coin): *coins with a ~ed edge.* **3.** (of cattle, crowds of people) move round and round in a confused way. '**~stone** *n.* either of the two round stones between which grain is ground; (fig.) a serious hindrance. **~er** *n.* man who owns or works a flour-~.

mil·len·ni·um [mɪ'lenɪəm] *n.* (pl. ~s, -nia [-ɪə]) **1.** 1,000 years. **2.** (fig.) future time of complete happiness for all.

mil·let ['mɪlɪt] *n.* (no pl.) grain plant with very small seeds.

mil·li- ['mɪlɪ-] *pref.* one thousandth part of: *~gram; ~metre.*

mil·li·ner ['mɪlɪnə*] *n.* person who makes or sells women's hats. **~y n.** (no pl.) (business of making or selling) women's hats; things needed for these.

mil·lion ['mɪljən] *n.* 1,000,000. **~aire** [ˌmɪljə'neə*] *n.* extremely rich man. **~th** ['mɪljənθ] *n. & adj.* 1,000,000th.

milt [mɪlt] *n.* (no pl.) (soft) roe¹ of male fish.

mime [maɪm] *v.i. & t. & n.* (act in a) simple kind of entertainment using gestures and facial movements but no words.

mim·ic ['mɪmɪk] *adj.* imitated or pretended; done in play: *~ warfare.* *n.* person imitating others, esp. in order to make fun of them. *v.t.* (p.t. & p.p. *-icked* ['mɪmɪkt]) **1.** imitate, esp. to cause amusement. **2.** be very like. **~ry n.** (no pl.) mimicking.

mi·mo·sa [mɪ'məʊzə] *n.* shrub with clusters of sweet-smelling, ball-like, yellow flowers.

min·a·ret ['mɪnəret] *n.* tall, slender spire (connected with a mosque) from which people are called to prayer. (See the picture at *mosque*.)

mince [mɪns] *v.t. & i.* **1.** cut up (meat, etc.) into small pieces. **2.** *not ~ matters,* speak bluntly; say frankly what one thinks. **3.** speak, walk, with unnatural and exaggerated care. *n.* (no pl.) ~d meat. '**~·meat** *n.* (no pl.) mixture of ~d dried fruit, sugar, suet, etc. ˌ~'pie *n.* small round pie filled with ~meat.

mind¹ [maɪnd] *n.* **1.** (no pl.) memory: *keep (bear) sth. in ~,* remember it; *call to ~,* recall to the memory; *put sb. in ~ of,* remind him of. **2.** what a person thinks; way of thinking, feeling, wishing; opinion; purpose: *make up one's ~,* come to a decision; *change one's ~,* change one's purpose or intention; *be*

in two ~s (about sth.), feel doubtful or hesitate; *know one's own ~,* know what one wants; *speak one's ~,* say plainly what one thinks; *be of one ~,* (of two or more persons) be in agreement; *have a good ~ to,* be almost decided or ready to; *take one's ~ off,* turn one's attention from. **3.** centre of one's thinking, reasoning, understanding, etc.: *out of one's ~,* not in one's right ~, mad; *presence of ~,* ability to decide or act quickly when there is danger, etc. **4.** (person with) mental ability: *one of the greatest ~s of the age.* **~ful adj.** *~ful of,* giving thought or care to. **~less adj** *~less of,* paying no attention to.

mind² [maɪnd] *v.t. & i.* **1.** take care of; attend to: *~ing the baby;* ~ the step, take care not to stumble over it. *M~ your own business!* Do not interfere in the affairs of others. *M~ (out)!* Be careful ~ (you) (i.e. please take note): *I have no objection,* ~ (you) but ... **2.** be troubled by; feel objection to: *Do you ~ my smoking? Would you ~ shutting the door* (i.e. please shut the door).

mind·ed ['maɪndɪd] *adj.* **1.** having a mind of a specified character: *absent-~; evil-~; strong-~.* **2.** disposed, inclined (*to do* sth.).

mine¹ [maɪn] *poss. pron. pred.* of or belonging to me.

mine² [maɪn] *n.* **1.** hole made in or under the earth to get coal, minerals, ores; (fig.) source (of knowledge). **2.** (tunnel for) charge of high explosive; metal case filled with high explosive for use in or on the sea, or (*land~*) dropped from the air or laid in or on the ground: *ships sunk by ~s. v.t. & i.* **1.** dig (coal, metals, etc.) from the ground. **2.** put ~s (2) (in the sea) or under (e.g. a fort); destroy, sink, or damage with a ~ (2). **3.** (also *under~*) make holes or tunnels under. '**~·field** *n.* (esp.) area of land or sea where ~s (2) have been laid. '**~ˌlay·er** ('~-ˌsweep·er) *n.* ship laying (sweeping up or destroying) ~s (2). **min·er n.** (esp.) man working in a ~ (1): *coal-~r.* **min·ing n.** (no pl.) process of getting minerals, etc. from ~s (1); (attrib.) *mining engineer; mining industry.*

min·er·al ['mɪnərəl] *n.* substance (e.g. coal) not vegetable or animal, got from the earth by mining, etc. ~ **oil n.** any oil of ~ origin. ~ **wa·ter n.** water containing gas (and often a flavouring), as *soda-water.*

min·er·al·o·gy [ˌmɪnə'rælədʒɪ] *n.* (no pl.) science of minerals. **min·er·al·o·gist n.** specialist in ~.

min·gle ['mɪŋgl] *v.t. & i.* mix (*with*): *truth ⁓d with falsehood*; *mingling with* (going about among) *the crowds*.

min·i ['mɪnɪ] *n.* (colloq.) **1.** woman's skirt, dress, or other garment ending well above the knees. **2.** anything miniature in size. **3.** (Gt. Brit., abbr. for) minicar. *adj.* (⁓) ending well above the knees; very short: *a ⁓skirt*.

min·i- ['mɪnɪ-] *pref.* very small, short, etc.: *⁓bus, ⁓cab, ⁓camera, ⁓car, ⁓computer, ⁓skirt*.

min·ia·ture ['mɪnətʃə*] *n.* very small picture of a person; small-scale copy or model of sth.; (attrib.) *⁓ railway*.

min·i·mize ['mɪnɪmaɪz] *v.t.* reduce to, estimate at, the smallest possible amount or degree.

min·i·mum ['mɪnɪməm] *n.* (pl. *-ma* [-mə], *⁓s*) & *adj.* (opp. *maximum*) least possible or recorded amount, degree, etc. (of): *the ⁓ temperature*; *⁓ wages*.

min·ing, see *mine².*

min·ion ['mɪnjən] *n.* slave; lowest servant.

min·is·ter ['mɪnɪstə*] *n.* **1.** person at the head of a department of State: *M⁓ for Defence*; *Prime M⁓*. **2.** person representing his government in a foreign country. **3.** Christian priest or clergyman. *v.i.* give help or service (*to*): *⁓ing to the sick*. **min·is·te·ri·al** [,mɪnɪ'stɪərɪəl] *adj.* of a ⁓ of State; of the Ministry; of a ⁓ of religion. **min·is·tra·tion** [,mɪnɪ'streɪʃn] *n.* giving of help or (esp. religious) service. **min·is·try** ['mɪnɪstrɪ] *n.* **1.** department of State under a ⁓ (1): *the Air Ministry*; *the Ministry of Finance*. **2.** all the ⁓s (1) forming a Government; the Cabinet. **3.** *the ministry*, the clerical (1) profession: *enter the ministry*, become a ⁓ (3). **4.** position of, time of being, duties of, a ⁓.

mink [mɪŋk] *n.* (valuable brown fur skin of a) small stoat-like animal.

min·now ['mɪnəʊ] *n.* sorts of very small freshwater fish.

mi·nor ['maɪnə*] *adj.* **1.** smaller; less important: *a broken leg and ⁓ injuries*. **2.** (in schools) younger of two brothers: *Jones ⁓*. **3.** ⁓ *scale*, (music) having one-and-a-half tones between the keynote and third note. *n.* person not yet legally of age (1). **⁓·i·ty** [maɪ'nɒrətɪ] *n.* **1.** (no pl.) state of being not legally of age (1). **2.** smaller number or part, esp. of a total of votes: *a ⁓ity government* (having a ⁓ity of the total number of seats in a legislative assembly). **3.** small group of persons differing from

others in race, religion, language, opinion, etc.

min·ster ['mɪnstə*] *n.* large or important church, esp. one that once belonged to a monastery.

min·strel ['mɪnstrəl] *n.* (formerly) travelling composer, player and singer of songs and ballads.

mint¹ [mɪnt] *n.* sort of plant whose leaves are used for flavouring.

mint² [mɪnt] *n.* place where coins are made, usu. under State authority. *v.t.* make (coins) by stamping metal.

min·u·et [,mɪnjʊ'et] *n.* (music for) slow, graceful dance for two persons.

mi·nus ['maɪnəs] *prep.* less; with the deduction of: $7 - 3$ is 4 ($7 - 3 = 4$); below zero. *adj.* **1.** (electr.) having a negative charge. **2.** (math.) negative: *the ⁓ sign*, the sign (—); *a ⁓ quantity*, a quantity less than 0 (e.g. $-21, -2x^2$). *n.* the sign (—); negative quantity; (fig.) disadvantage.

min·ute¹ ['mɪnɪt] *n.* **1.** one-sixtieth part of one hour. **2.** one-sixtieth part of a degree in the measurement of an angle. **3.** official record giving authority, advice, or making comments. **4.** (pl.) summary, records, of what is said and decided at a meeting, esp. of a society or committee. **'⁓·book** *n.* book for keeping ⁓s (4).

mi·nute² [maɪ'njuːt] *adj.* very small; giving small details: *a ⁓ description*.

mi·nu·ti·ae [maɪ'njuːʃiiː] *n. pl.* precise, trivial, or minor details.

minx [mɪŋks] *n.* sly, impertinent girl.

mir·a·cle ['mɪrəkl] *n.* **1.** act or event that does not follow the known laws of nature; remarkable and surprising event. **2.** remarkable specimen or example (of a quality): *a ⁓ of ingenuity*. **mi·rac·u·lous** [mɪ'rækjʊləs] *adj.* **mi·rac·u·lous·ly** *adv.*

mi·rage ['mɪrɑːʒ] *n.* **1.** effect, produced by air conditions, causing sth. distant to appear as if it were near, esp. in the desert. **2.** (fig.) any illusion.

mire ['maɪə*] *n.* (no pl.) wet ground; soft deep mud.

mir·ror ['mɪrə*] *n.* polished (formerly metal, now glass) surface reflecting images; looking-glass. *v.t.* reflect as a ⁓ does.

mirth [mɜːθ] *n.* (no pl.) being merry; laughter.

mis- [mɪs-] *pref.* bad(ly); wrong(ly); not: *misbehave*; *miscount*; *misinterpret*; *mismanage*; *mispronounce*; *misspell*, etc.

mis·ad·ven·ture [,mɪsəd'ventʃə*] *n.* (event caused by) bad luck.

mis·an·thrope ['mɪzənθrəʊp] *n.* person who hates mankind, avoids society.

mis·an·throp·ic [,mɪzən'θrɒpɪk] *adj.*

mis·ap·pre·hend ['mɪs,æprɪ'hend] *v.t.* misunderstand. **mis·ap·pre·hen·sion** ['mɪs,æprɪ'henʃn] *n.*

mis·car·riage [,mɪs'kærɪdʒ] *n.* 1. (no pl.) ~ *of justice*, mistake in judging or punishing. 2. failure to deliver to, or arrive at, a destination: ~ *of goods.* 3. delivery of a baby before it is able to live: *have a* ~.

mis·car·ry [,mɪs'kærɪ] *v.i.* 1. (of plans, etc.) fail; have a result different from what was hoped for. 2. (of letters, etc.) fail to arrive at the right destination. 3. give birth to a baby before it can live.

mis·cel·la·neous [,mɪsɪ'leɪnjəs] *adj.* of mixed sorts; having various qualities and characteristics. **mis·cel·la·ny** [mɪ'selənɪ] *n.* ~ collection (e.g. of writings on various subjects by various authors).

mis·chance [,mɪs'tʃɑːns] *n.* bad luck.

mis·chief ['mɪstʃɪf] *n.* 1. injury or damage done on purpose: *make* ~ *between,* cause ill feeling between (others) by gossip, etc. 2. foolish or thoughtless behaviour likely to cause trouble: *boys who are always getting into* ~. *She's up to* ~ *again.* 3. light-hearted desire to tease: *eyes full of* ~. **mis·chie·vous** ['mɪstʃɪvəs] *adj.* causing, engaged in, fond of, showing a spirit of, ~: *as mischievous as a monkey.*

mis·con·ceive [,mɪskən'siːv] *v.t. & i.* misunderstand (sb., a word); have a wrong idea or conception (*of*). **mis·con·cep·tion** [,mɪskən'sepʃn] *n. under a misconception.*

mis·con·duct [,mɪs'kɒndʌkt] *n.* (no pl.) wrong behaviour or conduct, esp. adultery; bad management. [,mɪskən'dʌkt] *v.t.* manage (a business, etc.) badly; behave (*oneself*) badly.

mis·con·strue [,mɪskən'struː] *v.t.* form a wrong idea of (sb.'s words, acts).

mis·cre·ant ['mɪskrɪənt] *n.* scoundrel.

mis·deal [,mɪs'diːl] *v.i. & t.* (p.t. & p.p. *-dealt*) deal (playing cards) wrongly. *n.* such a mistake.

mis·deed [,mɪs'diːd] *n.* wicked act; crime.

mis·de·mea·nour (U.S.A. **-nor**) [,mɪsdɪ'miːnə*] *n.* unlawful act of a not very serious sort.

mi·ser ['maɪzə*] *n.* person who loves wealth for its own sake and spends as little as possible. ~**·ly** *adj.*

mis·er·able ['mɪzərəbl] *adj.* 1. wretched; very unhappy; causing wretchedness and unhappiness. 2. poor in quality. **mis·er·ably** *adv.* **mis·ery** ['mɪz-**

əri] *n.* state of being ~; pain; suffering; poverty: *living in misery.*

mis·fire [,mɪs'faɪə*] *v.i.* (of a gun) fail to go off; (of a motor engine) fail to start. *n.* such a failure.

mis·fit ['mɪsfɪt] *n.* article of clothing that does not fit well; (fig.) person not well suited to his position, etc.

mis·for·tune [mɪs'fɔːtʃən] *n.* (happening caused by or marked by) bad luck.

mis·give [,mɪs'gɪv] *v.t.* (p.t. *-gave*, p.p. *-given*) fill with suspicion, doubt, or foreboding: *His mind misgave him.* **mis·giv·ing** [mɪs'gɪvɪŋ] *n.* doubt; distrust.

mis·guid·ed [,mɪs'gaɪdɪd] *adj.* foolish and wrong (because of bad guidance or influence).

mis·hap ['mɪshæp] *n.* unfortunate accident (usu. not serious).

mis·lay [,mɪs'leɪ] *v.t.* (p.t. & p.p. *-laid*) put (sth.) by chance where it cannot easily be found.

mis·lead [,mɪs'liːd] *v.t.* (p.t. & p.p. *-led*) lead wrongly; cause to be or do wrong; give a wrong idea to.

mis·no·mer [,mɪs'nəʊmə*] *n.* wrong use of a name or word.

mis·place [,mɪs'pleɪs] *v.t.* 1. put in a wrong place. 2. give (love, affections) wrongly or unwisely: ~*d confidence.*

mis·print [,mɪs'prɪnt] *v.t.* print wrongly. ['mɪsprɪnt] *n.* error in printing.

mis·quote [,mɪs'kwəʊt] *v.t.* quote wrongly. **mis·quo·ta·tion** [,mɪskwəʊ-'teɪʃn] *n.*

mis·rule [,mɪs'ruːl] *n.* (no pl.) bad government; disorder.

miss [mɪs] *v.t. & i.* (p.t. & p.p. ~*ed* [mɪst]) 1. fail to hit (hold, catch, reach, see, be at) what it is desired to hit, etc.: *fire at a lion and* ~ *it; try to catch a ball and* ~ *it;* ~ *a train;* ~ *the point of a joke.* 2. realize, learn, feel regret at, the absence of: *She'd* ~ *her gardener if he left.* 3. ~ *sth. out,* omit; fail to put in or say. *n.* failure to hit, etc.: *a lucky* ~, a fortunate escape. ~**·ing** *adj.* not to be found; not in the place where it ought to be: *a book with two pages* ~*ing; the dead, wounded, and* ~*ing* (i.e. soldiers in war); ~*ing persons* (who cannot be traced).

Miss [mɪs] *n.* title placed before the surname of an unmarried woman or girl.

mis·shap·en [,mɪs'ʃeɪpən] *adj.* (of the body) ill-shaped; deformed.

mis·sile ['mɪsaɪl] *n.* object thrown (e.g. a stone, a spear) or sent through the air (e.g. an arrow, a bomb) in order to hurt or damage; rocket propelled into the air (as a weapon, e.g. to destroy enemy aircraft): *ballistic* ~; *guided* ~.

mis·sion ['mɪʃn] *n.* **1.** (sending out of a) number of persons entrusted with special work, usu. abroad: *a trade* ~; *religious* ~s. **2.** work done by such persons; their building(s), organization, etc. **3.** special work which a person feels called upon to do: *his* ~ *in life.* **4.** special task or function assigned or undertaken: *a rescue* ~. **5.** (mil.) (esp.) dispatch of an aircraft or a spacecraft. ~**ary** ['mɪʃnərɪ] *n.* person sent to preach his religion, esp. to people ignorant of it. *attrib. adj.* of ~s or ~aries.

mis·sive ['mɪsɪv] *n.* (humor.) letter.

mis·spell [ˌmɪs'spel] *v.t.* (p.t. & p.p. ~ed or *-spelt*) spell wrongly. **mis·spell·ing** *n.*

mis·spent [ˌmɪs'spent, attrib. 'mɪs-spent] *adj.* wasted; foolishly spent.

mist [mɪst] *n.* water vapour in the air, less dense than fog: *hills hidden in* ~. ~**y** *adj.* (*-ier, -iest*) **1.** with ~: ~*y weather.* **2.** not clear: *a* ~*y idea.*

mis·take [mɪ'steɪk] *n.* wrong opinion, idea, or act; error: *by* ~, in error; as the result of carelessness, forgetfulness, etc. *v.t. & i.* (p.t. *-took*, p.p. *-taken*) **1.** be wrong, have a wrong idea, about: ~ *sb.'s meaning. You are mistaken.* **2.** ~ (*sb. or sth.*) *for*, wrongly suppose that (sb. or sth.) is another (person or thing).

mis·ter, see *Mr.*

mis·time [ˌmɪs'taɪm] *v.t.* say or do (sth.) at the wrong time: ~*d* (= inopportune) *intervention;* ~ *one's arrival.*

mis·tle·toe ['mɪsltəʊ] *n.* plant with small white berries, used for decoration at Christmas.

mis·tress ['mɪstrɪs] *n.* **1.** housewife in charge of a household. **2.** woman with knowledge or control (of sth.): *a* ~ *of needlework.* **3.** (Gt. Brit.) female schoolteacher. **4.** concubine.

mis·trust [ˌmɪs'trʌst] *v.t. & i. & n.* (no pl.) (feel) doubt or suspicion (about). ~**ful** *adj.* suspicious.

mis·un·der·stand   [ˌmɪsʌndə'stænd] *v.t.* (p.t. & p.p. *-stood*) take a wrong meaning from (instructions, messages, etc.); form a wrong opinion of (sb. or sth.). ~**ing** *n.* failure to understand rightly, esp. when this has led or may lead to ill feeling.

mis·use [ˌmɪs'juːz] *v.t.* use wrongly or for a wrong purpose; treat unkindly. [ˌmɪs'juːs] *n.* using wrongly; instance of this.

mite [maɪt] *n.* **1.** (old use) small coin. **2.** very small child. **3.** tiny insect-like creature: *cheese* ~s.

mit·i·gate ['mɪtɪgeɪt] *v.t.* make less severe, violent, or painful. **mit·i·ga·tion** [ˌmɪtɪ'geɪʃn] *n.* (no pl.).

mi·tre (U.S.A. **mi·ter**) ['maɪtə*] *n.* **1.** tall cap worn by bishops. **2.** ~(*-joint*), joint between two pieces of wood.

a bishop's mitre   a mitre-joint

mit·ten ['mɪtn] *n.* **1.** kind of glove covering four fingers together and thumb separately. **2.** covering for the back and palm of the hand only.

mix [mɪks] *v.t. & i.* (of different substances, people, etc.) put, bring, or come together so that the substances, etc. are no longer separate; make or prepare (sth.) by doing this: ~ *flour and sugar; oil and water do not* ~; ~ *a batter; be* ~*ed up in* (with) (e.g. politics), be involved in; *feel* ~*ed up* (about sth.), feel confused. ~**ed** [mɪkst] *adj.* of different sorts: ~*ed feelings;* ~*ed pickles;* ~*ed grill,* dish of various kinds of meat and vegetable cooked by grilling. ~**er** *n.* person or thing that ~es: *a food-*~*er.* ~**ture** ['mɪkstʃə*] *n.* **1.** (no pl.) ~ing; being ~ed. **2.** sth. that is ~ed: *a smoking* ~*ture* (made by ~ing different kinds of tobacco).

moan [məʊn] *v.i. & t. & n.* (utter, give, a) low sound of pain or regret or one suggesting distress.

moat [məʊt] *n.* deep, wide ditch filled with water, round a castle, etc. as a protection against attack.

mob [mɒb] *n.* **1.** disorderly crowd. **2.** *the* common people; *the* masses. *v.t.* (*-bb-*) crowd round (either to attack or to show admiration, etc.).

mo·bile ['məʊbaɪl] *adj.* moving, able to be moved, easily: ~ *troops;* (med.) ~ *clinic;* easily and often changing: ~ *features.* **mo·bil·i·ty** [məʊ'bɪlətɪ] *n.* (no pl.).

mo·bi·lize ['məʊbɪlaɪz] *v.t. & i.* collect together (forces, resources, etc.) and prepare for service or use, esp. in war. **mo·bi·li·za·tion** [ˌməʊbɪlaɪ'zeɪ-ʃn] *n.*

moc·ca·sin [ˈmɒkəsɪn] *n.* footwear of soft deerskin leather, as worn by N. American Indians.

mock [mɒk] *v.t. & i.* make fun of; ridicule (esp. by mimicking); ~ *at*, laugh at, make fun of. *attrib. adj.* not real or genuine: *a* ~ *battle*; ~ *turtle soup*. '~-**up** *n.* full-scale model of sth. (e.g. a new book) intended to show what it will look like when manufactured. ~**ing·ly** *adv.* ~**ery** *n.* **1.** (no pl.) ~ing; ridicule. **2.** sb. or sth. that is ~ed. **3.** bad or contemptible example (*of* sth.): *His trial was a* ~*ery of justice*.

mod [mɒd] *adj.* extremely up-to-date and fashionable in style of clothes, art, etc. *n.* ~ person, style, or fashion; *M~*, (Gt. Brit.) member of a teenage group in the 1960s distinguished by very neat and modern clothes: *M~s and Rockers*.

mode [məʊd] *n.* way in which sth. is done; style or fashion (of dress).

mod·el [ˈmɒdl] *n.* **1.** small-scale copy of sth.; design to be copied; design or style of a structure, esp. of a motor vehicle: *a 1980* ~ *of a car*; *a sports* ~. **2.** person or thing to be copied. **3.** mannequin. **4.** person employed by an artist as a ~ (2). **5.** (attrib.) deserving to be imitated: ~ *behaviour*; *a* ~ *husband*. *v.t. & i.* (-*ll*-, U.S.A. also -*l*-) **1.** shape (in some soft substance): ~*ling in clay*. **2.** make from a ~; take as a copy or example: ~ *one's behaviour upon* (sb. else's). **3.** act as a ~ (3, 4).

mod·er·ate [ˈmɒdərət] *adj.* **1.** not extreme, midway (in opinions, habits): ~ *in his opinions*. **2.** fairly large; fairly good: ~ *prices*; *a* ~ *appetite*. *n.* person with ~ opinions (esp. in politics). [ˈmɒdəreɪt] *v.t. & i.* make, become, less violent or extreme: ~ *one's demands* (*enthusiasm*). ~**ly** *adv.* to a ~ extent.

mod·er·a·tion [ˌmɒdəˈreɪʃn] *n.* (no pl.) quality of being ~: *moderation in food and drink*; *in moderation*, in a ~ way or amount. **mod·er·a·tor** [ˈmɒdəreɪtə*] *n.* **1.** arbitrator; mediator. **2.** substance used in a nuclear reactor to slow down neutrons.

mod·ern [ˈmɒdən] *adj.* **1.** of the present or recent times: ~ *history* (*languages*). **2.** new and up to date: ~ *ideas* (*methods*). ~**ize** *v.t. & i.* bring up to date; make suitable for present-day needs; adopt ~ ways.

mod·est [ˈmɒdɪst] *adj.* **1.** having, showing, a not too high opinion of one's merits, abilities, etc. **2.** not very large, fine, etc.: *a* ~ *demand*; *living in a* ~ *way*. **3.** taking, showing, care not to

do or say anything impure or improp er: ~ *in dress, speech, and behaviour* ~**·ly** *adv.* **mod·es·ty** *n.* (no pl.).

mod·i·cum [ˈmɒdɪkəm] *n.* (no pl. moderate amount.

mod·i·fy [ˈmɒdɪfaɪ] *v.t.* make change in; make less severe, violent, etc **mod·i·fi·ca·tion** [ˌmɒdɪfɪˈkeɪʃn] *n.*

mod·u·late [ˈmɒdjʊleɪt] *v.t.* make a change in the tone, pitch, or key of regulate; adjust. **mod·u·la·tion** [ˌmɒdjʊˈleɪʃn] *n.*

mod·ule [ˈmɒdjuːl] *n.* **1.** standard o unit of measurement. **2.** any in a serie of standardized units for use together self-contained, standardized, and inter changeable unit or component in a computer or other machine. **3.** self contained, self-supporting unit of a spacecraft: *command* ~, compartment of a spacecraft that contains the contro centre and living quarters; *lunar* ~ (to be detached from the spacecraft while in lunar orbit so that it may land on the surface of the moon).

Mo·ham·med·an [məʊˈhæmɪdən] see *Muhammadan*.

moist [mɔɪst] *adj.* slightly wet. ~**en** [ˈmɔɪsn] *v.t. & i.* make, become, ~ **mois·ture** [ˈmɔɪstʃə*] *n.* (no pl.) slight wetness; liquid in the form of vapour or in small drops on the surface of sth. **mois·tu·rize** [ˈmɔɪstʃəraɪz] *v.t.* make (esp. the skin) less dry (by use of a cosmetic).

mo·lar [ˈməʊlə*] *adj.* of the teeth used for grinding food. *n.* ~ tooth.

mo·las·ses [məʊˈlæsɪz] *n. pl.* (sing. v.) thick, dark syrup drained from raw sugar.

mole[1] [məʊl] *n.* small, dark-grey, fur covered animal living in tunnels which it makes in the ground. '~**hill** *n.* heap of earth thrown up by a ~.

mole[2] [məʊl] *n.* permanent, dark coloured spot on the skin.

mole[3] [məʊl] *n.* stone wall built in the sea as a breakwater or causeway.

mol·e·cule [ˈmɒlɪkjuːl] *n.* smallest unit into which a substance could be di vided without a change in its chemical nature. **mol·ec·u·lar** [məʊˈlekjʊlə*] *adj.*

mo·lest [məʊˈlest] *v.t.* trouble or annoy intentionally. **mo·les·ta·tion** [ˌməʊ le'steɪʃn] *n.* (no pl.).

mol·li·fy [ˈmɒlɪfaɪ] *v.t.* make (a person, his feelings) calm.

mol·lusc (U.S.A. -**lusk**) [ˈmɒləsk] *n.* one of a class of animals with soft bodies, some with shells (e.g. oysters, snails) and some without (e.g. slugs)

mol·ly·cod·dle ['mɒlɪˌkɒdl] *n.* person who takes too much care of his health, etc. *v.t.* take too much care of (oneself, sb.); pamper.

mol·ten, see **melt**.

mom [mɒm] *n.* (U.S.A., colloq.) = mother.

mo·ment ['məʊmənt] *n.* **1.** point of time: *in a* ~, very soon; *the* ~ (*that*), as soon as. **2.** (no pl.) importance: *affairs of great* ~. **mo·men·ta·ry** *adj.* lasting for, done in, a ~. **mo·men·tous** [məʊ-'mentəs] *adj.* very important or serious.

mo·men·tum [məʊ'mentəm] *n.* (no pl.) (scient.) quantity of motion of a moving body; (fig.) gain in force and speed caused by motion: *lose* (*gain*) ~.

mon·arch ['mɒnək] *n.* supreme ruler, esp. a king or an emperor. **mon·ar·chism** *n.* (no pl.). **mon·ar·chist** *n.* supporter of ~y. **mon·ar·chy** *n.* **1.** (no pl.) government by a ~. **2.** state ruled by a ~.

mon·as·tery ['mɒnəstərɪ] *n.* building in which monks live.

mo·nas·tic [mə'næstɪk] *adj.* of monasteries and monks.

Mon·day ['mʌndɪ] *n.* first day of the week.

mon·e·ta·ry ['mʌnɪtərɪ] *adj.* of money or coins.

mon·ey ['mʌnɪ] *n.* metal coin; (*paper* ~) official notes (4) printed with values and accepted as payment in place of coins. '~-,or·der *n.* official order (7) bought from a post office for money to be paid by another post office to a named person.

mon·goose ['mɒŋɡuːs] *n.* (pl. ~s [-sɪz]) small Indian animal clever at catching snakes.

mon·grel ['mʌŋɡrəl] *n.* dog of mixed breed; any plant or animal of mixed origin; (attrib) of mixed origin.

mon·i·tor ['mɒnɪtə*] *n.* **1.** schoolboy given authority over his fellows. **2.** person employed to listen to and report on foreign broadcasts. **3.** apparatus (1) for detecting radioactivity. **4.** television receiver used to select or check the picture picked up by a television camera. *v.t. & i.* act as a ~ (2, 3) (of).

monk [mʌŋk] *n.* one of a group of men living together under religious vows in a monastery.

mon·key ['mʌŋkɪ] *n.* (pl. ~s) mammal of a group of animals most closely allied to and resembling man. *v.i.* play mischievously (*about with* sth.). ~ busi·ness, (Gt. Brit. also) '~-tricks *ns.* (sl.) mischief. '~-nut *n.* peanut. '~-wrench *n.* wrench (3) with an adjustable jaw.

a monkey-wrench

mono ['mɒnəʊ] *adj. & n.* (pl. ~s) (colloq.) monophonic (reproduction, records, etc.).

mono- ['mɒnəʊ-] *pref.* one; single.

mono·chrome ['mɒnəkrəʊm] *n. & adj.* (painting) in one colour only.

mon·o·cle ['mɒnəkl] *n.* eyeglass for one eye only.

mo·nog·a·my [mɒ'nɒɡəmɪ] *n.* (no pl.) practice of being married to only one person at a time.

mono·gram ['mɒnəɡræm] *n.* two or more letters (esp. sb.'s initials) combined in one design. (See the picture on the left.)

mono·graph ['mɒnəɡrɑːf] *n.* written study of a subject, esp. a report on research.

mo·no·lith ['mɒnəlɪθ] *n.* single upright block of stone (as a pillar or monument). ~·ic *adj.*

mono·logue (U.S.A. **-log**) ['mɒnəlɒɡ] *n.* scene in a play, etc. in which only one person speaks.

mo·no·phon·ic [ˌmɒnəʊ'fɒnɪk] *adj.* of or relating to sound transmission, recording, or reproduction using only a single channel of transmission. (Cf. *stereophonic*).

mono·plane ['mɒnəʊpleɪn] *n.* aircraft with one wing on each side of the fuselage.

mo·nop·o·ly [mə'nɒpəlɪ] *n.* **1.** (possession of the) sole right to supply; supply or service thus controlled. **2.** complete possession of trade, talk, etc.: *In some countries tobacco is a government* ~. **mo·nop·o·list** *n.* person who has a ~. **mo·nop·o·lize** *v.t.* get, keep, a ~ of: *monopolize the conversation* (i.e. control it so that others cannot share).

mono·syl·la·ble ['mɒnəˌsɪləbl] *n.* word

a monogram

a monkey

of one syllable. **mono·syl·lab·ic** [ˌmɒnəʊsɪˈlæbɪk] *adj.*

mo·no·the·ism [ˈmɒnəʊθiːˌɪzəm] *n.* (no pl.) belief that there is only one God.

mono·tone [ˈmɒnətəʊn] *n.* (keeping a) level tone in talking or singing. **mo·not·o·nous** [məˈnɒtnəs] *adj.* (uninteresting because) unchanging. **mo·not·o·ny** [məˈnɒtnɪ] *n.* (no pl.) sameness; wearisome lack of variety.

mon·ox·ide [mɒˈnɒksaɪd] *n.* (chem.) oxide containing one atom of oxygen in the molecule: *carbon ~.*

mon·soon [mɒnˈsuːn] *n.* wind blowing in the Indian Ocean from S.W. in summer and from N.E. in winter.

mon·ster [ˈmɒnstə*] *n.* 1. wrongly-shaped animal or plant; person or thing of extraordinary shape, size, or qualities. 2. (in stories) imaginary creature (e.g. half animal, half bird). 3. very cruel person. *attrib. adj.* huge: *a ~ ship.* **mon·stros·i·ty** [mɒnˈstrɒsətɪ] *n.* state of being monstrous; ~ (1); outrageous thing. **mon·strous** [ˈmɒnstrəs] *adj.* 1. of or like a ~; of great size. 2. absurd; impossible: *monstrous demands.*

month [mʌnθ] *n.* any period of 28 days; one of the twelve parts into which a year is divided; period as from, e.g., 3 March to 3 April. **~·ly** *adj. & adv.* done, happening, once a ~; valid for one ~. *n.* periodical issued once a ~.

mon·u·ment [ˈmɒnjʊmənt] *n.* 1. building, column, statue, etc. serving to keep alive the memory of a person or event. 2. work of scholarship of permanent value. **mon·u·men·tal** [ˌmɒnjʊˈmentl] *adj.* 1. (of books, studies, etc.) of lasting value. 2. (of qualities, tasks, buildings) very great.

mood [muːd] *n.* state of mind or spirits. **~·y** *adj.* (-*ier*, -*iest*) having ~s that often change; gloomy. **~·i·ly** *adv.*

moon [muːn] *n.* *the ~,* the body (7) that moves round the earth once in a month, is illuminated by the sun and reflects some light to earth.

phases of the moon

moor[1] [mʊə*] *n.* area of open uncultivated land, esp. heather-covered land.

moor[2] [mʊə*] *v.t.* make (a boat, ship) secure (to the land or buoys) by means of cables, etc. **~·ings** *n. pl.* cables, etc. by which a ship is ~ed; place at which a ship is ~ed.

moose [muːs] *n.* (pl. ~) N. American sort of deer closely allied to or the same as the European elk.

moot [muːt] *adj.* ~ *point (question),* one about which there is uncertainty. *v.t.* raise, bring forward, for discussion.

mop [mɒp] *n.* 1. bundle of coarse strings, cloth, etc. fastened to a stick for cleaning floors, etc. 2. mass of thick untidy hair. *v.t.* (-*pp-*) clean with a ~; wipe up with, or as with, a ~: ~ *up,* clean up; (sl.) make an end of.

mope [məʊp] *v.i.* pity oneself; give way to sadness.

mo·ped [ˈməʊped] *n.* (Gt. Brit.) motorized bicycle.

mor·al [ˈmɒrəl] *adj.* 1. concerning principles of right and wrong. 2. good and virtuous: *a ~ life; ~ books.* 3. ~ *victory,* outcome of a struggle in which the weaker side is comforted because it has established the righteousness of its cause; ~ *certainty,* sth. so probable that there is little room for doubt. *n.* 1. that which a story, event, experience, etc. teaches. 2. (pl.) standards of behaviour; principles of right and wrong. **~·ist** *n.* person who points out ~s (1). **~·is·tic** [ˌmɒrəˈlɪstɪk] *adj.* concerned with ~s (2). **mo·ral·i·ty** [məˈrælətɪ] *n.* (no pl.) (standards, principles, of) good behaviour. **~·ize** *v.i. & t.* deal with ~ questions; show the ~ meaning of; point out ~s (2). **~·ly** *adv.*

mo·rale [mɒˈrɑːl] *n.* (no pl.) moral condition, esp. (of soldiers or workers) as regards discipline and confidence.

mo·rass [məˈræs] *n.* (liter.) stretch of low, soft, wet land; marsh; bog.

mor·a·to·ri·um [ˌmɒrəˈtɔːrɪəm] *n.* (pl. ~s, -ria [-rɪə]) legal authorization to delay payment of debts.

mor·bid [ˈmɔːbɪd] *adj.* 1. (med.) diseased: *a ~ growth* (e.g. a cancer). 2. (of sb.'s mind or ideas) unhealthy: *a ~ imagination.* 3. (of a person) having unhealthy or unnatural ideas and feelings. **~·ly** *adv.* **~·i·ty** [mɔːˈbɪdətɪ], **~·ness** *ns.* (no pl.) state of being ~.

mor·dant [ˈmɔːdənt] *adj.* biting; sarcastic.

more [mɔː*] *adj., n., & adv.* (contrasted with *less* and *fewer;* cf. *much, many, most*) I. *adj.* greater in number, quantity, quality, size, etc.; additional. II. *n.* greater amount, number, etc.; additional amount: *the ~ the better;* ~

about this later. What ~ do you want? May I have one ~? **III. adv. 1.** (forming the comparative degree of many adjectives and adverbs): *~ useful*; *~ easily*. **2.** to a greater extent; in a greater degree: *You should sleep ~ than you do at present*. **3.** again: *Do it once ~. Do you want to go there any ~?* **4.** *~ and ~*, increasingly; *~ or less*, about: *It's an hour's journey, ~ or less*; *be no ~*, be dead. **~·over** [mɔː'rəʊvə*] **adv.** (liter.) further; besides; in addition (to this).

morgue [mɔːg] **n.** building where bodies of persons found dead are kept until identified and claimed.

mor·i·bund ['mɒrɪbʌnd] **adj.** about to die or come to an end.

morn [mɔːn] **n.** (poet.) morning.

morn·ing ['mɔːnɪŋ] **n.** early part of the day between dawn and noon (or the midday meal). *~ coat*, man's tailcoat with the front sloped away; *~ watch*, (at sea) 4 a.m. to 8 a.m.

mo·roc·co [mə'rɒkəʊ] **n.** (no pl.) soft leather made from goatskins.

mo·rose [mə'rəʊs] **adj.** sullen; illtempered.

mor·phia ['mɔːfjə], **mor·phine** ['mɔːfiːn] **ns.** (no pl.) drug for relieving pain.

mor·row ['mɒrəʊ] **n.** *the ~*, (liter.) the next day (after the day or event indicated).

Morse [mɔːs] **n.** *~ (code)*, system of dots and dashes representing letters of the alphabet to be signalled by lamp, wireless, etc.

mor·sel ['mɔːsl] **n.** tiny piece (esp. *of* food); bite.

mor·tal ['mɔːtl] **adj. 1.** that must die; that cannot live for ever. **2.** causing death: *~ injuries*. **3.** lasting until death: *~ hatred*; *~ combat* (only ended by death). **4.** (sl.) very great; extreme: *in ~ fear of death*. **n.** human being. **~·ly adv. ~·i·ty** [mɔː'tælətɪ] **n.** (no pl.) **1.** being *~*. **2.** number of deaths caused by sth. (e.g. a disaster or disease). **3.** *~ity (rate)*, death-rate.

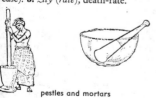

pestles and mortars

mor·tar ['mɔːtə*] **n. 1.** (no pl.) mixture of lime, sand, and water, used in building. **2.** bowl of hard material in which

substances are crushed to powder with a pestle. **3.** short gun for firing shells at high angles. **'~-board** **n. 1.** flat board with a short handle for holding *~* (1). **2.** square cap worn by members of a college.

a mortar-board

mort·gage ['mɔːgɪdʒ] **v.t.** give a creditor a claim on (property) as a security for payment of debt. **n.** act of mortgaging; agreement about this.

mor·ti·cian [mɔː'tɪʃn] **n.** (U.S.A.) = undertaker.

mor·ti·fy ['mɔːtɪfaɪ] **v.t. & i. 1.** cause (sb.) to be ashamed, humiliated, or hurt in his feelings: *mortified by sb.'s rudeness*; *a ~ing defeat*. **2.** *~ the flesh*, discipline bodily passions. **3.** (of flesh, e.g. round a wound) decay, be affected with gangrene. **mor·ti·fi·ca·tion** [ˌmɔːtɪfɪ'keɪʃn] **n.** (no pl.).

mor·tise, mor·tice ['mɔːtɪs] **n.** hole cut in a piece of wood, etc. to receive the end of another piece, esp. a tenon. **v.t.** join thus.

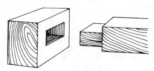

a mortise and tenon

mor·tu·ary ['mɔːtjʊərɪ] **n.** room or building to which dead bodies are taken to await burial.

mo·sa·ic [məʊ'zeɪɪk] **n. & adj.** (form or work of art) in which designs, pictures, etc. are made by fitting together bits of differently coloured stone, etc.

mosque [mɒsk] **n.** building in which Muslims worship Allah.

minaret

a mosque

mos·qui·to [məˈskiːtəʊ] *n.* (pl. *-oes*) small, flying, blood-sucking insect, esp. the sort spreading malaria.

moss [mɒs] *n.* sorts of small, green or yellow plant growing in thick masses on wet surfaces. **~y** *adj.* (*-ier, -iest*).

most [məʊst] *adj., n., & adv.* (contrasted with *least* and *fewest*; cf. *much, many, more*) **I. adj. & n. 1.** (the) greatest in number, quantity, etc.: *Which is ~, 3, 13, or 30? Those who have the ~ money are not always the happiest.* **2.** the majority of: *M~ people like children.* **3.** *at (the) ~*, not more than; *make the ~ of*, use to the best advantage; *for the ~ part*, almost all; in the main. **II. adv.** (forming the superlative degree of many adjectives and adverbs): *the ~ beautiful; ~ carefully. What pleased me ~ was his helpful nature. This is a ~ (= very) interesting book.* **~·ly** *adv.* chiefly; almost all; generally.

-most [-məʊst] *suff.* (forming adjs. with superlative sense from preps. or adjs. of position): *inmost; topmost.*

mote [məʊt] *n.* particle (esp. of dust).

mo·tel [məʊˈtel] *n.* hotel or group of cabins by the roadside, designed for the convenience of travellers by motor car.

moth [mɒθ] *n.* (sorts of) winged insect flying chiefly at night, attracted by lights.

moth·er [ˈmʌðə*] *n.* female parent. *~ country*, country in relation to its colonies; *~-of-pearl*, smooth, shining lining of some shells, esp. the pearl oyster; *~ tongue*, one's native language. *v.t.* watch over as a ~ does. **~·hood** *n.* (no pl.) state of being a ~. **~·less** *adj.* **~·ly** *adj.* having the tender qualities of a ~. **~·li·ness** *n.* (no pl.). **'~-in-law** *n.* (pl. *~s-in-law*) ~ of one's wife or husband.

mo·tif [məʊˈtiːf] *n.* main idea or design in a work of art.

mo·tion [ˈməʊʃn] *n.* **1.** (no pl.) (manner of) moving: *in ~, moving; put (set) in ~,* set going or working. *~ picture,* film (3). **2.** gesture; particular movement. **3.** proposal to be discussed and voted on at a meeting. **4.** emptying of the bowels. *v.t. & i.* direct (sb.) by a ~ (2); indicate by a gesture: *~ sb. in (away, to a seat). She ~ed to me to sit down.* **~·less** *adj.* not moving.

mo·tive [ˈməʊtɪv] *adj.* causing motion: *~ power. n.* that which causes sb. to act: *actuated by low and selfish ~s.* **mo·ti·vate** [ˈməʊtɪveɪt] *v.t.* give a ~ to; be a ~ of. **mo·ti·va·tion** [ˌməʊtɪˈveɪʃn] *n.*

mot·ley [ˈmɒtlɪ] *adj.* of various colours: *a ~ coat;* of various sorts: *a ~ crowd.*

mo·to-cross [ˈməʊtəʊkrɒs] *n.* cross-country motor-cycle race.

mo·tor [ˈməʊtə*] *n.* **1.** machine, esp. one worked by petrol or electricity, supplying motive power for a vehicle, lawn-mower or vessel. **2.** muscle or nerve producing motion. **3.** (attrib.) worked or driven by a ~: *~ bicycle (bike, boat, bus, car, coach, cycle, scooter, vehicle); ~-cyclist. v.i. & t.* travel, take (sb.), by ~ car. **~·ist** *n.* driver of a ~ car. **~·ize** *v.t.* equip (troops, etc.) with ~ transport; equip with a ~. **'~·way** *n.* (Gt. Brit.) road specially built for fast ~ traffic, usu. with dual carriageways.

mot·tled [ˈmɒtld] *adj.* irregularly marked with different colours.

mot·to [ˈmɒtəʊ] *n.* (pl. *-oes*) short sentence or phrase used as a guide or rule of behaviour.

mould¹ (U.S.A. **mold**) [məʊld] *n.* container into which liquid metal or a soft substance is put to take a desired shape; food (e.g. jelly) shaped in such a container. *v.t.* give a shape or form to: *~ a head in (out of) clay;* (fig.) *~ sb.'s character.*

mould² (U.S.A. **mold**) [məʊld] *n.* woolly or furry growth of fungi appearing on moist surfaces (e.g. leather, cheese). **~y** *adj.* (*-ier, -iest*) covered with, suggesting, ~: *~y bread; a ~y smell;* (fig.) out of date; old-fashioned.

mould³ (U.S.A. **mold**) [məʊld] *n.* (no pl.) soft, fine, loose, earth. **~·er** *v.i.* break up into ~; decay: *~ering ruins of a house.*

moult (U.S.A. **molt**) [məʊlt] *v.t. & i.* (of birds) lose (feathers) before a new growth. *n.* (no pl.) process or time of ~ing.

mound [maʊnd] *n.* mass of piled-up earth; small hill.

mount [maʊnt] *n.* **1.** (liter. except in proper names) mountain: *Mount (Mt.) Everest.* **2.** card, etc. that provides a margin for a picture or photograph fixed on it. **3.** horse, etc., on which a person rides or is to ride. *v.t. & i.* **1.** go up (a ladder, a hill); get on to (a horse, etc.); supply (sb.) with a horse: *the ~ed police. He ~ed (his horse) and rode off.* **2.** fix on to a card, stand, etc. for display or use: *~ pictures; ~ a gun (on a gun-carriage); ~ jewels (e.g. in gold).* **3.** *~ up,* become greater in amount: *Our living expenses are ~ing up.* **4.** *~ guard (over),* watch and protect; be on duty as a guard.

moun·tain [ˈmaʊntɪn] *n.* mass of very high land going up to a peak. **~·eer** [ˌmaʊntɪˈnɪə*] *n.* person who lives

muck

among ⁓s or is clever at climbing ⁓s. ⁓**eer·ing** *n.* (no pl.) climbing ⁓s (as a sport). ⁓**ous** ['maʊntɪnəs] *adj.* having many ⁓s; immense: ⁓*ous waves.* ⁓**range** *n.* series of ⁓s more or less in a line. '⁓**side** *n.* slope of a ⁓.

moun·te·bank ['maʊntɪbæŋk] *n.* sb. who persuades people by clever and humorous talk to buy worthless medicine, etc.

mourn [mɔːn] *v.t. & i.* feel or show sorrow for a death or loss: ⁓*ing the death of a friend*; ⁓*ing for (over) her dead child.* ⁓**er** *n.* person who ⁓s, esp. at a funeral. ⁓**ful** *adj.* sad. ⁓**ful·ly** *adv.* ⁓**ing** *n.* (no pl.) **1.** grief. **2.** (wearing of) black clothes as a sign of grief: *go into ⁓ing (for sb.).*

mouse [maʊs] *n.* (pl. mice [maɪs]) sorts of small rodent: *house-(field-)⁓.*

mice

mous·tache (U.S.A. **mus-**) [məˈstɑːʃ] *n.* hair on the upper lip.

mouth [maʊθ] *n.* (pl. ⁓s [maʊðz]) **1.** opening through which people and animals take in food; space behind this containing the tongue, etc. *down in the ⁓,* sad. **2.** opening or outlet (*of a bag, bottle, cave, tunnel, river, etc.*). [maʊð] *v.t. & i.* speak (words) with too much movement of the ⁓. ⁓**ful** *n.* as much as can be put into the ⁓ comfortably at one time. '⁓**-**'**or·gan** *n.* small musical wind instrument played by passing it along the lips. '⁓**·piece** *n.* **1.** part of a tobacco pipe or musical instrument placed against or between the lips. **2.** person, newspaper, etc. expressing the opinions of others.

move [muːv] *v.t. & i.* **1.** (cause to) change place or position: ⁓ *house,* take one's furniture, etc. to another house; ⁓ *in (out),* take one's furniture, etc. into (out of) a house, etc. **2.** ⁓ *along (on),* ⁓ to a new place or position; ⁓ *over (up),* adjust one's position to make room for others. **3.** work on the feelings of: ⁓*d to tears;* ⁓ *sb. to do sth.,* cause him to do sth. **4.** put forward for discussion and decision (at a meeting): *Mr. Chairman, I ⁓ that the money shall be used for library books.* **5.** cause (the bowels) to empty; (of the bowels) be emptied. *n.*

1. change of place or position: ⁓*s in a game of chess.* **2.** sth. (to be) done to achieve a purpose: *What's the next ⁓?* **3.** *on the ⁓,* moving about: *large enemy forces on the ⁓; make a ⁓,* (a) ⁓ to a different place; (b) begin to act; *get a ⁓ on,* (sl.) hurry up. **mov·able** ['muːvəbl] *adj.* **1.** that can be moved. **2.** changing date from year to year: *movable holidays. Easter is a movable feast. n.* (pl.) articles (as furniture) that may be removed from the house (contrasted with *fixtures*); personal property. ⁓**ment** *n.* **1.** (no pl.) moving or being ⁓d; activity. **2.** moving part of a machine or a particular group of such parts: *the ⁓ment of a clock.* **3.** united action and efforts of a group of people for a special purpose: *the ⁓ment to abolish slavery.* **4.** chief division of a musical work.

mov·ie ['muːvɪ] *n.* (U.S.A., colloq.) = film (3): *the ⁓s,* the cinema; the cinema industry: *feel like going to the ⁓s.*

mov·ing ['muːvɪŋ] *adj.* **1.** marked by or capable of movement: ⁓ *picture,* film (3). **2.** arousing or affecting the emotions. ⁓**ly** *adv.*

mow [məʊ] *v.t.* (p.t. ⁓ed, p.p. ⁓ed or ⁓n [məʊn]) cut (grass, etc.) with a scythe or machine (*lawn-⁓er*): ⁓*ing the lawn; new-⁓n hay;* (fig.) ⁓*n down by machine-gun fire.*

Mr, Mr. ['mɪstə*], **Mrs, Mrs.** ['mɪsɪz] *n.* title placed before the surname of a man, woman, who has no other title.

Ms. [mɪz] *n.* abbreviated title of *Miss* or *Mrs.,* used as the feminine of Mr. to avoid distinction between married and unmarried.

much [mʌtʃ] *adj.* (*more, most,* cf. *little*), *n.,* & *adv.* **I.** *adj. & n.* (used with sing. nouns; cf. *many,* used with pl. nouns) a lot (of), plenty (of), a good deal (of), a large quantity (of): *There isn't ⁓ food in the house, so we must go out and buy some. You have given me too ⁓, I can't eat it all.* as ⁓ *(as),* quantity equal to; same quantity as: *Give me as ⁓ as you did before. I've had as ⁓ trouble as I can bear.* **II.** *adv.* **1.** (modifying comparatives and superlatives): *He's ⁓ better today than yesterday. This is ⁓ the best essay* (far better than all others). **2.** (modifying past participles, etc.): *I'm very ⁓ afraid your child is seriously ill. I'm ⁓ annoyed at his behaviour.* **3.** greatly: ⁓ *to my surprise.* **4.** to a great extent or degree: *It doesn't matter ⁓ (⁓ matter). I don't like mangoes ⁓. She likes them very ⁓.*

muck [mʌk] *n.* (no pl.) **1.** farmyard

manure (animal droppings). **2.** dirt; anything looked upon as dirty or disgusting. *v.t. & i.* **1.** make dirty; remove ~ *out* from. **2.** ~ *sth. up*, (Gt. Brit., sl.) make a mess of it. **3.** ~ *about*, (Gt. Brit., sl.) spend time aimlessly. **~y** *adj.* (*-ier, -iest*) dirty.

mu·cous ['mjuːkəs] *adj.* of, covered with, mucus: ~ *membrane*, moist skin lining the nose, mouth, food canal.

mu·cus ['mjuːkəs] *n.* (no pl.) sticky or slimy liquid produced by the ~ membrane; slimy substance exuded by some animals, esp. fishes, snails, etc.

mud [mʌd] *n.* (no pl.) soft, wet earth. **~dy** *adj.* (*-ier, -iest*) full of, covered with, ~; (fig.) of ideas) confused. '**~-guard** *n.* curved strip covering the wheel of a bicycle, etc.

mud·dle ['mʌdl] *v.t. & i.* bring into confusion and disorder; make a mess of. *n.* (usu. no pl.) ~d state: *in a* ~.

mu·ez·zin [muːˈezɪn] *n.* man who calls the faithful to prayer from the minaret of a mosque.

muff [mʌf] *n.* covering, usu. a padded bag of fur, open at both ends, used by women to keep their hands warm.

muf·fin ['mʌfɪn] *n.* light, flat, round teacake, usu. eaten hot with butter.

muf·fle ['mʌfl] *v.t.* **1.** cover up for warmth: ~ (*oneself*) *up well* (e.g. by putting a scarf round the neck). **2.** make the sound of sth. (e.g. a bell or drum) dull by wrapping it up in cloth, etc. **~r** *n.* **1.** cloth or scarf worn round the neck for warmth. **2.** device (2) to deaden noise; (U.S.A.) silencer of a motor vehicle.

muf·ti ['mʌftɪ] *n.* *in* ~, (of sb. who normally wears uniform) wearing ordinary clothes.

mug¹ [mʌg] *n.* straight-sided drinking-vessel of china or metal with a handle, for use without a saucer: *a beer-*~.

mug² [mʌg] *n.* (Gt. Brit., sl.) simpleton.

mug³ [mʌg] *v.t.* (*-gg-*) rob with violence, esp. in a public place. **~ger** *n.* **~ging** *n.*

Mu·ham·mad·an, [məˈhæmɪdən], **Mo·ham·med·an** [məʊˈhæmɪdən] *n.* believer in Islam; Muslim. *adj.* of, relating to, Islam or Muhammad.

mu·lat·to [mjuːˈlætəʊ] *n.* (pl. *-os*, U.S.A. *-oes*) offspring of a Negro and a white person.

mul·ber·ry ['mʌlbərɪ] *n.* (fruit of) tree whose leaves are used for feeding silkworms.

mulch [mʌltʃ] *n.* mixture of wet straw, leaves, peat, etc., used to protect roots of plants, trees, etc. *v.t.* cover with ~.

mulct [mʌlkt] *v.t.* punish by means of a fine: ~ *sb. £10*; deprive (sb. *of*): ~*ed of his money*.

mule [mjuːl] *n.* offspring of a he-ass and a mare. **mul·ish** ['mjuːlɪʃ] *adj.* stubborn.

mull [mʌl] *v.t.* make (wine, beer) into a hot drink with sugar, spices, etc.: ~*ed claret* (*wine*).

mul·let ['mʌlɪt] *n.* sort of seafish, used as food.

mul·lion ['mʌlɪən] *n.* upright stone column between parts of a window.

mul·ti- ['mʌltɪ-] *pref.* having many (of). **~·far·i·ous** [ˌmʌltɪˈfeərɪəs] *adj.* many and various: ~*farious duties*. **~·lat·er·al** [ˌmʌltɪˈlætərəl] *adj.* (of a treaty, etc.) in which three or more states or parties participate. **~·lin·gual** [ˌmʌltɪˈlɪŋgwəl] *adj.* in or using many languages. **~·na·tion·al** [ˌmʌltɪˈnæʃənl] *adj.* operating in several countries.

mul·ti·ple ['mʌltɪpl] *adj.* having many parts. *n.* quantity that contains another quantity some number of times without remainder: *28 is a* ~ *of 7*.

mul·ti·ply ['mʌltɪplaɪ] *v.t. & i.* **1.** *6 multiplied by 5 is 30* ($6 \times 5 = 30$). **2.** produce a great number of: ~ *instances*. **3.** make or become great in number: *Rabbits soon* ~. **mul·ti·pli·ca·tion** [ˌmʌltɪplɪˈkeɪʃn] *n.* ~*ing* or being multiplied. **mul·ti·plic·i·ty** [ˌmʌltɪˈplɪsətɪ] *n.* (no pl.) great number or variety: *the multiplicity of his duties*.

mul·ti·ra·cial [ˌmʌltɪˈreɪʃl] *adj.* composed of, relating to, representing, various races of people: *a* ~ *country*.

mul·ti·stage [ˌmʌltɪˈsteɪdʒ] *adj.* (of a rocket, etc.) with parts that ignite (and fall away) in stages: *a* ~ *rocket*.

mul·ti·sto·rey [ˌmʌltɪˈstɔːrɪ] *adj.* having several storeys: *a* ~ *car-park*.

mul·ti·tude ['mʌltɪtjuːd] *n.* **1.** great number (esp. of people gathered together). **2.** *the* ~, the masses; the common people. **mul·ti·tu·di·nous** [ˌmʌltɪˈtjuːdɪnəs] *adj.* great in number.

mum¹ [mʌm] *int. & adj.* keep ~ *about* (*sth.*), say nothing about; keep secret. *M.'s the word!* Say nothing about it.

mum² [mʌm] *n.* (Gt. Brit., colloq.) mother.

mum·ble ['mʌmbl] *v.t. & i.* say sth., speak (one's words), indistinctly. *n.* ~d words: *His only answer was a* ~.

mum·mer ['mʌmə*] *n.* actor in an old form of drama without words. **~y** *n.* performance by ~s; (performance of) useless ceremonial (esp. religious).

mum·my¹ ['mʌmɪ] *n.* dead person preserved from decay by being embalmed, esp. as by the ancient Egyptians.

Egyptian mummies

mum·my² ['mʌmɪ] *n.* (Gt. Brit., colloq.) mother.

mumps [mʌmps] *n. pl.* (sing. v.) contagious disease causing painful swellings in the neck.

munch [mʌntʃ] *v.t. & i.* eat (food) with much movement of the jaw: ⁓*ing an apple.*

mun·dane ['mʌndeɪn] *adj.* worldly (contrasted with *spiritual*): ⁓ *affairs.*

mu·nic·i·pal [mjuːˈnɪsɪpl] *adj.* of a ⁓**i·ty** [mjuːˌnɪsɪˈpælətɪ] *n.* town or city governed by its own elected council; governing body (5) of such a town.

mu·nif·i·cent [mjuːˈnɪfɪsnt] *adj.* very generous. **mu·nif·i·cence** *n.* (no pl.).

mu·ni·tions [mjuːˈnɪʃnz] *n. pl.* military supplies, esp. guns, shells, etc.

mu·ral ['mjʊərəl] *adj.* of or on a wall: ⁓ *paintings. n.* ⁓ painting.

mur·der ['mɜːdə*] *n.* unlawful killing of a human being on purpose. *v.t.* kill (sb.) unlawfully and on purpose. ⁓**er** *n.* person guilty of ⁓. ⁓**ess** *n.* female ⁓er. ⁓**ous** ['mɜːdərəs] *adj.* planning, suggesting, designed for, ⁓: ⁓*ous weapons.*

murky ['mɜːkɪ] *adj.* (-ier, -iest) dark; gloomy.

mur·mur ['mɜːmə*] *v.t. & i. & n.* **1.** (make a) low, continuous, indistinct sound: *the* ⁓ *of bees; a* ⁓ *of pain; a stream* ⁓*ing over the stones.* **2.** say(ing) (sth.), talk(ing), in a low voice: ⁓*ing a prayer;* ⁓*ing against heavy taxes.*

mus·cle ['mʌsl] *n.* (band, bundle, of) elastic substance in an animal body that can be tightened or loosened to produce movement: *be* ⁓*-bound*, have stiff ⁓s through excessive exercise or training. **mus·cu·lar** ['mʌskjʊlə*] *adj.* of the ⁓s; having much ⁓.

muse [mjuːz] *v.i.* think deeply or dreamily (*on, upon, over*, sth.), ignoring what is happening around one.

muscles of the arm

mu·se·um [mjuːˈzɪəm] *n.* building in which objects illustrating art, history, science, etc. are displayed.

mush [mʌʃ] *n.* (no pl.) soft pulp; (U.S.A.) boiled cornmeal.

mush·room ['mʌʃrʊm] *n.* **1.** kind of fast-growing fungus that can be eaten. **2.** (attrib.) ⁓ *growth*, rapid development. *v.i.* **1.** gather ⁓s: *go* ⁓*ing*. **2.** spread or grow rapidly.

a mushroom (1)

mu·sic ['mjuːzɪk] *n.* (no pl.) **1.** (art of producing) pleasing combinations of sounds in rhythm and harmony; written or printed signs for these. **2.** *face the* ⁓, meet one's critics, face difficulties, etc. ⁓ **box** *n.* (U.S.A.) = musical box; juke-box. '⁓**hall** *n.* (Gt. Brit.) (building for) variety entertainment (singing, dancing, etc.).

mu·si·cal¹ ['mjuːzɪkl] *adj.* of, fond of, skilled in, music. ⁓ **box** *n.* (Gt. Brit.) box with an apparatus (1) that reproduces music mechanically when activated by clockwork. ⁓ **com·e·dy** *n.* light, dramatic entertainment with songs and dancing. ⁓**ly** *adv.*

mu·si·cal² ['mjuːzɪkl] *n.* musical comedy; musical film (3) (in which music has an essential part).

mu·si·cas·sette [ˌmjuːzɪkæˈset] *n.* small cassette of musical tape-recordings.

mu·si·cian [mjuːˈzɪʃn] *n.* person skilled in music; composer of music.

musk [mʌsk] *n.* (no pl.) substance obtained from male deer (⁓*-deer*), used in making perfumes. '⁓**-rat** *n.* rat-like water-animal of N. America.

mus·ket ['mʌskɪt] *n.* old style of gun, now replaced by the rifle. ⁓**ry** *n.* (no pl.) (science of, instruction in) shooting with rifles.

Muslim

Mus·lim ['mʊslɪm] *n.* believer in Islam; follower of Muhammad.

mus·lin ['mʌzlɪn] *n.* (no pl.) thin, fine, soft cotton cloth used for dresses, curtains, etc.

mus·sel ['mʌsl] *n.* mollusc with a black shell in two parts.

must [mʌst, məst] *v.aux.* (no infinitive, no participles; neg. ~ not, (colloq.) *mustn't* ['mʌsnt]) **1.** expressing a past, present, or future obligation: *I said I ~ go. I ~ go now. I ~ go next week. Why ~ you keep worrying about your money? You ~n't (= ~ not) do this* (i.e. you are not allowed to do it). **2.** expressing certainty or strong probability: *You ~ be hungry after your long walk. I think you ~ have made a mistake. n.* (colloq.) sth. that ~ be done, seen, heard, etc.: *This new book is a real ~.*

mus·tang ['mʌstæŋ] *n.* small wild or half-wild horse of the American plains.

mus·tard ['mʌstəd] *n.* plant; seeds of this crushed to a yellow powder; hot-tasting sauce made from this powder.

mus·ter ['mʌstə*] *n.* assembly or gathering of persons, esp. for review: *pass ~*, be considered satisfactory. *v.t. & i.* collect, call, come, together: *~ (up) one's courage*, overcome one's fears.

musty ['mʌstɪ] *adj.* (-ier, -iest) stale; smelling, tasting, mouldy.

mu·table ['mju:təbl] *adj.* likely to change; liable to change. **mu·ta·bil·i·ty** [,mju:tə'bɪlətɪ] *n.* (no pl.). **mu·ta·tion** [mju:'teɪʃn] *n.* change.

mute [mju:t] *adj.* **1.** silent; making no sound. **2.** (of a person) unable to speak; dumb. **3.** (of a letter in a word) not sounded (as the *b* in *dumb*). *n.* person who cannot speak.

mu·ti·late ['mju:tɪleɪt] *v.t.* damage by tearing, breaking, or cutting off a part. **mu·ti·la·tion** [,mju:tɪ'leɪʃn] *n.*

mu·ti·ny ['mju:tɪnɪ] *n.* (esp. of soldiers and sailors) open rising against authority. *v.i.* rise against authority; be guilty of ~. **mu·ti·neer** [,mju:tɪ'nɪə*] *n.* person guilty of ~. **mu·ti·nous** ['mju:tɪnəs] *adj.* rebellious.

mut·ter ['mʌtə*] *v.t. & i.* speak, say (sth.), in a low voice not meant to be heard: *~ing threats.* [the sheep.]

mut·ton ['mʌtn] *n.* (no pl.) meat from

mu·tu·al ['mju:tʃʊəl] *adj.* **1.** (of love, respect, etc.) shared, exchanged. **2.** (of feelings, opinions, etc.) held in common with others. **3.** common to two or more: *our ~ friend.* **~·ly** *adv.*

muz·zle ['mʌzl] *n.* **1.** nose and mouth of an animal (e.g. dog or fox). **2.** device (2) of straps or wires placed over an animal's ~ to prevent it from biting, etc. **3.** open end or mouth of a gun. *v.t.* put a ~ on (an animal); (fig.) prevent (a person, newspaper, etc.) from expressing views freely.

muz·zy ['mʌzɪ] *adj.* (-ier, -iest) confused in mind; dull; stupid from drinking.

my [maɪ] *poss. pron. attrib.* **1.** belonging to me. **2.** in a form of address: *My Lord. My dear (John).* **3.** in exclamations: *Oh, my!*

my·o·pia [maɪ'əʊpjə] *n.* (no pl.) short-sightedness. **my·op·ic** [maɪ'ɒpɪk] *adj.* short-sighted.

myr·i·ad ['mɪrɪəd] *n.* (poet. or rhet.) number beyond count.

myrrh [mɜ:*] *n.* sweet-smelling kind of gum or resin from trees, used for incense and perfumes.

myr·tle ['mɜ:tl] *n.* evergreen shrub with sweet-smelling white flowers and black berries.

my·self [maɪ'self] *pron.* (emphatic or refl. form): *I hurt ~. I ~ said so. I did it (all) by ~* (without help). (Cf. *herself, himself*).

mys·tery ['mɪstərɪ] *n.* **1.** sth. of which the cause or origin is hidden or impossible to understand. **2.** (no pl.) condition of being secret or obscure: *wrapped in ~.* **3.** (pl.) secret religious rites and ceremonies. **4.** ~ *play*, old play telling a Bible story. **mys·te·ri·ous** [mɪ'stɪərɪəs] *adj.* full of, suggesting, ~; wrapped in ~.

mys·tic ['mɪstɪk] *adj.* of hidden meaning or spiritual power; mysterious; causing feelings of awe and wonder. *n.* person who seeks union with God and, through that, the realization of truths beyond men's understanding. **mys·ti·cal** *adj.* = ~. **mys·ti·cal·ly** *adv.* **mys·ti·cism** ['mɪstɪsɪzəm] *n.* (no pl.) beliefs, experiences, of a ~.

mys·ti·fy ['mɪstɪfaɪ] *v.t.* puzzle; bewilder. **mys·ti·fi·ca·tion** [,mɪstɪfɪ'keɪʃn] *n.* ~ing; sth. that mystifies.

myth [mɪθ] *n.* **1.** story, handed down from olden times, containing the early beliefs of a race, esp. explanations of natural events. **2.** (no pl.) such stories collectively. **3.** false belief; non-existent person, thing, etc. **~·i·cal** ['mɪθɪkl] *adj.* of ~s; unreal; non-existent; fictitious. **my·thol·o·gy** [mɪ'θɒlədʒɪ] *n.* **1.** (no pl.) science or study of ~s. **2.** (no pl.) ~s collectively: *Greek ~ology.* **3.** body (6) or collection of ~s. **~·o·log·i·cal** [,mɪθə'lɒdʒɪkl] *adj.* **my·thol·o·gist** [mɪ'θɒlədʒɪst] *n.* student of ~ology.

N

na·dir ['neɪˌdɪə*] *n.* (no pl.) (opp. *zenith*) **1.** part of the sky directly under the observer. **2.** (fig.) lowest, weakest, point (of one's fortunes, hopes).

nag¹ [næg] *n.* (colloq.) small horse.

nag² [næg] *v.t. & i.* (-gg-) scold (sb., *at* sb.) continuously; annoy thus.

na·iad ['naɪæd] *n.* (pl. ~s, ~es [-iːz]) (Greek mythology) water-nymph.

nail [neɪl] *n.* **1.** layer of hard substance over the outer tip of a finger (*finger-~*) or toe (*toe-~*). **2.** piece of metal, pointed at one end and with a head at the other, (to be) hammered into articles to hold them together, or into a wall, etc. to hang sth. on. *on the ~*, at once; *hit the ~ on the head*, say or do the right thing. *v.t.* make fast with a ~ or ~s.

a finger-nail   a nail (2)

na·ive [nɑːˈiːv], **na·ive** [neɪv] *adj.* natural and innocent in speech and behaviour (e.g. because young or inexperienced). **~·ly** *adv.* **na·ive·ty** [nɑːˈiːvtɪ], **na·ive·ty** ['neɪvtɪ], **na·ive·té** [nɑːˈiːvteɪ] *n.* being ~; ~ remark, etc.

na·ked ['neɪkɪd] *adj.* without clothes on; bare; without the usual covering: *trees ~ of leaves*; *with the ~ eye*, without the help of a telescope, microscope, etc. **~·ly** *adv.* **~·ness** *n.* (no pl.).

name [neɪm] *n.* **1.** word(s) by which a person, animal, place, or other thing is known and spoken to or of: *in the ~ of*, with the authority of (e.g. the law); for the sake of (e.g. common

sense); *call sb. ~s*, call him insulting ~s (e.g. liar, coward); *not have a penny to one's ~*, be without money. **2.** (no pl.) reputation: *win a good ~ for oneself*. *v.t.* **1.** give a ~ to; say the ~ of: *~ sb. after*, give him the same ~ as. **2.** mention; state: *~ your price*, say what price you want. **~·less** *adj.* **1.** not having a ~; having an unknown ~. **2.** too bad to be ~d: *~less vices*. **3.** difficult or impossible to ~: *~less horror*. **~·ly** *adv.* that is to say: *Only one child, ~ly Mary, was absent*. '**~·sake** *n.* person or thing with the same ~ as another.

nan·ny ['nænɪ] *n.* **1.** (children's word for a) child's nurse. **2.** (also *~-goat*) female goat.

nap¹ [næp] *n.* short sleep (esp. during the day, not in bed). *v.i.* (-pp-) *catch sb. ~ping*, find him asleep; catch him unawares or off guard.

nap² [næp] *n.* (no pl.) surface of cloth, etc. consisting of soft, short hairs or fibres, smoothed and brushed up.

na·palm ['neɪpɑːm] *n.* (no pl.) ~ *bomb*, bomb containing petrol jelly.

nape [neɪp] *n.* back (of the neck).

naph·tha ['næfθə] *n.* (no pl.) liquid made from coal tar, used for burning, for cleaning clothes, etc. **~·lene** ['næfθəliːn] *n.* (no pl.) strong-smelling substance made from coal tar, used for keeping insects out of clothes, etc.

nap·kin ['næpkɪn] *n.* **1.** (also *table-~*) piece of cloth used at meals for protecting clothing, for wiping lips, etc. **2.** (U.S.A. *diaper*) (colloq. *nappy* ['næpɪ]) towel folded between a baby's legs.

nar·cis·sus [nɑːˈsɪsəs] *n.* (pl. -*si* [-saɪ], ~*es*) sorts of bulb plant with white or yellow flowers in spring.

nar·cot·ic [nɑːˈkɒtɪk] *n. & adj.* (kinds of drug) producing sleep or other insensible condition.

nar·rate [nəˈreɪt] *v.t.* tell (a story); give an account of. **nar·ra·tor** *n.* **nar·ra·tive** ['nærətɪv] *adj. & n.* (of, in the form of) story-telling; story.

nar·row ['nærəʊ] *adj.* **1.** measuring little across in comparison with length.

2. small; limited: *a ~ circle of friends*; *~ circumstances*, poverty. **3.** with a small margin: *a ~ escape from death*; *by a ~ majority*. **4.** strict; exact: *a ~ search*. **~·ly** *adv*. **1.** only just; with little to spare. **2.** closely; carefully. **,~·'mind·ed** *adj*. having no or little sympathy for other persons' opinions, beliefs, etc. **~·ness** *n*. (no pl.).

na·sal ['neɪzl] *adj*. of the nose; pronounced through the nose. *n*. ~ letter or sound. **~·ize** *v.t. & i.* make (a sound) ~; speak in a ~ manner.

nas·ty ['nɑːstɪ] *adj*. (-*ier*, -*iest*) **1.** dirty; unpleasant. **2.** threatening; dangerous; awkward (1). **nas·ti·ly** *adv*. **nas·ti·ness** *n*. (no pl.).

na·tal ['neɪtl] *adj*. of, from, one's birth.

na·tion ['neɪʃn] *n*. body (5) of people with a common language, history, and government. **~·wide**, throughout a ~. **~·al** ['næʃənl] *adj*. of, common to, a ~. *n*. person of a certain ~: *British ~als in South Africa*. **~·al·ism** ['næʃnəlɪzəm] *n*. (no pl.) **1.** political movement for ~al self-government. **2.** strong devotion to one's ~. **~·al·ist** ['næʃnəlɪst] *n*. supporter of ~alism (1). *adj*. = **~·al·is·tic** [,næʃnə'lɪstɪk] *adj*. supporting ~alism (1): *~alist(ic) movements in Africa*. **~·al·i·ty** [,næʃə'nælətɪ] *n*. being a member of a ~: *men of French ~ality*. **~·al·ize** ['næʃnəlaɪz] *v.t.* **1.** transfer (e.g. land) from private to State ownership. **2.** make into a ~. **~·al·iza·tion** [,næʃnəlaɪ'zeɪʃn] *n*.

na·tive ['neɪtɪv] *adj*. **1.** of the place, circumstances, etc., of one's birth: *This is my own, my ~ land!* **2.** (of qualities) belonging to a person by nature, not by education: *Rather instruct a lawyer to defend him he relied on his ~ wit*. **3.** (of plants and animals) belonging by origin (*to*): *plants ~ to America*. *n*. **1.** person belonging by birth to a place or country: *a ~ of Wales*. **2.** animal or plant natural to and having its origin in a certain region: *The kangaroo is a ~ of Australia*.

na·tiv·i·ty [nə'tɪvətɪ] *n*. birth. *the N~*, the birth of Jesus Christ: *a Nativity play* (about the N~).

nat·u·ral ['nætʃrəl] *adj*. **1.** of, concerned with, produced by, nature (1, 2): *~ forces* (e.g. storms); *~ gas*, gas found in the earth's crust, not manufactured; *~ history*, botany and zoology; *animals living in their ~* (i.e. wild) *state*. **2.** of, in agreement with, the nature (5) of a living thing: *a ~ orator*;

her ~ abilities. **3.** ordinary; normal; to be expected: *die a ~ death* (not by violence, etc.); *It is ~ for a bird to fly*. **4.** simple; not cultivated or self-conscious: *speaking in a ~ voice*; *~ behaviour*. **~·ly** *adv*. **1.** in a ~ (3, 4) way. **2.** by nature (5). **3.** of course; as might be expected. **~·ism** *n*. (no pl.) **1.** realism in art or literature. **2.** (phil.) doctrine that ~ causes and laws explain all phenomena. **~·ist** *n*. student of animals or plants.

nat·u·ral·ize ['nætʃrəlaɪz] *v.t. & i.* **1.** give (sb. from another country) rights of citizenship: *~ immigrants into the U.S.A.* **2.** take (a word) from one language into another. **3.** become ~d. **nat·u·ral·iza·tion** [,nætʃrəlaɪ'zeɪʃn] *n*. (no pl.).

na·ture ['neɪtʃə*] *n*. **1.** (no pl.) the whole universe and every created thing: *~ study*, study of plants, insects, animals, etc.; *~ worship* (e.g. of trees, oceans, wind). **2.** (no pl.) forces that control life, weather, etc. in the world: *mankind's struggle against ~*. **3.** (no pl.) simple life without civilization, cultivation, etc.: *in a state of ~*, naked. **4.** essential qualities of nonmaterial things: *studying the ~ of gases*. **5.** general characteristics of a living thing: *a girl with a kind ~*; *proud by ~*; *human ~*; *good ~*, kindness; unselfishness. *It is the ~ of dogs to bark*. **6.** sort; class: *things of this ~*; *in the ~ of*, almost the same as. **-na·tured** [-'neɪtʃəd] *adj*. good- (ill-) ~d, having a good (ill) ~ (5).

naught [nɔːt] *n*. nothing.

naughty ['nɔːtɪ] *adj*. (-*ier*, -*iest*) (of children, their behaviour, etc.) disobedient; causing trouble; bad; wrong. **naugh·ti·ly** *adv*. **naugh·ti·ness** *n*.

nau·sea ['nɔːsjə] *n*. (no pl.) feeling of sickness (e.g. caused by bad food) or disgust. **nau·se·ous** ['nɔːsɪəs] *adj*. disgusting. **nau·se·ate** ['nɔːsɪeɪt] *v.t. & i.* cause ~ to; feel sick (*at*): *nauseating food*.

nau·ti·cal ['nɔːtɪkl] *adj*. of ships, sailors, or navigation: *a ~ mile*, 6,080 feet (= 1,852 metres).

na·val ['neɪvl] *adj*. of a navy: *~ officers* (*warfare*, *battles*).

nave [neɪv] *n*. central part of a church where the congregation sits.

na·vel ['neɪvl] *n*. small depression in the surface of the belly.

nav·i·gate ['nævɪgeɪt] *v.t.* direct the course of (a ship or aircraft); sail or steam along (a river) or across (a sea). **nav·i·gable** ['nævɪgəbl] *adj*. that can be ~d; (of ships) in good condition for sailing, etc. **nav·i·ga·tion** [ˌnævɪ-ˈgeɪʃn] *n.* (no pl.) 1. science of navigating. 2. navigating; voyage: *inland navigation* (by canals and rivers). **nav·i·ga·tor** *n.* person who ~s or is qualified to ~; (esp.) person who explores by ship.

nav·vy [ˈnævɪ] *n.* (Gt. Brit.) unskilled workman employed in making roads, canals, railways, etc.

na·vy [ˈneɪvɪ] *n.* a country's warships; their officers and men. ~ *blue*, dark blue.

nay [neɪ] *adv.* (old use) no; not only that, but also: *I suspect, ~, I am certain, that ...*

near [nɪə*] *adv., prep., adj., & v.* **I. adv.** not far; to or at a short distance in space or time: *The summer holidays are drawing ~. as ~ as, ~ly*; closely: *as ~ as one can guess; ~ at hand,* (a) within easy reach; (b) not far in the future: *The examinations are ~ at hand. ~ by,* not far off: *He lives ~ by. ~by* (adj.). **II. prep.** close to: *Don't go ~ the edge of the cliff, you may fall over it. It's getting ~ dinner-time.* **III. adj.** 1. not far from; close to in space or time: *The station is quite ~. Can you tell me the ~est way to the police station? a ~ thing,* a narrow escape. 2. close in relationship; intimate: *She's a ~ relative of mine. They are our ~ and dear friends.* 3. (contrasted with *off*) on the side (of a vehicle or animal that runs) closer to the edge of the roadway (in Great Britain the left side). 4. ungenerous; niggardly. **IV. v.i. & t.** come ~ (to); approach: *a ship ~ing land. ~ly adv.* 1. almost: *~ly six o'clock.* 2. closely: *~ly related.* 3. *not ~ly (enough),* far from (enough). **~ness** *n.* (no pl.). **~-'sight·ed** *adj.* short-sighted.

neat [niːt] *adj.* 1. (liking to have everything) tidy, in good order with nothing out of place; done carefully: *a ~ worker (desk); ~ writing.* 2. simple and pleasant; in good taste; pleasing in shape or appearance: *a ~ dress; a ~ figure.* 3. cleverly said or done: *a ~ answer (trick).* 4. (of wines and spirits) unmixed with water: *drink one's whisky ~. ~ly adv. ~ness n.* (no pl.).

neb·u·la [ˈnebjʊlə] *n.* (pl. -lae [-liː], ~s) group of very distant stars, mass of gas, seen in the night sky as an indistinct patch of light. **neb·u·lous** [ˈnebjʊləs] *adj.* cloud-like; indistinct; vague.

nec·es·sary [ˈnesəsərɪ] *adj.* that has

to be done; that must be; that cannot be done without or escaped from: *Sleep is ~ to health. n.* (usu. pl.) things ~ *for living.* **nec·es·sar·i·ly** *adv.* as a ~ result. **ne·ces·si·tate** [nɪˈsesɪteɪt] *v.t.* make ~ necessary. **ne·ces·si·tous** [nɪˈsesɪtəs] *adj.* poor; needy. **ne·ces·si·ty** [nɪˈsesɪtɪ] *n.* 1. (no pl.) urgent need: *driven to steal by necessity; for use in case of necessity.* 2. sth. that is ~: *Food and warmth are necessities.* 3. (no pl.) poverty; hardship: *in necessity.*

neck [nek] *n.* 1. part of the body that connects the shoulders and the head: *~ and ~,* (of competitors in a race) running level, side by side; *~ or nothing,* with the alternative of complete victory or defeat; *~ and crop,* headlong; bodily. 2. anything like a ~ in shape: *the ~ of a bottle.* **'~·band** *n.* part of a shirt, etc. that goes round the ~. **~·lace** [ˈneklɪs] *n.* string of beads, pearls, etc. worn round the ~ as an ornament. **'~·line** *n.* line formed by the opening of a garment at the ~. **'~·tie** *n.* narrow band of material worn with a collar and knotted in front.

a necklace   a necktie

nec·tar [ˈnektə*] *n.* (no pl.) sweet liquid in flowers, gathered by bees.

née (U.S.A. **nee**) [neɪ] (Fr.) *adj.* (of a married woman) whose family name, before her marriage, was ...: *Mrs. Williams, née Jones.*

need [niːd] *v.t.* 1. want; require; be in ~ of; be necessary: *They ~ more food. His coat ~s mending.* 2. be obliged to: *N~ you go home yet? No, I ~ not (~n't). n.* 1. (no pl.) condition of being without sth. that is necessary: *in ~ of money.* 2. (no pl.) circumstances making sth. necessary: *no ~ to hurry.* 3. (no pl.) crisis; time of difficulty: *A friend in ~ is a friend indeed.* 4. sth. that is wanted or necessary: *earning enough for one's ~s.* **~·ful** *adj.* necessary. **~·less** *adj.* unnecessary. **~s** *adv.* (only in) *must ~s* or *~s must,* be compelled to, have to (do sth.). **~y** *adj.* (-ier, -iest) poor; not having what is necessary for living.

nee·dle ['niːdl] *n.* **1.** small, thin, pointed steel instrument with a hole (called *eye*) at one end for thread, used in sewing and darning. **2.** longer, thin, ~-like instrument without an eye, of wood, bone, steel, etc. for knitting, etc. **3.** pointer in a compass or on the dial of a meter or gauge. **4.** steel stylus used in recording and playing records² (4). **5.** ~-like part of a syringe. **6.** ~-like leaf (of pine and fir trees). '~·wom·an *n.* woman who does '~·work *n.* (no pl.) sewing.

ne'er [neə*] *adv.* (poet.) never. ~-do-well ['neəduːˌwel] *n.* useless or good-for-nothing person.

ne·ga·tion [nɪ'geɪʃn] *n.* (no pl.) act of denying: *Shaking the head is a sign of ~.*

neg·a·tive ['negətɪv] *adj.* **1.** (opp. *affirmative*) (of words and answers) indicating *no* or *not*: *a ~ answer.* **2.** (opp. *positive*) expressing the absence of clearly marked qualities: *~ criticism*; *~ virtue.* **3.** (math.) (of a quantity) that has to be subtracted from another or from zero (0): *~ quantities.* **4.** *~ electricity,* the kind produced at the cathode of a cell (4): *the ~ pole in a cell.* **5.** (photography) with light and dark reversed. *n.* **1.** ~ word or statement. **2.** (math.) ~ quantity. **3.** (photography) developed film or plate from which (positive) prints are made. *v.t.* **1.** prove (a theory, etc.) to be untrue. **2.** reject; neutralize (an effect).

ne·glect [nɪ'glekt] *v.t.* **1.** fail to pay attention to; disregard. **2.** leave undone (what one ought to do); omit (*to do* sth.). *n.* (no pl.) ~ing or being ~ed: *~ of duty*; *in a state of ~.* ~·ful *adj.*: *~ of duty*; *in the habit of ~ing.*

neg·li·gent ['neglɪdʒənt] *adj.* taking too little care (*of* one's duties, etc.). ~·ly *adv.* in a ~ manner: *be charged (1) with ~ly causing bodily harm.* **neg·li·gence** *n.* (no pl.). **neg·li·gi·ble** ['neglɪdʒəbl] *adj.* that need not be considered; of little or no importance or size.

ne·go·ti·ate [nɪ'gəʊʃɪeɪt] *v.i. & t.* **1.** discuss (sth. *with* sb.) in order to come to an agreement. **2.** arrange (*for* a sale, loan, etc.) by discussion; get or give money for (cheques, bonds, etc.). **3.** get past or over (an obstacle, etc.). **ne·go·ti·able** *adj.* that can be ~d; (of cheques, etc.) that can be exchanged for cash. **ne·go·ti·a·tor** *n.* person who ~s. **ne·go·ti·a·tion** [nɪˌgəʊʃɪ'eɪʃn] *n.*

Ne·gro ['niːgrəʊ] *n.* (pl. *-oes*) member (or, outside Africa, descendant) of one of the African races south of the Sahara. **Ne·gress** ['niːgrɪs] *n.* female ~.

neigh [neɪ] *v.i. & n.* (make) cry of a horse.

neigh·bour (U.S.A. **-bor**) ['neɪbə*] *n.* person living in a house, street, etc. near oneself; person, thing, or country that is near(est) another. ~·hood *n.* **1.** (people living in a) district; area near the place, etc. referred to: *in the ~hood of Leeds (the post office).* **2.** (no pl.) condition of being near. ~·ing *adj.* that border(s) upon: *~ing countries.* ~·ly *adj.* friendly. ~·li·ness *n.* (no pl.).

nei·ther ['naɪðə*] **I.** *adj. & pron.* (cf. *either*) not one nor the other (of two): *N~ statement is true. I like ~ of them.* **II.** *adv. & conj.* **1.** *~ ... nor*: *He ~ knows nor cares what happened. N~ you nor I could have done this.* **2.** nor; and not; no more than: *If you don't go, ~ shall I. I don't like it, ~ does she.*

nem·e·sis ['nemɪsɪs] *n.* (pl. *-ses* [-siːz]) just punishment for wrongdoing; deserved fate.

neo- [niːəʊ-] *pref.* new; later; revived. ~·lith·ic [ˌniːəʊ'lɪθɪk] *adj.* of the new or later stone age.

ne·ol·o·gism [niː'ɒlədʒɪzəm] *n.* coining of new words; new word, usage, or expression.

ne·on ['niːən] *n.* (no pl.) gas forming a very small proportion of the atmosphere, used in electric lamps: *~ lamp (light)*; *~ signs illuminated advertisements.*

neph·ew ['nevjuː] *n.* son of one's brother or sister.

nep·o·tism ['nepətɪzəm] *n.* (no pl.) the giving of special favour (esp. employment) by a person in high position to his relatives.

nerve [nɜːv] *n.* **1.** fibre or bundle of fibres carrying feelings and impulses between the brain and parts of the body. **2.** (pl.) condition of being easily excited, worried, irritated: *noises that get on my ~s* (i.e. worry me); *suffering from ~s*; *~-racking,* extremely trying on the ~s. **3.** (no pl.) quality of being bold, self-reliant, etc.: *have enough ~ to drive a racing car*; *lose one's ~,* become nervous (2). **4.** (old use) sinew: *strain every ~,* make the utmost effort (to do sth.). *v.t.* give strength to: *~ oneself for a task (to face trouble).* ~·less *adj.* without energy or strength.

ner·vous ['nɜːvəs] *adj.* **1.** of the ~s: *the nervous system*; *a nervous break-*

down. **2.** having or showing ~s (2).

nerv·y *adj.* (-ier, -iest) (colloq.) nervous (2).

-ness [-nɪs] *suff.* (forming ns. from adjs.) state or condition; instance of this: *bitterness; happiness; a kindness.*

nest [nest] *n.* **1.** place made or chosen by a bird for its eggs; kind of place in which certain living things have and keep their young: *a wasps' ~.* **2.** comfortable place: *a ~ of soft cushions.* **3.** number of like things (esp. boxes, tables) fitting one inside another. *v.i.* make and use a ~. '**~-egg** *n.* (fig.) sum of money saved for future use.

nes·tle ['nesl] *v.i. & t.* settle comfortably and warmly: *~ down among the cushions;* press oneself lovingly: *nestling closely to (up to) its mother.*

nest·ling ['nestlɪŋ] *n.* bird too young to leave the nest. (Cf. *fledgeling.*)

net¹ [net] *n.* open-work material of knotted string, hair, wire, etc.; such material made up for a special purpose: *fishing ~; tennis ~; mosquito ~.* *v.t.* (-tt-) catch (fish, animals, etc.) with or in a ~; cover (e.g. fruit trees) with a ~. **~ting** *n.* (no pl.) ~ material: *windows screened with wire ~ting.* '**~work** *n.* **1.** structure of cords or wires that cross at regular intervals and are knotted, etc. at the crossings. **2.** complex system of lines that cross: *a ~work of railways (canals).* **3.** connected system: *a ~work of radio stations; a spy ~work.*

net², nett [net] *adj.* remaining when nothing more is to be taken away: *~ profit* (when working expenses have been deducted); *~ price* (the lowest to be charged); *~ weight* (of the contents only). *v.t.* (-tt-) gain as a ~ profit: *It ~ted him nothing.*

neth·er ['neðə*] *adj.* (old use) lower.

net·tle ['netl] *n.* common wild plant with leaves that sting when touched. *v.t.* (fig.) make rather angry; annoy.

neu·ral·gia [ˌnjuə'rældʒə] *n.* sharp, jumping pain in the nerves, esp. of the face and head.

neu·rol·o·gy [ˌnjuə'rɒlədʒɪ] *n.* (no pl.) scientific study of the nervous system. **neu·rol·o·gist** *n.* expert in ~.

neu·ro·sis [ˌnjuə'rəusɪs] *n.* (pl. -ses [-siːz]) functional nervous disorder, esp. without organic change. **neu·rot·ic** [ˌnjuə'rɒtɪk] *n. & adj.* (person) suffering from nervous disorder; too nervous (person).

neu·ter ['njuːtə*] *adj.* (of plants) without male or female parts; (gram., of words) neither feminine nor masculine.

n. (esp.) ~ noun, adjective, pronoun, verb, or gender.

neu·tral ['njuːtrəl] *adj.* **1.** helping neither side in a war or quarrel; belonging to a ~ country: *~ territory.* **2.** having no definite characteristics, not clearly one (colour, etc.) nor another. **3.** (chem.) neither acid nor alkaline. *n.* ~ (1) person or country, etc.; ~ position of gears (3). **~i·ty** [njuːˈtrælətɪ] *n.* (no pl.) state of being ~, esp. in war. **~ize** ['njuːtrəlaɪz] *v.t.* **1.** make ~: *~ize a border territory.* **2.** take away the effect or special quality of sth. by means of sth. with an opposite effect or quality: *~ize a poison.*

neu·tron ['njuːtrɒn] *n.* elementary particle of about the same mass as a proton but without electric charge, forming part of the nucleus of an atom.

nev·er ['nevə*] *adv.* **1.** at no time; on no occasion. **2.** (an emphatic substitute for) not: *That will ~ happen if I can prevent it.* **3.** N~ mind! Don't worry about that. *Well, I ~!* How surprising! **~'more** *adv.* ~ again. **~the·less** [ˌnevəðə'les] *adv. & conj.* in spite of that; yet.

new [njuː] *adj.* **1.** not existing before; seen or heard of for the first time; recently introduced, etc. **2.** existing before, but only now discovered, etc. **3.** unfamiliar; freshly arrived. **4.** beginning again: *a ~ moon; a Happy N~ Year. adv.* ~ly; recently; just: *a ~-born baby; ~comers,* those recently arrived; *~fangled,* (derog.) ~, strange, and unwelcome; *~-laid eggs.* **~ly** *adv.* recently; in a ~ way. **~ness** *n.* (no pl.).

news [njuːz] *n. pl.* (usu. sing. v.) report or account of what has recently happened, of new facts, etc.: *a piece of interesting ~.* '**~a·gent** *n.* shopkeeper selling ~papers, periodicals, etc. '**~boy** *n.* boy selling ~papers on the street. '**~cast** *n.* radio or television broadcast of ~. '**~cast·er** *n.* radio or television broadcaster of ~. **~pa·per** ['njuːsˌpeɪpə*] *n.* set of printed and folded sheets containing ~, literary articles, etc., usu. one published daily. '**~pa·per·man** *n.* journalist. '**~read·er** *n.* ~caster. '**~reel** *n.* cinema film of recent events. '**~room** *n.* **1.** room where ~papers, etc. may be read. **2.** room where ~ is prepared for broadcasting. '**~stand** *n.* stall where ~papers, etc. are sold. '**~ven·dor** *n.* seller of ~papers.

newt [njuːt] *n.* small, lizard-like animal living in water.

next [nekst] **adj., n., adv., & prep.**
I. adj. & n. 1. coming nearest or immediately after, in space or order:
Take the ~ turning to the right. ~ door,
the ~ house: *Who lives ~ door? ~ door
to,* (fig.) almost. ~ *but one,* third in a
series. *I'm first, who's ~? ~ of kin; ~
please.* **2.** immediately following in
time: *We are going ~ Friday.* **II. adv.
1.** after this (or that); then: *When you
have finished this, what are you going
to do ~? What ~?* (to express surprise
or wonder). **2.** in the nearest place (to):
Come and sit ~ to me. **III. prep.** (old
use; = ~ to): *He placed his chair ~
hers.*

nib [nɪb] *n.* pointed, metal tip of a pen.
nib·ble ['nɪbl] *v.t. & i.* take tiny bites
(*at*): *fish nibbling (at) the bait. n.* the
act of nibbling (*at*).

nice [naɪs] *adj.* (~*r*, ~*st*) **1.** pleasant;
agreeable; good. **2.** needing care,
exactness (in judging, deciding sth.);
subtle. **3.** (ironic) disgraceful; bad:
a ~ mess. **4.** particular; fussy: *too ~
about one's food.* ~**·ly** *adv.* ~**·ty**
['naɪsətɪ] *n.* **1.** (no pl.) exactness;
quality of doing things with delicate
care: *~ty of judgement.* **2.** delicate
distinction: *the ~ties of criticism; to a
~ty,* without error or misjudgement.

a niche

niche [nɪtʃ] *n.* recess (often with a
shelf) in a wall, usu. for a statue or
ornament; (fig.) suitable or fitting
position: *find the right ~ for oneself*
(i.e. a position offering work that one
can do well).

nick [nɪk] *v.t. & n.* (make) a small,
V-shaped cut (in sth.), esp. as a record.
in the ~ of time, only just in time.

nick·el ['nɪkl] *n.* **1.** (no pl.) silver-white
metal used in alloys. **2.** (U.S.A.) coin
worth 5 cents.

nick·name ['nɪkneɪm] *n.* name given
in addition to or altered from or used
instead of the real name. *v.t.* give a
~ to.

nic·o·tine ['nɪkəti:n] *n.* (no pl.) poisonous substance in tobacco leaves.

niece [ni:s] *n.* daughter of one's
brother or sister.

nig·gard ['nɪgəd] *n.* mean, stingy
person. ~**·ly** *adj.* ungenerous; miserly.
nig·ger ['nɪgə*] *n.* (derog.) Negro.
nigh [naɪ] *adv. & prep.* (old use)
near (to).

night [naɪt] *n.* dark hours between one
day and the next: *all ~ (long),* throughout the whole ~. *Good ~!* (parting wish
on going to bed or going home late).
Have you had a good ~ (slept well)?
at ~, during the ~; ~ and day, continuously; *make a ~ of it,* pass the ~ in
pleasure-making, esp. at a party.
'~**·cap** *n.* (esp. alcoholic) drink taken
before going to bed. '~**·club** *n.* club
open at ~ for dancing, supper, entertainment, etc. '~**·dress,** '~**·gown** *ns.*
long, loose garment worn by a woman
or a child in bed. '~**·fall** *n.* (no pl.)
end of daylight. '~**·ie,** '~**·y** *n.* (colloq.)
~-dress. ~**·ly** *adj. & adv.* (done, happening) at ~ or every ~. '~**·mare** *n.*
terrible dream; horrible experience.
'~**·school** *n.* school that gives evening
lessons to persons who are working by
day. '~**·shirt** *n.* long, loose shirt
worn by a man or a boy in bed.
'~**·time** *n.* time from dusk to dawn:
in the ~-time, by ~. ,~'**watch·man** *n.*
man employed to be on guard (e.g. in
a factory) during the ~. '~**·work** *n.*
work that is done, or must be done,
by ~.

night·in·gale ['naɪtɪŋgeɪl] *n.* small
bird that sings sweetly at night as well
as during the day.

nil [nɪl] *n.* nothing: *The result of the
game was three-~.*

nim·ble ['nɪmbl] *adj.* (~*r*, ~*st*) quick-
moving: *as ~ as a goat;* (of the mind)
quick to understand; sharp. **nim·bly**
adv.

nin·com·poop ['nɪnkəmpu:p] *n.* fool.

nine [naɪn] *n. & adj.* 9. *a ~ days'
wonder,* sth. that excites attention for
a few days only. **ninth** [naɪnθ] *n. &
adj.* 9th; ¹/₉. ~**·teen** [,naɪn'ti:n] *n.
& adj.* 19. ~**·teenth** [,naɪn'ti:nθ] *n.
& adj.* 19th; ¹/₁₉. ~**·ty** ['naɪntɪ] *n. &
adj.* 90. **nine·ti·eth** ['naɪntɪɪθ] *n. &
adj.* 90th; ¹/₉₀.

nine·pins ['naɪnpɪnz] *n. pl.* (sing. v.)
game in which a ball is rolled along
the ground at nine bottle-shaped
pieces of wood.

nip¹ [nɪp] *n.* **1.** small, quick bite or
pinch. **2.** *a ~ in the air,* a feeling of
frost. *v.t. & i.* (*-pp-*) **1.** give a ~ to.
2. (of frost, etc.) stop the growth of:
~ in the bud, (esp. fig.) stop the
development of. **3.** (Gt. Brit., sl.)
move nimbly; hurry: *~ along (off, in).*

~·per *n.* **1.** (pl.) pincers, forceps, etc. **2.** (Gt. Brit., sl.) small child.

ip² [nɪp] *n.* small drink (esp. of brandy or other spirits).

ip·ple ['nɪpl] *n.* part of the breast through which milk comes; thing shaped like a ~.

i·tre (U.S.A. **ni·ter**) ['naɪtə*] *n.* (no pl.) salt obtained from potash, used in making gunpowder. **ni·trate** ['naɪ- treɪt] *n.* salt of nitric acid, esp. the kind used as fertilizer. **ni·tric** ['naɪtrɪk] *adj.* nitric acid, powerful acid that destroys most metals. **ni·tro·gen** ['naɪtrədʒən] *n.* (no pl.) gas without colour, taste, or smell, forming about four-fifths of the air. **ni·tro·glyc·er· ine** [ˌnaɪtrəʊ'ɡlɪsərɪn] *n.* (no pl.) pow- erful explosive.

o [nəʊ] *adj., adv., particle, & n.* **I. adj. 1.** not one; not any: *They have no food and will starve. We must go this way, because there is no other.* **2.** indicating the opposite of the follow- ing word: *He's no fool* (i.e. he's a clever man). *We got there in no time* (i.e. quickly). **3.** *No smoking!* Smoking is not allowed here. **II. adv.** (used with comparatives) not any: *We can go no farther,* we must stop here. **III. particle** (opp. *yes*) *Is it Monday to- day? No, it's Tuesday.* **IV. n.** (pl. *noes* [nəʊz]) the word or answer *no*; denial or refusal; negative vote: *the noes have it,* the negative voters are in the majority.

No. ['nʌmbə*] (abbr. for) number: *No.7.*

o·ble ['nəʊbl] *adj.* (~r, ~st) **1.** having, showing, high character and qualities. **2.** (of families) of high rank or birth: *men of ~ rank.* **3.** splendid; that excites admiration: ~ *buildings.* *n.* person of ~ (2) birth; peer. **no·bil·i·ty** [nəʊ'bɪlətɪ] *n.* (no pl.) **1.** *the* ~s as a class. **2.** quality of being ~. **no·bly** *adv.* '~·man, '~·wom·an *ns.* person of ~ (2) rank or birth; peer(ess).

o·body ['nəʊbədɪ] *pron.* not any- body; no person. *n.* person of no importance: *a mere* ~.

oc·tur·nal [nɒk'tɜːnl] *adj.* of, in, or done, active, or happening in, the night.

od [nɒd] *v.i. & t.* (-dd-) **1.** bow (the head) slightly and quickly as a sign of agreement or as a familiar greeting: *have a ~ding acquaintance with,* have a slight acquaintance with or knowledge of. **2.** let the head fall forward when sleepy or when falling asleep. *n.* ~ding movement (of the head). *the land of N~,* sleep.

No·el [nəʊ'el] *n.* Christmas.

noise [nɔɪz] *n.* sound, esp. loud, un- pleasant sound. ~**less** *adj.* silent. **noisy** *adj.* (-ier, -iest) making much ~; full of ~. **nois·i·ly** *adv.*

noi·some ['nɔɪsəm] *adj.* offensive; (esp. of smell) disgusting.

no·mad ['nəʊmæd] *n.* member of a tribe that travels about; wanderer. ~**ic** [nəʊ'mædɪk] *adj.* of ~s.

no·men·cla·ture [nəʊ'menklətʃə*] *n.* system of naming: *botanical* ~.

nom·i·nal ['nɒmɪnl] *adj.* **1.** existing, etc. in name or word only, not in fact: *the* ~ *ruler*; *the* ~ *value of shares.* **2.** *a* ~ *sum* (*rent*), one much below actual value given or received. ~**ly** *adv.*

nom·i·nate ['nɒmɪneɪt] *v.t.* put for- ward sb.'s name for election to a position: ~ *sb. for the Presidency.* **nom·i·na·tion** [ˌnɒmɪ'neɪʃn] *n.* (right of) nominating. **nom·i·na·tive** ['nɒmɪ- nətɪv] *adj. & n.* (gram.) (of the) form of a noun or adjective when it is the subject of a sentence: *nominative case.* **nom·i·nee** [ˌnɒmɪ'niː] *n.* person ~d.

non- [nɒn-] *pref.* who (that) is not, who (that) does not, etc.: *non-aggres- sion,* refraining from aggression or hostilities; *non-alignment,* (pol., of a State) principle or practice of not join- ing any one of the large groups of world powers; *non-aligned* (adj.); *non- combatant* (n. & adj.), (person) not taking part in fighting; *non-commis- sioned officers,* not having commissions (4); *non-committal,* not showing or giving a definite decision, etc.; *non- conformist,* Protestant not conforming to the ritual, etc. of an established (4) church; *non-fiction,* literary matter based directly on fact (opp. *novel, etc.*); *non-polluting,* not contaminating or defiling man's environment; *non-resi- dent* (n. & adj.), (person) not residing in: *non-resident students*; *non-skid,* (of tyres) specially constructed to resist skidding; *non-smoker,* (a) person who does not smoke; (b) compartment in a train, etc. where smoking is forbidden; *non-stop* (adj. & adv.), without a stop: *a non-stop train*; *fly non-stop*; *non-vio- lence,* policy of abstaining from the use of violence to gain one's ends.

nonce [nɒns] *n. for the* ~, for the present only.

non·cha·lant ['nɒnʃələnt] *adj.* not having, or not showing, interest or enthusiasm.

non·de·script ['nɒndɪskrɪpt] *n. & adj.* (person or thing) not easily classed, not having a definite character.

none [nʌn] *pron.* not any; not one: *Is there any beer in the house? No, (there's)* ~ *(at all). We invited several friends, but* ~ *came. N*~ *of them have (has) come yet.* *adv.* (only with comparatives and *too*) not at all: ~ *too plentiful;* ~ *the worse for his experiences.*

non·en·ti·ty [nɒ'nentətɪ] *n.* unimportant person.

non·plus [,nɒn'plʌs] *v.t.* (-ss-) surprise or puzzle (sb.) so much that he does not know what to do or say.

non·sense ['nɒnsəns] *n.* meaningless words; foolish talk, ideas, behaviour. **non·sen·si·cal** [nɒn'sensɪkl] *adj.*

noo·dle¹ ['nuːdl] *n.* (usu. pl.) mixture of flour and eggs prepared in long strips, used in soups, etc.

noo·dle² ['nuːdl] *n.* foolish person.

nook [nʊk] *n.* quiet, out-of-the-way place; inside corner.

noon [nuːn] *n.* 12 o'clock in the middle of the day. '~·day, '~·tide *ns.* (time about) ~.

no one ['nəʊwʌn] *pron.* nobody. *adj.* no single: ~ *person could do this.*

noose [nuːs] *n.* loop of rope (with a running knot) that becomes tighter when the rope is pulled: *the hangman's* ~.

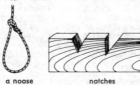

a noose   notches

nor [nɔː*] *conj.* 1. (after *neither* or *not*) and not: *I should like to have a holiday, but can find neither the time* ~ *the money. I have not the time* ~ *the money to go on holiday.* 2. and ... not: *He can't do it,* ~ *can I.*

norm [nɔːm] *n.* 1. standard; pattern; type. 2. amount of work required or expected: *fulfil one's* ~. 3. customary behaviour.

nor·mal ['nɔːml] *adj.* in agreement with what is representative, usual, or regular. *n.* (no pl.) *above (below)* ~, above (below) what is ~. ~·ly *adv.* ~·ize ['nɔːməlaɪz] *v.t.* make ~.

north [nɔːθ] *adv., n. & adj.* 1. (towards, at, near) one of the four cardinal points of the compass or the direction towards which the magnetic needle turns. 2. (attrib.) situated in, coming from, etc., the ~: *the N*~ *Pole; N*~ *American; N*~ *Sea.* ~·er·ly ['nɔːðəlɪ]

adj. & adv. (of winds) from the ~; towards the ~; in or to the ~. ~·ern ['nɔːðn] *adj.* in or of the ~. ~·ward(s) ['nɔːθwəd(z)] *adv.* towards the ~.

Nor·we·gian [nɔː'wiːdʒən] *n. & adj.* (native, inhabitant, or language) of Norway.

nose [nəʊz] *n.* 1. part of the face above the mouth, serving as the organ of smell. *pay through the* ~, pay a very high price; *poke one's* ~ *into sth.*, be inquisitive about it. 2. sense of smell. *v.i. & t.* 1. smell *(about, for);* discover by smelling: *The dog* ~*d out a rat.* 2. go forward carefully: *ship nosing (its way) through the ice.* '~·dive *v.i. & n.* (of an aircraft) (make a) quick descent with the ~ of the plane pointing to the earth. '~·gay *n.* bunch of cut flowers.

nosy, nos·ey *adj.* (-ier, -iest) inquisitive.

nos·tal·gia [nɒ'stældʒɪə] *n.* (no pl.) homesickness; sentimental longing *for* sth. one has known. **nos·tal·gic** [nɒ'stældʒɪk] *adj.* of, feeling, causing, ~.

nos·tril ['nɒstrəl] *n.* either of the two openings into the nose.

not [nɒt] *adv.* used to make a finite verb negative (often contracted to *n't* [-nt] as in *hasn't* ['hæznt]): *Have they gone yet? Haven't they gone yet? They have not gone yet.*

no·ta·ble ['nəʊtəbl] *adj.* deserving to be noticed; worthy of attention. **no·tably** *adv.* **no·ta·bil·i·ty** [,nəʊtə'bɪlətɪ] *n.* (esp.) important person.

no·ta·ry ['nəʊtərɪ] *n.* (often ~ *public*) official with authority to do certain kinds of legal business, esp. to record that he has witnessed the signing of legal documents.

no·ta·tion [nəʊ'teɪʃn] *n.* system of signs or symbols representing numbers, amounts, musical notes, etc. (e.g. Roman numerals, I, II, III, etc.).

notch [nɒtʃ] *v.t. & n.* (make a) V-shaped cut *(in or on* sth.). (See the picture.)

note [nəʊt] *n.* 1. short record (of facts, etc.) made to help the memory: ~*book* (in which to write ~s). 2. letter from one government to another; short letter: *a* ~ *of thanks;* ~*paper* (for writing letters on). 3. short comment on or explanation of a word or passage in a book. 4. written or printed promise to pay money: *bank*~*s; a £5* ~; *a promissory* ~. 5. single sound of a certain pitch and duration; sign (e.g. ♩, ♪) used to represent such a sound in printed music; any one of the keys of a piano or organ. **6.** quality (esp. of voice) showing the nature of sth., a feeling: *a ~ of self-satisfaction in his speech.* **7.** sign or mark used in writing and printing: *~ of exclamation* (!). **8.** (no pl.) distinction; importance: *a family of ~.* **9.** (no pl.) notice; attention: *worthy of ~. Take ~ of what I say.* **v.t. 1.** notice; pay attention to. **2.** ~ *down*, write down; make a ~ (1) of. **not·ed** ['nəʊtɪd] *adj.* well-known; famous. **~·wor·thy** ['nəʊt,wɜːðɪ] *adj.* deserving attention.

noth·ing ['nʌθɪŋ] *n.* not anything: *come to ~*, fail; have no result or success; *make ~ of*, (a) be unable to understand; (b) fail to use (e.g. opportunities); (c) treat as unimportant. *There is ~ for it but to ...*, the only possible way is to ...; we can only ... *adv.* not at all; in no way: *The house is ~ near as large as I expected.*

no·tice ['nəʊtɪs] *n.* **1.** (written or printed) news of sth. about to happen or sth. that has happened: *put up a ~*; *a ~-board.* **2.** (no pl.) warning, esp. warning given to or by sb. about the ending of an agreement (e.g. to a servant by an employer, to a tenant by the house-owner): *give a servant a month's ~*; *at short ~*, with little warning. **3.** short particulars of a new book, play, etc. in a periodical. **4.** (no pl.) attention: *Take no ~ of* (pay no attention to) *what they say. Bring it to the ~ of the manager. v.t.* take ~ of; see. **~·able** *adj.* easily seen or ~d.

no·ti·fy ['nəʊtɪfaɪ] *v.t.* give notice of; report *(to)*: *~ a loss to the police*; *~ the police of a loss.* **no·ti·fi·able** *adj.* that must be notified (esp. of certain diseases which must be reported to the health authorities). **no·ti·fi·ca·tion** [,nəʊtɪfɪ'keɪʃn] *n.*

no·tion ['nəʊʃn] *n.* **1.** idea; opinion. **2.** (pl.) (U.S.A.) small personal and clothing articles (as ribbons, etc.).

no·to·ri·ous [nəʊ'tɔːrɪəs] *adj.* widely known (esp. for sth. bad). **no·to·ri·ety** [,nəʊtə'raɪətɪ] *n.* (no pl.).

not·with·stand·ing [,nɒtwɪθ'stændɪŋ] *prep.* in spite of. *adv.* nevertheless; all the same. *conj.* although.

nought [nɔːt] *n.* (poet. or old use) nothing; figure 0.

noun [naʊn] *n.* (gram.) word by which a person, thing, quality, etc. is named; substantive.

nour·ish ['nʌrɪʃ] *v.t.* **1.** make or keep strong with food. **2.** have or encourage (hope, hatred, etc.). **~·ment** *n.* (no pl.) food; power of ~ing.

nov·el¹ ['nɒvl] *adj.* strange; of a new kind not previously known. **~·ty** *n.* **1.** (no pl.) newness; strangeness. **2.** previously unknown thing, idea, etc.; (pl.) new kinds of fancy goods, toys, etc.

nov·el² ['nɒvl] *n.* made-up story in prose, long enough to fill one or more books, about either imaginary or historical people. **~·ist** *n.* writer of ~s.

No·vem·ber [nəʊ'vembə*] *n.* eleventh month of the year.

nov·ice ['nɒvɪs] *n.* person who is still learning and who is without experience, esp. person who is to become a monk or a nun. **no·vi·ciate, no·vi·tiate** [nəʊ'vɪʃɪət] *n.* ~; period of being a ~.

now [naʊ] *adv., conj., & n.* **I.** *adv.* at the present time; in the present circumstances: *~ and again, ~ and then,* from time to time; sometimes. *N~ then! N~, ~!* (used as a friendly warning or protest). **II.** *conj.* through or because of the fact (that): *N~ (that) you mention it, I do remember seeing you at the theatre.* **III.** *n.* the present time or moment (chiefly after prepositions): *is there by (before, till) ~.* **~·a·days** ['naʊədeɪz] *adv.* in these days; at the present time.

no·where ['nəʊweə*] *adv.* not anywhere.

nox·ious ['nɒkʃəs] *adj.* harmful.

noz·zle ['nɒzl] *n.* metal end of a hose or bellows.

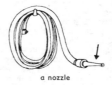

a nozzle

nu·cle·ar ['njuːklɪə*] *adj.* of, relating to, constituting, a nucleus (cf. *atomic*); using ~ energy: *~ disarmament, giving up of ~ weapons*; *~ energy*, energy obtained by ~ fission (see *fission*); *~ physics*, science dealing with the nuclei of atoms and atomic energy; *~ physicist*; *~ power*, (a) power derived from ~ energy: *a ~ power-station*; (b) country possessing ~ weapons, *~-powered* (adj.), (of ships) using ~ power; *~ reactor* (see *reactor*); *~ warfare*, atomic warfare; *~ weapons* (using ~ energy).

nu·cle·us ['njuːklɪəs] *n.* (pl. *nuclei* ['njuːklɪaɪ]) central part, round which other parts are grouped or round which other things collect.

nude [njuːd] *adj.* unclothed. *n.* ~ human figure (in art). **nud·ist** ['njuː-dɪst] *n.* person who believes that exposing the naked body to sun and air is beneficial.

nudge [nʌdʒ] *v.t.* push slightly with the elbow to attract attention. *n.* push given in this way.

nug·get ['nʌgɪt] *n.* lump of metal, esp. gold, as found in the earth.

nui·sance ['njuːsns] *n.* thing, person, act, etc. that causes trouble or offence.

null [nʌl] *adj.* of no effect or force: ~ *and void*, (law) without legal effect. **nul·li·fy** ['nʌlɪfaɪ] *v.t.* make ~ and void.

numb [nʌm] *v.t. & adj.* (make) without power to feel or move: *fingers ~(ed) with cold*; ~ *with grief*.

num·ber ['nʌmbə*] *n.* **1.** 1, 13, and 103 are ~s. **2.** quantity or amount: *a large ~ of people*; *fifteen in ~*; *times without ~*, very often. **3.** one issue of a periodical, esp. for one day, week, etc.: *the current ~*; *a back ~*, an old issue of a periodical, etc.; (fig., sl.) an out-of-date person or thing. **4.** dance, song, etc. for the stage. **5.** (gram.) class of word-forms including all singular or all plural, etc. words: *'does' is of the singular and 'men' is of the plural ~*. **6.** (pl.) arithmetic: *be good at ~s*. **7.** (pl.) numerical superiority: *win by ~s*. *v.t.* **1.** give a ~ to; put a ~ on. **2.** add up to. **3.** ~ (*sb.*) *among*, include him, regard him as being, among. **~·less** *adj.* more than can be counted. **'~-plate** *n.* (U.S.A. *license plate*) plate bearing the number of a registered vehicle.

nu·mer·al ['njuːmərəl] *n.* word or sign standing for a number. **nu·mer·a·tor** ['njuːməreɪtə*] *n.* number above the line in a fraction (e.g. 3 in ¾). **nu·mer·i·cal** [njuː'merɪkl] *adj.* of, in, connected with, numbers. **nu·mer·ous** ['njuːmərəs] *adj.* very many; great in number.

num·skull ['nʌmskʌl] *n.* stupid person.

nun [nʌn] *n.* woman who, after taking religious vows, lives, with other women, a secluded life in the service of God. **~·nery** *n.* house of nuns; convent.

nun·cio ['nʌnʃɪəʊ] *n.* (pl. ~s) ambassador or representative of the pope in a foreign country.

nup·tial ['nʌpʃl] *adj.* of marriage: ~ *bliss*. **~s** *n. pl.* wedding.

nurse [nɜːs] *n.* **1.** woman who looks after babies and small children for a living. **2.** person (usu. trained) who cares for people who are ill or injured: *hospital ~s. v.t.* **1.** act as a ~ (2): *nursing home*, (Gt. Brit.) private hospital, etc. **2.** feed (a baby) at the breast. **3.** hold (a baby) in the arms or on the lap. **4.** look after carefully, try to cause the growth of (e.g. young plants, a new business). **nur·sery** ['nɜːsərɪ] *n.* **1.** room for the special use of young children: *~ry rhymes*, poems or songs for young children; *~ry school* (for children under 5 years of age); *~ry slopes*, (skiing) slopes suitable for beginners. **2.** place where young plants and trees are raised. **'nur·sery·man** *n.* man who owns a ~ry (2).

nur·ture ['nɜːtʃə*] *n.* (no pl.) training; care; education (of children). *v.t.* give ~ to.

nut [nʌt] *n.* **1.** edible seed with a hard shell: *ground-~*, *pea~*, *wal~*. **2.** small piece of metal for screwing on to the end of a bolt. **'~·crack·ers** *n. pl.* device for cracking ~s. **'~·shell** *n. in a ~shell*, in the smallest possible space; in the fewest possible words.

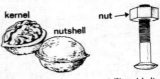

kernel   nut →

nutshell

a nut (1)   a nut (2) and bolt

nut·meg ['nʌtmeg] *n.* hard nut of an East Indian tree, grated to powder and used as a flavouring.

nu·tri·ment ['njuːtrɪmənt] *n.* nourishing food. **nu·tri·tion** [njuː'trɪʃn] *n.* (no pl.) process of supplying and receiving nourishment; science of food values. **nu·tri·tious** [njuː'trɪʃəs] *adj.* having high value as food; nourishing.

nuts [nʌts] *adj.* (sl.) crazy: *be ~ about sb. (sth.)*.

nuz·zle ['nʌzl] *v.i. & t.* press or rub the nose (*against, into*); press the nose against: *The horse ~d (against) my shoulder*.

ny·lon ['naɪlɒn] *n.* **1.** (no pl.) man-made fibre used for making stockings, blouses, ropes, brushes, etc. **2.** (pl.) ~ *stockings*.

nymph [nɪmf] *n.* (in Greek and Roman mythology) one of the lesser goddesses, living in rivers, trees, hills, etc.

O

O¹ [əʊ] *n.* (pl. *Os, O's*) (in quoting telephone numbers): *7506, 'seven five oh six'.*

O², **oh** [əʊ] *int.* cry of surprise, fear, etc.

oak [əʊk] *n.* (hard wood of) sorts of large tree common in many parts of the world.

oa·kum ['əʊkəm] *n.* (no pl.) loose fibre obtained by picking old ropes, used for filling spaces between boards of a ship.

oar [ɔ:*] *n.* pole with a flat blade used in rowing. **~s·man** ['ɔ:zmən] *n.* rower.

an oarsman rowing

oa·sis [əʊ'eisis] *n.* (pl. *oases* [-si:z]) fertile place, with water and trees, in a desert.

oath [əʊθ] *n.* (pl. **~s** [əʊðz]) 1. solemn undertaking with God's help to do sth.; solemn declaration that sth. is true: *take (make, swear) an ~; on (one's) ~*, having taken an ~. 2. wrongful use of God's name or of sacred words to express strong feeling; swear-word.

oats [əʊts] *n. pl.* (seed grains of a) plant grown in cool climates, providing food for men and horses: *sow one's wild ~,* (fig.) lead an immoral life as a young man. *oatmeal,* ground ~.

ob·du·rate ['ɒbdjʊərət] *adj.* stubborn. **ob·du·ra·cy** ['ɒbdjʊərəsɪ] *n.* (no pl.).

obe·di·ent [ə'bi:djənt] *adj.* doing, willing to do, what one is told to do. **~·ly** *adv.* **obe·di·ence** *n.* (no pl.) being *~: in obedience to.*

obei·sance [əʊ'beisəns] *n.* deep bow² (of respect or homage).

ob·e·lisk ['ɒbəlɪsk] *n.* tall, pointed,

four-sided stone pillar, as a monument or landmark.

obese [əʊ'bi:s] *adj.* (of persons) very fat. **obe·si·ty** [əʊ'bi:sətɪ] *n.* (no pl.).

obey [ə'beɪ] *v.t. & i.* do what one is told to do: *~ orders.*

obit·u·ary [ə'bɪtjʊərɪ] *n.* printed notice of sb.'s death, often with a short account of his life; (attrib.) *~ notices* (e.g. in a newspaper).

ob·ject¹ ['ɒbdʒɪkt] *n.* 1. sth. that can be seen or touched; material thing: *an ~-lesson,* lesson (to be) taught or learnt from an example before the learner. 2. person or thing to which action or feeling or thought is directed; purpose: *with no ~ in life; succeed in one's ~; time (distance, money) no ~,* time (etc.) need not be considered. 3. (gram.) noun or noun-equivalent governed by an active transitive verb or by a preposition.

ob·ject² [əb'dʒekt] *v.i.* say that one is not in favour of sth.; be opposed (*to*): *He ~ed to working on Sundays.* **ob·jec·tion** [əb'dʒekʃn] *n.* statement or feeling against sth.; cause of *~ing.* **ob·jec·tion·able** *adj.* likely to be *~ed* to; unpleasant: *an ~ionable smell.* **ob·jec·tor** *n.* person who *~s* (to sth.): *conscientious ~or* (see *conscientious* (1)).

ob·jec·tive [əb'dʒektɪv] *adj.* uninfluenced by thoughts and feelings; impersonal. *n.* 1. object aimed at; purpose; (esp. mil.) point to which armed forces are moving in order to capture it. 2. lens of a microscope or telescope, etc. closest to the object that is being looked at.

obla·tion [əʊ'bleɪʃn] *n.* offering made to God or a god.

ob·li·ga·tion [,ɒblɪ'geɪʃn] *n.* promise, duty, or condition that indicates what action ought to be taken (e.g. the power of the law, duty, a sense of what is right): *the ~s of good citizenship; under an ~ to sb. for his help* (i.e. feeling the need to repay him in some way). **oblig·a·to·ry** [ə'blɪgətərɪ] *adj.* that is necessary, required, by law, rule, or custom: *Is attendance at school obligatory?*

oblige [ə'blaɪdʒ] *v.t.* **1.** bind by a promise; require (sb. *to do* sth.). **2.** compel (sb. *to do* sth.): *He was ~d to sell his new car in order to pay his debt.* **3.** do sth. for sb. as a favour or in answer to a request: *I'm much ~d to you,* I'm grateful to you for what you've done. **oblig·ing** *adj.* willing to help.

oblique [ə'bli:k] *adj.* sloping; slanting: *an ~ angle,* any angle that is not a right angle (i.e. not 90°). (Cf. *acute* (5), *obtuse* (2).) **~·ly** *adv.*

oblit·er·ate [ə'blɪtəreɪt] *v.t.* rub or blot out; remove all signs of; destroy. **oblit·er·a·tion** [ə,blɪtə'reɪʃn] *n.* (no pl.).

obliv·i·on [ə'blɪvɪən] *n.* (no pl.) state of being quite forgotten: *sink (fall) into ~.* **obliv·i·ous** [ə'blɪvɪəs] *adj.* unaware (*of*); having no memory (*of*).

ob·long ['ɒblɒŋ] *n. & adj.* (figure) having four straight sides and angles of 90°, longer than it is wide.

ob·lo·quy ['ɒbləkwɪ] *n.* (no pl.) public shame or reproach.

ob·nox·ious [əb'nɒkʃəs] *adj.* offensive; nasty.

ob·scene [əb'si:n] *adj.* (of words, pictures, behaviour) likely to arouse indecent thoughts, esp. on sex. **ob·scen·i·ty** [əb'senətɪ] *n.* being ~; ~ language, etc.

ob·scure [əb'skjʊə*] *adj.* **1.** dark; hidden; not clearly seen or understood. **2.** not well known: *an ~ young poet.* *v.t.* make ~. **ob·scu·ri·ty** [əb'skjʊərətɪ] *n.*

ob·se·quies ['ɒbsɪkwɪz] *n. pl.* funeral ceremonies.

ob·se·qui·ous [əb'si:kwɪəs] *adj.* too eager to obey, serve, show respect.

ob·serve [əb'zɜ:v] *v.t. & i.* **1.** see and notice; watch carefully. **2.** pay attention to (laws, rules); celebrate (festivals, birthdays, anniversaries). **3.** say (*that*). **ob·serv·able** *adj.* that can be or that deserves to be ~d (1). **ob·ser·vance** *n.* **1.** (no pl.) observing (2) (of a law, festival, etc.). **2.** act performed as part of a ceremony, as a sign of respect or worship. **ob·ser·vant** *adj.* quick at noticing things; careful to ~ (2) (laws, rules, etc.). **ob·ser·va·tion** [,ɒbzə'veɪʃn] *n.* **1.** (no pl.) observing or being ~d: *keep sb. under observation,* watch him carefully; *criminals trying to avoid observation* (i.e. being seen). **2.** remark, statement (on what is ~d). **ob·ser·va·to·ry** [əb-

'zɜ:vətrɪ] *n.* building from which th sun and stars or other natural phenom ena may be ~d. **ob·serv·er** *n.* perso who ~s (1, 2).

ob·sess [əb'ses] *v.t.* (of a fear, fixe or false idea) continually distress occupy the mind of: *~ed by fear o unemployment.* **ob·ses·sion** [əb'seʃn *n.* (influence of) idea, feeling, etc that ~es sb.

ob·so·lete ['ɒbsəli:t] *adj.* no longer i use; out of date: *~ words (methods) **ob·so·les·cent** [,ɒbsəʊ'lesnt] *adj.* be coming ~.

ob·sta·cle ['ɒbstəkl] *n.* sth. in the wa that stops progress or makes it dif ficult.

ob·sti·nate ['ɒbstənət] *adj.* **1.** resistin argument or persuasion: *~ children **2.** not easily overcome: *~ resistanc (disease).* **~·ly** *adv.* **ob·sti·na·cy** ['ɒb stɪnəsɪ] *n.* (no pl.).

ob·struct [əb'strʌkt] *v.t.* be, get, pu sth., in the way of; block up (a road passage, etc.); hinder (free move ment); make (the development o progress of sth.) difficult. **ob·struc tion** [əb'strʌkʃn] *n.* (esp.) sth. that ~ **ob·struc·tive** *adj.* causing, likely t cause, ~ion.

ob·tain [əb'teɪn] *v.t. & i.* **1.** buy; hav lent or granted to oneself. **2.** get secure for oneself: *~ a position (ex perience, etc.).* **3.** (of rules, customs etc.) be established or in use. **~·abl adj.* that can be ~ed.

ob·trude [əb'tru:d] *v.t. & i.* push (oneself, one's opinions, etc.) forwar (*upon* sb.), esp. when unwanted. **ob tru·sive** [əb'tru:sɪv] *adj.*

ob·tuse [əb'tju:s] *adj.* **1.** blunt. **2.** (o an angle) between 90° and 180°. (Cf *acute* (5).) **3.** slow in understanding stupid. **~·ly** *adv.*

ob·verse ['ɒbvɜ:s] *n.* **1.** side of a coi or medal that bears the head or prin cipal design. (Cf. *reverse* (2).) **2.** fron or principal surface. **3.** counterpart o a fact or truth. **~·ly** [ɒb'vɜ:slɪ] *adv.*

ob·vi·ate ['ɒbvɪeɪt] *v.t.* get rid of, clea away (dangers, difficulties, etc.).

ob·vi·ous ['ɒbvɪəs] *adj.* easily seen o understood; plain; clear. **~·ly** *adv.*

oc·ca·sion [ə'keɪʒn] *n.* **1.** time at whic a particular event takes place; righ time (for sth.): *not an ~ (a suitabl time) for laughter; rise to the ~,* sho that one is equal to what needs to b done. **2.** (no pl.) reason; cause; need *There's no ~ for you to lose your temper **3.** immediate, inciting cause of sth (not the fundamental cause): *The rea

...*ause of the strike is not clear, but the* ... *was the dismissal of two workmen.* ...*.t.* be the ~ (2) of; cause: *Your late* ...*rrival ~ed anxiety.* **~·al** [ə'keɪʒənl] *adj.* infrequent: *pay sb. ~al visits.* **~·al·ly** *adv.* now and then; at intervals.

c·ci·dent ['ɒksɪdənt] *n.* the ~, (liter.) ...he West (Europe and America).

·cult [ɒ'kʌlt] *adj.* 1. hidden; secret. ...**.** mysterious; magical: *~ sciences* (e.g. ...strology).

·cu·py ['ɒkjʊpaɪ] *v.t.* 1. live in, be ...n possession of (a house, farm, etc.); ...ake and keep possession of (towns, countries, etc. in war). 2. take up, fill ...space, time, attention, the mind): ...*peeches ~ing two hours*; *anxieties that ...occupied my mind*; *~ing himself with his ...homework.* 3. place oneself in (a building, etc.), esp. as a political demonstration. 4. (esp. pass. or refl.) keep busy ...r engaged. **oc·cu·pi·er, oc·cu·pant** ['ɒkjʊpənt] *ns.* person who occupies ...house, etc. **oc·cu·pa·tion** [ˌɒkjʊ'peɪʃn] *n.* 1. (no pl.) act of ~ing (1) ...a house, country, etc.). 2. employment, business, trade, etc.; means of ...passing one's time. **oc·cu·pa·tion·al** [ˌɒkjʊ'peɪʃənl] *adj.* relating to or ...esulting from a particular occupation: *occupational therapy*, therapy by ...neans of activity.

·cur [ə'kɜː*] *v.i.* (-rr-) 1. take place; ...happen. 2. exist; to be found: *Which ...etter of the alphabet ~s most commonly?* **.** ~ *to*, come into (sb.'s mind): *When ...did the idea ~ to you? It ~red to me ...hat ... .* **~·rence** [ə'kʌrəns] *n.* happening: *an everyday ~rence*; *of frequent ...rence.*

:ean ['əʊʃn] *n.* vast body of water ...hat surrounds the land masses; one of ...he great seas that divide the continents.

chre (U.S.A. **ocher**) ['əʊkə*] *n.* (no ...l.) pale yellowish-brown colour.

clock [ə'klɒk] *particle* indicating ...he hour in telling the time: *What's ...he time? It's 5 ~.*

:·ta·gon ['ɒktəgən] *n.* plane figure ...with eight angles and sides. **oc·tag·o-** ...**al** [ɒk'tægənl] *adj.* eight-sided.

oc·tave ['ɒktɪv] *n.* (music) note that is six whole tones above or below a given note; interval of five whole tones and two semi-tones covered by a musical scale; note and its ~ sounding together.

Oc·to·ber [ɒk'təʊbə*] *n.* tenth month of the year.

oc·to·ge·na·ri·an [ˌɒktəʊdʒɪ'neərɪən] *n. & adj.* (person) aged between 80 and 89.

oc·to·pus ['ɒktəpəs] *n.* sea-animal with a soft body and eight arms (*tentacles*) provided with suckers. (See the picture.)

oc·u·lar ['ɒkjʊlə*] *adj.* of, for, by, the eyes; of seeing: *~ proof* (i.e. by being shown). **oc·u·list** ['ɒkjʊlɪst] *n.* eye-doctor.

odd [ɒd] *adj.* 1. (of numbers) not even: *1, 3, 5, 7 are ~ numbers.* 2. of one of a pair when the other is missing; of one or more of a set or series when not with the rest: *an ~ sock*; *two ~ volumes of an encyclopaedia.* 3. with a little extra: *twelve pounds ~* (more than £12 but less than £13). 4. strange; peculiar: *He's an ~ (~-looking) old man.* 5. *~ jobs*, various, unconnected bits of work; *at ~ times* (*moments*), at various and irregular times. **~·i·ty** ['ɒdɪtɪ] *n.* 1. (no pl.) quality of being ~ (4); strangeness. 2. peculiar person, thing, way of behaving, etc. **~·ly** *adv.* strangely: *~ly enough*, strange to say. **~·ments** *n. pl.* remnants; ~s and ends (see ~s (3)). **~s** *n. pl.* 1. chances in favour of or against sth. happening: *The ~s are against us* (*in our favour*). *The ~s are that ...*, it is likely that ... 2. *be at ~s* (*with*), be quarrelling (with). 3. *~s and ends*, small articles, bits and pieces, of various sorts.

ode [əʊd] *n.* poem, usu. in irregular metre and expressing noble feelings.

odi·ous ['əʊdjəs] *adj.* hateful; repulsive. **odi·um** ['əʊdjəm] *n.* (no pl.) widespread hatred.

odour (U.S.A. **odor**) ['əʊdə*] *n.* 1. smell. 2. (no pl.) *in good* (*bad*) *~* (*with*), having (not having) the favour and approval (of). **~·less** *adj.*

o'er ['əʊə*] *adv. & prep.* (poet.) over.

of [ɒv, əv] *prep.* 1. (indicating separation in space or time): *five miles south of Leeds*; (U.S.A.) *ten minutes* (a *quarter*) *of* (Gt. Brit. *to*) *twelve.* 2. (indicating authorship, origin): *the works of Shakespeare*; *a man of humble birth.* 3. (indicating cause): *die of grief.* 4. (indicating deliverance, loss): *be cured of a disease*; *be robbed of one's*

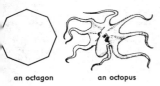

an octagon   an octopus

money. **5.** (indicating material): *a table of dark oak*. **6.** (indicating description): *a man of tall appearance*. **7.** (indicating an object): *a maker of pots*; *love of money*. **8.** (indicating a subject): *the love of a mother for her children*. **9.** (indicating portion or measure): *a sheet of paper*; *a yard of cloth*. **10.** (indicating relationship): *a friend of mine*; *a portrait of the queen*; *an offer of help*. **11.** (indicating time): *in days of old*; *of a Sunday*, on Sundays. **12.** by: *a man beloved of all his friends*. **13.** about: *I often think of you*.

off [ɒf] *prep., adv., & adj.* **I. prep. 1.** not on; (down or away) from: *He fell ~ the ladder*. *~ the record*, not to be recorded; confidential. **2.** (reducing, etc.): *Will you take 2½% ~ the price if I pay cash?* **3.** *~ duty*, free from duty (1). **4.** near to but not on; (of streets and roads) branching out from: *a house just ~ the main road*; *a road ~ the High Street*; *an island ~ the coast*. **5.** *~ colour*, unwell; *~ one's food* without appetite; *be ~ smoking*, do not smoke any more; *~ one's head*, mad; *~ the point*, irrelevant(ly). **II. adv. 1.** see *go ~*, *show ~*, etc. **2.** at or to a distance in space or time; away; departure; removal; separation: *The town is five miles ~. The holidays are only two weeks ~. Take ~ your coat. O~ with it!* Take it *~. I must be ~ now* (must leave now). *We're just ~ to America. We're ~, we've started. O~ we go!* We're starting. **3.** (contrasted with *on* (II, 4)) (indicating the ending of sth. arranged or planned): *The strike is ~.* **4.** (contrasted with *on* (II, 3)) disconnected; no longer available: *The electricity (gas, water) is ~. Switch ~ the light. Turn ~ the radio. That dish is ~, sir* (in a restaurant, no more of it is available though it is on the menu). **5.** (of food) no longer fresh: *This fish (meat) is ~.* **6.** (indicating completion): *Finish ~ that job before starting another*. **7.** (indicating absence or freedom from work or duty): *ask for a day ~*, ask for a day's holiday; *take the afternoon ~*; *take time ~*, stay away from work. **8.** (theatre) not on the stage: *voices ~.* **9.** *~ and on*, at times; at intervals; (badly) *well ~*, (not) rich. **III. adj. 1.** *the ~ side*, the further or far side. **2.** (of horses, vehicles) of the side further from the side of the road (in Great Britain the right side): *the ~ rear wheel*. (Cf. *near* (3).) **3.** *on the ~ chance*, on the improbable chance; *~ season*, period of little activity; *in one's ~ time*,

when one has no duties; in one's spar(e) time.

of·fal [ˈɒfl] *n.* (no pl.) **1.** those parts o(f) an animal (e.g. heart, liver, kidneys) that are considered less valuable tha(n) the flesh as food. **2.** waste parts of a(n) animal that has been cut up for foo(d).

of·fence (U.S.A. **of·fense**) [əˈfens] *n* **1.** wrongdoing; crime; sin; breakin(g) of a rule: *an ~ against God and ma(n)* (against the law, good manners). **2.** (n(o) pl.) hurting of sb.'s feelings; con(dition) of being hurt in one's feelings: *give ~ to sb.*; *quick to take ~*, easil(y) offended (2). **3.** that which annoys th(e) senses or which makes sb. angry. **4.** (no pl.) attacking: *weapons of ~.* **of fend** [əˈfend] *v.t. & i.* **1.** do wrong, commit an ~ (1) (against the law, cus(tom), etc.). **2.** give ~ (2) to; hurt th(e) feelings of. **3.** be displeasing to: *ugl(y) sounds that offend the ear.* **of·fend·e(r)** *n.* person who offends, esp. b(y) breaking the law. **of·fen·sive** [əˈfensɪv] *adj.* **1.** causing ~ (3): *an offensiv(e) smell*; *offensive language* (e.g. insults)(.) **2.** used for attacking; connected wit(h) attack: *an offensive weapon (war). n(.)* attack: *take the offensive*, go into at(-)tack. **of·fen·sive·ly** *adv.*

of·fer [ˈɒfə(r)] *v.t. & i.* **1.** hold out, pu(t) forward (a thing, suggestion, etc.), t(o) be taken or refused; say what one i(s) willing to pay, give, or exchange fo(r) sth. **2.** present to God: *~ prayers t(o) God*; *~ up prayers of thanksgiving.* **3.** attempt: *~ing no resistance.* **4.** occur, the first opportunity *(chance, occasion) that ~s* (that there is). *n.* statemen(t) *~ing* to do or give sth.; that which i(s) *~ed: make (accept) an ~*; *an ~ o(f) marriage*. *~ing n.* sth. *~ed* or present(-)ed, esp. the money collected at a church service. **~·to·ry** [ˈɒfətərɪ] *n(.)* money *~ing* in church.

off·hand [ˌɒfˈhænd] *adj.* without pre(-)vious thought or preparation; (o(f) behaviour) casual; careless; withou(t) enough respect: *in an ~ way. adv* without previous thought or prepara(-)tion: *I can't say ~.*

of·fice [ˈɒfɪs] *n.* **1.** (often pl.) room(s) used as a place of business, for cleric(al) work: *a lawyer's ~*; *working in an ~* (e.g. as a clerk, typist, etc.); *~ hours*, hours during which business is regu(-)larly conducted. **2.** (buildings of a) government department, including th(e) staff, their work and duties: *the Foreig(n) O~*; *the Home O~*. **3.** the wor(k) which it is sb.'s duty to do: *accep(t) (enter upon, leave, resign) ~* (esp. of a position in the government service): ~-bearer, ~-holder, person who holds a public ~. **4.** duty: *the ~ of chairman* (*host*). **5.** (pl.) attention; services; help: *through the good ~s* (kind help) *of a friend.* **6.** any occasional religious service: *O~ for the Dead*; certain prescribed forms of worship: *Divine O~.* '**~-boy** *n.* boy employed to do the less important duties in an ~ (1). **of·fi·cer** ['ɒfɪsə*] *n.* **1.** person appointed to command others in the armed forces, in merchant ships, aircraft, the police force, etc. **2.** person with a position of authority or trust, esp. in the government or civil service: *~s of state,* ministers in the government; *customs ~s; the ~s of a society* (e.g. the secretary).

of·fi·cial [ə'fɪʃl] *adj.* **1.** of a position of trust or authority; said, done, etc., with authority: *~ statements* (*records, uniform*). **2.** characteristic of, suitable for, persons holding office (3): *in an ~ style.* *n.* person holding a government position or engaged in public work: *government ~s.* **~·ly** *adv.* in an ~ manner; with ~ authority.

of·fi·ci·ate [ə'fɪʃɪeɪt] *v.i.* perform the duties of an office or position: *~ as chairman*; (of a priest or minister) *~ at a wedding.* **of·fi·cious** [ə'fɪʃəs] *adj.* too eager or ready to help, offer advice, use authority, etc.

off·set ['ɒfset] *v.t.* (-*tt*-; p.t. & p.p. -*set*) balance; compensate for.

off·shoot ['ɒfʃuːt] *n.* stem or branch growing from a main stem, etc.

off·side [,ɒf'saɪd] *attrib. adj. & adv.* (football, hockey) (of a player) in a position between the ball and the opponents' goal where the player may not play the ball.

off·spring ['ɒfsprɪŋ] *n.* (pl. ~) child (-ren); young of animals.

off·stage [,ɒf'steɪdʒ] *adj. & adv.* (theatre) not on the stage; not visible to the audience.

off·street ['ɒfstriːt] *adj.* (esp. of the parking of vehicles) not on the street: *~ parking.*

of·ten ['ɒfn] *adv.* (~er, ~est; *more, most*) **1.** many times; in a large proportion of cases. **2.** *How ~?* At what intervals? How many times? *as ~ as,* each time that.

ogle ['əʊgl] *v.i. & t.* look (*at* sb.) in a way suggesting love or longing; make eyes (*at*).

ogre ['əʊgə*] *n.* (in fairy-tales) cruel, man-eating giant.

oh, see O[1,2].

oil [ɔɪl] *n.* (sorts of) (usu. easily burning) liquid that does not mix with water, obtained from animals (*whale-~*), plants (*coconut ~*), or from wells (*petroleum*). *painted in ~s,* painted in ~-colours. *v.t.* put ~ on or into (parts of a machine, etc.). '**~-cake** *n.* (no pl.) cattle food made from seeds after ~ has been pressed out. '**~-,col·ours** *n. pl.* paint made from colouring matter and ~. '**~-field** *n.* area where mineral ~ is found. '**~-,paint·ing** *n.* **1.** (no pl.) art of painting in ~-colours. **2.** picture painted in ~-colours. '**~-skin** *n.* (coat, etc. of) cloth treated with ~ to make it keep out water. '**~-well** *n.* well from which mineral ~ is drawn. **~y** *adj.* (-ier, -iest) of, like, ~; covered with ~.

oint·ment ['ɔɪntmənt] *n.* medicinal paste made from oil or fat and used on the skin.

okay [,əʊ'keɪ] (abbr. O.K.) *adj. & adv.* (colloq.) all right; correct; approved. *v.t.* agree to; approve of. *n.* agreement; sanction.

old [əʊld] *adj.* (~er, ~est; see also *elder, eldest*) **1.** of age: *She's twenty-two years ~.* **2.** (contrasted with *young*) having lived a long time; past middle age: *~-age pension(er).* **3.** (contrasted with *new, modern, up-to-date*) belonging to past times; having been in existence or use for a long time. **4.** long known or familiar: *an ~ friend; my dear ~ boy* (a term of affection). **5.** having passed through a school: *an O~ Boys' Dance*; having had much experience: *an ~ hand at carpentry.* *n.* in days of ~, in past times. **~·en** ['əʊldən] *adj.* (liter.) *in ~en days* (*times*), in past times. **,~-'fash·ioned** *adj.* out of date; not according with modern ideas, tastes, etc.; keeping to ~ ways. '**~·ie** *n.* (colloq.) ~ person or thing.

ol·i·gar·chy ['ɒlɪgɑːkɪ] *n.* (country having) government by a small group of all-powerful persons; such a group.

ol·ive ['ɒlɪv] *n.* ~(-*tree*), (tree with a) small fruit with a stone-like seed. *hold out the ~-branch,* show that one is ready to discuss peace-making. *adj.* yellowish-green or yellowish-brown.

om·elette, om·elet ['ɒmlɪt] *n.* eggs beaten together, flavoured and fried.

omen ['əʊmen] *n.* (thing, happening, regarded as a) sign of sth. good or of evil fortune: *an ~ of success.* **om·i·nous** ['ɒmɪnəs] *adj.* of bad ~; threatening.

omit [ə'mɪt] *v.t.* (-*tt*-) **1.** fail (*to do* sth.): *~ to do one's homework.* **2.** leave out: *~ the next chapter,* not read it. **omis·sion** [əˈmɪʃn] *n.* ~ting; sth. ~ted.

om·ni·bus [ˈɒmnɪbəs] *n.* **1.** (former name for) bus. **2.** (attrib.) for many purposes: *an ~ bill*[2] *(3)*; containing many: *an ~ volume*, several books bound in one cover.

om·nip·o·tent [ɒmˈnɪpətənt] *adj.* having power over all: *the O~*, God. **om·nip·o·tence** *n.* (no pl.).

om·ni·scient [ɒmˈnɪsɪənt] *adj.* knowing all things: *the O~*, God. **om·ni·science** *n.* (no pl.).

om·niv·o·rous [ɒmˈnɪvərəs] *adj.* eating all kinds of food.

on [ɒn, ən] *prep. & adv.* **I.** *prep.* **1.** supported by; fastened to; covering (a surface); lying against; in contact with. **2.** (indicating time): *on Sundays*; *on 1st May*; *on that occasion*; *on my arrival*; *on time*, punctually. **3.** about: *a lecture on Shakespeare*. **4.** (indicating membership): *be on the committee*. **5.** (indicating direction) towards: *marched on London*; *drifting on the rocks (on shore)*. **6.** (expressing reason, basis, etc.): *based on fact*; *retire on a pension*. **7.** (indicating nearness): *a town on the coast*. **8.** (indicating occupation): *on business*; *be on holiday*. **9.** (indicating manner or state): *be on sale, on loan, on fire*. **II.** *adv.* **1.** (expressing progress): *They hurried on (i.e. forward). The time is getting on (i.e. late)*. **2.** (corresponding in meaning to the prep. (1) but omitting the noun): *Put your shoes on (i.e. on your feet). have nothing on*, be naked. *Put your coat on*. **3.** (contrasted with *off* (II, 4)): *Switch the light on*. **4.** (contrasted with *off* (II, 3)): *The strike is still on (has not ended yet)*. **5.** happening: *What's on (What's the programme) at the cinema this week?*

once [wʌns] *adv., conj., & n.* **I.** *adv.* **1.** on one occasion only; for one time: *I only went ~.* **2.** at some time in the past: *Once (upon a time) there was a princess*. **3.** ever; at all: *He didn't ~ offer to help me*. **4.** ~ *in a way (while)*, occasionally; ~ *and for all*, now and for the last time; *at ~*, now; immediately; *all at ~*, all together; suddenly. **II.** *conj.* from the moment that: *O~ you begin to feel afraid ...* **III.** *n.* one time or occasion: *For ~ you're right*.

on·com·ing [ˈɒnˌkʌmɪŋ] *n. & adj.* approach(ing): ~ *traffic*.

one [wʌn] *adj., pron., & n.* **I.** *adj.* **1.** single: ~ *book, two books, three books*. **2.** particular but undefined

single thing: *O~ day* (i.e. on a certain day that I have in mind) *we went to the Zoo*. ~ *morning in July*; *all in ~ direction*. **3.** single person or thing of the kind expressed or implied: ~ *of my friends. I read ~ of your books. It's all ~ to me*, I have no preference. *You can have ~ or the other, but not both*. **II.** *pron.* **1.** any person in a general way: *O~ should not do such an unkind thing as that* (i.e. nobody should do it). (Sometimes used as a third-person substitute for a pronoun of the first person: ~ *supposes you will come*.) **2.** individual of a particular kind: *the Holy O~*, God; *the Evil O~*, the Devil; *the absent ~* (member of the family not present); *the little ~s*, the children; *five young ~s* (e.g. five young birds); ~ *another*, each other: *They don't like ~ another*. ~ *by ~*, ~ *after another*, ~ at a time. **III.** *n.* **1.** figure 1: *a row of ~s* (i.e. 11111). **2.** single thing, person, or example: *by ~s and twos*; *the big man and the little ~*; *that ~ over there. Send me some good ~s. This is the ~ that is best*. **,~·'eyed** *adj.* having only ~ eye with which to see. **~·self** [wʌnˈself] *pron.* used by the speaker to refer to his own self or to persons in general: *O~ should not be too proud of ~self.* **,~·'sid·ed** *adj.* (esp.) concerned with, seeing, only ~ side: *a ~-sided argument*. **'~·time** *adj.* former. **'~·track** *adj.* (fig.) dominated by ~ interest, subject, etc.: *a ~-track mind*. **,~·'up** *adj.* ahead of another, as by one point; (fig.) in a position of advantage. **'~·way** *adj.* operating or moving in only ~ direction; (U.S.A.) of a ~ ticket) single not return; ~-*way street*, street in which traffic may pass in ~ direction only; ~-*way traffic*.

oner·ous [ˈɒnərəs] *adj.* needing effort; burdensome: ~ *duties*.

on·ion [ˈʌnjən] *n.* vegetable plant with a round root, having a sharp taste and smell.

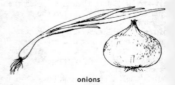

onions

on·look·er [ˈɒnˌlʊkə*] *n.* person who looks on at sth. happening.

on·ly [ˈəʊnlɪ] *adj., adv., & conj.* **I.** *attrib. adj.* (with a singular noun) that is the one single example; single; (with a plural noun) that are all examples; the best: *He's the ~ man (They are the ~ men) fit to take the responsibility.* **II.** *adv.* solely; no one more; nothing more: *Only men allowed to swim here. Only five men were hurt in the explosion. if ~* (see *if* (6)). **III.** *conj.* but one should add that: *The book would be helpful to you, ~ it's expensive.*

on·set ['ɒnset] *n.* **1.** attack. **2.** vigorous start: *the ~ of a disease.*

on·slaught ['ɒnslɔːt] *n.* furious attack (*on*).

onus ['əʊnəs] *n.* (no pl.) responsibility for, burden of, doing sth.: *The ~ of proof rests with you.*

on·ward ['ɒnwəd] *adj. & adv.* forward. ~s *adv.*

ooze [uːz] *n.* (no pl.) soft, liquid mud, esp. in a river-bed, at the bottom of a pond, etc. *v.i.* (of moisture, thick liquids) pass slowly through small openings: *blood oozing from a wound.* (fig.) *Their courage ~d away.*

opal ['əʊpl] *n.* precious stone in which changes of colour are seen.

opaque [əʊ'peɪk] *adj.* (*~r*, *~st*) **1.** not allowing light to pass through; that cannot be seen through. **2.** (fig.) obscure; dull.

open ['əʊpən] *adj.* **1.** not closed or enclosed, so that people and things can go in, out, or through; not covered in or over; spread out or unfolded; public, not restricted to a few people. **2.** (special uses with nouns): *in the ~ air*, out of doors; *with ~ arms*, with affection or joy; *an ~ boat*, one with no deck; *~ competitions (scholarships, etc.)*, not limited to any special persons but for anyone to enter; *the ~ country*, land where distant views can be seen; land not covered with forests, not built over, etc.; *keep ~ house*, be always ready to welcome visitors; *have an ~ mind*, be ready to consider new ideas, etc.; *in ~ order*, (of troops) widely spread out in a line; *an ~ question (verdict)*, one not settled or decided; *the ~ sea*, sea far from the land; *~ vowel*, vowel produced with a relatively wide ~ing of the mouth; *~ water*, free from ice. **3.** *~ to*, (a) willing to listen to (reasons, arguments) or to consider (an offer, etc.); (b) offering room or reason for (doubt). *n.* *the ~*, the ~ air; the ~ country; public notice or view. *v.t. & i.* **1.** make ~ or cause to be ~; unfasten; cut or make an ~ing in or a passage through. **2.** *~ out*, unfold; spread out; *~ up*, make ~; make possible the development of (a country, etc.). **3.** *~ fire (at, on)*, start shooting. **4.** start (a banking account, a debate); announce that (an exhibition, a meeting) may start. ~·**er** ['əʊpnə*] *n.* (esp.) device (2) for ~ing bottles, tins, etc.: *a tin-~er.* ~·**ing** ['əʊpnɪŋ] *n.* **1.** ~ space; way in or out. **2.** beginning. **3.** position (in a business firm, etc.) which is ~ or vacant: *no ~ings for stupid boys.* ~·**ly** *adv.* without secrecy; frankly. ~·'hand·ed *adj.* generous. ~·'heart·ed *adj.* frank; sincere. '~·work *n.* (no pl.) material (e.g. lace) with ~ings in it as in a net.

op·era ['ɒpərə] *n.* dramatic composition with music in which the words are sung. '~·glass·es *n. pl.* binoculars for use in a theatre. '~·house *n.* theatre for performances of ~s. **op·er·at·ic** [ˌɒpə'rætɪk] *adj.*

op·er·ate ['ɒpəreɪt] *v.t. & i.* **1.** (cause to) work, be in action, have an effect; manage: *~ a machine; machinery that ~s night and day; a machine ~d by electricity; a coin-~d juke-box.* **2.** *~ on sb.* (*for* sth.), perform a surgical operation (4) on. **op·er·able** ['ɒpərəbl] *adj.* that can be ~d; that can be treated by means of a surgical operation: *an operable tumour.* **op·er·a·tion** [ˌɒpə'reɪʃn] *n.* **1.** (no pl.) working; way in which sth. works: *in operation; come into operation*, become effective. **2.** piece of work; sth. (to be) done: *begin operations.* **3.** (pl.) movements of troops, ships, aircraft, etc. in warfare. **4.** cutting of the body by a surgeon (to remove diseased parts, etc.). **op·er·a·tive** ['ɒpərətɪv] *adj.* **1.** operating; effective. **2.** of surgical operations: *operative treatment.* *n.* worker, esp. in a factory. **op·er·a·tor** ['ɒpəreɪtə*] *n.* person who ~s sth.: *telegraph operators.*

opi·ate ['əʊpɪət] *n.* drug containing opium, used to relieve pain or help sb. to sleep.

opin·ion [ə'pɪnjən] *n.* **1.** belief or judgement not founded on complete knowledge; idea that sth. is probably true: *in my ~*, it seems likely to me that; *public ~*, what the majority of people think. **2.** professional estimate or advice: *get a lawyer's ~.* ~·**at·ed** [ə'pɪnjəneɪtɪd] *adj.* obstinate in one's ~s.

opi·um ['əʊpjəm] *n.* (no pl.) substance prepared from poppy juice, used to relieve pain, cause sleep, and as a drug to soothe the senses.

op·po·nent [ə'pəʊnənt] *n.* person

op·por·tune ['ɒpətjuːn] *adj.* **1.** (of time) favourable; good for a purpose. **2.** done, coming, at a favourable time. **op·por·tun·ist** *n.* person who is more anxious to gain an advantage than to consider whether he is gaining it fairly. **op·por·tu·ni·ty** [,ɒpə'tjuːnətɪ] *n.* favourable time or chance (*for* sth., *of* doing sth., *to do* sth.).

op·pose [ə'pəʊz] *v.t.* **1.** set oneself, fight, against (sb. or sth.). **2.** put forward as a contrast or opposite (*to*). **op·po·site** ['ɒpəzɪt] *adj.* **1.** facing: *the house opposite (to) mine.* **2.** entirely different; contrary: *in the opposite direction; the opposite sex. n.* word or thing that is opposite. **op·po·si·tion** [,ɒpə'zɪʃn] *n.* (no pl.) **1.** state of being opposite; resistance. **2.** *the Opposition,* members of the political party or parties opposing the Government.

op·press [ə'pres] *v.t.* **1.** rule unjustly or cruelly; keep down by unjust or cruel government. **2.** (fig.) weigh heavily on; cause to feel troubled or uncomfortable: *˷ed by the heat.* **op·pres·sion** [ə'preʃn] *n.* **op·pres·sive** *adj.* unjust; hard to bear: *˷ive laws; ˷ive weather (taxation).* **op·pres·sive·ly** *adv.* **op·pres·sor** *n.*

op·pro·bri·ous [ə'prəʊbrɪəs] *adj.* (of words, etc.) showing scorn or reproach. **op·pro·bri·um** [ə'prəʊbrɪəm] *n.* (no pl.) scorn; disgrace; public shame.

opt [ɒpt] *v.i.* make a choice (*for*): *˷ out (of),* choose not to participate (in): *˷ out of society.*

op·tic ['ɒptɪk] *adj.* of the eye or the sense of sight: *˷ nerve. n.* **1.** lens in an optical instrument. **2.** (pl., sing. v.) science of sight and esp. of the laws of light as its medium. **op·ti·cal** *adj.* of the sense of sight; for looking through; to help eyesight: *˷al instruments* (e.g. a microscope). **op·ti·cian** [ɒp'tɪʃn] *n.* person who makes or supplies *˷al* instruments, esp. spectacles (4).

op·ti·mism ['ɒptɪmɪzəm] *n.* (no pl.) belief that in the end good will triumph over evil; tendency to look upon the bright side of things; confidence in success. **op·ti·mist** *n.* optimistic person. **op·ti·mis·tic** [,ɒptɪ'mɪstɪk] *adj.* expecting the best; confident.

op·ti·mum ['ɒptɪməm] *adj. & n.* (pl. *-ma* [-mə]) best or most favourable (conditions): *˷ temperature.*

op·tion ['ɒpʃn] *n.* **1.** (no pl.) right or power of choosing. **2.** thing that is or may be chosen. **3.** (comm.) right to buy or sell sth. at a specified price within a specified period of time. **˷al** *adj.* that may be chosen or not as one wishes: *˷al subjects at school.* **˷al·ly** *adv.*

op·u·lent ['ɒpjʊlənt] *adj.* abundant; rich. **op·u·lence** *n.* (no pl.).

opus ['əʊpəs] *n.* (usu. no pl.) separate composition or set of compositions of a musician.

or [ɔː*, ə*] *conj.* **1.** (introducing an alternative): *Is it green or blue? either ... or* (see *either* (II, 2)); *or else,* otherwise; if not: *Hurry up, or else you will be late.* **2.** (introducing a word that explains, or means the same as, another): *100 new pence, or 1 pound.* **3.** (introducing all but the first of a series): *black or white or grey; black, white, or grey.*

-or [-ə*] *suff.* **1.** (forming ns.) sb. or sth. that carries out the action of the verb: *actor; elevator; governor.* **2.** (forming adjs. with comparative sense): *major; senior.*

or·a·cle ['ɒrəkl] *n.* **1.** (in ancient Greece) (answer given at a) place where questions about the future were asked of the gods; priest(ess) giving the answers. **2.** person considered able to give reliable guidance. **o·rac·u·lar** [ɒ'rækjʊlə*] *adj.* of or like an ˷; with a hidden meaning.

o·ral ['ɒrəl] *adj.* **1.** using the spoken, not the written, word: *an ˷ examination.* **2.** (anat.) of, by, for, the mouth *n.* (colloq.) ˷ examination. **˷·ly** *adv.*

or·ange ['ɒrɪndʒ] *n. & adj.* (evergreen tree with a) round, yellow, thick skinned juicy fruit; (of the) colour of an ˷ (between yellow and red). **˷·ade** [,ɒrɪndʒ'eɪd] *n.* drink made of ˷ juice synthetic substitute for this.

oranges an orang-utan

orang-utan [ɔː,ræŋuː'tæn], **orang-ou-tang** [ɔː,ræŋuː'tæŋ] *n.* large, long-armed ape of Borneo.

ora·tion [ɔː'reɪʃn] *n.* formal speech

made in public: *a funeral* ~. **or·a·tor**
['ɒrətə*] *n.* person who makes speeches, esp. a good speaker. **or·a·tor·i·cal**
[ˌɒrə'tɒrɪkl] *adj.* of speech-making.
or·a·to·ry ['ɒrətərɪ] *n.* **1.** (no pl.) art
of public speech-making. **2.** small
chapel for private worship or prayer.
or·a·to·rio [ˌɒrə'tɔːrɪəʊ] *n.* (pl. ~s)
musical composition for solo voices,
chorus, and orchestra, usu. with a
biblical subject.
orb [ɔːb] *n.* globe, esp. the sun, moon,
or one of the stars.
or·bit ['ɔːbɪt] *n.* path followed by a
heavenly body or a satellite, spacecraft, etc. round another: *the earth's* ~
round the sun; *satellites in* ~ *round the
earth.* *v.t. & i.* put into ~; move in
an ~ round (a body, etc.); (of a spacecraft, etc.) move in an ~; fly in a
circle: ~ *a satellite*; *a spacecraft* ~*ing
the moon*; *an aircraft* ~*ing over a
landing-field.* ~**al** ['ɔːbɪtl] *adj.* **1.** of
an ~ or ~s. **2.** (of a road) passing round
the outside of a city.
or·chard ['ɔːtʃəd] *n.* piece of ground
(usu. enclosed) with fruit-trees.
or·ches·tra ['ɔːkɪstrə] *n.* **1.** band of
persons playing musical instruments
(including stringed instruments) together. **2.** place in a theatre for an ~.
~**l** [ɔː'kestrəl] *adj.*
or·chid ['ɔːkɪd] *n.* sorts of plant, many
of which have flowers of bright colours
and unusual shapes.
or·dain [ɔː'deɪn] *v.t.* **1.** (of God, law,
authority) decide; give orders (*that*).
2. make (sb.) a priest or minister.
or·deal [ɔː'diːl] *n.* **1.** (no pl.) (in
former times) method of deciding sb.'s
guilt or innocence by requiring him
to pass a physical test, such as walking
through fire unharmed: ~ *by fire*; *trial
by* ~. **2.** any severe test of character or
endurance.
or·der ['ɔːdə*] *n.* **1.** (no pl.) way in
which things are placed in relation to
one another: *names in alphabetical* ~;
in ~ *of size.* **2.** (no pl.) condition in
which everything is carefully arranged; working condition: *in* ~, as it
should be; *machinery in good working*
~; *out of* ~, not functioning properly.
3. (no pl.) (condition brought about
by) good and firm government, obedience to the laws: *law and* ~, see *law*
(4); *keep* ~, enforce it. **4.** (no pl.) rules
usual at a public meeting: *called to* ~
by the Chairman (required to obey the
rules); *protest on a point of* ~. **5.** command given with authority: *obey* ~s;
by ~ *of the King.* **6.** request to supply

goods; the goods (to be) supplied:
an ~ *for two tons of flour*; *give an* ~ *for
goods*; *made to* ~, made according to
special or personal requirements; *on* ~,
asked for but not yet supplied. **7.** written direction (esp. to a bank or post
office) to pay money: *a postal* ~. **8.** (no
pl.) purpose; intention: *in* ~ *that*, so
that; with the intention that; *in* ~ *to
(do sth.)*, with the purpose of (doing
sth.). **9.** rank or class in society: *the* ~
of knights; group of people belonging
to or appointed to a special class (as an
honour): *the O*~ *of Merit*; badge, sign,
worn by members: *wearing his* ~s.
10. (pl.) authority given by a bishop
to perform church duties: *take holy* ~s,
become a priest; persons on whom
such ~s have been conferred: *the O*~
of Deacons. **11.** society of persons
living under religious rules, esp. a
brotherhood of monks. **12.** category of
classification of animals, plants, etc.
ranking above the family (4) and
below the class (1). *v.t.* **1.** give an ~
(5, 6, 7) to (sb.) or for (sth.). **2.** put
(sth.) in ~ (2); arrange. ~**ly** *adj.* **1.**
well-arranged; in good ~ (2). **2.** peaceful; well-behaved: *an* ~*ly crowd.* *n.*
(army) officer's messenger; hospital
attendant.
or·di·nal ['ɔːdɪnl] *n. & adj.* (number)
showing order or position in a series:
first, second, third are ~ *numbers.*
or·di·nance ['ɔːdɪnəns] *n.* order made
by an authority: ~*s of the City Council.*
or·di·nary ['ɔːdnrɪ] *adj.* normal; usual;
average: *out of the* ~, exceptional;
unusual. **or·di·nar·i·ly** ['ɔːdnrəlɪ]
adv.
or·di·na·tion [ˌɔːdɪ'neɪʃn] *n.* ceremony
of ordaining (2) (a priest or minister).
ord·nance ['ɔːdnəns] *n.* (no pl.) artillery. *Army O*~ *Department* (responsible for military supplies); ~ *survey
maps*, (Gt. Brit.) detailed maps of
Great Britain and Ireland made for
the Government.
ore [ɔː*] *n.* rock, earth, etc. from which
metal can be extracted.
or·gan ['ɔːgən] *n.* **1.** any part of an
animal body or plant serving an essential purpose: *the* ~s *of speech* (i.e. the
tongue, teeth, lips, etc.). **2.** means of
getting work done; organization. **3.**
means for making known what people
think: ~s *of public opinion* (e.g. newspapers, television, etc.). **4.** musical
instrument from which sounds are
produced by air forced through pipes,
played by keys pressed with the fingers
and pedals pressed with the feet:

~**-blower**, person who works the bellows of an ~; ~**-loft**, (in some churches, etc.) gallery where the ~ is placed. ~**·ic** [ɔː'gænɪk] *adj*. **1.** of the ~s of the body. **2.** having bodily ~s. **3.** of, relating to, or containing carbon compounds[1]; of, relating to, or dealt with by a branch (2) of chemistry concerned with the carbon compounds of living beings and most other carbon compounds: ~*ic chemistry*. **4.** *an* ~*ic whole*, an organized whole; *an* ~*ic part*, a structural part. ~**·ism** ['ɔːgənɪzəm] *n*. living being with parts that work together: (fig.) *the social* ~*ism*. ~**·ist** *n*. person who plays the ~ (4).

or·ga·nize ['ɔːgənaɪz] *v.t.* put into working order; arrange in a system; make preparations for: ~ *an army* (*an expedition, one's work*). ~**d** *adj*. highly ~d *forms of life*, having highly developed organs (1). **or·ga·ni·za·tion** [,ɔːgənaɪ'zeɪʃn] *n*. **1.** (no pl.) organizing or being ~d. **2.** ~d body of persons; ~d system. **or·ga·niz·er** *n*. person who is ~.

or·gy ['ɔːdʒɪ] *n*. occasion of wild merry-making, etc.: *a drunken* ~.

ori·ent[1] ['ɔːrɪənt] *n*. *the O*~, (liter.) countries east of the Mediterranean. **ori·en·tal** [,ɔːrɪ'entl] *adj*. of the O~: ~*al civilization* (*rugs*). *n*. *O*~*al*, native or inhabitant of the O~.

ori·ent[2] ['ɔːrɪent] *v.t.* **1.** place (a building, etc.) so as to face east. **2.** place or exactly determine the position of (sth.) with regard to the points of the compass; settle or find the bearings of (sth.): ~ *oneself*, (fig.) determine how one stands in relation to one's surroundings, etc.; make oneself familiar with a situation. **ori·en·tate** ['ɔːrɪenteɪt] *v.t.* = ~.

or·i·fice ['ɒrɪfɪs] *n*. outer opening; mouth of a cave, etc.

or·i·gin ['ɒrɪdʒɪn] *n*. starting-point; (person's) parentage: *of humble* ~. **orig·i·nate** [ə'rɪdʒəneɪt] *v.i. & t.* **1.** come into being. **2.** be the inventor of.

orig·i·nal [ə'rɪdʒənl] *adj*. **1.** first or earliest: *the* ~ *inhabitants*. **2.** newly formed or created; not copied or imitated: ~ *ideas*. **3.** able to produce new ideas, etc.: *an* ~ *mind*. *n*. **1.** that from which sth. is copied. **2.** (no pl.) language in which sth. was first written: *reading Homer in the* ~ (i.e. in Greek). **3.** eccentric person. ~**·ly** *adv*. ~**·i·ty** [ə,rɪdʒə'nælətɪ] *n*. (no pl.) quality of being ~; ability to create: *work that lacks* ~*ity*.

or·na·ment ['ɔːnəmənt] *n*. **1.** sth designed or used to add beauty to sth else. **2.** person, act, quality, etc adding beauty, charm, etc. (*to*) ['ɔːnəment] *v.t.* be an ~ to; mak● beautiful. **or·na·men·tal** [,ɔːnə'mentl] *adj*. of or for ~.

or·nate [ɔː'neɪt] *adj*. richly ornamented.

or·ni·thol·o·gy [,ɔːnɪ'θɒlədʒɪ] *n*. (n● pl.) scientific study of birds. **or·ni·thol·o·gist** *n*. expert in ~. **or·ni·tho·log·i·cal** [,ɔːnɪθə'lɒdʒɪkl] *adj*.

or·phan ['ɔːfn] *n*. child who has los● one or both of its parents by death *v.t.* cause to be an ~: ~*ed by war*. ~**·ag●** ['ɔːfənɪdʒ] *n*. institution for ~s.

or·tho·dox ['ɔːθədɒks] *adj*. (havin● opinions, beliefs, etc. that are) generally accepted or approved: *an* ~ member of the Church; ~ *beliefs*; ~ *behaviour*. ~**·y** *n*. (no pl.) being ~.

or·thog·ra·phy [ɔː'θɒgrəfɪ] *n*. (no pl.) system of spelling. **or·tho·graph·i·cal** [,ɔːθəʊ'græfɪk] *adj*.

os·cil·late ['ɒsɪleɪt] *v.t. & i.* (cause to) swing or move to and fro between two points, as a pendulum does.

osier ['əʊʒə*] *n*. kind of willow tree twigs of which are made into baskets

os·ten·si·ble [ɒ'stensəbl] *adj*. (of reasons, etc.) put forward in an attemp● to hide the real reason, etc. **os·ten·si·bly** *adv*.

os·ten·ta·tion [,ɒsten'teɪʃn] *n*. (no pl.) display (of wealth, learning, etc.) t● obtain admiration or envy. **os·ten·ta·tious** *adj*. fond of, showing, ~.

os·tler ['ɒslə*] *n*. man who looks afte● horses at an inn.

os·tra·cize ['ɒstrəsaɪz] *v.t.* banish from society; refuse to meet, talk to, etc **os·tra·cism** *n*. (no pl.).

os·trich ['ɒstrɪtʃ] *n*. (pl. ~*es*) large fast-running bird, unable to fly, bre● for its valuable tail feathers.

oth·er ['ʌðə*] *n*. (or *pron*.) & *adj* (person or thing) not the same as tha● already referred to: *the* ~, (sing.) th● second of two; *the* ~*s*, (pl.) with reference to two or more: *You tw● boys can go home, but (all) the* ~*s mus● stay here. Give this to Jack and tha● to the* ~ *boy. on the* ~ *hand*, introducing sth. in contrast to an earlier statement *the* ~ *day*, a few days ago; *every* ~ (a) all the ~s; (b) alternate; *second every* ~ *day*; ~ *than*, different from● *some day (time) or* ~, one day; some time. *adv*. ~*wise*; in a different way● *I could not treat him* ~ *than fairly* ~**·wise** ['ʌðəwaɪz] *adv*. differently; i●

different conditions; in ~ respects. *adj.* different.

ot·ter ['ɒtə*] *n.* fur-covered, fish-eating water-animal with four webbed feet; its fur.

ot·to·man ['ɒtəʊmən] *n.* long, cushioned seat without a back or arms, often used as a box.

ought [ɔːt] *v.aux.* (neg. ~ *not*, colloq. ~*n't*) **1.** (indicating obligation): *You ~ (~n't) to go.* **2.** (indicating what is advisable or right): *Your brother ~ to see (~ to have seen) a doctor at once.* **3.** (indicating probability): *If he started an hour ago he ~ to be here soon.*

ounce [aʊns] (abbr. *oz.*) *n.* unit of weight, one-sixteenth of a pound avoirdupois or one-twelfth of a pound troy (= 28.35 grams).

our ['aʊə*] *poss. pron. attrib.* of or belonging to us, that we are concerned with, etc. ~s ['aʊəz] *poss. pron. pred.* (the one or ones) belonging to us. ~selves [ˌaʊə'selvz] *pron. & refl.*

-our (U.S.A. **-or**) [-ə*] *suff.* (forming ns.) condition; activity: *colour*; *demeanour*.

-ous [-əs] *suff.* (forming adjs.) full of; abounding in; having; possessing the qualities of: *dangerous*; *murderous*; *poisonous*.

oust [aʊst] *v.t.* drive or push (sb.) out (*from* his employment, position, etc.).

out [aʊt] *adv.* away from (not in or at) a place; not in the usual condition; at an end; exhausted, etc.: ~ *of*, without; beyond; not in: ~ *of date*, old-fashioned; not now being used, etc.; ~*-of-date* (attrib. adj.); ~ *of breath*, breathless; breathing fast; ~ *of doors*, in the open air; ~ *of one's mind* (*senses*), mad; ~ *of temper*, angry; ~*-of-the-way*, remote; (fig.) uncommon; unusual; *have sth. ~ with sb.*, discuss a matter under dispute till an understanding is reached. *v.t. & i.* put out; (sl. or colloq.) eject by force; become known: *The truth will ~. ~·er* ['aʊtə*] *adj.* of or for the ~side; farther from the middle or inside: ~*er garments* (*wear*) (worn over other clothes); *the ~er suburbs*; ~*er space*, universe beyond the earth's atmosphere. ~*·er·most adj.* farthest from the inside or centre.

◆ut- [aʊt-] *pref.* **1.** located outside: *outhouse.* **2.** in a manner that goes beyond, surpasses, or excels: *outnumber*; *outrun.* **3.** various senses: *outcry*; *outspoken.*

◆ut·bid [ˌaʊt'bɪd] *v.t.* (-*dd*-; p.t. & p.p. -*bid*) bid (a1) higher than (sb. else) at a sale.

out·board ['aʊtbɔːd] *attrib. adj. & adv.* on or towards the outside of an aircraft, a ship, or vehicle: ~ *motor*, motor mounted (2) at the stern outside the boat.

out·bound ['aʊtbaʊnd] *adj.* (of ships) outward (2) bound.

out·break ['aʊtbreɪk] *n.* breaking out (see *break*, v. (2)) (of war, disease, etc.).

out·build·ing ['aʊtˌbɪldɪŋ] *n.* small building (e.g. shed, stable) separate from the main building.

out·burst ['aʊtbɜːst] *n.* bursting out (see *burst*, v. (2)) (of steam, anger, etc.).

out·cast ['aʊtkɑːst] *n. & adj.* (person or animal) driven out from home or society; homeless and friendless (vagabond).

out·class [ˌaʊt'klɑːs] *v.t.* be much better than; surpass.

out·come ['aʊtkʌm] *n.* effect or result of an event, of circumstances.

out·crop ['aʊtkrɒp] *n.* that part of a layer or vein (of rock, etc.) that can be seen above the ground's surface.

out·cry ['aʊtkraɪ] *n.* loud shout (of fear, etc.); public protest (*against*).

out·dis·tance [ˌaʊt'dɪstəns] *v.t.* travel faster than, and so leave (e.g. other runners in a race) far behind.

out·do [ˌaʊt'duː] *v.t.* (p.t. -*did*, p.p. -*done*) do more or better than: *not to be outdone*, not willing to let sb. else do better.

out·door ['aʊtdɔː*] *attrib. adj.* for, done in, the open air: ~ *games*; *live an ~ life.* ~s [ˌaʊt'dɔːz] *adv.* outside, in the open air.

out·er, out·er·most, see **out.**

out·face [ˌaʊt'feɪs] *v.t.* face boldly; stare at (sb.) until he turns his eyes away.

out·fit ['aʊtfɪt] *n.* **1.** all the clothing or articles needed for a purpose: *a camping ~*; *his school ~.* **2.** (colloq.) group of persons regarded as a unit; (U.S.A.) military unit. ~·ter *n.* shopkeeper selling (esp. men's) clothes.

out·flank [ˌaʊt'flæŋk] *v.t.* go or pass round the flank of (the enemy).

out·go·ing ['aʊtˌgəʊɪŋ] *adj.* going out; leaving: *the ~ tenant*; *the ~ ship* (*tide*).

out·grow [ˌaʊt'grəʊ] *v.t.* (p.t. -*grew*, p.p. -*grown*) grow too tall or too large for (e.g. one's clothes); grow faster or taller than (e.g. one's brother); leave behind, as one grows older (bad habits, childish interests, opinions, etc.).

out·growth ['aʊtgrəʊθ] *n.* **1.** natural development or product. **2.** that which grows out of sth.; offshoot.

out·house ['aʊthaʊs] *n.* stable, barn, etc. adjoining a main building.

out·ing ['aʊtɪŋ] *n.* go away from home for a short pleasure trip: *go for an ~; an ~ to the seaside.*

out·land·ish [aʊt'lændɪʃ] *adj.* looking or sounding strange or foreign.

out·last [,aʊt'lɑːst] *v.t.* last or live longer than.

out·law ['aʊtlɔː] *n.* (olden times) person punished by being placed outside the protection of the law; criminal. *v.t.* condemn (sb.) as an ~.

out·lay ['aʊtleɪ] *n.* spending; money spent (on materials, work, etc.).

out·let ['aʊtlet] *n.* **1.** way out for water, steam, etc.: *the ~ of a lake.* **2.** means of or occasion for releasing (one's feelings, energies, etc.).

out·line ['aʊtlaɪn] *n.* **1.** line(s) showing the shape or boundary: *a map in ~.* **2.** statement of the chief facts, points, etc.: *an ~ for an essay; an ~ of world history. v.t.* draw in ~ (1); give an ~ (2) of.

out·live [,aʊt'lɪv] *v.t.* live longer than; live until (sth.) is forgotten.

out·look ['aʊtlʊk] *n.* **1.** view on which one looks out. **2.** what seems likely to happen. **3.** person's way of looking at a problem, etc.

out·ly·ing ['aʊt,laɪɪŋ] *adj.* far from a centre: *~ villages.*

out·num·ber [,aʊt'nʌmbə*] *v.t.* be greater in number than.

out·pa·tient ['aʊt,peɪʃnt] *n.* person visiting a hospital for treatment but not lodged there. (Cf. *in*¹ (III, 1): *in patient.*)

out·post ['aʊtpəʊst] *n.* (soldiers in an) observation post far from the main body (5) of troops; outlying or frontier settlement.

out·put ['aʊtpʊt] *v.t.* (-tt-; p.t. & p.p. ~ or ~ted) (of a computer) supply (data (2), results, etc.). *n.* **1.** quantity of goods, etc. produced. **2.** power, energy, etc. produced; data (2) produced from a computer. **3.** place where energy, data (2), etc. leaves a system.

out·rage ['aʊtreɪdʒ] *n.* **1.** (act of) extreme violence or cruelty: *~s committed by the mob.* **2.** act that shocks public opinion: *an ~ upon decency. v.t.* be guilty of an ~ upon; do sth. that shocks (public opinion, etc.).

out·ra·geous [aʊt'reɪdʒəs] *adj.* shocking; very cruel, shameless, immoral. *~·ly adv.*

out·right [aʊt'raɪt] *adv.* **1.** openly, with nothing held back: *tell sb. ~ what one thinks.* **2.** completely; at one time: *buy a house ~* (i.e. not by instalments); *kill sb. ~.* ['aʊtraɪt] *adj.* positive; thorough: *an ~ denial.*

out·run [,aʊt'rʌn] *v.t.* (-nn-; p.t. *-ran*, p.p. *-run*) run faster or farther than; exceed.

out·set ['aʊtset] *n.* start: *at (from) the ~.*

out·side [,aʊt'saɪd] *n., adj., adv., & prep.* (contrasted with *inside*) **I.** *n.* **1.** outer side or surface; outer part. **2.** *at the ~, at the most.* **II.** *adj.* **1.** of, on, nearer, the ~. **2.** greatest possible or probable. **3.** not connected with or included in a group: *We shall need ~ help* (extra workers). **4.** (of a chance) very unlikely. **5.** (of a football player) positioned nearest to the edge of the field: *~ left (right).* **III.** *adv.* on or to the ~: *Let's go ~!* **IV.** *prep.* **1.** at or on the outer side of: *~ the house.* **2.** beyond the limits of. **out·sid·er** *n.* **1.** person who is not, or is not considered fit to be, a member of a group, society, etc. **2.** competitor thought to have no chance in a race or competition.

out·size(d) ['aʊtsaɪz(d)] *adjs.* (esp. of articles of clothing) unusually large.

out·skirts ['aʊtskɜːts] *n. pl.* borders or outlying parts, esp. of a town.

out·spok·en [,aʊt'spəʊkən] *adj.* saying freely what one thinks; frank.

out·spread [,aʊt'spred] *adj.* spread out; extended.

out·stand·ing [,aʊt'stændɪŋ] *adj.* **1.** in a position to be easily noticed; attracting notice: *~ features of the landscape.* **2.** (of problems, work, payments, etc.) still to be attended to.

out·stay [,aʊt'steɪ] *v.t.* stay longer than: *~ one's welcome,* stay too long.

out·stretched ['aʊtstretʃt] *adj.* stretched out; extended: *with ~ arms.*

out·strip [,aʊt'strɪp] *v.t.* (-pp-) do better than; pass (sb.) in a race, etc.

out·ward ['aʊtwəd] *adj.* **1.** of or on the outside. **2.** going out: *the ~ voyage.* *~(s) adv.* towards the outside; away from home or the centre. *~·ly adv.* on the surface; to all appearances.

out·weigh [,aʊt'weɪ] *v.t.* be greater in weight, value, or importance than.

out·wit [,aʊt'wɪt] *v.t.* (-tt-) get the better of by being cleverer or more cunning.

out·work ['aʊtwɜːk] *n.* part of a military defence system away from the centre: *the ~s of the castle.*

oval ['əʊvl] *n. & adj.* (plane¹ figure or outline that is) egg-shaped or shaped like an ellipse.

ova·tion [əʊ'veɪʃn] *n.* enthusiastic expression of welcome or approval.

ov·en ['ʌvn] *n.* enclosed, box-like space that is heated for baking food, etc.

over ['əʊvə*] *adv. & prep.* I. *adv.*
1. (indicating movement from an upright position, loss of balance, change from one side to the other, a twist): *fall ~, cross ~, change ~, roll ~ (and ~)*. 2. (indicating motion upwards and outwards): *boil ~*. 3. from beginning to end: *Think it (Read it) ~*. 4. (indicating repeated action): *Count it ~* (again). *(all) ~ again*, (do sth.) a second time; *~ and ~ again*, repeatedly. 5. remaining: *Is there any bread (left) ~?* 6. ended: *The meeting was ~ by ten o'clock*. 7. more than is usual or necessary (see *over-* (2)). 8. in characteristic manner: *that is James all ~*. 9. on the whole surface: *I ache all ~ my body*. 10. across (a street or other space or distance): *Take this ~ to the post office*. *swim ~ to the other side of the river*; *ask sb. ~* (to come as a visitor from a place not far off). II. *prep.* resting on, and partly or completely covering, a surface; at or to a level higher than, but not touching; in or across every part of; from one side to the other of; in command of: *ruling ~ a vast country*; throughout but not beyond: *stay ~ Sunday* (i.e. depart on Monday); more than: *speaking for ~ an hour*; *~ and above*, in addition to. *n.* (cricket) number of balls bowled in succession by each bowler in turn (4).
over- ['əʊvə*-] *pref.* 1. above; across: *overhead*; *overland*. 2. too (much): *overdose*; *overfull*; *overheated*; *overpolite*; *overtired*. 3. various senses: *overpower*; *overthrow*.
over·act [,əʊvər'ækt] *v.t. & i.* act in an exaggerated way: *~ing (in) his part*.
over·all[1] ['əʊvərɔːl] *adj.* from end to end; including everything: *~ length (measurements)*.
over·all[2] ['əʊvərɔːl] *n.* 1. (Gt. Brit.) loose-fitting garment worn over ordinary clothes to keep them clean. 2. (pl.) outer trousers of strong material, usu. with a bib and shoulder-straps, worn as a protection from dirt while working.
over·awe [,əʊvər'ɔː] *v.t.* overcome or restrain with awe.
over·bal·ance [,əʊvə'bæləns] *v.t. & i.* 1. (cause to) lose balance; fall over. 2. (esp. fig.) outweigh: *The losses ~d the gains*.
over·bear [,əʊvə'beə*] *v.t.* (p.t. *-bore*, p.p. *-borne*) overcome (by forcible argument, strong force, or authority): *objections overborne in the argument*. *~ing adj.* masterful; forcing others to one's will: *an ~ing manner*.

over·board ['əʊvəbɔːd] *adv.* over the side of a ship into the water: *fall ~*.
over·book [,əʊvə'bʊk] *v.t.* make more reservations for accommodations than are actually available in (an aircraft, a ship, or hotel, etc.).
over·cast ['əʊvəkɑːst] *adj.* (of the sky, and fig.) darkened (as) by clouds.
over·charge [,əʊvə'tʃɑːdʒ] *v.t. & i.* 1. charge (sb.) too high a price. 2. fill or load too heavily: *~ a gun*; *~ an electric circuit*.
over·coat ['əʊvəkəʊt] *n.* long coat worn out of doors over ordinary clothes in cold weather.
over·come [,əʊvə'kʌm] *v.t. & i.* (p.t. *-came*, p.p. *-come*) 1. get the better of; be too strong for: *~ the enemy (bad habits)*. 2. make weak: *be ~ by emotion*. 3. be victorious.
over·do [,əʊvə'duː] *v.t.* (p.t. *-did*, p.p. *-done*) do too much; exaggerate; cook (meat) too much.
over·draft ['əʊvədrɑːft] *n.* amount of money by which a bank account is overdrawn.
over·draw [,əʊvə'drɔː] *v.t. & i.* (p.t. *-drew*, p.p. *-drawn*) 1. draw a cheque for a sum in excess of (one's account at a bank). 2. exaggerate.
over·dress [,əʊvə'dres] *v.t. & i.* dress too showily.
over·due [,əʊvə'djuː] *adj.* beyond the time fixed (for arrival, payment, etc.).
over·flow [,əʊvə'fləʊ] *v.t. & i.* 1. flow over; flow over the edges or limits; flood; spread beyond the limits of: *a river ~ing its banks*. 2. (of kindness, harvest, etc.) be very abundant: *a heart ~ing with gratitude*. ['əʊvəfləʊ] *n.* flowing over; sth. that flows over: *the ~ of population*.
over·grown [,əʊvə'grəʊn] *adj.* 1. having grown too fast: *an ~ boy*. 2. covered (with sth. that has grown over): *flower-beds ~ with weeds*.
over·hang [,əʊvə'hæŋ] *v.t. & i.* (p.t. & p.p. *-hung*) stick out over; be over like a shelf: *~ing branches*; *cliffs ~ing a river*.
over·haul [,əʊvə'hɔːl] *v.t.* 1. examine thoroughly in order to learn about the condition of; put into good condition: *~ an engine*. 2. overtake. ['əʊvəhɔːl] *n.* thorough examination for repairs, etc.
over·head ['əʊvəhed] *adj.* 1. raised above the ground: *~ cables*; *an ~ railway* (built on supports above street level). 2. *~ expenses (charges)*, (comm.) those needed for carrying on a business (e.g. for rent, advertising, salaries, light, and heating), not manufacturing

costs. [ˌəʊvə'hed] *adv.* above one's head; in the sky: *the stars ~.*

over·hear [ˌəʊvə'hɪə*] *v.t.* (p.t. & p.p. -heard) hear without the knowledge of the speaker(s); hear what one is not intended to hear; hear by chance.

over·joyed [ˌəʊvə'dʒɔɪd] *adj.* greatly delighted (*at sth.*).

over·kill ['əʊvəkɪl] *n.* capacity greatly exceeding what is needed to annihilate the enemy.

over·land ['əʊvəlænd] *adj. &* [ˌəʊvə-'lænd] *adv.* (proceeding) by land (not by sea): *an ~ route; travel ~.*

over·lap [ˌəʊvə'læp] *v.t. & i.* (-pp-) partly cover and extend beyond one edge: *~ping tiles (boards).*

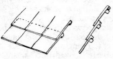

overlapping tiles

over·lay [ˌəʊvə'leɪ] *v.t.* (p.t. & p.p. -laid) put a coating or layer over the surface of.

over·leaf [ˌəʊvə'liːf] *adv.* on the other side of a leaf (of a book).

over·look [ˌəʊvə'lʊk] *v.t.* **1.** have a view of from above: *~ing the harbour.* **2.** fail to see or notice; pay no attention to: *~ an error.* **3.** let pass without punishing: *~ sb.'s wrongdoing.*

over·night [ˌəʊvə'naɪt] *adv.* **1.** on the night before: *get everything ready ~.* **2.** for the night: *Can you stay ~? adj.* during or for the night: *an ~ journey; an ~ stop.*

over·pass ['əʊvəpɑːs] *n.* flyover.

over·power [ˌəʊvə'paʊə*] *v.t.* overcome; be too strong for. *~ing adj.* too strong; very powerful: *an ~ing stink.*

over·rate [ˌəʊvə'reɪt] *v.t.* put too high a value on (e.g. sb.'s abilities).

over·reach [ˌəʊvə'riːtʃ] *v.t.* **1.** get the better of (by trickery). **2.** *~ oneself*, fail in one's object, damage one's own interests, by being too ambitious; *~ the mark*, go past it.

over·ride [ˌəʊvə'raɪd] *v.t.* (p.t. -rode, p.p. -ridden) prevail over (sb.'s opinions, decisions, wishes, claims, etc.).

over·rule [ˌəʊvə'ruːl] *v.t.* decide against (esp. by using one's higher authority): *objections ~d by the judge; ~d by the majority.*

over·run [ˌəʊvə'rʌn] *v.t.* (-nn-; p.t. -ran, p.p. -run) **1.** spread over and occupy or injure: *a country ~ by enemy*

troops; *a garden ~ with weeds.* **2.** g⟨ beyond (a limit): *speakers who ~ th⟨ time allowed.*

over·sea(s) [ˌəʊvə'siː(z)] *adjs.* (at, to from, for, places) across the sea: *~ education (trade, etc.).* *advs.* go *(live come from) overseas* (across the sea abroad).

over·see [ˌəʊvə'siː] *v.t.* (p.t. -saw, p.p -seen) look after, control (work, work men). *~r* ['əʊvəˌsɪə*] *n.* foreman.

over·sight ['əʊvəsaɪt] *n.* failure t⟨ notice sth.: *Your letter was unanswere⟨ through an ~.*

over·size(d) ['əʊvəsaɪz(d)] *adjs.* o⟨ more than the usual size.

over·sleep [ˌəʊvə'sliːp] *v.i. & refl* (p.t. & p.p. -slept) sleep too long; slee⟨ beyond the time for waking: *He over slept (himself) and was late for work*

over·state [ˌəʊvə'steɪt] *v.t.* state to⟨ much or more than is true about exaggerate. *~ment n.*

over·step [ˌəʊvə'step] *v.t.* (-pp-) g⟨ beyond: *~ one's authority.*

over·strung [ˌəʊvə'strʌŋ] *adj.* (of person, his nerves) intensely strained quickly and easily excited.

overt ['əʊvɜːt] *adj.* done openly publicly, not secretly. *~ly adv.*

over·take [ˌəʊvə'teɪk] *v.t.* (p.t. -took p.p. -taken) **1.** come or catch up with outstrip: *~ other cars on the road (ar rears of work).* **2.** (of storms, troubles etc.) come upon (sb.) suddenly, b⟨ surprise.

over·tax [ˌəʊvə'tæks] *v.t.* tax (1) to⟨ heavily; put too great a burden o⟨ strain on: *~ one's strength (patience)*

over·throw [ˌəʊvə'θrəʊ] *v.t.* (p.⟨ -threw, p.p. -thrown) defeat; put a⟨ end to; cause to fail or fall: *~ th⟨ government.* ['əʊvəθrəʊ] *n.* defeat fall; ruin.

over·time ['əʊvətaɪm] *n.* (no pl.) *&* *adv.* (time spent at work) after th⟨ usual hours: *earning extra for ~ working ~.*

over·ture ['əʊvəˌtjʊə*] *n.* **1.** (often pl esp. *make ~s to*) approach made *to* sb with the aim of starting discussions *peace ~s.* **2.** musical composition playe⟨ as an introduction to an opera or a⟨ a concert.

over·turn [ˌəʊvə'tɜːn] *v.t. & i.* **1** (cause) to turn over; upset: *He ~ed th⟨ boat. The boat ~ed.* **2.** (fig.) overthrow destroy.

over·weight ['əʊvəweɪt] *n.* excessiv⟨ or extra weight. [ˌəʊvə'weɪt] *adj.* be yond the weight allowed or normal *the luggage (that person) is ~.*

over·whelm [ˌəʊvəˈwelm] *v.t.* weigh down; submerge; overcome completely: ⁓ed by grief (*sb.'s kindness*); ⁓ed by the enemy's forces; an ⁓ing victory.

over·work [ˌəʊvəˈwɜːk] *v.t. & i.* (cause to) work too hard or too long: ⁓ oneself (*a horse*). *n.* (no pl.) excessive work.

over·wrought [ˌəʊvəˈrɔːt] *adj.* tired out by too much work or excitement; in a state of nervous illness.

owe [əʊ] *v.t. & i.* **1.** be in debt to (sb.) (*for* sth.); be in debt (*for* sth.): *owing £50 to one's tailor for an overcoat*; *owing one's tailor £50*; ⁓ *one's success to hard work*; *owing for his house.* **2.** be under obligation to give: ⁓ *loyalty to the king.* **ow·ing** *adj.* still to be paid. **ow·ing to** *prep.* because of.

owl [aʊl] *n.* night-flying bird with large eyes that lives on mice and small birds.

an owl　　　　　　an oyster

own [əʊn] *adj.* (used with possessives to give emphasis to the ownership or special character of sth.): *This is my pen; it's my ⁓ (pen), my very ⁓ and no one else's. This is all my ⁓ work* (i.e. nobody helped me). *hold one's ⁓*, keep one's position against attack; not be defeated or overcome; not lose strength; *on one's ⁓*, independent(ly); without a companion. *v.t. & i.* **1.** possess: ⁓ *a house.* **2.** agree; confess; recognize: ⁓ *that a claim is justified*; ⁓ *to having told a lie*; ⁓ *up (to a fault, etc.)*, confess (to it). **⁓·er** *n.* person who ⁓s (1) sth. **⁓·er·less** *adj.* having no (known) ⁓er: ⁓erless dogs. **⁓·er·ship** *n.* of uncertain ⁓ership.

ox [ɒks] *n.* (pl. oxen [ˈɒksn]) **1.** general name for domestic cattle. (Cf. *cow, bull, bullock.*) **2.** (esp.) fully grown bullock, used as a draught animal.

ox·i·da·tion [ˌɒksɪˈdeɪʃn] *n.* (chem.) act or process of oxidizing; state or result of being oxidized.

ox·ide [ˈɒksaɪd] *n.* compound of oxygen with another element: *iron* ⁓. **ox·i·dize** [ˈɒksɪdaɪz] *v.t. & i.* (cause to) combine with oxygen; make or become rusty. **ox·i·di·za·tion** [ˌɒksɪdaɪˈzeɪʃn] *n.*

ox·y·gen [ˈɒksɪdʒən] *n.* (no pl.) gas without smell, colour, or taste, necessary for life.

oys·ter [ˈɔɪstə*] *n.* kind of shellfish, eaten uncooked, whose shell sometimes contains a pearl. (See the picture.)

oz. [ˈaʊns(ɪz)] (abbr. for) ounce(s).

ozone [ˈəʊzəʊn] *n.* (no pl.) form of oxygen with a sharp, refreshing smell; (popular use) pure, refreshing air as at the seaside.

P

pa [pɑː] *n.* (colloq., abbr. for) papa.

pace [peɪs] *n.* **1.** (distance covered by the foot in a) single step in walking or running. **2.** rate of walking, running, or (fig.) progress: *keep ~ with* (sb.), (lit. or fig.) keep up with; progress at the same speed as. **3.** (esp. of horses) way of walking, running, etc.: *put sb. through his ~s*, (fig.) test his abilities, etc. *v.i. & t.* **1.** walk with slow or regular steps: *~ (up and down) a room.* **2.** measure by taking ~s: *~ out (off) a distance.*

pa·cif·ic [pəˈsɪfɪk] *adj.* peaceful; making or loving peace. **pac·i·fi·ca·tion** [ˌpæsɪfɪˈkeɪʃn] *n.* (no pl.) making or becoming peaceful; bringing about a state of peace. **pac·i·fism** [ˈpæsɪfɪzəm] *n.* (no pl.) principle that war should and could be abolished. **pac·i·fist** [ˈpæsɪfɪst] *n.* believer in pacifism. **pac·i·fy** [ˈpæsɪfaɪ] *v.t.* calm and quieten. **pac·i·fi·er** [ˈpæsɪfaɪə*] *n.* (esp. U.S.A.) dummy teat for babies.

pack [pæk] *n.* **1.** bundle of things tied or wrapped up together for carrying; (U.S.A.) = ~et: *a ~ of cigarettes.* *~-horse, ~-animal,* one used for carrying ~s. **2.** number of dogs kept for hunting (*a ~ of hounds*) or of wild animals (e.g. wolves) that go about together; (usu. derog.) number of persons or things: *a ~ of thieves (liars, lies).* **3.** complete set of (usu. 52) playing-cards. *v.t. & i.* **1.** put (things) into a box, bundle, bag, etc.; fill (a box, bag, etc.) with things: *~ing his clothes for a journey; ~ing his trunks; start ~ing for the holidays.* **2.** crush or crowd (into a place): *~ing people into a railway carriage; crowds ~ing into the cinemas.* **3.** put soft material into or round to keep sth. safe or to prevent loss or leakage: *glass ~ed in straw; ~ a leaking joint in a pipe.* **4.** *~ sb. off, send sb. ~ing,* send him away quickly. **~·age** [ˈpækɪdʒ] *n.* parcel; bundle; bale; compact assembly of various units or elements. *~age deal,* transaction agreed to as a whole (including the less favourable items). *~age holiday*

(*tour*) (with a fixed route at a fixed price). **~·et** [ˈpækɪt] *n.* small bundle, esp. of letters or papers: *a postal ~et; a ~et of cigarettes.* **~·ing** *n.* (no pl.) process of ~ing (goods); material used in ~ing (3). '**~·ing-case** *n.* (usu. wooden) case for ~ing goods in.

pact [pækt] *n.* agreement.

pad [pæd] *n.* **1.** cushion-like container filled with soft material, used to prevent damage, give comfort, improve the shape of sth., etc. **2.** guard for the leg, in cricket and other games. **3.** number of sheets of writing-paper fastened together along one edge. **4.** soft, fleshy underpart of the foot (of dogs, foxes, etc.). **5.** platform for the launching of rockets, etc.: *a launching ~.* *v.t.* (*-dd-*) **1.** put ~(s) (1) on or in **2.** (often *~ out*) make (a sentence, essay, book, etc.) longer by using unnecessary words or material. **~·ding** *n.* (no pl.) material used for making ~s (1).

pad·dle [ˈpædl] *n.* short oar with a broad blade at one or each end. *v.t. & i.* **1.** send (a canoe) through the water by using a ~ or ~s. **2.** walk with bare feet in water; move the hands about in water. '**~·,steam·er** *n.* ship with ~-wheels. '**~·wheel** *n.* wheel fitted with boards that strike the water in turn and so send the ship forward.

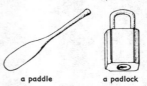

a paddle   a padlock

pad·dock [ˈpædək] *n.* small grass field (usu. for horses).

pad·dy [ˈpædɪ] *n.* (no pl.) growing rice; rice in the husk. '**~·field** *n.* rice-field.

pad·lock [ˈpædlɒk] *v.t. & n.* (fasten with a) removable lock that hangs by a pivoted hook and, when closed, holds sth. securely fastened.

pa·dre ['pɑːdrɪ] *n.* (army and navy, colloq.) chaplain; (colloq.) priest; clergyman.

pae·di·at·ric (U.S.A. **pe-**) [ˌpiːdɪ-ˈætrɪk] *adj.* of, relating to, children and their diseases. **~s** *n. pl.* (sg. or pl. v.) branch of medicine dealing with children and their diseases. **pae·di·a·tri·cian** [ˌpiːdɪə'trɪʃn], **pae·di·a·trist** ['piːdɪətrɪst] *ns.* (U.S.A. **pe-**) specialist in **~s**.

pa·gan ['peɪgən] *n. & adj.* (person who is) not a believer in one of the chief religions of the world. **~·ism** *n.* (no pl.) beliefs, practices, of **~s**.

page¹ [peɪdʒ] *n.* (one side of a) leaf of paper in a book, periodical, etc.

page² [peɪdʒ] *n.* (also **~-boy**) boy servant (in a club, hotel, etc.).

pag·eant ['pædʒənt] *n.* **1.** public entertainment, often outdoors, in which historical events are acted in the costume of the period. **2.** public celebration, esp. one in which there is a procession of persons in fine costumes (e.g. a coronation). **~·ry** *n.* rich, splendid display.

pa·go·da [pə'gəʊdə] *n.* (in India, Burma, China, Japan, etc.) sacred tower of several storeys.

a pagoda   a pail

paid, see *pay.*

pail [peɪl] *n.* bucket.

pain [peɪn] *n.* **1.** (no pl.) suffering of body or mind: *be in* **~**. **2.** particular or localized kind of bodily suffering: *a ~ in the left arm; ~s in the back.* **3.** (pl.) trouble: *take* **~s**, do one's best; work carefully. **4.** penalty: *on (under) ~ of (death),* with the risk of suffering (death). *v.t.* cause **~** to. **~ed** *adj.* distressed: *a ~ed look.* **~·ful** *adj.* causing **~** (*to* sb.). **~·ful·ly** *adv.* **~·less** *adj.* without **~**; causing no **~**. **~·less·ly** *adv.* '**~s·tak·ing** *adj.* taking trouble in doing sth.

paint [peɪnt] *n.* colouring matter (to be) mixed with oil or other liquid. *v.t. & i.* **1.** cover a surface with **~**: ~ *a door;* ~ *the town red,* (sl.) go out and celebrate

riotously. **2.** make a picture (of) with **~**: ~ *flowers.* **3.** colour with a cosmetic; apply a cosmetic to: ~ *one's mouth.* **4.** practice the art of **~ing**: ~ *for relaxation.* **5.** use cosmetics for adding colour: *She ~s heavily.* **~·er¹** *n.* person who **~s** (buildings, etc.); artist who **~s** (pictures). **~·ing** *n.* **~ed** picture; art of **~ing** pictures.

pain·ter² ['peɪntə*] *n.* rope by which a boat may be tied to a ship, pier, etc.

pair [peə*] *n.* **1.** two things of the same kind used together: *a ~ of shoes;* single article with two parts always joined: *a ~ of trousers (scissors).* **2.** two persons closely associated, e.g. a man and woman who are (about to be) married: *in ~s,* in twos. *v.t. & i.* form a ~ or **~s**; join in **~s**: *~ off,* arrange or go off in **~s**.

pa·ja·mas [pə'dʒɑːməz] (U.S.A.) = pyjamas.

pal [pæl] *n.* comrade; friend. *v.i.* (-ll-) ~ (*up*), (sl.) associate, become friendly (*with*).

pal·ace ['pælɪs] *n.* house of a ruler (e.g. a king) or a bishop; any large and splendid house. **pa·la·tial** [pə'leɪʃl] *adj.* of or like a **~**.

pal·ate ['pælət] *n.* **1.** roof of the mouth. **2.** sense of taste. **pal·at·able** ['pælə-təbl] *adj.* agreeable to the taste or the mind.

pa·la·ver [pə'lɑːvə*] *n.* conference, esp. between explorers and the people of the country. *v.i.* talk idly for a long time.

pale¹ [peɪl] *adj.* (**~r, ~st**) **1.** (of a person's face) having little colour; bloodless. **2.** (of colours) faint; not bright. *v.i.* become **~**; lose colour. **~·ness** *n.* (no pl.).

pale² [peɪl] *n.* **1.** long, pointed piece of wood used for fences. **2.** limits of what is considered good social behaviour: *beyond (outside) the* **~**. **pal·ing** *n.*, **pal·ings** *n. pl.* (fence of) **~s**.

palings

pal·ette ['pælət] *n.* board (with a hole for the thumb) on which an artist mixes his colours.

pal·i·sade [ˌpælɪ'seɪd] *n.* fence of strong, pointed, wooden stakes.

pall¹ [pɔːl] *v.i.* become uninteresting: *His long lecture ~ed on me.*

pall² [pɔːl] *n.* heavy cloth spread over a coffin; (fig.) any dark, heavy covering: *a ~ of smoke.*

pal·let¹ ['pælɪt], **pal·li·asse** ['pælɪæs] *ns.* straw-filled mattress for sleeping on.

pal·let² ['pælɪt] *n.* large, portable platform for storing or transporting goods (e.g. from a lorry into a train).

pal·li·ate ['pælɪeɪt] *v.t.* lessen the severity of (pain, disease); excuse the seriousness of (a crime, etc.). **pal·li·a·tion** [ˌpælɪ'eɪʃn] *n.* **pal·li·a·tive** ['pælɪətɪv] *n. & adj.* (sth.) serving to ~.

pal·lid ['pælɪd] *adj.* pale¹ (1); ill-looking.

pal·lor ['pælə*] *n.* (no pl.) paleness (of face).

palm¹ [pɑːm] *n.* inner part of the hand between wrist and fingers. *v.t. ~ sth. off on sb.,* persuade him, by trickery, to take sth. of little value. **~·ist** *n.* person who claims to tell a person's future by examining lines on his ~. **~·ist·ry** *n.* (no pl.) art of doing this.

palm² [pɑːm] *n.* **1.** sorts of tree growing in warm climates, with no branches and a mass of large, wide leaves at the top: *date-~; coconut ~.* **2.** ~-leaf as a symbol of victory: *carry off the ~,* be victorious or successful. *P~ Sunday,* Sunday before Easter. **~y** *adj.* (-ier, -iest) prosperous: *in my ~y days.*

pal·pa·ble ['pælpəbl] *adj.* that can be felt or touched; clear to the mind: *a ~ error.* **pal·pa·bly** *adv.*

pal·pi·tate ['pælpɪteɪt] *v.i.* (of the heart) beat rapidly; (of a person, his body) tremble (with terror, etc.). **pal·pi·ta·tion** [ˌpælpɪ'teɪʃn] *n.* palpitating of the heart (from disease, great efforts).

pal·ter ['pɔːltə*] *v.i. ~ with,* trifle with; be insincere when dealing with.

pal·try ['pɔːltrɪ] *adj.* (-ier, -iest) worthless; of no importance; contemptible.

pam·pas ['pæmpəs] *n. pl.* wide, treeless plains of S. America.

pam·per ['pæmpə*] *v.t.* indulge too much; be unduly kind to.

pamph·let ['pæmflɪt] *n.* small paper-covered book, esp. on a topical question. **pam·phle·teer** [ˌpæmflə'tɪə*] *n.* writer of ~s.

pan [pæn] *n.* flat dish, often shallow and without a cover, used for cooking and other household purposes. **'~·cake** *n.* batter fried in a pan (and usu. eaten hot).

pan- [pæn-] *pref.* of or for all: *pan-American.*

pan·a·cea [ˌpænə'sɪə] *n.* remedy for all diseases, troubles, etc.

pan·da ['pændə] *n.* bear-like, black-and-white mammal of Tibet. **~ car** *n.* (Gt. Brit.) police patrol car (with a broad, white stripe over the body (4)).

pan·de·mo·nium [ˌpændɪ'məʊnjəm] *n.* (scene of) wild and noisy disorder.

pan·der ['pændə*] *v.i. ~ to,* indulge (sb.); minister to (sb.'s) unworthy desires or tastes: *newspapers that ~ to our interest in crime.*

pane [peɪn] *n.* single sheet of glass in (a division of) a window.

pan·e·gyr·ic [ˌpænɪ'dʒɪrɪk] *n.* speech, piece of writing, praising a person or event.

pan·el ['pænl] *n.* **1.** separate part of the surface of a door, wall, ceiling, etc. usu. raised above or sunk below the surrounding area. **2.** board for controls and instruments: *control ~* (on a radio or television set); *instrument ~* (of an aircraft or motor vehicle). **3.** (list of names of) persons appointed to serve on a jury, take part in a discussion, a game, etc. on the radio or on television: *a ~ discussion (game).* *v.t.* (-ll-, U.S.A. also -l-) put ~s on or in. **~·ling** (U.S.A. **~·ing**) *n.* (no pl.) **~·led** work. **~·list** (U.S.A. **~·ist**) *n.* member of a discussion or advisory **~** (3) or of a radio or television **~** (3).

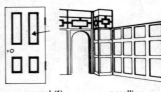

a panel (1)　　　　panelling

pang [pæŋ] *n.* sharp, sudden feeling of pain or remorse.

pan·ic ['pænɪk] *n.* unreasoning, uncontrolled, quickly-spreading fear. *adj.* (of fear) unreasoning. *v.t. & i.* (-ck-) affect or be affected with ~: *Don't ~!* **~·ky** *adj.* affected with ~. **'~-,strick·en** *adj.* overcome by ~; terrified.

pan·nier ['pænɪə*] *n.* **1.** one of a pair of baskets placed across the back of a horse or ass for carrying things in. **2.** one of a pair of bags on either side of the back of a bicycle or motor cycle.

pan·o·ply ['pænəplɪ] *n.* full suit of armour; (fig.) complete equipment.

pan·ora·ma [ˌpænə'rɑːmə] *n.* wide,

paradox

uninterrupted view; constantly changing scene: *the ~ of London life.*
pan·sy ['pænzɪ] *n.* flowering plant.

a pansy

pant [pænt] *v.t. & i.* **1.** take short, quick breaths. **2.** have a strong wish (*for* sth., *to do* sth.). **3.** say while ~ing: *~ing out his message. n.* short, quick breath; gasp.
pan·the·ism ['pænθɪːɪzəm] *n.* (no pl.) belief that God is in everything.
pan·ther ['pænθə*] *n.* leopard; (U.S.A.) puma.
pant·ies ['pæntɪz] *n. pl.* (colloq.) short knickers worn by women and girls; short trousers worn by children.
panti·hose, panty-hose ['pæntɪhəʊz] *n.* tights.
pan·to·mime ['pæntəmaɪm] *n.* **1.** drama, based on a fairy-tale, with music, dancing, and clowning. **2.** acting without words.
pan·try ['pæntrɪ] *n.* **1.** room in which silver, glass, table-linen, etc. are kept. **2.** room in which food is kept.
pants [pænts] *n. pl.* (colloq.) **1.** trousers: *pant(s) suit,* trouser suit; *pantskirt,* divided skirt resembling trousers. **2.** (Gt. Brit.) under~. **3.** panties.
pap [pæp] *n.* (no pl.) soft food for babies.
pa·pa [pə'pɑ:] *n.* (child's word for) father.
pa·pa·cy ['peɪpəsɪ] *n.* position of, authority of, the pope; system of government by popes. **pa·pal** ['peɪpl] *adj.* of the pope or the ~.
pa·pa·ya [pə'paɪə], **pa·paw** [pə'pɔ:], **paw·paw** ['pɔ:pɔ:] *ns.* tropical tree; its fruit, green outside and yellow inside.
pa·per ['peɪpə*] *n.* **1.** (no pl.) substance manufactured from wood-pulp, rags, etc. and used in sheets for writing, printing, wrapping, etc.: *a sheet of ~; a ~ bag.* **2.** newspaper. **3.** (pl.) documents showing who sb. is, what authority he has, etc. **4.** sth. written about a problem, etc. to be read aloud to a learned society, etc. **5.** set of examination questions on a given sub-

ject: *The biology ~ was difficult. v.t.* paste ~ on (walls, etc.). '~·back *n. & adj.* (book) bound in ~ covers (opp. *hardback*). '~·clip *n.* see *clip*[1]. '~·,hang·er *n.* man whose trade is to put wall~ on walls of rooms. '~·knife *n.* blunt one for slitting folded paper, etc. ~ mon·ey *n.* see *money*. '~·weight *n.* weight placed on loose ~s to prevent their being blown away.
pa·pier mâ·ché [ˌpæpjeɪ 'mæʃeɪ] (Fr.) *n.* (no pl.) paper pulped and used as a plastic material.
pa·pist ['peɪpɪst] *n.* (unfriendly word for a) member of the Roman Catholic Church.
pa·py·rus [pə'paɪərəs] *n.* **1.** (no pl.) (kind of paper made in ancient Egypt from a) tall water-plant or reed. **2.** (pl. -ri [pə'paɪəraɪ]) manuscript written on this.
par [pɑ:*] *n.* (no pl.) **1.** average or normal amount, degree, etc.: *above* (*at, below*) ~, (of shares) above (at, below) the original price. **2.** *on a ~ with,* equal to.
par·a·ble ['pærəbl] *n.* story designed to teach a moral lesson.
para·chute ['pærəʃuːt] *n.* apparatus (1) used for a jump from an aircraft or for dropping supplies. **para·chut·ist** *n.*

| a parachute | parallel lines | a parallel-ogram |

pa·rade [pə'reɪd] *v.t. & i.* **1.** gather (troops) together for drilling, etc.; march in procession with display. **2.** make a display of; try to attract attention to: *~ one's abilities. n.* **1.** parading of troops: *on ~. ~·ground,* area used for this. **2.** wide, often ornamental pathway, esp. on a sea front. **3.** display (of one's wealth, virtues, etc.) made to impress.
par·a·dise ['pærədaɪs] *n.* **1.** Garden of Eden. **2.** heaven. **3.** any place of perfect happiness.
par·a·dox ['pærədɒks] *n.* statement that seems to say sth. opposite to the truth but which may contain a truth

(e.g. 'More haste, less speed'). **~·i·cal** [,pærə'dɒksɪkl] *adj.*

par·af·fin ['pærəfɪn] *n.* (no pl.) ~ oil, oil obtained from coal or petroleum.

par·a·gon ['pærəgən] *n.* apparently perfect example of a person or thing.

para·graph ['pærəgrɑːf] *n.* division of a composition (usu. a group of several sentences dealing with one main idea) started on a new line.

par·a·keet ['pærəkiːt] *n.* sorts of small, long-tailed parrot.

par·al·lel ['pærəlel] *adj.* 1. (of lines) continuing at the same distance from one another; (of one line) having this relation (*to* another). 2. exactly corresponding (*to*). *n.* 1. ~ *of latitude*, line on a map ~ to the equator and passing through all places the same distance north or south of it. 2. person, event, etc. precisely similar (*to*). 3. comparison: *draw a* ~ *between* ... *v.t.* 1. be ~ to. 2. produce sth. as a ~ (2) of. **~·o·gram** [,pærə'leləʊgræm] *n.* four-sided plane figure with opposite sides ~. (See the picture at *parachute*.)

pa·ral·y·sis [pə'rælɪsɪs] *n.* (no pl.) loss of feeling or power to move in any or every part of the body. **par·a·lyse** (U.S.A. **-lyze**) ['pærəlaɪz] *v.t.* affect with ~; make helpless. **par·a·lyt·ic** [,pærə'lɪtɪk] *n. & adj.* (person) suffering from ~.

par·a·mount ['pærəmaʊnt] *adj.* of supreme importance; having supreme authority.

par·a·pet ['pærəpɪt] *n.* (usu. low) protective wall at the edge of a flat roof, side of a bridge, etc.

par·a·pher·na·lia [,pærəfə'neɪljə] *n. pl.* (sometimes sing. v.) numerous small possessions, tools, esp. concerning sb.'s hobby or technical work.

para·phrase ['pærəfreɪz] *v.t. & n.* (give a) restatement of the meaning of (a piece of writing) in other words.

par·a·site ['pærəsaɪt] *n.* 1. animal or plant living on or in another and getting its food from it. 2. person supported by another and giving him nothing in return.

para·sol ['pærəsɒl] *n.* light umbrella used as a sunshade.

para·troops ['pærətruːps] *n. pl.* airborne soldiers trained to land by parachute. **para·troop·er** ['pærətruːpə*] *n.* member of these.

par·cel ['pɑːsl] *n.* 1. thing(s) wrapped and tied up for carrying, sending by post, etc. 2. *part and* ~ *of,* an essential part of. *v.t.* (*-ll-,* U.S.A. also *-l-*) ~ *out,* divide; distribute.

parch [pɑːtʃ] *v.t. & i.* 1. (of heat, the sun, etc.) make (the throat, the land) dry. 2. dry or roast by heating: ~*ed peas.* 3. become hot and dry.

parch·ment ['pɑːtʃmənt] *n.* (manuscript on) writing material made from the skin of a sheep or goat; ~-like paper.

par·don ['pɑːdn] *v.t.* forgive; excuse. *n.* forgiveness. **~·able** *adj.* that can be ~ed. **~·ably** *adv.*

pare [peə*] *v.t.* cut away the outer part, edge, or skin of: ~ *sth. down,* (fig.) reduce (e.g. one's expenditure). **par·ing** ['peərɪŋ] *n.* sth. ~d off: *nail parings.*

par·ent ['peərənt] *n.* father or mother; (fig.) origin. **~·age** ['peərəntɪdʒ] *n.* (no pl.) *of unknown* ~*age* (having unknown ~s). **pa·ren·tal** [pə'rentl] *adj.* of a ~. **~·s-in-law** *n. pl.* father and mother of one's husband or wife.

pa·ren·the·sis [pə'renθɪsɪs] *n.* (pl. *-ses* [-siːz]) sentence within another sentence, marked off by commas, dashes, or brackets; (pl.) the brackets ( ), used to mark off a ~: *in parentheses.* **par·en·thet·i·cal** [,pærən'θetɪkl] *adj.*

pa·ri·ah ['pærɪə] *n.* outcast.

par·ish ['pærɪʃ] *n.* division of a county with its own church and clergyman; division of a county for local government: ~ *church (council).* **par·ish·io·ner** [pə'rɪʃənə*] *n.* person living in a (particular) ~, esp. a member of the ~ church.

par·i·ty ['pærətɪ] *n.* (no pl.) equality; being equal; being at par.

park [pɑːk] *n.* 1. public garden or recreation ground in a town. 2. area of grassland with trees round a large country house. 3. (*car-*)~, place where motor cars, etc. may be left for a time. 4. *national* ~, area of natural beauty (e.g. mountains, forest) set apart by the State for public enjoyment. *v.t.* put or leave (a motor car, etc.) in a public place or in a car-~.

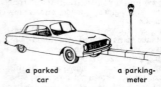

a parked car a parking-meter

par·ka ['pɑːkə] *n.* anorak.

park·ing ['pɑːkɪŋ] *n.* (no pl.) (area for the) leaving of motor cars, etc.: *Ample*

~ *is available.* no ~, ~ of motor cars, etc. is not allowed. **~ lot** *n.* (U.S.A.) outdoor car-park. '**~-,me·ter** *n.* coin-operated meter that registers the period for which a car is parked in a street. (See the picture.)

par·lance ['pɑːləns] *n. in common ~,* in the usual way of speaking.

par·ley ['pɑːlɪ] *n.* (pl. ~*s*) conference, esp. between leaders of opposed forces. *v.i.* discuss terms (*with* sb.).

par·lia·ment ['pɑːləmənt] *n.* (esp. in Great Britain and other countries with representative government) supreme law-making council or assembly, formed (in G.B.) of the House of Commons and the House of Lords. **par·lia·men·tar·i·an** [,pɑːləmən'teərɪən] *n.* person skilled in ~ary debate, rules, etc. **par·lia·men·ta·ry** [,pɑːlə'men-tərɪ] *adj.* of ~.

par·lour (U.S.A. **-lor**) ['pɑːlə*] *n.* sitting-room in a private house; private sitting-room at an inn. '**~-maid** *n.* female employee (in a private house) who waits at table. (Cf. *waitress*.)

pa·ro·chi·al [pə'rəʊkjəl] *adj.* of a parish; (fig.) limited; narrow: *a ~ outlook* (*mind*).

par·o·dy ['pærədɪ] *n.* (piece of) writing intended to amuse by imitating the style of writing used by sb. else; weak imitation. *v.t.* make a ~ of: *~ an author* (*a poem*). **par·o·dist** *n.*

pa·role [pə'rəʊl] *n.* prisoner's promise, if given freedom for a time without a guard, that he will return and not try to escape: *on ~,* liberated after making such a promise.

par·ox·ysm ['pærəksɪzəm] *n.* sudden attack or outburst (of pain, etc.).

par·quet ['pɑːkeɪ] *n.* flooring of wooden blocks fitted together like bricks to form a design.

par·ri·cide ['pærɪsaɪd] *n.* **1.** person who murders his father, near relation, or sovereign ruler. **2.** any of those crimes.

par·rot ['pærət] *n.* sorts of bird with a hooked bill and (usu.) brightly coloured feathers. Some kinds can be taught to imitate human speech; (fig.) person who repeats what others say.

par·ry ['pærɪ] *v.t.* turn aside (a blow, fig. a question).

parse [pɑːz] *v.t.* describe (a word, a sentence) grammatically and point out how the words are related.

par·si·mo·ny ['pɑːsɪmənɪ] *n.* (no pl.) (too much) care in the use of money,

goods, etc. **par·si·mo·ni·ous** [,pɑːsɪ-'məʊnjəs] *adj.* too economical.

pars·ley ['pɑːslɪ] *n.* garden plant whose leaves are used in sauces and for decorating food.

pars·nip ['pɑːsnɪp] *n.* sort of root vegetable.

par·son ['pɑːsn] *n.* parish priest; (colloq.) any (esp. Protestant) clergyman. **~·age** ['pɑːsnɪdʒ] *n.* ~'s house; vicarage.

part [pɑːt] *n.* **1.** some but not all of a thing or number of things: *for the most ~,* in most cases; mostly; *in ~,* in some degree. **2.** (pl.) *these* (*those*) ~*s,* this (that) ~ of the country; this (that) district. **3.** any one of a number of equal divisions: *A minute is the sixtieth ~ of an hour.* **4.** person's share in some activity; his duty or responsibility: *a man with a ~ in a play* (*in the recent conferences*); *on my* (*his,* etc.) ~*,* on the ~ *of Mr A.,* proceeding from, done by (me, him, Mr A.); *take ~ in* (an event, etc.), have a share in; help; *for my ~,* as far as I am concerned. **5.** what an actor in a play, cinema film, etc. says and does: *actors who are learning their ~s.* **6.** side in an agreement or dispute: *take sb.'s ~,* support him; approve of what he does, says, etc. **7.** *take sth. in good ~,* not be offended at it. **8.** essential part of a machine or other apparatus (1): (*spare*) ~*,* extra piece of a vehicle or machine, etc. (see *spare,* adj. (2)). **9.** division of a book, broadcast serial, etc., esp. as much as is issued or broadcast at one time: *a story in eight ~s.* **10.** (music) each of the melodies making up a harmony: *orchestra ~s*; melody for a particular voice or instrument: *the alto ~s.* **11.** ~ *of speech,* (gram.) one of the classes of words (e.g. noun, verb, adjective). *v.t. & i.* **1.** (cause to) separate or divide: ~ *a crowd. The crowd ~ed. Let's ~ friends* (i.e. separate without ill will). ~ *company* (*with*), (a) end a relationship (with); (b) disagree (with). **2.** ~ *one's hair,* make a dividing line by combing the hair in opposite ways. **3.** ~ *with,* give up; give away: *a man who won't ~ with his money.* **~·ing** *n.* (esp.) line where the hair is combed in opposite ways. **~·ly** *adv.* in ~; to some extent. '**~-song** *n.* song with different ~s for three or more voices to form a harmony. '**~-time** *adj. & adv.* for only ~ of the working week: *~-time teaching*; *working ~-time only.*

par·take [pɑː'teɪk] *v.i. & t.* (p.t. -*took,* p.p. -*taken*) **1.** have or take a share (*in* or *of* sth.). **2.** have some (*of* the food, drink, etc. provided): ~ *of a meal*. **3.** have some of the characteristics (*of* sth.).

par·tial ['pɑːʃl] *adj.* **1.** forming only a part; not complete: *a* ~ *success*. **2.** ~ *to*, having a liking or taste for. **3.** showing too much favour to one person or one side. **~·ly** *adv.* **par·tial·i·ty** [ˌpɑːʃɪ'ælətɪ] *n.* **1.** (no pl.) being ~ (3) in treatment, judgement, etc. **2.** special taste or liking (*for*).

par·tic·i·pate [pɑː'tɪsɪpeɪt] *v.i.* have a share, take part (*in* a common act, feeling, etc.): ~ *in sb.'s suffering*. **par·tic·i·pant** *n.* person who ~s. **par·tic·i·pa·tion** [pɑːˌtɪsɪ'peɪʃn] *n.* (no pl.).

par·ti·ci·ple ['pɑːtɪsɪpl] *n.* form of a verb: *'Writing' and 'written' are the present and past ~s of the verb 'write'.* **par·ti·cip·i·al** [ˌpɑːtɪ'sɪpɪəl] *adj.* of a ~: *participial adjective* (e.g. *loving* in 'a loving mother').

par·ti·cle ['pɑːtɪkl] *n.* **1.** very small bit: ~s *of dust.* **2.** (gram.) article (*a, an, the*), preposition or adverb (*up, in,* etc.), conjunction (*or*), or affix (*un-, in-, -ness, -ly*).

par·ti·col·oured ['pɑːtɪˌkʌləd] *adj.* differently coloured in different parts.

par·tic·u·lar [pə'tɪkjʊlə*] *adj.* **1.** relating to one as distinct from others: *in this* ~ *case.* **2.** special: *do sth. with* ~ *care; in* ~, especially. **3.** hard to satisfy: *very* ~ *about what he eats.* **4.** giving or showing great attention to detail: ~ *about what she wears.* **n.** detail: *go into* ~s, give details. **~·ize** *v.t.* give ~s of; name one by one. **~·ly** *adv.* especially; distinctly.

par·ti·san [ˌpɑːtɪ'zæn] *n.* **1.** person devoted to a party, group, or cause. **2.** member of an armed group that fights in secret against an enemy that has conquered its country.

par·ti·tion [pɑː'tɪʃn] *n.* **1.** (no pl.) division into parts: (pol.) *the* ~ *of Germany.* **2.** sth. that divides, esp. a thin wall between rooms, etc. **3.** part formed by dividing; section. *v.t.* divide: ~ed *off*, separated by means of a ~.

part·ner ['pɑːtnə*] *n.* **1.** person who takes part with another or others in some activity, esp. one of the owners of a business. **2.** one of two persons dancing together, playing tennis, cards, etc. together; husband or wife. *v.t.* be a ~ to. **~·ship** *n.* **1.** state of being a ~. **2.** joint business: *enter into* ~ship *with sb.*

par·tridge ['pɑːtrɪdʒ] *n.* sorts of bird of the same family as the pheasant; its flesh as food.

par·ty ['pɑːtɪ] *n.* **1.** body of persons united in opinion, in support of a cause, esp. in politics: *the* ~ *line*, the declared policy of a political ~. **2.** (no pl.) system of government based on political parties: *the* ~ *system; putting public interest before* ~. **3.** one of the persons or sides in a legal action, agreement, etc. **4.** group of persons travelling or working together: *a* ~ *line*, telephone line shared by two or more subscribers. **5.** meeting, by invitation, of a group of persons (e.g. at a private house) for pleasure: *a dinner* (*birthday, etc.*). ~. **6.** person taking part in or approving of an action: *a* ~ *to an action.* **7.** (humor.) person.

pass [pɑːs] *v.i. & t. & n.* **I.** *v.i. & t.* **1.** go past[2] (2), move towards and beyond (a person, place, or object): ~ing *through the village; after* ~ing *the post office.* **2.** give by handing: *P*~ (*me*) *the salt, please.* **3.** ~ *a remark*, speak (*about*); ~ *the time of day with*, give a greeting to. **4.** change (*from* one state of things to another); change (*into* another state of things). **5.** come to an end: *customs that are* ~ing. **6.** examine and accept; be examined and accepted (*in*): *The bill* ~ed. *Parliament* ~ed *the bill. The examiners* ~ed *the candidates. The boys* ~ed (*the examination*) *in French.* **7.** take place, be done or said (*between* persons). **8.** (of time) spend; be spent: *How shall we* ~ *the evening? Time* ~ed *quickly.* **9.** (cause to) circulate: *imprisoned for* ~ing *forged banknotes.* **10.** be beyond the range of; surpass: *a story that* ~es *belief.* **11.** give (an opinion, judgement, sentence *on* or *upon* sb. or sth.). **12.** (in football, etc.) kick, hand, or hit (the ball) to a player of one's own side. **13.** move; cause to go: ~ *one's hand across the forehead.* **14.** (with advs. & preps.) ~ *away*, die: *He* ~ed *away peacefully.* ~ *sb. or sth. by*, (a) go past, (b) pay no attention to; ~ *for*, be accepted as; ~ *off*, (a) (of events) take place without trouble: *The meeting of the strikers* ~ed *off quietly.* (b) disappear gradually; end: *The pain will soon* ~ *off.* (c) ~ *sth.* (*sb., oneself*) *off as*, represent falsely; get people to believe that (it, he, etc.) is sth. different; ~ *on*, (a) proceed on one's way; (b) die; (c) give or hand (sth. to sb. else): *a letter that was* ~ed *on to all the members of the family;* ~ *out*, (colloq.) faint; ~ *sth. or sb. over*,

pat

pay no attention to; overlook; ~ *through,* experience. **II.** *n.* **1.** success in satisfying examiners (without distinction or honours (7)): *a ~ in mathematics; a ~ degree.* **2.** (paper, ticket, etc. giving) permission or authority to travel, leave or enter a building, occupy a seat in a theatre, etc. **3.** (no pl.) serious condition: *Things have come to a sad (pretty) ~.* **4. come to ~,** happen; *bring to ~,* cause to happen. **5.** act of ~ing the ball from one player to another of the same team (in football, etc.). **6.** movement of the hand over or in front of sth. (as in conjuring, etc.). **7.** forward movement, blow (in fencing, etc.). **8.** narrow way over or between mountains. **~·able** ['pɑːsəbl] *adj.* **1.** (of roads, etc.) that can be ~ed over. **2.** that can be accepted as fairly good but not excellent. **~·ably** *adv.* '**~·book** *n.* (also *bank-book*) book with a customer's bank account record[2] (1). **pas·ser-by** [,pɑːsə'baɪ] *n.* (pl. *~ers-by*) person who goes past, esp. by chance. '**~·key** *n.* key opening a number of different locks. '**~·word** *n.* secret word which enables sb. to be known as a friend (e.g. by sentries).

pas·sage ['pæsɪdʒ] *n.* **1.** (no pl.) act of going past, through, or across; liberty or right to go through: *the ~ of time; bird of ~,* migratory bird. **2.** journey by sea or air: *book one's ~ to New York.* **3.** way through. **4.** (also *~way*) corridor. **5.** passing (6) of a bill so that it becomes law. **6.** short extract from a piece of writing.

pas·sen·ger ['pæsɪndʒə*] *n.* person being conveyed by bus, aircraft, train, ship, etc. **~ seat** *n.* (esp.) in motor vehicles the seat next to the driver's seat.

pas·sion ['pæʃn] *n.* **1.** (no pl.) strong feeling or enthusiasm, esp. of love, hate, or anger: *be filled with ~* (i.e. love) *for sb.* **2.** (with indef. art.) outburst of anger: *fly into a ~.* **3.** *the P~,* the suffering and death of Jesus. **~·ate** ['pæʃənət] *adj.* easily moved by ~; filled with, showing, ~.

pas·sive ['pæsɪv] *adj.* **1.** acted upon but not acting; not offering active resistance: *remain ~; ~ obedience; ~ resistance.* **2.** *~ voice,* (gram.) form used when the subject of the verb is affected, as in 'The letter *was written* yesterday'. *n.* (gram.) *~ voice.* **~·ly** *adv.* **pas·siv·i·ty** [pə'sɪvətɪ] *n.* (no pl.).

Pass·over ['pɑːs,əʊvə*] *n.* Jewish feast.

pass·port ['pɑːspɔːt] *n.* **1.** government document to be carried by a traveller abroad, giving personal particulars. **2.** (fig.) means of attaining (*to* favour, success, etc.).

past[1] [pɑːst] *adj.* of the time before the present; (gram.) expressing ~ action or state: *~ tense (participle).* *n.* **1.** ~ time; ~ events: *memories of the ~.* **2.** person's ~ life or experiences.

past[2] [pɑːst] *prep.* **1.** after: ~ *eleven o'clock.* **2.** up to and farther than: *walk ~ the church.* **3.** beyond: *pain that was ~ bearing* (too severe to be endured). *adv.* beyond in space; up to and farther than: *Walk (hurry, etc.) ~ and look the other way.*

paste [peɪst] *n.* (no pl.) **1.** soft mixture of flour, fat, etc. for making pastry. **2.** ~-like mixture made from meat, fish, etc. **3.** mixture of flour and water used for sticking things together, esp. paper on walls or boards. **4.** substance used in making artificial diamonds, etc. *v.t.* stick (things *down, together, on, etc.*) with ~ (3). '**~·board** *n.* (no pl.) cardboard.

pas·tel ['pæstel, attrib. 'pæstl] *n.* (picture drawn with) coloured chalk made into crayons: ~ *shades,* soft, light, delicate colours.

pas·teur·ize ['pæstəraɪz] *v.t.* rid (milk, etc.) from disease germs by using the heating method of Pasteur.

pas·tille ['pæstəl] *n.* small sweet, usu. containing medicine for the throat.

pas·time ['pɑːstaɪm] *n.* anything done to pass time pleasantly; game.

pas·tor ['pɑːstə*] *n.* minister (3) (esp. in a nonconformist church).

pas·tor·al ['pɑːstərəl] *adj.* **1.** of a bishop: ~ *letter* (to the members of his diocese); ~ *staff,* bishop's emblem, like a shepherd's staff or crook. **2.** of shepherds and country life: ~ *poetry.* *n.* ~ poem or drama.

past·ry ['peɪstrɪ] *n.* **1.** (no pl.) paste of flour, fat, etc. baked in an oven, with fruit, meat, etc. **2.** article(s) of food made wholly or partly of this (e.g. pie(s), tart(s), etc.).

pas·ture ['pɑːstʃə*] *n.* grassland for cattle; grass on such land. *v.t. & i.* put (cattle, sheep, etc.) on ~; (of animals) eat the grass on (a ~); graze. **pas·tur·age** ['pɑːstjʊrɪdʒ] *n.* = ~.

pasty[1] ['peɪstɪ] *adj.* (-ier, -iest) like paste (1). *a ~ complexion,* white and unhealthy.

pas·ty[2] ['pæstɪ] *n.* meat covered in paste (1) and baked.

pat[1] [pæt] *v.t. & i.* (-tt-) hit gently again and again with the open hand or with something flat; beat lightly

(*upon*): ~ *a dog*; ~ *sb. on the back*. **n.**
1. touch of this kind. **2.** small mass of
sth., esp. butter, shaped by ~ting it.
pat² [pæt] **adv.** at the right moment;
at once and without hesitation: *The
answer came ~.*

patch [pætʃ] **n. 1.** small piece of material put on over a hole or damaged
place. **2.** differently coloured part of
a surface: *a dog with a white ~ on its
neck.* **3.** small area of ground, esp. for
gardening: *the cabbage ~*; small area
of anything: *~es of fog.* **4.** *not a ~ on*,
not nearly so good as. **v.t. 1.** put a ~ or
~es on. **2.** ~ *up*, make roughly ready for
use: *an old ~ed-up motor bicycle*; *~ up
a quarrel*, (fig.) settle it for a time.
'~·work n. piece of material made of
bits of cloth of various sizes, shapes,
and colours sewn together. **~y adj.**
(-ier, -iest) (fig., of work) of uneven
quality.

pate [peɪt] **n.** (old use or colloq.)
head.

pa·tent¹ ['peɪtənt, 'pætənt] **adj. 1.** evi-
dent, easily seen: *It was ~ that he disliked
the idea.* **2.** *letters ~* (usu. ['pætənt]),
government authority to manufacture
sth. invented and protect it from imitation. **3.** protected by letters ~: *a ~
medicine*, one made and sold by one
manufacturer only. **4.** ~ *leather*, leather
with a hard, smooth, shiny surface.

pat·ent² ['peɪtənt, 'pætənt] **n. 1.**
(privilege granted by) letters ~. **2.**
sth. that is given legal protection by
letters ~ against imitation. **v.t.** obtain
a ~ for (an invention, etc.). **~·ee**
[,peɪtən'tiː, ,pætən'tiː] **n.** person to
whom a ~ has been granted.

pa·ter·nal [pə'tɜːnl] **adj. 1.** of or like
a father; fatherly. **2.** related through
the father: *~ aunt.* **~·ly adv. pa·ter·**
ni·ty [pə'tɜːnɪtɪ] **n.** (no pl.) **1.** being
a father; origin on the father's side:
paternity unknown. **2.** (fig.) source.

path [pɑːθ] **n.** (pl. ~s [pɑːðz]) **1.** (also
~way) way made (across fields, through
woods, etc.) by people walking. **2.**
(also *foot~*) prepared track for pedestrians along the side of a road. (Cf.
pavement.) **3.** line along which sth. or
sb. moves: *the moon's ~ round the
earth.* **'~·find·er n.** person who explores unknown regions to mark out a
new route; explorer. **'~·way n.** =
~ (1).

pa·thet·ic [pə'θetɪk] **adj.** sad; pitiful.
pa·thet·i·cal·ly adv.

pa·thol·o·gy [pə'θɒlədʒɪ] **n.** (no pl.)
science of diseases. **patho·log·i·cal**
[,pæθə'lɒdʒɪkl] **adj.** of ~; of the na-

ture of disease. **pa·thol·o·gist** [pə-
'θɒlədʒɪst] **n.** student of, expert in, ~.
pa·thos ['peɪθɒs] **n.** (no pl.) quality
in speech, writing, etc. that arouses
feelings of pity.

pa·tience ['peɪʃns] **n. 1.** (no pl.)
(power of) enduring trouble, suffering,
inconvenience, without complaining;
ability to wait for results, to solve
problems calmly and without haste,
etc.: *out of ~ with*, no longer able to
endure. **2.** (U.S.A. *solitaire*) kind of
card game (usu. for one person).

pa·tient ['peɪʃnt] **adj.** having or showing patience. **n.** person receiving
medical treatment.

pa·tri·arch ['peɪtrɪɑːk] **n. 1.** male head
of a family or tribe. **2.** old man who is
highly respected.

pa·tri·cian [pə'trɪʃn] **n. & adj.** (person) of noble birth (esp. of ancient
Rome).

pat·ri·cide ['pætrɪsaɪd] **n. 1.** killing of
one's father. **2.** person guilty of this.

pat·ri·mo·ny ['pætrɪmənɪ] **n.** property
inherited from one's father or ancestors.

pa·tri·ot ['peɪtrɪət] **n.** person who loves
and is ready to defend his country.
~·ic [,peɪtrɪ'ɒtɪk] **adj. pa·tri·o·tism**
['peɪtrɪətɪzəm] **n.** (no pl.) feelings and
qualities of a ~.

pa·trol [pə'trəʊl] **v.t. & i.** (-ll-) go
round (a camp, town, the streets, etc.)
to see that all is well, to look out (for
wrongdoers, the enemy, etc.). **n. 1.**
(no pl.) act of ~ling: *soldiers on ~*;
constant sea and air ~; *a (police) ~ car*;
~man (U.S.A.), policeman who ~s an
area; police constable. **2.** person(s),
ship(s), or aircraft on ~ duties: *An
Automobile Association* (abbr. *A.A.*)
~(man) helped us.

pa·tron ['peɪtrən] **n. 1.** person who
supports financially, etc. the artistic
or social work of a person or society.
2. regular customer (of a shop). **3.** ~
saint, saint regarded as protecting (a
church, town, travellers, etc.). **~·age**
['pætrənɪdʒ] **n. 1.** support, etc. given
by a ~ (1, 2). **2.** right of a ~ (1) to
appoint sb. to a position, to grant
privileges, etc. **3.** ~izing (2) manner.
~·ess ['peɪtrənɪs] **n.** female ~. **~·ize**
['pætrənaɪz] **v.t. 1.** be a ~ (1, 2) to.
2. treat (sb. whom one is helping,
talking to, etc.) as if he were an inferior person.

pat·ter¹ ['pætə*] **n.** (no pl.) sound of
quick, light taps or footsteps: *the ~ of
rain on a roof.* **v.i.** make this sound.

pat·ter² ['pætə*] **n.** (no pl.) **1.** kind of

talk, words, used by a class of people: *thieves'* ~. **2.** rapid talk of a conjurer or comedian.

pat·tern ['pætən] *n.* **1.** excellent example: *a* ~ *of all the virtues.* **2.** sth. serving as a model, esp. the shape of a garment, cut out in paper, used as a guide in dressmaking. **3.** sample, esp. a small piece of cloth. **4.** ornamental design (on a carpet, wallpaper, etc.). **5.** regular form or order: *behaviour* ~; *new* ~*s of education.*

pat·ty ['pætɪ] *n.* small pie with meat, oysters, etc. in it.

paunch [pɔ:ntʃ] *n.* fat belly.

pau·per ['pɔ:pə*] *n.* person with no income, esp. when he is supported by charity. ~**·ize** *v.t.* make a ~ of.

pause [pɔ:z] *n.* **1.** short interval or stop in the middle of (doing or saying sth.). **2.** *give* ~ *to,* cause (sb.) to stop and think. *v.i.* make a ~.

pave [peɪv] *v.t.* put flat stones, bricks, etc. on (a road, etc.): ~ *the way for,* (fig.) make conditions easy for. '~**ment** *n.* **1.** (U.S.A. *sidewalk*) ~d way at the side of a street for pedestrians: *a* ~*ment café.* **2.** (U.S.A.) hard surface for streets, roads, etc.; roadway.

pa·vil·ion [pə'vɪljən] *n.* **1.** ornamental building for concerts, dancing, etc. **2.** building on a sports ground for the use of players, spectators, etc. **3.** big tent.

paw [pɔ:] *n.* animal's foot that has claws or nails (opp. *hoof*): *a dog's* ~; (colloq.) hand. *v.t. & i.* **1.** (of animals) feel, scratch, with the ~(s): *be* ~*ed by a tiger*; *the cat* ~*ed at the mouse*; *the dog* ~*ed at the door.* **2.** (of a horse) strike (the ground) with a hoof. **3.** feel or touch clumsily, rudely, or indecently.

pawn¹ [pɔ:n] *n.* least valuable piece in the game of chess; (fig.) person made use of by others for their own advantage.

pawn² [pɔ:n] *v.t.* leave (clothing, jewellery, etc.) as pledge for money borrowed. *n.* (only) *in* ~, ~*ed*: *His watch is in* ~. '~**·bro·ker** *n.* person licensed to lend money at interest on the security of goods, etc. left with him. '~**·shop** *n.*

paw·paw, see *papaya.*

pay [peɪ] *v.t. & i.* (p.t. & p.p. *paid* [peɪd]) **1.** give (sb.) money for goods, etc.: ~ *sb. off,* ~ him his wages and discharge (4) him. **2.** suffer pain or punishment (*for* what one has done). **3.** give (attention *to* sth.); make (a call, a visit, *on* sb.); offer (a compliment

to sb.). **4.** ~ *out* (rope), let (it) pass out through the hands. *n.* (no pl.) money paid for regular work or services, esp. in the armed forces. '~**-day** *n.* day on which wages or salaries are (to be) paid. '~**-desk** *n.* place (e.g. in a supermarket) where one ~s the bill, wraps one's goods, and leaves. ~**ee** [peɪ'i:] *n.* person to whom money is (to be) paid. '~**mas·ter** *n.* officer in the army etc. responsible for ~. ~**·ment** *n.* **1.** (no pl.) ~ing or being paid. **2.** sum of money paid. **3.** (fig.) reward; punishment. '~**-,pack·et** *n.* (U.S.A. ~ *envelope*) envelope, etc. containing ~. ~ **phone,** U.S.A. ~ **sta·tion** *ns.* coin-operated telephone kiosk. '~**-roll** *n.* list of persons who receive regular ~ and of the amounts due to each.

pea [pi:] *n.* plant with seeds in pods, used as food; one of these seeds. '~**-nut** *n.* ground-nut.

peas in a pod

peace [pi:s] *n.* (no pl.) **1.** state of freedom from war and disorder: *at* ~ *with neighbouring countries; break the* ~, cause civil disorder, rioting, etc.; *keep the* ~, avoid or prevent disorder and strife. **2.** rest; quiet; calm: ~ *of mind; hold one's* ~, say nothing; stop talking. ~**·able** *adj.* not quarrelsome; ~**ful.** ~**·ably** *adv.* ~**·ful** *adj.* **1.** loving ~. **2.** calm; quiet. ~**·ful·ly** *adv.* '~**,mak·er** *n.* person who helps to bring about ~, to end quarrels. '~**-,of·fer·ing** *n.* sth. offered to show that one is willing to make ~.

peach [pi:tʃ] *n.* (tree with a) juicy, round fruit with delicate, yellowish-red skin and a rough, stone-like seed; yellowish-red colour.

pea·cock ['pi:kɒk] *n.* large male bird noted for its fine tail feathers. **pea·hen** ['pi:hen] *n.* female of ~.

a peacock   a pear

peak [piːk] *n*. **1.** pointed top, esp. of a móuntain. **2.** pointed front part of a cap, to shade the eyes. **3.** highest point or period of use: *at the ~ of his career*; *the ~ hours* (e.g. of traffic).

peal [piːl] *n*. **1.** loud ringing of a bell or of bells with different notes. **2.** set of bells tuned to be played together. **3.** loud echoing noise: *~s of thunder* (*laughter*). *v.t. & i.* (cause to) ring or sound loudly.

pear [peə*] *n*. (tree with) sweet juicy fruit, tapering towards the stalk¹. (See the picture at *peacock*.)

pearl [pɜːl] *n*. **1.** silvery-white gem that forms in some oyster shells, valued for its beauty. **2.** sth. that looks like a ~ (e.g. a dewdrop); sb. or sth. very precious.

peas·ant [ˈpeznt] *n*. (now used esp. of developing countries or former times) countryman working on the land, either for wages or on a very small farm which he rents or owns: *~ labour*. *~ry n. the ~*, all the ~s of a country; the ~s as a class.

peat [piːt] *n*. (no pl.) plant material partly decomposed by the action of water; piece of this cut out (to be) dried and burnt as fuel. *~y adj.* (*-ier*, *-iest*).

peb·ble [ˈpebl] *n*. small stone made smooth and round by rolling against other stones in the sea or a river.

pec·ca·dil·lo [ˌpekəˈdɪləʊ] *n*. (pl. *-loes*, *-los*) small unimportant weakness in a person's character; small fault.

peck¹ [pek] *n*. measure for dry goods (e.g. beans) equal to two gallons (= about 9 litres); (fig.) a lot: *a ~ of troubles*.

peck² [pek] *v.t. & i.* **1.** strike (*at*) with the beak; get by doing this: *hens ~ing corn*; make (a hole) by doing this. **2.** *~ at one's food*, (colloq.) eat only small bits of food; eat without appetite. *n*. stroke made by a bird with its beak; quick, carelessly given kiss. *~ish adj.* (colloq.) hungry.

pe·cu·liar [pɪˈkjuːljə*] *adj*. **1.** strange; unusual. **2.** special. **3.** *~ to*, used, adopted, practised, only by: *a style of dress ~ to this tribe*. *~ly adv.* *~·i·ty* [pɪˌkjuːlɪˈærətɪ] *n*. sth. strange or characteristic.   [money.\

pe·cu·ni·ary [pɪˈkjuːnjərɪ] *adj*. of∫

ped·a·gogue (U.S.A. *-gog*) [ˈpedəgɒg] *n*. (old use or derog.) schoolmaster; pedantic teacher. **ped·a·go·gy** [ˈpedəgɒdʒɪ] *n*. (no pl.) science of teaching. **ped·a·gog·ic** [ˌpedəˈgɒdʒɪk], **ped·a·gog·i·cal** *adjs*.

ped·al [ˈpedl] *n*. part of a machine or instrument (e.g. bicycle, sewing-machine, piano) worked by the foot or feet. *v.t. & i.* (*-ll-*, U.S.A. also *-l-*) work (a bicycle) by ~s; use a ~ or ~s (for playing an organ, riding a bicycle).

ped·ant [ˈpedənt] *n*. person who values book-learning, rules, etc. too highly. **pe·dan·tic** [pɪˈdæntɪk] *adj*. of a ~. *~·ry* [ˈpedəntrɪ] *n*. tiresome and unnecessary display of learning; too much insistence upon formal rules.

ped·dle [ˈpedl] *v.i. & t.* go from house to house, selling small articles. **ped·lar** (U.S.A. *~r*) [ˈpedlə*] *n*. person who does this.

ped·es·tal [ˈpedɪstl] *n*. base of a column; base for a statue or other work of art.

pe·des·tri·an [pɪˈdestrɪən] *n*. person walking in a street, etc.: *~ crossing*, street crossing specially marked, where ~s have priority over traffic; *~ precinct*, area in town where vehicles are not allowed. *adj*. **1.** going on foot; connected with walking. **2.** (of a person, what he says or writes) dull; uninspired.

pe·di·at·ric, etc. (U.S.A.), see *paediatric*, etc.

pedi·cab [ˈpedɪkæb] *n*. three-wheeled cab for two passengers and driver in some Asian countries).

ped·i·cure [ˈpedɪˌkjʊə*] *n*. **1.** (no pl.) care or treatment of the feet and toenails. **2.** chiropodist. *v.t.* give ~ treatment to.

ped·i·gree [ˈpedɪgriː] *n*. **1.** line of ancestors. **2.** (no pl.) ancient descent. **3.** (attrib.) *~ animals* (whose ~ is recorded).

ped·lar, see *peddle*.

pee [piː] (colloq.) *n*. urination; urine. *v.i.* urinate.

peek [piːk] *v.i.* peep (*at* sth.).

peel [piːl] *v.t. & i.* **1.** take the skin off (fruit, etc.). **2.** (of the skin of the body, wallpaper, the bark of a tree, etc.) come off in bits or strips. *n*. skin of fruit, potatoes, young shoots. *~ings n. pl.* pieces ~ed off: *potato ~ings*.

peep [piːp] *n*. **1.** short, quick look, often one taken secretly or inquisitively. **2.** look through a narrow opening (*~-hole*); incomplete view. **3.** first light (of day). *v.i.* take a ~ (*at*): *~ing from behind the curtains*. **2.** come into view slowly or partly: *The sun ~ed out from the clouds*.

peer¹ [pɪə*] *v.i.* look (*at*, *into*, sth.) closely, as if or when unable to see well.

peer² [pɪə*] *n.* **1.** person's equal in rank, merit, etc. **2.** (in Great Britain) nobleman; person with the right to sit in the House of Lords. **~·age** ['pɪərɪdʒ] *n.* the ~s (2); the rank of ~ (2): *raised to the ~age*; book with a list of ~s. **~·ess** ['pɪərɪs] *n.* female ~; wife of a ~ (2). **~·less** *adj.* without equal.

pee·vish ['piːvɪʃ] *adj.* irritable. **~·ly** *adv.*

peg [peg] *n.* **1.** wooden or metal pin or bolt used to fasten parts of woodwork, etc. together, to hang things on (e.g. *hat-~s*), to hold a rope (e.g. *tent-~s*), to fasten laundered clothes to a line

pegs (1)

(*clothes-~s*), to stop up a hole in a barrel, etc. *a square ~ in a round hole,* a person unfitted for his position. **2.** (Gt. Brit.) alcoholic drink, esp. whisky. *v.t. & i.* (*-gg-*) **1.** fasten with ~s: *~ a tent down.* **2.** (comm.) fix (prices, etc.) by regulation; keep (wages) steady. **3.** *~ away (at),* keep on working (at); *~ out,* (sl.) die.

Pe·king·ese [ˌpiːkɪŋˈiːz], **Pe·kin·ese** [ˌpiːkɪˈniːz] *n.* (pl. ~) small, snub²-nosed Chinese dog with long, silky hair.

pel·i·can ['pelɪkən] *n.* large water-bird with a long bill under which hangs a pouch.

pel·let ['pelɪt] *n.* **1.** small ball of sth. soft (e.g. wet paper, bread), made, for example, by rolling between the fingers; pill. **2.** small ball of lead for a gun.

pell-mell [ˌpelˈmel] *adv.* in a hurrying, disorderly manner.

pelt¹ [pelt] *n.* animal's skin with the hair or fur on it.

pelt² [pelt] *v.t. & i.* **1.** attack (with stones, mud, etc.). **2.** (of rain, etc.) beat down; fall heavily: *hail ~ing against the roof. It is ~ing with rain. n. at full ~,* at full speed.

the pelvis

pel·vis ['pelvɪs] *n.* (pl. *-ves* [-viːz], *~es*) cavity composed of the hip-bones and the lower part of the backbone, holding the bowel, bladder, etc.

pem·mi·can ['pemɪkən] *n.* (no pl.) dried, lean meat beaten and mixed into cakes (as) by N. American Indians.

pen¹ [pen] *n.* instrument for writing in ink, consisting of a metal nib in a holder (*~holder*), or (*fountain-~*) a nib fixed in a hollow container (*barrel*) of ink, or (*ball¹-~*) a tiny metal ball revolving at the end of a narrow tube filled with special ink. *v.t.* (*-nn-*) write (a letter, etc.). '**~-friend** *n.* friend with whom one corresponds, usu. without ever meeting. '**~·knife** *n.* small folding pocket-knife. '**~-man·ship** *n.* (no pl.) art or style of handwriting. '**~-name** *n.* literary pseudonym.

pen² [pen] *n.* small closed-in space for cattle, sheep, pigs, etc. *v.t.* (*-nn-*) *~ sb. up (in),* shut up in or as in a ~.

pe·nal ['piːnl] *adj.* connected with punishment: *~ laws; a ~ offence,* an offence for which there is a legal punishment; *~ servitude,* (hist.) imprisonment with hard labour. **~·ize** ['piːnəlaɪz] *v.t.* make (an act) ~; give a ~ty to (a player, competitor, etc.). **~·iza·tion** [ˌpiːnəlaɪˈzeɪʃn] *n.* **pen·al·ty** ['penltɪ] *n.* **1.** (no pl.) punishment for wrongdoing, for failure to obey rules or keep an agreement, etc. **2.** what is imposed as punishment, esp. payment of a fine, etc.; (fig.) suffering that wrongdoing brings. **3.** (in sport, competitions, etc.) loss of points, disadvantage, etc. imposed for breaking a rule.

pen·ance ['penəns] *n.* (no pl.) punishment that sb. imposes on himself to show repentance, as on the advice of a priest: *do ~ for one's sins.*

pence, see *penny.*

pen·cil ['pensl] *n.* instrument for drawing or writing with, especially a thin rod of wood enclosing a stick of graphite or coloured chalk sharpened to a point. *v.t.* (*-ll-*, U.S.A. also *-l-*) write or draw with a ~.

pen·dant ['pendənt] *n.* hanging ornament, esp. one fastened to a necklace, etc.

pend·ing ['pendɪŋ] *adj.* waiting to be settled or decided. *prep.* **1.** while waiting for (e.g. sb.'s arrival); until: *~ his return.* **2.** during the continuance of (e.g. discussions): *~ these negotiations.*

pen·du·lum ['pendjʊləm] *n.* weighted rod hung from a fixed point so that it swings freely, esp. one regulating the movement of a clock: *the swing of the ~,* (fig.) the movement (3) of public opinion from one extreme to the other.

a pendulum

a penguin

pen·e·trate ['penɪtreɪt] *v.t. & i.* **1.** make a way into or through; pierce; (fig.) see into or through. **2.** spread through: *bad smells that ~d (through) the building.* **pen·e·trat·ing** *adj.* (of a person, his mind) keen; able to see and understand quickly and clearly; (of cries, voices) piercing; loud and clear. **pen·e·tra·tion** [,penɪ'treɪʃn] *n.*

pen·guin ['peŋgwɪn] *n.* sea-bird of the Antarctic with wings used for swimming, not for flying.

pen·i·cil·lin [,penɪ'sɪlɪn] *n.* (no pl.) antibiotic drug that prevents the growth of certain disease-causing bacteria.

pen·in·su·la [pə'nɪnsjʊlə] *n.* area of land (e.g. Italy) almost surrounded by water. **~r** *adj.* of or like a ~.

pen·i·tence ['penɪtəns] *n.* sorrow and regret for wrongdoing. **pen·i·tent** *n.* person feeling regret. *adj.* feeling regret; showing ~: *penitent looks.* **pen·i·ten·tial** [,penɪ'tenʃl] *adj.* of ~ or of penance. **pen·i·ten·tia·ry** [,penɪ'tenʃərɪ] *n.* prison, esp. one in which reform of the prisoners is the chief aim; (U.S.A.) state or federal prison.

pen·nant ['penənt], **pen·non** ['penən] *ns.* long, narrow (usu. triangular) flag, as used on ships for signalling.

pen·ny ['penɪ] *n.* (pl. *pennies* for a number of coins, *pence* [pens] for value or cost) British coin worth one hundredth of an English pound: *(new) ~* (abbr. *p., p*). *These pears are 40p.* [pi:] *a pound.* **'~·worth, 'pen·n'orth** ['penəθ] *n.* as much as a ~ will buy. **pen·ni·less** *adj.* without money or property.

pen·sion ['penʃn] *n.* regular payment made by the State or by a former employer to sb. on completion of a term of service, or on retirement, disablement, etc. *v.t.* give a ~ to: *~ off.* **~** dismiss or allow to retire with a ~. **~·er** ['penʃənə*] *n.* person receiving a ~.

pen·sive ['pensɪv] *adj.* deep in thought.

pent [pent] *adj.* shut *in* or *up*; penned up: *~up feelings.*

pen·ta·gon ['pentəgən] *n.* plane figure with five sides and five internal angles.

pen·tath·lete [pen'tæθli:t] *n.* athlete who competes in a **pen·tath·lon** [pen'tæθlon] *n.* athletic contest in which each competitor takes part in five different events.

pent·house ['penthaʊs] *n.* **1.** sloping roof supported against a wall, esp. one for a shelter or shed. **2.** house or flat¹ built on the roof of a tall building.

pen·ul·ti·mate [pe'nʌltɪmət] *n. & adj.* (word, syllable, etc. that is) last but one.

pen·u·ry ['penjʊrɪ] *n.* (no pl.) poverty. **pe·nu·ri·ous** [pɪ'njʊərɪəs] *adj.* poor; not generous.

pe·o·ny ['pɪənɪ] *n.* garden plant with large round white, pink, or red flowers.

peo·ple ['pi:pl] *n.* (1 to 5 collective, never pl. in form but used with a pl. verb) **1.** persons in general. **2.** all those persons forming a State: *the English ~; government of the ~ by the ~ for the ~;* (attrib.) *the P.~'s Republic of China.* **3.** persons belonging to a place or forming a social class: *the ~ in the village.* **4.** *the ~,* those who are not nobles, not high in rank, position, etc. **5.** parents or other relatives: *Her ~ are all dead.* **6.** (with indef. art. and in pl.) tribe, race, or nation: *a brave and intelligent ~; the ~s of Asia; the English-speaking ~s. v.t.* fill with ~; put ~ in: *a thickly-~d district.*

pep [pep] *n.* (no pl.) (sl.) energy.

pep·per ['pepə*] *n.* **1.** (no pl.) hot-tasting powder made from the dried berries of certain plants, used with food. **2.** red, yellow, or green seed-pods of certain plants, used as a vegetable: *stuffed ~s. v.t.* **1.** add ~ to (food). **2.** ~ *sb. with* (stones, questions, etc.), pelt with. **'~·mint** *n.* **1.** (no pl.) (plant producing) hot-tasting oil, used in medicine and for flavouring sweets. **2.** sweet flavoured with ~mint. **~·y** *adj.* tasting of ~; (fig.) hot-tempered.

per [pɜ:*, pə*] *prep.* **1.** for each; in each: *~ annum* (year), *~ pound, ~ man, ~ cent* (hundred). **2.** by means of; by: *~ post.*

per·cent·age [pə'sentɪdʒ] *n.* rate or number per cent.

per·am·bu·la·tor [pə'ræmbjʊleɪtə*], **pram** [præm] *ns.* (U.S.A. *baby carriage*) four-wheeled, hand-pushed carriage for a baby.

per·ceive [pə'siːv] *v.t.* become aware of, esp. through the eyes or the mind. **per·cep·ti·ble** [pə'septəbl] *adj.* that can be ~d. **per·cep·ti·bly** *adv.* **per·cep·tion** [pə'sepʃn] *n.* (no pl.) act or power of perceiving. **per·cep·tive** [pə'septɪv] *adj.* having, connected with, perception.

perch [pɜːtʃ] *n.* **1.** bird's resting-place (e.g. a branch); rod or bar provided for this purpose. **2.** any high position occupied by a person or building. **3.** measure of distance, 5½ yards (= 5.03 metres). *v.i. & t.* **1.** alight or come to rest (*on*): *birds ~ing on boughs*; (of a person) take up a position (*on a high place*): *~ed on a high stool* (*on sb.'s shoulders*). **2.** (of a building) be situated: *~ed on the top of the hill.*

per·chance [pə'tʃɑːns] *adv.* (old use) perhaps; possibly; by chance.

per·co·late ['pɜːkəleɪt] *v.i. & t.* **1.** (of liquid) pass slowly (*through*); filter (*through*). **2.** cause (liquid, etc.) to ~. **per·co·la·tor** *n.* (esp.) apparatus (1) in which boiling water ~s through coffee.

per·cus·sion [pə'kʌʃn] *n.* striking together of two (usu. hard) objects; tapping² : ~ *instruments*, musical instruments played by ~ (e.g. drums). **~·ist** *n.* player of ~ instruments.

per·di·tion [pə'dɪʃn] *n.* (no pl.) complete ruin; everlasting damnation.

per·e·gri·na·tion [ˌperɪɡrɪ'neɪʃn] *n.* journey; travelling about.

pe·remp·to·ry [pə'remptərɪ] *adj.* (of commands) not to be disobeyed or questioned; (of a person, his manner) (too) commanding; insisting on obedience. **pe·remp·to·ri·ly** *adv.*

pe·ren·ni·al [pə'renjəl] *adj.* **1.** continuing throughout the whole year. **2.** lasting for a very long time. **3.** (of plants) living several years. *n.* ~ plant.

per·fect ['pɜːfɪkt] *adj.* **1.** complete; with everything needed. **2.** without fault; excellent. **3.** exact; precise: *a ~ circle.* **4.** entire: *a ~ stranger*; ~ *nonsense.* **5.** ~ *tense*, (gram.) tense denoting completed event or action viewed in relation to the present. *n.* ~ tense. [pə'fekt] *v.t.* make ~. **~·ly** *adv.* completely. **per·fec·tion** [pə'fekʃn] *n.* (no pl.) ~ing or being ~ed; ~ quality, person, etc.: *the ~ion of beauty*; *to ~ion*, completely.

per·fi·dy ['pɜːfɪdɪ] *n.* treachery; break-

ing of faith with sb.; treacherous act. **per·fid·i·ous** [pə'fɪdɪəs] *adj.* treacherous.

per·fo·rate ['pɜːfəreɪt] *v.t. & i.* make a hole or holes through, esp. a line of small holes in (paper) so that a part may be torn off easily. **per·fo·ra·tion** [ˌpɜːfə'reɪʃn] *n.* (esp.) line of holes made through paper (as between stamps).

per·force [pə'fɔːs] *adv.* of necessity.

per·form [pə'fɔːm] *v.t. & i.* **1.** do (a piece of work, sth. one is ordered to do, sth. one has promised to do, etc.). **2.** act (a play); play (music), sing, do tricks, etc., before an audience. **~·ance** *n.* **1.** (no pl.) ~ing. **2.** (esp.) sth. done or acted: *a fine ~ance.* **3.** ~ing of a play; concert: *two ~ances daily.* **~·er** *n.* person who ~s, esp. in a play or at a concert. **~·ing** *adj.* (of animals) trained to ~ stage tricks: *~ing elephants.*

per·fume ['pɜːfjuːm] *n.* (prepared liquid with a) sweet smell, esp. that of flowers. [pə'fjuːm] *v.t.* give a ~ to; put ~ on.

per·func·to·ry [pə'fʌŋktərɪ] *adj.* done as a duty but without care or interest; (of a person) doing things thus; casual. **per·func·to·ri·ly** *adv.*

per·go·la ['pɜːɡələ] *n.* structure of posts for climbing-plants shading a garden walk.

per·haps [pə'hæps, præps] *adv.* possibly; it may be.

per·il ['perəl] *n.* serious danger. **~·ous** *adj.* dangerous; risky.

pe·rim·e·ter [pə'rɪmɪtə*] *n.* (length of the) outer boundary of a closed figure.

pe·ri·od ['pɪərɪəd] *n.* **1.** length or portion of time marked off by events that recur (e.g. a month): *a lesson ~ of 45 minutes.* **2.** indefinite portion of time in the life of a person, nation, etc.: *the ~ of the French Revolution.* **3.** (gram.) complete sentence or statement, usu. complex. **4.** pause at the end of a sentence; mark (also called *full stop*) indicating this in writing. **~·ic** [ˌpɪərɪ'ɒdɪk] *adj.* occurring or appearing at regular intervals. **~·i·cal** *adj.* ~ic. *n.* ~ic publication (e.g. a magazine, a newspaper). **~·i·cal·ly** *adv.*

peri·pa·tet·ic [ˌperɪpə'tetɪk] *adj.* going about from place to place; wandering.

peri·scope ['perɪskəʊp] *n.* instrument with mirrors and lenses arranged to reflect a view down a tube, etc. so that the viewer may get a view as from a level above that of his eyes; used in submarines, trenches, etc. (See the picture on page 366.)

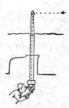

a periscope

per·ish ['perɪʃ] *v.t. & i.* **1.** (cause to) be destroyed, come to an end, die; decay. **2.** ~*ed with cold*, feeling very cold. **~·able** *adj.* (esp. of food) quickly or easily going bad.

peri·wig ['perɪwɪg] *n.* wig.

per·jure ['pɜːdʒə*] *v.refl.* ~ *oneself*, knowingly make a false statement after taking an oath to tell the truth. **~d** *adj.* having ~d oneself. **per·ju·ry** *n.* **1.** (no pl.) act of perjuring oneself. **2.** wilful false statement while on oath.

perk [pɜːk] *v.i. & t.* **1.** (of a person) ~ *up*, become lively and active. **2.** (of a horse, etc.) ~ *up* (*its head, tail*), lift up as a sign of interest, liveliness, etc. **~y** *adj.* (*-ier, -iest*) lively; showing interest or confidence. **~·i·ly** *adv.* **~·i·ness** *n.* (no pl.).

perm [pɜːm] *v.t. & n.* (colloq., abbr. for) (give a) permanent wave (to).

per·ma·nent ['pɜːmənənt] *adj.* going on for a long time; intended to last: *the ~ way*, railway track; ~ *wave*, style of hairdressing in which waves or curls are set in the hair so that they last several months. *n.* ~ wave. **~·ly** *adv.* **per·ma·nence** *n.* (no pl.) quality or state of being ~. **per·ma·nen·cy** *n.* **1.** (no pl.) permanence. **2.** ~ thing or arrangement.

per·me·ate ['pɜːmɪeɪt] *v.t. & i.* ~ (*through*), spread, pass, into every part (of). **per·me·able** ['pɜːmjəbl] *adj.* that can be ~d by fluids; porous.

per·mit [pə'mɪt] *v.t. & i.* (*-tt-*) **1.** allow: *Smoking not ~ted. P~ me to say that ...*; *weather ~ting*. **2.** ~ *of*, admit (3): *a situation that ~s of no delay*. ['pɜːmɪt] *n.* written authority to do sth., go somewhere, etc. **per·mis·si·ble** [pə'mɪsəbl] *adj.* which is ~ted. **per·mis·sion** [pə'mɪʃn] *n.* act of ~ting; formal consent. **per·mis·sive** [pə'mɪsɪv] *adj.* **1.** giving permission. **2.** tolerant, liberal, esp. in sexual matters: *the permissive society*.

per·mu·ta·tion [,pɜːmjuː'teɪʃn] *n.* change of the order in which a number of things are arranged.

per·ni·cious [pə'nɪʃəs] *adj.* harmful (*to*): ~ *influences* (*habits*).

per·nick·e·ty [pə'nɪkətɪ] *adj.* (colloq.) fussy; worrying about unimportant details.

per·ora·tion [,perə'reɪʃn] *n.* last part of a speech; summing up.

per·ox·ide [pə'rɒksaɪd] *n.* (no pl.) (esp.) chemical substance used as a disinfectant and for bleaching (e.g. hair).

per·pen·dic·u·lar [,pɜːpən'dɪkjʊlə*] *adj.* **1.** at an angle of 90° to (another line or surface). **2.** upright; crossing the horizontal at an angle of 90°. *n.* ~ line.

per·pe·trate ['pɜːpɪtreɪt] *v.t.* commit (a crime, an error); do (sth. wrong). **per·pe·tra·tor** *n.* **per·pe·tra·tion** [,pɜːpɪ'treɪʃn] *n.*

per·pet·u·al [pə'petʃʊəl] *adj.* **1.** never-ending; going on for a long time without stopping. **2.** often repeated. **~·ly** *adv.* **per·pet·u·ate** [pə'petʃʊeɪt] *v.t.* preserve from being forgotten or from going out of use. **per·pe·tu·ity** [,pɜːpɪ'tjuː:ɪtɪ] *n.* (no pl.) being ~: *in perpetuity*, for ever.

per·plex [pə'pleks] *v.t.* **1.** puzzle; bewilder. **2.** make (a question, etc.) more complex or confusing. **~ed** *adj.* **~·ed·ly** [pə'pleksɪdlɪ] *adv.* **~·i·ty** [pə'pleksətɪ] *n.* **1.** (no pl.) ~ed condition. **2.** ~ing thing.

per·qui·site ['pɜːkwɪzɪt] *n.* profit, allowance, etc. taken in addition to regular wages or salary.

per·se·cute ['pɜːsɪkjuːt] *v.t.* **1.** punish, treat cruelly, esp. because of religious beliefs. **2.** allow no peace to; worry (*with* questions, etc.). **per·se·cu·tor** *n.* **per·se·cu·tion** [,pɜːsɪ'kjuːʃn] *n.* persecuting or being ~d; instance of this.

per·se·vere [,pɜːsɪ'vɪə*] *v.i.* keep on steadily, continue (*at, in, with*). **per·se·ver·ance** [,pɜːsɪ'vɪərəns] *n.* (no pl.)

per·sist [pə'sɪst] *v.i.* **1.** ~ *in*, refuse, in spite of opposition, failure, etc., to make any change in (what one is doing, one's beliefs, etc.). **2.** continue to exist. **per·sis·tence** *n.* (no pl.). **per·sis·tent** *adj.* ~ing; continuing. **per·sis·tent·ly** *adv.*

per·son ['pɜːsn] *n.* **1.** man, woman, or child. **2.** living body of a ~: *attacks against the ~*, bodily attacks; *be present in ~*, be present oneself (not represented by sb. else). **3.** (gram.) one of three classes of personal pronouns, verb-forms, etc.: *first ~* (I, we), *second ~* (you), *third ~* (he, she, it, they).

~·**able** *adj.* good-looking. ~·**age** *n.* (important) ~. ~·**al** *adj.* **1.** private; individual; of a ~, not of a group: ~*al needs* (*opinions*). **2.** done, etc. by a ~ himself: *a ~al call* (*interview*). **3.** of a ~'s looks, abilities, qualities, etc.: ~*al beauty.* **4.** of the body: ~*al hygiene.* **5.** of, about, against, a ~: ~*al remarks.* ~·**al·ly** *adv.* **1.** in ~; oneself; not through others. **2.** as a ~. **3.** speaking for oneself: *P~ally I see no objection.* ~·**al·i·ty** [ˌpɜːsəˈnælətɪ] *n.* **1.** (no pl.) existence as a ~. **2.** qualities that make up a ~'s character: *a strong ~ality; a man with little ~ality.* **3.** ~ well known in certain circles: *a T.V. ~ality.* **4.** (pl.) impolite remarks about sb.'s looks, habits, etc. ~·**i·fy** [pɜːˈsɒnɪfaɪ] *v.t.* **1.** regard or represent (sth.) as a ~. **2.** be an example of (a quality). ~·**i·fi·ca·tion** [pɜːˌsɒnɪfɪˈkeɪʃn] *n.* ~·**nel** [ˌpɜːsəˈnel] *n.* (sing. or pl. v.) staff; ~s employed in any work, esp. public undertakings and the armed forces: *airline ~nel; military ~nel; ~nel department* (*manager*) (concerned with appointments of employees, relationships between individual employees, etc.).

per·spec·tive [pəˈspektɪv] *n.* **1.** (no pl.) art of drawing solid objects on a flat surface so as to give the right impression of their relative size, distance, etc. **2.** drawing so made. **3.** (no pl.) apparent relation between different aspects of a problem, etc.: *see sth. in the right ~.*

per·spi·ca·cious [ˌpɜːspɪˈkeɪʃəs] *adj.* quick to judge and understand. **per·spi·cac·i·ty** [ˌpɜːspɪˈkæsətɪ] *n.* (no pl.).

per·spic·u·ous [pəˈspɪkjuəs] *adj.* expressed clearly; expressing things clearly.

per·spire [pəˈspaɪə*] *v.i.* sweat. **per·spi·ra·tion** [ˌpɜːspəˈreɪʃn] *n.* (no pl.) sweat; sweating.

per·suade [pəˈsweɪd] *v.t.* cause (sb.) by reasoning (*to do* sth., etc.); convince (sb. *of* the truth of sth., *that* sth. is true, etc.). **per·sua·sion** [pəˈsweɪʒn] *n.* (no pl.) persuading; being ~d; conviction or belief. **per·sua·sive** [pəˈsweɪsɪv] *adj.* able to ~; convincing.

pert [pɜːt] *adj.* saucy; not showing proper respect: *a ~ child* (*answer*).

per·tain [pɜːˈteɪn] *v.i.* ~ *to*, belong to (as a part); have reference to.

per·ti·na·cious [ˌpɜːtɪˈneɪʃəs] *adj.* not easily giving up (what has been started); determined. **per·ti·nac·i·ty** [ˌpɜːtɪˈnæsətɪ] *n.* (no pl.).

per·ti·nent [ˈpɜːtɪnənt] *adj.* referring directly (*to* the question, etc.).

per·turb [pəˈtɜːb] *v.t.* trouble; make anxious: *~ing rumours.*

pe·ruke [pəˈruːk] *n.* (esp. hist.) long wig.

pe·ruse [pəˈruːz] *v.t.* read carefully. **pe·rus·al** *n.*

per·vade [pəˈveɪd] *v.t.* spread throughout; get into every part of. **per·va·sive** [pəˈveɪsɪv] *adj.* tending to ~: *pervasive ideas.*

per·verse [pəˈvɜːs] *adj.* **1.** (of persons) wilfully continuing in wrongdoing. **2.** (of behaviour) contrary to reason; (of circumstances) contrary (*to* one's wishes).

per·ver·sion [pəˈvɜːʃn] *n.* **1.** (no pl.) perverting or being perverted. **2.** perverted form: *sexual ~s.*

per·vert [pəˈvɜːt] *v.t.* **1.** turn (sth.) to a wrong use. **2.** cause (a person, his mind) to turn away from right behaviour, beliefs, etc. [ˈpɜːvɜːt] *n.* ~ed person.

pes·si·mism [ˈpesɪmɪzəm] *n.* (no pl.) tendency to believe that the worst thing is most likely to happen. **pes·si·mist** *n.* person subject to ~. **pes·si·mis·tic** (-**ti·cal·ly**) [ˌpesɪˈmɪstɪk (-əlɪ)] *adj.* (& *adv.*).

pest [pest] *n.* troublesome or destructive thing, animal, etc.: *garden ~s* (e.g. insects, snails, etc.); (old use) pestilence. **pes·ti·cide** [ˈpestɪsaɪd] *n.* substance used to destroy ~s.

pes·ter [ˈpestə*] *v.t.* trouble; annoy: *~ed with flies* (*requests for money*).

pes·ti·lence [ˈpestɪləns] *n.* fatal, infectious, quickly spreading disease. **pes·ti·len·tial** [ˌpestɪˈlenʃl] *adj.* **1.** causing injury or disease. **2.** (colloq.) annoying.

pes·tle [ˈpesl] *n.* instrument used for crushing substances in a mortar. (See the picture at *mortar.*)

pet[1] [pet] *n.* **1.** animal, etc. kept as a companion: *a ~ dog.* **2.** person treated as a favourite; sb. specially loved: *~ aversion,* sth. or sb. most disliked; *~ name,* name other than the real name, used affectionately. *v.t.* (-tt-) treat with affection; touch lovingly, esp. a person of the opposite sex.

pet[2] [pet] *n.* fit of ill temper, esp. about sth. unimportant. ~·**tish** *adj.*

pet·al [ˈpetl] *n.* one of the leaf-like divisions of a flower: *rose ~s.*

pe·ter [ˈpiːtə*] *v.i.* ~ *out,* come gradually to an end.

pe·ti·tion [pɪˈtɪʃn] *n.* prayer; earnest request, esp. one made to an authority and signed by a number of people.

v.t. & i. make a ~ to (sb. *for* sth.); ask humbly (*for* sth.). **~er** *n.*

pe·trel ['petrəl] *n.* long-winged, black and white sea-bird.

pet·ri·fy ['petrɪfaɪ] *v.t. & i.* (cause to) change into stone; (fig.) take away power to think, feel, act, etc. (through terror, surprise, etc.). **pet·ri·fac·tion** [ˌpetrɪ'fækʃn] *n.* **1.** (no pl.) ~ing or being petrified. **2.** petrified substance.

pet·rol ['petrəl] *n.* (no pl.) (U.S.A. *gasoline*) refined petroleum used to drive engines (in motor cars, etc.): ~ *station*, place where ~, etc. is sold to motorists. **pe·tro·leum** [pɪ'trəʊljəm] *n.* (no pl.) mineral oil from which ~, paraffin, etc. are obtained.

pet·ti·coat ['petɪkəʊt] *n.* woman's underskirt.

pet·ti·fog·ging ['petɪfɒgɪŋ] *adj.* (of persons) worrying about small and unimportant details; (of methods) concerned with small matters.

pet·ty ['petɪ] *adj.* (*-ier, -iest*) **1.** unimportant: ~ *troubles.* **2.** having or showing a narrow mind; mean: ~ *spite.* **3.** ~ *cash*, (comm.) money for or from small payments. **4.** ~ *officer*, naval officer below commissioned rank.

pet·u·lant ['petjʊlənt] *adj.* unreasonably impatient or irritable. **~ly** *adv.* **pet·u·lance** *n.* (no pl.).

pew [pju:] *n.* long bench with a back, usu. fixed to the floor, in a church.

pew·ter ['pju:tə*] *n.* (no pl.) grey alloy of tin and lead; vessels made of ~.

pha·lanx ['fælæŋks] *n.* (pl. ~*es, -langes* [fæ'lændʒi:z]) (in ancient Greece) body of soldiers in close ranks for fighting.

phan·tasm ['fæntæzəm] *n.* phantom. **phan·tas·mal** [fæn'tæzml] *adj.* of or like a ~. **phan·ta·sy** ['fæntəzɪ] *n.* fantasy.

phan·tom ['fæntəm] *n.* ghost; sth. without reality, as seen in a dream or vision.

Pha·raoh ['feərəʊ] *n.* title of the kings of ancient Egypt.

phar·ma·cy ['fɑːməsɪ] *n.* **1.** (no pl.) preparation and dispensing of medicines and drugs. **2.** chemist's shop, (U.S.A.) drugstore; dispensary. **phar·ma·cist** *n.* person skilled in or practising ~. **phar·ma·ceu·ti·cal** [ˌfɑːmə-'sjuːtɪkl] *adj.*

phase [feɪz] *n.* **1.** stage of development: *a* ~ *of history.* **2.** (of the moon) amount of bright surface visible from the earth (new moon, full moon, etc.). (Cf. *quarter* (8) and the picture at *moon*.)

pheas·ant ['feznt] *n.* long-tailed game-bird; its flesh as food.

a pheasant

phe·nom·e·non [fə'nɒmɪnən] *n.* (pl. *-ena* [-ɪnə]) **1.** thing that appears to or is perceived by the senses. **2.** remarkable or unusual person, thing, or happening. **phe·nom·e·nal** [fə'nɒm-ɪnl] *adj.* (esp.) extraordinary; unusual.

phi·al ['faɪəl] *n.* small bottle, esp. one for liquid medicine.

phi·lan·der [fɪ'lændə*] *v.i.* make love, be in the habit of making love, without serious intentions. **~er** *n.*

phi·lan·thro·py [fɪ'lænθrəpɪ] *n.* (no pl.) love of mankind; practice of helping other people, esp. those who are needy. **phi·lan·thro·pist** *n.* person who helps others, esp. those who are poor and in trouble. **phil·an·throp·ic** [ˌfɪlən'θrɒpɪk] *adj.* of ~; kind and helpful: *philanthropic institutions* (e.g. a home for blind people).

phi·lat·e·ly [fɪ'lætəlɪ] *n.* postage-stamp collecting. **phi·lat·e·list** *n.* stamp-collector.

phi·lol·o·gy [fɪ'lɒlədʒɪ] *n.* (no pl.) science of the nature and development of (a) language. **phi·lol·o·gist** *n.* student of, expert in, ~. **philo·log·i·cal** [ˌfɪlə'lɒdʒɪkl] *adj.* of ~.

phi·los·o·phy [fɪ'lɒsəfɪ] *n.* **1.** (no pl.) search for knowledge, esp. concerning nature and the meaning of existence. **2.** system of thought resulting from such a search. **3.** (no pl.) calm acceptance of events; self-control in the face of suffering or danger. **phi·los·o·pher** *n.* **1.** person studying ~ or having a system of ~. **2.** person whose mind is untroubled by his passions and hardships; person who lets reason govern his life. **philo·soph·i·cal** [ˌfɪlə'sɒfɪkl] *adj.* of, devoted to, ~; guided by ~; resigned. **phi·los·o·phize** [fɪ'lɒsəfaɪz] *v.i.* reason in the manner of a philosopher; speculate; theorize.

phlegm [flem] *n.* (no pl.) **1.** thick, semifluid substance forming on the skin of the throat and in the nose and brought up by coughing, etc. **2.** quality of being slow to act or feel emotion, interest, etc. **phleg·mat·ic** [fleg-'mætɪk] *adj.* having the quality of ~(2).

·ho·bia ['fəʊbjə] *n. & suff.* fear and dislike of. (See *hydro~*.)

·hoe·nix ['fiːnɪks] *n.* mythical bird.

·hon [fɒn] *n.* (phys.) unit of loudness of sounds.

·hone [fəʊn] *n. & v.t. & i.* (colloq.) telephone. '~**in** *n.* broadcast programme during which listeners or viewers telephone to the studio (3), etc. and participate.

·ho·net·ic [fəʊ'netɪk] *adj.* corresponding to the sounds of speech: ~ *spelling* (e.g. *flem* for *phlegm*); *a ~ language*, a language in which the same letters are always used for the same sounds. **~s** *n. pl.* (sing. v.) study and science of speech sounds and the symbols used to represent them. **pho·net·i·cal·ly** *adv.* **pho·ne·ti·cian** [ˌfəʊnɪ'tɪʃn] *n.* student of, expert in, ~s.

·ho·ney, pho·ny ['fəʊnɪ] *adj.* (-ier, -iest) (sl.) sham. *n.* ~ person.

·ho·no·graph ['fəʊnəgraːf] *n.* (U.S.A.) = record-player.

·hos·phate ['fɒsfeɪt] *n.* any salt of phosphorus, esp. fertilizer containing such salts.

·hos·pho·res·cent [ˌfɒsfə'resnt] *adj.* giving out a faint light without burning. **phos·pho·res·cence** *n.* (no pl.). **hos·phor·us** ['fɒsfərəs] *n.* (no pl.) yellowish, non-metallic element that catches fire easily and gives out a faint light in the dark.

·ho·to ['fəʊtəʊ] *n.* (pl. ~s) & *v.t.* (abbr. for) photograph.

·ho·to- ['fəʊtəʊ-] *pref.* light. '~**cell** *n.* ~electric cell. '~**cop·i·er** *n.* machine for ~copying documents. '~**copy** *v.t. & n.* (make a) copy of (a document, etc.) by a photographic method. **~·elec·tric cell** ['fəʊtəʊɪˌlektrɪk 'sel] *n.* cell or device (2) that emits an electric current when light falls on it (e.g. used to cause a door to open when sb. approaches it, to count objects passing before it, etc.).

ho·to·graph ['fəʊtəgraːf] *n.* picture made by means of the chemical action of light on a specially prepared glass plate or film. *v.t.* take a ~ of. **pho·tog·ra·pher** [fə'tɒgrəfə*] *n.* person who takes ~s. **pho·tog·ra·phy** [fə'tɒgrəfɪ] *n.* (no pl.) art or process of taking ~s. **~·ic** [ˌfəʊtə'græfɪk] *adj.* **~·i·cal·ly** *adv.*

hrase [freɪz] *n.* small group of words forming part of a sentence (e.g. *in the garden, in order to*). *v.t.* express in

words. **phras·al** ['freɪzl] *adj.* (gram.) consisting of a ~: *phrasal verbs* (e.g. *get up, look forward to*). **phra·se·ol·o·gy** [ˌfreɪzɪ'ɒlədʒɪ] *n.* (no pl.) wording; choice of words.

phys·ic ['fɪzɪk] *n.* (colloq.) medicine.

phys·i·cal ['fɪzɪkl] *adj.* **1.** of material (contrasted with moral and spiritual) things: *the ~ world.* **2.** ~ *geography,* of the earth's structure. **3.** of the body; bodily: ~ *education;* ~ *exercise* (e.g. walking); ~ *strength (beauty).* **4.** of the laws of nature: *It's a ~ impossibility to be in two places at once.* **~·ly** *adv.*

phy·si·cian [fɪ'zɪʃn] *n.* doctor of medicine and surgery.

phys·ics ['fɪzɪks] *n. pl.* (sing. v.) group of sciences dealing with matter and energy (e.g. heat, light, sound), but usu. excluding chemistry and biology. **phys·i·cist** ['fɪzɪsɪst] *n.* expert in ~.

phys·i·og·no·my [ˌfɪzɪ'ɒnəmɪ] *n.* (art of judging character from the) face; general features of a country.

phys·i·ol·o·gy [fɪzɪ'ɒlədʒɪ] *n.* (no pl.) science of the normal functions of living things. **phys·i·o·log·i·cal** [ˌfɪzɪə-'lɒdʒɪkl] *adj.* **phys·i·ol·o·gist** *n.* specialist in ~.

phy·sique [fɪ'ziːk] *n.* (no pl.) structure and development of the body: *a man of strong ~.*

a piano   a grand piano

pi·ano [pɪ'ænəʊ, 'pjɑːnəʊ] *n.* (pl. ~s) musical instrument with metal strings that sound when struck by hammers operated from a keyboard. **pi·a·nist** ['pɪənɪst] *n.* person who plays the ~. **pic·co·lo** ['pɪkələʊ] *n.* (pl. ~s) small flute.

pick[1] [pɪk] *n.* **1.** (also ~**axe**, U.S.A. ~**ax**)

a pick(axe)

heavy tool with an iron head having two sharp ends, used for breaking up

hard surfaces (e.g. brickwork, roads).
2. small, sharp-pointed instrument:
a tooth~.

pick² [pɪk] *v.t. & i.* **1.** take or gather
(flowers, fruit) from plants, bushes,
trees; get the meat off (a bone); tear
or separate with the fingers: *~ing rags;
~ing sth. to pieces; ~ at one's food,* eat
without interest or appetite. **2.** choose;
select: *~ only the best; ~ one's words; ~
one's way (steps) along a muddy road;
~ on sb.,* (a) nag at him; (b) single him
out, esp. for sth. unpleasant; *~ sth.
out,* distinguish it, choose it from,
among others. **3.** *~ up,* take hold of
and lift up (e.g. sth. on the floor);
acquire (e.g. bits of information);
take (sb., sth.) into a car, bus, etc. or
along with one; recover or regain one's
health (spirits, etc.); meet, talk to,
make the acquaintance of (sb.); *~ oneself up,* get to one's feet after a fall.
4. *~ sb.'s pocket,* steal sth. from his
pocket; *~ sb.'s brains,* use his ideas as
if they were one's own; *~ a lock,* open
it by using a pointed instrument, a
piece of wire, etc.; *~ a quarrel (with
sb.),* start one on purpose; *~ holes in
sth.,* point out the faults, etc. in it. *n.*
act of *~ing;* sth. that is *~ed* or
chosen: *the ~ of the bunch,* the best or
finest. **~-a-back** ['pɪkəbæk] *adv.*
(U.S.A. *piggyback*) (of the way a child
is carried) on sb.'s back or shoulders.
~ings *n. pl.* small bits left over; odds
and ends from which a profit may be
made; these profits. **~-me-up** ['pɪk-
miːʌp] *n.* sth. (e.g. a drink) that gives
new strength or cheerfulness. **'~-
pock·et** *n.* person who steals from a
person's pocket. **~-up** ['pɪkʌp] *n.* (pl.
~-ups) **1.** that part of a record-player

a record-player and pick-up

that holds the stylus (needle). **2.** small,
general-purpose van used by builders,
farmers, etc.

pick·et ['pɪkɪt] *n.* **1.** pointed stake, etc.
set upright in the ground. **2.** small
group of men on police duty or sent
out to watch the enemy, etc. **3.** one or
more workers on guard during a
strike, to try to stop others from going
to work. *v.t. & i.* **1.** put *~s* (1) round;

fasten (a horse) to a *~* (1). **2.** place *~*
(2) in or round. **3.** act as a *~* (3); place
~s (3) at.

pick·le ['pɪkl] *n.* **1.** (no pl.) salt water
vinegar, etc. for keeping meat, vegetables, etc. in good condition. **2.** (usu
pl.) vegetables kept in *~*. **3.** *in a (sad
etc.) ~,* in an embarrassing position; ir
a dirty state. *v.t.* preserve in, trea
with, *~* (1).

pic·nic ['pɪknɪk] *n.* pleasure trip on
which food is carried for eating out
doors. *v.i.* (*-ck-*) go on a *~*.

pic·to·ri·al [pɪk'tɔːrɪəl] *adj.* of, having
represented in, pictures.

pic·ture ['pɪktʃə*] *n.* **1.** painting
drawing, sketch, of sth., esp. as a worl
of art. **2.** beautiful person, thing, view
etc. **3.** *be the ~ of* (health, etc.), appea
to have (it) in a high degree. **4.** *in the ~*
fully informed or noticed. **5.** film (3)
the ~s, (Gt. Brit.) the cinema; *~-goer*
6. image on a television screen. *v.t*
make a *~* of; describe in words; have
or form a *~* of in one's mind; imagine

pic·tur·esque [ˌpɪktʃə'resk] *adj.* **1**
(of scenes, places, etc.) striking o
charming in appearance. **2.** (of a per
son, his language or behaviour) strik
ing; original; full of colour.

pid·gin ['pɪdʒɪn] *n.* *~ English,* mixture
of English and native words and idiom●
used in some parts of Asia, West Afri
ca, etc.

pie [paɪ] *n.* meat or fruit covered with
pastry and baked in a dish.

pie·bald ['paɪbɔːld] *adj.* (esp. of ●
horse) having white and dark patche
of irregular shape. *n.* *~* animal.

piece [piːs] *n.* **1.** part or bit of a soli●
substance: *in ~s,* broken; *come (take
break) to ~s.* **2.** separate instance o●
example: *a ~ of news (advice, luck
etc.).* **3.** unit or definite quantity ir
which goods are prepared for distribu
tion: *a ~ of cloth; sold only by the ~
~-goods* (esp. cotton and silk, ·i●
standard lengths). **4.** single composi
tion (in art, music, etc.): *a fine ~ o●
work (music, poetry, etc.).* **5.** single
thing out of a set: *a tea service o●
thirty ~s;* one of the wooden, metal
etc. objects moved on a board in such
games as chess. **6.** coin: *a fivepenny ~*
7. *pay by the ~s,* pay (a workman) by
the amount of work done, not by th●
time taken. *v.t.* put (parts, etc. *to
gether*); make by joining or adding *~*
together. **'~-meal** *adv.* (done) bit by
bit, a *~* at a time. **'~-work** *n.* worl
paid for according to the amount done
not by the time taken. **'~-,work·er** *n*

pier [pɪə*] *n.* **1.** structure of wood, iron, etc. built out into the sea as a landing-stage or for walking on for pleasure. **2.** pillar supporting a span (2) of a bridge, etc.; brickwork between windows or other openings.

pierce [pɪəs] *v.t. & i.* **1.** (of sharp-pointed instruments) go into or through; make (a hole) by doing this. **2.** (fig., of cold, pain, sounds, etc.) force a way into or through; affect deeply. **3.** penetrate (*through, into, etc.*).

pier·rot ['pɪərəʊ] *n.* member of a party of concert artistes who appear in loose, white clothes and tall caps.

a pierrot troupe with a piano

pi·ety ['paɪətɪ] *n.* (no pl.) being pious.
pif·fle ['pɪfl] *n.* (no pl.) (sl.) nonsense.
pig [pɪg] *n.* **1.** omnivorous mammal with a stout (3) body, short legs, bristly skin, and a long snout. **2.** (colloq.) dirty, greedy, or ill-mannered person. **3.** (sl., derog.) policeman. **4.** oblong mass of iron (~*-iron*) extracted from ore and shaped in a mould. ~**·gy**, ~**·gie** ['pɪgɪ] *n.* little ~. '~**·gy-back** *adv.* (U.S.A.) = pick-a-back. ¦~'**head·ed** *adj.* obstinate. '~**·sty** *n.* building for ~s. '~**·tail** *n.* plait of hair hanging down over the back of the neck.

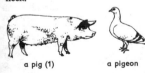

a pig (1)   a pigeon

pi·geon ['pɪdʒɪn] *n.* bird, wild or tame, of the dove family, some kinds being trained to carry letters. '~**-hole** *n.* one of a number of small, open boxes above a desk for keeping papers, etc. in. *v.t.* put (papers, etc.) in a ~-hole and forget them: (fig.) *The scheme was ~-holed* (i.e. consideration of it was postponed).

pig·ment ['pɪgmənt] *n.* (no pl.) colouring-matter for making dyes, paint, etc.; natural colouring-matter in the skin, hair, etc. of living beings.

pig·my, see *pygmy*.

pike¹ [paɪk] *n.* spear formerly used by soldiers fighting on foot: *as plain as a ~staff*, (fig.) easy to see or understand.

pike² [paɪk] *n.* large, fierce river-fish.

pil·chard ['pɪltʃəd] *n.* small sea-fish resembling the herring.

pile¹ [paɪl] *n.* heavy piece of timber driven into the ground, esp. under water, as a foundation for a building, etc. ~s. ¦~**·driv·er** *n.* machine for driving in ~s.

pile² [paɪl] *n.* **1.** number of things lying one upon another. **2.** large high building(s). **3.** *make a ~*, (colloq.) make a fortune. **4.** (*atomic*) ~, nuclear reactor. *v.t. & i.* **1.** put in a ~; make a ~ of: ~ *logs*; ~ *things up*. **2.** crowd *in, into,* or *on* a vehicle or *out of* a place, etc. **3.** ~ *up*, (a) accumulate; (b) (of vehicles) crash into each other. ~*-up* (n.), collision of several motor vehicles.

pile³ [paɪl] *n.* (no pl.) soft, thick, hair-like surface of velvet, some carpets, etc.

pil·fer ['pɪlfə*] *v.t. & i.* steal things of small value in small numbers or quantities.

pil·grim ['pɪlgrɪm] *n.* person who travels to a sacred place: ~*s to Mecca.* ~**·age** *n.* journey of a ~: *go on a ~age.*

pill [pɪl] *n.* small ball or tablet (4) of medicine for swallowing whole. *the ~,* oral contraceptive: *be on the ~,* be taking such ~s regularly.

pil·lage ['pɪlɪdʒ] *n. & v.t. & i.* plunder.

pil·lar ['pɪlə*] *n.* column, either as a support or as an ornament; (fig.) strong supporter (*of* a cause, organization, etc.). '~**-box** *n.* (Gt. Brit.) hollow ~ set up in the street in which letters are posted.

a pillar-box   a pineapple

pil·lion ['pɪljən] *n.* **1.** (hist.) seat for a second person behind the rider of a horse. **2.** seat for a passenger behind the driver of a motor bicycle: *ride ~* (be such a passenger).

pil·lo·ry ['pɪlərɪ] *n.* (hist.) wooden

framework in which the heads and hands of wrongdoers were secured as a punishment. *v.t.* (fig.) call public attention to faults, mistakes, etc.

pil·low ['pɪləʊ] *n.* soft cushion for the head, esp. in bed. '~·**case**, '~·**slip** *ns.* cotton or linen cover for a ~.

pi·lot ['paɪlət] *n.* **1.** person trained to take ships into or out of a harbour, up a river, etc. **2.** person trained to control aircraft in flight. **3.** (attrib.) experimental: ~ *scheme*, experiment for testing how sth. new would work, before it is used on a large scale. **4.** (fig.) guide. *v.t.* act as a ~ to.

pim·ple ['pɪmpl] *n.* small, hard, in-flamed spot on the skin.

pin [pɪn] *n.* short piece of stiff wire with a sharp point and a rounded head, used for fastening together pieces of cloth, paper, etc.: *a safety-~. don't care a ~*, don't care at all; ~*s and needles*, pricking sensation in the body caused by blood flowing again when circulation has been checked for a time. *v.t.* (-nn-) **1.** fasten (things *to-gether, up, to* sth., etc.) with a ~ or ~*s*: (fig.) ~ *one's hope on sb.* **2.** prevent from moving: ~*ned under the wrecked car*; ~ *sb. down* (to a promise, etc.), make him do what he ought to do. '~-**point** *v.t.* locate or aim with high precision; fix, determine, or establish with precision. '~-**prick** *n.* (fig.) small act, remark, etc. causing annoyance. '~-**up** *n.* (colloq.) picture of some favourite or famous person ~ned up on a wall, etc.: (attrib.) ~-*up girl.*

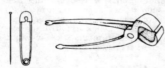

pins   (a pair of) pincers

pin·afore ['pɪnəfɔ:*] *n.* loose article of clothing worn over a dress to keep it clean.

pin·cers ['pɪnsəz] *n. pl.* (often *a pair of* ~) instrument for gripping things, pulling out nails, etc.

pinch [pɪntʃ] *v.t. & i.* **1.** take or have in a tight grip between the thumb and finger, or between two hard things that are pressed together: *He ~ed his finger in the doorway. He ~ed the top of the plant off.* **2.** be too tight; hurt by being too tight: *shoes that ~ (the feet).* **3.** *be ~ed for money*, have not

enough; ~*ed with cold*, suffering from the cold. **4.** (colloq.) steal; take with-out permission. *n.* **1.** painful squeeze; act of ~*ing* (1). (fig.) *feel the ~* (of poverty). **2.** amount that can be taken up with the thumb and finger: *a ~ of salt.* **3.** *at a ~*, if there is need and no other way is possible; *if it comes to the ~*, if it becomes absolutely neces-sary.

pine¹ [paɪn] *n.* kinds of evergreen tree with needle-shaped leaves (~-*needles*) and cones (~-*cones*); wood of this tree.

pine² [paɪn] *v.i.* **1.** waste *away* through sorrow or illness. **2.** have a strong desire (*for* sth., *to do* sth.).

pine·ap·ple ['paɪnˌæpl] *n.* (tropical plant with) sweet, juicy fruit. (See the picture at *pillar-box*.)

pin·ion¹ ['pɪnjən] *n.* bird's wing, esp. the outer joint; any flight-feather of a wing. *v.t.* hold or bind fast (sb.'s arms) to his sides.

pin·ion² ['pɪnjən] *n.* small cog-wheel with teeth fitting into those of a larger cog-wheel.

pink [pɪŋk] *n.* (no pl.) **1.** pale red colour. **2.** garden plant with sweet-scented flowers. **3.** *in the ~*, (sl.) very well. *adj.* of a pale red colour.

pin·nace ['pɪnɪs] *n.* ship's boat with (usu.) eight oarsmen; ship's boat driven by steam or petrol.

pin·na·cle ['pɪnəkl] *n.* **1.** tall, pointed ornament built on to a roof. **2.** (fig.) highest point: *at the ~ of his fame.*

pint [paɪnt] *n.* measure of capacity for liquids and certain dry goods, one-eighth of a gallon (= 0.57 litres, U.S.A. 0.47 litres): *a ~ of milk (of lentils).*

pi·o·neer [ˌpaɪə'nɪə*] *n.* **1.** person who goes first into a new or undeveloped country to settle or work there; first student of a new branch of study, etc.; explorer. **2.** (mil.) one of an advance party of soldiers (e.g. clearing or making roads). *v.i. & t.* act as a ~ (for).

pi·ous ['paɪəs] *adj.* **1.** having or show-ing deep love for religion. **2.** (old use) dutiful to parents. ~·**ly** *adv.*

pip¹ [pɪp] *n.* seed, esp. of a lemon, orange, apple, or pear.

pip² [pɪp] *n.* note of a time-signal on the telephone or radio.

pipe [paɪp] *n.* **1.** tube through which liquids or gases can flow. ~*line*, line of ~*s*, esp. for carrying petroleum from the well to distant places. **2.** musical wind instrument (tube with holes stopped with the fingers). **3.** *the ~s*,

pithy

bag⌣s. **4.** (sound of) whistle used by a boatswain. **5.** (tobacco-)⌣, tube with a bowl, used for smoking tobacco. **6.** (anat.) tubular organ in the body: wind⌣. *v.t. & i.* **1.** convey (water, etc.) through ⌣s (1). **2.** play (a tune) on a ⌣ (2, 3). **3.** summon (sailors) by blowing a ⌣ (4): ⌣ all hands on deck. **pip·er** *n.* player on a ⌣, esp. bag⌣s. **pip·ing** *n.* (no pl.) length of ⌣s (1), esp. for water and drains: ten feet of lead piping. *adj.* like the sound of a ⌣ (2, 3): a piping voice. *adv.* piping hot, hissing or very hot.

pi·quant ['pi:kənt] *adj.* pleasantly sharp to the taste; (fig.) pleasantly exciting to the mind. **pi·quan·cy** *n.* (no pl.).

pique [pi:k] *v.t.* **1.** hurt the pride or self-respect of. **2.** stir (the curiosity or interest). **3.** ⌣ oneself on (sth.), feel proud about. *n.* (no pl.) feeling one has when one's pride is hurt or one's curiosity is not satisfied; ill temper.

pi·rate ['paɪərət] *n.* **1.** sea-robber; sea-robbers' ship. **2.** person who infringes sb. else's copyright or other business rights, or who broadcasts without official authorization: (attrib.) a ⌣ radio station. *v.t.* reproduce (a book, etc.) without authority and for one's own profit. **pi·ra·cy** ['paɪərəsɪ] *n.*

pir·ou·ette [,pɪru'et] *n.* dancer's rapid turn on the point of the toe. *v.i.* make a ⌣ or series of ⌣s.

pis·tol ['pɪstl] *n.* small firearm held in one hand.

a piston inside a cylinder

pis·ton ['pɪstən] *n.* (in a pump or engine) short cylinder or round plate fitting closely inside another cylinder or tube in which it moves up and down or backwards and forwards to impart motion by means of a '⌣-rod *n.* rod to which a ⌣ is fixed. (See also the picture at cylinder.)

pit[1] [pɪt] *n.* **1.** deep hole in the earth, with steep sides, esp. one from which material is dug out: a chalk-⌣; a coal-⌣.

2. (Gt. Brit.) (people in) seats in the back part of the ground floor of a theatre. **3.** small dent in the skin, as left by smallpox, etc. **4.** hollow in an animal or plant body: ⌣ of the stomach, depression (2) below the bottom of the breastbone. **5.** hole in the floor of a garage or workshop from which the underside of motor vehicles can be examined and repaired. **6.** place at which racing cars stop for fuel, new tyres, etc. during a race. *v.t.* (-tt-) **1.** mark with ⌣s (3): a face ⌣ed with smallpox. **2.** match (a person or animal against) another in a fight, etc.: ⌣ one's strength against a rival. '⌣·fall *n.* ⌣ (1) with a covered opening, to trap wild animals; (fig.) unsuspected danger.

pit[2] [pɪt] *n.* (U.S.A.) stone (of fruit). *v.t.* (-tt-) (U.S.A.) remove the ⌣ from (a fruit).

pitch[1] [pɪtʃ] *v.t. & i.* **1.** put up (a tent, etc.). **2.** throw (a ball, etc.), esp. throw (sb. or sth. out, aside) with impatience or energetic dislike: P⌣ the drunkard out! **3.** (cause to) fall forwards or outwards: He (was) ⌣ed from the carriage. He ⌣ed on his head. **4.** (of a ship) move up and down as the bows rise and fall (cf. roll (4)). **5.** (music) set in a certain key: ⌣ a tune too high (in a lower key). **6.** ⌣ in, set to work with energy; ⌣ into, attack violently; ⌣ upon (sb.), select by chance. **7.** give a slope to (a roof). **8.** ⌣ed battle, battle for which two sides have made full preparations. *n.* **1.** (Gt. Brit.) place where sb. (esp. a street trader) usually does business. queer sb.'s ⌣, upset his plans. **2.** (cricket) part of the ground between the wickets. **3.** act of ⌣ing (2). **4.** amount of slope, esp. of a roof. **5.** (music and speech) degree of highness or lowness: the ⌣ of his voice. **6.** degree (of a quality): expectation raised to the highest ⌣. **7.** (of a ship) process of ⌣ing (4). '⌣·fork *n.* long-handled two-pointed fork for lifting hay, etc. *v.t.* lift or move with a ⌣fork.

pitch[2] [pɪtʃ] *n.* (no pl.) black, sticky substance made from coal tar or turpentine, used to fill cracks, cover roofs, etc. *v.t.* put ⌣ on. ⌣·'black, ⌣·'dark *adjs.* quite black or dark.

pitch·er[1] ['pɪtʃə*] *n.* large jug.

pitch·er[2] ['pɪtʃə*] *n.* (baseball) player who throws the ball.

pit·e·ous ['pɪtɪəs] *adj.* arousing pity.

pith [pɪθ] *n.* (no pl.) **1.** soft substance filling the stems of some plants. **2.** (fig.) most necessary or important part (of a speech, etc.). ⌣·y *adj.* (-ier, -iest) (esp.) full of forceful meaning; concise. **~·i·ly** *adv.*

pit·tance ['pɪtəns] *n.* low, insufficient payment or allowance (for work, etc.).

pity ['pɪtɪ] *n.* **1.** (no pl.) feeling of sorrow for the troubles, sufferings, etc. of another: *have* (*take*) ~ *on* (*sb.*), help (sb. in trouble). **2.** (event that gives) cause for regret or sorrow: *What a* ~ *that ... It's a thousand pities that ... v.t.* feel ~ for. **piti·able** ['pɪtɪəbl] *adj.* exciting ~; miserable; deserving only contempt. **piti·ful** *adj.* feeling ~; causing ~; arousing contempt. **piti·ful·ly** *adv.* **piti·less** *adj.* feeling no ~; merciless. **piti·less·ly** *adv.*

piv·ot ['pɪvət] *n.* central pin or point on which sth. turns; (fig.) sth. on which an argument or discussion depends. *v.t. & i.* **1.** place on, supply with, a ~. **2.** ~ *on*, turn as on a ~.

pix·ie, pixy ['pɪksɪ] *n.* small fairy.

plac·ard ['plækɑːd] *n.* sheet of paper with an announcement, displayed publicly. *v.t.* put ~s on (walls, etc.); make known by means of ~s.

pla·cate [plə'keɪt] *v.t.* soothe; take away (sb.'s) angry feelings.

place [pleɪs] *n.* **1.** particular part of space occupied by sth. or sb.; city, town, village, etc.; building or area of land used for a purpose that is stated: ~ *of worship*, church, etc.; ~s *of amusement*, cinemas, theatres, etc. **2.** *in* (*out of*) ~, in (not in) the right ~; *take* ~, (of an event) be held; happen; *give* ~ *to*, have one's ~ (or job) taken by; *in* ~ *of*, instead of. **3.** passage or part of a book, etc. reached in reading: *find* (*lose*) *one's* ~. **4.** work: *lose one's* ~, become unemployed. **5.** (in a competition) position among those whose success is recorded (e.g. the first three in a horse-race). **6.** position in social order, etc.: *keep sb. in his* ~, not allow him to be too familiar. *v.t.* **1.** put (sth.) in a certain ~; find a ~ for. **2.** give (an order to a tradesman) for (confidence in sb., etc.). **3.** give a ~ (5) to: *The horse I backed wasn't* ~*d.*

plac·id ['plæsɪd] *adj.* calm; untroubled; (of a person) not easily irritated. **~·ly** *adv.* **pla·cid·i·ty** [plæ'sɪdətɪ] *n.* (no pl.).

pla·gia·rize ['pleɪdʒəraɪz] *v.t.* take and use (e.g. in an essay) sb. else's ideas, words, etc. as if they were one's own. **pla·gia·rism** *n.* **pla·gia·rist** *n.*

plague [pleɪg] *n.* **1.** pestilence. **2.** cause of trouble, annoyance, or disaster: *a* ~ *of locusts. v.t.* annoy, esp. with repeated requests or questions.

plaice [pleɪs] *n.* kind of flat sea-fish.

plaid [plæd] *n.* long piece of woollen cloth worn over the shoulders by Scottish Highlanders.

plain[1] [pleɪn] *adj.* **1.** easy to see, hear, or understand: ~ *sailing*, (fig.) course of action that is simple and free from difficulties. **2.** simple; ordinary; without luxury or ornament: ~ *food* (*cooking*); *a* ~ *dress*; *a* ~ *blue dress* (i.e. of blue material without a design on it); *in* ~ *clothes*, (esp.) in ordinary clothes, not in uniform: *a* ~*-clothes policeman.* **3.** (of thoughts, actions, etc.) straightforward; frank: *in* ~ *words*; *to be* ~ *with you* (i.e. to speak openly); ~ *dealing.* **4.** (of sb.'s appearance) not pretty or handsome. *adv.* clearly. **~·ly** *adv.* **~·ness** *n.* (no pl.).

plain[2] [pleɪn] *n.* area of level country.

plain·tiff ['pleɪntɪf] *n.* person who brings an action in a lawcourt.

plain·tive ['pleɪntɪv] *adj.* sounding sad. **~·ly** *adv.*

plait [plæt] *v.t.* weave or twist (three or more lengths of hair, straw, etc.) under and over one another into one rope-like length. *n.* sth. made in this way: *wearing her hair in a* ~.

a plait

plan [plæn] *n.* **1.** outline drawing (of or for a building) showing the relative size, positions, etc. of the parts, esp. as if seen from above (cf. *elevation* (3)). **2.** diagram (of the parts of a machine). **3.** diagram showing how a garden, park, or other area of land has been, or is to be, laid out. **4.** arrangement for doing or using sth., considered in advance: ~s *for the summer holidays*; *working according to* ~. *v.t. & i.* (-*nn*-) make a ~ of or for; make ~s (*to do* sth.); consider and arrange in advance ~ (sth.) *out.* ~*ned economy*, economic system ~ned by government authorities.

plane[1] [pleɪn] *n.* **1.** flat or level surface

2. stage or level of development: *not in the same ~ as*, not at the same level (of thought, skill, etc.) as. **3.** tool with a blade (1) for smoothing wood, etc.

a plane¹ (3)

4. one of the main supporting surfaces of an aeroplane. **5.** aeroplane. *v.t. & i.* make smooth with a ~ (3): *~ down* (irregular surfaces). *adj.* perfectly flat; forming or lying along a ~ (1): *a ~ figure*; *~ geometry*.

plane² [pleɪn] *n.* sorts of tree with spreading branches and broad leaves.

plan·et ['plænɪt] *n.* one of the heavenly bodies (e.g. Mars) moving round the sun; one that moves round another ~ (as the moon moves round the earth).

plan·e·tary ['plænɪtəri] *adj.* of ~s.

plank [plæŋk] *n.* **1.** long, flat piece of timber; board. **2.** one of the items in a political platform (3). *v.t.* **1.** cover with ~s. **2.** ~ *sth. down*, (colloq.) put sth. down (e.g. money for a purchase) on a table, counter, etc.

plant [plɑːnt] *n.* **1.** living, growing thing other than an animal, esp. (*garden ~*) one with leaves, flowers, and roots, and smaller than a tree or shrub. **2.** machinery, etc. used in an industrial process, etc.: *The farm has its own lighting ~* (e.g. a generator for producing electric light). **3.** factory. *v.t.* **1.** put ~s in (a garden, etc.). **2.** put (bulbs, ~s, trees, etc.) in the ground to grow. **3.** place firmly in position: *~ oneself in the doorway*, stand there; *~ one's feet wide apart*, stand thus. **4.** establish (a colony); settle (a person) in a place as a colonist, etc. **plan·ta·tion** [plænˈteɪʃn] *n.* **1.** area of land ~ed with trees. **2.** large estate producing tea, tobacco, cotton, etc. **~·er** *n.* **1.** person growing crops on a ~ation (2): *coffee-(cotton-)~er*. **2.** machine for ~ing: *corn-~er*.

plaque [plɑːk] *n.* flat metal or porcelain plate on a wall as an ornament or as a memorial.

plas·ma ['plæzmə] *n.* colourless fluid of blood, lymph, or milk in which the corpuscles or fat-globules float: *blood ~*.

plas·ter ['plɑːstə*] *n.* **1.** (no pl.) paste of lime, sand, water, etc., used for coating walls and ceilings: *~ of Paris*, fine, white paste that becomes very hard when dry, used for making moulds, etc. *~ cast*, (a) mould made of ~ of Paris; (b) mould made with gauze and ~ of Paris to hold (esp.) a broken bone in place. **2.** medical preparation spread on a piece of cloth, etc. for use on the body (to relieve pain, cover a wound, etc.). (Cf. *sticking-~*.) *v.t.* **1.** put ~ (1) on (walls, etc.); put a ~ (2) on (the body). **2.** cover thickly (*with*): *hair ~ed with oil*. **~·er** *n.* workman who ~s walls, etc.

plas·tic ['plæstɪk] *adj.* **1.** (of materials) easily shaped: *Clay is a ~ substance.* (of goods) made of such materials: *~ bag (raincoats)*. **2.** of the art of modelling: *the ~ arts*; *~ surgery*. **3.** (fig.) easily bent or changed: *the ~ mind of a child*. *n.* substance derived from ~ material. *~s n. pl.* (sing. v.) (science of) ~ substances. **~·i·ty** [plæˈstɪsəti] *n.* (no pl.).

plate [pleɪt] *n.* **1.** circular, almost flat dish, usu. made of earthenware or china, from which food is eaten: *a dinner-(soup-)~*; *~·ful: a ~ of beef*. **2.** flat, thin sheet of metal, glass, etc., e.g. steel ~s for building ships, photographic ~s for use in cameras. *~ glass*, thick glass in large sheets for windows, etc. **3.** oblong piece of metal (usu. brass) with a person's, firm's, name, etc. fixed to the door or gate. **4.** (usu. photographic) book illustration printed separately from the text; metal, etc. ~ (2) of a page for use in reprinting. **5.** (collective sing.) (Gt. Brit.) gold or silver articles (e.g. spoons, dishes) for use at meals: *~-powder* (for cleaning such articles). **6.** (also *dental ~*) frame with artificial teeth, fitting the upper or lower jaw; (colloq.) denture. **7.** silver or gold cup as a prize for a (horse-)race; such a race. *v.t.* **1.** cover (a ship, etc.) with metal ~s (2). **2.** coat (one metal) with another: *silver-~d spoons*. **~·ful** *n.* amount that a ~ (1) holds.

pla·teau ['plætəʊ] *n.* (pl. ~x, ~s [-z]) expanse of level land high above sea-level.

plat·form ['plætfɔːm] *n.* **1.** flat surface built at a higher level than the railway lines at a station, for use by passengers. **2.** flat structure raised above floor-level for speakers in a hall, teachers in a classroom, etc. **3.** programme of a political party, esp. as stated before an election.

plat·ing ['pleɪtɪŋ] *n.* (esp.) thin coating of gold, silver, etc.

plat·i·num ['plætɪnəm] ***n.*** (no pl.) white, easily worked, heavy metal of great value.

plat·i·tude ['plætɪtju:d] ***n.*** statement that is obviously true, esp. one often heard before, but made as if it were new.

pla·toon [plə'tu:n] ***n.*** (mil.) tactical unit, subdivision of a company (6), commanded by a lieutenant.

plat·ter ['plætə*] ***n.*** (U.S.A. or old use) flat dish or plate, esp. for serving food.

plau·dit ['plɔ:dɪt] ***n.*** (usu. pl.) clapping, cry, etc. of approval or praise.

plau·si·ble ['plɔ:zɪbl] ***adj.*** **1.** (of excuses, arguments, etc.) seeming to be right or reasonable. **2.** (of persons) clever at producing ~ arguments, etc.: *a ~ rogue.* **plau·si·bil·i·ty** [ˌplɔ:zə'bɪlətɪ] ***n.***

play [pleɪ] ***v.i. & t.*** **1.** (contrasted with *work*) amuse oneself; have fun: *~ games.* **2.** perform (on a musical instrument): *~ the piano* (*violin*); act, take a part, in a stage drama: *~ing* (*the part of*) *Hamlet*; *~ the fool,* act foolishly; *~ the man,* be brave and honourable. **3.** (special uses with nouns): *~ a trick* (*a practical joke*) *on sb.,* perform, carry out, a trick against sb.; *~ tricks with sth.,* misuse it. **4.** (special uses with advs. & preps.): *~ at sth.,* do it in a not very serious spirit; *~ back,* reproduce (music, speech, etc.) from a tape, etc. after it has been recorded. *~-back* (n.), such reproduction of sound; *~ into sb.'s hands,* behave so that one gives him an advantage over oneself; *be ~ed out,* be tired out; have no strength or value left; *~ up,* (usu. imperative) put all one's energies into a game; *~ up to* (*sb.*), flatter him to win approval for oneself; *~ upon* (*sb.'s fears, etc.*), make use of them for one's own advantage; *~ with,* treat lightly; trifle with; allow the mind to think about. **5.** (of light, water) move about in a lively way: *sunlight ~ing on the water*; *fountains ~ing in the park.* **6.** send; be sent; direct (light, water, on or over sth.): *searchlights ~ing on the clouds*; *firemen ~ing their hoses on a burning building.* ***n.*** **1.** (no pl.) (contrasted with *work*) what is done for amusement; recreation: *in ~,* not seriously; *~ on words,* pun. **2.** drama for the stage: *the ~s of Shakespeare.* **3.** (no pl.) ~ing cards for money; gambling: *lose £50 in an hour's ~*; *high ~* (for large sums of money). **4.** (no pl.) ~ing of a game; manner of ~ing: *a lot of rough ~ in a football match*; *fair ~,* (fig.) equal conditions and treatment for all; *foul ~,* (fig.) treachery; violence. **5.** (no pl.) brisk, light, or fitful movement: *the ~ of sunlight on the water.* **6.** (no pl.) (space for) free and easy movement: *give one's fancy full ~,* allow one's imagination to be quite free; *a joint with too much ~,* one that is not tight enough. **7.** (no pl.) activity; operation: *come into ~,* begin to operate; *be in full ~,* be in full operation; *bring into ~,* bring into use. **~·er** ***n.*** **1.** person who ~s games. **2.** person who ~s a musical instrument. **3.** actor. **4.** mechanical device (2) for (re)producing sound: *a record-~er.* **'~·bill** ***n.*** theatre poster (1). **'~·boy** ***n.*** usu. rich man who is chiefly interested in enjoying himself. **'~ˌfel·low, '~-mate** ***ns.*** child who ~s with another. **~·ful** ***adj.*** full of fun; ready for ~; not serious. **~·ful·ly** ***adv.*** **'~ˌgo·er** ***n.*** person who often goes to the theatre. **'~·ground** ***n.*** piece of ground used for ~ing, esp. at a school. **'~·thing** ***n.*** toy. **'~·time** ***n.*** period for ~. **'~·wright** ***n.*** person who writes ~s for the theatre.

play·ing-card ['pleɪɪŋkɑ:d] ***n.*** oblong piece of thin cardboard used in games.

'play·ing-field ***n.*** field used in outdoor games.

plea [pli:] ***n.*** **1.** (law) statement made by or for a person charged in a lawcourt. **2.** request: *~s for help.* **3.** excuse offered for wrongdoing.

plead [pli:d] ***v.i. & t.*** **1.** make a plea (1); speak for either side in a lawcourt: *get a lawyer to ~ one's case*; *~ (not) guilty,* admit (deny) that one is guilty. **2.** ask earnestly: *~ for mercy*; *~ with sb. to show mercy.* **3.** offer as an excuse: *The thief ~ed poverty.*

pleas·ant ['pleznt] ***adj.*** giving pleasure; agreeable; friendly. **~·ly** ***adv.*** **~·ness** ***n.*** (no pl.). **~·ry** ***n.*** joking remark; humour.

please [pli:z] ***v.i. & t.*** **1.** give satisfaction (to); be agreeable (to); give pleasure (to): *be anxious to ~*; *(if you) ~,* polite word(s) used in making a request; *this will ~ you.* **2.** think fit; like; wish: *Take as many as you ~. Do as you ~.* **pleas·ing** ***adj.*** agreeable; giving pleasure.

plea·sure ['pleʒə*] ***n.*** **1.** (no pl.) feeling of being happy or satisfied: *take ~ in,* enjoy; *with ~,* willingly. **2.** thing that gives happiness. **plea·sur·able** ['pleʒərəbl] ***adj.*** giving ~.

pleat [pli:t] ***n.*** fold made by doubling cloth on itself. ***v.t.*** make ~s in: *a ~ed skirt.*

pleats   a pleated skirt

ple·be·ian [plɪ'biːən] *n. & adj.* (person who is) of the lower social classes.

leb·i·scite ['plebɪsɪt] *n.* (decision made upon a political question by the) votes of all qualified citizens.

ledge [pledʒ] *n.* **1.** sth. left with sb. to be kept by him until the giver has done sth. that he is under obligation to do; article left with a pawnbroker. **2.** sth. given as a sign of love, favour, approval, etc.; promise or agreement: *a ~ of my friendship*; *under ~ of secrecy*. *v.t.* **1.** give (sth.) as a ~; give (sb.) a promise, make an undertaking (to do sth.). **2.** drink the health of.

le·na·ry ['pliːnərɪ] *adj.* (of powers) unlimited; (of a meeting) attended by all who have the right to attend.

leni·po·ten·tia·ry [,plenɪpəʊ'tenʃərɪ] *n. & adj.* (person, e.g. representative, ambassador) having full power to act, make decisions, etc. (on behalf of his government, etc.).

len·ty ['plentɪ] *n.* (no pl.) more than enough (of): *~ of bread*; *there are ~ of oranges*; *food and drink in ~*; *we are in ~ of time*. **plen·ti·ful** *adj.* in large quantities or numbers. **plen·te·ous** ['plentjəs] *adj.* (liter.) plentiful.

leu·ri·sy ['plʊərəsɪ] *n.* (no pl.) serious illness in which the skin of the lungs and the chest wall is inflamed.

li·able ['plaɪəbl] *adj.* easily bent or twisted; (of the mind) easily influenced; open to suggestion. **pli·abil·i·ty** [,plaɪə'bɪlətɪ] *n.* (no pl.). **li·ant** ['plaɪənt] *adj.* pliable.

li·ers ['plaɪəz] *n. pl.* (often *a pair of ~*) tool, hinged like scissors, for holding, bending, turning, or twisting things.

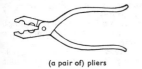

(a pair of) pliers

light[1] [plaɪt] *n.* sad or serious condition: *His affairs were in a sad ~*.
light[2] [plaɪt] *v.t.* *~ one's word*, give one's word; promise; *~ one's troth, ~*

oneself, (old use) engage oneself to be married or to marry.

plim·solls ['plɪmsəlz] *n. pl.* (U.S.A. *sneakers*) canvas sports shoes with a pliable rubber sole.

plinth [plɪnθ] *n.* square block or base supporting a column.

plod [plɒd] *v.i.* (-*dd*-) continue walking, working, etc. slowly but without resting: *~ding away at one's work*; *~ding along the road*. **~der** *n.* (esp.) slow but earnest worker.

plop [plɒp] *n.* sound as of a small object falling into water without a splash. *v.i.* (-*pp*-) make a ~; fall with a ~.

plot[1] [plɒt] *n.* small piece of land.

plot[2] [plɒt] *n.* **1.** plan or outline of the events in a story, esp. a novel or a drama. **2.** secret plan: *a ~ to overthrow the government*. *v.t.* (-*tt*-) **1.** make secret plans (4) (*to do* sth., *for* or *against* sth.): *~ sb.'s ruin*; *~ting against the State*. **2.** represent, mark the position of, sth. on a chart or graph: *~ a temperature curve*. **~ter** *n.*

plough (U.S.A. *plow*) [plaʊ] *n.* **1.** instrument for cutting and turning up the soil. **2.** instrument or device (2) resembling a ~: *a snow-~*. *v.t. & i.* **1.** break up (land) with a ~; use a ~. **2.** force (a way) through; advance laboriously: *a ship ~ing through the heavy waves*; *~ through a dull book*. **3.** (Gt. Brit., sl.) reject (a candidate) in an examination. '**~man** *n.* man who guides a ~. '**~share** *n.* blade (3) of a ~.

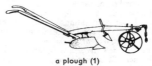

a plough (1)

pluck [plʌk] *v.t. & i.* **1.** pull the feathers off (a hen, goose, etc.). **2.** pick (flowers, fruit); pull (weeds, etc. *up* or *out*). **3.** snatch (*at* sth.); take hold of and pull (*at*). **4.** sound (the string of a musical instrument) by pulling at it. **5.** *~ up courage*, summon one's courage; overcome one's fears. *n.* (no pl.) courage; spirit: *a boy with plenty of ~*. **~y** *adj.* (-*ier*, -*iest*) brave. **~·i·ly** *adv.*

plug [plʌg] *n.* **1.** piece of wood, metal, etc. used to stop up a hole (e.g. in a barrel or wash-basin). **2.** device (2) for making a connection with a supply of electric current. **3.** sparking-~. *v.t.*

& i. (*-gg-*) **1.** stop up (a hole) with a ~ (1). **2.** ~ *away at*, (colloq.) work hard at. **3.** ~ *in*, make a connection with a ~ (2).

a plug (1)   an electric plug (2)   a sparking-plug (3)

plum [plʌm] *n.* **1.** (tree having a) soft, round, smooth-skinned fruit with a stone-like seed. **2.** sth. considered good and desirable, esp. well-paid employment. '~-ˌcake *n.* cake made with currants and raisins. ˌ~-'pud·ding *n.* **1.** boiled pudding containing currants, raisins, eggs, spices, etc., eaten at Christmas. **2.** ordinary pudding with raisins.

plum·age ['pluːmɪdʒ] *n.* (no pl.) bird's feathers.

plumb [plʌm] *n.* piece of lead tied to the end of a cord or rope (~-*line*) for finding the depth of water or testing whether a wall is perpendicular: *out of* ~, not perpendicular. *adv.* exactly. *v.t.* (fig.) get to the root of (a question, mystery).

plumb·er ['plʌmə*] *n.* man who fits pipes (for water, etc.) into buildings and repairs them. **plumb·ing** ['plʌm-ɪŋ] *n.* (no pl.) **1.** work of a ~. **2.** pipes, watertanks, etc. in a building.

plume [pluːm] *n.* feather, esp. one used for decorating; ornament of feathers; sth. suggesting a feather by its shape: *a* ~ *of steam. v.t.* **1.** (of a bird) ~ *itself* (*its feathers*), smooth the feathers. **2.** ~ *oneself* (*on*), congratulate oneself.

plump¹ [plʌmp] *adj.* (of an animal, a person) rounded; fat in a pleasant-looking way: ~ *cheeks. v.t. & i.* (often ~ *up* or *out*) make or become ~. ~·ness *n.* (no pl.).

plump² [plʌmp] *v.t. & i.* **1.** (cause to, allow to) fall, drop, suddenly and heavily: ~ (*oneself*) *down in a chair.* **2.** ~ *for*, choose, vote for, with confidence. *adv.* suddenly; abruptly.

plun·der ['plʌndə*] *v.t. & i.* take goods from (places) by force, rob (people), esp. during war or civil disorder. *n.* (no pl.) ~ing; goods taken. ~·er *n.*

plunge [plʌndʒ] *v.t. & i.* **1.** put (sth.), go, suddenly and with force, (*into*): *one's hand into water* (*a hole*); ~ *into a lake*; (fig.) ~ *a room into darkness* (e.g. by putting out the lights). **2.** (of a horse, a ship) move forward or downward violently. *n.* act of plunging (e.g. from a diving-platform into water): *take the* ~, (fig.) decide to do sth. risky or difficult.

plu·per·fect [ˌpluː'pɜːfɪkt] *adj.* (gram.) expressing action completed before some past time stated or implied (formed in English by *had* and a *p.p.*: *we had called*). *n.* ~ tense.

plu·ral ['plʊərəl] *n. & adj.* (form of word) used with reference to more than one: *The* ~ *of ox is oxen.*

plus [plʌs] *prep.* with the addition of: *Two* ~ *five is seven* (2+5 = 7); above zero. *adj.* **1.** additional; extra. **2.** (electr.) having a positive charge. **3.** (math.) positive: *the* ~ *sign*, the sign (+); *a* ~ *quantity*, a quantity greater than 0 (e.g. + 10). *n.* the sign (+) positive quantity; (fig.) advantage. ˌ~-'fours *n. pl.* wide, loose-fitting knickerbockers.

plush [plʌʃ] *n.* (no pl.) kind of silk or cotton cloth with a soft nap².

plu·toc·ra·cy [pluː'tɒkrəsɪ] *n.* (government by a) rich and powerful class. **plu·to·crat** ['pluːtəʊkræt] *n.* person who is powerful because of his wealth. **plu·to·crat·ic** [ˌpluːtəʊ'krætɪk] *adj.*

ply¹ [plaɪ] *n.* **1.** layer of wood or thickness of cloth: *three-*~ *wood.* ~*wood* thin, strong wood made by sticking several layers together with the grains (4) crosswise. **2.** one strand in wool, yarn, rope, etc.: *three-*~ *wool for knitting.*

ply² [plaɪ] *v.t. & i.* **1.** work with (an instrument): ~*ing her needle.* **2.** (of ships, buses, etc.) go regularly (*between*, *from ... to*): *ships that* ~ *between Glasgow and New York.* **3.** ~ *a trade*, work at it. **4.** ~ *sb. with*, keep him constantly supplied with (food and drink), questions, news, etc.).

pneu·mat·ic [njuː'mætɪk] *adj.* worked or driven by, filled with, compressed air: ~ *drills* (*tyres*).

pneu·mo·nia [njuː'məʊnjə] *n.* (no pl.) serious illness with inflammation of the lung(s).

poach¹ [pəʊtʃ] *v.t.* cook (an egg) by dropping the contents into boiling water: ~*ed eggs.*

poach² [pəʊtʃ] *v.t. & i.* (go on sb. else's land and) take (pheasants, hares, salmon, etc.) illegally. ~·er *n.*

pock [pɒk] *n.* spot on the skin caused

by smallpox: ~-*marked*, with pits left after smallpox.

ock·et ['pɒkɪt] *n.* **1.** small bag in an article of clothing for carrying things in. *in* (*out of*) ~, having gained (lost) money as the result of doing sth. **2.** string bag on a billiard table. **3.** hole, cavity in rock, etc. containing gold or ore. **4.** air ~. *v.t.* **1.** put in one's ~. **2.** keep (money, etc.) for oneself, esp. when this is wrong. **3.** hide, conceal: ~ *one's pride* (*feelings*). '~-**book** *n.* **1.** small notebook. **2.** leather case for paper money; wallet. **3.** (U.S.A.) woman's purse or handbag. '~-**knife** *n.* small knife with one or more folding blades (1) to be carried in a ~. '~-**mon·ey** *n.* money for small needs, esp. money given to children.

od [pɒd] *n.* long seed-vessel of various plants, esp. peas and beans. *v.t. & i.* (-*dd*-) take (peas, etc.) out of ~s; form ~s.

odgy ['pɒdʒɪ] *adj.* (-*ier*, -*iest*) (of a person) short and fat; (of a face) soft and fat.

o·em ['pəʊɪm] *n.* piece of writing in verse form, esp. one expressing deep feeling or noble thought in beautiful language. **po·et** ['pəʊɪt] *n.* writer of ~s. **po·et·ess** ['pəʊɪtɪs] *n.* female poet. **po·et·ic, po·et·i·cal** [pəʊ'etɪk(l)] *adjs.* of poets or poetry; in the form of verse: *poetic drama.* **po·et·ry** ['pəʊɪtrɪ] *n.* (no pl.) art of a poet; ~s; quality producing feeling like that produced by ~s: *the poetry of motion.*

oi·gnant ['pɔɪnənt] *adj.* **1.** sharp in taste or smell: ~ *sauces.* **2.** distressing to the feelings; deeply moving; keen: ~ *sorrow* (*regret, memories*).

oin·set·tia [pɔɪn'setɪə] *n.* plant with large, bright-red leaves like flower petals.

oint [pɔɪnt] *n.* **1.** sharp end (of a pin, pencil, cape², etc.). **2.** dot made by or as by the ~ of a pencil, etc. on paper: *a decimal* ~; *two* ~ *five* (2.5); *a full* ~, a full stop (cf. *full* (3)). **3.** mark, position (real or imagined), in space or time: ~ *of view*, position from which sth. is looked at; (fig.) way of looking at a question, etc.; *a* ~ *of departure*; *a turning-*~ *in his career*; *at this* ~, at this place or moment; *be on the* ~ *of doing sth.*, be about to do it; *when it comes to the* ~, when it is time for action or decision. **4.** mark on a scale; degree: *the boiling-*~. *of water. The cost of living has gone up five* ~s. **5.** one of thirty-two marks on the compass: ~s *of the compass* (e.g. N.N.E.). **6.**

chief idea, purpose, etc. of sth. said, done, planned, etc.: *miss* (*see*) *the* ~ *of a joke*; *come to the* ~, reach the most important part of an explanation, etc.; *carry* (*gain*) *one's* ~, persuade others to agree to one's purpose, etc.; *off* (*away from*) *the* ~; *to the* ~, concerned with what is being discussed, etc. **7.** detail, step, division, esp. one marking stages in the development of an argument, theory, etc.: *the first* ~ *of my argument*; *explain a theory,* ~ *by* ~. **8.** marked quality; characteristic: *What are her best* ~s *as a secretary?* **9.** unit for measuring scores in some games and sports: *score twenty* ~s. *The boxer won on* ~s (not by a knock-out). **11.** (pl.)

points

tapering movable rails by which a train can move from one track to another. *v.t. & i.* **1.** ~ *to*, show the position or direction of; indicate; suggest; be a sign of: *Everything* ~*ed to his guilt.* **2.** ~ *at*, direct attention to: ~ *a finger accusingly at sb.*; aim, direct, at: *The rocket was* ~*ed at* (*towards*) *the moon.* **3.** ~ *out*, call attention to, show, (a fact, *that* ...). **4.** make a ~ (1) on (e.g. a pencil); give sharpness to (advice, a moral). **5.** (of a dog) stand rigidly, usu. one foot raised, and with the muzzle ~ing in the direction of game. ,~-'**blank** *adj.* aimed, fired, at very close range; (fig., of sth. said, e.g. a refusal) in a way that leaves no room for doubt. *adv.* in a ~-blank manner. '~-,**du·ty** *n.* (Gt. Brit.) work of a policeman or traffic warden stationed at a particular ~ (e.g. to direct traffic, etc.). ~·**ed** *adj.* **1.** (fig.) directed definitely against a person or his behaviour: *a* ~*ed reproof*; *showing* ~*ed attentions to the pretty film star.* **2.** (of wit) sharp. ~·**er** *n.* **1.** stick used to ~ to things on a map, blackboard, etc. **2.** indicator on a dial. **3.** large, short-haired dog that hunts by scent and indicates the presence of game by ~ing (5). (See the picture on page 380.) ~·**less** *adj.* (fig.) meaningless; useless.

poise

a pointer (3)

poise [pɔɪz] *v.t. & i.* be or keep balanced; support in a particular place or manner. *n.* **1.** (no pl.) balance. **2.** way in which one carries oneself or holds one's head. **3.** (no pl.) (fig.) quiet self-confidence.

poi·son ['pɔɪzn] *n.* substance causing death or harm if absorbed by a living thing (animal or plant); (fig.) principle, idea, etc. that is harmful to society, etc. *v.t.* give ~ to; put ~ on; kill with ~; (fig.) injure morally. **~·er** *n.* **~·ous** *adj.*

poke [pəʊk] *v.t. & i.* **1.** push (with a stick, one's finger, etc.): ~ *the fire*; ~ *sth. in* (*down, etc.*). **2.** make (a hole) by pushing sth. in or through; get (a stick, etc.) *into* or *through* sth. by pushing. **3.** ~ *fun at*, make fun of. *n.* act of poking.

pok·er¹ ['pəʊkə*] *n.* metal bar for stirring or breaking up the coal in a fire.

po·ker² ['pəʊkə*] *n.* (no pl.) card-game for two or more players.

poky ['pəʊkɪ] *adj.* (*-ier, -iest*) (of a room, etc.) small; narrow.

po·lar ['pəʊlə*] *adj.* of or near the North or South Pole: ~ *bear*, the white kind living near the North Pole.

pole¹ [pəʊl] *n.* **1.** *North P~, South P~,* two ends of the earth's axis; two points in the sky about which the stars appear to turn; ~*-star*, star near the North P~ of the sky. **2.** either of the two ends of a magnet or the terminal points of an electric battery: *the negative* (*positive*) ~.

pole² [pəʊl] *n.* **1.** long, thick rod of wood or metal as used for supporting telegraph wires, tents, etc. or for flying a flag. **2.** unit for measuring distance: 5½ yards (= 5.03 metres). '~-,jump(·ing), '~-,vault(·ing) *ns.* jump(ing) over a high crossbar with the help of a long ~ held in the hands. '~-,vault·er *n.*

Pole [pəʊl] *n.* native or inhabitant of Poland.

po·lem·ic [pɒ'lemɪk] *adj. & n.* (of) dispute or argument.

po·lice [pə'liːs] *n.* (collective pl. ~, pl. v.) department of government, body (5) of men, concerned with the keeping of public order; *the ~,* the members of this body: *the ~ are on his track. v.t.* keep order in (a place) with ~, or as with ~. ~ **con·sta·ble** *n.* (Gt. Brit.) ~man of ordinary rank. **~-court** [pə'liːskɔːt] *n.* lawcourt for small offences. **~·man** [pə'liːsmən] *n.* member of the ~ force. **~-of·fi·cer** [pə'liːsˌɒfɪsə*] *n.* ~man or ~woman. ~ **sta·tion** *n.* office of the ~ in a district. **~·wom·an** [pə'liːsˌwʊmən] *n.* woman who is a member of the ~ force.

pol·i·cy¹ ['pɒlɪsɪ] *n.* **1.** plan of action, esp. one made by a government, business company, etc.: *foreign ~. Honesty is the best ~.* **2.** (no pl.) wise, sensible conduct.

pol·i·cy² ['pɒlɪsɪ] *n.* written statement of the terms of a contract of insurance.

po·lio ['pəʊlɪəʊ] *n.* (no pl.) (colloq. abbr. for) **po·lio·my·eli·tis** [ˌpəʊlɪəʊˌmaɪə'laɪtɪs] *n.* (no pl.) acute (4), infectious virus disease with inflammation of nerve cells in the grey matter of the spinal cord, often resulting in permanent paralysis.

pol·ish ['pɒlɪʃ] *v.t. & i.* **1.** make or become smooth and shiny by rubbing. **2.** (esp. in p.p.) improve in behaviour, intellectual interests, etc. **3.** ~ (*sth.*) *off*, finish quickly. *n.* **1.** (no pl.) (surface, etc., obtained by) ~ing. **2.** substance used for ~ing: *shoe-~.*

Pol·ish ['pəʊlɪʃ] *adj.* of Poland or the Poles. *n.* the language of Poland.

po·lite [pə'laɪt] *adj.* (~*r, ~st*) **1.** having, showing the possession of, good manners and consideration for other people. **2.** refined: ~ *society.* **~·ly** *adv.* **~·ness** *n.*

pol·i·tic ['pɒlɪtɪk] *adj.* **1.** (of persons) acting or judging wisely. **2.** (of actions) well-judged; prudent.

po·lit·i·cal [pə'lɪtɪkl] *adj.* of the State; of government; of public affairs; of politics: ~ *asylum,* protection given by a government to sb. who has left his own country for ~ reasons; ~ *economy,* economics; ~ *geography* (of boundaries, communications, etc.); ~ *prisoners* (imprisoned for opposing the government). **~·ly** *adv.*

pol·i·ti·cian [ˌpɒlɪ'tɪʃn] *n.* person taking part in politics or much interested in politics.

pol·i·tics ['pɒlɪtɪks] *n. pl.* (sing. or pl. v.) science or art of government; political views, affairs, questions, etc.: *party ~; local ~.*

poll [pəʊl] *n.* **1.** voting at an election; list of voters; counting of votes; place where voting takes place: *go to the ~;*

at the head of the ~ (i.e. having won). **2.** assessment of public opinion by putting questions to a representative selection of persons: *a (public) opinion* ~. **3.** (old use) head. *v.t. & i.* **1.** vote at an election; receive (a certain number of) votes. **2.** cut off the top of (the horns of animals); (= *pollard*) cut off the top of (a tree). '**~-tax** *n.* tax to be paid equally by every person. '**~-ing-booth** *n.* place where voters go to record votes.

pol·lard ['pɒləd] *v.t.* cut off the top of (a tree) so that a thick head of new branches grows out. *n.* ~ed tree.

pol·len ['pɒlən] *n.* (no pl.) fine powder (usu. yellow) formed on flowers, that fertilizes other flowers when carried to them by the wind, insects, etc. **pol·li·nate** ['pɒləneɪt] *v.t.* make fertile with ~.

pol·lute [pə'luːt] *v.t.* make dirty, foul, or filthy; contaminate or defile (man's environment): ~d *rivers (water)*. **pol·lu·tant** *n.* sth. that ~s. **pol·lut·er** *n.* person who ~s. **pol·lu·tion** [pə'luːʃn] *n.* polluting or being ~d; that which ~s.

po·lo ['pəʊləʊ] *n.* (no pl.) ball game played on horseback with mallets. '**~-neck** *n.* thick, round, turned-over collar: *a ~-neck sweater*.

poly- ['pɒlɪ-] *pref.* many. **po·lyg·a·my** [pə'lɪgəmɪ] *n.* (no pl.) (custom of) having more than one wife at the same time. **~·glot** ['pɒlɪglɒt] *adj.* knowing, using, written in, many languages. *n.* ~glot person or book. **~·gon** ['pɒlɪgən] *n.* figure with five or more straight sides. **~·syl·la·ble** ['pɒlɪ,sɪləbl] *n.* word of several (usu. more than three) syllables. **~·tech·nic** [,pɒlɪ'teknɪk] *n.* school where many, esp. technical subjects are taught.

pome·gran·ate ['pɒmɪ,grænɪt] *n.* (tree with) thick-skinned fruit that, when ripe, has a reddish centre full of seeds.

pom·mel ['pʌml] *n.* part of a saddle that sticks up at the front. *v.t.* (*-ll-*, U.S.A. also *-l-*) pummel.

pomp [pɒmp] *n.* (no pl.) splendid display, esp. at a public event.

pomp·ous ['pɒmpəs] *adj.* full of, showing, self-importance; over-dignified. **~·ly** *adv.* **pom·pos·i·ty** [pɒm-'pɒsətɪ] *n.*

pond [pɒnd] *n.* small area of still water, esp. one made or used as a drinking-place for cattle.

pon·der ['pɒndə*] *v.t. & i.* consider; be deep in thought.

pon·der·able ['pɒndərəbl] *adj.* that can be weighed or measured.

pon·der·ous ['pɒndərəs] *adj.* **1.** not moved or moving easily because of weight. **2.** (fig.) dull; tedious.

pon·iard ['pɒnjəd] *n.* dagger.

pon·tiff ['pɒntɪf] *n.* **1.** pope. **2.** (old use) chief priest; bishop.

pon·toon [pɒn'tuːn] *n.* **1.** flat-bottomed boat. **2.** one of a number of such boats, or a floating, hollow metal structure, supporting a roadway over a river, etc.: *a ~ bridge.*

po·ny ['pəʊnɪ] *n.* horse of small breed. '**~-tail** *n.* long hair tied at the back of the head, hanging down like a ~'s tail.

poo·dle ['puːdl] *n.* kind of dog with thick, curling hair, kept as a pet.

pooh [puː] *int.* expression of contempt. ,**~-'pooh** *v.t.* treat (an idea, etc.) with contempt.

pool[1] [puːl] *n.* **1.** small area of still water, esp. one naturally formed. **2.** water or other liquid on the floor, on a road, etc. **3.** part of a river where the water is quiet and deep. **4.** swimming-~.

pool[2] [puːl] *n.* **1.** (gambling) total of money staked by a group of gamblers: *football ~s.* **2.** arrangement by business firms to share business and divide profits; common fund or service provided by or shared among many. **3.** game for several players played on a billiard-table. *v.t.* put (money, etc.) together for the use of all who contribute: *They ~ed their savings and bought a car.*

poop [puːp] *n.* (raised deck at the) stern of a ship.

poor [pʊə*] *adj.* **1.** having little money; not having and not able to buy enough food, clothing, etc.: *the ~*, (pl.) ~ people. **2.** deserving or needing help or sympathy. **3.** small in quantity: *a ~ supply of teachers.* **4.** low in quality: ~ *soil (food); in ~ health.* '**~-house** *n.* (hist.) workhouse. ,**~-'spir·it·ed** *adj.* lacking in courage. **~·ly** *adv.* **1.** badly; with little success. **2.** ~*ly off,* having little money. *pred. adj.* ill; in ~ health: *be (looking) rather ~ly.* **~·ness** *n.* (no pl.) lack of some good quality: *the ~ness of the soil.* (Cf. *poverty.*)

pop[1] [pɒp] *v.t. & i.* (*-pp-*) **1.** (cause to) make a sharp, quick sound (as when a cork comes out of a bottle). **2.** (cause to) go or come (*in, out, etc.*) quickly: *always ~ping in and out; ~ping his head in at the door.* **3.** (U.S.A.) parch (maize) till it bursts open. ~*corn,* maize treated in this way. *n.* **1.** sharp sound like that heard when a cork is pulled out of a bottle. **2.** (colloq.) bottled drink with gas in it.

pop² [pɒp] *adj.* (colloq., abbr. for) popular: ~ *music* (*singers, song, records*) (e.g. those popular on radio and TV); ~ *group* (singers and players of ~ music). *n.* (colloq.) popular concert, record, music, song, etc. ~ **art** *n.* art form that uses everyday objects, such as comic strips, soup tins, posters, etc. as its subject matter.

pop³ [pɒp] *n.* (U.S.A., colloq.) = father.

pope [pəup] *n.* (Bishop of Rome as) head of the Roman Catholic Church.

pop-eyed ['pɒpaɪd] *adj.* (colloq.) having bulging eyes; having eyes wide open (with surprise, etc.).

pop·lar ['pɒplə*] *n.* (wood of) tall, straight, quickly-growing tree.

pop·lin ['pɒplɪn] *n.* (no pl.) cloth of silk and wool with raised lines on it; kind of strong, shiny cotton cloth used for shirts, etc.

pop·py ['pɒpɪ] *n.* sorts of plant, wild and cultivated, with large flowers, esp. red; from the juice of one sort opium is made.

pop·u·lace ['pɒpjʊləs] *n.* *the* ~, the common people; the general public.

pop·u·lar ['pɒpjʊlə*] *adj.* **1.** of or for the people: ~ *government*; ~ (i.e. low) *prices*. **2.** suited to the tastes, educational level, etc. of the general public: ~ *science*. **3.** liked and admired by the public: ~ *film actors*. ~**·i·ty** [,pɒpjʊ-'lærətɪ] *n.* (no pl.) condition of being ~ (3). ~**ize** *v.t.* make ~ (2, 3).

pop·u·late ['pɒpjʊleɪt] *v.t.* people. **pop·u·la·tion** [,pɒpjʊ'leɪʃn] *n.* (number of) people living in a place, country, etc. or a special section of them: *population explosion*, rapid increase of population of the world or a country. **pop·u·lous** ['pɒpjʊləs] *adj.* thickly ~d.

por·ce·lain ['pɔːsəlɪn] *n.* (no pl.) (articles, e.g. cups, plates, made of a) fine china with a coating of transparent material called *glaze*.

porch [pɔːtʃ] *n.* **1.** built-out, roofed doorway or entrance to a building. **2.** (U.S.A.) = veranda(h).

a porcupine

por·cu·pine ['pɔːkjʊpaɪn] *n.* small, rat-like animal covered with quills (2).

pore¹ [pɔː*] *n.* tiny opening in the skin through which sweat passes.

pore² [pɔː*] *v.i.* ~ *over*, study (a book, etc.) with close attention; ~ *upon*, give one's close attention to (problems).

pork [pɔːk] *n.* (no pl.) meat from a pig, esp. unsalted. (Cf. *ham, bacon*.)

porn [pɔːn], **por·no** ['pɔːnəʊ] *adjs.* (colloq., abbr. for) pornographic. *ns.* (no pl.) (colloq., abbr. for) **por·nog·ra·phy** [pɔː'nɒgrəfɪ] *n.* (no pl.) description or portrayal of any activity regarded as obscene, esp. sexual activity, in literature, films, etc.; such literature, etc. **por·no·graph·ic** [,pɔːnəʊ'græfɪk] *adj.*

po·rous ['pɔːrəs] *adj.* allowing liquid to pass through (as sandy soil does).

por·poise ['pɔːpəs] *n.* sea animal rather like a small whale, about five feet long and with a blunt, rounded snout.

por·ridge ['pɒrɪdʒ] *n.* (no pl.) soft food made by boiling oatmeal in water or milk.

port¹ [pɔːt] *n.* (town with a) harbour.

port² [pɔːt] *n.* **1.** doorway in a ship's side for loading or unloading. **2.** small glass window in a ship's side that closes a '~·hole *n.* opening for admission of light and air to a cabin in a ship.

port³ [pɔːt] *n.* left side of a ship or aircraft as one looks forward. *v.t.* turn (a ship's helm) to ~. (Cf. *starboard*.)

port⁴ [pɔːt] *n.* (also ~ *wine*) strong, sweet, dark-red wine of Portugal.

por·table ['pɔːtəbl] *adj.* that can be carried about; not heavy or fixed: *a* ~ *radio* (*television set, typewriter*). *n.* ~ object, esp. a ~ radio, television set, or typewriter.

por·tage ['pɔːtɪdʒ] *n.* (cost of) carrying goods, esp. when goods have to be carried overland between two rivers or parts of a river.

por·tal ['pɔːtl] *n.* doorway, esp. an imposing one of a large building.

port·cul·lis [,pɔːt'kʌlɪs] *n.* iron grating lowered in front of the gateway of castles, etc. to keep out attackers.

por·tend [pɔː'tend] *v.t.* be a sign or warning of (a future event, etc.). **por·tent** ['pɔːtent] *n.* thing, esp. sth. marvellous or mysterious, which ~s sth. **por·ten·tous** [pɔː'tentəs] *adj.* extraordinary; marvellous; (humor.) solemn.

por·ter¹ ['pɔːtə*] *n.* **1.** person whose work is to carry luggage, etc. at railway stations, hotels, etc. **2.** (U.S.A. *doorman*) person who tends¹ the door, esp. of large buildings, hotels, etc. **3.** (U.S.A.) attendant in a sleeping-car.

por·ter² ['pɔːtə*] *n.* dark-brown, bitter beer.

port·fo·lio [ˌpɔːt'fəʊlɪəʊ] *n.* (pl. ⁓s) **1.** holder (usu. leather) for loose papers, documents, etc. **2.** position as a Minister of State: *He resigned his* ⁓.

por·ti·co ['pɔːtɪkəʊ] *n.* (pl. -coes, -cos) roof supported by columns, esp. at the entrance of a building.

por·tion ['pɔːʃn] *n.* **1.** part, esp. a share, (to be) given when sth. is distributed. **2.** amount of food allotted to one person. *v.t.* divide into ⁓s.

port·ly ['pɔːtlɪ] *adj.* (usu. of elderly persons) stout.

port·man·teau [ˌpɔːt'mæntəʊ] *n.* (pl. ⁓s, ⁓x [-təʊz]) oblong, square-shouldered leather case for clothes, opening on a hinge into two equal parts.

por·trait ['pɔːtrɪt] *n.* painted picture, drawing, photograph, of a person or animal; vivid description in words.

por·trai·ture ['pɔːtrɪtʃə*] *n.* **1.** (no pl.) art of portraying. **2.** = ⁓. **por·tray** [pɔː'treɪ] *v.t.* make a picture of; describe vividly in words; act the part of. **por·tray·al** [pɔː'treɪəl] *n.* **1.** (no pl.) portraying. **2.** description.

Por·tu·guese [ˌpɔːtjuˈɡiːz] *n.* (pl. ⁓) & *adj.* (native, inhabitant, or language) of Portugal.

pose [pəʊz] *v.t. & i.* **1.** put (sb.) in a position before making a painting, photograph, etc. of him; take up such a position. **2.** behave in an affected way hoping to impress people; set oneself up (as): ⁓ *as an expert on art.* **3.** put forward (a difficult question or problem). *n.* **1.** position taken when posing (1) for a picture, etc. **2.** behaviour, attitude, intended to impress people. **pos·er** *n.* awkward or difficult question.

posh [pɒʃ] *adj.* (colloq.) smart; first-class.

po·si·tion [pə'zɪʃn] *n.* **1.** place where sth. or sb. is or stands, esp. in relation to others. **2.** right place for sth. or sb.: *in (out of)* ⁓. **3.** way in which the body is placed: *in a comfortable* ⁓. **4.** person's place or rank in relation to others, in employment, in society. **5.** job; employment. **6.** condition; circumstances: *not in a* ⁓ *to help,* unable to help. **7.** standpoint; views; opinions: *What's your* ⁓ *on this problem?*

pos·i·tive ['pɒzətɪv] *adj.* **1.** definite; sure; leaving no room for doubt: ⁓ *orders.* **2.** (of persons) quite certain, esp. about opinions: *Are you* ⁓ *it was after midnight?* **3.** practical and con-

structive; that definitely helps: *a* ⁓ *suggestion;* ⁓ *help.* **4.** (math.) greater than 0. *the* ⁓ *sign* (+). **5.** (electr.) that which is produced at the anode of a cell (4). **6.** (gram., of adjectives and adverbs) of the simple form, not the comparative or superlative degree. *n.* **1.** ⁓ (6) degree. **2.** photograph printed from a (negative) plate or film. ⁓**ly** *adv.* definitely.

pos·se ['pɒsɪ] *n.* **1.** body (5) of men sworn in by a sheriff to help in maintaining order. **2.** group of persons temporarily organized to make a search (e.g. for a criminal).

pos·sess [pə'zes] *v.t.* **1.** own; have. **2.** keep control over: ⁓ *one's soul in patience,* be patient. **3.** ⁓ *oneself of,* become the owner of; *be* ⁓*ed of,* own; have. **4.** *be* ⁓*ed,* be mad; be controlled by an evil spirit: *He fought like one* ⁓*ed.* **pos·ses·sion** [pə'zeʃn] *n.* **1.** (no pl.) ⁓ing: *in* ⁓*ion (of),* owning; having; *in the* ⁓*ion of,* owned by. **2.** (often pl.) property; sth. ⁓*ed: lose all one's* ⁓*ions.* **pos·ses·sive** [pə'zesɪv] *adj.* **1.** of ⁓*ion;* eager to ⁓ or retain. **2.** (gram.) showing ⁓*ion: the* ⁓*ive case* (e.g. *Tom's, the boy's, my*). **pos·ses·sor** *n.* owner.

pos·si·ble ['pɒsəbl] *adj.* **1.** that can be done; that can exist or happen. **2.** that is reasonable or satisfactory for a purpose: *a* ⁓ *answer to a problem.* **pos·si·bly** *adv.* **1.** by any possibility. **2.** perhaps. **pos·si·bil·i·ty** [ˌpɒsə'bɪlətɪ] *n.* **1.** (no pl.) state of being ⁓; (degree of) likelihood. **2.** sth. that is ⁓: *a scheme with great possibilities.*

post¹ [pəʊst] *n.* **1.** place where a soldier is on watch; place of duty; place occupied by soldiers, esp. a frontier fort. **2.** *last* ⁓, military bugle call sounded towards bedtime, and at funerals. **3.** trading station. **4.** position or appointment; job. *v.t.* put at a ⁓ (1): ⁓ *sentries at the gates;* send to a ⁓ (1).

post² [pəʊst] *n.* (U.S.A. *mail*) official conveyance and delivery of letters and parcels; one collection or distribution of letters, etc.; letters, etc. delivered at one time; ⁓ *office* or ⁓*al letter-box: take letters to the* ⁓; *send sth. by* ⁓. *v.t. & i.* **1.** send (letters, etc.) by ⁓; put (letters, etc.) in a letter-box or take to the ⁓ office for forwarding by ⁓. **2.** (hist.) travel by stages; make a quick journey: ⁓*ing from London to York.* **3.** ⁓ (*up*), (comm.) write items in a ledger: ⁓ (*up*) *export sales.* **4.** keep sb. ⁓*ed,* keep him supplied with news. ⁓**age** ['pəʊstɪdʒ] *n.* (no pl.) payment for the carrying of letters, etc.: *a* ⁓*age* *stamp* (see the picture at *stamp*). ~·al ['pəʊstəl] *adj.* of the ~ or ~ office: ~al order, official paper receipt for a small sum paid in by the sender to be cashed by the receiver at another ~ office in order to avoid sending money by ~. '~·box *n.* ~al letter-box. '~·card *n.* card for a short message to be sent by ~. '~·code *n.* (U.S.A. *zip code*) group of letters and numbers included in the ~al address, used to make the sorting and delivery of mail easier. ,~·'free *adj.* (U.S.A. ~-paid) without charge for ~age; (of a price) including a charge for ~age. ,~·'haste *adv.* in great haste. '~·man *n.* (U.S.A. *mailman*) man employed to deliver letters, etc. '~·mark *n.* official mark stamped on letters, etc. cancelling the ~age stamp(s). '~·mas·ter, '~·mis·tress *ns.* man, woman, in charge of a ~ office. P~ Of·fice *n.* public department or corporation in charge of the ~al service. ~ of·fice *n.* office, building, in which ~al work is carried on: ~-*office box*, numbered box in a ~ office where letters are kept until called for. ,~·'paid *adj.* with ~age already paid.

post[3] [pəʊst] *n.* upright piece of wood, metal, etc. supporting or marking sth.: *gate-~s*; *the winning-~*; *bed-~s*; *lamp-~s*. *v.t.* **1.** ~ *sth. up*, display publicly on a ~, on a notice-board, etc.: *P~ no bills!* **2.** make known by means of a ~ed notice: ~ *a ship as missing.* **3.** placard (a wall, etc.) with bills. ~·er *n.* **1.** public advertisement (to be) ~ed up (on a wall, etc.). **2.** large, printed picture (e.g. of a pop singer).

post- [pəʊst-] *pref.* after; later than. ,~·'date *v.t.* put on (a letter, cheque, etc.) a date later than the date of writing. ,~·'grad·u·ate *adj.* (of studies, etc.) done after having taken a degree. ~·hu·mous ['pɒstjʊməs] *adj.* (of a child) born after the death of its father; coming or happening after death; ~*humous fame.* ~·script ['pəʊsskrɪpt] *n.* (abbr. *P.S.*) sentence(s) added to a letter after the signature. ~·war [,pəʊst'wɔ:*, attrib. 'pəʊstwɔ:*] *adj.* after, later than, the (last) war.

poste res·tante [,pəʊst'restɑ̃:nt] *n.* post-office department to whose care letters may be addressed, to be kept until called for.

pos·te·ri·or [pɒ'stɪərɪə*] *adj.* **1.** later in time or order. **2.** placed behind; at the back. *n.* (sing. or pl.) buttocks.

pos·ter·i·ty [pɒ'sterətɪ] *n.* (no pl.) **1.** person's descendants (his children,

their children, etc.). **2.** those coming after; later generations.

pos·til·(l)ion [pə'stɪljən] *n.* man riding on one of the two or more horses pulling a carriage or coach.

post me·ri·di·em [,pəʊst me'rɪdɪəm] *adj.* (abbr. *p.m.*) between noon and midnight: *6.30 p.m.*

post·pone [,pəʊst'pəʊn] *v.t.* put off until another time. ~·ment *n.*

pos·tu·late ['pɒstjʊleɪt] *v.t.* demand, put forward, take for granted, as a necessary fact, as a basis for reasoning, etc. ['pɒstjʊlət] *n.* sth. ~d.

pos·ture ['pɒstʃə*] *n.* **1.** attitude of the body: *in a reclining ~*; muscular control of the body: *Good ~ helps you to keep well.* **2.** frame of mind; attitude. **3.** condition, state (of affairs, etc.). *v.i.* take up a ~: *a vain girl posturing before a mirror.* [flowers.]

po·sy ['pəʊzɪ] *n.* small bunch of cut flowers.

pot[1] [pɒt] *n.* **1.** round vessel of earthenware, glass, metal, etc. for holding things in, for cooking, etc.; contents of such a vessel: *a flower-~*; *a coffee-~*; *drink a ~ of tea*; *keep the ~ boiling*, (fig.) earn enough money to buy one's food, etc. **2.** (colloq.) large sum: *make a ~ (~s) of money.* *v.t.* (*-tt-*) **1.** put (meat, fish paste, etc.) in a ~ to preserve it. **2.** plant in a flower-~. '~·hole *n.* **1.** hole in a road made by rain and traffic. **2.** deep hole in rock (e.g. in limestone caves) by water. '~·hol·er *n.* explorer of ~-holes (2). ~ *luck n.* whatever is being prepared for a meal: *Come home with me and take ~ luck.* ~·ter *n.* maker of ~·tery *n.* **1.** (no pl.) ~s; earthenware. **2.** ~·ter's work or workshop.

pot[2] [pɒt] *n.* (no pl.) (sl.) marijuana.

po·ta·ble ['pəʊtəbl] *adj.* suitable for drinking.

pot·ash ['pɒtæʃ] *n.* (no pl.) substance used in making soap and glass, and as a fertilizer.

po·ta·to [pə'teɪtəʊ] *n.* (pl. *-oes*) plant with rounded tubers eaten as a vegetable; one of the tubers.

potatoes

o·tent ['pəʊtənt] *adj.* strong; powerful; effective: ~ *forces* (*reasons, charms*); ~ *drugs*; (of males) able to have sexual relations. **po·ten·cy** ['pəʊtənsɪ] *n.* (no pl.).   [person; ruler.\
o·ten·tate ['pəʊtənteɪt] *n.* powerful\
o·ten·tial [pə'tenʃl] *adj.* that can or may come into existence or action: *the ~ sales of a new book.*

o·tion ['pəʊʃn] *n.* drink of medicine, drug, or poison.

ot·ter¹, pot·ter·y, see *pot¹*.

ot·ter² ['pɒtə*] *v.i.* work (*at* sth.) with little energy; move (*about* from one little job to another.

ot·ty ['pɒtɪ] *adj.* (-*ier*, -*iest*) (Gt. Brit., sl.) (of jobs) unimportant; (of persons) mad (*about* sb. or sth.); strange in behaviour.

ouch [paʊtʃ] *n.* **1.** small bag (e.g. for pipe tobacco). **2.** bag-like formation (e.g. that in which a kangaroo carries its young); puffy area of skin (e.g. under the eyes of sick people).

oul·tice ['pəʊltɪs] *n.* soft mass of linseed, mustard, etc. heated and put on the skin to lessen pain, etc. *v.t.* put a ~ on.

oul·try ['pəʊltrɪ] *n.* (collective) hens, ducks, geese, etc. **poul·ter·er** ['pəʊltərə*] *n.* dealer in ~ and game.

ounce [paʊns] *v.i. & n.* (make a) sudden attack or downward swoop (*on*).

ound¹ [paʊnd] *n.* **1.** (abbr. *lb.*) unit of weight, 16 ounces avoirdupois (= 454 grams), 12 ounces troy (= 373 grams). **2.** (pl. ~, ~s) (symbol £) unit of money in Great Britain, 100 pence: *£5.*

ound² [paʊnd] *v.t. & i.* **1.** strike heavily and repeatedly (at, on): ~*ing* (*on*) *the piano*; ~*ing at the door with a stick.* **2.** crush to powder; break to pieces: *a ship ~ing* (*being ~ed*) *on the rocks.*

ound³ [paʊnd] *n.* closed area where stray cattle, (lost) animals, officially removed vehicles, etc. are kept until claimed.

our [pɔ:*] *v.t. & i.* **1.** (of liquids or substances that flow like liquids) (cause to) flow in a continuous stream: ~*ing tea out of a pot; sweat ~ing off his face*; (fig.) ~*ing out a story of misfortunes.* **2.** (of people) come (*in, out, etc.*) in large numbers: *people ~ing into the railway station.* **3.** (of rain) come down heavily: *a ~ing wet day. The rain ~ed down.*

out [paʊt] *v.t. & i.* push out (the lips), esp. when discontented, bad-tempered, etc. *n.* act of ~ing.

pov·er·ty ['pɒvətɪ] *n.* (no pl.) state of being poor. '~-,strick·en *adj.* very poor; looking very poor; shabby-looking.

pow·der ['paʊdə*] *n.* **1.** substance that has been crushed, rubbed, or worn to dust; special kind of ~, e.g. for use on the skin (*face-~*) or as a medicine. **2.** gun~. *v.t. & i.* put ~ on; use ~ on the face; make into ~. '~-,mag·a,zine *n.* place for storing gun~ and other explosives. '~-room *n.* ladies' cloak-room (2). ~ snow *n.* (no pl.) loose, dry snow. ~y *adj.* of, like, covered with, ~.

pow·er ['paʊə*] *n.* **1.** (no pl.) ability to do or act: *He gave me all the help in his ~.* **2.** (pl.) faculty of the body or mind: *My ~s are failing, I am becoming weak. tax one's ~s too much.* **3.** (no pl.) strength; force: *the ~ of a blow.* **4.** (no pl.) energy or force that can be used to do work: *water-~; electric ~; an engine of sixty horse~.* **5.** (no pl.) right; control; authority: *the ~ of the law; have sb. in one's ~,* be able to do what one wishes with him. **6.** person or organization having great authority or influence; State having great authority and influence in international affairs: *the Great P~s.* **7.** (math.) result obtained by multiplying a number or quantity by itself a certain number of times: *the fourth ~ of 3* (= 3^4 = $3 \times 3 \times 3 \times 3$ = 81). **8.** capacity to magnify: *the ~ of a lens; a telescope of high ~.* **~ed** *adj.* having, producing, propelled by means of, ~ (4): ~*ed aircraft; battery-~ed.* **~ful** *adj.* having or producing great ~. **~less** *adj.* without ~; unable (*to do* sth.). '~-house, ~ plant, '~-,sta·tion *ns.* place where ~ (4) (esp. electrical) is produced or distributed.

prac·tice (U.S.A. also **-tise**) ['præktɪs] *n.* **1.** (no pl.) performance; (habitual) action (contrasted with *theory*): *put a plan into ~.* **2.** way of doing sth. that is common or habitual; sth. done regularly: *the ~ of closing shops on Sundays.* **3.** (no pl.) frequent or regular repetition of sth. in order to become skilful: *in* (*out of*) ~, having (not having) lately practised. **4.** (no pl.) work of a doctor or lawyer: *retire from ~.* **5.** (collective) all those who consult a certain doctor or lawyer: *a doctor with a large ~* (i.e. many patients). **6.** *sharp ~*, not strictly honest or legal ways of doing business. **prac·ti·ca·ble** ['præk-tɪkəbl] *adj.* that can be put into ~; that can be done or used. **prac·ti·cal**

['præktɪkl] *adj.* **1.** concerned with ~ (1): *practical difficulties*; *a practical joke* (see *joke*). **2.** (of persons) clever at doing and making things; fond of action. **3.** useful; doing well what it is intended to do. **prac·ti·cal·ly** *adv.* **1.** in a practical manner. **2.** really. **3.** almost.

prac·tise (U.S.A. **-tice**) ['præktɪs] *v.t. & i.* **1.** do sth. repeatedly in order to become skilful: ~ *the piano.* **2.** make a custom of: ~ *early rising*; ~ *what one preaches* (2). **3.** ~ *the law* (*medicine*), work as a lawyer (a doctor). **~d** *adj.* skilled; having had much practice. **prac·ti·tion·er** [præk'tɪʃnə*] *n.* person practising medicine or the law: *general practitioner* (see *general* (1)).

prai·rie ['preərɪ] *n.* wide area of level land with grass but no trees, esp. in N. America.

praise [preɪz] *v.t.* **1.** speak with approval of; say that one admires. **2.** give honour and glory to (God). *n.* **1.** (no pl.) act of praising. **2.** (pl.) expressions of admiration: *sing sb.'s ~s*, ~ *him* enthusiastically. '~·wor·thy *adj.* deserving ~.

pram [præm] *n.* (Gt. Brit., abbr. for) perambulator.

prance [prɑ:ns] *v.i.* (of a horse) rise up on the hind legs and jump about; (of a person) jump or move about gaily; walk arrogantly.

prank [præŋk] *n.* playful or mischievous trick: *play a ~ on sb.*

prate [preɪt] *v.i. & t.* talk foolishly or boastfully; talk too much; say sth. in a prating manner.

prat·tle ['prætl] *v.i. & t.* talk, say sth., in a simple way; go on talking as a child does, about unimportant things. *n.* (no pl.) such talk.

prawn [prɔːn] *n.* shellfish like a large shrimp.

a prawn

pray [preɪ] *v.i. & t.* **1.** commune with God; offer thanks, make requests known (*to* God, *for* sth. or *for* the good of sb.). **2.** ask (sb.) (*for, to do* sth.) as a favour. **3.** (formal) if you please: *P~ don't speak so loud.* **~er** [preə*] *n.* ~·ing to God; thing ~ed for; form of worship (*Morning P~er*) or of words for use in ~ing: *the Lord's P~er.*

pre- [priː-, prɪ-] *pref.* before, as in *prefix, prepaid, pre-war.*

preach [priːtʃ] *v.t. & i.* **1.** deliver (a sermon); give a talk, esp. in church about religion or morals; give moral advice (*to*). **2.** recommend, urge, as right or desirable. **~er** *n.*

pre·am·ble [priː'æmbl] *n.* introduction to a talk, statement, piece of writing.

pre·car·i·ous [prɪ'keərɪəs] *adj.* uncertain; depending upon chance.

pre·cast [ˌpriː'kɑːst] *adj.* (esp. of concrete) cast into blocks ready for use in building: ~ *concrete segments.*

pre·cau·tion [prɪ'kɔːʃn] *n.* care taken in advance to avoid a risk: *take ~s against fire.* **~·ary** [prɪ'kɔːʃnərɪ] *adj.* for the sake of ~: ~*ary measures.*

pre·cede [priː'siːd] *v.t. & i.* come or go before (in time, place, or order).

pre·ced·ence [ˌpriː'siːdəns] *n.* (no pl.) (right to a) higher or earlier position: *a question which takes ~nce of (over) all others,* (that must be considered first).

prec·e·dent ['presɪdənt] *n.* earlier happening, decision, etc. taken as an example of or as a rule for what comes later.

pre·cept ['priːsept] *n.* rule or guide, esp. for behaviour.

pre·cinct ['priːsɪŋkt] *n.* **1.** space enclosed by outer walls or boundaries, esp. of a sacred or official building. **2.** (pl.) neighbourhood, environs (of a town). **3.** boundary. **4.** (U.S.A.) subdivision of a county, city, or ward: *an election ~*; *a police ~.* **5.** area in a town limited to a special use: *a pedestrian ~* (where motor traffic is prohibited).

pre·cious ['preʃəs] *adj.* **1.** of great value: *the ~ metals* (gold, silver, platinum); ~ *stone,* mineral material of great value that, when cut and polished, is used in jewellery. **2.** highly valued; dear (*to*).

prec·i·pice ['presɪpɪs] *n.* perpendicular or very steep face of a rock, cliff, or mountain.

pre·cip·i·tate [prɪ'sɪpɪteɪt] *v.t.* **1.** throw or send (stones, oneself) violently down from a height. **2.** cause (an event) to happen suddenly, quickly, or in haste. **3.** condense (vapour) into drops that fall as rain, dew, etc. **4.** (chem.) separate (solid matter) from a solution. [prɪ'sɪpɪtɪt] *n.* that which is ~d (4). [prɪ'sɪpɪtət] *adj.* violently hurried; hasty; (done, doing things) without enough thought. **pre·cip·i·ta·tion** [prɪˌsɪpɪ'teɪʃn] *n.* **1.** ~ action.

2. fall of rain, snow, etc.; amount of this.

pre·cip·i·tous [prɪˈsɪpɪtəs] *adj.* like a precipice; steep.

pré·cis [ˈpreɪsiː] *n.* (pl. ⁓ [ˈpreɪsiːz]) chief ideas, points, etc. of a speech or piece of writing restated in a shortened form.

pre·cise [prɪˈsaɪs] *adj.* **1.** exact; correctly stated; free from error. **2.** taking care to be exact, not to make errors. **⁓·ly** *adv.* (esp. in agreeing with sb.) quite so. **pre·ci·sion** [prɪˈsɪʒn] *n.* (no pl.) accuracy; freedom from error.

pre·clude [prɪˈkluːd] *v.t.* prevent (sb. *from doing* sth.); make impossible.

pre·co·cious [prɪˈkəʊʃəs] *adj.* (of a person) having some faculties developed earlier than is normal: *a ⁓ child*; (of actions, knowledge, etc.) marked by such development.

pre·con·ceive [ˌpriːkənˈsiːv] *v.t.* form (ideas, opinions) in advance (before getting knowledge or experience). **pre·con·cep·tion** [ˌpriːkənˈsepʃn] *n.* ⁓d idea.

pre·cur·sor [ˌpriːˈkɜːsə*] *n.* person or thing coming before, as a sign of what is to follow.

pred·a·to·ry [ˈpredətərɪ] *adj.* **1.** of plundering and robbery: ⁓ *tribesmen* (*habits*). **2.** (of animals) preying upon others.

pre·de·ces·sor [ˈpriːdɪsesə*] *n.* person who held a position before (the person mentioned).

pre·des·tine [ˌpriːˈdestɪn], **pre·des·ti·nate** [ˌpriːˈdestɪneɪt] *v.t.* settle or decide in advance.

pre·de·ter·mine [ˌpriːdɪˈtɜːmɪn] *v.t.* **1.** decide in advance. **2.** persuade or impel (sb.) in advance (*to* an action, *to do* sth.).

pre·dic·a·ment [prɪˈdɪkəmənt] *n.* awkward or unpleasant situation from which escape seems difficult.

pred·i·cate [ˈpredɪkeɪt] *v.t.* declare to be true or real. [ˈpredɪkət] *n.* (gram.) part of a statement that says sth. about the subject (e.g. *is beautiful* in *The girl is beautiful*). **pre·dic·a·tive** [prɪˈdɪkətɪv] *adj.* predicative adjective, one used only in a ⁓ (e.g. *asleep, alive*).

pre·dict [prɪˈdɪkt] *v.t.* say, tell in advance (sth. that will come, *that* sth. will happen): ⁓ *a good harvest* (*that it will rain*). **⁓·able** *adj.* that can be ⁓ed. **pre·dic·tion** [prɪˈdɪkʃn] *n.* ⁓ing; sth. ⁓ed.

pre·di·lec·tion [ˌpriːdɪˈlekʃn] *n.* special liking; preference (*for*).

pre·dis·pose [ˌpriːdɪsˈpəʊz] *v.t.* cause

(sb.) to be inclined or liable before the event (*to* sth., *to do* sth.). **pre·dis·po·si·tion** [ˈpriːˌdɪspəˈzɪʃn] *n.*

pre·dom·i·nant [prɪˈdɒmɪnənt] *adj.* having superior power or influence; prevailing or supreme (*over*); most noticeable. **pre·dom·i·nance** *n.* (no pl.). **pre·dom·i·nate** *v.i.* be ⁓ (*over*).

pre·em·i·nent [ˌpriːˈemɪnənt] *adj.* superior; best of all. **pre·em·i·nence** *n.* (no pl.).

pre·emp·tive [ˌpriːˈemptɪv] *adj.* a ⁓ strike, (mil.) a strike (3) against an enemy considered likely to attack.

preen [priːn] *v.t.* **1.** (of a bird) smooth (itself, its feathers) with its beak. **2.** (of a person) make (oneself) neat: ⁓ *oneself on*, (fig.) pride oneself on; be satisfied about.

pre·fab [ˈpriːfæb] *n.* (colloq., abbr. for) prefabricated building.

pre·fab·ri·cate [ˌpriːˈfæbrɪkeɪt] *v.t.* manufacture complete sections (of a house, ship, etc.) in advance of building, ready to be put together on the site.

pref·ace [ˈprefɪs] *n.* author's explanatory remarks at the beginning of a book. (Cf. *foreword*.) *v.t.* begin (a talk, etc. *with* sth.).

pre·fect [ˈpriːfekt] *n.* **1.** title of a governor in ancient Rome; title of a government official in France. **2.** (in some British schools) senior pupil given responsibility for keeping order, etc.

pre·fer [prɪˈfɜː*] *v.t.* (-rr-) **1.** choose rather; like better. **2.** put forward, submit (a complaint, request, etc.). **3.** appoint (sb. *to* a higher position). **⁓·able** [ˈprefərəbl] *adj.* superior (*to*); to be ⁓red. **⁓·ably** [ˈprefərəblɪ] *adv.* by choice or ⁓ence. **⁓·ence** [ˈprefərəns] *n.* **1.** ⁓ring; sth. ⁓red. **2.** favouring of one person, country, etc. more than another. **3.** ⁓*ence stock*, (Gt. Brit.) stock on which dividend payments must be made before profits are distributed to holders of ordinary stock. **⁓·en·tial** [ˌprefəˈrenʃl] *adj.* (esp. of taxes, tariffs) of or giving ⁓ence (2). **⁓·ment** *n.* (no pl.) giving or receiving a higher position (esp. in the Church).

pre·fix [ˈpriːfɪks] *n.* **1.** word or syllable (e.g. *hydro-, co-*) forming the first part of a compound word to add to or change the meaning. **2.** title placed before a name (e.g. *Mr.*). [ˌpriːˈfɪks] *v.t.* add a ⁓ to; add (a note, etc. *to* sth.) at the beginning.

preg·nant [ˈpreɡnənt] *adj.* **1.** (of a woman or female animal) carrying offspring in the process of develop-ment before birth. **2.** (of words, actions) full of meaning; important for the future. **preg·nan·cy** ['pregnənsɪ] **n.**

pre·his·tor·ic [,priːhɪ'stɒrɪk] **adj.** of the time before recorded history.

prej·u·dice ['predʒʊdɪs] **n. 1.** opinion, like or dislike, formed before one has adequate knowledge or experience: *a ~ against (in favour of) modern poetry.* **2.** (no pl.) (law) injury that results or may result from some action or judge-ment: *to the ~ of,* with (possible) in-jury to (sb.'s interests, etc.). **v.t. 1.** cause (sb.) to have a ~ (1). **2.** injure (sb.'s interests, etc.). **prej·u·di·cial** [,predʒʊ'dɪʃl] **adj.** causing ~ or injury (*to*).

prel·ate ['prelɪt] **n.** bishop or other churchman of equal or higher rank.

pre·lim·i·na·ry [prɪ'lɪmɪnərɪ] **adj.** coming first and preparing for what follows. **n.** (usu. pl.) ~ step, action, etc.

prel·ude ['preljuːd] **n.** introductory action or event; short piece of music that introduces a main work.

pre·ma·ture [,premə'tjʊə*] **adj.** done, happening, doing sth., before the right or usual time. **~·ly adv.**

pre·med·i·tate [,priː'medɪteɪt] **v.t.** consider, plan, (sth.) in advance: *a ~d crime.*

pre·mier ['premjə*] **adj.** first in posi-tion, importance, etc. **n.** prime minis-ter; head of a government.

pre·mière ['premɪeə*] **n.** first per-formance of or in a play, film, etc.

prem·ise ['premɪs] **n. 1.** (also *premiss*) statement on which reasoning is based. **2.** (pl.) house or building with its land.

pre·mi·um ['priːmjəm] **n.** (pl. ~*s*) **1.** amount or instalment paid for an in-surance policy or a lease. **2.** reward; bonus: *put a ~ on sth.,* make it profit-able for sb. (to do sth.), behave in a certain way). **3.** *at a ~,* (of stocks and shares) at more than the par value; (fig.) in high esteem.

pre·mo·ni·tion [,priːmə'nɪʃn] **n.** feel-ing of uneasiness considered as a warning (of approaching danger, etc.).

pre·oc·cu·py [,priː'ɒkjʊpaɪ] **v.t.** take all the attention of (sb., his mind) so that attention is not given to other matters: *preoccupied by (with) family troubles.* **pre·oc·cu·pa·tion** [priː,ɒkjʊ-'peɪʃn] **n.** (esp.) sth. that takes up all a person's thoughts.

pre·or·dain [,priːɔː'deɪn] **v.t.** deter-mine (2) in advance.

prep [prep] (schoolboy slang for) **n.**

preparation (1) (of lessons) and **adj.** *preparatory*: *~ school.*

pre·pare [prɪ'peə*] **v.t. & i. 1.** get or make ready: *~ one's lessons; ~ to do sth.; ~ for work.* **2.** *be ~d to,* be able and willing to. **prep·a·ra·tion** [,prepə-'reɪʃn] **n. 1.** (no pl.) preparing or being ~d; (time given to) preparing school lessons. **2.** (usu. pl.) thing done to get ready (*for* sth.): *make preparations, prepare (for).* **3.** kind of food, medi-cine, etc. specially ~d. **pre·par·a·to·ry** [prɪ'pærətərɪ] **adj.** introductory; needed for preparing: *preparatory measures; preparatory schools* (pre-paring pupils for entry to a higher school or (U.S.A.) college or uni-versity). **~d·ness** [prɪ'peədnɪs] **n.** (no pl.) being ~d.

pre·pay [,priː'peɪ] **v.t.** (p.t. & p.p. *-paid*) pay in advance.

pre·pon·der·ate [prɪ'pɒndəreɪt] **v.i.** be greater in number, strength, in-fluence, etc. **pre·pon·der·ant adj. pre·pon·der·ance n.** (no pl.).

prep·o·si·tion [,prepə'zɪʃn] **n.** (gram.) word used with a noun or pronoun to mark its relation with another word, as in: go *from* home; walk *to* school; swim *in* the river; a pound *of* tea. **~·al** [,prepə'zɪʃənl] **adj.** (gram.) *~al* phrase (e.g. *in front of*). **~·al·ly adv.**

pre·pos·sess·ing [,priːpə'zesɪŋ] **adj.** making a favourable impression; at-tractive. **pre·pos·ses·sion** [,priːpə-'zeʃn] **n.** favourable feeling formed in advance; prejudice.

pre·pos·ter·ous [prɪ'pɒstərəs] **adj.** completely contrary to reason or sense.

pre·req·ui·site [,priː'rekwɪzɪt] **n. & adj.** (thing) required as a previous condition (*for, of, to*): *Matriculation is a ~ of entrance to the university.*

pre·rog·a·tive [prɪ'rɒgətɪv] **n.** special right(s) or privilege(s) (of a ruler).

pres·age¹ ['presɪdʒ] **n.** feeling that sth. (usu. evil) will happen; sign looked upon as a warning.

pre·sage² ['presɪdʒ] **v.t.** be a sign of.

pre·school [,priː'skuːl] **adj.** of the period in a child's life from infancy to the age of five or six that precedes attendance at an elementary school: *a ~ child.* **n.** kindergarten.

pre·sci·ent ['presɪənt] **adj.** knowing about, able to see into, the future.

pre·scribe [prɪ'skraɪb] **v.t. & i. 1.** order the use of: *~d textbooks;* (esp.) order as a possible cure for illness: *The doctor ~d castor oil (complete rest).* **2.** say, with authority, what course of action, etc. is to be followed: *penalties*

~d by the law. **pre·scrip·tion** [prɪ-'skrɪpʃn] *n.* sth. ~d, esp. (written directions for preparing) medicine.

pres·ent¹ ['preznt] *adj.* 1. at the place referred to: ~ *company*, those who are here. 2. existing now: *the ~ government*. 3. not past or future: *at the ~ time*. (gram.) ~ *tense* (perfect, participle). *n.* ~ time; (gram.) ~ tense. *at ~*, now; for the ~, for now; until later. **pres·ence** ['prezns] *n.* (no pl.) 1. being ~ in a place: *in the presence of his friends*, with his friends there. 2. troops of one country stationed in another by mutual agreement: *the American presence abroad.* 3. *presence of mind*, ability to act quickly and sensibly in time of danger, etc. ~**ly** *adv.* 1. soon. 2. (U.S.A.) at the ~ time; now.

pres·ent² [prɪ'zent] *v.t.* 1. give; offer; put forward; submit: ~ *a cheque at the bank* (for payment); ~ *a petition to the mayor.* 2. introduce (sb., esp. to a person of high rank): *be ~ed at court.* 3. ~ *oneself*, appear, attend (for examination, trial, etc.). 4. hold (a rifle, etc.) in a certain way as a salute, etc.: *P~ arms!* ~**able** *adj.* fit to appear, be shown, etc. in public. **pres·en·ta·tion** [ˌprezənˈteɪʃn] *n.* ~ing or being ~ed; sth. ~ed, esp. at a public ceremony.

pres·ent³ ['preznt] *n.* sth. given; gift: *birthday ~s.*

pre·sen·ti·ment [prɪˈzentɪmənt] *n.* feeling that sth., esp. sth. bad, is about to happen.

pre·serve [prɪˈzɜːv] *v.t.* 1. keep safe; keep from danger, loss, risk of going bad, etc.: ~ *eggs*; ~ *one's eyesight.* 2. care for or protect land and rivers, with the animals, birds, and fish, esp. to prevent these from being taken by poachers. *n.* 1. woods, streams, etc. where animals, birds and fish are ~d: *a game¹* (5) ~; (pl., fig.) activities, interests, etc. looked upon as belonging specially to sb.: *poaching on sb. else's ~s.* 2. (usu pl.) jam. **pres·er·va·tion** [ˌprezəˈveɪʃn] *n.* (no pl.) 1. condition of sth. ~d: *in a good state of preservation* (i.e. well ~d). 2. act of preserving. **pre·ser·va·tive** [prɪˈzɜːvətɪv] *n. & adj.* (substance) used for preserving (e.g. food). **pre·serv·er** *n.* person or thing that ~s: *a life ~r.*

pre·side [prɪˈzaɪd] *v.i.* have, take, the position of authority (*over* a business, etc., *at* a meeting).

pres·i·den·cy ['prezɪdənsɪ] *n.* the ~, (term of) office of a president.

pres·i·dent ['prezɪdənt] *n.* 1. elected head of a republic. 2. head of certain government departments, of some business companies, colleges, societies, etc. **pres·i·den·tial** [ˌprezɪˈdenʃl] *adj.* of a ~ or his duties.

press¹ [pres] *v.t. & i.* 1. push against: ~ *the trigger of a gun* (*the button of an electric bell*); *crowds ~ing against the gates.* 2. use force or weight to make sth. flat, to get sth. into a smaller space, to get juice out of fruit, etc.: ~ *grapes* (to make wine); ~ *juice out of oranges*; ~ *clothes* (with an iron (2), to make them smooth). 3. keep close to and attack: ~ *the enemy*; ~ *an attack* (continue to attack vigorously). 4. ~ *for*, make repeated requests for. 5. *be ~ed for* (time, money, etc.), have hardly enough; be in great need of. 6. demand action or attention: *The matter is ~ing.* 7. *Time ~es*, there is no time to lose. 8. ~ *sb.'s hand*, grasp it to show affection, sympathy, etc. 9. ~ *sth. on sb.*, urge him again and again to take (e.g. food, money). *n.* 1. act of ~ing. 2. machine, apparatus (1), etc. for ~ing: *a hydraulic ~*; *a wine~.* 3. (also *printing-~*) machine for printing: *in the ~*, being printed. 4. business for printing (and sometimes publishing) books or newspapers. 5. *the ~*, printed periodicals; the newspapers generally; ~ *cutting* (U.S.A. ~ *clipping*), paragraph, article, etc. cut out from a newspaper. 6. pressure (of work, business, etc.). 7. crowd: *The boy was lost in the ~.* 8. cupboard for clothes, books, etc. ~**ing** *adj.* (of business) needing attention at once; (of persons, their requests) insistent. '~**man** *n.* (Gt. Brit.) journalist.

press² [pres] *v.t. & i.* 1. ~ *into service*, make use of because of urgent need. 2. (hist.) compel (sb.) to become a soldier or sailor.

pres·sure ['preʃə*] *n.* pressing; (amount of) force exerted continuously on or against sth. by sth. that touches it; compelling force or influence: *atmospheric ~*, weight of the atmosphere as measured by a barometer at a given point and time; *blood ~*, (a) varying ~ of blood in the vessels; (b) (colloq.) abnormally high value of this: *suffer from blood ~*; *high* (*low*) ~, (a) condition of the atmosphere with ~ above (below) the average; (b) (fig.) high (low) degree of activity, speed, etc.: *work at high* (*low*) ~. ~*cooker*, airtight container for cooking food quickly under high ~; ~ *gauge*, apparatus (1) for measuring the ~ of a liquid or gas at a given point; ~ *group*, organized group of members of an association, union, etc. that exerts its influence for the benefit of its members; ~ *suit*, inflatable suit for flying at high altitude. *bring* ~ *to bear on sb., put* ~ *on sb.*, do sth. that forces him (to do what is required). **pres·sur·ized** ['preʃəraɪzd] *adj.* (of aircraft cabins, etc.) constructed so that air-~, temperature, etc. in them can be adjusted for flying at great heights without discomfort.

pres·tige [pres'tiːʒ] *n.* (no pl.) respect resulting from the good reputation (of a person, nation, etc.); power or influence caused by this.

pre-stressed [ˌpriː'strest] *adj.* (of concrete) strengthened by means of stretched wires in it.

pre·sume [prɪ'zjuːm] *v.t. & i.* **1.** take for granted (*that*); suppose to be true. **2.** venture; dare: *May I ~ to advise you?* **3.** ~ *upon*, make a wrong use of, take an unfair advantage of (sb.'s kind nature, etc.). **pre·sump·tion** [prɪ'zʌmpʃn] *n.* **1.** sth. ~d (1); sth. that seems likely although there is no proof. **2.** (no pl.) behaviour that is too bold, that takes unfair advantage, etc.; arrogance. **pre·sump·tive** [prɪ'zʌmptɪv] *adj.* based on presumption (1): *the heir* ~, person who is the heir (to the throne, etc.) until sb. with a stronger claim is born. **pre·sump·tu·ous** [prɪ'zʌmptjʊəs] *adj.* (of behaviour, etc.) too bold or self-confident.

pre·sup·pose [ˌpriːsə'pəʊz] *v.t.* **1.** assume beforehand (*that*). **2.** require as a condition; imply: *Good health ~s enough sleep.* **pre·sup·po·si·tion** [ˌpriːsʌpə'zɪʃn] *n.* sth. ~d.

pre·tend [prɪ'tend] *v.t. & i.* **1.** make oneself appear (to be sth., to be doing sth.) either in play or to deceive others: ~ *to be asleep; children ~ing that they are grown-ups.* **2.** do this as an excuse or reason or to avoid danger, difficulty, etc.: ~ *sickness.* **3.** claim; say falsely: ~ *to like sb.* **4.** ~ *to*, put forward a (false) claim to. ~**er** *n.* person who ~s (4) to a position (e.g. the throne). **pre·tence** (U.S.A. **-tense**) [prɪ'tens] *n.* **1.** (no pl.) ~ing; make-believe. **2.** false claim or untrue reason; pretext. **pre·ten·sion** [prɪ'tenʃn] *n.* **1.** (often pl.) (statement of a) claim. **2.** (no pl.) being **pre·ten·tious** [prɪ'tenʃəs] *adj.* suggesting a claim to great merit or importance.

pre·ter- [ˌpriːtə*-] *pref.* beyond; outside the range of: ~*human*; ~*natural*.

pret·er·ite (U.S.A. **-it**) ['pretərɪt] *n. & adj.* ~ (*tense*), (gram.) (tense) expressing a past or completed action or state (e.g. *he went*).

pre·text ['priːtekst] *n.* false reason for an action: *under the* ~ *of (that).*

pret·ty ['prɪtɪ] *adj.* (-ier, -iest) pleasing and attractive without being beautiful or magnificent. *adv.* quite; rather: ~ *late (good).* **pret·ti·ly** *adv.* **pret·ti·ness** *n.* (no pl.).

pret·zel ['pretsl] *n.* crisp biscuit flavoured with salt, having the form of a loose knot, usu. eaten with beer.

pre·vail [prɪ'veɪl] *v.i.* **1.** gain victory (*over*); get control (*over*); fight successfully (*against*). **2.** be widespread; be generally seen, done, etc. **3.** ~ *upon* (sb. *to do* sth.), persuade. **prev·a·lent** ['prevələnt] *adj.* common, seen or done everywhere (at the time referred to): *the prevalent fashions.* **prev·a·lence** *n.* (no pl.) being prevalent: *the prevalence of influenza in winter.*

pre·var·i·cate [prɪ'værɪkeɪt] *v.i.* make untrue or partly untrue statements. **pre·var·i·ca·tion** [prɪˌværɪ'keɪʃn] *n.*

pre·vent [prɪ'vent] *v.t.* **1.** stop (sth.) from happening: ~ *an accident.* **2.** keep (sb. *from doing* sth.): ~ *sb. from falling.* ~**able** *adj.* that can be ~ed. **pre·ven·tion** *n.* (no pl.) act of ~ing. **pre·ven·tive** *adj.* serving to ~: ~*ive medicine.*

pre·vi·ous ['priːvjəs] *adj.* coming earlier in time or order: *a* ~ *conviction*[1]; *a* ~ *engagement*; ~ *to*, before. ~**ly** *adv.*

pre·war [ˌpriː'wɔː*, attrib. 'priːwɔː*] *adj.* before the (last) war.

prey [preɪ] *n.* (no pl.) **1.** animal, bird, etc. hunted for food by another: *beast (bird) of* ~ (e.g. a lion, an eagle), kind that kills and eats other animals or birds. **2.** *be a* ~ *to fears (disease, etc.)*, be always troubled by. *v.i.* ~ *upon*, (a) take, hunt, (other animals, etc.) as ~ (1); (b) plunder; (c) (of fears, disease, losses, etc.) trouble greatly.

price [praɪs] *n.* money for which sth. is (to be) sold or bought; that which must be done, given, or experienced to obtain or keep sth.: *the* ~ *of liberty (independence).* *v.t.* fix the ~ of sth.; mark (goods) with a ~. ~**less** *adj.* **1.** too valuable to be ~d. **2.** (sl.) most amusing; absurd.

prick [prɪk] *v.t. & i.* **1.** make a hole or mark in (sth.) with a sharp point: ~ *a toy balloon*; make (a hole or mark in sth.) in this way. **2.** hurt with a sharp point: ~ *one's finger with a needle.* **3.** cause sharp pain (to): *Thorns* ~. **4.** feel sharp pain: *My finger* ~s. **5.** ~ *up* *one's ears*, (esp. of dogs, horses) raise the ears; (fig., of persons) pay sharp attention. *n.* **1.** small mark or hole caused by the act of ‿ing. **2.** pain caused by ‿ing. **‿le** ['prɪkl] *n.* pointed growth on the stem, etc. of a plant or on the skin of some animals (e.g. a hedgehog). *v.t. & i.* give or have a ‿ing feeling. **‿ly** *adj.* (-ier, -iest) having ‿les; ‿ling: ‿ly *heat*, rash¹ with irritation of the skin caused by hot weather.

‿ride [praɪd] *n.* (no pl.) **1.** feeling of satisfaction arising from what one has done, or from persons, things, etc. one is concerned with: *take* ‿ *in one's work* (*the success of one's school, etc.*). **2.** object of such feeling: *a girl who is her mother's* ‿. **3.** (also *proper* ‿) self-respect; knowledge of one's own worth and character: ‿ *that prevented him from doing anything dishonourable.* **4.** too high an opinion of oneself, one's position, possessions, etc. *v.refl.* ‿ *oneself* (*up*)*on*, take ‿ in; be pleased and satisfied about.

‿riest [priːst] *n.* **1.** clergyman of a Christian Church, esp. one who is between a deacon and a bishop in the Church of England or the Roman Catholic Church. **2.** (of non-Christian religions) person trained to perform special acts of religion. **‿ess** *n.* female ‿ (2). **‿hood** *n.* whole body (5) of ‿s of one religion. **‿ly** *adj.* (-ier, -iest).

‿rig [prɪg] *n.* self-satisfied, self-righteous person. **‿gish** *adj.*

‿rim [prɪm] *adj.* (-mm-) neat; formal; disliking, showing a dislike of, anything improper: *a* ‿ *old lady.*

‿ri·ma ['priːmə] *adj.* first; chief. ‿ **bal·le·ri·na** ['priːmə ˌbæləˈriːnə] *n.* leading female dancer in a ballet company. ‿ **don·na** [ˌpriːməˈdɒnə] *n.* leading female singer in an opera.

‿ri·ma·cy ['praɪməsɪ] *n.* **1.** being of highest rank, quality, etc. **2.** position of an archbishop.

‿ri·ma·ry ['praɪmərɪ] *adj.* **1.** leading in time, order, or development: *of* ‿ (i.e. chief) *importance*; ‿ *education*; *a* ‿ *school.* **2.** ‿ *colours*, red, blue, and yellow, from which all others be obtained by mixing two or more.

‿ri·mate ['praɪmət] *n.* archbishop.

‿ri·mates [praɪˈmeɪtɪz] *n. pl.* (zool.) highest order (12) of mammals, including man, apes, monkeys, etc.

‿rime [praɪm] *adj.* **1.** chief; most important: ‿ *minister*, premier. **2.** of best quality: ‿ *beef.* **3.** ‿ *number*, number that cannot be divided exactly except by itself and the number 1

(e.g. 7, 17). *n.* first or finest part: *the* ‿ *of the year*; *in the* ‿ *of life*, the time when one's powers are fully developed. *v.t.* get ready for use or action: ‿ *a pump* (by putting water into it); *well* ‿*d with facts* (well supplied).

prim·er ['praɪmə*] *n.* first textbook of any school subject.

pri·me·val, pri·mae·val [praɪˈmiːvl] *adj.* **1.** of the earliest time in the world's history. **2.** very ancient: ‿ *forests.*

prim·i·tive ['prɪmɪtɪv] *adj.* of the earliest times; at an early stage of social development; simple: ‿ *man*; ‿ *weapons.*

prim·rose ['prɪmrəʊz] *n.* pale yellow (flower).

prince [prɪns] *n.* **1.** ruler, esp. of a small State. **2.** son or grandson of a sovereign. **prin·cess** [prɪnˈses, attrib. 'prɪnses] *n.* wife of a ‿; daughter or granddaughter of a sovereign. **‿ly** *adj.* (-ier, -iest) of or for a ‿; magnificent; very generous: *a* ‿*ly gift.*

prin·ci·pal ['prɪnsəpl] *adj.* highest in order of importance: *the* ‿ *towns of France.* *n.* **1.** head of certain organizations, esp. of some schools, colleges, and universities. **2.** person for whom another acts as an agent in business. **3.** money lent, put into a business, etc. on which interest is payable. **‿ly** *adv.* chiefly.

prin·ci·pal·i·ty [ˌprɪnsɪˈpælətɪ] *n.* country ruled by a prince (1): *the* ‿ *of Monaco.*

prin·ci·ple ['prɪnsəpl] *n.* **1.** basic truth; general law of cause and effect. **2.** guiding rule for behaviour: *Gambling is against my* ‿*s. on* ‿, because of, obeying, a ‿ (2), not because of self-interest, etc.; *a man of* ‿, an honest, upright man. **‿d** *adj.* (in compounds) following, having the kind of ‿ (2) indicated, as *high-*‿*d*, *loose-*‿*d.*

print [prɪnt] *v.t.* **1.** make marks on (paper, etc.) by pressing it with inked type, etc.; make (books, pictures, etc.) in this way: ‿*ed matter* (see *matter* (2)). **2.** make (a photograph) on paper, etc. from a negative film or plate. **3.** shape (one's letters, etc.) like those used in ‿. *n.* **1.** (no pl.) mark(s), letters, etc. made by ‿ing (1) on paper, etc.: *in* ‿, (of a book) ‿*ed* and on sale; *out of* ‿, (of a book) no more ‿*ed* copies available from the publisher. **2.** (any special kind of) ‿*ed* lettering: *in large, clear* ‿. **3.** (in compounds) mark made on a surface by sth. pressed on it:

finger~s. **4.** picture, design, etc. made by ~ing; photograph ~ed from a negative. **5.** (no pl.) cotton cloth with coloured designs, etc. ~ed on it. **~able** *adj.* (esp.) fit to be ~ed. **~er** *n.* workman who ~s books, etc.; owner of a ~ing business. '**~ing-ink** *n.* kind of ink used for ~ing on paper. '**~ing-office** *n.* place where ~ing is done. '**~ing-press** *n.* machine for ~ing books, etc.

pri·or[1] ['praɪə*] *adj.* earlier in time or order. *adv.* ~ *to*, before. **~·i·ty** [praɪ'ɒrətɪ] *n.* **1.** (no pl.) being ~; right to have or do sth. before others. **2.** an interest having ~ claim to consideration: *a ~ity project.*

pri·or[2] ['praɪə*] *n.* head of a religious order or house. **~·ess** *n.* female ~. **pri·o·ry** *n.* house governed by a ~ or ~ess.

prise, see *prize*[2].

prism ['prɪzəm] *n.* solid figure with similar, equal, and parallel ends, and whose sides are parallelograms; body with this form, esp. glass ~ that breaks up white light into the colours of the rainbow. **pris·mat·ic** [prɪz'mætɪk] *adj.* **1.** of the shape of a ~. **2.** (of colours) brilliant; varied.

a prism

pris·on ['prɪzn] *n.* **1.** building in which wrongdoers serve their sentences (2); place where a person is shut up against his will. **2.** (no pl.) confinement in such a building. **~·er** *n.* person held in ~ for crime, etc. or until tried in a lawcourt; person captured in war: *take a soldier ~er; a ~er of war.*

pri·vate ['praɪvɪt] *adj.* **1.** (opp. *public*) of, for the use of, concerning, one person or a group of persons, not people in general: *living on ~ means,* on an income not earned as salary, etc.; ~ *enterprise,* (a) business(es) not under State control; (b) (fig.) individual initiative; ~ *eye,* (colloq.) person undertaking special inquiries for pay; ~ *detective;* ~ *letter,* letter about personal, not business, matters; ~ *theatricals* (for family and friends). **2.** secret; kept secret: ~ *information.* **3.** having no official position: *a ~ person;* re-

tiring to ~ *life.* **4.** ~ *soldier,* ordinary soldier of the lowest rank. *n.* **1.** ~ soldier. **2.** *in ~,* confidentially; not in the presence of others. **~·ly** *adv.* in ~ alone. **pri·va·cy** ['prɪvəsɪ] *n.* (no pl.)

pri·va·tion [praɪ'veɪʃn] *n.* **1.** lack of the necessaries of life: *suffering many ~s.* **2.** state of being deprived of sth. *He found it a great ~ not being allowed to smoke in prison.*

priv·i·lege ['prɪvɪlɪdʒ] *n.* right or advantage available only to a person class, holder, of a certain position, etc ~**d** *adj.* having, granted, a ~ or ~s.

priv·y ['prɪvɪ] *adj.* (*-ier, -iest*) **1.** (old use, except in law) secret; private: ~ *to,* having private knowledge of. **2.** *P. Council,* committee of persons appointed by the sovereign, advising on some government business; ~ *purse* money provided by Parliament for a sovereign's personal use.

prize[1] [praɪz] *n.* **1.** sth. (to be) awarded to one who succeeds in a competition lottery, etc. **2.** sth. worth working for **3.** sth. (esp. a ship, its cargo) captured from the enemy in war. **4.** (attrib.) given as a ~; awarded a ~: *a ~ scholarship;* ~ *cattle.* *v.t.* value highly: *his most ~d possessions.* '**~-fight** *n.* boxing-match for which a money ~ is given '**~-ring** *n.* enclosed area in which a boxing-match for a ~ is fought; sport of ~-fighting.

prize[2], **prise** [praɪz] *v.t.* use force to get (a box, lid) (*open, up, off*).

pro[1] [prəʊ] *adj., n., & prep.* **I.** *adj.* ~ *and con(tra)* ['kɒn(trə)], (of arguments or reasons) for and against. **II.** *n.* (pl.) ~*s and con(tra)s,* arguments for and against. **III.** *prep.* ~ *and con(tra),* for and against.

pro[2] [prəʊ] *n.* (pl. ~s) (colloq., abbr. for) professional (player, etc.): *a golf ~.*

pro- [prəʊ-] *pref.* supporting; favouring: *~British.*

prob·able ['prɒbəbl] *adj.* likely to happen or to prove true or correct. **prob·ably** *adv.* **prob·abil·i·ty** [ˌprɒbə'bɪlətɪ] *n.* being ~; chance; sth. that is ~: *in all probability,* very probably; most likely.

pro·bate ['prəʊbeɪt] *n.* **1.** (no pl.) official process of proving that a will is drawn up in correct legal form. **2.** copy of a will with a certificate that it is correct.

pro·ba·tion [prə'beɪʃn] *n.* (no pl.) **1.** testing of a person's conduct, abilities, qualities, etc. before he is finally accepted for a position, admitted into a society, etc.: *two years' ~; on ~* (i.e.

undergoing ~). **2.** *the ~ system,* (law) the system by which (esp. young) offenders are allowed to go unpunished for their first offence while they continue to live an honest life; ~ *officer,* officer who watches over the behaviour of such offenders. **~·er** *n.* **1.** person on ~ (1), esp. a hospital nurse receiving training. **2.** offender under ~ (2).

‣**robe** [prəʊb] *n.* **1.** slender instrument with a blunt end, used by doctors for learning about the depth or direction of a wound, etc. **2.** (tech.) unmanned spacecraft that transmits information about its environment. *v.t.* examine with a ~; press a sharp instrument into; (fig.) inquire deeply into (sb.'s thought, the causes of sth.).

‣**ro·bi·ty** ['prəʊbətɪ] *n.* (no pl.) uprightness of character; straightforwardness.

‣**rob·lem** ['prɒbləm] *n.* question to be solved or decided, esp. sth. difficult: *mathematical ~s; a ~ child,* a child difficult to control. **~·at·ic, ~·at·i·cal** [ˌprɒbləˈmætɪk(l)] *adjs.* (esp. of a result) doubtful.

‣**ro·ce·dure** [prəˈsiːdʒə*] *n.* (regular) order of doing things, esp. in legal and political affairs.

‣**ro·ceed** [prəˈsiːd] *v.i.* **1.** go forward (*to* a place); continue, go on (*to do* sth., *with* one's work, etc.). **2.** come, arise (*from* a cause). **3.** take legal action (*against* sb.). **~·ing** *n.* **1.** action; sth. done or being done. **2.** (pl.) *take, start, legal ~ings* (*against* sb.), take legal action. **3.** (pl.) records (of the activities of a society, etc.). **~s** ['prəʊsiːdz] *n. pl.* financial results, profits, of an undertaking.

‣**ro·cess** ['prəʊses] *n.* **1.** connected series of actions, changes, etc.: *the ~ of digestion.* **2.** method, esp. one used in industry. **3.** (no pl.) forward movement; progress: *in ~ of time,* as time goes on; *in ~ of completion,* being completed. *v.t.* put (materials) through a ~ (2); treat in order to preserve: ~ *leather;* ~ *cheese;* ~ *tape* (*information*), (computer) put it through the system in order to obtain the required information.

‣**ro·ces·sion** [prəˈseʃn] *n.* number of persons, vehicles, etc. moving forward and following each other in an orderly way: *a funeral ~; march in ~ through the town.*

‣**ro·claim** [prəˈkleɪm] *v.t.* make known publicly or officially: ~ *a public holiday;* ~ *sb. king.* **proc·la·ma·tion**

[ˌprɒkləˈmeɪʃn] *n.* act of ~ing; sth. ~ed.

pro·cliv·i·ty [prəˈklɪvətɪ] *n.* tendency or inclination (*towards, to,* sth., *to do* sth., *for doing* sth.).

pro·cras·ti·nate [prəʊˈkræstɪneɪt] *v.i.* delay action. **pro·cras·ti·na·tion** [prəʊˌkræstɪˈneɪʃn] *n.* (no pl.).

proc·tor ['prɒktə*] *n.* university official with the duty of keeping students in order.

pro·cure [prəˈkjʊə*] *v.t.* **1.** obtain, esp. with care or effort. **2.** bring about; cause. **pro·cur·able** *adj.*

prod [prɒd] *v.t. & i.* (-dd-) push or poke (*at*) with sth. pointed: ~*ding* (*at*) *the animal with her umbrella. n.* poke or thrust.

prod·i·gal ['prɒdɪɡl] *adj.* wasteful (*of* sth.); spending or using too much (*of*). *n.* ~ person.

pro·di·gious [prəˈdɪdʒəs] *adj.* enormous; surprisingly great; wonderful.

prod·i·gy ['prɒdɪdʒɪ] *n.* sth. surprising because it seems contrary to the laws of nature; person who has unusual or remarkable abilities or who is a wonderful example of some quality: *a ~ of learning; an infant ~,* an extremely talented child.

pro·duce [prəˈdjuːs] *v.t.* **1.** put or bring forward to be looked at or examined: ~ *one's railway ticket when asked to do so;* ~ *evidence.* **2.** manufacture; make; create (works of art, etc.). **3.** bring forth, yield (crops, etc.); give birth to (young); lay (eggs). **4.** cause; bring about: *success ~d by long study.* **5.** (math.) make (a line) longer. **6.** bring before the public: ~ *a play,* organize its performance. **prod·uce** ['prɒdjuːs] *n.* (no pl.) sth. ~d, esp. by farming: *garden ~* (vegetables), etc.). **pro·duc·er** [prəˈdjuːsə*] *n.* **1.** person who ~s goods (contrasted with *consumer*). **2.** person responsible for the production of a play or film (apart from the directing of the actors); (Gt. Brit.) director of a play or broadcast performance. **prod·uct** ['prɒdʌkt] *n.* **1.** sth. ~d (by nature or by man): *farm products.* **2.** (math.) quantity obtained by multiplying numbers. **pro·duc·tion** [prəˈdʌkʃn] *n.* **1.** (no pl.) process of producing. **2.** sth. ~d. **3.** (no pl.) quantity ~d. **pro·duc·tive** [prəˈdʌktɪv] *adj.* **1.** able to ~; fertile: *productive land.* **2.** *productive of,* tending to ~: *discussions that are productive only of quarrels.* **prod·uc·tiv·i·ty** [ˌprɒdʌk-ˈtɪvətɪ] *n.* (no pl.) being productive;

capacity to ~; rate at which goods are ~d per man per hour.

pro·fane [prə'feɪn] *adj.* **1.** (contrasted with *holy, sacred*) worldly. **2.** having or showing contempt for God or sacred things: ~ *language* (*practices*); *a ~ man*. *v.t.* treat (sacred or holy places, things) with contempt, without proper reverence. ~**ly** *adv.* **pro·fan·i·ty** [prə'fænɪtɪ] *n.* ~ conduct or speech; (use of) swear-words.

pro·fess [prə'fes] *v.t.* **1.** declare that one has (beliefs, likes, ignorance, interests, etc.). **2.** have as one's profession: ~ *law* (*medicine*). **3.** claim; represent oneself (*to be, to do* sth.): *Don't* ~ *to be an expert* (*to have an expert's knowledge*), *a ~ed friend*, one who claims to be a friend, but is not. **pro·fes·sed·ly** [prə'fesɪdlɪ] *adv.* according to one's own account or claims.

pro·fes·sion [prə'feʃn] *n.* **1.** occupation, esp. one requiring advanced education and special training (e.g. the law, architecture, medicine, the Church). **2.** statement or declaration of belief, feeling, etc.: *a ~ of faith* (*friendship, loyalty*). ~**al** *adj.* **1.** of a profession (1): ~*al skill*; ~*al men* (e.g. lawyers, doctors). **2.** (opp. *amateur*) connected with, engaged in, the doing of sth. for payment or to make a living: ~*al football*(*ers*); ~*al musicians*. *n.* (opp. *amateur*) person who teaches or engages in some kind of sport for money; person who does sth. for payment that others do for pleasure: *turn* ~*al*, become a ~*al*.

pro·fes·sor [prə'fesə*] *n.* university teacher of the highest grade.

prof·fer ['prɒfə*] *v.t. & n.* offer.

pro·fi·cient [prə'fɪʃnt] *adj.* skilled; expert (*in* or *at* sth.). **pro·fi·cien·cy** *n.* (no pl.) being ~: *a certificate of proficiency in English*.

pro·file ['prəʊfaɪl] *n.* **1.** side view (e.g. of the face). **2.** edge or outline of sth. seen against a background. **3.** short biography, as given in a newspaper article, radio talk, etc.

prof·it ['prɒfɪt] *n.* **1.** (no pl.) advantage or good obtained from sth.: *gain* ~ *from one's studies*. **2.** money gained in business: *making a* ~ *of ten pence on every article sold*. *v.t. & i.* **1.** get ~ (*from*); bring ~ to. **2.** ~ *by*, be helped by; use to one's advantage: ~ *by sb. else's experience*. ~**·able** *adj.* bringing ~. **prof·i·teer** [,prɒfɪ'tɪə*] *v.i.* make large ~s, esp. by taking advantage of

times of difficulty or scarcity (e.g. in war). *n.* person who does this.

prof·li·gate ['prɒflɪgət] *adj.* **1.** (of a person, his behaviour) shamelessly immoral. **2.** (of the spending of money) reckless; very extravagant. *n.* ~ (1) person. **prof·li·ga·cy** *n.* (no pl.).

pro·found [prə'faʊnd] *adj.* **1.** deep: *a ~ sleep* (*sigh, interest*). **2.** needing, showing, having, great knowledge: ~ *books* (*writers, thinkers*). **3.** needing much thought or study to understand: ~ *mysteries*. ~**ly** *adv.* deeply; sincerely. **pro·fun·di·ty** [prə'fʌndɪtɪ] *n.*

pro·fuse [prə'fjuːs] *adj.* **1.** very plentiful or abundant: ~ *bleeding*; *my* ~ *thanks*. **2.** ~ *in* (*of*), giving, using, producing, very (or too) generously: *He was* ~ *in his apologies*. ~**ly** *adv.* **pro·fu·sion** [prə'fjuːʒn] *n.* (no pl.) great quantity: *roses growing in profusion*.

prog·e·ny ['prɒdʒənɪ] *n.* (collective sing.) offspring; descendants; children.

prog·no·sis [prɒg'nəʊsɪs] *n.* (pl. *-ses* [-siːz]) (med.) forecast of the probable course of a disease.

prog·nos·ti·cate [prɒg'nɒstɪkeɪt] *v.t.* foretell; predict. **prog·nos·ti·ca·tion** [prəg,nɒstɪ'keɪʃn] *n.* prediction.

pro·gramme (U.S.A. & computer **-gram**) ['prəʊgræm] *n.* **1.** list of items, events, etc. (e.g. for a concert, play at the theatre). **2.** plan of what is to be done: *political* ~*s. What's the* ~ *for tomorrow?* What are we going to do? **3.** coded series of information data (2) fed (3) into a computer. *v.t.* **1.** make a programme or plan of. **2.** (*-mm-*) supply (a computer) with a program: *programming language*, computer language. **pro·gram·mer** *n.* person who prepares a computer program.

prog·ress[1] ['prəʊgres] *n.* (no pl.) **1.** forward movement; advance: *making fast* ~. **2.** development: ~ *in civilization; now in* ~, now being done or carried on. **3.** improvement: *The patient is making good* ~ (is getting better).

pro·gress[2] [prəʊ'gres] *v.i.* make progress[1]. **pro·gres·sion** [prəʊ'greʃn] *n.* (no pl.) ~*ing: modes of* ~*ion* (e.g. crawling). **pro·gres·sive** [prəʊ'gresɪv] *adj.* **1.** making continuous forward movement. **2.** increasing by regular degrees: ~*ive taxation of incomes*. **3.** undergoing improvement; getting better (e.g. in civilization); supporting or favouring progress: *a* ~*ive nation* (*policy, political party*). **4.** contemporary: ~*ive music*. **5.** (gram., of tense) expressing action or state in progress: *am seeing, had been seeing*. *n.* person supporting a ~ive policy.

pro·hib·it [prə'hɪbɪt] *v.t.* forbid, prevent (by law, etc.) (sb. *from doing* sth.); order that sth. must not be done: *smoking ~ed*. **pro·hib·i·tive** *adj.* (esp. of prices) high enough to prevent purchase or use: ~*ive rents*. **pro·hi·bi·tion** [ˌprəʊɪ'bɪʃn] *n.* ~ing; order ~ing sth., esp. law ~ing the making or sale of alcoholic drinks.

proj·ect[1] ['prɒdʒekt] *n.* (plan for a) scheme or undertaking.

pro·ject[2] [prə'dʒekt] *v.t. & i.* **1.** make plans for: ~ *a new dam*. **2.** cause (a shadow, an outline, a picture from a film or slide) to fall on a surface (e.g. a wall or screen). **3.** stand out beyond the surface nearby: ~*ing eyebrows*. **pro·jec·tile** [prəʊ'dʒektaɪl] *n.* sth. (to be) shot forward, esp. from a gun; self-propelling missile (e.g. a rocket). **pro·jec·tion** [prə'dʒekʃn] *n.* **1.** ~ing (2, 3). **2.** sth. ~ed, esp. sth. that stands out; prominent part. **pro·jec·tion·ist** *n.* person who operates (1) a film ~or in a cinema (1). **pro·jec·tor** [prə'dʒektə*] *n.* apparatus (1) for ~ing pictures by rays of light on to a screen: *a film ~or; a slide-~or*.

pro·le·tar·i·at [ˌprəʊlɪ'teərɪət] *n.* whole body (5) of wage-earners, esp. manual workers. **pro·le·tar·i·an** *n. & adj.* (member) of the ~.

pro·lif·ic [prə'lɪfɪk] *adj.* producing much or many: *a ~ author* (writing many books); ~ *of new ideas*.

pro·lix ['prəʊlɪks] *adj.* (of a speaker, writer, speech, etc.) tedious; tiring because too long. ~·**i·ty** [prəʊ'lɪksətɪ] *n.* (no pl.).

pro·logue (U.S.A. **-log**) ['prəʊlɒg] *n.* **1.** introductory part of a poem; poem recited at the beginning of a play. **2.** (fig.) first of a series of events.

pro·long [prəʊ'lɒŋ] *v.t.* make longer. ~**ed** *adj.* continuing for a long time. **pro·lon·ga·tion** [ˌprəʊlɒŋ'geɪʃn] *n.* (esp.) part added to sth. to ~ it.

prom·e·nade [ˌprɒmə'nɑːd] *n.* (place suitable for, specially made for, a) walk or ride taken for pleasure in public; (Gt. Brit.) paved public walk at the seaside for this. *v.i. & t.* go up and down a ~; take (sb.) up and down a ~: ~ (*one's children*) *along the sea front*.

prom·i·nent ['prɒmɪnənt] *adj.* **1.** (of a part) standing out; projecting (3). **2.** easily seen. **3.** important; distinguished. **prom·i·nence** *n.* **1.** (no pl.) being ~. **2.** ~ part or place.

pro·mis·cu·ous [prə'mɪskjʊəs] *adj.* **1.** made up of a mixture; unsorted. **2.** without careful choice: ~ *friendships*. **pro·mis·cu·i·ty** [ˌprɒmɪ'skjuːətɪ] *n.* (no pl.) (state of) being ~.

prom·ise ['prɒmɪs] *n.* **1.** written or spoken undertaking to do or not to do sth., to give sth., etc.: *a ~ of help*; *make (keep, break) a ~*. **2.** (sth. that gives) hope of success or good results: *boys who show ~*, who are likely to be successful, etc. *v.t. & i.* **1.** make a ~ (1) to: ~ *help*; ~ *to do sth.*; ~ *that ...* **2.** give cause or hope for expecting: *clouds that ~ rain; a situation that ~s well*, seems likely to develop well. **prom·is·ing** *adj.* seeming likely to do well, to have good results, etc. **prom·is·so·ry** ['prɒmɪsərɪ] *adj. promissory note*, signed ~ to pay a stated sum of money.

prom·on·to·ry ['prɒməntrɪ] *n.* headland; high point of land standing out from the coast.

pro·mote [prə'məʊt] *v.t.* **1.** give (sb.) higher position or rank: ~*d manager*, ~*d to the position of manager*. **2.** (U.S.A.) advance (a pupil or student) from one class (3) or form (1) to the next higher one. **3.** help forward; encourage; support: ~ *peace* (*a plan for a new park*). **4.** help to organize and start (new business companies, etc.). **pro·mot·er** *n.* (esp.) person who ~s business companies, who is financially responsible for sporting events, theatrical productions, etc. **pro·mo·tion** [prə'məʊʃn] *n.*

prompt[1] [prɒmpt] *adj.* acting, done, sent, given, without delay: *a ~ answer*; ~ *to volunteer*. ~·**ly** *adv.* ~·**ness** *n.* (no pl.). **promp·ti·tude** ['prɒmptɪtjuːd] *n.* (no pl.).

prompt[2] [prɒmpt] *v.t.* **1.** cause or urge (sb. *to do* sth.): ~*ed by patriotism*. **2.** follow the text of a play and remind (actors), where necessary, of their lines. ~·**er** *n.* person who ~s actors.

pro·mul·gate ['prɒmlgeɪt] *v.t.* **1.** make public, announce officially (a decree, a new law, etc.). **2.** spread widely (beliefs, knowledge). **pro·mul·ga·tion** [ˌprɒml'geɪʃn] *n.* (no pl.).

prone [prəʊn] *adj.* (~*r*, ~*st*) **1.** (stretched out, lying) face downwards. **2.** ~ *to*, inclined to: ~ *to accident* (*error*).

prong [prɒŋ] *n.* each one of the pointed parts of a fork.

pro·noun ['prəʊnaʊn] *n.* (gram.) word used in place of a noun (e.g. *I, you,* *hers, mine, etc.*). **pro·nom·i·nal** [prəʊˈnɒmɪnl] *adj.*

pro·nounce [prəˈnaʊns] *v.t. & i.* **1.** say, make the sound of (a word, etc.). **2.** declare, announce (esp. sth. official): ~ *judgement* (*sentence*). **3.** give one's opinion (*on, for,* or *against, in favour of*, sth.). ~**able** *adj.* (of sounds, words) that can be ~d. ~**d** *adj.* definite; strongly marked. ~**ment** *n.* decision; formal statement of opinion. **pro·nun·ci·a·tion** [prəˌnʌnsɪ'eɪʃn] *n.* way of pronouncing a word; way in which sb. usually ~s his words.

proof [pruːf] *n.* **1.** fact(s), method(s), reasoning, etc. showing that sth. is true, that sth. is a fact: *supply ~(s) of a statement*; ~ *of the prisoner's guilt.* **2.** (no pl.) act of testing whether sth. is true, a fact, etc.: *capable of ~.* **3.** test; trial: *put sth. to the ~,* test it. **4.** trial copy of sth. printed, a picture, etc. for approval before other copies are printed: *galley ~,* ~ on a long slip of paper, for making corrections before division into pages. ~*reader,* person employed to read and correct ~s. ~*reading. adj.* giving safety or protection (*against* sth.): ~ *against temptation*; *a bomb-~ shelter; a rain-~ coat; heat-~, ladder-~, water~,* etc.

prop [prɒp] *n.* **1.** support used to keep sth. up: *pit-~s* (holding up the roof in a mine). **2.** person who supports sth. or sb.: *the ~ of his parents during their old age. v.t.* (*-pp-*) ~ (*up*), support; keep in position.

pro·pa·gan·da [ˌprɒpəˈɡændə] *n.* (no pl.) (means of, measures for, the) spreading of information, opinions, ideas, etc.: *health ~*; *political ~.*

prop·a·gate [ˈprɒpəɡeɪt] *v.t. & i.* **1.** increase the number of (plants, animals) by natural reproduction: ~ *by seed* (*cuttings*). **2.** spread (news, knowledge, etc.) more widely. **3.** (of animals, plants) reproduce; multiply. **prop·a·ga·tion** [ˌprɒpəˈɡeɪʃn] *n.* (no pl.) propagating or being ~d: *the propagation of disease by insects.*

pro·pel [prəˈpel] *v.t.* (*-ll-*) drive forward: *a ~ling pencil* (with lead moved

forward as the outer case is turned). ~**ler** *n.* shaft with blades (3) for ~ling a ship or aircraft.

prop·er [ˈprɒpə*] *adj.* **1.** right, correct, fitting (*for* doing sth., *to* do sth., *to* an occasion, etc.). **2.** in conformity with the conventions of society: ~ *behaviour.* **3.** rightly or strictly so named: *architecture* ~ (i.e. excluding, for example, the water-supply, etc.). **4.** ~ *noun* (*name*), name used for one special person, place, etc. (e.g. Mary). **5.** (colloq.) great; thorough: *a ~ mess.* ~**ly** *adv.* in a ~ manner: *behave ~ly*; *~ly* (i.e. strictly) *speaking.*

prop·er·ty [ˈprɒpətɪ] *n.* **1.** (no pl.) (collective) that which a person owns; possession(s). **2.** (esp.) land, land and building(s), or real estate. **3.** special quality belonging to sth.: *the ~ of dissolving grease.* **4.** (thea.) article of costume, furniture, etc. (not scenery) used on the stage in the performance of a play.

proph·e·cy [ˈprɒfɪsɪ] *n.* power of telling, statement of, what will happen in the future. **proph·e·sy** [ˈprɒfɪsaɪ] *v.t. & i.* **1.** say what will happen in the future: *prophesy war* (*that there will be war*). **2.** speak as a prophet; foretell future events: *He prophesied right.*

proph·et [ˈprɒfɪt] *n.* **1.** person who teaches religion and claims that his teaching comes to him directly from God: *the prophet Isaiah; Muhammad, the Prophet of Islam.* **2.** teacher of a new theory, cause, etc. **3.** person who tells what will happen in the future. **proph·et·ess** *n.* female prophet. **pro·phet·ic** [prəˈfetɪk] *adj.* of a prophet or of prophesying.

pro·phy·lac·tic [ˌprɒfɪˈlæktɪk] *n. & adj.* (substance, treatment) serving to protect from disease.

pro·pin·qui·ty [prəˈpɪŋkwɪtɪ] *n.* (no pl.) nearness (in time, place, relationship).

pro·pi·ti·ate [prəˈpɪʃɪeɪt] *v.t.* pacify; do sth. to take away the anger of; win the favour or support of. **pro·pi·ti·a·tion** [prəˌpɪʃɪ'eɪʃn] *n.* (no pl.). **pro·pi·tious** [prəˈpɪʃəs] *adj.* favourable; likely to bring success.

pro·por·tion [prəˈpɔːʃn] *n.* **1.** (no pl.) relationship of one thing to another in quantity, size, etc.; relation of a part to the whole: *wide in ~ to the height.* **2.** (often pl.) correct relation of parts or of the sizes of the several

a propeller

a protractor

parts: *a room of admirable ⁓s.* **3.** (pl.) size; measurements: *a coat of ample ⁓s.* **4.** part; share: *A large ⁓ of N. Africa is desert.* **5.** (math.) equality of relationship between two sets of numbers (e.g. 4 and 8, 6 and 12). *v.t.* put into ⁓ or right relationship: *⁓ what one spends to what one earns;* arrange the ⁓s of; divide into right shares. **⁓·al** [prə'pɔːʃənl] *adj.* in proper ⁓; corresponding in size, amount, etc. (*to*): *payment ⁓al to the work done.* **⁓·ate** [prə'pɔːʃnət] *adj.* ⁓al.

pro·pose [prə'pəʊz] *v.t. & i.* **1.** offer or put forward for consideration, as a suggestion, plan, or purpose: *⁓ an early start (to start early, that we start early).* **2.** offer marriage (*to* sb.). **3.** put forward (sb.'s name) for an office: *I ⁓ Mr. X for president.* **pro·pos·al** [prə'pəʊzl] *n.* **1.** sth. ⁓d; plan or scheme. **2.** offer (esp. of marriage). **prop·o·si·tion** [,prɒpə'zɪʃn] *n.* **1.** statement. **2.** question or problem (with or without the answer or solution). **3.** proposal.

pro·pound [prə'paʊnd] *v.t.* put forward for consideration or solution: *⁓ a theory (riddle).*

pro·pri·etary [prə'praɪətərɪ] *adj.* owned or controlled by sb.; held as property: *⁓ medicines* (patented); *⁓ name,* name the use of which is restricted by being a trade mark.

pro·pri·etor [prə'praɪətə*] *n.* person owning property; owner, esp. of a hotel, store, or land. **pro·pri·etress** *n.* female ⁓.

pro·pri·ety [prə'praɪətɪ] *n.* **1.** (no pl.) state of being proper (2) in behaviour. **2.** (pl.) details of correct conduct: *observe the proprieties.* **3.** (no pl.) correctness; suitability.

pro·pul·sion [prə'pʌlʃn] *n.* (no pl.) propelling force: *jet ⁓.*

pro ra·ta [,prəʊ'rɑːtə] *adv.* in proportion; according to the share, etc. of each.

pro·rogue [prə'rəʊg] *v.t.* bring (a session of Parliament, etc.) to an end for a time.

pro·sa·ic [prəʊ'zeɪɪk] *adj.* dull; uninteresting; commonplace.

pro·scribe [prəʊ'skraɪb] *v.t.* declare to be dangerous.

prose [prəʊz] *n.* (no pl.) language not in verse form. (Cf. *poetry.*)

pros·e·cute ['prɒsɪkjuːt] *v.t.* **1.** continue with (a trade, one's studies, an inquiry). **2.** start legal proceedings against: *Trespassers will be ⁓d.* **pros·e·cu·tion** [,prɒsɪ'kjuːʃn] *n.* **1.** (no pl.) act of prosecuting (1): *in the prosecu-*tion *of my inquiries.* **2.** prosecuting or being ⁓d (2). **3.** (law) prosecuting party (3): *the case for the prosecution.*

pros·e·cu·tor ['prɒsɪkjuːtə*] *n.* person who ⁓s (2): *public prosecutor,* person who ⁓s (2) on behalf of the State.

pros·e·lyte ['prɒsɪlaɪt] *n.* person converted to different religious, political, or other opinions or beliefs.

pros·o·dy ['prɒsədɪ] *n.* (no pl.) science of verse metres or rhythms.

pros·pect ['prɒspekt] *n.* **1.** wide view over land or sea or (fig.) before the mind, in the imagination. **2.** (pl.) sth. expected, hoped for, or looked forward to: *The ⁓s for a good crop¹ (1) are poor. Her ⁓s were brilliant.* **3.** (no pl.) hope; expectation: *not much ⁓ of recovering his health.* [prə'spekt] *v.t. & i.* search (a region) for mineral deposits (n. 2), etc.; search a region (*for*): *⁓ing for gold.* **pros·pec·tive** [prə'spektɪv] *adj.* hoped for; looked forward to: *⁓ive wealth; his ⁓ive bride.* **pros·pec·tor** [prə'spektə*] *n.* person who ⁓s (for gold, etc.).

pro·spec·tus [prə'spektəs] *n.* printed account giving details of and advertising sth. (e.g. a school, a new business enterprise, a book about to be published).

pros·per ['prɒspə*] *v.i. & t.* **1.** succeed; do well. **2.** (of God) cause to ⁓. **⁓·i·ty** [prɒ'sperətɪ] *n.* (no pl.) good fortune; state of being successful. **⁓·ous** ['prɒspərəs] *adj.* ⁓ing; successful; favourable.

pros·ti·tute ['prɒstɪtjuːt] *n.* person who offers herself (himself) for sexual intercourse, esp. for payment. *v.t.* put to wrong or immoral uses: *⁓ oneself (one's energies).* **pros·ti·tu·tion** [,prɒstɪ'tjuːʃn] *n.* (no pl.).

pros·trate ['prɒstreɪt] *adj.* lying stretched out on the ground, usu. face downward (e.g. because tired out, or to show submission, deep respect); overcome (with grief, etc.). [prɒ'streɪt] *v.t.* **1.** make ⁓: *trees ⁓d by the wind.* **2.** *⁓ oneself,* make oneself ⁓. **3.** *be ⁓d,* be overcome (with grief, etc.); be made helpless. **pros·tra·tion** [prɒ-'streɪʃn] *n.* (no pl.) (esp.) complete exhaustion.

prosy ['prəʊzɪ] *adj.* (*-ier, -iest*) dull; tedious. **pros·i·ly** *adv.* **pros·i·ness** *n.* (no pl.).

pro·tag·o·nist [prəʊ'tægənɪst] *n.* chief person in a contest, play, novel, etc.

pro·tect [prə'tekt] *v.t.* **1.** keep safe (*from, against,* danger, etc.); guard. **2.** help (home industry) by taxing imports. **pro·tec·tion** [prə'tekʃn] *n.* ~ing or being ~ed; person or thing that ~s. **pro·tec·tive** *adj.* giving ~ion: *the ~ive colouring of the tiger.* **pro·tec·tor** *n.* person who ~s; sth. made or designed to give ~ion. **pro·tec·tor·ate** [prə'tektərət] *n.* country under the ~ion of one of the great powers.

pro·té·gé (feminine -**gée**) ['prəʊteʒeɪ] *n.* person cared for by another; person to whom another gives protective help.

pro·tein ['prəʊtiːn] *n.* body-building substance essential to good health, in such foods as milk, eggs, meat.

pro·test [prə'test] *v.t. & i.* **1.** affirm strongly; declare against opposition (*that*): ~ing his innocence. **2.** raise an objection, say sth. (*against*). **3.** express disapproval, say that one is displeased, (*about*). ['prəʊtest] *n.* **1.** statement of disapproval, objection, or unwillingness: *do sth. under ~* (unwillingly, with the feeling that what one is doing is not right). **2.** (attrib.) expressing ~: *a ~ march*, a march by persons who object to official policy. **prot·es·ta·tion** [,prəʊtes'teɪʃn] *n.* ~ing; solemn declaration: ~ations of innocence (*friendship*).

Prot·es·tant ['protɪstənt] *n. & adj.* (member) of any of the Christian bodies (5) except the Roman Catholic and Eastern Churches. ~**·ism** *n.* (no pl.) systems, teaching, beliefs, etc. of the ~s; ~s as a body (5).

pro·to·col ['prəʊtəkɒl] *n.* **1.** first written form of an agreement (esp. between States), signed by those making it, in preparation for a treaty. **2.** (no pl.) code (2) of diplomatic or military etiquette and precedence.

pro·ton ['prəʊtɒn] *n.* unit of positive electricity forming part of an atom. (Cf. *electron*.)

pro·to·plasm ['prəʊtəʊplæzəm] *n.* colourless, jelly-like substance that is the material basis of life in animals and plants.

pro·to·type ['prəʊtəʊtaɪp] *n.* first or original example from which others have been or are to be copied or developed.

pro·tract [prə'trækt] *v.t.* prolong; lengthen the time taken by: *a ~ed visit* (*argument*). **pro·trac·tor** *n.* instrument for measuring angles. (See the picture at *propeller*.)

pro·trude [prə'truːd] *v.t. & i.* (cause to) stick out or project: ~ the tongue; *a shelf protruding from a wall.*

pro·tu·ber·ant [prə'tjuːbərənt] *adj.* curving or swelling outwards. **pro·**

tu·ber·ance *n.* sth. that is ~; bulge or swelling.

proud [praʊd] *adj.* **1.** having or showing pride (1, 3, 4): ~ of one's success; too ~ to ask for help. **2.** of or on which one may be justly ~: *a ~ day; a ~ sight.*

prove [pruːv] *v.t. & i.* (p.t. ~d, p.p. ~d, U.S.A., Scot., & liter. ~n ['pruː-vən]) **1.** supply proof of: ~ sb.'s guilt (*that he is guilty*). **2.** make certain of, by experiment or test: ~ sb.'s worth. **3.** be seen or found in the end (to be): *The new typist ~d (to be) useless.* **4.** (law) establish that (a will) is genuine and in order.

prov·en·der ['prɒvɪndə*] *n.* (no pl.) food for horses, cattle; fodder.

prov·erb ['prɒvɜːb] *n.* popular, short saying, with words of advice or warning. **pro·ver·bi·al** [prə'vɜːbjəl] *adj.* widely known and talked about. **pro·ver·bi·al·ly** *adv.*

pro·vide [prə'vaɪd] *v.t. & i.* **1.** give, supply (what is needed, esp. what a person needs in order to live): ~ for one's family; ~ one's children with clothes; ~d with all one wants. **2.** make ready, do what is necessary (*for* an event, *for* the future); take steps to guard (*against* danger, shortages, etc.). **pro·vid·ed** *conj.* on the condition or understanding (*that*). **pro·vid·ing** *conj.* ~d.

prov·i·dence ['prɒvɪdəns] *n.* (no pl.) **1.** (old use) care about future needs; thrift. **2.** P~, God; God's care for human beings and all He has created. **prov·i·den·tial** [,prɒvɪ'denʃl] *adj.* through, coming as from, P~: *a providential escape.*

prov·i·dent ['prɒvɪdənt] *adj.* (careful in) providing for future needs, esp. in old age: *a ~ fund for the staff.*

prov·ince ['prɒvɪns] *n.* **1.** large administrative division of a country. *the ~s*, all the country outside the capital. **2.** branch of learning; department: *the ~ of science; outside my ~*, not sth. with which I can or need deal. **pro·vin·cial** [prə'vɪnʃl] *adj.* **1.** of a ~. **2.** narrow in outlook; having, typical of, the speech, manners, views, etc. of a person living in the ~s. *n.* person from the ~s.

pro·vi·sion [prə'vɪʒn] *n.* **1.** (no pl.) providing; preparation (esp. for future needs): *make ~ for*, provide for. **2.** amount (*of* sth.) provided. **3.** (pl.) food; food supplies: *lay in a store of ~s; a ~ merchant*, a grocer. **4.** legal condition (e.g. a clause in a will). ~**al**

[prə'vɪʒənl] *adj.* for the present time only, and to be changed or replaced later: *the ~al government.* ~**al·ly** *adv.*

pro·vi·so [prə'vaɪzəʊ] *n.* (pl. *-os*, U.S.A. also *-oes*) (clause containing a) limitation (esp. in a legal document): *with the ~ that ...*

pro·voke [prə'vəʊk] *v.t.* 1. make angry; vex. 2. cause, arouse (discussion, laughter, etc.). 3. drive (sb. *to do* sth., *into doing* sth., *to* a state of anger, etc.). **pro·vok·ing** *adj.* annoying.

prov·o·ca·tion [ˌprɒvə'keɪʃn] *n.* provoking or being ~d; sth. that ~s: *under provocation,* when ~d. **pro·voc·a·tive** [prə'vɒkətɪv] *adj.* causing, likely to cause, anger, argument, interest, etc.

pro·vost ['prɒvəst] *n.* 1. head of certain colleges. 2. (in Scotland) mayor. 3. ~ *(marshal)* [prə'vəʊ], head of the military police.

prow [praʊ] *n.* pointed front of a ship or boat.

prow·ess ['praʊɪs] *n.* (no pl.) bravery; brave act(s); skill in fighting.

prowl [praʊl] *v.i.* go about cautiously looking for a chance to get food (as wild animals do), to steal, etc. *n. on the ~, ~ing.* ~ *car* (U.S.A.), squad car.

prox·im·i·ty [prɒk'sɪmətɪ] *n.* (no pl.) nearness.

proxy ['prɒksɪ] *n.* (document giving sb.) authority to represent or act for another (esp. in voting at an election); person given a ~.

prude [pru:d] *n.* person of extreme (often affected) propriety in behaviour or speech, esp. as regards sexual matters. **prud·ery** *n.* **prud·ish** *adj.*

pru·dent ['pru:dnt] *adj.* careful; acting only after careful thought or planning. ~**ly** *adv.* **pru·dence** *n.* (no pl.).

prune¹ [pru:n] *n.* dried plum.

prune² [pru:n] *v.t.* cut away parts of (trees, bushes, etc.) in order to control growth or shape; (fig.) take out unnecessary parts from.

pru·ri·ent ['prʊərɪənt] *adj.* having, showing, too much interest in matters of sex.

prus·sic ['prʌsɪk] *adj.* ~ *acid* (violent and deadly poison).

pry¹ [praɪ] *v.i.* ~ *into,* inquire too curiously into (other people's affairs or conduct).

pry² [praɪ] *v.t.* lift *up;* get *open* by force, esp. with a lever: (fig.) *~ a secret out of sb.*

psalm [sɑ:m] *n.* sacred song or hymn, esp. one of those (*the P~s*) in the Bible.

pseu·do- ['sju:dəʊ-] *pref.* false; seem-

ing to be, but not really being: *~-archaic.*

pseud·onym ['sju:dənɪm] *n.* name taken, esp. by a writer, instead of his real name. **pseud·on·y·mous** [sju:-'dɒnɪməs] *adj.*

pshaw [pʃɔ:] *int.* exclamation to indicate contempt, impatience, etc.

psy·che ['saɪkɪ] *n.* soul; mind.

psy·che·del·ic [ˌsaɪkɪ'delɪk] *adj.* 1. (of drugs) mind-expanding; hallucinogenic. 2. imitating the effects of ~ drugs: ~ *art (music).* *n.* (person who is addicted to a) ~ drug.

psy·chi·a·try [saɪ'kaɪətrɪ] *n.* (no pl.) study and treatment of mental illness. **psy·chi·a·trist** *n.* expert in ~. **psy·chi·at·ric** [ˌsaɪkɪ'ætrɪk] *adj.* of or relating to ~: *a psychiatric clinic.*

psy·chic, psy·chi·cal ['saɪkɪk(l)] *adjs.* of the soul or mind.

psy·cho·anal·y·sis [ˌsaɪkəʊə'næləsɪs] *n.* (no pl.) science of the mind and its processes, based on the division of the mind into the conscious and the unconscious.

psy·chol·o·gy [saɪ'kɒlədʒɪ] *n.* (no pl.) science, study, of the mind and its processes. **psy·chol·o·gist** *n.* expert in ~. **psy·cho·log·i·cal** [ˌsaɪkə'lɒdʒɪkl] *adj.* **psy·cho·log·i·cal·ly** *adv.*

psy·cho·path ['saɪkəʊpæθ] *n.* mentally ill or unstable person, esp. one with abnormal social behaviour.

psy·cho·sis [saɪ'kəʊsɪs] *n.* (pl. *-ses* [-si:z]) severe mental derangement.

psy·cho·ther·a·py [ˌsaɪkəʊ'θerəpɪ] *n.* (no pl.) treatment of mental or emotional disorder (3) by psychological methods.

pto·maine ['təʊmeɪn] *n.* poison that is found in decaying animal and vegetable matter.

pub [pʌb] *n.* (colloq., abbr. for) public house.

pu·ber·ty ['pju:bətɪ] *n.* (no pl.) age at which a person becomes physically able to be a parent.

pub·lic ['pʌblɪk] *adj.* (opp. *private*) of, for, connected with, owned by, done for or done by, known to, people in general: *a ~ library (park); a matter of ~ knowledge* (i.e. known to all). ~ *house,* inn; (Gt. Brit.) house (not a hotel or club) whose chief business is to sell alcoholic drinks to be consumed on the premises; ~ *relations,* (esp. good) relations between a person, firm, or institution and the ~; ~ *relations officer,* person employed in ~ relations and issuing information to newspapers, etc.; ~ *school,* (in England) type of boarding-school for older pupils, supported by endowments and managed by a board of governors; ~ **elementary and secondary schools**, government-controlled schools providing free education; ~ **spirit**, readiness to work for the welfare of the community. *n. the* ~, people in general; people of a particular class: *the theatre-going (reading)* ~; *in* ~, openly, not in private or in secret. **~·ly** *adv.* in ~; openly.

pub·li·can *n.* (Gt. Brit.) keeper of a ~ house. **pub·li·cist** ['pʌblɪsɪst] *n.* newspaperman who writes on questions of ~ interest; expert in international law. **pub·lic·i·ty** [pʌb'lɪsətɪ] *n.* (no pl.) **1.** state of being known to, seen by, everyone: *avoid ~ity.* **2.** advertisement; (measures (6) used for the) obtaining of ~ notice: *a ~ity campaign.* **pub·li·cize** ['pʌblɪsaɪz] *v.t.* give ~ity (2) to.

pub·li·ca·tion [,pʌblɪ'keɪʃn] *n.* **1.** (no pl.) act of publishing. **2.** sth. published (e.g. a book or periodical).

pub·lish ['pʌblɪʃ] *v.t.* **1.** make known to the public: ~ *the news.* **2.** have (a book, periodical, etc.) printed and announce that it is for sale. **~·er** *n.* **1.** person whose business is the ~ing of books, etc. **2.** (U.S.A.) owner of a newspaper or periodical.

puck[1] [pʌk] *n.* hard rubber disc used in ice hockey.

puck[2] [pʌk] *n.* mischievous sprite.

puck·er ['pʌkə*] *v.t. & i.* ~ (*up*), draw together into small folds or wrinkles. *n.* small fold or wrinkle.

pud·ding ['pʊdɪŋ] *n.* **1.** dish of food, usu. a soft, sweet mixture, served as part of a meal, generally eaten after the meat course. **2.** kind of sausage.

pud·dle ['pʌdl] *n.* small, dirty pool of rain-water, esp. on a road.

pu·er·ile ['pjʊəraɪl] *adj.* childish; suitable only for a child.

puff [pʌf] *n.* **1.** (sound of a) short, quick sending out of breath or wind; amount of steam, smoke, etc. sent out at one time. **2.** (also *powder-~*) piece or ball of soft material for putting powder on the skin. **3.** ~ *pastry*, light and flaky pastry. *v.i. & t.* **1.** send out ~s (1); move along with ~s (1); breathe quickly (as after running); (of smoke, steam, etc.) come out in ~s (1): *The train ~ed out of the station. He ~ed at his cigar. He ~ed (= blew) out the candle.* **2.** cause to swell out with air: *~ing out his chest with pride; ~ed up*, filled with pride; conceited. **~y** *adj.* (-*ier*, -*iest*) easily made short of breath (by

running, etc.); swollen: ~*y under the eyes.*

puf·fin ['pʌfɪn] *n.* N. Atlantic sea-bird with a large bill.

pu·gi·list ['pjuːdʒɪlɪst] *n.* boxer; fighter. **pu·gi·lism** *n.* (no pl.) boxing.

pug·na·cious [pʌg'neɪʃəs] *adj.* fond of in the habit of, fighting. **pug·nac·i·ty** [pʌg'næsətɪ] *n.* (no pl.).

pull [pʊl] *v.t. & i.* **1.** (opp. *push*) take hold of and use force upon (sth. or sb.) so as to bring it (him) closer to oneself, or to take it along as one moves, or to remove it from where it is fixed: *~ up a weed; have a tooth ~ed out;* ~ *a cart.* **2.** (with advs.): ~ (*sb. or sth.*) *about,* ~ in different directions treat roughly; ~ *sth. down,* destroy it break it down; ~ *sb. down,* (of illness) make him weak; ~ *in,* (a) (of a train) enter a station; (b) (of a vehicle) move to the side of a road or move off the road; ~ *sth. off,* (fig.) be successful in winning or achieving it; ~ *over* (U.S.A.), ~ in (b); ~ *round,* recover from illness, etc.; ~ *sb. round,* help him to recover from illness, etc.; ~ *through,* come safely through illness, misfortune, etc.; ~ *oneself together,* get control of oneself, one's feelings, etc.; ~ *up,* stop; ~ (*sth. or sb.*) *up,* cause to stop. **3.** (with nouns): ~ *a face,* show dislike, disgust, disappointment, etc.; ~ *one's weight,* do one's fair share of work with others; ~ *sb.'s leg,* try to deceive him in order to have a joke. *n.* **1.** act of ~ing; force used in ~ing. **2.** take a ~ *at the bottle,* drink from it. **3.** spell[3] of rowing: *a short ~ on the lake.* **4.** handle, etc. that is to be ~ed: *a bell-~.* **5.** power to get help or attention through influence (e.g. with people in high positions). **'~·over** *n.* knitted garment ~ed on over the head.

pul·let ['pʊlɪt] *n.* young hen.

pul·ley ['pʊlɪ] *n.* (pl. ~s) wheel with rope or chain, used for lifting things. **'~-block** *n.* wooden block in which a ~ is fixed.

a pulley(-block and tackle)

pulp [pʌlp] *n.* (no pl.) **1.** soft, fleshy part of fruit. **2.** soft mass of other material, esp. of wood fibre as used for making paper. *v.t. & i.* make into ~ or like ~; become (like) ~; take out the ~ from. **~y** *adj.* (*-ier*, *-iest*) resembling or consisting of ~.

ul·pit ['pʊlpɪt] *n.* small, raised, and enclosed structure in a church, used by the preacher.

ul·sate [pʌl'seɪt] *v.i.* expand and contract by turns; throb; vibrate; quiver[1].

ulse [pʌls] *n.* **1.** regular beat of the arteries (e.g. as felt at the wrist) as the blood is pumped through them by the heart. **2.** any regular rhythm.

ul·ver·ize ['pʌlvəraɪz] *v.t. & i.* **1.** grind to powder; (fig.) smash completely. **2.** become powder or dust.

u·ma ['pju:mə] *n.* (U.S.A. *cougar*) large, brown American animal of the cat family.

um·ice ['pʌmɪs] *n.* (no pl.) (also ~stone) light, porous stone (lava) used for cleaning and polishing.

um·mel ['pʌml] *v.t.* (*-ll-*, U.S.A. also *-l-*) beat repeatedly with the fist(s).

ump[1] [pʌmp] *n.* machine for forcing liquid, gas, or air into or out of sth. (e.g. water from a well, air into a tyre).

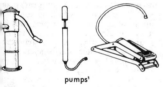

pumps[1]

v.t. & i. **1.** force (water, etc.) (*out*, *up*, *into* sth.); make (a tyre, etc.) full (of air, etc.), by using a ~. **2.** use a ~.

ump[2] [pʌmp] *n.* sort of light shoe, usu. without fastening, worn for dancing.

ump·kin ['pʌmpkɪn] *n.* (plant with a) large, round, yellow fruit with many seeds in it, used as a vegetable.

un [pʌn] *n.* humorous use of words that sound alike or of words with two meanings. *v.i.* (*-nn-*) make ~s; make a ~ (*on*, *upon*, another word).

unch[1] [pʌntʃ] *v.t.* strike hard with the fist. *n.* blow given with the fist.

unch[2] [pʌntʃ] *n.* tool, machine, for making holes (e.g. in leather or bus tickets). *v.t.* use a ~ to make a hole (in sth.): ~ *tickets*; ~ *holes in cards*; ~(*ed*) *card* (*tape*) (with holes ~ed in for conveying instructions to a computer, etc.).

punch[3] [pʌntʃ] *n.* drink made of wine, hot water, lemon juice, etc.

Punch [pʌntʃ] *n.* grotesque, humpbacked figure in the puppet-show called ~ *and Judy.* as pleased (*proud*) *as* ~, showing great pleasure (pride).

punc·til·i·ous [pʌŋk'tɪlɪəs] *adj.* very careful to carry out correctly details of conduct and ceremony; careful in performing duties. **~·ly** *adv.*

punc·tu·al ['pʌŋktjʊəl] *adj.* neither early nor late; coming, doing sth., at the right time; (of a person) in the habit of being ~. **~·ly** *adv.* **~·i·ty** [,pʌŋktjʊ'ælətɪ] *n.* (no pl.).

punc·tu·ate ['pʌŋktjʊeɪt] *v.t.* **1.** put marks (e.g. . , : ;) into a piece of writing. **2.** interrupt from time to time: *a speech* ~*d with cheers.* **punc·tu·a·tion** [,pʌŋktjʊ'eɪʃn] *n.* (no pl.) art or practice of punctuating: *punctuation mark*, stop (n. 4).

punc·ture ['pʌŋktʃə*] *n.* small hole (esp. in a bicycle or car tyre) made by sth. pointed. *v.t. & i.* make (get) a ~ in: ~ *an abscess*; *a* ~*d tyre.*

pun·gent ['pʌndʒənt] *adj.* (of smells, tastes, fig., of remarks, etc.) sharp; biting; stinging.

pun·ish ['pʌnɪʃ] *v.t.* **1.** cause (sb.) suffering or inflict a penalty for wrongdoing. **2.** treat roughly; knock about. **~·able** *adj.* that can be ~ed by law or right: *a* ~*able offence.* **~·ment** *n.* **1.** (no pl.) ~ing or being ~ed. **2.** penalty inflicted for wrongdoing.

pu·ni·tive ['pju:nətɪv] *adj.* (intended for) punishing: *a* ~ *expedition.*

a punt

punk [pʌŋk] *n.* **1.** (colloq.) worthless stuff; rubbish. **2.** (colloq.) worthless person; young ruffian. **3.** (Gt. Brit.) member of the ~ (2) movement. *adj.* **1.** (colloq.) worthless; rotten. **2.** (Gt. Brit.) of a movement among certain young people in the late 1970ies who are opposed to modern materialistic society and who express this by an eccentric outward appearance (e.g. painted faces, safety-pins worn through the nose, etc.) and in loud, lively music (called ~ *rock*) that is often accompanied by violence, rude language, etc.

punt [pʌnt] *n.* flat-bottomed boat with square ends, moved by pushing a long pole against the river-bed. (See the picture on page 401.) *v.t. & i.* move (a ~) in this way; carry (sb. or sth.) in a ~; go in a ~. [and weak.]

pu·ny ['pju:nɪ] *adj.* (*-ier, -iest*) small

pup [pʌp] *n.* (abbr. for) puppy.

pu·pa ['pju:pə] *n.* (pl. *-pae* [-pi:], ~s) chrysalis.

pu·pil[1] ['pju:pl] *n.* young person who is being taught at school or by a private teacher. (Cf. *student.*)

pu·pil[2] ['pju:pl] *n.* (anat.) circular opening in the centre of the eye, regulating the passage of light.

pup·pet ['pʌpɪt] *n.* doll or small figure of an animal, etc. with jointed limbs moved by wires, etc.: *a ~-show;* (fig.) person, etc. controlled completely by another: *a ~ government.*

pup·py ['pʌpɪ] *n.* **1.** young dog. **2.** conceited young man.

pur·chase ['pɜ:tʃəs] *v.t.* buy. *n.* **1.** (no pl.) buying. **2.** sth. bought.

pure [pjʊə*] *adj.* (~r, ~st) **1.** unmixed with any other substance, etc.: ~ *water.* **2.** clean; without evil or sin: ~ *in body and mind.* **3.** (of sounds) clear and distinct. **4.** complete: ~ *nonsense,* nothing but nonsense; *a ~ accident,* one caused completely by chance, no one being to blame. **5.** ~ *mathematics (science)* (dealing with theory only, not applied). **~·ly** *adv.* (esp.) entirely; completely; merely. **~·ness,** **pu·ri·ty** ['pjʊərətɪ] *ns.* (no pl.). **pu·ri·fy** ['pjʊərɪfaɪ] *v.t.* make ~. **pu·ri·fi·ca·tion** [ˌpjʊərɪfɪ-'keɪʃn] *n.* (no pl.). **pur·ist** *n.* person paying great attention to correct use of words, grammar, style, etc.

purge [pɜ:dʒ] *v.t.* **1.** make clean or free (*of, from,* physical or moral impurity). **2.** empty (the bowels) of waste matter by means of medicine. **3.** rid (a political party, etc.) of persons regarded as undesirable. *n.* purging; medicine for purging. **pur·ga·tive** ['pɜ:ɡətɪv] *n. & adj.* (substance) having the power to ~ (2). **pur·ga·to·ry** ['pɜ:ɡətərɪ] *n.* **1.** (esp. in the Roman Catholic Church) place in which souls after death are purified by temporary suffering before entering heaven. **2.** any place or state of temporary suffering or expiation.

pu·ri·tan ['pjʊərɪtən] *n.* **1.** P~, (16th and 17th centuries) member of a division of the Protestant Church that

wanted simpler forms of church cere mony. **2.** person who is strict in moral and religion. *adj.* of or like a P~ or ~ **~·i·cal** [ˌpjʊərɪ'tænɪkl] *adj.* strict an severe.

pur·lieus ['pɜ:lju:z] *n. pl.* ground districts, bordering on (a place); out skirts (of a town, etc.).

pur·loin [pɜ:'lɔɪn] *v.t.* (formal) stea

pur·ple ['pɜ:pl] *n.* (no pl.) *& adj* (colour) of red and blue mixed to gether. *the ~,* the ~ robes of a Roma emperor or a cardinal.

pur·port ['pɜ:pət] *n.* general mean ing or intention of sth. said or written likely explanation of a person's action etc. *v.t.* **1.** seem to mean. **2.** clair (to be); be intended or designed (to be

pur·pose ['pɜ:pəs] *n.* **1.** what one mean to do, get, be, etc.; plan; intentior **2.** that for which a thing is designed **3.** (no pl.) determination; power o forming plans and keeping to them *weak of ~.* **4.** *on ~,* by intention, not b chance; *to little (no) ~,* with little (n result or effect; *to the ~,* useful fo one's ~; *to the point; serve one's ~* b satisfactory. *v.t.* have as a ~ (1). **~·fu** *adj.* having a conscious ~ (1). **~·l** *adv.* on ~.

purr [pɜ:*] *v.i. & t.* **1.** (of a cat) mak a low, continuous, vibrating sound a a sign of contentment or pleasure; (a car engine, etc.) make a simila sound. **2.** utter, express (content ment, words) thus. *n.* this sound.

purse [pɜ:s] *n.* **1.** small bag, usu. o leather, for money. **2.** sum of mone collected or offered as a prize, gif etc. **3.** (U.S.A.) = handbag. *v.t.* (*up*), draw (the lips) together in tin folds or wrinkles.

purs·er ['pɜ:sə*] *n.* officer responsibl for ship's accounts, stores, etc.

pur·su·ance [pə'sjuːəns] *n. in ~ of,* i the carrying out of or performance o (one's duties, a plan, etc.).

pur·sue [pə'sjuː] *v.t.* **1.** go after i order to catch up with, capture, o kill: ~ *a robber (game).* **2.** go on with work at: ~ *one's studies after leavin school.* **3.** have as an aim or a purpose ~ *pleasure.* **pur·suit** [pə'sjuːt] *n.* **1.** (n pl.) pursuing: *in pursuit of rabbit.* **2.** sth. at which one works or to whic one gives one's time: *engaged in literar pursuits.* [ing pus.]

pu·ru·lent ['pjʊərʊlənt] *adj.* contain

pur·vey [pə'veɪ] *v.t. & i.* suppl (food) (*to*) customers; supply provi sions (*for*): *a firm ~ing (meat) for th Navy.* **~·or** *n.*

our·view ['pɜːvjuː] *n.* range of operation or activity; extent.

us [pʌs] *n.* (no pl.) thick, yellowish-white liquid formed in and coming out from a poisoned place in the body.

ush [puʃ] *v.t. & i.* **1.** (opp. *pull*) use force on (sth. or sb.) so as to cause it (him) to move away; move (sth. or sb.) *up, over, etc.* in this way; exert pressure (*against*): ~ *a button* (e.g. to ring a bell); ~ *a door open.* **2.** ~ *on* (*along, forward*), go on with one's journey, one's work, etc.; *be ~ed for* (time, etc.), have hardly enough for one's needs. **3.** (fig.) urge, force, or drive (sb., oneself, *to do* sth.); force (one's goods, etc.) on the attention of other persons. **4.** sell (drugs) illegally. *n.* **1.** act of ~ing; vigorous effort. **2.** (no pl.) determination to make one's way, attract attention, etc.: *have enough ~ to succeed.* **3.** *at a ~,* if compelled by need or circumstances. **~·er** *n.* **1.** ~ing (3) person. **2.** illegal seller of drugs.

uss [pus] *n.* (word used for, or to call, a) cat or kitten. **~y(-cat)** ['pusɪ(kæt)] *n.* (child's word for a) cat or kitten.

ut¹ [put] *v.t.* (*-tt-*; p.t. & p.p. ~) **1.** cause to be in a certain place or position or in a certain relation or condition. **2.** (with advs.): *be much ~ about,* be troubled or worried; ~ (*an idea, etc.*) *across sb.,* persuade him to accept it or approve of it; ~ *sth. away,* into the proper place, the place where it is usually kept; ~ *back,* move (the hands of a clock) backwards to an earlier time; slow down or delay the development of sth.; ~ *by,* save for future use; ~ *down,* (a) write down; (b) enter the name of (sb.) on a list, esp. as a subscriber; (c) attribute to: ~ *it down to his ignorance;* (d) snub¹; *a ~down* (n.), a snub¹; (e) suppress (e.g. a rebellion) by force or (e.g. gambling) by authority; ~ *sb. down as,* consider him to be; ~ *forth,* exert (e.g. all one's strength); ~ *forward,* ~ (a theory, etc.) before people for their consideration; ~ *in,* (a) advance (a claim); (b) pass or spend (time); (c) submit (a document); (d) make a stop (at a port); ~ *in for,* apply for (a position); ~ *in an appearance,* show oneself (*at* a meeting, etc.); ~ *off,* postpone; make the time (of an event, for doing sth.) later; ~ *sb. off,* make excuses and try to evade doing sth. one has promised to do or that one ought to do for sb.; ~ *sb. off his game,* cause him to play badly by taking his attention from it; ~ *sb. off his food,* cause him not to want it; ~ *on,* (a) clothe oneself with: ~ *one's coat, etc. on;* (b) give oneself, pretend to have (a certain appearance, etc.); (c) move (the hands of a clock) forward; (d) arrange for, make available (e.g. extra trains); (e) increase (e.g. speed); (f) add to: ~ *on weight,* get heavier; (g) bet (money) on; ~ *sb. on,* (colloq.) deceive him; *~·on* (n.), act, statement, etc. meant to deceive as. naïve or credulous; prank; hoax; ~ *it on,* (colloq.) exaggerate (emotion, effort); overcharge; ~ *out,* (a) cause (sth.) to stop burning; (b) cause (sb.) to be troubled, inconvenienced, or annoyed; (c) (of ships) move out (from harbour, etc.); ~ *sth. through,* complete it successfully; get it done; connect (e.g. by telephone); ~ *up,* (a) raise; (b) offer (a prayer); (c) offer (goods) for sale; (d) pack (goods) (*in* boxes, barrels, etc.); (e) provide, obtain, food and lodging (*at*); (f) give (sb.'s name) as a candidate, esp. for election by voting; ~ *up a fight,* not give way without a struggle; ~ *sb. up to sth.,* suggest it to him; tell him about it; ~ *up with,* endure, bear patiently, without protest. **3.** (in phrases): ~ *an end to,* cause to end; *be hard ~ to it,* be in difficult or embarrassed circumstances; ~ *to death,* kill; ~ *sb. in mind of,* cause him to recall; ~ *sb. in the wrong,* cause him to feel or seem at fault; ~ *sth. in hand,* make a start in doing sth. **4.** state; express in words: *I ~ the matter clearly to them.*

put², see *putt.*

pu·tre·fy ['pjuːtrɪfaɪ] *v.t. & i.* (cause to) become rotten or putrid. **pu·tre·fac·tion** [ˌpjuːtrɪ'fækʃn] *n.* **pu·tres·cent** [pjuː'tresnt] *adj.* becoming **pu·trid** ['pjuːtrɪd] *adj.* having gone rotten; decomposed and ill-smelling: *putrid fish.*

putt, put² [pʌt] *v.i. & t.* (*-tt-*) strike (a golf-ball) gently with a club (*~ing-iron*) so that it rolls across a smooth grass area (*~ing-green*) towards or into a hole. *n.* such a stroke.

put·ty ['pʌtɪ] *n.* (no pl.) soft paste of powder and oil used for fixing glass in window frames, etc. *v.t.* fix with ~.

puz·zle ['pʌzl] *n.* **1.** question, problem, difficult to understand or answer. **2.** problem (e.g. a *crossword ~*) or toy (e.g. a *jigsaw ~*) designed to test a person's knowledge or skill. **3.** (no pl.) bewilderment; perplexity: *be in a ~ about sth. v.t. & i.* **1.** cause (sb.) to be

perplexed; make hard thought necessary. **2.** ~ *over a problem,* think deeply
about it; ~ *sth. out,* (try to) find the
answer or solution by hard thought.

pyg·my, pig·my ['pɪgmɪ] *n.* member
of a race of very short persons in
Africa; (attrib.) small; insignificant.

py·ja·mas (U.S.A. **pa-**) [pə'dʒɑːməz]
n. pl. loose-fitting jacket and trousers
for sleeping in.

py·lon ['paɪlən] *n.* tall steel framework
for supporting power cables.

pyr·a·mid ['pɪrəmɪd] *n.* solid figure
with a triangular or square base and
sloping sides meeting at a point; structure with this shape, esp. one of those

built in ancient Egypt; pile of objects
in the form of a ~.

a pyramid   Egyptian pyramids

pyre ['paɪə*] *n.* large pile of wood for
burning a dead body.

py·thon ['paɪθn] *n.* large snake that
kills its prey by twisting itself round
it and crushing it.

Q

quack¹ [kwæk] *v.i. & n.* (make the) cry of a duck.

quack² [kwæk] *n.* person dishonestly claiming to have knowledge and skill, esp. in medicine; (attrib.) of, used by, sold by, such persons: *a ~ doctor; ~ remedies.*

quad·ran·gle ['kwɒdræŋgl] *n.* plane figure with four sides, esp. a square or rectangle; space in the form of a ~ wholly or nearly surrounded by buildings, esp. in a college. **qua·dran·gu·lar** [kwɒ'dræŋgjʊlə*] *adj.* in the form of a ~.

quad·rant ['kwɒdrənt] *n.* **1.** fourth part of a circle or its circumference. **2.** instrument used for measuring angles (of altitude) in astronomy, navigation, etc.

quad·ri·lat·er·al [ˌkwɒdrɪ'lætərəl] *adj. & n.* four-sided (plane figure).

quad·ru·ped ['kwɒdrʊped] *n.* four-footed animal.

qua·dru·ple ['kwɒdrʊpl] *adj.* made up of four parts; agreed to by four persons, parties, etc.: *~ alliance. n.* number or amount four times as great as another. *v.t. & i.* multiply by 4. **~t** ['kwɒdrʊplɪt] *n.* (usu. pl.) one of four babies born at one birth: *one of the ~ts.*

quaff [kwɑːf] *v.t. & i.* (liter.) drink deeply.

quag·mire ['kwægmaɪə*] *n.* area of soft, wet land; bog; marsh.

quail¹ [kweɪl] *n.* (pl. ~s, collective pl. ~) game bird similar to a partridge.

a quail¹

quail² [kweɪl] *v.i.* feel or show fear (*at, before,* danger, etc.).

quaint [kweɪnt] *adj.* attractive or pleasing because unusual or old-fashioned. **~ly** *adv.* **~ness** *n.* (no pl.).

quake [kweɪk] *v.i.* (of the earth) shake; tremble; (of a person) tremble (*with* fear, cold, etc.). *n.* (colloq.) earth~.

Quak·er ['kweɪkə*] *n.* (popular name) member of the Society of Friends, a Christian group holding informal meetings instead of formal church services and strictly opposed to violence and war.

qual·i·fy ['kwɒlɪfaɪ] *v.t. & i.* **1.** provide with the necessary qualities, entitle (*to do sth., for doing sth., for* a post, as a doctor, etc.): *Her training qualifies her for this job.* **2.** limit; make less inclusive, less general: *~ a general statement.* **3.** (gram.) describe; name the qualities of: *Adjectives ~ nouns.* **4.** describe (*as*): *~ sb. as selfish.* **5.** fulfil the necessary conditions (*for* a profession, *as* a teacher, etc.): *Are you qualified to teach English?* **qual·i·fi·ca·tion** [ˌkwɒlɪfɪ'keɪʃn] *n.* **1.** training, test, etc. that qualifies (1) a person; document awarded at the end of such training: *a doctor's qualifications.* **2.** sth. that qualifies (2) or limits: *accept a statement without qualifications.*

qual·i·ty ['kwɒlətɪ] *n.* **1.** (degree, esp. high degree, of) goodness or worth: *material of the best ~; a poor ~ of cloth.* **2.** sth. that is special in or that distinguishes a person or thing: *One ~ of pine-wood is that it can be sawn easily. aim at ~ rather than quantity.* **3.** (old use) high social position. **qual·i·ta·tive** ['kwɒlɪtətɪv] *adj.* relating to ~: (chem.) *qualitative analysis.*

qualm [kwɑːm] *n.* **1.** feeling of doubt (esp. about whether one is doing or has done right); misgiving: *He feels no ~s about lying.* **2.** temporary feeling of sickness in the stomach.

quan·da·ry ['kwɒndərɪ] *n.* state of doubt or perplexity.

quan·ti·ty ['kwɒntətɪ] *n.* **1.** property of things that can be measured (e.g. size, weight, number): *prefer quality to ~.* **2.** certain amount or number; (often pl.) large amount or num-

ber: *buy things in* ~ (*in large quantities*).
3. *an unknown* ~ (math., in an equation);
(fig.) person or thing whose action
cannot be foreseen. **quan·ti·ta·tive**
['kwɒntɪtətɪv] *adj.* relating to ~.

quar·an·tine ['kwɒrəntiːn] *n.* (period
of) separation from others until it is
known that there is no danger of
spreading disease: *be (kept) in* ~ *for a
week. v.t.* put or keep in ~: ~*d because
of yellow fever.*

quar·rel ['kwɒrəl] *n.* **1.** angry argument; violent disagreement: *have a* ~
with sb. over (about) sth.; pick a ~. **2.**
cause for being angry; reason for
protest or complaint. *v.i.* (*-ll-*, U.S.A.
also *-l-*) have, take part in, a ~ (*with
sb., about* sth.); ~ *with*, find fault with;
refuse to accept. ~**some** *adj.* in the
habit of ~ling; fond of ~ling.

quar·ry¹ ['kwɒrɪ] *n.* place, usually
open to the air, where stone, slate, etc.
is obtained (for building, etc.). *v.t. &
i.* get (stone, etc.) from a ~; (fig.) search
for (facts, evidence, etc.) in old newspapers, records, etc.; diligently search
old files, records, etc.

quar·ry² ['kwɒrɪ] *n.* animal, bird, etc.
that is hunted; (fig.) any object of
search or pursuit.

quart [kwɔːt] *n.* measure of capacity
for liquids, equal to two pints (= 1.14
litre).

quar·ter ['kwɔːtə*] *n.* **1.** fourth part
(¹/₄); one of four equal or corresponding parts: *a* ~ *of an hour; an hour and
a* ~; *the first* ~ *of this century* (1901-25).
2. point of time 15 minutes before or
after the full hour: *a* ~ *past ten; a* ~ *to*
(U.S.A. *of) nine.* **3.** period of three
months for which rent, etc. must be
paid. **4.** joint of meat including a leg:
a ~ *of mutton.* **5.** direction; district;
source of supply, help, information,
etc.: *men running from all* ~*s; travel in
every* ~ *of the globe* (i.e. everywhere).
6. (U.S.A.) (coin worth) 25 cents. **7.**
division of a town, esp. one occupied
by a special class of people: *the business* ~; *the Chinese* ~ *of San Francisco.*
8. one-fourth of a lunar month; the
moon's phase at the end of the first
or third week. **9.** (Gt. Brit.) grain-
measure of 8 bushels (= 290.78 litres).
10. one-fourth of a hundredweight,
28 lb. (= 12.71 kilograms), (U.S.A.)
25 lb. (= 11.35 kilograms). **11.** mercy
to a defeated enemy: *give (receive, ask
for)* ~. **12.** (pl.) lodgings; place to stay
in: *take up* ~*s with a friend*; (esp.) place
where soldiers are lodged: *All troops
to return to* ~*s at once.* **13.** *at close* ~*s,*

close together. **14.** after part of a ship's
side. **15.** appointed post for sailors on
a ship, esp. for fighting. *v.t.* **1.** divide
into ~s (1). **2.** find lodgings for; place
(soldiers) in lodgings. '~**day** *n.* one
of four days in the year on which rents
and other three-monthly accounts are
due. '~**deck** *n.* part of the upper deck
of a warship reserved for officers. ~**ly**
adj. & adv. (happening) once in each
three months. *n.* periodical published
~ly. '~**mas·ter** *n.* army officer in
charge of stores, etc.; petty officer in
charge of steering the ship, signals, etc.

quar·tet(te) [kwɔː'tet] *n.* (piece of
music for) four players or singers.

quartz [kwɔːts] *n.* (no pl.) hard mineral,
now used in making very exact time-
keeping instruments: ~ *clock (watch)*
(operated by vibrations of a ~ crystal).

qua·si- ['kweɪsaɪ-] *pref.* seeming(ly);
half: *a quasi-official position.*

quat·rain ['kwɒtreɪn] *n.* verse of four
lines.

qua·ver ['kweɪvə*] *v.i. & t.* **1.** (of the
voice or a sound) shake; tremble. **2.**
say or sing in a shaking voice. *n.* **1.**
~ing sound. **2.** musical note half as
long as a crotchet.

quay [kiː] *n.* solid, stationary landing-
place, usu. built of stone or iron where
ships can be loaded and unloaded.

a quay

quea·sy ['kwiːzɪ] *adj.* **1.** (of food) causing a feeling of sickness in the stomach.
2. (of the stomach) easily upset. **3.** (of
a person) easily made sick. **4.** (fig., of
a person or his conscience) over-
scrupulous; over-delicate.

queen [kwiːn] *n.* **1.** wife of a king. **2.**
female ruler. **3.** ~ *bee (wasp, ant)*, fertile,
egg-producing bee (wasp, ant). **4.**
woman or sth. personified as a woman
regarded as pre-eminent among a
group. **5.** piece in chess. **6.** (sl.) male
homosexual. ~**ly** *adj.* of, like, suitable for, a ~.

queer [kwɪə*] *adj.* **1.** strange; odd;
unusual; eccentric. **2.** causing doubt
or suspicion. **3.** (colloq.) unwell; faint.
4. (sl.) homosexual. *v.t.* (sl.) put out
of order; cause to go wrong (see
pitch¹ (n. 1)). ~**ly** *adv.* ~**ness** *n.*

quite

quell [kwel] *v.t.* (poet. and rhet.) subdue (a rebellion, etc.).

quench [kwentʃ] *v.t.* **1.** put out (flames, fire). **2.** satisfy (thirst). **3.** put an end to (hope, etc.). **4.** cool (steel, etc.) in water.

quer·u·lous ['kwerʊləs] *adj.* full of complaints; fretful. ⁓·ly *adv.* ⁓·ness *n.*

que·ry ['kwɪərɪ] *n.* **1.** question, esp. one raising a doubt about the truth of sth. **2.** the mark (?) put against sth. as a sign of doubt. *v.t. & i.* ask (*if, whether*); express doubt about; put the mark (?) against.

quest [kwest] *n.* search (*for* sth.): *in* ⁓ *of,* (old use or liter.) seeking for; trying to find.

ques·tion ['kwestʃən] *n.* **1.** sentence that by word order, use of interrogative words (*where, why,* etc.) or intonation asks for information, permission, etc., and expects an answer. ⁓ *mark,* the mark (?); ⁓-*master,* chairman of a broadcast quiz, etc. **2.** sth. about which there is discussion; sth. that needs to be decided; inquiry; problem: *out of the* ⁓, impossible. *It is only a* ⁓ *of time, it will certainly come* (happen, etc.) *sooner or later.* (*the man,* etc.) *in* ⁓, being talked about. **3.** (putting forward of) doubt, objection: *beyond* (*all*) (*without*) ⁓, without doubt; *call sth. in* ⁓, raise objections to; express doubt about. *v.t. & i.* **1.** ask a ⁓ or ⁓s of. **2.** express or feel doubt about. ⁓·able ['kwestʃənəbl] *adj.* which may be ⁓ed (2). ⁓ **mark** *n.* the sign (?). ⁓·naire [ˌkwestɪə'neə*] *n.* list of ⁓s to be answered by a number of people, esp. to get facts, information about their views.

queue [kjuː] *n.* **1.** line of people waiting for their turn (e.g. to get on a bus, buy sth., etc.): *jump the* ⁓, take precedence of other people waiting in a ⁓. **2.** line of vehicles waiting to proceed. **3.** plait of hair or wig hanging down the back of the neck. *v.i.* (often ⁓ *up*) get into, be in, a ⁓.

quib·ble ['kwɪbl] *n.* use of ambiguous or irrelevant language to evade the main point of an argument. *v.i.* use ⁓s; argue about small points or differences: ⁓ *over sth.*

quick [kwɪk] *adj.* **1.** moving fast; done in a short time; able to move fast and do things in a short time: *Be* ⁓ *about it!* Hurry up! **2.** lively; bright; active; prompt: ⁓ *to understand; a* ⁓ *ear for music;* ⁓-*witted,* ⁓ at seeing and making jokes, etc.; ⁓ at understanding things; ⁓ *to take offence,* ⁓-*tempered,* easily

made angry. **3.** (old use) living: *the* ⁓ *and the dead.* *n.* sensitive flesh below the skin, esp. the nails: *cut sb. to the* ⁓, (fig.) hurt his feelings deeply. *adv.* = ⁓·ly *adv.* ⁓·ness *n.* ⁓·en ['kwɪkən] *v.t. & i.* **1.** make or become ⁓er. **2.** make or become more lively or active. '⁓·lime *n.* (no pl.) unslaked lime (see *lime*[1]). '⁓·sand *n.* (area of) loose, wet, deep sand which sucks down men, animals, etc. that try to walk on it. '⁓·set *adj.* (of a hedge) made of living plants, esp. hawthorn (not stakes). '⁓·sil·ver *n.* (no pl.) mercury.

quid[1] [kwɪd] *n.* lump of tobacco to be chewed.

quid[2] [kwɪd] *n.* (pl. ⁓) (Gt. Brit., sl.) pound (sterling).

qui·es·cent [kwaɪ'esnt] *adj.* at rest; motionless; passive. ⁓·ly *adv.* **qui·es·cence** *n.* (no pl.).

qui·et ['kwaɪət] *adj.* **1.** with little or no movement or sound: *a* ⁓ *sea* (*evening*). **2.** free from excitement, trouble, anxiety: *a* ⁓ *life* (*mind*). **3.** gentle; not rough (in disposition): ⁓ *children.* **4.** (of colours) not bright. **5.** not open or revealed: ⁓ *resentment; keep sth.* ⁓, keep it secret; *on the* ⁓, (sl.) *on the q.t.* [ˌkjuː'tiː], secretly. *n.* state of being ⁓: *live in peace and* ⁓; *an hour's* ⁓. *v.t. & i.* (more usu. ⁓·en ['kwaɪətn]) make or become ⁓. ⁓·ly *adv.* ⁓·ness *n.* **qui·etude** ['kwaɪɪtjuːd] *n.* stillness; calmness.

quill [kwɪl] *n.* **1.** large wing or tail feather; (hollow stem of) such a feather as formerly used for writing with. **2.** long, sharp, stiff spine of a porcupine.

quilt [kwɪlt] *n.* padded bed-covering.

quince [kwɪns] *n.* (tree with a) hard, acid, pear-shaped fruit.

qui·nine [kwɪ'niːn] *n.* bitter liquid made from the bark of a tree and used as a medicine for fevers.

quin·tes·sence [kwɪn'tesns] *n.* perfect example: *the* ⁓ *of politeness.*

quin·tet(te) [kwɪn'tet] *n.* (piece of music for) group of five players or singers.

quip [kwɪp] *n.* **1.** clever, witty, or sarcastic remark or saying. **2.** quibble.

quire ['kwaɪə*] *n.* twenty-four sheets of writing-paper.

quit [kwɪt] *v.t. & i.* (-*tt*-; p.t. & p.p. ⁓ted or ⁓) **1.** go away from; leave. **2.** stop (doing sth.). **3.** (old use, refl.) acquit: *They* ⁓ted *themselves well.* *pred. adj.* free; clear: *be* ⁓ *of,* be free of; be no longer burdened with.

quite [kwaɪt] *adv.* **1.** completely;

altogether: *I ~ agree.* **2.** rather; somewhat; to some extent: *~ cool this evening. He's ~ a scholar.* **3.** really; truly; actually: *~ an achievement.* **4.** *~ (so),* (in answers) expressing understanding or agreement.

quits [kwɪts] *pred. adj. be ~,* be on even terms (*with* sb. by paying a debt of money, punishment, etc.).

quiv·er¹ [ˈkwɪvə*] *v.t. & i.* (cause to) tremble slightly or vibrate: *leaves ~ing in the wind; in a ~ing voice.* *n.* *~ing* sound or motion.

quiv·er² [ˈkwɪvə*] *n.* archer's case for carrying arrows.

qui vive [ˌkiːˈviːv] (Fr.) *n. on the ~,* on the alert; watchful.

quix·ot·ic [kwɪkˈsɒtɪk] *adj.* romantic, idealistic, imaginative, but utterly impractical, and regardless of one's own material interests. **quix·ot·i·cal·ly** *adv.*

quiz [kwɪz] *v.t.* (-zz-) **1.** ask questions of, as a test of knowledge. **2.** (old use) make fun of; stare at curiously through an eyeglass. *n.* (pl. *~zes*) general test of knowledge; test of knowledge in radio or television as an entertainment. **~·zi·cal** [ˈkwɪzɪkl] *adj.* **1.** comical; causing amusement. **2.** teasing: *a ~zical smile.* **~·zi·cal·ly** *adv.*

quod [kwɒd] *n.* (Gt. Brit., sl.) prison.

quoit [kɔɪt] *n.* ring (of metal, rubber, rope) to be thrown to encircle an iron peg; (pl.) this game.

quo·rum [ˈkwɔːrəm] *n.* number of persons who must, by the rules, be present at a meeting (of a committee, etc.) before its proceedings can have authority.

quo·ta [ˈkwəʊtə] *n.* proportional part of a fixed total amount or quantity (e.g. quantity of goods allowed to be imported or exported, or number of immigrants allowed to enter a country, etc.).

quote [kwəʊt] *v.t.* **1.** repeat, write (words used by another); repeat or write words (*from* a book, etc.). **2.** give (a reference, etc.) to support a statement: *~ a recent instance.* **3.** enclose (words) within quotation marks. **4.** name, mention (a price). **quo·ta·tion** [kwəʊˈteɪʃn] *n.* **1.** passage ~d (1) from a book, etc. *quotation marks,* the marks (' ' or " ") placed before and after the words ~d. **2.** amount stated as the current price of an article: *the quotations from the Stock Exchange.* **3.** estimate of the cost of a piece of work.

quoth [kwəʊθ] *v.t.* (old use) said.

quo·tient [ˈkwəʊʃnt] *n.* number obtained by dividing one number by another.

R

rab·bi ['ræbaɪ] *n.* teacher of the Jewish law; (title of a) spiritual leader of a Jewish congregation.

rab·bit ['ræbɪt] *n.* small animal of the hare family living in a burrow.

rab·ble ['ræbl] *n.* **1.** disorderly crowd; mob. ~*-rouser,* person who stirs up the passions of the mob for political change. **2.** *the ~,* (derog.) the lower classes; the common people.

ra·bid ['ræbɪd] *adj.* **1.** furious; unreasoning; fanatical; violent. **2.** (of dogs) affected with rabies; mad.

ra·bies ['reɪbiːz] *n.* (no pl.) disease causing madness in dogs, wolves, etc.; hydrophobia.

race¹ [reɪs] *n.* **1.** contest or competition in speed (e.g. in running, sailing, driving, etc.): *the ~s,* series of these for dogs, horses, etc. **2.** strong, fast current of water in the sea, a river, etc. *v.i. & t.* **1.** run a ~ (1) (*with* sb., *against* time, etc.). **2.** cause (a horse, etc.) to take part in a ~ (1). **3.** (cause to) move at great speed. **rac·ing** *n.* (no pl.) (esp.) horse-racing; car racing: *a racing car.* '~*-course n.* ground or track prepared for horse-~s. '~*-horse n.* horse specially bred for racing.

race² [reɪs] *n.* **1.** any of several subdivisions of mankind characterized by distinctive physical traits, esp. colour of skin, shape of eyes and nose, etc.: *the Negroid (white) ~.* **2.** group of people having a common culture, history, language, etc.: *Anglo-Saxon ~.* **3.** main division of any living creatures: *the human ~,* mankind; *the feathered ~,* (humor.) birds. **ra·cial** ['reɪʃl] *adj.* of or related to ~².

rack¹ [ræk] *n.* **1.** wooden or metal framework for holding food (esp. hay) for animals. **2.** framework with bars, marked

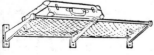

a luggage rack (3)

pegs, etc. for holding things, hanging things on, etc.: *a plate-~; a hat-~.* **3.** shelf in a railway carriage, bus, etc. for light luggage. **4.** instrument formerly used for torturing a victim by stretching: *on the ~,* (fig.) in distress or under strain. **5.** rod, bar, or rail with teeth or cogs into which the teeth on a wheel fit (as used on special railways up steep hillsides). *v.t.* **1.** torture by stretching on the ~ (4); cause severe pain to: *~ed with grief; a ~ing headache.* **2.** ~ *one's brains (for* an answer, etc.), make great mental efforts.

rack² [ræk] *n.* (only in) *go to ~ and ruin,* fall into a ruined state.

rack·et¹ ['rækɪt] *n.* **1.** uproar; loud noise. **2.** time of social activity, hurry, and bustle. **3.** dishonest way of getting money by deceiving or threatening people, selling worthless goods, etc. **4.** ordeal; trying experience: *stand the ~,* come successfully through a test; accept the consequences of sth. ~·**eer** [ˌrækɪˈtɪə*] *n.* person engaged in a ~ (3).

rack·et², rac·quet ['rækɪt] *n.* **1.** light bat used for hitting the ball in tennis and other games. **2.** (pl., usu. sing. v.) ball-game for two or four players in a four-walled court.

a racket² (1)

racy ['reɪsɪ] *adj.* **1.** (of speech or writing) vivid; vigorous. **2.** having strongly marked characteristics. **3.** natural; unspoiled. **ra·ci·ly** *adv.*

ra·dar ['reɪdɑː*] *n.* (no pl.) radio apparatus that indicates on a screen solid objects that come within its range, used by pilots, etc., esp. in fog or darkness.

ra·di·ant ['reɪdjənt] *adj.* **1.** sending out rays of light; shining. **2.** (of a persón's looks, eyes) bright; showing joy or love. **3.** (phys.) transmitted by radiation. **~ly** *adv.* **ra·di·ance** *n.* (no pl.).

ra·di·ate ['reɪdɪeɪt] *v.t. & i.* **1.** send out rays of (light or heat); come or go out in rays: *a stove radiating warmth*; *heat radiating from a stove.* **2.** give out, show (joy, etc.). **3.** spread out like radii *from* a centre. **ra·di·a·tion** [,reɪdɪ'eɪʃn] *n.* radiating; emission of energy in rays. **2.** sth. ~d. **ra·di·a·tor** ['reɪdɪeɪtə*] *n.* **1.** apparatus for radiating heat, esp. heat from steam or hot water supplied through pipes or from electric current. **2.** device for cooling a motor vehicle's engine.

radiators

rad·i·cal ['rædɪkl] *adj.* **1.** of or from the root or base; fundamental: ~ (i.e. thorough and complete) *reforms.* **2.** (pol.) favouring fundamental reforms: *the R~ Party.* **3.** (math.) relating to the root of a number or quantity. *n.* person with ~ (2) opinions; member of the R~ Party. **~ly** *adv.*

ra·dii, see *radius.*

ra·dio ['reɪdɪəʊ] *n.* (pl. ~s) **1.** wireless telegraphy or telephony: *send a message by* ~; broadcasting: (attrib.) ~ *programme.* **2.** (also ~ *set*) apparatus for receiving broadcast programmes or (as on ships, aircraft, etc.) for receiving and transmitting ~ messages: *a portable* ~. **3.** broadcasting station: *R~ Luxembourg.* *v.t. & i.* send by ~. **'~gram** *n.* combined ~ set and recordplayer.

ra·dio- ['reɪdɪəʊ-] *pref.* of rays or radium. **~·ac·tive** [,reɪdɪəʊ'æktɪv] *adj.* (of such metals as radium and uranium) having the property of sending out rays which pass through solids and produce electrical effects. **~·ac·tiv·i·ty** [,reɪdɪəʊæk'tɪvətɪ] *n.* **'~graph** *n.* X-ray photograph. **ra·di·og·ra·phy** [,reɪdɪ'ɒgrəfɪ] *n.* (no pl.).

rad·ish ['rædɪʃ] *n.* small salad plant with edible root.

ra·di·um ['reɪdɪəm] *n.* (no pl.) radioactive metal used in the treatment of some diseases (e.g. cancer).

ra·di·us ['reɪdjəs] *n.* (pl. *-dii* [-dɪaɪ]) **1.** (length of a) straight line from the centre of a circle or sphere to any point on the circumference or surface. **2.** circular area measured by its ~.

raf·fia ['ræfɪə] *n.* (no pl.) fibre from the leaf-stalks of a kind of palm, used for making baskets, hats, etc.

raf·fle ['ræfl] *n.* sale of an article by a lottery, esp. for charity. *v.t.* sell (sth.) by this method.

raft [rɑːft] *n.* flat, floating platform of rough timber or other buoyant material for the transportation of persons or things, esp. as a substitute for a boat in emergencies.

raf·ter ['rɑːftə*] *n.* one of the sloping beams forming the framework of a roof, supporting tiles, slates, etc.

rag[1] [ræg] *n.* **1.** odd bit of cloth. **2.** (pl.) old or torn clothes: *dressed in* ~*s*; *glad* ~*s*, (colloq.) best clothes; evening dress. **3.** (humor.) newspaper which one considers contemptible. **4.** scrap; (irregular) piece: *not a* ~ *of evidence.* **5.** old, waste pieces of cloth as material for paper. **~·a·muf·fin** ['rægə,mʌfɪn] *n.* dirty person, esp. small boy dressed in ~*s*. **~·ged** ['rægɪd] *adj.* **1.** (with clothes) badly torn or in ~*s*. **2.** having rough or irregular edges or outlines or surfaces: *a dog with a* ~*ged coat of hair.* **3.** (of work, etc.) imperfect; faulty.

rag[2] [ræg] *v.t.* (*-gg-*) (sl.) tease; play practical jokes on. *n.* ~ging.

rage [reɪdʒ] *n.* **1.** (outburst of) furious anger; violence: *be in (fly into) a* ~, be (become) uncontrollably angry. **2.** strong desire (*for* sth.). **3.** (*all) the* ~, the fashion. *v.i.* be violently angry; (of storms, etc.) be violent.

raid [reɪd] *v.t. & i. & n.* (make a) sudden attack (*on*) or surprise visit (to): *a* ~ *on a bank*; *air* ~*s on London.* **~·er** *n.* person, ship, aircraft, etc. making a ~.

rail[1] [reɪl] *n.* **1.** wood or metal bar or rod, or continuous series of such bars or rods used as part of a fence, as a protection against contact or falling over, as a means to hang things on, etc. **2.** steel bar or continuous line of such bars forming one side of a track for trains or trams: *send sth. by* ~; *travel by* ~; *go off the* ~*s*, (of a train, etc.) leave the track; (fig.) become out of order, out of control. *v.t.* put ~*s* (1) round; shut (*in*, *off*), separate, by means of ~*s* (1). **~·ing** *n.* (often pl.) fence made with ~*s* (e.g. at the side of steps). **'~·road** (U.S.A.), **'~·way**

ns. track on which trains run; system of such tracks, with the locomotives, cars, waggons, etc. and the organization controlling everything: *modernize the ~way.*

rail² [reɪl] *v.i.* complain, speak angrily (*against, at,* sth. or sb.). **~·lery** ['reɪlərɪ] *n.* good-humoured teasing.

rai·ment ['reɪmənt] *n.* (no pl.) (liter.) clothing.

rain [reɪn] *n.* **1.** water falling in drops from the sky; fall of such drops: *walk in the ~; ~ or shine,* whether it ~s or not. *There was a heavy ~ in the morning.* **2.** thick, fast fall of sth. like ~: *a ~ of bullets;* (fig.) *a ~ of congratulations.* **3.** *the ~s,* the rainy season in some tropical countries. *v.t. & i.* **1.** *It is ~ing, ~ is falling. It never ~s but it pours* (e.g. if one misfortune comes, another will follow). **2.** come, fall, send (*down upon*), like ~: *tears ~ing down his cheeks.* **~·bow** ['reɪnbəʊ] *n.* many-coloured arch formed in the sky or in spray when the sun shines through falling drops of water. '**~·fall** *n.* **1.** amount of ~ falling within a given time and area (e.g. as measured in inches or cm of depth per annum). **2.** shower (1). '**~·gauge** *n.* instrument for measuring ~fall. '**~·proof** *adj.* able to keep ~ out. (*-ier, -iest*) having much ~: *~y weather; save sth. for a ~y day,* put (esp. money) aside for a possible time of need.

raise [reɪz] *v.t.* **1.** lift up (e.g. a weight, one's hat, one's voice, etc.); make (e.g. prices, the temperature, sb.'s hopes, etc.) higher; erect or build (e.g. a monument). **2.** cause to rise or appear: *buses raising clouds of dust; ~ Cain* (*hell, the devil, the roof*), (sl.) cause an uproar; start a big row. **3.** bring up for attention or discussion: *~ a new point; ~ a question* (*a protest*). **4.** grow or produce (crops); breed (sheep, cattle, etc.); bring up (a family). **5.** get or bring together; manage to get: *~ an army* (*a loan, money for the holidays*). **6.** *~ a siege* (*blockade*), end it.

rai·sin ['reɪzn] *n.* dried grape (as used in cakes, etc.).

a rake¹

rake¹ [reɪk] *n.* long-handled tool with teeth (2), used for drawing together dead leaves, straw, hay, etc. or for smoothing soil or gravel. *v.t. & i.* **1.** use a ~ on (soil, etc.) for smoothing. **2.** get (sth. *together, up, out, etc.*) with or as with a ~. **3.** search (*through* or *over* old records, papers, etc.) for facts, etc. ~ *sth. up,* bring to people's knowledge (sth. forgotten, e.g. a charge of wrongdoing). **4.** fire with guns at (a ship, etc.) from end to end.

rake² [reɪk] *n.* dissolute man.

rak·ish ['reɪkɪʃ] *adj.* **1.** (of a ship) looking as if built for speed. **2.** smart; jaunty; dashing: *a hat worn at a ~ angle.* **3.** of or like a rake².

ral·ly¹ ['rælɪ] *v.t. & i.* **1.** (cause to) come together, esp. after defeat or confusion, or in the face of threats or danger, to make new efforts. **2.** give new strength to; (cause to) recover (health, strength): *The patient is ~ing. ~ one's spirits* (*wits*). *n.* **1.** ~ing. **2.** public meeting, esp. to support a cause: *a political ~.* **3.** competition for motor vehicles, esp. over public roads. **4.** (tennis, etc.) exchange of several strokes before a point is scored.

ral·ly² ['rælɪ] *v.t.* tease in a good-humoured way; make fun of.

ram [ræm] *n.* **1.** male sheep. **2.** implement for striking or pushing with great force, e.g. the falling weight of a pile-driving machine. *v.t.* (*-mm-*) strike and push heavily. '**~·rod** *n.* iron rod for ~ming gunpowder, etc. into old-fashioned guns.

ram·ble ['ræmbl] *v.i.* walk for pleasure, with no special destination; (fig.) wander in one's talk, not keeping to the subject. *n.* rambling walk. **~r** *n.* person who ~s; climbing rose. **ram·bling** *adj.* (esp. of buildings, streets, towns) extending in various directions irregularly, as if built without planning; (fig., of a speech, essay, etc.) disconnected.

ram·i·fy ['ræmɪfaɪ] *v.i. & t.* form or produce branches; make or become a network. **ram·i·fi·ca·tion** [ˌræmɪfɪ-'keɪʃn] *n.*

ramp¹ [ræmp] *n.* rising bank of earth; sloping way from one level to another.

ramp² [ræmp] *n.* (sl.) attempt to obtain much too high a price; swindle.

ram·page [ræm'peɪdʒ] *v.i.* rush about in excitement or rage. *n. on the ~,* rampaging.

ram·pant ['ræmpənt] *adj.* **1.** (esp. of diseases, social evils) unchecked; beyond control. **2.** (heraldry, esp. of a lion) on the hind legs.

ram·part ['ræmpɑːt] *n.* wide bank of

earth, often with a wall, built to defend a fort, etc.

ram·shack·le ['ræm,ʃækl] *adj.* almost collapsing: *a ~ old house.*

ran, see **run**[1].

ranch [rɑːntʃ, U.S.A. ræntʃ] *n.* (in N. America) large farm, esp. for raising cattle, horses, or sheep, but also for fruit, chickens, etc. **~·er** *n.*

ran·cid ['rænsɪd] *adj.* **1.** (esp. of fat, butter) having gone bad; ill-smelling. **2.** with the smell or taste of stale fat or butter.

ran·cour (U.S.A. **-cor**) ['ræŋkə*] *n.* deep and long-lasting feeling of bitterness; spitefulness. **ran·cor·ous** ['ræŋkərəs] *adj.*

ran·dom ['rændəm] *n. at ~,* without aim or system: *chosen at ~. adj.* done or made at *~: ~ remarks; a ~ selection.*

rang, see **ring**[2] (v.).

range [reɪndʒ] *n.* **1.** row, line, or series of things: *a ~ of mountains (cliffs).* **2.** area of ground with targets for firing at: *a rifle-~.* **3.** distance to which a gun will shoot or to which a shell, etc. can be fired: *in (beyond, out of) ~;* distance between a gun, etc. and the target: *at short (long) ~.* **4.** extent; distance between limits: *a wide ~ of prices (colours); the annual ~ of temperature* (e.g. from —20°C to 35°C); *the ~ of her voice* (i.e. between her top and bottom notes). **5.** area over which plants are found growing or in which animals are found living. **6.** area included in or concerned with sth.: *a subject that is outside my ~,* one that I know nothing about. **7.** cooking-stove, with a flat metal top and an oven. *v.t. & i.* **1.** put in a row or rows; arrange in order. **2.** go, move, wander *(over, through, etc.* the woods, hills, etc.). **3.** extend; run in a line: *a boundary ranging N. and S.* **4.** vary between limits: *prices ranging from £4 to £7 (between £4 and £7).* **5.** put, take one's place, in a specified situation, group, or company: *men who ~d themselves with (against, on the side of) the rebels.*

'~-,find·er *n.* **1.** instrument for measuring the distance of sth. to be fired at. **2.** camera attachment for measuring the distance between camera and object.

rank[1] [ræŋk] *n.* **1.** line of persons or things: *a taxi-~.* **2.** (army) number of soldiers placed side by side: *the ~s, the ~ and file,* common soldiers, privates and corporals. (fig.) ordinary, undistinguished people. **3.** position in a scale, esp. grade in the armed forces:

promoted to the ~ of captain; people of all ~s. *v.t. & i.* **1.** put or arrange in a ~ or ~s. **2.** have, give (sb.), a certain ~ (3) compared with others: *~ (sb.) with the world's greatest actors.*

rank[2] [ræŋk] *adj.* **1.** (of plants) growing too luxuriantly; with excessive foliage. **2.** (of land) choked with weeds. **3.** having a bad, strong taste or smell; offensive: *~ tobacco.* **4.** unmistakably bad: *a ~ traitor.*

ran·kle ['ræŋkl] *v.i.* continue to be a painful or bitter memory: *insults that ~d in her mind.*

ran·sack ['rænsæk] *v.t.* **1.** search (a place, etc.) thoroughly *(for* sth.). **2.** rob; plunder *(of* things): *the enemy ~ed the town.*

ran·som ['rænsəm] *n.* freeing of a captive upon payment; the sum of money, etc. paid: *hold sb. to ~,* hold him captive and demand ~. *v.t.* obtain the freedom of (sb.), set (sb.) free, in exchange for ~.

rant [rænt] *v.i. & t.* speak wildly, violently, or boastingly; say or recite (sth.) noisily and theatrically: *a bad actor ~ing his words.* **~·er** *n.*

rap[1] [ræp] *v.t. & i.* (-*pp-*) **1.** knock (1) repeatedly: *sb. ~ping at the window.* **2.** *~ sth. out,* say sth. suddenly or sharply; (of a spirit (2) summoned by a medium (4)) express sth. by *~s. n.* **1.** (sound of a) knock. **2.** light, quick blow: *a ~ on or over the knuckles* (punishment for a child); (fig.) reproof. **3.** (sl.) blame; consequences: *take the ~ (for* sth.).

rap[2] [ræp] *n. not care a ~,* not care at all.

ra·pa·cious [rə'peɪʃəs] *adj.* greedy (esp. for money). **ra·pac·i·ty** [rə-'pæsətɪ] *n.* (no pl.) greed; avarice.

rape[1] [reɪp] *v.t.* **1.** (poet.) seize and carry off by force. **2.** force (a woman or girl) to have sexual intercourse. *n.* act of raping.

rape[2] [reɪp] *n.* plant grown as food for sheep and pigs; plant grown for the oil obtained from its seeds.

rap·id ['ræpɪd] *adj.* **1.** quick. **2.** (of a slope) steep. *n.* (usu. pl.) part of a river where a steep slope makes the water flow fast. **~·ly** *adv.* **ra·pid·i·ty** [rə'pɪdətɪ] *n.* (no pl.).

ra·pi·er ['reɪpjə*] *n.* light, slim sword used in fencing[2].

rapt [ræpt] *adj.* so deep in thought, so carried away by feelings, that one is unaware of other things: *~ in a book; listening with ~ attention.* **rap·ture** ['ræptʃə*] *n.* ecstatic joy or delight:

(pl.) *be in* (*go into*) ⁓ures (*over, about, sth.*), *be* (*become*) extremely happy or enthusiastic. **rap·tur·ous** *adj.*

rare¹ [reə*] *adj.* (⁓*r,* ⁓*st*) **1.** unusual; uncommon; not often happening, seen, etc.: *It is very* ⁓ *for him to let me wait.* **2.** unusually good: *They had* ⁓ *fun together.* **3.** (of a substance, esp. the atmosphere) thin; not dense. **⁓·ly** *adv.* seldom. **⁓·fied** ['reərɪfaɪd] *adj.* = ⁓ (3): *the* ⁓*fied air of the mountain tops.* **rar·i·ty** ['reərətɪ] *n.* being ⁓ (1, 3); ⁓ (1) thing.

rare² [reə*] *adj.* (of meat) underdone; not completely cooked.

ras·cal ['rɑːskəl] *n.* **1.** dishonest person. **2.** (playfully) mischievous person (esp. a child), fond of playing tricks.

rase, see *raze.*

rash¹ [ræʃ] *n.* (breaking out of, patch of) tiny red spots on the skin.

rash² [ræʃ] *adj.* too hasty; overbold; done, doing things, without enough thought of the consequences. **⁓·ly** *adv.* **⁓·ness** *n.* (no pl.).

rash·er ['ræʃə*] *n.* slice of bacon or ham (to be) fried.

rasp [rɑːsp] *n.* metal tool like a coarse file with surfaces covered with sharp points, used for scraping. *v.t. & i.* **1.** scrape with a ⁓. **2.** make a grating sound; (fig.) have an irritating effect on (nerves).

rasp·ber·ry ['rɑːzbərɪ] *n.* (bush with) small, sweet, red or yellow berries.

rat [ræt] *n.* animal like, but larger than, a mouse: *smell a* ⁓, (fig.) suspect that sth. wrong is being done.

a rat   a ratchet

ratch·et ['rætʃɪt] *n.* toothed wheel provided with a spring catch that allows the wheel to turn in one direction only.

rate¹ [reɪt] *n.* **1.** standard or way of reckoning, obtained by bringing two numbers or amounts into relationship: *walking at the* ⁓ *of 3 miles an hour*; *buy things at the* ⁓ *of 40p. a hundred*; *an annual* (*birth*) *death* ⁓ *of 25 per 1,000*; ⁓ *of exchange,* relationship between two currencies. **2.** *at this* ⁓, if this is true; if this state of affairs continues; *at any* ⁓, in any case; whatever happens. **3.** tax on property paid to the local authorities for local purposes: *the* ⁓s,

these payments collectively; *the water-*⁓. **4.** *first* ⁓, excellent; *second* ⁓, fairly good; *third* ⁓, rather poor; (attrib.) *a first-*⁓ *book.* *v.t. & i.* **1.** judge or estimate the quality or value of; consider. **2.** value (property) for the purpose of assessing ⁓s (3) on.

rate² [reɪt] *v.t. & i.* scold.

rath·er ['rɑːðə*] *adv.* **1.** more willingly; by preference: *Don't come today, I would* ⁓ *you came* (would prefer you to come) *tomorrow.* **2.** more precisely: *late last night, or* ⁓ *this morning.* **3.** somewhat: *that* ⁓ *tall boy over there*; *its* ⁓ *a pity*; *a* ⁓ *good result,* ⁓ *a good result.* **4.** (colloq., in answers) most certainly; indeed so: A. *Are you comfortable?* B. *Yes,* ⁓!

rat·i·fy ['rætɪfaɪ] *v.t.* confirm (an agreement) by signature or other formality. **rat·i·fi·ca·tion** [,rætɪfɪ'keɪʃn] *n.* (no pl.).

rat·ing ['reɪtɪŋ] *n.* **1.** class, classification (e.g. of yachts by tonnage, engines by horsepower, etc.). **2.** (in the Navy) person's position or class as recorded in the ship's books; non-commissioned sailor. **3.** index of popularity of radio or television programmes.

ra·tio ['reɪʃɪəʊ] *n.* relation between two amounts expressed by the number of times one contains the other: *The* ⁓*s 1 to 5 and 20 to 100 are the same.*

ra·tion ['ræʃn] *n.* fixed quantity, esp. of food, allowed to one person; (usu. pl.) fixed allowance of food, esp. for soldiers and sailors. *v.t.* limit (people, goods) to ⁓s.

ra·tio·nal ['ræʃənl] *adj.* of reason or reasoning; able to reason; sensible; that can be tested by reason: ⁓ *conduct* (*explanations*). **⁓·ly** *adv.*

rat·tle ['rætl] *v.t. & i.* **1.** (cause to) make short, sharp sounds quickly, one after the other: *windows that* ⁓ *in the wind.* **2.** talk, say, or repeat sth., quickly and in a thoughtless or lively way: ⁓ *off a poem one has learnt by heart.* **3.** move, fall, travel fast and with a rattling noise: *A cart full of milk-bottles* ⁓*d past.* *n.* **1.** (baby's toy producing a) rattling noise. **2.** set of horny rings in a ⁓snake's tail. '**⁓·snake** *n.* poisonous American snake that makes a rattling noise with its tail.

rau·cous ['rɔːkəs] *adj.* (of sounds) harsh; rough; hoarse.

rav·age ['rævɪdʒ] *v.t. & i.* **1.** destroy; damage badly: *forests* ⁓*d by fire.* **2.** rob, plunder, with violence. *n.* **1.** destruction; devastation; (usu. pl.) destructive effects (of): *the* ⁓*s of time.*

rave [reɪv] *v.i.* **1.** talk wildly, violently, angrily. **2.** talk with exaggerated enthusiasm (*of, about*). **3.** (of the sea, wind, etc.) roar; rage. **rav·ings** *n. pl.* foolish or wild talk (e.g. of a madman).

rav·el ['rævl] *v.t. & i.* (-*ll*-, U.S.A. also -*l*-) **1.** (of knitted or woven things) separate into threads; become un-twisted; fray: *Bind the edge so that it will not ~.* **2.** cause (threads, hair, etc.) to be twisted together; (fig.) make confused.

ra·ven ['reɪvn] *n.* large, black bird like a crow. *adj.* (esp. of hair) glossy black.

rav·en·ous ['rævənəs] *adj.* **1.** very hungry. **2.** greedy.

ra·vine [rə'viːn] *n.* deep, narrow valley.

rav·ish ['rævɪʃ] *v.t.* **1.** fill with delight: *a ~ing view.* **2.** (old use) seize and carry off. **3.** rape (a woman or girl).

raw [rɔː] *adj.* **1.** uncooked. **2.** in the natural state, not manufactured or prepared for use: *~ hides* (not yet tanned); *~ materials.* **3.** (of persons) untrained; unskilled; inexperienced: *~ recruits.* **4.** (of the weather) damp and cold. **5.** (of a place on the flesh) with the skin rubbed off; sore and painful; (of a wound) unhealed; bloody. **6.** harsh; unjust: *get a ~ deal.*

ray [reɪ] *n.* **1.** line, beam, of radiant light, heat, energy: *the ~s of the sun;* *X-~s.* **2.** any one of a number of lines coming out from a centre.

ray·on ['reɪɒn] *n.* silk-like material made from cellulose.

raze, rase [reɪz] *v.t.* destroy completely (towns, buildings), esp. by levelling them to the ground.

ra·zor ['reɪzə*] *n.* instrument with a sharp blade, used for shaving.

re [riː] *prep.* (law) in the matter of; concerning.

re- [riː-] *pref.* **1.** again: *reappear; re-count.* **2.** again and in a different way: *rearrange.*

reach [riːtʃ] *v.t. & i.* **1.** stretch (the hand): *~ out one's hand for sth.;* *~ for a book.* **2.** stretch out the hand for and take (sth.); get and give (sth.) to: *Please ~ me that book.* **3.** get to; go as far as: *~ London* (*the end of a chapter*); *as far as the eye can ~. n.* **1.** (extent or distance of) *~ing: within easy ~ of London; out of ~; beyond the ~ of all help.* **2.** straight stretch, esp. of a river, between two bends.

re·act [rɪ'ækt] *v.i.* **1.** have an effect (*on* the person or thing acting): *Applause ~s upon a speaker* (e.g. has the effect of giving him confidence). **2.** *~ to,* behave differently, be changed, as the result of being acted upon: *Children ~ to kind treatment by becoming more self-confident.* **3.** *~ against,* respond to sth. with a feeling of dislike: *~ing against flattery.* **re·ac·tion** [rɪ'ækʃn] *n.* **1.** action or state resulting from, or in response to, sth., esp. a return of an earlier condition after a period of the opposite condition: *After these days of excitement, there was a ~ion* (e.g. a period when life seemed dull). **2.** responsive feeling: *What was her ~ion to your story?* **3.** tendency to oppose change and progress, esp. in politics. **4.** (chem.) action of one agent upon another. **re·ac·tion·ary** [rɪ'ækʃnərɪ] *n. & adj.* (person) supporting polit-ical *~ion*; (person) opposing prog-ress. **re·ac·tor** [rɪ'æktə*] *n. nuclear ~or,* apparatus (1) for the controlled production of nuclear energy.

read [riːd] *v.t. & i.* (p.t. & p.p. ~ [red]) **1.** look at and (be able to) understand (sth. written or printed); say (aloud or silently) what is written or printed: *The girl can neither ~ nor write. He has ~ many books. She was ~ing a story to the children.* **2.** study (a subject, esp. at a university): *~ing physics at Cambridge.* **3.** give a certain impression; seem (good, bad, etc.) when *~: The play ~s well.* **4.** *~ be-tween the lines* (see *line¹* (9)). **5.** (of instruments) indicate: *What does the thermometer ~? n.* period of time given to *~ing: having a quiet ~. ~·able adj.* capable of being *~;* that is easy or pleasant to *~. ~·er* **1.** person who *~s,* esp. one who *~s* a great deal. **2.** person employed by a publishing company to *~* and evaluate books offered for publication. **3.** printer's proof-corrector. **4.** person who *~s* parts of a service in church. **5.** school *~ing-book.* **6.** university teacher junior to a professor. **~·ing** *n.* **1.** knowledge, esp. of books: *a man of wide ~ing.* **2.** way in which sth. is interpreted or understood: *my solicitor's ~ing of this clause in the agreement* (i.e. what he says it means). **3.** figure of measure-ment, etc. as shown on a dial, scale, etc.: *the ~ing on my thermometer is 23° C.* **4.** alternative wording of a pas-sage in an author's original text that has occurred in copying or reprinting.

ready ['redɪ] *adj.* **1.** in the condition needed for use; in the condition for doing sth.; willing (to do sth.): *~ for school; ~ to start; get things ~; make ~,* prepare. **2.** quick; prompt: *be too ~*

with excuses. *He always has a ~ answer.*
3. within reach; easily available: *have
a gun ~* (near at hand); *~ money,*
money in the form of coins and notes,
which can be used for payment at the
time goods are bought; cash payment;
~ reckoner, book of answers to various
common calculations needed in business, etc., *~-made,* (esp. of clothes)
made in standard sizes, not made
specially to the wearer's measurements; (fig., of ideas, etc.) unoriginal;
commonplace. *v.t.* make ~; prepare.
read·i·ly *adv.* willingly; without
difficulty or trouble. **read·i·ness** *n.*
(no pl.) **1.** *in readiness for, ~* (1) for.
2. willingness. **3.** quickness.

re·al [rɪəl] *adj.* **1.** existing in fact; not
imagined or supposed; not made up
or artificial: *~ silk (gold); the ~* (i.e.
true) *reason; a ~* (i.e. complete,
thorough) *cure.* **2.** *~ estate,* (law) land
and buildings. **~·ism** ['rɪəlɪzəm] *n.*
(no pl.) **1.** (in art and literature) showing of ~ life, facts, etc. in a true way,
without glossing over what is ugly and
painful. **2.** behaviour based on the
facing of facts and disregard of sentiment and convention. **~·is·tic** [ˌrɪə-
'lɪstɪk] *adj.* marked by ~ism (1); concerned with what is ~ and practical;
not sentimental. **~·i·ty** [rɪ'ælətɪ] *n.*
1. quality of being ~: *in ~ity,* in actual
fact. **2.** sth. ~; sth. actually seen, experienced, etc.: *the grim ~ities of war.*
3. resemblance to what is ~: *show sth.
with perfect ~ity.* **~·ly** *adv.* truly; in
fact: *~ly!* (expression of surprise or
censure); *~? is that so? do you mean it?*
real·ize ['rɪəlaɪz] *v.t.* **1.** be fully conscious of; understand: *~ one's mistake;
~ that one is wrong.* **2.** convert (a hope,
plan, etc.) into a fact: *~ one's ambitions.*
3. exchange (property, business shares,
etc.) for money; (of property, etc.)
obtain as a price for or profit (*on*).
re·al·iza·tion [ˌrɪəlaɪ'zeɪʃn] *n.* (no pl.).
realm [relm] *n.* **1.** kingdom. **2.** region,
sphere, domain (of knowledge, imagi-
nation, etc.).
re·al·tor ['rɪəltə*] *n.* (U.S.A.) = estate
agent.
ream [riːm] *n.* 480 sheets or 20 quires
of paper.
reap [riːp] *v.t. & i.* **1.** cut (grain, etc.);
gather in a crop of grain from (a field,
etc.). **2.** (fig.) get as a return or result.
~·er *n.* person or machine that ~s.
rear[1] [rɪə*] *n.* **1.** back part: *The office
is in the ~ of the house. The garage is
at the ~ of the house* (behind the house).
2. last part of an army, fleet, etc.:

attack the enemy in the ~ (from behind);
bring up the ~, come (be) last. **3.**
(attrib.) at the back: *leave the bus by
the ~ entrance.* ˌ~-'ad·mi·ral *n.* naval
officer below a vice-admiral. '~·guard
n. soldiers guarding the ~ (2). '~-
lamp, '~-light *ns.* (usu. a) red light
at the ~ of a motor car, etc. '~-ˌview
'mir·ror *n.* mirror that enables the
driver of a vehicle to see the traffic,
etc. behind.
rear[2] [rɪə*] *v.t. & i.* **1.** cause or help
to grow; bring up; take care of; foster:
~ poultry; ~ a family. **2.** (esp. of a
horse) rise on the hind legs. **3.** (rhet.)
raise; lift up (the head). **4.** (rhet.) set
up; build (e.g. an altar).
rea·son ['riːzn] *n.* **1.** (fact put forward
or serving as) cause of or justification for sth.: *my ~ for saying
so; the ~ why I said so; by ~ of,*
because of; *with ~,* rightly. **2.** power
of the mind to understand, form
opinions, etc.: *It stands to ~ (that),* it
is clear to the mind (that); sensible
people agree (that); *do anything in ~*
(anything moderate or sensible); *listen
to ~,* allow oneself to be persuaded;
bring sb. to ~, make sb. give up his
resistance or his foolish activities; *lose
one's ~,* go mad. *v.i. & t.* **1.** make use
of one's ~ (2) (*about* sth.). **2.** argue,
use ~s (1) (*with* sb.) in order to convince him. **3.** put forward as an argument: *He ~ed that ... .* **4.** ~ *sb. into* (*out
of*) *doing sth.,* persuade him by argument to do (not to do) sth. **5.** ~ *sth.
out,* think (a problem, etc.) through
logically. **~·able** ['riːznəbl] *adj.* **1.**
having ordinary common sense; able
to ~. **2.** acting, done, in accordance
with ~ (2); willing to listen to ~. **3.**
moderate; neither more nor less than
seems right or acceptable: *a ~able
excuse (price).* **~·ably** *adv.*
re·as·sure [ˌriːə'ʃʊə*] *v.t.* remove the
fears or doubts of (sb.). **re·as·sur·ance**
n. (no pl.).
re·bate ['riːbeɪt] *n.* sum of money by
which a payment may be reduced;
discount.
re·bel [rɪ'bel] *v.i.* (-*ll*-) **1.** take up
arms to fight (*against* the government).
2. show resistance; protest strongly:
*children who ~ against too much home-
work.* **reb·el** ['rebl] *n.* person who
~s; (attrib.) *the ~ army.* **~·lion** [rɪ-
'beljən] *n.* ~ling, esp. an armed rising
against a government. **~·lious**
[rɪ'beljəs] *adj.* acting like a ~; taking
part in a ~lion; not easily controlled:
a child with a ~lious temper.

re·bound [rɪ'baʊnd] *v.i.* spring or bounce back after hitting sth. ['riː- baʊnd] *n.* act of ~ing.

re·buff [rɪ'bʌf] *n.* blunt refusal of an offer of, or request for, friendship, help, etc.; snub[1]. *v.t.* give a ~ to.

re·buke [rɪ'bjuːk] *v.t.* speak severely to (sb. for doing wrong, etc.); reprove. *n.* words used in rebuking sb.; reproof.

re·but [rɪ'bʌt] *v.t.* (-tt-) prove (a charge, piece of evidence, etc.) to be false. ~tal [rɪ'bʌtl] *n.*

re·cal·ci·trant [rɪ'kælsɪtrənt] *adj.* disobedient; resisting authority.

re·call [rɪ'kɔːl] *v.t.* 1. summon back (e.g. an ambassador). 2. bring back (an event, etc.) to the mind. 3. take back; revoke (an order, a decision). *n.* 1. summons to return, esp. to an ambassador to return to his own country. 2. *beyond* (*past*) ~, that cannot be brought back or revoked.

re·cant [rɪ'kænt] *v.t. & i.* give up (an opinion, a belief); take back (a statement) as being false. **re·can·ta·tion** [ˌriːkæn'teɪʃn] *n.*

re·ca·pit·u·late [ˌriːkə'pɪtjʊleɪt] *v.t. & i.* repeat, go through again, the chief points of (an argument, etc.). **re·ca·pit·u·la·tion** ['riːkəˌpɪtjʊ'leɪʃn] *n.*

re·cast [ˌriː'kɑːst] *v.t.* (p.t. & p.p. -*cast*) 1. give a new shape or arrangement to: ~ *a sentence.* 2. change the cast of (a play, a film, etc.).

re·cede [rɪ'siːd] *v.i.* 1. (appear to) go back or away from the observer or from an earlier position. 2. become less in character or value. 3. slope away from the front or from the observer: *a receding chin.* 4. withdraw (*from* a promise, an opinion, etc.).

re·ceipt [rɪ'siːt] *n.* 1. receiving or being received: *on* ~ *of the news.* 2. (pl.) money received (in a business, etc.). 3. written statement that sth. (esp. money) has been received. 4. (old use) recipe. *v.t.* give a ~ for or acknowledge the ~ of; mark as paid: *the* ~*ed bill had been returned.*

re·ceive [rɪ'siːv] *v.t. & i.* 1. accept; take or get (sth. offered, sent, etc.): ~ *insults* (*punishment, a warm welcome*). 2. allow to enter; (formally) see, welcome, or entertain (guests, a delegation, etc.). ~**d** *adj.* widely accepted as correct: *the* ~*d opinion* (*text*).

re·ceiv·er *n.* 1. person who ~s, esp. stolen goods. 2. device (2) for receiving sth., esp. that part of a telephone that is held to the ear; radio or television receiving apparatus (1): *a radio* ~. **re·ceiv·ing-set** [rɪ'siːvɪŋset] *n.* apparatus (1) for receiving radio or television signals; ~r (2).

re·cent ['riːsnt] *adj.* (having existed, been made, happened) not long before; begun not long ago. ~**ly** *adv.*

re·cep·ta·cle [rɪ'septəkl] *n.* container or holder in which things may be put away or out of sight.

re·cep·tion [rɪ'sepʃn] *n.* 1. receiving or being received, esp. of a person into a place or company: *prepare the rooms for the* ~ *of the guests*; ~ *desk* (in a hotel). 2. formal party: *a wedding* ~. 3. manner of being received: *The play met with an unfriendly* ~ *from the critics. The politician was given a warm* ~. 4. receiving of radio or television signals; quality of reproduction of these signals: *Is radio* ~ *good in your district?* **re·cep·tive** [rɪ'septɪv] *adj.* quick or ready to receive new ideas, suggestions, etc.

re·cess [rɪ'ses] *n.* 1. period of time when work is stopped (e.g. when Parliament, the lawcourts, are not in session). 2. part of a room where the wall is set back from the main part; alcove. 3. dark or secret inner place or part: *the* ~*es of a cave*; *in the inmost* ~*es of the heart.* **re·ces·sion** [rɪ'seʃn] *n.* (temporary) decline in economic activity.

rec·i·pe ['resɪpɪ] *n.* directions for preparing (a cake, a dish of food, a medical remedy, etc.) or for getting any result.

re·cip·i·ent [rɪ'sɪpɪənt] *n.* person who receives sth.

re·cip·ro·cal [rɪ'sɪprəkl] *adj.* given and received in return; mutual: ~ *help* (*gifts, affection*).

re·cip·ro·cate [rɪ'sɪprəkeɪt] *v.t. & i.* 1. (of two persons) give and receive, each to and from each. 2. give in return. 3. (of parts of a machine) (cause to) move backwards and forwards in a straight line (e.g. the piston of an engine).

re·cite [rɪ'saɪt] *v.t. & i.* 1. say (esp. poems) aloud from memory. 2. give a list of, tell one by one (names, facts, etc.). **re·cit·al** [rɪ'saɪtl] *n.* 1. detailed account of a number of connected events: *the recital of his complaints* (*adventures*). 2. musical performance by one person or a small group or of the works of one composer. **rec·i·ta·tion** [ˌresɪ'teɪʃn] *n.* 1. reciting. 2. a public delivery of prose or poetry learnt by heart. 3. sth. (to be) ~d (e.g. a poem).

reck·less ['reklɪs] *adj.* rash; not thinking of the consequences.

reck·on ['rekən] *v.t. & i.* **1.** find out (the quantity, number, cost, etc.) by working with numbers: ~ *up*, add up; ~ *in*, include, take into account, when ~ing. **2.** ~ *with*, take into account; settle accounts with. **3.** look upon (*as*); be of the opinion, suppose (*that*). **4.** ~ (*up*)*on*, depend on; base one's hopes or plans on. **~·ing** ['reknɪŋ] *n.* (esp.) bill (for charges at a hotel, restaurant, etc.). *day of* ~*ing*, time when one's acts (esp. wrongdoing) must be accounted for; *out in one's* ~*ing*, mistaken in one's calculations or expectations.

re·claim [rɪ'kleɪm] *v.t.* **1.** bring back (waste land, etc.) to a useful condition, a state of cultivation, etc. **2.** request that sth. be returned. **3.** reform. **rec·la·ma·tion** [,reklə'meɪʃn] *n.* (no pl.).

re·cline [rɪ'klaɪn] *v.i. & t.* be, place oneself, in a position of rest; put (one's arms, etc.) in a resting position; lie down or back.

re·cluse [rɪ'kluːs] *n.* person who lives alone and avoids others.

rec·og·nize ['rekəgnaɪz] *v.t.* **1.** know, (be able to) identify again, (sb. or sth.) that one has seen, heard, etc. before: *I* ~ *that tune.* **2.** be willing to accept (sb. or sth.) as what he or it claims to be: *refuse to* ~ *a new government.* **3.** be ready to admit; be aware: ~ *that one is not qualified for a post;* ~ *the danger of an undertaking.* **4.** acknowledge: *His long years of service have been* ~*d.* **rec·og·ni·tion** [,rekəg'nɪʃn] *n.* recognizing or being ~d: *He was given a medal in recognition of his services.*

re·coil [rɪ'kɔɪl] *v.i.* **1.** jump back (*from*, e.g. in fear). **2.** (of a gun) kick back (when fired). **3.** ~ (*up*)*on*, (fig.) react. ['riːkɔɪl] *n.* act of ~ing.

rec·ol·lect [,rekə'lekt] *v.t. & i.* call back to the mind; succeed in remembering. **rec·ol·lec·tion** [,rekə'lekʃn] *n.* **1.** time over which the memory goes back: *It happened within my* ~*ion.* **2.** sth. ~ed; a memory: ~*ions of one's childhood.* **3.** act or power of ~ing.

rec·om·mend [,rekə'mend] *v.t.* **1.** speak favourably of; say that one thinks sth. is good (*for* sth.) or that sb. is fitted (*for* a post, etc., *as* a teacher, etc.). **2.** suggest as wise or suitable; advise: *I* ~ *you to do what your doctor says.* **3.** (of a quality, etc.) cause to be or appear pleasing, satisfactory: *His bad conduct does not* ~ *him.* **rec·om·men·da·tion** [,rekəmen'deɪʃn] *n.* **1.**

act of ~ing. **2.** statement, letter, etc. that ~s sb. or sth.

rec·om·pense ['rekəmpens] *v.t.* reward or punish; make payment to: ~ *sb. for his trouble;* ~ *good with evil;* ~ *sb. for a loss.* *n.* reward; payment.

rec·on·cile ['rekənsaɪl] *v.t.* **1.** cause (persons) to become friends after they have quarrelled. **2.** settle (quarrels); bring (differing opinions) into harmony; cause to agree: ~ *what sb. says with the facts.* **3.** ~ *oneself to sth., be* ~*d to sth.,* overcome one's objection to sth.; resign oneself to sth. **rec·on·cil·i·a·tion** [,rekənsɪlɪ'eɪʃn] *n.*

re·con·dite [rɪ'kɒndaɪt] *adj.* (of knowledge) little known; obscure; (of an author) having ~ knowledge.

re·con·di·tion [,riːkən'dɪʃn] *v.t.* put into good condition again.

re·con·nais·sance [rɪ'kɒnɪsəns] *n.* act or instance of reconnoitring.

re·con·noi·tre (U.S.A. **-ter**) [,rekə'nɔɪtə*] *v.t. & i.* go to or near (a place or area occupied by enemy forces) to learn about their position, strength, etc.

re·cord¹ [rɪ'kɔːd] *v.t.* **1.** set down in writing for reference. **2.** preserve for later use, by writing or in other ways (e.g. by means of photographs, tape- ~ers, ~² (4), etc.): *The radio programme was* ~*ed. The volume* ~*s the history of the regiment.* **3.** (of an instrument) mark or indicate on a scale, etc.: *What temperature does the thermometer* ~*?* **~·er** *n.* apparatus (1) that ~*s* (2): *tape-*~*er; video* ~*er.*

re·cord² ['rekɔːd] *n.* **1.** written account of facts, events, etc.: *a* ~ *of attendance.* **2.** state of being ~ed (1), esp. as evidence of sth.: *on* ~, ~*ed* (1); *bear* ~ *to,* give evidence supporting the truth of; *off the* ~, not for publication; unofficial(ly). **3.** facts known about the past of sb. or sth.: *an airline with a bad* ~ (e.g. many accidents to its aircraft). **4.** disc on which music, etc. has been ~ed (2). **5.** limit, score, point, attainment, mark, etc. (high or low), not reached before; (esp. in sport) the best yet done: *break* (*beat*) *the* ~, do better (worse) than ever before. **6.** (attrib.) that is a ~ (5): *a* ~ *rice crop; a* ~ *score.*

re·cord·ing [rɪ'kɔːdɪŋ] *n.* programme, piece of music, etc. registered for reproduction: *a good* ~ *of an opera.*

rec·ord-play·er ['rekɔːd,pleɪə*] *n.* instrument for the reproduction of sound from discs. (See the picture at *pick-up.*)

re·count[1] [rɪ'kaʊnt] *v.t.* give an account of; tell.

re·count[2] [,riː'kaʊnt] *v.t. &* ['riː'kaʊnt] *n.* count(ing) again.

re·coup [rɪ'kuːp] *v.t.* compensate (sb., oneself, *for*, loss, etc.); make up for.

re·course [rɪ'kɔːs] *n.* (no pl.) 1. *have ~ to*, turn to for help; seek help from. 2. sb. or sth. turned to for help.

re·cov·er [rɪ'kʌvə*] *v.t. & i.* 1. get back (sth. lost, etc.); get back the use of (one's sight, hearing, etc.): *~ consciousness*. 2. become well, happy, etc. again: *~ from an illness*. 3. *~ oneself*, regain control of oneself; become calm or normal. **~y** *n.* (no pl.).

rec·re·a·tion [,rekrɪ'eɪʃn] *n.* (form of) play or amusement; relaxation of body and mind; sth. that pleasantly occupies one's time after work is done.

re·crim·i·na·tion [rɪ,krɪmɪ'neɪʃn] *n.* accusation in return for one already made.

re·cru·des·cence [,riːkruː'desns] *n.* (of disease, violence, etc.) breaking out again; new outburst.

re·cruit [rɪ'kruːt] *n.* new member of a society, group, etc., esp. a soldier in his early days of training. *v.t. & i.* 1. get *~s* for; get (sb.) as a *~*. 2. get a sufficient quantity or store of; bring back to what is usual: *~ supplies (one's strength)*.

rec·tan·gle ['rek,tæŋgl] *n.* plane, four-sided figure with four right angles, esp. one with adjacent sides unequal. **rec·tan·gu·lar** [rek'tæŋgjʊlə*] *adj.* in the shape of a *~*.

rec·ti·fy ['rektɪfaɪ] *v.t.* put right; take out mistakes from. **rec·ti·fi·ca·tion** [,rektɪfɪ'keɪʃn] *n.*

rec·ti·tude ['rektɪtjuːd] *n.* (no pl.) honesty; upright or straightforward behaviour.

rec·tor ['rektə*] *n.* 1. (Church of England) clergyman in charge of a parish the tithes of which were not withdrawn (e.g. to a monastery or university) or at or after the time when the English Church separated from the Church of Rome. (Cf. *vicar*.) 2. head of certain universities, colleges, etc. **~y** *n.* *~'s* residence.

re·cum·bent [rɪ'kʌmbənt] *adj.* (esp. of a person) lying down.

re·cu·per·ate [rɪ'kjuːpəreɪt] *v.t. & i.* make or become strong again after illness, exhaustion, loss, etc. **re·cu·per·a·tion** [rɪ,kjuːpə'reɪʃn] *n.* (no pl.).

re·cur [rɪ'kɜː*] *v.i.* (-rr-) 1. come, happen, again; be repeated. 2. go back (*to* sth.) in words or thought: *~ring*

to what I said yesterday. 3. (of ideas, etc.) come back (*to* one's mind, etc.). **~rence** [rɪ'kʌrəns] *n.* *~ring*; repetition: *Let there be no ~rence of this mistake*. **~rent** [rɪ'kʌrənt] *adj.* *~ring* frequently or regularly.

red [red] *adj.* (-dd-) 1. of the colour of fresh blood, rubies, human lips, etc.; of shades varying from crimson to light brown and orange: *~ roses; ~ hair; ~ with anger*, flushed in the face; *with ~ hands*, with hands stained with blood; *~ eyes*, bloodshot; sore with weeping; *see ~*, be filled with fury. 2. radically left politically; communist. 3. *R.~*, Russian; Soviet: *the R.~ Army. n.* 1. (no pl.) *~* colour. 2. (no pl.) *~* clothes: *dressed in ~*. 3. debtor side of an account: *be in the ~*, be in debt. 4. person radically left politically; anarchist; communist. '**~breast** *n.* robin (a bird). '**~brick (uni'ver·si·ty)** *n.* university founded near the end of the 19th century, lacking the prestige of Oxford and Cambridge. **R.~ Cres·cent** *n.* organization like the R.~ Cross in Muslim countries. **R.~ Cross** *n.* (emblem of an) international organization concerned with the treatment of the sick and wounded in war, and with the relief of suffering caused by natural disasters. **~den** ['redn] *v.t. & i.* make or become *~*. **~dish** ['redɪʃ] *adj.* somewhat *~*; tinged with *~*. **~'hand·ed** *adj.* take (catch) *sb. ~handed* (in the act of doing sth. wrong). **R.~ In·di·an** *n.* N. American Indian. **~-'let·ter 'day** *n.* day with *~* letter(s) in the calendar; (fig.) memorable day because of some happy or important event. **~ rag** *n.* (fig.) sth. that excites a person's anger (like sth. *~* enrages a bull). '**~skin** *n.* (old name for) R.~ Indian. **~ tape** *n.* excessive use of formalities in public business.

re·deem [rɪ'diːm] *v.t.* 1. get (sth.) back by payment or by doing sth.: *~ a pawned watch (one's honour)*. 2. perform (a promise, obligation). 3. set free by payment; rescue: *~ a slave (prisoner)*; (by Jesus) make free from sin. 4. compensate: *his ~ing feature*, the feature or quality which balances his faults, etc. **the R.~er** *n.* Jesus Christ. **re·demp·tion** [rɪ'dempʃn] *n.* *~ing* or being *~ed*; deliverance or rescue (esp. from evil ways): *past redemption*, too bad to be *~ed* (3).

re·do [,riː'duː] *v.t. & i.* (p.t. -did, p.p. -done) do again.

red·o·lent ['redəʊlənt] *adj.* *~ of (with)*,

(a) smelling of; scented with; (b) (fig.) reminiscent of; suggestive of.

re·double [ˌriː'dʌbl] *v.t. & i.* make or become greater or stronger.

re·doubt·able [rɪ'daʊtəbl] *adj.* formidable; to be feared.

re·dound [rɪ'daʊnd] *v.i.* contribute greatly in the end (*to* one's credit, advantage, etc.); promote.

re·dress [rɪ'dres] *v.t.* 1. set (a wrong) right again; make up for; do sth. that compensates for (a wrong). 2. ~ *the balance*, make them equal again. *n.* (no pl.) act of ~ing; sth. (e.g. payment) that ~es.

re·duce [rɪ'djuːs] *v.t. & i.* 1. make less; make smaller in size, amount, extent, price, etc.: ~ *speed* (*one's expenses*, *etc.*). 2. ~ *to*, bring or get to a certain condition, state, way of living, etc.: ~ *a class of noisy children to order*; ~ *a sergeant to the ranks*, make him a private again; *be living in ~d circumstances*, in (comparative) poverty. 3. change (to another form): ~ *pounds to pence* (*wood* &c. *to pulp*). **re·duc·tion** [rɪ'dʌkʃn] *n.* 1. reducing or being ~d: *a reduction in price*; *price reductions*; *sell sth. at a reduction*. 2. copy, on a smaller scale, of a picture, map, etc.

re·dun·dant [rɪ'dʌndənt] *adj.* superfluous; beyond what is needed: ~ *labour*, surplus workers. **re·dun·dan·cy** *n.* *redundancy pay*(*ment*), money paid by an employer to a ~ worker.

reed [riːd] *n.* 1. (tall, firm stem or stalk of) water or marsh plant: *a broken ~*, (fig.) an unreliable person or thing; (collective) a growth or mass of ~s, or ~s used as material for thatching. 2. (in wind instruments, organs) part that vibrates to produce sound. ~**y** *adj.* 1. full of ~s (1). 2. (of sounds, voices) shrill.

reef[1] [riːf] *n.* that part of a sail that can be rolled up or folded so as to reduce its area. *v.t.* reduce the area of (a sail) by rolling up or folding part of it. '~-**knot** *n.* ordinary double knot.

reef[2] [riːf] *n.* ridge of rock, shingle, etc. just below or above the surface of the sea: *wrecked on a ~*.

reef·er ['riːfə] *n.* marijuana cigarette.

reek [riːk] *n.* strong, bad smell (e.g. of stale tobacco smoke). *v.i.* 1. smell strongly and unpleasantly (*of*). 2. ~ *with*, be covered (with sweat, blood, etc.).

reel[1] [riːl] *n.* cylinder, roller, or similar device on which cotton, wire, photographic film, etc. is wound: *off the ~*, (fig.) without a pause; in rapid succes-

sion. *v.t.* roll or wind on to, or with the help of, a ~; take (sth.) *off*, draw (sth.) *in* or *up*, by means of a ~: ~ *off* (*a story, etc.*), tell quickly and easily.

reel[2] [riːl] *v.i.* 1. walk or stand unsteadily, moving from side to side. 2. be dizzy; (of things) seem to be going round: *The street ~ed before my eyes.* 3. be shaken physically or mentally: *His mind ~ed when he heard the news.*

reel[3] [riːl] *n.* (music for a) lively Scottish dance.

re·en·try [riː'entrɪ] *n.* act of entering again; (of a spacecraft, missile) act of re-entering the earth's atmosphere after travel in space.

re·fec·to·ry [rɪ'fektərɪ] *n.* dining-hall (in a monastery, convent, college, etc.).

re·fer [rɪ'fɜː*] *v.t. & i.* (-*rr*-) 1. send, take, hand over (*to* sb. or sth.) to be dealt with, decided, etc.: ~ *a dispute to the United Nations*; ~ *sb. to the Manager*. 2. turn to, go to, for information, etc.: ~ *to one's notes*. 3. ~ *to*, (of a speaker) speak of; allude to: *I was not ~ring to you*. 4. ~ *to*, (of a statement, a remark, etc.) be directed to; apply to: *What I have said ~s to all of you*. 5. ~ *sth. to sth.*, consider as the cause. **ref·er·ee** [ˌrefə'riː] *n.* 1. person to whom questions, disputes, etc. are ~red for decision or settlement. 2. (in football, boxing, etc.) person chosen to enforce rules and settle disputes. *v.i. & t.* act as ~ee (for). **ref·er·ence** ['refrəns] *n.* 1. (instance of) ~ring: *a ~ence book* (e.g. a dictionary); *a ~ence library* (where books may be consulted but not taken away). 2. allusion: *make ~ence to a conversation*. 3. (person willing to make a) statement about a person's character or abilities: *excellent ~ences from former employers*. 4. note, direction, etc. telling where certain information may be found: *a cross-~ence*, one to another passage in the same book for further information; *~ence marks*, marks used to refer the reader to the place (e.g. a footnote) where further information may be found. 5. *in* (*with*) *~ence to*, concerning; about; *without ~ence to*, irrespective of. **ref·er·en·dum** [ˌrefə'rendəm] *n.* (pl. ~s, -*da* [-də]) the ~ring (1) of a political question to a direct vote of the citizens.

re·fill ['riːfɪl] *n.* renewed filling; material, etc. used for this. [ˌriː'fɪl] *v.t.* fill again; provide a new filling for.

re·fine [rɪ'faɪn] *v.t. & i.* 1. free (e.g. gold, sugar) from other substances; make or become pure. 2. cause to be more cultured, polished in manners; get rid of what is coarse or vulgar: ~d speech (tastes, manners). **3.** ~ (up)on, improve by giving more attention to details. **~·ment** *n.* **1.** refining or being ~d. **2.** purity of feeling, taste, language, etc.; delicacy of manners. **3.** example of such ~d feeling, taste, etc.; delicate or ingenious development of sth.: ~ments of cruelty (meaning). **re·fin·ery** *n.* place, building, etc. where sth. is ~d (1): a sugar ~ry.

re·fit [ˌriːˈfit] *v.t. & i.* (-tt-) make (a ship, etc.) ready for use again by renewing or repairing; (of a ship) be made fit for further voyages. [often ˈriːfit] *n.* ~ting.

re·flect [rɪˈflekt] *v.t. & i.* **1.** (of a surface) throw back (light, heat, sound); (of a mirror, etc.) send back an image of. **2.** express; show the nature of: sad looks that ~ed the thoughts passing through his mind. **3.** (of actions, results) bring (credit or discredit upon). **4.** ~ (up)on, hurt the good reputation of; bring discredit (up)on: Such behaviour ~s upon his honesty (suggests that he is dishonest). **5.** consider; think (on, that, how, etc.). **re·flec·tion** (Gt. Brit. also **re·flex·ion**) [rɪˈflekʃn] *n.* **1.** ~ing or being ~ed. **2.** sth. ~ed, esp. an image ~ed in a mirror or still water. **2.** thought; (re)consideration: lost in ~ion; on ~ion, after careful thought. **3.** expression of a thought in speech or writing; idea arising in the mind: ~ions on the political situation in Europe. **4.** expression of blame: cast a ~ion upon sb. **5.** sth. that brings discredit. **re·flec·tive** *adj.* thoughtful; in the habit of ~ing (5). **re·flec·tor** *n.* sth. that ~s (1).

re·flex [ˈriːfleks] *adj.* **1.** ~ action, action that is independent of the will (e.g. a sneeze, shivering). **2.** ~ camera, camera in which the image is reflected onto a screen for focusing. *n.* ~ action. **~·ion** *n.* see reflection.

re·flex·ive [rɪˈfleksɪv] *n. & adj.* (word or form) relating to an action directed back upon the agent: a ~ verb (e.g. cut oneself); a ~ pronoun (e.g. manifest itself).

re·form¹ [rɪˈfɔːm] *v.t. & i.* make or become better by removing or putting right what is bad or wrong: ~ the world (a sinner, one's character). *n.* ~ing; removal of vices, imperfections, etc.; change made with this purpose in view. **ref·or·ma·tion** [ˌrefəˈmeɪʃn] *n.* **1.** ~ing or being ~ed; change for the better in political, social or reli-

gious affairs. **2.** the R~ation, the 16th-century movement for ~ of the Roman Catholic Church which led to the establishment of the R~ed or Protestant Churches. **re·for·ma·to·ry** [rɪˈfɔːmətəri] *adj.* tending to, designed to, ~. *n.* (U.S.A. or hist.) school or institution for ~ing young offenders against the law. **~·er** *n.* person actively supporting ~s.

re·form² [ˌriːˈfɔːm] *v.t. & i.* form again.

re·fract [rɪˈfrækt] *v.t.* (of water, glass, etc.) bend aside (a ray of light) when it enters obliquely from another medium: Light is ~ed when it enters a prism. **re·frac·tion** [rɪˈfrækʃn] *n.* (no pl.)

re·frac·to·ry [rɪˈfræktəri] *adj.* **1.** resisting control, discipline, etc.; (of disease) not yielding to treatment. **2.** (of substances, esp. metals) hard to fuse, melt, or work.

re·frain¹ [rɪˈfreɪn] *v.i.* hold oneself back (from sth., from doing sth.).

re·frain² [rɪˈfreɪn] *n.* lines of a song which are repeated, esp. at the end of each verse.

re·fresh [rɪˈfreʃ] *v.t. & i.* give new strength to; make fresh: ~ oneself with a cup of tea (a warm bath). **2.** ~ one's memory, freshen it up by referring to notes, etc. **3.** take ~ment. **~·er** *n.* sth. that ~es; (colloq.) drink. ~er course, course giving instructions in modern methods, newer techniques, etc. **~·ing** *adj.* **1.** strengthening; restoring freshness, vitality, energy, etc.: a ~ing sleep (breeze). **2.** giving an unexpected, pleasant sensation: ~ing innocence. **~·ment** *n.* **1.** (no pl.) ~ing or being ~ed. **2.** (often pl.) that which ~es, esp. food or drink.

re·frig·er·ate [rɪˈfrɪdʒəreɪt] *v.t.* make cool or cold; preserve (food) by keeping it very cold. **re·frig·er·a·tor** *n.* cabinet or room in which food is kept cold. **re·frig·er·a·tion** [rɪˌfrɪdʒəˈreɪʃn] *n.* (no pl.).

ref·uge [ˈrefjuːdʒ] *n.* (place giving) shelter or protection from trouble, danger, or pursuit. **ref·u·gee** [ˌrefjuːˈdʒiː] *n.* person taking ~, esp. in a foreign country from political or religious persecution, or from war, floods, etc.

re·fund [riːˈfʌnd] *v.t.* pay back (money to sb.). [ˈriːfʌnd] *n.* money ~ed.

re·fuse¹ [rɪˈfjuːz] *v.t. & i.* say 'no' to (offer, gift, request, etc.); show unwillingness to accept (sth. offered), to do (sth. that one is asked to do): They ~d to help. He was ~d admittance. **re-**

fus·al [rɪ'fjuːzl] *n.* **1.** refusing. **2.** (*first*) *refusal*, right of deciding whether to accept or ~ sth. before it is offered to others.

ref·use[2] ['refjuːs] *n.* waste or worthless material.

re·fute [rɪ'fjuːt] *v.t.* prove (statements, opinions, etc.) to be wrong or mistaken; prove (sb.) wrong in his opinions, etc. **ref·u·ta·tion** [,refjuː-'teɪʃn] *n.* **1.** (no pl.) refuting. **2.** counter-argument.

re·gain [rɪ'geɪn] *v.t.* **1.** get possession of again: ~ *consciousness.* **2.** get back to (a place or position).

re·gal ['riːgl] *adj.* of, for, fit for, by, a king or queen. ~·**ly** *adv.*

re·gale [rɪ'geɪl] *v.t.* & *i.* give pleasure or delight to (sb., oneself) (*with* food, drink, etc.); feast oneself (*on* sth.).

re·ga·lia [rɪ'geɪljə] *n. pl.* emblems (crown, sceptre, etc.) of royalty; emblems or decorations of an order (e.g. of the Freemasons).

re·gard [rɪ'gɑːd] *v.t.* **1.** look closely at. **2.** consider: ~ *sb. with awe;* ~*ed as the best dentist in the town.* **3.** look upon mentally: ~ *it as madness;* ~ *sth. with horror.* **4.** pay attention to; respect: *he never* ~*s my advice* (*wishes*). **5.** *as* ~*s,* ~*ing,* concerning; with reference to. *n.* **1.** long, steady, or significant look: *His* ~ *was fixed on the horizon.* **2.** point attended to; respect: *in* (*with*) ~ *to,* with respect to; concerning; *in this* ~, in respect of this point. **3.** attention; concern; consideration: *with little* ~ *for the feelings of others.* **4.** respect; esteem; kindly feeling: *win sb.'s* ~; *held in high* ~. **5.** (pl.) (esp. at the end of a letter) kindly thoughts and wishes: *give my kind* ~*s to your mother.* ~·**ful** *adj.* ~ *ful of,* paying attention to; taking into account. ~·**less** *adj.* ~*less of,* paying no attention to; without taking into account; in spite of.

re·gat·ta [rɪ'gætə] *n.* meeting for boat races (rowing-boats, yachts, etc.).

re·gen·er·ate [rɪ'dʒenəreɪt] *v.t.* & *i.* **1.** reform spiritually; raise morally. **2.** give new strength or life to; restore to original strength or properties. **3.** grow again. **re·gen·er·a·tion** [rɪ,dʒenə-'reɪʃn] *n.* (no pl.).

re·gent ['riːdʒənt] *n.* & *adj.* (person) performing the duties of a ruler who is too young, old, ill, etc., or who is absent: *the Prince R*~. **re·gen·cy** ['riːdʒənsɪ] *n.* (time of) office of a ~: *the Regency* (in Great Britain 1810—20). **re·gime, ré·gime** [reɪ'ʒiːm] *n.* method or system of government or of ad-

ministration; prevailing system of things.

reg·i·ment ['redʒɪmənt] *n.* **1.** permanent unit of an army divided into companies, troops, or batteries, commanded by a colonel. **2.** large number (*of*). ['redʒɪment] *v.t.* organize; discipline. **reg·i·men·ta·tion** [,redʒɪmen'teɪʃn] *n.* (no pl.) subjection to control; strict political or other discipline.

re·gion ['riːdʒən] *n.* area or division with or without definite boundaries or characteristics: *the Arctic* ~*s; in the* ~ *of the heart.* ~·**al** *adj.* of ~*s: a* ~*al geography.* ~·**al·ly** *adv.*

reg·is·ter ['redʒɪstə*] *n.* **1.** (book containing a) record or list (e.g. of births, marriages, or deaths). **2.** mechanical device recording speed, force, numbers, etc.: *a cash* ~. **3.** range of a voice or musical instrument. *v.t.* & *i.* **1.** make a written record of, in a list. **2.** put or get sb.'s name, one's own name, on a ~ (e.g. at a hotel). **3.** (of instruments, e.g. a thermometer) indicate; record[1]. **4.** (of sb.'s face) show (a feeling). **5.** send (a letter, parcel) by special post, paying a fee which ensures compensation in case of loss. **reg·is·trar** [,redʒɪ'strɑː*] *n.* person who keeps ~s or records[2], esp. for a university or a town counsel. **reg·is·tra·tion** [,redʒɪ'streɪʃn] *n.* **reg·is·try** ['redʒɪstrɪ] *n.* place where ~s are kept: *registry* (sometimes *register*) *office,* place for marriages before a registrar (without a religious ceremony).

re·gret [rɪ'gret] *n.* **1.** feeling of sadness at the loss of sth., or of annoyance or disappointment because sth. has or has not been done. **2.** (usu. pl.) (in polite refusals of invitations, etc.): *refuse with many* ~*s. v.t.* (-*tt-*) have ~ for; be sorry (*that*). ~·**ful** *adj.* sad; sorry. ~·**ful·ly** *adv.* ~·**ta·ble** *adj.* to be ~*ted.*

reg·u·lar ['regjʊlə*] *adj.* **1.** evenly arranged; symmetrical; systematic: ~ *teeth* (*features*). **2.** coming, happening, done, again and again at even intervals: ~ *breathing.* **3.** normal; orderly: *a man of* ~ *habits.* **4.** properly qualified; not amateur; full-time or professional: *a* ~ *doctor* (not a quack); *the* ~ *army.* **5.** in keeping with standards of correctness (e.g. of etiquette). **6.** (gram.) having normal type of inflexion: *The verb 'take' is not* ~. **7.** (colloq.) complete; thorough: *He's a* ~ *rascal. n.* **1.** soldier of the ~ army. **2.** (colloq.) ~ customer, client, etc. ~·**i·ty** [,regjʊ-'lærətɪ] *n.* (no pl.). ~·**ize** ['regjʊləraɪz] *v.t.* make lawful or correct. ~ly *adv.* in a ~ manner; at ~ intervals or times.

reg·u·late [ˈregjuleit] *v.t.* **1.** control by means of a system or by a rule. **2.** adjust (an apparatus, a mechanism) to obtain a desired result: ~ *a clock.* **reg·u·la·tion** [ˌregjuˈleiʃn] *n.* **1.** (no pl.) regulating or being ~d. **2.** rule; order; authoritative direction. **3.** (attrib.) correct, as required by rules: *regulation dress.* **reg·u·la·tor** *n.* person or thing that ~s, esp. that part of a clock, machine, etc. that ~s (2) (speed, etc.).

re·ha·bil·i·tate [ˌriːəˈbiliteit] *v.t.* **1.** restore (e.g. old buildings) to a good condition. **2.** restore (sb.) to former rank, position, or reputation. **3.** bring back to a normal life by special treatment (after illness, imprisonment, etc.).

re·hearse [riˈhɜːs] *v.t. & i.* **1.** practise (a play, etc.) for public performance. **2.** say over again; give an account of: ~ *the day's happenings.* **re·hears·al** *n.* **1.** (no pl.) rehearsing. **2.** trial performance of a play, etc.: *dress rehearsal,* (final) rehearsal in costume and with scenery.

reign [rein] *n.* **1.** (period of) rule: *the ~ of George VI.* **2.** (fig.) dominance: *the ~ of reason.* *v.i.* **1.** rule (over). **2.** prevail: *Silence ~s, all is quiet.*

re·im·burse [ˌriːimˈbɜːs] *v.t.* repay (a person who has spent money, the amount spent). ~·ment *n.* repayment of expenses.

rein [rein] *n.* (often pl.) long, narrow strap fastened to the bit of a bridle for controlling a horse: *give a horse the ~s,* let it go its own way; *give free ~(s) (the ~s) to sb. (sth.),* let sb. (sth.) have free scope; *keep a tight ~ on (sb., sth.),* allow little freedom to; *assume (drop) the ~s of government,* assume (give up) office. *v.t.* control with, or as with, ~s.

rein·deer [ˈreindiə*] *n.* (pl. ~) kind of large deer used in Lapland for transport, etc.

re·in·force [ˌriːinˈfɔːs] *v.t.* make stronger by adding or supplying more material, men, etc.; increase the size, thickness, etc. of. ~·ment *n.* **1.** (no pl.) reinforcing or being ~d. **2.** sth. that ~s; (esp. in pl.) men, ships, etc. sent to ~.

re·in·state [ˌriːinˈsteit] *v.t.* put back, establish, in a former position or condition. ~·ment *n.*

re·it·er·ate [riˈitəreit] *v.t.* say or do again several times. **re·it·er·a·tion** [riːˌitəˈreiʃn] *n.*

re·ject [riˈdʒekt] *v.t.* **1.** put aside,

throw away, as not fit to be kept. **2.** refuse to accept: ~ *an offer.* [ˈriːdʒekt] *n.* ~ed article. **re·jec·tion** [riˈdʒekʃn] *n.*

re·joice [riˈdʒɔis] *v.i. & t.* be or make glad; show signs of great happiness: ~ *at your success; success that ~d your parents.* **re·joic·ing** *n.* **1.** (no pl.) happiness; joy. **2.** (pl.) celebration(s); merry-making.

re·join[1] [riˈdʒɔin] *v.i. & t.* **1.** answer. **2.** (law) reply to a charge or plea. ~·der *n.* answer.

re·join[2] [ˌriːˈdʒɔin] *v.t. & i.* join (together) again.

re·ju·ve·nate [riˈdʒuːvineit] *v.t. & i.* make or become young again in nature or appearance. **re·ju·ve·na·tion** [riˌdʒuːviˈneiʃn] *n.* (no pl.).

re·lapse [riˈlæps] *v.i.* fall back (*into* bad ways, error, illness, weakness, etc.). *n.* falling back, esp. after recovering from illness.

re·late [riˈleit] *v.t. & i.* **1.** tell (a story); give an account of (facts, adventures, etc.). **2.** connect in thought or meaning: ~ *results to (with) their causes.* **3.** have reference (*to*); stand in some relation (*to*): *She is interested in nothing except what ~s to herself.* **re·lat·ed** *adj.* connected (esp. by family) (*to*).

re·la·tion [riˈleiʃn] *n.* **1.** (no pl.) relating (1). **2.** sth. related (1) (a tale, a narrative, an account, etc.). **3.** connection; what there is between one thing, person, idea, etc. and another or others: *the ~ between mother and child; the ~s expressed by prepositions* (e.g. time, place, direction); *effort and expense that bear no ~ (that are out of all ~) to the results* (i.e. are not proportional to the results); *in ~ to,* as regards; concerning. **4.** (often pl.) dealings; what one person, group, country, etc. has to do with another: *have business ~s with a firm in London; friendly ~s between countries.* **5.** relative (n. 1). ~·ship *n.* **1.** ~ (3). **2.** state of being related. **3.** condition of belonging to the same family; kinship.

rel·a·tive [ˈrelətiv] *adj.* **1.** ~ *to,* referring to; having a connection with: *the facts ~ to this problem.* **2.** comparative: *the ~ advantages of two methods. They are living in ~ comfort* (i.e. compared with other people, or with themselves at an earlier time). **3.** considered in relation (3) to each other: *the ~ duties of a ruler and his subjects.* **4.** (gram.) ~ *pronoun* (e.g. *whom* in 'the man whom I met'); ~ *adverb* (e.g. *where* in 'the place where I met him'); ~ clause, clause joined to the antecedent by a ~ word. **n. 1.** person to whom one is related (an uncle, aunt, cousin, nephew, etc.). **2.** (gram.) ~ pronoun or adverb. **~ly** adv. comparatively; in proportion (to).

re·lax [rɪ'læks] v.t. & i. **1.** (cause to) become less tight or stiff; (allow to) become less severe or strict: ~ the muscles (discipline). **2.** cast off social restraint, nervous tension, etc.; seek rest or recreation. **~ation** [ˌriːlæk-'seɪʃn] **n. 1.** ~ing or being ~ed. **2.** (esp.) recreation.

re·lay n. 1. ['riːleɪ] supply of fresh horses to replace tired ones; gang of men, supply of material, etc. similarly used: working in ~s; ~ race, race between two or more teams, each member of the team running one section of the total distance. **2.** [ˌriː'leɪ] device (2) to receive, reinforce, and transmit broadcast programmes, telegraph messages, etc.; ~ed broadcast programme. [riː'leɪ] v.t. (p.t. & p.p. ~ed) send on further (e.g. a broadcast programme received from another station).

re·lease [rɪ'liːs] v.t. **1.** allow to go; set free; unfasten: ~ sb. from prison (from a promise); ~ the handbrake (of a car). **2.** allow (news) to be known or published; allow (a film) to be exhibited publicly. **n. 1.** (no pl.) releasing or being ~d. **2.** handle, lever, etc. that ~s part of a machine.

rel·e·gate ['relɪgeɪt] v.t. **1.** hand over (a question, task, etc., to sb. for decision, etc.). **2.** dismiss to a lower position or condition. **rel·e·ga·tion** [ˌrelɪ-'geɪʃn] **n.** (no pl.).

re·lent [rɪ'lent] v.i. become less harsh; begin to show mercy. **~less** adj. without pity.

rel·e·vant ['relɪvənt] adj. connected with what is being discussed. **rel·e·vance, rel·e·van·cy ns.**

re·li·able [rɪ'laɪəbl] adj. that can be relied upon. **re·li·ably** adv. **re·li·abil·i·ty** [rɪˌlaɪə'bɪlətɪ] **n.** (no pl.).

re·li·ance [rɪ'laɪəns] **n. 1.** (no pl.) trust. **2.** person or thing depended upon. **re·li·ant** adj. having trust; trusting.

rel·ic ['relɪk] **n. 1.** part of the body, dress, etc. of a saint, kept after his death as an object of reverence. **2.** sth. that has survived from the past and that serves to keep memories alive. **3.** (pl.) dead person's body; what has survived destruction or decay.

re·lief¹ [rɪ'liːf] **n.** (no pl.) **1.** lessening or ending or removal of pain, anxiety,

etc.: a sigh of ~; the medicine brought some ~. **2.** that which brings ~ (1); food, clothes, money, etc. (to be) given to people in trouble: a ~ fund. R~ was sent to those made homeless by the floods. **3.** sth. that adds interest to what would, without it, be dull or monotonous. **4.** freedom from duty (esp. keeping watch); person(s) replacing other person(s) on duty.

re·lief² [rɪ'liːf] **n. 1.** (no pl.) method of carving or moulding in which a design or figure stands out from the surface. **2.** design or carving made in this way. **3.** (no pl.) (lit. or fig.) degree of clearness or outline: standing out in sharp ~ (i.e. clearly). **4.** (no pl.) (in drawing, etc.) appearance of being done in ~ by the use of colour, shading, etc.: a ~ map, map showing hills, valleys, etc. by shading and colouring, not only by contour lines.

re·lieve [rɪ'liːv] v.t. **1.** give or bring relief¹ to: ~ one's feelings, provide an outlet for them (e.g. by crying or swearing); ~ nature (oneself), empty the bladder or bowels. **2.** ~ sb. of sth., take it from him; (humor.) steal it from him. **3.** take the place of (sb. on duty).

re·li·gion [rɪ'lɪdʒən] **n. 1.** (no pl.) belief in the existence of a supernatural power as creator and controller of the universe. **2.** system of faith and worship based on such belief: the Christian (Muslim, Buddhist) ~. **re·li·gious** [rɪ'lɪdʒəs] adj. **1.** of ~. **2.** (of a person) devout; god-fearing. **3.** conscientious: with religious exactitude.

re·lin·quish [rɪ'lɪŋkwɪʃ] v.t. give up (e.g. hope); let go (e.g. one's hold of sth.).

rel·ish ['relɪʃ] **n. 1.** special taste or flavour; sth. that gives or has an attractive flavour or quality. **2.** liking (for). v.t. enjoy; get pleasure from.

re·luc·tant [rɪ'lʌktənt] adj. (slow to do sth. because) unwilling. **re·luc·tance n.** (no pl.).

re·ly [rɪ'laɪ] v.i. ~ (up)on, depend upon (sb., sth.) for help.

re·main [rɪ'meɪn] v.i. **1.** be still present after a part has gone or has been taken away. **2.** continue in some place or condition; continue to be. **~der** [rɪ-'meɪndə*] **n.** that which ~s; those who ~; the rest. **re·mains n. pl. 1.** what is left (e.g. of a meal). **2.** ruins (e.g. of ancient Rome). **3.** dead body.

re·mand [rɪ'mɑːnd] v.t. send (an accused person) back to prison (from a court of law) until more evidence is obtained. *n.* (no pl.) ~ing or being ~ed: *detention on* ~.

re·mark [rɪ'mɑːk] *v.t. & i.* **1.** notice; see. **2.** say (*that*); comment (*on, upon*). *n.* **1.** notice; looking at: *nothing worthy of* ~. **2.** comment; sth. said. **~·able** *adj.* out of the ordinary; deserving notice. **~·ably** *adv.*

rem·e·dy ['remɪdɪ] *n.* cure (for a disease, etc.); method of, sth. used for, putting right sth. that is wrong. *v.t.* provide a ~ for; put right. **re·me·di·al** [rɪ'miːdjəl] *adj.* providing a ~: *remedial measures.*

re·mem·ber [rɪ'membə*] *v.t. & i.* **1.** keep or have in the memory; call back to the mind; not forget. **2.** ~ *sb. to* (sb. else), give or carry greetings to. **3.** make a present to; tip: *He ~ed us in his will.* **re·mem·brance** [rɪ'membrəns] *n.* **1.** (no pl.) ~ing or being ~ed; memory: *in remembrance of.* **2.** sth. given or kept in memory of sb. or sth. **3.** (pl.) regards (5), greetings (sent in a letter or by a third person).

re·mind [rɪ'maɪnd] *v.t.* cause (sb.) to remember (*to do* sth., *that*); cause (sb.) to think (*of* sth. or sb.). **~·er** *n.* sth. (e.g. a letter) that helps sb. to remember sth.

rem·i·nis·cence [ˌremɪ'nɪsns] *n.* **1.** (no pl.) remembering; recalling of past experiences. **2.** (pl.) account of what sb. remembers: *~s of the days when he was a sailor.* **3.** sth. that is suggestive (*of* sth. else). **rem·i·nis·cent** *adj.* **1.** reminding one (*of*); suggestive (*of*). **2.** remembering the past: *become reminiscent.*

re·miss [rɪ'mɪs] *adj.* careless; not doing one's duty properly: ~ *in one's duties.* **~·ness** *n.* (no pl.).

re·mis·sion [rɪ'mɪʃn] *n.* **1.** (no pl.) pardon or forgiveness (of sins, by God). **2.** freeing (from debt, punishment, etc.). **3.** (no pl.) lessening or weakening (of pain, efforts, etc.).

re·mit [rɪ'mɪt] *v.t. & i.* (-tt-) **1.** (of God) forgive (sins). **2.** free sb. from (a debt, punishment, etc.). **3.** send (money, etc.) by post. **4.** make or become less: ~ *one's efforts.* **5.** take or send (a question to be decided) (*to* some authority). **~·tance** *n.* **1.** (no pl.) sending of money. **2.** sum of money sent.

rem·nant ['remnənt] *n.* **1.** small part that remains. **2.** (esp.) piece of cloth left after the greater part has been sold or used.

re·mon·strate ['remənstreɪt] *v.i.* make a protest (*against* sth.); argue in pro-

test (*with* sb., *about* sth., *that*). **re·mon·strance** [rɪ'mɒnstrəns] *n.* **1.** (no pl.) remonstrating. **2.** protest (*against*).

re·morse [rɪ'mɔːs] *n.* (no pl.) deep, bitter regret for wrongdoing; compunction: *without* ~, merciless(ly). **~·ful** *adj.* feeling ~. **~·less** *adj.* without ~.

re·mote [rɪ'məʊt] *adj.* (~r, ~st) **1.** far away in space or time: ~ *control,* control of apparatus (1) from a distance by means of radio signals, etc. **2.** widely separated (in feeling, interests, etc. *from*). **3.** (esp. in the superl.) slight: *a* ~ *possibility; not the ~st idea.* **4.** reserved; aloof.

re·move [rɪ'muːv] *v.t. & i.* **1.** take off or away from the place occupied; take to another place: ~ *one's hat (one's hand from sb.'s shoulder*); ~ *a boy from school.* **2.** get rid of: ~ *doubts (fears*); ~ *stains (nail varnish*). **3.** dismiss (from office). **4.** (usu. *move*) change one's dwelling-place; go to live elsewhere. **5.** ~*d,* (of cousins) different by a generation: *cousin once* ~*d,* cousin's child. **remov·able** *adj.* (e.g. of officials) that can be ~d (from office at any time). **re·mov·al** [rɪ'muːvl] *n.* act of removing: *a removal van* (for removing furniture).

re·mu·ner·ate [rɪ'mjuːnəreɪt] *v.t.* pay (sb.) for work or services; reward. **re·mu·ner·a·tion** [rɪˌmjuːnə'reɪʃn] *n.* (no pl.) payment; reward. **re·mu·ner·a·tive** [rɪ'mjuːnərətɪv] *adj.* profitable.

re·nais·sance [rə'neɪsəns] *n.* **1.** *the R.~,* (period of) revival of art and literature in Europe in the 14th, 15th, and 16th centuries, based on ancient Greek learning. **2.** any similar revival.

rend [rend] *v.t. & i.* (p.t. & p.p. *rent* [rent]) (liter.) **1.** pull or divide forcibly: *a country rent (in two*) *by civil war.* **2.** tear or pull (*off, away*) violently.

ren·der ['rendə*] *v.t.* **1.** give in return or exchange, or as sth. due: ~ *thanks to God;* ~ *good for evil;* ~ *help to those in need.* **2.** present; offer; send in (an account for payment). **3.** perform or sing (a piece of music); give a performance of (e.g. a drama, a character in a drama); give a translation of (*in* another language). **4.** cause to be (in some condition): ~*ed helpless by an accident.* **5.** melt (fat); clarify or extract by melting: ~ (*down*) *lard.*

ren·dez·vous ['rɒndɪvuː] *n.* (pl. ~) **1.** (place decided upon for a) meeting at a time agreed upon. **2.** place where people often meet.

re·new [rɪ'njuː] *v.t.* **1.** make (as good

as) new; restore to its original condition; put new vigour into. 2. replace (sth.) with a new thing of the same sort: *snakes ⏜ing their skins*. 3. get, make, say, or give again: *⏜ a lease (an attack, an acquaintance)*. **⏜·al** *n.* **1.** (no pl.) ⏜ing or being ⏜ed. **2.** sth. ⏜ed.

re·nounce [rɪˈnaʊns] *v.t.* **1.** say that one will no longer have anything to do with, that one no longer recognizes (sb. or sth. having a claim to one's care, affection, etc.). **2.** declare formally to give up (a claim, right, privilege, etc.). **re·nun·ci·a·tion** [rɪˌnʌnsɪˈeɪʃn] *n.* (no pl.).

ren·o·vate [ˈrenəʊveɪt] *v.t.* restore (e.g. old buildings) to good or strong condition. **ren·o·va·tion** [ˌrenəʊˈveɪʃn] *n.*

re·nown [rɪˈnaʊn] *n.* (no pl.) fame. **⏜ed** *adj.* famous.

rent[1], see *rend*.

rent[2] [rent] *n.* torn place (in cloth, etc.); (also fig.) split.

rent[3] [rent] *n.* regular payment for the use of land, a building, a room or rooms, machinery, etc. *v.t. & i.* occupy or use for ⏜; allow (land, rooms, etc.) to be occupied or used for ⏜. **⏜·al** *n.* amount of ⏜ paid or received.

re·nun·ci·a·tion, see *renounce*.

re·pair[1] [rɪˈpeə*] *v.t.* **1.** mend; put (sth. damaged or worn) into good condition: *⏜ the roads (an engine, a skirt)*. **2.** put right; make up for: *⏜ a wrong*. *n.* **1.** (no pl.) ⏜ing or being ⏜ed: *road under ⏜*. **2.** work or process of ⏜ing. **3.** (no pl.) good condition; relative condition for working or using: *The car is in (out of) ⏜. The car is in good (bad) ⏜*. **⏜·able** *adj.* that can be ⏜ed. **⏜·er** *n.* person who ⏜s sth.: *shoe ⏜er*. **rep·a·ra·ble** [ˈrepərəbl] *adj.* (esp. of losses) that can be made good. **rep·a·ra·tion** [ˌrepəˈreɪʃn] *n.* **1.** (no pl.) act of compensating for loss or damage. **2.** (pl.) compensation for war damage payable by a defeated nation.

re·pair[2] [rɪˈpeə*] *v.i.* go (*to*) (esp. frequently or in large numbers).

rep·ar·tee [ˌrepɑːˈtiː] *n.* witty, clever answer(s).

re·past [rɪˈpɑːst] *n.* (formal) meal.

re·pa·tri·ate [riːˈpætrɪeɪt] *v.t.* send or bring (sb.) back to his own country. *n.* ⏜d person. **re·pa·tri·a·tion** [ˌriːpætrɪˈeɪʃn] *n.*

re·pay [riːˈpeɪ] *v.t. & i.* (p.t. & p.p. -*paid*) pay back (money, etc.); give in return for: *⏜ sb.'s kindness (sb. for his kindness)*. **⏜·ment** *n.*

re·peal [rɪˈpiːl] *v.t.* revoke, annul (a law, etc.). *n.* ⏜ing.

re·peat [rɪˈpiːt] *v.t. & i.* **1.** say or do again: *⏜ a word (a mistake)*; *⏜ oneself*, say or do what one has already said or done before. **2.** say (what sb. else has said or what one has learnt by heart). **3.** (of food) be tasted intermittently for some time after being swallowed. **4.** (of numbers) recur; appear again. **⏜·ed·ly** *adv.* again and again. **rep·e·ti·tion** [ˌrepɪˈtɪʃn] *n.* **1.** (no pl.) ⏜ing or being ⏜ed. **2.** sth. ⏜ed. **3.** further occurrence.

re·pel [rɪˈpel] *v.t.* (-*ll*-) **1.** drive back or away: *⏜ the enemy (a temptation)*. **2.** cause a feeling of dislike: *⏜led by his long beard*. **⏜·lent** *adj.* tending to ⏜: *water-⏜lent*; unattractive; uninviting.

re·pent [rɪˈpent] *v.t. & i.* wish one had not done (sth.); be or feel sorry (esp. about wrongdoing); regret: *⏜ (of) one's sins*. **re·pen·tance** [rɪˈpentəns] *n.* (no pl.) regret for wrongdoing. **re·pen·tant** *adj.* feeling or showing ⏜ance.

re·per·cus·sion [ˌriːpəˈkʌʃn] *n.* **1.** (no pl.) coming or springing back (after striking sth. with force). **2.** echoing sound. **3.** (usu. pl.) far-reaching and indirect effect of an event.

rep·er·toire [ˈrepətwɑː*] *n.* plays, songs, pieces, etc., that a theatrical company, actor, musician, etc. is prepared to perform.

rep·er·to·ry [ˈrepətərɪ] *n.* **1.** repertoire. **2.** store or collection, esp. of information, facts, etc.

rep·e·ti·tion, see *repeat*.

re·pine [rɪˈpaɪn] *v.i.* be discontented.

re·place [rɪˈpleɪs] *v.t.* **1.** put back in its place. **2.** take the place of: *Have buses ⏜d trams in your town?* **3.** ⏜ sth. by (with) sth., supply sth. as a substitute for sth.: *⏜ butter by margarine*. **⏜·able** *adj.* that can be ⏜d.

re·play [ˌriːˈpleɪ] *v.t.* play (a match[2], recording, etc.) over again. [ˈriːpleɪ] *n.* ⏜ing (of a match[2], dance, etc.).

re·plen·ish [rɪˈplenɪʃ] *v.t.* fill up (sth.) again (*with*): *⏜ one's wardrobe with new clothes*.

re·plete [rɪˈpliːt] *adj.* filled: *⏜ with food*; well provided (*with*). **re·ple·tion** [rɪˈpliːʃn] *n.* (no pl.) being ⏜.

rep·li·ca [ˈreplɪkə] *n.* exact copy, esp. one made by an artist of one of his own pictures.

re·ply [rɪˈplaɪ] *v.i. & t.* give as an answer (*to*), in word or action: *He did not ⏜ (to my question). He replied* *that he had not seen her. They replied to the enemy's fire.* **n.** act of ~ing; what is replied: *They gave no ~. What did they say in ~?*

re·port [rɪ'pɔːt] **v.t. & i. 1.** give an account of (sth. seen, heard, done, etc.); give as news: ~ *speeches made in Parliament.* ~*ed speech,* (gram.) speech as it is ~ed with the necessary changes of pronouns, tenses, etc. **2.** go to sb., go somewhere, and say that one has come, that one is ready for work, etc.: ~ *to the manager.* **3.** make a complaint against (sb.) or about (sth.) (*to* sb. in authority): *The soldier was ~ed for insolence.* **n. 1.** account of, statement about, sth. heard, seen, done, etc. **2.** common or general talk; rumour. **3.** periodical statement on pupil's work, conduct, etc. by the teachers. **4.** way sb. or sth. is spoken about; repute. **5.** noise of an explosion: *the ~ of a gun.* ~**·er** **n.** person who ~s for a newspaper, the radio, television, etc.

re·pose¹ [rɪ'pəʊz] **v.t. & i. 1.** rest; give rest or support to: *A girl was reposing in the hammock.* **2.** be supported or based (*on*). **n.** (no pl.) **1.** rest; sleep. **2.** quietness; restful or quiet behaviour or appearance.

re·pose² [rɪ'pəʊz] **v.t.** place or put (trust, belief, confidence, etc.) *in.*

re·pos·i·to·ry [rɪ'pɒzɪtərɪ] **n.** place where things are or may be stored.

rep·re·hen·si·ble [ˌreprɪ'hensəbl] **adj.** deserving reproof.

rep·re·sent [ˌreprɪ'zent] **v.t. 1.** be, give, make, a picture, sign, symbol, or example of: *a painting that ~s the Garden of Eden.* **2.** declare to be; describe (*as*): ~ *oneself as an expert.* **3.** make clear; explain: ~ *one's grievances to the management.* **4.** act or speak for; be an agent for; be M.P. for. **5.** act (a play, etc.), play the part of, on the stage. **rep·re·sen·ta·tion** [ˌreprɪzen'teɪʃn] **n. rep·re·sen·ta·tive** [ˌreprɪ'zentətɪv] **adj. 1.** typical; serving as an example of a class or group; containing examples of a number of classes or groups: *models ~ative of primitive tools.* **2.** consisting of elected deputies: ~*ative government.* **n. 1.** example, typical specimen (*of* a group or class). **2.** person elected to ~ (4) others: *House of R~atives,* lower house of the U.S. Congress.

re·press [rɪ'pres] **v.t.** keep or put down or under; prevent from finding an outlet: ~ *an impulse* (*a sneeze*). **re·pres·sion** [rɪ'preʃn] **n. re·pres·sive** **adj.**

re·prieve [rɪ'priːv] **v.t. 1.** postpone or remit the punishment of (esp. sb. condemned to death). **2.** give relief to for a short time (from trouble, danger, etc.). **n. 1.** (order giving authority for) postponement or remission of punishment (esp. by death). **2.** temporary relief (from trouble, danger, etc.).

rep·ri·mand ['reprɪmɑːnd] **v.t.** reprove (sb.) severely or officially. **n.** severe or official reproof.

re·pri·sal [rɪ'praɪzl] **n. 1.** (no pl.) paying back injury with injury. **2.** act of retaliation against an enemy.

re·proach [rɪ'prəʊtʃ] **v.t.** find fault with (sb.) (*for, with,* sth.); blame; censure: ~ *sb. for being late; I have nothing to ~ myself with* (i.e. I don't feel that I am in the wrong). **n. 1.** (no pl.) ~ing. **2.** word, phrase, etc. that ~es: *heap ~es on sb.* **3.** sth. that may bring disgrace or discredit. **4.** (no pl.) state of disgrace or discredit: *above* (*beyond*) ~, perfect; blameless. ~**·ful** **adj.** full of, expressing, ~.

rep·ro·bate ['reprəbeɪt] **v.t.** disapprove strongly of. **adj. & n.** immoral, unprincipled (person).

re·pro·duce [ˌriːprə'djuːs] **v.t. & i. 1.** copy; cause to be seen, heard, etc., again: ~ *music from a record.* **2.** produce offspring; bring about a natural increase: *plants that ~ by spores* (e.g. ferns). **3.** grow anew (lost part of the body, etc.). **re·pro·duc·tion** [ˌriːprə'dʌkʃn] **n. 1.** (no pl.) process of reproducing. **2.** sth. ~d (1); copy of sth., esp. of a work of art. **re·pro·duc·tive** [ˌriːprə'dʌktɪv] **adj.**

re·proof [rɪ'pruːf] **n.** (words of) blame or disapproval. **re·prove** [rɪ'pruːv] **v.t.** find fault with; say sharp words to.

rep·tile ['reptaɪl] **n.** cold-blooded animal that creeps or crawls (e.g. a lizard, tortoise, or snake).

re·pub·lic [rɪ'pʌblɪk] **n.** (country with a) system of government in which the elected representatives of the people are supreme and the head of the government (the president) is elected. **re·pub·li·can** **adj.** of a ~. **n.** person who favours a ~an government. *R~an,* (U.S.A.) member of the R~an Party (one of the two main political parties in the U.S.A.). (Cf. *democrat(ic)*).

re·pu·di·ate [rɪ'pjuːdɪeɪt] **v.t. 1.** refuse to accept or acknowledge (a statement, sb.'s authority, etc.). **2.** refuse to pay (a debt, etc.). **3.** say that one will have nothing more to do with: ~ *a wicked son.* **re·pu·di·a·tion** [rɪˌpjuːdɪ'eɪʃn] **n.**

re·pug·nant [rɪ'pʌgnənt] **adj.** distasteful; causing a feeling of dislike or opposition. **re·pug·nance** *n.* (no pl.) strong dislike (*to* sth.).

re·pulse [rɪ'pʌls] *v.t.* **1.** drive back (the enemy); resist (an attack) successfully. **2.** refuse to accept (help, friendly offers); treat (sb. offering help, etc.) coldly; rebuff (sb.). *n.* repulsing or being ~d. **re·pul·sion** [rɪ'pʌlʃn] *n.* (no pl.) **1.** feeling of dislike or distaste. **2.** (phys.) tendency of bodies to repel each other. **re·pul·sive** [rɪ'pʌlsɪv] *adj.* **1.** causing strong dislike. **2.** (phys.) exercising repulsion; repelling.

rep·u·ta·tion [ˌrepjʊ'teɪʃn] *n.* (no pl.) general opinion about the character, qualities, etc. of sb. or sth.: *a man of high ~; live up to one's ~*, act as people expect one to act. **rep·u·table** ['repjʊtəbl] *adj.* respectable; of excellent ~. **re·pute** [rɪ'pjuːt] *n.* (good or bad) ~. **re·put·ed** [rɪ'pjuːtɪd] *adj.* **1.** generally considered (*to be*). **2.** generally considered to be (but with a certain element of doubt): *his reputed father.*

re·quest [rɪ'kwest] *n.* **1.** (no pl.) asking or being asked: *do sth. at sb.'s ~; on* (*by*) ~, in response to an expressed wish. **2.** expressed desire: *make a ~ for sth. There have been many ~s for this product.* **3.** thing asked for. **4.** state of being asked for; demand: *in ~*, often asked for. *v.t.* make a ~ (*for* sth., *that*).

re·qui·em ['rekwɪem] *n.* (music for) Mass for the dead.

re·quire [rɪ'kwaɪə*] *v.t.* **1.** need; depend on for success, etc. **2.** order (sb. to do sth.). **3.** demand (as a right or by authority). ~**ment** *n.*

req·ui·site ['rekwɪzɪt] *n. & adj.* (thing) needed or required.

req·ui·si·tion [ˌrekwɪ'zɪʃn] *n.* (esp. formal and usually written) demand for the supply of (food, etc.) or use of (houses, etc.). *v.t.* make a ~ for.

re·quite [rɪ'kwaɪt] *v.t.* pay back; reward or avenge. **re·quit·al** *n.* (no pl.) repayment.

re·scind [rɪ'sɪnd] *v.t.* cancel (a law, etc.).

res·cue ['reskjuː] *v.t.* deliver from danger or harm; set free (from captivity, the power of enemies, etc.). *n.* rescuing or being ~d: *come* (*go*) *to the ~* (*to sb.'s ~*).

re·search [rɪ'sɜːtʃ] *n.* investigation undertaken in order to discover new facts: *be engaged in ~; ~ workers. v.i.* make ~es.

re·sem·ble [rɪ'zembl] *v.t.* be like; be

similar to. **re·sem·blance** [rɪ'zembləns] *n.* (point of) likeness.

re·sent [rɪ'zent] *v.t.* feel bitter, indignant, or angry at: ~ *being called stupid.* ~**ful** *adj.* feeling or showing ~ment; inclined to ~. ~**ment** *n.* (no pl.).

re·serve [rɪ'zɜːv] *v.t.* **1.** store, keep back, for later use or occasion. **2.** set apart (*for* sb.'s special use, or *for* a special purpose): *This room is ~d for children* (*television*). **3.** secure possession of or right to use: ~ *a room at a hotel. n.* **1.** sth. that is being or has been stored for later use: *the bank's ~s* (of money). **2.** (no pl.) state of being unused but available: *have some money in ~.* **3.** (sing. or pl.) military forces kept back to be used when needed. **4.** area of land set apart for a special purpose: *a game ~* (e.g. in Africa, for wild animals). **5.** condition that limits or restricts: *accept a statement without ~*, believe every word of it; ~ *price*, (esp. at an auction) lowest price that will be accepted. **6.** (no pl.) self-control in speech and behaviour; keeping silent or saying little; not showing one's feelings: *break through sb.'s ~*, get him to talk and be more sociable. **res·er·va·tion** [ˌrezə'veɪʃn] *n.* **1.** (no pl.) reserving or being ~d. **2.** express or tacit limitation or exception: *without reservation*, without any limiting condition. **3.** (U.S.A.) area of land ~d, esp. for the exclusive use of the Indians. **4.** booking (e.g. of a seat in a train, a room in a hotel, a berth on a ship, etc.). ~**d** *adj.* avoiding familiarity or intimacy; uncommunicative.

res·er·voir ['rezəvwɑː*] *n.* **1.** place (often an artificial lake) where water is stored (e.g. for supplying a town). **2.** any receptacle for holding a liquid. **3.** (fig.) supply (*of* facts, knowledge).

re·shuf·fle [ˌriː'ʃʌfl] *v.t.* shuffle again. *n. a Cabinet ~*, a redistribution of posts among Cabinet ministers.

re·side [rɪ'zaɪd] *v.i.* **1.** have one's home (*in, at,* etc.). **2.** (of power, right, etc.) be present *in*. **res·i·dence** ['rezɪdəns] *n.* **1.** (no pl.) residing: *take up one's ~nce in a place*, start to live there. **2.** building in which one ~s. **res·i·dent** ['rezɪdənt] *adj.* residing: *the ~nt population* (i.e. excluding visitors). *n.* **1.** person who ~s in a place (contrasted with a visitor). **2.** *R~nt*, British government agent in some States. **res·i·den·cy** ['rezɪdənsɪ] *n.* ~nce of a British political representative. **res·i·den·tial** [ˌrezɪ'denʃl] *adj.* of ~nce; of, with, private houses: *the ~ntial part of the town* (contrasted with the business or industrial parts).

res·i·due ['rezıdju:] *n.* that which remains after a part is taken or used.

re·sign [rı'zaın] *v.t. & i.* 1. give up (a position, claim, etc.). 2. *~ oneself to,* submit to; be ready to accept or endure without protest. *~ed adj.* having or showing patient acceptance of sth.

res·ig·na·tion [,rezıg'neıʃn] *n.* 1. *~ing* a position; letter to one's employer, stating this. 2. being *~ed* to conditions.

re·sil·ience [rı'zılıəns] *n.* (no pl.) quality or property of quickly recovering the original shape or condition after being pulled, pressed, crushed, etc. **re·sil·ient** *adj.* having or showing *~*.

res·in ['rezın] *n.* sticky substance that flows out from plants when cut or injured, esp. from fir and pine trees.

re·sist [rı'zıst] *v.t. & i.* 1. oppose; use force against in order to prevent the advance of. 2. be undamaged or unaffected by: *a kind of glass dish that ~s heat* (i.e. that does not crack or break in a hot oven). 3. keep oneself back from. **re·sis·tance** [rı'zıstəns] *n.* (no pl.) 1. (power of) *~ing: make (offer) no ~ance; ~ance (movement),* underground organization in a conquered country *~ing* the occupying power. 2. opposing force: *take the line of least ~ance,* (fig.) adopt the easiest way or method. **re·sis·tant** *adj.* having or showing *~*ance (to): *heat-~ant.* *~·less adj.* that cannot be *~ed.*

res·o·lute ['rezəlu:t] *adj.* fixed in determination or purpose; firm.

res·o·lu·tion [,rezə'lu:ʃn] *n.* 1. (no pl.) quality of being resolute. 2. sth. that is resolved (1); formal expression of opinion by a legislative body or a public meeting: *pass a ~.* 3. determination: *good ~s,* intentions for good conduct, etc. 4. separation into components.

re·solve [rı'zɒlv] *v.t. & i.* 1. decide; determine (*that, to do* sth.): *He ~d to succeed.* 2. put an end to (doubts, difficulties, etc.) by providing the answer. 3. (of a legislative body, public meeting, etc.) pass by vote the decision (*that*). 4. break up, separate (*into* parts). *n.* determination; sth. *~d* (1).

res·o·nant ['rezənənt] *adj.* 1. (of sounds) resounding; continuing to resound. 2. tending to prolong sounds by vibration: *~ walls.* 3. (of places) resounding. **res·o·nance** *n.*

re·sort [rı'zɔ:t] *v.i.* 1. make use of for help or to gain one's purpose; turn for aid *to: ~ to force.* 2. go often (*to a place*). *n.* 1. *~ing* (1): *in the last ~,* as a last attempt; when all else has failed. 2. thing or person *~ed* (1) to. 3. place visited frequently or by large numbers of people: *a seaside (health) ~.*

re·sound [rı'zaʊnd] *v.i. & t.* 1. (of a voice, instrument, sound) echo and re-echo; fill a place with sound. 2. (of a place) be filled with; echo back (sound). 3. (fig., of fame, an event, etc.) be much talked of.

re·source [rı'sɔ:s] *n.* 1. (pl.) wealth, supplies of goods, etc. that a person or country has or can use: *natural ~s,* minerals, water-power, etc. 2. sth. that helps in doing sth., that one can turn to for help, support, etc.: *be at the end of one's ~s.* 3. pastime (e.g. reading, music, etc.). 4. (no pl.) skill in finding *~s* (2): *a man of ~.* *~·ful adj.* good or quick at finding *~s* (2).

re·spect [rı'spekt] *n.* 1. (no pl.) honour; high opinion or regard: *pay (show) ~ to one's teachers.* 2. (no pl.) attention; consideration: *have ~ for the needs of the public.* 3. (no pl.) reference; relation: *with ~ to,* concerning; *without ~ to,* leaving out of the question; paying no attention to. 4. (pl.) greetings: *Give my ~s to your father. pay one's ~s to sb.,* pay sb. a polite visit. 5. detail; particular; point; aspect: *in ~ of,* as regards; *in this one ~; in some (all, no, many) ~s.* *v.t.* 1. have *~* (1, 2) for: *~ one's elders.* 2. treat with consideration; refrain from interfering with, etc.: *~ a person's feelings (wishes); ~ the law.* *~·able adj.* 1. deserving *~* (1, 2). 2. (of a person) of good social standing, reputation, etc.; (of clothes, behaviour, etc.) suitable for such persons; proper; decent. 3. fairly high in degree or amount: *a ~able income.* *~·ably adv.* *~·abil·i·ty* [rı,spektə'bılətı] *n.* (no pl.) being *~*able (2). *~·ful adj.* showing *~* (to). *~·ing prep.* with regard to. **re·spec·tive** [rı'spektıv] *adj.* for, belonging to, of, each of those in question: *He invited his three colleagues with their ~ive wives.* **re·spec·tive·ly** *adv.* separately or in turn, and in the order mentioned: *Tom, Dick, and Harry are 12, 14, and 15 years old, ~ively.*

re·spire [rı'spaıə*] *v.i.* breathe; breathe in and out. **res·pi·ra·tor** ['respəreıtə*] *n.* apparatus for breathing through to prevent the inhalation of poisonous gases, etc. **re·spi·ra·to·ry** [rı'spaıərətərı] *adj.* of breathing;

respiratory organs (diseases). **res·pi·ra·tion** [ˌrespəˈreɪʃn] *n.*

re·spite [ˈrespaɪt] *n.* **1.** time of relief or rest (*from* toil, suffering, anything unpleasant). **2.** postponement or delay permitted in the suffering of a penalty or the discharge of an obligation. *v.t.* give a ~ to.

re·splen·dent [rɪˈsplendənt] *adj.* very bright; splendid. **re·splen·dence** *n.* (no pl.).

re·spond [rɪˈspɒnd] *v.i.* **1.** answer: ~ *to a question.* **2.** act in answer to. **3.** react (*to*): ~ *to kindness* (*a medicine*). **re·sponse** [rɪˈspɒns] *n.* ~ing; answer; reaction. **re·spon·sive** *adj.* answering; ~ing easily or quickly.

re·spon·si·ble [rɪˈspɒnsəbl] *adj.* **1.** (of persons) legally or morally liable *for* the care of sth. or sb., in a position where one can be blamed for loss, failure, etc.: *Who is* ~ *for the organization of the meeting?* be ~ (*to*), have to give an account of what one does (*to* sb.). **2.** being the cause or source of: *Poor visibility was* ~ *for the car accident.* **3.** trustworthy; reliable; dependable: *Give the task to a* ~ *person.* **4.** (of work, a position, etc.) requiring **re·spon·si·bil·i·ty** [rɪˌspɒnsəˈbɪlətɪ] *n.* **1.** (no pl.) being ~: *He did it on his own responsibility* (i.e. without being told or authorized to do it). **2.** sth. for which a person is ~; duty: *the heavy responsibilities of the prime minister.*

rest¹ [rest] *n.* **1.** (no pl.) condition of being free from activity, movement, disturbance; (period of) quiet or sleep: *at* ~, (a) not moving; not agitated or troubled; (b) dead; *be laid to* ~, be buried; *set sb.'s mind at* ~, calm him; relieve him of doubt, anxiety, etc. **2.** sth. used as a support: *a head-*~. **3.** (music) (sign marking an) interval of silence. **4.** establishment for the accommodation of a particular class or group: *sailors'* ~. *v.i. & t.* **1.** be still or quiet; be free from activity, movement, disturbance, etc. **2.** give a ~ to: ~ *one's horse;* ~ *one's eyes.* **3.** (cause to) be supported (*on* or *against* sth.): ~ *one's elbows on the table.* ~**ful** *adj.* quiet; peaceful; giving ~ or a feeling of ~. ~**less** *adj.* never still or quiet; unable to ~.

rest² [rest] *n.* (always *the* ~) **1.** what is left and (*all*) *the* ~ *of it,* and everything else that might be mentioned; *for the* ~, as regards anything beyond what has been mentioned. **2.** the others.

rest³ [rest] *v.i.* **1.** remain, continue to be, in some condition or position: *You*

may ~ *assured that ...* **2.** depend: *A great deal* ~*s on his answer.* **3.** ~ *with,* be left in the hands or charge of: *It* ~*s with you to decide,* you are the one who must decide.

res·tau·rant [ˈrestərɔ̃ːŋ, ˈrestərɒnt] *n.* place where meals can be bought and eaten.

res·ti·tu·tion [ˌrestɪˈtjuːʃn] *n.* (no pl.) restoring (of sth. stolen, etc.) to its owner.

res·tive [ˈrestɪv] *adj.* **1.** (of horses) refusing to move forward; stubbornly moving backwards or sideways. **2.** (of persons) resisting control or discipline.

re·store [rɪˈstɔː*] *v.t.* **1.** give back (sth. stolen, etc.). **2.** bring back into use (e.g. old customs). **3.** put (sb.) back into a former position. **4.** (attempt to) bring back to the original state by repairing, rebuilding, etc. (e.g. an old building, painting, etc.). **5.** make well or normal again: ~*d to health.* **res·to·ra·tion** [ˌrestəˈreɪʃn] *n.* **1.** (no pl.) restoring or being ~*d.* **2.** *the Restoration,* (the period of) the re-establishment of the monarchy in England.

re·strain [rɪˈstreɪn] *v.t.* hold back; keep under control; prevent (sb. or sth. *from doing* sth., etc.). ~**t** *n.* **1.** (no pl.) ~ing or being ~ed: *without* ~*t,* freely; copiously. **2.** (no pl.) confinement, esp. because of insanity: *put sb. under* ~*t.* **3.** sth. that ~s.

re·strict [rɪˈstrɪkt] *v.t.* limit; keep within limits. **re·stric·tion** [rɪˈstrɪkʃn] *n.* **1.** (no pl.) ~ing or being ~ed. **2.** sth. that ~s. **re·stric·tive** *adj.* ~ing; tending to ~.

re·sult [rɪˈzʌlt] *n.* **1.** that which is produced by an activity or other cause; outcome; effect. **2.** sth. obtained by calculation. *v.i.* **1.** happen as a consequence (*from* conditions, causes, etc.). **2.** end in a specified manner: ~ *in failure.*

re·sume [rɪˈzjuːm] *v.t.* **1.** go on after stopping for a time. **2.** take or occupy again: ~ *one's seat.* **re·sump·tion** [rɪˈzʌmpʃn] *n.*

res·ur·rect [ˌrezəˈrekt] *v.t.* **1.** take up from the grave. **2.** bring back into use or to the memory. **3.** dig up. **res·ur·rec·tion** [ˌrezəˈrekʃn] *n.* **1.** *the R~ion,* the rising of Jesus from the tomb; the rising of all the dead on the Last Day. **2.** revival after disuse or inactivity.

re·sus·ci·tate [rɪˈsʌsɪteɪt] *v.t. & i.* bring or come back to consciousness (e.g. sb. nearly drowned, etc.). **re·sus·ci·ta·tion** [rɪˌsʌsɪˈteɪʃn] *n.* (no pl.)

re·tail [ˈriːteɪl] *n.* selling of goods to

the general public, not for resale (cf. *wholesale*): *sell by* ~; ~ *prices.* [ri:'teɪl] *v.t. & i.* **1.** sell (goods) by ~. **2.** (of goods) be sold by ~ (*at* or *for* a price). **3.** relate (gossip, etc.) in detail to others. ~**er** [ri:'teɪlə*] *n.* tradesman who sells by ~.

re·tain [rɪ'teɪn] *v.t.* **1.** keep; continue to have or hold; keep in place: *a pot that does not* ~ *water.* **2.** get the services of (esp. a barrister) by payment. ~**er** *n.* **1.** (old use) servant of sb. of high rank. **2.** fee paid to ~ sb.'s services.

re·tal·i·ate [rɪ'tælɪeɪt] *v.i. & t.* return the same sort of ill-treatment as one has received (*upon, against,* sb.); repay (an injury, insult, etc.) in kind. **re·tal·i·a·tion** [rɪ,tælɪ'eɪʃn] *n.* (no pl.).

re·tard [rɪ'tɑːd] *v.t.* check; hinder (esp. progress, development). ~**ed** *adj.* backward in mental development.

retch [retʃ] *v.i.* make the sound and motion of vomiting but without the result.

re·ten·tive [rɪ'tentɪv] *adj.* having the power of retaining (1) things. **re·ten·tion** [rɪ'tenʃn] *n.* (no pl.) retaining or being retained.

ret·i·cent ['retɪsənt] *adj.* (in the habit of) saying little; not saying all that is known or felt; reserved. **ret·i·cence** *n.*

ret·i·nue ['retɪnjuː] *n.* number of persons (servants, officers, etc.) travelling with a person of high rank.

re·tire [rɪ'taɪə*] *v.i. & t.* **1.** withdraw, go away (*from* a place, *from* company, *to* a place). **2.** give up one's work, business, or position: ~ *on a pension*; cause (sb.) to do this. **3.** go to bed. ~**d** *adj.* **1.** having ~d (2): *a* ~*d civil servant.* **2.** quiet; secluded. ~**ment** *n.* condition of being ~d: *live in* (*go into*) ~*ment.* **re·tir·ing** *adj.* avoiding society; reserved.

re·tort¹ [rɪ'tɔːt] *v.i. & t.* answer back quickly and sharply (esp. to an accusation or challenge); get equal with sb. by returning (insults, attacks, etc.). *n.* such an answer.

re·tort² [rɪ'tɔːt] *n.* vessel with a long, narrow neck bent downwards, used for distilling liquids.

re·touch [,riː'tʌtʃ] *v.t.* improve (a photograph, painting, etc.) by making small changes.

re·trace [rɪ'treɪs] *v.t.* **1.** go back over or along: ~ *one's steps.* **2.** go over (past actions, etc.) in one's mind.

re·tract [rɪ'trækt] *v.t. & i.* **1.** take back or withdraw (a statement, an offer, or opinion). **2.** draw (a part of the body, the undercarriage of an air-craft, etc.) back or in; be drawn back or in. ~**able** *adj.* that can be ~ed.

re·treat [rɪ'triːt] *v.i.* go back; withdraw: *force the enemy to* ~. *n.* **1.** act of ~ing: *in full* ~; *make good one's* ~, ~ safely; *beat a* ~, (fig.) withdraw from an undertaking. **2.** signal for ~ing: *sound the* ~ (e.g. on a bugle or drum). **3.** (place for a) period of quiet and rest: *go into* ~.

re·trench [rɪ'trentʃ] *v.t. & i.* cut down, reduce (expenses, etc.); economize. ~**ment** *n.*

ret·ri·bu·tion [,retrɪ'bjuːʃn] *n.* (no pl.) deserved punishment.

re·trieve [rɪ'triːv] *v.t. & i.* **1.** get possession of again. **2.** make good; put right (an error). **3.** restore to a flourishing state (esp. one's fortunes). **4.** (of specially trained dogs) find and bring in (killed or wounded game, etc.). **re·triev·er** *n.* breed of dog used for retrieving (4).

retro-, **re·tro-** [,retrəʊ-, 'retrəʊ-] *pref.* backwards; back again.

re·tro·ac·tive [,retrəʊ'æktɪv] *adj.* retrospective.

ret·ro·grade ['retrəʊgreɪd] *adj.* directed backwards; becoming worse; likely to cause worse conditions, etc.

re·tro·gres·sion [,retrəʊ'greʃn] *n.* return to a less advanced state. **re·tro·gres·sive** [,retrəʊ'gresɪv] *adj.*

re·tro·spect ['retrəʊspekt] *n.* (no pl.) review of past events, etc.: *in* ~, when looking back (at sth. in the past). **re·tro·spec·tion** [,retrəʊ'spekʃn] *n.* **re·tro·spec·tive** [,retrəʊ'spektɪv] *adj.* **1.** looking back on past events, etc. **2.** (of laws, etc.) applying to the past: ~*ive legislation.*

re·turn [rɪ'tɜːn] *v.i. & t.* **1.** come or go back. **2.** give, put, send, pay, back: ~ *a borrowed book.* **3.** say in reply. **4.** (of a constituency) send (sb.) as representative to Parliament. *n.* **1.** ~ing or being ~ed: *on his* ~ *home*; *by* ~, by the next post out; *in* ~ (*for*), as repayment or in exchange; *many happy* ~*s* (*of the day*) (phrase used as a birthday or festival greeting). *a* ~ *ticket,* ticket for a journey to a place and back again. **2.** (often pl.) profit (on an investment or undertaking). **3.** official report or statement: *the election* ~*s.* ~**able** *adj.* that can be, or is to be, ~ed.

re·union [,riː'juːnjən] *n.* **1.** (no pl.) reuniting or being reunited. **2.** (esp.) meeting of old friends, former colleagues, relatives, etc. after a long separation. **re·unite** [,riːjuː'naɪt] *v.t. & i.* bring or come together again.

ev [rev] *v.t. & i.* (*-vv-*) ~ (*up*), (colloq.) increase the speed of revolutions in (an engine). *n.* (colloq.) revolution (of an engine).

e·veal [rɪ'viːl] *v.t.* allow or cause to be seen; make known (a secret, a truth, etc.). **rev·e·la·tion** [,revə'leɪʃn] *n.* **1.** (no pl.) ~ing. **2.** sth. ~ed, esp. a piece of surprising knowledge.

e·veil·le [rɪ'væli] *n.* (in the army) signal to men to get up in the morning: *sound the ~.*

ev·el ['revl] *v.i.* (*-ll-*, U.S.A. also *-l-*) **1.** make merry; have a gay, lively time. **2.** ~ *in*, take great pleasure in. *n.* joyful merry-making. **~·ry** *n.* wild or noisy merry-making.

ev·e·la·tion, see *reveal*.

e·venge [rɪ'vendʒ] *v.t.* **1.** do sth. to get satisfaction for (a wrong): ~ *an insult*; ~ *one's friend* (i.e. do equal harm to the person who did wrong to one's friend). **2.** *be ~d, ~ oneself* (*on* sb. *for* sth.), inflict injury in return for injury inflicted on oneself. *n.* **1.** (no pl.) act of revenging; desire to ~. **2.** (sport) opportunity given for reversing a former result by a return game, etc. **~·ful** *adj.* feeling or showing a desire for ~: *~ful looks.*

ev·e·nue ['revənjuː] *n.* **1.** (no pl.) income, esp. the total annual income of the State; government department charged with the collection of such income: *Inland R~*, income from government taxes, etc.; ~ *officer*, customs and excise officer. **2.** (pl.) collective items of such income.

e·ver·ber·ate [rɪ'vɜːbəreɪt] *v.t. & i.* (esp. of sound) send back; be sent back. **re·ver·ber·a·tion** [rɪ,vɜːbə'reɪʃn] *n.*

e·vere [rɪ'vɪə*] *v.t.* have deep respect for; regard as sacred. **rev·er·ence** ['revərəns] *n.* deep respect; feeling of wonder and awe: *hold sb.* (*sth.*) *in ~nce.* *v.t.* treat with ~nce. **rev·er·end** ['revərənd] *adj.* **1.** deserving to be treated with respect (because of age, character, etc.). **2.** *the R~nd* (usu. shortened in writing to *the Rev.*), used as a title for clergymen: *The Rev. T. Wells*; *R~nd Mother*, Mother Superior of a convent. **rev·er·ent** ['revərənt] *adj.* feeling or showing ~nce. **rev·er·en·tial** [,revə'renʃl] *adj.* caused or marked by ~nce.

ev·er·ie ['revərɪ] *n.* (state of enjoying) dreamy, pleasant thoughts: *lost in ~*; *indulge in ~s about the future.*

e·verse [rɪ'vɜːs] *adj.* contrary or opposite in character, order, or direc-

tion: *the ~ side of a record²* (4); ~ *gear*, used to make a vehicle move backwards. *n.* **1.** (no pl.) reverse; contrary: *do the ~ of what one is asked to do.* **2.** ~ side (of cloth, a coin, medal, etc.). (Cf. *obverse* (1.).) **3.** defeat; change to bad fortune: *suffer a financial ~.* **4.** mechanism or device that ~s sth.: *put the car into ~. v.t. & i.* **1.** turn (sth.) the other way round or up or inside out: ~ *one's policy*; ~ *the charges*, (teleph.) let the person to whom the call is made pay for it; ~ *arms*, carry rifles so that they point downwards. **2.** (cause to) go in the opposite direction. **3.** change the order or position of. **4.** revoke, annul (decree, act, decision, etc.). **re·ver·sal** [rɪ'vɜːsl] *n.* reversing or being ~d. **re·vers·ible** [rɪ'vɜːsəbl] *adj.* that can be ~d (esp. of cloth, either side of which can be used on the outside).

re·vert [rɪ'vɜːt] *v.i.* return (*to* a former state, problem, an earlier question, etc.).

re·view [rɪ'vjuː] *v.t. & i.* **1.** consider or examine again; go over again in the mind: ~ *last week's lesson.* **2.** inspect formally (troops, a fleet, etc.). **3.** write an account of (new books, etc.) for periodicals, etc. *n.* **1.** act of ~ing. **2.** critical account of a new book, play, film, etc. **3.** periodical with articles on current events, ~s of new books, etc.

re·vile [rɪ'vaɪl] *v.t. & i.* swear at; call bad names; talk abusively.

re·vise [rɪ'vaɪz] *v.t.* reconsider; read through carefully, esp. in order to correct and improve. **re·vi·sion** [rɪ'vɪʒn] *n.* revising or being ~d; ~d version.

re·vive [rɪ'vaɪv] *v.t. & i.* **1.** come or bring back to consciousness, strength, health, or an earlier state: *flowers that ~ in water. Our hopes ~d.* **2.** come, bring, into use again: ~ *old customs.* **re·viv·al** [rɪ'vaɪvl] *n.* **1.** reviving or being ~d: *the Revival of Learning*, the Renaissance. **2.** (esp.) (meetings intended to produce an) increase of interest in religion. **re·viv·al·ist** [rɪ'vaɪvəlɪst] person organizing a revival (2).

re·voke [rɪ'vəʊk] *v.t.* repeal; cancel; withdraw (a decree, etc.). **re·vo·cable** ['revəkəbl] *adj.* that can be ~d. **re·vo·ca·tion** [,revə'keɪʃn] *n.*

re·volt [rɪ'vəʊlt] *v.i. & t.* **1.** rise in rebellion. **2.** be filled with disgust or horror (*at* or *against* a crime, a stink, etc.). **3.** cause a feeling of disgust or horror in: *sights that ~ed all who saw* *them.* ***n.*** **1.** (no pl.) act of ⁓ing. **2.** rebellion; rising.

rev·o·lu·tion [ˌrevə'luːʃn] ***n.*** **1.** revolving or journeying round: *the ⁓ of the earth round the sun.* **2.** complete turn of a wheel: *sixty-five ⁓s a minute.* **3.** complete change (in conditions, ways of doing things, esp. in methods of government when caused by the overthrow of one system by force): *the Industrial R⁓; the French R⁓.* **⁓·ary** ***adj.*** of a ⁓ (3); bringing, causing, favouring, great (and often violent) changes. ***n.*** supporter of (political) ⁓. **⁓·ize** ***v.t.*** make a complete change in.

re·volve [rɪ'vɒlv] ***v.t. & i.*** **1.** (cause to) go round in a circle: *A wheel ⁓s round its axis. a revolving door.* **2.** turn over in the mind; think about all sides of (a problem, etc.).

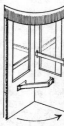

a revolving door

re·volv·er [rɪ'vɒlvə*] ***n.*** pistol that can be fired a number of times without being reloaded.

re·vue [rɪ'vjuː] ***n.*** theatrical entertainment of songs, dances, satire on current events, etc.

re·vul·sion [rɪ'vʌlʃn] ***n.*** (no pl.) sudden and complete change of feeling.

re·ward [rɪ'wɔːd] ***n.*** sth. offered, given, or obtained in return for work or services, or for the restoration of lost or stolen property, or for the capture of a criminal, etc. ***v.t.*** give a ⁓ to (sb. *for* sth.).

rhap·so·dy ['ræpsədɪ] ***n.*** **1.** enthusiastic expression of delight (in speech, poetry, music). **2.** (music) composition in irregular form.

rhet·o·ric ['retərɪk] ***n.*** (no pl.) **1.** (art of) using words impressively in speech and writing. **2.** language with much display and ornamentation (often with the implication of exaggeration and insincerity). **rhe·tor·i·cal** [rɪ'tɒrɪkl] ***adj.*** in, using, a style designed to impress or persuade; artificial or ex-

aggerated in language. *a ⁓al question,* one asked for the sake of effect (2), not because an answer is needed or expected. **rhet·o·ri·cian** [ˌretə'rɪʃən] ***n.*** person skilled in ⁓ (1) or fond of ⁓al language.

rheu·ma·tism ['ruːmətɪzəm] ***n.*** (no pl.) painful disease marked by stiffness and inflammation of muscles and joints. **rheu·mat·ic** [ruː'mætɪk] ***adj.*** of ⁓; causing, caused by, ⁓; suffering from, liable to have, ⁓.

rhi·noc·er·os [raɪ'nɒsərəs] ***n.*** (pl. ⁓es, collective pl. ⁓) thick-skinned animal of Africa and Asia having one or two upright horns on its nose.

a rhinoceros

rhu·barb ['ruːbɑːb] ***n.*** (plant with) thick, juicy stalks which are cooked and used like fruit.

rhyme [raɪm] ***n.*** **1.** (no pl.) sameness of sound in endings of words, esp. at ends of lines of verse (e.g. *sea, key, rhyme, time*). **2.** verse(s) with ⁓: *nursery ⁓s,* poems or songs for small children. **3.** word that ⁓s with another. ***v.i. & t.*** **1.** (of words or lines of verse) be in ⁓: *'father' ⁓s with 'rather'.* **2.** use (a word) as a ⁓: *Poets ⁓ 'love' with 'above'.* **3.** write verse(s) with ⁓. **⁓d** ***adj.*** having ⁓s

rhythm ['rɪðəm] ***n.*** **1.** (no pl.) regular succession of weak and strong stresses, accents, sounds, or movements (in speech, music, dancing, etc.); regular recurrence of events, etc.: *the ⁓ of the tides.* **2.** particular pattern of this kind *exciting ⁓s of drum music.* **rhyth·mic, rhyth·mi·cal** ['rɪðmɪk(l)] ***adjs.***

rib [rɪb] ***n.*** **1.** any one of the curved bones extending from the backbone round the chest to the front of the body. **2.** sth. like a rib in form, position, or use as a supporting or strengthening part, as e.g. curved timber in the sides of a ship, a thick vein in a leaf, etc. **⁓bed** [rɪbd] ***adj.*** marked by, strengthened with, ⁓s.

rib·ald ['rɪbəld] ***adj.*** (of a person) using indecent or irreverent language (of talk, laughter, etc.) coarse; mocking. **⁓·ry** ***n.*** ⁓ language or talk.

·ib·bon ['rɪbən] *n.* **1.** (length or piece of) silk or other material woven in a long, narrow strip or band, used for ornamenting, for tying things, etc. **2.** sth. like a ~: *a typewriter ~.* **3.** strip of satin or other material being or representing a medal, or worn to indicate membership of an order, a club, college, etc.

·ice [raɪs] *n.* (plant with) white grain used as food.

·ich [rɪtʃ] *adj.* **1.** having much money or property. **2.** (of clothes, jewels, furniture, etc.) costly; splendid. **3.** (of land, etc.) producing much; abundant (*in*). **4.** (of food) containing much fat, many eggs, etc. **5.** (of colours, sounds, etc.) deep; strong; full. **~·es** ['rɪtʃɪz] *n. pl.* wealth; abundance. **~·ly** *adv.* **1.** in a ~ (2) manner. **2.** fully: (esp.) *~ly deserved.* **~·ness** *n.* (no pl.) quality of being ~.

·ick [rɪk] *n.* pile of hay, straw, etc. regularly built (and usu. thatched or otherwise covered to protect it from the rain). *v.t.* make into a ~.

·ick·ets ['rɪkɪts] *n.* (sg. or pl. v.) disease of childhood, marked by softening and malformation of the bones.

·ick·ety ['rɪkəti] *adj.* weak, esp. in the joints; likely to break and collapse: *~ furniture.*

·ick·shaw ['rɪkʃɔ:] *n.* two-wheeled carriage pulled by a man.

·ic·o·chet ['rɪkəʃeɪ] *n.* **1.** (no pl.) jumping or skipping movement (of a stone, bullet, etc.) after hitting the ground, a wall, the surface of water, etc. **2.** hit made after this. *v.i.* (*-t-, -tt-*) (of a projectile) skip or bound off.

·id [rɪd] *v.t.* (p.t. ~ or old use ~*ded*, p.p. ~) make free (of): *~ a house of mice; get ~ of a cough. I was glad to be ~ of him.* **~·dance** ['rɪdəns] *n.* (no pl.) clearing away; being free from: *good ~dance,* a welcome relief to be ~ of sb. or sth.

·id·den ['rɪdn] p.p. of *ride.* (esp. in compounds) oppressed or dominated by: *disease-~ slums.*

·id·dle¹ ['rɪdl] *n.* puzzling question; puzzling thing, situation, person, etc.

·id·dle² ['rɪdl] *n.* coarse sieve (for stones, earth, etc.). *v.t.* **1.** pass (material) through a ~. **2.** make many holes in (sth.) (e.g. by firing bullets into it).

·ide [raɪd] *v.i. & t.* (p.t. *rode* [rəʊd], p.p. *ridden* ['rɪdn]) **1.** sit on (a horse, bicycle, etc.) and be carried along; sit on and control: *riding (on) a camel.* **2.**

be carried along (*in* a bus, train, etc.). **3.** be supported by; float on water: *a ship riding at anchor.* *n.* **1.** journey on horseback, on a bicycle, as a passenger in a car, bus, train, etc.: *go for a ~; take sb. for a ~,* (sl.) deceive him. **2.** path through a wood or forest, with a soft surface suitable for riding a horse on but not for vehicles. **rid·er** *n.* **1.** person who ~s a horse, etc. **2.** additional observation following a statement, verdict, etc.

ridge [rɪdʒ] *n.* **1.** raised line where two sloping surfaces meet: *the ~ of a roof (the ~ of the nose).* **2.** long, narrow stretch of high land along the tops of a line of hills; long mountain-range; watershed. **3.** raised, narrow strip (e.g. on ploughed land, between the furrows). *v.t.* make into, cover with, ~s.

rid·i·cule ['rɪdɪkju:l] *v.t.* cause (sb. or sth.) to appear foolish; make fun of. *n.* (no pl.) holding or being held as an object of derision or mockery. **ri·dic·u·lous** [rɪ'dɪkjʊləs] *adj.* deserving to be laughed at; absurd; unreasonable.

rife [raɪf] *pred. adj.* **1.** widespread; common. **2.** ~ *with,* having many or much; full of: *a country ~ with superstition.*

riff-raff ['rɪfræf] *n.* ill-behaved people of the lowest class.

ri·fle¹ ['raɪfl] *v.t.* search and rob: *The thieves ~d every drawer in the house.*

ri·fle² ['raɪfl] *v.t.* cut spiral grooves in (the barrel of a gun). *n.* gun with a long ~d barrel.

rift [rɪft] *n.* split or crack: *a ~ in the clouds.*

rig [rɪɡ] *v.t.* (*-gg-*) **1.** supply (a ship) with masts, ~ging, sails, etc. **2.** ~ *sb. out (with sth.),* (a) provide with necessary clothes, equipment, etc.; (b) dress up; ~ *sth. up,* (a) assemble or adjust parts of (an aircraft, etc.); (b) make, put together, quickly or with any materials available: *~ up a shelter.* *n.* **1.** way in which a ship's masts, sails, etc. are arranged. **2.** (colloq.) style of dress; clothing; person's general appearance resulting from his clothing. **3.** equipment put together for a special purpose: *oil-~.* **~·ging** *n.* (no pl.) all the ropes, etc. that support a ship's masts and sails.

right¹ [raɪt] *adj. & n. & adv.* (opp. *left²*) **I.** *adj. & n.* (of, in, on, the) side of the body that is towards the east when one faces the north: *In Britain traffic keeps to the left, not to the ~, side of the road. Take the first turning to the ~. the R~,* (pol.) the conservative or reactionary group(s), party or parties. **II. adv.** to the ~ side: *He looked neither ~ nor left.* **~-'hand·ed adj.** using the ~ hand more often and more easily than the left. **R~ist n.** supporter of the doctrines of the R~.

right² [raɪt] **adj.** (opp. *wrong*) **1.** (of conduct, etc.) just; morally good; according to law or duty. **2.** *the ~ side* (of cloth, etc.), the side intended to be seen. **3.** true; correct; satisfactory: *the ~ time*; *on the ~ road*; *the ~ man for the job.* **4.** ~ *angle*, one of 90°: *These two roads cross at ~ angles.* **n. 1.** that which is ~: *know the difference between ~ and wrong*; *be in the ~*, have justice or truth on one's side. **2.** sth. to which one has a just claim; sth. one may do or have by law: *by ~(s)*, justly; correctly; *by ~ of*, because of; on account of; *~ of way*, (a) ~ established by usage to pass over another's ground; (b) (in road traffic) precedence in passing granted to one vehicle, etc. with regard to another. **v.t.** put, bring, or come back, into the ~, or an upright, condition; make sth. ~ again. **~·ful adj. 1.** according to law or justice: *the ~ful owner (king).* **2.** (of actions) justifiable. **~·ly adv.** justly; correctly: *if I am ~ly informed.*

right³ [raɪt] **adv. 1.** straight; directly: *Go ~ on until you get to the church.* *~ away*, immediately: *I'll go (come) ~ away.* **2.** completely; all the way: *turn ~ round*; *a ~-about turn*, a turn continued until one is facing in the opposite direction. **3.** exactly: *~ in the middle.*

righ·teous [ˈraɪtʃəs] **adj. 1.** doing what is morally right; obeying the law. **2.** morally justifiable. **~·ly adv. ~·ness n.** (no pl.)

rig·id [ˈrɪdʒɪd] **adj. 1.** stiff; unbending; that cannot be bent. **2.** firm; strict; not changing; not to be changed: *a ~ rule*; *~ discipline.* **~·ly adv. ri·gid·i·ty** [rɪˈdʒɪdətɪ] **n.** (no pl.).

rig·ma·role [ˈrɪgmərəʊl] **n.** long, wandering story or statement that does not mean much.

rig·our (U.S.A. **-or**) [ˈrɪgə*] **n. 1.** (no pl.) sternness; strictness. **2.** (often pl.) severe conditions (of climate, etc.). **rig·or·ous** [ˈrɪgərəs] **adj.** stern; strict. **2.** harsh; severe.

rile [raɪl] **v.t.** (colloq.) make angry.

rim [rɪm] **n. 1.** raised or thickened edge, esp. of sth. circular: *the ~ of a bowl.* **2.** outer ring of a wheel's framework (to which a tyre is fitted). **3.** border round the lenses of spec-

tacles. **v.t.** (-*mm-*) make or be a ~ for; provide with a ~: *a pool ~med with flowers.*

rind [raɪnd] **n. 1.** hard, outside skin or covering (of some fruits, e.g. melons, or of bacon and cheese). **2.** bark of a tree or plant.

ring¹ [rɪŋ] **n. 1.** circle: *have ~s round one's eyes*; *puff out ~s of smoke*; *children dancing in a ~*; *make (run) ~s round sb.*, move, do things, very much faster or better than sb. **2.** circular band: *a wedding-~*; *a key-~* (on which keys are carried). **3.** enclosed space for a circus, boxing matches, a cattle-show, etc. **4.** group of persons who combine for a selfish purpose (e.g. to control prices). **5.** betting at races: *the ~*, bookmakers. **v.t.** (p.t. & p.p. *~ed*) **1.** surround; put a ~ round or over. **2.** put a ~ in the nose of (a bull, etc.) or on the leg of (a bird, etc.). **'~·lead·er n.** person who leads others in a rising against authority. **~ road n.** road round a large town for the use of through traffic. **'~·worm n.** (no pl.) skin disease appearing in round, red patches.

ring² [rɪŋ] **v.i. & t.** (p.t. *rang* [ræŋ]) p.p. *rung* [rʌŋ]) **1.** give out a clear, musical sound as when metal vibrates: *The telephone bell rang.* **2.** cause sth. (esp. a bell) to ~; do this in order to get attention, give a warning, etc.: *~ for the waiter.* *That ~s a bell*, (fig., colloq.) that reminds one of sth. **3.** ~ (*sb.*) *up*, get into communication by telephone; *~ off*, end a telephone conversation. **4.** announce (the hour, etc.) by the sound of a bell, etc.: *~ the changes (on sth.)*, (fig.) do or use sth. in all possible different ways. **5.** (of a place) resound (*with*). **6.** (of the ears) be filled with a humming sound. **n.** *~ing* (1) sound.

ring·let [ˈrɪŋlɪt] **n.** small curl of hair.

rink [rɪŋk] **n.** sheet of artificial ice for skating; specially made floor for roller-skating.

rinse [rɪns] **v.t.** (often *~ out*) wash with clean water in order to remove unwanted substances: *~ the clothes*; *~ out the soap*; *~ out the teapot.* **n. 1.** act of rinsing: *Give your hair a good ~.* **2.** solution for tinting the hair.

ri·ot [ˈraɪət] **n. 1.** violent outbreak of lawlessness by people in a district. **2.** (no pl.) noisy, uncontrolled behaviour (e.g. by students making merry): *run ~*, throw off discipline; be out of control. **3.** (no pl.) unrestrained indulgence in or display of sth. **v.i. 1.**

take part in a ~. **2.** indulge (*in*); revel (*in*). **~·er** *n.* person who ~s. **~·ous** *adj.* taking part in a ~; disorderly.

rip [rɪp] *v.t. & i.* (*-pp-*) **1.** pull, tear, or cut (sth.) quickly and violently (to get it off, out, open, etc.): ~ *a letter open*; ~ *the cover off*; ~ *a piece of cloth in two.* **2.** (of material) be ~ped. *n.* torn place; long cut.

ripe [raɪp] *adj.* (~*r*, ~*st*) **1.** (of fruit, grain, etc.) ready to be gathered and used. **2.** fully developed: ~ *judgement.* **3.** ~ *for*, ready for (e.g. mischief). **rip·en** ['raɪpən] *v.t. & i.* (cause to) become ~.

rip·ple ['rɪpl] *n.* (sound of) small wave(s) (esp. travelling along the surface); gentle sound that rises and falls: *a ~ of laughter*; wavy or crinkled appearance in hair, etc. *v.t. & i.* (cause to) move in ~s; make ~s in; (cause to) rise and fall gently.

rise [raɪz] *v.i.* (p.t. *rose* [rəuz], p.p. ~*n* ['rɪzn]) **1.** get up from a lying, sitting, or kneeling position; get out of bed. **2.** go or come up or higher; reach a high(er) level or position or amount: *Prices have ~n considerably. The flood is still rising. The smoke rose straight up. He's likely to ~ in the world.* **3.** (of the sun, moon, stars) appear above the horizon. **4.** come to the surface: *bubbles rising from the bottom of a pond.* **5.** come to life (*again, from the dead*). **6.** have as a starting-point: *The river ~s in Turkey.* **7.** rebel (*against* the government, etc.). **8.** (of Parliament, a committee, etc.) adjourn (2). *n.* **1.** small hill; upward slope. **2.** upward progress; increase (in value, temperature, wages, etc.): *on the ~, increasing.* **3.** *give ~ to,* be the cause of. **4.** movement of fish to the surface. *get* (*take*) *a ~ out of sb.,* cause him to show annoyance or weakness (usu. by good-natured teasing). **ris·ing** *adj. the rising generation,* the young people who are growing up; *rising twelve,* getting near the age of twelve. *n.* (esp.) rebellion.

risk [rɪsk] *n.* possibility or chance of meeting danger, suffering loss or injury, etc.: *take* (*run*) ~s; *at the ~ of one's life*; *at ~,* exposed to danger. *v.t.* expose to the chance of danger, injury, or loss: ~ *one's neck* (i.e. one's life); take the chance of: ~ *failure.* **~y** *adj.* (*-ier, -iest*)

ris·qué ['riːskeɪ] *adj.* (of a remark, joke, story, etc.) slightly indecent.

ris·sole ['rɪsəul] *n.* small ball of minced meat or fish, mixed with breadcrumbs, potato, etc. and fried.

rite [raɪt] *n.* act or ceremony, esp. in religious services: ~s *of baptism.* **rit·u·al** ['rɪtʃuəl] *n.* system of ~s. *adj.* of or connected with ~s: *the ritual dances of an African tribe.*

ri·val ['raɪvl] *n.* **1.** person who competes with another (because he wants the same thing, or to be or do better than the other): *business ~s*; (attrib.) ~ *shops. v.t.* (*-ll-*, U.S.A. also *-l-*) be a ~ of; claim to be (almost) as good as. **~·ry** *n.* being ~s; competition.

riv·er ['rɪvə*] *n.* **1.** natural stream of water flowing to the sea, etc.: *the ~ Nile.* **2.** great flow: *a ~ of tears* (*blood*).

riv·et ['rɪvɪt] *n.* metal pin or bolt for fastening metal plates (in a ship's sides, etc.). *v.t.* **1.** fasten with ~s. **2.** fix, concentrate (one's eyes, attention, etc. *on, upon*); attract (attention, etc.).

rivets

riv·u·let ['rɪvjulɪt] *n.* small stream.

road [rəud] *n.* **1.** specially prepared track, between places, for the use of pedestrians, riders, vehicles, etc.: *on the ~,* travelling (esp. as a commercial traveller or a vagrant); *take the ~,* start a journey; *one for the ~,* (colloq.) final drink before departure. **2.** one's way or route: *in my* (*your, etc.*) ~, in my (etc.) way. **3.** way of getting (*to*): *the ~ to ruin* (*success*); *royal ~ to,* way of attaining (sth.) without trouble. **4.** (usu. pl.) stretch of water near the shore where ships can ride at anchor. '**~-block** *n.* obstruction on a ~ set up by the army or the police to stop or slow down traffic for questioning, etc. '**~-ˌmet·al** *n.* broken stone for making or repairing ~s. '**~·side** *n.* border of a ~. ~ *sign n.* sign giving information to drivers, etc. '**~·stead** *n.* = ~ (4). '**~·way** *n.* (usu. *the ~way*) that part of a ~ used by traffic (contrasted with the footpath or pavement). '**~·works** *n. pl.* construction or repair of ~s. '**~·wor·thy** *adj.* (of motor vehicles, etc.) fit to be used on the ~s; (of persons) fit to travel.

roam [rəum] *v.i. & t.* wander (over or through).

roan [rəun] *adj.* (of animals) with a coat in which the chief colour, esp. brown, is thickly mixed with grey or white. *n.* ~ horse, etc.

roar [rɔː*] *n.* loud, deep sound as of a

lion, the sea, thunder, a person in pain, etc.: ~s *of laughter* (*applause*); *set the table in a* ~, make the company at table laugh loud. *v.i. & t.* **1.** make such sounds: *They* ~*ed with laughter* (*pain*). **2.** shout, say, sing (*out*) (commands, an oath, a song, etc.).

roast [rəʊst] *v.t. & i.* **1.** cook, be cooked, over or in front of a fire or (of meat) in an oven. **2.** heat, be heated: ~ *coffee-beans.* **3.** expose or be exposed to fire or great heat: *She likes to lie in the sun and* ~. *n.* ~ed meat. *attrib. adj.* that has been ~ed: ~ *beef* (*pork*).

rob [rɒb] *v.t.* (-bb-) **1.** deprive (sb.) *of* his property; take property from (a place) unlawfully (and often by force): ~ *sb. of his wallet*; ~ *a bank.* **2.** deprive (sb.) *of* what is due to him: *They* ~*bed him of his inheritance.* ~**ber** *n.* ~**bery** *n.* act of ~bing: *daylight* ~*bery*, charging of excessive prices.

robe [rəʊb] *n.* **1.** long, loose outer garment. **2.** (often pl.) long, loose garment worn as an indication of rank, office, profession, etc.: *the king in his* ~*s of state. v.t. & i.* put a ~ or ~s on.

rob·in ['rɒbɪn] *n.* (also ~ *redbreast*) small bird with a red breast.

ro·bot ['rəʊbɒt] *n.* mechanism made to act like a man; machine-like person.

ro·bust [rəʊ'bʌst] *adj.* vigorous; healthy; (of the mind, etc.) sensible; straightforward.

rock[1] [rɒk] *n.* **1.** (no pl.) solid, stony part of the earth's crust: *a house with a foundation built on* ~. **2.** mass of ~ standing out from the earth's surface or the sea-floor: *as firm as a* ~; *on the* ~*s*, (a) (colloq., of a marriage) likely to break up soon; (b) (colloq.) very short of money; (c) (of drinks) served with ice cubes. **3.** large, detached stone; boulder: ~*s falling down the mountainside.* ~**'bot·tom** *attrib. adj.* (of prices) the lowest. '~**·gar·den,** ~**·ery** ['rɒkərɪ] *n.* (part of a) garden laid out among ~s for growing mountain plants, etc. ~**y** *adj.* (-ier, -iest) full of ~s; hard like ~.

rock[2] [rɒk] *v.t. & i.* **1.** (cause to) sway, swing, etc. backwards and forwards or from side to side: ~ *a baby to sleep.* **2.** dance to ~ music. **3.** shake: *The town was* ~*ed by an earthquake. n.* ~*ing motion.* ~('*n'roll*), (popular dance to) music with a heavy beat. ~**er** *n.* **1.** one of the curved wooden bars on which a ~ing chair or ~ing horse ~s. **2.** (U.S.A.) = ~ing chair. **3.** (Gt. Brit., in the 1960's) leather-jacketed teenager

on a motor bike. **4.** *off one's* ~*er,* (sl.) crazy. '~**·ing-chair** *n.* chair mounted on ~ers. '~**·ing-horse** *n.* wooden horse on ~ers for a child.

rock·et ['rɒkɪt] *n.* tube-shaped case filled with fast-burning material, which launches itself into the air (as a firework, a signal of distress, or a self-propelled projectile, or is used to launch a spacecraft, etc.). *v.i.* go up fast like a ~.

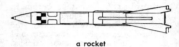

a rocket

rod [rɒd] *n.* **1.** thin, straight piece of wood or metal: *curtain-*~*s*; *a fishing-*~; *piston-*~. **2.** stick used for punishing. **3.** measure of length, $5\frac{1}{2}$ yards (= 5.03 metres).

rode, see *ride* (v.).

ro·dent ['rəʊdənt] *n.* animal (e.g. a rat, rabbit, squirrel) that gnaws things.

ro·deo [rəʊ'deɪəʊ, U.S.A. 'rəʊdɪəʊ] *n.* (pl. ~s) **1.** rounding up of cattle for marking them. **2.** public exhibition of cowboy skills (e.g. catching cattle with ropes, riding untamed horses, etc.).

roe[1] [rəʊ] *n.* **1.** (*hard*) ~, mass of eggs in a female fish. **2.** (*soft*) ~, mass of sperm in a male fish; milt.

roe[2] [rəʊ] *n.* (pl. ~s, collective pl. ~) small kind of deer.

rogue [rəʊg] *n.* rascal. **rogu·ery** ['rəʊgərɪ] *n.* **1.** conduct of a ~. **2.** playful mischief. **rogu·ish** ['rəʊgɪʃ] *adj.* (esp.) playfully mischievous.

rois·ter·er ['rɔɪstərə*] *n.* rough, noisy merry-maker.

role, rôle [rəʊl] *n.* actor's part in a play; person's task or duty in an undertaking.

roll [rəʊl] *v.t. & i.* **1.** (cause to) move along on wheels or by turning over and over: ~ *a barrel. The coin* ~*ed under the table.* **2.** make into the shape of a ball or cylinder: ~ *string into a ball*; ~ *up a map (the carpet)*; ~ *oneself up in a blanket.* **3.** make flat or smooth by pressing with a ~ing cylinder of wood, metal, etc.: ~ *out pastry*; ~*ed gold*, thin coating of gold on another metal. **4.** rock or sway from side to side; walk with a swaying gait: *The ship was* ~*ing in the storm.* **5.** (of surfaces) have long slopes that rise and fall: *miles of* ~*ing country.* **6.** move with a rise and fall: *The waves* ~*ed in to the* *beach.* **7.** come or go in some direction: *The years ⁓ed by.* **8.** (cause to) move from side to side: *His eyes ⁓ed strangely.* **9.** make, utter, be uttered with, long, deep sounds as of thunder: *The thunder ⁓ed in the distance.* **10.** ⁓ *in*, come in large numbers; *be ⁓ing in* (*money*, *etc.*), have plenty of; ⁓ *up*, appear on the scene; join a group. *n.* **1.** sth. made roughly into the shape of a cylinder by being ⁓ed (2) or folded; sth. in this shape, however formed: *a ⁓ of cloth; a man with ⁓s of fat on him.* **2.** ⁓ing (4) movement: *the heavy ⁓ of a ship.* **3.** ⁓ing (9) sound: *a ⁓ of drums.* **4.** official list, esp. of names: *call the ⁓,* read the names to check who is present. **5.** ⁓ (*of bread*), *bread ⁓,* small quantity of bread baked in the shape of a ball. **⁓·er** *n.* **1.** cylinder-shaped object of wood, metal, rubber, etc., usu. part of a machine, for pressing, smoothing, crushing, printing, road-making, etc. **2.** revolving cylinder of wood, metal, etc. over or on which sth. is moved. '⁓·er-skates *n. pl.* skates with four small wheels for use on a smooth floor. '⁓·ing-pin *n.* ⁓er about one foot long used for ⁓ing out dough, etc. '⁓·ing-stock *n.* railway's coaches, wagons, etc. '⁓·neck *n.* long, turtle-necked collar made to be ⁓ed over: (attrib.) *a ⁓-neck pullover.*

rol·lick·ing ['rɒlɪkɪŋ] *adj.* noisy and jolly.

Ro·man ['rəʊmən] *adj.* **1.** of (esp. ancient) Rome: ⁓ *numerals* (e.g. I, II, IV, X = 1, 2, 4, 10). **2.** ⁓ (*Catholic*), of the Church of Rome. *n.* **1.** citizen of ancient Rome. **2.** (pl.) Christians of ancient Rome. **3.** ⁓ Catholic.

ro·mance [rəʊ'mæns] *n.* **1.** story or novel of adventure; love story, esp. one in which the events are quite unlike real life. **2.** real experience, esp. a love affair, considered to be remarkable or worth description: *Their meeting was quite a ⁓.* **ro·man·tic** [rəʊ'mæntɪk] *adj.* **1.** (of persons) having ideas, feelings, etc. remote from experience and real life; imaginative. **2.** of, like, suggesting, ⁓: *romantic scenes* (*tales, lives*). **3.** (in art, literature, music) marked by feeling rather than by intellect (opp. *classic, classical*).

romp [rɒmp] *v.i.* **1.** (esp. of children) play about, esp. running, jumping, and being rather rough. **2.** win, succeed, etc. without apparent effort. *n.* **1.** child fond of ⁓ing. **2.** rough, noisy play. **⁓·er** *n.* (sing. or pl.) loose-fitting garment worn by a child for ⁓ing.

roof [ruːf] *n.* top covering of a building, tent, bus, etc. *raise the ⁓,* (colloq.) (a) make a great noise; (b) become very angry. *v.t.* put a ⁓ on; be a ⁓ for.

rook[1] [rʊk] *n.* large, black bird like a crow. **⁓·ery** *n.* **1.** (group of trees with a) colony of ⁓s. **2.** colony of penguins or seals.

rook[2] [rʊk] *n.* person who cheats when gambling, esp. at cards and dice. *v.t.* **1.** swindle, esp. at cards and dice. **2.** charge (sb.) far too high a price.

rook[3] [rʊk] *n.* piece in chess (also called a *castle*).

room [ruːm] *n.* **1.** one of the separate divisions of a building, enclosed by its floor, ceiling, and walls; (pl.) set of these occupied by one person or family. (Cf. *apartments.*) **2.** (no pl.) space that is or might be occupied, or that is enough for a purpose: *make ⁓ for sth.* (sb.). *Standing ⁓ only.* **3.** (no pl.) scope, opportunity (*for* improvement, etc.). **⁓·ed** *adj. a three-⁓ed house*, a house with three ⁓s. **⁓·y** *adj.* (-*ier, -iest*) having much ⁓ (2) in it.

roost [ruːst] *n.* branch, pole, etc. on which a bird rests, esp. one for hens to sleep or rest on; hen-house, esp. that part of it where fowls sleep. *v.i.* sleep on a ⁓. **⁓·er** *n.* domestic cock.

root[1] [ruːt] *n.* **1.** that part of a plant, tree, etc. that is normally in the soil and that takes water and food from it: *take* (*strike*) ⁓, send down a ⁓; begin to grow; (fig.) become established; ⁓ *and branch,* thoroughly; radically. **2.** (also ⁓-*crop*) plant with a ⁓ used as food (e.g. carrot, turnip, etc.). **3.** that part of a hair, tooth, the tongue, a finger-nail, etc. that is like a ⁓ in function, position, etc. **4.** (fig.) that from which sth. grows; source: *get to the ⁓ of the trouble.* **5.** (gram.) (part of a) word on which other forms of that word are based. **6.** (math.) quantity that, when multiplied by itself a certain number of times, produces a given quantity: *4 is the square ⁓ of 16. v.t. & i.* **1.** (of plants, cuttings, etc.) (cause to) send out ⁓s and begin to grow. **2.** ⁓ *sth. up* (*out*), pull or dig up together with the ⁓s; (fig.) get rid of completely. **3.** cause to stand fixed and unmoving: *⁓ed to the spot.* **4.** (usu. in p.p.) (of ideas, principles, etc.) firmly established.

root[2] [ruːt] *v.i. & t.* **1.** (of pigs, etc.) turn up the ground with the snout, etc. in search of food. **2.** (of persons) search for; turn things over when searching: ⁓ (*sth.*) *out,* find by searching.

rope [rəʊp] *n.* **1.** (piece or length of) thick, strong cord or wire made by twisting finer cords or wires together: *the* ~, noose for hanging a condemned person; *the* ~*s,* (a) the cords used to enclose a prize-ring, etc.; (b) the special techniques or procedures involved: *know the* ~*s,* know how to set about some activity or business. **2.** number of things twisted together or threaded on a line together: *a* ~ *of onions* (*pearls*). *v.t.* **1.** tie (*up, together*) with ~. **2.** enclose, mark *off,* with a rope. **3.** ~ *sb. in,* (fig.) get him to help in some activity.

ro·sa·ry [ˈrəʊzərɪ] *n.* **1.** form of prayer in the Roman Catholic Church. **2.** string of beads for keeping count of these prayers. **3.** rose-garden.

rose[1], see **rise** (v.).

rose[2] [rəʊz] *n.* **1.** sweet-smelling flower (white, red, yellow, pink), growing on a bush with thorny stems.

a rose

2. pinkish-red colour. *see things through* ~*-coloured spectacles,* see them as bright and hopeful. **3.** sth. shaped like or suggesting a ~. **ro·sette** [rəʊˈzet] *n.* ~-shaped ornament. '~·**wood** *n.* (no pl.) hard, dark-red wood. **rosy** [ˈrəʊzɪ] *adj.* (-ier, -iest) **1.** (esp. of a person's cheeks) bright; reddish. **2.** (fig.) bright: *a rosy future.*

ros·trum [ˈrɒstrəm] *n.* (pl. ~*s,-tra* [-trə]) platform or pulpit for public speaking.

rot [rɒt] *v.i. & t.* (-tt-) **1.** go bad by natural process: *fruit* ~*ting on the ground.* **2.** (fig., of society, etc.) gradually perish by lack of vigour or activity; (of prisoners, etc.) waste away. **3.** cause to decay; make ~ten. **4.** (sl.) talk nonsense; make fun (of). *n.* (no pl.) **1.** decay; condition of being bad: *a tree affected by* ~. **2.** (sl.) nonsense: *Don't talk* ~*!* ~·**ten** [ˈrɒtn] *adj.* **1.** decayed; having ~ted: ~*ten eggs.* **2.** (sl.) bad; disagreeable.

ro·ta·ry [ˈrəʊtərɪ] *adj.* **1.** (of motion) round a central point. **2.** (of an engine) working by ~ motion.

ro·tate [rəʊˈteɪt] *v.t. & i.* **1.** (cause to) move round a central point. **2.** (cause to) take turns or come in succession. **ro·ta·tion** [rəʊˈteɪʃn] *n.* **1.** (no pl.) rotating or being ~d. **2.** complete turning. **3.** regular recurrence of things or events in succession: *in rotation,* in turn.

ro·tor [ˈrəʊtə*] *n.* rotating blade(s) (3) of a helicopter; rotary part of a machine.

rot·ten, see **rot.**

ro·tund [rəʊˈtʌnd] *adj.* **1.** (of a person, his face) round and fat. **2.** (of the voice) rich and deep. **ro·tun·di·ty** [rəʊˈtʌndətɪ] *n.* **ro·tun·da** [rəʊˈtʌndə] *n.* round building, esp. one with a dome.

rouge [ruːʒ] *n.* red substance for colouring the cheeks or lips. *v.i. & t.* put ~ on (the face).

rough [rʌf] *adj.* **1.** not level, smooth, or polished; of irregular surface; (of roads, etc.) not easy to walk or ride on. **2.** not calm or gentle; moving or acting violently: ~ *children* (*behaviour*); *a* ~ *sea.* **3.** made or done without attention to detail, esp. as a first attempt: *a* ~ *sketch* (*translation*). **4.** (of sounds) harsh: *in a* ~ *voice.* **5.** without comfort or conveniences: *the* ~ *life of an explorer.* *n.* **1.** ~ *state;* ~ *ground;* ~ *surface;* unpleasantness; hardship: *take the* ~ *with the smooth,* accept the unpleasant things as well as the pleasant things; *in the* ~, in an unfinished state. **2.** rowdy; hooligan. *v.t.* **1.** make ~: ~ (*hair, etc.*) *up,* make untidy; ~ *sb. up,* (sl.) attack him violently. **2.** ~ *sth. out,* make a ~ (3) plan or outline. **3.** ~ *it,* do without the usual comforts of life (e.g. while camping). *adv.* in a ~ manner: *treat sb.* ~; *play* ~. ~-**and**-**'ready** *adj.* good enough for ordinary purposes; lacking finish and refinement. '~·**cast** *n.* plaster containing pebbles or gravel, applied to outside walls. ~·**en** *v.t. & i.* make or become ~. ~·'**hew** *v.t.* shape ~*ly:* ~*-hewn,* (fig., of persons) lacking polish; uncultivated. ~·**ly** *adv.* **1.** in a ~ manner. **2.** approximately; about: *It will cost* ~*ly £25.* ~·**shod** [ˈrʌfʃɒd] *adj.* (of a horse) with shoes provided with special nails to prevent slipping: *ride* ~*shod over,* (fig.) treat harshly or contemptuously.

rou·lette [ruːˈlet] *n.* (no pl.) gambling game played with a revolving wheel or disc.

round [raʊnd] *adj.* **1.** shaped like a circle or ball: *a* ~ *table* (*window, head*). **2.** done with or involving circular motion: *a* ~ *trip,* (a) a circular trip;

b) (U.S.A.) a trip to a certain place nd back again by the same route. **3.** omplete; full; entire: ~ *numbers*, umbers given without odd units; ~ *igures*, figures given as an estimate; *~ dozen; a good, ~ sum (of money)*, a onsiderable sum. *n.* **1.** sth. ~; whole lice of bread; sandwich made from whole slices of bread. **2.** rung of a adder. **3.** regular series or succession r distribution (of duties, pleasures, tc.): *the daily ~*, the ordinary occupaions of the day; *the postman's ~*; *go make)* one's *~s*, make one's usual isits, esp. of inspection; *go the ~(s)*, of news, etc.) be passed on. **4.** (amount f ammunition needed for firing a) ingle shot: *a ~ of ammunition*; *have nly five ~s left*. **5.** one stage in a ompetition: *a fight (boxing-match) of en ~s*. **6.** allowance of sth. distributed r measured out; one of a set or series: *ay for a ~ of drinks*; *~ after ~ of heers*. *adv.* **1.** in a circle or in a half-ircle: *look ~* (i.e. behind); *all the ear ~*, throughout the year. **2.** (so as o be) in a circle: *a crowd soon gathered ~*. **3.** from one (person, place, point, tc.) to another: *Hand these papers ~*. *ot enough food to go ~* (i.e. not enough or everyone). **4.** by a longer route: *Ve came the long way ~* (i.e. not by the lirect route). **5.** to or from a place where sb. is or will be: *Come ~ and see ne some time*. *prep.* **1.** (expressing poition) on all sides of; so as to encircle r enclose: *a town with a wall ~ it*. **2.** expressing movement) in a circular ath that comes back to the starting-oint): *work ~ the clock* (all day and ll night); *fly ~ the world*. **3.** so as to ollow the curving line of: *follow sb. ~ a corner*. **4.** in all directions from or vith regard to: *the fields ~ the village*. *She looked ~ the room*. *v.t. & i.* **1.** nake or become ~: *stones ~ed by the ction of water*. **2.** go ~: *~ a corner*. **3.** *~ sth. off*, make it complete; add a uitable finish; *~ up* (esp. animals), get hem together; *~ up* (*down*) (a figure, rice, etc.), bring it to a whole number; *~ (up)on* sb., turn on him and attack

a roundabout (2)

him (in words or action). **~-about** ['raʊndəbaʊt] *adj.* not going or coming by, or using the shortest or most direct way: *I heard the news in a ~about way*. *n.* **1.** merry-go-round. **2.** circular enclosure at a road junction, causing traffic to go ~ instead of across. **~·ly** *adv.* **1.** with vigour. **2.** bluntly: *tell sb. ~ly that he is behaving badly*. '**~·s·man** *n.* tradesman or his employee going ~ (to customers' houses) to ask for orders and to deliver goods.

rouse [raʊz] *v.t. & i.* **1.** wake (*up*). **2.** cause (sb.) to be more active, interested, etc.: *~ sb. to action*; *~d to anger* (made angry) *by insults*; *rousing cheers*.

rout[1] [raʊt] *v.t. & n.* (cause) complete defeat and disorderly flight.

rout[2] [raʊt] *v.t. & i.* *~ sb. out*, force him out (of bed, etc.).

route [ruːt] *n.* way taken or planned from one place to another. *~ **march** n.* march made by soldiers in training.

rou·tine [ruːˈtiːn] *n.* fixed and regular way of doing things: *a matter of ~*; *the ~* (i.e. usual) *procedure*.

rove [rəʊv] *v.i.* roam; wander. **rov·er** *n.*

row[1] [rəʊ] *n.* line of persons or things: *a ~ of houses*; (esp.) line of seats: *sitting in the front ~*.

row[2] [rəʊ] *v.t. & i.* move (a boat) by using oars; carry or take (sb. or sth.) in a boat with oars: *~ sb. across a river*. *n.* journey or outing in a ~ing-boat: *go for a ~*. *~·er n.* person who ~s a boat. '**~(·ing)-boat** *n.* boat moved by the use of oars. *~·lock* ['rɒlək] *n.* pivot for an oar on the side of a boat.

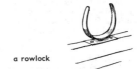

a rowlock

row[3] [raʊ] *n.* (colloq.) **1.** noisy or violent argument or quarrel: *have a ~ with one's neighbours*. **2.** (no pl.) uproar; noisy disturbance. **3.** instance of being reprimanded: *get into a ~ for being late at the office*.

row·dy ['raʊdɪ] *adj.* (-*ier*, -*iest*) rough and noisy. *n.* ~ person. **row·di·ly** *adv.* **row·di·ness**, **~ism** *ns.* (no pl.) ~ behaviour.

roy·al ['rɔɪəl] *adj.* of, like, suitable for, supported by, belonging to the family of, a king or queen: *His R~ Highness*; *the R~ Navy*. *~·ly adv.* **~·ist** *n.* supporter of a king or queen as an institution or of the ~ side in a civil war, etc. **~ty** *n.* **1.** (no pl.) ~ persons: *in the presence of ~ty.* **2.** (no pl.) position, dignity, power, etc. of a ~ person. **3.** payment of money by a mining or oil company to the owner of land: *oil ~ties;* sum (to be) paid to the owner of a copyright or patent.

rub [rʌb] *v.t. & i.* (-bb-) **1.** move (one thing) backwards and forwards on the surface of (another): ~ *one's hands with soap;* ~ *one's hands together;* ~ *oil on the skin;* ~ *sth. out* (*off*), remove (esp. marks) by ~bing; ~ *shoulders with* (*people*), meet and mix with. **2.** dry, clean, polish, bring a surface to a certain condition, by ~bing: ~ *up the silver spoons;* ~ *up your French,* (fig.) freshen your knowledge of it. **3.** slide (sth.) *against, in, on, over,* sth. with friction: *The tyre is ~bing against the kerbstone.* *n.* **1.** act of ~bing. **2.** difficulty; cause of trouble: *there's the ~.*

rub·ber[1] ['rʌbə*] *n.* **1.** (no pl.) elastic substance made from the juice of certain trees or made chemically and used for making tyres, balls, etc. **2.** piece of ~ material for rubbing out pencil-marks. **3.** person or thing that rubs.

rub·ber[2] ['rʌbə*] *n.* (cards) three successive games between the same sides: *win the ~,* win two games in succession or two out of three.

rub·bish ['rʌbɪʃ] *n.* **1.** waste material; things thrown away or destroyed as worthless. **2.** nonsense.

rub·ble ['rʌbl] *n.* (no pl.) bits of broken stone, rock, or brickwork.

ru·bi·cund ['ru:bɪkənd] *adj.* (of a person's face) ruddy.

ru·bric ['ru:brɪk] *n.* title or heading printed in red or special type, esp. a direction given in a prayer-book.

ru·by ['ru:bɪ] *n.* red jewel; deep-red colour. *adj.* (-ier, -iest) deep-red.

ruck[1] [rʌk] *n. the* (*common*) ~, ordinary, commonplace people or things.

ruck[2] [rʌk] *n.* irregular fold or crease (esp. in cloth). *v.t. & i.* (often ~ *up*) make into ~s; be pulled into ~s.

ruck·sack ['rʌksæk] *n.* canvas bag strapped on one's back.

ruc·tion ['rʌkʃn] *n.* (colloq.) quarrel; disturbance; row[3].

rud·der ['rʌdə*] *n.* flat, broad piece of wood or metal hinged on the stern of a boat or ship, or on the rear of an aeroplane, for steering.

rud·dy ['rʌdɪ] *adj.* (-ier, -iest) (of the face) red, as showing good health: ~ *cheeks.*

rude [ru:d] *adj.* (~r, ~st) **1.** (of a person, his behaviour, speech, etc.) in polite; not showing respect or con sideration. **2.** startling; violent; roug get a ~ shock. **3.** primitive; withou refinement: *our ~ forefathers.* roughly made; simple: *the ~ ornamen made by the Saxons.* **~·ly** *adv.* **~·ne** *n.* (no pl.)

ru·di·ment ['ru:dɪmənt] *n.* **1.** (p first steps or stages (of an art science). **2.** imperfect beginning ~ sth. that will develop or might, und different conditions, have develope imperfectly developed part or orga **ru·di·men·ta·ry** [,ru:dɪ'mentərɪ] *ad* **1.** elementary. **2.** undeveloped; havir stopped at an early stage.

rue [ru:] *v.t.* repent of; think of wit sadness or regret. **~·ful** *adj.* expressin or causing (mock) sorrow or compa sion.

ruff [rʌf] *n.* **1.** ring of differently co oured or marked feathers round bird's neck, or of hair round an an mal's neck. **2.** wide, stiff frill worn a a collar in the 16th century.

ruf·fi·an ['rʌfjən] *n.* violent, cruel ma

ruf·fle ['rʌfl] *v.t. & i.* disturb th peace, calm, or smoothness of: *easi ~d,* easily annoyed or put out of ten per. *n.* strip of material gathered int folds; frill used to ornament a dres

rug [rʌg] *n.* **1.** floor mat of thic material. **2.** thick, usu. woollen, cove ing or wrap: *a travelling~.*

Rug·by ['rʌgbɪ] *n.* (no pl.) ~ *footbal* form of football played by two team of usu. fifteen players using an ova shaped ball which may be kicked carried.

rug·ged ['rʌgɪd] *adj.* **1.** rough; ur even; rocky: *a ~ coast.* **2.** irregula wrinkled: ~ *features.* **3.** rough, bi kindly and honest: *a ~ old peasant' manners.*

rug·ger ['rʌgə*] *n.* (no pl.) (sl.) Rugb football.

ru·in ['ruɪn] *n.* **1.** (no pl.) destructio overthrow; serious damage: *the ~ c my hopes; bring sb. or sth. to ~.* **2.** (pl.) cause of this: *Gambling was his ~* **3.** (no pl.) state of being decaye destroyed, collapsed: *The church ha fallen into ~.* **4.** sth., esp. a building that has fallen to pieces: *The old for is now only a ~. The building is in ~ v.t.* cause the ~ of: *crops ~ed by th storm; be ~ed,* have lost one's property position, etc. **ru·i·na·tion** [ruɪ'neɪʃ *n.* (no pl.) being ~ed; bringing to **~·ous** *adj.* causing ~; in ~s.

rule [ru:l] *n.* **1.** law or custom that guides or controls behaviour or action; decision made by an organization, etc. about what must or must not be done: *obey the ~s of the game*; *the ~(s) of the road*, custom regulating the side to be taken by vehicles, ships, etc. when meeting or passing each other; *work to ~*, follow the ~s of one's occupation pedantically to reduce efficiency, usu. as a protest. **2.** sth. that is usually done; habit: *Make it a ~ to read one English book a week. as a ~*, usually; more often than not. **3.** (no pl.) government; authority: *the ~ of the people*; *under French ~*. **4.** strip of wood, metal, etc., used to measure: *a foot-~* (12 inches long). *v.t. & i.* **1.** govern; have authority (*over*): *~ the country*; *~ over a large empire.* **2.** give as a decision (*that*): *~ sth. out*, declare that it cannot be considered, etc. **3.** make (a line or lines) on paper with a ~r; make parallel lines on (paper) with a ~r: *~ sth. off*, separate it by ruling a line.
rul·er *n.* **1.** person who ~s (1). **2.** straight strip of wood, metal, etc., used for drawing straight lines. **rul·ing** *adj.* predominant; prevalent. *n.* (esp.) decision made by sb. in authority (e.g. a judge).
rum[1] [rʌm] *n.* (no pl.) alcoholic drink made from sugar-cane juice.
rum[2] [rʌm] *adj.* (-*mm*-) (sl.) queer; odd.
rum·ble ['rʌmbl] *v.i. & n.* (make a) deep, heavy, continuous sound: *thunder (gun-fire) rumbling in the distance.*
ru·mi·nant ['ru:mɪnənt] *n. & adj.* (animal) that chews the cud (e.g. cows, deer, etc.). **ru·mi·nate** ['ru:mɪneɪt] *v.i.* **1.** turn over in the mind; meditate. **2.** (of animals) chew the cud.
rum·mage ['rʌmɪdʒ] *v.i. & t.* turn things over, move things about, while looking for sth.: *~ in a drawer*; *~ through old papers. ~ sale n.* sale of old articles for charity; jumble sale.
ru·mour (U.S.A. **ru·mor**) ['ru:mə*] *n.* hearsay: *according to ~. v.t.* report by way of ~: *It is ~ed that ...*
rump [rʌmp] *n.* animal's buttocks.
rum·ple ['rʌmpl] *v.t.* crease; crumple.
rum·pus ['rʌmpəs] *n.* (no pl.) (sl.) disturbance; noise; uproar.
run[1] [rʌn] *v.i. & t.* (-*nn*-; p.t. **ran** [ræn], p.p. **~**) **1.** (of men and animals) move with quick steps, faster than when walking. **2.** (of vehicles) go along; make a journey; (of public conveyances, e.g. buses, etc.) ply (2): *The buses ~ every ten minutes.* **3.** (of machines, etc.) keep going; be in action; be in

working order: *leave the engine ~ning.* **4.** (of liquids) flow; cause to flow: *leave the water (the tap) ~ning.* **5.** become; get: *~ into debt*; *~ short of money*; *supplies ~ning low.* **6.** (cause to) pass or move quickly or lightly (over, through, etc.): *A shiver ran down his spine. Doubts kept ~ning through his mind. He ran his fingers over the keys of the piano. She ran a comb through her hair. He ran his eyes over the page.* **7.** (of roads, lines, etc.) go; extend: *The road ~s due north. Shelves ran round two walls.* **8.** (of colours in a material) spread when wet: *Will the dye ~ when the blouse is washed?* **9.** force; cause (sth.) to go (against, into, through): *~ a splinter into one's finger*; *~ one's head against a wall.* **10.** control, manage (a business, a theatre, the home). **11.** (of a play in the theatre) continue to be performed; (of an agreement) continue in force; (of the sale of books) reach: *The book ran into (through) six editions.* **12.** expose oneself to; be open to: *~ a risk*, take the chance. **13.** have a tendency or common characteristic: *Short-sightedness ~s in the family.* **14.** get (goods) into a country illegally: *engaged in ~ning contraband.* **15.** be a candidate (*for*). (Cf. **stand for**.) **16.** cause to ~ (a horse in a race). **17.** (of a series of words, musical notes) have, be in, a certain order: *How does the verse ~?* **18.** (of woven or knitted materials) become unwoven; drop stitches. **19.** be on the average; tend to be: *prices ~ning high.* **20.** (with advs. & preps.): *~ across (sb. or sth.)*, meet or find by chance; *~ after (sb.)*, try to catch; *~ away*, (esp.) try to escape; leave; *~ away with* (a lot of money, etc.), use it up; *~ down*, (of a clock, etc.) stop because the spring is unwound; *be ~ down*, (of a person) be tired, exhausted; *~ (sb.) down*, say unkind things about him; *~ sb. in*, (of the police) arrest him and take him into custody; *~ sth. in*, (esp. the engine of a car) bring it into good working order by carefully ~ning it; *~ into*, collide with; meet unexpectedly; *~ on*, be joined together; continue; talk continuously; *~ out (of)*, become exhausted; have no more; *~ over*, (of a vessel or its contents) overflow; *~ over (sb.)*, knock down and pass over: *The child was ~ over by a bus. ~ up (a flag)*, raise; *~ up (a bill, etc.)*, let (the bill, etc.) grow larger. '**~·away** *n.* person who ~s away. *adj.* (horse, person, etc.) ~ning away: *a ~away slave.* **~·ner** *n.* **1.** person, animal, etc. that ~s. **2.** (in compounds) smuggler: *gun-~ners.* **3.** messenger. **4.** part on which sth. slides: *the ~ners of a sledge.* **5.** stem coming from a plant and taking root: *strawberry ~ners.* **6.** long piece of cloth (for a sideboard, etc.); long piece of carpet. **,~·ner-'up** *n.* person taking the second place in a competition. **,~·ning** *adj.* **1.** done, made, carried on, while ~ning: *a ~ning jump.* **2.** continuous; uninterrupted: *a ~ning commentary,* a description given while the event is taking place. **3.** (after a plural noun) in succession: *five times (nights) ~ning.* **4.** (of water) flowing. **5.** (of sores) with liquid or pus coming out. *n.* in (*out of*) *the ~ning,* having (not having) a chance of success in a race, etc.; *make the ~ning,* be the leading ~ner; set the pace. **run²** [rʌn] *n.* **1.** act of ~ning; outing or journey in a car, train, etc.: *go for a ~; on the ~,* ~ning away; continuously busy. **2.** (usu. large, enclosed) space for domestic animals: *a chicken (cattle) ~.* **3.** quick fall: *prices coming down with a ~.* **4.** series of performances: *The play had a ~ of six months.* **5.** unit of score in cricket and baseball. **6.** period; succession: *a ~ of ill luck; in the long ~,* finally. **7.** permission to make free use (*of*): *have (give sb.) the ~ of the house.* **8.** ~ *on,* demand for: *a ~ on the bank,* a rush by many people to withdraw money. **9.** common, average, ordinary, type or class: *the common ~ of mankind,* ordinary, average people. **10.** general direction or trend: *the ~ of events.* **11.** (music) series of notes sung or played quickly and in the order of the scale. **12.** (U.S.A.) = ladder (2). **'~·way** *n.* (esp.) track on which aircraft take off and land.

rung¹, see *ring²* (v.).

rung² [rʌŋ] *n.* cross-piece forming a step in a ladder or joining the legs of a chair to strengthen it.

rup·ture ['rʌptʃə*] *n.* act of breaking apart or bursting; (fig.) ending of friendly relations. *v.t. & i.* break (e.g a blood-vessel); end (a connection, etc.).

ru·ral ['ruərəl] *adj.* in, of, characteristic of, suitable for, the country: ~ *life* (*customs*).

ruse [ruːz] *n.* trick; deceitful way of doing or getting sth.

rush¹ [rʌʃ] *v.t. & i.* **1.** (cause to) go or come with violence or speed: *~ing fresh troops to the front; ~ing out of school.* **2.** act quickly and without enough thought; force (sb.) into hasty action. **3.** capture by a sudden attack; get through, over, into, etc. by pressing eagerly forward: ~ *the gates of the sports ground.* *n.* **1.** rapid, headlong movement; sudden advance: *swept away by the ~ of the flood.* **2.** sudden demand; sudden or intense activity: *the ~-hour* (when, in a big town, everyone is travelling to or from work): (attrib.) *be caught in the ~-hour traffic.*

rush² [rʌʃ] *n.* (tall stem of a) marsh plant.

rusk [rʌsk] *n.* piece of bread baked hard and crisp; kind of crisp biscuit.

rus·set ['rʌsɪt] *n.* **1.** (no pl.) reddish brown. **2.** apple with rough, ~-coloured skin. *adj.* reddish-brown.

Rus·sian ['rʌʃən] *n. & adj.* (native, inhabitant, or language) of Russia.

rust [rʌst] *n.* (no pl.) reddish-brown coating formed on iron by the action of water and air. *v.t. & i.* (cause to) become covered with ~; (fig.) become poor in quality because not used. ~**y** *adj.* (*-ier, -iest*) covered with ~; (fig., of a person) out of practice (3); (fig.) impaired by neglect or disuse.

rus·tic ['rʌstɪk] *adj.* **1.** characteristic of country people (contrasted with smart city people); simple; artless; unsophisticated. **2.** rough; unrefined; boorish. **3.** of rude or country workmanship. *n.* peasant; simple country person.

rus·tle ['rʌsl] *n.* (no pl.) gentle, light sound (as of dry leaves moved by a breeze). *v.t. & i.* (cause to) make this sound; move with such a sound.

rut [rʌt] *n.* **1.** line or track made by wheel(s) in soft ground. **2.** (fig.) fixed practice (2); regular course; monotonous routine: *get into a ~,* get into a fixed way of living so that it becomes difficult to change. *v.t.* (*-tt-*) (esp. in p.p.) form ~s (1) in: *the ~ted surface of a road.*

ruth·less ['ruːθlɪs] *adj.* cruel; without pity; showing no mercy.

rye [raɪ] *n.* (no pl.) (plant with) grain used for making flour and as animal fodder.

S

Sab·bath ['sæbəθ] *n.* weekly day of rest, Saturday for Jews, Sunday for Christians.

sa·ble ['seɪbl] *n.* (valuable fur of a) small, dark-coated animal. *adj.* (liter.) black.

sab·o·tage ['sæbətɑːʒ] *n.* wilful damaging of machinery, materials, etc. during an industrial or political dispute, or during war. *v.t.* commit ~ on; wreck (a plan, etc.). **sab·o·teur** [,sæbə-'tɜː*] *n.* person who commits ~.

sa·bre (U.S.A. **sa·ber**) ['seɪbə*] *n.* heavy cavalry sword with a curved blade.

sa·chet ['sæʃeɪ] *n.* small, perfumed bag, used to scent clothes, etc.

sack[1] [sæk] *n.* 1. large bag of strong material (for heavy goods, e.g. coal, flour, potatoes). 2. quantity held by a ~. *v.t.* put (things) into ~s. '**~cloth** *n.* (no pl.) coarse material of flax or hemp: *in ~cloth and ashes*, (fig.) showing regret and grief. ~**ing** *n.* ~cloth.

sack[2] [sæk] *v.t.* (colloq.) dismiss (sb.) from employment. *n.* (colloq.) dismissal: *get the ~*, be dismissed; *give sb. the ~*, dismiss him.

sack[3] [sæk] *v.t.* rob, plunder violently (a town, etc. captured in war). *n.* (usu. no pl.) act of plundering (a captured town, etc.): *the ~ of Rome.*

sac·ra·ment ['sækrəmənt] *n.* solemn religious ceremony in the Christian Church (e.g. baptism, marriage); (esp.) *the ~, the Blessed or Holy S~,* Holy Communion. **sac·ra·men·tal** [,sækrə'mentl] *adj.* of a ~: *the ~al wine.*

sa·cred ['seɪkrɪd] *adj.* 1. of God; connected with religion: *a ~ building* (e.g. a church); ~ *music.* 2. solemn: *a ~ promise.* 3. (to be) treated with great respect or reverence: *the ~ cows of India. Nothing is ~ to them,* they respect nothing. ~**ly** *adv.* ~**ness** *n.* (no pl.).

sac·ri·fice ['sækrɪfaɪs] *n.* 1. offering of sth. precious to a god; the thing offered: *the ~ of an ox to Jupiter.* 2. giving up of sth. of value to oneself for a special purpose or to benefit sb.

else: *parents who make ~s* (go without things) *in order to educate their children.* 3. sth. given up in this way. 4. sell sth. at a ~, sell it below its true value. *v.t. & i.* make a ~; give up as a ~ (2): *He ~d his life to save the child from drowning.* **sac·ri·fi·cial** [,sækrɪ-'fɪʃl] *adj.* of, like, a ~.

sac·ri·lege ['sækrɪlɪdʒ] *n.* (no pl.) disrespectful treatment of, injury to, what should be sacred. **sac·ri·le·gious** [,sækrɪ'lɪdʒəs] *adj.*

sac·ro·sanct ['sækrəusæŋkt] *adj.* (to be) protected from all harm, because sacred or holy.

sad [sæd] *adj.* (-dd-) unhappy; causing unhappy feelings. ~**ly** *adv.* ~**ness** *n.* (no pl.). ~**den** ['sædn] *v.t. & i.* make or become sad.

sad·dle ['sædl] *n.* 1. leather seat for a rider on a horse or bicycle. 2. line or ridge of high land rising at each end to a high point. *v.t.* 1. put a ~ on (a horse). 2. put a heavy responsibility on (sb.): *~d with big debts.* '**~bag** *n.* one of a pair of bags laid over a horse's back; small bag (e.g. for tools) hung on a bicycle ~. ~**r** *n.* maker of ~s and leather goods for horses.

sa·dism ['seɪdɪzəm] *n.* enjoyment of cruelty; cruelty inflicted for pleasure. **sa·dist** *n.* person who gets pleasure from cruelty. **sa·dis·tic** [sə'dɪstɪk] *adj.*

sa·fa·ri [sə'fɑːrɪ] *n.* overland journey or (esp. hunting) expedition or organized tour to game reserves (for people on holiday), esp. in East and Central Africa: *go on ~; ~ park,* area where wild animals (e.g. lions) are kept in the open for viewing.

safe [seɪf] *adj.* (~r, ~st) 1. ~ *(from),* free from, protected from, danger. 2. unhurt or undamaged: ~ *and sound.* 3. not causing or likely to cause harm or danger: *travelling at a ~ speed.* 4. cautious; not taking risks: *a ~ driver; on the ~ side,* with more precaution than may be necessary. *n.* 1. metal chest, with a strong lock, for keeping valuables in. 2. cool, airy cupboard

for food: *a meat-~.* **~ con·duct** *n.*
(document giving the) right to visit
or pass through a dangerous area, esp.
in time of war. '**~·guard** *n.* something
that gives protection or prevents harm.
v.t. protect. **~ keep·ing** *n.* (no pl.)
care; keeping ~. **~·ly** *adv.*

safe·ty ['seɪftɪ] *n.* (no pl.) being safe;
freedom from danger: *play for ~*, take
no risks; *in ~*, safely; *~-glass*, glass that
does not splinter when broken; *~
match*, match that ignites only when
rubbed on a specially prepared surface; *~-pin*, pin with a guard (6) for
the point; *~ razor*, razor with a guard
(6) to prevent the blade (1) from cutting the skin; *~-valve*, valve that re-
leases pressure when it becomes too
great; (fig.) way of releasing feelings
of anger, etc. harmlessly.

sag [sæg] *v.i.* (*-gg-*) **1.** sink or curve
down in the middle under weight or
pressure: *a ~ging roof.* **2.** hang down
unevenly; hang sideways. *n.* (degree
of) ~ging.

sa·ga ['sɑːgə] *n.* **1.** old story of heroic
deeds, esp. of Icelandic or Norwegian
heroes. **2.** series of connected books,
esp. novels, giving the history of a
family, etc.: '*The Forsyte S.~*' by *John
Galsworthy.*

sa·ga·cious [sə'geɪʃəs] *adj.* showing
wisdom, common sense, or (of animals) intelligence. **sa·gac·i·ty** [sə-
'gæsətɪ] *n.* (no pl.) sound judgement.

sage[1] [seɪdʒ] *adj.* (*~r, ~st*) wise. *n.* wise
man; man who is believed to be wise.
~·ly *adv.*

sage[2] [seɪdʒ] *n.* (no pl.) garden plant
with grey-green leaves, used to flavour
food.

sa·go ['seɪgəʊ] *n.* (no pl.) starchy food,
in the form of hard, white grains,
made from the pith of certain palm-
trees.

sa·hib ['sɑːb] *n.* (Indian title) sir;
gentleman.

said, see *say* (v.).

sail [seɪl] *n.* **1.** sheet of canvas spread
to catch the wind and move a boat or
ship forward: *under ~*, with *~s* spread;
in full ~, with all *~s* spread; *set ~*, begin a voyage. **2.** set of boards attached
to the arm of a windmill to catch the
wind. **3.** (rarely pl.) (short) excursion
on water for pleasure: *go for a ~.* **4.**
(pl. *~*) *~ing-ship: a fleet of fifty ~.*
v.i. & t. **1.** move forward across the
sea, a lake, etc. by means of a *~* or *~s*
or engine-power. **2.** begin a voyage.
3. voyage across or on: *~ the Pacific.*
4. control (a boat). **5.** (of birds, clouds,

the moon) move smoothly like a ship
with *~s.* '**~·boat** (U.S.A.). '**~·ing-boat**
ns. boat propelled by *~s.* '**~·ing-ship**,
'**~·ing-,ves·sel** *ns.* (opp. *steamer*) ship
propelled by *~s.* **~·or** *n.* **1.** seaman;
member of a ship's crew. **2.** *a bad
(good) ~or*, a person (not) usually seasick in rough weather.

saint [seɪnt, sənt, sɪnt, snt] *n.* **1.** holy
person. **2.** person declared by the
Church to have won by his holy living
on earth a place in Heaven. **~·ed** *adj.*
declared to be, regarded as, a *~.* **~·ly**
adj. (*-ier, -iest*) very holy or good;
like a *~.* **~·li·ness** *n.* (no pl.).

saith [seθ] old form of *says.*

sake [seɪk] *n. for the ~ of, for my (your,
the country's, etc.) ~*, for the welfare
or interest of; because of an interest in
or desire for: *be patient for the ~ of
peace.*

sal·able, see *saleable.*

sal·ad ['sæləd] *n.* **1.** uncooked (and
usu. green) vegetables (lettuce, onion,
celery, etc.) prepared as food: *~-dress-
ing*, mixture of oil, vinegar, cream, etc.
used with *~s.* **2.** mixture of different
kinds of cold food prepared with
fruits or vegetables and a *~-dressing*:
fish ~; chicken ~. **3.** *fruit ~*, mixed
sliced fruits. **4.** (no pl.) lettuce, endive,
etc. suitable for eating raw.

sal·a·ry ['sælərɪ] *n.* (usu. monthly or
quarterly) payment for regular employment on a yearly basis: *a ~ of
£2,100 per annum.* (Cf. *weekly wage.*)
sal·a·ried *adj.* receiving a *~.*

sale [seɪl] *n.* **1.** (no pl.) exchange of
goods or property for money; act of
selling sth.: *on (for) ~*, offered for purchase. **2.** instance of selling sth. **3.**
offering of goods at low prices for a
period (to get rid of old stock, etc.):
the winter (summer) ~. **4.** occasion
when goods or property are put up
for *~ by auction.* **~·able, sal·able**
['seɪləbl] *adj.* suitable for selling;
likely to sell. '**~s·man**, '**~s·wom·an**
ns. man, woman, selling goods in a
shop or (on behalf of wholesalers) to
shopkeepers. '**~s·man·ship** *n.* (no pl.)
skill in selling goods.

sa·lient ['seɪlɪənt] *adj.* outstanding;
easily noticed: *the ~ points of a speech.*
n. forward wedge driven into the
enemy's battle front.

sa·line ['seɪlaɪn] *adj.* containing salt.

sa·li·va [sə'laɪvə] *n.* (no pl.) natural
liquid present in the mouth; spittle.

sal·low ['sæləʊ] *adj.* (of the skin) of an
unhealthy yellow colour.

sal·ly ['sælɪ] *n.* **1.** sudden breaking-out

by soldiers who are surrounded by the enemy: *make a successful ~*. **2.** witty remark. *v.i.* **1.** make a ~ (1). **2.** ~ *forth* (*out*) go out (on a journey, for a walk).

salm·on ['sæmən] *n.* (pl. usu. ~) large fish valued for food; the colour of ~ flesh, orange-pink.

sa·lon ['sælɔ̃:ŋ] *n.* **1.** large room for entertaining guests. **2.** stylish business establishment or shop: *a beauty-~*.

sa·loon [sə'luːn] *n.* **1.** room for social use in a ship, public house, etc.: *the ship's dining-~*; *the ~ bar* (Gt. Brit., for drinks in a hotel, etc.). **2.** (Gt. Brit.) public room(s) for a specified purpose: *a billiard-(hairdressing-, shooting-)~*. **3.** (U.S.A.) place where alcoholic drinks are bought and drunk; bar (8). (Cf. *pub(lic house)*.) **4.** ~ (*car*), (U.S.A. *sedan*) motor car with wholly enclosed seating space for 4 — 7 passengers.

salt [sɔːlt] *n.* **1.** (no pl.) white substance obtained from mines, present in sea-water, used to flavour and preserve food: *~-cellar* ['sɔːlt,selə*]; vessel containing ~ for table use. *take (a statement) with a grain of ~*, feel doubt about whether it is altogether true; *not worth one's ~*, not deserving one's pay; *the ~ of the earth*, the finest citizens. **2.** (chem.) chemical compound of a metal and an acid. **3.** *an old ~*, an experienced sailor. *v.t.* put ~ on or in food. *adj.* (also ~*y*) **1.** (opp. *fresh* (3)) impregnated with, containing, tasting of, cured (3) or preserved or seasoned with, ~: ~ *butter*; ~ *water*, sea-water, etc.; *~-water*, of, or living in, the sea: *~-water fish*. **2.** (fig., of tears, grief, etc.) bitter.

sa·lu·bri·ous [sə'luːbrɪəs] *adj.* (esp. of climate) health-giving.

sal·u·tary ['sæljʊtərɪ] *adj.* having a good effect (on body or mind): ~ *exercise (advice)*.

sal·u·ta·tion [,sæljuː'teɪʃn] *n.* (act or expression of) greeting: *raise one's hat in ~*.

a salute

a sash-window

sa·lute [sə'luːt] *n.* sth. done to welcome sb. or to show respect or honour, esp.

(*military ~*) the raising of the hand to the forehead, the firing of guns, the lowering and raising of a flag. *v.t. & i.* **1.** make a ~ to (sb.). **2.** greet (with a bow, by raising the hat, etc.).

sal·vage ['sælvɪdʒ] *n.* (no pl.) **1.** saving of property from loss (by fire or other disaster). **2.** (payment due for saving) such property. **3.** waste materials (e.g. paper, to be collected and re-used). *v.t.* save from loss in a fire, wreck, etc.

sal·va·tion [sæl'veɪʃn] *n.* (no pl.) **1.** act of saving, state of having been saved, from the power of sin. *S~ Army*, religious and missionary body (5) organized in a semi-military way to campaign for Christ and help the poor. **2.** that which saves sb. from loss, disaster, etc.

salve [sælv] *n.* **1.** oily substance used on wounds, sores, or burns. **2.** (fig.) sth. that comforts wounded feelings or soothes an uneasy conscience. *v.t.* **1.** (old use) put ~ (1) on. **2.** be a ~ (2) to.

sal·ver ['sælvə*] *n.* tray, usu. round and made of silver or other metal, on which letters, drinks, etc. are presented.

sal·vo ['sælvəʊ] *n.* (pl. *-oes*, *-os*) firing of a number of guns together (e.g. as a salute).

same [seɪm] *adj. & pron.* (with def. art.) **1.** unchanged; not different; identical: *We have lived in the ~ house for twenty years. He is the ~ age as his wife.* **2.** *come to the ~ thing*, make no difference; *be all (just) the ~ to*, make no difference to; *at the ~ time*, however; nevertheless; yet. *adv. the ~*, in the same way: *If you leave me I shall never feel the ~ again. all the ~*, in spite of that; although that is the case.

sam·ple ['sɑːmpl] *n.* specimen; one of a number, part of a whole, taken to show what the rest is like. *v.t.* take a ~ or ~s of; test a part of.

san·a·to·ri·um [,sænə'tɔːrɪəm] *n.* (pl. *~s*, *-ria* [-rɪə]) (U.S.A. also *sanitarium*) hospital, esp. one for people with weak lungs or for convalescent people.

sanc·ti·fy ['sæŋktɪfaɪ] *v.t.* make holy; set apart as sacred. **sanc·ti·fi·ca·tion** [,sæŋktɪfɪ'keɪʃn] *n.* (no pl.).

sanc·ti·mo·nious [,sæŋktɪ'məʊnjəs] *adj.* making a show of sanctity.

sanc·tion ['sæŋkʃn] *n.* **1.** (no pl.) right or permission given by authority to do sth. **2.** (no pl.) approval, encouragement (of behaviour, etc.), by general custom or tradition. **3.** penalty intended to restore respect for law or authority: ~s *against aggressors*. *v.t.* give ~ (1, 2) to.

sanc·ti·ty ['sæŋktətɪ] *n.* 1. (no pl.) holiness; sacredness. 2. (pl.) sacred obligations, feelings, etc.: *the sanctities of the home.*

sanc·tu·ary ['sæŋktjʊərɪ] *n.* 1. holy or sacred place, esp. a church, etc. 2. (hist.) place (esp. the church altar) where persons were protected, by Church law, from arrest or violence; place of refuge: *Great Britain, the ~ of political refugees.* 3. (no pl.) (right of offering) freedom from arrest, etc.: *seek (take) ~.* 4. area where birds and wild animals are left undisturbed: *a bird ~.*

sanc·tum ['sæŋktəm] *n.* 1. holy place. 2. (colloq.) person's private room or study.

sand [sænd] *n.* 1. (no pl.) tiny grains of worn rock as seen on the sea-shore, in deserts, etc. 2. *the ~s,* expanse of ~ exposed at low tide. '**~·bag** *n.* bag filled with ~, used as a defence. '**~·bank** *n.* deposit (2) of ~ forming a shallow place in a river or the sea. '**~·hill** *n.* dune. '**~ı·pa·per** *n.* (no pl.) strong paper with ~ glued to it, used for rubbing rough surfaces smooth. '**~·pit** *n.* enclosure filled partly with ~ for children to play in. '**~·stone** *n.* rock formed mostly of ~. **~·y** *adj.* (-ier, -iest) 1. covered with ~. 2. (esp. of hair) yellowish-red.

san·dal ['sændl] *n.* kind of shoe made of a sole with straps to hold it on the foot.

a sandal

sand·wich ['sænwɪdʒ] *n.* two slices of bread with meat, etc. between. ~*-man,* man walking about the streets with two advertisement boards (~*-boards*), one hanging over his chest, the other over his back. *v.t.* put (one thing or person) between two others, esp. where there is little space.

sane [seɪn] *adj.* (~*r, ~st*) 1. healthy in mind; not mad. 2. sensible: ~ *views* (*policies*). **~·ly** *adv.*

sang, see *sing.*

sang-froid [,sɑ̃:ŋ'frwɑː] (Fr.) *n.* (no pl.) calmness in face of danger.

san·gui·na·ry ['sæŋgwɪnərɪ] *adj.* 1. with much bloodshed: *a ~ battle.* 2. fond of bloodshed; delighting in cruel acts: *a ~ ruler.*

san·guine ['sæŋgwɪn] *adj.* 1. hopeful; optimistic. 2. red-faced.

san·i·tar·i·um [,sænɪ'teərɪəm] *n.* (pl. ~*s, -ria* [-rɪə]) (U.S.A.) = sanatorium.

san·i·tary ['sænɪtərɪ] *adj.* 1. clean; free from dirt that might cause disease: ~ *conditions.* 2. of, concerned with, the protection of health. **san·i·ta·tion** [,sænɪ'teɪʃn] *n.* (no pl.) arrangements to give ~ conditions (e.g. for the removal of sewage).

san·i·ty ['sænɪtɪ] *n.* (no pl.) being sane; soundness of judgement.

sank, see *sink* (v.).

San·ta Claus [,sæntə'klɔːz] *n.* person said to fill children's stockings with presents on the night before Christmas.

sap¹ [sæp] *n.* (no pl.) liquid in a plant, carrying necessary food to all parts. *v.t.* (-pp-) drain (wood) of ~; (fig.) weaken; take away the life and strength of: ~*ped by disease* (*an unhealthy climate*). **~·ling** ['sæplɪŋ] *n.* young tree. **~·py** *adj.* (-ier, -iest) full of ~; young and vigorous.

sap² [sæp] *n.* tunnel or covered trench made to get nearer to the enemy. *v.i. & t.* (-pp-) make a ~; weaken (a wall, etc.) by digging under it; (fig.) destroy (sb.'s faith, confidence, etc.). **~·per** *n.* soldier engaged in engineering work (e.g. road and bridge building).

sap·phire ['sæfaɪə*] *n.* clear, bright blue jewel.

sar·casm ['sɑːkæzəm] *n.* 1. (no pl.) (use of) bitter remarks intended to wound the feelings. 2. such a remark. **sar·cas·tic** [sɑː'kæstɪk] *adj.* of, using, ~. **sar·cas·ti·cal·ly** *adv.*

sar·coph·a·gus [sɑː'kɒfəgəs] *n.* (pl. *-gi* [-gaɪ], ~*es*) stone coffin, esp. as used in ancient times.

sar·dine [sɑː'diːn] *n.* small fish, (usu.) tinned in oil: *packed like ~s,* (fig.) crowded close together.

sar·don·ic [sɑː'dɒnɪk] *adj.* scornful; mocking. **sar·don·i·cal·ly** *adv.*

sa·ri ['sɑːrɪ] *n.* length of cotton or silk material draped round the body, worn by Hindu women. (See the picture on page 447.)

sa·rong [sə'rɒŋ] *n.* broad strip of material wrapped round the middle of the body to form a loose skirt, as worn by Malays.

sar·to·ri·al [sɑː'tɔːrɪəl] *adj.* of tailors and their work; of men's clothing.

sash¹ [sæʃ] *n.* narrow strip of cloth worn over clothing round the waist or one shoulder for ornament or as part of a uniform.

sash² [sæʃ] *n.* ~-*window*, window that slides up and down (cf. *casement* and see the picture at *salute*). ~-*cord*, ~-*line*, cord (with weight) running over a pulley to keep the window balanced in any desired position.

a sari

sat, see *sit*.

Sa·tan ['seɪtən] *n.* the Evil One; the Devil. ~·**ic** [sə'tænɪk] *adj.* of ~; wicked.

satch·el ['sætʃl] *n.* leather or canvas bag, as for school-books.

sate [seɪt] *v.t.* satiate.

sat·el·lite ['sætəlaɪt] *n.* **1.** planet moving round another: *The moon is a ~ of the earth.* **2.** artificial object (e.g. a spacecraft) put in orbit round the earth or another planet. **3.** (fig.) person, State, depending upon and taking the lead from another: ~ *town*, smaller town built to take the excess population of a larger town near it.

sa·ti·ate ['seɪʃɪeɪt] *v.t.* satisfy (too) fully: ~*d with food* (*pleasure*). **sa·ti·ety** [sə'taɪətɪ] *n.* (no pl.) condition or feeling of being ~*d*.

sat·in ['sætɪn] *n.* (no pl.) silk material smooth and shiny on one side. *adj.* like ~.

sat·ire ['sætaɪə*] *n.* form of writing holding up a person or society to ridicule or showing the foolishness of an idea, custom, etc.; piece of writing that does this. **sa·tir·i·cal** [sə'tɪrɪkl] *adj.* **sa·tir·i·cal·ly** *adv.* **sat·i·rist** ['sætərɪst] *n.* writer of ~(s). **sat·i·rize** ['sætəraɪz] *v.t.* attack with ~(s).

sat·is·fy ['sætɪsfaɪ] *v.t. & i.* **1.** give (sb.) what he wants or needs; make contented. **2.** be enough for (one's needs); be equal to (what one hopes or desires). **3.** convince (sb., oneself, of sth., *that* ...). **sat·is·fac·tion** [,sætɪs-'fækʃn] *n.* ~*ing* or being satisfied; sth. that satisfies; feeling of pleasure. **sat·is·fac·to·ry** [,sætɪs'fæktərɪ] *adj.* giving pleasure or satisfaction; ~*ing* a need or desire; good enough for a purpose. **sat·is·fac·to·ri·ly** *adv.*

sat·u·rate ['sætʃəreɪt] *v.t.* **1.** make thoroughly wet; soak with moisture (or, fig., *with* learning, prejudice, etc.). **2.** (chem.) cause (one substance) to absorb the greatest possible amount of another: *a ~d solution of salt.* **sat·u·ra·tion** [,sætʃə'reɪʃn] *n.* (no pl.).

Sat·ur·day ['sætədɪ] *n.* sixth day of the week.

sat·ur·nine ['sætənaɪn] *adj.* gloomy.

sa·tyr ['sætə*] *n.* (in Greek and Roman mythology) immortal creature, half man and half animal.

sauce [sɔːs] *n.* **1.** liquid served with food to give it extra flavour. **2.** (no pl.) (colloq.) impudence. **saucy** *adj.* (*-ier, -iest*) impudent. **sauc·i·ly** *adv.*

sauce·pan ['sɔːspən] *n.* deep, round, metal cooking-pot, usu. with a lid and a handle.

sau·cer ['sɔːsə*] *n.* small, circular dish on which a cup stands.

saun·ter ['sɔːntə*] *v.i.* walk in a leisurely way. *n.* leisurely walk.

sau·sage ['sɒsɪdʒ] *n.* chopped-up meat, etc. flavoured and stuffed into a tube of skin; one section of such a tube.

sav·age ['sævɪdʒ] *adj.* **1.** in a primitive or uncivilized state: ~ *tribes* (*countries*). **2.** fierce; cruel. *n.* ~ person. ~·**ry** ['sævɪdʒrɪ] *n.* (no pl.) ~ (1) condition; ~ (2) behaviour.

sa·van·na(h) [sə'vænə] *n.* treeless plain, esp. of Central America.

sa·vant ['sævənt] *n.* man of great learning, esp. a distinguished scientist.

save [seɪv] *v.t. & i.* **1.** make or keep safe (from loss, injury, etc.): ~ *sb. from drowning*; ~ *sb.'s life*; ~ *a person from himself* (from the results of his own foolishness). **2.** keep or store for future use (esp. ~ *up*, of money): ~ *half your salary*; ~ *some of the meat for tomorrow.* **3.** avoid; make unnecessary: *If you walk, you'll ~ spending money on bus fares.* **4.** keep (sb.) from the necessity to use (money, etc.): *That will ~ me a lot of trouble.* **5.** (in the Christian religion) set free from the power of (or eternal punishment for) sin. *prep. & conj.* except: *all ~ him.* **sav·ing** *adj.* the saving grace of (*humour*, etc.), the one good quality that redeems sb.

from other bad qualities. *n.* **1.** way of saving; amount that is ⁓d: *a saving of time and money.* **2.** (pl.) money ⁓d up: *Keep your savings in the bank.* **sav·ings bank** *n.* bank that holds, gives interest on, small savings (2).

sav·iour (U.S.A. **-ior**) ['seɪvjə*] *n.* person who rescues, saves, sb. from danger. *The S⁓, Our S⁓,* Jesus Christ.

sa·vour (U.S.A. **sa·vor**) ['seɪvə*] *n.* taste or flavour (*of* sth.); suggestion (*of* a quality). *v.i.* ⁓ *of,* suggest the presence of: *His answer ⁓s of impertinence.* **⁓y** *n. & adj.* (food dish) having a sharp or salt, not a sweet, taste.

saw¹, see *see¹.*

saw² [sɔː] *n.* wood- or metal-cutting tool with a tooth-edged steel blade. *v.t. & i.* (p.t. ⁓ed, p.p. ⁓n [sɔːn] or ⁓ed) use a ⁓: ⁓ *sth. up,* cut it into pieces with a ⁓. '⁓·dust *n.* (no pl.) tiny bits of wood falling off when wood is ⁓n. '⁓·mill *n.* workshop, etc. where wood is ⁓n by machinery. '⁓·yer ['sɔːjə*] *n.* man whose work is ⁓ing wood.

sax·o·phone ['sæksəfəʊn] *n.* musical wind instrument made of brass. **sax·o·phon·ist** [sæk'sɒfənɪst] *n.* ⁓ player.

say [seɪ] *v.t. & i.* (pres. t., 3rd person sing. ⁓s [sez], p.t. & p.p. said [sed]) **1.** use one's voice to utter (words, sentences); speak; talk: *S⁓ 'Thank you' when you are given something. Now ⁓ it again.* **2.** *What do you ⁓ to ...?* What do you think about (the suggestion, etc.)? *go without ⁓ing,* be obvious; *that is to ⁓,* in other words; *they ⁓, it is said,* rumour has it (*that*). *n. have (⁓) one's ⁓,* state one's opinions, views; *have a ⁓ in the matter,* have an opportunity to share in a discussion, decision, etc. **⁓·ing** *n.* common remark: *It was a ⁓ing of his that ...*

scab [skæb] *n.* **1.** dry crust formed over a wound or sore. **2.** (no pl.) skin disease, esp. of sheep. **3.** blackleg. **⁓·by** *adj.* (-ier, -iest) covered with ⁓s.

scab·bard ['skæbəd] *n.* case for the blade of a sword, dagger, or bayonet.

sca·bies ['skeɪbiːz] *n.* (no pl.) kind of skin disease.

scaf·fold ['skæfəld] *n.* **1.** structure put up for workmen and materials around a building that is being erected or repaired. **2.** platform on which criminals are executed. **⁓·ing** *n.* (no pl.) (materials for a) ⁓ (e.g. poles, planks, steel tubes).

scald [skɔːld] *v.t.* **1.** hurt with hot liquid or steam: ⁓ *one's hand with hot*

fat; ⁓ing tears, tears of bitter grief. **2.** clean (dishes, etc.) with boiling water or steam. **3.** heat (milk) almost to boiling-point. *n.* injury from hot liquid or steam.

scale¹ [skeɪl] *n.* **1.** series of marks at regular intervals for the purpose of measuring (as on a ruler or a thermometer). **2.** system of units for measuring: *the decimal ⁓.* **3.** tool or instrument marked for measuring. **4.** arrangement in steps or degrees: *a ⁓ of wages; a person who is high in the social ⁓.* **5.** proportion between the size of sth. and the map, plan, diagram, etc. that represents it: *a map on the ⁓ of one inch to a mile.* **6.** relative size, extent, etc.: *making preparations on a large ⁓.* **7.** (music) series of tones arranged in order of pitch, esp. a series of eight starting on a keynote. *v.t.* **1.** climb (a wall, cliff, etc.) (with a ladder, etc.). **2.** make a copy or representation of, according to a certain ⁓ (5). **3.** ⁓ *up* (*down*), increase (decrease) by a certain proportion: *All prices* (*wages*) *were ⁓d up ten per cent.*

scale² [skeɪl] *n.* **1.** one of the two pans of a balance. **2.** (pl. often *a pair of* ⁓s) simple balance; instrument for measuring weight. *turn the ⁓(s),* decide the result of sth. that is in doubt; *hold the ⁓s even,* judge fairly (between).

scales² (2)

scale³ [skeɪl] *n.* **1.** one of the thin, flat plates of hard material covering the skin of many fishes and reptiles. **2.** plate or thin outer piece resembling a fish-⁓ on an organic or other object (e.g. a flake of skin, a scab, a flake of rust on iron). **3.** (no pl.) chalky deposit inside boilers, water-pipes, or on teeth. *v.t. & i.* **1.** take ⁓s from (a fish). **2.** come (*off*) in flakes: *paint scaling off a wall.* **scaly** *adj.* (-ier, -iest) covered with, composed of, scale(s).

scal·ly·wag ['skælɪwæg] *n.* scamp.

scalp [skælp] *n.* skin and hair of the top of the head. *v.t.* cut the ⁓ off.

scalp·el ['skælpəl] *n.* small knife used by surgeons.

scamp [skæmp] *n.* (derog. or playfully) worthless person; rascal. *v.t.* do (work) carelessly or too quickly.

scam·per ['skæmpə*] *v.i.* (esp. of small animals, e.g. mice and rabbits, when frightened, or of children and dogs at play) run quickly. *n.* short, quick run: *take the dog for a ~*.

scan [skæn] *v.t. & i.* (*-nn-*) **1.** look at attentively; run the eyes over every part of: *~ the horizon* (*sb.'s proposals*). **2.** look at quickly but not very thoroughly: *~ the morning papers* (2). **3.** test the metre of (a line of verse) by noting the division into feet (see *foot* (6)). **4.** (of a line of verse) be metrically correct. **5.** traverse (a particular area) with controlled radar, etc. beams in search of sth. **6.** examine all parts of to detect radioactivity. **7.** resolve (4) (a television picture) into its elements of light and shade for transmission (1). **~·ning** *n.* (no pl.) (med.) method for detecting abnormalities in the body by the use of special photographic instruments that record[1] (3) the movement of an administered (3) radioactive substance as it passes through the organs, etc.

scan·dal ['skændl] *n.* **1.** (actions, behaviour, etc. that cause) general feeling of indignation; shameful or disgraceful action. **2.** (no pl.) harmful gossip; unkind talk that hurts sb.'s reputation: *Don't talk* (*listen to*) *~*. **~·ize** ['skændəlaiz] *v.t.* shock; fill with indignation; offend moral feelings, etc. **~·ous** ['skændələs] *adj.* **1.** very wrong; shocking. **2.** (of reports, rumours) containing *~* (2). **3.** (of persons) fond of spreading *~* (2): *~ous neighbours.*

Scan·di·na·vian [,skændɪ'neɪvjən] *n. & adj.* (native, inhabitant, or family of languages) of Scandinavia.

scant [skænt] *adj.* (having) hardly enough: *~ of breath*; *pay ~ attention to what sb. says.* **~·y** *adj.* (*-ier*, *-iest*) barely sufficient; small in size or amount. **~·i·ly** *adv.*

-scape [-skeɪp] *suff.* (forming ns.) view or picture of a specified type of scene: *landscape.*

scape·goat ['skeɪpɡəʊt] *n.* person blamed or punished for the mistake(s) or wrongdoing of others.

scar [skɑ:*] *n.* mark remaining on the surface (of skin, furniture) as the result of injury or damage. *v.t. & i.* (*-rr-*) **1.** mark with a *~* or *~s*: *an arm ~red by numerous vaccinations.* **2.** heal over; form a *~* or *~s* (on): *The cut on her thumb soon ~red over.*

scar·ab ['skærəb] *n.* kinds of beetle; carving in the shape of a *~*.

scarce [skeəs] *adj.* (*~r*, *~st*) **1.** rare; not

available in sufficient quantity: *Eggs were ~ here last winter.* **2.** uncommon; not often seen or found. **~·ly** *adv.* not quite; almost not; barely: *S~ly anyone knows what happened.* **scar·ci·ty** *n.*

a scarab

scare [skeə*] *v.t. & i.* frighten; become frightened. *n.* fright; state of widespread alarm: *The news from X caused a war ~.* **'~·crow** *n.* figure made of sticks and old clothes, put in a field to frighten birds from crops. **'~·mon·ger** *n.* person who starts a *~*.

scarf [skɑ:f] *n.* (pl. *scarves* [skɑ:vz], *~s*) long strip of material (silk, wool, etc.) worn over the shoulders, round the neck, or over the hair.

scar·let ['skɑ:lət] *n.* (no pl.) *& adj.* bright red. *~ fever*, infectious disease that causes *~* marks on the skin.

scath·ing ['skeɪðɪŋ] *adj.* (of words, criticism, etc.) harsh; cutting.

scat·ter ['skætə*] *v.t. & i.* **1.** send, go, in different directions. **2.** throw or put here and there: *~ seed*; *~ sand on an icy road.* **'~·brain** *n.* thoughtless (2), flighty person. **'~·brained** *adj.* **~ed** *adj.* not situated together: *~ed villages.*

scav·en·ger ['skævɪndʒə*] *n.* **1.** animal or bird (e.g. a vulture) that lives on decaying flesh. **2.** (Gt. Brit.) streetcleaner.

sce·nar·io [sɪ'nɑ:rɪəʊ] *n.* (pl. *~s*) outline of events, details of scenes, etc. in a drama, esp. for a film production.

scene [si:n] *n.* **1.** place of an actual or imagined event: *the ~ of a famous battle.* **2.** view; sth. that is seen: *boats in the harbour making a pretty ~*; *go abroad for a change of ~.* **3.** one of the parts, shorter than an act, into which a play is divided: *Act I, S~ ii.* **4.** painted background, woodwork, canvas, etc. on the stage of a theatre, representing a place: *behind the ~s*, at the back of the stage, hidden from the audience, and so (fig., of a person) having information about matters not known by the general public. **5.** angry outburst; noisy argument; display of bad temper in the presence of other people: *Don't make a ~.* **sce·nery** ['si:nərɪ] *n.* (no pl.) **1.** stage ~ (4). **2.** general natural features of a district: *mountain ~ry.* **sce·nic** ['si:nɪk] *adj.* of ~ry.

scent [sent] *n.* **1.** smell, esp. of sth. pleasant: *the ~ of roses.* **2.** (no pl.) (usu. liquid) preparation made from flowers; perfume: *a bottle of ~. She put some ~ on her hair.* **3.** (usu. no pl.) smell left by an animal by which dogs can follow its track: *on (off) the ~,* following (not following) the right ~; *throw sb. off the ~,* (fig.) mislead him, deceive him, by giving wrong suggestions, etc. **4.** (no pl.) sense of smell (in dogs, etc.): *hunt by ~. v.t.* **1.** learn the presence of by smell: *My dog ~ed a fox.* **2.** (fig.) suspect; become aware of: *~ a plot (crime).* **3.** put ~ (2) on. **4.** give a ~ (1) to.

scep·tic (U.S.A. **skep-**) ['skeptɪk] *n.* person who doubts whether sth. is true, esp. one who doubts the truth of religious teachings. **scep·ti·cal** (U.S.A. **skep-**) *adj.* **scep·ti·cal·ly** (U.S.A. **skep-**) *adv.* **scep·ti·cism** (U.S.A. **skep-**) ['skeptɪsɪzəm] *n.* (no pl.) doubting state of mind.

scep·tre (U.S.A. **-ter**) ['septə*] *n.* rod or staff carried by a ruler as a sign of power or authority.

sched·ule ['ʃedju:l] *n.* list or statement of details, esp. of times for doing things; programme for work; (U.S.A.) = timetable: *on (behind) ~,* on (not on) time: *The train arrived on ~. according to ~,* as planned. *v.t.* make a ~ of: put in a ~: *~d flight (service),* (e.g. of aircraft) flying according to regular timetables.

scheme [ski:m] *n.* **1.** arrangement; ordered system: *a colour ~* (e.g. for a room, so that colours of curtains, rugs, etc. are in harmony). **2.** plan or design for work or activity: *a ~* (i.e. syllabus) *for the term's work.* **3.** secret and dishonest plan. *v.i. & t.* make a ~ or ~s, esp. dishonest (*for* sth., *to do* sth.); make a ~ or ~s for. **schem·er** *n.* **schem·ing** *adj.* (esp.) (of a person) making dishonest ~s.

schism ['sɪzəm] *n.* **1.** (no pl.) division (esp. of a Church) into groups, esp. because of difference of opinion. **2.** offence of causing such a division. **schis·mat·ic** [sɪz'mætɪk] *adj.* causing, likely to cause, ~.

schizo·phre·nia [ˌskɪtsəʊ'fri:njə] *n.* mental disorder marked by lack of

association between thoughts, feelings, and actions. **schizo·phre·nic** [ˌskɪtsəʊ-'frenɪk] *adj.* of ~. *n.* person suffering from ~.

schnor·kel, see *snorkel.*

schol·ar ['skɒlə*] *n.* **1.** (old use) boy or girl at school. **2.** student who, after a competitive examination, is awarded money or other help so that he may attend school or college: *a Rhodes ~.* **3.** person with much knowledge (usu. of a particular subject): *Professor X, the famous Greek ~. ~·ly adj.* having or showing much learning; of or befitting a ~ (3); fond of learning. **~·ship** *n.* **1.** (no pl.) learning or knowledge obtained by study. **2.** money given to a ~ (2) so that he may continue his studies. **scho·las·tic** [skə'læstɪk] *adj.* of schools or education.

school¹ [sku:l] *n.* **1.** building, institution, where children or adults are taught; all the pupils in a ~: *at ~,* attending lessons; *at* (U.S.A. *in*) *~,* in the course of being educated in a ~; *go to ~,* attend lessons in a ~. *S~ begins at 8 a.m. S~ is over.* **2.** group of persons having the same principles or characteristics (e.g. of technique) or influenced by the same teacher, esp. a group of artists: *the Dutch ~ of painting. v.t.* train; control; discipline: *~ed by adversity.* **~ age** *n.* (no pl.) period of life in which children normally attend ~. (attrib.) *~-age children.* **'~-bag** *n.* bag for carrying books, etc. to or from ~. **'~-book** *n.* book used in ~. **'~-boy** *n.* boy at ~. **~ bus** *n.* bus taking children to or from ~. **'~-days** *n. pl.* time of being at ~, esp. as looked back upon. **'~-fel·low, '~-mate** *ns.* one educated or being educated at the same ~ as another. **'~-girl** *n.* girl at ~. **~·ing** *n.* (no pl.) education at ~. **'~-mas·ter, '~-mis·tress** *ns.* man, woman, teaching in a ~. **'~-room** *n.* room used for lessons. **'~-time** *n.* lesson-time at ~ or at home; ~-days.

school² [sku:l] *n.* large number (*of* fish) swimming together: *a ~ of whales.*

a schooner

schoo·ner ['skuːnə*] *n.* kind of sailing-ship with two or more masts. *prairie ~*, large, covered wagon used by early settlers for crossing the prairies.

a prairie schooner

schuss [ʃʊs] *v.i. & n.* (make a) straight, downhill run on skis.

sci·ence ['saɪəns] *n.* **1.** (no pl.) knowledge arranged in a system, esp. knowledge obtained by observation and testing of facts. **2.** branch of such knowledge (e.g. physics, chemistry, biology). *~ fiction*, fiction based on recent or imagined scientific discoveries, frequently dealing with space travel, life on other planets, etc. **3.** (no pl.) skill; expertness (e.g. in sport).

sci·en·tif·ic [ˌsaɪən'tɪfɪk] *adj.* **1.** of, for, connected with, used in, ~; guided by the rules of ~: *scientific farming.* **2.** having, using, needing, skill or expert knowledge: *a scientific boxer.* **sci·en·tif·i·cal·ly** *adv.* **sci·en·tist** ['saɪəntɪst] *n.* person expert in one of the natural or physical ~s.

sci-fi [ˌsaɪ'faɪ] *n.* (no pl.) (colloq., abbr. for) science (2) fiction.

scin·til·late ['sɪntɪleɪt] *v.i.* sparkle.

sci·on ['saɪən] *n.* young member of (usu. an old or a noble family).

scis·sors ['sɪzəz] *n. pl.* (often *a pair of ~*) cutting instrument with two blades (1) that cut as they come together.

scoff [skɒf] *v.i.* speak contemptuously; mock (*at*). *n.* **1.** mocking words. **2.** laughing-stock. **~·er** *n.*

scold [skəʊld] *v.t. & i.* blame (sb.) with angry words; speak angrily in protest. *n.* woman who ~s. **~·ing** *n.* harsh or severe rebuke: *get* (*give sb.*) *a ~ing.*

scone [skɒn] *n.* soft, flat cake of barley meal or wheat flour baked quickly.

scoop [skuːp] *n.* **1.** (sorts of) deep, shovel-like tool for taking up and moving quantities of flour, sand, earth,

a scoop (1)

etc.; long-handled, ladle-shaped tool for dipping out liquid; such a part of a machine with that purpose. **2.** piece of news obtained and published by one newspaper before others. *v.t.* **1.** lift (*up, out*) with, or as with, a ~. **2.** make (a hole or a hollow *in* sth.) as with a ~.

scoot [skuːt] *v.i.* run off quickly.

scoot·er ['skuːtə*] *n.* **1.** child's toy propelled by foot and consisting of two wheels, a footboard, and a long steering-handle. **2.** (also *motor ~*) motor cycle with small wheels and a low saddle.

a scooter (1)

scope [skəʊp] *n.* (no pl.) **1.** outlook; range of action or observation. **2.** opportunity; outlet: *work that gives ~ for one's abilities.*

scorch [skɔːtʃ] *v.t. & i.* **1.** burn or discolour the surface of (sth.) with dry heat; become ~ed. **2.** (sl., of motorists, cyclists, etc.) travel (*along*) at very high speed. **~·ing** *adj.* very hot. *adv.* extremely hot: *~ing hot.*

score¹ [skɔː*] *n.* **1.** cut or scratch made on a surface; line drawn on a board for the purpose of keeping a record². **2.** record² kept by ~s (1), esp. of money owing: *run up a ~*, get into debt; *pay off* (*wipe off, settle*) *old ~s*, (fig.) get even with someone for past offences; *have one's revenge.* **3.** (record² of) points, goals, runs, etc. made by a team or player in sport. **4.** *on the ~ of,* because of; *on that ~,* as far as that point is concerned. **5.** copy of orchestral, etc. music showing what each instrument is to play, each voice to sing. *v.t. & i.* **1.** make (cuts, scratches, lines) on: *a composition ~d with corrections in red ink.* **2.** make or keep a record² (esp. for games). **3.** make as points in a game, etc.: *~ a goal; a batsman who failed to ~.* **4.** win an advantage; do well: *~ off sb.,* (colloq.) get the better of him (in an argument, etc.). **5.** write, in a ~ (5), instrumental or vocal parts for a musical composition. **scor·er** *n.* (esp.) person who keeps the ~ (3) (e.g. for a game of cricket).

score² [skɔː*] *n.* (set of) twenty: *three ~ and ten,* 70.

scorn [skɔːn] *n.* (no pl.) **1.** contempt; feeling that sb. or sth. deserves no respect. **2.** person, action, etc. that is despised or looked down on. *v.t.* **1.** feel or show contempt for: *We ~ liars.* **2.** refuse, be unwilling (*to do* sth.), because it is wrong or unworthy. **~·ful** *adj.* showing or feeling ~. **~·ful·ly** *adv.*

scor·pi·on ['skɔːpjən] *n.* small animal of the spider group with a poisonous sting in its long tail.

Scotch [skɒtʃ] *adj.* of Scotland or its inhabitants. *n.* **1.** form of English used in Scotland. *the ~,* (pl.) the people of Scotland. **2.** ~ whisky. '**~·man**, '**~·wom·an** *ns.* native of Scotland.

scot-free [,skɒt'friː] *adv.* go (*get off, escape*) ~ (unharmed, unpunished).

Scot·tish ['skɒtɪʃ] *adj.* Scotch.

scoun·drel ['skaʊndrəl] *n.* wicked person. **~·ly** *adj.* wicked.

scour¹ ['skaʊə*] *v.t.* **1.** rub (a dirty surface) bright or clean. **2.** get (rust, marks, etc. *off, out, away*) by rubbing. *n.* act of ~ing.

scour² ['skaʊə*] *v.t.* go rapidly into every part of (a place) looking (*for* sb. or sth.): *~ing the woods for a lost child.*

scourge [skɜːdʒ] *n.* whip for punishment; (fig.) cause of suffering (e.g. an outbreak of disease). *v.t.* whip; punish; (fig.) bring pain or suffering to.

scout¹ [skaʊt] *n.* **1.** person (not a spy), ship, or small, fast aircraft sent out to get information about the enemy's movements, strength, etc. **2.** (*Boy*) *S~,* member of the world-wide organization (*S~ Association*) for boys intended to develop character and teach self-reliance, discipline, and public spirit. *Girl S~* (U.S.A.), Girl Guide. **3.** (Gt.

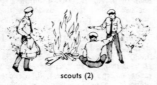

scouts (2)

Brit.) patrolman of a motoring organization helping motorists on the roads (cf. *patrol* (2)). **4.** person employed to look out for talented performers (e.g. in sport, the theatre, etc.): *a talent ~. v.i.* go out as a ~ (1): *~ about, ~ round (for),* go about looking (for things or people wanted).

scout² [skaʊt] *v.t.* consider (an idea or suggestion) worthless or ridiculous.

scowl [skaʊl] *v.i. & n.* (have a) bad-tempered look on the face.

scrag·gy ['skrægɪ] *adj.* (*-ier, -iest*) thin and bony.

scram·ble· ['skræmbl] *v.i. & t.* **1.** climb or crawl (*up, over, along, into, etc.*): *~ up a cliff.* **2.** struggle with others (*for* sth.). **3.** cook (eggs) by beating them and then heating them in melted butter. *n.* **1.** climb or walk over or through obstacles, rough ground, etc. **2.** rough struggle (*for* sth.).

scrap¹ [skræp] *n.* **1.** small (usu. unwanted) piece. **2.** (no pl.) waste or unwanted articles, esp. those of value only for the material they contain: *~-iron,* articles of iron and steel to be melted down. **3.** (pl.) odds and ends; bits of uneaten food. **4.** picture, etc. cut from a book or newspaper for keeping in a collection. *v.t.* (*-pp-*) throw away as useless or worn out. '**~-book** *n.* book of blank pages on to which pictures, etc. cut from newspapers, etc. are pasted. '**~-heap** *n.* pile of waste or unwanted material or articles. **~·py** *adj.* (*-ier, -iest*) made up of bits; not complete or properly arranged.

scrap² [skræp] *n. & v.i.* (*-pp-*) (sl.) fight (*with*).

scrape [skreɪp] *v.t. & i.* **1.** make clean, smooth, or level by drawing or pushing the hard edge of a tool, or sth. rough, along the surface; remove (mud, grease, paint, etc.) in this way: *~ paint off the door.* **2.** injure or damage by scraping. **3.** go, get, through or past another object, touching or almost touching it: *~ along a wall; branches scraping against the window; ~ through an examination,* (fig.) only just pass. **4.** collect with effort or difficulty: *~ up enough money to pay the rent.* **5.** rub with a harsh or rough sound. **6.** make by scraping (1): *~ (out) a hole in the sand.* *n.* **1.** act or sound of scraping. **2.** ~d place. **3.** awkward situation resulting from foolish behaviour: *a boy who is always getting into ~s.* **scrap·er** *n.* tool used for scraping.

scratch [skrætʃ] *v.t. & i.* **1.** make lines on or in a surface with sth. pointed or sharp; break or cut lightly (a surface) in this way: *~ the paint on a door; ~ out a word* (with a knife, or by drawing a line through it); *a cat that ~es.* **2.** make (a hole) by ~ing. **3.** rub (the skin) with the finger-nails, etc. to relieve itching: *~ one's head.* **4.** draw or write carelessly. **5.** rub with a harsh

noise; make a harsh noise: *This pen
～es.* **6.** withdraw (a horse, a candidate,
oneself) from a contest. *n.* **1.** mark,
cut, injury, sound, made by ～ing:
escape without a ～ (i.e. quite unhurt).
2. (no pl.) period or act of ～ing (3).
3. (no pl.) starting line for a race: *start
from ～*, (fig.) start from the beginning
or without any advantages; *come up
to ～*, (fig.) be ready to do what one is
expected or required to do. *adj.* done
or formed with whatever is available:
a ～ team (collected hastily); *a ～ dinner.*
～y adj. (-ier, -iest) (of drawings, writing) done carelessly; (of a pen) that
makes a ～ing noise.
scrawl [skrɔːl] *v.i. & t.* write or draw
quickly and carelessly. *n.* ～ed writing;
sth. ～ed.
scream [skriːm] *v.i. & t.* **1.** give a loud,
sharp cry of, or as of, fear or pain; cry
(sth.) in a loud, high voice: *～ with
laughter*, laugh in a noisy, uncontrolled way. **2.** (of the wind, machines,
etc.) make a loud, shrill noise. *n.* loud,
shrill, piercing cry or noise.
screech [skriːtʃ] *v.i. & t.* **1.** make a
harsh, piercing sound. **2.** scream in
anger or pain; cry out in high tones:
monkeys ～ing in the trees. *n.* ～ing cry or
noise.
screed [skriːd] *n.* long (and usu. uninteresting) letter.

a screen (1)

a scroll

screen [skriːn] *n.* **1.** (often movable)
upright framework, often made so as
to fold, used to hide sb. or sth. from
view or to protect from draughts or
too much heat or light, etc. **2.** anything that gives shelter or protection
as a ～ (1) does: *a ～ of trees* (hiding a
house from the road); *a smoke ～* (used
in war to hide ships, etc. from the
enemy). **3.** frame with fine wire netting (*～-window, ～-door*) to keep out
flies, mosquitoes, etc. **4.** sieve (for
coal, gravel, etc.). **5.** smooth surface
on to which slides, films, television
pictures, etc. are projected; (attrib.) of
the cinema: *～ actor*; *～-play*, script (2)
of a film; *the ～*, moving pictures
collectively. *v.t.* **1.** shelter, protect,

hide from view, with a ～ (1, 2); (fig.)
protect (sb.) from punishment, blame,
discovery, etc. **2.** provide (windows,
a house, etc.) with wire ～s (3). **3.**
separate (coal, etc.) into different
sizes by passing through a ～ (4). **4.**
(pol.) investigate (sb.'s) past history
in order to judge his loyalty, etc. to
the State. **5.** examine (sb.) to judge his
qualifications for a post, etc. **6.** show
(an object, film, slide, etc.) on a ～ (5);
make a cinema film of.
screw [skruː] *n.* **1.** metal peg with a
spiral groove round its length driven
into wood, metal, etc. by twisting
under pressure, for fastening and
holding things together. **2.** sth. turned
like a ～ and used for exerting pressure,
tightening, etc.: *put the ～ on sb.*, (fig.)
use one's power to force him to do
sth. **3.** action of turning; turn: *give it
another ～.* **4.** propeller of a ship or an
aircraft (*air～*). *v.t. & i.* **1.** fasten or
tighten with a ～ or ～s (1): *S～ down
the lid.* **2.** twist round: *～ the lid of a
jar on (off); ～* (i.e. turn) *one's head
round.* **3.** *～ up one's eyes (mouth, face),*
cause the skin there to wrinkle; *～ up
one's courage*, overcome one's fears.
4. exert pressure; force (*out of*).
'～＿driv·er *n.* tool for turning ～s (1).

a screw (1)

a scrubbing-brush

scrib·ble ['skrɪbl] *v.i. & t.* write
hastily or carelessly; make meaningless marks on paper, etc. *n.* sth. ～d.
scribe [skraɪb] *n.* professional letter-
writer; (Bible) teacher of Jewish law.
scrim·mage ['skrɪmɪdʒ] *n.* confused
struggle. *v.i.* take part in a ～.
script [skrɪpt] *n.* **1.** (no pl.) (opp.
print) handwriting; type that imitates
handwriting. **2.** (abbr. for) manuscript
or typescript, esp. of an actor's part
in a play, a talk to be broadcast, etc.
scrip·ture ['skrɪptʃə*] *n.* **1.** *The (Holy)
S～s, S～,* the Bible. **2.** sacred writings
of a religion. **scrip·tur·al** *adj.* based
on the Bible.
scroll [skrəʊl] *n.* roll of paper or parchment for writing on; ancient book written on a ～. (See the picture at *screen.*)
scrub[1] [skrʌb] *n.* (no pl.) (land covered
with) trees and bushes of poor quality;
brushwood. **～by adj.** (-ier, -iest) **1.**
insignificant; stunted. **2.** unshaven:
a ～by chin.

scrub² [skrʌb] *v.t. & i.* (-*bb*-) clean by rubbing hard, esp. with a stiff brush, soap, and water. *n.* ~bing. '~**bing-brush**,(U.S.A.)~**brush** *ns.* stiff brush for ~bing floors. (See the p. at *screw*.)

scruff [skrʌf] *n.* back of the neck, esp. of an animal, when used for grasping or lifting: *take by the* ~ *of the neck.* ~**y** *adj.* (-*ier*, -*iest*) untidy and rough looking.

scru·ple ['skru:pl] *n.* (hesitation caused by) uneasiness of conscience: *Have you no* ~*s about borrowing things without permission? v.i.* ~ *to do sth.*, have ~s about doing it. **scru·pu·lous** ['skru:pjuləs] *adj.* **1.** careful to do nothing morally wrong. **2.** paying great attention to small points (esp. of conscience).

scru·ti·ny ['skru:tɪnɪ] *n.* thorough and detailed examination. **scru·ti·nize** *v.t.* make a ~ of.

scuf·fle ['skʌfl] *n.* rough, confused fight or struggle. *v.i.* take part in a ~.

scull [skʌl] *n.* one of a pair of oars used together; single oar used with a twisting stroke at the stern of a boat. *v.t. & i.* row (a boat) with ~s or propel (a boat) with one ~ at the stern.

scul·lery ['skʌlərɪ] *n.* room in which pots, pans, dishes, etc. are washed.

sculp·ture ['skʌlptʃə*] *n.* **1.** (no pl.) art of making representations in stone, wood, metal, etc. by carving, modelling, etc. **2.** (piece of) such work. *v.t. & i.* make a ~ of; ornament with ~: *a* ~*d column.* **sculp·tor** ['skʌlptə*] *n.* artist who makes ~s. **sculp·tur·al** ['skʌlptʃərəl] *adj.*

scum [skʌm] *n.* (no pl.) **1.** froth or dirty substance that comes to the surface of a boiling liquid, a pond, etc. **2.** (fig.) worst or seemingly worthless part (*of* the population, etc.). ~**my** *adj.* (-*ier*, -*iest*) of, like, containing, ~.

scup·per ['skʌpə*] *n.* opening in a ship's side for draining water from the deck.

scurf [skɜ:f] *n.* (no pl.) small bits of dead skin, esp. on the scalp, loosened as new skin grows. ~**y** *adj.* (-*ier*, -*iest*) having, covered with, ~.

scur·ri·lous ['skʌrɪləs] *adj.* using, full of, violent words of abuse: *a* ~ *attack on the Council.*

scur·ry ['skʌrɪ] *v.i.* run, esp. with short, quick steps. *n.* (no pl.) act or sound of ~ing.

scur·vy ['skɜ:vɪ] *adj.* (-*ier*, -*iest*) contemptible: *a* ~ *trick. n.* (no pl.) disease caused by lack of fresh fruit and vegetables to eat.

scut·tle¹ ['skʌtl] *n.* (also *coal-*~) container for a supply of coal at the fireside.

a coal-scuttle

scut·tle² ['skʌtl] *v.t.* make, open, a hole in (a ship) below the water-line, esp. to sink it and so prevent its being captured by the enemy.

scut·tle³ ['skʌtl] *v.i.* scurry (*off*, *away*).

scythe [saɪð] *n.* tool with a long, slightly curved blade (1) on a long, wooden pole, for cutting long grass, etc. *v.t.* cut with a ~.

a scythe

sea [si:] *n.* **1.** (any part of the) expanse of salt water that surrounds the continents (cf. *ocean*); name given to certain large areas of inland water, e.g. the Black S~, the Caspian S~, the Dead S~ (cf. *Lake Victoria*, *Lake Erie*): *by* ~, in a ship; *go to* ~, become a sailor; *put* (*out*) *to* ~, leave land or harbour; (*all*) *at* ~, (fig.) puzzled; at a loss. **2.** big wave coming over a ship, etc.: *swept overboard by a huge* ~. **3.** large area or stretch (*of* sth.); large quantity: *a* ~ *of upturned faces.* '~**board** *n.* coast region. '~**borne** *adj.* (of trade) carried in ships. '~**far-ing** *adj.* of work or voyages on the ~. '~**fish** *n.* (opp. *freshwater fish*). ~ **front** *n.* part of a town facing the ~. '~**gull** *n.* common ~bird with long wings. '~**legs** *n. pl. get one's* ~*legs*, become used to the heaving motion of a ship. '~-,**lev·el** *n.* level of the ~'s surface used in reckoning height of land and depth of ~. '~,**li·on** *n.* large seal of the Pacific Ocean. ~**man** ['si:mən] *n.* sailor, esp. one who is not an officer. '~,**man·ship** *n.* (no pl.) art of, skill in, managing a ship. '~**plane** *n.* aircraft constructed so that it can come down on and rise from water. '⁓·port *n.* town with a harbour. ⁓ pow·er *n.* 1. (no pl.) ability to control and use the ⁓s (by means of naval strength). 2. State having this power. '⁓·shore *n.* land at the ⁓'s edge. '⁓·sick *adj.* sick from the motion of a ship. '⁓·sick·ness *n.* (no pl.). '⁓-side *n. & adj.* (place, town) by the ⁓. '⁓-ur·chin *n.* small ⁓-animal of globular form with a shell covered with sharp spines (2). '⁓·ward *adj.* towards the ⁓. '⁓·wards *adv.* '⁓-ˌwa·ter *n.* (no pl.) water from the ⁓. '⁓·weed *n.* plant(s) growing in the ⁓ or on rocks washed by the ⁓. '⁓ˌwor·thy *adj.* (of ships) fit for a voyage; well built.

seal[1] [siːl] *n.* 1. piece of wax, lead, etc. often stamped with a design, attached to a document to show that it is genuine, or to a letter, box, door, etc. to guard against its being opened by unauthorized persons: *under ⁓ of secrecy*, (fig.) subject to secrecy on stated grounds. 2. piece of metal, etc. on which is the design to be stamped on a ⁓. *v.t.* 1. put a ⁓ (1) on; stamp a ⁓ (1). 2. close tightly: ⁓ *a crack in a pipe*; ⁓ *a jar of fruit* (i.e. make it airtight). 3. ⁓ *a bargain*, settle it. *His fate is* ⁓*ed* (is definitely decided). '⁓·ing-wax *n.* kind of wax, melted to ⁓ letters, etc.

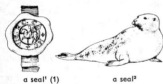

a seal[1] (1)   a seal[2]

seal[2] [siːl] *n.* fish-eating sea-animal valued for its fur.

seam [siːm] *n.* 1. line where two edges, esp. of cloth or leather, are turned back and sewn together. 2. layer of coal, etc. between layers of other material (e.g. rock, clay). 3. line or mark like a ⁓ (1). *v.t.* (esp. in the p.p., of the face) ⁓*ed with*, marked with (lines, scars, etc.). ⁓·**stress** ['semstrɪs], **semp·stress** ['sempstrɪs] *ns.* woman who makes a living by sewing. ⁓**y** *adj.* (*-ier, -iest*) *the* ⁓*y side* (*of life*), (the evils of) poverty, crime, etc.

sear [sɪə*] *v.t.* burn the surface of, esp. with a heated iron; (fig.) make (sb.'s heart) hard and unfeeling.

search [sɜːtʃ] *v.t. & i.* 1. examine, look carefully at, through, or into (*for*, in order to find) sth. or sb.: ⁓ *a criminal to see what he has in his pockets*. 2. go deeply into; go into every part of: *a* ⁓*ing wind*. *n.* act of ⁓*ing: go in* ⁓ *of a missing child*. ⁓·**ing** *adj.* (of a look) taking in all details; (of a test, etc.) thorough. '⁓·**light** *n.* powerful electric lamp for ⁓*ing* the sky, sea, etc. '⁓-ˌpar·ty *n.* number of persons going out to look for sb. or sth. that is lost or concealed. '⁓-ˌwar·rant *n.* official authority given to policemen when it is necessary to ⁓ a house (for stolen goods, etc.).

sea·son ['siːzn] *n.* 1. one of the divisions of the year according to the weather (e.g. spring, summer, etc.): *the dry* (*rainy*) ⁓. 2. period suitable or normal for sth.: *the football* ⁓; *the nesting* ⁓; *the dead* (*off*) ⁓, (at holiday resorts, etc.) the time when there are very few guests; *the holiday* ⁓; *in* (*out of*) ⁓, (of fish, fruit, etc.) to be had (not to be had) in good condition and at ordinary prices; *in* ⁓ *and out of* ⁓, at all times. 3. period (in a town) when most of the social events take place. 4. *for a* ⁓, (old use) for a short time. *v.t. & i.* 1. make or become suitable for use (through the effects of time, the weather, or treatment): *well-*⁓*ed wood*, wood that has become dry and hard. 2. flavour (food) (with salt, pepper, etc.). ⁓·**able** *adj.* 1. (of the weather) of the kind to be expected at the right time of year. 2. (of help, advice, gifts, etc.) coming at the right time; opportune. ⁓·**al** ['siːzənl] *adj.* dependent on the ⁓s (1); changing with the ⁓s (1): ⁓*al occupations* (e.g. fruit picking). ⁓·**ing** *n.* sth. that adds flavour (e.g. salt). '⁓-ˌtick·et *n.* ticket giving the owner the right to travel between two places or to go to a place of amusement, etc. as often as he wishes during a certain period.

seat [siːt] *n.* 1. sth. made or used for sitting on (e.g. a chair, box, rug): *take a* ⁓, sit down; *a* ⁓*-belt*, a belt fastened to the sides of a ⁓ in a passenger vehicle or aircraft, designed to hold a person steady in his ⁓. 2. part of a chair, stool, etc. on which one sits. 3. part of the body (the *buttocks*) on which one sits; part of a garment (e.g. of trousers, a skirt) covering this. 4. place in which one has the right to sit: *have a* ⁓ *in Parliament* (i.e. be a member). 5. *country* ⁓, large house with land, in the country. 6. place where sth. is or is carried on: *the* ⁓ *of government*; *a* ⁓ *of learning* (e.g. a university). *v.t.* **1.** ~ *oneself, be* ~*ed,* sit down. *Please be* ~*ed, ladies and gentlemen.* **2.** have ~s for: *a hall that* ~*s 200.*

se·cede [sɪ'siːd] *v.i.* (of a group) withdraw from membership (of a church, federation, etc.). **se·ces·sion** [sɪ'seʃn] *n.*

se·clude [sɪ'kluːd] *v.t.* keep (a person, oneself) apart from the company of others: *lead a* ~*d life.* **se·clud·ed** *adj.* (esp. of a place) hidden away; solitary. **se·clu·sion** [sɪ'kluːʒn] *n.* (no pl.) secluding or being ~d; ~d place; retirement: *live in seclusion.*

sec·ond[1] ['sekənd] *adj.* **1.** next after the first in position, time, order, etc.: ~ *to none,* surpassed by no other; ~ *childhood,* old age when accompanied by mental weakness; ~ *floor,* the one above the first (i.e. Gt. Brit. two floors, U.S.A. one floor, above the ground); ~ *lieutenant,* lowest commissioned rank in the army; ~ *sight,* ability to see future events or events happening at a distance as if present. **2.** additional; extra: *a* ~ *pair of gloves;* ~ *name,* surname; ~ *nature,* acquired tendency that has become instinctive; ~ *thoughts,* opinion or resolution formed on reconsideration. **3.** another; of the same kind as one that has gone before: *a* ~ *Napoleon.* *n.* **1.** person or thing that comes next after the first. **2.** person who supports or helps another in a duel or a boxing-match. **3.** (pl.) goods below the best quality. *v.t.* **1.** support (esp. in a duel or boxing-match). **2.** (at a meeting) speak in support of a motion (after it has been proposed). **3.** [sɪ'kɒnd] (Gt. Brit., esp. mil.) take (sb.) from his ordinary duty and give him a special duty. '~-**best** *adj.* next after the best. '~-**class** *adj.* of the class next after the first; inferior. *adv.* by the ~ class: *travel* ~-*class.* '~-**hand** *adj.* **1.** already used by sb. else: ~-*hand clothes (books).* (Cf. *used* (1).) **2.** (of news, knowledge) obtained from others, not based on personal observation, etc. '~-**rate** *adj.* not of the best quality.

sec·ond[2] ['sekənd] *n.* **1.** sixtieth part of a minute of time or angular measurement (indicated by the mark ″): *the* ~ *hand of a watch.* **2.** (colloq.) moment; short time: *wait a* ~.

sec·on·dary ['sekəndərɪ] *adj.* following what is first or primary: ~ *school (education)* (between the primary school and the university); less important than what is chief or first.

se·cre·cy ['siːkrəsɪ] *n.* (no pl.) **1.** keeping things secret; ability to do this. **2.** state of being (kept) secret.

se·cret ['siːkrɪt] *adj.* **1.** (to be) kept from the knowledge or view of others; of which others have no knowledge: *a* ~ *marriage;* ~ *agent,* member of the S~ Service (if he works for one's own government) (cf. *spy*); S~ *Service,* government department concerned with espionage and counter-espionage. **2.** (of a place) secluded. **3.** (of a person) ~ive. *n.* **1.** sth. ~: *keep a* ~, not tell anyone else; *in the* ~, among those allowed to know it. **2.** hidden cause; explanation; way of doing sth., that is not widely known: *What is the* ~ *of his success?* **3.** (no pl.) secrecy: *in* ~, ~ly. ~·**ly** *adv.* in a ~ manner. ~·**ive** ['siːkrətɪv] *adj.* having the habit of keeping things ~; needlessly reserved.

sec·re·tary ['sekrətrɪ] *n.* **1.** person employed to send letters, keep papers and records[2], make business arrangements and appointments, etc. for another or for an organization. **2.** S~ *of State,* (Gt. Brit.) minister in charge of a major government department; (U.S.A.) = Foreign (2) S~. **sec·re·tar·i·al** [,sekrə'teərɪəl] *adj.* of a ~ or a ~'s work. **sec·re·tar·i·at** [,sekrə-'teərɪət] *n.* **1.** office of a ~. **2.** staff of secretaries.

se·crete [sɪ'kriːt] *v.t.* **1.** put or keep in a secret place. **2.** produce by secretion (1). **se·cre·tion** [sɪ'kriːʃn] *n.* **1.** (no pl.) (physiol.) process by which certain substances in a plant or animal body are separated (from sap or blood, etc.) for use or as waste matter. **2.** substance ~d (e.g. saliva, bile).

sect [sekt] *n.* group of people united by (esp. religious) beliefs or opinions that differ from those more generally accepted. **sec·tar·i·an** [sek'teərɪən] *n. & adj.* (member, supporter) of a ~ or ~s.

sec·tion ['sekʃn] *n.* **1.** part cut off; slice. **2.** one of a number of completed parts to be put together to make a structure: *fit together the* ~s *of a shed.*

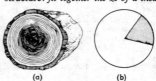

(a) (b)

(a) a cross-section of a tree trunk

(b) a sector of a circle

457

seed

3. division of a piece of writing (often indicated by the ~-mark §), of a town, country, or community: *the residential (shopping)* ~ (= *area*). **4.** (also *cross*-~) view or representation of sth. seen as if cut straight through. ~·al ['sekʃənl] *adj.* **1.** made or supplied in ~s (2): *a ~al bookcase.* **2.** of a ~ or ~s (3): *~al jealousies* (e.g. between ~s of a community).

sec·tor ['sektə*] *n.* **1.** (mil.) one of the areas into which a battle area is divided for the purpose of controlling operations; similar portion of any activity: *the public and private ~s of industry.* **2.** (geom.) part of a circle lying between two straight lines drawn from the centre to the circumference.

sec·u·lar ['sekjələ*] *adj.* worldly or material, not religious or spiritual: ~ *art* (*music, education*).

se·cure [sɪ'kjʊə*] *adj.* **1.** safe (*from* or *against* risk, etc.). **2.** firmly or tightly fixed; not likely to slip or break. *v.t.* **1.** make ~: *a ~ village from* (*against*) *floods by building embankments.* **2.** make fast¹: *~ the doors and windows.* **3.** obtain: *~ tickets for a concert.* ~·ly *adv.*

se·cu·ri·ty [sɪ'kjʊərətɪ] *n.* **1.** (sth. that provides) safety: ~ *risk,* person of doubtful loyalty to the State. **2.** sth. valuable (e.g. a life-insurance policy) given as a pledge for the repayment of a promise or undertaking. **3.** document, certificate, etc. showing ownership of property (esp. bonds, stocks, and shares).

se·dan [sɪ'dæn] *n.* **1.** (also ~-*chair*) covered chair carried on poles by two men, used in the 17th and 18th centuries. **2.** (U.S.A.) = saloon (car).

a sedan-chair

se·date [sɪ'deɪt] *adj.* (of a person, his behaviour) calm; serious; grave. ~·ly *adv.*

sed·a·tive ['sedətɪv] *n. & adj.* (medicine, drug) tending to calm the nerves.

sed·en·tary ['sedntərɪ] *adj.* (of work) done sitting down (at a desk, etc.); (of persons) spending much of their time seated: *lead a ~ life.*

sed·i·ment ['sedɪmənt] *n.* matter (sand, gravel, mud, dirt) that settles to the bottom of a liquid (e.g. mud left on fields after a river has been in flood over them).

se·di·tion [sɪ'dɪʃn] *n.* (no pl.) words, actions, intended to make people rebel against authority. **se·di·tious** [sɪ'dɪʃəs] *adj.*

se·duce [sɪ'djuːs] *v.t.* persuade (sb.) to do wrong (e.g. by offering money); (esp.) persuade (a woman) to give up her chastity. **se·duc·er** *n.* **se·duc·tion** [sɪ'dʌkʃn] *n.* **1.** seducing or being ~d. **2.** sth. very attractive and tempting. **se·duc·tive** [sɪ'dʌktɪv] *adj.* alluring; captivating.

sed·u·lous ['sedjʊləs] *adj.* persevering; done with persistence.

see¹ [siː] *v.i. & t.* (p.t. *saw* [sɔː], p.p. *~n* [siːn]) **1.** have (use) the power of sight. **2.** understand; learn. **3.** attend to; take care: *S~ that the windows are fastened.* **4.** receive a call from; give an interview to; visit: *I can't ~ you today.* ~ *a doctor.* (*I'll*) *be ~ing you!* ~ *you (later)!* (colloq.) '*Goodbye!*' (till we meet again). **5.** (with advs. & preps.): ~ *about,* attend to; take steps to do (sth.) or to get (sth.); ~ *after,* look after; attend to; ~ *into,* inquire into; ~ *sb. off,* go to a railway station, an airport, a ship, etc. to ~ sb. start a journey; ~ *sb. out,* go with him to the door when he is leaving; ~ *through* (*sb.* or *sth.*), (fig.) not be deceived by; ~ (*sb.* or *sth.*) *through,* support for as long as is necessary; ~ *through* (adj.), (esp. of clothing) transparent; ~ *to,* attend to; ~ *to it that,* take care, make certain, that. **6.** (with ns. & adjs.): ~ *the back of sb.,* get rid of him; ~ *the last of,* have done with; ~ *life,* have wide experience of many kinds of activity, etc.; ~ *the sights,* visit notable places, etc. as a sightseer; ~ *double,* see two things where there is only one; ~ *red,* become violently angry. **7.** (various uses): *I'll ~,* I will consider the matter. *Let me ~,* give me time to think or recall.

see² [siː] *n.* district under a bishop. *the Holy S~,* the papacy.

seed [siːd] *n.* (pl. ~*s,* ~) **1.** flowering plant's element of life, from which another plant can grow: *run* (*go*) *to ~,* stop flowering and produce ~; (fig.) become careless of one's appearance and clothes. **2.** cause, origin (*of* a tendency, development). **3.** (no pl.) semen. **4.** ~ed player: *No. 3* ~, the third best. *v.i. & t.* **1.** (of plants) produce ~. **2.** sow with ~. **3.** take the ~ out of (e.g. dried fruit). **4.** ~ed players, (esp. tennis) tested and proved of high standard. **~·less** *adj.* having no ~: *~less raisins.* **~·ling** *n.* plant newly grown from a ~. **'~s·man** *n.* dealer in ~s. **~·y** *adj.* (*-ier, -iest*) **1.** full of ~. **2.** shabby. **3.** (colloq.) unwell.

seek [si:k] *v.t. & i.* (p.t. & p.p. *sought* [sɔ:t]) **1.** look for; try to find: *~ shelter*; *~ safety in flight.* **2.** *~ for*, look for. **3.** *~ to do sth.*, try to do sth. **4.** *sought after*, wanted; in demand.

seem [si:m] *v.i.* have or give the impression or appearance of being or doing; appear to be: *Things far off ~ (to be) small.* **~·ing** *adj.* apparent but perhaps not real: *his ~ing friendship.* **~·ing·ly** *adv.* in appearance; apparently.

seem·ly ['si:mlɪ] *adj.* (*-ier, -iest*) (of behaviour) proper or correct (for the occasion or circumstances); decent; decorous.

seen, see *see*[1].

seep [si:p] *v.i.* (of liquids) ooze out or through; trickle. **~·age** ['si:pɪdʒ] *n.* (no pl.).

seer ['si:ə*] *n.* person claiming to see into the future; prophet.

see·saw ['si:sɔ:] *n.* (game played on a) long board and pivot with a person astride each end that can rise and fall alternately; up-and-down or to-and-fro motion. *v.i.* move or play in this way.

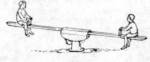

a seesaw

seethe [si:ð] *v.i.* (fig.) boil; bubble over; be agitated: *seething with anger*; *streets seething with people.*

seg·ment ['seɡmənt] *n.* **1.** part cut off or marked off by a line: (geom.) *a ~ of a circle.* **2.** division or section: *a ~ of an orange.*

seg·re·gate ['seɡrɪɡeɪt] *v.t.* **1.** separate, put apart, from others. **2.** enforce racial segregation on (persons) or in (a community, etc.). **seg·re·ga·tion** [,seɡrɪ'ɡeɪʃn] *n.* (no pl.) segregating or being ~d: *racial segregation.* **seg-**

re·ga·tion·ist [,seɡrɪ'ɡeɪʃənɪst] *n.* person who believes in or practises segregation, esp. of races.

seis·mic ['saɪzmɪk] *adj.* of earthquakes. **seis·mo·graph** ['saɪzməɡrɑ:f] *n.* instrument that records[1] the strength and the distance away of an earthquake.

seize [si:z] *v.t. & i.* **1.** take possession of (property, etc.) by law: *~ sb.'s goods for payment of debt.* **2.** take hold of, suddenly and violently: *~ a thief by the collar*; *~ an opportunity*, (fig.) use it promptly. **3.** *~ upon an idea*, see and use it. **sei·zure** ['si:ʒə*] *n.* **1.** seizing. **2.** sudden attack of illness (esp. of heart trouble or apoplexy).

sel·dom ['seldəm] *adv.* rarely; not often: *She was ~ seen there.*

se·lect [sɪ'lekt] *v.t.* choose (as being the most suitable, etc.). *adj.* **1.** carefully chosen. **2.** (of a school, society, etc.) of or for carefully chosen persons; not open to all. **se·lec·tion** [sɪ'lekʃn] *n.* **1.** (no pl.) ~ing. **2.** collection or group of ~ed things or examples; number of things from which to ~. **se·lec·tive** *adj.* having the power to ~. **se·lec·tor** *n.* (esp.) member of a committee ~ing a sports team.

self [self] *n.* (pl. *selves* [selvz]) **1.** (no pl.) person's nature, special qualities, own individuality: *one's better ~*, one's better nature. **2.** interests, etc. considered from one's own point of view: *a woman with no thought of ~*, an unselfish woman.

self- [self-] *pref.* short for *itself, myself, himself, oneself, etc.*, as in *~-taught*, taught by oneself, *~-control*, control of oneself. **,~-as'ser·tive** *adj.* insisting on one's own claims; pushing oneself forward. **,~-as'ser·tion** *n.* (no pl.). **,~-'cen·tred** *adj.* interested chiefly in oneself, one's own affairs. **,~-'col·oured** *adj.* of the same colour all over. **,~-com'mand** *n.* (no pl.) power of commanding one's feelings. **,~-'con·fi·dence** *n.* (no pl.) belief in one's own abilities. **,~-'con·fi·dent** *adj.* **,~-'con·scious** *adj.* (esp.) shy, unnatural in behaviour because unable to forget oneself. **,~-con'tained** *adj.* **1.** (esp. of a flat) complete in itself and with its own private entrance. **2.** (of a person) reserved. **,~-de'fence** *n.* (no pl.) defence of one's own body, property, rights, etc. **,~-de'ni·al** *n.* (no pl.) voluntary sacrifice of pleasures to save money, etc. **,~-de,ter·mi'na·tion** *n.* (no pl.) (esp.) right of a nation to decide the kind of government it shall have. ,~-em'ployed *adj.* working as the owner of a business, etc. ,~-'ev·i·dent *adj.* clear without proof or more evidence. ,~-im'por·tant *adj.* pompous; having too high an opinion of oneself. ,~-in'dul·gent *adj.* giving way to desires for one's own comfort, pleasures, etc. '~-made *adj.* (esp. of persons) having succeeded by their own efforts, esp. after beginning life without money, education, or influence. ,~-'pity *n.* (no pl.) exaggerated pity for oneself. ,~-pos'sessed *adj.* calm; cool; confident. ,~-pos-'ses·sion *n.* (no pl.) coolness; composure. '~-,pres·er'va·tion *n.* (no pl.) (instinct for) keeping oneself from harm or destruction. ,~-re'li·ant *adj.* having or showing confidence in one's own powers, etc. ,~-re'li·ance *n.* (no pl.). ,~-re'spect *n.* (no pl.) proper regard for one's own character and reputation. ,~-'right·eous *adj.* convinced of one's own goodness; feeling that one is better than others. ,~-'sac·ri·fice *n.* giving up of one's own interests for the sake of other persons. '~-same *adj.* the very same. ,~-'sat·is·fied *adj.* showing (undue) satisfaction with oneself or one's achievements. '~-,sat·is·fac·tion *n.* (no pl.). ,~'seek·ing *adj. & n.* (no pl.) selfish (behaviour). ,~-'ser·vice (esp. *attrib.*) *adj.* helping oneself: (a) (of restaurants, shops) having goods, etc. on counters, shelves, etc. from which customers serve themselves and pay as they leave at a cashier's desk; (b) (of a garage) one at which customers fill their cars with petrol and then pay the charge at a counter. ,~-'sown *adj.* (of plants) growing from seed dropped by a plant. ,~-'styled *adj.* using a name, title, etc. to which one has no right. ,~-suf'fi·cient *adj.* needing no help from others; overconfident. ,~-'will *n.* (no pl.) wilfulness. ,~-'willed *adj.* obstinate; refusing advice or guidance.

self·ish ['selfɪʃ] *adj.* chiefly thinking of or interested in one's own needs and welfare; without care for others. ~·ly *adv.* ~·ness *n.* (no pl.).

sell [sel] *v.t. & i.* (p.t. & p.p. **sold** [səʊld]) **1.** give in exchange for money: ~ off, ~ (stocks of goods) cheaply; ~ out, ~ (part or all of one's share in a business); ~ all of one's stock (of sth.); ~ (sb.) up, ~ his goods for payment of debt. **2.** (of shopkeepers, etc.) keep stocks for sale; (of goods) be sold; find buyers. ~·er *n.* person who ~s: a

book~er; sth. that is sold, esp. a best ~er, a book that ~s (2) in large numbers.

sel·vage, sel·vedge ['selvɪdʒ] *n.* edge of cloth woven so that threads do not unravel.

selves, see *self.*

sem·a·phore ['seməfɔ:*] *n.* **1.** (no pl.) system for sending signals by using arms on a post or flags held in the hands. **2.** mechanical device (2) with red and green lights on movable arms, used for signalling on railways. *v.t. & i.* signal or send (messages) by ~.

sem·blance ['sembləns] *n.* likeness; appearance.

se·men ['si:mən] *n.* (no pl.) fertilizing, sperm-bearing fluid of a male animal.

se·mes·ter [sɪ'mestə*] *n.* (esp. in Germany and U.S.A.) half of a university year. (Cf. Gt. Brit. *term* (1).)

semi- ['semɪ] *pref.* **1.** half of: a ~circle. **2.** almost; partly: ~-civilized; ~-conscious; ~-official; ~fluid; ~-solid. **3.** occurring, published, etc. twice in (a year, etc.): ~-annual; a ~-weekly. ,~'co·lon *n.* the sign (;) used in writing and printing. ,~-de'tached *adj.* (of a house) joined to another on one side only. ,~'fi·nal *n.* last match (contest) but one in a competition. ,~'fi·nal·ist *n.* player, team, in the ~finals.

sem·i·nar ['semɪnɑ:*] *n.* class of students in a university, studying a problem and meeting for discussions with a teacher.

sem·i·nary ['semɪnərɪ] *n.* Roman Catholic training college for priests.

Se·mit·ic [sɪ'mɪtɪk] *adj.* **1.** of a branch of the language family that includes Hebrew and Arabic. **2.** of the Jews.

semp·stress, see *seamstress.*

sen·ate ['senɪt] *n.* **1.** Upper House (usu. smaller) of the two parts of Parliament, esp. in France and U.S.A. **2.** governing council of some universities. **3.** highest council of state in ancient Rome. **sen·a·tor** ['senətə*] *n.* member of a ~ (1, 3).

send [send] *v.t. & i.* (p.t. & p.p. **sent** [sent]) **1.** cause (sb. or sth.) to go, come, or be carried; get (sb. or sth.) taken: ~ *away*, ~ to a distance; dismiss (a servant, etc.); ~ *for*, ask or order sb. to come; ask or order that sth. shall be sent; ~ *forth*, produce (leaves, etc.); ~ *in*, enter (one's name, work, etc. *for* a competition, an exhibition, etc.); ~ *off* (letters, goods), dispatch; ~ *on*, forward; ~ *in* advance (e.g. one's luggage); ~ *out*, give forth (light, heat);

distribute (circulars, etc.) by post, messengers, etc.; ~ word, ~ news, a message, etc. **2.** cause to become: ~ sb. mad. **~·er** n. person or thing that ~s: (on a letter) ... return to ~er. **'~-off** n. meeting (e.g. at a railway station) of a traveller's friends to wish him a good journey, to show respect, etc.

se·nile ['si:naɪl] adj. showing signs of, caused by, old age. **se·nil·i·ty** [sɪ-'nɪlɪtɪ] n. (no pl.) weakness (of body or mind) in old age.

se·nior ['si:njə*] adj. **1.** (often ~ to) older in years; higher in rank, authority, etc. **2.** (after a person's name) indicating the elder person with the same name: Tom Brown, S~ (abbr. Sen.). n. **1.** ~ person: She is my ~ by three years. **2.** (U.S.A.) student in his or her fourth year at high school or college. **~·i·ty** [ˌsiːnɪ'ɒrɪtɪ] n. (no pl.) condition of being ~ (in age, rank, etc.).

sen·sa·tion [sen'seɪʃn] n. **1.** feeling: a ~ of warmth (smoothness, dizziness). **2.** (sth. that causes) deep interest or excitement. **~·al** [sen'seɪʃənl] adj. causing deep interest: a ~al crime; (of newspapers, etc.) presenting news in a manner designed to cause excitement.

sense [sens] n. **1.** any one of the special powers of the body by which a person is conscious of things: sight, hearing, smell, taste, and feeling. **2.** (no pl.) feeling; consciousness: a ~ of pleasure (shame). **3.** (no pl.) power of judging; judgement; practical wisdom: a man of ~; have ~ enough not to waste money on useless things. **4.** (no pl.) appreciation or understanding of the value or worth (of): a ~ of humour; the moral ~; my ~ of duty. **5.** meaning: a word with several ~s; make ~, have a meaning that can be understood. **6.** (pl.) normal state of mind: out of one's ~s, mad; bring sb. to his ~s, get him to stop behaving foolishly; come to one's ~s, stop behaving foolishly. v.t. be vaguely aware of: ~ danger. **~·less** adj. **1.** foolish. **2.** unconscious.

sen·si·bil·i·ty [ˌsensɪ'bɪlɪtɪ] n. **1.** (no pl.) power of feeling, esp. delicate emotional impressions. **2.** (pl.) tendency to feel offended, etc.; susceptibility.

sen·si·ble ['sensəbl] adj. **1.** having or showing good sense (3): a ~ answer. **2.** aware (of).

sen·si·tive ['sensɪtɪv] adj. **1.** quick to receive impressions: ~ skin. The eyes are ~ to light. **2.** easily hurt in the spirit

or offended: ~ to criticism. **3.** (of instruments) able to record small changes. **4.** (of photographic film, paper, etc.) affected by light. **sen·si·tiv·i·ty** [sensɪ'tɪvɪtɪ] n. (no pl.) quality, degree, of being ~. **sen·si·tize** ['sensɪtaɪz] v.t. make (film, paper, etc.) ~ (4) (for photographic purposes).

sen·sor ['sensə*] n. device (2) that responds to a physical stimulus (as heat, light, or a particular motion) and transmits a resulting impulse (e.g. for operating a control).

sen·so·ry ['sensərɪ] adj. of the senses (1) or sensation (1).

sen·su·al ['sensjʊəl] adj. of, given up to, the pleasures of the senses only; self-indulgent in regard to food and drink and sexual enjoyment. **~·ist** n. ~ person. **sen·su·ous** ['sensjʊəs] adj. affecting, noticed by, appealing to, the senses.

sent, see send.

sen·tence ['sentəns] n. **1.** (gram.) words, esp. with subject and predicate, that form a statement, question, or request, making complete sense. (Cf. clause, phrase.) **2.** (statement by a judge, etc. of) punishment: under ~ of death. v.t. state that (sb.) is to have a certain punishment: ~ a thief to six months' imprisonment.

sen·ten·tious [sen'tenʃəs] adj. having, putting on, an air of wisdom; pompous.

sen·tient ['senʃnt] adj. that feels or is able to feel.

sen·ti·ment ['sentɪmənt] n. **1.** mental feeling (e.g. of admiration, pity, loyalty). **2.** (no pl.) (tendency to be moved by) (a display of) tender feeling (instead of reason). **3.** expression of feeling; opinion or point of view. **sen·ti·men·tal** [ˌsentɪ'mentl] adj. easily moved by, full of, tender feelings; designed to have an effect on the feelings: ~al girls (novels); for ~al reasons. **sen·ti·men·tal·ist** [ˌsentɪ'mentəlɪst] n. person moved by ~ rather than by reason. **sen·ti·men·tal·i·ty** [ˌsentɪmen'tælətɪ] n. (no pl.) false or exaggerated ~.

sen·ti·nel ['sentɪnl] n. sentry.

sen·try ['sentrɪ] n. soldier keeping watch or guard. **'~-box** n. hut or cabin for a ~. **'~-go** n. duty of pacing up and down as a ~: on ~-go.

sep·a·rate ['seprət] adj. apart; not joined; distinct; individual: keep this ~ (from the others). ['sepəreɪt] v.t. & i. **1.** make, keep, or become ~: ~ the *sheep from the goats.* **2.** (of a number of people) go in different ways. **sep·a·rable** ['sepərəbl] *adj.* that can be ~d. **sep·a·ra·tion** [,sepə'reɪʃn] *n.* (period of) being ~d; act of separating.

se·pia ['siːpjə] *n.* (no pl.) dark brown (paint).

Sep·tem·ber [sep'tembə*] *n.* ninth month of the year.

sep·tic ['septɪk] *adj.* infected; causing, caused by, infection (with disease germs): ~ *poisoning.*

sep·tu·a·ge·nar·i·an ['septjuədʒɪ-'neərɪən] *n. & adj.* (person) aged between 70 and 79.

sep·ul·chre (U.S.A. **-cher**) ['sepəlkə*] *n.* tomb: *the Holy S~,* that of Jesus Christ. **se·pul·chral** [sɪ'pʌlkrəl] *adj.* **1.** of a ~; of burial. **2.** (of a voice, etc.) deep and mournful.

se·quel ['siːkwəl] *n.* **1.** that which follows or arises out of (an earlier happening): *in the ~,* later on. **2.** later story, film, etc. about the same people.

se·quence ['siːkwəns] *n.* a following on; connected line of events, ideas, etc.: *in ~,* one after another; in order.

se·ques·ter [sɪ'kwestə*] *v.t.* keep (sb.) away or apart from other people; withdraw (oneself) to a quiet place: *a ~ed life.*

ser·aph ['serəf] *n.* (pl. ~s, ~im [-ɪm]) angel. **se·raph·ic** [se'ræfɪk] *adj.* angelic; happy and beautiful as a ~.

ser·e·nade [,serə'neɪd] *n.* music (intended to be) sung or played outdoors at night. *v.t.* sing or play a ~ to (sb.).

se·rene [sɪ'riːn] *adj.* clear and calm. **~·ly** *adv.* **se·ren·i·ty** [sɪ'renətɪ] *n.* (no pl.).

serf [sɜːf] *n.* (in olden times) person not allowed to leave the land on which he worked. **~·dom** *n.* (no pl.) social system under which land was cultivated by ~s; ~'s condition of life.

serge [sɜːdʒ] *n.* (no pl.) hard-wearing, woollen cloth.

ser·geant ['sɑːdʒənt] *n.* **1.** non-commissioned army officer above a corporal and below a ~-major. **2.** (Gt. Brit.) police-officer with rank below that of an inspector (2). **'~-'ma·jor** *n.* warrant-officer, between a non-commissioned and a commissioned army officer.

se·ri·al ['sɪərɪəl] *adj.* **1.** of, in, forming, a series: *the ~ number of a banknote.* **2.** (of a story, etc.) appearing in parts (in a periodical, on radio, television, etc.). *n.* ~ play, story, etc. **~·ly** *adv.* **~·ize** *v.t.* publish, produce, in ~ form.

se·ries ['sɪərɪːz] *n.* (pl. ~) **1.** number of

things, events, etc. each of which is related in some way to the others, esp. to the one before it. **2.** succession: *a ~ of wet days.*

se·ri·ous ['sɪərɪəs] *adj.* **1.** solemn; thoughtful; not frivolous. **2.** important because of possible danger: *a ~ illness (situation).* **3.** in earnest; sincere; not playful. **~·ly** *adv.* **~·ness** *n.* (no pl.).

ser·mon ['sɜːmən] *n.* spoken or written address on a religious or moral subject, esp. one given in church.

ser·pent ['sɜːpənt] *n.* snake. **ser·pen·tine** ['sɜːpəntaɪn] *adj.* curving and twisting like a ~: *the ~ine windings of a river (road).*

ser·ried ['serɪd] *adj.* (of persons in lines or ranks) close together.

se·rum ['sɪərəm] *n.* (pl. *sera* [-rə], ~s) **1.** (no pl.) watery part of the blood. **2.** such a fluid taken from the blood of an animal that has been made immune to a disease, used for inoculation.

ser·vant ['sɜːvənt] *n.* wage-earning person, esp. one engaged to do housework, etc.; member of a (company's, etc.) staff. *public ~,* State official; *civil ~,* member of the Civil Service.

serve [sɜːv] *v.t. & i.* **1.** work for; be a servant to (sb.): *serving as cook (gardener, etc.).* **2.** perform duties (for): ~ *one's country in Parliament;* ~ *a year in the Army;* ~ *on* (be a member of) *a committee.* **3.** attend to (customers in a shop, etc.); supply (*with* goods or services); place (food, etc.) on the table for a meal; give (food, etc.) to people at a meal: *Dinner is ~d. S~ the coffee in the next room.* **4.** be satisfactory for a need or purpose: *a box that ~d as a seat; an excuse that will not ~* (that is not good enough). **5.** act towards, treat (sb. in a certain way): ~ *sb. shamefully,* behave badly towards him. *It ~s him right,* this is a suitable punishment for or consequence of his behaviour. **6.** ~ *one's time (apprenticeship),* pass the usual or normal number of years (learning a trade, etc.); go through one's term of office, etc. **7.** ~ *time,* ~ *a sentence,* undergo a period of imprisonment. **8.** (law) deliver (a summons, etc.) to the person named in it: ~ *a summons on sb.;* ~ *sb. with a writ.* **9.** (tennis, etc.) put the ball into play: ~ *a ball;* ~ *well* (badly).

ser·vice ['sɜːvɪs] *n.* **1.** (no pl.) being a servant; position as a servant: *go into ~,* become a domestic servant. **2.** department or branch of public work, government employment, etc.: *the*

Civil (Diplomatic) S~; the fighting ~s, the Navy, Army, Air Force; *on active ~,* engaged on military duties in time of war; *~ dress (rifle, etc.),* military dress, etc. **3.** sth. done to help or benefit another: *get the ~s of a doctor (lawyer); his ~s to the State.* **4.** (no pl.) benefit; use; advantage: *at your ~,* ready and willing to do what you want; ready for you to use. **5.** system or arrangement that supplies public needs, esp. for communications: *a bus (train, etc.) ~; the postal (telephone) ~.* **6.** form of worship and prayer to God: *three ~s every Sunday*; religious ceremony for a special purpose: *the marriage (burial) ~.* **7.** complete set of plates, dishes, etc. for use at table: *a tea (dinner) ~ of 50 pieces.* **8.** (no pl.) act or work of serving food and drink (in hotels, etc.); work done by domestic servants, hotel staff, etc.: *add 10% to the bill for ~; make a ~ charge; a ~ flat,* one whose rent includes the cost of cleaning, etc. **9.** (no pl.) expert help or advice given by manufacturers, etc. after the sale of an article: *send the car in for ~. ~ station,* petrol station that also offers general ~ (e.g. greasing, checking of brakes, etc.). **10.** (tennis, etc.) act of serving the ball; manner of doing this; person's turn to serve; game in which one serves. *v.t.* keep in (9) for; put into, keep in, good order: *Cars ~d here.* **~·able** ['sɜːvɪsəbl] *adj.* **1.** able to help. **2.** strong and lasting.

ser·vi·ette [ˌsɜːvɪ'et] *n.* table-napkin.

ser·vile ['sɜːvaɪl] *adj.* **1.** of or like slaves. **2.** suggesting the attitude of a slave to his master: *~ flattery.* **ser·vil·i·ty** [sɜː'vɪlətɪ] *n.* (no pl.).

ser·vi·tude ['sɜːvɪtjuːd] *n.* (no pl.) condition of being forced to work for others and of having no freedom.

ses·sion ['seʃn] *n.* **1.** (meeting of a) lawcourt, law-making body (5), etc.; time occupied by discussions at such a meeting: *in ~,* assembled for business, etc. **2.** single, uninterrupted meeting for other purposes: *a recording ~* (for recording material on discs or tapes).

set[1] [set] *v.t. & i.* (-*tt*-; p.t. & p.p. ~) **1.** put or place (sth. in a certain position, condition, or relation): *~ a box on its end; ~ a stake in the ground.* **2.** (of the sun, etc.) go down below the horizon. **3.** (with preps. & advs.): *~ about one's work, ~ about doing sth.,* make a start; *~ apart, ~ aside,* put separately; reserve; *~ sb. or sth. back,* stop

or slow down the progress of; move back (e.g. the hands of a clock); *~ (sb.) down,* (of a vehicle, the driver) allow (a passenger) to get out; *~ forth,* start a journey; state clearly (e.g. one's views); *~ in,* (of a type of weather, a disease, etc.) start and seem likely to continue; (of tides, winds) begin to flow (in towards the shore); *~ off,* (a) start a journey; (b) explode (a mine, firework, etc.); (c) cause (sb.) to begin laughing (talking, etc.); (d) make more striking by contrast: *a large hat ~ting off a pretty little face; ~ on sb.,* attack him; *~ (sb. or sth.) on,* cause or urge to attack; *~ out,* start a journey, etc.; *~ sth. out,* make known (e.g. reasons); put on view; *~ to,* begin vigorously (to do sth.); begin fighting; *~ up,* begin business (*as a carpenter,* etc.); *~ (sb or sth.) up,* (a) get (sb.) started (*in* business); (b) get a business started; (c) make (sb.) strong after an illness, etc.; (d) arrange (type) in order ready for printing; (e) put forward (e.g. a defence); *well ~ up (with),* well provided; *~ upon,* attack. **4.** (with certain objects): *~ a (broken) bone,* bring the parts together so that they may unite; *~ a clock (watch),* move the hands to show a certain time; *~ eggs,* place them under a hen; *~ (sb.) an example,* show, by one's own behaviour, how others should behave; *never ~ eyes on,* never see; *~ one's face against (sth.),* be firmly opposed to; *~ a fashion,* start one to be copied; *~ fire (a light) to sth.,* cause it to begin burning; *~ one's hair,* fix it while damp so that it dries in the desired style; *~ one's heart on (sth.),* direct and fix one's hopes on; *~ a hen,* place it on eggs (for hatching); *~ one's name (hand, seal, etc.) (to a document),* sign or seal; *~ the pace,* go at a pace that others must keep up with; *~ sail,* begin a voyage; *~ a saw,* (sharpen and) adjust its teeth; *~ much (little, etc.) store by sth.,* value it greatly (little, etc.); *~ the table,* lay it ready with plates, etc.; *~ one's teeth,* close the jaws tightly; (fig.) show firm determination; *~ a trap (for),* arrange or adjust it to catch a mouse, etc.; (fig.) do sth. to discover a dishonest person, etc. **5.** cause (sb. or sth.) to be in a certain state, relation, etc.: *~ sth. straight; ~ a prisoner free; ~ sb.'s doubts at rest (sb.'s mind at ease); ~ sb. at his ease; ~ sb. (the law) at defiance; ~ things to rights,* restore them to order. **6.** cause (sb.) to do sth.; give as a task, etc.: *~ (sb.) a difficult problem; ~ the* *men to chop wood.* **7.** (of liquids, soft substances, etc.) become hard or solid: *The mortar (jam, jelly) hasn't ~ yet.* **8.** (of plants, esp. fruit-trees, their blossom) form or develop fruit. **9.** put (a jewel, etc.) firmly in gold or in a framework (e.g. of other jewels). **10.** *~ sth. to music*, compose a tune for (words, a verse, etc.). **11.** (of a hunting dog) stand motionless with the muzzle pointing to indicate the presence of game. **12.** (special uses of the passive past participle): *~ fair*, (of the weather) good and unlikely to change; *~ fast*, tightly fixed; unable to move; *a ~ lunch* (at a restaurant, etc., there being no choice of dishes); *a ~ time (date)* (arranged in advance); *a ~ smile (look)* (fixed; unchanging); *~ opinions* (fixed); *~ in one's ways*, having fixed habits; *a ~ book*, a book on which an examination will be held.

et² [set] *n.* **1.** (no pl.) direction (of current, wind, tide); tendency (of opinion). **2.** number of things of a similar kind, that go together: *a ~ of golf-clubs*; *a tea (dinner) ~*, service (7); *a ~ of (false) teeth.* **3.** group of people of a social type: *the jet (racing) ~.* **4.** (math.) collection of things having a common property: *~ theory*, study of *~s* without regard to the nature of their individual constituents. **5.** radio or television receiver. **6.** (no pl.) position or angle; posture: *the ~ of sb.'s head (shoulders).* **7.** young plant, cutting, or bulb ready to be planted. **8.** group of games in tennis. **9.** place prepared for a scene in a film or play: *Everyone to be on the ~ at 8.30 a.m.* **10.** *make a dead ~ at*, attack vigorously; try to win the friendship of. **11.** *~ting of the hair: a shampoo and ~.* **'~-back** *n.* (cause of a) check to progress or development. **~ square** *n.* triangular piece of wood, etc. for drawing lines at certain angles (e.g. 30°, 60°,

a set square

and 90°). **~ting** *n.* **1.** framework in which sth. (e.g. a jewel) is fixed. (See *set¹* (9).) **2.** music composed for a poem, etc. **3.** place, scene, etc. considered as the background or framework of a story, event, etc. **,~-'to** *n.* (pl. *~s*) fight; argument. **et-tee** [se'ti:] *n.* long, soft seat like a

sofa, with sides and a back, for two or more persons.

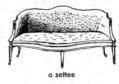

a settee

set·ter ['setə*] *n.* breed of long-haired dog trained to stand motionless on scenting game.

a setter

set·tle¹ ['setl] *n.* long, wooden seat with arms and a high back, the seat often being the lid of a chest.
set·tle² ['setl] *v.t. & i.* **1.** (often *~ down*) (cause to) come to rest: *~ (oneself) down in an armchair*; (cause to) become used to a new way of life or occupation: *~ down to a new job*; *~ one's son in business*; *married and ~d down.* **2.** make or become calm, untroubled: *I can't ~ (down) to anything* (i.e. I am restless). *let the excitement ~ down*; *a period of ~d weather.* **3.** make one's home (in, at): *~ in the country.* **4.** go to and live *in* (as colonists); establish colonists in: *The Dutch ~d in S. Africa.* **5.** reach an agreement about; decide: *That ~s the matter. Nothing is ~d yet. ~ one's affairs* (e.g. by making one's will); *~ (up)on*, decide or resolve (to do sth., have sth., etc.). **6.** pay (a debt, etc.): *~ a hotel bill*; *~ up*; *~ with your creditors*, come to an arrangement with them about debts; *have an account to ~ with sb.*, (fig.) have some unpleasant business to discuss. **7.** (of dust, etc. in the air, solid substances in a liquid, etc.) (cause to) sink to the floor, the ground, the bottom of a container, etc.: *The rain ~d the dust. The dust ~d on the floor.* **8.** (of a liquid) (cause to) become clear (as sediment, etc. *~s* (7)). **9.** (of the

settlement

ground, the foundation of a building, etc.) sink gradually to a lower level. **10.** (law) give (sb. property, etc.) for use during his lifetime: ~ *part of one's estate on one's son*. **~·ment** *n*. **1.** act of settling (an argument, a debt, etc.). **2.** (statement of) property, etc. ~d (10) on sb.: *a marriage ~ment*. **3.** group of colonists; new colony; process of settling (4) colonists. **4.** group of persons engaged in social welfare work in a slum area: *~ments in the East End of London*. **~·r** *n*. person who ~s (4) in a new country: *the English, German, French, etc. ~rs in N. America.*

sev·en ['sevn] *n. & adj.* 7. **~·th** ['sevnθ] *n. & adj.* 7th; ¹/₇. *in the ~th heaven*, extremely happy. **~·teen** [,sevn'ti:n] *n. & adj.* 17. **~·teenth** [,sevn'ti:nθ] *n. & adj.* 17th; ¹/₁₇. **~·ty** ['sevntɪ] *n. & adj.* 70. **~·ti·eth** ['sevntɪɪθ] *n. & adj.* 70th; ¹/₇₀.

sev·er ['sevə*] *v.t. & i.* **1.** cut (e.g. a rope) in two; break off (relations, a friendship). **2.** (of a rope, etc.) break.

sev·er·al ['sevrəl] *adj.* **1.** three or rather more; some. **2.** separate; individual: *They went their ~ ways*, each went his own way. *pron.* a moderate number; not many; some. **~·ly** *adv.* separately.

se·vere [sɪ'vɪə*] *adj.* (~*r*, ~*st*) **1.** stern; unkind; strict. **2.** (of the weather, a disease) violent; harsh. **3.** (of a test) hard. **4.** (of style, etc.) simple; without ornament. **~·ly** *adv.* **se·ver·i·ty** [sɪ'verətɪ] *n.*

sew [səʊ] *v.t. & i.* (p.t. ~ed, p.p. ~ed or ~n [səʊn]) work with a needle and thread; fasten with stitches; make (a garment) by stitching. **~·ing** *n*. (no pl.) act of ~ing; work (e.g. clothes) being ~n. **'~·ing-ma,chine** *n.* machine for ~ing and stitching.

sew·age ['sju:ɪdʒ] *n.* (no pl.) waste matter carried away in sewers.

sew·er [sjʊə*] *n.* large, usu. underground, drain that collects and carries away water and organic waste matter from buildings and roadways. **~·age** ['sjʊərɪdʒ] *n.* (no pl.) waste removal by ~s; system of ~s.

sewn, see *sew*.

sex [seks] *n.* **1.** being male or female; males or females collectively: ~ *appeal*, attractiveness of a person of one ~ to the other. **2.** (no pl.) ~ual activity and everything connected with it: *a film with too much ~ in it*. **~·u·al** ['seksjʊəl] *adj.* of ~ or the ~es: ~*ual intercourse*, physical union of male and female persons. **~·u·al·ly** *adv.* **~·y** *adj.* (-*ier, -iest*) ~ually attractive.

sex·a·ge·nar·i·an [,seksədʒɪ'neərɪən] *n. & adj.* (person) aged between 6 and 69.

sex·tant ['sekstənt] *n.* instrument use for measuring the altitude of the su etc. (in order to determine a ship position).

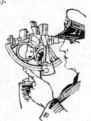

a sextant

sex·ton ['sekstən] *n.* man who take care of a church building, digs grave rings the church bell, etc.

shab·by ['ʃæbɪ] *adj.* (-*ier, -iest*) **1.** i bad condition because much worn, etc.; wearing ~ clothes. **2.** (behaviour) mean; unfair. **shab·bi·** *adv.*

shack [ʃæk] *n.* small, roughly built hu or shelter.

shack·le ['ʃækl] *n.* one of a pair of iro rings joined by a chain for fastenin a prisoner's wrists or ankles; (pl (fig.) sth. that prevents freedom action. *v.t.* put ~s on; (fig.) preve from acting freely.

shade [ʃeɪd] *n.* **1.** (no pl.) partly dar area sheltered from direct rays of ligh *sitting in the ~*. **2.** (no pl.) darker part(of a picture, etc.: *not enough light an ~ in your drawing*. **3.** degree or dept of colour: *various ~s of colour*. **4.** degre of difference: *a word with many ~s meaning*. **5.** sth. (e.g. for a lamp, calle a *lamp~*) that shuts out light or lesser its brightness; (U.S.A.) = blind (pl.) (U.S.A.) = sun-glasses. **6.** ghos (pl.) the Greek underworld or hom of spirits. *v.t. & i.* **1.** keep direct ray of light from: *He ~d his eyes with h hand*. **2.** cover (a light, lamp, etc. **3.** darken (parts of a drawing, etc.) give an appearance of solidity, et **4.** change by degrees (*into, from ... to* pink shading into red. **shady** *adj.* (-*ie -iest*) **1.** giving ~ from sunlight; in th ~: *the shady side of a street*. **2.** (colloq of behaviour) of doubtful honesty.

shad·ow ['ʃædəʊ] *n.* **1.** area of shad dark shape, thrown on the ground, o a wall, floor, etc. by sth. that cuts off the direct rays of light. **2.** dark patch or area: *have ~s under the eyes.* **3.** (no pl.) slightest trace: *without a ~ of doubt.* **4.** person's inseparable attendant or companion. *v.t.* **1.** darken. **2.** keep a secret watch on; follow all the movements of (e.g. a suspected criminal). **~y** *adj.* (*-ier, -iest*) of or like a ~.

haft [ʃɑːft] *n.* **1.** long, slender stem of an arrow or spear. **2.** long handle of an axe, etc. **3.** one of the two wooden poles between which a horse is harnessed to pull a cart, etc. **4.** long, narrow space, usu. vertical (e.g. for a lift in a building, for ventilation, for going down into a coal-mine, etc). **5.** main part of a column (1). **6.** bar or rod joining parts of a machine or causing parts to turn.

hag·gy [ˈʃægɪ] *adj.* (*-ier, -iest*) **1.** rough and coarse: *~ eyebrows.* **2.** covered with ~ hair: *a ~ dog.*

hake [ʃeɪk] *v.t. & i.* (p.t. **shook** [ʃʊk], p.p. **shaken** [ˈʃeɪkən]) **1.** (cause to) move from side to side, up and down, forwards and backwards: *~ one's head,* move it from side to side to indicate 'No' or doubt, disapproval, etc.; *~ hands (with sb.),* take sb.'s hand at meeting or parting, or to show sympathy, etc.; *~ off* (e.g. a cold, a bad habit), get free from. **2.** shock; trouble; weaken: *~ sb.'s faith (courage); ~e ~n by bad news.* **3.** (of sb.'s voice) tremble; become weak or faltering from old age, strong feeling). *n.* shaking or being ~n. **shak·er** *n.* vessel used for shaking: *a cocktail-~r.* **shaky** *adj.* (*-ier, -iest*) **1.** (of a person, his movements) unsteady. **2.** (of things) unsafe; unreliable. **shak·i·ly** *adv.*

hale [ʃeɪl] *n.* (no pl.) soft rock that splits easily into thin layers.

hall [ʃæl, ʃəl] *v.aux.* (pres. t. ~ or 'll after I or we); past t. *should* [ʃʊd] or *'d* (after I or we); neg. ~ *not,* colloq. **han't** [ʃɑːnt], *should not,* colloq. **houldn't** [ˈʃʊdnt]) **1.** (used in expressing the future tense (cf. *will*)): *We ~ arrive tomorrow. S~ we come tomorrow? I told him that I should see him the following day.* **2.** (used in expressing) (a) the speaker's determination: *You say you won't go, but I say ou ~ go.* (b) a promise: *If you work well today you ~ go home early.* **3.** (used in statements or questions concerning wishes, commands, duties, etc.): *S~ I = Do you want me to) open the window? You shouldn't* (= ought not ») *behave like that.* **4.** (used in ex-

pressing purpose (cf. *may, might*)): *I lent him an umbrella so that he should not get wet.* **5.** (used in reported speech): (*He said, 'You will fail'.*) *He told me that I should fail.* **6.** (*should* is used to express probability or expectation): *She should be here by now.* **7.** (*should* is used after *how, why,* etc.): *How should I know? Why should he go there?*

shal·low [ˈʃæləʊ] *adj.* of little depth: *~ water; a ~ dish;* (fig.) not earnest or serious: *~ talk.* *n.* (often pl.) ~ place in a river, lake, etc.

shalt [ʃælt, ʃəlt] *v.* old form of *shall* used with 'thou': *Thou ~ not steal.*

sham [ʃæm] *v.t. & i.* (*-mm-*) pretend: *~ming illness (sleep).* *n.* person who ~s; sth. intended to deceive: *His kindness is only a ~* (i.e. he is not really kind). *adj.* false; pretended: *a ~ fight* (as in training).

sham·ble [ˈʃæmbl] *v.i.* walk unsteadily without lifting the feet enough. *n.* shambling gait.

sham·bles [ˈʃæmblz] *n. pl.* (usu. sing. v.) **1.** scene of bloodshed: *the place became a ~.* **2.** (colloq.) place or scene of complete disorder.

shame [ʃeɪm] *n.* (no pl.) **1.** distressed feeling; loss of self-respect, caused by wrong or dishonourable or foolish behaviour (of oneself, one's family, etc.); capacity for experiencing this feeling: *be quite without ~.* **2.** dishonour: *bring ~ on one's family; put sb. to ~,* cause him to be disgraced. **3.** sth. unworthy; sth. that causes ~: *What a ~ to deceive the old man!* *v.t.* **1.** cause ~ (2) to; cause (sb.) to feel ~ (1). **2.** frighten or force (sb. *into* or *out of doing* sth.) by causing him to feel ~. **~'faced** *adj.* showing ~; looking distressed through ~. **~'faced·ly** *adv.* **~ful** *adj.* causing or bringing ~. **~ful·ly** *adv.* **~less** *adj.* feeling no ~; done without ~. **~less·ly** *adv.*

a shamrock

sham·poo [ʃæmˈpuː] *n.* (special soap, powder, etc. for a) washing of the hair: *a ~ and set.* *v.t.* wash (the hair of the head).

sham·rock [ˈʃæmrɒk] *n.* clover-like

plant with (usu.) three leaves on each stem.

shank [ʃæŋk] *n.* **1.** leg, esp. from knee to ankle. **2.** straight, slender part of an anchor, key, spoon, etc.

shan't, see *shall*.

shan·ty[1] [ˈʃæntɪ] *n.* poorly made house or shed.

shan·ty[2] [ˈʃæntɪ] *n.* sailor's song.

shape [ʃeɪp] *n.* outward form; appearance; outline: *The Earth has the same ~ as an orange. in any ~ or form*, of any kind; in any way; *take ~*, (of ideas, etc.) become orderly, well arranged; (of plans, buildings) approach completion. *v.t. & i.* **1.** give a certain ~ to. **2.** take ~; develop: *plans that are shaping well* (i.e. are promising (2)); *~ up*, get into ~; ready oneself. **~·less** *adj.* without a clear or graceful ~; without order. **~·ly** *adj.* well ~d; having a pleasing ~.

share[1] [ʃeə*] *n.* **1.** part or division that sb. has in, receives from, or gives to a stock (7) held by several or many persons, or that he contributes to a fund, expenses, etc.: *go ~s in*, divide (*with* others); become part owner (*with* others). **2.** (no pl.) part taken by sb. in an action, undertaking, etc. **3.** one of the equal parts into which the capital of a business company is divided, giving (to the owner of *preference ~s*) a right to a fixed rate of dividend or (to the owner of *ordinary ~s*) a right to part of the profits. *v.t. & i.* **1.** give a ~ of to others; divide and distribute. **2.** have or use (*with*): *~ a hotel bedroom with a stranger*. **3.** have a ~ (*in*): *Let me ~ in the cost of the outing.* '**~·hold·er** *n.* owner of ~s in a business company. '**~-out** *n.* distribution (among members of a group).

share[2] [ʃeə*] *n.* blade (1) of a plough.

shark [ʃɑːk] *n.* large sea-fish that eats other fish and is dangerous to bathers, etc.

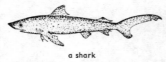

a shark

sharp [ʃɑːp] *adj.* **1.** with a good cutting edge; not blunt: *a ~ knife*; with a fine point: *a ~ needle.* **2.** well-defined; clearcut; distinct: *a ~ outline.* **3.** (of curves, slopes, bends) abrupt; changing direction quickly: *a ~ curve in the road.* **4.** (of sounds) shrill; piercing: *a ~ cry*

of distress. **5.** quickly aware of things ~ *eyes*; *a ~ sense of smell (hearing).* (of feelings, taste) keen; suggestin cutting or pricking: *a ~ pain*; *a sau with a ~ flavour.* **7.** harsh; severe: *rebukes.* **8.** quick in mind: *a ~ chila a ~-witted boy.* **9.** quick; brisk: *a walk*; *a ~* (i.e. violent) *struggle.* **1** quick to take advantage; unscrupu lous: *a ~ lawyer*; *~ practice.* **11.** (musi above the normal pitch; (of a not raised half a tone in pitch: *C ~ r* (music) (the symbol # used to indicat a) note that is raised half a tone: ~ *and flats. adv.* **1.** punctually: *at o'clock ~.* **2.** suddenly; abruptly: *turn to the left.* **3.** (music) above the tru pitch: *sing ~.* **~·en** [ˈʃɑːpən] *v.t. &* make or become ~(er). **~·en·e** [ˈʃɑːpnə*] *n.* sth. that ~ens: *a penci ~ener.* **~·er** *n.* swindler, esp. (*card-~e* person who makes a living by cheatin at cards. **~·ly** *adv.* **~·ness** *n.* (no pl.

shat·ter [ˈʃætə*] *v.t. & i.* **1.** brea suddenly into small pieces. **2.** (fig end (sb.'s hopes); shock (sb.'s nerves

shave [ʃeɪv] *v.t. & i.* (p.t. *~d*, p.p. ~ or, esp. as adj., *~n* [ˈʃeɪvn]) **1.** cut (hai off the chin, etc. with a razor. **2.** c off (a thin layer, slice, etc.). **3.** pa very close to, almost touching. *n.* shaving (of the face). **2.** *a close* (*narrou ~*, a fortunate escape from disaste injury, loss, etc. **shav·en** [ˈʃeɪvn] *ad* (in compounds): *clean-~n*, *well-~* having been ~d clean, well. **shav·er** *n* **1.** (also *dry-~r*) razor with an electr motor. **2.** (colloq.) lad; youngste *a young ~r.* '**shav·ing-brush** *n.* brus for spreading lather over the fac before shaving. **shav·ings** *n. pl.* thi slices ~d off wood, esp. with a plan (3). (Cf. *sawdust.*)

shawl [ʃɔːl] *n.* large (usu. square) piec of material worn about the shoulde or head by women or wrapped roun a baby.

she [ʃiː, ʃɪ] *pron.* female person, an mal, etc. previously referred to. *attri adj.* female: *a ~-goat. n.* femal woman: *This cat is a ~, not a he.*

sheaf [ʃiːf] *n.* (pl. *sheaves* [ʃiːvz]) bund of corn, barley, etc. stalks tied t gether after reaping; bundle of paper etc.

shear [ʃɪə*] *v.t.* (p.t. *~ed*, p.p. sho [ʃɔːn] or *~ed*) cut the wool off (a shee with ~s: *a sheep shorn of its wool. ~ n. pl.* (often *a pair of ~s*) large scisso of various kinds for *~ing* sheep, cuttin cloth, grass, etc.

sheath [ʃiːθ] *n.* (pl. *~s* [ʃiːðz]) **1.** ca

for the blade (1) of a sword, dagger, or tool. **2.** long, folded covering, esp. as part of a plant. ~e [ʃiːð] *v.t.* **1.** put (a sword, etc.) into a ~. **2.** encase in protective material: ~*e a ship's bottom with copper.*

sheaves, see *sheaf.*

shed¹ [ʃed] *n.* building, roughly made structure, used for storing things, sheltering animals, etc.

a shed¹

shed² [ʃed] *v.t.* (-dd-; p.t. & p.p. ~) **1.** let (tears, leaves, feathers, etc.) fall or come off: ~ *tears,* weep; *trees* ~*ding their leaves.* **2.** cause (blood) to flow: ~ *sb.'s blood,* kill or wound him. **3.** give forth: *a fire that* ~*s warmth;* ~ *light on,* (fig.) help to explain (sth. obscure).

sheen [ʃiːn] *n.* (no pl.) shiny quality (of a surface).

sheep [ʃiːp] *n.* (collective pl. ~) grass-eating animal kept for its flesh as food (*mutton*) and its wool. '~-**dog** *n.* dog trained to help a shepherd to look after ~. '~-**fold** *n.* enclosure for ~. ~**ish** *adj.* awkwardly self-conscious; timid like a ~.

sheer¹ [ʃɪə*] *adj.* **1.** complete; thorough; absolute: ~ *nonsense; a* ~ *waste of time.* **2.** (of textiles, etc.) finely woven and almost transparent: *stockings of* ~ *silk.* **3.** straight up or down: *a* ~ *drop of fifty feet. adv.* straight up or down.

sheer² [ʃɪə*] *v.i.* (esp. of a ship) change direction.

sheet [ʃiːt] *n.* **1.** large piece of linen or cotton cloth, esp. for a bed. **2.** broad, thin, flat piece (*of glass, iron, paper,* etc.): ~ *copper* (*iron, metal*) (rolled or hammered into thin ~s). **3.** wide expanse (*of water, ice,* etc.). **4.** cord fastened to the lower corner of a sail, used to hold and regulate it. ~**ing** *n.* (no pl.) material (e.g. cotton, linen) used for ~s. ~ **light·ning** *n.* (no pl.) lightning that comes in ~-like flashes of diffused brightness, not in zigzags.

sheik(h) [ʃeɪk] *n.* Arab chieftain.

shelf [ʃelf] *n.* (pl. *shelves* [ʃelvz]) **1.** level board fastened at right angles

to a wall, or in a bookcase, cupboard, etc. to stand things on. **2.** ~-like piece of rock on a cliff, mountainside, etc.

shelve [ʃelv] *v.t. & i.* **1.** put on a ~; (fig., of problems, etc.) postpone dealing with. **2.** (of land, the sea-shore) slope gradually.

a shelf (1)

shell [ʃel] *n.* **1.** hard, outer covering of bird's eggs, nuts, some seeds and fruits, and of some water animals (called ~*fish,* e.g. oysters, lobsters). **2.** outer structure, walls, of an unfinished or ruined building. **3.** metal case, filled with explosive, to be fired from a large gun. *v.t. & i.* **1.** take out of, be released from, a ~ (1): ~*ing peas.* **2.** fire ~s (3) at (from artillery). **3.** ~ *out,* (sl.) pay for, give (money) for, sth. '~-**fish** *n.* see ~ (1). '~-**shock** *n.* nervous or mental disorder caused by the noise and blast of bursting ~s (3).

shel·ter ['ʃeltə*] *n.* **1.** (no pl.) condition of being protected or safe (e.g. from rain, the heat of the sun, danger). **2.** sth. that gives safety or protection, esp. from the weather: *a bus* ~, a roofed enclosure at a bus stop; *an air-raid* ~. *v.t. & i.* **1.** give ~ to; protect. **2.** take ~ (*in, under,* etc. sth.; *from* the rain, etc.).

shelve, shelves, see *shelf.*

shep·herd ['ʃepəd] *n.* man who takes care of sheep. *the Good S~,* Jesus Christ. *v.t.* take care of; guide or direct (people) like sheep.

sher·iff ['ʃerɪf] *n.* **1.** chief officer of the Crown in counties and certain cities, with legal and ceremonial duties. **2.** (U.S.A.) officer with power to enforce law and order in his county.

sher·ry ['ʃerɪ] *n.* kinds of yellow or brown wine from Spain.

shield [ʃiːld] *n.* **1.** piece of armour (leather, steel, etc.) carried on the arm to protect the body in a fight. **2.** sth. designed to keep out dust, wind, etc., to protect from danger (e.g. in a machine) or damage. **3.** (fig.) person who protects. **4.** design in the shape of a ~ (1) in a coat of arms. *v.t.* protect;

keep safe; (fig.) save (sb.) from punishment or suffering.

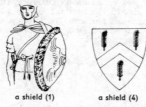

a shield (1)　　a shield (4)

the side; ～ *oars*, take them out of the water into the boat. **3.** agree to serve in a ～ for a voyage: *He ～ped as a*

ships

shift [ʃɪft] *v.t. & i.* **1.** move, be moved, from one place to another: ～ *the scenes* (on the stage of a theatre); ～ *the blame* (*on*) *to sb. else.* **2.** ～ *for oneself*, manage to get a living, look after oneself, without help from others. *n.* **1.** change; group of workmen who start work as another group finishes; period for which such a group works: *on the day* (*night*) ～; *doing an eight-hour* ～. **2.** way of evading a difficulty; trick; scheme. **3.** changed way of dealing with a situation: *make* ～ (*to do* sth.), do as well as one can without proper materials, tools, etc. **～·less** *adj.* without ability to find ways of succeeding. **～y** *adj.* (*-ier*, *-iest*) untrustworthy; apt to use tricks.

shil·ling [ˈʃɪlɪŋ] *n.* former British coin, value 12 pence (= 5 new pence, 5 p.): *a* ～*'s-worth*, as much as a ～ will buy.

shim·mer [ˈʃɪmə*] *v.i. & n.* (no pl.) (shine with a) wavering, soft light: *moonlight* ～*ing on the lake*; *the* ～ *of pearls.*

shin [ʃɪn] *n.* front of the leg between the knee and the ankle.

shine [ʃaɪn] *v.i. & t.* (p.t. & p.p. shone [ʃɒn]) **1.** give out or reflect light; be bright; (colloq., p.t. & p.p. ～*d*) make bright; polish. **2.** (fig.) be good (*at* or in sth.): *He doesn't* ～ *at tennis.* *n.* (no pl.) polish; brightness; (U.S.A.) polishing (of shoes, etc.). **shiny** *adj.* (*-ier*, *-iest*).

shin·gle¹ [ˈʃɪŋgl] *n.* (no pl.) small, smooth pebbles on (or from) the seashore.

shin·gle² [ˈʃɪŋgl] *n.* small, flat, square or oblong piece of thin wood used (like tiles) for covering a roof or wall. *v.t.* cover (a roof, etc.) with ～s.

ship [ʃɪp] *n.* **1.** seagoing vessel of considerable size: *a sailing-*～; *a steam-*～. **2.** spacecraft; (U.S.A.) = aircraft. *v.t. & i.* (*-pp-*) **1.** put, take or send (goods, etc.) in a ～. **2.** ～ *water*, (at sea) be flooded by water breaking over

steward. **'～·mate** *n.* fellow sailor in a ～. **～·ment** *n.* **1.** (no pl.) putting of goods on a ～. **2.** amount of goods ～ped at one time. **～·per** *n.* person who arranges for goods to be ～ped. **～·ping** *n.* (no pl.) all the ～s of a country, port, etc. **'～·shape** *adj.* in good order. **'～·wreck** *n.* loss or destruction of a ～ at sea by storm, etc. *v.t. & i.* (cause to) suffer ～wreck. **'～·wright** *n.* ～-builder. **'～·yard** *n.* place where ～s are built.

-ship [-ʃɪp] *suff.* (forming abstract ns.) **1.** state or quality of being; status; office: *friendship*; *hardship*; *membership*; *ownership*; *professorship.* **2.** skill: *horsemanship.*

shire [ˈʃaɪə*] *n.* county (chiefly in compounds [-ʃə*], as *Yorkshire*).

shirk [ʃɜːk] *v.t. & i.* avoid, try to escape (doing sth., responsibility, duty, sth. unpleasant, etc.). **～·er** *n.*

shirt [ʃɜːt] *n.* man's loose-fitting garment of cotton, etc. for the upper part of the body, usu. worn under a jacket: *in one's* ～*-sleeves*, with no jacket on.

shit [ʃɪt] (vulgar) *v.i.* (*-tt-*) empty the bowels. *int.* Rubbish! *n.* (no pl.) **1.** excrement. **2.** nonsense. **3.** contemptible person.

shiv·er¹ [ˈʃɪvə*] *v.i.* tremble, esp. from cold or fear. *n.* ～*ing.*

shiv·er² [ˈʃɪvə*] *n.* (usu. pl.) one of many small, broken pieces (of glass, etc.). *v.t. & i.* break into ～s.

shoal¹ [ʃəʊl] *n.* great number of fish swimming together: *a* ～ *of herring.*

shoal² [ʃəʊl] *n.* shallow place in the sea, esp. where there are sandbanks.

shock¹ [ʃɒk] *n.* number of sheaves of grain placed together and supporting each other in a field to dry after harvest.

shock² [ʃɒk] *n.* (usu. *a* ～ *of hair*) rough, untidy mass of hair (on sb.'s head). **'～·head·ed** *adj.* with such hair.

shock³ [ʃɒk] *n.* **1.** violent blow or shaking caused by a collision or explosion: ~ *absorber*, device (2) on a vehicle, etc. for absorbing ~s, vibrations, etc. **2.** (*electric*) ~, disturbing effect of the passage of electric current through the body. **3.** sudden and violent disturbance of the feelings or the nervous system (caused by strong emotion, bad news, severe injury, etc.); condition caused by this: *suffering from* ~. *v.t.* (of news, etc.) cause ~ (3) to; fill with surprised disgust, horror, etc. ~·er *n.* (colloq.) person or thing that ~s, esp. a sensational novel or drama. ~·ing *adj.* very bad or wrong: ~*ing behaviour*; causing ~ (3).

shod, see *shoe* (v.).

shod·dy [ˈʃɒdɪ] *adj.* (-ier, -iest) of worse quality than it seems to be; below standard: *a* ~ *piece of work.*

shoe [ʃuː] *n.* outer covering for the foot, esp. one that does not reach above the ankle (cf. *boot, slipper, sandal*).

shoes

v.t. (p.t. & p.p. *shod* [ʃɒd]) **1.** put ~s on (a horse). **2.** (esp. p.p.): *well* (*poorly*) *shod for wet weather*, having, wearing, strong (poor) ~s. 'shoe·horn *n.* device (2) for getting the heel easily into a tight-fitting ~. 'shoe·lace, 'shoe·string *ns.* cord for lacing ~s.

shone, see *shine* (v.).

shoo [ʃuː] *int.* cry used for driving away birds, etc. *v.t.* drive (birds, etc. *off, away*) by crying 'S~!'

shook, see *shake* (v.).

shoot [ʃuːt] *v.i. & t.* (p.t. & p.p. *shot* [ʃɒt]) **1.** move, come, go, send, suddenly or quickly (*out, in, up, forth,* etc.): *flames* ~*ing up from a burning house. The snake shot out its tongue.* **2.** (of plants, bushes) sprout; send out new leaves, etc. from a stem. **3.** (of pain) pass with a stabbing sensation (*through, up,* an arm, etc.): ~*ing pains. The pain shot up his arm.* **4.** (of boats) move, be moved, rapidly over or through: ~ *the rapids*; (sl.) pass (the traffic-lights at red). **5.** (with a rifle, etc.) fire (4) a bullet from it; loose (an arrow); hit with a shell, bullet, arrow, etc.; wound or kill (sb.) by doing this: ~ *a lion*; *be shot in the leg*; ~ *away all one's ammunition.* **6.** (fig., sl.) inject

(a drug). **7.** take a cinema picture of (a scene). *n.* **1.** new, young growth on a plant or bush. **2.** chute. ~·ing *n.* (no pl.) act of ~*ing* a gun, etc.; right of ~*ing* (birds, etc.) over sb.'s land. '~·ing-gal·ler·y *n.* place for ~*ing* at targets with firearms. '~·ing-range *n.* ground with butts² for rifle practice. ~·ing star *n.* meteor.

shop [ʃɒp] *n.* **1.** (U.S.A. *store*) building or room where goods are shown and sold to the public: ~ *assistant*, (Gt. Brit.) sb. employed to serve customers in a ~. **2.** (no pl.) one's profession, trade, or business; things connected with it: *talk* ~, talk about one's profession, work, etc. **3.** (also *work*~) place where goods, esp. machines, are manufactured or repaired. *closed* (*open*) ~, works where only (not only) trade-union members are accepted. *v.i.* (-*pp*-) go to ~s (1) to buy things (often *go* ~*ping*). ~·ping *n.* (no pl.) *have some* ~*ping to do*; *a* ~*ping centre*, part of a town where there are ~s, markets, etc. close together. '~·keep·er *n.* owner of a retail ~. '~-lift·er *n.* person who steals things from ~s while pretending to be a customer. '~-lift·ing *n.* ~-'soiled (Gt. Brit.), ~-'worn *adjs.* damaged or dirty as the result of being put on view or handled in a ~. ~-'stew·ard *n.* trade-union official in a workshop. '~·walk·er *n.* (U.S.A. *floorwalker*) person who directs customers to the right counters, departments, etc. in a large ~.

shore¹ [ʃɔː*] *n.* land bordering the sea, a lake, etc.: *on* ~, on land.

shore² [ʃɔː*] *n.* wooden support placed against a shaky wall or the side of a ship on ~¹. *v.t.* ~ *up*, support with a ~ or ~s.

shorn, see *shear.*

short [ʃɔːt] *adj.* **1.** (opp. *long, tall*) measuring little from end to end in space or time. **2.** less than the usual, stated, or required (amount, distance, weight, etc.): *The shopkeeper was fined for giving* ~ *weight* (*measure*). *a factory working* ~ *time* (fewer hours per day, fewer days per week, than usual); *a* ~ *cut,* a way of getting somewhere, doing sth., quicker than usual; ~ *of,* not having enough of: ~ *of money*; ~ *of breath,* (quickly becoming) breathless. **3.** (of a person) saying as little as possible; (of what he says) expressed in few words: *He* (*His answer*) *was* ~ *and to the point. for* ~, as a ~er form (of a name): *Benjamin, called 'Ben' for* ~. *in* ~, in a few words (used after

a longer description or explanation).
4. (of cake, pastry) easily breaking or
crumbling. *adj.* **1.** suddenly; abruptly: *stop* ~; *pull up* ~. **2.** *come (fall)*
~ *of*, fail to reach (what is required,
expected, etc.); *apart from*; *cut (sb. or sth.)* ~,
(a) interrupt; (b) make ~(er). **~age**
['ʃɔːtɪdʒ] *n.* condition of not having
enough: *food* ~*ages*; *a* ~*age of rice.*
~'com·ing *n.* (usu. pl.) fault; failure
to be as good as is required or expected. ~ **drink** *n.* small quantity (e.g.
of whisky, gin, etc.) served in a comparatively small glass. **~·en** ['ʃɔːtn] *v.t.*
& i. make or become ~(er). **~·en·ing**
n. (no pl.) fat (lard, butter, etc.) used
in making cakes, pastry, etc. '**~·hand**
n. (no pl.) system of rapid writing
using special signs. **~·'hand·ed** *adj.*
having not enough workers. **~·'lived**
adj. brief. **~·ly** *adv.* **1.** in a ~ time;
soon: ~*ly before (after)*, a ~ time before (after). **2.** briefly; in a few words.
3. sharply; curtly. **~·ness** *n.* (no pl.).
~s *n. pl.* ~ trousers extending to or
above the knees. **~·'sight·ed** *adj.* **1.**
unable to see things at a distance
clearly. **2.** (fig.) not thinking sufficiently of future needs, etc. ~ **sto·ry**
n. prose narrative ~er than a novel.
~·'tem·pered *adj.* easily made angry.
~·'wind·ed *adj.* (easily made) breathless.

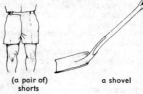

(a pair of) shorts   a shovel

shot[1] [ʃɒt] *n.* **1.** (sound of the) firing
of a gun, etc. *(do sth.) like a* ~, at once;
without hesitation; *off like a* ~, off at
great speed. **2.** attempt to hit sth.,
hitting sth. (e.g. with a stone); attempt to do sth., answer a question,
etc.: *Let me have a* ~ (i.e. try). **3.** that
which is fired from a gun, esp. (pl.
unchanged) a quantity of tiny balls of
lead contained in the cartridge of a
sporting gun (instead of a single bullet). **4.** heavy iron ball thrown in an
athletic competition called the ~*·put*:
putting the ~; ~*·putter.* **5.** person who
shoots, with reference to his skill: *a
good (poor)* ~. **6.** hypodermic injection
of a drug. **7.** photograph; film se-

quence photographed by one cine-
camera: *exterior* ~*s.* '**~·gun** *n.* sporting gun firing ~ (3).
shot[2] [ʃɒt] *adj.* (of cloth) woven or
dyed so as to show different colours
when looked at from different angles.
shot[3], see **shoot** (v.).
should, see **shall**.
shoul·der ['ʃəʊldə*] *n.* **1.** that part of
the body of a human being or animal
where an arm or foreleg is joined to
the trunk, or where the wing of a bird
joins its neck: *They were standing* ~
to ~ (side by side, close together).
straight from the ~, (fig., of a rebuke,
etc.) frankly put. **2.** (pl.) top part
of the back (1, 2). **3.** animal's foreleg
as meat. **4.** ~-like part (of a bottle,
mountain, etc.). *v.t.* **1.** take on one's
~(s). **2.** push with the ~: ~ *one's way
through a crowd.* '**~·blade** *n.* one of
the two flat bones of the ~s, behind
and below the neck.
shout [ʃaʊt] *n.* loud call or cry. *v.i.*
& t. give a ~; speak, say (sth.), in a
loud voice.
shove [ʃʌv] *v.t. & i. & n.* push.
shov·el ['ʃʌvl] *n.* spade-like tool, used
for moving coal, sand, snow, etc. (See
the p. on the left.) *v.t.* (-*ll*-, U.S.A.
also -*l*-) **1.** take (*up*), move, with a ~.
2. make, clear (a path, etc.), with a ~.
~·ful *n.*
show [ʃəʊ] *v.t. & i.* (p.t. ~*ed*, p.p. ~*n*,
rarely *shewn* [ʃəʊn]) **1.** allow to be
seen; bring before the sight; be visible
or noticeable. **2.** (with advs.): ~ *sb. in
(out)*, lead him to a room (out to the
doorway of a building); ~ *off*, make a
display of one's accomplishments,
powers, possessions, etc.; ~ *sth. off*,
display it to advantage; help to make
its beauty, etc. noticeable; ~ *up*,
(colloq.) be present (at a meeting,
etc.); ~ *(sb. or sth.) up*, make the truth
about (sb. or sth. dishonest, etc.)
known to others. **3.** (with nouns): ~
fight, give signs of being ready to fight;
~ *one's hand*, make known one's plans;
~ *kindness (mercy)* (give, grant); ~ *the
way*, (fig.) set an example. *n.* **1.** (no
pl.) ~*ing: a* ~ *of hands*, (voting by a)
raising of hands for or against (a
proposal). **2.** collection of things
publicly displayed, esp. for competition: *a flower-*~; *a travelling-*~ *of wild
animals*; *on* ~, exhibited. **3.** display (of
one's possessions, abilities, etc.) for
effect, to impress others: *a room
furnished for* ~, *not for comfort.* **4.**
(colloq.) public entertainment, theatrical performance, etc.: *put up a good*

~, perform, do, well. **5.** (sl.) sth. going on; undertaking: *give the (whole)* ~ *away*, let people know what is being done or planned. ~ **busi·ness**, (sl.) **~·biz** ['ʃəʊbɪz] *ns.* the entertainment profession. '**~-case** *n.* glazed case in which goods, etc. are displayed. '**~-down** *n.* settlement of a quarrel, etc. in an open, direct way. ~**·ing** *n.* (usu. no pl.) *on one's own* ~*ing*, as made clear by oneself; *make a poor* ~*ing*, give a poor impression. '**~-,jump·ing** *n.* (no pl.) (in a competition) jumping on horseback over barriers, fences, etc. '**~-,jump·er** *n.* '**~·man** *n.* organizer of public entertainments, esp. a circus. '**~·man·ship** *n.* (no pl.) art of attracting public attention (e.g. to what one is trying to sell). '**~-room**, '**~-,win·dow** *ns.* one in which goods are displayed. ~**y** *adj.* (-ier, -iest) likely to attract attention; (too much) decorated; (too) brightly coloured. ~**·i·ly** *adv.*

show·er ['ʃaʊə*] *n.* **1.** short fall of rain, etc.; large number of things, arriving together: *a* ~ *of sparks (arrows, leaves, etc.).* **2.** (also ~*-bath*) (taking of a bath by standing under a) ~ or spray of water coming from a pipe fixed overhead. *v.i. & t.* fall, send, give, in a ~. ~**y** *adj.* (of the weather) with frequent ~s.

shrank, see *shrink.*

shrap·nel ['ʃræpnl] *n.* shell that scatters bullets or pieces of metal when it explodes.

shred [ʃred] *n.* strip or piece cut or torn or broken off sth.; fragment: *torn to* ~*s*; *not a* ~ *of evidence against the accused man. v.t. & i.* (-dd-) make into ~s; mince.

shrew [ʃruː] *n.* **1.** bad-tempered, scolding woman. **2.** small, mouse-like animal. ~**·ish** *adj.* sharp-tongued.

shrewd [ʃruːd] *adj.* **1.** having, showing, sound judgement and common sense. **2.** (of a guess) near the truth. ~**·ly** *adv.* ~**·ness** *n.* (no pl.).

shriek [ʃriːk] *v.i. & t. & n.* scream.

shrift [ʃrɪft] *n.* (no pl.) *give sb. (get) short* ~, little time (to prepare for punishment, get sth. done, etc.).

shrill [ʃrɪl] *adj.* (of sounds, etc.) sharp; piercing; high-pitched.

shrimp [ʃrɪmp] *n.* (pl. ~s, ~) **1.** small shellfish, cooked as food. **2.** very small person. *v.i. go* ~*ing*, catch ~s in nets.

shrine [ʃraɪn] *n.* **1.** tomb or casket containing holy relics. **2.** building or place associated with sth. or sb. especially respected.

shrink [ʃrɪŋk] *v.i. & t.* (p.t. *shrank* [ʃræŋk] or *shrunk* [ʃrʌŋk], p.p. *shrunk* or, as adj., *shrunken* ['ʃrʌŋkən]) **1.** become or make less, smaller (esp. of cloth through wetting). **2.** move back, show unwillingness to do sth. (*from* fear, shame, because it is unpleasant). ~**·age** ['ʃrɪŋkɪdʒ] *n.* (no pl.) process of ~ing; degree of ~ing.

a shrimp (1)

shriv·el ['ʃrɪvl] *v.t. & i.* (-ll-, U.S.A. also -l-) (cause to) become dried or curled up (through heat, frost, dryness, old age).

shroud [ʃraʊd] *n.* **1.** cloth or sheet wrapped round a corpse. **2.** sth. that covers and hides: *a* ~ *of mist.* **3.** (pl.) ropes supporting a ship's mast. *v.t.* wrap or cover in a ~.

Shrove Tues·day [,ʃrəʊv 'tjuːzdɪ] *n.* day before Ash Wednesday.

shrub [ʃrʌb] *n.* plant with a woody stem, lower than a tree and (usu.) with several separate stems from the root. ~**·bery** ['ʃrʌbərɪ] *n.* place planted with ~s.

shrug [ʃrʌg] *v.t. & i.* (-gg-) lift (the shoulders) slightly (to show indifference, doubt, etc.). *n.* such a movement.

shrunk(·en), see *shrink.*

shud·der ['ʃʌdə*] *v.i.* shake; tremble with fear or disgust: ~ *at the sight of* ... *n.* uncontrollable trembling.

shuf·fle ['ʃʌfl] *v.i. & t. & i.* **1.** walk (*along*) without raising the feet properly. **2.** mix (playing-cards) before dealing; put (papers, etc.) into disorder. **3.** do sth. in a careless way: ~ *into one's clothes*; ~ *one's clothes on (off)*; ~ *through one's work. n.* shuffling movement; shuffling of cards.

shun [ʃʌn] *v.t.* (-nn-) keep away from; avoid: ~ *temptation (publicity).*

shunt [ʃʌnt] *v.t. & i.* send (a railway wagon, etc.) from one track to another; (of a train, etc.) be ~ed to a siding.

shut [ʃʌt] *v.t. & i.* (-*tt*-; p.t. & p.p.
~) **1.** move (e.g. a door, the lips)
so as to close an opening; (of a window,
door, etc.) become closed; keep (sb.
or sth. *out*) (e.g. by closing a door,
etc.). **2.** (with advs.): ~ *down*, (of a
factory, etc.) stop work; *be* ~ *in*, (of a
building, etc.) be cut off (from view,
from easy access, etc., e.g. by trees,
other high buildings, etc.); ~ *off*, stop
the supply of (gas, water, etc.); *be* ~
off from, be kept away, be separated,
from (society, etc.); ~ *out*, keep out;
exclude (landscape, etc.) from view;
~ *up*, fasten doors, windows, etc. in a
building (for safety); (sl., esp. imper.)
stop talking; make (sb.) stop talking.
shut·ter [ˈʃʌtə*] *n.* **1.** movable cover
(wooden board or screen) for a window
(to keep out light or thieves): *put up
the* ~*s*, close a shop; stop doing business. **2.** (in a camera) device (2) that
opens to allow light to pass through
the lens.

a shuttle (1)

shut·tle [ˈʃʌtl] *n.* **1.** part of a loom or
sewing-machine that carries the thread
from side to side. **2.** train, bus, etc.
going to and fro between places not
far apart on a ~ *service*. **3.** (*space*) ~,
space vehicle for repeated use (e.g.
to transport men and materials to a
space station). *v.t. & i.* (cause to)
move to and fro like a ~. 'ˌ~·cock *n.*

a shuttlecock

cork with a ring of feathers, struck to
and fro across a net in games like bad-
minton, etc.
shy[1] [ʃaɪ] *adj.* (~*er* or *shier*, ~*est* or
shiest) **1.** (of persons) self-conscious
and uncomfortable in the presence of
others. **2.** (of behaviour) showing such
self-consciousness: *a* ~ *look* (*smile*). **3.**
(of animals) unwilling to be seen. **4.** *fight* ~ *of*, be inclined to avoid. *v.i.* (of a horse) turn

aside in fear or alarm: *The horse shied
at a white object in the hedge.* ~·ly *adv.*
~·ness *n.* (no pl.).
shy[2] [ʃaɪ] *v.t. & n.* (colloq.) throw.
sick [sɪk] *adj.* **1.** (pred. only) *be* ~,
throw up food from the stomach;
sea~ *on the first day of the voyage*; *feel*
~, feel that one is about to throw up
food from the stomach. **2.** unwell; ill:
fall ~, become ill; *go* ~, (mil.) report to
the doctor for medical treatment.
the ~ (pl.) those who are ill. **3.** ~ *at*
(*about*), feeling regret or annoyance
at; ~ *for*, filled with a longing for; ~ *of*,
tired of. ~·en [ˈsɪkn] *v.i. & t.* **1.** be
~*ening for*, be in the first stages of (an
illness). **2.** become or make tired (*of*),
disgusted. ~·en·ing *adj.* disgusting;
unpleasant: *a* ~*ening smell.* ~·ly *adj.*
(-*ier*, -*iest*) **1.** causing a ~ feeling. **2.**
frequently in bad health; weak: *a* ~*ly
child.* **3.** suggesting unhappiness or illness: *a* ~*ly smile.* ~·ness *n.* ill health;
illness.
sick·le [ˈsɪkl] *n.* short-handled tool
with a curved blade (1) for cutting
grass, wheat, etc.
side [saɪd] *n.* **1.** one of the flat or fairly
flat surfaces of an object; one of these
that is not the top or bottom: *a box
has a top, a bottom, and four* ~*s*; either
of the two surfaces of a piece of paper,
cloth, or other very thin, flat object;
more or less vertical outer or inner
surface: *the* ~ *of a cave or mountain*;
the two surfaces of a house or the
human body that are not the front or
the back of it; (math.) one of the lines
enclosing a square or a triangle: *on all
~s, on every* ~, everywhere around;
by the ~ *of*, (fig.) compared with; ~ *by*
~, touching or close together; *put sth.
on one* ~, put it away; save it for future
use. **2.** part of an object, area, space,
etc. away, at a distance, from the
observer's right or left: *the left* (*right*)
~ (*of the street*). **3.** one of two groups
of opponents in politics, war, games,
etc.: *off* (*on*) ~, (football, etc.) in a position (for receiving or playing the ball)
that is (is not) contrary to the rules;
take ~*s* (*with*), support (sb., a party)
in a dispute. **4.** (no pl.) (sl.) pretence
of being superior or important: *He
puts on too much* ~. *v.i.* (only in) ~
with, support (in a dispute). 'ˌ~·board
n. table, usu. with drawers and cupboards, placed against the wall of a
dining-room. 'ˌ~·burns *n. pl.* ~
whiskers. 'ˌ~·car *n.* small, one-wheeled
car fastened to the ~ of a motor cycle
sid·ed [ˈsaɪdɪd] *adj.* having a specified

number of ~s: *a four-~d structure.*
'**~-dish** *n.* extra dish or course at a
meal. '**~-,is·sue** *n.* question of less importance (in relation to the main one).
'**~-light** *n.* one of two small lamps at
the front of a motor car; (fig.) sth. that
throws extra, incidental, light on a
problem. '**~-line** *n.* occupation that is
not one's main work; class of goods
sold in addition to the chief classes of
goods; (pl.) (ground bordering the)
lines at the ~s of a football field,
tennis-court, etc. '**~-long** *adj. & adv.*
(directed) to or from one ~: *a ~long
glance.* '**~-road** *n.* minor road joining
or branching off a main road. '**~-,sad·**
dle *n.* woman's saddle, made so that
both feet may be on the same ~ of the
horse. *adv.* on a ~-saddle. '**~-show** *n.*
small show at a fair or exhibition;
activity of small importance in relation
to the main activity. '**~-step** *v.t. & n.*
(avoid by taking a) sudden step to one
~. '**~-street** *n.* street lying aside from
the main streets or roads. '**~-track** *n.*
siding. *v.t.* postpone or avoid discussion of (a proposal, etc.); turn (sb.)
away from his main purpose to sth.
less important. '**~-walk** *n.* (U.S.A.;
Gt. Brit. = *pavement*) paved way at
the ~ of a street for pedestrians: *a
~walk café.* **~·ways** *adv.* to, towards,
from, the ~; with the ~ or edge first.
'**~-,whis·kers** *n. pl.* whiskers grown
on the cheeks, usu. worn long.

sid·ing ['saɪdɪŋ] *n.* short railway track
at the side of the main line.

si·dle ['saɪdl] *v.i.* walk (*up to, away
from,* sb.) in a shy or nervous way.

siege [siːdʒ] *n.* (period of) operations
of armed forces to capture a fortified
place: *lay ~ to,* besiege.

si·es·ta [sɪ'estə] *n.* afternoon rest, esp.
as taken in hot countries.

sieve [sɪv] *n.* utensil with wire network
to separate finer grains from coarse
grains, or solids from liquids.

sift [sɪft] *v.t. & i.* **1.** separate by putting
through a sieve: *~ ashes from cinders;
~ evidence,* (fig.) examine it carefully.
2. shake through a sieve: *~ sugar on
to a cake.*

sigh [saɪ] *v.i. & t.* **1.** take a deep breath
that can be heard (showing sadness,
tiredness, relief, etc.); (of the wind)
make a ~-like sound. **2.** ~ *for,* feel a
longing for. **3.** express, utter, with ~s.
n. act or sound of ~ing.

sight [saɪt] *n.* **1.** (no pl.) (power of) seeing: *lose one's ~,* become blind; *have
long (short* or *near) ~,* be able to see
things well only at long (short) range;

know sb. (*only*) *by ~* (by appearance,
not as an acquaintance); *lose ~ of,* see
no longer; (fig.) be out of touch with;
fail to keep in mind; *catch ~ of,* begin
to see; succeed in seeing; *at* (*on*) *~,* as
soon as (sth. or sb.) is seen; *in* (*out of*)
~, that can (cannot) be seen. **2.** (no
pl.) opinion: *Do what is right in your
own ~.* **3.** sth. seen or to be seen, esp.
sth. remarkable; (pl.) noteworthy
buildings, places, etc. in a town or
district: *Come and see the ~s of London.*
4. (no pl.) *a ~,* (colloq.) a person or
thing that excites ridicule or unfavourable comment: *What a ~ she looks in
that old dress!* **5.** device (2) helping to
aim or observe when using a rifle,
telescope, etc.; observation taken with
such a device. *v.t.* **1.** catch ~ of; see
(by coming near to): *~ land.* **2.** observe
(a star, etc.) by using ~ (5); adjust the
~s (5) of a gun, etc. **~·ed** *adj.* having
the kind of ~ (1) indicated: *long-~ed;
short-~ed.* **~·less** *adj.* blind[1]. '**~·see·ing**
n. going about to see places, etc.
'**~·se·er** *n.* person visiting the ~s (3)
of a town, etc.

sign [saɪn] *n.* **1.** mark, object, used to
represent sth.: *mathematical ~s* (e.g.
+, −, ×, ÷). **2.** word(s), design, etc.
on a board or plate to warn sb. of or
direct sb. towards sth.: *traffic ~s* (e.g.
to give warning of a speed limit). **3.**
sth. that gives evidence, points to the
existence or likelihood, of sth.: *~s of
suffering on a person's face.* **4.** movement of the hand, head, etc. used with
or instead of words: *~ language* (used
by deaf and dumb persons). **5.** ~board.
v.t. & i. **1.** write one's name on (a
letter, document, etc.) to show that
one is the writer or that one agrees
with the contents: *~ away,* give up
(rights, property, etc.) by *~ing one's
name; ~ on* (*up*), ~ an agreement about
employment. **2.** make known (to sb.)
an order or request by using ~s (4):
The policeman ~ed to (*for*) *us to stop.*
'**~·board** *n.* board with a notice or
advertisement on it (e.g. one giving
the name of an inn). '**~·post** *n.* post
showing names and directions of
towns, villages, etc.

sig·nal[1] ['sɪgnl] *n.* **1.** (making of a)
sign, movement, (showing of a)
light, to give warning, instructions,
news, etc., esp. to sb. at a distance.
2. *railway ~,* post, etc. for ~s to drivers
of trains. **3.** event that is a starting-
point for a series of events. **4.** (electr.)
electrical impulse(s) or radio wave(s)
transmitted as a ~. *v.i. & t.* (-*ll*-,

U.S.A. also -*l*-) **1.** make a ~ or ~s (*to sb.*, *to do sth.*, *that*). **2.** use ~s. **3.** send (news) by ~(s). '**~-box** *n.* (U.S.A. ~ *tower*) building on a railway from which railway ~s are worked. **~·ler** (U.S.A. also **~·er**) *n.* person who sends and receives ~s in the Army. '**~·man** *n.* person who sends and receives ~s (on railways, in the Navy, etc.).

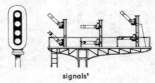

signals¹

sig·nal² ['sɪgnl] *attrib. adj.* remarkable; outstanding: *win a ~ victory*. **~·ly** *adv.* **~·ize** *v.t.* make (an event) ~.

sig·na·to·ry ['sɪgnətərɪ] *n. & adj.* (person, country) that has signed an agreement.

sig·na·ture ['sɪgnətʃə*] *n.* **1.** person's name signed by himself. **2.** ~ *tune*, special tune used in broadcasting to announce a particular programme, etc.

sig·ni·fy ['sɪgnɪfaɪ] *v.t. & i.* **1.** show by a sign; make known: ~ *one's approval*. **2.** mean; be a sign of. **3.** ~ *much* (*little*), be of much (little) importance. **sig·nif·i·cance** [sɪg'nɪfɪkəns] *n.* (no pl.) meaning; importance. **sig·nif·i·cant** *adj.* important; having a special or suggestive meaning. **sig·ni·fi·ca·tion** [,sɪgnɪfɪ'keɪʃn] *n.* (exact) meaning (of a word).

si·lage ['saɪlɪdʒ] *n.* (no pl.) green cattle food stored in a silo.

si·lence ['saɪləns] *n.* (no pl.) condition of being quiet or silent: *listen to sb. in* ~. *v.t.* make (sb. or sth.) silent; cause to be quiet. **si·lenc·er** *n.* device (2) that reduces the noise made by the exhaust of a petrol engine, the report (5) of a gun, etc. **si·lent** *adj.* **1.** making no or little sound; still; without sound: *a silent film* (without a sound-track); *the silent majority*, people of moderate opinions who rarely make themselves heard. **2.** saying little or nothing; giving no answer, no news. **si·lent·ly** *adv.*

sil·hou·ette [,sɪlu:'et] *n.* picture in solid black showing only the shape; shape of sth. or sb. seen against a light background. *v.t.* show or make a ~ of: *a mountain ~d against the sky at daybreak*.

sil·i·con ['sɪlɪkən] *n.* (no pl.) non-metallic element found in quartz, sandstone, etc., used esp. in alloys.

silk [sɪlk] *n.* (no pl.) thin, soft thread from the cocoons of certain insects; material made from this; made of ~: ~ *stockings*. **~·en** ['sɪlkən] *adj.* (liter.) soft and smooth: ~*en hair*; *a* ~*en voice*. '**~·worm** *n.* caterpillar that produces ~. **~·y** *adj.* (-*ier*, -*iest*) soft, shiny, smooth, like ~.

sill [sɪl] *n.* shelf, block of wood or stone at the base of a window.

sil·ly ['sɪlɪ] *adj.* (-*ier*, -*iest*) foolish; weak-minded. **sil·li·ness** *n.* (no pl.).

si·lo ['saɪləʊ] *n.* (pl. ~s) airtight structure in which green food (*silage*) for farm animals is stored.

silt [sɪlt] *n.* (no pl.) sand, mud, etc. deposited by moving water (at the mouth of a river, in a harbour, etc.). *v.t. & i.* (of a harbour, etc.) (cause to) become stopped (*up*) with ~.

sil·van, syl·van ['sɪlvən] *adj.* of trees or a wood (2); rural.

sil·ver ['sɪlvə*] *n.* (no pl.) **1.** shining, white metal used for making coins, ornaments, spoons, etc. **2.** things made of ~, esp. ~ coins and table ~ (spoons, forks, dishes, etc.). **3.** (attrib.) ~-coloured; (of sounds) soft and clear. *v.t.* coat with ~ or material like ~; make (sth.) bright like ~. **~·y** *adj.* like ~; clear-toned.

sim·i·lar ['sɪmɪlə*] *adj.* like; of the same sort: ~ *to*, almost the same as. **~·ly** *adv.* **~·i·ty** [,sɪmɪ'lærətɪ] *n.* likeness.

sim·i·le ['sɪmɪlɪ] *n.* (use of) comparison of one thing to another (e.g. 'He is as brave as a lion').

sim·mer ['sɪmə*] *v.i. & t.* **1.** be, keep (a pot, food, etc.), almost at boiling-point. **2.** be filled with (anger, etc.) that is just kept under control: ~*ing with rage*.

sim·per ['sɪmpə*] *v.i. & n.* (give a) silly, self-conscious smile.

sim·ple ['sɪmpl] *adj.* (~*r*, ~*st*) **1.** unmixed; not divided into parts; having only a small number of parts: *a* ~ *substance*; *a* ~ *machine*. **2.** plain; not much decorated or ornamented: ~ *food* (*cooking*); ~ *buildings*; *the* ~ *life*, a way of living without luxuries and artificial amusements, etc. **3.** not highly developed: ~ *forms of plant life*. **4.** easily done or understood; not causing trouble: *a* ~ *task*; *written in* ~ *language*. **5.** innocent; straightforward: *behave in a pleasant and* ~ *way*. **6.** foolish; inexperienced. **7.** with nothing added; absolute: *a* ~ *fact*; *the truth, pure and*

~. **~·ton** ['sɪmpltən] *n.* foolish, easily-deceived person. **sim·plic·i·ty** [sɪm-'plɪsətɪ] *n.* (no pl.) state of being ~. **sim·pli·fy** ['sɪmplɪfaɪ] *v.t.* make ~(r); make easier to understand or deal with. **sim·pli·fi·ca·tion** [ˌsɪmplɪfɪ-'keɪʃn] *n.* simplifying; sth. that is simplified. **sim·ply** *adv.* **1.** in a ~ manner. **2.** absolutely. **3.** only.

sim·u·late ['sɪmjʊleɪt] *v.t.* pretend to be; pretend to have or feel. **sim·u·la·tor** *n.* apparatus (1) designed to provide under test conditions phenomena like those occurring in real operations. **si·mul·ta·neous** [ˌsɪməl'teɪnjəs] *adj.* happening or done at the same time.

sin [sɪn] *n.* **1.** breaking of, act that breaks, God's laws. **2.** sth. looked upon as contrary to good manners, common sense, etc.: *It's a ~ to make the children do too much homework.* *v.i.* (-nn-) commit ~; do wrong. **~·ful** *adj.* wicked. **~·less** *adj.* free from ~. **~·ner** *n.* person who ~s.

since [sɪns] *adv.* **1.** (with the perfect tenses) after a date in the past; before the present time; between some time in the past and the present time: *Last Tuesday he went out for a walk and has not been seen ~. ever ~: I met him ten years ago and have admired him ever ~.* **2.** ago: *She left here many years ~.* *prep.* during a period of time after: *We haven't met ~ her marriage.* *conj.* **1.** from the past time when: *Where have you been ~ I last saw you? It is just a week ~ we arrived here.* **2.** as: *S~ we have no money we can't buy anything.*

sin·cere [sɪn'sɪə*] *adj.* **1.** (of feelings, behaviour) genuine; not pretended. **2.** (of a person) straightforward; not in the habit of expressing feelings that are not genuine. **~·ly** *adv.* in a ~ manner. *yours ~ly* (used before the signature at the end of a letter to an acquaintance or a friend). **sin·cer·i·ty** [sɪn'serətɪ] *n.* (no pl.).

si·ne·cure ['saɪnɪˌkjʊə*] *n.* position for which one receives credit or payment without having to work or take responsibility; easy, well-paid job.

sin·ew ['sɪnjuː] *n.* **1.** tendon (strong cord) joining a muscle to a bone. **2.** (pl.) muscles; energy; physical strength; (fig.) framework; resources: *~s of war,* money. **~y** *adj.* having strong ~s; (fig.) strong and firm; tough.

sing [sɪŋ] *v.i.* & *t.* (p.t. *sang* [sæŋ], p.p. *sung* [sʌŋ]) **1.** make continuous musical sounds (*tunes*) with the voice;

utter words or sentences set to a tune: ~ *out,* call loudly (*for*); ~ *up,* ~ with more force. **2.** make a whistling or humming sound: *The kettle is ~ing on the fire.* **3.** (often ~ *of*) celebrate in poetry. **~·er** *n.* person who ~s, esp. in public. **'~·song** *n.* **1.** *in a ~song,* in a rising and falling tone of monotonous regularity. **2.** meeting of friends to ~ songs together.

singe [sɪndʒ] *v.t.* & *i.* **1.** burn off the tips or ends, esp. of hair. **2.** blacken the surface of (cloth, etc.) by burning.

sin·gle ['sɪŋgl] *adj.* **1.** one only: ~ *ticket,* for a journey to a place, not there and back. **2.** for the use of, used for, done by, one person, etc.: *a ~ bed;* ~ *room,* bedroom for one person. **3.** unmarried. *n.* **1.** (tennis) game with one person on each side. **2.** record[2] (4) with only one short song on each side (cf. *long-playing*). *v.t.* ~ *out,* select from others (for special attention, etc.). **ˌ~-'hand·ed** *adj.* & *adv.* without help from others. **ˌ~-'mind·ed** *adj.* intent on, devoted to, one cause or purpose. **sin·gly** *adv.* one by one; by oneself.

sin·glet ['sɪŋglɪt] *n.* (Gt. Brit.) undershirt; vest.

sin·gu·lar ['sɪŋgjʊlə*] *adj.* **1.** uncommon; strange. **2.** outstanding (courage, etc.). **3.** (gram.) of the form used in speaking of one person or thing. *n.* ~ (3) form (of a word). **~·ly** *adv.* **~·i·ty** [ˌsɪŋgjʊ'lærətɪ] *n.* sth. that is ~ (1); quality of being ~ (1).

sin·is·ter ['sɪnɪstə*] *adj.* **1.** suggesting evil or coming misfortune: *a ~ beginning.* **2.** showing ill will: *a ~ face.*

sink [sɪŋk] *v.i.* & *t.* (p.t. *sank* [sæŋk], p.p. *sunk* [sʌŋk]) **1.** go down, esp. below the horizon or surface of a liquid or a soft substance; cause or allow (a ship) to ~. **2.** slope downwards; become lower or weaker: *The foundations have sunk.* (fig.) *His heart sank at the news.* **3.** make by digging, etc.: ~ *a well.* **4.** (of liquids, and fig.) go deep (*into*): *The rain sank into the dry ground. The warning sank into his mind.* **5.** put (money) into an undertaking, esp. one from which it cannot easily be taken out again. *n.* fixed basin (of stone, porcelain, etc.) with a drain for taking off water, used for washing dishes, etc. **~·able** *adj.* that can be sunk. **~·er** *n.* (esp.) lead weight for ~ing a fishing-line or net. **~·ing** *adj.* *~ing feeling,* feeling in the stomach caused by hunger or fear; *~ing fund,* money from revenue put aside by a government, business company, etc. for gradual repayment of a debt.

sin·u·ous ['sɪnjʊəs] *adj.* winding; full of curves and twists.

sip [sɪp] *v.t. & i.* (-*pp*-) drink, taking (the liquid in) a very small quantity at a time. *n.* (quantity taken in) one act of ˷ping.

si·phon, sy·phon ['saɪfn] *n.* **1.** bent or curved tube so arranged that liquid will flow up and then down through it. **2.** bottle from which soda-water, etc. can be forced out by pressure of gas in it. *v.t. & i.* (cause to) draw (out, off) through a ˷.

a siphon   a soda-siphon

sir [sɜ:*] *n.* **1.** respectful form of address to a man, used in speaking and writing: *Good morning, sir. Dear Sir,* … (Cf. *madam.*) **2.** prefix to the name of a knight or baronet: *Sir* [sə*] *Walter Scott.*

sire ['saɪə*] *n.* **1.** (old use) father or male ancestor. **2.** (old use) title of respect used when addressing a king or emperor. **3.** male parent of an animal, esp. a horse.

si·ren ['saɪərən] *n.* **1.** (in Greek mythology) one of a number of winged women whose songs charmed sailors and caused their destruction. **2.** woman who attracts and is dangerous to men. **3.** ship's whistle for sending warnings and signals; device (2) for producing a loud, shrill noise (as a warning, etc.).

sir·loin ['sɜ:lɔɪn] *n.* best part of loin of beef.

sir·up, see *syrup.*

si·sal ['saɪsl] *n.* (no pl.) plant with strong fibre used for making rope.

sis·sy ['sɪsɪ] *adj. & n.* (typical of an) effeminate or (a) cowardly person.

sis·ter ['sɪstə*] *n.* **1.** daughter of the same parents as oneself or another person referred to. **2.** (Gt. Brit.) senior hospital nurse. **3.** member of a ˷hood; nun: *S˷s of Mercy.* **4.** (attrib.) of the same design, type, etc.: ˷ *ships.* ˷**hood** *n.* society of women who devote themselves to charitable work or who live together in a religious order (11). '˷**-in-law** *n.* (pl. ˷*s-in-law*) ˷ of one's wife or husband; wife of one's brother. ˷**ly** *adj.* of or like a ˷.

sit [sɪt] *v.i. & t.* (-*tt*-; p.t. & p.p. *sat* [sæt]) **1.** rest the body on the buttocks. **2.** (with advs. & preps.): ˷ *down,* take a seat; ˷*-down strike,* strike by workers who refuse to leave the place where they are working until their demands are considered or satisfied; ˷ *down under* (insults, etc.), suffer without complaint; ˷ *for,* represent (a town, etc.) in Parliament; ˷ *for an examination,* take an examination; ˷ *for one's portrait,* have one's portrait painted while sitting before an artist; ˷ *in,* demonstrate by occupying a place as a protest against sth.; ˷*-in* (n.); ˷ *on a committee, etc.,* be a member of one; ˷ *(up)on a question, etc.,* (of a jury, etc.) inquire into it; ˷ *(up)on sb.,* (sl.) snub him; ˷ *out* (a *play*), remain to the end; ˷ *up,* take an upright position after lying flat; not go to bed (until later than the usual time); *make sb.* ˷ *up,* (colloq.) shock or surprise him; rouse him to activity. **3.** (of Parliament, a court of law, a committee, etc.) hold meetings, etc. **4.** keep one's seat on (a horse). **5.** (of clothing) fit: *a coat that ˷s well* (loosely, etc.) *on sb.* **6.** (of birds) perch; (of hens) be on a nest, covering eggs in order to hatch them. ˷**·ting** *n.* (esp.) time during which a court of law, Parliament, etc., ˷s (3), or during which a person is engaged on one task: *finish reading a book at one ˷ting.* '˷**·ting-room** *n.* room for general use.

si·tar [sɪ'tɑ:*] *n.* Indian stringed musical instrument played with the fingers.

site [saɪt] *n.* place where sth. was, is, or is to be: *the ˷ of a battle; a ˷ for a new school; a building* (caravan) ˷.

sit·u·at·ed ['sɪtjʊeɪtɪd] *adj.* (of a town, building, etc.) placed; (of a person) in (certain) circumstances. **sit·u·a·tion** [,sɪtjʊ'eɪʃn] *n.* **1.** position (of a town, building, etc.). **2.** condition, state of affairs, esp. at a certain time. **3.** work, employment, esp. as a domestic servant.

six [sɪks] *n. & adj.* **6.** *at ˷es and sevens,* in confusion. ˷**·pence** ['sɪkspəns] *n.* British coin still in circulation, value formerly ˷ pennies, now 2½ p. ˷**th** [sɪksθ] *n. & adj.* 6th; ¹/₆. ˷**·teen** [,sɪks'ti:n] *n. & adj.* 16. ˷**·teenth** [,sɪks'ti:nθ] *n. & adj.* 16th; ¹/₁₆. ˷**·ty** ['sɪkstɪ] *n. & adj.* 60. ˷**·ti·eth** ['sɪkstɪɪθ] *n. & adj.* 60th; ¹/₆₀.

size¹ [saɪz] *n.* **1.** (no pl.) degree of largeness or smallness: *about the ˷ of,* about as large as; *of some ˷,* fairly large. **2.** one of the standard and (usu.) numbered ⁓s in which articles of clothing, etc. are made: ⁓ *six shoes.* **v.t. 1.** arrange in ⁓s. **2.** ⁓ *up,* form an opinion or a judgement of. **siz·able** *adj.* of a fairly large ⁓.

size² [saɪz] *n.* (no pl.) sticky substance used to glaze textiles, paper, etc.

sized [saɪzd] *adj.* having a certain size: *medium-*⁓.

siz·zle ['sɪzl] **v.i. & n.** (colloq.) (make the) hissing sound as of sth. cooking in fat.

skate¹ [skeɪt] *n.* one of a pair of sharp-edged steel blades to be fastened to a boot for moving smoothly over ice. **v.i.** move, perform, on ⁓s. (Cf. *roller-*⁓s.)

a skate¹   skiing

'⁓·board *n.* small surf-board mounted (2) on roller-⁓ wheels, used by ⁓*board-ers* to career over the concrete while standing on the board. **skat·er** *n.* person who ⁓s. **skat·ing** *n.* **'skat·ing-rink** *n.* specially prepared surface for skating.

skate² [skeɪt] *n.* large, flat seafish, valued as food.

a skate²

skein [skeɪn] *n.* length of silk or wool yarn coiled into a bundle.

skel·e·ton ['skelɪtn] *n.* **1.** bones of an animal body in the same relative posi-tions as in life. **2.** hard framework of an animal or plant. **3.** framework of a building or of an organization, plan, theory, etc. **4.** (attrib.) ⁓ *key,* key that will open a number of different locks; ⁓ *staff* (*crew, etc.*), one reduced to the smallest possible number needed for maintenance.

skep·tic, etc. (U.S.A.), see *sceptic.*

sketch [sketʃ] *n.* **1.** rough, quickly-made drawing. **2.** short account or description. **3.** short, humorous play or piece of writing. **v.t. & i.** make a ⁓ of: ⁓ *sth. out,* give a rough plan of it. **⁓y** *adj.* (-*ier,* -*iest*) done roughly and without detail or care; incomplete. **⁓·i·ly** *adv.*

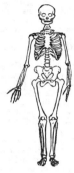

a skeleton (1)

skew·er ['skjʊə*] *n.* pointed stick of wood or metal for holding meat to-gether while cooking. **v.t.** fasten with, or as with, a ⁓.

ski [skiː] *n.* (pl. ⁓s, ⁓) one of a pair of long, narrow strips of wood, metal, etc., strapped to the boots, for moving over snow. **v.i.** move over snow on ⁓s. (See the picture at *skate¹.*) **'⁓-bob** *n.* kind of bicycle frame with ⁓s in place of wheels. **⁓-er** *n.* person who ⁓s. **'⁓-,jump(·ing)** *n.* jump(ing) after getting up speed on a downward slope. **'⁓-lift** *n.* lift (2) for carrying ⁓ers up a slope, usu. on seats hung from an overhead cable. **'⁓-run** *n.* slope suit-able for ⁓ing as a sport.

skid [skɪd] *n.* **1.** piece of wood or metal fixed under the wheel of a cart, etc. to prevent it from turning, and in this way check the speed when going downhill. **2.** slipping movement of the wheels of a car, etc. on a slippery road. **v.i.** (-*dd-*) (of a car, etc.) move or slip (sideways).

skiff [skɪf] *n.* small, light boat, esp. one rowed or sculled by one person.

skill [skɪl] *n.* **1.** (no pl.) ability to do sth. well and expertly. **2.** particular kind of ⁓. **⁓ed** *adj.* trained; ex-perienced: ⁓*ed workmen;* needing ⁓: ⁓*ed work.* **skil·ful** (U.S.A. **skill-**) *adj.* having or showing ⁓. **skil·ful·ly** (U.S.A. **skill-**) *adv.*

skim [skɪm] *v.t. & i.* (*-mm-*) **1.** remove the cream, scum, etc. from the surface of (a liquid): ~ *the cream off*; ~ *the milk.* **2.** move lightly over (a surface), not touching or only occasionally touching it: *a bird ~ming* (*over*) *a lake.* **3.** read through sth. quickly, noting only the chief points. ~ **milk** *n.* milk from which the cream has been ~med.

skimp [skɪmp] *v.t. & i.* supply, use, less than enough of what is needed.

skin [skɪn] *n.* **1.** (no pl.) elastic substance forming the outer covering of the body of a person or animal. **2.** animal ~ with or without the hair or fur; material made from this; hide². **3.** outer covering of a fruit, plant, sausage, etc.: *banana ~s.* **4.** thin film that forms on boiled milk. **5.** container made of ~ for holding liquids, etc. *v.t. & i.* (*-nn-*) take the ~ off. ~-'**deep** *adj.* not going deep; of or on the surface only. '~-**dive** *v.i.* swim deep below the surface of water, usu. with a face mask, flippers, and an aqualung. '~-,**div·er** *n.* person who does this, esp. as a sport. '~-,**div·ing** *n.* (no pl.). '~-**flint** *n.* miser. ~**ny** *adj.* (*-ier, -iest*) having little flesh.

skip [skɪp] *v.i. & t.* (*-pp-*) **1.** jump lightly and quickly: ~ *out of the way of the bus.* **2.** jump over a rope that is turned over the head and under the feet as one jumps. **3.** go from one point to another; (esp.) go from one part of a book, etc. to another without reading what is between: ~ *the next chapter. n.* ~ping movement. ~

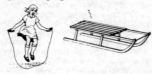

skipping (2)   a sled(ge) or toboggan

skip·per [ˈskɪpə*] *n.* **1.** captain, esp. of a small merchant ship. **2.** captain of an aircraft. **3.** captain of a team in games.

skir·mish [ˈskɜːmɪʃ] *n.* (usu. unplanned) fight between small parts of armies or fleets.

skirt [skɜːt] *n.* **1.** woman's loose garment that hangs from the waist. **2.** part of a dress, etc. below the waist. **3.** (pl.) outskirts. *v.t. & i.* be on, pass along, the ~s (3) of. '~-**ing-board** *n.* (Gt. Brit.) board fixed along the bottom of the walls of a room.

skit [skɪt] *n.* short piece of humorous writing, short play, copying and making fun of sth. or sb.

skit·tish [ˈskɪtɪʃ] *adj.* (of horses and persons) lively; full of play and fun.

skit·tle [ˈskɪtl] *n.* one of the bottle-shaped pieces of wood to be knocked down by a ball rolled towards them in the game of ~s.

skulk [skʌlk] *v.i.* hide, move secretly, through cowardice, or to avoid work or duty, or with an evil purpose.

skull [skʌl] *n.* bony framework of the head. '~-**cap** *n.* brimless, close-fitting cap.

skunk [skʌŋk] *n.* small N. American animal that sends out a bad-smelling liquid when attacked; its fur.

a skunk

sky [skaɪ] *n.* the space in which we see the sun, moon, stars, and clouds. '~-**dive** *v.i.* dive from an aircraft in a long, free fall as a sport, often performing various manœuvres before opening the parachute. '~-,**div·ing** *n.* (no pl.). ,~-'**high** *adj. & adv.* up in(to) the ~. ~**jack** [ˈskaɪdʒæk] *v.t.* (sl.) hijack (an aircraft). *n.* ~jacking. '~,**jack·er** *n.* '~-**lark** *n.* small bird that sings as it flies high into the ~. '~-**light** *n.* window in a roof. '~-**line** *n.* outline of things (mountains, buildings, etc.) seen against the ~. '~,**scrap·er** *n.* very tall building.

slab [slæb] *n.* thick, flat piece (of stone or other solid substance).

slack [slæk] *adj.* **1.** giving little care or attention to one's work; having or showing little energy. **2.** dull; inactive; with not much business or work needing to be done. **3.** loose; not tight: *a ~ rope. n.* **1.** *the ~,* that part of a rope, etc. that hangs loosely. **2.** coal-dust. **3.** (pl.) loose-fitting trousers. *v.i.* be lazy or careless in one's work: ~ *off* (*up*), reduce speed; do less work. ~**en** [ˈslækən] *v.t. & i.* make or become slower, looser, or less active. ~**er** *n.* (colloq.) sb. who tries to avoid his proper share of work. ~**ly** *adv.* ~**ness** *n.* (no pl.).

slag [slæg] *n.* (no pl.) waste matter remaining when metal has been extracted from ore.

slain, see *slay.*

slake [sleɪk] *v.t.* **1.** satisfy or make less strong (thirst, desire for revenge, etc.). **2.** change the chemical nature of (lime¹) by adding water.

sla·lom ['slɑːləm] *n.* **1.** ski-race down a zigzag course marked out by poles with flags: *a giant ~.* **2.** obstacle race in canoes.

slam [slæm] *v.t. & i.* (-mm-) **1.** shut violently: ~ *the door. The door ~med.* **2.** put (*down*); throw or knock with force: ~ *sth. down. n.* noise of a door, window, etc. being ~med.

slan·der ['slɑːndə*] *v.t. & n.* (make a) false statement that damages a person's reputation. **~ous** *adj.* making such statements; containing ~s.

slang [slæŋ] *n.* (no pl.) **1.** words, meanings, phrases, commonly used in talk but not suitable for good writing or serious occasions. **2.** kind of ~ used by a trade or social group: *schoolboy ~.* **3.** (attrib.) ~ *words. v.t. & i.* use scolding language (to). **~y** *adj.* (-ier, -iest) fond of using ~; full of ~; of the nature of ~: ~y *expressions.*

slant [slɑːnt] *v.i. & t.* slope. *n.* slope: *on a* (*the*) ~, ~ing; sloping.

slap [slæp] *n.* quick blow with the open hand or with sth. flat. *v.t.* (-pp-) **1.** hit with a ~. **2.** put (sth. *down*) with a ~ping noise. '**~dash** *adj.* (*& adv.*) careless(ly); reckless(ly). '**~stick** *n.* boisterous comedy of the roughest kind: (attrib.) ~*stick comedy.*

slash [slæʃ] *v.t. & i.* make long cuts in (or *at*) sth. with a sweeping stroke; strike with a whip. *n.* act of ~ing; long cut.

slat [slæt] *n.* long, thin, narrow piece of wood, metal, or plastic material, esp. used in venetian blinds.

slate [sleɪt] *n.* **1.** (no pl.) kind of blue-grey stone that splits easily into thin, smooth, flat layers. **2.** square or oblong piece of this used for roofs. **3.** sheet of ~ in a wooden frame for writing on: *a clean ~,* (fig.) *a good record²* (3). **4.** (no pl.) colour of ~; blue-grey. *v.t.* **1.** cover (a roof) with ~s. **2.** (Gt. Brit., colloq.) criticize severely. **slaty** *adj.* (-ier, -iest) like, containing, ~.

slat·tern ['slætən] *n.* dirty, untidily dressed woman. **~ly** *adj.*

slaugh·ter ['slɔːtə*] *v.t.* kill (an animal) for food; kill (people) in great numbers. *n.* (no pl.) killing of animals for food or of many people (in war). '**~house** *n.* place where animals are killed for food.

slave [sleɪv] *n.* **1.** person who is the property of another and bound to serve him; person compelled to work very hard for someone else. **2.** *a ~ to* (*of*), sb. completely in the power of, under the control of, an impulse, habit, etc. *v.i.* work hard (*at* sth., *for* a living, etc.). '**~·driv·er** *n.* man in charge of ~s; employer, etc. forcing those under him to work very hard. **slav·er** *n.* ship or person trading in ~s. **slav·ery** ['sleɪvərɪ] *n.* (no pl.) condition of being a ~; custom of having ~s; hard, esp. badly paid, employment. **slav·ish** *adj.* **1.** in the manner of ~s; (esp.) weak and submissive. **2.** without originality: *a slavish imitation.* **slav·ish·ly** *adv.*

slay [sleɪ] *v.t.* (p.t. *slew* [sluː], p.p. *slain* [sleɪn]) kill; murder.

sled [sled] (U.S.A.), **sledge** [sledʒ] *ns.* vehicle with runners (4) (long, narrow strips of wood or metal) instead of wheels, used on snow. *v.i. & t.* (-dd-) travel, carry, by ~. (See the picture at *skip.*)

sledge(-ham·mer) ['sledʒ(ˌhæmə*)] *n.* heavy hammer used by blacksmiths.

sleek [sliːk] *adj.* **1.** (of hair, an animal's fur, etc.) soft and smooth. **2.** (of a person or animal) having ~ hair or fur. **3.** (of a person, his behaviour) over-anxious to please. *v.t.* make ~ (1); smooth with the hand.

sleep [sliːp] *n.* (no pl.) completely restful and inactive condition of the body such as that which normally comes each night for several hours in bed; period of this: *have a good ~; go to ~, fall asleep. v.i. & t.* (p.t. & p.p. *slept* [slept]) **1.** rest in the condition of ~; be or fall asleep. **2.** ~ *sth. off,* recover from (e.g. a headache) by ~ing. **3.** (of a hotel, etc.) have enough beds for: *a hotel that can ~ sixty guests.* **~·er** *n.* **1.** person who ~s: *a heavy* (*light*) ~*er.* **2.** wooden beam, etc. as a support for railway lines. **3.** (bed in a) ~ing-car(riage). '**~·ing-bag** *n.* warmly lined, waterproof bag for ~ing in, esp. out of doors. '**~·ing-car,** '**~·ing-·car·riage** *ns.* railway carriage with beds or berths. **~·ing part·ner** *n.* person who puts money into a business but plays no active part in it. '**~·ing-pill** *n.* medicine to cause a person to ~. **~·less** *adj.* without ~; unable to get ~: *a ~less night.* **~·less·ly** *adv.* **~·less·ness** *n.* (no pl.). '**~·walk·er** *n.* person who walks while asleep. **~y** *adj.* (-ier, -iest) **1.** needing, ready for, ~: *feel ~y.*

~yhead, ~y or inattentive person (esp. as a form of address). **2.** inactive: *a ~y village*. **~·i·ly** *adv*. **~·i·ness** *n*. (no pl.).

sleet [sli:t] *n*. (no pl.) falling snow or hail mixed with rain. *v.i. It was ~ing*, ~ was falling.

sleeve [sli:v] *n*. that part of a garment that covers the arm. *laugh up one's ~*, be secretly amused; *have sth. up one's ~*, have an idea, plan, etc. that one keeps secret for future use.

sleigh [sleɪ] *n*. sledge, esp. one drawn by a horse.

sleight [slaɪt] *n*. (only in) *~-of-hand*, expertness in using the hand(s) in performing tricks, in juggling, etc.

slen·der ['slendə*] *adj*. **1.** small in width or circumference compared with height or length: *a ~ stem*. **2.** not fat; graceful: *a ~ girl*; *a ~ waist*. **3.** slight; small; inadequate: *a ~ chance of success*.

slept, see *sleep* (v.).

sleuth [slu:θ] *n*. detective. '**~-hound** *n*. dog that follows a scent; bloodhound; (fig.) detective.

slew[1], see *slay*.

slew[2], **slue** [slu:] *v.i. & t.* force or turn *round* into a new direction.

slice [slaɪs] *n*. **1.** thin, wide, flat piece cut off sth., esp. bread, meat, large fruit, or cake. **2.** utensil with a wide, flat surface for cutting, serving, or lifting (e.g. cooked fish). *v.t. & i.* cut into ~s; cut (a piece *off*).

slick [slɪk] *adj*. (colloq.) **1.** smooth. **2.** (of a person, his manners) too smooth; tricky.

slide [slaɪd] *v.t. & i.* (p.t. & p.p. *slid* [slɪd]) **1.** (cause to) move smoothly, slip along, over a polished surface, ice, etc.: *children sliding on the ice*. **2.** (of things) move easily and smoothly: *drawers that ~ in and out. The book slid from my knee to the floor*. **3.** *let things ~*, not trouble about things. **4.** pass gradually, without being aware (*into* a condition, e.g. dishonesty). *n*. **1.** act of sliding (1). **2.** smooth stretch of ice, hard snow, etc. on which to ~ (1). **3.** smooth slope down which things or persons can ~ (1). **4.** mounted (2) picture to be slid into a *~-projector* and shown on a screen. **5.** glass plate on which is placed sth. to be examined under a microscope. **6.** part of a machine, etc. that ~s. **7.** ~ *rule*, rule with a sliding part, used for mathematical calculations. **slid·ing scale** *n*. scale by which one thing (e.g. salary) goes up or down in relation to changes in sth. else (e.g. cost of living).

a slide rule

slight[1] [slaɪt] *adj*. **1.** slim; slender. **2.** small; not serious or important: *a ~ headache*. **~·ly** *adv*. (esp.) a little: *~ly better*.

slight[2] [slaɪt] *v.t.* treat (sb.) without proper respect or courtesy. *n*. (behaviour, words, showing a) lack of proper respect.

slim [slɪm] *adj*. (-mm-) **1.** slender. **2.** small; insufficient: *a ~ attendance (excuse)*. *v.i.* (-mm-) eat less, take physical exercise, etc. to reduce one's weight and become ~ (1).

slime [slaɪm] *n*. (no pl.) **1.** soft, thick mud. **2.** sticky substance from snails, etc. **slimy** *adj*. (-ier, -iest) of, like, covered with, ~.

sling [slɪŋ] *n*. band of material, rope, chain, etc. looped round an object (e.g. a broken arm, a barrel) to support or lift it; short strap of leather, etc. to throw stones to a distance. *v.t.* (p.t. & p.p. *slung* [slʌŋ]) **1.** throw with force: *~ stones at a window*. **2.** support (sth.) so that it can swing, be lifted, etc.: *~ a hammock between two trees; with his gun slung over his shoulder*.

a sling

slink [slɪŋk] *v.i.* (p.t. & p.p. *slunk* [slʌŋk]) go (*about, away, by, off*) in a secret, guilty, or ashamed manner.

slip [slɪp] *v.i. & t.* (-pp-) **1.** lose one's balance; fall or almost fall as the result of this: *He ~ped and broke his leg*. **2.** go or move quietly or quickly, esp. without attracting attention: *He ~ped past me. The years ~ped by*. **3.** move, get away, escape, fall, by being hard to hold or by not being held firmly: *The fish ~ped out of my fingers. The blanket ~ped off the bed*. **4.** put; pull on or push off with a quick, easy movement: *~ into (out of) a dress; ~ a coat on (off); ~ a coin into sb.'s hand*.

5. make a small mistake, esp. by being careless: ~ *in one's grammar*; ~ *up*, (colloq.) make a mistake. **6.** move smoothly and effortlessly; go with a sliding motion: *a ship ~ping through the water.* **7.** escape, get free, from: *The dog ~ped its collar. It ~ped my memory.* ***n.*** **1.** act of ~ping. *give sb. the ~,* get away from him. **2.** small mistake: ~ *of the pen* (*tongue*), error in writing (speaking). **3.** loose cover for a pillow, etc. **4.** kind of petticoat. **5.** *gym-~,* girl's garment for gymnastic exercises. **6.** narrow strip of paper. **7.** young, slender person: *a ~ of a girl.* '**~-knot** ***n.*** knot that ~s along its own cord to form a noose that becomes tight. **~·per** ***n.*** loose-fitting, light shoe worn indoors. **~·pery** ***adj.*** (also *-ier, -iest*) **1.** smooth, wet, polished, so that it is difficult to hold, to stand on, or to move on: *a ~pery road*; (fig., of a subject) requiring tactful handling. **2.** (of persons) unreliable; unscrupulous: *a ~pery customer.* '**~-road** ***n.*** (Gt. Brit.) road for joining or leaving a motorway. '**~-shod** ***adj.*** slovenly; careless.

slit [slɪt] ***n.*** long, narrow cut, tear, or opening. ***v.t.*** (*-tt-*; p.t. & p.p. ~) make a ~ in; cut or tear into narrow pieces; open (an envelope, etc.) by ~ting.

slith·er ['slɪðə*] ***v.i.*** slide.

slob·ber ['slɒbə*] ***v.i. & t.*** **1.** let spittle run from the mouth; make wet with spittle. **2.** ~ *over* (*sb.* or *sth.*), show foolish or excessive love or admiration for.

slo·gan ['sləʊgən] ***n.*** striking and easily remembered phrase used to advertise sth. or to make clear the aim(s) of a group, organization, campaign, etc.; party watchword: *political ~s.*

sloop [sluːp] ***n.*** **1.** small, one-masted sailing-ship. **2.** small warship used for anti-submarine escort duty.

slop [slɒp] ***v.i. & t.*** (*-pp-*) **1.** (of liquids) spill over the edge. **2.** cause (liquid) to do this: ~ *coffee on the table.* **~s** ***n. pl.*** **1.** dirty waste water from the kitchen, etc. **2.** liquid food (e.g. milk, soup), esp. for sick people. '**~·ba·sin** ***n.*** (Gt. Brit.) bowl into which the dregs of teacups are emptied at table. **~·py** ***adj.*** (*-ier, -iest*) **1.** wet and dirty with rain or ~s (1): *~py roads.* **2.** (of food) consisting of ~s (2); watery and disagreeable. **3.** (of a person) foolishly sentimental; (of sentiment) foolish and weak. **4.** (colloq.) careless; untidy.

slope [sləʊp] ***n.*** **1.** slanting line, position or direction, at an angle of less than 90° to the earth's surface or to

some other line or flat surface: *the ~ of the roof.* **2.** area of rising or falling ground. ***v.i. & t.*** have a ~; cause to ~; give a ~ to. ~ *arms,* (mil.) place and hold the rifle in a sloping position on the left shoulder.

slot [slɒt] ***n.*** narrow opening through which sth. (e.g. a coin) is to be put. ***v.t.*** (*-tt-*) make a ~ or ~s in. '**~-ma-,chine** ***n.*** machine from which, e.g. matches, a ticket, can be obtained by putting a coin through a ~.

sloth [sləʊθ] ***n.*** **1.** (no pl.) laziness; idleness. **2.** S. American mammal that lives in the branches of trees and moves very slowly.

a sloth (2)

slouch [slaʊtʃ] ***v.i.*** stand, sit, move, in a lazy, tired way.

slough[1] [slaʊ] ***n.*** swamp; marsh.

slough[2] [slʌf] ***n.*** cast-off skin of a snake. ***v.t. & i.*** put, come, or throw (*off*).

slov·en·ly ['slʌvnlɪ] ***adj.*** dirty, untidy, or careless (in dress, habits, work, etc.). **slov·en** ***n.*** ~ person. **slov·en·li·ness** ***n.*** (no pl.).

slow [sləʊ] ***adj.*** **1.** taking a long time; not quick; at less than the usual speed: ~ *lane,* lane (5) for ~-moving traffic; ~ *motion,* operation or speed of film in which actions, etc. appear much ~er than usual. **2.** dull; not quick at learning; not lively enough: *What a ~ entertainment!* **3.** (usu. pred.) (of a watch or clock) showing a time that is earlier than the correct time: *My watch is four minutes ~.* ***v.t. & i.*** (cause to) go at a ~er speed than before: *The train ~ed down.* ***adv.*** at a low speed; less active: *Go ~ till you feel better. Go ~er or you will fall. go ~,* (of workers, etc.) work ~ly as a protest, or in order to get attention to demands, etc. *go-slow* (n.). '**~-coach** ***n.*** person who acts or thinks ~ly. '**~-down** ***n.*** action of ~ing down; go-~. **~·ly** ***adv.*** *Try to walk more ~ly.* **~·ness** ***n.*** (no pl.).

sludge [slʌdʒ] ***n.*** (no pl.) thick mud; thick, dirty oil or grease.

slue, see *slew²*.

slug¹ [slʌg] *n.* slow-moving creature like a snail but without a shell.

a slug¹

slug² [slʌg] *n.* bullet of irregular shape.

slug·gard ['slʌgəd] *n.* lazy, slow-moving person. **slug·gish** ['slʌgɪʃ] *adj.* inactive; slow-moving.

sluice [sluːs] *n.* **1.** apparatus (1) (*~-gate*, *~-valve*) for regulating the level of water by controlling the flow into or out of (a canal, lake, etc.). **2.** current of water through a ~. **3.** artificial water-channel, esp. for washing ore; thorough washing with a stream of water. *v.t. & i.* **1.** send a stream of water over; wash with a stream of water. **2.** (of water) come (*out*) in a stream.

slum [slʌm] *n.* **1.** street of poor, dirty, crowded houses. **2.** (pl.) part of a town where there are ~s (1).

slum·ber ['slʌmbə*] *v.i. & t. & n.* (liter., rhet., or fig.) sleep.

slump [slʌmp] *v.i.* **1.** drop or fall heavily (*down, into, to*). **2.** (of prices, trade, activity) fall steeply or suddenly. *n.* period of time during which prices, trade activity, etc. have ~ed.

slung, see *sling* (v.).

slunk, see *slink*.

slur [slɜː*] *v.t. & i.* (*-rr-*) **1.** join (words, syllables, musical notes, etc.) so that they cannot be separately distinguished. **2.** ~ *over*, deal quickly with in the hope of concealing: ~ *over sb.'s faults. n.* **1.** reproach; sth. that damages one's reputation. **2.** act of ~ring sounds.

slush [slʌʃ] *n.* (no pl.) soft, melting snow; slimy mud.

slut [slʌt] *n.* slovenly woman.

sly [slaɪ] *adj.* (*~er, ~est*) **1.** deceitful; keeping or doing things secretly; seeming to have, suggesting, secret knowledge: *a ~ look; on the ~,* secretly. **2.** playfully mischievous.

smack¹ [smæk] *n.* (sound of a) blow given with the open hand. *v.t.* **1.** strike with the open hand. **2.** ~ *one's lips,* make a ~ing sound with the lips to show pleasure (at food, etc.). *adv.* in a sudden and violent way: *run ~ into a brick wall.*

smack² [smæk] *n.* sort of small sailing-boat for fishing.

smack³ [smæk] *v.i. & n.* (have a) slight flavour or suggestion (*of*).

small [smɔːl] *adj.* not large: *Lions are large, dogs are ~, and rats are ~er still. look (feel) ~,* (fig.) look (feel) foolish or humbled. *~ change,* coins of ~ value. *the ~ hours,* the early hours (1 a.m. to 4 a.m.). *~ talk,* talk about unimportant things. *on the ~ side,* a little too ~. *adv.* into ~ pieces: *chop it ~. n.* **1.** *the* slenderest part: *the ~ of the back.* **2.** (pl.) (Gt. Brit., colloq.) ~ articles of laundry. *~ arms n. pl.* weapons light enough to be carried in the hand. **'~-pox** *n.* (no pl.) serious, contagious disease that leaves permanent marks on the skin.

smart¹ [smɑːt] *v.i. & n.* (no pl.) (feel or cause) sharp pain (in body or mind).

smart² [smɑːt] *adj.* **1.** bright; new-looking; clean; well-dressed. **2.** clever; skilful; having a good, quick brain. **3.** fashionable. **4.** (of a walk) quick; brisk. **5.** severe: *a ~ blow (punishment).* **~·en** ['smɑːtn] *v.t. & i.* ~*en up,* make or become ~ (1). **~·ly** *adv.* **~·ness** *n.* (no pl.).

smash [smæʃ] *v.t. & i.* **1.** break, be broken, into pieces: ~ *up,* break violently. **2.** rush, force a way, violently (*into, through, etc.*): *The car ~ed into a wall.* **3.** defeat utterly: ~ *the enemy;* ~ *a record,* (sport) set up a better record. **4.** (of a business firm) go bankrupt. *n.* **1.** (sound of) ~ing; violent fall, blow, collision; accident. **2.** bankruptcy. **3.** (attrib.) ~ *hit,* (sl.) sth. (e.g. a new song, film, etc.) that is at once very successful. **~·ing** *adj.* (colloq.) unusually good; excellent.

smat·ter·ing ['smætərɪŋ] *n.* (usu. no pl.) *a ~ of,* a slight knowledge of (a subject).

smear [smɪə*] *v.t. & i.* **1.** cover or mark with sth. oily or sticky. **2.** make dirty, greasy marks on. **3.** (of wet ink, etc.) spread and make dirty marks, etc. *n.* mark made by ~ing.

smell [smel] *n.* **1.** (no pl.) that one of the five senses that is special to the nose. **2.** that which is noticed by means of the nose; bad or unpleasant quality that affects the nose: *What a ~! v.t. & i.* (p.t. & p.p. *smelt* [smelt]) **1.** be aware of by means of the sense of ~; use the nose for its special purpose of detecting a ~; sniff in order to enjoy, etc. the ~ of sth.: ~ *of,* have the ~ of; suggest: *His breath ~s of beer.* ~ *out,* discover by means of the sense of ~; (fig.) discover (a secret, etc.) by careful inquiry. **2.** give out a ~: *The flowers*

~ *sweet. The dinner ~s good.* **'~-ing-salts** *n. pl.* sharp-~ing substance used to relieve headache or faintness. **~y** *adj.* (*-ier, -iest*) (colloq.) having a bad ~.

smelt [smelt] *v.t.* melt (ore); separate (metal) from ore by doing this.

smile [smaɪl] *n.* have a pleased, happy expression on the face. *v.i. & t.* **1.** give a ~ or ~s: ~ (*up*)*on,* (fig.) look with favour or approval on. **2.** express with a ~: ~ *a welcome.* **smil·ing·ly** *adv.* with a ~.

smirch [smɜːtʃ] *v.t.* make dirty; (fig.) dishonour. *n.* (fig.) stain (on one's reputation).

smirk [smɜːk] *n.* habitual or silly, self-satisfied smile. *v.i.* smile thus.

smite [smaɪt] *v.t. & i.* (p.t. *smote* [sməʊt], p.p. *smitten* ['smɪtn]) (liter. or humor. only) **1.** strike; hit hard. *smitten by* (*with*), deeply attracted by; attacked by (an illness). **2.** defeat utterly.

smith [smɪθ] *n.* worker in iron or other metals, esp. a black~. **~y** ['smɪðɪ] *n.* black~'s workshop.

smock [smɒk] *n.* loose garment like an overall.

smog [smɒg] *n.* (no pl.) mixture of fog and smoke.

smoke [sməʊk] *n.* **1.** (no pl.) black, grey, etc. vapour that can be seen coming from a burning substance with particles of carbon. (Cf. *steam.*) *end in ~,* have no satisfying result. **2.** act of smoking tobacco; (sl.) cigar; cigarette. *v.i. & t.* **1.** give out ~. **2.** (of a fire or fireplace) send out ~ into the room. **3.** breathe in and out the ~ of burning tobacco from a cigarette, cigar, or pipe between one's lips. **4.** dry and preserve (meat, fish) with ~. **5.** stain, darken, or dry with ~: ~*d glasses.* **6.** drive *out* with ~; send ~ on to (insects, plants). **smok·er** *n.* person who ~s tobacco; railway carriage in which passengers may smoke (3). **'smok·ing·carriage (-car, -compart·ment)** *ns.* one reserved for ~rs on a railway-train. **smoky** *adj.* (*-ier, -iest*) **1.** giving out ~; full of ~: *smoky chimneys.* **2.** like ~ in taste, appearance, etc. **~·less** *adj.* burning without ~: ~*less coal*; free from ~: *a ~less atmosphere.* **'~-screen** *n.* cloud of ~ intended to hide military or naval operations. **'~-stack** *n.* tall factory chimney; outlet for ~ and steam from a steamship or railway engine.

smooth [smuːð] *adj.* **1.** having a surface like that of glass; (of the sea) without waves; (of movement) free from shaking, bumping, etc. **2.** (of a liquid mixture) free from lumps; well-beaten or -mixed. **3.** (of sounds, speech) flowing easily. **4.** (of a person, his manner or words) flattering; pleasant but perhaps insincere. *v.t. & i.* **1.** make ~ (often ~ *down, out*). **2.** free from difficulties, troubles, etc.: ~ *away sb.'s objections.* **~·ly** *adv.* **~·ness** *n.* (no pl.). **'~-faced** *adj.* pleasant in behaviour and appearance but insincere. **'~·spo·ken, '~-tongued** *adjs.* using ~ (4) words.

smote, see *smite.*

smooth·er ['smʌðə*] *v.t. & i.* **1.** cause the death of, by stopping the breath of or by keeping air from. **2.** cover thickly or completely: ~*ed in dust*; ~ *a child with kisses.* **3.** keep back, suppress (a yawn, one's anger, etc.). **4.** put out (a fire), cause (a fire) to burn slowly, by covering it with ashes, sand, etc.

smoul·der (U.S.A. **smol-**) ['sməʊldə*] *v.i.* burn slowly without flame. *n.* (no pl.) ~ing fire.

smudge [smʌdʒ] *n.* dirty mark, esp. one where wet ink has been rubbed. *v.t. & i.* make a ~ on; mark with ~s; (of ink, drawing, etc.) become smeared or blurred.

smug [smʌg] *adj.* (*-gg-*) self-satisfied; too fond of comfort and respectability. **~·ly** *adv.*

smug·gle ['smʌgl] *v.t. & i.* **1.** get (goods) secretly and illegally (*into, out of,* a country, *through* the customs, etc.). **2.** take (sth. or sb.) secretly (*into, etc.*): ~ *a letter to sb. in prison.* **~r** *n.*

smut [smʌt] *n.* (mark or stain made by a) bit of soot, dirt from burning coal, etc. **~·ty** *adj.* (*-ier, -iest*) dirty with ~s; (fig.) improper: ~*ty stories.*

snack [snæk] *n.* light, usu. hurriedly eaten, meal. **'~-bar** *n.* place where ~s are served, usu. at a counter[1].

snag [snæg] *n.* rough or sharp object, root of a tree, hidden rock, that may be a source of danger; (fig.) unexpected hindrance or difficulty.

snail [sneɪl] *n.* kinds of small, soft animal, most of them with a spiral shell, as shown here.

a snail

snake [sneɪk] *n.* long, legless, crawling reptile, some of which are poisonous. (See the picture at *coil*.) **snaky** *adj.* (*-ier, -iest*) of or like a ~; infested with ~s.

snap [snæp] *v.t. & i.* (*-pp-*) **1.** make a sudden, often noisy, bite (*at*); (try to) snatch (*at* sth.). **2.** say (sth.), speak, sharply: ~ *at sb.*, speak to sb. sharply; ~ *sb.'s head off*, speak suddenly and impatiently to him. **3.** break with a sharp noise; open or close with a sudden, cracking noise; make a sharp noise: ~ *one's fingers*. **4.** take a ~shot of. *n.* **1.** act or sound of ~ping. **2.** *a cold* ~, a sudden, short period of cold weather. **3.** ~shot. **4.** (attrib.) done quickly and without much warning: *a* ~ *election* (*vote*). *adv.* with a ~ (1). **~·pish** *adj.* inclined to ~ (2), to be ill tempered. **~·py** *adj.* (*-ier, -iest*) lively. '**~·shot** *n.* casual, informal photograph taken with a hand camera.

snare [sneə*] *n.* trap, esp. one with a noose, for catching small animals and birds; (fig.) trick; temptation. *v.t.* catch in a ~.

snarl [snɑːl] *v.i. & t.* (of dogs) show the teeth and growl; (of persons) speak or say in an angry way. *n.* act or sound of ~ing.

snatch [snætʃ] *v.t. & i.* **1.** put out the hand suddenly and take: ~ *sth. up* (*down, away, off, etc.*). **2.** ~ *at*, try to get by ~ing. **3.** get quickly or when the chance occurs: ~ *an hour's sleep.* *n.* **1.** sudden stretching out of the hand to get sth. **2.** short outburst or period (*of* sth.): ~*es of song.*

sneak [sniːk] *v.i. & t.* **1.** go quietly and secretly (*away, in, off, etc.*). **2.** (sl.) take away (sb. else's property) without permission. *n.* cowardly, treacherous person. **~·ers** *n. pl.* (chiefly U.S.A.) = plimsolls.

sneer [snɪə*] *v.i. & n.* (show contempt by a) scornful smile or words: ~ *at sb.* or *sth.* **~·ing·ly** *adv.*

sneeze [sniːz] *n.* sudden, uncontrollable outburst of air through the nose and mouth. *v.i.* make a ~.

sniff [snɪf] *v.i. & t.* **1.** draw air in through the nose so that there is a sound; do this (~ *at*) to show disapproval or contempt. **2.** draw (sth.) in through the nose as one breathes: ~ *up powdered medicine*; smell by doing this: *dogs* ~*ing* (*at*) *a lamppost*. *n.* act or sound of ~ing; breath (*of* air, etc.). **snif·fle** ['snɪfl] *v.i.* snuffle.

snig·ger ['snɪɡə*] *n.* half-suppressed

laugh, esp. at sth. improper. *v.i.* laugh in this way (*at* or *over* sth.).

snip [snɪp] *v.t. & i.* (*-pp-*) cut with scissors: ~ *the ends off.* *n.* cut made by ~ping; sth. ~ped off.

snipe[1] [snaɪp] *n.* (*pl.* ~s, ~) game[1] (5) bird with a long bill, living in marshes.

a snipe[1]

a snow-shoe

snipe[2] [snaɪp] *v.i. & t.* shoot (*at* sb.) from a hiding-place or in darkness; kill or wound by firing shots in this way. **snip·er** *n.* person who ~s.

snip·pet ['snɪpɪt] *n.* small piece cut off; (pl.) small bits (*of* information, news, etc.).

sniv·el ['snɪvl] *v.i.* (*-ll-*, U.S.A. also *-l-*) cry with pretended grief, sorrow, or fear; whine. *n.* tearful state or talk.

snob [snɒb] *n.* person who pays too much respect to social position or wealth. **~·bery** *n.* **~·bish** *adj.* **~·bish·ly** *adv.* **~·bish·ness** *n.*

snoop [snuːp] *v.i.* (colloq.) pry into other persons' affairs. **~·er** *n.* person who does this.

snooze [snuːz] *v.i. & n.* (colloq.) (take a) short sleep, esp. in the daytime.

snore [snɔː*] *v.i.* breathe roughly and noisily while sleeping. *n.* sound of snoring.

snor·kel ['snɔːkl], **schnor·kel** ['ʃnɔːkl] *n.* device (2) for supplying air to a submerged submarine; breathing-tube for an underwater swimmer.

snort [snɔːt] *v.i. & t.* force air violently out through the nose; do this (*of* sb.) *with* impatience, contempt, etc.; express (defiance, etc.) by ~ing; throw *out* (words) with ~ing. *n.* act or·sound of ~ing.

snout [snaʊt] *n.* nose (and mouth) of an animal, esp. a pig; pointed front of sth. like an animal's ~.

snow [snəʊ] *n.* (no pl.) frozen vapour falling from the sky in light, white flakes; mass of such flakes on the ground, etc. *v.i. & t.* **1.** (of ~) come down from the sky. **2.** come or send (*down*, etc.) like ~, in large quantities. **3.** *be* ~*ed up* (*in*), be prevented by ~ from going out. '**~·ball** *n.* lump of ~ pressed together for throwing in play; (fig.) sth. that increases quickly in

social

size as it moves forward. **'~-bound adj.** unable to travel because of heavy falls of ~. **'~-capped (-clad, -,covered) adjs.** (of mountains) covered at the top with ~. **'~-drift n.** bank of ~ heaped up by wind. **'~-drop n.** bulb plant with small, white flowers in early spring. **'~-fall n.** (esp.) amount of ~ that falls on one occasion or on a given area within a given period of time. **'~-flake n.** feather-like piece of falling ~. **'~-man n.** figure of a man made of ~ by children. **'~-plough n.** device (2) for pushing ~ from roads and railways. **'~-shoe n.** frame with leather straps for walking on soft, deep ~. (See the picture at *snipe*¹.) **'~-storm n.** heavy fall of ~, esp. with wind. **,~-'white adj.** white as ~. **~y adj.** (-*ier*, -*iest*) of or like ~; covered with ~.

snub¹ [snʌb] **v.t.** (-*bb*-) treat (esp. a younger or less senior person) with cold behaviour or contempt; reject (an offer) thus **n.** ~bing words or behaviour.

snub² [snʌb] **adj.** a ~ nose, (~-nosed, with) a short, thick, slightly turned-up nose.

snuff¹ [snʌf] **v.i. & t.** sniff. **n.** (no pl.) powdered tobacco to be taken up into the nose by sniffing. **'~-,col·oured adj.** brownish-yellow.

snuff² [snʌf] **v.t. & i. 1.** cut or pinch off the end of the wick of (a candle); put *out* (a candle light) by doing this. **2.** ~ *out*, (sl.) die.

snuf·fle ['snʌfl] **v.i.** make sniffing sounds; breathe noisily, talk through the nose, esp. when it is partly stopped up. **n.** act or sound of snuffling.

snug [snʌg] **adj.** (-*gg*-) **1.** warm and comfortable; sheltered. **2.** neat and tidy; rightly or conveniently placed or arranged. **~gle** ['snʌgl] **v.i. & t.** lie or get (close to sb.) so as to be warm or comfortable: ~*gle up to sb.*; draw (a child, etc.) close to one: *She ~gled the child close to her.*

so [səʊ] **adv. 1.** to such an extent: *Why are you so unkind? He is not so stupid as that. He was so ill that we had to call a doctor. Now we have come so far* (as far as this), *we may as well go all the way. so long as,* on condition that: *You may borrow the book, so long as you keep it clean. so far from,* instead of: *So far from helping, he hindered us.* **2.** in this (that) way: *As you treat me, so will I treat you. Stand so* (like this). *so that,* (a) in order that: *Speak clearly, so that we can hear you.*

(b) with the result that: *He remained still, so that people thought he had died. so as to,* in order to: *I will hurry, so as not to delay you.* **3.** (used instead of a word, phrase, etc.): *I told you so!* (That is what I told you.) **4.** also: *You are learning English and so are they.* **5.** *or so,* about: *She is forty or so* (about forty). **conj. 1.** therefore; that is why: *She asked me to go, so I went.* **2.** (as an exclamation): *So you've come back at last!* **so-and-so** ['səʊənsəʊ] **n. 1.** sb. or sth. not (needing to be) named. **2.** disliked or contemptible person. **,so-'called adj.** called or named thus (esp. without good reason).

soak [səʊk] **v.i. & t. 1.** become wet through by being in liquid or by absorbing liquid: *Let the clothes ~ in soapy water.* **2.** cause (sth.) to absorb as much liquid as possible: ~ *bread in milk* (*dirty clothes in water*). **3.** (of rain, etc.) make very wet; enter, pass (*through, into, etc.*). **4.** ~ *up,* (of substances) take up, absorb (liquid). **n.** act of ~ing.

soap [səʊp] **n.** fatty substance used with water to remove dirt by washing and scrubbing: *a bar* (*cake*) *of* ~; *soft* ~, (fig.) flattery. **v.t.** rub ~ on; wash with ~. **'~-,bub·ble n.** filmy ball of ~y water with changing colours, full of air. **'~-suds n. pl.** mass of foam or lather made from ~ and water. **~y adj.** (-*ier*, -*iest*) of or like ~; (fig.) over-anxious to please.

soar [sɔ:*] **v.i.** go, float high, in the air; rise beyond what is ordinary: *a ~ing eagle. Prices ~ed.*

sob [sɒb] **v.i. & t.** (-*bb*-) draw in the breath sharply and irregularly from sorrow or pain, esp. while crying; say (sth.) while doing this. **n.** act or sound of ~bing.

so·ber ['səʊbə*] **adj. 1.** self-controlled; temperate; serious in thought, etc.; calm. **2.** avoiding drunkenness; not drunk. **3.** (of colours) not bright. **v.t. & i.** make or become ~. **so·bri·ety** [səʊ'braɪətɪ] **n.** (no pl.) quality or condition of being ~.

soc·cer ['sɒkə*] **n.** (no pl.) (colloq.) Association football.

so·cia·ble ['səʊʃəbl] **adj.** fond of the company of others; friendly; showing friendliness. **so·cia·bly adv. so·cia·bil·i·ty** [,səʊʃə'bɪlətɪ] **n.** (no pl.).

so·cial ['səʊʃl] **adj. 1.** living in groups, not separately. **2.** of people living in communities; of relations (4) between persons or communities: ~ *customs*; ~ *reform*; ~ *security*, government provisions for helping people who are unemployed, disabled, ill, etc.; ~ welfare; ~ worker. **3.** of or in society: *one's* ~ *equals* (i.e. persons of the same class in a society (1)). *n.* friendly meeting, esp. one organized by a church. **~·ism** *n.* (no pl.) theory that land, transport, the chief industries, natural resources, etc. should be owned and managed by the State or public bodies in the interests of the community as a whole. **~·ist** *n.* supporter of, believer in, ~ism. *adj.* (also ~istic) of, tending towards, ~ism. **~·ize** ['səʊʃəlaɪz] *v.t.* make ~istic; transfer to public ownership. **~·iza·tion** [ˌsəʊ-ʃəlaɪ'zeɪʃn] *n.* (no pl.).

so·ci·e·ty [sə'saɪətɪ] *n.* **1.** social community; persons living together as a group or as a nation. **2.** (no pl.) organization, customs, etc. of such a group. **3.** (no pl.) people of fashion or distinction in a place, district, country, etc.; the upper classes. **4.** (no pl.) company; companionship: *spend an evening in the* ~ *of one's friends.* **5.** organization of persons formed with a purpose; club; association: *the school debating* ~.

so·ci·ol·o·gy [ˌsəʊsɪ'ɒlədʒɪ] *n.* (no pl.) science of the nature and growth of society and social behaviour. **so·ci·ol·o·gist** *n.* expert in ~.

sock [sɒk] *n.* **1.** short stocking not reaching the knee. **2.** loose sole put inside a shoe.

sock·et ['sɒkɪt] *n.* hollow into which sth. fits or in which sth. turns.

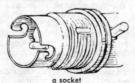

a socket

sod [sɒd] *n.* **1.** (no pl.) surface of grassland with the roots and earth. **2.** piece of this cut from the ground.

so·da ['səʊdə] *n.* (no pl.) common chemical substance used in making soap, glass, etc. *washing-*~ (for softening water, cleaning, etc.); *baking-*~ (used in cooking); *~-water*, water charged with gas to make it bubble. '**~·foun·tain** *n.* (U.S.A.) counter from which ~-water, ices, etc. are served.

sod·den ['sɒdn] *adj.* **1.** wet through: *clothes* ~ *with rain.* **2.** (of bread, etc.) heavy and dough-like. **3.** stupid through too much drinking of alcohol.

so·di·um ['səʊdjəm] *n.* (no pl.) silver-white metal occurring naturally only in compounds.

so·fa ['səʊfə] *n.* long, cushioned seat, with a back and arms, for two or three persons to sit or one to lie on.

a sofa

soft [sɒft] *adj.* **1.** not hard: *Our car got stuck in the* ~, *wet soil.* **2.** (of cloth, hair, skin, etc.) smooth; delicate. **3.** (of light, colours) not bright; restful to the eyes. **4.** (of sounds) subdued; not loud. **5.** (of words, answers, etc.) mild; intended to please. **6.** (of air, weather, etc.) mild. **7.** (of water) free from mineral salts and therefore good for washing. **8.** sympathetic; compassionate: *have a* ~ *heart; have a* ~ *spot for sb.,* be fond of him. **9.** (sl.) easy: *a* ~ *job.* **10.** ~ *drinks,* cold, non-alcoholic drinks, esp. fruit juices. **11.** (colloq.) silly. **~·en** ['sɒfn] *v.t. & i.* make or become ~. **~·ly** *adv.* '**~·ware** *n.* data (2), programs, etc. not forming parts of a computer but used for its operation (opp. *hardware* (2)).

sog·gy ['sɒgɪ] *adj.* (*-ier, -iest*) (esp. of ground) heavy with water.

soil[1] [sɔɪl] *n.* ground; earth, esp. the earth in which plants grow.

soil[2] [sɔɪl] *v.t. & i.* make or become dirty.

so·journ ['sɒdʒɜːn] *v.i. & n.* (make a) stay (*with* sb., *at* or *in*) for a time.

so·lace ['sɒləs] *n.* (that which gives) comfort or relief (when one is in trouble, pain, etc.). *v.t.* give ~ to.

so·lar ['səʊlə*] *adj.* of the sun.

sold, see *sell.*

sol·der ['sɒldə*] *n.* (no pl.) easily melted metal used to join surfaces of harder metals, wires, etc. *v.t.* join with ~. '**~·ing-·i·ron** *n.* tool used for ~ing.

sol·dier ['səʊldʒə*] *n.* member of an army. **~·ly, ~·like** *adjs.* like a ~; smart, brave, etc.

sole[1] [səʊl] *n.* under part of the foot, or of a sock, shoe, etc. *v.t.* fasten a ~ on (a shoe, etc.).

sole[2] [səʊl] *n.* flat sea-fish with a delicate flavour. (See the picture.)

sole[3] [səʊl] *adj.* **1.** one and only; single.

some

2. restricted to one person, etc.: *have the ~ right of selling this article.* **~·ly** *adv.* **1.** alone. **2.** only.

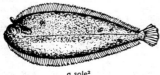

a sole²

so·le·cism ['sɒlɪsɪzəm] *n.* error in the use of language; offence against good manners.

sol·emn ['sɒləm] *adj.* **1.** performed with religious or other ceremony; causing deep thought or respect. **2.** serious-looking; grave; important. **~·ly** *adv.* **so·lem·ni·ty** [sə'lemnətɪ] *n.* **1.** (no pl.) seriousness; gravity. **2.** ~ ceremony.

sol·em·nize ['sɒləmnaɪz] *v.t.* perform (a religious ceremony, esp. a wedding) with the usual rites; make ~.

sol-fa [,sɒl'fɑː] *n.* system of syllables each representing a musical note.

so·lic·it [sə'lɪsɪt] *v.t. & i.* ask (*for*) earnestly or repeatedly: *~ sb. for help; ~ sb.'s help* (*trade*).

so·lic·i·tor [sə'lɪsɪtə*] *n.* lawyer who prepares legal documents (e.g. wills), advises his clients on legal matters, and speaks on their behalf in lower courts. (Cf. *barrister.*)

so·lic·i·tous [sə'lɪsɪtəs] *adj.* troubled, anxious (*about*); eager (*to do* sth.). **so·lic·i·tude** [sə'lɪsɪtjuːd] *n.* (no pl.) being ~; anxiety; concern.

sol·id ['sɒlɪd] *adj.* **1.** not in the form of a liquid or gas; not (easily) changing its shape when pressed. **2.** without holes or spaces; not hollow. **3.** of strong or firm material or construction: *~ buildings.* **4.** (math.) having three dimensions (length, breadth, and thickness): *a ~ figure* (e.g. a cube). **5.** firm, hard, or compact in substance: *~ ground.* **6.** that can be depended on: *~ arguments; a ~ business firm.* **7.** firmly united in support of sth.; unanimous: *~ in defence of the country.* **8.** of the same substance throughout: *~ gold.* **9.** continuous; without a break: *waiting for a ~ hour.* *n.* **1.** body or substance that is ~, not a liquid or a gas. **2.** (math.) body or object having three dimensions. **~·ly** *adv.* **sol·i·dar·i·ty** [,sɒlɪ'dærətɪ] *n.* (no pl.) unity resulting from common interests or feelings: *national ~arity in the face of danger.* **so·lid·i·fy** [sə'lɪdɪfaɪ] *v.t. & i.* make or become ~, hard, or firm. **so·lid·i·ty** [sə'lɪdətɪ] *n.* (no pl.) quality of being ~.

so·lil·o·quy [sə'lɪləkwɪ] *n.* act of speaking one's thoughts aloud; (thea.) speech in which a character speaks his thoughts without addressing a listener. **so·lil·o·quize** [sə'lɪləkwaɪz] *v.i.* talk to oneself.

sol·i·taire [,sɒlɪ'teə*] *n.* **1.** single gem set¹ (9) alone. **2.** (U.S.A.) = patience (2).

sol·i·tary ['sɒlɪtərɪ] *adj.* **1.** (living) alone; without companions; lonely. **2.** only one. **3.** (of places) seldom visited. **sol·i·tude** ['sɒlɪtjuːd] *n.* being ~; ~ place.

so·lo ['səʊləʊ] *n.* (pl. ~s, -li [-liː]) piece of music (to be) performed by one person. *adv.* alone. **~·ist** *n.* person who performs a ~.

sol·stice ['sɒlstɪs] *n.* either of the two times each year when day and night are equally long.

sol·u·ble ['sɒljʊbl] *adj.* **1.** that can be dissolved (*in* a liquid). **2.** that can be solved or explained. **sol·u·bil·i·ty** [,sɒljʊ'bɪlətɪ] *n.* (no pl.).

so·lu·tion [sə'luːʃn] *n.* **1.** answer (*to* a question, etc.); way of dealing with a difficulty, etc. **2.** process of dissolving a solid or gas in a liquid; the liquid that results: *a ~ of salt in water.*

solve [sɒlv] *v.t.* find the answer to (a problem, etc.); find a way out of (a difficulty, etc.).

sol·vent ['sɒlvənt] *adj.* **1.** (of a substance, usu. a liquid) able to dissolve other substances. **2.** having money enough to pay one's debts. *n.* **~** (1) substance: *Petrol is a ~ of grease.* **sol·ven·cy** *n.* (no pl.) being ~ (2).

som·bre ['sɒmbə*] *adj.* dark-coloured; gloomy; dismal.

some [sʌm, səm] *adj. & pron.* **I.** *adj.* **1.** (cf. *any*) (used with a material noun to indicate an amount or quantity that is not fixed): *Won't you have ~ (any) sugar with your cereal?* **2.** (cf. *any*) (used as a plural of *a, an, one*): *Have they any children? Yes, they have ~, but I don't know how many. No, they haven't any.* **3.** (used with *more*): *Do you want ~ (any) more writing-paper?* **4.** (used to indicate an unknown person, place, etc.): *He's staying at ~ hotel (or other) in London.* **5.** considerable quantity of: *I shall be away ~ (a fairly long) time.* **6.** about; approximately: *They invited ~ twenty people.* **II.** *pron.* (~ *of* and *any of* are equivalent to *a few of, a little of, part of*): *S~ of* *these books are dirty. S~ of this paper is torn.* **~·body** ['sʌmbədɪ] *pron.* **1.** ~ (indefinite) person. **2.** person of importance: *He's ~body in his own town, if not elsewhere.* **~·how** ['sʌmhaʊ] *adv.* in ~ way (or other): *I shall get it ~how (or other).* **~·one** ['sʌmwʌn] *pron.* ~body. **~·thing** ['sʌmθɪŋ] *pron.* an object, event, etc. (of an indefinite nature): *There is ~thing moving behind the trees. There's ~thing in what he says. or ~thing, or ~ unspecified alternative possibility: He's an actor or ~thing. ~thing of, to ~ extent: He's ~thing of an expert on this subject.* (Cf. *anything.*) **~·times** ['sʌmtaɪmz] *adv.* from time to time; now and then: *We ~times go to the cinema. S~times I travel by train, at other times I take the car.* **~·what** ['sʌmwɒt] *adv.* in ~ degree; rather. **~·where** ['sʌmweə*] *adv.* in, at, to, some place: *You will find the book ~where in his office.* (Cf. *anywhere.*)

-some [-səm] *suff.* **1.** (forming adjs.) productive of; likely to: *quarrelsome*; *tiresome.* **2.** (forming ns. from numerals) group of: *foursome.*

som·er·sault ['sʌməsɔːlt] *n.* leap or fall in which one turns heels over head before landing on one's feet. *v.i.* turn a ~.

som·no·lent ['sɒmnələnt] *adj.* sleepy; almost asleep; causing sleep. **som·no·lence** *n.* (no pl.).

son [sʌn] *n.* male child of a parent. **'~-in-law** *n.* (pl. ~s-in-law) daughter's husband.

so·na·ta [sə'nɑːtə] *n.* musical composition with three or four movements, for one or two instruments.

sonde [sɒnd] *n.* device (2) sent up to obtain information about atmospheric conditions.

song [sɒŋ] *n.* **1.** (no pl.) singing; music for, or produced by, the voice. *for a ~,* very cheaply. *nothing to make a ~ (and dance) about,* (colloq.) of little or no importance. **2.** musical cry of some birds: *a ~bird.* **3.** short poem set to music or meant to be sung. **4.** (no pl.) poetry; verse.

son·ic ['sɒnɪk] *adj.* relating to sound, sound-waves, or the speed of sound. *~ bang (boom),* noise made when an aircraft exceeds the speed of sound.

son·net ['sɒnɪt] *n.* kind of poem containing 14 lines, each of 10 syllables, and with a formal pattern of rhymes.

so·no·rous [sə'nɔːrəs] *adj.* **1.** having a full, deep sound. **2.** (of language, style, etc.) making a deep impression.

soon [suːn] *adv.* **1.** not long after the present time or the time spoken of; in a short time. **2.** early. **3.** *as ~ as,* at the moment that; when; not later than; *no ~er ... than,* immediately when or after. **4.** *would (just) as ~ (would ~er),* would with equal (with more) pleasure or willingness.

soot [sʊt] *n.* (no pl.) black powder in smoke, or left by smoke on surfaces. **~y** *adj.* (-ier, -iest).

soothe [suːð] *v.t.* **1.** make (a person, his nerves) quiet or calm. **2.** make (pains, aches) less sharp or severe. **sooth·ing·ly** *adv.*

sooth·say·er ['suːθˌseɪə*] *n.* fortune-teller.

sop [sɒp] *n.* **1.** piece of bread, etc. soaked in milk, soup, etc. **2.** sth. offered to sb. to prevent trouble or to give temporary satisfaction. *v.t.* (-pp-) soak (bread, etc. in milk, gravy, etc.); take (up) liquid, etc. **~·ping** *adj.* wet through.

soph·ism ['sɒfɪzəm] *n.* false reasoning intended to deceive. **soph·ist** ['sɒfɪst] *n.* person who uses clever but misleading arguments. **so·phis·ti·cat·ed** [sə'fɪstɪkeɪtɪd] *adj.* having lost natural simplicity; (of apparatus, etc.) with the latest technical developments and refinements; (of mental activity) refined; intellectually appealing. **so·phis·ti·ca·tion** [səˌfɪstɪ'keɪʃn] *n.* (no pl.).

soph·o·more ['sɒfəmɔː*] *n.* (U.S.A.) student in his second year at college or high school.

so·po·rif·ic [ˌsɒpə'rɪfɪk] *n. & adj.* (substance, drink, etc.) producing sleep.

sop·py ['sɒpɪ] *adj.* (-ier, -iest) **1.** very wet. **2.** (colloq.) too sentimental.

so·pra·no [sə'prɑːnəʊ] *n.* (pl. ~s, -ni [-niː]) (woman or child with the) highest singing voice. *adj.* relating to such a voice.

sor·cer·er ['sɔːsərə*] *n.* man who practises magic with the help of evil spirits. **sor·cer·ess** *n.* female ~. **sor·cery** ['sɔːsərɪ] *n.* (no pl.) witchcraft.

sor·did ['sɔːdɪd] *adj.* **1.** (of conditions) wretched; shabby; comfortless. **2.** (of persons, behaviour, etc.) contemptible; prompted by self-interest or meanness.

sore [sɔː*] *adj.* (~r, ~st) **1.** (of a part of the body) tender and painful; hurting when touched or used: *a ~ knee (throat).* **2.** filled with sorrow: *a ~ heart.* **3.** causing sorrow or annoyance: *a ~ point (subject),* one that hurts the feelings when talked about. **4.** (old use, also as an adv.) grievous(ly): *in ~ need*; *~ oppressed*. **n.** ~ place on the body; (fig.) ~ subject; painful memory. **~·ly** *adv.* greatly; severely: *~ly tempted*.

sor·rel ['sɒrəl] **n. 1.** (no pl.) light reddish-brown colour. **2.** horse of this colour. **adj.** of a light reddish-brown colour.

sor·row ['sɒrəʊ] **n.** (cause of) grief or sadness; regret. **v.i.** feel ~ (*at, over, for,* sth.). **~·ful** *adj.* **~·ful·ly** *adv.*

sor·ry ['sɒrɪ] **adj.** (-ier, -iest) **1.** (pred. only) feeling regret or sadness: *be ~ for (about) sth.*; *~ to hear that*; *feel ~ for,* feel sympathy for. **2.** (attrib.) pitiful: *in a ~ state*; worthless: *a ~ excuse*.

sort [sɔːt] **n. 1.** group or class of persons or things that are alike in some ways: *What ~ of people does he think we are?* of *~s* (colloq.), of a *~,* not fully deserving the name; *~ of,* (colloq.) rather; to some extent: *He ~ of threatened me. after a ~, in a ~,* to a certain extent. **2.** *a good ~,* (esp.) a person who is likable, who has good qualities. **3.** *out of ~s,* (colloq.) feeling unwell; in low spirits. **v.t.** (often *~ out*) arrange in groups (according to size, quality, destination, etc.): *~ing letters*; separate things of one ~ from others: *~ out the good apples from the bad*; *give me some time to ~ that (things) out,* (fig., to find a solution). **~·er n.** (esp.) post-office worker who *~s* letters.

SOS [ˌesəʊ'es] **n.** message for help (sent by radio, etc.) from a ship, aircraft, etc. when in danger; any urgent call for help.

sot [sɒt] **n.** habitual drunkard.

sough [saʊ] **v.i. & i.** (make a) moaning or sighing sound (as of the wind in trees, etc.).

sought, see *seek.*

soul [səʊl] **n. 1.** non-material part of a human being, believed to exist for ever. **2.** person's real self, the centre of his feelings, thoughts, etc. **3.** person: *not a ~ to be seen*; person regarded with familiarity, pity, contempt, etc.: *He's a good ~. Poor little ~.* **4.** person regarded as the pattern or personification of some virtue or quality: *He is the ~ of honour.* **5.** *the life and ~ of sth.,* (person looked upon as) the animating part of sth. **6.** (no pl.) quality that arouses emotion, esp. as exemplified in Negro music, art, and other cultural manifestations. Originally the term was used by Negro jazz musicians to describe the deeply felt quality of spiritual and gospel music when it

appeared in jazz: *~ music.* **~·ful adj.** having, affecting, showing, deep feeling: *~ful looks.* **~·less adj.** without higher or deep feelings.

sound¹ [saʊnd] **n. 1.** that which can be heard: *the ~ of voices*; *within ~ of the guns,* near enough to hear them; *vowel (consonant) ~s.* **2.** (no pl.) mental impression produced by sth. stated or read: *I don't like the ~ of it.* **v.i. & t. 1.** produce ~ from; make (sth.) produce ~: *~ a trumpet.* **2.** utter. **3.** pronounce. **4.** give notice of: *~ an alarm.* **5.** give forth ~: *the trumpet ~ed.* **6.** make a certain impression on the ear or the mind: *His explanation ~s reasonable.* **7.** test, examine (e.g. with an instrument, tool, etc., and by listening): *~ the wheels of a railway coach. The doctor ~ed my chest.* **~·bar·ri·er n.** point at which an aircraft's speed equals that of *~*-waves, causing a sonic boom. **'~·film n.** talking film. **'~·proof adj.** that *~s* cannot pass into or through: *a ~-proof room (ceiling).* **'~·track n.** narrow strip on the side of a cinema film for recording ~.

sound² [saʊnd] **n.** narrow passage of water joining two larger areas of water; inlet of the sea. **v.t. & i. 1.** test and measure the depth of (the sea, etc.) with a lead weight on a rope (called a *~ing-line*); find the depth of water in (a ship's hold) with a *~ing-rod.* **2.** get records of temperature, humidity, pressure, etc. from (the upper atmosphere) with a *~ing-balloon* or a sonde. **3.** ~ *sb. (out),* (fig.) try (esp. in a cautious or reserved manner) to learn his views (*on* or *about* a subject).

sound³ [saʊnd] **adj. 1.** healthy; in good condition: *~ fruit (teeth).* **2.** dependable; based on reason; prudent: *a ~ argument (policy).* **3.** thorough; complete: *a ~ sleep (thrashing).* **4.** financially secure: *a ~ firm.* **adv.** ~·ly: *~ asleep,* in a deep sleep. **~·ly adv. 1.** in a ~ manner: *sleep ~ly.* **2.** thoroughly. **~·ness n.** (no pl.).

soup [suːp] **n.** liquid food made by boiling meat, vegetables, etc. in water. *in the ~,* (colloq.) in trouble. **v.t.** ~ *(up),* (colloq.) increase the power of (an engine): *a ~ed-up car.*

sour ['saʊə*] **adj. 1.** having a sharp, acid taste (like that of unripe fruit). **2.** (of milk, etc.) having a taste of fermentation. **3.** bad-tempered; sharp-tongued. **v.t. & i.** make or become ~ (2, 3). **~·ly adv. ~·ness n.** (no pl.).

source [sɔːs] **n. 1.** starting-point of a river. **2.** place from which sth. comes

or is got; origin: *news from a reliable ~.*
3. original document, etc. serving as
material for a study: *~ material.*

souse [saʊs] *v.t.* **1.** throw into water;
throw water over. **2.** put (fish, etc.)
into salted water, vinegar, etc. to
preserve it. **3.** *~d,* (p.p.) (sl.) drunk.

south [saʊθ] *adv., n., & adj.* **1.** (towards, at, near) one of the four cardinal points of the compass, or the
direction towards which the magnetic
needle turns. **2.** (attrib.) situated in,
coming from, etc. the ~: *the S~ Pole;
S~ America; S~ Sea.* **~·er·ly** [ˈsʌðəlɪ]
adj. & adv. (of winds) from the ~;
towards the ~; in or to the ~. **~·ern**
[ˈsʌðən] *adj.* in or of the ~. **~·ward(s)**
[ˈsaʊθwəd(z)] *adv.* towards the ~.

sou·ve·nir [ˌsuːvəˈnɪə*] *n.* sth. taken,
bought, or received as a gift, and kept
as a reminder of a person, place, or
event.

sou'·west·er [saʊˈwestə*] *n.* **1.** strong
S.W. wind. **2.** oilskin hat with a wide
flap at the back to protect the neck.

sov·er·eign [ˈsɒvrɪn] *adj.* **1.** (of power)
highest; without limit. **2.** (of a state,
a ruler) having ~ power. **3.** excellent;
of proved or undoubted value: *no ~
remedy for leprosy.* *n.* **1.** ruler, esp. a
king, queen, or emperor. **2.** British
gold coin (not now in general circulation). **~·ty** *n.* (no pl.) ~ power.

so·vi·et [ˈsəʊvɪət] *n.* one of the councils
of workers, etc. in any part of the
U.S.S.R. (Union of S~ Socialist
Republics); any of the higher groups
to which these councils give authority,
forming part of the system of government of the U.S.S.R.: *S~ Russia; the
S~ Union.*

sow[1] [səʊ] *v.t. & i.* (p.t. *~ed* [səʊd],
p.p. *~n* [səʊn] or *~ed*) put (seed)
in the ground; plant (land *with* seed).

sow[2] [saʊ] *n.* female pig.

soya (bean) [ˈsɔɪə (biːn)] *n.* plant
grown as food and for the oil obtained
from its seeds.

spa [spaː] *n.* (place where there is a)
spring of mineral water having medicinal properties.

space [speɪs] *n.* **1.** (no pl.) that in
which all objects exist or move: *The
universe exists in ~.* **2.** interval or
distance between two or more objects:
*the ~s between printed words; separated
by a ~ of ten feet.* **3.** area or volume: *an
open ~,* land, esp. in or near a town,
not built on. **4.** (no pl.) limited or unoccupied place or area: *not enough ~ in
this classroom for thirty desks.* **5.** (no pl.)
period of time: *in the ~ of ten years.*

v.t. place (esp. words, letters) with
regular ~s (2) between: *~ out,* put more
or wider ~s between. '**~·bar** *n.* bar in
a typewriter for making ~s (2) be-
tween words, etc. '**~·craft**, '**~·ship** *ns.*
vehicle for travelling in ~. **~ flight** *n.*
flight beyond the earth's atmosphere.
~ sta·tion *n.* artificial satellite used as
a base for operations in ~. '**~·suit** *n.*
suit with air supply and other provisions to make life in free ~ possible
for its wearer. **~ walk** *n.* act of moving
in ~ outside a ~craft. **spa·cious**
[ˈspeɪʃəs] *adj.* having much ~; roomy.

spade [speɪd] *n.* **1.** tool for digging.
call a ~ a ~, speak plainly or bluntly.
2. (one of a) suit of playing-cards with
black figures shaped like an inverted
heart with a short stem. *v.t.* (often *~
up*) dig with a ~. '**~·work** *n.* hard
work needed at the start of an undertaking.

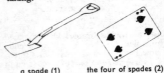

a spade (1)   the four of spades (2)

spa·ghet·ti [spəˈgetɪ] *n.* thin kind of
macaroni.

span [spæn] *n.* **1.** distance (about 9
inches or 23 centimetres) between the
tips of a person's thumb and little
finger when stretched out. **2.** distance
or part between supports of an arch:
*a bridge that crosses the river in a single
~.* **3.** distance between the wing tips of
an aeroplane. **4.** length in time, from
beginning to end of sth.: *our ~ of life.*
v.t. (*-nn-*) **1.** extend across (from side
to side): *a river ~ned by many bridges.*
2. measure by ~s (1).

a spaniel

span·gle [ˈspæŋgl] *n.* tiny disc of shining metal, esp. one of many, used for

ornament on a dress, etc. *v.t.* cover with, or as with, ~s: *the sky ~d with stars.*

Span·iard ['spænjəd] *n.* native or inhabitant of Spain.

span·iel ['spænjəl] *n.* (breed of) dog with long, silky hair and large, drooping ears. (See the picture.)

Span·ish ['spænɪʃ] *adj.* of Spain; of, written or spoken in, the ~ language. *n.* the language of the ~ people. *the ~,* (pl.) the people of Spain.

spank [spæŋk] *v.t.* 1. punish (a child) by slapping on the buttocks with the open hand. 2. (esp. of a horse or ship) move (*along*) at a good pace. *n.* slap. *~ing n.* slapping on the buttocks. *adj.* (colloq.) excellent; (of a trot, pace, etc.) brisk; (of a breeze) fresh; strong.

span·ner ['spænə*] *n.* tool for gripping and turning nuts (2).

spanners

spar[1] [spɑ:*] *n.* strong pole used for a ship's mast, yard, etc.

spar[2] [spɑ:*] *v.i.* (-rr-) make the motions of attack and defence with the fists (as in boxing); (fig.) dispute or argue. *~ring partner,* man with whom a boxer ~s as part of his training.

spare [speə*] *v.t. & i.* 1. refrain from hurting, killing, or wounding; show mercy to: ~ *sb.'s life.* 2. refrain from inflicting; relieve of the necessity of doing, etc.: *They wanted to ~ her the trouble.* 3. use economically or frugally: *~ no pains (expense),* do everything that hard work (money) can do; *not ~ oneself,* use all one's energy. 4. dispense with; do without: *Can you ~ me a minute (pound)? We can't ~ the time for a holiday at present. Can you ~ me a gallon of petrol?* have enough and *to ~,* have more than is needed. *adj.* 1. additional to what is needed: *I have no ~ time (cash),* no time (money) that I need not use. 2. kept in reserve for use when needed: *a ~ tyre; ~ parts* (for a machine, etc. to replace broken or worn-out parts); *a ~ room* (esp. one kept for guests). 3. (of persons) thin; lean. 4. small in quantity: *a ~ meal (diet). n.* ~ (2) part for a machine, etc.

spar·ing *adj.* economical: *Be sparing*

with the butter, we haven't much left. **spar·ing·ly** *adv.*

spark [spɑ:k] *n.* tiny, glowing bit thrown off from a burning substance or still present in ashes, etc., or produced by striking hard metal and stone together; flash of light produced by the breaking of an electric current; (fig.) sign of life, energy, etc.; flash of wit. *v.i.* give out ~s. '*~-plug,* (esp. Gt. Brit.) '*~-ing-plug ns.* device (2) for firing the gas in a petrol engine, etc. (See the picture at *plug.*)

spar·kle ['spɑ:kl] *v.i. & n.* (send out) flashes of light; gleam.

spar·row ['spærəʊ] *n.* small, brownish-grey bird common near houses.

sparse [spɑ:s] *adj.* thinly scattered: *a ~ population;* not dense or thick: *a ~ beard.* *~ly adv.* **spar·si·ty** ['spɑ:sətɪ] *n.* (no pl.).

Spar·tan ['spɑ:tn] *n. & adj.* (person) caring little for comfort; unafraid of pain or hardship; (of living conditions) hard because very simple.

spasm ['spæzəm] *n.* 1. sudden and involuntary tightening of the muscles. 2. sudden fit of pain, outburst of grief, etc. **spas·mod·ic** [spæz'mɒdɪk] *adj.* 1. taking place, done, at irregular intervals. 2. caused by, affected by, ~s (1).

spat, see *spit*[2] (v.).

spa·tial ['speɪʃl] *adj.* of, in relation to, existing in, space.

spat·ter ['spætə*] *v.t. & i.* 1. scatter (a liquid, mud, etc.) here and there in small drops; splash (sb. *with* mud, etc.). 2. (of a liquid) fall here and there in small drops. *n.* ~ing; splash.

spawn [spɔ:n] *n.* (no pl.) 1. eggs of fish and certain water-animals (e.g. frogs). 2. thread-like matter from which fungi grow. *v.i. & t.* 1. produce ~. 2. (fig.) produce or generate in large numbers.

speak [spi:k] *v.i. & t.* (p.t. *spoke* [spəʊk], p.p. *spoken* ['spəʊkən]) say sth. aloud in one's ordinary (not a singing) voice; have a conversation: ~ *to sb. about sth.;* know and be able to use (a language); address an audience; make a speech: ~ *out (up),* (a) ~ loud(er); (b) give one's views openly; ~ *one's mind,* say exactly what one thinks, even if it is unwelcome to the hearer(s); *nothing to ~ of,* nothing worth mentioning; not much; *so to ~,* as one might say; *not on ~ing terms with,* no longer friendly with; ~ *well for,* be evidence in favour of; *a ~ing likeness,* (of a portrait, etc.) one that is life-like. *~er n.* (esp.) person ~ing in public;

(the S.er) presiding officer of the House of Commons.

spear [spɪə*] *n.* weapon with a metal point on a long shaft. *v.t.* pierce, wound, make a hole in, with a ~.

spear·mint ['spɪəmɪnt] *n.* aromatic variety of mint, used in cooking and to flavour chewing-gum.

spe·cial ['speʃl] *adj.* **1.** of a particular or certain sort; not common, usual, or general; of or for a certain person, thing, purpose, etc.: ~ *constable*, man enrolled to help the ordinary police in time of need; ~ *delivery*, delivery of mail by a ~ messenger outside the regularly scheduled hours; ~ *train*, extra train for a ~ purpose. **2.** especial; exceptional in degree, amount, intensity, etc.: *give sb.* ~ *treatment*. **~·ist** ['speʃəlɪst] *n.* person who is an expert in a ~ branch of work, esp. in medicine: *a ~ist in diseases of the ear.*

spe·ci·al·i·ty [ˌspeʃɪ'ælətɪ] *n.* **1.** ~ quality or characteristic of sb. or sth. **2.** (also ~ty) work, article, product, etc. for which a person, place, etc. is well known. **~·ize** ['speʃəlaɪz] *v.i. & t.* **1.** be or become a ~ist *(in* sth.); give ~ or particular attention to. **2.** adapt for a particular purpose. **~·iza·tion** [ˌspeʃəlaɪ'zeɪʃn] *n.* **~·ty** *n.* ~ity (2).

spe·cie ['spiːʃɪ] *n.* (no pl.) money in the form of coins (not banknotes).

spe·cies ['spiːʃiːz] *n.* (pl. ~) **1.** group having some common characteristics. **2.** (biol.) division of a genus: *the (human)* ~, mankind. **3.** sort; kind.

spe·cif·ic [spɪ'sɪfɪk] *adj.* **1.** detailed and precise: ~ *orders*. **2.** relating to one particular thing, etc.; not general: *to be used for a ~ purpose*; *a ~ remedy* (for one particular disease). *n.* ~ remedy.

spec·i·fy ['spesɪfaɪ] *v.t.* mention definitely; give the name or details of; include in the ~ations. **spec·i·fi·ca·tion** [ˌspesɪfɪ'keɪʃn] *n.* **1.** (no pl.) specifying. **2.** (usu. pl.) details, instructions, etc. for the design, materials, etc. of sth. to be made or done.

spec·i·men ['spesɪmɪn] *n.* **1.** sample; one of a class as an example: ~s *of rocks and ores*. **2.** part taken to represent the whole: ~ *pages of a new book*. **3.** portion of material for use in testing: *supply a ~ of one's urine*. **4.** (colloq., usu. derog.) sb. or sth. regarded with contempt or amusement.

spe·cious ['spiːʃəs] *adj.* seeming true or right but not really so.

speck [spek] *n.* **1.** small spot of dirt or colour. **2.** particle; tiny bit (of dust, etc.). **3.** spot of rottenness in fruit.

~**ed** *adj.* marked with ~s. **~·le** ['spekl] *n.* small mark or spot, esp. one of many, distinct in colour, on the skin, feathers, etc. **~·led** ['spekld] *adj.* marked with ~les: *a ~led hen.*

spec·ta·cle ['spektəkl] *n.* **1.** public display, procession, etc., esp. one with ceremony. **2.** sth. seen; sth. taking place before the eyes, esp. sth. fine, remarkable, or noteworthy: *The sunset was a tremendous* ~. *make a* ~ *of oneself*, behave, dress, etc. ridiculously. **3.** (often *a pair of* ~s) pair of lenses to correct or assist defective eyesight or to protect the eyes. **specs** *n. pl.* (colloq.) ~s (3). **spec·tac·u·lar** [spek-'tækjʊlə*] *adj.* making a fine ~ (1, 2); attracting public attention. **spec·ta·tor** [spek'teɪtə*] *n.* onlooker.

spec·tre (U.S.A. **-ter**) ['spektə*] *n.* ghost; haunting fear of future trouble, etc. **spec·tral** ['spektrəl] *adj.* **1.** of or like a ~. **2.** of spectra or the spectrum.

spec·trum ['spektrəm] *n.* (pl. *-tra* [-trə]) **1.** image of a band of colours (as seen in a rainbow) formed by rays of light which have passed through a prism. **2.** (fig.) entire range or sequence.

spec·u·late ['spekjʊleɪt] *v.i.* **1.** consider, form opinions (without having complete knowledge) *(about, on, upon,* sth.); guess *(how* to do sth., etc.). **2.** buy and sell goods, stocks and shares, etc. with risk of loss and hope of profit through changes in their market value: ~ *in oil (shares)*. **spec·u·la·tor** *n.* person who ~s (2). **spec·u·la·tion** [ˌspekjʊ'leɪʃn] *n.* **1.** speculating (1); meditation; opinion reached thus; guess. **2.** speculating (2); speculative investment or transaction. **spec·u·la·tive** ['spekjʊlətɪv] *adj.* concerned with speculation (1, 2); involving risk of loss.

sped, see *speed* (v.).

speech [spiːtʃ] *n.* **1.** (no pl.) power, act, manner, of speaking. **2.** talk given in public: *make a* ~. **'~-day** *n.* annual school celebration with ~es and distribution of prizes. **~·less** *adj.* unable to speak, esp. because of deep feeling.

speed [spiːd] *n.* **1.** rate of moving: *travelling at full* ~; *at a* ~ *of thirty miles an hour*; *exceed the* ~ *limit*, go faster than the law allows. **2.** rapidity of movement; swiftness. *more haste, less* ~, too much haste may result in delay. **3.** (phot.) sensitivity of film to light. *v.t. & i.* (p.t. & p.p. **sped** [sped]) **1.** (cause to) go quickly: *cars ~ing past*

the school; ~ *an arrow from the bow.*
2. (old use) *God ~ you! May God make
you prosper.* **3.** (of motorists) travel
at an illegal or dangerous ~. **4.** (p.t. &
p.p. ~*ed*) regulate the ~ of (an engine,
etc.); cause to go at a fixed ~: ~ *sth. up,
cause sth. to work at a greater ~*; ~ *up
the train service.* '~·**boat** *n.* motor boat
designed for high ~. ~**ing** *n.* (of
motorists) travelling at an illegal or
dangerous ~: *He was fined for ~ing.*
~**·om·e·ter** [spi'dɒmɪtə] *n.* instrument recording the ~ of a motor car,
etc. '~·**way** *n.* **1.** racing track for
motor cycles, etc. **2.** (U.S.A.) road or
track for fast motor traffic. ~**y** *adj.*
(-ier, -iest) quick; coming, done,
without delay. ~**·i·ly** *adv.*

spell[1] [spel] *v.t. & i.* (p.t. & p.p. *spelt*
[spelt] or ~*ed*) **1.** name or write the
letters of (a word) in their proper
order: ~ *sth. out,* (a) make out (words,
writing) laboriously letter by letter;
(b) (fig.) explain sth. in detail. **2.** (of letters) form (a word) when put together
in a particular order: *D-O-G ~s dog.*
3. have as a consequence: *Does laziness
always ~ failure in life?* ~**ing** *n.* way
a word is spelt.

spell[2] [spel] *n.* **1.** words used as a
charm, supposed to have magic power.
2. overpowering attraction: *under a ~,*
mastered or controlled by, or as by,
a ~. '~·**bound** *adj.* with the attention
held by, or as by, a ~: *The speaker held
his audience ~bound.*

spell[3] [spel] *n.* period of time: *a ~ of
cold weather*; period of activity or duty,
esp. one at which two or more persons take turns.

spelt, see *spell*[1].

spend [spend] *v.t. & i.* (p.t. & p.p.
spent [spent]) **1.** pay out (money) for
goods, services, etc. **2.** use up (energy,
time, material, etc.). **3.** pass (time):
~ *a weekend in Paris.* '~·**thrift** *n.* person who wastes money. **spent** *adj.*
exhausted.

sperm [spɜːm] *n.* (no pl.) fertilizing
fluid of a male animal. ~ **whale** *n.*
whale valuable for a white, fatty substance, used for candles, etc.

spew [spjuː] *v.t. & i.* (liter. or fig.)
vomit.

sphere [sfɪə*] *n.* **1.** form of a ball or
globe; star; planet; (liter.) the heav-
ens; the sky. **2.** person's existence,
activities, surroundings, etc.: *distinguished in many ~s.* **3.** range; extent: ~
of influence, area where a country
claims, or is allowed, special rights.
spher·i·cal ['sferɪkl] *adj.* shaped like

a ~. **spher·oid** ['sfɪərɔɪd] *n.* body almost spherical.

sphinx [sfɪŋks] *n.* stone statue in Egypt
with a lion's body and a woman's
head; person who keeps his thoughts
and intentions secret.

spice [spaɪs] *n.* **1.** sorts of substances
(e.g. pepper, ginger, nutmeg) used to
flavour food. **2.** (no pl.) (fig.) interesting flavour, suggestion, or trace (*of*):
a ~ of humour (danger). *v.t.* add flavour
to (sth.) with, or as with, ~. **spicy**
adj. (-ier, -iest) of, flavoured with, ~;
(fig.) somewhat scandalous; improper:
a spicy story.

spick [spɪk] *adj.* (only in) ~ *and span,*
bright, clean, and tidy.

spi·der ['spaɪdə*] *n.* (sorts of) creature
with eight legs. Most sorts spin webs
(see the picture at *web*), in which
insects are caught.

spike [spaɪk] *n.* **1.** sharp point; pointed
piece of metal (e.g. on iron railings
or on running-shoes). **2.** ear of grain
(e.g. corn); long, pointed cluster of
flowers on a single stem. *v.t.* **1.** put
~s on (shoes, etc.). **2.** pierce or injure
with a ~.

spill[1] [spɪl] *v.t. & i.* (p.t. & p.p. *spilt*
[spɪlt] or ~*ed*) **1.** (of liquid, powder,
substance in small particles) (allow
to) run over the side of the container:
Don't ~ the milk. ~ the beans, disclose
a secret thereby ruining a surprise or
plan; ~ *blood,* be guilty of killing sb.
2. (of a horse, carriage, etc.) upset;
cause (the rider, a passenger, etc.) to
fall. *n.* fall from a horse, carriage, etc.

spill[2] [spɪl] *n.* thin strip of wood,
rolled or twisted piece of paper, used
to light candles, etc.

spin [spɪn] *v.t. & i.* (-nn-; p.t. *spun*
[spʌn] or old use *span* [spæn], p.p.
spun) **1.** form (thread) by twisting
wool, cotton, etc.; draw out and twist
(wool, cotton, etc.) into threads; make
(yarn) in this way. **2.** form by means
of threads: *spiders ~ning their webs.* **3.**
(fig.) produce, compose (a narrative,
etc.): ~ *a yarn,* tell a story. **4.** ~ *sth.
out,* make it last for a long time; prolong it: *He spun the project out for over
two years.* **5.** (cause to) go round and
round: ~ *a top*; *my head was ~ning,*
I felt dizzy. *n.* **1.** ~ning motion, esp.
as given to the ball in some games.
2. short drive in a motor car, ride on
a cycle, etc.: *go for a ~.* ~**·dle** ['spɪndl]
n. **1.** thin rod used for twisting and
winding thread. **2.** bar or pin that
turns round, or on which sth. turns.
~**·dly** *adj.* (-ier, -iest) long and thin.

,~-'dri·er *n.* device (2) that uses centrifugal force to dry laundered clothes. ,~-'dry *v.t.* dry in a ~-drier. '~·ning-wheel *n.* simple household machine for ~ning (1) on a ~dle turned by a large wheel.

spin·ach ['spɪnɪdʒ] *n.* (no pl.) plant with green leaves used as a vegetable.

spine [spaɪn] *n.* **1.** backbone. **2.** one of the sharp needle-like parts on some plants (e.g. a cactus) and animals (e.g. a porcupine). **3.** back of a book that faces outward on a shelf. spi·nal ['spaɪnl] *adj.* of the ~ (1): *the spinal column*, the backbone; *the spinal c(h)ord*, nerve-fibres in the ~. ~·less *adj.* having no ~ (1); (fig.) without courage to make decisions. spiny *adj.* (-ier, -iest) having ~s (2).

spin·et [spɪ'net] *n.* old type of keyboard instrument like a harpsichord.

spin·ster ['spɪnstə*] *n.* **1.** (esp. legal or official use) unmarried woman. **2.** woman past the common age for marrying or thought unlikely to marry.

spi·ral ['spaɪərəl] *adj. & n.* (in the form of an) advancing or ascending continuous curve winding round a central point: *a ~ staircase.* *v.i.* (-ll-, U.S.A. also -l-) move in a ~.

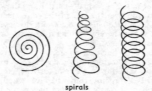

spirals

spire ['spaɪə*] *n.* tall, pointed structure rising above a tower (esp. of a church). (See the picture on page 504.)

spir·it ['spɪrɪt] *n.* **1.** soul; immaterial, intellectual, or moral part of man: *in (the) ~*, inwardly. **2.** the soul thought of as separate from the body: *the abode of ~s* (i.e. where the ~s of dead persons are). **3.** fairy; elf; goblin. **4.** (no pl.) quality of courage, vigour, liveliness: *a man of ~*; *put more ~ into one's work.* **5.** (no pl.) mental or moral attitude; mood: *done in a ~ of mischief.* **6.** person considered from the intellectual, moral, or emotional point of view: *He is one of the leading ~s of the reform movement.* **7.** (no pl.) real meaning or purpose underlying a law, etc.: *Obey the ~, not the letter, of a law.* **8.** (pl.) state of mind (as being happy, hopeful, etc., or the opposite): *in high ~s,*

cheerful; *in poor (low) ~s*, out of ~s, sad; depressed. **9.** (no pl.) animating influence or principle; mental or moral tendency: *They cannot resist the ~ of the age (times).* **10.** (pl.) distilled alcoholic drinks (e.g. whisky, brandy). **11.** industrial alcohol. ~-*lamp*, one in which this is burned. ~-*level*, instrument for testing whether a surface is horizontal. **12.** (chem.) solution in alcohol. *v.t.* take (sb. or sth. *away, off*) secretly or mysteriously. ~·ed *adj.* full of ~ (4); lively; courageous. ~·less *adj.* without energy or courage; depressed. spir·i·tu·al ['spɪrɪtjuəl] *adj.* **1.** of the ~ (1) or soul; of religion, not of material things. **2.** caring much for things of the ~ (1). *n.* (*Negro ~ual*) religious song characteristic of N. American Negroes. spir·i·tu·al·ism *n.* (no pl.) belief in the possibility of receiving messages from the ~s of the dead; practice of attempting to do this. spir·i·tu·al·ist *n.* believer in ~ualism. spir·i·tu·ous ['spɪrɪtjuəs] *adj.* (of liquids) containing distilled alcohol.

spit¹ [spɪt] *n.* thin, pointed rod for sticking meat onto for roasting. *v.t.* (-tt-) fix or stick with a ~.

spit² [spɪt] *v.i. & t.* (-tt-; p.t. & p.p. *spat* [spæt]) **1.** force liquid from the mouth; force (blood, food, saliva, etc. *out*) from the mouth: *She spat in the man's face. The baby spat out the spinach. ~ it out,* (colloq.) speak without further delay. **2.** (of a cat, etc.) make an angry, ~ting noise; utter (oaths, curses, etc.) sharply. **3.** *the ~ting image of* (see n. 3). *n.* **1.** act of ~ting. **2.** (no pl.) ~tle. **3.** *the dead ~ of, the ~ and image of,* the exact counterpart or likeness of. '~·fire *n.* hot-tempered person. ~·tle *n.* (no pl.) liquid produced in the mouth. ~·toon [spɪ'tu:n] *n.* pan to ~ into.

spite [spaɪt] *n.* **1.** (no pl.) ill will; desire to cause pain or damage: *done from (out of) ~.* **2.** grudge: *have a ~ against sb.* **3.** *in ~ of,* notwithstanding; not being, not to be, prevented by: *They went out in ~ of the rain. v.t.* injure or annoy because of ~. ~·ful *adj.* having, showing, ~. ~·ful·ly *adv.*

splash [splæʃ] *v.t. & i.* **1.** cause (a liquid) to fly about in drops; (of a liquid) fly about and fall in drops. **2.** make (sb. or sth.) wet by ~ing. **3.** move, fall, etc. (*along, across, into,* sth.) so that there is ~ing: *~ing (their way) across the stream; ~ing into the swimming-pool; ~ down,* (of a spacecraft) land in water, esp. in the sea, after a space flight. *n.* (sound, spot, or mark made by) ⁓ing. make a ⁓, (fig.) attract attention by making a show (esp. of one's wealth). '⁓-**down** *n.* landing of a spacecraft in the sea.

splay [spleɪ] *v.i. & t.* (of an opening) slope outwards; become, make, wider. *adj.* turned outward, esp. in an awkward or ungainly manner. '⁓-**foot** *n.* broad, flat foot turned outward. '⁓-,**foot·ed** *adj.*

spleen [spliːn] *n.* 1. organ in the abdomen that causes changes in the blood. 2. (no pl.) bad temper: *vent one's ⁓ on sb.*; *in a fit of ⁓.*

splen·did ['splendɪd] *adj.* 1. magnificent: *a ⁓ sunset (house, victory).* 2. (colloq.) excellent; very fine: *a ⁓ idea.* **splen·dour** (U.S.A. -**dor**) ['splendə*] *n.* magnificence; brightness.

splice [splaɪs] *v.t.* join (two ends of rope, etc.) by weaving the strands of one into the strands of the other; join

a spliced rope

(two pieces of wood) by fastening them so that they overlap. *n.* join made by splicing.

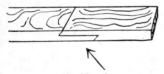

a spliced board

splint [splɪnt] *n.* strip of wood, etc. bound to an arm, leg, etc. to keep a broken bone in the right position.

splin·ter ['splɪntə*] *n.* sharp-pointed or sharp-edged bit of hard material (wood, stone, glass, etc.) split, torn, or broken off a larger piece. *⁓ group (party)*, (pol.) group of persons who have broken away from their party. *v.t. & i.* break into ⁓s; come (*off*) as a ⁓.

split [splɪt] *v.t. & i.* (-*tt*-; p.t. & p.p. ⁓) 1. break, cause to break, be broken, into two or more parts, esp. from end to end along the line of

natural division: *⁓ting logs; wood that ⁓s easily.* 2. divide: *The enemy were unwise to ⁓ their forces. ⁓ the cost of the party.* 3. break (*open*) by bursting. 4. *⁓ one's sides*, laugh violently; *a ⁓ting headache*, a very severe one; *⁓ hairs*, make very fine distinctions (in an argument, etc.); *⁓ on sb.*, (sl.) give away his secret; give information about him. *n.* ⁓ting; crack or tear made by ⁓ting; separation or division resulting from ⁓ting.

splut·ter ['splʌtə*] *v.i. & t.* 1. speak quickly and confusedly (from excitement, etc.). 2. utter (words, a threat, etc.) hastily and confusedly or indistinctly. 3. sound as if spitting.

spoil [spɔɪl] *v.t. & i.* (p.t. & p.p. ⁓t or ⁓ed) 1. make useless or unsatisfactory: *fruit ⁓t by insects; holidays ⁓t by bad weather.* 2. harm the character or temper by wrong upbringing or lack of discipline: *parents who ⁓ their children.* 3. pay great attention to the comfort and wishes of: *His wife ⁓s him.* 4. (of food, etc.) become bad, unfit for use. 5. *be ⁓ing for*, be eager for (a fight, etc.). *n.* (usu. pl. or collective sing.) 1. stolen goods; plunder. 2. profits gained from political power, etc. '⁓-**sport** *n.* person who ⁓s the enjoyment of others.

spoke[1], see *speak.*

spoke[2] [spəʊk] *n.* 1. any one of the bars or wires connecting the hub (centre) of a wheel with the rim (outer edge). *put a ⁓ in sb.'s wheel*, prevent him from carrying out his plans. 2. rung of a ladder.

spo·ken, see *speak.*

spokes·man ['spəʊksmən] *n.* person speaking, chosen to speak, on behalf of a group.

sponge [spʌndʒ] *n.* 1. kinds of simple sea-animal. 2. its light structure of soft elastic material full of holes and able to absorb water easily; one of these, or sth. of similar fabric, used for washing, cleaning, etc. *throw up the ⁓*, admit

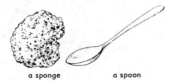

a sponge   a spoon

defeat or failure. *v.t. & i.* 1. wash, clean, wipe, with a ⁓; take (*up* liquid) with a ⁓. 2. *⁓ on sb.*, live on sb., get money from sb., without giving anything in return; ~ sth. from sb., get sth. by sponging. '~-cake n. soft, light, yellow cake. spong·er n. person who ~s (2) on others. spongy adj. (-ier, -iest) soft, porous, and elastic like a ~: spongy, moss-covered land.

spon·sor ['spɒnsə*] n. 1. person (e.g. a godfather or godmother) making himself responsible for another. 2. person who first puts forward or guarantees a proposal; person, firm, etc. paying for a commercial radio or television programme. v.t. act as a ~ for.

spon·ta·ne·ous [spɒn'teɪnjəs] adj. done, happening, from natural impulse, not caused or suggested from outside: a ~ offer of assistance. ~ combustion, burning caused by chemical changes, etc. inside the material, not by the application of fire from outside.

spoof [spu:f] v.t. & n. (sl.) hoax.

spook [spu:k] n. (humor.) ghost.

spool [spu:l] n. reel (for thread, wire, photographic film, etc.).

spoon [spu:n] n. utensil used for stirring, serving, and taking up food, etc. (See the picture at sponge.) v.t. take (up, out) with a ~. '~-feed v.t. (p.t. & p.p. -fed) 1. feed from a spoon. 2. give (sb.) excessive help or teaching, thereby precluding the necessity to act or think for himself. ~ful n. as much as a ~ can hold.

spoor [spʊə*] n. track or scent of an animal, enabling it to be followed.

spo·rad·ic [spə'rædɪk] adj. occurring, seen, only here and there or occasionally.

spore [spɔ:*] n. germ, single cell, by which a flowerless plant (e.g. a fern) reproduces itself.

sport [spɔ:t] n. 1. (no pl.) activity engaged in, esp. outdoors, for amusement or exercise. 2. particular form of such activity (e.g. swimming, wrestling, fishing, or games such as football). 3. (pl.) meeting for athletic contests: the school ~s. 4. (no pl.) fun: make ~ of sb., make him seem ridiculous; say sth. in ~, in fun; not seriously. 5. (colloq.) ~sman (2). v.i. & t. 1. play about; amuse oneself: a kitten ~ing with its tail. 2. (colloq.) have or wear for proud display: ~ a moustache (a diamond ring). ~ing adj. 1. of ~. 2. fond of, interested in, ~. 3. willing to take a risk of losing; involving risk of losing: a ~ing offer. ~ive adj. playful. ~s car n. open, low-built motor car designed for high speed. '~s·man n. 1. person who takes part in, is fond

of, ~. 2. (also ~) person who plays fairly, who is willing to take risks, and is cheerful if he loses. '~s·man·like adj. fair and honourable; ready to obey the rules. '~s·man·ship n. ~s writ·er n. person who writes (esp. as a journalist) on ~s.

spot [spɒt] n. 1. small (esp. round) mark different in colour from what it is on: white dress material with red ~s. 2. dirty mark or stain. 3. small, red place, blemish, on the skin. 4. (fig.) moral blemish: There isn't a ~ on her reputation. 5. particular place or area: the ~ where he was murdered; do sth. on the ~, do it there and then; the man on the ~, the man present at the place in question. 6. ~ cash, payment on delivery of goods; ~ prices, prices quoted for such payment. v.t. & i. (-tt-) 1. mark, become marked, with ~s: desks ~ted with ink. 2. pick out, recognize, see (one thing or person out of many): ~ a friend in a crowd; ~ the winner in a race, pick out the winner before the start. ~less adj. (esp.) quite clean. '~light n. (lamp giving a) strong light directed on to a particular place or person (esp. on the stage of a theatre). ~ted adj. (esp. zool.) marked with ~s. ~ty adj. (-ier, iest) marked with ~s: a ~ty face.

spouse [spaʊz] n. (law or old use) husband or wife.

spout [spaʊt] n. 1. pipe (1) or lip through or from which liquid pours (e.g. for carrying rainwater from a roof, or tea from a teapot). 2. stream of liquid coming out with great force. v.i. & t. 1. (of liquid) come or send out with force: water ~ing from a broken pipe. 2. (colloq.) speak, recite (verses, etc.), pompously.

sprain [spreɪn] v.t. injure (a joint, e.g. in the wrist or leg) by twisting violently so that there is pain and swelling. n. injury so caused.

sprang, see spring[1] (v.).

sprat [spræt] n. small sea-fish used as food.

sprawl [sprɔ:l] v.i. 1. sit or lie with the arms and legs loosely spread out; fall so that one lies in this way: be sent ~ing in the mud. 2. (of plants, handwriting, town, etc.) spread out loosely and irregularly. n. ~ing position.

spray[1] [spreɪ] n. 1. (no pl.) liquid sent through the air in tiny drops (by the wind or through an apparatus (1)). 2. kinds of liquid preparation (e.g. a perfume, disinfectant) to be applied in the form of ~ through an atomizer or similar apparatus (1). **3.** atomizer or similar apparatus (1) for applying such a liquid. *v.t.* scatter ~ on: ~ *mosquitoes (a fruit-tree).* **~·er** *n.* apparatus (1) for ~ing.

spray(er)s

pray² [sprei] *n.* small branch of a tree or plant, esp. one with leaves and flowers; ornament in similar form.

pread [spred] *v.t. & i.* (p.t. & p.p. ~) **1.** extend the surface or width of sth. by unfolding or unrolling; cover by doing this: ~ *a cloth on a table (a table with a cloth);* ~ *out a map (one's arms).* **2.** put (a substance) on a surface and extend by flattening, etc.; cover by doing this: ~ *butter on bread (bread with butter).* **3.** extend in time: *payments* ~ *over six months.* **4.** (cause to) become more widely extended or distributed: *water ~ing over the floor; disease* ~ *by flies; a rumour ~ing through the district.* *n.* **1.** extent; breadth: the ~ *of a bird's wings.* **2.** ~ing (4); extension: *the* ~ *of education (disease).* **3.** (colloq.) feast; table covered with food. **4.** cloth cover ~ over a table or bed. **5.** various kinds of paste (to be) ~ on bread, etc.

pree [spri:] *n.* lively frolic: *have a* ~, have a lively, merry time; *be on the* ~, be having a ~; *buying (shopping, spending)* ~, bout of lavish spending of money.

prig [sprig] *n.* small twig (*of a plant or tree*) with leaves, etc.

pright·ly ['spraitli] *adj.* (-ier, -iest) lively; brisk.

pring¹ [spriŋ] *v.i. & t.* (p.t. *sprang* [spræŋ], p.p. *sprung* [sprʌŋ]) **1.** jump suddenly from the ground; move suddenly (*up, down, out, etc.*) from rest or concealment: ~ *to one's feet;* ~ *out of bed.* **2.** (often ~ *up*) appear; grow up quickly from the ground or from a stem, etc.: *weeds ~ing up everywhere.* **3.** arise or come (*from*). **4.** bring forward suddenly: ~ *a surprise on sb.* **5.** ~ *a trap (a mine),* cause it to go off (burst). **6.** (of wood) split or crack. ~ *a leak,* (of a ship) crack or burst so that water enters. *n.* **1.** act of ~ing (1);

~ing (1) movement. **2.** (place where there is) water coming up from the ground. **3.** device of twisted, bent, or coiled metal or wire that tends to return to its shape or position when pulled or pushed: *the* ~*s of a motor car.*

a spring¹ (3)

4. (no pl.) elastic quality: *rubber bands that have lost their* ~. **5.** cause or origin. **6.** (attrib.) containing, resting on, a ~ or ~s (3): *a* ~ *bed with a* ~ *mattress; a* ~ *balance; a* ~*-board* (e.g. for diving from). **7.** ~*-tide* (opp. of *neap-tide*), very high tide after full and new moon. **~y** *adj.* (-ier, -iest) elastic.

spring² [spriŋ] *n.* season of the year in which vegetation sprouts; season between winter and summer. '~·time *n.* season of ~.

sprin·kle ['spriŋkl] *v.t. & i.* direct, throw, a shower of (sand, water, flour, etc.) on to (a surface): ~ *water on a dusty road,* ~ *a dusty road with water;* rain lightly. *n.* small shower. **~·r** *n.* (esp.) apparatus (1) for sprinkling water. **sprin·kling** *n.* small quantity or number (e.g. of people at a meeting).

sprint [sprint] *v.i.* run a short distance at full speed. *n.* such a run; (esp.) burst of speed at the end of a race.

sprite [sprait] *n.* elf; fairy.

sprock·et ['sprokit] *n.* each of several teeth on a wheel engaging with the links of a chain, etc. '~·wheel *n.* such a wheel (e.g. as on a bicycle).

sprout [spraut] *v.i. & t.* **1.** start to grow; put out leaves, etc.: *weeds ~ing everywhere.* **2.** cause to grow: *The rain ~ed the corn.* **3.** develop, produce (hair, horns, etc.). *n.* shoot, newly ~ed part, of a plant, etc. *Brussels ~s,* edible buds from the stem of a cabbage-like plant.

spruce¹ [spru:s] *adj.* neat and smart in dress and appearance. *v.t. & i.* ~ (*oneself*) *up,* make oneself ~.

spruce² [spru:s] *n.* kinds of fir-tree.

sprung, see *spring¹* (v.).

spry [sprai] *adj.* lively; nimble.

spud [spʌd] *n.* (colloq.) potato.

spume [spju:m] *n.* (no pl.) foam.

spun, see *spin* (v.).

spur [spɜ:*] *n.* **1.** sharp-toothed wheel worn on the heel of a rider's boot and used to make a horse go faster. **2.** (fig.) sth. that urges a person on to activity:

act on the ~ *of the moment* (on a sudden impulse). **3.** sharp, hard projection at the back of a cock's leg. **4.** ridge extending from a mountain or hill. *v.t.* (*-rr-*) urge on with, or as with, ~s (1, 2).

spurs (1, 3)

spu·ri·ous ['spjʊərɪəs] *adj.* false; not genuine.

spurn [spɜ:n] *v.t.* reject or refuse contemptuously; treat with contempt.

spurt [spɜ:t] *v.i.* **1.** (of liquid, flame, etc.) come (*out*) in a sudden burst. **2.** make a sudden, short, and violent effort, esp. in a race or other contest. *n.* sudden bursting forth: ~s *of water* (*flame, energy*).

sput·ter ['spʌtə*] *v.i. & t.* **1.** make a series of spitting sounds: *sausages* ~*ing in the frying-pan.* **2.** splutter.

spy [spaɪ] *n.* **1.** person who tries to get secret information, esp. about the military affairs of other countries (called a 'spy' if he works for a foreign government) (cf. *secret agent*). **2.** person who secretly watches the movements and activities of others. *v.i. & t.* **1.** ~ (*up*)*on*, watch secretly; act as a ~ on. **2.** see; observe; discover. '~**·glass** *n.* small telescope.

squab·ble ['skwɒbl] *v.i.* quarrel noisily (about sth. unimportant). *n.* noisy quarrel.

squad [skwɒd] *n.* small group of soldiers, police, etc. working or being trained together. ~ *car*, (U.S.A.) police car having a radio link (3) with headquarters; *homicide* ~, (U.S.A.) group of police-officers who investigate homicides.

squad·ron ['skwɒdrən] *n.* **1.** division of a cavalry regiment (120—200 men). **2.** number of warships or military aircraft forming a unit.

squal·id ['skwɒlɪd] *adj.* dirty; wretched; uncared-for. **squa·lor** ['skwɒlə*] *n.* (no pl.) ~ condition.

squall [skwɔ:l] *n.* **1.** loud cry of pain or fear (esp. from a baby or child). **2.** sudden, violent wind, often with rain or snow. *v.i.* utter ~s (1).

squan·der ['skwɒndə*] *v.t.* waste (time, money, etc.).

square [skweə*] *n.* **1.** plane figure with four equal sides and four right angles. **2.** object with the shape of a ~. **3.** space in a town, with buildings round it. **4.** result obtained when a number is multiplied by itself: *The* ~ *of 7 is 49* **5.** instrument for obtaining or testing right angles: *out of* ~, not at right angles. **6.** (sl.) conventional or old-fashioned person (considered to be out of touch with current trends. *adj.* **1.** having the shape of a ~ (1). **2.** having or forming a right angle: ~ *corner* (*shoulders*). **3.** level or parallel (*with*) **4.** (of dealings, business, etc.) fair honest: *a* ~ *deal*, a fair bargain equality of opportunity. **5.** (of accounts, etc.) balanced: *get* ~ *with sb.* settle accounts with, pay debts to, (fig. have one's revenge on, him. **6.** connected with a number multiplied by itself: ~ *inch* (*foot, etc.*), area equal to that of a ~ with sides of one inch (foot etc.); ~ *root* (*of 16*), number which when multiplied by itself equals (16) ~ *measure* (expressed in ~ feet, metres etc.). **7.** thorough; uncompromising *meet with a* ~ *refusal*; *a* ~ *meal*, one that is satisfying because there is enough good food. **8.** (sl.) conventional; old-fashioned. *adv.* ~ly. *v.t & i.* **1.** make ~. **2.** cause one line surface, etc. to be at right angles to another: ~ *a length of timber.* **3.** make straight or level: ~ *one's shoulders.* **4** get the ~ (4) of (a number); multiply a number by itself. **4.** mark (*off*) in ~s **6.** (often ~ *up*) settle, balance (accounts). **7.** ~ *with*, make or be consistent with: ~ *your practice with you principles.* **8.** (colloq.) bribe. ~**·ly** *adv* ~**·ness** *n.* (no pl.).

squash[1] [skwɒʃ] *v.t. & i.* **1.** crush press flat or *into* a small space. **2.** snub *n.* **1.** number of persons ~ed together **2.** *lemon* (*orange, etc.*) ~, drink made from lemon, etc. juice. **3.** ~ (*rackets*) game played with rackets and a smal rubber ball in a walled court.

squash[2] [skwɒʃ] *n.* (pl. ~) kinds o gourd, like a pumpkin, used as food

squat [skwɒt] *v.i.* (*-tt-*) sit on one' heels; (colloq.) sit (*down*). *adj.* (of a person, etc.) short and thick. ~**·ter** *n* person who occupies public land, a unoccupied building, etc. withou legal right; (in Australia) sheep-farmer.

squaw [skwɔ:] *n.* N. American Indian woman or wife.

squawk [skwɔ:k] *v.i. & n.* (esp. o birds) (utter a) loud, harsh cry; (make a) loud complaint.

squeak [skwiːk] *n.* **1.** short, shrill cry (e.g. of a mouse) or similar sound (e.g. from an unoiled hinge). **2.** *a narrow ~*, a narrow escape from danger or failure. *v.i. & t.* make a ~; say in a ~ing voice.

squeal [skwiːl] *n.* shrill cry or sound, longer and louder than a squeak, and indicating terror or pain. *v.i. & t.* give a ~; say in a ~ing voice.

squea·mish [ˈskwiːmɪʃ] *adj.* **1.** having a delicate stomach and easily made sick; feeling sick. **2.** too particular or strict about what is right; easily disgusted or offended.

squeeze [skwiːz] *v.t. & i.* press on from the opposite side or from all sides; change the shape, size, etc. of sth. by doing this; get juice, water, etc. (*out of* sth.) by doing this; force (*into, etc.*) by pressing; get (money, etc. *out of* sb.) by extortion, entreaty etc.: ~ *a lemon*; ~ *the juice out*; ~ (*one's way*) *through a crowd* (*into a crowded bus*); ~ *sb.'s hand*, press it to show sympathy, etc. *The blackmailers will ~ the last penny out of their victim. n.* act of squeezing; condition of being ~d; sth. obtained by squeezing; close fit. **squeez·er** *n.* a lemon-~r.

squelch [skweltʃ] *v.i. & t.* make a sucking sound as when feet are lifted from stiff, sticky mud.

squib [skwɪb] *n.* small firework that burns with a hissing sound and finally explodes.

squint [skwɪnt] *v.i.* **1.** have the eyes turned in different directions; be cross-eyed. **2.** look sideways or with half-shut eyes or through a narrow opening (*at, through*). *n.* **1.** ~ing position of the eyeballs: *a man with a ~.* **2.** (colloq.) look, glance (*at*).

squire [ˈskwaɪə*] *n.* **1.** (in England) chief landowner in a country parish. **2.** (in olden times) knight's attendant.

squirm [skwɜːm] *v.i.* twist the body, wriggle (from discomfort, shame, etc.).

a squirrel

squir·rel [ˈskwɪrəl] *n.* small, bushytailed animal with red or grey fur, living in trees.

squirt [skwɜːt] *v.t. & i.* (of liquid or powder) force out, be forced out, in a thin stream or jet. *n.* instrument for ~ing liquid, etc.; jet of liquid, etc.

stab [stæb] *v.t. & i.* (-*bb*-) **1.** pierce or wound with a sharp-pointed weapon or instrument; push (a knife, etc.) into. **2.** produce a sensation as of being ~bed: ~*bing pains in the back. n.* ~bing blow.

sta·ble[1] [ˈsteɪbl] *n.* building in which horses are kept. *v.t.* put or keep (horses) in a ~.

sta·ble[2] [ˈsteɪbl] *adj.* firm; fixed; not likely to move or change. **sta·bil·i·ty** [stəˈbɪlətɪ] *n.* (no pl.) quality of being ~. **sta·bi·lize** [ˈsteɪbɪlaɪz] *v.t. & i.* make or become ~. **sta·bi·li·za·tion** [ˌsteɪbɪlaɪˈzeɪʃn] *n.* (no pl.).

stac·ca·to [stəˈkɑːtəʊ] *adj. & adv.* (of music) (to be played) with each successive note clear and detached.

stack [stæk] *n.* **1.** large pile of hay, straw, etc., usu. with a sloping, thatched top, for storage. **2.** (neatly arranged) pile (*of* books, wood, etc.). **3.** (also chimney-~) tall factory chimney; number of chimneys side by side on a roof. **4.** ~*s of* (*food, etc.*), (colloq.) great quantities of. *v.t.* make into a ~ or ~s; pile up.

sta·di·um [ˈsteɪdjəm] *n.* (pl. ~s) enclosed area of land for games, athletic competitions, etc., usu. with stands for spectators.

staff [stɑːf] *n.* **1.** strong stick used as a support when walking, etc.; such a ~ as a sign of office or authority. **2.** pole serving as a support: *a flag~.* **3.** group of assistants working under a manager or head: *the headmaster and his ~* (i.e. the teachers); *the editorial ~ of a newspaper.* **4.** group of senior army officers engaged in organization but not in actual fighting; (attrib.) ~ *officers.* **5.** (pl. *staves* [steɪvz]) (music) set of five parallel lines on or between which notes are written. *v.t.* provide with a ~ (3).

stag [stæg] *n.* male deer.

stage [steɪdʒ] *n.* **1.** raised platform or structure, esp. the platform on which the actors perform in a theatre; (fig.) scene of action. **2.** theatrical work; the profession of acting: *go on the ~*, become an actor; ~ *direction*, instruction in the text of a play to actors about their positions, movements, etc.; ~ *fright*, nervousness felt when facing an audience; ~*manager*, person who superintends the production of a play, supervises the rehearsals, and is in complete charge of the ~

during a performance. **3.** point, period, or step in development: *a plan in its early ~s*; *at an early ~ in our history.* **4.** journey, distance, between two stopping-places along a road or route: *by easy ~s.* *v.t.* put (a play) on the ~ (1); arrange (an event) to take place dramatically. '**~·coach** *n.* (hist.) horse-drawn public vehicle which carried passengers (and mail) by ~s (4) on a regular route. **stag·er** *n.* *old ~r,* person of long experience. **stag·ing** *n.* **1.** scaffolding. **2.** (method of) presenting a play on the stage of a theatre.

stag·ger ['stægə*] *v.i. & t.* **1.** walk or move unsteadily (from weakness, a heavy burden, drunkenness, etc.); (of a blow) cause (sb.) to do this. **2.** (of news, etc.) shock deeply; cause worry or confusion to: *~ed by the high cost of living* (*the difficulty of the examination questions*). **3.** arrange (times of events, etc.) so that they occur one after another: *~ annual holidays.* *n.* *~ing* movement.

stag·nant ['stægnənt] *adj.* **1.** (of water) without current or tide; still and stale. **2.** (fig.) unchanging; inactive. **stag·nate** [stæg'neɪt] *v.i.* be ~; (fig.) be or become dull through disuse, etc.

stain [steɪn] *v.t. & i.* **1.** (of liquids, other substances) change the colour of; make coloured patches or dirty marks on: *blood-~ed fingers*; *a table-cloth ~ed with gravy.* **2.** colour (wood, fabrics, etc.) with a substance that penetrates the material. **3.** colour (glass) during manufacture: *~ed-glass windows.* **4.** (of material) become discoloured or soiled: *a dress that ~s easily.* *n.* **1.** liquid used for ~ing (2) wood, etc. **2.** ~ed place; dirty mark or patch: *ink ~s*; (fig.) *a ~ on one's reputation.* **~·less** *adj.* **1.** without a ~: *a ~less* (i.e. pure) *reputation.* **2.** (esp. of a certain kind of steel alloy) that resists rust and ~s.

stair [steə*] *n.* (often pl.) (any one of a) series of fixed steps leading from one floor of a building to another: *sitting on the bottom ~.* '**~·case** *n.* (part of a building containing a) flight[1] (5) of ~s.

stake [steɪk] *n.* **1.** strong, pointed stick (to be) driven into the ground as a post, a support for sth., etc. **2.** post, as used in olden times, to which a person was tied before being burnt to death as a punishment (for heresy): *condemned to the ~.* **3.** sum of money risked on the unknown result of a

future event (e.g. a horse-race). *at ~,* in danger of being lost; risked. *v.t.* **1.** support with a ~ (1). **2.** mark *out* or *off* with ~s (1): *~ out a claim* (to land). **3.** risk (money, one's hopes, etc. *on*). '**~·hold·er** *n.* person with whom ~s (3) are deposited until the result is known.

sta·lac·tite ['stæləktaɪt] *n.* pencil-shaped deposit of lime[1] growing downwards from the roof of a cave as water drips from it. **sta·lag·mite** ['stæləg-maɪt] *n.* similar deposit mounting upwards from the floor of a cave as water containing lime[1] drips on to it from above.

stalactites (above) and stalagmites

stale [steɪl] *adj.* (*~r, ~st*) **1.** (of food) dry and unappetizing because not fresh. **2.** uninteresting because heard before: *~ news* (*jokes*).

stale·mate ['steɪlmeɪt] *n.* position of the pieces in chess in which no further move is possible; (fig.) any stage of a dispute at which further action by either side appears impossible.

stalk[1] [stɔːk] *n.* non-woody part of a plant that supports a flower or flowers, a leaf or leaves, or a fruit or fruits.

stalk[2] [stɔːk] *v.i. & t.* **1.** walk with slow, stiff strides, esp. in a proud, self-important, or grim way. **2.** pursue (game, an enemy, etc.) stealthily.

stall [stɔːl] *n.* **1.** compartment for one animal in a stable or cattle-shed. **2.** small, open-fronted shop; table, etc. used by a trader in a market, on a street, in a railway station, etc.: *a flower-~*; *a book-~.* **3.** (usu. pl.) (Gt. Brit.) seat in the part of a theatre nearest to the stage: *orchestra ~s,* front rows of ~s. *v.t. & i.* **1.** place or keep (an animal) in a ~ (1). **2.** (of a motor-car engine) (cause to) fail to keep going through insufficient power or speed. **3.** (of aircraft) cause to be, become, out of control through loss of speed.

stal·lion ['stæljən] *n.* male horse, esp. one used for breeding.

stal·wart ['stɔːlwət] *adj.* tall and strong; solidly built; firm and resolved: *~ supporters.*

sta·men ['steɪmen] *n.* male part of a flower, bearing pollen.

stam·i·na ['stæmɪnə] *n.* (no pl.) reserve of energy enabling a person or animal to work hard for a long time.

stam·mer ['stæmə*] *v.i. & t.* speak haltingly with a tendency to repeat certain sounds or syllables (e.g. 'g-g-give me that b-b-book'); say sth. in this confused or hesitating way: ~ *out a request. n.* (tendency to) ~*ing* talk. ~**·er** *n.*

stamp [stæmp] *v.t. & i.* **1.** put (one's foot) down with force (on sth.): ~*ing about the room*; ~ *sth. down (flat)*; ~ *out a fire*; ~ *on a spider*; (fig.) ~ *out* (put an end to) *a disease (a rebellion).* **2.** print (design, lettering, etc.) by using a ~ (2) on paper, cloth, etc.: ~ *one's address on an envelope (an envelope with one's address)*; ~ *a pattern on cloth.* **3.** crush (ores, etc.). **4.** put a (postage) ~ (4) on (a letter, etc.). **5.** (of behaviour, etc.) ~ *sb. as,* characterize him as (having a certain quality, etc.): *His opinions* ~ *him as a man of high principles. n.* **1.** act of ~*ing* (1) with the foot. **2.** instrument used for ~*ing* (2) designs, etc.: *a rubber* ~ *of your name and address.* **3.** design, word(s), etc. made by ~*ing* (2) on a surface; (fig.) characteristic mark or quality: *a face that bears the* ~ *of suffering.* **4.** piece of printed paper stuck on envelopes, etc. to show the postage paid, or the duty paid on legal documents. **5.** character; kind: *men of that* ~.

a postage stamp

an office stamp

stam·pede [stæm'piːd] *n.* sudden rush of frightened people or animals. *v.i. & t.* take part in a ~; cause to ~.

stanch[1] [stɑːntʃ], **staunch**[2] [stɔːntʃ] *v.t.* check the flow of (esp. blood); stop the flow of blood from (a wound).

stanch[2], see *staunch*[1].

stan·chion ['stɑːnʃn] *n.* upright post supporting sth.

stand [stænd] *v.i. & t.* (p.t. & p.p. *stood* [stʊd]) **1.** have, take, keep, an upright position: ~ *up,* rise to the feet. **2.** be of a certain height when ~*ing*: *He* ~*s five foot ten.* **3.** remain without change: *Let the words* ~. **4.** place (sth.)

upright: *S*~ *them in a row. S*~ *the ladder against the wall.* **5.** endure; undergo: *can't* ~ *the hot weather*; ~ *his trial for theft.* **6.** be in a certain condition or situation: *We* ~ *in need of help. as affairs now* ~. ~ *well with* (be well thought of by) *one's employer. I* ~ *corrected,* I accept the correction of my views. **7.** (colloq.) provide and pay for: ~ *drinks all round,* pay for drinks for everyone; ~ *sb. a good dinner.* **8.** ~ *a (good, poor, etc.) chance (of sth.),* have a prospect (of sth.); ~ *one's ground,* not give way to force, argument, etc. *It* ~*s to reason (that),* all reasonable persons must agree. ~ *on ceremony,* pay too much attention to formalities of behaviour; ~ *to win (lose),* be in a position where one is likely to win (lose). **9.** (with advs. & preps.) ~ *back,* move back; ~ *by,* (a) be an inactive onlooker; (b) be ready (for action); (c) support, side with (sb.); (d) be faithful to (a promise, etc.); ~ *for,* (a) represent: *£* ~*s for 'pound'; the Christian religion and all it* ~*s for*; (b) be a candidate for (Parliament, an office, etc.); (c) support, contend for (a principle, etc.); (d) (colloq.) tolerate; ~ *off,* remain at a distance; ~ *out,* (a) be easily seen above or among others; (b) continue to resist; continue firm (*against or for* sth.); ~ *up for,* defend the cause of; support (a person, cause); ~ *up to,* face boldly; show readiness to fight; (of materials) remain in good condition despite (hard wear, etc.). *n.* **1.** stopping of motion or progress: *come to a* ~, stop; *bring (sth. or sb.) to a* ~, cause to stop. **2.** *make a* ~, fight in defence (*for or against* sb. or sth.). **3.** position taken up: *take one's* ~, base one's argument, point of view, etc. (*on or upon* sth.). **4.** small piece of furniture, support, etc. on or in which things may be placed: *an umbrella-*~; *a music-*~; *an ink*~. **5.** stall in a market, etc.: *a news-*~ (from which newspapers, etc. are sold). **6.** *cab-*~, place in a street, etc. where cabs ~ in line waiting to be hired. **7.** structure (usu. sloping) where people may ~ or sit to watch races, sports meetings, etc. **8.** (U.S.A.) = witness-box: *take the* ~. '~**-by** *n.* sb. or sth. that one can depend on. ~**·ing** *n.* (no pl.) **1.** duration: *of long* ~*ing,* that has existed for a long time. **2.** established position or reputation: *men of high* ~*ing.* **adj.** established and permanent; ready for use: *a* ~*ing army; a* ~*ing order* (for sth. to be done or delivered regularly). **⁓-off·ish** [ˌstænd'ɒfɪʃ] *adj.* cold and distant in behaviour. **'⁓·point** *n.* point of view. **'⁓·still** *n.* stop: *come to* (*bring to, be at*) *a* ⁓*still.*

stan·dard ['stændəd] *n.* **1.** flag, esp. one to which loyalty is given or asked. **2.** (often attrib.) sth. used as a test or measure for weights, lengths, qualities, etc. or for the required degree of excellence: *the* ⁓ *of height required for army recruits*; ⁓ *weights and measures*; ⁓ *authors* (of long-established reputation); *a high* ⁓ *of living*; *work that is not up to* ⁓ (not so good as is required); ⁓ *time* (as officially adopted for a country or part of it); *S⁓ English,* form of English speech used by the majority of educated English-speaking people. **3.** (often attrib.) upright support: *a* ⁓ *lamp* (on a tall support with its base on the floor). **4.** class in a primary school. **⁓·ize** *v.t.* make of one size, shape, quality, etc. according to fixed ⁓*s* (2): *Motor-car parts are usually ⁓ized.* **⁓·iza·tion** [ˌstændədaɪ'zeɪʃn] *n.* (no pl.).

stank, see *stink* (v.).

stan·za ['stænzə] *n.* group of rhymed lines forming a division of a poem.

sta·ple¹ ['steɪpl] *n.* U-shaped metal bar with pointed ends, hammered into a wall, etc. to hold sth. (see the picture at *hasp*); piece of wire for fastening sheets of paper together.

sta·ple² ['steɪpl] *n.* **1.** chief sort of article or goods produced or traded in: *Cotton is one of the* ⁓*s of Egypt.* **2.** chief material or element (of sth.); (attrib.) forming the ⁓: *the* ⁓ *product of Brazil* (i.e. coffee).

star [stɑː*] *n.* **1.** any one of the bodies in space seen as distant points of light in the sky at night, esp. one that is not a planet. **2.** figure or design suggesting a ⁓ by its shape; asterisk (* *): *S⁓s and Stripes,* flag of the U.S.A.; *the S⁓-Spangled Banner,* (a) the flag of the U.S.A.; (b) the national anthem of the U.S.A. **3.** person famous as an author, singer, actor, actress, etc.: *film* ⁓*s.* **4.** planet or other heavenly body regarded as influencing a person's fortune, etc.: *born under a lucky* ⁓. *v.t. & i.* (*-rr-*) **1.** mark or decorate with a ⁓ or ⁓*s.* **2.** be a ⁓ (3) actor, etc. (*in* a play or film). **⁓·ry** *adj.* lighted by, shining like, ⁓*s.* **'⁓·fish** *n.* ⁓-shaped sea-animal.

star·board ['stɑːbəd] *n.* right side of a ship or aircraft from the point of view of a person looking forward (cf. *port³*).

starch [stɑːtʃ] *n.* (no pl.) **1.** white, tasteless substance, plentiful in potatoes, grain, etc. **2.** this substance prepared in powder form and used for stiffening cotton clothes, etc. *v.t.* make (e.g. shirt collars) stiff with ⁓. **⁓·y** *adj.* (*-ier, -iest*) of or like ⁓; containing ⁓; (fig.) stiff; formal.

stare [steə*] *v.i. & t.* look (*at*) fixedly; (of eyes) be wide open; look at in this way: ⁓ *sb. into silence*; ⁓ *him in the face*, ⁓ *at his face*; (of an object) be right in front of him. *n.* staring look.

star·ing *adj.* (of colours, etc.) too conspicuous.

stark [stɑːk] *adj.* **1.** stiff, esp. in death. **2.** complete. *adv.* completely: ⁓ *naked.*

star·ling ['stɑːlɪŋ] *n.* small bird with black, brown-spotted plumage.

start [stɑːt] *v.i. & t.* **1.** set out; begin a journey; begin an activity, etc.: *At last the train* ⁓*ed. S⁓ work at nine o'clock. It* ⁓*ed to rain* (⁓*ed raining*). *to* ⁓ *with,* (a) in the first place, before anything else is considered; (b) at the beginning. **2.** (cause to) come into existence; set going: *Who* ⁓*ed the fire? How did the fire* ⁓? **3.** make a sudden movement (from fear, surprise, etc.): *He* ⁓*ed from his seat.* ⁓ *back* (*forward, aside, etc.*). **4.** issue, flow, enter, with sudden force: *Tears* ⁓*ed to her eyes. His eyes* ⁓*ed from their sockets,* they bulged. *n.* **1.** act of ⁓ing (1): *make an early* ⁓; *the* ⁓ *of a race; for a* ⁓, (colloq.) *to* ⁓ *with.* **2.** sudden movement of fear, surprise, etc. **3.** amount of time or distance by which one person ⁓*s* (1) in front of competitors; advantageous position: *We gave the small boy a* ⁓ *of ten yards. get the* ⁓ *of sb.,* gain advantage over him. **4.** *by fits and* ⁓*s,* irregularly.

star·tle ['stɑːtl] *v.t.* give a shock or surprise to; cause to move or jump.

starve [stɑːv] *v.t. & i.* (cause to) suffer or die from hunger: ⁓ *the enemy into submission,* force them to submit from lack of food; *be starving* (*for food*), (colloq.) be very hungry; *be* ⁓*d of,* ⁓ *for,* (fig.) long for; be in great need of. **star·va·tion** [stɑː'veɪʃn] *n.* (no pl.).

state¹ [steɪt] *n.* **1.** (no pl.) condition in which sth. or sb. is (in circumstances, appearance, mind, health, etc.): *in a poor* ⁓ *of health; a* ⁓ *of emergency. The house was in a dirty* ⁓. *What a* ⁓ *he's in!* How anxious, dirty, untidy, etc. he is! **2.** (no pl.) rank in society; position in life. **3.** (no pl.) (often attrib.) pomp; ceremonial formality: *The Queen drove through the streets in* ⁓ *to* *open Parliament. the* ~ *coach* (used e.g. by a ruler on ceremonial occasions); *lie in* ~, (of a dead person) be placed on view in a public place before burial. **4.** (often *S*~) organized political community with its apparatus of government; territory in which this exists; such a community forming part of a federal republic: *Railways in Great Britain belong to the S*~*. the S*~ *of New York; the United S*~*s of America,* (colloq.) *the S*~*s.* **5.** (no pl.) civil government: *Church and S*~*.* ~**·ly** *adj.* (*-ier, -iest*) dignified. '~**·room** *n.* private sleeping-compartment in a ship. ~**s·man** ['steɪtsmən] *n.* person who takes an important part in the management of S~ affairs. '~**s·man·like** *adj.* gifted with, showing, wisdom and a broadminded outlook in public affairs. '~**s·man·ship** *n.* (no pl.) skill and wisdom in managing public affairs.

state[2] [steɪt] *v.t.* express in words, esp. carefully, fully, and clearly: ~ *one's views (reasons)*; ~ *that (why, how).* **stat·ed** *adj.* made known; announced: *at* ~*d times.* ~**·ment** *n.* **1.** (no pl.) expression in words. **2.** stating of facts, views, a problem, etc.: *make (issue) a* ~*ment; a bank* ~*ment.*

stat·ic ['stætɪk] *adj.* at rest; in a state of balance.

sta·tion ['steɪʃn] *n.* **1.** position (to be) taken up by sb. or sth. for some purpose. **2.** establishment where a public service is provided: *a police (broadcasting, radar, fire)* ~. **3.** stopping-place for railway trains, buses, etc.; buildings, offices, etc. connected with it: *a railway (bus, goods, etc.)* ~. **4.** social position: *people in all* ~*s of life.* **5.** military or naval base; those living there. *v.t.* put (sb.), oneself, a military or naval force, etc.) at or in a specified location. '~**·,mas·ter** *n.* man in charge of a railway ~. ~ **wag·on** *n.* (U.S.A.) = estate car.

a station wagon

sta·tion·ary ['steɪʃnərɪ] *adj.* **1.** not intended to be moved about. **2.** not moving or changing.

sta·tio·ner ['steɪʃnə*] *n.* dealer in ~**y** *n.* (no pl.) writing-materials.

sta·tis·tics [stə'tɪstɪks] *n. pl.* **1.** numerical facts collected and arranged for comparison, etc. **2.** (sing. v.) science of ~. **sta·tis·ti·cal** [stə'tɪstɪkl] *adj.* of ~. **stat·is·ti·cian** [,stætɪ'stɪʃn] *n.* person expert in ~.

stat·ue ['stætjuː] *n.* figure of a person, animal, etc. in wood, stone, bronze, etc. **stat·u·esque** [,stætjʊ'esk] *adj.* like a ~, esp. in having clear-cut outlines, in being motionless, etc. **stat·u·ette** [,stætjʊ'et] *n.* small ~.

stat·ure ['stætʃə*] *n.* (no pl.) (person's) height.

sta·tus ['steɪtəs] *n.* (no pl.) **1.** person's legal, social, or professional position in relation to others. **2.** position of affairs.

stat·ute ['stætjuːt] *n.* (written) law passed by Parliament or other lawmaking body. **stat·u·to·ry** ['stætjʊtərɪ] *adj.* fixed, done, required, by ~.

staunch[1] [stɔːntʃ], **stanch**[2] [stɑːntʃ] *adj.* (of a friend, supporter, etc.) trustworthy; loyal; firm.

staunch[2], see *stanch*[1].

stave [steɪv] *n.* **1.** one of the curved pieces of wood used for the sides of a barrel, tub, etc. **2.** see *staff* (5). *v.t.* (p.t. & p.p. ~*d or stove* [stəʊv]) **1.** ~ *in*, break; smash; make a hole in. **2.** ~ *off*, keep off, delay (danger, disaster, etc.).

stay[1] [steɪ] *v.i. & t.* **1.** be, keep, remain (at a place, in a position or condition): ~ *where you are*; ~ *in the house*; ~ *up late*, not go to bed until late; ~ *single*, not marry; ~ *put*, (colloq.) remain where placed; *has come (is here) to* ~, (colloq.) must be regarded as permanent. **2.** live for a time (e.g. as a guest): ~ *at a hotel*; ~ *with friends.* **3.** stop; delay; postpone; check: ~ *the progress of a disease.* **4.** endure; be able to continue (work, etc.): ~*ing-power*, endurance. *n.* **1.** (period of) ~*ing* (2): *a short* ~ *at a friend's house.* **2.** (law) suspension of judicial proceedings.

stay[2] [steɪ] *n.* rope or wire supporting a mast, pole, etc.; (fig.) support.

stead [sted] *n.* (no pl.) **1.** *in sb.'s* ~, in his place; instead of him. **2.** *stand sb. in good* ~, be useful or helpful to him in time of need.

stead·fast ['stedfəst] *adj.* firm and unchanging; keeping firm (*to*).

stead·y ['stedɪ] *adj.* (*-ier, -iest*) **1.** standing firm; balanced; not likely to fall over. **2.** regular in movement, speed, direction, etc.: *a* ~ *wind; a* ~ *rate of progress.* **3.** regular in behaviour, habits, etc.: *a* ~ *young man.* **4.** constant; unchanging: *a* ~ *faith (purpose).*

v.t. & i. make or become ~; keep ~.
stead·i·ly *adv.* **stead·i·ness** *n.*

steak [steɪk] *n.* (thick slice of) meat or
fish for frying, grilling, etc.

steal [stiːl] *v.t. & i.* (p.t. **stole** [stəʊl],
p.p. **stolen** ['stəʊlən]) **1.** take (sb. else's
property) secretly, without right, unlawfully. **2.** move, come, or go (*in, out,
away, etc.*), secretly and quietly. **3.**
obtain by surprise or a trick: ~ *a march
on sb.*, do sth. before him and so win
an advantage over him.

stealth [stelθ] *n.* (no pl.) *do sth. by* ~,
do sth. secretly. **~y** *adj.* (*-ier, -iest*)
doing sth., done, quietly and secretly.
~·i·ly *adv.*

steam [stiːm] *n.* (no pl.) gas or vapour
into which boiling water changes:
~-heated buildings. get up ~, increase
pressure of ~ in an engine; (fig.) collect
one's energy; become excited or angry;
let off ~, (fig.) release surplus energy
or emotion. *v.i. & t.* **1.** give out ~.
2. move, work, etc. (as if) under the
power of ~: *a ship* ~*ing up the Red
Sea.* **3.** cook, soften, clean, by means
of ~. **'~-,en·gine, '~-,ship** *ns.* engine,
ship, worked or driven by pressure of
~. **~·er** *n.* **1.** ~ship. **2.** vessel in which
food is cooked by being ~ed. **~y** *adj.*
(*-ier, -iest*) of, like, full of, ~.

steel [stiːl] *n.* (no pl.) hard alloy of iron
and carbon or other elements, used for
knives, tools, machines, etc. *v.t.* make
(*oneself, one's will*) strongly determined (*to do sth., against sth.*).
'~·works *n. pl.* (often sing. v.) factory
where ~ is manufactured. **~y** *adj.*
(*-ier, -iest*) like ~ in hardness, brightness, etc. **'~·yard** *n.* apparatus for
weighing, with a short arm to take
the object to be weighed, and a long,
graduated arm along which a weight
slides.

a steeple   a step-ladder

(a) the spire
(b) the tower

steep¹ [stiːp] *adj.* **1.** (of a slope) rising
or falling sharply. **2.** (of a roof, etc.)
with a ~ slope. **3.** (colloq., of a
demand) unreasonable.

steep² [stiːp] *v.t. & i.* soak.

stee·ple ['stiːpl] *n.* high church tower,
with a spire. **'~·chase** *n.* cross-country
horse-race or race on foot with obstacles such as hedges and ditches.
'~·jack *n.* workman who climbs and
repairs ~s and other high structures.

steer¹ [stɪə*] *n.* young bullock.

steer² [stɪə*] *v.t. & i.* direct the course
of (a boat, motor car, etc.): ~ *clear of*,
(fig.) take care to avoid. **~ing-wheel**,
wheel for controlling the front wheels
of a motor vehicle, mounted (2) on a
~ing-column. **'~s·man** *n.* man who ~s
a ship.

steer·age ['stɪərɪdʒ] *n.* (no pl.) **1.** (act
of) steering. **2.** part of a ship for passengers travelling at the lowest fares.

stel·lar ['stelə*] *adj.* of the stars.

stem¹ [stem] *n.* **1.** part of a plant coming up from the roots. **2.** part of a leaf,
flower, or fruit that joins it to the
main stalk, branch, etc. **3.** anything
that joins like a ~ (e.g. the part of a
wineglass between the bowl and the
base). **4.** main part of a word (e.g. *man*
in un*man*ly) from which other words
are made by additions. **5.** main upright timber at the bow of a ship:
from ~ *to stern*, from end to end of a
ship. *v.i.* (*-mm-*) ~ *from*, arise from;
have as origin.

stem² [stem] *v.t.* (*-mm-*) **1.** check,
stop, dam up (a current of water, etc.).
2. make progress against the resistance
of (the tide, etc.).

stench [stentʃ] *n.* bad smell.

sten·cil ['stensl] *n.* thin sheet of metal,
cardboard, waxed paper, etc. with
letters, designs, etc. cut through it;
lettering, designs, etc. printed by
inking paper, etc. through a ~. *v.t.*
(*-ll-*, U.S.A. also *-l-*) produce (letters,
figures, designs, etc.) by means of a ~.

ste·nog·ra·phy [stə'nɒɡrəfɪ] *n.* shorthand. **ste·nog·ra·pher** *n.* writer of
shorthand.

sten·to·ri·an [sten'tɔːrɪən] *adj.* (of a
voice) loud and strong.

step [step] *v.i. & t.* (*-pp-*) **1.** move the
foot, or one foot after the other, forward, or in the direction indicated:
~ *on to (off) the platform*; ~ *into a boat*;
~ *across a stream*; ~ *aside*, move to one
side; (fig.) let sb. else take one's place;
~ *out*, walk quickly; ~ *on the gas*
(colloq. *on it*), press down the accelerator pedal to increase speed;
(fig.) hurry. **2.** walk by ~ping: *S~* (i.e.
come) *this way, please.* **3.** ~ *up* (production, etc.), raise; increase. *n.* **1.** act
of ~ping once; distance covered by
doing this: *walking with slow* ~*s*; ~ *by*

~, gradually. **2.** (also *foot~*) sound made by sb. walking. **3.** person's way of walking (seen or heard): *I recognize his ~.* **4.** *in (out of)* ~, putting (not putting) the same foot to the ground at the same time as others (in walking, marching, dancing); (fig.) conforming (not conforming) to what others are doing. **5.** place for the foot when going from one level to another: *Mind the ~s down into the cellar.* **6.** *(a pair of)* ~s, *~-ladder*, folding ladder with flat ~s (not rungs). (See the picture on page 504.) **7.** one action in a series of actions designed to effect a purpose: *take ~s to prevent illness; a false ~*, a mistaken action. **8.** grade; rank; promotion.

step- [step-] *pref.* '~₁**broth·er**, '~₁**sis·ter** *ns.* child of an earlier marriage of one's ~father or ~mother. '~·**child**, '~₁**daugh·ter**, '~·**son** *ns.* child of an earlier marriage of one's wife or husband. '~₁**fa·ther**, '~₁**moth·er** *ns.* later husband, wife, of one of one's parents.

steppe [step] *n.* level, treeless plain, esp. in S.E. Europe and central Asia.

ste·reo·pho·nic [ˌsterɪəʊˈfɒnɪk], (colloq.) **ste·reo** [ˈsterɪəʊ] *adjs.* of or relating to sound transmission, recording, or reproduction using two or more transmission channels so that the sound reaches the listener from more than one direction and thus seems more realistic. (Cf. *monophonic.*)

ste·reo·scope [ˈsterɪəskəʊp] *n.* apparatus by which two photographs of sth., taken from slightly different angles, are seen as if united and with the effect of depth and solidity. **ste·reo·scop·ic** [ˌsterɪəˈskɒpɪk] *adj.*

ste·reo·type [ˈsterɪətaɪp] *n.* **1.** (process of printing from a) printing-plate cast from a mould of a piece of printing set in type. **2.** (fig.) phrase, idea, belief, etc. now unchanging and formalized. *v.t.* **1.** make ~s of; print by the use of ~s. **2.** (fig.) give a fixed form to: ~*d*, (of phrases, ideas, etc.) fixed in form; used and repeated without change; unoriginal.

ster·ile [ˈsteraɪl] *adj.* **1.** (opp. *fertile* (2)) not producing, not able to produce, seeds or offspring. **2.** (of land) barren. **3.** (fig.) having no result. **4.** free from living germs. **ste·ril·i·ty** [steˈrɪlətɪ] *n.* (no pl.) being ~. **ster·il·ize** [ˈsterəlaɪz] *v.t.* make ~. **ster·il·iza·tion** [ˌsterəlaɪˈzeɪʃn] *n.* (no pl.).

ster·ling [ˈstɜːlɪŋ] *adj.* **1.** (of gold and silver) of standard value and purity.

2. (fig.) genuine; of solid worth: *a ~ fellow.* *n.* British money: *payable in ~.*

stern¹ [stɜːn] *adj.* **1.** demanding or enforcing obedience. **2.** (of face, looks, etc.) severe; strict. ~·**ly** *adv.* ~·**ness** *n.* (no pl.).

stern² [stɜːn] *n.* rear end of a ship or boat.

stetho·scope [ˈsteθəskəʊp] *n.* instrument used by doctors for listening to the beating of the heart, sounds of breathing, etc.

a stethoscope

ste·ve·dore [ˈstiːvədɔː*] *n.* firm or individual engaged in the loading or unloading of a vessel.

stew [stjuː] *v.t. & i.* cook, be cooked, slowly in water or juice, in a closed dish, etc. *let sb. ~ in his own juice*, do nothing to help him (when he is in trouble for which he is himself responsible). *n.* **1.** dish of ~ed meat, etc. **2.** *in a ~*, (colloq.) in a nervous, anxious condition.

stew·ard [stjʊəd] *n.* **1.** man who arranges for the supply of food, etc. in a club, college, etc. **2.** attendant for passengers in a ship or aircraft: *the baggage (cabin, deck, etc.) ~.* **3.** man responsible for organizing details of a dance, public meeting, show, etc. **4.** man who manages another's property, esp. a large house or estate. ~·**ess** *n.* female ~, esp. in a ship or aircraft. ~·**ship** *n.* (no pl.) rank, duties, period of office, of a ~ (4).

stick¹ [stɪk] *n.* **1.** thin branch, broken, cut, or fallen from a tree or bush: *gather ~s to make a fire.* **2.** such a branch cut to convenient length for use in walking, etc.: *He cannot walk without a ~. give sb. the ~*, punish him with a cane. **3.** rod-shaped piece *(of* chalk, sealing-wax, dynamite, celery, etc.). *v.t.* support with ~s: ~ *peas.*

stick² [stɪk] *v.t. & i.* (p.t. & p.p. **stuck** [stʌk]) **1.** push (sth. pointed) *(into, through, etc.)*: ~ *a fork into a potato.* **2.** (of sth. pointed) be, remain, in a position by the point: *a needle stuck in the cushion; find a nail ~ing in a tyre.* **3.** (cause to) be or become joined or fastened with, or as with, paste, glue, etc.: ~ *a stamp on a letter; the stamps* have stuck (*together*); *be stuck with* (*sb., sth.*), (colloq.) be unable to get rid of. **4.** (colloq.) put (in some position), esp. quickly or carelessly: ~ *papers in a drawer. He stuck his hands in his pockets.* **5.** be or become fixed; fail to work properly: *the key stuck in the lock* (could not be turned or withdrawn). **6.** (with advs. & preps.): ~ *at*, stop short of; hesitate at: ~ *at trifles*; ~ *at nothing*, be ready to do anything, however difficult, wrong, etc. it may be; ~ *out*, (cause to) project, stand out: *with his chest stuck out. Don't* ~ *your tongue out at me.* ~ *out for*, refuse to give way until one gets (e.g. a higher salary); ~ *it out*, (colloq.) endure hardship, etc. to the end; ~ *to*, be faithful to (one's word, a friend); continue at (a task, etc.); ~ *up for*, defend; support. **'~·ing‑plas·ter** *n.* plaster for ~ing on and protecting a cut, injury, etc. **~·y** *adj.* (-*ier*, -*iest*) that ~s (3) or tends to ~ (3) to anything that touches it. **~·i·ly** *adv.* **~·i·ness** *n.*

stick·ler ['stɪklə*] *n. a* ~ *for*, a person who insists upon the importance of (accuracy, discipline, formality, etc.).

stiff [stɪf] *adj.* **1.** not easily bent or changed in shape: *a* ~ (i.e. starched) *collar; a* ~ *leg; feel* ~ *in the joints.* **2.** hard to stir, work, move, etc.: *mix flour and milk to a* ~ *paste;* hard to do; difficult: *a* ~ *climb.* **3.** (of behaviour, etc.) formal; cold. **4.** (of a breeze, of alcoholic drinks) strong; (of a price, penalty, etc.) high. *adv.* thoroughly; to the point of exhaustion: *He bored me* ~, he bored me very much. *I was scared* ~, I was very badly scared. *n.* (sl.) corpse. **stif·fen** ['stɪfn] *v.t. & i.* make or become ~(er). **~·ly** *adv.* **~·ness** *n.* (no pl.).

sti·fle ['staɪfl] *v.t. & i.* **1.** smother; make breathing difficult or impossible: *The heat in Calcutta was stifling.* **2.** suppress (e.g. a rebellion, a yawn, a cry, etc.).

stig·ma ['stɪgmə] *n.* (esp. fig.) mark of shame or disgrace. **~·tize** ['stɪgmətaɪz] *v.t.* ~*tize sb. as*, describe him scornfully as (e.g. a liar, coward).

stile [staɪl] *n.* step(s) for climbing over a fence. (See the picture.)

sti·let·to [stɪ'letəʊ] *n.* (pl. -*os*, -*oes*) small dagger. ~ *heel*, (on women's shoes) high, thin heel, usu. made of metal.

still¹ [stɪl] *adj. & adv.* without movement or sound; quiet: *stand* ~. ~ *life*, picture of fruit, flowers, etc. *n.* **1.** (no pl.) deep silence: *in the* ~ *of night.*

2. ordinary photograph, esp. a single shot¹ (7) from a cinema film (e.g. as used for advertising in the press). *v.t.* (lit.) make calm; cause to be at rest. **'~·born** *adj.* dead when born. **~·ness** *n.* (no pl.).

still² [stɪl] *adv.* **1.** even up to this or that (past, present, or future) time: *He has* (*had*) *been working all day but* ~ *has* (*had*) *not finished.* **2.** (with a comp.) even; yet; in a greater degree: *This is good but that is better* ~ (~ *better*).

still³ [stɪl] *n.* apparatus for making liquors (brandy, whisky, etc.) by distilling.

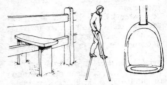

a stile   (a pair of) stilts   a stirrup

stilt [stɪlt] *n.* one of a pair of poles, each with a rest for the foot, enabling the user to walk at a distance above the ground. (See the picture above.) **~·ed** *adj.* (of talk, writing, behaviour, etc.) stiff and unnatural; too formal.

stim·u·lant ['stɪmjʊlənt] *n.* drink (e.g. coffee, brandy), drug, etc. that increases bodily or mental activity; sth. that spurs one on (e.g. praise, joy, hope).

stim·u·late ['stɪmjʊleɪt] *v.t.* excite; rouse; quicken thought or feeling: ~ *sb. to activity* (*to work harder*). **stim·u·lat·ing** *adj.* **stim·u·lus** ['stɪmjʊləs] (pl. -*li* [-laɪ]) *n.* sth. that ~s.

sting [stɪŋ] *n.* **1.** sharp, often poisonous, pointed organ (1) of some insects (e.g. bees, wasps, gnats). **2.** stiff, sharp hair of nettle, etc. causing pain on contact with the skin. **3.** sharp pain caused by the ~ of an insect or by touching nettles, etc.; place of a wound made by a ~. **4.** (fig.) any sharp pain of the body or mind: *the* ~ *of the wind* (*of hunger, criticism*). *v.t. & i.* (p.t. & p.p. *stung* [stʌŋ]) **1.** prick or wound with or as with a ~; have the power to ~. **2.** cause sharp pain (to). **3.** (of parts of the body) feel sharp pain.

stin·gy ['stɪndʒɪ] *adj.* (-*ier*, -*iest*) **1.** spending, using, or giving unwillingly; niggardly: ~ *with the sugar.* **2.** scanty: *a* ~ *allowance from his father.*

stink [stɪŋk] *v.i.* (p.t. *stank* [stæŋk] or *stunk* [stʌŋk], p.p. *stunk*) *& n.* (have a) nasty or offensive smell: *They* ~ *of garlic. He* ~*s of money*, (sl.) he is immensely rich.

stint [stɪnt] *v.t. & i.* keep (sb.) to a small allowance; supply or give (sth.) in niggardly amount or grudgingly: *She* ~*ed herself of food in order to give the children enough. n. without* ~, freely; without limit; without sparing any effort.

sti·pend ['staɪpend] *n.* (esp. clergyman's) salary.

stip·ple ['stɪpl] *v.t.* draw or paint with dots instead of lines, etc.

stip·u·late ['stɪpjʊleɪt] *v.t. & i.* 1. state, put forward, as a necessary condition (*that*). 2. ~ *for*, insist upon (as part of an agreement): ~ *for the best materials to be used.* **stip·u·la·tion** [ˌstɪpjʊ'leɪʃn] *n.* sth. ~d; condition.

stir [stɜː*] *v.i. & t.* (-rr-) 1. be moving; cause to move: *The wind* ~*red the leaves. Nobody in the house was* ~*ring.* 2. move a spoon, etc. round and round in a liquid, etc. in order to mix it thoroughly: ~ *milk into a cake mixture.* 3. (often ~ *up*) excite: ~ *the blood*; *a story that* ~*red* (*up*) *one's feelings. n.* 1. slightest movement: *not a* ~. 2. commotion; excitement; sensation: *Her new novel made quite a* ~. ~**·ring** *adj.* exciting.

stir·rup ['stɪrəp] *n.* foot-rest, hanging down from a saddle, for the rider of a horse. (See the picture on page 506.)

stitch [stɪtʃ] *n.* 1. (in sewing) the passing of a needle and thread in and out of cloth, etc.; (in knitting, etc.) one complete turn of the wool, etc. over the needle. 2. thread, etc. seen between two successive holes made by a needle; result of a single movement with a threaded needle, knitting-needle, etc.: *take the* ~*es out of a wound*; *a* ~ *in time saves nine*, (proverb) a small piece of work done now may save a lot of work later. 3. (no pl.) sudden, sharp pain in the side caused by running, etc. *v.t. & i.* sew; put ~*es in or on.

stoat [stəʊt] *n.* small, furry animal larger than a rat; weasel; ermine.

stock [stɒk] *n.* 1. lower part of a tree trunk. 2. base, support, or handle of an instrument, tool, etc.: *the* ~ *of a rifle* (*plough*). 3. (no pl.) line of ancestry: *a woman of Irish* ~. *He comes of farming* ~. 4. store of goods available for sale, distribution, or use, esp. goods kept by a trader or shopkeeper:

be in (*out of*) ~, be available (not available); *take* ~, examine and list goods in ~; *take* ~ *of*, (fig.) review (a situation); estimate (sb.'s abilities, etc.); *a good* ~ *of information.* 5. (no pl.) (also *live*~ ['laɪvstɒk]) farm animals: ~*-farmer*; ~*-breeding.* 6. (no pl.) liquid in which bones, meat, fish, vegetables, etc. have been stewed, used for making soup, gravy, etc. 7. money lent to a government in return for interest; shares[1] (3) in the capital of a business company: ~ *exchange*, place where ~s and shares are bought and sold. 8. (attrib.) usually kept in ~ (4) (and therefore regularly available): ~ *sizes in hats* (commonly or regularly used); (fig.) always available and perpetually repeated without fresh thought or originality; hackneyed: ~ *arguments* (*jokes*). 9. *the* ~*s*, framework with holes for the feet in which wrongdoers were formerly locked in a sitting position. 10. (pl.) framework supporting a ship while it is being built or repaired. 11. sorts of sweet-smelling garden flower. *v.t.* 1. (of a shop, etc.) have a ~ (4) of; keep in ~: *Do you* ~ *bowler hats?* 2. supply or equip (*with*): ~ *a farm with animals and machinery.* '~**·bro·ker** *n.* man whose business is the buying and selling of ~(s) (7). ˌ~**-in-'trade** *n.* (no pl.) things needed for sb.'s business, trade, activity, etc. '~**·pil·ing** *n.* process of building up ~s (4) of raw materials, etc. to be held in reserve, esp. for war purposes. ˌ~**-'still** *adv.* motionless. '~**·yard** *n.* enclosure where cattle are kept temporarily (e.g. before being slaughtered or marketed).

stock·ade [stɒ'keɪd] *n.* line or wall of upright stakes, built as a defence. *v.t.* put a ~ round.

stock·ing ['stɒkɪŋ] *n.* tight-fitting covering of nylon, silk, cotton, wool, etc. for the foot and leg, reaching to or above the knee: *a pair of* ~s.

stocky ['stɒkɪ] *adj.* (-ier, -iest) (of persons, animals, plants) short, strong, and stout.

stodgy ['stɒdʒɪ] *adj.* (-ier, -iest) 1. (of food) heavy and solid. 2. (of books, etc.) uninterestingly written.

sto·ic ['stəʊɪk] *n.* person who has great self-control, who bears pain and discomfort without complaint. ~**al** *adj.* of or like a ~. ~**al·ly** *adv.* ~**ism** ['stəʊɪsɪzəm] *n.* (no pl.) patient and uncomplaining endurance of suffering, etc.

stoke [stəʊk] *v.t. & i.* put coal, etc.

on the fire of (an engine, furnace, etc.); attend to a fire or furnace. **'∼·hole, '∼·hold** *ns.* place where a ship's furnaces are ∼d. **stok·er** *n.* workman who ∼s a furnace, etc.; mechanical device for doing this.

stole¹, sto·len, see **steal.**

stole² [stəʊl] *n.* **1.** strip of silk, etc. worn (round the neck with the ends hanging down in front) by priests of some Christian Churches during services. **2.** woman's shoulder wrap.

stol·id ['stɒlɪd] *adj.* not easily excited; slow to show the feelings.

stom·ach ['stʌmək] *n.* **1.** baglike enlargement of the alimentary canal into which food passes to be digested. **2.** belly; abdomen. **3.** (no pl.) appetite. **4.** (no pl.) inclination; liking: *I have no ∼ for this trip.* *v.t.* (usu. neg. or interr.) endure; put up with: *I can't ∼ his jokes.*

stone [stəʊn] *n.* **1.** (no pl.) solid mineral matter other than metal; rock: *a house built of ∼; a ∼ house.* **2.** piece of this of any shape, usu. broken off: *a heap of ∼s; cut one's foot on a sharp ∼; leave no ∼ unturned* (to do sth.), try every possible means; *throw ∼s or a ∼ at,* (fig.) attack the character of sb. **3.** jewel: *precious ∼s.* **4.** piece of ∼ of a definite shape for a special purpose: *a paving ∼.* **5.** hard shell and seed in such fruits as the peach, plum, cherry. **6.** (pl. ∼) (Gt. Brit.) unit of weight, 14 lb. *v.t.* **1.** throw ∼s at (sb. in order to kill or injure). **2.** take ∼s (5) out of (fruit). **,∼-'blind (-'dead, -'deaf)** *adjs.* completely blind, etc. **'∼,ma·son** *n.* man who cuts ∼, prepares, and builds with ∼. **∼'s throw** *n.* short distance: *within a ∼'s throw (of),* very close (to). **'∼-ware** *n.* (no pl.) pottery made from flint and clay. **stony** *adj.* (-*ier,* -*iest*) **1.** having or covered with many ∼s. **2.** hard, cold, and unsympathetic: *a stony heart.*

stood, see **stand** (v.).

stool [stuːl] *n.* **1.** seat without a back or arms, usu. for one person. **2.** (usu. *foot∼*) low support on which to rest the feet.

stoop [stuːp] *v.i. & t.* **1.** bend the body forwards and downwards; bend the neck so that the head is forward and down: *∼ing with old age; ∼ to pick sth. up.* **2.** (fig.) lower oneself morally: *∼ to cheating.* *n.* (no pl.) ∼ing position of the body: *walk with a ∼.*

stop [stɒp] *v.t. & i.* (-*pp*-) **1.** put an end to (the movement or progress of sb. or sth.); prevent; hinder; discontinue; come to rest; halt: *∼ a car; ∼ dead,* cease abruptly; *∼ off (over),* break one's journey; *∼off, ∼over* (ns.). **2.** fill or close (a hole, an opening, etc.): *∼ a decayed tooth; ∼ a leak in a pipe; ∼ up a mouse-hole; ∼ one's ears* (e.g. by covering them with the hands). **3.** discontinue (payment of): *∼ sb.'s wages; ∼ (payment of) a cheque,* order the bank not to cash it; *the firm has ∼ped payment,* has declared itself not solvent (2). **4.** stay, remain (*at home, in bed, etc.*). **5.** (music) produce the desired note(s) by pressing the fingers on strings (of a violin, etc.) or over holes (in a flute, etc.). *n.* **1.** ∼ping or being ∼ped: *The train came to a sudden ∼. put a ∼ to sth.,* bring sth. to a ∼, cause it to ∼ or end. **2.** place where buses, etc. ∼ regularly: *the nearest bus-∼.* **3.** (in a flute, etc.) lever or key for altering the pitch¹ (5); (in an organ (4)) set of pipes producing tones of one quality (e.g. of a bassoon); knob that brings this into action. **4.** (in writing, printing) punctuation mark, esp. comma, semicolon, colon, or *full* (3) ∼. **5.** device (e.g. a peg) that ∼s the movement of sth. at a fixed point. **'∼·cock** *n.* valve for controlling the flow of liquid or gas through a pipe. **'∼·gap** *n.* thing or person filling the place of another for a time. **∼·page** ['stɒpɪdʒ] *n.* condition of being ∼ped up; obstruction; interruption. **∼·per** *n.* cork or plug for closing an opening, esp. the mouth of a bottle. **'∼-press** *n.* (Gt. Brit.) latest news added to a newspaper already on the printing machines. **'∼-watch** *n.* watch with a hand that can be started and ∼ped when desired, used to time events such as races to a fraction of a second.

store [stɔː*] *n.* **1.** quantity or supply of sth. kept for use as needed. **2.** (no pl.) *in ∼,* (a) kept ready for future use; (b) destined (*for*); coming to: *trouble in ∼ for that careless assistant.* **3.** device (2) in a computer for storing and retrieving data (2) or instructions. **4.** (pl.) goods, etc. of a particular kind or for a special purpose: *naval and military ∼s.* **5.** place where goods are kept; warehouse. **6.** (pl.) shop selling many varieties of goods; (U.S.A.) (sing.) any kind of shop: *a clothing ∼.* **7.** *set (no) great ∼ by (on) (sth.),* consider of great (little) value or importance. *v.t.* **1.** (often ∼ *up*) collect, keep, for future use. **2.** put (e.g. furniture) in a warehouse for safe keeping. **3.** fill, supply (*with*): *∼ the shed with wood*

(*one's mind with facts*). **stor·age**
['stɔːrɪdʒ] *n.* (no pl.) (space used for,
money charged for, the) storing of
goods, etc.: *cold storage*, storage in a
refrigerator: *fish kept in cold storage.*
'**ᴖ·house** *n.* **1.** warehouse. **2.** (fig.)
abundant supply or source: *This book
is a ᴖhouse of information.*

sto·rey, sto·ry² ['stɔːrɪ] *n.* (pl. **-reys,
-ries**) floor or level in a building: *a
house of two ᴖs* (i.e. with rooms on
the ground floor and one floor upstairs):
upper ᴖ, (humor.) the brain. **(-)'sto·
reyed, (-)'sto·ried** *adj.* having ᴖs
(stories): *a two-ᴖed (two -storied) house.*

stork [stɔːk] *n.* large, long-legged wad-
ing bird, usu. white except for black
wing-tips, a long, reddish bill, and
red feet.

storm [stɔːm] *n.* **1.** violent weather
conditions: *a thunder- (snow-, sand-,
etc.)ᴖ; a ᴖ in a teacup,* (fig.) much
excitement about sth. trivial. **2.** violent
outburst of feeling: *a ᴖ of protest, etc.*
3. *take (a place) by ᴖ,* capture by a sudden and violent attack. *v.i. & t.* **1.**
shout angrily *(at).* **2.** force (a way)
into (a building, etc.); capture (a place)
by sudden and violent attack. **ᴖy** *adj.*
(**-ier, -iest**). **ᴖ·i·ly** *adv.*

sto·ry¹ ['stɔːrɪ] *n.* **1.** account of real
events: *the ᴖ of Columbus.* **2.** account
of imaginary events: *a ghost ᴖ.* **3.**
(colloq. or children's language) lie;
untrue statement.

sto·ry², see *storey.*

stout [staʊt] *adj.* **1.** strong, thick, not
easily broken or worn out: *ᴖ shoes.*
2. determined and brave: *ᴖ companions;*
ᴖ-hearted. **3.** (of a person) rather fat.
n. (no pl.) kind of strong, dark beer.
ᴖ·ly *adv.* in a ᴖ (2) manner.

stove¹ [staʊv] *n.* enclosed apparatus
for producing heat for cooking, warming rooms, etc.

stove², see *stave* (v.).

stow [staʊ] *v.t.* pack, esp. carefully and
closely: *ᴖ cargo in a ship's holds; ᴖ a
trunk with clothes.* '**ᴖ·away** *n.* person
who hides himself in a ship or aircraft
(until after it leaves) in order to make
a journey without paying.

strad·dle ['strædl] *v.i. & t.* **1.** stand
with the legs wide apart. **2.** sit or stand
across (sth.) with the legs widely
separated: *ᴖ a ditch (a horse).*

strag·gle ['strægl] *v.i.* **1.** grow, spread,
in an irregular or untidy way: *a strag-
gling village; vines that ᴖd over the
fences.* **2.** drop behind while on the
march. **ᴖr** *n.* person who ᴖs (2).

straight [streɪt] *adj.* **1.** without a curve

or bend; extending in one direction:
a ᴖ line (road); ᴖ hair (without curls).
2. parallel to (sth. else, esp. the
horizon): *Put your hat on ᴖ.* **3.** in good
order; tidy: *Put your desk ᴖ before you
leave.* **4.** (of a person, his behaviour,
etc.) honest; frank; upright: *Give me a
ᴖ answer.* **5.** *a ᴖ fight,* (in politics) a
contest in which there are only two
candidates; *keep a ᴖ face,* refrain from
smiling or laughing. *adv.* **1.** in a ᴖ
line; by or in the shortest way; without delay: *Come ᴖ home.* **2.** *ᴖ away
(off),* (colloq.) at once; without delay;
ᴖ on (across, in, out, etc.), directly on,
etc.; *say sth. ᴖ out,* openly, without
hesitation. **3.** *go ᴖ,* (fig.) live an honest
life (esp. after having been dishonest).
n. **1.** *ᴖ condition: out of the ᴖ,* crooked.
2. straight part of sth., esp. the final
part of a racecourse. **ᴖ·en** ['streɪtn]
v.t. & i. make or become ᴖ. **ᴖ'for·
ward** *adj.* **1.** honest; upright. **2.** simple; easy to do or understand.

strain [streɪn] *v.t. & i.* **1.** stretch
tightly by pulling *(at): ᴖ (at) a rope.*
2. make the greatest possible use
of; make great efforts; exert one's
powers; injure or weaken by doing
this: *ᴖ every nerve (to do sth.),* do one's
utmost; *ᴖ one's eyes in poor light; ᴖ
one's heart,* injure it by over-exertion;
ᴖing at the oars. **3.** (fig.) stretch beyond
its proper limit; twist from the true
purpose or meaning: *ᴖ the truth,* say
sth. that is almost a lie. **4.** hold (sb.)
tightly *(to* oneself, *in* one's arms, etc.).
5. pass (liquids) through a cloth, a
network of fine wire, etc. to separate
solid matter: *ᴖ the soup. n.* **1.** condition of being stretched; force exerted:
The rope broke under the ᴖ. **2.** sth. that
tests and ᴖs one's powers; severe
demand on one's strength, etc.: *the ᴖ
of sleepless nights; a ᴖ on the nerves.*
3. (no pl.) exhaustion; fatigue: *suffering from over-ᴖ.* **4.** sprain; injury
caused by twisting a joint. **5.** (pl.)
music, song, or verse (of the kind indicated): *the ᴖs of an organ.* **6.** manner
of speaking or writing: *in a cheerful ᴖ.*
7. tendency in sb.'s character: *a ᴖ of
insanity in the family.* **ᴖed** *adj.* (esp.
of feelings and behaviour) forced; unnatural: *ᴖed relations* (marked by great
tension through loss of patience, irri-
tability, etc.). **ᴖer** *n.* sieve, filter, or
similar device for ᴖing (5) liquids.

strait [streɪt] *n.* **1.** (sing. or pl.)
narrow passage of water connecting
two seas or two large bodies of water:
the Sᴖ of Gibraltar. **2.** (usu. pl.)

trouble; difficulty: *in great ~s*; *in financial ~s*. *adj.* (old use) narrow; limited: *~-jacket*, long-sleeved, strong jacket put on violent persons to bind the arms. *~-laced*, severely moral (2). **~·en** ['streɪtn] *v.t.* *in ~ened circumstances*, in poverty.

strand[1] [strænd] *n.* (poet. or rhet.) sandy shore of a lake, sea, or river. *v.i. & t.* **1.** (of a ship) run aground. **2.** *be ~ed*, (fig.) be left helpless, without money, friends, etc.: *~ed in a foreign country*.

strand[2] [strænd] *n.* any one of the threads, wires, yarns, etc. twisted together into a rope or cable, or in a textile material; tress of hair; (fig.) element in any composite whole.

strange [streɪndʒ] *adj.* (*~r, ~st*) **1.** not seen, heard, known, or experienced before; foreign; unfamiliar; surprising: *feel ~*, not be in one's usual condition, esp. feel dizzy; *~ to say*, it is surprising that. **2.** (pred.) unaccustomed (*to*). **~·ly** *adv.* **~·ness** *n.* **strang·er** *n.* person one does not know; person in a place or in company that he does not know.

stran·gle ['stræŋgl] *v.t.* kill by squeezing the throat of; hinder the breathing of. **'~·hold** *n.* (usu. lit. or fig.) deadly grip. **stran·gu·la·tion** [ˌstræŋgju-'leɪʃn] *n.* (no pl.).

strap [stræp] *n.* strip of leather or other flexible material used to fasten things together, to keep sth. (e.g. a wrist-watch) in place, etc.: *a shoulder-~*. *v.t.* (*-pp-*) **1.** fasten or hold in place with a ~ or ~s. **2.** beat with a ~. **~·ping** *adj.* (esp. of a person) tall and strong.

stra·ta, see *stratum*.

strat·a·gem ['strætədʒəm] *n.* (use of a) trick or device to deceive sb., esp. the enemy in war.

strat·e·gy ['strætɪdʒɪ] *n.* **1.** (no pl.) art of planning operations in war, esp. the movements of armies and navies into favourable positions for fighting. **2.** instance of or plan formed according to this. **stra·te·gic** [strə'tiːdʒɪk] *adj.* of, by, serving the purpose of, ~. **strat·e·gist** ['strætɪdʒɪst] *n.* expert in ~.

strato·sphere ['strætəʊˌsfɪə*] *n.* upper portion of the atmosphere, beginning about seven miles above the earth.

stra·tum ['strɑːtəm] *n.* (pl. *-ta* [-tə]) horizontal layer of rock, etc. in the earth's crust; (fig.) social class or division.

straw [strɔː] *n.* **1.** (no pl.) dry, cut stalks of grain as material for thatching, mats, hats, fodder, etc.: *a roof thatched*

with ~. **2.** single stalk or piece of ~; hollow tube originally of ~ for sucking drink through. *the last ~*, slight addition to a task, burden, etc. that makes it intolerable; *catch at a ~*, try to seize any chance, however small, in the hope of escaping from danger, etc.

straw·ber·ry ['strɔːbərɪ] *n.* (plant having) juicy, edible, red fruit covered with tiny, yellow seeds.

stray [streɪ] *v.i.* wander (*from* the right path, *from* one's companions, etc.); lose one's way; become distracted (*from* a point, an argument, etc.). *adj.* **1.** having ~ed: *~ cats*. **2.** occasional; seen or happening now and then. *n.* *~ed* animal or person (esp. a child): *waifs and ~s*, homeless children.

streak [striːk] *n.* **1.** long, thin, usu. irregular line or band: *~s of lean and fat* (in meat); *like a ~ of lightning* (i.e. very fast). **2.** trace (*of* some quality): *a ~ of vanity* (cruelty). **3.** brief period: *a ~ of good luck*. *v.t.* mark with ~(s). **~·y** *adj.* (*-ier, -iest*) marked with, having, ~s.

stream [striːm] *n.* **1.** river. **2.** steady flow or current (of liquid, gas, persons, things, etc.): *go with the ~*, (fig.) act, think, etc. as the majority does. *v.i.* **1.** move as a ~; flow freely: *crowds ~ing out of the cinemas*. **2.** float or wave (in the wind): *flags ~ing* (out) *in the wind*. **~·er** *n.* long, narrow flag; long, narrow ribbon attached at one end and floating or waving at the other. **'~·lined** *adj.* (of a car, aircraft, etc.) designed to offer least resistance to the flow of air, etc.; simplified for efficiency.

street [striːt] *n.* town or village road, with houses on one side or both: *in the ~*; *not in the same ~ with*, (colloq.) not nearly as good as. **'~·car** *n.* (U.S.A.) = tram(car).

strength [streŋθ] *n.* (no pl.) **1.** quality of being strong. *on the ~ of*, relying on. **2.** that which makes sb. or sth. strong: *His ~ is endurance*. **3.** power measured by the number of persons present or persons who can be used: *The enemy were in* (great) *~*. **~·en** ['streŋθn] *v.t. & i.* make or become strong(er).

stren·u·ous ['strenjʊəs] *adj.* using or needing great effort; energetic: *~ work(ers)*.

stress [stres] *n.* **1.** (no pl.) pressure; conditions causing hardship, etc.: *under the ~ of poverty* (fear); *driven by ~ of weather*; *times of ~*, times of trouble and danger. **2.** weight or force (*on*): *a school that lays ~ on foreign languages*. **3.** (result of) extra force, used in speaking, on a particular word or syllable: *The ~ is on the first syllable.* **4.** (mech.) force exerted between two bodies or between parts of one body. *v.t.* put ~ on; emphasize.

stretch [stretʃ] *v.t. & i.* **1.** make wider, longer, or tighter by pulling; be or become wider, etc. when pulled: *S~ the rope tight. Rubber ~es easily.* ~ *one's arms,* extend them (e.g. after sleeping); ~ *one's legs,* go for a short walk as a relief from sitting, etc. for a long time; ~ *out one's arm for a book.* **2.** ~ *oneself out (on),* lie at full length (on). **3.** make (a word, law, etc.) include or cover more than is strictly right: ~ *a point (in sb.'s favour),* treat (him) more favourably than is right or usual. **4.** extend: *forests ~ing for hundreds of miles.* *n.* **1.** act of ~ing or being ~ed. **2.** unbroken or continuous period of time or extent of country, etc.: *at a ~,* continuously. **3.** (sl.) term of imprisonment. **~·er** *n.* framework (of poles, canvas, etc.) for carrying a sick or injured person.

a stretcher

strew [stru:] *v.t.* (p.t. ~ed, p.p. ~ed or ~n [stru:n]) scatter (sand, flowers, etc.) *over* a surface; (partly) cover (a surface) *with* sand, etc.

strick·en ['strɪkən] *adj.* affected or overcome: *terror-~.*

strict [strɪkt] *adj.* **1.** stern; demanding obedience. **2.** clearly and exactly defined or limited: *in the ~ sense of the word; the ~ truth.* **3.** requiring exact observance: *in ~ confidence; a ~ rule against smoking.* **~·ly** *adv.* in a ~ manner: *~ly speaking,* if the words are used in their ~ sense. **~·ness** *n.* (no pl.).

stric·ture ['strɪktʃə*] *n.* (usu. pl.) severe criticism or blame (*on, upon*).

stride [straɪd] *v.i. & t.* (p.t. strode [strəʊd], p.p. stridden ['strɪdn]) **1.** walk with long steps. **2.** pass (*over* or *across* sth.) with one step. *n.* (distance covered in) one, long step. *take sth. in one's ~,* do it without special effort; *make great ~s,* make rapid progress.

stri·dent ['straɪdnt] *adj.* (of sounds) shrill; loud and harsh.

strife [straɪf] *n.* (no pl.) quarrelling; state of conflict.

strike [straɪk] *v.i. & t.* (p.t. & p.p. struck [strʌk]) **1.** hit; aim a blow (*at*): ~ *sb. on the chin;* ~ *at the root of the trouble.* **2.** (with advs.): ~ *off (out),* cross out (a word, etc.) by drawing a line through it; ~ *out,* (a) use one's arms and legs vigorously in swimming: ~ *out for the shore;* (b) follow a new or independent path, a new form of activity: ~ *out for oneself,* begin a new activity, esp. start business on one's own account; ~ *up,* begin (playing music, singing, etc.); start (a friendship, conversation, etc.). **3.** (cause to) sound by striking: *The clock struck four.* **4.** lower, take down (a flag, sail, tent). **5.** make (a coin, medal, etc.) by stamping out of metal. **6.** produce (a light) by striking or scraping: ~ *a match,* light it by scraping. **7.** find; discover; arrive at: ~ *an average,* reach one (*between* amounts); ~ *a bargain,* make one; ~ *a balance,* balance accounts; ~ *gold;* ~ *oil,* (a) discover oil by drilling; (b) (fig.) have good fortune; ~ *it rich,* find a source of prosperity; ~ *the right path through the forest.* **8.** set out, go (in a certain direction): *We struck (out) across the fields.* **9.** ~ *terror (fear, etc.) into (sb.),* fill (sb.) with terror, etc.; *be struck dumb (blind, etc.),* be suddenly made dumb, etc. **10.** impress; have an effect upon the mind; attract the attention of: *How does the plan ~ you?* **11.** (of an idea) occur to (sb. suddenly). **12.** (of workers) stop working in order to get better conditions (e.g. higher pay or shorter hours) or in protest against sth. **13.** (of plants) (cause to) grow roots: *The cutting soon struck (root).* *n.* **1.** act of striking (12): *The workers are on ~.* **2.** act of striking (oil, etc.) in the earth. **3.** act of striking (1); (mil.) attack, esp. from the air. **'~·break·er** *n.* worker who takes the place of one on ~. **strik·er** *n.* **1.** worker on ~. **2.** (football) front-line player. **strik·ing** *adj.* attracting attention; unusual.

string [strɪŋ] *n.* **1.** (piece or length of) fine cord or other material used for tying things, keeping things in place, etc. **2.** series of things threaded on a ~: *a ~ of beads;* number of things in, or as in, a line: *a ~ of buses (lies).* **3.** tightly-stretched length of cord, gut, or wire (e.g. in a violin or piano) for producing musical sounds: *the ~s,* musical instruments of the violin family in an orchestra. **4.** ~s (1) used for causing puppets to move: *pull the ~s,* control the actions of others (as if they were puppets). *v.t. & i.* (p.t. & p.p. *strung* [strʌŋ]) **1.** put a ~ on (a violin, a tennis racket, etc.). **2.** put (beads, etc.) on a ~. **3.** tie or hang on a ~, etc.: ~ *lanterns among the trees for a garden party*; put (facts, etc.) together. **4.** *strung (up)*, *highly strung*, *high-strung*, (of a person, his senses, nerves, etc.) made tense, ready, excited, etc. **~y** *adj.* (-*ier*, -*iest*) like ~: ~*y meat* (full of tough, ~-like fibres).

strin·gent ['strɪndʒənt] *adj.* (of rules, etc.) strict; that must be obeyed.

strip [strɪp] *v.t. & i.* (-*pp*-) **1.** take off (clothes, covering, etc.): ~ *the bark off a tree*; ~ (*off one's clothes*) *and jump into a lake*. **2.** deprive (sb. or sth.) of (belongings, rights, contents, equipment, etc.): ~*ped of all his wealth.* *n.* long, narrow piece (of material, land, etc.).

stripe [straɪp] *n.* **1.** long, narrow band (usually of uniform breadth) on a surface from which it differs in colour or material: *the tiger's ~s*; *the Stars and S~s* (the flag of the U.S.A.). **2.** (often V-shaped) badge worn on a uniform showing rank (of a soldier, etc.).

strip·ling ['strɪplɪŋ] *n.* young man not yet fully grown.

strive [straɪv] *v.i.* (p.t. *strove* [strəʊv], p.p. ~*n* ['strɪvn]) **1.** struggle (*with*, *against*). **2.** make great efforts (*to do* sth., *for* sth.).

strode, see *stride* (v.).

stroke[1] [strəʊk] *n.* **1.** blow: *the ~ of a hammer*. **2.** one of a series of regularly repeated movements, esp. as a way of swimming or rowing: *swimming with a slow ~*; *a strong ~* (in rowing). **3.** single movement of the hand(s) or arm(s), esp. in games (e.g. cricket). **4.** (mark made by a) single movement of a pen or brush: *with one ~ of the pen*. **5.** single effort: *a good ~ of business*; *not do a ~ of work all day*; *a ~ of luck*, a piece of good fortune. **6.** sound made by a bell striking the hours: *on the ~ of three*, at three o'clock. **7.** sudden attack of illness caused by the bursting of a blood-vessel in the brain, with loss of feeling, power to move, etc.: *suffering from a ~*. **8.** oarsman who regulates the stroke (2) for the others in a boat. *v.t.* act as ~ (8).

stroke[2] [strəʊk] *v.t.* pass the hand along a surface, usu. again and again: ~ *a cat.* *n.* act of stroking; stroking movement.

stroll [strəʊl] *v.i. & n.* (go for a) quiet, unhurried walk.

strong [strɒŋ] *adj.* **1.** (opp. *weak*) having power to resist; not easily hurt, damaged, broken, etc.; having great power of body, mind, or spirit: *as ~ as a horse*; ~ *eyes (nerves)*; *going ~*, (sl.) continuing (an activity) vigorously, in good health, etc. **2.** having much of the flavouring substance in relation to the water, etc.: ~ *coffee*; *a ~ solution*. **3.** ~ *drink*, containing alcohol (esp. spirits). **4.** having a considerable effect on the mind or senses: ~ *language*, forcible (esp. abusive or blasphemous) expressions; *a ~ smell of gas*. **5.** ~ *verb*, verb that forms the past tense by a vowel change (e.g. *sing*, *sang*), not by adding -(*e*)*d* or -*t*. **~·ly** *adv.* '**~-box** *n.* small chest that is ~ly built for keeping valuables. '**~·hold** *n.* fort or fortified building; (fig.) place where a cause is ~ly supported. '**~-room** *n.* fireproof room with thick walls and (usu.) a thick steel door (e.g. in a bank) designed to protect valuables against fire and theft.

strove, see *strive*.

struck, see *strike* (v.).

struc·ture ['strʌktʃə*] *n.* **1.** (no pl.) way in which sth. is built, put together, organized, etc. **2.** building; any complex whole; framework or essential parts of a building, etc. **struc·tur·al** ['strʌktʃərəl] *adj.* of a ~, esp. the framework: *structural alterations*.

strug·gle ['strʌgl] *v.i.* fight, make violent efforts (*to get free, to do* sth.; *for*, *against*, sth., etc.). *n.* struggling; great effort; contest.

strum [strʌm] *v.i. & t.* (-*mm*-) play (on a stringed instrument) carelessly or without skill.

strung, see *string* (v.).

strut[1] [strʌt] *v.i.* (-*tt*-) walk (*about*, *around*, *etc.*) in a stiff, self-satisfied way. *n.* such a way of walking.

strut[2] [strʌt] *n.* piece of wood or metal used as a support, esp. in a framework.

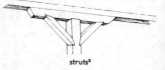

struts[2]

stub [stʌb] *n.* short, remaining end of a pencil, cigarette, etc.; counterfoil of a cheque, receipt, etc. *v.t.* (-*bb*-) **1.** ~

one's toe, strike it against sth. **2.** ~ (*out*), extinguish (a cigarette, etc.) by pressing it against sth. hard.

stub·ble ['stʌbl] *n.* (no pl.) **1.** ends of grain plants left in the ground after harvest. **2.** short, stiff growth of beard.

stub·born ['stʌbən] *adj.* obstinate; difficult to deal with.

stub·by ['stʌbɪ] *adj.* (*-ier, -iest*) short and thick: ~ *fingers*.

stuc·co ['stʌkəʊ] *n.* (pl. *-os, -oes*) (sorts of) plaster or cement, used for covering and decorating ceilings or wall surfaces.

stuck, see *stick²*.

stud¹ [stʌd] *n.* **1.** small, button-like device put through two buttonholes to fasten a collar, shirt-front, etc. **2.** large-headed nail or knob, usu. one of many, on the surface of sth. (e.g. a door) as an ornament or (e.g. on the sole of a boot) for protection; small object projecting slightly from the road-surface as a marker, etc.: *reflector* ~*s*, pieces of glass, etc. used on roadsides and reflecting light from headlamps at night. *v.t.* (*-dd-*) set with ~s to strengthen or decorate: ~*ded with* (*jewels, etc.*), having (jewels, etc.) set or scattered in or on the surface.

stud² [stʌd] *n.* number of horses kept by one owner for a special purpose, esp. racing or breeding: ~(*-horse*), stallion.

stu·dent ['stju:dnt] *n.* **1.** person who is studying at a university or another place of higher education or technical training: *medical* ~*s*; (U.S.A. also) *pupil¹*. **2.** anyone who is devoting himself to some branch of learning.

stu·dio ['stju:dɪəʊ] *n.* (pl. ~*s*) **1.** well-lit workroom of a painter, sculptor, photographer, etc. ~ *couch*, couch that can be used as a bed. **2.** hall, etc. where cinema films are made. **3.** room from which radio or television programmes are broadcast.

study ['stʌdɪ] *v.t. & i.* **1.** give time and attention to learning or discovering sth.: ~ *medicine*; ~*ing to be an engineer.* **2.** examine carefully: ~ *a map.* **3.** give care and consideration to: ~ *the wishes of one's friends.* **4.** (in p.p.) intentional: *a studied insult. n.* **1.** (sing. or pl.) ~*ing* (1): *make a* ~ *of history*; *begin one's studies.* **2.** room used by sb. for ~*ing*, reading, writing, etc. **3.** sketch, etc. made for practice or experiment. **4.** sth. that attracts investigation; sth. that is (to be) investigated. **5.** *be in a brown* ~, be too absorbed in thought to observe what is going on.

stu·dious ['stju:djəs] *adj.* **1.** having or showing the habit of ~*ing.* **2.** painstaking.

stuff [stʌf] *n.* **1.** material or substance. **2.** (no pl.) material of which the name is uncertain, unknown, unimportant; material of poor quality; woollen cloth. *v.t.* **1.** press (sth.) tightly (*into*); fill (sth.) tightly (*with*): ~ *feathers into a bag* (*a bag with feathers*). **2.** fill (fowl, rolled meat, etc.) with minced seasoning, etc. before cooking: *a* ~*ed turkey.* **3.** fill out the skin of (a bird or animal) with material to restore its original shape. **4.** cause (a person, an animal) to eat as much as possible: ~ *oneself*, eat greedily. ~*·ing n.* (no pl.) material with which to ~ (e.g. cushions, birds, animals, etc.). ~*y adj.* (*-ier, -iest*) (of a room) badly ventilated.

stul·ti·fy ['stʌltɪfaɪ] *v.t.* cause to seem foolish or to be useless.

stum·ble ['stʌmbl] *v.i.* **1.** strike the foot against sth. and almost fall. **2.** ~ (*up*)*on*, find by chance. **3.** speak in a hesitating way, with pauses and mistakes. *n.* act of stumbling. '**stum·bling-block** *n.* sth. causing difficulty or hesitation.

stump [stʌmp] *n.* **1.** part of a tree remaining in the ground when the trunk has fallen or has been cut down. **2.** anything remaining after the main part has been cut or broken or has worn off (e.g. an amputated limb, a broken or decayed tooth, the stub of a pencil, cigar, etc.). **3.** (cricket) one of the three upright sticks (cf. *wicket*) at which the

stumps (3) and bails² forming a wicket

ball is bowled. *v.i. & t.* **1.** walk (*along, about, etc.*) with stiff, heavy movements. **2.** (colloq.) be too hard for; leave at a loss: *The question* ~*ed me.* **3.** (cricket) end the innings of (a batsman) by touching the ~*s* (3) with the ball while the batsman is out of position. ~*y adj.* (*-ier, -iest*) short and thick.

stun [stʌn] *v.t.* (*-nn-*) **1.** make unconscious by a blow, esp. one on the head. **2.** shock: ~*ned by the bad news.* ~*·ning adj.* (colloq.) extremely beautiful or attractive; splendid.

stung, see *sting* (v.).

stunk, see *stink* (v.).

stunt[1] [stʌnt] *v.t.* stop or check the growth or development of.

stunt[2] [stʌnt] *n.* (colloq.) sth. remarkable done to attract attention; act of bodily skill, often dangerous: ~ *man*, person employed to take an actor's place in performing dangerous ~s.

stu·pe·fy ['stjuːpɪfaɪ] *v.t.* make (sb.'s mind or senses) dull; make clear thought impossible: *stupefied with drink* (*amazement*). **stu·pe·fac·tion** [ˌstjuːpɪˈfækʃn] *n.* (no pl.).

stu·pen·dous [stjuːˈpendəs] *adj.* tremendous; amazing (in size, degree).

stu·pid ['stjuːpɪd] *adj.* slow-thinking; foolish. ~·i·ty [stjuːˈpɪdətɪ] *n.* (no pl.).

stu·por ['stjuːpə*] *n.* almost unconscious condition caused by shock, drugs, drink, etc.

stur·dy ['stɜːdɪ] *adj.* (-*ier*, -*iest*) strong and solid; vigorous. **stur·di·ly** *adv.* **stur·di·ness** *n.* (no pl.).

stur·geon ['stɜːdʒən] *n.* kinds of large fish valued as food and esp. for their roe[1] that is made into caviare.

stut·ter ['stʌtə*] *v.i. & t.* stammer.

sty[1] [staɪ] *n.* pigsty.

sty[2], **stye** [staɪ] *n.* inflamed swelling on the edge of an eyelid.

style [staɪl] *n.* 1. manner of writing or speaking (contrasted with the subject-matter); manner of doing anything, esp. when it is characteristic of an artist or a period of art, etc. 2. (no pl.) quality that marks out anything done or made as superior, fashionable, or distinctive: *do things in* ~, not in a commonplace way. 3. fashion in dress: *the latest* ~ *in coats.* 4. general appearance, form, or design; kind or sort: *made in three* ~s. 5. right title (to be) used when addressing sb. *v.t.* 1. describe by a certain name or ~ (5): *He should be* ~*d 'Right Honourable'.* 2. design. **styl·ish** ['staɪlɪʃ] *adj.* having ~ (2); fashionable. **styl·ist** ['staɪlɪst] *n.* 1. person, esp. a writer, who has or aims at a good literary ~. 2. person who designs fashionable ~s or makes things according to these: *a hair-stylist.* **sty·lis·tic** [staɪˈlɪstɪk] *adj.* of ~ in writing.

sty·lus ['staɪləs] *n.* (pl. -*li* [-laɪ], ~*es*) (esp.) tiny, pointed sapphire or diamond used to cut grooves in records[2] (4) or to reproduce sound from records.

suave [swɑːv] *adj.* smooth in manner; agreeably polite.

sub- [sʌb-] *pref.* 1. (with names of officials or official organizations) deputy or junior: *sub-lieutenant*; *subcommittee.* 2. not quite; not altogether: *subhuman*; *subtropical.* 3. forming a division between two others: *a sub-species.*

sub·al·tern ['sʌbltən] *n.* commissioned army officer of lower rank than a captain.

sub·con·scious [ˌsʌbˈkɒnʃəs] *adj. & n.* (no pl.) (of) mental activities of which we are not (wholly) aware.

sub·con·ti·nent [ˌsʌbˈkɒntɪnənt] *n.* mass of land, large enough to be regarded as a separate continent but forming part of a larger mass: *the S~*, India and Pakistan.

sub·cul·ture ['sʌbˌkʌltʃə*] *n.* cultural group within a larger culture.

sub·di·vide [ˌsʌbdɪˈvaɪd] *v.t. & i.* divide into further divisions. **sub·di·vi·sion** ['sʌbdɪˌvɪʒn] *n.*

sub·due [səbˈdjuː] *v.t.* 1. overcome; bring under control. 2. make quieter; softer, less strong: ~*d light.*

sub·head·ing ['sʌbˌhedɪŋ] *n.* words showing the contents of part of an article, etc. (in a newspaper, etc.).

sub·ject ['sʌbdʒɪkt] *n.* 1. any member of a State except the supreme ruler: *British* ~s. 2. sth. (to be) talked or written about or studied: *the* ~ *of an essay*; *change the* ~, talk about sth. different; ~*-matter*, matter treated of in a book, etc. 3. person, animal, or thing (to be) treated or dealt with: *a* ~ *for experiment.* 4. circumstance, person, or thing that gives cause for specified feeling or action: *a* ~ *for pity.* 5. person with specified (usu. undesirable) tendencies: *a hysterical* ~. 6. (gram.) word(s) in a sentence about which sth. is predicated. *adj.* 1. under foreign government or protection: ~ *races* (*nations*); ~ *to*, owing obedience to. 2. ~ *to*, having a tendency to; liable to: *traffic* ~ *to delays in bad weather.* 3. (also as adv.): ~ *to*, conditional(ly) on: ~ *to your approval.* [səbˈdʒekt] *v.t.* 1. bring, get (a country, nation, person) under control. 2. cause to undergo or experience; expose: ~ *oneself* (*one's friends*) *to criticism.* **sub·jec·tion** [səbˈdʒekʃn] *n.* (no pl.) 1. ~*ing* (1): *the* ~*ion of the rebels.* 2. being ~*ed* (1). **sub·jec·tive** [səbˈdʒektɪv] *adj.* 1. (of ideas, feelings, etc.) existing in the mind; not objective. 2. (gram.) of the ~.

sub·ju·gate ['sʌbdʒʊgeɪt] *v.t.* subdue (1); conquer. **sub·ju·ga·tion** [ˌsʌbdʒʊˈgeɪʃn] *n.* (no pl.).

sub·let [ˌsʌb'let] *v.t. & i.* (-*tt*-) rent to sb. else (a room, house, etc. of which one is a tenant).

sub·lieu·ten·ant [ˌsʌblef'tenənt] *n.* (Gt. Brit.) naval officer with rank next below that of a lieutenant.

sub·lime [sə'blaɪm] *adj.* of the greatest and highest sort; causing wonder or reverence: ~ *scenery*. **sub·lim·i·ty** [sə'blɪmətɪ] *n.*

sub·ma·rine [ˌsʌbmə'riːn] *n. & adj.* (ship able to operate) under the surface of the sea.

sub·merge [səb'mɜːdʒ] *v.t. & i.* 1. put under water; cover with water. 2. sink out of sight; (of submarines) go down under water.

sub·mit [səb'mɪt] *v.t. & i.* (-*tt*-) 1. put (*oneself*) under the control of another. 2. put forward for opinion, discussion, decision, etc.: ~ *plans* (*reports, etc.*) *to sb.* 3. suggest (*that*). 4. surrender; give in: ~ *to the enemy.* **sub·mis·sion** [səb'mɪʃn] *n.* 1. (no pl.) ~ting. 2. theory, etc. ~ted (2). **sub·mis·sive** [səb'mɪsɪv] *adj.* yielding to power or authority; obedient.

sub·nor·mal [ˌsʌb'nɔːml] *adj.* below normal.

sub·or·di·nate [sə'bɔːdnət] *adj.* 1. junior in rank or position (*to*). 2. less important. 3. ~ *clause*, (gram.) one that is introduced by a conjunction and serves as a noun, adjective, or adverb. *n.* sb. in a ~ position; sb. working under another. [sə'bɔːdɪneɪt] *v.t.* treat as ~; make ~ (*to*).

sub·scribe [səb'skraɪb] *v.t. & i.* 1. (agree to) pay (a sum of money) in common with other persons (*to a cause, for* sth.): ~ *£5 to a flood relief fund.* 2. ~ *to*, agree to take (a newspaper, etc.) regularly for a specified time: ~ *for a book*, agree before it is published to pay for a copy or copies. 3. ~ *to* (views, opinions, etc.), agree with (them). **sub·scrib·er** *n.* **sub·scrip·tion** [səb'skrɪpʃn] *n.* 1. (no pl.) subscribing or being ~d. 2. money ~d (for charity, for receiving a newspaper, etc.) or paid for membership of a club. 3. offer of a reduced price to those who order a book before it is published.

sub·se·quent ['sʌbsɪkwənt] *adj.* later; following. ~**ly** *adv.* afterwards.

sub·ser·vi·ent [səb'sɜːvjənt] *adj.* giving too much respect.

sub·side [səb'saɪd] *v.i.* 1. (of flood water) sink to a lower or to the normal level. 2. (of land) sink. 3. (of buildings) settle lower down in the ground. 4. (of winds, passions, etc.) become quiet

after being violent. **sub·si·dence** [səb'saɪdns] *n.*

sub·sid·iary [səb'sɪdjərɪ] *adj.* 1. serving as a help or a support (*to*) but not of first importance. 2. ~ *company*, one controlled by a larger one. *n.* ~ thing or person; ~ company.

sub·si·dy ['sʌbsɪdɪ] *n.* money granted, esp. by a government or society, to an industry or other cause needing help, or to an ally in war, or (e.g. *food subsidies*) to keep prices at a desired level. **sub·si·dize** ['sʌbsɪdaɪz] *v.t.* give a ~ to.

sub·sist [səb'sɪst] *v.i.* exist; be kept in existence (*on* food). **sub·sis·tence** [səb'sɪstəns] *n.* (no pl.) existence; means of existing: *my means of ~ence*, how I make a living.

sub·stance ['sʌbstəns] *n.* 1. material; particular kind of matter: *Iron is a hard ~.* 2. (no pl.) most important part, chief or real meaning, of sth. (e.g. of a speech or argument). 3. (no pl.) firmness; solidity. 4. (no pl.) money; property: *a man of ~.* **sub·stan·tial** [səb'stænʃl] *adj.* 1. strongly or solidly built or made. 2. real; having physical existence. 3. large; considerable: *a substantial meal* (*improvement*). 4. wealthy. 5. *in substantial agreement*, agreeing on all important points. **sub·stan·ti·ate** [səb'stænʃɪeɪt] *v.t.* give facts to support (a claim, statement, etc.).

sub·stan·tive ['sʌbstəntɪv] *n.* (gram.) noun.

sub·sti·tute ['sʌbstɪtjuːt] *n.* person or thing taking the place of or acting for another. *v.t. & i.* put, use, or serve as a ~ (*for*). **sub·sti·tu·tion** [ˌsʌbstɪ'tjuːʃn] *n.*

sub·ter·fuge ['sʌbtəfjuːdʒ] *n.* trick, excuse, esp. one used to evade trouble or sth. unpleasant.

sub·ter·ra·nean [ˌsʌbtə'reɪnjən] *adj.* underground.

sub·ti·tle ['sʌbˌtaɪtl] *n.* secondary title (of a book); translation of the dialogue of a foreign language film, printed on the film.

sub·tle ['sʌtl] *adj.* (~*r*, ~*st*) 1. difficult to perceive or describe because fine or delicate; mysterious: *a ~ charm* (*flavour*); ~ *humour* (*smiles*). 2. quick and clever at seeing or making delicate differences; sensitive: *a ~ observer* (*critic*). 3. ingenious; elaborate; complex: *a ~ argument* (*design*). ~**ty** *n.* 1. (no pl.) quality of being ~. 2. fine distinction; piece of hair-splitting.

sub·tract [səb'trækt] *v.t.* take (a number, quantity) away (*from another* number, etc.). **sub·trac·tion** [səb-'trækʃn] **n.**

sub·urb ['sʌbɜ:b] **n.** outlying district of a town or city. **sub·ur·ban** [sə-'bɜ:bən] **adj.** of or in a ~: *an shops.*

sub·vert [səb'vɜ:t] **v.t.** destroy, overthrow (religion, a government, etc.) by weakening the people's trust or belief. **sub·ver·sive** [səb'vɜ:sɪv] **adj.** tending to ~.

sub·way ['sʌbweɪ] **n. 1.** underground passage or tunnel, esp. one to enable people to get from one side of a busy street to the other. **2.** (U.S.A.) = underground (1).

suc·ceed [sək'si:d] **v.i. & t. 1.** do what one is trying to do; gain one's purpose: ~ *in (passing)* an examination. **2.** do well; go well; have a good result: *The plan ~ed.* **3.** come next after and take the place of: *Who ~ed him as Prime Minister?* **4.** ~ *to,* inherit; have (a title, position, property) on the death of the owner: ~ *to the throne.* **suc·cess** [sək'ses] **n. 1.** (no pl.) ~ing; outcome of an undertaking; accomplishment of what was aimed at; good fortune: *meet with success.* **2.** person or thing that ~s: *The book was a great success.* **suc·cess·ful adj.** having success (*in*). **suc·ces·sion** [sək'seʃn] **n. 1.** (no pl.) coming of one thing after another in time or order: *the succession of the seasons; in succession,* one after the other. **2.** number of things in succession: *a succession of wet days.* **3.** (no pl.) (right of) ~ing (4) to a title, to property, etc.; persons having this right: *first in succession to the throne.* **suc·ces·sive** [sək'sesɪv] **adj.** coming one after the other in an uninterrupted sequence: *win five successive games.* **suc·ces·sor** [sək'sesə*] **n.** person or thing that ~s (3,4) another.

suc·cinct [sək'sɪŋkt] **adj.** expressed briefly and clearly.

suc·cour (U.S.A. **-cor**) ['sʌkə*] **n.** help given in time of need. **v.t.** give ~ to.

suc·cu·lent ['sʌkjʊlənt] **adj.** (of fruit) juicy; (of plants) having thick and fleshy stems and leaves. **suc·cu·lence n.** (no pl.).

suc·cumb [sə'kʌm] **v.i.** yield (*to* a temptation, etc.); die.

such [sʌtʃ] **adj. 1.** of the same kind or degree (*as*): *I have never seen ~ heavy rain as this.* **2.** *You can borrow my bicycle,* ~ *as it is* (suggesting that it is not a good one). *His illness is not ~ as to cause* (not of a kind that might cause) *anxiety.* **3.** *His rudeness was ~ that* (was so marked that) *his parents were ashamed.* **4.** *Don't be in ~* (so great)

a hurry. ***pron.*** ~ persons or things: *I haven't many books on that subject, but ~ as I have* (those that I have) *I will lend you. He's a good businessman and is recognized as ~* (i.e. as a good businessman).

suck [sʌk] **v.t. & i. 1.** draw (liquid) into the mouth by the use of the lip muscles: ~ *the juice from an orange;* ~ *an orange dry;* ~ *(milk from) the mother's breast; (fig.)* ~ *in knowledge.* **2.** hold (sth.) in the mouth and lick, roll about, squeeze, etc. with the tongue: ~ *one's thumb (a toffee).* **3.** take (liquid in or *up*); absorb: *plants ~ing up moisture from the soil.* **n.** act or process of ~ing. **~le** ['sʌkl] **v.t.** feed with milk from the breast or udder. **~ling n.** baby or young animal still being ~led by its mother.

suck·er ['sʌkə*] **n. 1.** unwanted shoot (1) coming up from an underground root or stem, not from the main plant. **2.** organ in some animals enabling them to rest on a surface by suction.

suc·tion ['sʌkʃn] **n.** (no pl.) **1.** action of sucking; removal of air, liquid, etc. from a vessel or cavity so as to produce a partial vacuum and enable air pressure from outside to force in liquid, dust, etc.: *Some pumps and all vacuum cleaners work by ~.* **2.** similar process enabling sth. (e.g. a concave rubber disc) to be held in contact with a surface by means of a vacuum.

sud·den ['sʌdn] **adj.** happening, coming, done, quickly or unexpectedly. **n.** *all of a ~,* unexpectedly. **~ly adv.**

suds [sʌdz] **n. pl.** froth, mass of tiny bubbles, on soapy water.

sue [sju:] **v.t. & i.** (p.t. & p.p. ~d; pres. p. *suing* ['sju:ɪŋ]) **1.** make a legal claim against: ~ *one's employer for unpaid wages.* **2.** beg; ask: ~ *(the enemy) for peace; suing for mercy.*

suede [sweɪd] **n.** kind of soft leather used for making gloves, shoes, etc.

su·et ['sjʊɪt] **n.** (no pl.) solid fat covering the kidneys of sheep and oxen, used in cooking.

suf·fer ['sʌfə*] **v.i. & t. 1.** feel or have pain, loss, etc.; experience, undergo (sth. unpleasant): ~ *from* (often have) *headaches. His business ~ed during the war.* ~ *pain (defeat).* **2.** allow; tolerate: *We can't ~ such insolence.* **~ance n.** (no pl.) permission implied by absence of objection: *He's here on ~ance* (allowed to be here but not wanted). **~ing n.** pain; (pl.) feelings of pain; painful experiences.

suf·fice [sə'faɪs] *v.i. & t.* be enough: *Will that ~ for your needs (~ you)?*

suf·fi·cient [sə'fɪʃənt] *adj.* enough.

suf·fi·cien·cy *n.* (no pl.) sufficient quantity (*of*).

suf·fix ['sʌfɪks] *n.* letter(s) or syllable(s) added at the end of a word to make another word (e.g. *y* added to *rust* to make *rusty*).

suf·fo·cate ['sʌfəkeɪt] *v.t. & i.* choke; kill by stopping the breathing of; cause or have difficulty in breathing. **suf·fo·ca·tion** [,sʌfə'keɪʃn] *n.* (no pl.).

suf·frage ['sʌfrɪdʒ] *n.* (right to) vote in elections.

suf·fuse [sə'fjuːz] *v.t.* (esp. of colours, tears) spread slowly over the surface of: *the evening sky ~d with crimson.*

sug·ar ['ʃʊgə*] *n.* sweet substance obtained from various plants, esp. the *~-cane* and the *~-beet. v.t.* sweeten or mix with ~. **~y** *adj.* tasting of ~; (fig., of music, etc.) too sweet.

sug·gest [sə'dʒest] *v.t.* 1. propose; put forward for consideration, as a possibility: *~ a visit to the theatre (that we should go to the theatre).* 2. bring (an idea, etc.) into the mind: *The look on his face ~ed fear* (caused others to think he was frightened). **sug·ges·tion** [sə'dʒestʃn] *n.* 1. (no pl.) ~ing: *on your ~ion.* 2. idea, plan, etc. that is ~ed. 3. slight indication: *speaking with a ~ion of a foreign accent.* **sug·ges·tive** *adj.* tending to bring ideas, etc. to the mind: *a ~ive lecture;* ~ing sth. indecent.

sui·cide ['sjʊɪsaɪd] *n.* 1. self-murder; instance of this: *commit ~.* 2. person who intentionally kills himself. 3. (no pl.) action destructive to one's own interests. **sui·ci·dal** [sjʊɪ'saɪdl] *adj.* of ~; (fig.) very harmful to one's own interests.

suit [suːt] *n.* 1. set of articles of outer clothing of the same material: *a ~ of armour; man's ~,* jacket (, waistcoat,) and trousers; *woman's ~,* coat and skirt. 2. request made to a superior, esp. to a ruler. 3. (also *law~*) case in a lawcourt. 4. any of the four sets of cards (spades, hearts, diamonds, clubs) used in many card games: *follow ~,* (a) play a card of the ~ that has been led; (b) (fig.) do what someone else does. 5. asking a woman's hand in marriage. *v.t.* 1. satisfy; meet the needs of; be convenient to or right for: *Does the climate ~ you?* 2. (esp. of clothes, hair-style, etc.) look well on; be appropriate for: *That hat doesn't ~ you.* 3. ~ *sth. to,* make fit or appropriate: ~ *the punishment to the crime;* ~ *the action to the word,* carry out the promise or threat at once. 4. (p.p.) *be ~ed for (to),* be fitted: *Is he ~ed for teaching (to be a teacher)* (i.e. is he the right sort of man)? **~able** ['suːtəbl] *adj.* right for the purpose or occasion. **~ably** *adv.* **~abil·i·ty** [,suːtə'bɪlətɪ] *n.* **'~-case** *n.* portable, flat-sided case for carrying one's clothes, etc. when one is travelling. **~or** *n.* 1. person bringing a law~. 2. man courting a woman.

suite [swiːt] *n.* 1. personal attendants of an important person (e.g. a ruler). 2. complete set of matching articles of furniture: *a bedroom ~.* 3. set of rooms (e.g. in a hotel).

sulk [sʌlk] *v.i.* be in a bad temper and show this by refusing to talk, etc. **~s** *n. pl. the ~s,* condition of ~ing. **~y** *adj.* (-ier, -iest) ~ing; having a tendency to ~. **~i·ly** *adv.*

sul·len ['sʌlən] *adj.* 1. silently bad-tempered; unforgiving. 2. (of the sky, etc.) dark and gloomy.

sul·ly ['sʌlɪ] *v.t.* stain or discredit (sb.'s reputation, etc.).

sul·phur (U.S.A. **-fur**) ['sʌlfə*] *n.* (no pl.) light-yellow, non-metallic element that burns with a blue flame and a strong smell. **sul·phu·ric** (U.S.A. **sulfu-**) [sʌl'fjʊərɪk] *adj.*

sul·tan ['sʌltən] *n.* Muslim ruler.

sul·try ['sʌltrɪ] *adj.* (-ier, -iest) 1. (of the weather) hot and airless. 2. (of a person's temper) passionate.

sum [sʌm] *n.* 1. total obtained by adding together numbers or amounts. 2. amount of money. 3. problem in arithmetic: *good at ~s; do a ~ in one's head.* 4. *in ~,* in a few words. *v.t. & i.* (-mm-) ~ *up,* (a) give the total of; (b) express briefly (the chief points of what has been said, etc.); (c) form a judgement or opinion of. **~ma·ry** ['sʌmərɪ] *n.* brief account of the chief points. *adj.* done or given without delay or attention to small matters: *~mary justice.* **~ma·rize** ['sʌməraɪz] *v.t.* be or make a ~mary of.

sum·mer ['sʌmə*] *n.* (in temperate climates the) warmest season of the year. **'~-house** *n.* garden shelter with seats. ~ **school** *n.* course of lectures during the ~ vacations, esp. at a university. **'~-time** *n.* 1. (also *~time*) weather or season of ~. 2. ~ *time,* daylight saving time.

sum·mit ['sʌmɪt] *n.* highest point; top: (fig.) *the ~ of his ambition; a ~ meeting,* one between heads of governments.

sum·mon ['sʌmən] *v.t.* **1.** demand the presence of; call upon to appear, esp. in a lawcourt; call (people) together for a meeting, etc.: ~ *Parliament.* **2.** ~ *up,* gather together (one's energy, courage) (*to do* sth., *for* a task, etc.). **~s** *n.* **1.** order to appear before a judge. **2.** command to do sth. or appear somewhere. *v.t.* serve a ~s (1) on.

sump [sʌmp] *n.* **1.** inner casing of a petrol engine, containing oil. **2.** hole, pit, or well into which waste liquid drains.

sump·tu·ous ['sʌmptjʊəs] *adj.* costly-looking; magnificent: *a ~ feast.*

sun [sʌn] *n.* **1.** heavenly body from which the earth gets warmth and light. **2.** light or warmth from the ~, or both: *have the ~ in one's eyes; sitting in the ~.* **3.** any fixed star with satellites. *v.t. & i.* (-*nn-*) put in the rays of the ~; expose (oneself) to the rays of the ~: *The cat was ~ning itself on the path.* '~·blind *n.* shade or awning fixed outside a window. '~·burn *n.* tanning or inflammation of the skin caused by exposure to the ~. '~·di·al *n.* device that shows the time by the shadow of a rod or plate on a dial (1). '~·down

a sunblind   a sundial

n. ~set. '~·flow·er *n.* tall plant with large, yellow flowers. '~·glass·es *n. pl.* tinted glasses to protect the eyes from the ~. '~·lit *adj.* lighted by the ~. ~ny *adj.* (-*ier,* -*iest*) **1.** bright with ~light. **2.** (fig.) cheerful: *her ~ny smiles.* '~·rise *n.* (time of the) ~'s appearance above the horizon. '~·set *n.* (time of the) ~'s disappearance below the horizon; colours seen in the sky at this time. '~·shade *n.* **1.** sort of umbrella used for keeping off ~-light; parasol. **2.** awning. **3.** (pl.) (esp. U.S.A.) = ~glasses. '~·shine *n.* (no pl.) light of the ~. '~·spot *n.* dark patch on the ~ at times. '~·stroke *n.* (no pl.) illness caused by excessive exposure to the ~.

sun·dae ['sʌndeɪ] *n.* portion of ice-cream served with crushed fruit, nuts, etc.

Sun·day ['sʌndɪ] *n.* seventh day of the week, observed by Christians as a day

of rest and worship: *a month of ~s,* an indefinitely long period; ~ *school,* one held on ~ for religious teaching.

sun·dry ['sʌndrɪ] *adj.* various; several: *all and ~,* everybody collectively and individually. **sun·dries** *n. pl.* various small items not separately named.

sung, see *sing.*

sunk, see *sink* (v.). **~·en** ['sʌnkən] *adj.* (esp. of sb.'s face or cheeks) fallen in; hollow-looking.

su·per ['su:pə*] *adj.* (sl.) splendid; excellent.

su·per- ['su:pə*-] *pref.* **1.** more or greater than: *superhuman; superman; supernormal; superstar.* **2.** to an unusually high degree: *supercharged; superheated; superabundant.* **3.** above; on the top: *superimpose.*

su·per·an·nu·ate [ˌsu:pə'rænjʊeɪt] *v.t.* give a pension to (an employee) when he is old or unable to work; dismiss (sb.) because of age or weakness. **su·per·an·nu·a·tion** ['su:pəˌrænjʊ'eɪʃn] *n.*

su·perb [sju:'pɜ:b] *adj.* magnificent.

su·per·cil·ious [ˌsu:pə'sɪlɪəs] *adj.* showing contemptuous indifference.

su·per·fi·cial [ˌsu:pə'fɪʃl] *adj.* **1.** of or on the surface only; not going deep: *a ~ wound.* **2.** not thorough or profound: *a ~ book (knowledge of sth.).* **~ly** *adv.*

su·per·fine [ˌsu:pə'faɪn] *adj.* **1.** unusually fine in quality. **2.** excessively refined.

su·per·flu·ous [su:'pɜ:flʊəs] *adj.* more than is needed or wanted. **su·per·flu·ity** [ˌsu:pə'flʊətɪ] *n.* ~ quantity.

su·per·in·tend [ˌsu:pərɪn'tend] *v.t. & i.* manage; watch and direct (work, etc.). **su·per·in·ten·dence** *n.* (no pl.). **su·per·in·ten·dent** *n.* **1.** person who ~s; manager. **2.** police officer above the rank of chief inspector.

su·pe·ri·or [su:'pɪərɪə*] *adj.* **1.** better than the average: ~ *cloth;* ~ *grades of coffee.* **2.** greater in number: *The enemy attacked with ~ forces (were in ~ numbers).* **3.** ~ *to,* better than; higher in rank or position than; not influenced by, not giving way to (e.g. flattery, temptation, etc.). **4.** priggish; supercilious. *n.* **1.** person of higher rank, authority, etc. than another or who is better, etc. than another (*in* sth.). **2.** *S~,* head of a monastery or convent: *Father S~,* abbot; *Mother S~,* abbess. **~·i·ty** [su:ˌpɪərɪ'ɒrətɪ] *n.* (no pl.).

su·per·la·tive [su:'pɜ:lətɪv] *adj.* **1.** of the highest degree or quality: *a man of ~ wisdom.* **2.** *the ~ degree,* (gram.)

the form of an adjective and adverb expressing the highest degree (e.g. *best, most foolishly*). *n.* (gram.) ⁓ degree or form.

su·per·mar·ket [ˈsuːpəˌmɑːkɪt] *n.* large self-service store for food, household articles, etc.

su·per·nat·u·ral [ˌsuːpəˈnætʃrəl] *adj.* spiritual; of that which is not controlled or explained by physical laws.

su·per·nu·mer·ary [ˌsuːpəˈnjuːmərərɪ] *n. & adj.* (sb. or sth.) in excess of the normal number; (person) engaged for extra work; (actor) having a small part but nothing to say.

su·per·sede [ˌsuːpəˈsiːd] *v.t.* take the place of; put or use sb. or sth. in the place of: *Buses have* ⁓*d trams in most cities.*

su·per·son·ic [ˌsuːpəˈsɒnɪk] *adj.* (of speeds) greater than that of sound; (of aircraft) able to fly at such speed.

su·per·sti·tion [ˌsuːpəˈstɪʃn] *n.* 1. unreasoning belief in, fear of, what is unknown or mysterious, esp. belief in magic. 2. idea, practice, etc. founded on such belief. **su·per·sti·tious** [ˌsuːpəˈstɪʃəs] *adj.* of, showing, resulting from, ⁓; believing in ⁓s.

su·per·struc·ture [ˈsuːpəˌstrʌktʃə*] *n.* structure built on sth. else; parts of a ship above the main deck.

su·per·vene [ˌsuːpəˈviːn] *v.i.* come or happen as an interruption of or a change from a condition or process.

su·per·vise [ˈsuːpəvaɪz] *v.t.* watch and direct (work, workers, an organization). **su·per·vi·sor** *n.* **su·per·vi·sion** [ˌsuːpəˈvɪʒn] *n.* (no pl.).

su·pine [sjuːˈpaɪn] *adj.* 1. lying flat on the back. 2. inactive; slow to act.

sup·per [ˈsʌpə*] *n.* meal taken at the end of the day, esp. one that is less formal and substantial than dinner.

sup·plant [səˈplɑːnt] *v.t.* 1. supersede: *Trams are being* ⁓*ed by buses.* 2. take the place of (sb.), esp. after getting him out of office, etc. by unfair means: ⁓ *a rival.*

sup·ple [ˈsʌpl] *adj.* easily bent; not stiff: *the* ⁓ *limbs of a child; a* ⁓ *mind,* (fig.) quick to respond to ideas.

sup·ple·ment [ˈsʌplɪmənt] *n.* 1. sth. added later to improve or complete (e.g. a dictionary). 2. extra and separate addition to a periodical. [ˈsʌplɪment] *v.t.* make additions to. **sup·ple·men·ta·ry** [ˌsʌplɪˈmentərɪ] *adj.* additional; extra: ⁓*ary estimates.*

sup·pli·cate [ˈsʌplɪkeɪt] *v. & i.* ask (sb.) humbly and earnestly (*for* sth.). **sup·pli·ant** [ˈsʌplɪənt] *n. & adj.* (person) asking humbly for sth.

sup·ply [səˈplaɪ] *v.t.* 1. give or provide (sth. needed or asked for): ⁓ *customers with food (food for the children).* 2. meet (a need): ⁓ *the need for more houses. n.* 1. (no pl.) ⁓ing. 2. that which is supplied; stock or amount of sth. that is obtainable: ⁓ *and demand,* quantities available and quantities asked for. 3. (pl.) (esp.) stores necessary for some public, esp. military need. **sup·pli·er** *n.* person or firm ⁓ing goods, etc.

sup·port [səˈpɔːt] *v.t.* 1. bear the weight of; hold up or keep in place. 2. strengthen; help (sb. or sth.) to go on: ⁓ *a claim (a hospital, a political party).* 3. provide for; supply (a person, one's family) with food, clothes, etc. 4. endure. *n.* 1. (no pl.) ⁓ing or being ⁓ed: *in* ⁓ *of,* in order to help or to promote. 2. sb. or sth. that ⁓s. ⁓·er *n.* person who ⁓s; device (2) that ⁓s.

sup·pose [səˈpəʊz] *v.t.* 1. let it be thought that; take it as a fact that: *S*⁓ *the world were flat.* 2. guess; think: *What do you* ⁓ *he wanted?* 3. require as a condition; imply: *Creation* ⁓*s a creator.* 4. (forming an imperative, or used to make suggestions): *S*⁓ *we go* (i.e. let's go) *for a swim. S*⁓ *you have another try.* 5. *be* ⁓*d to,* (a) be expected to: *You're* ⁓*d to know the rules.* (b) (in the neg.) (colloq.) not be allowed to: *You're not* ⁓*d to read this letter.* ⁓**d** *adj.* accepted as being so: *his* ⁓*d generosity.* **sup·pos·ed·ly** [səˈpəʊzɪdlɪ] *adv.* as is (or was) ⁓d. **sup·pos·ing** *conj.* if. **sup·po·si·tion** [ˌsʌpəˈzɪʃn] *n.* 1. (no pl.) supposing: *based on supposition.* 2. sth. ⁓d; guess.

sup·press [səˈpres] *v.t.* 1. put an end to the activity or existence of: ⁓ *a rising (the slave-trade, etc.).* 2. prevent from being seen or known: ⁓ *a yawn (the news).* **sup·pres·sion** *n.*

sup·pu·rate [ˈsʌpjʊəreɪt] *v.i.* form pus.

su·preme [sʊˈpriːm] *adj.* highest in rank or authority; of the greatest importance or value. *the S*⁓ *Being,* God. ⁓·**ly** *adv.* **su·prem·a·cy** [sʊˈpreməsɪ] *n.* (no pl.) being ⁓; highest authority.

sur·charge [ˈsɜːtʃɑːdʒ] *n.* payment demanded in addition to the usual charge (e.g. as a penalty for an understamped letter). [sɜːˈtʃɑːdʒ] *v.t.* make an additional charge to or for.

sure [ʃʊə*] *adj.* (⁓*r,* ⁓*st*) 1. ⁓ *of,* ⁓ *that,* free from doubt; certain: *feel* ⁓ *of oneself,* feel self-confident. 2. *be* ⁓ *to* (come, etc.), do not fail to (come, etc.); *make* ⁓, satisfy oneself; do what is needed in order to feel certain, to get sth., etc. **3.** proved or tested; trustworthy: *a ~ remedy*; *a ~ messenger*. **adv.** *~ enough*, certainly; as expected; *as ~ as*, as certain as. **~ly adv. 1.** with certainty or safety. **2.** if experience or probability can be trusted. **~ty** ['ʃʊərətɪ] **n.** (sth. given as a) guarantee; person who makes himself responsible for the conduct or debt(s) of another: *stand ~ty for sb.*

surf [sɜːf] **n.** (no pl.) waves breaking in white foam on the sea-shore, on sandbanks, or on reefs. **'~-board n.** long, narrow board used in *~ing*. **'~-boat n.** boat specially built for use in *~*. **~ing**, **'~-ˌrid·ing ns.** sport of riding the *~* on a *~*-board.

sur·face ['sɜːfɪs] **n. 1.** the outside of any object, etc.; any of the sides of an object; the top of a liquid: *a smooth ~*. *The submarine rose to the ~*. **2.** outward appearance; what is seen or learnt from a quick view or consideration. **v.i.** (e.g. of a submarine) rise to the *~* of the sea.

sur·feit ['sɜːfɪt] **n.** too much of anything, esp. food and drink; feeling of discomfort, caused by a *~*. **v.t. & i.** overfeed; overeat (*oneself on* sth.); (cause to) take too much of something.

surge [sɜːdʒ] **v.i.** move forward, roll on, in or like waves: *The floods ~d over the valley. The crowds ~d out of the railway station.* **n.** (forward rush of) waves; a wave; surging motion: *the ~ of the ocean*; (fig.) *a ~ of anger*.

sur·geon ['sɜːdʒən] **n.** doctor who performs operations: *a heart ~*. **sur·gery** ['sɜːdʒərɪ] **n. 1.** (no pl.) treatment of injuries and diseases by a *~*. **2.** doctor's room where patients come to consult him. **sur·gi·cal** ['sɜːdʒɪkl] **adj.** of, by, or for surgery.

sur·ly ['sɜːlɪ] **adj.** (*-ier, -iest*) bad-tempered and unfriendly. **sur·li·ness n.** (no pl.).

sur·mise [sɜːˈmaɪz] **v.t. & i. &** ['sɜːmaɪz] **n.** guess; conjecture.

sur·mount [sɜːˈmaʊnt] **v.t. 1.** overcome (difficulties, etc.); get over (obstacles). **2.** *be ~ed by (with)*, have on or over the top.

sur·name ['sɜːneɪm] **n.** name common to all members of a family.

sur·pass [səˈpɑːs] **v.t.** do or be better than; exceed.

sur·plice ['sɜːplɪs] **n.** loose-fitting (usu. white) gown with wide sleeves worn by some priests and choristers during church services.

sur·plus ['sɜːpləs] **n.** amount (esp.

money) that remains after needs have been supplied; excess of receipts over expenditure. (Cf. *deficit*.)

a surplice

sur·prise [səˈpraɪz] **n.** (feeling caused by) sth. sudden or unexpected. **v.t. 1.** give a feeling of *~* to. **2.** *be ~d*, experience *~*. **3.** come upon (sb., the enemy) unexpectedly, without previous warning. **sur·pris·ing adj.** causing *~*.

sur·ren·der [səˈrendə*] **v.t. & i. 1.** give up (oneself, a ship, town, etc.) (*to* the enemy, the police, etc.). **2.** give up possession of (freedom, liberty. etc. *to* sb.). **3.** *~ oneself to*, yield or give way to (a habit, an emotion such as despair, etc.). **n.** (no pl.) *~ing* or being *~ed*.

sur·rep·ti·tious [ˌsʌrəpˈtɪʃəs] **adj.** (of actions) done secretly or stealthily.

sur·round [səˈraʊnd] **v.t.** be, go, all round; shut in on all sides. **~ings n. pl.** everything around and about a place; conditions that may affect a person: *living in pleasant ~ings*.

sur·tax ['sɜːtæks] **n.** additional tax on high personal incomes.

sur·vey [səˈveɪ] **v.t. 1.** take a general view of. **2.** examine the general condition of sth.: *~ the international situation*. **3.** measure and map out the position, size, boundaries, etc. of (land, a country, coast, etc.). ['sɜːveɪ] **n. 1.** general view. **2.** piece of land-*~ing*; map or record[2] (1) of this. **~·or** [səˈveɪə*] **n. 1.** person whose business is the *~ing* of land or buildings. **2.** official inspector.

sur·vive [səˈvaɪv] **v.i. & t.** continue to live or exist; live or exist longer than; remain alive after: *those who ~d the earthquake.* **sur·viv·al** [səˈvaɪvl] **n. 1.** (no pl.) surviving. **2.** person, custom, belief, etc. that has *~d* but is looked upon as belonging to past times. **sur·viv·or** *n.* person who has ～d: *the survivors of a shipwreck.*

sus·cep·ti·ble [səˈseptəbl] *adj.* **1.** easily influenced by feelings: *a girl with a ～ nature.* **2.** ～ *to,* affected by; sensitive to: ～ *to flattery (pain, etc.).* **3.** ～ *of,* that can receive or be given: ～ *of proof.* **sus·cep·ti·bil·i·ty** [səˌseptəˈbɪlətɪ] *n.* **1.** (no pl.) being ～. **2.** (pl.) sensitive feelings of a person.

sus·pect [səˈspekt] *v.t.* **1.** have an idea or feeling (concerning the possible existence of): *He ～ed that the enemy were hiding among the trees. He ～ed an ambush.* **2.** feel doubt about: ～ *the truth of an account.* **3.** have a feeling that sb. may be guilty (of): ～*ed of telling lies.* [ˈsʌspekt] *n.* person ～ed of wrongdoing. [ˈsʌspekt] *pred. adj.* of doubtful character; ～ed.

sus·pend [səˈspend] *v.t.* **1.** hang up: ～ *a lamp from the ceiling.* **2.** (p.p.) ～*ed,* (of solid particles, in the air, in a liquid) sustained somewhere between top and bottom: *dust (smoke) ～ed in the still air.* **3.** stop for a time: ～ *payment,* stop payment (e.g. when bankrupt, etc.). **4.** announce that (sb.) cannot be allowed to perform his duties, enjoy privileges, etc. for a time. **5.** delay; keep in an undecided state for a time: ～ *judgement.* ～**er** *n.* (*a pair of*) ～*ers,* (Gt. Brit.) elastic band, etc. to hold up socks or stockings; (U.S.A.) = braces. **sus·pen·sion** [səˈspenʃn] *n.* (no pl.) **1.** ～*ing* or being ～*ed:* *suspension bridge,* bridge ～*ed* on or by means of steel cables. **2.** means by which a vehicle is supported on its axles.

a suspension bridge

sus·pense [səˈspens] *n.* (no pl.) anxious uncertainty (about news, events, decisions, etc.): *keep sb. in ～,* keep him waiting for news about sth.

sus·pi·cion [səˈspɪʃn] *n.* **1.** feeling of a person who suspects; feeling that sth. is wrong. **2.** suspecting or being suspected: *above ～,* too obviously good, honest, etc. that ～ is out of the question. **3.** (no pl.) slight taste or suggestion (of). **sus·pi·cious** [səˈspɪʃəs] *adj.* having, showing, or causing ～. **sus·tain** [səˈsteɪn] *v.t.* **1.** keep from

falling or sinking. **2.** (enable to) keep up or last: ～*ing food* (that gives strength); ～ *an argument* (attempt). **3.** suffer: ～ *a loss* (defeat). **4.** (law) decide in favour of; admit; uphold. **sus·te·nance** [ˈsʌstɪnəns] *n.* (no pl.) (nourishing quality in) food and drink.

su·ze·rain [ˈsuːzəreɪn] *n.* State or ruler in relation to another country over which it or he has some control or authority.

swab [swɒb] *n.* **1.** mop or pad for cleaning. **2.** absorbent pad for medical use; specimen (e.g. of mucus) so taken. *v.t.* (-bb-) clean with a ～; take (*up* liquid) with a ～.

swag·ger [ˈswægə*] *v.i.* walk or behave in a self-important or self-satisfied manner.

swal·low¹ [ˈswɒləʊ] *v.t. & i.* **1.** cause or allow to go down one's throat: ～ *one's lunch,* eat it quickly; work the muscles of the throat as when ～*ing* sth. (esp. under emotional stress): *He ～ed hard and turned away.* **2.** take in; use (*up*); absorb: *earnings that were ～ed up by doctors' bills.* **3.** (fig.) ～ *a story,* believe it too easily; ～ *an insult,* accept it meekly; ～ *one's anger,* not show it; ～ *one's words,* take them back; express regret for them. *n.* **1.** act of ～*ing.* **2.** amount ～*ed* at one time.

swal·low² [ˈswɒləʊ] *n.* kinds of small, fast-flying, fork-tailed bird associated with summer.

swam, see *swim* (v.).

swamp [swɒmp] *n.* (area of) soft, wet land; marsh. *v.t.* **1.** flood, soak (e.g. a boat, the people or things in it) with water. **2.** (fig.) overwhelm (*with*): ～*ed with work* (orders for goods, etc.). ～**y** *adj.* (-ier, -iest).

swan [swɒn] *n.* large, graceful, long-necked (usu. white) water-bird.

swank [swæŋk] *v.i.* (colloq.) swagger; behave or talk boastfully; show off.

swap, swop [swɒp] *v.t. & i.* (-pp-) (colloq.) exchange by barter: ～ *chocolate for cigarettes;* ～ *places with sb.,* exchange seats; ～ *partners.*

swarm¹ [swɔːm] *n.* **1.** colony, large number, of insects, birds, etc. moving about together: *a ～ of ants* (bees). **2.** (pl.) large numbers (*of children, etc.*). *v.i.* **1.** (of bees) fly off together in a body from a hive to start a new colony. **2.** be present in large numbers; move in a ～: *People ～ed into the cinemas.* **3.** be ～*ing with,* ～ *with,* be crowded, filled, or covered with: *a dog ～ing with fleas. The zoo ～ed with visitors.*

swarm² [swɔːm] *v.i. & t.* climb (*up*

a tree, rope, etc.) by clasping with the hands and legs alternately.

swarthy ['swɔːðɪ] *adj.* (*-ier*, *-iest*) dark(-complexioned).

swas·ti·ka ['swɒstɪkə] *n.* symbol or ornament in the form of a cross, as shown here: 卐.

swat [swɒt] *v.t.* (*-tt-*) (colloq.) hit with a quick, hard blow: ~ *a fly*.

swathe [sweɪð] *v.t.* wrap or bind up: *His leg was ~d in bandages.*

sway [sweɪ] *v.t. & i.* **1.** (cause to) move, first to one side and then to the other: *The branches ~ed in the wind.* **2.** control or influence; govern the direction of: *~ed by his feelings; a speech that ~ed the voters.* *n.* (no pl.) **1.** ~ing movement. **2.** rule; control: *under the ~ of a dictator.*

swear [sweə*] *v.t. & i.* (p.t. *swore* [swɔː*], p.p. *sworn* [swɔːn]) **1.** say solemnly or with emphasis: ~ *to do sth.*; ~ *that one will do sth.* **2.** take an oath; cause (sb.) to take an oath: ~ *a witness*; ~ *sb. to secrecy.* **3.** ~ *by sth.*, (a) appeal to as a witness and guarantee of the oath; (b) (colloq.) use and have great confidence in (e.g. a medicine); ~ *off sth.*, declare that one will give up (smoking, etc.). **4.** use curses and profane language. '**~word** *n.* word used in ~ing (4).

sweat [swet] *n.* **1.** (no pl.) moisture that is given off by the body through the skin. **2.** condition of a person or animal when covered with ~: *in a ~.* **3.** (no pl.) ~-like moisture on a surface (e.g. condensation on an inner wall). **4.** (no pl.) (colloq.) hard work. *v.i. & t.* **1.** give out ~; (fig.) be in a state of terror or suffering. **2.** work hard. **3.** make (an athlete, a horse) ~ (by exercise). **4.** make (sb.) work very hard at starvation wages under poor conditions: *~ed labour.* '**~er** *n.* knitted jacket or jersey, usu. of thick wool. **~y** *adj.* (*-ier*, *-iest*) (e.g. of clothes) wet with, smelling of, ~.

Swede [swiːd] *n.* native or inhabitant of Sweden.

Swed·ish ['swiːdɪʃ] *n. & adj.* (language) of Sweden or its inhabitants.

sweep [swiːp] *v.t. & i.* (p.t. & p.p. *swept* [swept]) **1.** clear away (dust, dirt, etc.) with a brush or broom; clean by doing this: ~ *up the dust*; ~ *a floor* (*a chimney*). **2.** move or pass quickly over or along, esp. so as to overcome or remove anything in the way: *Houses were swept away by the floods. The waves swept me off my feet.* **3.** extend in an unbroken line or curve or expanse: *The coast ~s northwards.* **4.** pass lightly across or along; pass (eyes, hands, etc.) quickly along or over: *The searchlights swept the sky. Her dress swept the ground.* **5.** move in a stately manner: *She swept out of the room.* *n.* **1.** act of ~ing with, or as with, a broom: *Give the room a good ~. make a clean ~* (of sth.), (fig.) get rid of (e.g. sth. old or outdated). **2.** ~ing movement: *with a ~ of his arm.* **3.** long, curving stretch of country, of a road, or a river. **4.** range of sth. moving or moved in a wide curve: *Don't go within the ~ of the scythe.* **5.** (also *chimney-~*) man whose work is ~ing soot from chimneys. '**~er** *n.* person or thing that ~s: *street-~ers; carpet-~er.* **~ing** *adj.* far-reaching; taking in very much: *~ing changes; a ~ing statement* (regardless of limitations or exceptions). '**~stake** *n.*, '**~stakes** *n. pl.* (usu. sing. v.) form of gambling, esp. on a horse-race.

sweet [swiːt] *adj.* **1.** tasting like sugar or honey: *have a ~ tooth, like ~ things.* **2.** fresh and pure: ~ *milk.* **3.** pleasant or attractive: *a ~ scent* (*voice*); *a ~ temper; a ~ little boy.* *n.* **1.** dish of ~ food (tart², pudding, etc.) as one course of a meal. **2.** ~meat. **3.** (pl.) delights; pleasures. **4.** (as a form of address) darling. **~en** ['swiːtn] *v.t. & i.* make or become ~. **~en·ing** *n.* substance that ~ens. '**~heart** *n.* either of a pair of lovers. '**~meat** *n.* piece of ~-tasting food, usu. consisting chiefly of sugar or chocolate with flavouring or filling, or of fruit preserved in sugar.

swell [swel] *v.t. & i.* (p.t. *~ed* [sweld], p.p. *swollen* ['swəʊlən] or *~ed*) **1.** (cause to) become greater in volume, thickness, or force: *Wood often ~s when wet.* (fig.) *He* (*His heart*) *was ~ing with pride. suffering from a ~ed* (*swollen*) *head.* (sl., from conceit). **2.** ~ (*out*), (cause to) have a curved surface: *sails ~ing out in the wind; the wind ~ed the sails.* *n.* **1.** gradual increase of sound: *the ~ of an organ.* **2.** (no pl.) slow rise and fall of the sea's surface after a storm. **3.** (colloq.) smartly dressed person; person of distinction or ability. *adj.* (colloq.) **1.** fashionably dressed; smart; distinguished. **2.** fine; splendid. **~ing** *n.* swollen place on the body (e.g. as a result of a blow or of a diseased tooth).

swel·ter ['sweltə*] *v.i.* be uncomfortably warm; suffer from the heat.

swept, see *sweep* (v.).

swerve [swɜːv] *v.t. & i.* (cause to) change direction suddenly: *The car ⁓d to avoid knocking the boy down.* *n.* swerving movement.

swift[1] [swɪft] *adj.* quick. ⁓·**ly** *adv.* ⁓·**ness** *n.* (no pl.).

swift[2] [swɪft] *n.* small, insect-eating bird with long wings, similar to a swallow.

swill [swɪl] *v.t. & i.* (often ⁓ *out*) rinse. *n.* **1.** rinsing. **2.** (no pl.) (partly) liquid, edible refuse as pig-food.

swim [swɪm] *v.i. & t.* (-*mm*-; p.t. *swam* [swæm], p.p. *swum* [swʌm]) **1.** move the body through water by using arms, legs, fins, the tail, etc.; cross by ⁓ming: *Fish ⁓. ⁓ (across) the river;* go ⁓ming; ⁓ming-pool, artificial pool[1] suitable for ⁓ming in. **2.** be covered (*with*), overflowing (*with*), or (as if) floating (*in* or *on*): *eyes ⁓ming with tears; meat ⁓ming in gravy.* **3.** seem to be moving round and round; have a dizzy feeling: *The room swam before his eyes. His head swam. n.* **1.** act of ⁓ming (1): *go for a ⁓.* **2.** *be in* (*out of*) *the ⁓,* be (not be) taking part in, aware of, what is going on. ⁓·**ming·ly** *adv.* easily and without trouble: *getting along ⁓mingly.*

swin·dle ['swɪndl] *v.t. & i.* cheat (sb. *out of* money, etc.); get (money, etc. *out of* sb.) by cheating. *n.* piece of swindling; sth. sold, etc. that is less valuable than it is described to be. ⁓**r** *n.* person who ⁓s.

swine [swaɪn] *n.* (pl. ⁓) **1.** (U.S.A., formal, or zool.) pig. **2.** person of greedy or bestial habits.

swing [swɪŋ] *v.t. & i.* (p.t. & p.p. *swung* [swʌŋ]) **1.** (of sth. fixed at one end or side) (cause to) move forwards and backwards or in a curve: *⁓ing one's arms. The door swung open.* **2.** walk or run with a free, easy movement: *soldiers advancing at a ⁓ing trot.* **3.** (cause to) turn in a curve: *The car swung round the corner.* **4.** (sl.) be lively or up to date. *n.* **1.** ⁓ing movement or

a swing (4)

walk. **2.** strong rhythm: *go with a ⁓,* go easily, without trouble; *in full ⁓,* active; in full operation. **3.** ⁓ (*music*),

(1930's) orchestral jazz, usually played by big bands. **4.** seat held by ropes or chains for ⁓ing on; spell of ⁓ing on such a seat. ⁓**er** *n.* (sl.) youthful and lively person who keeps up with the latest fashions, etc.

swirl [swɜːl] *v.t. & i.* (of liquid, air, dust, etc.) (cause to) move or flow at varying speeds, with twists and turns: *dust ⁓ing about the streets. n.* ⁓ing movement; eddy.

swish [swɪʃ] *v.t. & i.* **1.** move (sth.) through the air with a hissing or brushing sound; cut (sth. *off*) in this way. **2.** make, move with, a sound like that of a cane or a whip cutting the air. *n.* sound of, sound suggesting, a cane or whip being ⁓ed.

switch [swɪtʃ] *n.* **1.** device for making and breaking a connection at railway points (to allow trains to go from one track to another). **2.** device for making and breaking an electric circuit. **3.** thin, flexible twig or stick (e.g. one for whipping a horse). *v.t. & i.* **1.** turn (an electric current *off*, *on*) by means of a ⁓ (2). **2.** move (a train, tram) on to another track. **3.** (fig.) turn (one's thoughts, a conversation) from one subject to another. **4.** whip with a ⁓ (3). **5.** swing (sth.) round suddenly; snatch (sth.) suddenly: *The horse ⁓ed its tail. He ⁓ed it out of my hand.* '⁓·**back** *n.* (also ⁓*back railway*) railway that twists and turns up and down steep slopes, esp. one in an amusement park. '⁓·**board** *n.* panel with numerous ⁓es (2), esp. for making connections by telephone, or operating electric circuits.

a switch (2)   a swivel

swiv·el ['swɪvl] *n.* coupling between two parts that allows one part to revolve without turning the other: *a ⁓ chair* (with a seat rotating on a pivot). *v.t. & i.* (-*ll*-, U.S.A. also -*l*-) turn on, or as on, a ⁓.

swol·len, p.p. of *swell* (esp. when used as an adj.): *a ⁓ ankle.*

swoon [swuːn] *v.i. & n.* faint(ing fit).

swoop [swuːp] *v.i.* come with a rush: *The eagle ⁓ed (down) on its prey. n.* ⁓ing movement; sudden attempt to snatch and carry off sth.

swop, see *swap.*

sword [sɔːd] *n.* long steel blade fixed in a hilt, used as a weapon: *put to the ~, kill; cross ~s with,* (fig.) dispute with. **'~-fish** *n.* large sea-fish with a long, ~-like upper jaw. **'~s·man** *n.* man skilled in the use of a ~.

swore, sworn, see *swear.*

swot [swɒt] *v.i. & t.* (*-tt-*) (sl.) study hard: *~ a subject up,* study it hurriedly. *n.* 1. person who ~s. 2. hard work.

swum, see *swim* (v.).

swung, see *swing* (v.).

syc·a·more ['sɪkəmɔː*] *n.* 1. ~ (*maple*), large maple grown for its shade and timber. 2. (U.S.A.) = plane-tree.

syl·lable ['sɪləbl] *n.* unit of pronunciation uttered without interruption and containing usu. one vowel sound; word or division of a word with one vowel sound in it: *Arithmetic is a word of four ~s.* **syl·lab·ic** [sɪ'læbɪk] *adj.* of or in ~s.

syl·la·bus ['sɪləbəs] *n.* (pl. ~es, *-bi* [-baɪ]) outline or summary of a course of studies; programme of school lessons.

syl·lo·gism ['sɪlədʒɪzəm] *n.* form of reasoning in which a conclusion is reached from two statements, e.g.: *All men must die; I am a man; therefore I must die.*

syl·van, see *silvan.*

sym·bol ['sɪmbl] *n.* sign, mark, object, etc. looked upon as representing or recalling sth.: *The cross is the ~ of Christianity.* +, —, ×, *and* ÷ *are common mathematical ~s.* **~·ic** [sɪm-'bɒlɪk] *adj.* of, using, used as, a ~. **~·i·cal·ly** *adv.* **~·ize** ['sɪmbəlaɪz] *v.t.* be a ~ of; make use of a ~ or ~s for.

sym·me·try ['sɪmɪtrɪ] *n.* (no pl.) (beauty resulting from the) right proportion of parts; quality of harmony or balance (in size, design, etc.) between parts. **sym·met·ri·cal** [sɪ'metrɪkl] *adj.* having ~; (of a design, etc.) having (usu. two) exactly similar parts on either side of a dividing line.

sym·pa·thy ['sɪmpəθɪ] *n.* (no pl.) 1. (capacity for) sharing the feelings of others; tendency to share, state of sharing, sb.'s emotion or sensation or condition. 2. mental participation with sb.('s trouble); compassion: *feel ~ for sb.* 3. agreement in opinion or desire: *in ~ with,* agreeing with; approving of (e.g. a proposal). **sym·pa·thet·ic** [ˌsɪmpə'θetɪk] *adj.* having or showing ~; caused by ~. **sym·pa·thize** ['sɪmpəθaɪz] *v.i.* feel or express ~ (*with*).

sym·pho·ny ['sɪmfənɪ] *n.* elaborate musical composition in three or four parts for (usu. a large) orchestra. **sym·phon·ic** [sɪm'fɒnɪk] *adj.* of, for, pertaining to, having the character of, a ~.

sym·po·sium [sɪm'pəʊzjəm] *n.* (pl. *-sia* [-zjə], ~s) meeting at which several speakers discuss a topic (before an audience); a collection of opinions on a subject, esp. one published by a periodical, etc.

symp·tom ['sɪmptəm] *n.* 1. change in the body's condition that indicates illness. 2. sign of the existence of sth. **~·at·ic** [ˌsɪmptə'mætɪk] *adj.* serving as a ~ (*of*).

syn·a·gogue (U.S.A. **-gog**) ['sɪnəgɒg] *n.* (building used for an) assembly of Jews for religious teaching and worship.

syn·chro·nize ['sɪŋkrənaɪz] *v.t. & i.* (cause to) happen at the same time; agree in time, speed, etc. (*with*). *~ watches,* make them show exactly the same time; *a film,* make the dialogue, music, etc. exactly simultaneous with the action. **syn·chro·ni·za·tion** [ˌsɪŋkrənar'zeɪʃn] *n.* (no pl.).

syn·di·cate ['sɪndɪkɪt] *n.* 1. combination of commercial firms associated to promote a common interest. 2. agency that buys literary articles, photographs, etc. and distributes them for simultaneous publication in a number of periodicals. 3. group of people controlling organized crime, etc.

syn·od ['sɪnəd] *n.* meeting of church officers to discuss and decide questions of policy, government, teaching, etc.

syn·onym ['sɪnənɪm] *n.* word with the same meaning as another in the same language. **syn·on·y·mous** [sɪ'nɒnɪməs] *adj.*

syn·op·sis [sɪ'nɒpsɪs] *n.* (pl. *-ses* [-siːz]) summary or outline (of a book, play, etc.).

syn·tax ['sɪntæks] *n.* (no pl.) (rules for) sentence-building.

syn·the·sis ['sɪnθɪsɪs] *n.* (pl. *-ses* [-siːz]) combination of separate parts, substances, etc. into a whole or into a system; that which results from this process. **syn·thet·ic** [sɪn'θetɪk] *adj.* produced by ~; (of substances) artificially made: *synthetic rubber.*

sy·phon, see *siphon.*

sy·ringe ['sɪrɪndʒ] *n.* device for drawing in liquid by suction and forcing it out again in a fine stream, used for washing out wounds, injecting liquids into the body, in spraying plants, etc.

a syringe

syr·up (U.S.A. also **sir·up**) [ˈsɪrəp] *n.* (no pl.) **1.** thick, sweet liquid made from sugar-cane juice or by boiling sugar with water. **2.** medicine in the form of a thick, sweet liquid.

sys·tem [ˈsɪstəm] *n.* **1.** group of things or parts working together in a regular relation: *the nervous ~.* **2.** ordered set of principles, ideas, etc.: *a ~ of government.* **3.** human body: *Too much alcohol is bad for the ~.* **4.** (no pl.) orderly methods: *work without ~.* **~·at·ic** [ˌsɪstɪˈmætɪk] *adj.* methodical; based on a ~. **~·at·i·cal·ly** *adv.*

T

tab [tæb] *n.* **1.** small piece or strip of cloth, etc. fixed to a garment, etc. as a badge, distinguishing mark, or (as a loop) for hanging up a coat. **2.** (colloq.) account; check.

ta·ble ['teɪbl] *n.* **1.** piece of furniture with a flat top and (usu. four) legs: *a dining-~*; *at ~*, while having a meal. **2.** (no pl.) people seated at a ~: *His talk amused the whole ~*. **3.** (no pl.) food provided at ~: *keep a good ~*, provide good meals. **4.** list, orderly arrangement, of facts, information, etc.: *~ of contents*; *multiplication ~s*. '*~-cloth n.* cloth (to be) spread over a ~. '*~-land n.* plateau. '*~-spoon n.* large spoon for serving food on to plates at ~.

ta·ble d'hôte [,tɑːblˈdəʊt] (Fr.) *n.* ~ *dinner*, restaurant or hotel meal at a fixed price.

tab·let ['tæblɪt] *n.* **1.** flat sheet of wood, stone, etc., for cutting words on (e.g. as used by the ancient Romans). **2.** flat surface with words cut or written on it (e.g. one fixed to a wall in memory of sb. or sth.). **3.** number of sheets of writing-paper fastened together along one edge. **4.** lump of hard soap; small, flat, hard piece of prepared medicine; flat, hard sweet.

a mural tablet (2)

ta·boo, ta·bu [təˈbuː] *n.* act or thing that (esp. primitive) religion or custom regards as forbidden, not to be touched, spoken of, etc. *adj.* forbidden; consecrated. *v.t.* put under a ~; forbid or prohibit: *a subject that was ~ed*.

tab·u·lar ['tæbjʊlə*] *adj.* arranged or displayed in tables (4). **tab·u·late** ['tæbjʊleɪt] *v.t.* arrange (facts, figures, etc.) in ~ form.

ta·chom·e·ter [tæˈkɒmɪtə*] *n.* instrument for measuring speed of rotation, esp. of the engine of a vehicle.

tac·it ['tæsɪt] *adj.* unspoken; understood without being put into words: *~ agreement (consent)*.

tac·i·turn ['tæsɪtɜːn] *adj.* (in the habit of) saying very little. **tac·i·tur·ni·ty** [,tæsɪˈtɜːnətɪ] *n.* (no pl.).

tack [tæk] *n.* **1.** short, flat-headed nail. **2.** long, loose stitch used in fastening pieces of cloth together loosely or temporarily. **3.** sailing-ship's direction as fixed by the direction of the wind and the position of the sails: *on the port (starboard) ~*, with the wind on the port (starboard) side; *on the right (wrong) ~*, (fig.) following a wise (unwise) course of action. **4.** (no pl.) (among sailors) *hard ~*, hard ship-biscuit. *v.t. & i.* **1.** fasten (*down*) with ~s (1). **2.** fasten with ~s (2). **3.** sail a zigzag course.

tack·le ['tækl] *n.* **1.** set of ropes and pulleys for working a ship's sails, or for lifting weights, etc. **2.** (no pl.) equipment, apparatus (1), for doing sth.: *fishing-~*. **3.** act of tackling (3) in football, etc. *v.t. & i.* **1.** deal with, attack (a problem, a piece of work). **2.** seize, lay hold of (e.g. a thief). **3.** (football, etc.) obstruct, intercept, or seize and stop (a player running with the ball).

tackling (3)

tact [tækt] *n.* (no pl.) (use of) skill and understanding shown by sb. who

take

handles people and situations successfully and without causing offence. ~·**ful**(·**ly**) *adj.* (*adv.*) ~·**less**(·**ly**) *adj.* (*adv.*)

tac·tics ['tæktɪks] *n. pl.* (often sing. v.) art of placing or moving fighting forces for or during battle (cf. *strategy*); (fig.) plan(s) or method(s) for carrying out a policy. **tac·ti·cal** ['tæktɪkl] *adj.* of ~. **tac·ti·cian** [tæk'tɪʃn] *n.* expert in ~.

tad·pole ['tædpəʊl] *n.* young of the frog or toad before full development.

a tadpole   a tail

taf·fe·ta ['tæfɪtə] *n.* (no pl.) thin, shiny, rather stiff silk material.

taff·rail ['tæfreɪl] *n.* rail round a ship's stern.

tag [tæg] *n.* **1.** loose or ragged end. **2.** metal or plastic point at the end of a string, shoe-lace, etc. **3.** label (e.g. for showing prices, addresses). **4.** phrase or sentence often quoted: *Latin ~s*. **5.** (no pl.) children's game in which one child chases and tries to touch another, who then becomes the pursuer. *v.t. & i.* (-*gg*-) **1.** join (sth., esp. a piece of writing, *to* or *on to* sth. else). **2.** follow closely: *children ~ging after their mother*. **3.** fasten a ~ (3) to.

tail [teɪl] *n.* **1.** movable part at the end of the body of an animal, bird, fish, or reptile. **2.** sth. like a ~ in position: *the ~ of a kite (comet, an aircraft)*. ~**coat**, man's morning or evening coat with a long skirt divided at the back into ~s and cut away in front; ~-**lamp**, ~-**light**, one at the end of a train, car, or other vehicle. **3.** (usu. pl.) side of a coin not having the monarch's head on it: (in spinning a coin to decide sth.) *heads or ~s? v.t. & i.* ~ (*sb., after sb.*), follow close behind; ~ *away* (*off*), become smaller in number, size, etc.

tai·lor ['teɪlə*] *n.* maker of suits and overcoats, esp. for men. *v.t.* cut out and sew: *a well-~ed man* (with well-made clothes); ~-**made**, (esp. of a woman's dress) made by a ~, with special attention to exact fit.

taint [teɪnt] *n.* trace of some bad quality, decay, or infection. *v.t. & i.* make or become infected: ~*ed meat*.

take [teɪk] *v.t. & i.* (p.t. **took** [tʊk], p.p. ~*n* ['teɪkən]) **1.** get hold of with the hand(s), etc. or with an instrument, etc. (cf. *leave*, *let go of*): ~ *sb.'s hand*; ~ *sth.* (*up*) *with one's fingers*; ~ *hold of sth.*, hold it; seize it. **2.** capture; catch (sb. or sth.) by surprise or pursuit; win; become ill with (a disease); attract: ~ *a fortress*; ~ *500 prisoners*; *a rabbit ~n in a trap*; ~ *first prize in a competition*; ~ *cold*, become ill with a cold; *be ~n ill*; ~ *fire*, begin to burn; ~ (i.e. attract) *the fancy*; *not much ~n with* (i.e. attracted by) *the idea.* **3.** carry, accompany (sb. or sth.): ~ *a letter to the post*; ~ *a friend home in one's car*; ~ *a box upstairs.* **4.** have; eat or drink; give, allow, or get for oneself: ~ *a bath* (*a holiday*, *dinner*, *some medicine*, *a deep breath*); ~ *pride* (*an interest*) *in one's work*; ~ *a seat*, sit down; *this seat is ~n*; ~ (i.e. hire) *a taxi*; ~ (i.e. rent) *a seaside cottage for the holidays.* **5.** accept; receive; subscribe to: *I will ~ £5 for it. Which newspaper do you ~?* **6.** make a record[2] (1): ~ *notes of a lecture*; ~ *a photograph.* **7.** need: *The work took four hours. It ~s two to make a quarrel.* **8.** suppose; conclude: *I took him to be an honest man.* ~ *sth. for granted*, accept it as true, certain to happen. **9.** (with advs. & preps.): ~ *after* (*sb.*), resemble (a parent or relation) in looks, etc.; ~ *sth. back*, (esp.) withdraw sth. one has said; ~ (*sth.*) *down*, lower; write down (notes, etc.); ~ *sb. down*, lower his pride; ~ (*sb.*) *in*, receive (him) as a guest, etc.; (fig.) get the better of by a trick; ~ (*sth.*) *in*, (a) receive into the mind; understand; (b) see at a glance; (c) pay for and receive (a newspaper, etc.) regularly; (d) reduce the area, width, etc. of (e.g. a garment); (e) include or comprise; ~ (*sb.* or *sth.*) *for*, consider to be; esp. wrongly suppose to be: *He was ~n for an Englishman.* ~ *off*, (a) (of aircraft) start a flight; ~-*off* (n.); (b) (fig.) ridicule by imitation; ~ *on*, (a) undertake (work); (b) engage (workers); (c) assume (a quality or appearance); ~ *out*, obtain (an insurance policy, a licence, a summons, etc.); remove (a stain); ~ (*sth.*) *over*, succeed to the management or ownership of; accept the transfer of (duties, etc.): *When does the new manager ~ over?* ~-*over* (n.), assumption of control, esp. of a business, etc.; ~ *to*, (a) adopt as a habit or practice: ~ *to gardening on retirement*; (b) use, go to, as a means of escape: ~ *to flight*; ~ *to one's heels*; ~ *to the woods*; ~ *to the boats* (abandon ship); (c) conceive a liking for: *I took* *to the man at once.* ~ *up,* (a) absorb; (b) dissolve; (c) occupy (time, space); (d) begin to give one's attention to; (e) proceed to deal with. **10.** (esp. of vaccine) have effect; act. *n.* amount (of fish, etc.) ~ *n* (2). **tak·ing** *adj.* attractive. *n.* (pl.) money ~*n* by a shop, etc. during a stated period; gains.

tale [teɪl] *n.* **1.** story: *fairy-~s.* **2.** report; account: *tell ~s,* tell about sb.'s wrongdoing.

tal·ent ['tælənt] *n.* **1.** natural power to do sth.; ability: *a man of great ~; a ~ for painting.* **2.** people with ~: *local ~.* **~·ed** *adj.* having ~.

tal·is·man ['tælɪzmən] *n.* (pl. ~*s*) sth. considered as bringing luck; charm (2).

talk [tɔːk] *v.i. & t.* say things; speak to give information (*to*); discuss matters (*with*); have the power of speech: *Some parrots can ~.* ~ *sth. over,* discuss it; ~ *sb. out of doing sth.,* persuade him not to do it; ~ *sb. round,* get his support or agreement to. *n.* **1.** ~*ing;* informal lecture. **2.** *small ~,* conversation on unimportant subjects; *the ~ of the town,* sth. or sb. everyone is ~*ing* about. **~·ative** ['tɔːkətɪv] *adj.* liking to ~ a lot. **~·ing** *adj.* having the power of speech; expressive: ~*ing eyes;* ~*ing film* (*picture*), cinema film with audible dialogue, songs, etc. recorded on a sound-track. ~ *show n.* television show in which guest celebrities are interviewed.

tall [tɔːl] *adj.* **1.** (esp. of persons) of more than ordinary height: *a ~ man; six foot ~.* **2.** *a ~ story,* one that is difficult to believe; *a ~ order,* a task difficult to perform; an unreasonable request.

tal·low ['tæləʊ] *n.* (no pl.) hard (esp. animal) fat used for making candles, etc.

tal·ly ['tælɪ] *v.i.* (of stories, amounts, etc.) correspond; agree. *n.* reckoning.

tal·ly-ho [,tælɪ'həʊ] *int.* huntsman's cry on catching sight of the fox.

tal·on ['tælən] *n.* claw of a bird of prey (e.g. an eagle).

tame [teɪm] *adj.* (~*r,* ~*st*) **1.** (of animals) used to living with human beings; not wild or fierce. **2.** dull; uninteresting. *v.t.* make ~. **tam·er** *n.* person who ~*s* wild animals: *a lion-~r.*

tam·per ['tæmpə*] *v.i.* meddle or interfere (*with*).

tan [tæn] *n. & adj.* yellowish-brown; brown colour of sunburnt skin. *v.t. & i.* (-*nn-*) **1.** make (an animal's skin) into leather. **2.** make or become brown with sunburn. **~·ner** *n.* workman who

~*s* skins. **~·nery** *n.* place where skins are ~*ned.*

tan·dem ['tændəm] *n.* ~ (*bicycle*), bicycle for two persons to ride on, one behind the other.

tang [tæŋ] *n.* sharp taste or smell.

tan·gent ['tændʒənt] *n.* straight line touching but not cutting a curve. *go* (*fly*) *off at a ~,* change suddenly from one line of thought, action, etc. to another.

tan·ger·ine [,tændʒə'riːn] *n.* **1.** ~ (*orange*), small, sweet, loose-skinned orange. **2.** (no pl.) its deep, orange-yellow colour.

tan·gi·ble ['tændʒəbl] *adj.* **1.** that can be touched. **2.** clear and definite: ~ *proof.*

tan·gle ['tæŋgl] *n.* confused mass (of string, hair, etc.). *v.t. & i.* make or become disordered.

tan·go ['tæŋgəʊ] *n.* (pl. ~*s*) slow S. American dance for two persons.

tank [tæŋk] *n.* **1.** (usu. large) container for liquid or gas: *the petrol ~ of a motor car.* **2.** armoured fighting vehicle. **~·er** *n.* ship or aircraft with ~*s* for carrying esp. mineral oils; lorry with a large cylindrical ~ for carrying oil, milk, etc.

a tank (2)

tan·kard ['tæŋkəd] *n.* metal mug, esp. one for beer.

tan·ta·lize ['tæntəlaɪz] *v.t.* raise hopes that are to be disappointed; keep just out of reach sth. that sb. desires.

tan·ta·mount ['tæntəmaʊnt] *adj.* (only in) ~ *to,* equal in effect to.

tan·trum ['tæntrəm] *n.* (pl. ~*s*) fit of bad temper or anger: *in one of his ~s.*

a tap¹

tap¹ [tæp] *n.* (U.S.A. *faucet*) device (2 for controlling the flow of a liquid o gas from a pipe, barrel, etc.: *on* ~, (of beer, etc.) in a barrel with a ~; (fig.) ready for use. *v.t.* (-*pp*-) **1.** let liquid out from (through a ~ in a barrel); cut (the bark of a tree) and get (sap, etc.): ~*ping rubber trees*. **2.** (fig.) try to obtain (money, information, etc.) from: ~ *a friend for a loan*; ~ *the telephone wires*, make a connection in order to listen secretly to conversations.

ap² [tæp] *n.* quick, light blow. *v.t. & i.* (-*pp*-) give a ~ or ~*s*: ~ *one's foot on the floor*; ~ *at* (*on*) *the door*; ~ *sb. on the shoulder*.

ape [teɪp] *n.* **1.** long, narrow strip of cloth, paper, etc., used for tying up parcels, in dressmaking, etc., or stretched across a racing-track at the finishing-line. **2.** narrow strip of paper on which telegraph instruments automatically print news, etc. **3.** (*magnetic*) ~, impregnated or coated plastic strip, used to record¹ (2) sound¹ or vision. *v.t.* **1.** fasten, tie up, with ~. **2.** record¹ (2) (sound¹, etc.) on a magnetic ~. ~ **deck** *n.* ~-recorder (without amplifiers and loudspeakers) as a component in a hi-fi equipment. '~-,mea·sure *n.* ~ graduated for measuring things with. '~-re,cord·er *n.* apparatus (1) that records¹ (2) sounds¹, etc. on magnetic ~ and afterwards reproduces them. '~-re,cord·ing *n.* such a record² or reproduction. '~-worm *n.* long, flat worm that lodges in the intestines of man and animals.

a·per¹ ['teɪpə*] *n.* length of thread with a thin coating of wax, burnt to give a light.

a·per² ['teɪpə*] *v.t. & i.* make or become gradually narrower towards one end: ~*ing fingers*; *one end* ~*ing off to a point*.

ap·es·try ['tæpɪstrɪ] *n.* cloth with designs or pictures made by weaving coloured threads into it, used esp. for hanging on walls.

ar [tɑː*] *n.* (no pl.) black substance, thick and sticky when melted, obtained from coal. *v.t.* (-*rr*-) coat with ~. ~**ry** *adj.* (-*ier*, -*iest*). ~**mac** ['tɑːmæk] *n.* mixture of ~ and crushed stone used for road surfaces or runways on airfields.

ar·dy ['tɑːdɪ] *adj.* (-*ier*, -*iest*) late; slow. **tar·di·ly** *adv.* **tar·di·ness** *n.* (no pl.).

ar·get ['tɑːgɪt] *n.* **1.** sth. to be aimed at. **2.** thing, plan, etc. against which criticism, etc. is directed.

ar·iff ['tærɪf] *n.* **1.** list of fixed charges, esp. for meals, rooms, etc. at a hotel. **2.** list of taxes on goods imported or (less often) exported; tax on a particular class of imported goods.

tar·mac, see *tar*.

tar·nish ['tɑːnɪʃ] *v.i. & t.* (esp. of metal surfaces) lose, cause loss of, brightness.

tar·pau·lin [tɑː'pɔːlɪn] *n.* (sheet or cover of) canvas made waterproof, esp. with tar.

tar·ry¹ ['tærɪ] *v.i.* (liter.) wait (*for*); be slow or late in coming, going, or appearing; stay (*at, in*, etc.).

tar·ry² ['tɑːrɪ] see *tar*.

tart¹ [tɑːt] *adj.* acid; sharp in taste; (fig.) sharp: *a* ~ *answer*. ~**ly** *adv.*

tart² [tɑːt] *n.* **1.** fruit pie. **2.** circle of pastry with fruit or jam on it.

tar·tan ['tɑːtən] *n.* **1.** (no pl.) Scottish woollen fabric woven with coloured crossing stripes. **2.** particular pattern of ~.

task [tɑːsk] *n.* piece of (esp. hard) work (to be) done. *take sb. to* ~, scold him (*for, about,* sth.). ~ (of a ~) put a strain on (sb.'s powers). ~ **force** *n.* specially organized unit for a special purpose. '~,mas·ter, '~,mis·tress *ns.* person who imposes hard ~s on others.

tas·sel ['tæsl] *n.* bunch of threads, etc. tied together at one end and hanging from a flag, hat, etc. as an ornament. ~**led** (U.S.A. ~**ed**) *adj.* having ~s.

taste [teɪst] *n.* **1.** sense by which flavour is known: *sweet to the* ~. **2.** quality of substances made known by this sense (e.g. by putting on the tongue): *Sugar has a sweet* ~. **3.** (usu. no pl.) small quantity (*of* sth. to eat or drink): *a* ~ *of wine.* **4.** liking or preference (*for*): *He has a* ~ *for modern art. not to my* ~, not to my liking. **5.** (no pl.) ability to enjoy beauty, esp. in art and literature; ability to choose and use the best kind of behaviour, etc.: *a man of* ~; *in good* (*bad*) ~, pleasing (displeasing) to people with ~ (5). *v.t. & i.* **1.** be aware of the ~ (2) of sth. **2.** (of food, etc.) have a particular ~ (2): *It* ~*s sour. It* ~*s of onions.* **3.** test the ~ (2) of: *The cook* ~*d the soup.* **4.** experience: ~ *the joys of freedom.* ~**ful** *adj.* showing good ~ (5); *in good* ~. ~**ful·ly** *adv.* ~**less** *adj.* **1.** (of food) having little or no flavour. **2.** without ~ (5); in bad ~. ~**less·ly** *adv.* **tasty** *adj.* (-*ier*, -*iest*) pleasing to the ~ (1).

ta·ta [,tæ'tɑː] *int.* (childish or colloq.) goodbye.

tat·ter ['tætə*] *n.* (usu. pl.) rag; piece of cloth, paper, etc. torn off or hanging loosely from sth.: *in* ⁓*s*, in rags or torn strips. ⁓**ed** *adj.* ragged.

tat·tle ['tætl] *v.i.* chatter; prattle; gossip. *n.* (no pl.) trivial talk or gossip.

tat·too¹ [tə'tuː] *v.t.* mark (sb.'s skin) with permanent designs or patterns by pricking it and inserting colouring matter. *n.* (pl. ⁓*s*) such a mark.

tat·too² [tə'tuː] *n.* (pl. ⁓*s*) **1.** (no pl.) beating of a drum or drums to call soldiers back to quarters: *beat* (*sound*) *the* ⁓. **2.** public entertainment with music, marching, etc. by soldiers. **3.** continuous tapping with fingers, etc.: *beat a* ⁓ *on the table.*

taught, see **teach.**

taunt [tɔːnt] *n.* remark intended to hurt sb.'s feelings. *v.t.* attack (sb.) with ⁓*s*: ⁓ *a man with having failed.* ⁓**ing·ly** *adv.*

taut [tɔːt] *adj.* (of ropes, nerves, etc.) tightly stretched; tense. ⁓**ly** *adv.*

tau·tol·o·gy [tɔː'tɒlədʒɪ] *n.* (no pl.) saying of the same thing again in different words.

tav·ern ['tævən] *n.* (old use) inn.

taw·dry ['tɔːdrɪ] *adj.* (*-ier, -iest*) showy, brightly coloured or decorated, but in bad taste.

taw·ny ['tɔːnɪ] *adj.* (*-ier, -iest*) brownish-yellow.

tax [tæks] *n.* **1.** sum of money (to be) paid by citizens (according to income, value of purchases, etc.) to the government for public purposes. **2.** *a* ⁓ *on* (one's strength, patience, etc.), sth. that put a strain or a burden on. *v.t.* **1.** put a ⁓ (1) on; get a ⁓: ⁓ *sugar* (*the rich*). **2.** be a ⁓ (2) on (one's patience, memory, etc.). **3.** ⁓ *sb. with sth.*, accuse him of: *They* ⁓*ed me with having neglected the work.* ⁓**·able** *adj.* that can be ⁓ed (1). ⁓**·a·tion** [tæk'seɪʃn] *n.* (no pl.) system of raising money by ⁓es; ⁓es (to be) paid. ⁓**·'free** *adj.* (of goods) not ⁓ed; (of dividends, etc.) after payment of a ⁓ by the company. ⁓ **ha·ven** *n.* country, etc. where income ⁓ is low. '⁓**pay·er** *n.* person who pays ⁓es. ⁓ **re·turn** *n.* declaration of one's income for purposes of ⁓a-tion.

taxi ['tæksɪ] *n.* (pl. ⁓*s* ['tæksɪz]) (rarely ⁓*-cab*) motor car, usu. with a ⁓meter, that may be hired. *v.i. & t.* **1.** go in a ⁓. **2.** (of aircraft) (cause to) move on wheels on the ground: *The plane* ⁓*ed across the tarmac.* '⁓**·driv·er** *n.* driver of a ⁓. '⁓**me·ter** *n.* (usu. *meter*) device(2) that automatically records¹(3) the fare for a journey in a ⁓. '⁓**·rank** *n.* place where ⁓s wait to be hired.

taxi·der·my ['tæksɪdɜːmɪ] *n.* (no pl.) art of preparing and stuffing the skins of animals, birds, and fish so that they look as they did when living. **taxi·der·mist** *n.* person who practises ⁓.

tea [tiː] *n.* **1.** (no pl.) (dried leaves of an) evergreen shrub of eastern Asia; drink made by pouring boiling water on these leaves. **2.** occasion (in the late afternoon) on which ⁓ is drunk: *high* ⁓, *meal* (with ⁓ to drink) taken in the early evening in place of a later supper or dinner. '⁓**-bag** *n.* filter paperbag holding enough ⁓-leaves for one ⁓cup. '⁓**-cloth** *n.* **1.** small cloth for a ⁓-table. **2.** cloth for drying dishes, etc. '⁓**-set.** '⁓**-ser·vice** *ns.* number of cups, saucers, plates, with ⁓pot, milk jug, etc., usu. of the same pattern, for use at ⁓ (2). '⁓**-things** *n. pl.* cups, plates etc. needed for serving ⁓ (2).

teach [tiːtʃ] *v.t. & i.* (p.t. & p.p. *taught* [tɔːt]) give instruction to (sb.); cause (sb.) to know or be able to do (sth.); give lessons at school; do this for a living. ⁓**·er** *n.* person who ⁓es. '⁓**-in** *n.* series of lectures and discussions on an important political or social issue (e.g. as held by university ⁓ers and students). ⁓**·ing** *n.* **1.** (no pl.) work of a ⁓er. **2.** (esp.) that which is taught: *the* ⁓*ing*(*s*) *of Christ.*

teak [tiːk] *n.* **1.** large tree of India, Burma, Malaysia, etc. **2.** (no pl.) its hard wood used in shipbuilding, etc.

team [tiːm] *n.* **1.** two or more oxen, horses, etc. pulling a cart, plough, etc. together. **2.** number of persons playing together and forming one side in certain games (e.g. football or cricket). '⁓**-work** *n.* (no pl.) combined effort; organized co-operation.

tear¹ [teə*] *v.t. & i.* (p.t. *tore* [tɔː*] p.p. *torn* [tɔːn]) **1.** pull sharply apart or to pieces; make (a hole in sth.) by pulling sharply: ⁓ *a piece of paper in two* (*to pieces, to bits*); ⁓ *up,* ⁓ *into small pieces*; ⁓ *a dress on a nail; a torn coat.* **2.** cause (sth.) to be *down, off* etc. by pulling sharply: ⁓ *a page out of a book*; ⁓ *down a notice.* **3.** (usu. passive) destroy the peace of: *a country torn by civil war.* **4.** become torn: *Paper* ⁓*s easily.* **5.** go in excitement or at a great speed: *children* ⁓*ing out of school.* *n.* torn place (e.g. in a coat).

tear² [tɪə*] *n.* drop of salty water, coming from the eye: *in* ⁓*s,* crying. ⁓**ful** *adj.* crying; wet with ⁓*s*: *a* ⁓*ful face.* ⁓**ful·ly** *adv.* '⁓**-jerk·er** *n.* (colloq.) song, story, film, etc. tha[t] evokes extravagant sadness or sympathy.

tease [ti:z] *v.t.* make fun of (sb.) playfully or unkindly; worry with jokes, questions, etc.; annoy: *It's unkind to ~ a child because he stutters.* *n.* person fond of teasing others. **teas·er** *n.* 1. teasing person. 2. (colloq.) difficult question or task. **teas·ing·ly** *adv.*

teat [ti:t] *n.* nipple.

tech·ni·cal ['teknɪkl] *adj.* of, connected with, special to, one of the mechanical or industrial arts (e.g. printing, weaving) or with the methods used by experts: *~ terms*; *the ~ skill of a pianist.* **~·i·ty** [,teknɪ'kælətɪ] *n.* ~ word, phrase, point, etc. **tech·ni·cian** [tek'nɪʃn] *n.* person expert in the technique of a particular art or craft; highly skilled craftsman. **tech·nique** [tek'ni:k] *n.* method of doing sth. expertly, esp. mechanical skill (often contrasted with feeling or expression, e.g. in music and art). **tech·nol·o·gy** [tek'nɒlədʒɪ] *n.* (no pl.) (science of) practical and industrial arts; systematic application of knowledge to practical tasks in industry.

Ted·dy bear ['tedɪ beə*] *n.* child's toy bear. **Ted·dy boy** *n.* (Gt. Brit., colloq., in the 1950's) member of a gang usu. dressed in early twentieth century style.

te·di·ous ['ti:djəs] *adj.* slow and uninteresting: *a ~ lecture.* **te·di·um** ['ti:djəm] *n.* (no pl.) ~ state; boredom; monotony.

teem [ti:m] *v.i.* 1. be present in great numbers. 2. ~ *with*, have in great numbers: *rivers ~ing with fish.*

teens [ti:nz] *n. pl.* the numbers 13 to 19: *girls in their ~* (13 to 19 years of age). **teen·ag·er** ['ti:n,eɪdʒə*] *n.* person in his (her) ~.

teeth, see **tooth**.

teethe [ti:ð] *v.i.* (of a baby) be getting its first teeth.

tee·to·tal [ti:'təʊtl] *adj.* of, advocating, total abstinence from alcoholic drinks. **~·ler** (U.S.A. **~·er**) *n.* person who refuses alcoholic drinks.

tele- ['telɪ-] *pref.* 1. long distance. 2. ~vision. **~·cam·era** ['telɪ,kæmərə] *n.* ~vision camera. **~·cast** ['telɪkɑːst] *v.t.* (p.t. & p.p. *-cast* or *-casted*) & *n.* (transmit a) ~vision broadcast. **'~,cast·er** *n.* ~vision broadcaster. **~·com·mu·ni·ca·tion** ['telɪkə,mju:nɪ'keɪʃn] *n.* communication over long distances by cable, ~graph, ~phone, radio, or ~vision sent by ~. **~·gram** ['telɪɡræm] *n.* message sent by ~graph.

~·graph ['telɪɡrɑːf] *n.* means of, apparatus (1) for, sending messages by the use of electric current along wires or by wireless. *v.t. & i.* send (news, etc.) by ~graph. **te·leg·ra·pher** [tɪ'leɡrəfə*], **te·leg·ra·phist** [tɪ'leɡrəfɪst] *ns.* person trained to send and receive messages by ~graph. **~·graph·ic** [,telɪ'ɡræfɪk] *adj.* **te·leg·ra·phy** [tɪ'leɡrəfɪ] *n.* use, science, of the ~graph. **~·phone** ['telɪfəʊn] *n.* (abbr. *phone*) means, apparatus (1), for talking to sb. at a distance by using electric current or radio: *~phone booth (kiosk)*, small enclosure with a coin-operated ~phone for public use. *v.t. & i.* send (news, etc.) by ~phone; use the ~phone. **~·print·er** ['telɪ,prɪntə*], (U.S.A.) **~·type·writ·er** [,telɪ'taɪp,raɪtə*] *ns.* ~graph instrument for transmitting messages by typing. **~·vi·sion** ['telɪ,vɪʒn] *n.* (abbr. *T.V.* or Gt. Brit., colloq. *telly*) 1. (no pl.) process of transmitting a view of events, plays, etc. (while these are taking place, or from films or tapes) by radio to a distant ~vision receiving set with synchronized sound[1]. 2. *~vision (set)*, apparatus (1) for receiving and showing this transmission. **~·vise** ['telɪvaɪz] *v.t.* send views of (an event, a play, etc.) by ~vision.

te·lep·a·thy [tɪ'lepəθɪ] *n.* (no pl.) direct communication of thoughts or feelings from one mind to another at a distance without the use of signs, sounds, or words.

tele·scope ['telɪskəʊp] *n.* tube-like instrument with lenses for making distant objects appear nearer and larger. *v.t. & i.* make or become shorter by means of or in the manner of sections that slide one within the other. **tele·scop·ic** [,telɪ'skɒpɪk] *adj.* 1. of, containing, able to be seen with, a ~. 2. having sections that slide one within the other: *a telescopic aerial.*

tel·ex, Tel·ex ['teleks] *n.* (no pl.) system of communication using teleprinters. *v.t.* send, communicate with, by ~.

tell [tel] *v.t. & i.* (p.t. & p.p. *told* [təʊld]) 1. make known (in spoken or written words); inform about (one's name, etc.); relate (a story, etc.); utter (a lie, etc.); order: *T~ her to go away.* 2. (esp. with *can*, *be able to*) know apart; distinguish: *Can you ~ the difference between them? Can you ~ Mary from her twin sister?* 3. *there is no ~ing* (what will happen, etc.), it is impossible to say. 4. have a marked effect

teller

(*upon*); influence the result of: *All this hard work is* ~*ing on him* (is affecting his health). **5.** (old use) count: ~ *one's beads*, say one's prayers with a rosary; *all told*, altogether; ~ *off*, count one by one and give orders (*for a task, to do sth.*); (colloq.) scold. **~·er** *n.* **1.** person who receives and pays out money over a bank counter. **2.** man who counts votes (e.g. in the House of Commons). **~·ing** *adj.* effective: *a* ~*ing speech.* **'~·tale** *n. & attrib. adj.* (person) making known a secret, sb.'s feelings, etc.

tel·ly ['telɪ] *n.* (Gt. Brit., colloq.) television (set).

te·mer·i·ty [tɪ'merətɪ] *n.* (no pl.) rashness.

tem·per ['tempə*] *n.* **1.** degree of hardness, toughness, elasticity, of a substance, esp. of steel. **2.** state or condition of the mind: *in a good* (*bad*) ~, calm and pleasant (angry); *keep* (*lose*) *one's* ~, keep (fail to keep) one's anger under control; *out of* ~ (*with*), angry. *v.t. & i.* **1.** give the required ~ (1) to (steel, etc.) by heating and cooling, etc. **2.** soften or modify (sth. *with*): *~ justice with mercy*, be merciful when giving a just punishment. **~ed** *adj.* (in compounds) having or showing a given kind of ~ (2): *a sweet-~ed child.*

tem·per·a·ment ['tempərəmənt] *n.* person's disposition or nature, esp. as this affects his way of thinking, feeling, and behaving: *a girl with a nervous* (*an artistic*) ~. **tem·per·a·men·tal** [,tempərə'mentl] *adj.* **1.** caused by ~: *a boy with a ~al dislike of study.* **2.** easily excited; having quickly-changing moods.

tem·per·ance ['tempərəns] *n.* (no pl.) moderation, self-control, in speech, behaviour, and (esp.) in the use of alcoholic drinks. **tem·per·ate** ['tempərət] *adj.* **1.** showing, behaving with, ~. **2.** (of climate, parts of the world) free from extremes of heat and cold.

tem·per·a·ture ['temprətʃə*] *n.* degree of heat or cold: *take sb.'s* ~, measure it with a thermometer; *have a* ~, have a fever.

tem·pest ['tempɪst] *n.* violent storm. **tem·pes·tu·ous** [tem'pestjʊəs] *adj.* (of the weather, also fig.) violent.

tem·ple¹ ['templ] *n.* building (esp. in ancient times) dedicated to a god; place of worship.

tem·ple² ['templ] *n.* flat part of either side of the head between the forehead and the ear.

tem·po ['tempəʊ] *n.* (pl. ~s, -pi [-piː])

1. speed at which music is (to be) played. **2.** rate of motion or activity.

tem·po·ral ['tempərəl] *adj.* **1.** of, existing in, time. **2.** of this physical life only, not spiritual.

tem·po·rary ['tempərərɪ] *adj.* lasting for, designed to be used for, a short time only: ~ *employment.* **tem·po·ra·ri·ly** *adv.*

tem·po·rize ['tempəraɪz] *v.i.* delay making a decision, giving an answer, stating one's purpose, etc.; act so as to gain time.

tempt [tempt] *v.t.* **1.** (try to) persuade (sb.) to do sth. wrong or foolish. **2.** attract (sb.) to have or do sth.: *The weather* ~*ed him to go for a swim.* **temp·ta·tion** [temp'teɪʃn] *n.* ~*ing* or being ~*ed*; sth. that ~*s.* ~·**er** *n.* (esp.) *the T~er*, Satan. **~·ing·ly** *adv.*

ten [ten] *n. & adj.* 10. **~·th** [tenθ] *n. & adj.* 10th; ¹/₁₀. **'~·pins** *n. pl.* (sing. v.) game similar to ninepins but using ten bottle-shaped pieces of wood.

ten·able ['tenəbl] *adj.* **1.** that can be defended successfully: *a fortress* (*position, an argument*) *that is* ~. **2.** (of an office or post¹ (4)) that can be held (*by sb. for* a certain period).

te·na·cious [tɪ'neɪʃəs] *adj.* holding tightly; refusing to let go *of*: *a* ~ *memory*; ~ *of our liberties.* **te·nac·i·ty** [tɪ'næsətɪ] *n.* (no pl.).

ten·ant ['tenənt] *n.* person who pays rent for the use of land, a building, room, etc. *v.t.* (usu. pass.) ~*ed*, used by a ~. **ten·an·cy** ['tenənsɪ] *n.* (no pl.) use of land, etc. as a ~; length of time during which a ~ uses land, etc.

tend¹ [tend] *v.t.* watch over, take care of (e.g. people who are ill).

tend² [tend] *v.i.* **1.** have a ~*ency*: *Prices are* ~*ing upwards.* **2.** move or be directed: *Their steps* ~*ed towards the bridge.* **ten·den·cy** ['tendənsɪ] *n.* turning or inclination (*to, towards, to do* sth.): *Your work shows a* ~*ency to improve.*

ten·der¹ ['tendə*] *n.* **1.** wagon for coal and water behind a steam locomotive. **2.** small ship attending a larger one to carry stores, put on or take off passengers, etc. **3.** person who looks after sth.: *a bar~.*

ten·der² ['tendə*] *v.t. & i.* **1.** offer ~ *payment* (of a debt); ~ *one's service* (*resignation*). **2.** make an offer (to carry out work, supply goods, etc.): ~ *for the construction of a bridge*, submit an offer to do it for a stated price. *n.* **1.** statement of the price at which one offers to supply goods or services, t do sth. **2.** sth. offered: *legal* ~, form of money that must by law be accepted in payment of a debt.

en·der³ ['tendə*] *adj.* **1.** delicate; easily hurt or damaged; quickly feeling pain. **2.** (of meat) easily chewed; not tough. **3.** kind; loving: ~ *looks*. **~·ly** *adv.* **~·ness** *n.* (no pl.).

en·don ['tendən] *n.* tough, thick cord that joins muscle to bone.

en·dril ['tendrɪl] *n.* thread-like part of a climbing plant (e.g. a vine) that twists round any support near by.

en·e·ment ['tenɪmənt] *n.* dwelling-house, esp. a large one for the use of many families at low rents.

en·et ['tiːnet] *n.* principle; belief; doctrine.

en·nis ['tenɪs] *n.* (no pl.) game for two or four players who hit a ball backwards and forwards over a net.

en·on ['tenən] *n.* end of a piece of wood shaped to go into a mortise to make a joint. (See the p. at *mortise*.)

en·or¹ ['tenə*] *n.* (usu. no pl.) general routine or direction (*of* one's life); general meaning or thread (*of* a speech, etc.).

en·or² ['tenə*] *n.* (musical part for or person having the) highest normal adult male voice. (See *alto*.) [time.\

ense¹ [tens] *n.* verb form that shows⌡

ense² [tens] *adj.* (~*r*, ~*st*) **1.** tightly stretched. **2.** showing or feeling excitement, etc.: *faces* ~ *with anxiety*. **~·ly** *adv.* **~·ness**, **ten·si·ty** ['tensatɪ] *ns.* (no pl.).

en·sile [tensaɪl] *adj.* **1.** of tension. **2.** capable of being stretched.

en·sion ['tenʃn] *n.* (no pl.) **1.** state of, degree of, being tense: *the* ~ *of a violin string*. **2.** condition when feelings are tense, when relations between two persons, groups, states, etc. are strained: *political* ~.

ent [tent] *n.* shelter made of canvas supported by poles and ropes.

en·ta·cle ['tentəkl] *n.* slender, flexible, snake-like, boneless part of certain animals (e.g. the octopus), used for feeling, holding, moving, etc.

en·ta·tive ['tentətɪv] *adj.* made or done as a trial, to see the effect: *only a* ~ *suggestion*. **~·ly** *adv.*

en·ter·hooks ['tentəhʊks] *n. pl.* (only in) *on* ~, in a state of anxious suspense.

enth, see **ten**.

en·u·ous ['tenjʊəs] *adj.* thin; flimsy.

en·ure ['tenjʊə*] *n.* (period of, time of, conditions of) holding (e.g. a political office) or using (land): ~ *of office*; *security of* ~.

tep·id ['tepɪd] *adj.* lukewarm.

ter·cen·te·na·ry [ˌtɜːsen'tiːnərɪ] *n.* (celebration of the) 300th anniversary of an event.

ter·cen·ten·ni·al [ˌtɜːsen'tenjəl] *adj.* lasting, happening every, 300 years. *n.* 300th anniversary.

term [tɜːm] *n.* **1.** fixed or limited period of time: *a* ~ *of imprisonment*; period during which lawcourts, schools, etc. are open. **2.** (pl.) conditions offered or agreed to: ~*s of surrender*; *come to* ~*s*, *make* ~*s (with sb.)*, reach an agreement; *inquire about* ~*s* (i.e. prices) *for a stay at a hotel*. **3.** (pl.) relations: *on good* ~*s with sb.*, friendly with him. **4.** word(s) expressing a definite idea, etc., esp. in a branch of study: *scientific* ~*s*. **5.** (pl.) mode of expression: *in* ~*s of high praise*; *in abusive* ~*s*. *v.t.* name; give a certain ~ (4) to.

ter·mi·na·ble ['tɜːmɪnəbl] *adj.* that can be ended.

ter·mi·nal ['tɜːmɪnl] *adj.* **1.** of, taking place, each term (1): ~ *examinations*. **2.** of, forming, the point or place at either end (e.g. of a railway). *n.* **1.** ~ part or point, esp. the point of connection for closing an electric circuit. **2.** terminus for railway trains or long-distance buses; building (in a town) used by passengers departing for or arriving from an airport.

ter·mi·nate ['tɜːmɪneɪt] *v.t. & i.* come to an end; put an end to: ~ *in*, have at the end. **ter·mi·na·tion** [ˌtɜːmɪ'neɪʃn] *n.* ending (e.g. of a contract or word).

ter·mi·nol·o·gy [ˌtɜːmɪ'nɒlədʒɪ] *n.* system of names or terms (4) used in a science or art: *grammatical* ~.

ter·mi·nus ['tɜːmɪnəs] *n.* (pl. *-ni* [-naɪ], *-nuses* [-nəsɪz]) station at the end of a railway; end of a tram, bus, or air route.

ter·mite ['tɜːmaɪt] *n.* ant-like insect (often called *white ant*) that causes great damage to wood, etc.

ter·race ['terəs] *n.* **1.** level(led) piece of ground on a slope. **2.** continuous row of houses, esp. along the top of a slope. ~*d adj.* cut into ~*s*; having ~*s*: *a* ~*d lawn*.

ter·ra·cot·ta [ˌterə'kɒtə] *n.* (no pl.) hard, reddish-brown pottery.

ter·ra fir·ma [ˌterə 'fɜːmə] (Latin) *n.* (no pl.) dry land; solid ground.

ter·rain [te'reɪn] *n.* stretch of country, esp. as regards its physical features.

ter·res·tri·al [tɪ'restrɪəl] *adj.* of, on, living on, the earth or land.

ter·ri·ble ['terəbl] *adj.* causing great

fear, sorrow, or discomfort. **ter·ri·bly** *adv.* (sl.) very (much).

ter·ri·er ['terɪə*] *n.* kinds of small, active dog.

ter·rif·ic [tə'rɪfɪk] *adj.* **1.** causing fear; terrible. **2.** (colloq.) very great; extreme.

ter·ri·fy ['terɪfaɪ] *v.t.* fill with fear.

ter·ri·to·ri·al [,terɪ'tɔːrɪəl] *adj.* of land, esp. land forming a division of a country: ~ *waters,* the sea near a country's coast.

ter·ri·to·ry ['terɪtərɪ] *n.* **1.** land, esp. land under one ruler or government: *Portuguese ~ in Africa.* **2.** land or district, esp. its extent: *a business salesman who has a large ~ to travel.* **3.** (U.S.A.) district not yet admitted to the full rights of a State but having its own legislature.

ter·ror ['terə*] *n.* (person, thing, etc. causing) great fear. **~ism** *n.* (no pl.) use of ~, violence, etc., esp. for political purposes. **~ist** *n.* person who uses violence, etc. to cause ~ for political ends. **~ize** *v.t.* fill with ~, coerce, by threats or acts of violence.

terse [tɜːs] *adj.* (~r, ~st) (of speech, style, speakers) brief and to the point (6). **~ly** *adv.*

test [test] *n.* examination or trial (of sth.) to find its quality, value, composition, etc.; trial or examination (e.g. of sb.'s powers or knowledge): *put sth. to the* ~. ~ *drive,* drive in a motor vehicle one thinks of buying to determine its qualities, etc. **~-drive** (v.t.); ~ *pilot,* pilot who takes newly-built aircraft on ~ *flights. v.t.* **1.** put to the ~; examine: ~ *ore for gold.* **2.** be a ~ of: *The long climb ~ed our powers of endurance.* **'~-tube** *n.* slender glass tube, closed at one end, used in chemical ~s: ~*-tube baby,* baby started outside the body and then planted inside a female to develop naturally.

test-tubes

tes·ta·ment ['testəmənt] *n.* **1.** (often *last will and ~*) see *will*³ (6). **2.** *Old T~, New T~,* (the) two main divisions of the Bible.

tes·ti·fy ['testɪfaɪ] *v.t. & i.* **1.** give evidence (in a court of law *against, on behalf of, that*). **2.** state publicly,

declare (*that*). **3.** ~ *to,* be a sign o evidence of: *Your work testifies to you ability.*

tes·ti·mo·ni·al [,testɪ'məʊnjəl] *n.* **1** written statement testifying to a pe son's merits, abilities, qualifications etc. **2.** sth. given to sb. to show ap preciation of services, usu. sth. sub scribed for by several or many person

tes·ti·mo·ny ['testɪmənɪ] *n.* (no pl. statement, esp. in a court of law testifying that sth. is true; proof o evidence; open declarations or state ments.

tes·ty ['testɪ] *adj.* (*-ier, -iest*) easil annoyed.

tête-à-tête [,teɪtɑː'teɪt] (Fr.) *n.* privat meeting between two persons; thei talk.

teth·er ['teðə*] *n.* rope or chain b which an animal is fastened whil grazing: *at the end of one's ~,* (fig.) a the end of one's powers, resources etc. *v.t.* fasten with a ~.

text [tekst] *n.* **1.** (no pl.) main body o a book (contrasted with notes, an in dex, etc.). **2.** sentence, esp. of Scrip ture, as the subject of a sermon or dis cussion. **'~book** *n.* book giving in struction in a branch of learning.

tex·tile ['tekstaɪl] *attrib. adj.* of th making of cloth: *the ~ industry.* woven material; material suitable fo spinning and weaving.

tex·ture ['tekstʃə*] *n.* **1.** arrange ment of the threads in a textile fabri *cloth with a loose ~.* **2.** structure o substance, esp. when felt or looked a

than [ðæn, ðən] *conj.* **1.** (introducin the second part of a comparison *John is taller ~ Jack.* **2.** *no(ne) other* not any other person but: *I met no(n other ~ my old friend Philip toda nothing else ~,* only; entirely: *It w nothing else ~ bad luck that they lo the game.*

thank [θæŋk] *v.t.* express gratitude (sb. *for* sth.). **~s** *n. pl.* **1.** words gratitude. **2.** (colloq.) you (i.e. 'Pleas accept my ~s'). **~s to,** as the result o because of; *give ~s,* (esp.) ~ God fo food, etc.; say grace. **~ful** *adj.* **~ful** *adv.* **~less** *adj.* (esp. of actions) fo which no ~s are offered: *a ~less tas* **~less·ly** *adv.* **'~s₁giv·ing** *n.* (form o prayer used in) expression of ~s God (e.g. for victory in war, th harvest).

that [ðæt] *adj. & pron.* (pl. *tho* [ðəʊz]) (contrasted with *this, thes* **1.** *Look at ~ man (those men) ov there. This photograph is much clear* *than ~ (one).* **2.** *My new car is of a different make from ~ which I had before. Those who want to go swimming must put their names down on the list.* **adv.** *(colloq.)* to such a degree; so: *I couldn't walk ~ far* (i.e. as far as ~). [ðət, ðæt] **rel. pron.** *(pl. ~) The letter ~ came this morning is from my father. Give help to anyone ~ needs it.* (Cf. *which, who.*) **conj. 1.** *I will see ~ a meal is ready for you when you get home tonight.* **2.** *Bring it to the light, so ~ I can see it better.* **3.** *His manners are so bad ~ nobody invites him to a party.* **4.** *You may go on condition ~ you will not come home alone.* **5.** (in exclamations): *Oh, ~ I could see you again! How I wish it were possible for us to meet again!*

thatch [θætʃ] **n. 1.** (roof-covering of) dried straw, reeds, etc. **2.** (colloq.) thick hair of the head. **v.t.** cover (a roof, etc.) with ~.

a thatched roof

thaw [θɔː] **v.i. & t. 1.** *It is ~ing, the* temperature has risen above freezing-point, snow and ice are beginning to melt. **2.** (cause anything frozen to) become liquid or soft again. **3.** (of persons, their behaviour) (cause to) become less formal, more friendly. **n.** (usu. no pl.) (state of the weather causing) ~ing.

the [ðə, (before vowel sounds) ðɪ, (strong form) ðiː] **def. art.** weak form of *this, that, these, those.* **adv.** by so much; by that amount: ~ *more he has,* ~ *more he wants.*

the·atre (U.S.A. **-ater**) ['θɪətə*] **n. 1.** building for the acting of plays. **2.** hall or room with seats in rows rising one behind another for lectures, scientific demonstrations, etc. **3.** *operating ~,* room in a hospital where surgical operations are performed. **4.** (usu. no pl.) *the ~,* drama; the writing and acting of plays. **the·at·ri·cal** [θɪ-'ætrɪkl] **adj. 1.** of or for the ~ (1): *theatrical scenery.* **2.** (of behaviour, etc.) unnatural; exaggerated; designed for effect.

thee [ðiː] **pron.** object form of *thou.*

theft [θeft] **n.** (act of) stealing.

their [ðeə*] **poss. pron. attrib.** of them: *They have lost ~ dog.* **~s** [ðeəz] **poss. pron. pred.** *That dog is not ~s, it's ours.*

the·ism ['θiːɪzəm] **n.** (no pl.) belief in the existence of a God who has made himself known to mankind. **the·ist n.** believer in ~.

them, see *they.*

theme [θiːm] **n. 1.** subject of a talk or piece of writing. **2.** (music) short tune that is repeated, expand-ed, etc. (e.g. in a sonata or sym-phony). **3.** ~ *song,* song that is so often repeated in a musical play, film, etc. that it characterizes the pro-duction or one of the performers.

then [ðen] **adv. & conj.** **1.** at that time (past or future): *We were living in Scotland ~. Will you still be here ~? from ~,* from that time onwards. **2.** next; after that; afterwards: *We'll go to Paris first, ~ to Rome.* **3.** in that case: *You say you feel ill; ~ why don't you call the doctor?* **4.** and also: *T~ there's James, oughtn't he to come, too?* **5.** (in warning, protesting, to call attention): *Now then ...* **adj.** existing, etc. at that time: *the ~ king.* **n.** that time: *before (till, by, from) ~; since ~,* between that time and now.

thence [ðens] **adv.** from there. ˌ~'**forth,** ˌ~'**for·ward** **advs.** from that time on-wards.

the·ol·o·gy [θɪ'ɒlədʒɪ] **n.** (no pl.) science of the nature of God and of the foundations of religious belief. **theo·lo·gian** [θɪə'ləʊdʒjən] **n.** person skilled in ~. **theo·log·i·cal** [θɪə'lɒdʒɪkl] **adj.**

the·o·rem ['θɪərəm] **n. 1.** statement that reasoning shows to be true. **2.** (math.) statement that a reasoned proof is required for.

the·o·ry ['θɪərɪ] **n. 1.** (explanation of) general principles of an art or science (contrasted with *practice*). **2.** reasoned supposition put forward to explain facts or events: *Darwin's ~ of evolu-tion.* **3.** conjecture; speculation: *In ~, four things could happen,* there are four possibilities. **the·o·ret·ic, -i·cal** [θɪə'retɪk(l)] **adjs.** based on ~, not on practice or experience. **the·o·rize** ['θɪəraɪz] **v.i.** make theories (*about*). **the·o·rist n.** person who forms theories.

ther·a·peu·tic [ˌθerə'pjuːtɪk] **adj.** con-nected with the art of healing, the cure of diseases. **ther·a·peu·ti·cal·ly adv.** **~s n. pl.** (usu. sing. v.) branch of medicine dealing with the application of remedies for diseases.

ther·a·py ['θerəpɪ] *n.* medical treatment of a disease. **ther·a·pist** *n.* specialist in ~.

there [ðeə*] *adv.* (contrasted with *here*) **1.** in, at, or to that place: *Put my box down* ~. **2.** *T*~ *goes the fox. T*~ *it goes.* **3.** calling attention: *There's a hole in your shoe. Hallo* ~*! Look out,* ~*!* **4.** with *seem, appear,* etc.: *T*~ *seems to be no escape. T*~ *appears to be nobody here.* **5.** (used to introduce a sentence): *T*~ *is no doubt about it.* *n.* that place or position; that point: *take it from* ~; *pass by* ~; *somewhere near* ~. *int.* (in comforting): (*T*~), ~, *dry your tears!* (in triumph): *T*~, *now, I was right!* (in dismay): *T*~, *I've upset the ink! I've upset the ink!* **'~·abouts** *adv.* near that place, number, quantity, etc. **,~'af·ter** *adv.* afterwards. **,~'by** *adv.* by that means; in that way. **'~·fore** *adv.* for that reason. **,~·up'on** *adv.* then; as the result of that.

therm [θɜːm] *n.* unit of heat. **ther·mal** ['θɜːml] *adj.* of heat: ~*al springs,* springs of warm or hot water.

ther·mo- ['θɜːməʊ-] *pref.* of heat; of temperature: *thermometer; thermostat.*

ther·mom·e·ter [θə'mɒmɪtə*] *n.* instrument for measuring temperature.

ther·mo·stat ['θɜːməʊstæt] *n.* device (2) for automatically regulating temperature by cutting off and restoring the supply of heat (e.g. in central heating).

these, see *this.*

the·sis ['θiːsɪs] *n.* (pl. *-ses* ['θiːsiːz]) statement or theory (to be) put forward and supported by arguments, esp. a written essay submitted for a university degree.

thews [θjuːz] *n. pl.* muscles; sinews.

they [ðeɪ] *pron.* subject form pl. of *he, she, it.* **them** [ðem, ðəm] *pron.* object form of *they.*

thick [θɪk] *adj.* **1.** (opp. *thin*) of comparatively great (or of a given) measurement, from one side to the other or from the upper surface to the lower surface: *a* ~ *line;* ~ *ice; three inches* ~. **2.** having a large number of units close together: ~ *hair; a* ~ *forest.* **3.** (of liquids, the atmosphere) semi-solid; not clear: ~ *soup; a* ~ *fog.* **4.** ~ *with,* full of; holding a mass of: *air* ~ *with dust* (*snow*). **5.** (of the voice) indistinct (e.g. because one has a cold). **6.** (colloq.) intimate: *as* ~ *as thieves,* very friendly. *n.* (no pl.) ~*est part; part where activity is greatest: in the* ~ *of the fight; through* ~ *and thin,* whatever

the conditions may be. *adv.* ~*ly: come* ~ *and fast,* come quickly and in large numbers. **~·en.**['θɪkən] *v.t. & i.* make or become ~. **'~·head·ed** *adj.* stupid. **~·ly** *adv.* **~·ness** *n.* **1.** (no pl.) being ~. **2.** (esp.) layer. **'~·set** *adj.* **1.** (of a person) short and stout. **2.** closely massed or planted. **'~·skinned** *adj.* (fig.) not easily hurt by insults, reproaches, etc.; without delicate feelings.

thick·et ['θɪkɪt] *n.* mass of trees, shrubs, undergrowth, growing thickly together.

thief [θiːf] *n.* (pl. *thieves* [θiːvz]) person who steals, esp. secretly and without violence. (Cf. *robber, burglar.*) **thieve** [θiːv] *v.t. & i.* steal.

thigh [θaɪ] *n.* part of the leg above the knee.

thim·ble ['θɪmbl] *n.* cap (of metal, etc.) used to protect the end of the finger when pushing a needle through cloth, etc. **~·ful** *n.* (colloq.) sip (*of* liquid).

a thimble   a thistle

thin [θɪn] *adj.* (-nn-) **1.** (opp. *thick*) having opposite surfaces close together; of small diameter: *a* ~ *sheet of paper; a* ~ *piece of string.* **2.** having not much flesh: ~ *in the face.* **3.** not full or closely packed or copious: *a* ~ *audience;* ~ *hair.* **4.** (of liquids, e.g. soup) watery; without much substance. **5.** *a* ~ *excuse,* (colloq.) an excuse that is easily seen through; *have a* ~ *time,* (sl.) have a dull or uncomfortable time. *v.t. & i.* (-nn-) make or become ~: ~ *the plants out,* take out some so that the rest grow better. *n.* (no pl.) *through thick and* ~, through bad times as well as good. **~·(·ly)** *advs.* **~·ness** *n.* (no pl.). **'~·skinned** *adj.* sensitive (to criticism, etc.); easily offended.

thine [ðaɪn] *poss. pron.* (old use) your(s) (sing.).

thing [θɪŋ] *n.* **1.** any material object: *A rose is a lovely ~.* **2.** (pl.) general conditions or circumstances: *T~s are getting better every day.* **3.** (pl.) *your (his, etc.) ~s,* belongings, esp. clothes: *Have you packed your ~s yet?* **4.** (no pl.) *the (very) ~,* just what is needed, or what is considered right or usual: *not at all the ~ to do. This is the very ~ I wanted.*

think [θɪŋk] *v.t. & i.* (p.t. & p.p. *thought* [θɔːt]) **1.** use the mind in order to form an opinion, etc. **2.** consider; be of the opinion: *~ highly (well, little, nothing) (sb. or sth.),* have a high (good, etc.) opinion of; *~ nothing of (doing sth.)* (e.g. walking thirty miles), consider it not unusual or remarkable; *~ better of (doing sth.),* reconsider (and give up); *~ sth. out,* consider carefully and make a plan; *~ sth. over,* consider further before deciding it.

third [θɜːd] *n. & adj.* 3rd; ¹/₃. *~·ly adv.* '*~·rate adj.* of poor quality. **T~ World** *n.* (no pl.) developing countries that are not politically aligned with the great power blocs.

thirst [θɜːst] *n.* (no pl.) **1.** feeling caused by a desire or need to drink; suffering caused by this: *die of ~.* **2.** (fig.) strong desire (*for* knowledge, etc.). *v.i.* have ~; (fig.) be eager (*for* revenge, etc.). *~y adj.* (*-ier, -iest*) having or causing ~: *~y work. ~·i·ly adv.*

thir·teen [,θɜːˈtiːn] *n. & adj.* 13. *~th* [,θɜːˈtiːnθ] *n. & adj.* 13th; ¹/₁₃. **thir·ty** [ˈθɜːtɪ] *n. & adj.* 30. **thir·ti·eth** [ˈθɜːtɪɪθ] *n. & adj.* 30th; ¹/₃₀.

this [ðɪs] *adj. & pron.* (pl. *these* [ðiːz]) (contrasted with *that, those*): *Look at ~ picture here, and then at that picture over there. T~ is by far the better picture. adv.* (colloq.) to such a degree; so: *about ~ high; have come ~ far* (i.e. as far as ~).

this·tle [ˈθɪsl] *n.* (sorts of) wild plant with prickly leaves and yellow, white, or purple flowers. (See the picture at *thimble.*) '*~·down n.* (no pl.) ~ seed(s).

thith·er [ˈðɪðə*] *adv.* (old use) to that place; in that direction.

thong [θɒŋ] *n.* narrow strip of leather (e.g. as reins, a whip).

tho·rax [ˈθɔːræks] *n.* middle of the three main sections of an insect.

thorn [θɔːn] *n.* **1.** sharp-pointed growth on the stem of a plant. **2.** shrub or bush with ~s (e.g. *haw~*). *~y adj.* (*-ier, -iest*) **1.** having ~s. **2.** (fig., of questions, etc.) full of trouble and difficulty; causing argument.

thor·ough [ˈθʌrə] *adj.* complete in

every way; not forgetting or overlooking anything; detailed: *give the room a ~ cleaning; a ~ worker; receive ~ instruction in English. ~·ly adv. ~·ness n.* (no pl.). '*~·bred n. & adj.* (animal, esp. a horse) of pure breed. '*~·fare n.* street or road, esp. one much used by traffic: *No ~fare,* warning that a road is private or that one end is closed. '*~·go·ing adj.* complete.

thou [ðaʊ] *pron.* (old or liter. form of) you (sing.).

though, tho' [ðaʊ] *conj.* (also *although*) **1.** in spite of the fact that: *T~ poor, he was always neatly dressed.* **2.** even if: *T~ you hate me, I will serve you faithfully.* **3.** *as ~,* as if. **4.** and yet; all the same: *I'll try, ~ I don't think I shall succeed. adv.* but yet; however: *I wish you had told me, ~.*

thought¹, see **think**.

thought² [θɔːt] *n.* **1.** (no pl.) (power, process, way, of) thinking: *lost in ~; modern ~; take ~ for,* be concerned about. **2.** idea, opinion, intention, formed by thinking: *He had no ~ of* (i.e. no intention of) *causing you anxiety. ~·ful adj.* **1.** full of ~; showing ~: *~ful looks.* **2.** considerate; thinking of, showing ~ for, the needs of others. *~·ful·ly adv. ~·ful·ness n.* (no pl.). *~·less adj.* **1.** selfish; inconsiderate (*of* others). **2.** unthinking; careless. *~·less·ly adv. ~·less·ness n.*

thou·sand [ˈθaʊznd] *n. & adj.* 1,000. *~th* [ˈθaʊzntθ] *n. & adj.* 1,000th; ¹/₁,₀₀₀.

thrall [θrɔːl] *n.* (often fig.) (condition of being a) slave: *a ~ to drink.* **thral·dom** (U.S.A. also *~·dom) n.* (no pl.) slavery.

thrash [θræʃ] *v.t. & i.* **1.** beat with a stick, whip, etc. **2.** defeat. **3.** *~ out* (a problem), discuss thoroughly. **4.** thresh. *~·ing n.* beating; defeat: *give sb. (get) a good ~ing.*

thread [θred] *n.* **1.** length of spun cotton, silk, flax, wool, etc., esp. for use in sewing and weaving. **2.** chain or line (*of* thought, an argument, etc.). **3.** spiral ridge round a screw. *v.t.* **1.** put ~ through (a needle); put (beads, etc.) on a ~. **2.** make (*one's way*) through (a crowd of people, etc.), by going in and out among them. '*~·bare adj.* **1.** (of cloth) worn thin; shabby. **2.** (fig., of arguments, etc.) old; much used and therefore uninteresting.

threat [θret] *n.* **1.** statement of an intention to punish or hurt sb., esp. if he does not do as one wishes. **2.** sign or warning of coming trouble, danger, etc.: *a ~ of rain in the sky.* **~·en** ['θretn] *v.t. & i.* **1.** use a ~ or ~s to: *~en sb. with sth.; ~en to shoot sb.* **2.** give warning of (danger, trouble, etc.): *clouds that ~en rain.* **3.** (of sth. unpleasant) seem likely to come. **~·en·ing·ly** *adv.*

three [θriː] *n. & adj.* **3.** *~-'lane adj.* (of a road) marked out for ~ lines of traffic. *~·pence* ['θrepəns] *n.* (Gt. Brit.) sum of ~ pence (= 3 p., old currency 3 d.). *~·pen·ny* ['θrepəni] *adj.* (Gt. Brit.) costing or worth 3 p. (old currency 3 d.). *'~·ply,* see *ply¹. ~'score n.* sixty.

thresh [θreʃ] *v.t. & i.* beat the grain out of (wheat, etc.); beat wheat, etc. for this purpose.

thresh·old ['θreʃhəʊld] *n.* stone or plank under a doorway; (fig.) start; beginning: *on the ~ of your career as a teacher.*

threw, see *throw* (v.).

thrice [θraɪs] *adv.* three times.

thrift [θrɪft] *n.* (no pl.) care, economy, in the use of money or goods. *~y adj.* (-ier, -iest) using ~; economical.

thrill [θrɪl] *n.* (experience causing) excited feeling passing like a wave along the nerves. *v.i. & t.* **1.** feel a ~ or ~s: *~ with pleasure.* **2.** cause a ~ or ~s in: *a play that ~ed the audience.* *~·er n.* exciting story, play, or film.

thrive [θraɪv] *v.i.* (p.t. *throve* [θrəʊv], p.p. *~n* ['θrɪvn]) succeed; grow strong or healthy: *Children ~ on good food.*

throat [θrəʊt] *n.* **1.** front part of the neck. **2.** passage in the neck through which food passes to the stomach and air to the lungs. *~y adj.* (-ier, -iest) (of the voice) thick (as when one has a cold); guttural.

throb [θrɒb] *v.i.* (-bb-) (of the heart, pulse, etc.) beat, esp. more rapidly than usual: *~bing with excitement; a wound ~bing with pain.* *n.* *~bing;* vibration.

throe [θrəʊ] *n.* (usu. pl.) sharp pain (e.g. of childbirth). *in the ~s of,* (colloq.) struggling with.

throne [θrəʊn] *n.* **1.** ceremonial chair or seat of a king, queen, bishop, etc.; (fig.) royal authority. **2.** *the T~,* the sovereign.

throng [θrɒŋ] *n. & v.i. & t.* crowd.

throt·tle ['θrɒtl] *v.t.* **1.** seize (sb.) by the throat and stop his breathing. **2.** control the flow of petrol, etc. to an engine. *n.* (also *~-valve*) valve controlling the flow of petrol, etc. to an engine.

through, thro' (U.S.A. **thru**) [θruː] *prep.* **1.** (of places) from end to end or side to side of; entering at one side, on one surface, etc. and coming out at the other: *The River Thames flows ~ London. The road goes* (right) *~ the forest.* **2.** (fig.) *We must go ~* (i.e. examine) *the accounts.* **3.** (of time) from beginning to end of: *He will not live ~ the night,* he will die before morning. **4.** (indicating the cause, etc.): *The accident happened ~ no fault of yours.* **5.** (U.S.A.) up to and including: *from Monday ~ Friday. adv.* **1.** from end to end, side to side, beginning to end: *I've read the letter ~ twice and cannot understand it.* **2.** to the end; till complete: *see a job ~.* **3.** all the way: *Does this train go ~ to Bombay?* (Also as adj., modifying the noun): *a ~ train to Bombay; ~ traffic,* road traffic that is going ~ a place (contrasted with local traffic). **4.** connected by telephone: *Can you put me ~ to the manager?* *~·out* [θruː'aʊt] *adv. & prep.* in every part (of); from end to end (of). *'~·way,* (U.S.A. also) *'thru·way n.* thoroughfare, esp. expressway.

throve, see *thrive.*

throw [θrəʊ] *v.t. & i.* (p.t. *threw* [θruː], p.p. *~n* [θrəʊn]) **1.** cause (sth.) to go through the air, usu. with force, by a movement of the arm or by mechanical means. **2.** put (articles of clothing) *on, off, over,* etc., quickly or carelessly. **3.** move (one's arms, legs, etc.) *out, up, down,* violently: *~ one's chest out* (*one's arms about*). **4.** (of a horse) cause the rider to fall to the ground; (of a wrestler) force an opponent to the floor. **5.** (in phrases): *~ away,* lose by foolishness or neglect: *~ away one's advantages; ~-away* (n. & adj.), (sth.) to be ~n away after (one) use; *~ back,* (usu. pass.) compel to rely on; *~* (sth.) *in,* (a) give (sth.) extra, without addition to the price; (b) put in (a remark, etc.) casually; *~ oneself into* (an activity), take part in with vigour and enthusiasm; *~ off,* get rid of; become free from; *~ open,* make (e.g. a competition) open to all persons; *~ out,* (a) make (a suggestion); give (a hint) in a casual way; (b) reject (a bill); *~ over,* abandon (a plan, a friend); *~ up,* (a) vomit (food); (b) resign from (a position). *n. ~ing* or being *~n;* distance to which sth. is or can be ~n: *within a stone's ~,* quite near.

thru, see *through.*

thrum [θrʌm] *v.t. & i.* (-mm-) play

(a stringed instrument) by pulling the strings, esp. carelessly or idly.

thrush [θrʌʃ] *n.* (sorts of) song-bird.

thrust [θrʌst] *v.t. & i.* (p.t. & p.p. ~) push suddenly or violently; make a forward stroke with a sword, etc. *n.* **1.** act of ~ing; (in war) strong attempt to push forward into the enemy's lines (11), etc. **2.** (no pl.) (tech.) forward force exerted by a propeller, jet, etc.

thud [θʌd] *v.i.* (-dd-) *& n.* (strike, fall with, a) dull sound as of a blow on sth. soft.

thug [θʌg] *n.* violent criminal.

thumb [θʌm] *n.* short, thick finger set apart from the other four. *under sb.'s* ~, under his influence and control; *rule of* ~, rule based on experience or practice. *v.t. & i.* **1.** turn over (pages, etc.); make dirty by doing this: *a well-~ed book.* **2.** ~ *a lift,* (try to) get a free ride in a vehicle (by signalling to the driver). '~·**tack** *n.* (U.S.A.) = drawing-pin.

thump [θʌmp] *v.t. & i.* strike heavily, esp. with the fist(s); (of the heart) beat fast. *n.* (sound of a) heavy blow.

thun·der [ˈθʌndə*] *n.* **1.** (no pl.) loud noise coming after lightning. **2.** loud noise like or suggesting ~: *the* ~ *of the guns. v.i. & i.* **1.** *It* ~*ed,* there was ~. **2.** make a loud noise like ~: *sb.* ~*ing at the door.* **3.** speak in a loud voice; make an attack (*against*). '~·**bolt** *n.* lightning and crash of ~; (fig.) unexpected and destructive event. '~·**clap** *n.* crash of ~; (fig.) sudden, terrible event or news. '~·**storm** *n.* storm of ~ and lightning, usu. with heavy rain. '~·**struck** *adj.* amazed. ~**y** *adj.* (of weather) giving signs of ~.

Thurs·day [ˈθɜːzdɪ] *n.* fourth day of the week.

thus [ðʌs] *adv.* in this way; so: ~ *far,* to this point.

thwart[1] [θwɔːt] *v.t.* obstruct a person or his plans.

thwart[2] [θwɔːt] *n.* seat across a rowing-boat for an oarsman.

thy [ðaɪ] *poss. pron. attrib.* (old use) your (sing.).

thyme [taɪm] *n.* plant with sweet-smelling leaves, used to flavour food.

ti·ara [tɪˈɑːrə] *n.* ornamental coronet for a woman; crown worn by the pope.

tick[1] [tɪk] *n.* **1.** light, regular sound, esp. of a clock or watch. **2.** small mark (often √) put against names, figures, etc. in a list or to show that sth. is correct. **3.** *on* ~, (colloq.) on credit. *v.i. & t.* **1.** (of a clock, etc.) make ~s

(1). **2.** put a ~ (2) against: ~ (*off*) *the items in a list.* **3.** ~ *sb. off,* (sl.) rebuke him. ~·**er** *n.* (colloq.) watch; (humor.) heart. '~·**er-tape** *n.* telegraphic tape.

tick[2] [tɪk] *n.* small insect that fastens itself on the skin (e.g. of dogs) and sucks blood.

tick[3] [tɪk] *n.* **1.** cover or case of a mattress or pillow. **2.** (no pl.) (also ~*ing*) material used for this.

tick·et [ˈtɪkɪt] *n.* card, piece of paper, giving the holder the right to travel in a train, bus, etc. or to a seat in a theatre, etc. or showing the cost of sth. *v.t.* put a ~ on (esp. sth. to be sold).

tick·le [ˈtɪkl] *v.t. & i.* **1.** excite the nerves of the skin by touching or rubbing lightly, esp. at sensitive parts, often so as to cause laughter: ~ *sb. in the ribs. The rough blanket* ~*s (me).* **2.** have an itching feeling (as of being ~d): *My nose* ~*s.* **3.** please (one's sense of humour or of taste): ~*d to death,* ~*d pink,* (colloq.) extremely amused, etc. *n.* act of tickling sb.; sensation of being ~d. **tick·lish** *adj.* **1.** (of a person) easily made to laugh or wriggle when ~d. **2.** (of a problem, piece of work) needing delicate care or caution.

tide [taɪd] *n.* **1.** regular rise and fall in the level of the sea, caused by the attraction of the moon: *at high (low)* ~; *washed up by the* ~. **2.** flow or tendency (of opinion, public feeling, etc.). *v.t.* ~ *over,* get over, enable (sb.) to get over (a period of difficulty, etc.): *Will £10* ~ *you over until you get your wages?* **tid·al** [ˈtaɪdl] *adj.* of the ~(s): *a tidal wave,* a great wave such as may accompany an earthquake.

tid·ings [ˈtaɪdɪŋz] *n. pl.* (sing. or pl. v.) (liter.) news.

ti·dy [ˈtaɪdɪ] *adj.* (-ier, -iest) neat; orderly: *a* ~ *room (person);* ~ *habits. v.t. & i.* (often ~ *up*) make ~. **ti·di·ly** *adv.* **ti·di·ness** *n.* (no pl.).

tie [taɪ] *v.t. & i.* (pres. p. *tying,* p.t. & p.p. ~*d*) **1.** fasten with string, etc.: ~ *a man's feet together;* ~ *up a parcel.* **2.** make a (knot). **3.** (fig., of conditions in an agreement, etc.) restrict; limit the freedom of. **4.** (of players, teams; often ~ *with*) make the same score (as). **5.** ~ *in (up),* (cause to) agree or be closely associated *with;* ~ *up,* (a) invest (money) so that it is not easily available; (b) ensure that (property, etc.) can be used, sold, etc. only under certain (usu. legal) conditions. *n.* **1.** sth. used for fastening; rod or beam holding parts of a structure together;

(U.S.A.) = railway sleeper (2). **2.** (fig.) sth. that holds people together: *~s of friendship*; *family ~s.* **3.** sth. that takes up one's attention and limits one's freedom of action: *Small children are often a ~.* **4.** equal score in a game, etc.: *The match ended in a ~.* **5.** neck~.

tier [tɪə*] *n.* row (esp. of seats), shelf, etc., esp. one of a number rising in parallel lines.

tiff [tɪf] *n.* slight quarrel.

ti·ger ['taɪgə*] *n.* large, fierce animal of Asia, yellow-skinned with black stripes. **ti·gress** ['taɪgrɪs] *n.* female ~.

tight [taɪt] *adj.* **1.** fixed or fitting closely: *a ~ cork.* **2.** (of knots, etc.) not easily unfastened: *~ ropes.* **4.** fully stretched: *~ ropes.* **4.** closely or firmly put together or packed so that all the space is occupied: *Stuff the cushions until they are ~.* **5.** produced by or needing pressure: *a ~ squeeze*; *in a ~ corner* (*place*), (fig.) in a dangerous or difficult situation from which escape is difficult; *a ~ fit*, (fig.) condition in which there is no room for any more things, etc. **6.** (in compounds, as *air~*, *water~*, etc.) made so that air, water, etc. can neither enter nor escape. *adv.* ~ly. **~en** ['taɪtn] *v.t. & i.* (often *~en up*) make or become ~ (not loose): *~en one's belt.* **'~·fist·ed** *adj.* mean; ungenerous. **'~·rope** *n.* rope on which acrobats perform. **~s** *n. pl.* skin-~ garment as worn by dancers, acrobats, etc.; woman's close-fitting garment covering the legs and body up to the waist, worn in place of stockings. **~·ly** *adv.* **~ness** *n.* (no pl.).

tile [taɪl] *n.* square or oblong plate of baked clay for covering roofs, etc. *v.t.* cover (a roof, etc.) with ~s.

till¹ [tɪl] *prep. & conj.* until.

till² [tɪl] *n.* money-drawer in a shop; cash register.

till³ [tɪl] *v.t.* cultivate (land). **~·er** *n.*

til·ler ['tɪlə*] *n.* handle fixed to the rudder of a small boat.

tilt [tɪlt] *v.t. & i.* **1.** (cause to) come into a sloping position: *T~ the barrel up* (to empty it, etc.). *The table ~ed.* **2.** (in former times, of men on horseback) ride *at* one another with lances; (fig.) attack in speech or writing: *~ing at gamblers.* *n.* **1.** ~ing (1); sloping position. **2.** act of ~ing (2) with lances: (*at*) *full ~*, at full speed and with great force.

tim·ber ['tɪmbə*] *n.* **1.** (no pl.) wood prepared for use in building, etc. **2.** beam forming a support (e.g. in a roof or a ship). **3.** (no pl.) trees large enough for use as ~ (1). **~ed** *adj.* (of buildings) made of ~ or with a framework of ~.

tim·bre ['tæmbrə] *n.* characteristic quality of sound produced by a particular voice or instrument.

time [taɪm] *n.* **1.** (no pl.) all the days of the past, present, and future; the passing of all the days and years, taken as a whole: *The world exists in space and ~.* **2.** (no pl.) portion or measure of ~; point of ~ stated in hours and minutes: *The ~ is five o'clock.* **3.** *in ~*, (a) early enough: *We are in ~ for the meeting.* (b) after a period of ~; in the future: *You will speak English in ~* (c) *in good ~*, early; in due course; (d) *in no ~*, very soon; very quickly; *at one ~*, during a certain period of ~ in the past; *at the same ~*, yet; even if that is true; *from ~ to ~*, occasionally; *~ and* (*~*) *again*, repeatedly; often; *~ out of mind*, period of ~ further back than memory can go; (*work*) *against ~*, (work) fast because ~ is limited. **4.** (pl.) multiplied by: *Three ~s five is fifteen.* **5.** (often pl.) period of ~ associated with sth. or sb.: *in ancient ~s*; *the ~(s) of the Stuarts* (i.e. when the Stuart kings ruled). **6.** (often pl.) conditions of life, circumstances, etc., of a period: *T~s are good* (*bad*). *T~s have changed.* *have a good ~*, enjoy oneself. **7.** system of measuring ~: *Greenwich ~*; *summer ~* (see *daylight saving ~*). **8.** length of a musical note; speed at which a piece of music is played; style of musical movement according to the number of beats in a bar: *in* (*out of*) *~*, in (not in) accordance with the ~ of the music; *beat ~*, show the ~ of music by movements of the hand, etc.; *keep ~*, sing or dance in ~. *v.t.* **1.** choose, arrange, or decide the ~ for (sth. to happen). **2.** measure the ~ taken by (e.g. a runner) or for (e.g. a race). **'~·card**, **'~·clock** *ns.* one for recording workmen's hours of work. **'~·hon·oured** *adj.* respected because old. **~·less** *adj.* unending. **~·ly** *adj.* coming, occurring, at the right ~, when needed, etc **'~·ta·ble** *n.* scheme of school work etc.; (book with) list of ~s at which things are to be done, esp. of arrivals and departures of trains, ships, etc **'~·work** *n.* (no pl.) work for which payment is by the hour or day. (Cf. *piece-work*.)

tim·id ['tɪmɪd] *adj.* easily frightened **~·ly** *adv.* **ti·mid·i·ty** [tɪ'mɪdətɪ], **~·ness** *ns.* (no pl.).

tim·o·rous(·ly) [ˈtɪmərəs(lɪ)] *adj.* (*adv.*) timid(ly).

tin [tɪn] *n.* **1.** (no pl.) soft, white metal used for coating iron sheets. **2.** (U.S.A. *can²* (2)) ~-plated container for food, etc., esp. one sealed so as to be airtight; its contents: *a ~ of sardines.* *v.t.* (*-nn-*) **1.** coat (sheet iron, etc.) with ~. **2.** pack (food, tobacco, etc.) in ~s (2). '~-,open·er *n.* (Gt. Brit.) tool for opening ~s. **~ plate** *n.* (no pl.) sheet iron coated with ~.

tinc·ture [ˈtɪŋktʃə*] *n.* **1.** medical substance dissolved in alcohol. **2.** small amount, trace, suggestion (*of*).

tin·der [ˈtɪndə*] *n.* (no pl.) material that easily catches fire from a spark.

tinge [tɪndʒ] *v.t.* **1.** colour slightly (*with* red, etc.). **2.** affect slightly: *admiration ~d with envy.* *n.* slight colouring or mixture (*of*).

tin·gle [ˈtɪŋgl] *v.i. & n.* (have a) pricking or stinging feeling in the skin: (fig.) *tingling with excitement.*

tin·ker [ˈtɪŋkə*] *n.* tin-plate worker who travels from place to place and repairs kettles, pans, etc. *v.i.* (try to) do repairs, usu. without expert knowledge: ~ *with (~ away at) sth.*

tin·kle [ˈtɪŋkl] *v.t. & i.* (cause to) make a succession of slight, ringing sounds (e.g. of a small bell). *n.* (no pl.) such sounds: *the ~ of a bell.*

tin·sel [ˈtɪnsl] *n.* (no pl.) glittering, metallic substance made in sheets, strips, and threads, used for ornament; (fig.) cheap, showy brilliance.

tint [tɪnt] *n.* (esp. pale) shade or variety of colour: *~s of green in the sky.* *v.t.* give a ~ to; put a ~ on.

ti·ny [ˈtaɪnɪ] *adj.* (*-ier, -iest*) very small.

-tion [-ʃn] *suff.* (forming ns. with vs.) **1.** act or state of ...ing: *action; addition; opposition.* **2.** condition of being ...ed: *exhaustion.* **-tion·al** [-ʃənl] *adj.*

tip¹ [tɪp] *n.* **1.** pointed or thin end of sth.: *the ~s of one's fingers.* **2.** small piece put on the end of sth.: *~ of a cigarette.* *v.t.* (*-pp-*) supply with a ~ (2): *filter-~ped cigarettes.* '~-toe *v.i. & adv.* (walk quietly, be) on the ~s of one's toes: *standing on ~toe; ~toe out of the room.* ,~'top *adj.* (& *adv.*) excellent(ly).

tip² [tɪp] *v.t. & i.* (*-pp-*) **1.** (often ~ *up, over*) (cause to) lean or slant, rise on one side or at one end; (cause to) overbalance or overturn: *He was ~ped out of the cart into the ditch.* **2.** empty (the contents of sth.) *out of* or *into* by ~ping: *T~ the water out of the pail.*

n. (Gt. Brit.) place where rubbish, etc. may be ~ped (2); dump.

tip³ [tɪp] *v.t.* (*-pp-*) **1.** touch or strike lightly: *His bat just ~ped the ball.* **2.** give or hand (sth. to sb.) in an informal way; give a ~ (2) to: *He ~ped the porter handsomely.* ~ *sb. off*, (fig.) give him a warning, a hint, or inside information; *a ~-off*, a hint. *n.* **1.** light blow; tap. **2.** gift of extra money to a porter, waiter, etc. for personal services. **3.** piece of advice on how to do sth., esp. of secret information about the probable winner of a horse-race, on the future value of business shares, etc. **~ster** [ˈtɪpstə*] *n.* person who gives ~s (3) about races.

tip·ple [ˈtɪpl] *v.i. & t.* be in the habit of taking much alcoholic liquor; drink (wine, etc.). *n.* (no pl.) (colloq.) alcoholic drink. **~r** *n.* person who ~s.

tip·sy [ˈtɪpsɪ] *adj.* (*-ier, -iest*) intoxicated.

tip·toe, see *tip¹*.

tip·top, see *tip¹*.

ti·rade [taɪˈreɪd] *n.* long, angry or scolding speech.

tire¹, see *tyre.*

tire² [ˈtaɪə*] *v.t. & i.* make or become weary, in need of rest, or uninterested: ~ *of*, lose interest in. **~d** *adj.* weary in body or mind: *~d out*, exhausted. **~less** *adj.* not easily ~d; ceaseless: *a ~less worker; ~less energy.* **~some** *adj.* troublesome.

ti·ro, ty·ro [ˈtaɪərəʊ] *n.* (pl. ~s) beginner; person with little experience.

tis·sue [ˈtɪʃuː] *n.* **1.** any fine, woven fabric. **2.** any of the substances forming part of an animal or plant: *skin (nervous, muscular) ~.* **3.** (fig.) web or network (*of* lies, etc.). **4.** (also ~-*paper*) thin, soft paper used for wrapping, paper handkerchiefs, etc.: *toilet (face) ~s.*

tit¹ [tɪt] *n.* small bird, of various kinds (e.g. blue ~, coal-~, ~mouse).

tit² [tɪt] *n.* (only in) ~ *for tat*, blow for blow.

ti·tan·ic [taɪˈtænɪk] *adj.* immense.

tit·bit (U.S.A. tid-) [ˈtɪtbɪt, U.S.A. ˈtɪd-] *n.* choice and attractive bit (*of* food, news, etc.).

tithe [taɪð] *n.* tenth part of farm produce formerly given by ancient custom for the support of (Church of England) parish priests.

ti·tle [ˈtaɪtl] *n.* **1.** name of a book, poem, picture, etc. **2.** word used to show a person's rank or occupation (e.g. Lord, Prince, Professor). **3.** right (*to* sth., *to do* sth.), esp. (law) right to the possession of property. **~d** *adj.* having a ~ (2) of nobility. **'~-deed** *n.* document proving a ~ (3) to property. **'~-page** *n.* page of a book that gives the ~ (1), author's name, etc.

tit·ter ['tɪtə*] *v.i. & n.* (give a) silly, half-suppressed little laugh.

tit·tle-tat·tle ['tɪtl̩,tætl̩] *n. & v.i.* gossip.

tit·u·lar ['tɪtjʊlə*] *adj.* existing in name but not having authority or duties: *the ~ ruler.*

to [tuː, tʊ, tə] *prep.* **1.** in the direction of; towards: *walk to the station; fall to the ground.* **2.** towards (a condition, quality, etc.): *go to sleep; slow to anger.* **3.** (introducing the indirect object): *Give it to her.* **4.** towards (a time, the end of a period, etc.): *a quarter to two; from Monday to Friday; stay to the end of the play.* **5.** (indicating a comparison): *prefer walking to climbing; win by six goals to three.* **particle 1.** (marking the infinitive): *He wants me to go.* **2.** (as a substitute for the infinitive): *I meant to call but had no time to.* [tuː] *adv.* **1.** to or in the usual or required position, esp. a closed position: *Please push the door to.* **2.** *to and fro,* backwards and forwards; from side to side.

toad [təʊd] *n.* frog-like animal that lives chiefly on land. **'~·stool** *n.* (usu. poisonous) kind of umbrella-shaped fungus.

a toad

toady ['təʊdɪ] *v.t. & i. & n.* flatter(er), esp. in the hope of gain.

toast[1] [təʊst] *n.* (no pl.) sliced bread made brown and crisp by being held in front of heat. *v.t. & i.* **1.** heat (sliced bread, etc.) in this way. **2.** warm (oneself, one's feet, etc.) before a fire. **~·er** *n.* electrical device (2) for ~ing bread.

toast[2] [təʊst] *v.t.* drink to the health, happiness, success, etc. or in honour of: *~ the bride and bridegroom.* *n.* act of ~ing; words spoken before drinking; person, etc. ~ed.

to·bac·co [təˈbækəʊ] *n.* (pl. ~s) (plant having) leaves (to be) dried and used for smoking (in pipes, cigarettes, etc.). **~·nist** [təˈbækənɪst] *n.* shopkeeper who sells ~, cigarettes, etc.

to·bog·gan [təˈbɒgən] *n.* long, narrow sledge for sporting purposes. (See the picture at *skip.*) *v.i.* go down a snow- or ice-covered slope on a ~.

toc·sin ['tɒksɪn] *n.* (bell rung to give a) signal of alarm.

to·day [təˈdeɪ] *adv. & n.* (on) this day; (at) this present period or age (3).

tod·dle ['tɒdl̩] *v.i.* walk with short, uncertain steps as a baby does. **~r** *n.* baby who can ~.

tod·dy ['tɒdɪ] *n.* sweetened (and spiced) drink of alcoholic spirits and hot water.

to-do [təˈduː] *n.* fuss; commotion: *What a ~!* What a lot of excitement and talk!

toe [təʊ] *n.* **1.** one of the five divisions of the front part of the foot; similar part in an animal's foot. **2.** part of a sock, shoe, etc. covering the ~s. *v.t.* touch, reach, with the ~s: *~ the line,* stand with the ~s on the starting-line ready for a race; (fig.) obey orders given to one as a member of a group.

tof·fee, tof·fy ['tɒfɪ] *n.* (piece of a) hard, sticky sweet made by boiling sugar, fat, etc.

to·geth·er [təˈgeðə*] *adv.* **1.** one with another; in company: *They went to the jeweller's ~ and bought a wedding ring. ~ with,* as well as; in addition to; also: *They bought a hairbrush, ~ with a case to keep it in.* **2.** at the same time: *troubles that come ~.* **3.** without interruption: *talk for hours ~.*

toil [tɔɪl] *v.i.* **1.** work hard (*at* a task). **2.** move with difficulty (*up* a mountain, *through,* etc.). *n.* (no pl.) hard work. **~·er** *n.* person who ~s (1).

toi·let ['tɔɪlɪt] *n.* **1.** process of dressing, arranging the hair, etc.: *She spends only five minutes on her ~.* **2.** (old use) (style of) dress or costume. **3.** (attrib.) of or for the ~: *~ articles; a ~-set,* brush, comb, hand-mirror, etc. **4.** (room containing a) lavatory; water-closet. **~-paper,** paper for use in the lavatory.

toils [tɔɪlz] *n. pl.* nets; snares: *caught in the ~ of the law.*

to·ken ['təʊkən] *n.* **1.** sign, evidence, guarantee, or mark (of sth.): *in ~ of,* as evidence of. **2.** *~ payment,* payment of a small part of what is owed, made to show that the debt is recognized. *~ strike,* brief strike as a warning.

told, see *tell.*

tol·er·ate ['tɒləreɪt] *v.t.* allow or endure without protest. **tol·er·able** ['tɒlərəbl̩] *adj.* **1.** that can be ~d. **2.** fairly good **tol·er·ance** *n.* (no pl.) quality of tolerating opinions, customs, behav-

iour, etc. different from one's own.
tol·er·ant *adj.* having or showing
tolerance. **tol·er·a·tion** [ˌtɒləˈreɪʃn] *n.*
(no pl.) tolerance, esp. the practice of
allowing religious freedom.

toll[1] [təʊl] *n.* **1.** payment required or
made for the use of a road, bridge,
harbour, etc. **2.** (fig.) sth. paid, lost,
or suffered: *the ~ of the roads*, deaths
and injuries from traffic accidents;
take ~ of, take or destroy a part of:
*The war took a heavy ~ of the nation's
manhood.* '**~-bar**, '**~-gate** *ns.* one at
which a ~ (1) must be paid. '**~-call** *n.*
telephone call for which the charge is
higher than for a local call. '**~-road** *n.*
road maintained by means of ~s collected on it.

toll[2] [təʊl] *v.i.* & *t.* **1.** (of a bell) ring
with slow, regular strokes: *~ing for
sb.'s death.* **2.** cause (a bell) to ring in
this way. *n.* (no pl.) sound made by
the ~ing of a bell.

tom·a·hawk ['tɒməhɔːk] *n.* light axe
used as a tool and weapon by N.
American Indians.

to·ma·to [təˈmɑːtəʊ] *n.* (pl. *-oes*) (plant
with) soft, juicy, red or yellow fruit
usually eaten with meat and in salads:
(attrib.) ~ *juice.*

tomb [tuːm] *n.* place for a dead body,
dug in the ground, cut out of rock,
etc., esp. one with a monument over
it. '**~·stone** *n.* stone set up over a ~.

tom·boy ['tɒmbɔɪ] *n.* girl who likes
rough, noisy games.

tom(-cat) ['tɒm(kæt)] *n.* male cat.

tome [təʊm] *n.* large, heavy book.

tom·fool [ˌtɒmˈfuːl] *n.* fool. **~·ery** *n.*
senseless behaviour; stupid joke.

to·mor·row [təˈmɒrəʊ] *adv.* & *n.* (on)
the day after today.

tom-tom ['tɒmtɒm] *n.* Indian, African,
or Asian drum, beaten with the hands.

ton [tʌn] *n.* **1.** measure of weight (Gt.
Brit. 2,240 lb. = 1016 kg; U.S.A.
2,000 lb. = 907,18 kg). *metric ~,*
1000 kg. **2.** (colloq.) large number or
amount: *~s of money.* **3.** (Gt. Brit.,
sl.) speed of 100 m.p.h. *~-up* (attrib.
adj.): *~-up boys,* motor-cyclists who
travel at high speed.

tone [təʊn] *n.* **1.** sound, esp. with
reference to its quality: *the sweet ~(s)
of a violin; speak in an angry (entreat-
ing, etc.) ~.* **2.** (contrasted with *stress*)
rise or fall of the voice in speaking.
3. (music) any of the five larger intervals between one note and the next
which, with two semi·~s, make up an
octave. **4.** (no pl.) general spirit,
character, morale, of a community:

the ~ of the school. **5.** shade (of colour);
degree (of light). *v.t.* & *i.* **1.** give a
particular ~ of sound or colour to: *~
down,* make or become less intense; *~
up,* make or become higher, brighter,
in ~. **2.** (esp. of colours) be in harmony
(*with*). '**~-arm** *n.* tubular arm that
connects the pick-up of a record-
player to the amplifier. **~ed** *adj.* having a particular kind of ~ (1): *silver-~d
trumpets.* **~·less** *adj.* dull; lifeless:
in a ~less voice.

tongs [tɒŋz] *n. pl.* (often *a pair of ~*)
tool for taking up and holding (a piece
of coal, a lump of sugar, a block of
ice, etc.).

tongue [tʌŋ] *n.* **1.** movable organ in
the mouth, used in talking, tasting,
and licking. *have one's ~ in one's cheek,*
say sth. that one does not mean to be
taken seriously; *hold one's ~,* be silent.
2. language: *our mother ~.* **3.** sth. like
a ~: *the ~ of a bell; ~s of flame.* '**~-tied**
adj. unable to speak, esp. through fear
or shyness.

ton·ic ['tɒnɪk] *n.* & *adj.* **1.** (sth., esp.
medicine) giving strength or energy:
*the ~ quality of sea air; a bottle of ~;
~ water,* non-alcoholic drink with
quinine. **2.** (music) keynote. ~ **sol-fa**
[ˌtɒnɪk sɒlˈfɑː] (in teaching singing)
method of showing musical notes by
means of syllables (e.g. *sol, fa, doh*).

to·night [təˈnaɪt] *adv.* & *n.* (on) the
night of today.

ton·nage ['tʌnɪdʒ] *n.* **1.** internal cubic
capacity or cargo-carrying capacity of
a ship in tons. **2.** total ~ (1) of a country's merchant shipping. **3.** charge per
ton on cargo, etc. for transport.

ton·sil ['tɒnsl] *n.* either of two small,
oval masses of tissue in the throat.
~·li·tis [ˌtɒnsɪˈlaɪtɪs] *n.* (no pl.) inflammation of the ~s.

ton·sure ['tɒnʃə*] *n.* shaving of the top
of the head of a person about to become a priest or monk; part so shaved.

too [tuː] *adv.* **1.** also; in addition; as
well. **2.** moreover. **3.** in a higher degree than is wanted, bearable, etc.

took, see **take** (v.).

tool [tuːl] *n.* **1.** implement held in the
hand(s) and used by workmen (e.g.
gardeners, carpenters, builders). (Cf.
instrument.) *machine ~, ~* operated by
power, used for working on metal,
wood, etc. **2.** person who is used by
another for dishonest purposes.

toot [tuːt] *n.* short, sharp warning
sound from a horn, trumpet, etc.
v.t. & *i.* (cause to) give out a ~ or ~s.

tooth [tuːθ] *n.* (pl. *teeth* [tiːθ]) **1.** each of

the small, white, bony structures rooted in the jaws, used for biting and chewing. *fight ~ and nail*, fight bitterly, with all one's force; *in the teeth of*, against the full force of. 2. ~-like part, esp. of a comb, saw, or rake[1]. '**~ache** *n.* (no pl.) continuous pain in a ~ or teeth. '**~less** *adj.* without teeth. **~some** *adj.* (of food) pleasant to the taste.

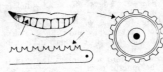

teeth

top¹ [tɒp] *n.* 1. (usu. no pl.) highest part or point. 2. utmost degree; fullest capacity: *~ secret*, of the highest secrecy; *at the ~ of his voice*, as loudly as possible. 3. (attrib.) of or at the ~; highest in position or degree: *the ~ shelf*; *at ~ speed*; *~ hat*, man's silk hat. *v.t.* (*-pp-*) 1. provide a ~ for; be a ~ to. 2. reach the ~ of (e.g. a slope); be at the ~ of. 3. cut the ~(s) off (e.g. plants). '**~coat** *n.* overcoat. '**~heavy** *adj.* too heavy at the ~ in relation to the bottom. **~less** *adj.* (of a woman's garment) leaving the breasts bare: *a ~less bathing-suit*; (of a woman) wearing such a garment: *~less waitresses*. '**~mast** *n.* upper part of a mast. '**~most** *adj.* highest. **~ping** *adj.* (Gt. Brit., sl.) excellent.

top² [tɒp] *n.* toy that spins and balances on a point. (*sleep*) *like a ~*, soundly.

to·paz ['təʊpæz] *n.* semi-precious stone, usu. yellow.

top·ic ['tɒpɪk] *n.* subject for discussion. **top·i·cal** *adj.* of present interest: *~al news*.

to·pog·ra·phy [tə'pɒɡrəfɪ] *n.* (description of the) features (e.g. rivers, roads, etc.) of a place or district. **to·po·graph·i·cal** [ˌtɒpə'ɡræfɪkl] *adj.*

top·ple ['tɒpl] *v.t. & i.* (cause to) be unsteady and overturn.

top·sy-tur·vy [ˌtɒpsɪ'tɜːvɪ] *adj. & adv.* upside down; in confusion.

torch [tɔːtʃ] *n.* 1. piece of wood treated with oil, etc., used as a flaming light; (fig.) sth. that gives enlightenment: *the ~ of learning*. 2. (Gt. Brit.) battery-operated hand-light.

tore, see *tear¹* (v.).

tor·ment ['tɔːment] *n.* (cause of) severe bodily or mental suffering. [tɔː'ment] *v.t.* cause severe suffering to; annoy. **tor·men·tor** [tɔː'mentə*] *n.*

torn, see *tear¹* (v.).

tor·na·do [tɔː'neɪdəʊ] *n.* (pl. *-oes*, *-os*) violent local (thunder)storm, esp. in W. Africa and U.S.A.; whirlwind.

tor·pe·do [tɔː'piːdəʊ] *n.* (pl. *-oes*) cigar-shaped, self-propelled shell filled with explosive, aimed at ships and launched to travel below the surface of the sea. *v.t.* strike, damage, sink, with a ~. **~-boat** *n.* small, fast warship from which ~es are fired.

tor·pid ['tɔːpɪd] *adj.* 1. dull and slow; inactive. 2. (of animals that hibernate) not moving or feeling. **~i·ty** [tɔː'pɪdətɪ], **tor·por** ['tɔːpə*] *ns.* (no pl.) ~ condition.

tor·rent ['tɒrənt] *n.* violent, rushing stream of liquid, esp. water: *rain falling in ~s*; (fig.) violent outburst (of angry words, etc.). **tor·ren·tial** [tə'renʃl] *adj.* of, like, caused by, a ~: *~ial rain*.

tor·rid ['tɒrɪd] *adj.* (of the weather, a country) very hot; tropical: *the ~ zone*.

tor·so ['tɔːsəʊ] *n.* (pl. *~s*) human trunk; (esp.) statue of the human body without head, arms, and legs.

tor·toise ['tɔːtəs] *n.* slow-moving, four-legged land (or freshwater) animal with a hard shell. **~-shell** ['tɔːtəʃel] *n.* yellowish-brown outer shell of some sea-turtles, used for making combs, etc.

a tortoise

tor·tu·ous ['tɔːtjʊəs] *adj.* full of twists and bends; (fig.) not straightforward.

tor·ture ['tɔːtʃə*] *v.t. & n.* (cause) severe suffering (to): *~ a man to make him confess*; *suffer ~ from toothache*. **tor·tur·er** *n.*

To·ry ['tɔːrɪ] *n. & adj.* (colloq. or derog.) Conservative.

toss [tɒs] *v.t. & i.* 1. (cause to) move restlessly from side to side or up and down: *Ships ~ing about on the stormy sea*. 2. throw up into or through the air: *~ one's hat on a shelf*. *The horse ~ed its rider*. 3. *~ (up)* a coin, spin a coin up into the air and guess which side (head or tail) will be on top when it falls; ~ *for it*, decide sth. by doing this. **4.** ~ *one's head*, jerk it up and back (to suggest contempt or indifference). **5.** ~ *sth. off*, drink it straight down. *n.* **1.** ~ing movement: *a ~ of the head.* **2.** *win* (*lose*) *the* ~, guess rightly (wrongly) when a coin is ~ed up; *a ~-up*, sth. of which the outcome depends upon chance.

tot¹ [tɒt] *n.* **1.** very small child. **2.** (colloq.) small portion of spirits (e.g. rum).

tot² [tɒt] *v.t. & i.* (-*tt*-) add up: *expenses ~ting up to £5.*

to·tal ['təʊtl] *adj.* complete; entire: *his ~ debts. n.* ~ amount: *a ~ of £20. v.t. & i.* (-*ll*-, U.S.A. also -*l*-) find the ~ of; reach the ~ of; amount to. ~**·ly** *adv.* completely.

to·tal·i·tar·i·an [ˌtəʊtælɪ'teərɪən] *adj.* ~ *State*, State in which only one political party is allowed and no rival loyalties are recognized (2).

to·tal·iza·tor ['təʊtəlaɪzeɪtə*] *n.* machine for registering the number of bets (esp. on horses or greyhounds) and money due to backers.

tote [təʊt] *n.* (sl., abbr. for) totalizator.

to·tem ['təʊtəm] *n.* (carved or painted representation of a) natural object, esp. an animal, considered, esp. by N. American Indians, to have a close connection with a family group. '~**·pole** *n.* pole or pillar on which a ~ is carved or painted.

tot·ter ['tɒtə*] *v.i.* **1.** walk with weak, unsteady steps. **2.** be almost falling. ~**y** *adj.* unsteady.

touch [tʌtʃ] *v.i. & t.* **1.** (of two or more objects) not be entirely separate, one from the other(s); (cause to) be in contact with; put a finger, hand, etc. on or against. **2.** affect a person or his feelings; concern: *The sad story ~ed us* (*our hearts*). **3.** (usu. in neg.) compare with; be equal to: *No one can ~ him as an actor of tragic roles.* **4.** (with advs. & preps.): ~ *at*, (of a ship) visit (a port) for a short stay; ~ *down*, (of an aircraft) come down to land; ~*down* (n.); ~ (*up*)*on*, say sth. about, refer to (a subject) briefly; ~ *up*, make small changes in (a picture, piece of writing, etc.) to improve it. *n.* **1.** act or fact of ~ing. **2.** (no pl.) (sense giving) feeling by ~ing: *soft* (*rough, etc.*) *to the* ~. **3.** stroke made with a pen, brush, etc.: *add a few finishing ~es to a painting.* **4.** slight quantity, trace (*of* sth.): *a ~ of frost in the air.* **5.** (no pl.) connec-

tion: *in* (*out of*) ~ (*with*), in (not in) regular communication; having (not having) information about: *in ~ with old friends; lose ~* (*with*), get out of ~ (with). **6.** style or manner of ~ing the keys, strings, etc. of a musical instrument, of workmanship (in art): *the ~ of a master* (i.e. expert style). ~**-and-go** [ˌtʌtʃən'gəʊ] *adj.* of uncertain outcome: *It was ~-and-go whether he would arrive in time.* ~**ed** *pred. adj.* **1.** moved (see *move* (3)). **2.** slightly mad. ~**ing** *adj.* arousing pity or sympathy. *prep.* (old use or liter.) concerning. '~**·stone** *n.* sth. used as a test or standard (of purity, etc.). ~**y** *adj.* (-*ier*, -*iest*) easily or quickly offended. ~**·i·ness** *n.* (no pl.).

tough [tʌf] *adj.* **1.** (of meat) hard to cut or to get one's teeth into. **2.** not easily cut, broken, or worn out: ~ *leather.* **3.** strong; able to endure hardships: ~ *soldiers.* **4.** (of work, problems) difficult: *a ~ job.* **5.** (of persons) rough and violent: *a ~ criminal. n.* ~ (5) man. ~**en** ['tʌfn] *v.t. & i.* make or become ~.

tour [tʊə*] *n.* journey out and home again during which several or many places are visited. *v.t. & i.* make a ~ (of): ~ *Europe.* ~**ism** *n.* (no pl.) organized ~ing; business of providing holidays, ~s, hotels, etc. for ~ists. ~**ist** *n.* person making a ~ for pleasure.

tour·na·ment ['tʊənəmənt] *n.* **1.** series of contests of skill between a number of players: *a tennis* (*chess*) ~. **2.** (hist.) contest between armed knights on horseback. **tour·ney** ['tʊənɪ] *n.* ~ (2).

tour·ni·quet ['tʊənɪkeɪ] *n.* device (2) for stopping a flow of blood through an artery by twisting sth. tightly around a limb.

a tourniquet

tou·sle ['taʊzl] *v.t.* put (esp. the hair) into disorder by pulling it about, rubbing it, etc.

tout [taʊt] *n.* person who worries others to buy sth., use his services, etc., esp. one who sells information about racehorses. *v.i.* act as a ~: ~*ing for custom.*

tow¹ [təʊ] *v.t.* pull (a ship, motor car, etc.) along by a rope or chain: ~ *a broken-down car to a garage.* *n.* ~*ing* or being ~*ed:* *have* (*take*) *in* ~, (fig.) be accompanied by (take possession of) (sb.). '~(·ing)-path *n.* path along the side of a river or canal for use in ~*ing.*

tow² [təʊ] *n.* (no pl.) broken fibres of flax, hemp, etc. (for rope, etc.).

to-ward(s) [tə'wɔːd(z)] *prep.* **1.** in the direction of; approaching. **2.** (of time) near. **3.** for the purpose of (helping). **4.** as regards; in relation to.

tow-el ['taʊəl] *n.* cloth for drying oneself after washing, for drying dishes, etc. *v.t. & i.* (*-ll-*, U.S.A. also *-l-*) dry or rub (oneself) with a ~; use a ~.

tow-er ['taʊə*] *n.* tall, strong building containing offices, dwelling-places, etc.; tall part of a building, usu. square or round, esp. as part of a castle or church. (See the picture on page 504.) *v.i.* ~ (*over*, *above*), rise to a great height, be very tall, esp. in relation to the height of the surroundings: ~ *above*, (fig.) greatly exceed in ability, moral qualities, etc.; *in a* ~*ing rage*, violently angry.

town [taʊn] *n.* **1.** place (bigger than a village) with streets, shops, houses, etc. where people live in large numbers. (Cf. *country* (4).) **2.** (no pl.) the people of a ~: *The whole* ~ *was talking about it.* **3.** business, shopping, etc. part of a ~ (contrasted with the suburbs, etc.): *go to* ~ *to do some shopping.* **4.** nearest big centre of population, esp. (in England) London. ~ **hall** *n.* building with offices of local government and usu. a hall for public events (e.g. meetings, concerts).

tox-ic ['tɒksɪk] *adj.* of, caused by, poison; poisonous. **tox-in** ['tɒksɪn] *n.* poisonous substance, esp. one formed in plants and animals.

toy [tɔɪ] *n.* child's plaything. *attrib. adj.* that is a ~: *a* ~ *soldier* (made of lead, etc.); ~ *dogs*, small kinds kept as pets. *v.i.* ~ *with* (*sth.*), (a) handle absent-mindedly; (b) think not very seriously about it: ~ *with the idea of buying a horse.*

trace [treɪs] *v.t.* **1.** outline; mark (*out*): ~ *out the plan of a house.* **2.** copy, e.g. by drawing on transparent *tracing-paper* the lines, etc. of (a map, design, etc.) placed underneath. **3.** follow or discover (sb. or sth.) by observing marks, tracks, bits of evidence, etc.:

~ *a rumour back to the person who started it.* *n.* **1.** mark, sign, etc. showing that sb. or sth. has been present, that sth. has existed or happened: ~*s of an ancient civilization.* **2.** small, least possible, amount (*of sth.*): *not a* ~ *of fear in his character.* **trac-ing** *n.* copy (of a map, etc.) made by tracing (2).

trac-ery ['treɪsərɪ] *n.* ornamental arrangement of designs (e.g. as made by frost on glass, or of stonework in a church window).

tracery   a tractor

track [træk] *n.* **1.** line or series of marks left by a cart, person, animal, etc. in passing along: ~*s in the snow; on the* ~ *of*, in pursuit of; *make* ~*s for,* (sl.) go towards. **2.** path made by frequent use: *off the* ~, (lit. or fig.) on a wrong path or course of action; away from the subject. **3.** course; line taken by sth.: *the* ~ *of a comet* (*storm*). **4.** set of rails for trains, etc.: *single* (*double*) ~, one pair (two pairs) of rails. **5.** endless belt used instead of wheels on some tractors, tanks, etc. (hence ~*ed vehicles*). **6.** prepared path for racing: *a running-*~, *a racing-*~. *v.t.* follow (an animal, etc.) along its ~*s* (1): ~ *down a bear* (find by ~*ing*). ~*·er dog* *n.* police dog used to ~ fugitives. ~ **events** *n. pl.* certain athletic contests (e.g. running races) contrasted with *field events.* ~*·less adj.* having no ~*s* (2). ~ **suit** *n.* suit worn by athletes during training, etc. to keep warm.

tract¹ [trækt] *n.* stretch or area (*of* forest, farm land, water, etc.).

tract² [trækt] *n.* short, printed essay on sth., esp. a moral or religious subject.

trac-table ['træktəbl] *adj.* easily controlled or guided.

trac-tion ['trækʃn] *n.* (no pl.) (power used in) pulling or drawing sth. over a surface: *electric* (*steam*) ~. ~*-engine*, engine used for pulling heavy loads.

trac-tor ['træktə*] *n.* powerful motor vehicle used for pulling ploughs or other heavy equipment. (See the picture.)

trade [treɪd] *n.* **1.** buying and selling

of goods; exchange of goods for money or other goods; particular branch of this: *the cotton (book)* ~; ~ *mark*, design, special name, etc. used to distinguish a manufacturer's goods from others; ~ *wind*, strong wind blowing always towards the equator from the S.E. and N.E. **2.** occupation; way of making a living, esp. a handicraft: *He's a carpenter (shoemaker, tailor) by* ~. **3.** the people, organizations, etc. engaged in a ~: ~ *union*, ~s *union*, organized association of workers in a ~ or group of ~s, formed to protect their interests, improve their conditions, etc.; ~*unionist*, member of a ~ union. *v.i. & t.* **1.** engage in ~ (1): *trading in furs*; ~ (i.e. barter) *furs for tools*. **2.** ~ *(up)on*, take a wrong advantage of, use (sb.'s sympathy, one's good reputation), in order to get sth. **trad·er** *n.* merchant. **'~s·man** *n.* shopkeeper.

tra·di·tion [trəˈdɪʃn] *n.* (handing down from generation to generation of) opinions, beliefs, customs, etc.; opinion, belief, etc. handed down from the past. ~**al** *adj.*

tra·duce [trəˈdjuːs] *v.t.* slander.

traf·fic [ˈtræfɪk] *n.* (no pl.) **1.** (movement of) people and vehicles along roads and streets. **2.** transport business done by a railway, shipping line, etc. **3.** trading: *illegal drug* ~. *v.i.* (-*ck*-) ~ *in*, trade in. ~ **block**, ~ **jam** *ns.* large number of motor vehicles, etc. held up and unable to move on. ~ **is·land** *n.* paved, etc. area in a road to direct ~ and provide refuge for pedestrians crossing. '~**-light(s)**, '~**-ˌsig·nal** *ns.* mechanical signal that controls road ~ by coloured lights. ~ **war·den** *n.* (Gt. Brit.) person assisting the police in controlling the movement of road ~ and esp. the parking of vehicles at parking-meters, etc.

traf·fi·ca·tor [ˈtræfɪkeɪtə*] *n.* (Gt. Brit.) (also *traffic indicator*) device (2) on a motor vehicle to indicate the direction in which the vehicle is about to turn.

trag·e·dy [ˈtrædʒɪdɪ] *n.* **1.** play for the theatre, etc., branch of drama, of a serious and solemn kind, usu. with a sad ending. **2.** sad event or experience in real life. **tra·ge·dian** [trəˈdʒiːdjən] *n.* writer of, actor in, ~ (1). **trag·ic** [ˈtrædʒɪk] *adj.* of ~ (1); very sad. **trag·i·cal·ly** *adv.*

trail [treɪl] *n.* **1.** line, mark(s), traces, left by sb. or sth. that has passed by: *a ~ of smoke* (from a steam-engine); a

~ *of destruction* (left by a violent storm, etc.). **2.** track or scent followed in hunting: *(The hounds were) hot on the* ~, close behind. **3.** path through rough country. *v.t. & i.* **1.** pull or be pulled along behind: *a child* ~*ing a toy cart*; *a long dress* ~*ing on the ground*. **2.** follow the ~ of: ~ *a wild animal (a criminal)*. **3.** (of plants) grow along or over the ground, down a wall, etc. **4.** walk wearily *(along, etc.)*. ~**er** *n.* **1.** vehicle towed by another (e.g. a small cart, a caravan): ~*er park*, caravan park. **2.** ~*ing plant*. **3.** series of short extracts from a cinema or television film to advertise it in advance.

a trailer (1)

train [treɪn] *v.t. & i.* **1.** give teaching and practice to (e.g. a child, a soldier, an animal) in order to bring to a desired standard of behaviour, efficiency, or physical condition: ~ *children to be good citizens*; ~ *a horse for a race*; a *shortage of* ~*ed nurses*. **2.** cause (a plant) to grow in a required direction. **3.** ~ *a gun (up)on*, aim it at. *n.* **1.** (engine and) railway coaches, wagons, etc. joined together. **2.** number of persons, animals, carriages, etc. moving in a line: *a* ~ *of camels*. **3.** series or chain *(of thoughts, ideas, events)*. **4.** group of attendants travelling with a king, etc. **5.** part of a long dress or robe that trails on the ground. **6.** line of gunpowder leading to a mine, etc.; (hence) *in* ~, in readiness. ~**ee** [treɪˈniː] *n.* person receiving (usu. industrial) ~*ing*. ~**er** *n.* person who ~s (1) (athletes, animals for the circus, racehorses, etc.). ~**ing** *n.* (no pl.) ~*ing* or being ~*ed*: *in (out of)* ~*ing*, in (not in) good physical condition (for some athletic activity). ~*ing-college (-school)*, (esp.) one for ~*ing* teachers.

trait [treɪ] *n.* distinguishing quality or characteristic.

trai·tor [ˈtreɪtə*] *n.* person who betrays a friend, is disloyal to his country, a cause, etc. ~**ous** *adj.* **trai·tress** [ˈtreɪtrɪs] *n.* female ~.

tra·jec·to·ry ['trædʒɪktərɪ] *n.* curved path of a projectile (e.g. a bullet, missile).

tram [træm] *n.* (also ~car; U.S.A. = *streetcar*) electric car running on rails (usu.) along public roads or streets. '~-line, '~way *ns.* (Gt. Brit.) line of rails for ~s.

a tram(car)

tram·mel ['træml] *v.t.* (-ll-, U.S.A. also -l-) hamper; make progress difficult. *n.* (usu. pl.) sth. that ~s: *the ~s of routine.*

tramp [træmp] *v.i. & t.* 1. walk with heavy steps. 2. walk (esp. for a long distance); walk through or over: ~ *through Wales;* ~ *the hills.* *n.* 1. (no pl.) sound of heavy footsteps (e.g. of soldiers marching). 2. long walk. 3. person (usu. homeless) who goes from place to place and does no regular work. 4. (sl.) prostitute. 5. (also ~-ship, ~-steamer) cargo boat that goes to any port(s) where cargo can be picked up.

tram·ple ['træmpl] *v.t. & i.* crush heavily (on); crush under the feet: ~ *the flowers;* ~ *the grass down.*

tram·po·line ['træmpəlɪn] *n.* canvas sheet connected by springs[1] (n. 3) to a horizontal frame, used by acrobats, etc.

trance [trɑːns] *n.* 1. sleep-like condition. 2. abnormal, dreamy state.

tran·quil ['træŋkwɪl] *adj.* calm; quiet. ~·ly *adv.* ~·li·ty (U.S.A. also ~·i·ty) [træŋ'kwɪlətɪ] *n.* (no pl.) ~ state. ~·lize (U.S.A. also ~·ize) ['træŋkwɪlaɪz] *v.t.* make ~, esp. by a drug, etc. ~·liz·er (U.S.A. also ~·iz·er) *n.* drug that ~lizes, esp. one that reduces anxiety and tension.

trans- [træns-] *pref.* 1. across; on or to the other side of: *transatlantic; transcontinental.* 2. into another state or place: *transcribe; transform; transplant.* 3. through: *translucent.*

trans·act [træn'zækt] *v.t.* do, conduct (business *with* sb.). **trans·ac·tion** [træn'zækʃn] *n.* 1. (~ing of a) piece of business. 2. (pl.) (records[2] (1) of) proceedings of a society (5), esp. lectures to a learned society.

trans·al·pine [,trænz'ælpaɪn] *adj.* be-yond the Alps, esp. as viewed from Italy.

tran·scend [træn'send] *v.t.* be or go beyond or outside the range of (experience, imagination). **tran·scen·dent** *adj.* surpassing: *of ~ent genius.*

tran·scribe [træn'skraɪb] *v.t.* copy in writing, esp. write (sth.) in full from shorthand notes. **tran·script** ['trænskrɪpt] *n.* sth. ~d. **tran·scrip·tion** [træn'skrɪpʃn] *n.* transcribing; sth. ~d, esp. into a special form of writing: *phonetic transcription.*

tran·sept ['trænsept] *n.* (either end of the) shorter part of a cross-shaped church.

trans·fer [træns'fɜː*] *v.t. & i.* (-rr-) 1. change position; move *from* one place *to* another. 2. hand over (property, etc.) to sb. 3. (of a person) move or be moved from one occupation, position, etc. to another. ['trænsfɜː*] *n.* ~ring or being ~red; document ~ring sb. or sth. ~ *fee,* (esp.) sum paid for a ~ of a professional footballer to another club; ~ *list,* list of footballers available for ~. ~·able *adj.* that can be ~red. ~·ence ['trænsfərəns] *n.* ~ring, esp. from one job to another.

trans·fig·ure [træns'fɪgə*] *v.t.* change the shape or appearance of, esp. so as to make glorious or exalted. **trans·fig·u·ra·tion** [,trænsfɪgjʊ'reɪʃn] *n.* change of this sort, esp. the *Transfiguration,* that of Jesus, as described in the Bible (Matthew 17).

trans·fix [træns'fɪks] *v.t.* 1. pierce (with a pointed weapon, etc.). 2. cause (sb.) to be unable to move, think, etc.: ~ed with fear *(surprise).*

trans·form [træns'fɔːm] *v.t. & i.* change the shape, appearance, quality, or nature (of). **trans·for·ma·tion** [,trænsfə'meɪʃn] *n.* ~·er *n.* (esp.) apparatus (1) that increases or decreases the voltage of an electric current.

trans·fuse [træns'fjuːz] *v.t.* transfer (sth., esp. blood) from one living person to another. **trans·fu·sion** [træns'fjuːʒn] *n.* transfusing, esp. of blood: *The patient had several blood transfusions.*

trans·gress [træns'gres] *v.t. & i.* 1. overstep bounds; break (a law, treaty, an agreement). 2. do wrong; sin. **trans·gres·sion** [træns'greʃn] *n.* **trans·gres·sor** *n.* wrongdoer; sinner.

tran·sient ['trænzɪənt] *adj.* lasting for a short time only; brief.

tran·sis·tor [træn'sɪstə*] *n.* electronic device (2), much smaller than a valve (3), used in radio sets, etc.: *a ~ radio.* ~·ize *v.t.* equip with ~s.

tran·sit ['trænsɪt] *n.* (no pl.) conveying or being conveyed across, over, or through: *lost (delayed) in ~* (while being taken or carried from one place to another).

tran·si·tion [træn'sɪʒn] *n.* change from one condition or set of circumstances to another.

tran·si·tive ['trænsɪtɪv] *adj.* (gram.) characterized by having or containing a direct object: *a ~ verb.*

tran·si·to·ry ['trænsɪtərɪ] *adj.* transient.

trans·late [træns'leɪt] *v.t.* give the meaning of (sth. said or written) in another language. **trans·la·tion** [træns'leɪʃn] *n.* process of translating; sth. ~d. **trans·la·tor** *n.* person who ~s, esp. sth. written. (Cf. *interpreter*.)

trans·lu·cent [trænz'luːsnt] *adj.* allowing light to pass through, but not transparent.

trans·mit [trænz'mɪt] *v.t.* (-tt-) **1.** pass or hand on; send on: *~ a message by radio*; *~ a disease*. **2.** let through or along: *Iron ~s heat.* **trans·mis·sion** [trænz'mɪʃn] *n.* **1.** (no pl.) ~ting or being ~ted. **2.** part of a motor engine that ~s power to turn the axle(s). **~·ter** *n.* (esp.) part of a telegraph, radio apparatus, for sending out signals, radio programmes, etc.

trans·par·ent [træns'pærənt] *adj.* **1.** that can be seen through, like clear glass. **2.** unmistakable or undoubted: *a ~ lie.* **3.** clear; easily understood: *a ~ style.* **trans·par·ence, trans·par·en·cy** *ns.* (no pl.).

tran·spire [træn'spaɪə*] *v.i. & t.* **1.** (of an event, a secret) become known; come to light. **2.** (colloq.) happen. **3.** (of the body, plants) give off, pass off (moisture, vapour).

trans·plant [træns'plɑːnt] *v.t.* take up (plants, etc. with their roots) and plant in another place. ['trænsplɑːnt] *n.* replacement (by surgical operation) of a diseased organ with a healthy one from another body: *a heart (kidney) ~.* **trans·plan·ta·tion** [ˌtrænsplɑːn'teɪʃn] *n.*

trans·port [træn'spɔːt] *v.t.* **1.** carry (persons, goods) from one place to another. **2.** (in former times) send (a criminal) to a distant colony as punishment. **3.** *be ~ed with*, be overcome with (joy, etc.). ['trænspɔːt] *n.* **1.** (no pl.) ~ing (1). **2.** (attrib.) of or for ~ing (1): *London's ~ system.* **3.** ship, aircraft, for carrying soldiers. **4.** (often pl.) *in a ~* (*in ~s*) *of delight* (*rage, etc.*), carried away by strong feelings of pleasure,

rage, etc. **trans·por·ta·tion** [ˌtrænspɔː'teɪʃn] *n.* (no pl.) (esp.) ~ing (2) or being ~ed (2). **~·er** *n.* person or thing that ~s or serves as a means of ~ation.

trans·pose [træns'pəʊz] *v.t.* cause (two or more things) to change places. **trans·po·si·tion** [ˌtrænspə'zɪʃn] *n.*

trans·verse ['trænzvɜːs] *adj.* lying or placed across. **~·ly** *adv.*

trap [træp] *n.* **1.** device (2) for catching animals, etc. **2.** plan or trick for making a person do or say sth. he does not wish to do or say: *set a ~ to catch a thief*; *fall into a ~*, be caught by a trick. **3.** light, two-wheeled carriage pulled by a horse or pony. *v.t.* (-pp-) take in a ~ (1, 2); capture by a trick. **'~·door** *n.* door in a floor or roof. **~·per** *n.* man who ~s animals for their skins.

tra·peze [trə'piːz] *n.* horizontal bar or rod supported by two ropes, used by acrobats and persons doing physical training.

trap·pings ['træpɪŋz] *n. pl.* ornaments or decorations, esp. as a sign of public office: *the ~ of royalty.*

trash [træʃ] *n.* (no pl.) **1.** worthless material or writing; rubbish; refuse². **2.** worthless person(s): *white ~* (U.S.A.), (derog.) poor white population in the Southern States. **~·y** *adj.* (-ier, -iest) worthless.

trav·el ['trævl] *v.i. & t.* (-ll-, U.S.A. also -l-) **1.** make (esp. long) journeys. **2.** go; move: *Light ~s faster than sound.* *n.* **1.** (no pl.) ~ling; *fond of ~.* **2.** (pl.) journeys, esp. to other countries: *Is he back from his ~s yet?* **~ agen·cy, ~ bu·reau** *ns.* one making arrangements for ~lers by selling tickets, reserving accommodation, etc. **~ agent** *n.* person making such arrangements for ~lers. **~·ing sales·man** *n.* (U.S.A.) = commercial ~ler. **~·ler** (U.S.A. also **~·er**) *n.* **1.** person who ~s. **2.** commercial ~ler. **~·ogue** (U.S.A. also **-og**) ['trævəlɒg] *n.* film or illustrated lecture on ~.

tra·verse ['trævəs] *v.t.* travel, pass, or lie across.

trav·es·ty ['trævɪstɪ] *n.* imitation or description of sth. that is, often on purpose, unlike and inferior to the real thing: *His trial was a ~ of justice.* *v.t.* make or be a ~ of.

trawl [trɔːl] *v.i. & t. & n.* (go fishing with, drag along the sea-bottom, a) large, wide-mouthed net (also called **~-net**). **~·er** *n.* boat used in ~ing.

tray [treɪ] *n.* flat piece of wood, metal,

etc. with raised edges, for holding small, light things: *a tea-*~; *a pen-*~.

treach·er·ous ['tretʃərəs] *adj.* 1. false or disloyal (to a friend, a cause, etc.). 2. deceptive; not to be relied on: *The ice (My memory) is* ~. **treach·ery** ['tretʃərɪ] *n.* being ~; ~ act(s).

trea·cle ['triːkl] *n.* (no pl.) thick, sticky, dark liquid produced while sugar is being refined.

tread [tred] *v.i. & t.* (p.t. *trod* [trɒd], p.p. *trodden* ['trɒdn]) 1. walk, put the foot or feet down (*on*): ~ *on sb.'s toes.* 2. stamp or crush *in, down,* etc. with the feet: ~ *out a fire in the grass.* 3. make by walking: *The cattle had trodden a path to the river. n.* 1. way or sound of walking: *with a heavy (loud)* ~. 2. part of a step or stair on which the foot is placed. 3. moulded part of a tyre that touches the ground.

trea·dle ['tredl] *n.* pedal or lever that drives a machine (e.g. a sewing-machine) and is worked by pressure of the foot or feet. *v.i.* work a ~.

trea·son ['triːzn] *n.* (no pl.) treachery to one's ruler or government; disloyalty. ~·**able** *adj.* having the nature of ~.

trea·sure ['treʒə*] *n.* (store of) gold and silver, jewels, etc.; wealth; highly valued object or person: *art* ~*s. v.t.* 1. store up for future use; keep; remember: ~ (*up*) *old letters.* 2. value highly. **trea·sur·er** *n.* person in charge of money, etc. belonging to a society, etc. **trea·sury** ['treʒərɪ] *n.* 1. department of government that controls a country's public money. 2. place where ~s are kept; funds of a society, organization, etc.

treat [triːt] *v.t. & i.* 1. act or behave towards: ~ *sb. kindly*; ~ *sb. as (if he were) a child.* 2. consider: ~ *sth. lightly (as a joke).* 3. discuss; deal with: *He* ~*ed the subject thoroughly.* 4. (of a lecture, book, etc.) ~ *of,* be about: *The essay* ~*s of insect pests.* 5. give medical or surgical care to (a person, disease). 6. put (a substance) through a process (in manufacture, etc.): ~ *a substance with acid.* 7. ~ *sb. to sth.,* supply him with (food or drink, entertainment, etc.) at one's own expense: ~ *a friend to a good dinner.* 8. discuss or arrange terms (*with*). *n.* 1. pleasure, esp. sth. not often enjoyed: *What a* ~ *to get out of the noisy town!* 2. ~*ing* of others to food, etc.: *stand* ~, bear the expense of the entertainment. **trea·tise** ['triː-tɪz] *n.* book, etc. that deals carefully and methodically with a subject.

~·**ment** *n.* way of ~ing sb. or sth.; particular kind of medical ~ment.

trea·ty ['triːtɪ] *n.* agreement made and signed between States: *a peace* ~, *a* ~ *of peace*; *a trade* ~.

tre·ble¹ ['trebl] *v.t. & i. & adj.* (make or become) three times as much, etc.

tre·ble² ['trebl] *n.* (boy's voice, instrument, that takes the) highest part in music. *adj.* of or for the ~.

tree [triː] *n.* perennial plant with a single, self-supporting trunk of wood with (usu.) no branches for some distance above the ground. *family* ~, diagram or list showing or giving family descent.

a tree　　　a trestle-table

trek [trek] *v.i.* (-*kk*-) go on a long journey, esp. by ox-wagon or similarly with animals: *pony-*~*king. n.* such a journey; any long, hard journey.

trel·lis ['trelɪs] *n.* upright framework of strips of wood, etc. crossing one another (e.g. for supporting climbing plants).

trem·ble ['trembl] *v.i.* shake (with fear, anger, cold, etc.); be agitated or worried. *n.* trembling; shudder.

tre·men·dous [trɪ'mendəs] *adj.* very great; enormous. ~·**ly** *adv.*

trem·or ['tremə*] *n.* 1. shaking or trembling. 2. thrill (of fear, excitement, etc.).

trem·u·lous ['tremjʊləs] *adj.* trembling; timid; nervous.

trench [trentʃ] *n.* ditch dug in the ground (e.g. for draining off water, or as a protection for soldiers against the enemy's fire). *v.t. & i.* make a ~ or ~es in.

trench·ant ['trentʃənt] *adj.* (of language) vigorous; decisive.

trend [trend] *n.* general direction; tendency. *v.i.* have a certain ~: *The coast* ~*s (towards the) south.* ~·**y** *adj.* (-*ier,* -*iest*) (Gt. Brit., colloq.) showing, following, the latest ~ of fashion, etc.

trep·i·da·tion [ˌtrepɪ'deɪʃn] *n.* (no pl.) alarm; excited state of mind.

tres·pass ['trespəs] *v.i.* 1. ~ (*on* or *upon*), go on to privately-owned land without right or permission; (fig.) encroach (*upon sb.'s time, hospitality,*

etc.). **2.** (old use) do wrong (*against*).
n. act of ⌐ing. ⌐·**er** *n.*

tress [tres] *n.* portion or lock of hair
on the head; (pl.) long hair (esp. of a
woman's or girl's head).

tres·tle ['tresl] *n.* horizontal bar with
two divergent pairs of legs, used as a
support for a table top, a workman's
bench, etc. ⌐-*bridge*, bridge supported
by a timber or metal framework;
⌐-*table*, table made by laying a board
or boards on ⌐s. (See the picture at
tree.)

tri- [traɪ-] *pref.* three.

tri·al ['traɪəl] *n.* **1.** testing; test: *a ⌐ of
strength; give sth. a ⌐*, use it to learn
whether it is good, useful, etc.;
(attrib.) *a ⌐ flight* (e.g. of a new aircraft, to test it); *on ⌐*, for the purpose
of testing. **2.** sth. or sb. troublesome
or annoying: *a boy who is a ⌐ to his
teachers*. **3.** examination before a judge
(and jury): *on ⌐ for theft*.

tri·an·gle ['traɪæŋgl] *n.* **1.** plane figure
with three straight sides; any three
points not in a straight line. **2.** musical
instrument made of a steel rod in the
shape of a ⌐, struck with a steel rod.

tri·an·gu·lar [traɪ'æŋgjʊlə*] *adj.* **1.**
in the shape of a ⌐. **2.** in which three
persons, etc. take part.

tribe [traɪb] *n.* racial group, esp. one
united by language and customs, living
as a community under one or more
chiefs. ⌐s·**man** *n.* member of a ⌐.
trib·al ['traɪbl] *adj.*

trib·u·la·tion [ˌtrɪbjuˈleɪʃn] *n.* great
trouble; (cause of) grief.

tri·bu·nal [traɪˈbjuːnl] *n.* place of
judgement; board (3) of officials or
judges appointed for special duty (e.g.
to hear appeals against high rents,
military service, etc.).

trib·ute ['trɪbjuːt] *n.* **1.** (usu. regular)
payment that one government or ruler
exacts from another. **2.** sth. done, said,
or given to show respect or admiration: *pay ⌐ to the founders of a school*.
trib·u·tary ['trɪbjʊtərɪ] *n. & adj.* **1.**
(country, ruler, etc.) paying ⌐ (1) to
another. **2.** (river) flowing into another.

trice¹ [traɪs] *v.t.* ⌐ *up*, pull up and tie
(a sail) in place.

trice² [traɪs] *n.* (only in) *in a ⌐*, in an
instant; at once.

trick [trɪk] *n.* **1.** sth. done in order to
deceive, to outwit or outdo sb.; sth.
done to make a person appear ridiculous: *play a ⌐ on sb.* **2.** mischievous or
foolish act; practical joke: *The children
are always up to mad ⌐s. a dirty
(shabby) ⌐*, a contemptible action. **3.**

action, usu. needing skill or practice,
done to deceive and amuse people:
card (conjuring) ⌐s. **4.** way of behaving
that is peculiar to a person: *He has a
⌐ of pulling his left ear when he's
thinking.* **5.** right way of doing sth.,
usu. a way that must be learnt by
practice: *There's a ⌐ in it. You'll soon
get the ⌐ of it.* **6.** (cards played in)
one round (of bridge, etc.): *take (win)
a ⌐*, win one round. *v.t.* deceive by
⌐ (1): *⌐ sb. out of sth. (into doing sth.).*
⌐·**er·y** *n.* (no pl.) deception; cheating.
⌐·**ster** ['trɪkstə*] *n.* person who has
the habit of ⌐ing (1) people. ⌐·**y** *adj.*
(*-ier, -iest*) **1.** (of persons, their actions)
deceptive. **2.** (of work, etc.) requiring
skill; full of hidden difficulties.

trick·le ['trɪkl] *v.t. & i.* (of liquid)
(cause to) flow in drops or in a thin
stream. *n.* weak or thin flow: *The
stream had shrunk to a ⌐.*

tri·col·our (U.S.A. -or) ['trɪkələ*] *n.*
flag (e.g. the French flag) with three
equal bands of different colours.

tri·cy·cle ['traɪsɪkl] *n.* three-wheeled
cycle.

tri·dent ['traɪdənt] *n.* spear with three
points.

tri·en·ni·al [traɪ'enjəl] *adj.* lasting for,
happening or done every, three years.
n. ⌐ plant.

tri·fle ['traɪfl] *n.* **1.** thing, event, etc.
of little value or importance. **2.** small
amount, esp. of money. **3.** *a ⌐* (adv.),
somewhat; a little: *The skirt is a ⌐
too long.* **4.** sweet dish of cake, jam,
cream, etc. *v.i. & t.* **1.** talk or act
lightly, without serious purpose: *He's
not a man to be ⌐d with.* **2.** ⌐ *away*,
waste: *⌐ away a whole hour.* **tri·fling**
adj. unimportant.

trig·ger ['trɪgə*] *n.* lever for releasing
a spring, esp. of a firearm.

trig·o·nom·e·try [ˌtrɪgəˈnɒmɪtrɪ] *n.*
(no pl.) branch of mathematics that
deals with the relations between sides
and angles of triangles.

tri·lat·er·al [ˌtraɪˈlætərəl] *adj.* three-
sided: *a ⌐ treaty.*

trill [trɪl] *n.* shaking or quavering
sound made by the voice, etc. *v.i. &
t.* say, sing, or play with a ⌐.

tril·lion ['trɪljən] *n. & adj.* (Gt. Brit.)
one million × million × million;
(U.S.A.) one million × million.

tril·o·gy ['trɪlədʒɪ] *n.* group of three
plays, operas, novels, etc., each complete in itself but with a common subject.

trim [trɪm] *adj.* (*-mm-*) in good order;
neat and tidy. *v.t.* (*-mm-*) **1.** make ⌐,

esp. by taking or cutting away uneven, irregular, or unwanted parts: ~ *a hedge (one's beard, the wick of a lamp)*. **2.** decorate or ornament (a hat, dress, etc. with lace, etc.). **3.** adjust the balance of (a boat, an aircraft) by arranging the position of cargo, passengers, etc.; arrange (sails) to suit the wind. *n.* (no pl.) state or degree of preparedness (*for* sth.); fitness: *get into ~ for the sports meeting. ~* **ming** *n.* (esp.) material (lace, ribbon, etc.) for ~ming (2) dresses or hats.

trin·i·ty ['trɪnɪtɪ] *n.* group of three. *the T~,* (in Christian teaching) union of Father, Son, and Holy Ghost; one God.

trin·ket ['trɪŋkɪt] *n.* small jewel or ornament, of little value.

trio ['triːəʊ] *n.* (pl. ~s) group of three; (musical composition for) group of three singers or players.

trip [trɪp] *v.i. & t.* (-pp-) **1.** run with quick light steps. **2.** (cause to) stumble; (almost) fall after striking the foot on sth.: ~ *over the root of a tree.* **3.** (often ~ *up*), make a mistake; (cause sb. to) fall. *n.* **1.** journey, esp. for pleasure. **2.** fall or stumble. **3.** (colloq.) visionary experience caused by a psychedelic drug: *a bad ~,* hallucinations, pain, etc. caused by taking a psychedelic drug. **~·per** *n.* (Gt. Brit.) person making a (usu. short) ~ (1) for pleasure: *weekend ~pers.*

tri·par·tite [,traɪ'pɑːtaɪt] *adj.* **1.** (of an agreement) in which three parties have a share. **2.** having three parts.

tripe [traɪp] *n.* (no pl.) **1.** part of a cow's stomach used as food. **2.** (sl.) worthless talk, writing, ideas.

tri·ple ['trɪpl] *adj.* made up of three (parts or parties (3)). *v.t. & i.* make, become, be, three times as much or as many: ~ *your income.*

trip·let ['trɪplɪt] *n.* **1.** one of three children born at one birth. **2.** (pl.) three such children. **3.** set of three.

trip·li·cate ['trɪplɪkət] *adj.* of which there are three alike made. *n.* one of three like things, esp. documents: *in ~,* one original and two copies. ['trɪplɪkeɪt] *v.t.* make in ~.

tri·pod ['traɪpɒd] *n.* three-legged support (e.g. for a camera).

tri·sect [traɪ'sekt] *v.t.* divide (a line, angle, etc.) into three (esp. equal) parts.

trite [traɪt] *adj.* (of remarks, ideas, feelings) commonplace; not new.

tri·umph ['traɪəmf] *n.* (joy or satisfaction at) success or victory: *return home in ~; shouts of ~. v.i.* win a victory (*over*); exult (*over*); show joy because of success. **tri·um·phal** [traɪ'ʌmfl] *adj.* of, for, a ~; expressing ~. **tri·um·phant** [traɪ'ʌmfənt] *adj.* (rejoicing at) having ~ed.

tri·um·vir [trɪ'ʌmvə*] *n.* (pl. ~s, ~i [trɪ'ʊmvɪriː]) (in ancient Rome) each of three men holding an office jointly. **tri·um·vi·rate** [traɪ'ʌmvɪrət] *n.* office of a ~; body (5) of ~s or of a group of any three persons.

triv·i·al ['trɪvɪəl] *adj.* **1.** of small value or importance. **2.** (of persons) trifling. **~·i·ty** [,trɪvɪ'ælətɪ] *n.* ~ thing, idea, etc.

trod(·den), see *tread* (v.).

trog·lo·dyte ['trɒɡlədaɪt] *n.* cave-dweller in ancient times.

troi·ka ['trɔɪkə] *n.* **1.** Russian vehicle drawn by three horses abreast. **2.** group of three administrators or political leaders; triumvirate.

trol·ley ['trɒlɪ] *n.* (pl. ~s), **trol·ly** ['trɒlɪ] *n.* (pl. -ies) **1.** (Gt. Brit.) two- or four-wheeled handcart; (also *tea-~*) small table, running on castors (1), for serving refreshments. **2.** (Gt. Brit.) small, low truck running on rails. **3.** small contact wheel between a tramcar or bus (*~bus*) and an overhead cable.

trom·bone [trɒm'bəʊn] *n.* large, loud, brass wind instrument with a sliding tube.

a trombone   a trumpet

troop [truːp] *n.* **1.** group of persons or animals, esp. when moving: ~*s of children; a ~ of antelopes.* **2.** unit of cavalry. **3.** (pl.) soldiers. *v.i.* come or go together in a group: *children ~ing out of school.* **~·er** *n.* **1.** soldier in a cavalry regiment. **2.** (U.S.A.) mounted policeman, now usu. using a motor vehicle. '**~-ship** *n.* ship to carry soldiers.

tro·phy ['trəʊfɪ] *n.* sth. gained, awarded, or kept in memory of a victory or success (e.g. in hunting, games, etc.): *a tennis ~*.

trop·ic ['trɒpɪk] *n.* **1.** line of latitude 23° 27′ north (*T~ of Cancer*) or south (*T~ of Capricorn*) of the equator. **2.** *the ~s*, the part of the world between these lines. **trop·i·cal** *adj.* of, or as of, the ~s: *~al fruit*; *~al temperatures*.

trot [trɒt] *v.i. & t.* (*-tt-*) **1.** (of horses, etc.) go at a pace faster than a walk but not so fast as a gallop. **2.** (of a person) run with short steps. **3.** cause to ~. *n.* (no pl.) *~ting* pace; period of *~ting*: *at a steady ~*; *go for a ~*.

troth [trəʊθ] *n.* (no pl.) (old use) plight one's ~, promise to marry.

trou·ble ['trʌbl] *v.t. & i.* **1.** cause worry, discomfort, anxiety, or inconvenience to: *~d by bad news (with a cough)*. **2.** *May I trouble you (for sth., to do sth.)? Will you please (give me ..., do sth.)?* **3.** give oneself worry or inconvenience: *Don't ~ to do that. Don't ~ about that. n.* **1.** (person or happening causing) worry, anxiety, discomfort, unhappiness, possible punishment: *be in ~, get into ~*, do, have done, sth. likely to bring ~. **2.** (no pl.) extra work; effort; difficulty: *It will be no ~. have ~ with one's lessons*, find them difficult; *take ~ (to do sth., with or over sth.)*, take pains; use great care. **3.** (pl.) public disturbances; political or social unrest: *labour ~s* (e.g. strikes). **4.** faulty operation: *engine ~*. **5.** disease: *kidney ~*. '*~-*,**mak·er** *n.* person who stirs up discontent. *~some adj.* causing ~; needing much care.

trough [trɒf] *n.* **1.** long, open box for animals to feed or drink from or for kneading dough for bread. **2.** hollow in the sea's surface between two waves.

trounce [traʊns] *v.t.* beat; thrash; defeat.

troupe [tru:p] *n.* company, esp. of actors or members of a circus.

trou·ser ['traʊzə*] *n.* **1.** (pl.) (often a *pair of ~s*) outer garment for the legs, reaching from waist to ankles. **2.** (attrib.) of, for, ~s: *~ pockets*. '*~-*suit *n.* woman's suit of ~s and jacket.

trous·seau ['tru:səʊ] *n.* outfit of clothing, etc. for a bride.

trout [traʊt] *n.* (pl. ~) freshwater fish valued as food.

trow·el ['traʊəl] *n.* **1.** flat-bladed tool for spreading mortar on bricks, plaster on walls, etc. **2.** hand-tool with a scoop for lifting plants, etc.

troy [trɔɪ] *n.* (no pl.) British system of weights, used for gold and silver, in which 1 pound = 12 ounces.

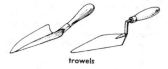

trowels

tru·ant ['tru:ənt] *n.* child who stays away from school without good reason: *play ~, be a ~*. **tru·an·cy** ['tru:ənsɪ] *n.* **1.** (no pl.) state of being ~. **2.** act or instance of playing ~.

truce [tru:s] *n.* (agreement for the) stopping of fighting for a time (e.g. to take away the wounded).

truck¹ [trʌk] *n.* **1.** (Gt. Brit.) open railway wagon for heavy goods (e.g. coal). **2.** railway porter's barrow. **3.** lorry.

truck² [trʌk] *n.* (no pl.) **1.** barter; exchange: *have no ~ with*, have no dealings with; have nothing to do with. **2.** (U.S.A.) market-garden produce: *~ farm (garden)*.

truck·le ['trʌkl] *v.i. ~ to*, submit to in a servile or cowardly way.

tru·cu·lent ['trʌkjʊlənt] *adj.* looking for, desiring, a fight; ready to make trouble. *~ly adv.* **tru·cu·lence, tru·cu·len·cy** *ns.*

trudge [trʌdʒ] *v.i. & t.* walk wearily or heavily: *trudging through deep snow*; *~ 15 miles. n.* long tiring walk.

true [tru:] *adj.* (*~r, ~st*) **1.** in accordance or agreement with fact: *come ~*, (of a hope or dream) become fact; happen. **2.** loyal, faithful (*to* a friend, etc.). **3.** genuine; rightly so named. **4.** correct: *a ~ copy*. **tru·ism** ['tru:-ɪzəm] *n.* statement that is obviously ~ and need not have been made. **tru·ly** *adv.* **1.** sincerely. **2.** truthfully. **3.** certainly; genuinely: *a truly brave action*.

trump [trʌmp] *n.* playing-card of a suit temporarily ranking above others: *turn up ~s*, (fig., colloq.) turn out better than was expected; have a stroke of luck. *v.t. ~ up*, invent (an excuse, a false story, etc.) to deceive sb.

trum·pery ['trʌmpərɪ] *adj.* showy, but of little value: *~ ornaments*.

trum·pet ['trʌmpɪt] *n.* **1.** musical wind instrument of brass (see the picture at *trombone*): *blow one's own ~*, (fig.) praise oneself. **2.** sth. shaped like a ~. *v.i.* blow a ~ or (e.g. of an elephant) make a ~-sound. *~·er n.*

trun·cate [trʌŋˈkeɪt] *v.t.* shorten by cutting the top, tip, or end from.

trun·cheon [ˈtrʌntʃən] *n.* short, thick club (e.g. used by the police).

trun·dle [ˈtrʌndl] *v.t. & i.* (of sth. heavy or awkward in shape) roll along: *tanks (2) trundling along.*

trunk [trʌŋk] *n.* **1.** main stem of a tree. **2.** body without head, arms, or legs. **3.** large box for holding clothes, etc. while travelling. **4.** long nose of an elephant. **5.** (U.S.A.) = boot (2) of a motor car. **6.** (pl.) short, close-fitting breeches worn by men for swimming, boxing, etc. **7.** (attrib.) ~-call, telephone call to a distant place. '~-line, (a) main line of a railway; (b) telephone cable for ~-calls. ~-road, important main road.

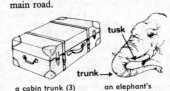

a cabin trunk (3)   an elephant's
                      trunk (4) and tusks

truss [trʌs] *n.* **1.** (Gt. Brit.) bundle (of hay or straw). **2.** framework supporting a roof, bridge, etc. *v.t.* bind or fasten: ~ (up) *a chicken*, pin the wings to the body before roasting it.

trust [trʌst] *n.* **1.** (no pl.) confidence, strong belief, in the goodness, strength, reliability, of sth. or sb.: *on* ~, without proof; on credit. **2.** person or thing confided in. **3.** (no pl.) responsibility: *a position of great* ~. **4.** (law) property held and managed by one or more persons (~*ees*) for another's benefit; legal relation (*in a* ~) between the ~*ee*(s) and the property; such property. **5.** association of business firms to achieve some special object. *v.i. & t.* **1.** have ~ (1) in: ~ *in God.* **2.** give into the care of: *T*~ *your business affairs to me. T*~ *me with your affairs.* **3.** allow credit to a customer, etc. **4.** hope: *I* ~ *you will be able to help us.* **5.** allow (sb.) to have sth., to do sth., without a feeling of doubt or anxiety. ~·**ee** [ˌtrʌsˈtiː] *n.* person who has charge of property in ~ (4) or of the business affairs of an institution. ~·**ee·ship** *n.* position of ~*ee*; (esp.) responsibility for a territory, granted by the United Nations. ~·**ful** *adj.* ready to ~ others; not suspicious. ~·**ing** *adj.* having or showing ~ (1).

~·**wor·thy** *adj.* deserving ~ (1); dependable. ~**y** *adj.* (-ier, -iest) (old use) ~worthy.

truth [truːθ] *n.* (pl. ~s [-ðz]) **1.** (no pl.) quality or state of being true. **2.** (no pl.) that which is true: *tell the* ~. **3.** fact, belief, etc. accepted as true: *the* ~*s of religion.* ~·**ful** *adj.* **1.** (of persons) in the habit of telling the ~. **2.** (of statements) true.

try [traɪ] *v.i. & t.* **1.** make an attempt. **2.** ~ *for*, make an attempt to get (esp. a position). **3.** use sth., do sth., as an experiment or test, to see whether it is satisfactory: *Have you tried quinine?* ~ *sth. on*, put on (a garment, a shoe, etc.) to see whether it fits, looks well, etc.; ~ *one's hand at sth.*, make a first attempt at it; ~ *sth. out*, use or experiment in order to test. **4.** inquire into (a case) in a lawcourt: *He was tried and found guilty of theft.* **5.** cause annoyance or suffering (to); afflict; strain: ~ *sb.'s patience (courage). Small print tries the eyes.* *n.* attempt: *Let me have a* ~. ~·**ing** *adj.* causing trouble or annoyance; difficult to endure.

tryst [trɪst] *n.* (old use) (time and place for, agreement to have, a) meeting, esp. between lovers.

tset·se [ˈtsetsɪ] *n.* (in tropical Africa) fly whose bite causes (often fatal) disease in man and animals.

T-shirt [ˈtiːʃɜːt] *n.* short-sleeved, close-fitting, collarless usu. cotton shirt worn informally.

tub [tʌb] *n.* **1.** large, open vessel, usu. round and made of wood, metal, or plastic. **2.** (colloq.) bath-~; bath: *have a cold* ~. ~·**by** *adj.* (-ier, -iest) short, fat, and round.

tube [tjuːb] *n.* **1.** long, hollow cylinder (e.g. of glass or rubber). **2.** soft metal container with a screw-cap, used for toothpaste, etc. **3.** (colloq.) underground railway (in London). **4.** (U.S.A.) valve for use in radio or television sets. **5.** (anat., zool.) hollow, ~-shaped organ or vessel: *the bronchial* ~*s.* **tub·ing** *n.* (no pl.) length of ~: *two yards of rubber tubing.* **tu·bu·lar** [ˈtjuːbjʊlə*] *adj.* ~-shaped; having ~s: *a tubular boiler.*

tu·ber [ˈtjuːbə*] *n.* thick, swollen part, formed on a stem underground, from which new plants will grow (e.g. a potato).

tu·ber·cu·lo·sis [tjuːˌbɜːkjʊˈləʊsɪs] *n.* (no pl.) wasting disease affecting various parts of the body's tissues, esp. the lungs. **tu·ber·cu·lar** [tjuːˈbɜːkjʊlə*], **tu·ber·cu·lous** *adjs.* of, affected by, ~.

tuck [tʌk] *n.* **1.** flat, stitched fold of material in a garment, for shortening or for ornament. **2.** (no pl.) (Gt. Brit., sl.) food, esp. cakes and sweets. *v.t. & i.* **1.** roll, fold, or push (e.g. part of one's clothing) into a more convenient or secure position. **2.** ~ *sb.* (*oneself*) *up* (*in*), cover warmly by pulling bedclothes over, round, etc. **3.** ~ *in*, (colloq.) eat heartily. '~-**shop** *n.* shop (for school-children) selling sweets, pastries, etc.

-tude [-tjuːd] *suff.* (forming abstract ns.) *altitude*; *gratitude*; *solitude*.

Tues·day ['tjuːzdɪ] *n.* second day of the week.

tuft [tʌft] *n.* bunch of hair, bristles, grass, feathers, etc. growing closely or held firmly together at one end.

tug [tʌg] *v.i. & t.* (-gg-) pull hard or violently; pull (*at* sth.). *n.* **1.** sudden or violent pull. **2.** (also ~*boat*) small, powerful boat for towing ships, etc. ~-**of-war** [ˌtʌgəv'wɔː*] *n.* competition in which two teams pull against each other on a rope.

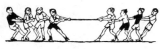

a tug-of-war

tu·ition [tjuː'ɪʃn] *n.* (no pl.) (fee for) teaching.

tu·lip ['tjuːlɪp] *n.* bulb plant having, in spring, a large, upturned, bell-shaped flower.

tum·ble ['tʌmbl] *v.i. & t.* **1.** fall, esp. quickly or violently: ~ *down the stairs*; ~ *off a bicycle*. **2.** cause to fall: *The earthquake ~d us out of bed. n.* fall. '~-**down** *attrib. adj.* (of buildings) unsafe; likely to collapse.

tum·bler ['tʌmblə*] *n.* **1.** drinking-glass with no stem. **2.** acrobat.

tum·brel ['tʌmbrəl], **tum·bril** ['tʌmbrɪl] *n.* cart, esp. of the kind that carried prisoners to the guillotine during the French Revolution.

tum·my ['tʌmɪ] *n.* (colloq.) stomach.

tu·mour (U.S.A. **tu·mor**) ['tjuːmə*] *n.* diseased growth in some part of the body.

tu·mult ['tjuːmʌlt] *n.* **1.** uproar; disturbance. **2.** mental excitement: *He* (*His mind*) *was in a* ~. **tu·mul·tu·ous** [tjuː'mʌltjʊəs] *adj.* disorderly; noisy and violent.

tun [tʌn] *n.* large cask for beer, wine, etc.; measure of capacity (252 gallons).

tu·na ['tuːnə] *n.* (pl. ~, ~s) tunny; its flesh as food.

tun·dra ['tʌndrə] *n.* treeless plain, often marshy land, in the arctic regions; partially frozen desert.

tune [tjuːn] *n.* **1.** succession of notes forming a melody (of a song, hymn, etc.). **2.** correct pitch; agreement or harmony: *sing* (*play*) *in* (*out of*) ~, sing (play) so that the notes are correctly (not correctly) pitched. **3.** (no pl.) (fig.) harmony: *be in* (*out of*) ~ *with one's companions* (*surroundings*), be happy (not happy) with them. *v.t. & i.* **1.** adjust strings, etc. of a musical instrument to the right pitch. **2.** ~ *up*, (of an orchestra) put the instruments in ~. **3.** ~ *in*, adjust a radio receiver so as to get the programme from the station required. **tun·er** *n.* **1.** person who ~s musical instruments: *a piano-* ~*r*. **2.** (part of) a radio, etc. that receives the signals. ~**ful** *adj.* having a pleasing ~.

tu·nic ['tjuːnɪk] *n.* close-fitting, military-style jacket.

tun·nel ['tʌnl] *n.* underground passage, esp. through a hill, etc. for a road, railway, canal, etc. *v.t. & i.* (-ll-, U.S.A. also -l-) dig a ~ through (sth.); dig a ~ (*through, into*) sth.

tun·ny ['tʌnɪ] *n.* (pl. -nies, ~) large sea-fish used as food.

tup·pence ['tʌpəns] *n.* (Gt. Brit.) twopence. **tup·pen·ny** ['tʌpnɪ] *adj.* (Gt. Brit.) twopenny.

tur·ban ['tɜːbən] *n.* man's head-dress made by winding a length of cloth round the head; woman's head-dress resembling a ~.

tur·bid ['tɜːbɪd] *adj.* (of liquids) thick; muddy; not clear.

tur·bine ['tɜːbaɪn] *n.* engine or motor whose driving-wheel is turned by a strong current of water, steam, or air.

tur·bot ['tɜːbət] *n.* large, flat seafish valued as food.

tur·bu·lent ['tɜːbjʊlənt] *adj.* violent; disorderly; uncontrolled: ~ *waves* (*passions, mobs*). **tur·bu·lence** *n.*

tu·reen [tə'riːn] *n.* deep dish with a lid, from which soup, vegetables, etc. are served at table.

turf [tɜːf] *n.* (pl. ~s, turves [-vz]) **1.** (no pl.) soil-surface with grass roots growing in it. **2.** piece of ~ cut out. **3.** (no pl.) *the* ~, the racecourse; the occupation or profession of horse-racing. *v.t.* cover with ~.

tur·gid ['tɜːdʒɪd] *adj.* **1.** swollen (e.g. by disease). **2.** (of language) pompous; full of high-sounding words.

tur·key ['tɜːkɪ] *n.* (pl. ~s) large bird used as food.

a turkey

tur·moil ['tɜːmɔɪl] *n.* noise; confusion.

turn [tɜːn] *v.t. & i.* **1.** (cause to) move round a point; (cause to) move so as to face in a different direction. **2.** (with advs. & preps.): ~ *about*, ~ so as to face in the opposite direction; ~ *down*, (a) fold down: ~ *down a collar*; ~ *down the bedclothes*; (b) reduce the volume of (sound, etc.) by ~ing a knob, etc.; (c) reduce (the flame of a lamp, etc.) by ~ing a tap, etc.; (d) (fig.) reject (an offer, the person making it); ~ *in*, (colloq.) go to bed; ~ *sb. in*, surrender him to the police; ~ *off*, change direction; leave (one road) for another; ~ *off (on)*, stop (start) the flow of (water, electric current, etc.) by ~ing a tap, switch, etc.; ~ *out*, (a) stop the flow of (gas) by ~ing a tap; (b) expel; put out by force; (c) produce (goods); (d) empty (drawers, one's pockets, a room, etc., e.g. when searching for sth. or when cleaning); (e) (cause to) go or come out for some purpose: *The whole village ~ed out to welcome him.* (f) prove to be; be in the end: *The day ~ed out wet.* ~ *over*, give the control of (a business, etc. *to sb.*); ~ *to*, go to (*sb. or sth.*, esp. for help, comfort); begin work; ~ *up*, (a) (of persons) arrive; (b) (of objects) be found, esp. by chance; (c) (of a chance, etc.) appear. **3.** (cause to) change in nature, quality, etc.: *Frost ~s water into ice. The milk has ~ed* (become sour). *His hair is ~ing grey.* **4.** shape (sth.) while it is ~ing on a lathe. **5.** remake a garment (e.g. a coat) so that the inner surface is the outer surface. **6.** reach and pass: *He has not ~ed forty yet. It has just ~ed two o'clock.* **7.** (with nouns): ~ *sb.'s brain*, make him mad; ~ *the corner*, (fig.) pass a crisis successfully; ~ *sb.'s head*, make him too vain; ~ *one's hand to*, be able to do; ~ *one's stomach*, make one (want to) vomit. *n.* **1.** ~ing movement. **2.** change of direction: ~s *in the road.* **3.** change in condition: *Affairs took*

a ~ for the better (became better). **4.** occasion or opportunity for doing sth., esp. in one's proper order among others: *wait* (*until it is*) *one's ~*; *in ~*; ~ *and ~ about*, (of two persons) first one and then the other; *by ~s*, (of individuals or groups) in rotation; alternately: *laugh and cry by ~s. She went hot and cold by ~s. out of ~*, before or after the right or regular time; *take ~s at* (*sth.*), do it in ~. **5.** short period of activity: *take a ~ at the oars; go for a ~* (= a walk) *in the park.* **6.** performance (e.g. a song or dance) by one person or a group of persons, forming part of an entertainment. **7.** (*do sb.*) *a good* (*bad*) ~, a kind (an unkind) act. **8.** natural tendency: *a boy with a mechanical ~*, a boy interested in, clever at, mechanical things. **9.** *serve one's ~*, be satisfactory for one's purpose; *done to a ~*, cooked enough but not too much. '~·coat *n.* person who changes his opinions or the party he supports. ~·er *n.* person who works a lathe. ~·ing *n.* place where a road ~s, esp. where one road branches off from another; such a branch road. '~·ing-point *n.* place or point at which sb. or sth. ~s (1); (fig.) crisis. '~·out *n.* attendance of people at a meeting, etc.; general appearance of a person's equipment; act of emptying sth. (e.g. a room) out; that which is moved out in this way. '~·over *n.* amount of business done (usu. within a named period of time). '~·pike *n.* **1.** (hist.) toll-gate. **2.** (U.S.A.) toll-road for fast traffic. '~·stile *n.* revolving gate that admits only one person at a time. '~·ta·ble *n.* flat, circular, revolving platform, e.g. one on which a locomotive is turned round, or on which records[2] (4) are played. '~·up *n.* **1.** sth. ~ed up, (esp. Gt. Brit.) the lower end of a trouser leg. **2.** (colloq.) unexpected event.

tur·nip ['tɜːnɪp] *n.* (plant with a) large round root used as a vegetable and as food for cattle.

tur·pen·tine ['tɜːpəntaɪn] *n.* (no pl.) oil obtained from certain trees, used for mixing paint and varnish, and in medicine.

tur·pi·tude ['tɜːpɪtjuːd] *n.* (no pl.) wickedness.

tur·quoise ['tɜːkwɔɪz] *n.* (colour of a) greenish-blue precious stone.

tur·ret ['tʌrɪt] *n.* **1.** small tower, usu. at the corner of a building. **2.** steel structure protecting gunners, often made so as to revolve with the gun(s).

tur·tle ['tɜːtl] *n.* sea-animal with a soft body protected by a hard shell like that of a tortoise. **turn** ~, (of a ship) turn upside down; capsize. '**~-neck** *n.* high, close-fitting collar, esp. of a sweater. '**~-necked** *adj.* having such a collar.

turves, see *turf.*

tusk [tʌsk] *n.* long, pointed tooth, esp. one coming out from the mouth as in the elephant or walrus. (See the pictures at *trunk* and *walrus.*)

tus·sle ['tʌsl] *v.i. & n.* (have a) hard fight or struggle (*with*).

tu·tor ['tjuːtə*] *n.* **1.** private teacher. **2.** (Gt. Brit.) university teacher who guides the studies of a number of students. *v.t. & i.* act as ~ to (sb.). **tu·to·ri·al** [tjuː'tɔːrɪəl] *adj.* of a ~ or his duties: ~*ial classes.* *n.* period of individual instruction given by a college ~.

twad·dle ['twɒdl] *n.* (no pl.) foolish talk.

twain [tweɪn] *n.* (old use) two.

twang [twæŋ] *n.* sound of a tight string or wire being plucked. *v.t. & i.* (cause sth. to) make this sound.

tweak [twiːk] *v.t. & n.* pinch and twist.

tweed [twiːd] *n.* **1.** (no pl.) thick, soft, woollen cloth, usu. woven of mixed colours. **2.** (pl.) cloths or clothes of ~.

tweez·ers ['twiːzəz] *n. pl.* (often *a pair of* ~) small pair of pincers for picking up or pulling out very small things.

(a pair of) tweezers

twelve [twelv] *n. & adj.* 12. **twelfth** [twelfθ] *n. & adj.* 12th; ¹/₁₂.

twen·ty ['twentɪ] *n. & adj.* 20. **twen·ti·eth** ['twentɪɪθ] *n. & adj.* 20th; ¹/₂₀.

twice [twaɪs] *adv.* two times.

twid·dle ['twɪdl] *v.t. & i.* twist or turn idly or aimlessly: ~ *one's thumbs.*

twig [twɪg] *n.* small, woody shoot on a branch (of a tree or bush).

twi·light ['twaɪlaɪt] *n.* (no pl.) faint half-light before sunrise or after sunset.

twill [twɪl] *n.* (no pl.) textile fabric woven so that fine diagonal lines or ribs appear on the surface. ~**ed** *adj.* (of cloth) woven in this way.

twin [twɪn] *n.* **1.** either of two children born together of the same mother; (attrib.) ~ *brothers.* **2.** (usu. attrib.) (thing) completely like and associated with another: *a steamer with* ~ *screws* (two identical propellers); ~ *beds,* two identical single beds; ~*-engined,* having two engines; *a* ~ *set,* woman's matching cardigan and jumper; ~ *towns,* two towns (usu. in different countries) establishing special links.

twine [twaɪn] *n.* (no pl.) thin string made by twisting two or more strands² together. *v.t. & i.* twist; wind: ~ *flowers into a wreath.*

twinge [twɪndʒ] *n.* sudden, sharp pain: *a* ~ *of toothache* (*conscience*).

twin·kle ['twɪŋkl] *v.i.* shine with a light that gleams unsteadily: *stars twinkling in the sky; eyes twinkling with fun.* *n.* **1.** (no pl.) twinkling light. **2.** twitching of the eyelid; sparkle, gleam, of the eyes: *a mischievous* ~ *in the old man's eyes.* **twin·kling** *n.* (no pl.) *in a twinkling,* in an instant.

twirl [twɜːl] *v.t. & i.* (cause to) rotate quickly.

twist [twɪst] *v.t. & i.* **1.** wind or turn (a number of strands², etc.) one about another. **2.** turn the two ends of sth. in opposite directions; turn one end of sth.: ~ *the cap off a fountain-pen.* **3.** force (sb.'s words, etc.) out of their true meaning. **4.** (e.g. of a road) turn and curve in different directions. *n.* **1.** ~*ing* or being ~*ed.* **2.** sth. made by ~*ing;* thread, rope, yarn, etc. made by ~*ing* two or more strands² about one another. **3.** peculiar tendency of mind or character: *a man with a criminal* ~. ~**er** *n.* dishonest person. ~**y** *adj.* (-*ier,* -*iest*) full of ~s; (fig.) dishonest.

twit [twɪt] *v.t.* (-*tt*-) tease (sb. *with* having made a mistake, etc.).

twitch [twɪtʃ] *n.* **1.** sudden, quick, usu. uncontrollable movement of a muscle. **2.** sudden, quick pull. *v.i. & t.* **1.** make a ~: *His nose* ~*ed as he passed the kitchen door. The horse* ~*ed its ears.* **2.** jerk: *The wind* ~*ed the paper out of her hand.*

twit·ter ['twɪtə*] *v.i.* (of birds) chirp; make a succession of soft, short sounds. *n.* such sounds. *in a* ~, (colloq.) in a nervous or an excited state.

two [tuː] *n. & adj.* 2. ~*-piece,* suit of clothes or a woman's bathing-suit consisting of ~ separate parts of similar or matching material; (attrib.) *a* ~*-piece suit;* ~*-ply,* (wool, etc.) of ~ strands² or thicknesses: *a* ~*-ply carpet;* ~*-seater,* vehicle or aircraft with ~ seats. ~**pence** ['tʌpəns] *n.* (Gt. Brit.) sum of ~ pence (= 2 p., old currency 2 d.). ~**pen·ny** ['tʌpnɪ] *adj.* (Gt. Brit.) costing or worth 2 p. (old currency 2 d.).

-ty [-tɪ] *suff.* (forming ns.) denoting quality or condition: *cruelty*; *loyalty*; *penalty*.

ty·coon [taɪˈkuːn] *n.* (colloq.) wealthy and powerful businessman: *oil ~s.*

type [taɪp] *n.* **1.** person, thing, event, etc. considered as an example of its class or group. **2.** class or group considered to have common characteristics: *men of this ~.* **3.** (no pl.) letters, etc. cast in a block of metal, for use in printing; any form of these: *in large ~*; *italic ~. v.i. & t.* write with a ~writer: *~ a letter. She ~s well.* '~-ˌset·ter *n.* worker or machine that sets ~ (3) for printing. '~·write *v.t. & i.* (p.t. *-wrote*, p.p. *-written*) (usu. *type*) use a ~writer: *a ~written letter.* '~·writ·er *n.* machine with which one

a typewriter

prints letters on paper, using the fingers on a keyboard. **typ·i·cal** ['tɪpɪkl] *adj.* ~ *(of)*, serving as a ~; representative or characteristic. **typ·i·cal·ly** *adv.* **typ·i·fy** ['tɪpɪfaɪ] *v.t.* be a symbol of; be representative of. **typ·ist** ['taɪpɪst] *n.* person who ~s, esp. in order to earn a living. **ty·pog·ra·phy** [taɪˈpɒɡrəfɪ] *n.* (no pl.) art or style of printing.

ty·phoid ['taɪfɔɪd] *n.* (no pl.) (often ~ *fever*) serious disease that attacks the intestines. **ty·phus** ['taɪfəs] *n.* (no pl.) disease causing red spots on the body and great weakness.

ty·phoon [taɪˈfuːn] *n.* violent hurricane occurring in the E. Asian seas.

ty·rant ['taɪərənt] *n.* cruel or unjust ruler, esp. one who has obtained complete power by force. **ty·ran·ni·cal** [tɪˈrænɪkl], **tyr·an·nous** ['tɪrənəs] *adjs.* acting like a ~; of a ~. **tyr·an·nize** ['tɪrənaɪz] *v.i. & t.* rule cruelly and unjustly: *tyrannize over the weak*; *tyrannize one's family.* **tyr·an·ny** ['tɪrənɪ] *n.* cruel and unjust use of power; government by a ~.

tyre (U.S.A. **tire**) ['taɪə*] *n.* band of metal or rubber round the rim of a wheel.

ty·ro, see *tiro*.

U

ubiq·ui·tous [ju:'bɪkwɪtəs] *adj.* present everywhere or in several places at the same time. **ubiq·ui·ty** *n.* (no pl.) quality of being ~.

U-boat ['ju:bəʊt] *n.* German submarine.

ud·der ['ʌdə*] *n.* organ of a cow, goat, etc. from which milk comes.

ug·ly ['ʌglɪ] *adj.* (-ier, -iest) 1. unpleasant to look at; hideous. 2. threatening: *The sky looks* ~ (i.e. suggests bad weather). *an* ~ *customer,* a dangerous person.

uku·le·le [,ju:kə'leɪlɪ] *n.* small, four-stringed guitar as used in Hawaii.

a ukulele

ul·cer ['ʌlsə*] *n.* open sore forming poisonous matter.

ul·te·ri·or [ʌl'tɪərɪə*] *adj.* situated beyond; beyond what is at first seen or said: ~ *motives,* motives other than those expressed.

ul·ti·mate ['ʌltɪmət] *adj.* last; furthest; basic: ~ *principles* (*truths, etc.*). ~·ly *adv.* finally.

ul·ti·ma·tum [,ʌltɪ'meɪtəm] *n.* (pl. ~s, -ta [-tə]) final statement of conditions to be accepted without discussion, esp. one that threatens war if the conditions are not accepted.

ul·tra- ['ʌltrə-] *pref.* beyond what is reasonable, natural, or usual; excessively: *ultra-conservative; ultra-critical; ultra-modern; ultraviolet.*

ul·tra-left [,ʌltrə'left] *adj.* (pol.) extremely radical.

ul·tra·ma·rine [,ʌltrəmə'ri:n] *adj. & n.* (no pl.) brilliant pure blue (colour).

um·brage ['ʌmbrɪdʒ] *n.* (no pl.) feeling that one has been treated unfairly or without proper respect: *take* ~ (*at*).

um·brel·la [ʌm'brelə] *n.* folding frame (with stick and handle), covered with silk, cotton, etc. used to shelter the person holding it from rain or sun.

um·pire ['ʌmpaɪə*] *n.* person chosen or asked to act as judge in a dispute, or to see that the rules of a game (e.g. cricket) are followed by the players. (Cf. *referee* for football and boxing.) *v.t. & i.* act as ~ (in).

ump·teen [,ʌmp'ti:n] *adj.* (sl.) a large number of. ~**th** [,ʌmp'ti:nθ] *adj. for the* ~**th** *time,* for I don't know how many times.

un- [ʌn-] *pref.* 1. (before adjs. and advs.) not: *unable; unbecoming; uncertain*(*ly*); *uncontrollable; uncontrollably; unfair; unmanly; unsuitable; unsuitably; unwanted.* 2. (before vs.) do the opposite of, reverse the action of, what is indicated by the verb: *uncover; undress; unlock; unscrew; untie.* 3. (before ns.) indicating absence of: *uncertainty; untruth; unwillingness.*

un·abat·ed [,ʌnə'beɪtɪd] *adj.* (of a storm, etc.) (continuing) as strong, violent, etc. as before.

un·ac·count·able [,ʌnə'kaʊntəbl] *adj.* strange; for which no explanation can be found.

unan·i·mous [ju:'nænɪməs] *adj.* 1. in complete agreement: *a* ~ *vote.* 2. all holding the same opinion: *We are* ~ *in our support of the policy.* ~·ly *adv.* **una·nim·i·ty** [,ju:nə'nɪmətɪ] *n.* (no pl.) complete agreement or unity.

un·as·sum·ing [,ʌnə'sju:mɪŋ] *adj.* not pushing oneself forward; not drawing attention to oneself; modest.

un·awares [,ʌnə'weəz] *adv.* by surprise; unexpectedly; without being aware.

un·bal·anced [,ʌn'bælənst] *adj.* (esp. of a person, his mind) not quite sane.

un·bend [,ʌn'bend] *v.t. & i.* (p.t. & p.p. *unbent*) (esp.) relax; become less stiff or formal in behaviour.

un·bo·som [,ʌn'bʊzəm] *v.t.* ~ *oneself,* confide one's troubles, etc. (*to* sb.).

un·bri·dled [,ʌn'braɪdld] *adj.* (esp.) uncontrolled; violent (rage, etc.).

un·bur·den [,ʌn'bɜ:dn] *v.t.* (esp.) ~

oneself, get relief by confessing sth., telling one's troubles (*to* sb.).

un·called-for [ˌʌnˈkɔːldfɔː*] *adj.* neither desirable nor necessary.

un·can·ny [ʌnˈkænɪ] *adj.* unnatural; mysterious.

un·cle [ˈʌŋkl] *n.* brother of one's father or mother; husband of one's aunt.

un·com·mon [ʌnˈkɒmən] *adj.* not common; unusual; remarkable.

un·con·di·tion·al [ˌʌnkənˈdɪʃənl] *adj.* not subject to conditions; absolute: ~ *surrender.*

un·con·scio·nable [ʌnˈkɒnʃnəbl] *adj.* unreasonable: *for an* ~ *time.*

un·con·scious [ʌnˈkɒnʃəs] *adj.* 1. having lost consciousness. 2. not intentional: *an* ~ *action.*

un·couth [ʌnˈkuːθ] *adj.* (of persons, their behaviour) rough, awkward, clumsy, or uncultured.

unc·tion [ˈʌŋkʃn] *n.* (no pl.) 1. act of anointing with oil, esp. as a religious rite. 2. pretended (insincere) earnestness in speaking, in tone of voice.

unc·tu·ous [ˈʌŋktjʊəs] *adj.* insincere in speech or manner.

un·der [ˈʌndə*] *prep.* 1. in or to a position lower than: ~ *the bridge* (*table*). 2. in and covered by: ~ *the water.* 3. less than: ~ *age,* not yet 18; under the legal age for sth. 4. ~ *discussion* (*repair, etc.*), being discussed, etc.; ~ *protest,* unwillingly; after protesting; ~ *fire,* (being) fired at; ~ *orders,* having received orders, been ordered (*to do* sth. etc.); *marching* ~ (= weighed down by) *a heavy load of equipment.* *adv.* in or to a lower place: *The ship went* ~ (i.e. sank).

un·der- [ˈʌndə*-] *pref.* 1. (before ns.) worn or placed under: *underclothes; underclothing; undergarment; undercarriage* (aircraft's landing gear). 2. (before vs.) not sufficiently; not so much as is necessary: *undercharge; underestimate; underrate; understamp; undervalue.* 3. lower in rank; subordinate: ~*gardener;* ~*secretary.*

un·der·cur·rent [ˈʌndəˌkʌrənt] *n.* current flowing below the surface; (fig.) tendency (of thought or feeling) lying below what is first seen: *an* ~ *of opposition* (*melancholy*).

un·der·cut [ˌʌndəˈkʌt] *v.t.* (-*tt-*; p.t. & p.p. -*cut*) offer goods, services, at a lower price than (competitors).

un·der·de·vel·oped [ˌʌndədɪˈveləpt] *adj.* not yet fully developed: ~ *muscles;* ~ *countries.*

un·der·dog [ˈʌndədɒg] *n.* poor and helpless person usually oppressed by others.

un·der·done [ˌʌndəˈdʌn, attrib. ˈʌndədʌn] *adj.* (esp. of meat) not completely cooked throughout.

un·der·go [ˌʌndəˈgəʊ] *v.t.* (p.t. -*went,* p.p. -*gone*) 1. experience (hardship, trials, suffering). 2. go through (a process).

un·der·grad·u·ate [ˌʌndəˈgrædjʊət] *n.* university student working for a bachelor's degree: (attrib.) ~ *studies.*

un·der·ground [ˈʌndəgraʊnd] *adj.* below the ground; (fig., esp. pol.) secret; hidden. [ˌʌndəˈgraʊnd] *adv.* below the ground; (fig., esp. pol.) in(to) secrecy or hiding. [ˈʌndəgraʊnd] *n.* 1. (U.S.A. *subway*) railway situated below the surface. 2. any group, organization, or movement whose activities are outside the established society or culture.

un·der·growth [ˈʌndəgrəʊθ] *n.* (no pl.) shrubs, bushes, low trees, growing under taller trees.

un·der·hand [ˌʌndəˈhænd] *adj.* & *adv.* 1. (bowling in cricket) with the hand kept below the shoulder. 2. deceitful(ly); sly(ly).

un·der·lie [ˌʌndəˈlaɪ] *v.t.* (p.t. -*lay,* p.p. -*lain;* pres. p. -*lying*) (esp.) be the foundation of (a theory, etc.).

un·der·line [ˌʌndəˈlaɪn] *v.t.* draw a line under (a word, etc.); (fig.) emphasize.

un·der·ling [ˈʌndəlɪŋ] *n.* (usu. derog.) person in an unimportant position under another.

un·der·mine [ˌʌndəˈmaɪn] *v.t.* 1. make a hollow or tunnel under; weaken at the base: *cliffs* ~*d by the sea.* 2. weaken gradually: ~ *sb.'s authority; health* ~*d by overwork.*

un·der·neath [ˌʌndəˈniːθ] *adv.* & *prep.* under; at or to a lower place; below.

un·der·pants [ˈʌndəpænts] *n. pl.* undergarment covering the lower part of the body and part of the thighs.

un·der·pass [ˈʌndəpɑːs] *n.* section of a road that goes under another road or railway.

un·der·pin [ˌʌndəˈpɪn] *v.t.* (-*nn-*) put timber, stones, etc. under (a wall) to support it.

un·der·priv·i·leged [ˌʌndəˈprɪvɪlɪdʒd] *adj.* less privileged than others; not enjoying the normal standard of living or rights in a society.

un·der·sell [ˌʌndəˈsell] *v.t.* (p.t. & p.p. -*sold*) sell (goods) at a lower price than (competitors).

un·der·side [ˈʌndəsaɪd] *n.* lower or under side or surface.

un·der·signed [ˌʌndəˈsaɪnd] *adj.* ~, the person(s) signing below.

un·der·stand [ˌʌndəˈstænd] *v.t. & i.* (p.t. & p.p. *-stood*) **1.** know the meaning, nature, explanation, of (sth.): *make oneself understood,* make one's meaning clear. **2.** learn (from information received): *I ~ (that) you are now married.* **3.** supply (a word or words) mentally. **~·able** *adj.* that can be understood. **~ing** *adj.* (good at) ~ing or realizing other persons' feelings, points of view, etc. *n.* **1.** (no pl.) power of clear thought. **2.** (no pl.) capacity for sympathizing, seeing from another person's point of view, etc. **3.** agreement; realization of another's views or feelings towards oneself: *reach (come to) an ~ing with sb.* **4.** condition: *on this ~ing; on the ~ing that.*

un·der·state [ˌʌndəˈsteɪt] *v.t.* belittle (the importance, value, significance, etc. of sth.) in description. **~·ment** *n.*

un·der·study [ˈʌndəˌstʌdɪ] *n.* person learning to, able to, take the place of another (esp. an actor). *v.t.* act as ~ for; rehearse a part so as to ~ for (sb.).

un·der·take [ˌʌndəˈteɪk] *v.t.* (p.t. *-took*, p.p. *-taken*) **1.** make oneself responsible for: *~ a task; ~ to do sth.* **2.** start (a piece of work). **3.** affirm; promise (*that, to do* sth.). **un·der·tak·ing** *n.* **1.** work that one has undertaken (1) to do. **2.** promise.

un·der·tak·er [ˈʌndəˌteɪkə*] *n.* person whose business is to prepare the dead for burial or cremation and manage funerals.

un·der·tone [ˈʌndətəʊn] *n.* **1.** low, quiet tone: *talk in ~s,* with subdued voices. **2.** underlying quality: *an ~ of* hostility.

un·der·tow [ˈʌndətəʊ] *n.* current caused by the backward flow of a wave after breaking on the beach.

un·der·wa·ter [ˈʌndəˌwɔːtə*] *adj.* below the surface of the water.

un·der·wear [ˈʌndəweə*] *n.* (no pl.) underclothing.

un·der·world [ˈʌndəwɜːld] *n.* **1.** (in Greek mythology) place of the departed spirits of the dead. **2.** part of society that lives by vice and crime.

un·der·write [ˌʌndəˈraɪt] *v.t.* (p.t. *-wrote*, p.p. *-written*) undertake (3) to bear all or part of possible loss (by signing an agreement about insurance, esp. of ships). **un·der·writ·er** [ˈʌndəˌraɪtə*] *n.*

un·de·vel·oped [ˌʌndɪˈveləpt] *adj.* not developed: *~ land,* land not yet used (for agriculture, industry, etc.).

un·dies [ˈʌndɪz] *n. pl.* (colloq.) (esp. women's) underclothes.

un·do [ˌʌnˈduː] *v.t.* (p.t. *-did,* p.p. *-done*) **1.** untie, unfasten (knots, buttons, etc.). **2.** destroy the result of; bring back the state of affairs that existed before: *He has undone all the good work of his predecessor.* **3.** *be undone,* be brought to ruin or disaster. **~·ing** *n.* (cause of) ruin: *Drink was his ~ing.*

un·dock [ˌʌnˈdɒk] *v.t. & i.* disconnect (orbiting spacecraft).

un·due [ˌʌnˈdjuː] *adj.* improper; more than is right: *with ~ haste.* **un·du·ly** *adv.*

un·du·late [ˈʌndjʊleɪt] *v.t. & i.* (of surfaces) (cause to) have a wavy motion or look: *a field of wheat undulating in the breeze.*

un·earth [ˌʌnˈɜːθ] *v.t.* discover and bring to light; uncover (e.g. by digging): *~ a fox (a buried treasure); ~ new facts about the life of Nelson.*

un·earth·ly [ʌnˈɜːθlɪ] *adj.* **1.** supernatural. **2.** mysterious; ghostly; frightening: *~ screams.* **3.** (colloq.) unreasonably early or inconvenient: *getting up at an ~ hour.*

un·easy [ʌnˈiːzɪ] *adj.* uncomfortable in body or mind; troubled or anxious. **un·eas·i·ly** *adv.*

un·em·ployed [ˌʌnɪmˈplɔɪd] *adj.* not in use; having no employment; temporarily out of work: *the ~.* **un·em·ploy·ment** *n.* (no pl.) state of being ~.

un·err·ing [ˌʌnˈɜːrɪŋ] *adj.* accurate: *with ~ aim.*

un·ex·am·pled [ˌʌnɪgˈzɑːmpld] *adj.* of which there is no other example that can be compared with it: *years of ~ prosperity.*

un·fail·ing [ʌnˈfeɪlɪŋ] *adj.* **1.** never coming to an end. **2.** always to be depended upon; loyal: *an ~ friend.*

un·fold [ʌnˈfəʊld] *v.t. & i.* (esp. fig.) reveal, make known (one's intentions, etc.): *as the story ~s (itself).*

un·found·ed [ˌʌnˈfaʊndɪd] *adj.* without foundation: *~ (i.e. false) rumours.*

un·frock [ˌʌnˈfrɒk] *v.t.* dismiss from the priesthood (for bad conduct).

un·gain·ly [ʌnˈgeɪnlɪ] *adj.* clumsy; awkward; ungraceful.

un·gov·ern·able [ˌʌnˈgʌvənəbl] *adj.* that cannot be kept under control: *an ~ temper.*

un·guard·ed [ˌʌnˈgɑːdɪd] *adj.* (esp. of a statement) careless; allowing sth. secret to become known.

un·heard-of [ˌʌn'hɜːdɒv] *adj.* extraordinary; without earlier example.

un·hinged [ˌʌn'hɪndʒd] *adj.* (of a person, his mind) unbalanced.

uni- ['juːnɪ-] *pref.* one; the same: *uniform*; *unicolour(ed)*.

uni·corn ['juːnɪkɔːn] *n.* (in old stories) horse-like animal with one long horn in the middle of its forehead.

a unicorn (right)

uni·form ['juːnɪfɔːm] *adj.* the same; never varying: *of ~ length*; *to be kept at a ~ temperature*. *n.* (style of) dress worn by all members of an organization, etc. (e.g. the armed forces, the police). **~·ly** *adv.* **uni·for·mi·ty** [ˌjuːnɪ'fɔːmətɪ] *n.* (no pl.) ~ condition.

uni·fy ['juːnɪfaɪ] *v.t.* 1. form into one; unite. 2. make uniform. **uni·fi·ca·tion** [ˌjuːnɪfɪ'keɪʃn] *n.* (no pl.) ~ing: *The unification of Europe is vital to peace.*

un·im·peach·able [ˌʌnɪm'piːtʃəbl] *adj.* that cannot be questioned or doubted: *~ honesty.*

union ['juːnjən] *n.* 1. uniting or being united; joining or being joined (e.g. of two or three towns into one, of two persons in marriage). 2. (no pl.) agreement or harmony: *in perfect ~.* 3. group, association, etc. formed by the uniting of persons, smaller groups, etc.: *a trade ~*; *the Soviet U~*; *the U~ Jack*, the British flag. 4. (Gt. Brit., hist.) workhouse. **~·ist** *n.* member of a trade ~.

unique [juː'niːk] *adj.* having no like or equal; being the only one of its sort. **~·ly** *adv.* **~·ness** *n.* (no pl.).

uni·son ['juːnɪzn] *n.* (no pl.) concord or agreement: *acting in ~*; *sing in ~*, all singing the same notes, not harmonizing.

unit ['juːnɪt] *n.* 1. single person, or thing, or group regarded as complete in itself: *The family is often taken as the ~ of society.* 2. quantity or amount used as a standard of measurement: *The metre is a ~ of length.* 3. (math.) the number 1. 4. device (2) with a specified function forming an element in a complex mechanism: *~ furniture*, articles of furniture of similar design, materials, etc. to be used together.

unite [juː'naɪt] *v.t. & i.* 1. make or become one; join together. 2. act or work together: *Let us ~ in fighting disease and poverty!* **unit·ed** *adj.* the *U~d Kingdom*, Great Britain and Northern Ireland; *a ~d family*; *a ~d effort.* **uni·ty** ['juːnətɪ] *n.* 1. state of being ~d; (an) arrangement of parts to form a complete whole. 2. (no pl.) harmony, agreement (of aims, feelings, etc.).

uni·verse ['juːnɪvɜːs] *n. the ~,* everything that exists everywhere; all the stars, planets, etc.; the whole creation and the Creator; all mankind. **uni·ver·sal** [ˌjuːnɪ'vɜːsl] *adj.* of or for all; used by, done by, affecting, all: *a universal rule*, a rule with no exceptions; *the universal misery caused by world wars.* **uni·ver·sal·ly** *adv.*

uni·ver·si·ty [ˌjuːnɪ'vɜːsətɪ] *n.* (colleges, buildings, etc. of an) institution giving more advanced education than is given in schools, awarding degrees, and engaging in research; members of this collectively.

un·kempt [ˌʌn'kempt] *adj.* untidy; (esp. of the hair) uncombed.

un·less [ən'les] *conj.* if not; except when.

un·let·tered [ˌʌn'letəd] *adj.* uneducated; unable to read.

un·looked-for [ʌn'lʊktfɔː*] *adj.* unexpected.

un·man [ˌʌn'mæn] *v.t.* (-nn-) weaken the courage and self-control of. **~ned** *adj.* having no crew aboard: *an ~ned aircraft (spacecraft).*

un·matched [ˌʌn'mætʃt] *adj.* without an equal.

un·mean·ing [ˌʌn'miːnɪŋ] *adj.* without meaning or purpose.

un·men·tion·able [ʌn'menʃnəbl] *adj.* so bad, etc. that it cannot even be spoken of.

un·mis·tak·able [ˌʌnmɪ'steɪkəbl] *adj.* clear; about which no mistake is possible.

un·mit·i·gat·ed [ʌn'mɪtɪgeɪtɪd] *adj.* complete; absolute: *an ~ scoundrel.*

un·nerve [ˌʌn'nɜːv] *v.t.* cause to lose self-control, power of decision, or courage.

un·par·lia·men·ta·ry [ˌʌnˌpɑːlə'mentərɪ] *adj.* (of language, conduct) not suitable (e.g. because abusive, disorderly) for parliament.

un·pleas·ant [ʌn'pleznt] *adj.* not pleasant; disagreeable. ~·**ness** *n.* quarrel; bad feeling (between persons).

un·prec·e·dent·ed [ʌn'presɪdentɪd] *adj.* without precedent.

un·pre·tend·ing [ˌʌnprɪ'tendɪŋ], **un·pre·ten·tious** [ˌʌnprɪ'tenʃəs] *adjs.* not trying to seem important; modest.

un·prin·ci·pled [ʌn'prɪnsəpld] *adj.* without moral principles; dishonest.

un·pro·fes·sion·al [ˌʌnprə'feʃənl] *adj.* (esp. of conduct) contrary to the rules or customs of a profession.

un·rav·el [ʌn'rævl] *v.t. & i.* (-*ll*-, U.S.A. also -*l*-) **1.** separate the threads of; pull or become separate: *The cuff of my sleeve has* ~*led.* **2.** make clear, solve (a mystery, etc.).

un·re·mit·ting [ˌʌnrɪ'mɪtɪŋ] *adj.* unceasing: ~ *care.*

un·re·quit·ed [ˌʌnrɪ'kwaɪtɪd] *adj.* (of love, etc.) not returned or returned in kind.

un·rest [ˌʌn'rest] *n.* (no pl.) (esp.) disturbed condition(s): *social* ~ (e.g. caused by unemployment); *political* ~.

un·ru·ly [ʌn'ruːlɪ] *adj.* (-*ier*, -*iest*) not easily controlled; disorderly.

un·sa·voury (U.S.A.-**vory**) [ˌʌn'seɪvərɪ] *adj.* (esp. of scandal, a story) nasty; disgusting.

un·scathed [ˌʌn'skeɪðd] *adj.* unharmed; unhurt.

un·scru·pu·lous [ʌn'skruːpjʊləs] *adj.* not guided by conscience; not held back by scruples from doing wrong.

un·seat [ˌʌn'siːt] *v.t.* **1.** remove from office: *Mr. X was* ~*ed at the general election* (lost his seat in Parliament). **2.** *be* ~*ed,* be thrown from a horse.

un·seen [ˌʌn'siːn] *adj.* not seen; invisible. *n.* passage to be translated, without preparation, from a foreign language into one's own: *English* ~*s.*

un·set·tle [ˌʌn'setl] *v.t.* make troubled, anxious or uncertain: ~*d weather,* uncertain, changeable weather.

un·sight·ly [ʌn'saɪtlɪ] *adj.* displeasing to the eye: ~ *advertisements in the countryside.*

un·sound [ˌʌn'saʊnd] *adj.* (esp.) *of* ~ *mind,* unbalanced in mind.

un·speak·able [ʌn'spiːkəbl] *adj.* that cannot be described in words: ~ *joy* (*wickedness*).

un·strung [ˌʌn'strʌŋ] *adj.* (esp.) with little or no control over the nerves, mind, or feelings.

un·stud·ied [ˌʌn'stʌdɪd] *adj.* (of behaviour) natural; not aimed at impressing other persons.

un·think·able [ʌn'θɪŋkəbl] *adj.* such as one cannot have any real idea of; belief in; (colloq.) not to be considered.

un·think·ing [ˌʌn'θɪŋkɪŋ] *adj.* thoughtless; done, etc. without thought of the effect.

un·til [ən'tɪl] *prep. & conj.* up to (the time when): *Wait* ~ *tomorrow. Wait* ~ *his return. Go straight on* ~ *you come to the post office and then turn left.*

un·time·ly [ʌn'taɪmlɪ] *adj.* coming at a wrong or unsuitable time or too soon: ~ *remarks.*

un·to ['ʌntʊ, -tə] *prep.* (old use) to.

un·told [ˌʌn'təʊld] *adj.* (esp.) too much or too many to be measured, counted, etc.: *a man of* ~ *wealth.*

un·to·ward [ˌʌntə'wɔːd] *adj.* unfavourable; unfortunate.

un·used[1] [ˌʌn'juːzd] *adj.* not made use of.

un·used[2] [ˌʌn'juːst] *adj.* ~ *to,* not accustomed to.

un·ut·ter·able [ʌn'ʌtərəbl] *adj.* that cannot be expressed in words: ~ *joy.*

un·var·nished [ˌʌn'vɑːnɪʃt] *adj.* (esp.) *the* ~ *truth* (plain and straightforward); *an* ~ *account of sth.*

un·wield·y [ʌn'wiːldɪ] *adj.* awkward to move or control because of size, shape, or weight.

un·wit·ting [ʌn'wɪtɪŋ] *adj.* unknowing; unaware; unintentional.

up [ʌp] *adv. & prep., adv. particle.* **1.** (e.g. *stand up, blow up,* see under the verbs) to or in an erect or vertical position: *John's already up* (i.e. out of bed). *up and about,* out of bed and active (after sleep or illness). **2.** to or in a high(er) or (more) important place, degree, etc.: *Pull your socks up. Are you going up to London* (i.e. from the country) *soon? go up and down,* go backwards and forwards, higher and lower. **3.** *up to,* (a) occupied or busy with: *What's he up to? He's up to no good,* he is doing sth. wrong, etc.; (b) equal to: *not up to much,* not very good. *I don't feel up to doing much,* I don't feel well enough to do much; (c) as far as: *up to now;* (d) required from: *It's up to me* ... **4.** *What's up?* What's going on? What's the matter? *The game's up, it's all up,* we're beaten; we've lost. **5.** (with vs. to indicate completeness, finality): *The stream has dried up* (has become completely dry). *eat everything up; time's up,* the allowed time is ended. **6.** (with vs. to indicate an increase in intensity, etc.): *Speak up!* Speak with more force.

Hurry up! n. ups and downs, (fig.) changes of fortune.

up- [ʌp-] *pref.* in an upward direction: *an upturned nose; the up-stroke* (e.g. of the pen when writing the letter 1); *the up train* (to London); *with upraised hands.*

up·braid [ʌp'breɪd] *v.t.* scold.

up·bring·ing ['ʌpˌbrɪŋɪŋ] *n.* (no pl.) training and education during childhood.

up-coun·try [ˌʌp'kʌntrɪ] *adj. &* [ʌp-'kʌntrɪ] *adv.* towards the interior; inland: ~ *districts; live* ~.

up·date [ʌp'deɪt] *v.t.* bring up to date: ~ *a dictionary.*

up·heav·al [ʌp'hiːvl] *n.* great and sudden change (fig., in conditions).

up·hill [ˌʌp'hɪl] *adj.* sloping up; ascending; (fig.) difficult; needing effort: *an* ~ *task. adv.* up a slope: *walk* ~.

up·hold [ʌp'həʊld] *v.t.* (p.t. & p.p. *upheld*) support (a decision).

up·hol·ster [ʌp'həʊlstə*] *v.t.* provide (seats, etc.) with padding, springs, covering material, etc.; provide (a room) with carpets, curtains, cushioned seats, etc. ~·**er** *n.* person whose trade is to ~. ~**y** *n.* (no pl.) (materials used in, business of) ~ing.

up·keep ['ʌpkiːp] *n.* (no pl.) (cost of) keeping sth. in good condition.

up·land ['ʌplənd] *n.* (often pl.) high part(s) of a country; (attrib.) *an* ~ *region.*

up·lift [ʌp'lɪft] *v.t.* (fig.) raise (spiritually or emotionally).

up·on [ə'pɒn] *prep.* on: *once* ~ *a time;* ~ *my word.*

up·per ['ʌpə*] *adj.* higher. *get (have) the* ~ *hand,* get (have) control, an advantage, (over sb.). *the U~ House,* the House of Lords. *n.* part of a shoe or boot above the sole. '~·**most** *adj.* highest. *adv.* on, to, at, the top or surface.

up·right [ˌʌp'raɪt] *adj.* 1. erect; placed vertically (at right angles to the ground): *an* ~ *post.* 2. ['ʌpraɪt] honourable; straightforward in behaviour: *an* ~ *man. adv.* in an ~ manner or position. ['ʌpraɪt] *n.* ~ support in a structure. ~**·ly** *adv.*

up·ris·ing ['ʌpˌraɪzɪŋ] *n.* revolt.

up·roar ['ʌprɔː*] *n.* (no pl.) outburst of noise and excitement: *The meeting ended in (an)* ~. ~**·i·ous** [ʌp'rɔːrɪəs] *adj.* very noisy: *an* ~*ious meeting* (esp. with much loud laughter).

up·root [ʌp'ruːt] *v.t.* pull up (sth.) with its root(s).

up·set [ʌp'set] *v.t. & i.* (-tt-; p.t. & p.p. *upset*) 1. overturn: *Don't* ~ *the boat. The boat* ~. *Who has* ~ *the milk?* 2. trouble; cause (sth. or sb.) to be disturbed: ~ *the enemy's plans. Don't* ~ *your stomach by eating too much rich food. The news quite* ~ *her. n.* ~*ting or* being ~.

up·shot ['ʌpʃɒt] *n.* (no pl.) result or outcome: *What was the* ~ *of it all?*

up·side-down [ˌʌpsaɪd'daʊn] *adv.* with the upper side underneath or at the bottom; (fig.) in disorder.

up·stairs [ˌʌp'steəz] *adv.* to or on a higher floor. ['ʌpsteəz] *attrib. adj. an* ~ *room.*

up·start ['ʌpstɑːt] *n.* (often attrib.) person who has risen suddenly from a humble position, esp. one whose behaviour causes resentment.

up·stream [ˌʌp'striːm] *adv.* up a river; against the current.

up·take ['ʌpteɪk] *n. quick (slow) on (in) the* ~, quick (slow) to see the point of sth. said, to understand what is meant.

up·tight ['ʌptaɪt] *adj.* (colloq.) extremely tense; nervous; angry.

up-to-date [ˌʌptə'deɪt] *attrib. adj.* (pred. *up to date*) of the present time, of the newest sort.

up·ward ['ʌpwəd] *adj.* moving or directed up: *the* ~ *trend of prices.* ~**(s)** *adv.* towards a higher place, etc. ~ *of,* more than.

ura·ni·um [juˈreɪnjəm] *n.* (no pl.) heavy, white metal with radioactive properties, a source of atomic energy

ur·ban ['ɜːbən] *adj.* of or in a town. ~ *districts;* ~ *guerrilla* (operating in towns by kidnapping, etc.). ~**·ize** *v.t.* change from a rural to an ~ character.

ur·bane [ɜː'beɪn] *adj.* polite; polished in manners. ~**·ly** *adv.* **ur·ban·i·ty** [ɜː'bænətɪ] *n.*

ur·chin ['ɜːtʃɪn] *n.* troublesome small boy, esp. one who roams the streets.

-ure [-jʊə*, -jə*] *suff.* (forming ns.) 1. act; process: *enclosure; exposure; seizure.* 2. office; function: *judicature.* 3. body (5) performing such a function: *legislature.*

urge [ɜːdʒ] *v.t.* 1. push or drive (sth. or sb.) (*on, onward, forward*): ~ *one's horse on.* 2. request (sb.) earnestly, try to persuade (sb. *to do* sth.). 3. press (*upon* sb.) requests and arguments: *He* ~*d upon his pupils the importance of hard work. n.* strong desire: *He has an* ~ *to travel.* **ur·gen·cy** ['ɜːdʒənsɪ] *n.* (no pl.) need for, importance of, haste or prompt action. **ur·gent** ['ɜ:dʒənt] *adj.* needing prompt decision or action; (of a person, his voice, etc.) showing that sth. is ⁓nt. **ur·gent·ly** *adv.*

urine ['jʊərɪn] *n.* (no pl.) waste liquid that collects in the bladder and is discharged from the body. **uri·nate** ['jʊərɪneɪt] *v.i.* discharge ⁓.

urn [ɜ:n] *n.* **1.** vase, usu. with stem and base, esp. as used for holding the ashes of a person whose body has been cremated. **2.** large metal container in which a drink such as tea or coffee is made or kept warm (in restaurants, canteens, etc.).

us, see *we.*

us·age ['ju:zɪdʒ] *n.* **1.** (no pl.) way of using sth.: *Machines soon wear out under rough* ⁓. **2.** sth. commonly said or done; general custom or practice.

use [ju:z] *v.t.* (p.t. & p.p. ⁓d [ju:zd]) **1.** employ for a purpose: *a knife to cut bread.* **2.** ⁓ *up,* consume the whole of: *We've* ⁓d *up all our oil, we have no oil left.* **3.** behave towards: *U⁓ others as you would like them to* ⁓ *you.* **4.** (indicating a constant or frequent practice in the past, or the existence of something in the past): ⁓d *to* ['ju:sttə]: *He* ⁓d *to play football when he was a boy. There* ⁓d *to be a theatre at this corner years ago.* [ju:s] *n.* **1.** purpose for which sth. or sb. may be employed; work that sth. or sb. is able to do: *a tool with many* ⁓s. **2.** (no pl.) using or being ⁓d: *in* ⁓, being ⁓d; *come into* ⁓, begin to be ⁓d; *go (fall) out of* ⁓, be no longer ⁓d. **3.** (no pl.) value; advantage: *Is this of any* ⁓ *to you?* **4.** (no pl.) power of using: *lose the* ⁓ *of one's legs.* **5.** right to ⁓: *have the* ⁓ *of a good library.* ⁓**d** *adj.* **1.** [ju:zd] (of clothes, vehicles, etc.) no longer new; second-hand: ⁓*d cars.* **2.** [ju:st] ⁓*d to,* having become familiar with by habit or custom: *be (become, get)* ⁓*d to sth.* ⁓**ful** *adj.* helpful. ⁓**ful·ly** *adv.* ⁓**ful·ness** *n.* (no pl.). ⁓**less** ['ju:s-] *adj.* worthless. ⁓**less·ly** *adv.* ⁓**less·ness** *n.* (no pl.). **us·er** ['ju:zə*] *n.* person who ⁓s sth.: *How many telephone* ⁓rs *are there in your town?*

ush·er ['ʌʃə*] *n.* **1.** person who shows people to their seats in theatres, cinemas, etc. **2.** doorkeeper in a lawcourt, etc. **3.** (old use) assistant schoolmaster. *v.t.* go with (sb.) as ⁓ (1); take (*into* a room, etc.): *I was* ⁓*ed in by the servant.* ⁓**ette** [ˌʌʃəˈret] *n.* female ⁓ (1), esp. in a cinema.

usu·al ['ju:ʒʊəl] *adj.* such as commonly happens; customary. ⁓**ly** *adv.*

usurp [ju:'zɜ:p] *v.t.* take (sb.'s power, authority, position) wrongfully. ⁓**er** *n.* person who ⁓s (e.g. the throne).

usu·ry ['ju:ʒʊrɪ] *n.* (no pl.) (practice of) lending money, esp. at a rate of interest generally considered to be too high; such high interest. **usu·rer** ['ju:ʒərə*] *n.* person whose business is ⁓.

uten·sil [ju:'tensl] *n.* tool, instrument, etc., esp. for use in the house: *kitchen* ⁓*s* (pots, pans, brushes).

util·i·ty [ju:'tɪlɪtɪ] *n.* **1.** (no pl.) quality of being useful. **2.** *public utilities,* public services, etc. supplying water, gas, electricity; bus or railway services, etc. **util·i·tar·i·an** [ˌju:tɪlɪ'teərɪən] *adj.* for use rather than for decoration, etc. **uti·lize** ['ju:tɪlaɪz] *v.t.* make use of; find a use for. **uti·li·za·tion** [ˌju:tɪlaɪ'zeɪʃn] *n.* (no pl.).

ut·most ['ʌtməʊst] *adj.* **1.** furthest: *the* ⁓ *ends of the earth.* **2.** greatest: *in the* ⁓ *danger. n.* (no pl.) the most that is possible: *do one's* ⁓; *enjoy oneself to the* ⁓.

Uto·pia [ju:'təʊpjə] *n.* imaginary perfect social and political system. **Uto·pi·an, uto·pi·an** *adj.* attractive and desirable but impracticable.

ut·ter[1] ['ʌtə*] *attrib. adj.* complete; total: ⁓ *darkness.* ⁓**ly** *adv.*

ut·ter[2] ['ʌtə*] *v.t.* send out (a sound) so as to be heard: ⁓ *a sigh (a cry of pain)*; say: *the last words she* ⁓*ed.* ⁓**ance** ['ʌtərəns] *n.* **1.** (no pl.) way of speaking: *a clear* ⁓*ance.* **2.** (no pl.) give ⁓*ance to one's feelings,* express them in words. **3.** sth. said.

ut·ter·most ['ʌtəməʊst] *adj. & n.* (no pl.) utmost.

U-turn ['ju:tɜ:n] *n.* turn of 180° by a vehicle so as to face in the opposite direction without reversing.

V

va·cant ['veɪkənt] *adj.* **1.** empty: ~ space. **2.** not occupied by anyone: *a ~ room* (in a hotel). *The position is ~* (i.e. there is no one to do the work). **3.** (of the mind) unoccupied with thought; (of the eyes, looks, etc.) showing no signs of thought or interest. **~·ly** *adv.* **va·can·cy** *n.* **1.** empty space. **2.** (no pl.) being ~ (3). **3.** position in business, etc. for which sb. is needed: *good vacancies for clerks and typists.*

va·cate [və'keɪt] *v.t.* give up living in (a house, rooms, etc.); leave unoccupied: ~ *one's seat.*

va·ca·tion [və'keɪʃn] *n.* **1.** vacating (e.g. of a position). **2.** weeks during which universities and lawcourts stop work. **3.** (esp. U.S.A.) period of holidays: *on ~,* on holiday. *v.i.* (U.S.A.) take or spend a ~ (3) (*at, in*).

vac·ci·nate ['væksɪneɪt] *v.t.* protect (sb.) against smallpox, etc. by injecting vaccine (e.g. into the arm). **vac·ci·na·tion** [,væksɪ'neɪʃn] *n.* **vac·cine** ['væksi:n] *n.* preparation of disease germs (or viruses) used for the protection of persons against smallpox and some other diseases.

vac·il·late ['væsɪleɪt] *v.i.* waver, hesitate, be uncertain (*in opinion,* etc., *between* different opinions, etc.). **vac·il·la·tion** [,væsɪ'leɪʃn] *n.*

vac·u·ous ['vækjʊəs] *adj.* vacant (3).

vac·u·um ['vækjʊəm] *n.* (pl. *-ua* [-ʊə], *~s*) space completely empty of substance or air; space in a container from which air has been pumped out: ~ *cleaner,* apparatus (1) that takes up dust, dirt, etc. by suction; ~ *flask* (*bottle*), (Gt. Brit.) flask with two walls having a ~ between them, for keeping contents at an unchanging temperature.

vag·a·bond ['vægəbɒnd] *adj.* having no fixed living-place; habitually wandering: *lead a ~ life; ~ gipsies. n. ~* person; tramp.

va·ga·ry ['veɪgərɪ] *n.* strange, unusual act or idea, esp. one for which there seems to be no good reason: *the vagaries of fashion.*

va·grant ['veɪgrənt] *adj.* leading a wandering life: ~ *tribes. n. ~* person; vagabond; tramp. **va·gran·cy** *n.* (no pl.) being a ~.

vague [veɪg] *adj.* (*~r, ~st*) **1.** not clear; indistinct: ~ *outlines;* ~ *demands.* **2.** (of persons, their looks, etc.) uncertain (about needs, intentions, etc.). **~·ly** *adv.* **~·ness** *n.*

vain [veɪn] *adj.* **1.** without use, value, meaning, or result: *a ~ attempt.* **2.** having too high an opinion of one's looks or abilities, etc.; conceited. **3.** *in ~,* without the desired result: *Our efforts were in ~.* **~·ly** *adv.* **~·glo·ry** *n.* (no pl.) extreme vanity or pride in oneself. **~·glo·ri·ous** *adj.*

vale [veɪl] *n.* (old use or poet. except in place-names) valley.

val·en·tine ['væləntaɪn] *n.* (letter, card, etc. often sent anonymously on St. V.~'s Day, 14 Feb., to a) sweetheart.

va·le·ri·an [və'lɪərɪən] *n.* plant with pink or white flowers and a strong smell liked by cats; root of this used in medicine.

va·let ['vælɪt] *n.* manservant who looks after his employer's clothes.

val·iant ['væljənt] *adj.* brave.

val·id ['vælɪd] *adj.* **1.** (law) effective because made or done with the correct formalities: *The claim (marriage) was not ~.* **2.** (of contracts, etc.) having force in law: ~ *for three months.* **3.** (of arguments, reasons, etc.) well-based; sound. **~·ly** *adv.* **val·i·date** ['vælɪdeɪt] *v.t.* make ~. **va·lid·i·ty** [və'lɪdətɪ] *n.* (no pl.).

va·lise [və'li:z] *n.* bag for clothes, etc. during a journey; kitbag.

val·ley ['vælɪ] *n.* (pl. *~s*) stretch of land between hills or mountains, often with a river flowing through it.

val·our (U.S.A. *-or*) ['vælə*] *n.* (no pl.) bravery, esp. in war. **val·or·ous** *adj.*

val·ue ['vælju:] *n.* **1.** (no pl.) quality of being useful or desirable. **2.** worth of sth. in terms of money or other goods for which it can be exchanged: *good ~ for one's money.* **~-added tax,** tax on the rise in ~ of an article at each stage of its production. **3.** (no pl.) what sth. is considered to be worth: *I've been offered £15 for the ring but its ~ is much higher.* *v.t.* **1.** estimate the money ~ of. **2.** have a high opinion of: *I ~ your advice.* **valu·able** ['væljuəbl] *adj.* of much ~. *n.* (usu. pl.) thing(s) of much ~ (e.g. jewels, gold objects). **val·u·a·tion** [,vælju'eɪʃn] *n.* process of deciding the ~ (3); the ~ (3) decided upon.

valve [vælv] *n.* **1.** (sorts of) mechanical device (2) for controlling the flow of air, liquid, gas, etc. into a tube, pipe, etc. **2.** structure in the heart or in a blood-vessel allowing the blood to flow in one direction only. **3.** (U.S.A. *tube*) vacuum tube (used in radio and television sets, etc.).

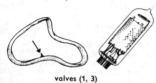

valves (1, 3)

van¹ [væn] *n.* **1.** covered or roofed vehicle for conveying goods by road: *the baker's ~*; *a furniture ~.* **2.** (Gt. Brit.) roofed railway carriage for goods or luggage: *the luggage ~.*

van² [væn] *n.* **1.** front or leading part of an army or fleet in battle. **2.** those persons who lead a procession or (fig.) a movement: *in the ~ of scientific progress.* '**~·guard** *n.* advance party of an army, etc. as a guard against surprise attacks, etc.

van·dal ['vændl] *n.* person who wilfully destroys or damages works of art, spoils the beauties of nature, etc. **~·ism** ['vændəlɪzəm] *n.* (no pl.).

vane [veɪn] *n.* **1.** arrow, etc. on the top of a building, turned by the wind so as to show its direction. **2.** blade (3) of a propeller, sail of a windmill, etc.

va·nil·la [və'nɪlə] *n.* **1.** (pods or beans of a) plant with sweet-smelling flowers. **2.** (no pl.) flavouring substance from ~ beans: *~ custard (ice).*

van·ish ['vænɪʃ] *v.i.* **1.** disappear suddenly; fade away gradually. **2.** go out of existence.

van·i·ty ['vænətɪ] *n.* **1.** (no pl.) conceit; having too high an opinion of one's looks, abilities, etc. **2.** worthlessness; quality of being unsatisfying, without

true value; worthless thing or act: *the ~ of earthly greatness; the vanities of life.*

van·quish ['væŋkwɪʃ] *v.t.* defeat.

van·tage ['vɑːntɪdʒ] *n.* advantage; superiority in a contest.

va·pid ['væpɪd] *adj.* tasteless; uninteresting. **~·i·ty** [və'pɪdətɪ] *n.*

va·pour (U.S.A. **va·por**) ['veɪpə*] *n.* (no pl.) steam; mist; gaseous form of a substance that is normally liquid or solid. **va·por·ize** ['veɪpəraɪz] *v.t. & i.* (cause to) change into ~.

vari..., see *vary.*

var·i·cose ['værɪkəʊs] *adj.* ~ *vein,* permanently swollen or enlarged vein.

var·nish ['vɑːnɪʃ] *n.* (liquid used to give a) hard, shiny, transparent coating on the surface of wood, metal, etc.; other preparation for a similar purpose: *nail ~,* (Gt. Brit.) ~ for fingernails. *v.t.* put ~ on.

var·si·ty ['vɑːsətɪ] *n.* (Gt. Brit., colloq.) university.

vary ['veərɪ] *v.i. & t.* be, become, or make different: *~ing prices.* **vari·able** *adj.* ~ing; changeable; that can be changed. **vari·abil·i·ty** [,veərɪə'bɪlətɪ] *n.* (no pl.). **vari·ance** *n.* (no pl.) ~ing; condition of being in disagreement: *at variance with.* **vari·ant** *adj.* different or alternative: *'Tire' and 'tyre' are variant spellings. n.* variant form (esp. of a word, its spelling). **vari·a·tion** [,veərɪ-'eɪʃn] *n.* (degree of) ~ing: *variations of temperature; with little variation of speed.* **var·ied** *adj.* **1.** of different sorts. **2.** continually or often changing: *a varied career.* **var·ie·gat·ed** ['veərɪgeɪtɪd] *adj.* marked irregularly with differently coloured patches. **va·ri·ety** [və'raɪətɪ] *n.* **1.** (no pl.) quality of not being all the same or not the same at all times: *We want more variety in our food.* **2.** (no pl.) number or group of different things: *for a variety of reasons.* **3.** division of a species. **4.** (no pl.) kind of entertainment: *variety show,* stage entertainment of songs, dances, short plays, etc. **var·i·ous** ['veərɪəs] *adj.* different; several: *for various reasons.*

vase [vɑːz] *n.* vessel of glass, pottery, etc., used for holding flowers or as an ornament.

vas·sal ['væsl] *n.* person who, in former times, held land in return for military help to the owner of the land. **~·age** ['væsəlɪdʒ] *n.* (no pl.) condition of being a ~.

vast [vɑːst] *adj.* immense; extensive.

vat [væt] *n.* tank or great vessel for

holding liquids, esp. in brewing, dyeing, and tanning.

vaude·ville ['vəudəvɪl] *n.* (no pl.) variety (4).

vault[1] [vɔ:lt] *n.* **1.** arched roof; series of arches forming a roof. **2.** underground room or cellar, esp. for storing wine or valuables. **3.** burial chamber. **~ed** *adj.* having, built with, ~s.

a vaulted roof

vault[2] [vɔ:lt] *v.i. & t.* jump in a single movement, with the hand(s) resting on sth. or with the help of a pole: ~ (*over*) *a fence*; ~ *on to a horse*; ~*ing-horse*, (gymnastics) wooden block for use in ~*ing*. *n.* jump made in this way.

vaunt [vɔ:nt] *v.i. & t. & n.* boast. (no pl.) meat from a calf.

veal [vi:l] *n.* (no pl.) meat from a calf.

veer [vɪə*] *v.i.* (esp. of wind, fig. of opinion, talk) change direction: *The wind ~ed round to the north.*

veg·e·ta·ble ['vedʒtəbl] *adj.* of, from, relating to, plants or plant life: *the ~ kingdom*; ~ *oils*. *n.* plant, esp. of the sort used for food (e.g. potatoes, beans, carrots, cabbages). **veg·e·tar·i·an** [,vedʒɪ'teərɪən] *n.* person who does not eat meat; (attrib.) of ~s: *a vegetarian diet.* **veg·e·ta·tion** [,vedʒɪ'teɪʃn] *n.* (no pl.) plant life in general; all the plants growing in a place or area: *tropical vegetation.*

ve·he·ment ['vi:ɪmənt] *adj.* (of feelings) strong; eager; (of persons, their speech, etc.) filled with, showing, strong or eager feeling. **ve·he·mence** *n.* (no pl.).

ve·hi·cle ['vi:ɪkl] *n.* **1.** any conveyance (usu. wheeled, but also a sledge) for goods or passengers on land. **2.** means by which thought, feeling, etc. can be conveyed: *use the newspapers as a ~ for political views.* **ve·hic·u·lar** [vɪ'hɪkjʊlə*] *adj.* of transport ~s: *This road is closed to vehicular traffic.*

veil [veɪl] *n.* **1.** covering of fine net or other material to protect or hide a woman's face, or as part of a head-dress. *take the ~*, become a nun. **2.** sth. that hides: *a ~ of mist. v.t.* put a ~ over; (fig.) conceal: ~ *one's distrust.*

vein [veɪn] *n.* **1.** blood-vessel along which blood flows from all parts of the body to the heart (cf. *artery*). **2.** one of the ~-like lines in a leaf, in the wing of an insect; coloured line in some kinds of stone (e.g. marble). **3.** crack or fissure in rock, filled with coal, ore, etc. **4.** distinctive character or tendency; mood; state of mind: *a ~ of melancholy in sb.'s character. He talked in a merry ~ for several minutes.*

the veins of a leaf

veld(t) [velt] *n.* (stretch of) rocky grass-land of the S. African plateau.

vel·lum ['veləm] *n.* (no pl.) parchment.

ve·loc·i·ty [vɪ'lɒsɪtɪ] *n.* (no pl.) (of objects) rate of motion; speed.

vel·vet ['velvɪt] *n.* (no pl.) cloth made of silk, cotton, nylon, etc. with thick, soft nap[2] on one side; (attrib.) made of ~; soft like ~: *a ~ frock.* **~y** *adj.* soft and smooth like ~.

ve·nal ['vi:nl] *adj.* **1.** (of persons) willing to do wrong for money. **2.** (of conduct, etc.) influenced by, done for, (possible) payment.

vend [vend] *v.t.* **1.** (law) sell. **2.** offer (small wares) for sale: ~*ing-machine*, coin-operated machine for the sale of small articles (e.g. cigarettes, food, etc.). **~er** *n.* seller. **ven·dor** *n.* **1.** (esp. law) seller. *news-~or*, seller of newspapers, etc. **2.** vending-machine.

ven·det·ta [ven'detə] *n.* quarrel between families in which each commits murders in revenge for previous murders.

ve·neer [və'nɪə*] *n.* **1.** thin layer of fine quality wood glued to the surface of cheaper wood (for furniture, etc.). **2.** (fig.) surface appearance (of politeness, civilization, etc.) covering the true nature. *v.t.* put a ~ (1) on (wood, etc.).

ven·er·able ['venərəbl] *adj.* deserving respect because of age, character, associations, etc. **ven·er·ate** ['venəreɪt] *v.t.* regard with deep respect. **ven·er·a·tion** [,venə'reɪʃn] *n.* (no pl.) deep respect.

Ve·ne·tian [və'ni:ʃn] *adj.* of Venice. *v~ blind*, window blind of many horizontal slats that may be adjusted so as to admit or exclude light and air

ven·geance ['vendʒəns] *n.* (no pl.) **1.** revenge; return of injury for injury: *take ~ upon sb.*, have one's revenge. **2.** *with a ~*, thoroughly; very much: *It's raining with a ~.* **venge·ful** ['vendʒful] *adj.* desiring ~.

ve·nial ['viːnjəl] *adj.* (of a sin or error) excusable; not serious.

ven·i·son ['venzn] *n.* (no pl.) deer meat.

ven·om ['venəm] *n.* (no pl.) **1.** poison of snakes, etc. **2.** hate; spite; ill feeling. **~·ous** *adj.* deadly; spiteful.

vent [vent] *n.* **1.** (also *~-hole*) hole serving as an inlet or outlet for air, gas, liquid, etc. **2.** (no pl.) (fig.) outlet for one's feelings: *give ~ to one's feelings*, express them. *v.t.* provide an outlet for.

ven·ti·late ['ventɪleɪt] *v.t.* **1.** cause air to move freely in and out of: *~ a room.* **2.** make (a question, a grievance) widely known and cause it to be discussed. **ven·ti·la·tion** [ˌventɪ'leɪʃn] *n.* (no pl.). **ven·ti·la·tor** *n.* device (2) for ventilating (1).

ven·tril·o·quism [ven'trɪləkwɪzəm] *n.* (no pl.) art of producing voice-sounds so that they seem to come from a person or place at a distance from the speaker. **ven·tril·o·quist** *n.* person skilled in this art.

ven·ture ['ventʃə*] *n.* undertaking in which there is risk: *at a ~*, without definite aim; trusting to chance. *v.t. & i.* **1.** take the risk of danger or loss; be brave enough (*to do sth.*): *~ near the edge of a cliff.* **2.** put forward (an opinion); go so far as; dare: *I ~ to say that ...*; *if I may ~ to disagree.* **~·some** *adj.* ready to take risks; daring; (of acts) risky.

ve·ra·cious [vəˈreɪʃəs] *adj.* true; truthful. **ve·rac·i·ty** [vəˈræsɪtɪ] *n.* (no pl.).

ve·ran·da(h) [vəˈrændə] *n.* (U.S.A. also *porch* (2)) roofed and floored open space along the side(s) of a house, etc.

verb [vɜːb] *n.* word or phrase indicating what sb. or sth. does, what state sb. or sth. is in, what is becoming of sth. or sb.

ver·bal ['vɜːbl] *adj.* **1.** of or in words: *a ~ error.* **2.** spoken, not written: *a ~ message.* **3.** word for word: *a ~ translation.* **4.** of verbs: *~ noun*, verb form used as a noun (e.g. *dancing* in '*Dancing is good exercise*'). **~·ly** *adv.* in spoken words, not in writing.

ver·ba·tim [vɜː'beɪtɪm] *adv. & adj.* word for word; exactly as spoken or written: *a speech reported ~*; *a ~ report.*

ver·bose [vɜː'bəʊs] *adj.* using, con-

taining, more words than are needed.

ver·bos·i·ty [vɜː'bɒsətɪ] *n.* (no pl.).

ver·dant ['vɜːdənt] *adj.* (esp. of grass, fields, etc.) fresh and green. **ver·dure** ['vɜːdʒə*] *n.* (no pl.) greenness of growing things; fresh, green growth.

ver·dict ['vɜːdɪkt] *n.* **1.** decision reached by a jury on a question of fact in a law case. **2.** decision or opinion given after a test, etc.: *the ~ of the electors.*

ver·di·gris ['vɜːdɪgrɪs] *n.* (no pl.) green substance formed on copper surfaces.

verge [vɜːdʒ] *n.* **1.** border (e.g. strip of grassy ground at the side of a road); edge of a lawn. **2.** (no pl.) *be on the ~ of doing sth.*, be about to do it. *v.i.* **1.** incline: *The sun was verging towards the horizon.* **2.** *~ upon*, be near to: *The country was verging upon bankruptcy.*

verg·er ['vɜːdʒə*] *n.* person who shows people to their seats in an Anglican church.

ver·i·fy ['verɪfaɪ] *v.t.* **1.** test the truth or accuracy of (statements, etc.). **2.** (of an event, etc.) show the truth of (sth. said, etc.). **ver·i·fi·able** *adj.* that can be verified. **ver·i·fi·ca·tion** [ˌverɪfɪ'keɪʃn] *n.*

ver·i·ly ['verɪlɪ] *adv.* (old use) truly.

ver·i·si·mil·i·tude [ˌverɪsɪ'mɪlɪtjuːd] *n.* appearance, semblance, of truth; sth. that seems true.

ver·i·table ['verɪtəbl] *adj.* real; rightly named.

ver·i·ty ['verətɪ] *n.* **1.** (no pl.) truth (of a statement, etc.). **2.** true statement; sth. that really exists.

ver·mi·cel·li [ˌvɜːmɪ'selɪ] *n.* (no pl.) paste of white flour made into long, slender threads.

ver·mi·form ['vɜːmɪfɔːm] *adj.* worm-shaped: *~ appendix.*

ver·mil·ion [vəˈmɪljən] *adj. & n.* (no pl.) bright red (colour).

ver·min ['vɜːmɪn] *n.* (usu. treated as pl.) **1.** wild animals (e.g. rats) harmful to plants, birds, etc. **2.** insects (e.g. lice) sometimes found on the bodies of human beings or animals. **~·ous** *adj.* **1.** infested with fleas, lice, etc. **2.** caused by insect ~: *~ous diseases.*

ver·nac·u·lar [vəˈnækjʊlə*] *adj.* (of a word, a language) of the country in question: *the ~ languages of India.* *n.* language or dialect of a country or district.

ver·nal ['vɜːnl] *adj.* (liter.) of, in, as in, the season of spring.

ver·sa·tile ['vɜːsətaɪl] *adj.* interested in and clever at many different things. **ver·sa·til·i·ty** [ˌvɜːsə'tɪlətɪ] *n.* (no pl.).

verse [vɜːs] *n.* **1.** (no pl.) (form of) writing arranged in groups of lines, each conforming to a pattern of accented and unaccented syllables and often having a rhyming syllable at the end: *written in* ~; *prose and* ~. **2.** one line of ~ (1). **3.** group of such lines forming a unit in a poem, hymn, etc.: *a poem of five* ~*s*. **4.** one of the short, numbered divisions of a chapter in the Bible.

versed [vɜːst] *adj.* ~ *in*, skilled or experienced in.

ver·sion ['vɜːʃn] *n.* **1.** translation into another language: *a new* ~ *of the Bible.* **2.** account of an event, etc. from the point of view of one person, etc.: *contradictory* ~*s of what was said.*

ver·sus ['vɜːsəs] *prep.* (Latin) (in law and sport, often shortened to *v.* or *vs.* in writing and print) against.

ver·te·bra ['vɜːtɪbrə] *n.* (pl. -*brae* [-briː]) each segment of the backbone; (pl.) backbone. **ver·te·brate** ['vɜːtɪbrət] *n. & adj.* (animal, bird, etc.) having a backbone.

ver·ti·cal ['vɜːtɪkl] *adj.* at right angles to the earth's surface or to another line (cf. *horizontal*): *a* ~ *line* (*cliff*); *a* ~ *take-off aircraft* (able to rise ~*ly*, not needing a runway).

ver·ti·go ['vɜːtɪɡəʊ] *n.* (no pl.) dizziness.

verve [vɜːv] *n.* (no pl.) spirit and force in the work of an artist, writer, musician.

very ['verɪ] *adv.* to a great extent; to a marked degree: ~ *good*, ~ *well*, excellent(ly). *attrib. adj.* **1.** actually this and no other: *in this* ~ *place*; *the* ~ *thing I wanted.* **2.** extreme: *at the* ~ *beginning.*

ves·pers ['vespəz] *n. pl.* church service in the evening; evensong.

ves·sel ['vesl] *n.* **1.** container for liquids (e.g. a bucket, bottle, cup). **2.** ship or large boat. **3.** (esp.) blood-~.

vest [vest] *n.* **1.** (Gt. Brit.) garment worn on the upper part of the body next to the skin. **2.** (Gt. Brit., trade use; U.S.A.) = waistcoat.

ves·ti·bule ['vestɪbjuːl] *n.* lobby or entrance hall of a building (e.g. where hats and coats may be left).

ves·tige ['vestɪdʒ] *n.* trace or sign; small remaining bit that is evidence of what once existed: *Not a* ~ *of the castle remained.*

vest·ment ['vestmənt] *n.* garment, esp. one worn by a priest in church; ceremonial robe. **ves·try** ['vestrɪ] *n.* **1.** part of a church where ~*s* are kept. **2.** parish committee of ratepayers.

vet[1] [vet] *n.* (colloq., abbr. for) veterinary surgeon. *v.t.* (-*tt*-) (colloq.) **1.** give (sb.) a medical examination. **2.** examine closely (a piece of writing, a candidate, etc.).

vet[2] [vet] *n. & adj.* (U.S.A., colloq., abbr. for) veteran.

vet·er·an ['vetərən] *n.* person having had much or long experience, esp. as a soldier; (U.S.A.) any ex-service man. *attrib. adj.* of a ~; composed of ~*s*: *a* ~ *teacher*; *a* ~ *car*, (Gt. Brit.) a car made before 1916 or 1905.

vet·er·i·nary ['vetərɪnərɪ] *adj.* of or concerned with the diseases of animals: (Gt. Brit.) *a* ~ *surgeon* (*college*). *n.* (Gt. Brit.) ~ surgeon. **vet·er·i·nar·i·an** [ˌvetərɪˈneərɪən] *n.* (U.S.A.) = ~ surgeon.

ve·to ['viːtəʊ] *n.* (pl. -*oes*) right to prevent a bill from becoming law; right to reject or forbid sth.; statement rejecting or prohibiting sth.: *put a* ~ *on sth.*, forbid it. *v.t.* use a ~ against; prohibit: *The meeting was* ~*ed by the president.*

vex [veks] *v.t.* annoy; distress; trouble. *a* ~*ed question*, difficult question causing much discussion. ~**·a·tion** [vekˈseɪʃn] *n.* being ~*ed*; sth. that ~*es*. ~**·a·tious** [vekˈseɪʃəs] *adj.* annoying: ~*atious regulations.*

via ['vaɪə] *prep.* (Latin) by way of: *travel from London to Paris* ~ *Dover.*

via·duct ['vaɪədʌkt] *n.* bridge with arches carrying a road or railway across a valley or low ground.

vi·al ['vaɪəl] *n.* small, usu. cylindrical vessel for holding liquid medicines.

vi·brate [vaɪˈbreɪt] *v.t. & i.* **1.** (cause to) move rapidly and continuously backwards and forwards like the string of a violin: *The building* ~*s whenever a lorry passes.* **2.** (of stretched strings, the voice) throb: *a voice vibrating with passion.* **vi·brant** ['vaɪbrənt] *adj.* vibrating: *the vibrant notes of a cello.* **vi·bra·tion** [vaɪˈbreɪʃn] *n.* vibrating movement.

vic·ar ['vɪkə*] *n.* (Church of England) clergyman in charge of a church and the parish belonging to it, who receives a yearly payment for his duties. ~**·age** ['vɪkərɪdʒ] *n.* ~'*s* residence.

vi·car·i·ous [vɪˈkeərɪəs] *adj.* done, undergone, by one person for another or others.

vice[1] [vaɪs] *n.* **1.** (any particular kind of) evil conduct or immorality. **2.** (in a horse) bad habit (e.g. kicking) that makes control difficult.

vice[2] (U.S.A. **vise**) [vaɪs] *n.* apparatus

(1) with strong jaws in which things can be held tightly while being worked upon.

a vice²

vice- [vaɪs-] *pref.* acting for (another); holding rank next below: *vice-admiral*; *vice-chairman*; *vice-president*. **~·roy** ['vaɪsrɔɪ] *n.* (formerly) person governing a colony, etc. as the sovereign's representative. **~·re·gal** [ˌvaɪs'riːgl] *adj.* of a ~roy.

vi·ce ver·sa [ˌvaɪsɪ'vɜːsə] *adv.* (Latin) the other way round: *We gossip about them and* ~ (i.e. they gossip about us).

vi·cin·i·ty [vɪ'sɪnəti] *n.* 1. (no pl.) nearness. 2. neighbourhood: *in close* ~ *to the school; no school in the* ~.

vi·cious ['vɪʃəs] *adj.* 1. of vice¹; given up to vice¹: *a* ~ *man* (*life, habit*). 2. spiteful: *a* ~ *look* (*kick, temper*). 3. (of a horse) having bad habits such as biting and kicking. 4. having faults: *a* ~ *argument.* **~·ly** *adv.*

vi·cis·si·tude [vɪ'sɪsɪtjuːd] *n.* change, esp. in sb.'s fortunes.

vic·tim ['vɪktɪm] *n.* 1. living creature killed and offered as a religious sacrifice. 2. person, animal, etc. suffering injury, pain, loss, etc. because of circumstances, an event, the ill will of sb. else, etc.: *He is the* ~ *of his own foolishness* (*his brother's anger*). **~·ize** *v.t.* make a ~ of (sb.).

vic·tor ['vɪktə*] *n.* person who conquers or wins. **vic·to·ry** *n.* success (in a battle, contest, game, etc.). **vic·to·ri·ous** [vɪk'tɔːrɪəs] *adj.* having gained ~y.

vict·ual ['vɪtl] *n.* (usu. pl.) food and drink; provisions. *v.t. & i.* (*-ll-*, U.S.A. also *-l-*) 1. supply with ~s: ~ *a ship.* 2. obtain stores. **~·ler** (U.S.A. also **~·er**) ['vɪtlə*] *n.* trader in ~s.

vid·eo ['vɪdɪəʊ] *n.* (pl. ~s) (U.S.A.) = television. *adj.* relating to or used in the transmission or reception of photographic images: ~ *cassette*, cassette of ~ tape used in cassette television; ~ (*cassette*) *recorder*; ~ *disc*, disc for recording sound and images for use in television sets in the same way ~ cassettes are used; ~ *tape* (n.), magnetic tape for recording sound and vision (e.g. of television programmes); ~ (*-tape*) *recordings*; ~*-tape* (v.t.), make a recording on magnetic tape of (e.g. a television programme).

vie [vaɪ] *v.i.* (pres. p. *vying*) rival or compete (*with*): *vying with one another for the first place.*

view [vjuː] *n.* 1. (no pl.) state of seeing or being seen; range of vision; sight (of): *be in* ~, *come into* ~ (in(to) a position where (it) can be seen); *on* ~, being shown or exhibited. 2. sth. (to be) looked at, esp. a stretch of natural scenery: *a house with a* ~. 3. opinion: *We take a serious* ~ *of his conduct, it is, in our opinion, bad. in* ~ *of*, considering; taking into account. 4. purpose; plan; intention: *fall in with* (*meet*) *sb.'s* ~*s*, agree with his wishes; *with a* ~ *to*, with intention to. *v.t. & i.* look at; examine; consider; watch television. **~·er** *n.* 1. (esp.) person who watches television. 2. optical device (2) for looking at slides (4), etc. **~·find·er** *n.* part of a camera showing the extent of a picture. **~·point** *n.* point (3) of ~.

vig·il ['vɪdʒɪl] *n.* staying awake to keep watch or to pray. **vig·i·lance** *n.* (no pl.) keeping watch; watchfulness. **vig·i·lant** *adj.* watchful.

vig·our (U.S.A. **-or**) ['vɪgə*] *n.* (no pl.) mental or physical strength; energy. **vig·or·ous** ['vɪgərəs] *adj.* strong; energetic.

vile [vaɪl] *adj.* 1. shameful and disgusting: ~ *habits* (*language*). 2. (colloq.) bad: ~ *weather.* **vil·i·fy** ['vɪlɪfaɪ] *v.t.* slander; say evil things about (sb.).

vil·la ['vɪlə] *n.* house in its own grounds or garden, esp. one on the outskirts of a town.

vil·lage ['vɪlɪdʒ] *n.* place smaller than a town, where there are houses, shops, etc. **vil·lag·er** *n.* inhabitant of a ~.

vil·lain ['vɪlən] *n.* (esp. in drama) wrongdoer; wicked man; (colloq., used playfully) rascal: *the little* ~. **~·ous** *adj.* very bad. **~·y** *n.* evil conduct or act.

vim [vɪm] *n.* (no pl.) (colloq.) energy.

vin·di·cate ['vɪndɪkeɪt] *v.t.* justify (sb., etc.) by evidence or argument; show or prove the truth, justice, etc. of (sth. that has been attacked or disputed). **vin·di·ca·tion** [ˌvɪndɪ'keɪʃn] *n.*

vin·dic·tive [vɪn'dɪktɪv] *adj.* unforgiving; having or showing a desire for revenge.

vine [vaɪn] *n.* climbing plant, esp. the kind that bears grapes. **~·yard** ['vɪnjəd] *n.* area of land planted with grape-~s, esp. for wine-making.

vin·e·gar ['vɪnɪgə*] *n.* acid liquid

(from malt or wine) used in cooking for flavouring and preserving food.

vin·tage ['vɪntɪdʒ] *n.* **1.** (period of) grape harvesting. **2.** (wine from) grapes of a particular year: *of the ~ of 1925; a rare old ~* (of high quality). *adj.* of high quality, esp. from the past: *a ~ car*, (Gt. Brit.) a car made between 1917 and 1930.

vi·o·la[1] [vɪ'əʊlə] *n.* tenor violin of larger size than the ordinary violin.

vi·o·la[2] ['vaɪələ] *n.* kinds of plant resembling the pansy and violet.

vi·o·late ['vaɪəleɪt] *v.t.* **1.** break (an oath, a treaty, etc.); act contrary to (what one's conscience tells one to do, etc.). **2.** act towards (a sacred place, sb.'s seclusion etc.) without proper respect. **vi·o·la·tion** [ˌvaɪə'leɪʃn] *n.*

vi·o·lent ['vaɪələnt] *adj.* **1.** using, showing, accompanied by, great force: *a ~ wind* (*attack*); *~ passions.* **2.** caused by *~ attack*: *~ death.* **3.** severe: *~ toothache.* *~·ly adv.* **vi·o·lence** *n.* (no pl.) being *~*; *~ conduct*: *crimes of violence; an outbreak of violence* (= rioting).

vi·o·let ['vaɪəlɪt] *n.* **1.** small, wild or garden plant with sweet-smelling flowers. **2.** (no pl.) bluish-purple colour of *~s.* *adj.* blue-red.

vi·o·lin [ˌvaɪə'lɪn] *n.* four-stringed musical instrument played with a bow. *~ist* ['vaɪəlɪnɪst] *n.* player of a *~*.

playing the violin   a viper

vi·o·lon·cel·lo [ˌvaɪələn'tʃeləʊ] *n.* (pl. *~s*) (abbr. *cello*) large-sized violin, deeper in tone, played while held between the knees. **vi·o·lon·cel·list** *n.* (abbr. *cellist*) player of a *~*.

vi·per ['vaɪpə*] *n.* small, poisonous snake, esp. the *common ~* or adder.

vir·gin ['vɜːdʒɪn] *n.* girl or woman (and in recent use, man) who has not experienced sexual union. *adj.* **1.** pure and untouched: *~ snow.* **2.** in the original condition; unused: *~ soil* (*forests*). *~·al adj.* of, like, a *~*; pure. *~·i·ty* [və'dʒɪnətɪ] *n.* (no pl.).

vir·ile ['vɪraɪl] *adj.* having or showing strength, energy, manly qualities; having the powers of a full-grown man. **vi·ril·i·ty** [vɪ'rɪlətɪ] *n.* (no pl.).

vir·tu·al ['vɜːtʃʊəl] *adj.* being in fact, acting as, what is described, but not accepted openly or in name as such: *the ~ head of the business; a ~ defeat.* *~·ly adv.*

vir·tue ['vɜːtjuː] *n.* **1.** (any particular kind of) goodness or excellence (e.g. patience). **2.** (no pl.) chastity, esp. of a woman. **3.** *by* (*in*) *~ of*, because of. **vir·tu·ous** ['vɜːtʃʊəs] *adj.* having, showing, *~*; (of a woman) chaste. **vir·tu·ous·ly** *adv.*

vir·u·lent ['vɪrʊlənt] *adj.* (of poison) strong; deadly; (of ill feeling, hatred) bitter; (of words, etc.) full of ill feeling; (of diseases, sores) poisonous. **vir·u·lence** *n.* (no pl.).

vi·rus ['vaɪərəs] *n.* poisonous element causing spread of infectious disease: *the ~ of influenza.*

vi·sa ['viːzə] *n.* stamp or signature put on a passport to show that it has been examined and approved by the officials of the foreign country that the owner intends to visit (*entrance* or *entry ~*) or leave (*exit ~*). *v.t.* put a *~* on.

vis·age ['vɪzɪdʒ] *n.* (liter.) face.

vis-a-vis [ˌviːzɑː'viː] *prep. & adv.* (Fr.) facing (one another).

vis·cid ['vɪsɪd], **vis·cous** ['vɪskəs] *adjs.* sticky; semifluid.

vis·count ['vaɪkaʊnt] *n.* British nobleman higher in rank than a baron, lower than an earl.

vise, see *vice*[2].

vis·ible ['vɪzəbl] *adj.* that can be seen; that is in sight. **vis·i·bil·i·ty** [ˌvɪzɪ'bɪlətɪ] *n.* (no pl.) being *~*; (esp.) condition of the atmosphere for seeing things at a distance.

vi·sion ['vɪʒn] *n.* **1.** (no pl.) power of seeing or imagining. **2.** sth. seen, esp. during sleep or in imagination: *have a ~ of the future.* *~·ary* ['vɪʒnərɪ] *adj.* **1.** existing only in the imagination; not practical or possible: *~ary ideas* (*plans, scenes*). **2.** (of persons) having *~ary* ideas; dreamy. *n. ~ary* (2) person.

vis·it ['vɪzɪt] *v.t. & i.* **1.** go to see (sb.); go to (a place) for a time. **2.** (biblical use) (*upon* a person) punish; give punishment for (a sin): *~ the sins of the fathers upon the children. n.* act of *~ing* (1); time of *~ing*: *pay sb. a ~; on a short ~ to an aunt.* *~ing n.* paying *~s*; making calls: *~ing hours at a hospital; be on ~ing terms with sb.,* know sb. well enough to *~ him.* **vis·i·tor** *n.* person who *~s* (1). **vis·i·ta·tion** [ˌvɪzɪ'teɪʃn] *n.* (esp.) trouble, disaster, looked upon as punishment from God.

vi·sor, **vi·zor** ['vaɪzə*] *n.* **1.** front piece of a helmet, esp. the movable upper piece. **2.** peak of a cap. **3.** fixed or movable oblong shield at the top of a windscreen in a vehicle to protect the eyes from bright sunshine.

vis·ta ['vɪstə] *n.* long, narrow view; (fig.) series of events looked back on or forward to.

vi·su·al ['vɪzjʊəl] *adj.* concerned with, used in, seeing: ~ *aids in teaching* (e.g. pictures, cinema films). ~·**ize** *v.t.* bring (sth.) as a picture before the mind.

vi·tal ['vaɪtl] *adj.* **1.** of, connected with, necessary for, living: *wounded in a ~ part.* **2.** supreme: *of ~ importance.* ~·**ly** *adv.* ~·**i·ty** [vaɪˈtælətɪ] *n.* (no pl.) **1.** ~ power; capacity to endure. **2.** liveliness; driving force. ~·**ize** *v.t.* fill with ~ity; put vigour into.

vi·ta·min ['vɪtəmɪn] *n.* sorts of substance, present in certain foods, that are essential to good health.

vi·ti·ate ['vɪʃɪeɪt] *v.t.* lower the quality of; weaken or destroy the force of.

vit·ri·ol ['vɪtrɪəl] *n.* (no pl.) sulphuric acid. ~·**ic** [ˌvɪtrɪˈblɪk] *adj.* (fig., of words, feelings) biting; full of invective.

vi·tu·per·ate [vɪˈtjuːpəreɪt] *v.t.* abuse in words; curse. **vi·tu·per·a·tive** [vɪˈtjuːpərətɪv] *adj.* abusive. **vi·tu·per·a·tion** [vɪˌtjuːpəˈreɪʃn] *n.*

vi·va·cious [vɪˈveɪʃəs] *adj.* lively; high-spirited. **vi·vac·i·ty** [vɪˈvæsətɪ] *n.* (no pl.)

vi·va vo·ce [ˌvaɪvəˈvəʊsɪ] *adj.* (& *adv.*) (Latin) oral(ly). *n.* oral (part of an) examination.

viv·id ['vɪvɪd] *adj.* **1.** (of colours, etc.) intense; bright. **2.** (of descriptions) giving a clear and distinct picture. **3.** lively: *a ~ imagination.* ~·**ly** *adv.*

vivi·sect [ˌvɪvɪˈsekt] *v.t.* cut up or experiment on (living animals) for scientific research. **vivi·sec·tion** [ˌvɪvɪˈsekʃn] *n.*

vix·en ['vɪksn] *n.* female fox.

viz. [vɪˈdiːlɪset, vɪz] (Latin, usu. read as *namely* ['neɪmlɪ]) *adv.* that is to say; namely.

vi·zor, see *visor*.

vo·cab·u·lary [vəʊˈkæbjʊlərɪ] *n.* **1.** book containing a list of words; list of words used in a book, etc., usu. with definitions or translations. **2.** total number of words used in a language; (range of) words known to or used by a person, by sb. in a profession.

vo·cal ['vəʊkl] *adj.* of, for, with, or using, the voice: ~ *c(h)ords,* string-like structure in the throat, with edges vibrating in an airstream to produce voice; *the ~ organs,* the tongue, lips, etc.; ~ *music* (to be sung). ~·**ist** *n.* singer.

vo·ca·tion [vəʊˈkeɪʃn] *n.* **1.** (no pl.) feeling that one is called to (and qualified for) a certain kind of work, esp. social or religious work, or occupation. **2.** person's trade or profession. ~·**al** [vəʊˈkeɪʃənl] *adj.* of or for a ~ (2): ~*al guidance,* advice on the choice of a ~ (2).

vod·ka ['vɒdkə] *n.* strong, Russian alcoholic drink distilled from rye.

vogue [vəʊg] *n.* fashion (1): *in ~,* in fashion; *all the ~,* popular everywhere; *have a great ~,* be popular or fashionable.

voice [vɔɪs] *n.* **1.** sounds made when speaking or singing; power of making such sounds: *He has lost his ~,* he cannot speak or sing (e.g. because of a bad cold). **2.** (no pl.) (right to give an) opinion: *I have no ~ in the matter.* **3.** (no pl.) (phonetics) sound produced by vibration of the vocal c(h)ords, not with breath only. **4.** (gram.) see *active* (*passive*) ~. *v.t.* **1.** put into words: *The spokesman ~d the feelings of the crowd.* **2.** (phonetics) (esp. p.p.) utter with ~ (3): ~*d sounds.* ~·**over** *n.* narration in a film not accompanied by the picture of the speaker.

void [vɔɪd] *adj.* **1.** empty. **2.** ~ *of,* without. **3.** (law) (often *null and ~*) without force; invalid.

vol·a·tile ['vɒlətaɪl] *adj.* (of a liquid) that easily changes into gas or vapour; (of a person) lively; gay; changeable.

vol·ca·no [vɒlˈkeɪnəʊ] *n.* (pl. -oes, -os) mountain with an opening or openings through which gases, lava, ashes, etc. come up from below the earth's crust (cf. *crater*). **vol·can·ic** [vɒlˈkænɪk] *adj.* of, from, like, a ~.

vo·li·tion [vəʊˈlɪʃn] *n.* (no pl.) act, power, of using one's will, of choosing, making a decision: *do sth. of (by) one's own ~.*

vol·ley ['vɒlɪ] *n.* **1.** hurling or shooting of a number of missiles (stones, arrows, bullets, etc.) together. **2.** number of oaths, curses, questions, directed together, or in quick succession, at sb. **3.** (tennis) return of the ball before it touches the ground. '~·**ball** *n.* (no pl.) game in which players on each side of a high net keep a ball in motion by hitting it with their hands back and forth over the net without letting it touch the ground.

volt [vəʊlt] *n.* unit of electrical force. **~·age** ['vəʊltɪdʒ] *n.* electrical force measured in ~s.

vol·u·ble ['vɒljʊbl] *adj.* talking, able to talk, very quickly and easily; (of speech) fluent. **vol·u·bly** *adv.* **vol·u·bil·i·ty** [,vɒljʊ'bɪlətɪ] *n.* (no pl.).

vol·ume ['vɒljuːm] *n.* **1.** book, esp. one of a set of books. **2.** (no pl.) amount of space occupied by a substance, a liquid, or a gas. **3.** large mass, amount, or quantity: *the ~ of work*; *the ~ of traffic*; (esp. pl.) rounded masses of steam or smoke: *~s of black smoke*. **4.** (no pl.) (of sound) loudness; sonority: *a voice of great ~*. **vo·lu·mi·nous** [və'ljuːmɪnəs] *adj.* **1.** (of writing) great in quantity; (of a writer) producing much. **2.** spacious; occupying much space: *a voluminous correspondence*.

vol·un·tary ['vɒləntərɪ] *adj.* **1.** done, doing, or ready to do things willingly, without being compelled: *~ helpers*; *a ~ statement*. **2.** carried on, supported, by *~* work and gifts. **vol·un·tar·i·ly** *adv.*

vol·un·teer [,vɒlən'tɪə*] *n.* **1.** person who offers to do sth., esp. sth. unpleasant or dangerous. **2.** soldier who is not conscripted. *v.t. & i.* come forward as a *~*; offer (help, service, *to do* sth.).

vo·lup·tuous [və'lʌptjʊəs] *adj.* of, for, arousing, given up to, sensuous or sensual pleasure.

vom·it ['vɒmɪt] *v.t. & i.* **1.** bring back from the stomach through the mouth. **2.** send out in large quantities: *factory chimneys ~ing smoke*. *n.* (no pl.) food that has been ~ed.

vo·ra·cious [və'reɪʃəs] *adj.* very hungry or greedy; desiring much: *a ~ reader*. **vo·rac·i·ty** [vɒ'ræsətɪ] *n.* (no pl.).

vor·tex ['vɔːteks] *n.* (pl. -*tices* [-tɪsiːz], *~es*) water or wind circling violently; quickly circling mass.

vote [vəʊt] *n.* **1.** (right to) expression of opinion or will, given by persons for or against sb. or sth., esp. by ballot or by putting up of hands: *put sth. to the ~*, decide it by asking for ~s. **2.** total number of ~s (to be) given to a political party, etc.: *The Labour ~ is expected to decrease*. *v.i. & t.* **1.** give a ~ (1) (*for* or *against* sth. or sb.); announce

a proposal (*that ...*). **2.** approve by ~s: *~ a sum of money for education*. **3.** (colloq.) declare by general agreement: *The new teacher was ~d a fine fellow*. **vot·er** *n.* person with the right to *~* in elections.

vouch [vaʊtʃ] *v.i. ~ for* (sb. or sth.), be responsible for (a person, his honesty, the truth of a statement, etc.). **~·er** *n.* receipt or document showing payment of money or correctness of accounts, etc.

vouch·safe [vaʊtʃ'seɪf] *v.t.* be kind enough to give (sth.) or *to do* (sth.): *~ a reply*; *~ to help*.

vow [vaʊ] *n.* solemn promise or undertaking: *marriage ~s*; *under a ~ of silence*, having promised not to speak about sth.; *break a ~. v.t. & i.* promise solemnly; make a ~ (*that ..., to do* sth.).

vow·el ['vaʊəl] *n.* **1.** vocal sound made without audible stopping of the breath. **2.** letter or symbol used to represent such a sound (e.g. the letters *a, e, i, o, u*, the symbols ɪ, ʌ, and ə).

voy·age ['vɔɪɪdʒ] *v.i. & n.* (make a) journey by ship: *a ~ up the Nile*.

vul·can·ite ['vʌlkənaɪt] *n.* (no pl.) hard plastic made from rubber and sulphur. **vul·can·ize** ['vʌlkənaɪz] *v.t.* treat (rubber) with sulphur at great heat to harden it.

vul·gar ['vʌlgə*] *adj.* ill-mannered; in bad taste (5); rough and noisy: *~ language*. **~·i·ty** [vʌl'gærətɪ] *n. ~* behaviour.

vul·ner·able ['vʌlnərəbl] *adj.* that is liable to be damaged; that may be wounded or hurt; not protected against attack.

a vulture

vul·ture ['vʌltʃə*] *n.* large bird, usu. with head and neck almost bare of feathers, that lives on the flesh of dead animals.

vy·ing, see *vie.*

W

wad [wɒd] *n.* **1.** lump of soft material for keeping things apart or in place, or to stop up a hole. **2.** number of papers or banknotes pressed or rolled together. *v.t.* (-*dd*-) put a ~ or ~s or ~ding into or round sth. **~·ding** *n.* (no pl.) soft material, esp. raw cotton, used for packing, lining² things, etc.

wad·dle ['wɒdl] *v.i.* walk with slow steps and a sideways roll, as a duck does. *n.* (no pl.) this kind of walk.

wade [weɪd] *v.i. & t.* walk (*through* water, *across* a stream, etc.); (fig.) make one's way with effort (*through* a book). **wad·ers** *n. pl.* high rubber boots used by men when fishing in rivers.

wa·di ['wɒdɪ] *n.* (in northern Africa and the Middle East) rocky water-course, dry except after heavy rain.

wa·fer ['weɪfə*] *n.* thin, flat biscuit (e.g. as eaten with ice cream).

waf·fle ['wɒfl] *n.* small cake made of batter³ baked in a ~-iron (usu. two shallow metal pans hinged together).

waft [wɑːft] *v.t.* carry lightly and smoothly through the air.

wag [wæg] *v.t. & i.* (-*gg*-) (cause to) move from side to side or up and down: *The dog ~ged its tail. set chins* (*tongues*) ~*ging*, cause people to talk (esp. scandal). *n.* **1.** ~ging movement. **2.** merry person fond of making practical jokes.

wage¹ [weɪdʒ] *n.* (usu. pl.) payment made or received (usu. weekly) for work or services (cf. *salary, fee*). **'~-,earn·er** *n.* person who works for ~s. **~ freeze** *n.* severe control, fixing, or stabilization of ~s. **'~-,pack·et** *n.* pay-packet.

wage² [weɪdʒ] *v.t.* carry on, engage in (war, a campaign).

wa·ger ['weɪdʒə*] *v.t. & i.* bet. *n.* bet: *lay* (*make*) *a* ~.

wag·gle ['wægl] *v.t. & i.* wag.

wag·on (esp. Gt. Brit.) **wag·gon** ['wægən] *n.* **1.** four-wheeled vehicle for carrying goods, pulled by horses or oxen. **2.** (U.S.A. *freight car*) open railway truck (e.g. for coal).

waif [weɪf] *n.* homeless person, esp. a child; homeless cat or dog.

wail [weɪl] *v.i. & t.* cry or complain with a loud, usu. high, voice: ~ (*over*) *one's misfortunes*; (of the wind) sound like a person ~ing. *n.* ~ing cry; complaint.

wain·scot ['weɪnskət] *n.* wooden panelling on the lower part of the walls of a room.

waist [weɪst] *n.* part of the body between the ribs and hips; part of a garment that goes round the ~. **~·coat** ['weɪskəut] *n.* (Gt. Brit.) close-fitting, sleeveless upper garment reaching to the ~ and buttoned down the front.

wait [weɪt] *v.i. & t.* **1.** stay where one is, delay acting, until sb. or sth. comes or until sth. happens: ~ *for sb.*; ~ *until the rain stops*; ~ *to see what happens*; ~ *up*, stay up; not go to bed. **2.** ~ *upon* (*sb.*), act as a servant to; fetch and carry things for; ~ *at table*, serve food, carry away dishes, etc. *n.* act or time of ~ing: *We had a long ~ for the bus. lie in* ~ (*for*), be in hiding in order to attack, etc. **~·er, ~·ress** ['weɪtrɪs] *ns.* man, woman, who ~s at table in a restaurant, hotel, etc. **'~-ing-room** *n.* room provided for persons to ~ in, esp. by a doctor, etc., or at a railway or bus station.

waive [weɪv] *v.t.* give up (a right or claim); not insist upon.

wake¹ [weɪk] *v.t. & i.* (p.t. *woke* [wəuk] or ~*d*, p.p. ~*d, woke*, or *woken* ['wəukən]) **1.** (often ~ *up*) (cause to) stop sleeping. **2.** stir up (sb.); rouse: ~ *memories.* **~·ful** *adj.* unable to sleep; with little sleep: *pass a ~ful night.* **wak·en** ['weɪkən] *v.t. & i.* = ~.

wake² [weɪk] *n.* track left by a ship on water. *in the* ~ *of*, after; following.

walk [wɔːk] *v.i. & t.* **1.** (of persons) move by putting forward each foot in turn, without having both feet off the ground at once (cf. *run*); (of animals) move forward at their slowest pace (cf. *trot, gallop*). **2.** ~ *away* (*off*) *with*, (colloq.) carry off; steal; win easily; ~ *off*, depart (esp. abruptly); ~ *out,* depart suddenly and angrily; go on strike; ~-out (n.), (esp.) (workers') strike; ~ out on sb., desert him; leave him at a time when he is expecting help, etc.; ~ up to, come near to (sb.). 3. cause to ~: ~ a horse up a hill. n. 1. journey on foot, esp. for pleasure or exercise; manner or style of ~ing. 2. path for ~ing: numerous pleasant ~s in the district. 3. ~ of life, person's social position, trade, or profession. '~-,over n. (colloq.) easy victory (because there is no, or only weak, opposition). '~-up n. & adj. (U.S.A.) (building) without a lift and with access to the upper floors only by stairs: a ~-up apartment (flat).

walk·ie-talk·ie [,wɔːkɪ'tɔːkɪ] n. portable radio transmitting- and receiving-set.

wall [wɔːl] n. continuous, vertical, and strong structure of stone, brick, concrete, wood, etc. forming one of the sides of a room or building, or enclosing a garden, courtyard, etc. with one's back to the ~, fighting where escape or retreat is impossible; go to the ~, be pushed aside as weak or helpless. v.t. close (up an opening, e.g. a window) with a ~ of bricks, etc. '~,flow·er n. garden plant with sweet-smelling yellow or dark-red flowers. '~,pa·per n. decorative paper used to cover the ~s of a room.

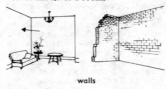

walls

wal·la·by ['wɒləbɪ] n. (sorts of) small kangaroo.

wal·let ['wɒlɪt] n. 1. folding pocket-case, usu. of leather, for papers, bank-notes, etc. 2. (old use) bag for food, etc. carried on a journey.

wal·low ['wɒləʊ] v.i. roll about (in mud, etc.) as a pig does.

wal·nut ['wɔːlnʌt] n. (tree producing) edible nut in a hard shell; wood of this tree, used for making furniture.

wal·rus ['wɔːlrəs] n. large sea-animal with two tusks pointing down from the mouth. (See the picture.)

waltz [wɔːls] n. (music in ³/₄ time for a) ballroom dance. v.i. dance a ~.

wan [wɒn] adj. (-nn-) (of a person, his looks, etc.) looking ill or tired; (of

light, the sky) pale; not bright. ~·ly adv.

wand [wɒnd] n. 1. baton (2). 2. thin stick or rod, esp. as used by a fairy or a magician (e.g. in a pantomime).

a walrus

wan·der ['wɒndə*] v.i. & t. 1. go from place to place without any special plan; leave the right path or road. 2. be absent-minded; allow the thoughts to go from subject to subject. ~·er n. ~·ings n. pl.

wane [weɪn] v.i. 1. (of the moon) show a smaller bright area after full moon (cf. wax¹). 2. become less or weaker: His influence has ~d. n. process of waning: on the ~.

wan·gle ['wæŋgl] v.t. (sl.) get, arrange (sth.) by cajolery or trickery.

want [wɒnt] v.t. & i. 1. require; be in need of. 2. be ~ing, be missing or lacking: A few pages of this book are ~ing. He is ~ing in courtesy (is not polite). 3. wish for; have a desire for: ~ for nothing, have all one needs; ~ed (by the police) (because suspected to be a criminal, etc.). n. 1. (no pl.) lack; scarcity; state of being absent: The plants died for ~ of water. 2. (no pl.) need; absence of a necessary thing: He's always in ~ of money. 3. (usu. pl.) desire for sth. held necessary to life, happiness, success, etc.: a man of few ~s; thing so desired: we can supply your ~s. ~·ing prep. without; in the absence of.

wan·ton ['wɒntən] adj. 1. playful: ~ breezes. 2. uncontrolled; disorderly: a ~ growth of weeds. 3. wilful; serving no useful purpose; done without good reason: ~ damage (insults). 4. immoral; unchaste: ~ thoughts. n. (esp.) ~ (4) woman. ~·ly adv. in a ~ (3) manner.

war [wɔː*] n. use of armed force, (period of) fighting, between nations or groups: declare (make) ~ on; be at ~ (with); go to ~ against; have been in the ~s, (colloq.) have been injured, etc.; cold ~, unfriendly relations between nations. v.i. (-rr-) fight; make ~: ~ against neighbouring countries. '~·fare n. (no pl.) making ~; condition of being at ~; fighting: the horrors of *modern* ~*fare*; *chemical* (*psychological*) ~*fare*. '~·**head** *n*. explosive head of a missile, torpedo, etc. '~·**like** *adj*. ready for ~; suggesting ~; fond of ~. '~-**path** *n*. (only in) *on the* ~*path*, ready for, engaged in, a fight or quarrel. ~**ring** *adj*. (of tendencies, etc.) not in harmony; rival. '~·**ship** *n*. ship armed[2] (1) for use in ~. '~-**worn** *adj*. exhausted by ~.

war·ble ['wɔːbl] *v.i. & t.* (esp. of birds) sing, esp. with a gentle trilling note. *n*. warbling; bird's song.

ward [wɔːd] *n*. **1**. young person under the guardianship of an older person or of law authorities. **2**. *keep watch and* ~, guard or protect. **3**. division of a town for purposes of government. **4**. division of, separate room in, a building, esp. a prison or hospital: *the fever* (*isolation*) ~. *v.t.* ~ *off*, keep away, avoid (a blow, danger, etc.).

war·den ['wɔːdn] *n*. person having control or authority (e.g. the heads of some colleges and schools in Great Britain, persons in charge of hostels): *a traffic* ~ (cf. *traffic*). ~**er**, ~**ress** ['wɔːdrɪs] *ns*. man, woman, acting as guard in a prison. '~·**room** *n*. room for use by a warship's officers.

-ward [-wəd] *suff*. (forming adjs. or advs.) having specified direction or tendency: *backward*; *downward*; *eastward*; *homeward*; *toward*.

ward·robe ['wɔːdrəʊb] *n*. cupboard-like piece of furniture in which to hang up clothes; a person's stock of clothes.

-wards [-wədz] *suff*. (forming advs.) to or in the direction of: *backwards*; *downwards*; *eastwards*; *homewards*; *towards*.

ware [weə*] *n*. **1**. (chiefly in compounds) manufactured goods: *glass*~; *silver*~; *iron*~; *tin*~. **2**. (pl.) articles offered for sale. '~·**house** *n*. building for storing goods, furniture, etc. *v.t.* store in a ~house.

war·i·ly, see *wary*.

warm [wɔːm] *adj*. having a sufficient degree of heat to be comfortable to the body (between *cool* and *hot*); (of clothing) serving to keep the body ~; (of relationships, behaviour between persons) kindly; enthusiastic; affectionate: *a* ~ *welcome*; *make things* ~ *for sb.*, make things unpleasant for him; make trouble for him; punish him. *v.t. & i.* (often ~ *up*) make or become ~; (fig.) become more enthusiastic about what one is doing or saying. *n*. (usu. no pl.) act of ~ing: *Come by the fire and have*

a ~. ~**ly** *adv*. ,~-'**blood·ed** *adj*. (of animals) having ~ blood (contrasted with snakes, etc.); (fig.) having feelings which are quickly excited. ,~-'**heart-ed** *adj*. kind and sympathetic. ~**th** [wɔːmθ] *n*. (no pl.) state of being ~; (fig.) excitement; passion.

warn [wɔːn] *v.t.* make (sb.) aware of possible danger or unpleasantness. ~**ing** *n*. that which ~s; words, happening, etc. that ~.

warp [wɔːp] *v.t. & i.* (cause to) become bent or twisted from the usual or natural shape: *The hot sun* ~*ed the boards*. (fig.) *His mind is* ~*ed*. *n*. **1**. part (e.g. of a board) in a ~ed state. **2**. long threads over and under which other threads (the *weft*) are passed when cloth is woven on a loom.

war·rant ['wɒrənt] *n*. **1**. (no pl.) justification; sth. giving right or authority (for action, etc.): *He has no* ~ *for saying so*. **2**. written order giving official authority for sth.: *a* ~ *to arrest a suspected criminal*; *sign his death-*~. **3**. certificate appointing a man as a ~-officer. *v.t.* **1**. be a ~ (1) for. **2**. guarantee (the quality, etc. of goods). '~-,**of·fi·cer** *n*. member of the armed forces (e.g. sergeant-major) of the highest rank below commissioned officers.

war·ren ['wɒrən] *n*. area of land with many rabbit holes.

war·rior ['wɒrɪə*] *n*. (liter.) soldier.

wart [wɔːt] *n*. small, tough growth on the skin.

wary ['weərɪ] *adj*. (*-ier, -iest*) cautious; in the habit of looking out for possible danger or trouble: ~ *of giving offence*. **war·i·ly** *adv*.

was, see *be*.

wash [wɒʃ] *v.t. & i.* **1**. make clean with or in water or other liquid: ~ (*sth.*) *out* (*off*), remove by ~ing; ~ *up*, (esp.) ~ dishes, cutlery, etc. after a meal. **2**. (of materials) be capable of being ~ed without damage: *Does this stuff* ~ *well?* **3**. (of the sea, a river, etc.) flow past or against; carry (sth.) *away*, *off*, etc.: ~*ed overboard by a big wave*; *wood* ~*ed up on the beach by the tide*. *n*. **1**. (no pl.) act of ~ing; being ~ed: *give the car a* ~. **2**. (no pl.) clothing, bed-sheets, etc. to be ~ed or being ~ed; place where they are ~ed: *All my shirts are at the* ~. *She was hanging out the* ~. **3**. (no pl.) wake[2]; swirl of water, waves (e.g. made by the passage of a ship). **4**. (no pl.) thin, weak, or inferior liquid food: *this soup is a mere* ~. **5**. (in compounds) liquid prepared for a special kind of ~ing: white~ (for walls); mouth~ (disinfectant). ~-and-'wear adj. (of garments) not needing to be ironed after ~ing. '~-ba·sin n. basin for ~ing one's face and hands. '~-cloth n. (U.S.A.) = face-flannel; face-cloth. ~·er n. 1. machine for ~ing clothes. 2. small, flat ring of rubber or leather for making a joint or screw tight. ~ing n. = ~ (n. 2). '~-ing-ma,chine n. machine for ~ing clothes. '~-,leath·er n. soft leather for cleaning and polishing. '~-out n. carrying away of earth, rock, etc. by floods: trains delayed by a ~-out; (colloq.) useless or unsuccessful person, thing, event, etc. '~-room n. (U.S.A.) = lavatory. ~y adj. (-ier, -iest) (of colour) pale; (of liquids, etc.) thin; watery.

wasp [wɒsp] n. flying insect with a narrow waist and a powerful sting in the tail. ~·ish adj. ill-tempered.

wast [wɒst] v. (old form) thou ~, you were.

waste [weɪst] adj. 1. (of land) that is not, cannot be, used; no longer of use; barren: lay ~, ravage; reclaim ~ land. 2. useless; thrown away because not wanted: ~ paper, ~ products, useless by-products of a manufacturing process. v.t. & i. 1. make no use of; use with no good purpose; use more of (sth.) than is necessary: ~ one's time and money; ~ water. 2. make (land) ~. 3. (cause to) lose strength by degrees: He's wasting away. n. 1. wasting or being ~d: a ~ of energy (time); run (go) to ~, be ~d. 2. ~ material; bits and pieces remaining and unwanted. 3. area of ~ land: the ~s of the Sahara. **wast·age** ['weɪstɪdʒ] n. (no pl.) amount ~d; loss by ~. ~·ful adj. causing ~; using more than is needed. ~-'pa·per ,bas·ket, (esp. U.S.A.) '~,bas·ket ns. basket or other container for discarded scraps of paper, etc. '~-pipe n. pipe for carrying away ~ water (e.g. from a kitchen sink). **wast·er, wast·rel** ['weɪstrəl] ns. ~ful, good-for-nothing person.

watch[1] [wɒtʃ] v.t. & i. 1. look at; keep the eyes on; look out (for sb. or sth. expected, danger, etc.); be on guard (over sth.). 2. (old use) remain awake: ~ at the bedside of a sick child. n. 1. act of ~ing, esp. to see that all is well: keep ~, look out for danger; on the ~ (for), ~ing for sb. or sth., esp. possible danger. 2. (usu. no pl.) (in former times) body of men, called ~men, employed to go through the streets and protect people, their prop-

erty, esp. at night. 3. (in ships) period of duty (4 or 2 hours) for part of the crew: the middle ~, midnight to 4 a.m.; the men working in such a ~. '~-dog n. dog kept to protect property. ~·ful adj. on the ~. '~·man n. 1. see ~ (n. 2). 2. (modern use) man employed to guard a building (e.g. a bank) against thieves, etc., esp. at night. '~·word n. 1. password. 2. slogan.

watch[2] [wɒtʃ] n. small timepiece that can be carried in the pocket or worn on the wrist.

wa·ter ['wɔːtə*] n. 1. liquid as in rivers, seas, etc.: rain-~; by ~, by boat, ship, etc.; under ~, flooded; get into (be in) hot ~, get into (have) trouble because of foolish behaviour, etc.; throw cold ~ on (a plan, etc.), discourage (it); hold ~, (of a theory) be sound when tested. 2. state of the tide: at high (low) ~; in low ~, (fig.) short of money. 3. (often pl.) mass of ~: The ~s of the lake pour out over the rocks. 4. solution, etc. of a substance in ~: soda-~; rose-~. v.t. & i. 1. put ~ on. 2. give ~ to (e.g. a horse). 3. (of the eyes or mouth) fill with ~, have much liquid: The smoke made my eyes ~. The smell made my mouth ~, made me want (the food, etc.). 4. add ~ to: ~ the milk; ~ sth. down, (fig.) weaken it. '~-,can·non n. high-pressure hose[1] for shooting a powerful jet of water to disperse a crowd, etc. '~-,clos·et n. (or W.C. [,dʌblju:'si:]) small room where waste from the body is washed down a drain-pipe by ~ from a cistern. '~-,col·our n. 1. (pl.) paints (to be) mixed with ~, not with oil. 2. picture painted with ~-colours. 3. art of painting such pictures. '~-course n. (channel of) small river. '~-cress n. plant that grows in ~, with hot-tasting leaves. ~ed adj. (of silk) having a pattern of wavy lines. '~-fall n. fall of ~ (e.g. in a river over a cliff or over rocks). '~·fowl n. (collective pl.) ~-birds, esp. swimming game-birds. '~-front n. part of a town beside a river, lake, or harbour. '~-ing-can n. vessel with a long spout and often a perforated sprinkler, used for ~ing plants. '~-ing-place n. 1. spa. 2. pool, etc. where animals go for ~. 3. seaside town visited by people for holidays. '~-,lev·el n. (height of the) surface of ~ in a reservoir or other body of ~. '~-,lily n. plant with broad, flat, floating leaves and white, blue, yellow, or red flowers. '~-line n. line along which the surface of the ~ touches the ship's side. '**~·logged** *adj.* **1.** (of wood, a boat, etc.) so full of ~ that it can hardly float. **2.** (of ground) swampy;

water-lilies

very wet. '**~·mark** *n.* paper manufacturer's design, seen when the paper is held against the light. '**~·mel·on** *n.* large, smooth-skinned melon with juicy pink or red flesh inside. '**~·proof** *n. & adj.* (coat) that does not let ~ through. *v.t.* make (sth.) ~proof. '**~·shed** *n.* line of high land separating river systems. '**~·ski** *n.* one of a pair of skis on which a person towed by a fast motor boat can skim (2) the surface of ~. *v.i.* move over ~ on ~-skis. '**~·spout** *n.* (esp.) gyrating column of ~ and spray formed by a whirlwind between the sea and a cloud. '**~·tight** *adj.* made, fastened, etc. so that ~ cannot get out or in; (fig., of an agreement, etc.) drawn up so that there is no escape from any of the provisions, etc. '**~·wave** *n.* wave in the hair produced by the use of ~. '**~·way** *n.* navigable channel. '**~·works** *n. pl.* (often sing. v.) system of reservoirs, pipes, etc. for supplying ~ to a town or area. **~y** *adj.* of or like ~; containing too much ~; (of colour) pale.

watt [wɒt] *n.* unit of electrical power.

wat·tle ['wɒtl] *n.* structure of sticks or twigs intertwined with thicker sticks at right angles, used for fences, walls, etc.: ~ *and daub*, this structure covered with clay, for walls or roofs.

wave [weɪv] *v.i. & t.* **1.** move or be moved to and fro, up and down, as a flag moves in the wind. **2.** cause (sth.) to move in this way: ~ *one's hand* (to *sb.*); ~ *one's umbrella*; make a signal to sb. by this means: ~ *sb. on* (*away, etc.*). **3.** (of a line or surface, of hair) be, lie, or grow in a series of curves; be wavy; cause to be like this. *n.* **1.** long ridge of water, esp. on the sea, between two hollows (or troughs, furrows); such a ridge curling over and breaking on the shore. **2.** act of waving; waving movement: *a* ~ *of the hand.* **3.** curve

like a ~ of the sea: *the* ~*s in her hair.* **4.** steady increase and spreading (of sth.): *a* ~ *of enthusiasm* (*indignation*); *a crime* ~; *a heat* (*cold*) ~, a period of weather much hotter (colder) than usual. **5.** ~-like motion by which heat, light, sound, or electricity is spread or carried. '**~·length** *n.* distance between the highest point (crest) of one ~ and that of the next, esp. with reference to wireless telegraphy. **wavy** ['weɪvɪ] *adj.* (-*ier*, -*iest*) having ~-like curves: *a wavy line.*

wa·ver ['weɪvə*] *v.i.* **1.** move uncertainly or unsteadily: ~*ing shadows.* **2.** hesitate (*between* two opinions, etc.). **3.** (of troops, etc.) show signs of giving way, become unsteady in attack or defence.

wax[1] [wæks] *v.i.* **1.** (esp. of the moon) show a larger bright area (cf. *wane*). **2.** (old use) become (indignant, merry, etc.).

wax[2] [wæks] *n.* (no pl.) **1.** soft, yellow substance made by bees and used by them for honeycomb cells; this substance made white and pure, used for making candles, for modelling, etc. **2.** substance similar to bees~ (e.g. paraffin ~, sealing-~). *v.t.* cover, polish, treat, with ~. **~·en** ['wæksən] *adj.* of or like ~. '**~·work** *n.* human figure modelled in ~.

way [weɪ] *n.* **1.** road, street, path, etc.; esp. in compounds: *high~, rail~; live across* (*over*) *the* ~, live on the other side of the street or road; *pave the* ~ *for,* (fig.) prepare (people) for. **2.** route, road (to be) used *from* one place *to* another: *the quickest* ~ *from A to B; lose one's* ~; *buy some bread on the* ~ *home.* **3.** direction: *look this* ~; *go that* ~; *the wrong* ~ *round,* facing the wrong direction. **4.** (no pl.) distance: *We're a long* ~ *from home.* **5.** method or plan; course of action: *the right* ~ *to do it; do it in this* ~; ~*s and means,* (esp.) methods of providing money for sth. needed. **6.** (often pl.) method of behaving; habit or custom: *British* ~*s of living. It's not his* ~ *to be mean. She has winning* ~*s* (i.e. behaves so as to win the confidence and affection of people). **7.** respect; point or detail: *They're in no* ~ *similar. He's clever in some* ~*s.* **8.** (no pl.) space or freedom for movement: *You're in my* ~. *Get out of the* ~. *All traffic must make* ~ *for the fire-engine.* **9.** (phrases): *by the* ~ (often used to introduce a remark not connected with the subject of conversation); *by* ~ *of,* for the purpose of:

by ~ of introduction; in the course of: *by ~ of business*; *in a ~*, to some extent or degree; *in a bad (etc.) ~*, in a bad condition, very ill, etc.; *in a small ~*, on a small scale; *have (get) one's own ~*, have (do, get) what one wants; *give ~*, break, bend, yield *(under, to)*. **10.** (no pl.) progress; forward movement: *make one's ~ home*; *gather (lose) ~*, (of ships) gain (lose) speed; *be under ~*, (of ships) be moving forward. **11.** (no pl.) structure of heavy timber down which a newly-built ship slides into the water. '~**far·er** *n.* (liter.) person travelling on foot. '~**side** *adj. & n.* (of, at, the) side of the road: *~side flowers (inns)*.

way·lay [ˌweɪ'leɪ] *v.t.* (p.t. & p.p. -laid) (wait somewhere to) attack, rob, or speak to (sb.) as he passes.

-ways [-weɪz] *suff.* (forming advs.) in such a way, course, direction, or manner: *lengthways*; *sideways*.

way·ward ['weɪwəd] *adj.* self-willed; not easily controlled or guided.

we [wiː, wɪ] *pron.* (object form *us* [ʌs]) used by a speaker or writer in referring to himself and another or others.

weak [wiːk] *adj.* **1.** (opp. *strong*) below the usual strength of strength; easily bent or broken; unable to resist attack, hard wear, or use. **2.** (of a solution) having little of some substance in relation to the water, etc.: *~ beer (tea)*; *a ~ solution*. **3.** (of the senses) below normal: *~ sight*. **4.** *~ verb*, (gram.) verb that forms the past tense and p.p. by the addition of -*ed*, -*d*, or -*t* (e.g. *walked*, *dealt*). *~***en** ['wiːkən] *v.t. & i.* make or become *~*(er). *'~-'***kneed** *adj.* (fig.) *~* in character; lacking determination. *~***ling** ['wiːklɪŋ] *n. ~* person or animal. *~***ly** *adj.* (*-ier*, *-iest*) delicate in health; sickly. *adv.* in a *~* manner. *ˌ~-'***mind·ed** *adj.* (esp.) easily influenced by others. *~***ness** *n.* **1.** (no pl.) state of being *~*. **2.** fault or defect of character. **3.** *have a ~ness for*, a special or foolish liking for.

weal [wiːl] *n.* mark on the skin made by a blow from a stick, whip, etc.

wealth [welθ] *n.* (no pl.) **1.** (possession of a) great amount of money, property, etc.; riches. **2.** great amount or number (*of*): *a ~ of illustrations*. *~***y** *adj.* (*-ier*, *-iest*) having *~* (1); rich.

wean [wiːn] *v.t.* **1.** accustom (a baby, a young animal) to food other than its mother's milk. **2.** cause (sb.) to turn away (*from* bad habits, companions, etc.).

weap·on ['wepən] *n.* sth. designed for,

used for, fighting or struggling (e.g. guns, fists, a strike by workmen).

wear [weə*] *v.t. & i.* (p.t. *wore* [wɔː*], p.p. *worn* [wɔːn]) **1.** have on the body or (of looks) on the face: *He was ~ing a hat (spectacles, a troubled look, a beard, a ring on his finger, heavy shoes)*. *~ one's hair long*, allow it to be long. **2.** (cause to) become less useful, be in a certain condition, etc. by being used: *This material has worn thin. My socks have worn into holes. The steps (The inscription on the stone) have worn away.* **3.** (be of a sort to) endure continued use; remain in a certain condition: *Good leather will ~ for years. This cloth has worn well (badly).* **4.** (fig. uses with advs.): *~ off*, pass away: *The feeling of strangeness soon wore off*. *~ on*, (of time) pass slowly away; *~ out*, make or become exhausted: *His patience wore out (was worn out) at last. worn out by hard work. n.* (no pl.) **1.** use as clothing: *a suit for everyday ~*; *showing signs of ~* (i.e. no longer new-looking); *the worse for ~*, having been worn or used a long time and no longer in a good and useful condition. **2.** damage or loss of quality from use: *The carpets are showing ~*. *(fair) ~ and tear*, damage, loss in value, resulting from (normal) use. **3.** (esp. in compounds) things to *~* (1): *beach ~*; *foot~*; *ski~*; *sports~*; *under~*; *a shop selling children's ~*.

wea·ry ['wɪərɪ] *adj.* (*-ier*, *-iest*) **1.** tired. **2.** causing tiredness: *a ~ journey*. *v.t. & i.* make or become *~*. **wea·ri·ly** *adv.* **wea·ri·ness** *n.* (no pl.). **wea·ri·some** *adj.* tiring; long and dull.

wea·sel ['wiːzl] *n.* small, fierce animal with red-brown fur, living on rats and rabbits, birds' eggs, etc.

weath·er ['weðə*] *n.* conditions over a particular area and time with reference to sunshine, temperature, wind, rain, etc. *v.t. & i.* **1.** come safely through (a storm, a crisis). **2.** become affected by the *~*: *rocks ~ed by wind and water*; *leave wood to ~* (i.e. season (v. 1)). *'~-ˌ***beat·en** *adj.* (of sb.'s face) showing the result of exposure to sun, wind, etc. *'~-***bound** *adj.* unable to make or continue a journey because of bad *~*. *'~-***cock**, *'~-***vane** *ns.* device (2), often in the shape of a cock, turning with the wind and showing its direction.

weave [wiːv] *v.t. & i.* (p.t. *wove* [wəʊv], p.p. *woven* ['wəʊvn]) **1.** make (by hand or by machine) (threads) into cloth, etc.; make (cloth, etc.)

from threads. **2.** make (garlands, baskets, etc.) by a similar process; (fig.) put together, compose (a story, romance, etc.) from incidents. **n.** style of weaving: *a loose (coarse, plain, etc.)* ~. **weav·er** *n.* person whose occupation is weaving cloth at a loom¹.

web [web] *n.* **1.** network (usu. fig.): *a ~ of lies.* **2.** sth. made of threads by some creatures: *a spider's* ~. **3.** skin joining the toes of water-birds, bats, and some water-animals (e.g. frogs): ~**-footed**, ~**-toed** (adjs.). **~bed** [webd] *adj.* having ~s (3) between the toes. **~·bing** *n.* (no pl.) band of coarse woven material used in belts, seats of chairs, etc.

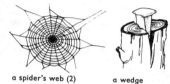

a spider's web (2)   a wedge

wed [wed] *v.t. & i.* (-dd-) marry. ~**ded to**, devoted to (e.g. a hobby, an opinion). **~·ding** *n.* marriage ceremony. '**~·lock** *n.* (no pl.) state of being married.

wedge [wedʒ] *n.* V-shaped piece, esp. of wood or metal, for splitting or securing. *the thin end of the* ~, a small change or demand likely to lead to big changes or demands. *v.t.* fix tightly (as) with a ~; fasten (sth.) tightly with a ~.

Wednes·day ['wenzdɪ] *n.* third day of the week.

wee [wi:] *adj.* very small: *a ~ bit.*

weed [wi:d] *n.* wild plant growing where it is not wanted (e.g. in a garden, a field of wheat, etc.): *a garden running to* ~s (overgrown with ~s). ~**-killer**, substance used to destroy ~s. *v.t. & i.* **1.** take ~s out of (the ground). **2.** ~ **out**, remove, get rid of (what is of lower value than the rest). **~y** *adj.* (-ier, -iest) **1.** with many ~s growing. **2.** tall, thin, and weak: *~y young men.*

weeds [wi:dz] *n. pl.* (usu. *widow's* ~) mourning (= black clothes) as worn by widows.

week [wi:k] *n.* **1.** any period of seven days; (esp.) seven days from Sunday-Monday midnight to Sunday-Monday midnight. **2.** the six working days (i.e. except Sunday). '**~·day** *n.* any day except Sunday. '**~·end** *n.* Saturday and Sunday (as a period of rest or

holiday): *a ~-end visit.* **~·ly** *adj. & adv.* (happening) once a ~, every ~; of, for, lasting, a ~: *a ~ly wage of £60*; *~ly visits.* **n.** periodical published once a ~.

weep [wi:p] *v.i. & t.* (p.t. & p.p. *wept* [wept]) cry; let tears fall from the eyes: ~*ing for joy*; ~*ing over her dead son.* **n.** fit or spell of ~ing. **~·ing** *adj.* (of trees, esp. birch and willow) with branches drooping gracefully: ~*ing willows.*

wee·vil ['wi:vɪl] *n.* small beetle with a hard shell, feeding on nuts, grain, and other seeds.

weft [weft] *n.* cross-threads taken over and under the warp in weaving.

weigh [weɪ] *v.t. & i.* **1.** learn how heavy sth. is. **2.** show a certain measure when put on a scale, etc.: *The box ~s 10 pounds.* **3.** compare, balance, the value or importance of (one thing *with* or *against* another): ~ *the consequences*; ~ *one's words*, choose them carefully. **4.** ~ *with*, have an effect upon; appear important to. **5.** ~ (*sth.* or *sb.*) *down*, pull down by being heavy; (fig.) make troubled or anxious; ~ *upon*, (fig.) be heavy on. **6.** ~ *anchor*, raise it and begin a voyage. ~

weight [weɪt] *n.* **1.** (no pl.) force with which a body tends towards the centre of the earth. **2.** (no pl.) how heavy a body is; this expressed in some scale (e.g. in tons, kilograms) as measured on a weighing-machine, etc.: *Are bananas sold by ~ or at so much a piece?* **3.** piece of metal of a certain ~ used in weighing things (*an ounce, 100 grams,* ~) or in a machine (e.g. *a clock worked by ~s*). ~**-lifter**, person who lifts great ~s in competitions or as an exercise; ~**-lifting**, athletic sport or exercise of lifting great ~s. **4.** (no pl.) (degree of) importance or influence: *arguments of great* ~. *v.t.* **1.** put a ~ (3) on; make heavy. **2.** ~ *down*, burden with: *He was ~ed down with packages.* **~y** *adj.* (-ier, -iest) **1.** of great ~; burdensome. **2.** influential; important: *~y arguments.*

weir [wɪə*] *n.* wall or similar structure built across a river to control the flow of water.

weird [wɪəd] *adj.* **1.** unnatural; unearthly. **2.** (colloq.) strange; difficult to explain or understand. **~·ly** *adv.*

wel·come ['welkəm] *adj.* **1.** received with, giving, pleasure: *a ~ visitor (rest).* *make sb.* ~, show him that his coming is ~. **2.** *you are ~ to ...*, it gives me pleasure to give (lend, etc.) you ...;

you're ~, no thanks are required. **n.** words, behaviour, etc. used when sb. arrives, when an offer is received, etc.: *We had a warm (cold, enthusiastic)* ~. **v.t.** show pleasure or satisfaction at the arrival of sb. or sth.; greet (in the way indicated): ~ *a suggestion (warmly, coldly).*

weld [weld] **v.t. & i. 1.** join or unite (pieces of metal, usu. heated) by hammering, pressing together, etc.; make (material into sth.) by doing this. **2.** (of iron, etc.) be capable of being ~ed. **n.** ~ed joint. **~·er n.**

wel·fare ['welfeə*] **n.** (no pl.) condition of having good health, a comfortable home, etc. *W~ State*, state in which the ~ of all classes is aided by national insurance, medical services, old-age pensions, etc.; ~ *work*, organized efforts to improve the conditions of living for the poor, etc.; ~ *worker*, person engaged in ~ work.

well[1] [wel] **n. 1.** shaft (4), usu. lined with brick or stone, sunk in the ground for a water-supply (see the picture at *windlass*). **2.** hole bored for mineral oil: *an oil-*~. **3.** (old use, or in place-names) spring or fountain of water. **4.** deep, enclosed space in a building, often from roof to basement, for a staircase or lift. **v.i.** (liter.) flow (*up, out*) as water flows from a ~ (3).

well[2] [wel] (*better* ['betə*], *best* [best]) **adj. 1.** in good health: *be (look, feel)* ~; in a satisfactory condition: *Is all* ~ *with you?* (Are you happy, etc.?) **2.** *it would be* ~ *to*, it would be wise or desirable to; ~ *and good*, all right, I agree (accept). **adv. 1.** in a good, right, or satisfactory manner: *children behaving* ~; ~*-behaved children*; *speak English* ~; with approval: *We think* ~ *of him.* **2.** *as* ~ *(as)*, in addition (to); also. **3.** *be* ~ *out of* (sth.), be the happier because not concerned with. **4.** with good reason: *You may* ~ *be surprised.* **5.** *We may as* ~ *(begin now, etc.)*, there is no reason why we should not. **n.** (no pl.) *wish sb.* ~, wish him success; *let* ~ *alone*, not change what is already satisfactory. **int.** expressing surprise, expectation, acceptance, etc.

well- [wel-] **pref.** well[2] (adv.). ~-'be·ing **n.** (no pl.) welfare; health, happiness, and prosperity. ~-'born **adj.** of a family with good social position. ~-con'nect·ed **adj.** ~-born. ~-dis·posed [,weldɪ'spəuzd] **adj.** having kind feelings (*towards*); ready to help. ~-'do·ing **n.** (no pl.) good deeds. ~-in'ten·tioned, ~-'mean·ing, ~-

'meant **adjs.** having, resulting from, good intentions. ~-'nigh **adv.** almost. ~-'timed **adj.** done, said, etc. at a suitable time. ~-to-'do **adj.** wealthy. ~-'tried **adj.** (of methods, remedies) tested and proved useful. ~-'worn **adj.** much used.

wel·ling·tons ['welɪŋtənz] **n. pl.** high boots reaching to the knees.

Welsh [welʃ] **n. & adj.** (the language) of the people of Wales. *the* ~, (pl.) the people of Wales. ~ *rabbit (rarebit)*, dish of melted cheese on hot toast.

welt [welt] **n. 1.** strip of thick leather to which the sole and the upper part of a shoe are stitched. **2.** weal.

wel·ter ['weltə*] **v.i.** wallow. **n.** confused mixture or state (*of*).

wench [wentʃ] **n.** (old use) girl or young woman, esp. a household servant.

wend [wend] **v.t.** ~ *one's way* (home, etc.), (liter.) go; make one's way.

went, see *go* (v.).

wept, see *weep* (v.).

were, see *be*.

wert [wɜːt] **v.** (old form) *thou* ~, you were.

west [west] **n.** (no pl.) that part of the horizon where the sun is seen to set; that part of the world, of a country, etc. in this direction; cardinal point of the compass that is on the left of a person facing north. *the W~*, (a) the part of the U.S.A. lying ~ of the Mississippi; (b) (pol.) the non-Communist States of Europe and America. **adj.** situated in the ~; towards, at, in the direction of, the ~; coming from the ~: *the W~ Indies*; *the* ~ *African peoples*; *a* ~ *wind*. **adv.** to, towards, the ~: *sail* ~ *from Southampton to New York.* ~·er·ly **adj. & adv.** (of direction) towards the ~; (of winds) from the ~. ~·ern **adj.** of, in, from, characteristic of, the ~: *western civilization*, that of Europe and America. ~·ern·ize **v.t.** introduce ~ern civilization (in)to. ~·ward **adj.** towards the ~. ~·ward(s) **adv.**

wet [wet] **adj.** (-tt-) **1.** covered or soaked with water. **2.** rainy: *a* ~ *day.* **n.** moisture; rain: *Come in out of the* ~. **v.t.** (-tt-; p.t. & p.p. ~ or ~ted) make ~. ~·ting **n.** becoming or being made ~: *get a* ~*ting.* ~-nurse **n.** woman who suckles another woman's child.

weth·er ['weðə*] **n.** castrated ram (1).

whack [wæk] **v.t.** strike (sb. or sth.) with a blow hard enough to be heard. **n.** (sound of a) sharp blow.

whale [weɪl] *n.* largest sea-animal in existence, valued for its oil. '∼·**bone** *n.* thin, horny, springy substance from the upper jaw of some kinds of ∼. **whal·er** *n.* ship or man engaged in hunting ∼s.

wharf [wɔːf] *n.* (pl. ∼s, *wharves* [wɔːvz]) wooden or stone structure at which ships are moored for (un)loading cargo. ∼**age** ['wɔːfɪdʒ] *n.* (no pl.) (payment for) use of a ∼.

what [wɒt] *adj.* **1.** (cf. *which*) (asking for one or more out of several people or things to be identified): *W∼ books have you read on this subject? W∼ time is it? W∼ authors do you like best?* **2.** (exclamatory): *W∼ a fool you are!* ***pron.*** ∼ thing(s): *W∼ would you like for breakfast? ∼ for,* for ∼ purpose? *W∼'s the weather like?* ***rel. pron.*** that which; the thing(s) which: *Do ∼ you think is right.* ***adv.*** to what extent or degree: *W∼ does he care? W∼ does it matter.* ∼ *with,* on account of (usu. more than one thing): ∼ *with unemployment and high prices.* ∼'**ev·er** ***pron.*** *W∼ever (service) you give, give it willingly.* ∼*ever he says, it does not matter* ∼ *he says; no doubt ∼ever, no doubt at all.*

wheat [wiːt] *n.* (plant producing) grain from which flour (as used for bread, etc.) is made. ∼**en** ['wiːtn] *adj.* of (coarse) ∼ flour: ∼*en bread.*

whee·dle ['wiːdl] *v.t.* make oneself pleasant to sb., flatter or coax, to get sth. one wants: *The child ∼d 50 pence out of her father (∼d her father into giving her 50 pence).*

wheel [wiːl] *n.* circular frame or disc that turns on an axle (in a machine, on a bicycle, cart, motor car, etc.): *at the ∼, driving a car, etc.; steering a ship.*

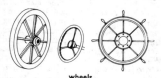

wheels

v.t. & i. **1.** push or pull (sth. on ∼s, e.g. a barrow); convey (sth.) in a handcart, etc. **2.** (cause to) turn in a curve or a circle. '∼·**bar·row** *n.* small one-∼ed vehicle with two legs and two handles, for moving small loads. ∼'**chair** *n.* chair with large ∼s for the use of sb. unable to walk. ∼·**wright**

['wiːlraɪt] *n.* man who makes and repairs ∼s.

wheeze [wiːz] *v.i. & t.* breathe noisily, esp. with a whistling sound in the chest or windpipe; (of a pump, etc.) make a similar sound: ∼ *(sth.) out,* utter with such sounds. **wheezy** *adj.* (-*ier*, -*iest*).

whelp [welp] *n.* **1.** young dog; (old use) young lion, tiger, bear, wolf, etc.; cub. **2.** ill-bred boy or young man.

when [wen] *adv.* **1.** at what time? on what occasion?: *W∼ can you come to see us?* **2.** (after *day, time,* etc.) at or on which: *Sunday is the day ∼ I am least busy.* ***conj.*** **1.** at or during the time that: *It was late ∼ we arrived.* **2.** although: *He stands ∼ he might sit down.* **3.** since; considering that: *Why should I be polite to him ∼ he is rude to me?* **4.** at or during which time: *I will come and see you ∼ I have an hour to spare.* ∼'**ev·er** *adv.* at every time ∼.

whence [wens] *adv.* (old use) **1.** (in questions) from what place or cause? **2.** (in statements) from which place. **3.** to the place from which: *Return ∼ you came.*

where [weə*] *adv.* **1.** in or to what place or position?; in what direction?: *W∼ does she live? W∼ are you going to (does he come from)?* **2.** what place?: *W∼ does the place ∼ I was born.* **4.** in, at, to, the place in which: *I found my car ∼ I had left it.* ∼·**abouts** [ˌweərə'baʊts] *adv.* in or near what place. ['weərəbaʊts] *n.* (sing. or pl. v.) place where sb. or sth. is. ∼'**as** *conj.* taking into consideration that; but in contrast. '∼·**fore** *adv.* (old use) why. ***conj.*** for which reason; why. ∼·**up'on** *adv.* after which; and then. **wher'ev·er** *adv.* in, to, at, whatever place; at those places ∼. ∼·**with·al** ['weəwɪðɔːl] *n.* (no pl.) (colloq.) money with which to do sth.: *I haven't the ∼withal to marry.*

whet [wet] *v.t.* (-*tt*-) sharpen (a knife, etc.); (fig.) excite (the appetite, interest, etc.). '∼·**stone** *n.* stone for ∼ting edged tools.

wheth·er ['weðə*] *conj.* **1.** (cf. *if,* introducing an indirect question): *I don't know ∼ I can come or not.* **2.** (introducing an infinitive phrase): *I don't know ∼ to accept or refuse.*

whey [weɪ] *n.* (no pl.) liquid part of sour milk after separation of curds (for making cheese).

which [wɪtʃ] *adj.* (cf. *what*). *W∼ way shall we go, to the right or to the left of the wood? Tell me ∼ books on my* *shelf you would like to borrow.* **pron. 1.** ~ thing(s); ~ person(s): *W~ is taller, Tom or Dick?* **2. rel. pron.** (referring to things, not persons): *This river, ~ flows through London, is called the Thames. The hotel at ~ we stayed was the cheapest in the town.* (Cf. *that.*) **~'ev·er pron. & adj.** any one or ones (of a limited number, esp. two).

whiff [wɪf] **n.** slight breath (of air, smoke, etc.); smell: *the ~ of a cigar.*

Whig [wɪg] **n. & adj.** (Gt. Brit., hist.) Liberal (opp. *Tory*).

while [waɪl] **conj. 1.** during the time that; for as long as; at the same time as: *W~ there's life there's hope. W~ in London he studied music.* **2.** (implying a contrast) whereas. **3.** although: *W~ I admire your courage, I think you ought not to go on this dangerous journey.* **n.** (period of) time: *Where have you been all this ~? once in a ~, occasionally; worth one's ~,* repaying the time, effort, etc. needed. **v.t.** ~ *away the time,* pass the time pleasantly.

whim [wɪm] **n.** sudden desire or idea, often sth. unusual or unreasoning.

whim·per ['wɪmpə*] **v.i. & t. & n.** (make a or utter with a) weak cry of pain or fear (e.g. as of a baby when ill).

whim·sy, whim·sey ['wɪmzɪ] **n.** (pl. -sies, -seys) whim; fanciful idea or wish. **whim·si·cal** ['wɪmzɪkl] **adj.** full of whimsies; odd; quaint.

whine [waɪn] **n.** low, long-drawn, complaining cry (e.g. made by a miserable dog or child). **v.i. & t.** make, say (sth.) with, such a cry; ask (for help, etc.) in a piteous way.

whin·ny ['wɪnɪ] **n.** gentle neigh made by a horse to show pleasure. **v.i.** make this sound.

whip [wɪp] **n.** length of cord, strip of leather, etc. fastened to a handle, used for urging a horse on or for punishing. *have the ~ hand of (over) (sb.),* have mastery over; be in a position to control. **v.t. & i.** (-pp-) **1.** strike with a ~. **2.** beat (eggs, cream, etc.) with a fork, etc. to mix thoroughly and make stiff: *~ped cream.* **3.** move or take suddenly: *~ out a knife; ~ off your coat.* **~ping n.** beating with a ~ as punishment. **~ping-top n.** top².

whir(r) [wɜː] **n.** (no pl.) sound (as) of bird's wings moving quickly or of wheels, etc. turning fast. **v.i.** (-rr-) make such sound.

whirl [wɜːl] **v.t. & i. 1.** (cause to) move quickly round and round: *fallen leaves ~ing in the wind.* **2.** (of the brain,

the senses) be giddy; seem to ~. **3.** take, be taken, rapidly (*off, away,* etc.) in a car, etc. **n.** (no pl.) **1.** ~ing movement: *a ~ of dust;* (fig.) *my thoughts are in a ~.* **2.** bustling activity: *the ~ of modern life.* **'~·pool n.** place where there are ~ing currents of water. **'~·wind n.** swift, circling current of air.

whisk [wɪsk] **n. 1.** small brush for removing dust, flies, etc. **2.** metal device (2) (e.g. coiled wire) for whipping (2) eggs, etc. **3.** light, brushing movement (e.g. of a horse's tail). **v.t. & i. 1.** brush (*off, away,* etc.) lightly and quickly. **2.** take (sb. or sth.), go (*off, away*), quickly and suddenly: *He was ~ed off to prison. I was ~ed up to my room in a lift.* **3.** wave or move quickly: *The cow ~ed her tail.*

whisk·er ['wɪskə*] **n. 1.** (usu. pl.) hair left to grow down the sides of a man's face (cf. *beard, moustache*). **2.** one of the long, stiff hairs growing near the mouth of a cat, etc.

whis·key ['wɪskɪ] **n.** (pl. ~s) (U.S.A. and Irish spelling of) whisky.

whis·ky ['wɪskɪ] **n.** (pl. -kies) strong alcoholic drink distilled from grain, esp. from malted barley; drink of this: *Three whiskies, please.*

whis·per ['wɪspə*] **v.i. & t.** speak, say (sth.), very softly, using the breath but not the vocal c(h)ords; (of leaves, the wind, etc.) make soft sounds. **n.** ~ing sound; sth. ~ed; (esp.) sth. ~ed secretly; a rumour.

whist [wɪst] **n.** (no pl.) card-game for four players.

whis·tle ['wɪsl] **n. 1.** (usu. high) clear note made by forcing a stream of air or steam through a small opening, or by the wind; musical sound made by birds. **2.** instrument for producing such sounds: *a steam-~; the referee's ~.* **v.i. & t.** make a ~ (1) (e.g. by blowing through the rounded lips or by using a ~ (2)); make a musical series of notes in this way: *~ a tune;* make a signal (*to sb., to a dog, etc.*) with such sounds.

Whit [wɪt], see *Whitsun.*

white [waɪt] **adj.** (~r, ~st) of the colour of fresh snow or the paper on which this book is printed (opp. *black*). *the ~ flag,* the symbol of surrender. *a ~ lie,* a lie considered to be harmless, esp. one told for the sake of being polite. **n. 1.** (no pl.) ~ colour. **2.** ~ man. **3.** ~ part of the eyeball. **4.** colourless liquid in an egg, ~ when boiled or fried (cf. *yolk*). **whit·en** ['waɪtn] **v.t. & i.** make or become ~(r). **whit·ing n.** (no pl.)

powdered ~ chalk used in ~wash.
~ **cof·fee** *n.* coffee with milk or cream.
|~-'**col·lar** *adj.* of, relating to, the
class of salaried employees not engaged in manual labour. '~·**wash** *n.*
(no pl.) mixture of powdered chalk or
lime and water used for coating walls,
ceilings, etc. *v.t.* put ~wash on; (fig.)
try to make (sb., his reputation) appear blameless. ~ **wa·ter** *n.* foamy
water (as in rapids, waterfalls, etc.).
Whit·ey ['waɪtɪ] *n.* (pl. ~s) (usu.
derog.) ~ person; ~ persons collectively.

whith·er ['wɪðə*] *adv.* (old use)
where.

Whit·sun ['wɪtsən] *n.* (also *Whit Sunday*) 7th Sunday after Easter. ~·**tide**
n. ~ and the weekend or the following
week (often called *Whit Monday*, etc.).

whit·tle ['wɪtl] *v.t. & i.* (often ~ *down*
or *away*) cut thin slices or strips off
(wood); cut (*at* sth.) in this way; (fig.)
reduce by degrees: ~ *down the salaries.*

whiz(z) [wɪz] *v.i.* (-zz-) *& n.* (no pl.)
(make the) sound of sth. rushing
through the air: *An arrow ~ed past
my ear.*

who [huː] *pron.* (object form ~**m**
[huːm], colloq. ~; possessive ~**se**
[huːz]) (used as the subject, and only
of persons) what person(s): *W~ is
that man? W~ are those men? Do you
know ~ she is? Do you know ~(m) you
are speaking to? To ~m did you give
it?* (formal style), *W~ did you give
it to?* (colloq.). [huː; hʊ] *rel. pron.*
*This is the man ~ asked to see you. My
son, ~m you met last week, wants to
see you again.* |~'**dun·(n)it** *n.* (colloq.)
(= ~ *done it*, illiterate for ~ *did it?*)
detective or mystery story, play or
film. ~'**ev·er** *pron.* any person ~; the
person ~.

whole [həʊl] *adj.* **1.** (attrib.) all that
there is of; complete: *the ~ truth*, all
the truth; *his ~ energies*, all his energies. **2.** undamaged; unbroken: *escape
with a ~ skin; not a ~* (i.e. uncracked
or unbroken) *plate in the house.* **3.**
complete; entire: *cook a ~ sheep; rain
for three ~ days; a ~ number*, a number
without a fraction. *n.* **1.** sth. complete:
A ~ is greater than any of its parts. **2.**
all there is of sth.: *He lost the ~ of his
money.* **3.** *as a ~,* (considered) all together, not separately; *on the ~,* taking
everything into consideration. |~-
'**heart·ed(ly)** *adj.* (*& adv.*) (in a
manner) not weakened by doubt or
hesitation. '~·**sale** *n.* (cf. *retail*) selling
of goods (esp. in large quantities) to
shopkeepers, etc. for resale to the
public: *sell by ~sale;* ~*sale prices. adj.
& adv.* by or relating to ~sale; at a
~sale price; (fig.) on a large scale: *a
~sale slaughter took place.* ~·**some** *adj.*
healthy; favourable to the health:
~*some food (surroundings).* **whol·ly**
['həʊlɪ] *adv.* completely.

whom, see *who*.

whoop [huːp] *n.* loud cry: ~*s of joy.*
'~·**ing cough** *n.* (no pl.) children's
disease with short violent coughs
after long indrawing of breath.

whore [hɔː*] *n.* prostitute.

whose, see *who*.

why [waɪ] *adv.* for what reason?: *W~
are you so late? The reason ~ he did it
is not clear. int.* (indicating surprise):
W~, even a child knows that!; (indicating protest): *W~, I could have told you
the answer if you had asked me.*

wick [wɪk] *n.* (length of) thread that
runs through a candle; strip of woven
material by which oil in an oil-lamp
or stove is drawn up to burn.

wick·ed ['wɪkɪd] *adj.* **1.** (of a person,
his acts) bad; wrong; immoral. **2.**
spiteful; intended to injure: ~ *rumours.*
3. playfully mischievous. ~·**ly** *adv.*
~·**ness** *n.*

wick·er ['wɪkə*] *n.* (no pl.) (usu.
attrib.) twigs or canes woven together,
usu. for baskets or furniture: *a ~ chair.*
'~·**work** *n.* (no pl.) things made of ~.

wick·et ['wɪkɪt] *n.* **1.** (also ~*-door*, ~*-gate*)
small door or gate, esp. one at the side
of, or made in, a larger one. **2.** small
opening (e.g. one with a sliding window) at which tickets, etc. are sold. **3.**
(cricket) three stumps (3) (with cross-
pieces called *bails²*) at which the ball
is bowled; stretch of grass between
the two ~s: *A soft ~ helps the bowlers.
take a ~,* defeat a batsman. '~·**keep·er**
n. player stationed behind the ~ (3).

wide [waɪd] *adj.* (~*r*, ~*st*) **1.** measuring
much from side to side or in com-
parison with length; broad: *a ~ road;
sixty feet ~.* **2.** of great extent: *a man
with ~ interests* (i.e. in many subjects).
3. ~ *of,* far from (what is aimed at or
desired): *Your answer was ~ of the
mark. adv.* **1.** in many directions:
searching far and ~. **2.** fully: ~ *open;* ~
awake. **3.** ~ *apart,* with ~ space(s) between. **4.** far from what is aimed at:
The arrow fell ~ (of the mark). ~·**ly** *adv.*
1. at ~ intervals. **2.** to a large extent.
3. over a large area. **wid·en** ['waɪdn]
v.t. & i. make or become ~(r). '~·
spread *adj.* (esp.) found, distributed, over a large area.

wid·ow ['wɪdəʊ] *n.* woman who has not married again after her husband's death. **~·er** *n.* man who has not married again after his wife's death. **~ed** *adj.* made a ~ or ~er: ~ed by the war.

width [wɪdθ] *n.* **1.** (no pl.) quality of being wide. **2.** measurement from side to side: *ten feet in* ~. **3.** piece of material of a certain ~ (2): *join two ~s of cloth.*

wield [wi:ld] *v.t.* have and use: ~ *an axe*; (fig.) ~ *control (authority).*

wife [waɪf] *n.* (pl. *wives* [waɪvz]) married woman, esp. in relation to her husband: *Smith and his* ~.

wig [wɪg] *n.* head-covering of false hair (e.g. as worn by judges in law-courts, by actors, etc.).

the wig of a judge

wig·gle ['wɪgl] *v.t. & i.* (cause to) move with quick, short, side-to-side movements: *The baby* ~*d its toes.*

wild [waɪld] *adj.* **1.** (of animals) living in natural conditions (e.g. lions and tigers); not tamed; (of plants) growing in natural conditions; not cultivated. **2.** not civilized. **3.** uncultivated; unsettled: ~ *and mountainous areas.* **4.** disorderly; out of control: *a room in* ~ *disorder*; *a* ~ *fellow*; *run* ~, grow unchecked, undisciplined, or untrained. **5.** violent; uncontrolled; stormy: ~ *seas (weather)*; ~ *with anger*; *driven* ~ *with anxiety.* **6.** reckless; done or said without proper thought or care: ~ *schemes (guesses).* **7.** *be* ~ *about sth. or sb.*, *be* ~ *to do sth.*, (colloq.) have a strong desire for, love of, etc. *adv.* without care or control. *n.* (pl.) uncultivated and (often) unpeopled areas: *the* ~*s of Africa.* **~·ly** *adv.* **~·ness** *n.* '**~cat attrib. adj. 1.** reckless; financially unsound: ~*cat schemes.* **2.** ~*cat strike*, sudden, unofficial, and irresponsible strike (by workers). '**~·fire** *n.* (only in) *spread like* ~*fire*, (of news, etc.) spread very quickly. '**~·life** *n.* (no pl.) ~ animals collectively.

wil·der·ness ['wɪldənɪs] *n.* (usu. no pl.) wild, uncultivated, waste land; desert.

wile [waɪl] *n.* (usu. pl.) trick; bit of cunning: *the* ~*s of the Devil.* *v.t.* entice, trick (sb. *away*, *into doing* sth.).

wil·ful (U.S.A. also **will-**) ['wɪlful] *adj.* **1.** (of a person) obstinate; determined to have one's own way. **2.** (of bad acts) done on purpose: ~ *murder.* **~·ly** *adv.*

will[1] [wɪl] *v.aux.* (pres. t. ~, colloq. '*ll* [l] , p.t. *would* [wʊd, wəd], colloq. '*d* [d] ; neg. ~ *not*, colloq. *won't* [wəʊnt], *would not*, colloq. *wouldn't* ['wʊdnt]) **1.** (used in the future tense (cf. *shall*): *you*, *he*, *they*, ~ *go.* **2.** (used in the 1st person to express willingness, etc.): *All right, I* ~ *come.* **3.** (in requests): *W~ you (Won't you) come in?* **4.** (indicating strong purpose, etc.): *She* ~ *have her own way.* **5.** (in refusing): *I won't let you go.* **6.** (*would* is used in the 2nd and 3rd persons in conditional statements and questions): *If a car had no brakes there would soon be an accident. would rather* (see *rather* (1)).

will[2] [wɪl] *v.t.* (p.t. *would* [wʊd], no other forms used) **1.** (old use) wish: *Let him do what he* ~. **2.** (expressing wishes): *Would that it were true*, I wish it were true. **3.** make use of one's mental power in an attempt to do or get sth.: *We cannot achieve success merely by* ~*ing it.* **4.** (p.t. & p.p. ~*ed*) leave (property, etc. *to*) by means of a testament (or *will*[3] (6)): *He* ~*ed most of his money to charities.*

will[3] [wɪl] *n.* **1.** (no pl.) mental power by which a person can direct his thoughts and actions, and influence those of others. **2.** (also ~*-power*) control exercised over oneself, one's impulses: *have no* ~ *of one's own.* **3.** (no pl.) determination; desire; purpose: *work (do sth.) with a* ~. *He always has his* ~, *do sth. of one's own free* ~. *God's* ~ *be done. married against her* ~ (i.e. to sb. she did not wish to marry). **4.** *at* ~, whenever and however one pleases. **5.** *good (ill)* ~, kind (unkind) feeling towards others. **6.** (often *last* '~ *and testament*) statement in writing saying how sb. wishes his property to be distributed after his death. **~·ful** *adj.* (U.S.A.) = wilful.

wil·lies ['wɪlɪz] *n. pl.* (sl.) nervous feeling of discomfort or fear: *It gives me the* ~.

will·ing ['wɪlɪŋ] *adj.* **1.** ready to help, to do what is needed: ~ *workers*; ~ *to work.* **2.** done, given, etc. readily, without hesitation: ~ *obedience.* **~·ly** *adv.* **~·ness** *n.* (no pl.).

will-o'-the-wisp [ˌwɪləðəˈwɪsp] *n.*

(fig.) sth. or sb. that one pursues unsuccessfully because it or he is difficult to grasp or reach.

wil·low ['wɪləʊ] *n.* (wood of) tree with thin, easily-bent branches. **~y** *adj.* (of persons) slender and graceful in movement.

wil·ly-nil·ly [,wɪlɪ'nɪlɪ] *adv.* whether one likes it or not.

wilt[1] [wɪlt] *v.* (old form) *thou* ~, you will.

wilt[2] [wɪlt] *v.t. & i.* (of plants, etc.) (cause to) droop, lose freshness.

wily ['waɪlɪ] *adj.* (-ier, -iest) full of wiles; cunning: *as* ~ *as a fox.*

win [wɪn] *v.t. & i.* (-nn-; p.t. & p.p. *won* [wʌn]) **1.** get by means of hard work, perseverance, etc., as the result of competition, etc.; do best in (*a fight,* etc.): ~ *a race* (*a battle, a scholarship, a prize, fame and fortune*). *Which team won?* **2.** persuade (sb.) by argument, etc. (*to do sth.*): ~ (*sb.*) *over*, overcome his objections to sth. **3.** reach by effort: ~ *the summit* (*shore*). *n.* success in a game, competition, etc. **~ner** *n.* person, animal, thing, that ~s. **~ning** *adj.* (esp. of looks, behaviour) attractive; likely to win favour, etc.: *a* ~*ning smile;* ~*ning ways.* ~*nings n. pl.* (esp.) money won in gambling.

wince [wɪns] *v.i. & n.* (make a) sudden movement (in fear or pain): *He* ~*d at the insult.*

winch [wɪntʃ] *n.* windlass.

wind[1] [wɪnd] *n.* **1.** air blowing along as the result of natural forces: *A cold* ~ *blew from the north. The* ~ *carried my hat away. in the* ~, being secretly planned or going forward; (*see, find out*) *how the* ~ *blows*, what people are thinking, what is likely to happen; *take the* ~ *out of sb.'s sails*, prevent him from doing or saying sth. by doing or saying it first. **2.** (no pl.) breath needed for running, etc.: *The runner soon lost his* ~. **3.** (no pl.) scent carried by the ~ (1): *get* ~ *of*, (fig.) get news of; suspect. **4.** (no pl.) gas formed in the bowels and causing discomfort: *suffer from* ~. **5.** (no pl.) meaningless or valueless talk. **6.** (no pl.) (sound of) orchestral ~ instruments. *v.t.* **1.** cause to be out of breath: *The blow* ~*ed me.* **2.** rest (a horse that is out of breath). '**~·fall** *n.* fruit blown down by the ~; (fig.) unexpected piece of good fortune, esp. money, coming to sb. ~ **in·stru·ment** *n.* musical instrument (e.g. a trumpet or flute) from which sound is produced by forcing air through it. '**~·mill** *n.* mill worked by the ~ acting

on large, wooden sails, used for grinding grain or pumping up water. '**~·pipe** *n.* passage for air from the throat to the lungs. '**~·screen**, (U.S.A.) '**~·shield** *ns.* window in front of the driver's seat in a motor car, etc. '**~·tun·nel** *n.* structure through which air is forced (at controlled speeds) to study its effects on the model of an aircraft, etc. standing in the passage. '**~·ward** *adj. & adv.* on or to the side from which the ~ blows (opp. *leeward*). ~**y** *adj.* (-ier, -iest) **1.** with much ~: *a* ~*y day*; open to the ~: *a* ~*y cliff.* **2.** (fig.) wordy; empty: ~*y talk* (speaker).

wind[2] [waɪnd] *v.t. & i.* (p.t. & p.p. *wound* [waʊnd]) **1.** (cause to) move in a curving, circular, spiral, or twisting manner: *The river* ~*s* (*its way*) *to the sea. a* ~*ing staircase.* **2.** twist (string, wool, yarn, etc.) into a ball or round or on to sth. (e.g. a reel). **3.** turn (a handle, e.g. of a ~*lass*); raise (sth.) by doing this: ~ *up ore from a mine;* ~ (*up*), tighten the spring of (a clock, etc.) to put or keep its works in motion. **4.** ~ *up*, come or bring to an end: *It's time for him to* ~ *up his speech.* ~ *up a business company* (*one's affairs*), put everything in order before bringing to an end; ~*-up* (*n.*), conclusion; finish. **5.** *be wound up*, be tense with (excitement, etc.). *n.* bend or twist; single turn in ~*ing* string, a clock, etc. '**~·ing-sheet** *n.* sheet (to be) wound round a corpse.

wind[3] [waɪnd] *v.t.* (p.t. & p.p. ~*ed* or *wound* [waʊnd]) blow or sound (a horn, a bugle, a call *on* a horn, etc.).

wind·lass ['wɪndləs] *n.* machine for lifting or pulling.

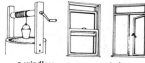

a windlass   windows

win·dow ['wɪndəʊ] *n.* opening in a wall, etc. to let in light and air; framed pane(s) of glass for or in a ~ opening: *Please shut the* ~. ~ **shade** *n.* (U.S.A.) = *blind*[2]. '**~·shop·ping** *n.* (no pl.) looking at the goods displayed in the shop-~s without going inside to buy sth.: *go* ~*-shopping.*

wine [waɪn] *n.* alcoholic drink made from the juice of grapes; ~-like drink made from other fruits or plants.

wing [wɪŋ] *n.* **1.** one of the organs of a bird or insect by which it flies; one of the flat surfaces on each side of an aircraft that support it in the air. *on the ~*, in flight; *under sb.'s ~*, (of a person) cared for by, protected by, sb. **2.** part of a building, army, etc. stretching out at the side: *build a new ~ to a hospital.* **3.** (U.S.A. *fender*) mudguard of a motor vehicle. **4.** (pol.) extreme section of a political party. **5.** (pl.) sides of the stage in a theatre (not visible to the audience).

a wing (1)   the wings (5)

wink [wɪŋk] *v.i. & t.* **1.** shut and open (one's eyes or, usu., one eye) quickly; do this (with one eye *at* sb.) as a private signal or hint (e.g. of amusement). **2.** *~ at* (sth.), deliberately ignore (misconduct). *n.* **1.** act of ~ing, esp. as a hint or signal. **2.** *forty ~s*, a short sleep (esp. during the day); *not sleep a ~, not have a ~ of sleep*, not sleep at all.

win·ner, win·ning(s), see **win**.

win·now [ˈwɪnəʊ] *v.t.* **1.** use a stream of air to separate dry, outer coverings from (grain). **2.** (fig.) separate what is true, good, useful, etc. from what is false, worthless, etc.

win·ter [ˈwɪntə*] *n.* season between autumn and spring, when (except in the tropics) the weather is usually cold. *v.i.* pass the ~: *~ in the south.* **win·try** *adj.* (-ier, -iest) of or like ~; cold: *a wintry sky.*

wipe [waɪp] *v.t.* **1.** clean or dry (sth.) by rubbing with a cloth, etc.: *~ the dishes; ~ sth. dry; ~ your tears away.* **2.** *~ off*, remove by wiping; *~ out*, clean the inside of; remove (e.g. a mark or fig. disgrace); destroy completely; *~ up*, soak up (liquid) by wiping. *n.* act of wiping. **wip·er** *n.* sth. that ~s or is used for wiping: *windscreen-~r*, rubber strip mechanically moved to and fro across a windscreen to remove rain-water, etc.

wire [waɪə*] *n.* **1.** (piece or length of) strong metal thread: *telephone ~s.* **2.** (colloq.) telegram. *v.t. & i.* **1.** fasten (sth.) with ~. **2.** put ~(s) into: *~ a house for electric current.* **3.** (colloq.) telegraph. **wir·ing** [ˈwaɪərɪŋ] *n.* (no pl.)

system of ~s for carrying electric current in a house, apparatus (1), etc. **wiry** [ˈwaɪərɪ] *adj.* (-ier, -iest) (esp. of persons) lean and with strong sinews.

wire·less [ˈwaɪəlɪs] *adj.* without the use of wires: *~ telegraphy. n.* (no pl.) **1.** ~ telegraphy or telegram. **2.** (Gt. Brit.) radio receiving set or broadcast or programme: *listen to a concert on (over) the ~.*

wise[1] [waɪz] *adj.* (~r, ~st) having or showing experience, knowledge, good judgement, prudence, etc.: *~ men (acts).* **~·ly** *adv.* **wis·dom** [ˈwɪzdəm] *n.* (no pl.) **1.** quality of being ~. *wisdom tooth*, back tooth usu. cut (5) at about 20 years of age. **2.** ~ thoughts, sayings, etc.: *the wisdom of our ancestors.* **~·acre** [ˈwaɪzˌeɪkə*] *n.* person who tries to seem much ~r than he really is. **wise**[2] [waɪz] *n.* (no pl.) (old use) *in no ~, in this ~*, in no (this) way.

-wise [-waɪz] *suff.* (forming adjs. and advs.) **1.** in the manner of: *clockwise; crabwise; lengthwise.* **2.** in respect of: *moneywise.*

wish [wɪʃ] *v.t. & i.* **1.** have as an unfulfilled desire or a desire that cannot be fulfilled: *I ~ I knew.* **2.** want: *When do you ~ to leave (~ me to leave)?* **3.** hope or desire (sth.) for (sb.): *~ sb. a pleasant journey.* **4.** *~ for*, desire to have; pray for: *can't ~ for anything better; have everything you can ~ (for).* *n.* **1.** desire; longing: *in obedience to your ~es.* **2.** *with all good ~es, ~ing (3)* you well. **~·ful** *adj.* *~ful thinking*, thinking that sth. is true merely because one ~es it were true.

wisp [wɪsp] *n.* small bundle or twist (of straw, hair, etc.); spiral (of smoke).

wist·ful [ˈwɪstfʊl] *adj.* having, moved by, showing, an unsatisfied and often vague desire: *~ eyes.* **~·ly** *adv.*

wit [wɪt] *n.* **1.** intelligence; quickness of mind: *have one's ~s about one*, be quick to see what is happening, ready to act; *be at one's ~'s (~s') end*, not know what to do or say; *live by one's ~s*, live by clever, not always honest, methods. **2.** (person noted for) clever and humorous expression of ideas: *conversation full of ~.* **~·ti·cism** [ˈwɪtɪsɪzəm] *n.* humorous remark. **~·ty** *adj.* (-ier, -iest) full of humour. **~·ti·ly** *adv.*

witch [wɪtʃ] *n.* woman said to use magic, esp. for evil purposes. **'~·craft** *n.* (no pl.) use of such magic. **'~·doc·tor** *n.* male ~. **~·ery** *n.* (no pl.) **1.** ~craft. **2.** fascination; charm.

with [wɪð] *prep.* **1.** having; carrying:

a coat ~ four pockets; *a man ~ a bad arm (no hat on)*. **2.** to indicate what is used; having as material or contents: *writing ~ a pen*; *fill a barrow ~ sand*. **3.** (to indicate accompaniment or relationship): *live ~ one's parents*; *mix one thing ~ another*; *~ it*, (colloq.) up-to-date; progressive; following the latest fashions; *~it* (adj.), (colloq.) fashionably up-to-date: *a ~it man of the jet-set age*; *in ~*, in association *~*; mixed up *~*: *He's in ~ the wrong crowd*. *not ~ you*, (colloq.) unable to follow your meaning. **4.** (to indicate opposition): *fight ~, argue ~, sb*. **5.** (to indicate manner): *do sth. ~ pleasure*. **6.** at the same time as; in the same way as: *A tree's shadow moves ~ the sun*. **7.** in regard to; concerning: *Be patient ~ children*. **8.** (to indicate care, charge, or possession): *Leave the baby ~ its grandmother. I have no money ~ me*. **9.** (to indicate separation): *I parted ~ her after many years*. **10.** (to indicate support, agreement): *Are you ~ me or against me in this matter?*

with·draw [wɪð'drɔː] *v.t. & i.* (p.t. -drew, p.p. -drawn) **1.** pull or draw back. **2.** take out or away: *~ savings from the bank*; *~ a child from school*. **3.** take back (a statement, an accusation, an offer). **4.** (cause to) move or go back or away: *~ troops from a place*. **~·al** [wɪð'drɔːəl] *n.* *~n adj.* unsociable; emotionally detached.

with·er [ˈwɪðə*] *v.t. & i.* **1.** (often *~ up, away*) (cause to) become dry, faded, or dead: *The hot summer ~ed (up) the grass. The flowers ~ed*. **2.** cause (sb.) to be covered with shame or confusion: *She gave him a ~ing look*.

with·hold [wɪð'həʊld] *v.t.* (p.t. & p.p. -held) keep back; refuse to give.

with·in [wɪ'ðɪn] *adv.* (old use or liter.) inside. *prep.* inside; not beyond: *remain ~ call (reach)*, remain near by; *~ hearing*, near enough to hear or be heard; *~ an hour*, in less than an hour; *~ a mile of the airport* (not more than a mile away); *live ~ one's income* (not spend more).

with·out [wɪ'ðaʊt] *adv.* (old use or liter.) outside. *prep.* not having; lacking.

with·stand [wɪð'stænd] *v.t.* (p.t. & p.p. -stood) resist; hold out against (pressure, attack).

wit·ness [ˈwɪtnɪs] *n.* **1.** (often *eye~*) person present at an event; person who gives evidence under oath in a lawcourt. *~-box*, (U.S.A.) *~ stand*, enclosure in a lawcourt from which *~es*

give evidence. **2.** (no pl.) evidence; what is said about sb. or an event. *bear ~ to sb.'s character*, speak about it from knowledge. **3.** person who adds his own signature to a document to testify that another person's signature on it is genuine. **4.** sb. or sth. that is a sign or proof of sth.: *My clothes are a ~ of my poverty*. *v.t. & i.* **1.** be a *~* (3) to (an agreement, etc.). **2.** be a *~* (1) of (an event). **3.** give *~* (2) (in a lawcourt, etc.). **4.** be a *~* (4) of (sth.).

wit·ti·cism, wit·ty, see *wit*.

wit·ting·ly [ˈwɪtɪŋlɪ] *adv.* consciously; knowingly; on purpose.

wives, see *wife*.

wiz·ard [ˈwɪzəd] *n.* **1.** magician. **2.** person with amazing abilities: *He's a ~ at mathematics*.

wiz·ened [ˈwɪznd] *adj.* (esp. of the face) wrinkled; shrivelled.

wob·ble [ˈwɒbl] *v.t. & i.* (cause to) move unsteadily from side to side; (fig.) be uncertain (in opinions, in making decisions, etc.). **wob·bly** *adj.* (-ier, -iest).

woe [wəʊ] *n.* **1.** (no pl.) sorrow; grief; distress: *a tale of ~*. **2.** (pl.) causes of *~*: *poverty, illness, and other ~s*. **~·ful** *adj.* sorrowful; causing *~*

woke, wok·en, see *wake*[1].

wolf [wʊlf] *n.* (pl. *wolves* [wʊlvz]) wild, flesh-eating animal of the dog family, hunting in packs. *keep the ~ from the door*, be able to buy enough food, etc. for oneself and one's family. *v.t. ~ one's food*, eat it quickly and greedily.

wom·an [ˈwʊmən] *n.* (pl. *women* [ˈwɪmɪn]) **1.** adult female human being. *Women's Lib(eration)*, movement of women calling for liberation from domestic duties and all forms of male domination. *~'s (women's) rights*, position of legal and social equality with men. **2.** the female sex; any *~*. **3.** (attrib.) female: *~ doctor (driver, friend)*; *a ~ novelist*, (pl.) *women novelists*. **~·hood** *n.* (no pl.) women in general; state of being a *~*: *reach ~hood*. **~·ish** *adj.* (of a man) like a *~* (in feeling, behaviour, etc.); (of things) more suitable for women than men. **~·ly** *adj.* (often -ier, -iest) proper to a *~*: *~ly modesty*.

womb [wuːm] *n.* (anat.) organ in a woman and other female mammals in which offspring is held and nourished while developing before birth.

wom·en, see *woman*.

won, see *win* (v.).

won·der [ˈwʌndə*] *n.* feeling caused by sth. unusual or surprising; thing or event causing such a feeling: *look at sth. in* ~; *be filled with* ~; *no* ~ *that* ..., it is not surprising that ...; *for a* ~, it is surprising (that); *work* ~s, produce amazing results. *v.i. & t.* **1.** feel ~ (*at*). **2.** ask oneself (*about sth., who, what, why, whether, etc.*). ~**ful** *adj.* causing ~; remarkable. ~**ment** *n.* (no pl.) surprise. **won·drous** ['wʌndrəs] *adj.* (old use or liter.) ~ful.

wont [wəʊnt] *n.* (no pl.) what sb. is accustomed to doing: *He went to bed much later than was his* ~. **pred. adj.** *he was* ~ *to* ..., it was his custom to ... ~**ed** *attrib. adj.* customary; usual.

won't, see *will*[1].

woo [wuː] *v.t.* **1.** ~ *a woman,* try to win her love; pay court (5) to her. **2.** try to win (fame, fortune, sleep).

wood [wʊd] *n.* **1.** hard, solid substance of a tree inside the bark. **2.** (often pl.) area of land covered with growing trees. *out of the* ~, free from troubles or difficulties. '~**cut** *n.* print from a design or picture cut on a block of ~. ~**ed** *adj.* covered with ~s (2). ~**en** ['wʊdn] *adj.* made of ~; (fig.) stiff, clumsy, as if made of ~. '~**land** *n.* (no pl.) tree-covered land. '~**peck·er** *n.* bird that clings to the bark of trees and pecks[2] (1) to find insects. '~-

a woodpecker

wind *n.* wind instrument (usu.) of ~ in an orchestra. '~**work** *n.* (no pl.) **1.** things made of ~, esp. the ~en parts of a building. **2.** carpentry. ~**y** *adj.* (*-ier, -iest*) **1.** ~ed. **2.** of or like ~.

wool [wʊl] *n.* (no pl.) soft, curly hair of sheep, goats, camels, and some other animals; thread, yarn, cloth, clothing, made from this. ~**len** (U.S.A. also ~**en**) ['wʊlən] *adj.* made of ~. *n.* (usu. pl.) cloth, etc. made of ~. ~**ly** (U.S.A. also ~**y**) *adj.* (*-ier, -iest*) **1.** made of, looking like, covered with, ~: ~*ly hair; a* ~*ly coat.* **2.** (fig., of ideas, arguments) not clear. *n.* knitted ~len garment.

word [wɜːd] *n.* **1.** unit of language as spoken, written, or printed: *put one's thoughts into* ~s. **2.** sth. said; talk; statement: *have a* ~ *with sb.,* speak to him; *have* ~s (*with sb.*), quarrel; *by* ~ *of mouth,* in spoken ~s, not in writing; *take sb. at his* ~, act on the belief that he means what he has said. **3.** (no pl.) news: *Leave* ~ *for me at the office. Send me* ~ *tomorrow.* **4.** (no pl.) promise; assurance: *break (keep, give sb.) one's* ~; *be as good as one's* ~, do all one has promised. **5.** (no pl.) command; order: *His* ~ *is law. v.t.* express in ~s: *How shall we* ~ *the letter?* ~**ing** *n.* (no pl.) choice of ~s to express meaning. ~**·'per·fect** *adj.* knowing, able to repeat, sth. (e.g. a part in a play) perfectly. ~**y** *adj.* (*-ier, -iest*) using, expressed in, a large number of ~s, esp. unnecessary ~s.

wore, see *wear* (v.).

work [wɜːk] *n.* **1.** (no pl.) use of physical or mental powers with the purpose of doing or making sth. (esp. contrasted with play or amusement); use of energy supplied by steam, electricity, etc.: *Machines do much of the* ~ *formerly done by man. set (get) to* ~, begin doing sth.; *make short* ~ *of sth.,* finish it quickly. **2.** (no pl.) what a person does to earn a living; employment: *in (out of)* ~, having (not having) employment; *at* ~, at one's place of employment; *busy with one's* ~. **3.** (no pl.) sth. (to be) done by ~ (1): *have a lot of* ~ *to do.* **4.** (no pl.) things needed or used for ~: *She took her* ~ (e.g. sewing) *into the garden.* **5.** (no pl.) sth. produced by ~: *the* ~ *of silversmiths;* also in compounds, as *needle*~, *stone*~, *wood*~. **6.** product of the intellect or imagination: *a* ~ *of art; the* ~s (i.e. plays and poems) *of Shakespeare.* **7.** (pl.) moving parts of a machine (e.g. a clock): *sth. wrong with the* ~s. **8.** (pl., often sing. v.) building(s) where industrial or manufacturing processes are carried on: *gas*~s; *an iron*~s. *The* ~s *is (are) closed.* **9.** *public* ~s, the building of roads, embankments, etc. by government authorities. *v.i. & t.* (p.t. & p.p. ~ed or old use or liter. **wrought** [rɔːt]) **1.** do ~; engage in physical or mental activity: ~ *40 hours a week;* ~*ing hard all day;* ~ *to rule* (see *rule* (1)). **2.** (of a machine, apparatus, bodily organ) be in operation; do what it is required or designed to do: *The lift (bell, etc.) is not* ~*ing.* **3.** (of a plan, method, etc.) have the desired outcome; be successful: *Will the method* ~? **4.** cause to ~; set in motion: *He* ~s his wife too hard. *The machines are ⌄ed by electricity.* **5.** produce as the result of effort; perform: ~ *miracles* (*a cure, harm, mischief*); ~ *out* (i.e. plan) *a scheme.* **6.** (cause to) move or go, usu. by degrees and often with difficulty (*in, out, through,* or *into* some condition): *The screw has ⌄ed loose. Can you ~ the stone into position? The men ⌄ed their way forward.* ~ *into,* introduce (e.g. a few jokes into a lecture); ~ *off,* get rid of; deal with: ~ *off one's superfluous energy;* ~ *up,* create by degrees: ~ *up a business;* excite: ~ *up sb.'s feelings* (*a rebellion*). **7.** ~ *out,* (a) be capable of being solved; (b) be, turn out, in the end: *How will things ~ out? The problem will not ~ out. The total ⌄s out at £20.* ~ *sth. out,* (a) calculate; (b) get results for; (c) plan; develop in detail; (d) solve; (e) exhaust by using: *I can't ~ out this algebra problem. They've ⌄ed out new methods. The silver mine is now ⌄ed out.* **8.** make or shape by hammering, kneading, etc.: ~ *clay,* knead it with water. **9.** cause a change to come about in; have (esp. a disturbing) influence *upon: The sufferings of the refugees ⌄ed upon our feelings. The idea ⌄ed like madness in his brain.* **10.** make by stitching; embroider: ~ *a design on a cushion cover.* ~**·able** *adj.* that can be ⌄ed; practicable: *a ⌄able scheme.* ~**·a·day** ['wɜːkədeɪ] *adj.* commonplace; dull: *a ⌄aday life.* '~**-,bag,** '~**-,bas·ket,** '~**-,box** *ns.* one for holding (esp. needle⌄) materials. ~**·er** *n.* person who ⌄s; *man.* '~**·house** *n.* (Gt. Brit., hist.) public institution for homeless people; (U.S.A.) house of correction for petty offenders. ~**·ing** *n.* (esp.) (part of a) mine or quarry. '~**·man** *n.* man who earns a living by physical labour or in a factory, etc. '~**·man·like** *adj.* characteristic of a good ⌄man. '~**·man·ship** *n.* (no pl.) quality as seen in sth. made: *articles of poor ⌄manship.* '~**·shop** *n.* room or building where things, esp. machines, are made or repaired.

world [wɜːld] *n.* **1.** the earth, its countries and people. **2.** persons, institutions, etc. connected with a special class of people or of interests: *the ~ of sport; the academic ~.* **3.** *the Old W⌄,* Europe, Asia, and Africa; *the New W⌄,* America. **4.** *a ~ of,* a great amount of; *for all the ~ like,* like in every way; *be* (*feel*) *on top of the ~,* feel elated (because of success, etc.); *sth. out of this ~,* sth. sublime. ~**·ly**

adj. **1.** material: *my ⌄ly goods,* my property. **2.** (contrasted with *spiritual*) of this ~: *⌄ly pleasures.*

worm [wɜːm] *n.* kinds of small, boneless, limbless, creeping creature, esp. (*earth⌄*) the kind living in the ground. *v.t.* (often ~ *oneself,* ~ *one's way*) go or get slowly (*through, into*); win by perseverance and patience, etc.: ~ *one's way into favour;* ~ *a secret out of sb.* '~**·eat·en** *adj.* (of wood, etc.) full of holes made by ⌄s; (fig.) antiquated.

worn, see **wear** (v.).

wor·ry ['wʌrɪ] *v.t. & i.* **1.** trouble; give (sb.) ˈno peace of mind: ~ *sb. with foolish questions;* ~ *sb. to do sth.* **2.** be troubled; be anxious or uneasy: *Don't ~ about trifles. not to ~,* there is no need to ~. **3.** (usu. of dogs) seize and shake with the teeth: *The dog was ⌄ing a rat. n.* **1.** (usu. pl.) sth. that worries; cause of anxiety: *Is your life full of worries?* **2.** (no pl.) condition of being troubled: *show signs of* ~.

worse [wɜːs] *adj. & adv.* (comp. of *bad(ly)*): *Your work is bad but hers is* ~. *He behaved far ~ than she did. the ~ for wear,* in a bad condition as the result of being worn or used; (fig.) exhausted; ~ *off,* poorer; less well treated. *n.* (no pl.) sth. ~: *a change for the* ~. **wors·en** ['wɜːsn] *v.t. & i.* make or become ~.

wor·ship ['wɜːʃɪp] *n.* (no pl.) **1.** reverence and respect paid to God: *public* ~, church service; *place of* ~, church or chapel. **2.** admiration and respect shown to or felt for sb. or sth.: *hero-*~. **3.** *your* (*his*) *W⌄,* title of respect used to (of) a magistrate or mayor. *v.t. & i.* (-*pp*-, U.S.A. also -*p*-) **1.** give ~ (1, 2) to. **2.** attend church service. ~**·per** (U.S.A. also ~**·er**) *n.*

worst [wɜːst] *adj. & adv.* (superl. of *bad(ly)*): *the ~ film I've ever seen. n.* (no pl.) ~ part, state, event, etc.: *at* (*the*) ~, if the ~ thing happens; *get the ~ of it,* be defeated. *If the ~ comes to the ~,* if things are as bad as they possibly can be.

wor·sted ['wʊstɪd] *n.* (no pl.) twisted woollen yarn or thread; cloth made of this.

worth [wɜːθ] *pred. adj.* **1.** having a certain value; of value equal to: *That's not ~ more than £10. for what it is ~,* without any guarantee or promise concerning it. **2.** possessing: *He died ~ £5,000.* **3.** giving a satisfactory return or reward for: *The book is well ~ reading. It was ~ it* (~ *our while*) (~ *the* money, time, etc. given to it.) *n.* (no pl.) value; what sb. or sth. is ~: *a discovery of great ~; a pound's ~* [wəθ] *of stamps,* as many as £1 will buy. ~**·less** *adj.* ¸~'**while** *adj.* that is ~ the time, money, etc. needed: *a ~while experiment.*

wor·thy ['wɜːðɪ] *adj.* (-ier, -iest) **1.** deserving (support, etc): ~ *of respect; a ~ cause* (i.e. one deserving support). **2.** deserving respect: *a ~ gentleman.* **wor·thi·ly** *adv.*

would, see *will¹* and *will².*

wound¹ [waʊnd] *v.* see *wind²* (v.) and *wind³.*

wound² [wuːnd] *n.* **1.** hurt or injury to the body caused by cutting, shooting, tearing, etc., esp. as the result of attack. **2.** pain given to a person's feelings: *a ~ to his pride.* **3.** injury to a plant, tree, etc. in which the bark is cut or torn: *give a ~ to: ten killed and fifty ~ed in the battle* (cf. *injured* in an accident).

wove, wo·ven, see *weave* (v.).

wran·gle ['ræŋgl] *v.i. & n.* (take part in a) noisy or angry argument.

wrap [ræp] *v.t. & i.* (-pp-) **1.** (often ~ *up*) put (soft material, a blanket, etc.) round; cover or roll up (*in* paper or other soft material, etc.). **2.** *be ~ped up in,* (a) be packed or enclosed in; (b) (fig.) be concealed in: *The affair is ~ped up in mystery.* (c) be deeply interested in: *be ~ped up in one's studies;* (d) be deeply devoted to. *n.* extra outer garment or covering (e.g. a scarf, cloak, rug). ¸~**·around** *n. & adj.* (object) that extends round sth.: *a ~around skirt.* ~**·per** *n.* **1.** paper enclosing a newspaper, periodical, etc. for posting; paper enclosing a sweet, chocolate, etc.; detachable paper cover of a book. **2.** light dressing-gown. ~**·ping** *n.* (material for) covering or packing.

wrath [rɒθ] *n.* (no pl.) (liter.) deep anger; strong indignation. ~**·ful** *adj.* angry.

wreath [riːθ] *n.* (pl. ~s [riːðz]) **1.** flowers or leaves twisted or woven together in a circle (worn on the head, or placed on a coffin, a grave, a memorial, etc.). **2.** ring or curling line (*of* smoke, etc.). ~**e** [riːð] *v.t. & i.* encircle; cover: *hills ~ed in mist; a face ~ed in smiles,* a smiling face; form (flowers, etc.) into a ~; (of smoke, mist, etc.) move in the shape of a ~.

wreck [rek] *n.* **1.** ruin or destruction, esp. of a ship. **2.** ship that has suffered destruction or that has sunk. **3.** motor car, building, etc. that has been badly damaged or that has fallen into ruin. **4.** person whose health has been destroyed. *v.t.* cause the ~ of: *The ships (My hopes) were ~ed.* ~**·age** ['rekɪdʒ] *n.* (no pl.) ~ed material; fragments: *The ~age of the aircraft was scattered over a wide area.* ~**ed** *adj.* (of sailors, etc.) having suffered ship~. ~**er** *n.* **1.** person whose work is the recovery of a ~ed ship or its contents. **2.** person whose work is the demolition of old buildings (cf. *housebreaker*). **3.** (U.S.A.) vehicle with hoisting apparatus and equipment for towing ~ed or disabled vehicles.

wren [ren] *n.* small, usu. brown, short-winged song-bird.

wrench [rentʃ] *n.* **1.** sudden and violent twist or pull. **2.** (pain caused by) sad parting or separation. **3.** tool for gripping and turning nuts, bolts, etc.; spanner. *v.t.* **1.** twist or pull violently: ~ *sth. off (away, open).* **2.** injure (e.g. one's ankle) by twisting.

wrest [rest] *v.t.* **1.** take (sth.) violently away (*from*): *I ~ed the knife from him (out of his hand).* **2.** get by effort or with difficulty: ~ *a living from the soil.*

wres·tle ['resl] *v.i. & t.* struggle (*with sb.*) (as a sporting contest) in an effort to throw (him) down without hitting (him); (fig.) ~ *with a problem.* ~**r** *n.* person who ~s, esp. in sport.

wretch [retʃ] *n.* **1.** unfortunate and miserable person. **2.** contemptible, mean person. ~**ed** ['retʃɪd] *adj.* **1.** miserable; likely to cause misery: *living in ~ed conditions.* **2.** of poor quality; bad: ~*ed food* (*weather*). ~**ed·ness** *n.* (no pl.).

wrig·gle ['rɪgl] *v.i. & t.* **1.** twist and turn (the body or a part of it); move along by twisting: *children who ~ in their seats. The fish ~d out of my fingers.* **2.** (fig.) ~ *out of* (*doing sth., a difficulty*), escape from. *n.* wriggling movement.

wring [rɪŋ] *v.t.* (p.t. & p.p. **wrung** [rʌŋ]) **1.** twist; squeeze: ~ *sb.'s hand,* press it with emotion; ~ *one's hands,* sqeeze them together (indicating great sorrow, distress, etc.); ~ *a chicken's neck* (to kill it). **2.** twist and squeeze tightly; force (esp. water *out*) by doing this: ~ (*out*) *wet clothes;* ~ *water out of a cloth;* (fig.) ~ *money* (*a confession*) *out of sb.,* get it by persuasion, etc.; ~*ing wet,* (of clothes, etc.) so wet that water can be wrung out of them. ~**er** *n.* mangle¹.

wrin·kle ['rɪŋkl] *n.* small fold or line

in the skin (esp. of the kind produced by age) or on the surface of sth. (e.g. a dress): *iron out the ⁓s. v.t. & i.* make or get ⁓s in: ⁓ *(up) one's fore-head.*

wrist [rist] *n.* joint between the hand and the arm. **⁓·let** ['ristlit] *n.* band or ornament for the ⁓. **'⁓-watch** *n.* watch worn on a strap, etc. round the ⁓.

writ [rit] *n.* **1.** written order issued in the name of a ruler or sb. in authority to an official or other person to do or not to do sth.: *a ⁓ for the arrest of sb.* **2.** *Holy W⁓,* the Bible.

write [rait] *v.i. & t.* (p.t. *wrote* [rəut], p.p. *written* ['ritn]) **1.** make letters or other symbols on a surface, esp. with a pencil or pen on paper: *learn to read and ⁓.* **2.** put down (on paper) by means of words, etc.: *⁓ (down) the address*; *⁓ out a cheque*; *⁓ up,* (esp.) describe, write about (an event, etc.), esp. praising. **3.** do the work of an author; compose (sth.) for publication: *⁓ a novel.* **writ·er** *n.* person who ⁓s, esp. an author or journalist. **writ·ing** *n.* **1.** (no pl.) (in the senses of the verb): *put sth. down in writing*; *writing materials, pen(s), pencil(s),* and *writing-paper,* etc. for writing with or on. **2.** handwriting. **3.** (usu. pl.) literary work: *the writings of Swift.*

writhe [raið] *v.i.* twist or roll about in pain; (fig.) suffer mental agony: *⁓ under insults.*

writ·ten, see *write.*

wrong [rɒŋ] *adj.* (opp. *right²*) **1.** not morally right; unjust: *It is ⁓ to lie.* **2.** mistaken; unsuitable; improper: *They came the ⁓ way. He gave the ⁓ answer. You're doing it the ⁓ way. on the ⁓ side of (50, etc.),* older than. **3.** out of order; in a bad condition: *There's something ⁓ with that radio. What's ⁓ with you? adv.* in a ⁓ manner: *You've spelt my name ⁓* (cf. *⁓ly). go ⁓,* (a) take a ⁓ road; (b) (of plans) have a poor result; (c) get out of order; (d) take to evil ways. *n.* **1.** (no pl.) what is morally ⁓; in-justice. **2.** instance of unjust treat-ment: *You've done me a great ⁓ by blaming me for this. in the ⁓,* having done or said sth. ⁓; in error; *put sb. in the ⁓,* cause him to seem in the ⁓. *v.t.* do ⁓ to; treat (sb.) unjustly; be unfair to. **⁓·do·ing** *n.* doing ⁓; crime; sin. **⁓·ful** *adj.* unjust; unlawful. **⁓·ful·ly** *adv.* **⁓·ly** *adv.* (esp. with a p.p.) *I was ⁓ly informed.*

wrote, see *write.*

wroth [rəuθ] *pred. adj.* (liter. or humor.) angry.

wrought [rɔːt] (old p.t. & p.p. of *work*) **1.** ⁓ *iron,* forged or rolled iron, not cast iron. **2.** *in a ⁓-up state,* with the feelings excited or disturbed.

wrung, see *wring.*

wry [rai] *adj.* (-ier, -iest) pulled or twisted out of shape: *make a ⁓ face* (usu. showing disgust, disappoint-ment).

X

Xmas ['krisməs] *n.* common abbrevia-tion (not used in speaking) for *Christ-mas.*

X-ray [ˌeks'rei] *n.* **1.** (pl.) short-wave rays that penetrate solids and make it

possible to see into or through them. **2.** photograph taken by this means: (attrib.) *an ⁓ photograph (picture)*; *have an ⁓ (examination). v.t.* examine, photograph, or treat with ⁓s.

Y

-y [-ɪ] *suff.* **1.** (forming adjs.) (a) from ns.: like; covered with; having the character of; composed of: *funny*; *icy*; *muddy*; *smoky*; *woolly*; (b) from vs.: tending or inclined to: *sleepy*; *sticky*. **2.** (forming ns.) denoting (a) state, condition, or quality: *courtesy*; *glory*; (b) activity; place of business: *laundry*; (c) specified action: *entreaty*; *inquiry*. **3.** (forming diminutive ns., pet names, etc.): *daddy*; *granny*.

yacht [jɒt] *n.* **1.** light sailing-boat built specially for racing. **2.** small (usu. privately-owned) (motor-driven vessel or sailing-ship, used for pleasure-cruising. [Asia.]

yak [jæk] *n.* long-haired ox of Central

yam [jæm] *n.* climbing plant of tropical countries; its tuber as food.

yap [jæp] *v.i.* (-pp-) *& n.* (utter a) short, sharp bark (as of an excited puppy).

yard¹ [jɑːd] *n.* **1.** unit of length, 3 feet or 36 inches (= 91,44 centimetres). **2.** pole fastened to a mast for supporting a sail. '**~-arm** *n.* either end of a ~ (2).

yard² [jɑːd] *n.* **1.** (usu. unroofed,) enclosed or partly enclosed space near or round a building or buildings, often with a paved or stone floor: *the school ~* (playground); *a farm~*. **2.** (U.S.A.) garden of a house. **3.** enclosure for a special purpose: *railway-~s, marshalling ~s* (where goods trains are made up and coaches, etc. stored). (See also *dock~, ship~*).

yarn [jɑːn] *n.* **1.** (no pl.) thread prepared for knitting, weaving, etc., esp. woollen thread. **2.** (colloq.) story; traveller's tale: *spin a ~*, tell or make up a story. *v.i.* tell ~s (2).

yawn [jɔːn] *v.i. & t.* **1.** open the mouth wide and breathe in deeply, as when needing sleep or when bored. **2.** utter, say, with a ~. **3.** be wide open: *a ~ing gulf*. *n.* act of ~ing (1).

ye¹ [jiː] *pron.* (old form of) you: *How d'ye do?*

ye² [jiː] *adj.* (old form of) the: *Ye olde Bull and Bush* (as an inn sign).

yea [jeɪ] *adv. & int.* (old use) yes.

year [jɜː*] *n.* **1.** time taken by the earth in making one revolution round the sun, 365¼ days. **2.** period from 1 January to 31 December; period of the same length but starting on a different day: *be ten ~s of age*; *the academic ~*; *leap ~* (see *leap*). **~·ling** ['jɜːlɪŋ] *n.* animal between one and two years old. **~·ly** *adj. & adv.* (taking place) every ~; once every ~.

yearn [jɜːn] *v.i.* have a strong desire (*for, to do* sth.). **~·ing** *n.* longing (*after, for*). **~·ing·ly** *adv.*

yeast [jiːst] *n.* substance used in the brewing of beer and the making of bread; added to the dough it produces gas and so makes the bread light² (4).

yell [jel] *v.i. & t. & n.* (utter a) loud cry of pain, excitement, etc.; say (sth.) in a ~ing voice.

yel·low ['jeləʊ] *n.* (no pl.) *& adj.* colour of gold or the yolk of a hen's egg. *~ fever*, tropical disease causing the skin to turn ~; *the ~ press*, newspapers that present news in a sensational way. *v.t. & i.* (cause to) become ~.

yelp [jelp] *v.i. & n.* (esp. of dogs) (utter a) short, sharp cry (of pain, anger, or excitement).

yeo·man ['jəʊmən] *n.* (pl. -men) (old use) working farmer who owned his land. *do ~('s) service*, give valuable help in time of need. **~·ry** *n.* (no pl.) (Gt. Brit., hist.) cavalry force of volunteers raised from the ~ class.

yes [jes] *particle* (contrasted with *no*) indicating agreement, consent, etc. *n.* the word or answer *yes*.

yes·ter·day ['jestədɪ] *adv. & n.* (on) the day before today.

yet [jet] *adv.* by this or that time; up to now; up to then; so far; still; at some future time. (Cf. *already*.) *conj.* but still; nevertheless.

yew [juː] *n.* (also *~-tree*) evergreen tree with dark-green leaves; its wood.

yield [jiːld] *v.t. & i.* **1.** give a natural product, a result, or profit: *trees that ~ fruit*; *investments ~ing 10 per cent.*

2. give way, esp. to force; surrender: ~ *a town to the enemy*; ~ *to temptation*. **3.** ~ *to none*, refuse to admit that anyone else is more fond of, zealous for, etc. **n.** amount produced: *the* ~ *per acre*. ~**ing adj.** easily giving way or bending; (fig.) not obstinate.

yo·ghurt, yo·gurt [ˈjɒgət] **n.** fermented, semi-solid, sourish, curd-like food made from milk.

yoke [jəʊk] **n. 1.** shaped piece of wood placed across the necks of oxen pulling a cart, plough, etc. **2.** (pl. ~) two oxen working together: *three* ~ *of oxen*. **3.** *pass* (*come*) *under the* ~, acknowledge and accept defeat; *throw off the* ~ (*of servitude, etc.*), rebel, refuse to obey. **4.** piece of wood shaped to fit a person's shoulders, used to support the weight of buckets, etc. **5.** part of a dress, etc. fitting the shoulders and the upper part of the chest. **v.t. 1.** put a ~ (1) on (oxen). **2.** ~*d to*, united to.

(a) yoke (1, 2)

yo·kel [ˈjəʊkl] **n.** simple-minded countryman.

yolk [jəʊk] **n.** yellow part of an egg.

yon [jɒn], **yon·der** [ˈjɒndə*] **adj. & adv.** (that is, that can be seen) over there.

yore [jɔː*] **n.** (no pl.) (liter.) *of* ~, of olden days; of the past.

you [juː, jʊ] **pron. 1.** person(s) addressed: *Y~ are my friend(s)*. **2.** any person: *Y~ never know who may become* ~*r enemy* (one never knows who ...). ~**'re** [jʊə*] ~ are.

your [jɔː*] **poss. pron. attrib.** belonging to, relating to, you: *This is* ~ *book*. ~**s** [jɔːz] **poss. pron. pred.** of you: *This book is* ~*s* (belongs to you). ~**self** [jɔːˈself] **pron.** (pl. ~*selves* [-selvz]) **1.** refl. form: *Did you hurt* ~*self when you fell down?* **2.** *You* ~*self said so* (nobody else). **3.** *You sat by* ~*self* (alone). *Did you do it by* ~*self* (without help)? **4.** in your normal state of health or mind: *You are quite* ~*self again*.

young [jʌŋ] **adj. 1.** (contrasted with *old*) not far advanced in life, growth, etc.; of recent birth or origin: *a* ~ *woman* (*tree, animal, nation, etc.*). **2.** still near its beginning: *The night is still* ~. **n.** (collective) ~ offspring: *the* ~, ~ people; ~ ones (of animals and birds). ~**ish adj.** fairly ~. ~**ster** [ˈjʌŋstə*] **n.** child, esp. a boy; ~ person.

youth [juːθ] **n.** (pl. ~*s* [juːðz]) **1.** (no pl.) state or time of being young. **2.** young man; (collective pl.) young people: *the* ~ *of the nation*; *a* ~ *hostel*. ~**ful adj.** young; having the qualities, etc. of young people: ~*ful appearance*.

Yu·go·slav, Ju·go·slav [ˌjuːgəʊˈslɑːv] **n. & adj.** (native or inhabitant) of Yugoslavia. **Yu·go·sla·vi·an, J-** [ˌjuːgəʊˈslɑːvjən] **adj.** of Yugoslavia or the ~s.

yule [juːl] **n.** (also ~-*tide*) Christmas.

Z

zeal [ziːl] *n.* (no pl.) enthusiasm; warm interest (*for* a cause, one's work, etc.). **~ot** ['zelət] *n.* person who shows much ~ for a cause, religion, etc.; fanatic. **~ous** ['zeləs] *adj.* having, showing, acting with, ~. **~ous·ly** *adv.*

ze·bra ['ziːbrə] *n.* horse-like, wild animal of Africa, with dark and white stripes on its body. **~ cross·ing** *n.* (Gt. Brit.) street crossing marked with broad, white stripes where pedestrians have priority over vehicles.

ze·nith ['zenɪθ] *n.* (no pl.) (opp. *nadir*) **1.** part of the sky directly above the observer. **2.** (fig.) highest point (of one's fame, fortune).

zeph·yr ['zefə*] *n.* west wind; (poet.) soft, gentle breeze.

ze·ro ['zɪərəʊ] *n.* **1.** figure 0; nought. **2.** point between the positive (+) and negative (−) on a scale, esp. a thermometer.

zest [zest] *n.* (no pl.) **1.** great interest or pleasure. **2.** pleasing or stimulating quality or flavour: *The possible danger gave* (*a*) ~ *to the adventure.*

zig·zag ['zɪgzæg] *n.* line or path that turns right and left alternately at sharp (equal or unequal) angles: (attrib.) *a ~ path up the hillside.* *adv.* in a ~. *v.i.* (*-gg-*) go in a ~ course.

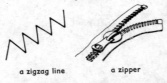

a zigzag line   a zipper

zinc [zɪŋk] *n.* (no pl.) white metal used in alloys, and for coating sheet iron for roofing, etc.

zip [zɪp] *n.* sound as of a bullet going through the air. *v.t. & i.* (*-pp-*) fasten up with a ~-fastener. **~ code** *n.* (U.S.A.) five-digit number used to identify each postal delivery area in the U.S.A. '~(-,fast·en·er), ~·per ns. device (2) for locking together two toothed metal or plastic edges by means of a sliding tab, used for fastening bags, dresses, etc.

zo·di·ac ['zəʊdɪæk] *n.* belt of the sky in which the sun, moon, and planets move, divided into twelve parts called *the signs of the* ~.

zone [zəʊn] *n.* **1.** belt or band round sth. and distinguished from it by colour, appearance, etc. **2.** one of the five parts into which the earth is divided by imaginary lines parallel to the equator (the *torrid*, the *N. & S. temperate*, and the *arctic* or *frigid ~s*). **3.** area with particular features, purpose, or use: *the war* ~; *the ~ of submarine activity; parking* ~*s; smokeless* ~*s.* **zon·al** ['zəʊnl] *adj.* of, arranged in, ~s.

zoo [zuː] *n.* zoological gardens.

zo·ol·o·gy [zəʊ'ɒlədʒɪ] *n.* (no pl.) science of the structure, forms, and distribution of animals. **zo·o·log·i·cal** [,zəʊə'lɒdʒɪkl] *adj.* of ~: *zoological gardens*, park (usu. public) in which many kinds of animals are kept for exhibition. **zo·ol·o·gist** [zəʊ'ɒlədʒɪst] *n.* expert in ~.

zoom [zuːm] *v.i.* **1.** move with a loud, low hum or buzz. **2.** (of an aircraft) move upwards at high speed and a steep angle. **3.** (of a camera) move toward or away from an object rapidly so that the image appears to come closer to or to move away from the observer. *n.* **1.** sudden upward flight of an aircraft. **2.** (attrib.) ~ *lens*, (on a camera) lens with continuously variable focal length.

Appendices

British and American Abbreviations

A

A. (Gt. Brit., of films: certified as suitable for adults but possibly not for children.)

a. acre.

A.A. anti-aircraft; (Gt. Brit.) Automobile Association; (Gt. Brit., of films: to be seen only by persons over 14).

A.A.A. (Gt. Brit.) Amateur Athletic Association; (U.S.A.) American Automobile Association.

a.a.r. against all risks.

A.A.U. (U.S.A.) Amateur Athletic Union.

A.B. able-bodied seaman.

AB (U.S.A.) Bachelor of Arts.

abbr. abbreviated; abbreviation.

ABC American Broadcasting Company.

A.C. alternating current.

a/c account.

acc. according to; account.

acct. account.

A.D. Anno Domini (Latin = (in the year) since the birth of Christ).

add. address.

Adm. Admiral.

advt. advertisement.

AEC Atomic Energy Commission.

AEF American Expeditionary Forces.

AFL-CIO American Federation of Labor and Congress of Industrial Organizations.

AFN American Forces Network.

Afr. Africa; African.

aftn. afternoon.

Ala. Alabama.

Alas. Alaska.

Am. America; American.

AM (U.S.A.) = M.A.

a.m. ante meridiem (Latin = before noon).

AMA American Medical Association.

amp. ampere.

A.P. Associated Press.

approx. approximate(ly).

appx. appendix.

Apr. April.

ARC American Red Cross.

Ariz. Arizona.

Ark. Arkansas.

A.R.P. Air-Raid Precautions.

arr. arrival; arrives.

art. article.

AS anti-submarine.

ASA American Standards Association.

Asst. Assistant.

asst'd assorted.

Aug. August.

auth. author(ess).

av. average.

A.V. Audio-Visual; Authorized Version (of the Bible).

avdp. avoirdupois.

Av(e). Avenue.

AWOL absent without leave.

B

b. born.

B.A. Bachelor of Arts; British Academy; British Airways.

Barr. Barrister.

Bart. Baronet.

B.B.C. British Broadcasting Corporation.

bbl. barrels (esp. of oil).

B.C. Before Christ; British Columbia; British Council.

bd. bound.

B.E. bill of exchange.

Beds. Bedfordshire.

Berks. Berkshire.

B.F.N. British Forces Network.

bk. book.

B.L. bill of lading; British Library.

bl. barrel.

bldg(s). building(s).

B.Lit(t). Bachelor of Letters, Bachelor of Literature.

bls. bales.

Blvd. Boulevard.

B.M. Bachelor of Medicine; British Museum.

B.M.A. British Medical Association.

B.Mus. Bachelor of Music.

B.O. body odour; Box Office; Branch Office.

B.o.T. (Gt. Brit.) Board of Trade.

B.P. boiling-point.

B.Pharm. Bachelor of Pharmacy.

Abbreviations

B.Phil. Bachelor of Philosophy.
B.R. British Rail(ways).
Br. British; Brother.
B.R.C.S. British Red Cross Society.
Brig. Brigadier.
Brit. Britain; British.
Bros. Brothers (esp. in the title of firms).
BS (U.S.A.) Bachelor of Science.
B.S. British Standard.
B.Sc. (Gt. Brit.) Bachelor of Science.
B.S.T. British Standard Time; British Summer Time.
Bt. Baronet.
B.th.u., B.t.u. British thermal unit(s).
bu. bushel(s).
Bucks. Buckinghamshire.

C

C. Celsius; Centigrade.
c. cent(s); century; circa (= about); cubic.
ca. circa (= about).
C.A. (Gt. Brit.) chartered accountant.
C/A current account.
Cal(if). California.
Cambs. Cambridgeshire.
Can. Canada; Canadian.
Capt. Captain.
CARE Co-operative for American Relief Everywhere.
Cath. Catholic.
C.B. Companion (of the Order) of the Bath.
C.B.C. Canadian Broadcasting Corporation.
CBD (U.S.A.) cash before delivery.
C.B.E. (Gt. Brit.) Commander (of the Order) of the British Empire.
CBS (U.S.A.) Columbia Broadcasting System.
C.C. continuous current; County Council(lor).
c.c. cubic centimetre(s).
C.E. Church of England; civil engineer.
CENTO Central Treaty Organization.
cert. certificate; certified.
C.E.T. Central European Time.
cf. confer (= compare).
ch. chapter.
Ches. Cheshire.
C.I. Channel Islands.
CIA (U.S.A.) Central Intelligence Agency.
C.I.D. (Gt. Brit.) Criminal Investigation Department.
c.i.f. cost, insurance, freight.
C.-in-C. Commander-in-Chief.
cl. centilitre(s); class.
cm centimetre(s).

C.N.D. Campaign for Nuclear Disarmament.
C.O. Commanding Officer; conscientious objector.
Co. company; county.
c/o (used in addressing letters to sb. in the) care of ...
C.O.D. cash (U.S.A. collect) on delivery.
C. of E. Church of England; Council of Europe.
Col. Colonel.
Coll. College.
Colo. Colorado.
Conn. Connecticut.
Cons. (Gt. Brit.) Conservative (political party).
cont. contents; continued.
Co-op Co-operative (Society).
Corn. Cornwall.
Corp. Corporal; (U.S.A.) Corporation.
C.P. Cape Province; Communist Party.
cp. compare.
CPA (U.S.A.) certified public accountant.
C.S. Civil Servant; Civil Service.
CST (U.S.A.) Central Standard Time.
ct cent.
cu. cubic.
C.U.P. Cambridge University Press.
c.w.o. cash with order.
cwt. hundredweight.

D

d. died; denarius (Latin, former British coin = penny, pence).
D.A. deposit account.
DA (U.S.A.) district attorney.
D.C., d.c. direct current.
DC (U.S.A.) District of Columbia.
Dec. December.
deg. degree(s).
Del. Delaware.
Dem (U.S.A.) Democrat; Democratic.
dep. departs; departure; deputy.
Dept. Department.
Dir. Director.
disc. discount.
dist. distance; district.
D.J. dinner-jacket; disc jockey.
D.Lit(t). Doctor of Letters, Doctor of Literature.
D.M. Doctor of Medicine.
D.Mus. Doctor of Music.
do. ditto.
doc. document.
dol. dollar(s).
Dors. Dorsetshire.
doz. dozen(s).
D.P. displaced person; data processing.
D.Phil. Doctor of Philosophy.

Dpt. Department.
Dr. Doctor; debtor.
D.Sc. Doctor of Science.
DST (U.S.A.) Daylight Saving Time.
dupl. duplicate.
Dur. Durham.
dwt. pennyweight.
dz. dozen(s).

E

E. east(ern); English.
E.C. European Community; East Central.
E.C.E. Economic Commission for Europe.
Ed., ed. edition; edited (by); editor.
EDP electronic data processing.
E.E.C. European Economic Community (the Common Market).
E.F.T.A. European Free Trade Association.
e.g. exempli gratia (Latin = for instance, for example).
EMS European Monetary System.
encl. enclosed; enclosure(s).
Eng. Engineer(ing); England; English.
E.R. Elizabeth Regina (Queen Elizabeth).
E.S.P. extra-sensory perception.
Esq. Esquire.
E.S.R.O. European Space Research Organization.
Ess. Essex.
est. established; estimated.
EST Eastern Standard Time.
etc., &c. et cetera, and the rest, and so on.
Euratom European Atomic Energy Community.
excl. exclusive; excluding.

F

F. Fahrenheit; Fellow.
f. fathom; female; feminine; foot; feet; following.
F.A. (Gt. Brit.) Football Association.
Fahr. Fahrenheit.
F.A.O. Food and Agriculture Organization.
FBI (U.S.A.) Federal Bureau of Investigation.
F.B.I. Federation of British Industries.
FCC (U.S.A.) Federal Communications Commission.
Feb. February.
FIFA Fédération Internationale de Football Association (Fr. = International Football Federation).
fig. figure(s).
Fla. Florida.
fm. fathom(s).

F.O. (Gt. Brit.) Foreign Office.
f.o.b. free on board.
f.o.r. free on rail.
F.P. freezing-point.
Fr. France; French.
fr. franc(s).
Fri. Friday.
ft. foot; feet.
FTC (U.S.A.) Federal Trade Commission.
fur. furlong(s).

G

g. gram(s); guinea (= 105 p.); grain(s).
G.A. general agent; general assembly.
Ga. Georgia.
gal. gallon(s).
G.A.T.T. General Agreement on Tariffs and Trade.
G.B. Great Britain.
G.B.S. George Bernard Shaw.
G.C.B. Knight Grand Cross (of the Order) of the Bath.
Gen. General.
gen. general(ly).
Ger. German; Germany.
G.I. government issue (American private soldier).
G.L.C. Greater London Council.
Glos. Gloucestershire.
G.M.T. Greenwich Mean Time.
gns. guineas.
GOP (U.S.A.) Grand Old Party (the Republican Party).
Gov. Government; Governor.
G.P. general practitioner.
G.P.O. General Post Office.
gr. grain(s); gram(s); gross.
grad. graduate(d).
gr.wt. gross weight.
gs. guineas.
guar. guaranteed.

H

h. hour(s).
Hants. Hampshire.
H.B.M. His (Her) Britannic Majesty.
H.C. (Gt. Brit.) House of Commons.
H.C.J. (Gt. Brit.) High Court of Justice.
H.E. high explosive.
Heref. Herefordshire.
Herts. Hertfordshire.
H.F. high frequency; (Gt. Brit.) Home Fleet; (Gt. Brit.) Home Forces.
hf. half.
H.L. (Gt. Brit.) House of Lords.
H.M. His (Her) Majesty.
H.M.S. His (Her) Majesty's Service; His (Her) Majesty's Ship (Steamer).
H.M.S.O. His (Her) Majesty's Stationery Office.

Abbreviations

H.O. (Gt. Brit.) Home Office.
Hon. Honorary; Honourable.
h.p. horsepower; high pressure; hire-purchase.
H.Q. Headquarters.
HR (U.S.A.) House of Representatives.
H.R.H. His (Her) Royal Highness.
hrs. hours.
H.T. high tension.
H.W.M. high-water mark.

I

I. Island; Isle.
Ia., IA Iowa.
I.A.T.A. International Air Transport Association.
ib(id). ibidem (Latin = in the same place).
I.B.M. International Business Machines.
I.C.A.O. International Civil Aviation Organization.
I.C.B.M. intercontinental ballistic missile.
I.C.F.T.U. International Confederation of Free Trade Unions.
I.C.J. International Court of Justice.
I.D. Intelligence Department.
ID Idaho.
i.e. id est (Latin = that is to say).
Ill. Illinois.
I.L.O. International Labour Organization.
I.L.P. (Gt. Brit.) Independent Labour Party.
I.M.F. International Monetary Fund.
Imp. Imperial.
in. inch(es).
Inc. (U.S.A.) Incorporated.
incl. inclusive; including.
Ind. Indiana.
inst. instant.
I.O.C. International Olympic Committee.
I.O.M. Isle of Man.
IOU I owe you.
I.O.W. Isle of Wight.
IPA International Phonetic Association.
I.Q. intelligence quotient.
I.R.A. Irish Republican Army.
I.R.C. International Red Cross.
Ire. Ireland.
I.S.O. International Organization for Standardization.
I.T.O. International Trade Organization.
ITV (Gt. Brit.) independent television.
I.U.S. International Union of Students.
I.U.S.Y. International Union of Socialist Youth.

J

J. Judge; Justice.
Jan. January.
J.C. Jesus Christ.
J.P. Justice of the Peace.
Jr. Junior (Latin = the younger).
Jul. July.
Jun. June.
Jun(r). Junior (Latin = the younger).

K

Kans. Kansas.
K.C. King's Counsel.
K.C.B. Knight Commander (of the Order) of the Bath.
kg kilogram(s).
kHz kilohertz.
K.K.K. Ku-Klux-Klan.
km kilometre(s).
K.O. knock-out.
k.p.h. kilometres per hour.
kW kilowatt(s).
Ky., KY Kentucky.

L

l. left; line; litre(s).
£ pound sterling.
La., LA Louisiana.
LA Los Angeles.
£A Australian pound.
Lancs. Lancashire.
lang. language.
lat. latitude.
lb. pound(s).
L.C. letter of credit.
L.C.J. (Gt. Brit.) Lord Chief Justice.
Ld. Lord.
Leics. Leicestershire.
Lincs. Lincolnshire.
L.J. (Gt. Brit.) Lord Justice.
ll. lines.
LMT (U.S.A.) local mean time.
long. longitude.
L.P. long-playing (record); Labour Party; low pressure.
l.p. low pressure.
LSD lysergic acid diethylamide (drug inducing hallucinations).
L.S.O. London Symphony Orchestra.
L.T. low tension.
Lt. Lieutenant.
Lt.-Col. Lieutenant-Colonel.
Ltd. limited.
Lt.-Gen. Lieutenant-General.

M

m. male; masculine; married; metre(s); mile(s); minute(s).
M.A. Master of Arts.

Maj. Major.
Maj.-Gen. Major-General.
Mar. March.
Mass. Massachusetts.
max. maximum.
M.B. Medicinae Baccalaureus (Latin = Bachelor of Medicine).
M.C. Master of Ceremonies; (U.S.A.) Member of Congress.
M.D. Medicinae Doctor (Latin = Doctor of Medicine).
Md. Maryland.
Me. Maine.
med. medical; medicine; medieval.
mg milligram(s).
mi. (U.S.A.) mile(s).
Mich. Michigan.
Middx. Middlesex.
min. minute(s); minimum.
Minn. Minnesota.
Miss. Mississippi.
mm millimetre(s).
M.O. money order.
Mo. Missouri.
Mon. Monday.
Mont. Montana.
MP, M.P. Member of Parliament; Military Police.
m.p.h. miles per hour.
M.Pharm. Master of Pharmacy.
Mr Mister.
Mrs Mistress.
MS. manuscript.
M.S. motor ship.
Ms, Ms. [mɪz] (title of a woman, used without distinction between married and unmarried).
M.Sc. Master of Science.
M.S.L. mean sea level.
MSS. manuscripts.
Mt. Mount.

N

N. north(ern).
n. noon.
N.A.A.F.I. (Gt. Brit.) Navy, Army, and Air Force Institute.
NASA (U.S.A.) National Aeronautics and Space Administration.
nat. national; natural.
NATO North Atlantic Treaty Organization.
NBC (U.S.A.) National Broadcasting Company.
N.C. North Carolina.
N.C.O. non-commissioned officer.
N.D(ak). North Dakota.
N.E. northeast(ern).
Neb(r). Nebraska.
neg. negative.
Nev. Nevada.

N.H. New Hampshire.
N.H.S. (Gt. Brit.) National Health Service.
N.J. New Jersey.
N.M(ex). New Mexico.
No. (U.S.A.) North; number.
Norf. Norfolk.
Northants. Northamptonshire.
Northumb. Northumberland.
Nos. numbers.
Notts. Nottinghamshire.
Nov. November.
N.T. New Testament.
nt.wt. net weight.
N.W. northwest(ern).
N.Y. New York.
N.Y.C. New York City.
N.Z. New Zealand.

O

O. Ohio; order.
o/a on account (of).
OAS Organization of American States.
OAU Organization of African Unity.
ob. obiit (Latin = died).
Oct. October.
O.E.C.D. Organization for Economic Co-operation and Development.
O.H.M.S. On His (Her) Majesty's Service.
O.K. all right; "I agree".
Okla. Oklahoma.
O.P.E.C. Organization of Petroleum Exporting Countries.
Ore(g). Oregon.
O.T. Old Testament.
O.U.P. Oxford University Press.
Oxon. Oxfordshire.
oz. ounce(s).

P

p. page; penny; pence.
Pa. Pennsylvania.
p.a. per annum (Latin = yearly).
Pan Am Pan-American (World Airways Incorporated).
par. paragraph.
P.C. police constable; (Gt. Brit.) Privy Councillor; (U.S.A.) Peace Corps.
p.c. per cent; post card.
P.D. Police Department; per diem (Latin = by the day).
pd. paid.
P.E.N., PEN Club Poets, Playwrights, Editors, Essayists, and Novelists (International Association of Writers).
Penn(a). Pennsylvania.
Ph.D. Philosophiae Doctor (Latin = Doctor of Philosophy).
P.M. Prime Minister.
p.m. post meridiem (Latin = after noon).
P.M.G. Postmaster General.

Abbreviations

P.O. Post Office; postal order.
P.O.Box post-office box.
p.o.d. pay on delivery.
P.O.O. post-office order.
pop. population.
pos. positive.
P.O.S.B. Post-Office Savings Bank.
P.O.W. prisoner of war.
pp. pages.
P.R. public relations; Puerto Rico.
pref. preface.
Pres. President.
Prof. Professor.
prol. prologue.
Prot. Protestant.
P.S. Police Sergeant; postscript.
P.T. physical training.
pt. part; pint; point; port.
P.T.A. Parent-Teacher Association.
Pte. (Gt. Brit.) Private (soldier).
P.T.I. Physical Training Instructor.
P.T.O. please turn over.
Pvt. (U.S.A.) Private (soldier).
P.W. prisoner of war.
PX (U.S.A.) Post Exchange.

Q

Q.C. Queen's Counsel.
qr. quarter(s).
qt. quart(s).
qu. query.
quot. quotation.
q.v. quod vide (Latin = which see).
qy. query.

R

R. Railway; Regina (= Queen); River; Royal; (U.S.A.) Republican.
r. right.
R.A. Royal Academy.
R.A.C. Royal Automobile Club.
R.A.F. Royal Air Force.
R.C. Red Cross; Roman Catholic.
Rd. Road.
rd. rod.
recd. received.
ref. reference.
regd. registered.
Regt. Regiment.
Rep (U.S.A.) Representative (in Congress); Republican.
rep representative; repertory (theatre or company).
resp. respective(ly).
ret(d). retired.
Rev(d). Reverend.
R.I. Rhode Island.
R.M. Royal Mail; Royal Marines.
R.M.A. Royal Military Academy.
R.N. Royal Navy.
R.P. reply paid.

r.p.m. revolutions per minute.
RR (U.S.A.) railroad.
R.S. Royal Society.
R.S.P.C.A. Royal Society for the Prevention of Cruelty to Animals.
R.S.V.P. répondez s'il vous plaît (Fr. = please reply).
R.T. radio telegraphy; radio telephony.
Rt.Hon. (Gt. Brit.) Right Honourable.
Ry. Railway.

S

S. south; southern.
s. second(s); shilling(s).
S.A. South Africa; South America; Salvation Army.
SACEUR Supreme Allied Commander Europe.
Salop. Shropshire.
SALT Strategic Arms Limitation Talks.
Sat. Saturday.
S.C. South Carolina.
Sch. school.
S.D(ak). South Dakota.
S.E. southeast(ern).
SEATO South-East Asia Treaty Organization.
Sec. Secretary.
sec. second(s).
Sen(r). Senior (Latin = the elder).
Sept. September.
S(er)gt. Sergeant.
S.F. science fiction.
sh. shilling(s).
SHAPE Supreme Headquarters Allied Powers Europe.
S.M. Sergeant-Major.
Soc. Society.
Som(s). Somersetshire.
Sq. Square.
sq. square.
sq.ft. square foot.
sq.in. square inch.
Sr. Senior (Latin = the elder).
S.S. steamship.
St. Saint; Street.
st. stone (14 lb.).
Sta. Station.
Staffs. Staffordshire.
S.T.D. subscriber trunk dialling.
St.Ex. Stock Exchange.
stg. sterling.
sub. substitute.
Suff. Suffolk.
Sun. Sunday.
suppl. supplement.
Supt. Superintendent.
Suss. Sussex.
S.W. southwest(ern).
Sx. Sussex.
Sy. Surrey.

T

t. ton(s).
T.B. tuberculosis.
Tenn. Tennessee.
Tex. Texas.
tgm. telegram.
T.G.W.U. (Gt. Brit.) Transport and General Workers' Union.
Thur(s). Thursday.
T.M.O. telegraph money order.
T.N.T. trinitrotoluene (a powerful explosive).
T.O. Telegraph (Telephone) Office; turnover.
T.P.O. Travelling Post Office.
T.R.H. Their Royal Highnesses.
T.U. Trade Union.
T.U.C. (Gt. Brit.) Trades Union Congress.
Tue(s). Tuesday.
TV, T.V. television.
T.W.A. (U.S.A.) Trans World Airlines.

U

U. universal (of films: open to all persons).
UFO, U.F.O. unidentified flying object.
U.H.F. ultra-high frequency.
U.K. United Kingdom (England, Scotland, Wales, and N. Ireland).
ult. ultimo (Latin = last day of the month).
UN, U.N. United Nations.
UNESCO United Nations Educational, Scientific, and Cultural Organization.
UNICEF United Nations International Children's Emergency Fund, United Nations Children's Fund.
UNO, U.N.O. United Nations Organization.
UNSC United Nations Security Council.
UP (U.S.A.) United Press.
UPI United Press International.
US, U.S. United States.
USA, U.S.A. United States of America; United States Army.
USAF, U.S.A.F. United States Air Force.
USN, U.S.N. United States Navy.
USS, U.S.S. United States Ship.
U.S.S.R. Union of Soviet Socialist Republics.
Ut. Utah.
U.V. ultraviolet.

V

V volt(s).
v. verse; versus (Latin = against); vide (Latin = see).
Va., VA Virginia.
V.A.T. value-added tax.
V.D. venereal disease.
V.H.F. very high frequency.
VIP, V.I.P. very important person.
Vis. Viscount(ess).
viz. videlicet (Latin = namely).
vol. volume.
vols. volumes.
vs. versus (Latin = against).
Vt. Vermont.
V.T.O.(L.) vertical take-off (and landing).
v.v. vice versa (Latin = conversely).

W

W. west(ern).
W., w. watt(s).
Warks. Warwickshire.
Wash. Washington.
WASP (U.S.A.) White Anglo-Saxon Protestant.
W.C. West Central; water-closet.
Wed. Wednesday.
W.F.T.U. World Federation of Trade Unions.
WHO, W.H.O. World Health Organization.
W.I. West Indies.
Wilts. Wiltshire.
Wis. Wisconsin.
WL, w.l. wave-length.
WT wireless telegraphy (telephony).
wt. weight.
W.Va. West Virginia.
Wyo. Wyoming.

X

X (Gt. Brit., of films: not suitable for persons under 18).
Xmas Christmas.

Y

yd(s). yard(s).
Y.H.(A.) Youth Hostel(s' Association).
Y.M.C.A. Young Men's Christian Association.
Yorks. Yorkshire.
yr(s). year(s).
Y.W.C.A. Young Women's Christian Association.

Spelling and Pronunciation
of Proper Names

A

Ab·er·deen [ˌæbə'diːn]; Ab·er·deen-shire [ˌæbə'diːnʃə*].
Ab·ou·kir [ˌæbuː'kɪə*].
Abra·ham ['eɪbrəhæm] m.
Ab·ys·sin·ia [ˌæbɪ'sɪnjə].
Achil·les [ə'kɪliːz].
Ad·al·bert ['ædəlbəːt] m.
Ad·am ['ædəm] m.
Ad·di·son ['ædɪsn].
Ad·e·laide ['ædəleɪd].
Aden ['eɪdn].
Ad·i·ron·dacks [ˌædɪ'rɒndæks] pl.
Adri·at·ic Sea [ˌeɪdrɪ'ætɪk 'siː].
Ae·ge·an Sea [iː'dʒiːən 'siː].
Aes·chy·lus ['iːskɪləs].
Ae·sop ['iːsɒp].
Af·ghan·i·stan [æf'gænɪstæn].
Af·ri·ca ['æfrɪkə].
Ag·a·tha ['ægəθə] f.
Aix-la-Chapelle [ˌeɪkslɑː'ʃæ'pel].
Al·a·bama [ˌælə'bæmə].
Alas·ka [ə'læskə].
Al·ba·nia [æl'beɪnjə].
Al·ba·ny ['ɔːlbənɪ].
Al·bert ['ælbət] m.
Al·ber·ta [æl'bɜːtə].
Al·der·ney ['ɔːldənɪ].
Al·der·shot ['ɔːldəʃɒt].
Aleu·tian Is·lands [ə'luːʃjən 'aɪləndz] pl.
Al·ex·an·der [ˌælɪg'zaːndə] m.
Al·ex·an·dra [ˌælɪg'zaːndrə] f.
Al·fred ['ælfrɪd] m.
Al·ge·ria [æl'dʒɪərɪə].
Al·ger·non ['ældʒənən] m.
Algiers [æl'dʒɪəz].
Al·ice ['ælɪs] f.
Al·le·ghe·ny ['ælɪgenɪ].
Al·sace [æl'sæs], Al·sa·tia [æl'seɪʃjə].
Am·a·zon ['æməzən].
Ame·lia [ə'miːljə] f.
Amer·i·ca [ə'merɪkə].
Amy ['eɪmɪ] f.
An·des ['ændiːz] pl.
An·dor·ra [æn'dɔːrə].
An·drew ['ændruː] m.
An·gle·sey ['æŋglsɪ].
An·glia ['æŋglɪə].
An·go·la [æŋ'gəʊlə].

An·gus ['æŋgəs].
An·nap·o·lis [ə'næpəlɪs].
Ann(e) [æn] f.
Ant·arc·ti·ca [ænt'ɑːktɪkə].
An·tho·ny ['æntənɪ] m.
An·til·les [æn'tɪliːz] pl.
An·trim ['æntrɪm].
Ant·werp ['æntwɜːp].
Ap·en·nines ['æpɪnaɪnz] pl.
Ap·pa·la·chians [ˌæpə'leɪtʃjənz] pl.
Ara·bia [ə'reɪbɪə].
Ar·chi·bald ['ɑːtʃɪbɔːld] m.
Ar·chi·me·des [ˌɑːkɪ'miːdiːz].
Arc·tic ['ɑːktɪk].
Ar·den ['ɑːdn].
Ar·gen·ti·na [ˌɑːdʒən'tiːnə], Ar·gen·tine ['ɑːdʒəntaɪn].
Ar·gyll(·shire) [ɑː'gaɪl(ʃə*)].
Ar·is·toph·a·nes [ˌærɪ'stɒfəniːz].
Ar·is·tot·le ['ærɪstɒtl].
Ar·i·zo·na [ˌærɪ'zəʊnə].
Ar·kan·sas ['ɑːkənsɔː].
Ar·ling·ton ['ɑːlɪŋtən].
Ar·magh [ɑː'mɑː].
Ar·me·nia [ɑː'miːnjə].
Ar·thur ['ɑːθə*] m.
As·cot ['æskət].
Asia ['eɪʃə]: ~ Minor.
As·syr·ia [ə'sɪrɪə].
As·tra·khan [ˌæstrə'kæn].
Ath·ens ['æθɪnz].
At·lan·ta [ət'læntə].
At·lan·tic (Ocean) [ət'læntɪk ('əʊʃn)].
Auck·land ['ɔːklənd].
Au·den ['ɔːdn].
Au·gus·ta [ɔː'gʌstə].
Au·gus·tus [ɔː'gʌstəs] m.
Aus·ten ['ɒstɪn].
Aus·tin ['ɒstɪn].
Aus·tra·lia [ɒ'streɪljə].
Aus·tria ['ɒstrɪə].
Avon ['eɪvən].
Ax·min·ster ['æksmɪnstə*].
Ayr(·shire) ['eə*(ʃə*)].
Azores [ə'zɔːz] pl.

B

Bab·y·lon ['bæbɪlən].
Ba·con ['beɪkən].
Ba·den-Pow·ell [ˌbeɪdn'pəʊəl].

Ba·ha·mas [bə'hɑːməz] *pl.*
Bah·rain, Bah·rein [bɑː'reɪn].
Bal·dwin ['bɔːldwɪn] *m.*
Bâle [bɑːl].
Bal·four ['bælfə*].
Bal·kans ['bɔːlkənz] *pl.*
Bal·mor·al [bæl'mɒrəl].
Bal·tic Sea ['bɔːltɪk 'siː].
Bal·ti·more ['bɔːltɪmɔː*].
Ban·gla·desh [ˌbæŋglə'deʃ].
Bar·ba·dos [bɑː'beɪdəʊz].
Bar·thol·o·mew [bɑː'θɒləmjuː] *m.*
Bath [bɑːθ].
Bat·on Rouge [ˌbætən'ruːʒ].
Bat·ter·sea ['bætəsɪ].
Ba·var·ia [bə'veərɪə].
Bea·cons·field ['biːkənzfiːld].
Be·atrice ['bɪətrɪs] *f.*
Bea·ver·brook ['biːvəbrʊk].
Beck·et ['bekɪt].
Beck·y ['bekɪ] *f.*
Bed·ford ['bedfəd]; Bed·ford·shire ['bedfədʃə*].
Bel·fast [ˌbel'fɑːst].
Bel·gium ['beldʒəm].
Bel·grade [ˌbel'greɪd].
Bel·gra·via [bel'greɪvjə].
Be·lize [be'liːz].
Ben [ben] *m.*
Ben·e·dict ['benɪdɪkt] *m.*
Ben·gal [ˌbeŋ'gɔːl].
Ben·ja·min ['bendʒəmɪn] *m.*
Ben Ne·vis [ˌben 'nevɪs].
Berke·ley ['bɑːklɪ, U.S.A. 'bɜːklɪ].
Berk·shire ['bɑːkʃə*].
Ber·lin [bɜː'lɪn].
Ber·mu·das [bə'mjuːdəz] *pl.*
Ber·nard ['bɜːnəd] *m.*
Berne [bɜːn].
Bern·stein ['bɜːnstaɪn].
Ber·tha ['bɜːθə] *f.*
Ber·wick(·shire) ['berɪk(ʃə*)].
Bess, Bes·sy ['bes(ɪ)], Bet·sey ['betsɪ], Bet·ty ['betɪ] *f.*
Bill, Bil·ly ['bɪl(ɪ)] *m.*
Bir·ken·head ['bɜːkənhed].
Bir·ming·ham ['bɜːmɪŋəm].
Bis·cay ['bɪskeɪ]: *Bay of* ~.
Bis·marck ['bɪzmɑːk].
Blooms·bury ['bluːmzbərɪ].
Bob [bɒb] *m.*
Bo·he·mia [bəʊ'hiːmjə].
Boi·se ['bɔɪsiː].
Bol·eyn ['bʊlɪn]: *Anne* ~.
Bo·liv·ia [bə'lɪvɪə].
Bom·bay [ˌbɒm'beɪ].
Bo·na·parte ['bəʊnəpɑːt].
Booth [buːð].
Bos·ton ['bɒstən].
Bo·tswa·na [bʊ'tswɑːnə].
Bourne·mouth ['bɔːnməθ].
Brad·ford ['brædfəd].

Bra·zil [brə'zɪl].
Breck·nock(·shire) ['breknɒk(ʃə*)].
Brid·get ['brɪdʒɪt] *f.*
Brigh·ton ['braɪtn].
Bris·tol ['brɪstl].
Brit·ain ['brɪtn]: *Great* ~.
Bri·tan·nia [brɪ'tænjə].
Brit·ta·ny ['brɪtənɪ].
Brit·ten ['brɪtn].
Broad·way ['brɔːdweɪ].
Bron·të ['brɒntɪ].
Brook·lyn ['brʊklɪn].
Brow·ning ['braʊnɪŋ].
Bruges [bruːʒ].
Bruns·wick ['brʌnzwɪk].
Brus·sels ['brʌslz].
Bu·chan·an [bjuː'kænən].
Bu·cha·rest [ˌbjuːkə'rest].
Bud·dha ['bʊdə].
Bul·gar·ia [bʌl'geərɪə].
Bur·gun·dy ['bɜːgəndɪ].
Bur·ma ['bɜːmə].
Burns [bɜːnz].
Bu·run·di [bʊ'rʊndɪ].
Bute(·shire) ['bjuːt(ʃə*)].
By·ron ['baɪərən].

C

Caer·nar·von(·shire) [kə'nɑːvən(ʃə*)].
Cae·sar ['siːzə*].
Cain [keɪn].
Cai·ro ['kaɪərəʊ].
Caith·ness ['keɪθnes].
Ca·lais ['kæleɪ].
Cal·cut·ta [kæl'kʌtə].
Cal·i·for·nia [ˌkælɪ'fɔːnjə].
Cam·bo·dia [kæm'bəʊdjə].
Cam·bridge ['keɪmbrɪdʒ]; Cam·bridge·shire ['keɪmbrɪdʒʃə*].
Cam·er·oon [ˌkæməruːn].
Can·a·da ['kænədə].
Ca·nary Is·lands [kə'neərɪ 'aɪləndz] *pl.*
Can·ber·ra ['kænbərə].
Can·ter·bury ['kæntəbərɪ].
Cape Ca·nav·er·al ['keɪp kə'nævərəl].
Cape Town ['keɪptaʊn].
Cape Verde Is·lands [keɪp'vɜːd 'aɪləndz] *pl.*
Ca·pri ['kæpriː].
Car·diff ['kɑːdɪf].
Car·di·gan(·shire) ['kɑːdɪgən(ʃə*)].
Ca·rin·thia [kə'rɪnθɪə].
Car·lyle [kɑː'laɪl].
Car·mar·then(·shire) [kə'mɑːðn (-ʃə*)].
Car·ne·gie [kɑː'negɪ].
Car·o·line ['kærəlaɪn] *f.*
Car·pa·thi·ans [kɑː'peɪθjənz] *pl.*
Car·rie ['kærɪ] *f.*
Car·son City ['kɑːsn 'sɪtɪ].
Car·ter ['kɑːtə*].

Cath·er·ine ['kæθərɪn] f.
Cax·ton ['kækstən].
Ce·cil ['sesl] m.
Cec·i·ly ['sɪsɪlɪ] f.
Cey·lon [sɪ'lɒn].
Chad [tʃæd].
Cham·ber·lain ['tʃeɪmbəlɪn].
Char·ing Cross [ˌtʃærɪŋ'krɒs].
Char·le·magne ['ʃɑːləmeɪn].
Charles [tʃɑːlz] m.
Charles·ton ['tʃɑːlstən].
Char·lotte ['ʃɑːlət] f.
Chau·cer ['tʃɔːsə*].
Chel·sea ['tʃelsɪ].
Chel·ten·ham ['tʃeltnəm].
Chesh·ire ['tʃeʃə*].
Ches·ter·field ['tʃestəfiːld].
Chev·i·ot Hills ['tʃevɪət 'hɪlz] pl.
Chey·enne [ʃaɪ'æn].
Chi·ca·go [ʃɪ'kɑːgəʊ].
Chile ['tʃɪlɪ].
Chi·na ['tʃaɪnə].
Chip·pen·dale ['tʃɪpəndeɪl].
Chris·tian ['krɪstjən] m.
Chris·ti·na [krɪ'stiːnə] f.
Chris·to·pher ['krɪstəfə*] m.
Chrys·ler ['kraɪzlə*].
Chur·chill ['tʃɜːtʃɪl].
Cin·cin·nati [ˌsɪnsɪ'nætɪ].
Cis·sie ['sɪsɪ] f.
Clack·man·nan(·shire) [klæk'mænən (-ʃə*)].
Clap·ham ['klæpəm].
Clara ['kleərə], **Clare** [kleə*] f.
Clar·en·don ['klærəndən].
Cle·o·pat·ra [klɪə'pætrə].
Cleve·land ['kliːvlənd].
Clwyd ['kluːɪd].
Clyde [klaɪd].
Cole·ridge ['kəʊlərɪdʒ].
Co·logne [kə'ləʊn].
Co·lom·bia [kə'lɒmbɪə].
Co·lom·bo [kə'lʌmbəʊ].
Col·o·ra·do [ˌkɒlə'rɑːdəʊ].
Co·lum·bia [kə'lʌmbɪə].
Co·lum·bus [kə'lʌmbəs].
Com·o·ro Is·lands ['kɒmərəʊ 'aɪləndz] pl.
Con·cord ['kɒŋkɔːd].
Con·go ['kɒŋgəʊ].
Con·nect·i·cut [kə'netɪkət].
Con·stance ['kɒnstəns] f.
Con·stance ['kɒnstəns]: Lake of ~.
Con·stan·ti·no·ple [ˌkɒnstæntɪ'nəʊpl].
Cook [kʊk].
Coo·per ['kuːpə*].
Co·pen·ha·gen [ˌkəʊpn'heɪgən].
Co·di·lle·ras [ˌkɒdɪ'ljeərəs] pl.
Cor·inth ['kɒrɪnθ].
Cor·ne·lia [kɔː'niːljə] f.
Corn·wall ['kɔːnwəl].
Cos·ta Ri·ca [ˌkɒstə'riːkə].

Cov·ent Gar·den ['kɒvənt 'gɑːdn].
Cov·en·try ['kɒvəntrɪ].
Crete [kriːt].
Cri·mea [kraɪ'mɪə].
Crom·well ['krɒmwəl].
Cru·soe ['kruːsəʊ].
Cu·ba ['kjuːbə].
Cum·ber·land ['kʌmbələnd].
Cum·bria ['kʌmbrɪə].
Cy·prus ['saɪprəs].
Czecho·slo·va·kia [ˌtʃekəʊsləʊ'vækɪə].

D

Da·ho·mey [də'həʊmɪ].
Dal·ma·tia [dæl'meɪʃjə].
Dam·o·cles ['dæməkliːz].
Dan·iel ['dænjəl] m.
Dan·ube ['dænjuːb].
Dar·da·nelles [ˌdɑːdə'nelz] pl.
Dar·jee·ling [dɑː'dʒiːlɪŋ].
Dart·moor ['dɑːtˌmʊə*].
Dar·win ['dɑːwɪn].
Da·vid ['deɪvɪd] m.
Dee [diː].
De·foe [dɪ'fəʊ].
Del·a·ware ['deləweə*].
Den·bigh(·shire) ['denbɪ(ʃə*)].
Den·mark ['denmɑːk].
Den·ver ['denvə*].
Der·by(·shire) ['dɑːbɪ(ʃə*)].
Des Moines [dɪ'mɔɪn].
De·troit [də'trɔɪt].
Dev·on(·shire) ['devn(ʃə*)].
Dew·ey ['djuːɪ].
Di·ana [daɪ'ænə] f.
Dick [dɪk] m.
Dick·ens ['dɪkɪnz].
Dis·rae·li [dɪs'reɪlɪ].
Dol·ly ['dɒlɪ] f.
Do·min·i·can Re·pub·lic [də'mɪnɪkən rɪ'pʌblɪk].
Don·ald ['dɒnld] m.
Donne [dʌn, dɒn].
Don Qui·xote [ˌdɒn 'kwɪksət].
Dor·o·thy ['dɒrəθɪ] f.
Dor·set(·shire) ['dɔːsɪt(ʃə*)].
Dos Pas·sos [ˌdɒs 'pæsɒs].
Doug·las ['dʌgləs] m.
Do·ver ['dəʊvə*].
Down [daʊn].
Down·ing Street ['daʊnɪŋ 'striːt].
Drei·ser ['draɪsə].
Dry·den ['draɪdn].
Dub·lin ['dʌblɪn].
Dul·wich ['dʌlɪdʒ].
Dum·bar·ton(·shire) [dʌm'bɑːtn (-ʃə*)].
Dum·fries and Gal·lo·way [dʌm-'friːsən 'gæləweɪ]; **Dum·fries·shire** [dʌm'friːsʃə*].

Dun·kirk [dʌnˈkɜːk].
Dur·ban [ˈdɜːbən].
Dur·ham [ˈdʌrəm].
Dy·fed [ˈdʌvɪd].

E

East Lo·thi·an [ˈiːst ˈləʊðjən].
Ec·ua·dor [ˈekwədɔː*].
Ed·die [ˈedɪ] m.
Ed·in·burgh [ˈedɪnbərə].
Ed·i·son [ˈedɪsn].
Ed·mund [ˈedmənd] m.
Ed·ward [ˈedwəd] m.
Egypt [ˈiːdʒɪpt].
Ei·leen [ˈaɪliːn] f.
Eire [ˈeərə].
Ei·sen·how·er [ˈaɪznˌhaʊə*].
El·ea·nor [ˈelɪnə*] f.
Eli·jah [ɪˈlaɪdʒə] m.
El·i·nor [ˈelɪnə*] f.
El·iot [ˈeljət].
Eliz·a·beth [ɪˈlɪzəbəθ] f.
El·lis Is·land [ˈelɪs ˈaɪlənd].
El Sal·va·dor [el ˈsælvədɔː*].
Em·er·son [ˈeməsn].
Em·i·ly [ˈemɪlɪ] f.
Eng·land [ˈɪŋɡlənd].
Enid [ˈiːnɪd] f.
Enoch [ˈiːnɒk] m.
Ep·som [ˈepsəm].
Equa·to·ri·al Gui·nea [ˌekwəˈtɔːrɪəl ˈɡɪnɪ].
Erie [ˈɪərɪ].
Er·nest [ˈɜːnɪst] m.
Es·sex [ˈesɪks].
Eth·el [ˈeθl] f.
Ethi·o·pia [ˌiːθɪˈəʊpjə].
Eton [ˈiːtn].
Eu·gene [juːˈʒeɪn] m.
Eu·ge·nia [juːˈdʒiːnjə] f.
Eu·phra·tes [juːˈfreɪtiːz].
Eur·asia [jʊəˈreɪʃə].
Eu·rip·ides [jʊəˈrɪpɪdiːz].
Eu·rope [ˈjʊərəp].
Eu·stace [ˈjuːstəs] m.
Ev·ans [ˈevənz].
Eve [iːv] f.
Eve·lyn [ˈiːvlɪn] f.

F

Falk·land Is·lands [ˈfɔːklənd ˈaɪləndz] pl.
Fal·staff [ˈfɔːlstɑːf].
Far·a·day [ˈfærədɪ].
Faulk·ner [ˈfɔːknə*].
Fawkes [fɔːks].
Fe·li·cia [fəˈlɪsɪə] f.
Fe·lix [ˈfiːlɪks] m.
Fer·man·agh [fəˈmænə].
Fiel·ding [ˈfiːldɪŋ].

Fife(·shire) [ˈfaɪf(ʃə*)].
Fi·ji [ˌfiːˈdʒiː].
Fin·land [ˈfɪnlənd].
Firth of Forth [ˈfɜːθəvˈfɔːθ].
Fitz·ger·ald [fɪtsˈdʒerəld].
Flan·ders [ˈflɑːndəz].
Flem·ing [ˈflemɪŋ].
Flint(·shire) [ˈflɪnt(ʃə*)].
Flor·ence [ˈflɒrəns].
Flor·i·da [ˈflɒrɪdə].
Folke·stone [ˈfəʊkstən].
Ford [fɔːd].
For·syth [fɔːˈsaɪθ].
Foth·er·ing·hay [ˈfɒðərɪŋɡeɪ].
France [frɑːns].
Fran·ces [ˈfrɑːnsɪs] f.
Fran·cis [ˈfrɑːnsɪs] m.
Frank·fort [ˈfræŋkfət].
Frank·lin [ˈfræŋklɪn].
Fred(·dy) [ˈfred(ɪ)] m.
Fred·er·ic(k) [ˈfredrɪk] m.
Ful·ton [ˈfʊltən].

G

Ga·bon [ɡæˈbɒn].
Gains·bor·ough [ˈɡeɪnzbərə].
Gal·lup [ˈɡæləp].
Gals·wor·thy [ˈɡɔːlzwɜːðɪ].
Gam·bia [ˈɡæmbɪə].
Gan·ges [ˈɡændʒiːz].
Ga·za Strip [ˈɡɑːzə ˈstrɪp].
Ge·ne·va [dʒɪˈniːvə].
Gen·oa [ˈdʒenəʊə].
Geof·frey [ˈdʒefrɪ] m.
George [dʒɔːdʒ] m.
Geor·gia [ˈdʒɔːdʒə].
Ger·ald [ˈdʒerəld] m.
Ger·al·dine [ˈdʒerəldiːn] f.
Ger·ma·ny [ˈdʒɜːmənɪ].
Gersh·win [ˈɡɜːʃwɪn].
Ger·trude [ˈɡɜːtruːd] f.
Get·tys·burg [ˈɡetɪzbɜːɡ].
Gha·na [ˈɡɑːnə].
Ghent [ɡent].
Gi·bral·tar [dʒɪˈbrɔːltə*].
Giles [dʒaɪlz] m.
Gill [ɡɪl] f.
Gins·berg [ˈɡɪnzbɜːɡ].
Glad·stone [ˈɡlædstən].
Gla·mor·gan(·shire) [ɡləˈmɔːɡən (-ʃə*)].
Glas·gow [ˈɡlɑːsɡəʊ].
Glouces·ter(·shire) [ˈɡlɒstə*(ʃə*)].
Go·li·ath [ɡəʊˈlaɪəθ].
Gor·don [ˈɡɔːdn].
Goth·am [ˈɡəʊtəm].
Gra·ham [ˈɡreɪəm] m.
Gram·pi·an [ˈɡræmpjən].
Grand Can·yon [ɡrændˈkænjən].
Greece [ɡriːs].
Greene [ɡriːn].

Green·land ['griːnlənd].
Green·wich ['grɪnɪdʒ].
Greg·o·ry ['gregərɪ] *m.*
Gre·na·da [gre'neɪdə].
Gri·sons ['griːzɔ̃ːŋ].
Gros·ve·nor ['grəʊvnə*].
Gua·te·ma·la [ˌgwætɪ'mɑːlə].
Guern·sey ['gɜːnzɪ].
Guin·ea ['gɪnɪ].
Guin·e·vere ['gwɪnɪˌvɪə*].
Guin·ness ['gɪnɪs].
Gul·li·ver ['gʌlɪvə*].
Guy [gaɪ] *m.*
Guy·ana [gaɪ'ænə].
Gwen·do·len, Gwen·do·lyn ['gwendəlɪn] *f.*
Gwy·nedd ['gwɪnəð].

H

Hague [heɪg]: *the ~.*
Hai·ti ['heɪtɪ].
Hal·i·fax ['hælɪfæks].
Ham·il·ton ['hæmltən].
Ham·let ['hæmlɪt].
Ham·mer·smith ['hæməsmɪθ].
Hamp·shire ['hæmpʃə*].
Hamp·stead ['hæmpstɪd].
Han·no·ver ['hænəʊvə*].
Har·dy ['hɑːdɪ].
Har·old ['hærəld] *m.*
Har·ris·burg ['hærɪsbɜːg].
Har·row ['hærəʊ].
Har·ry ['hærɪ] *m.*
Hart·ford ['hɑːtfəd].
Har·vard Uni·ver·si·ty ['hɑːvəd ˌjuːnɪ'vɜːsətɪ].
Har·wich ['hærɪdʒ].
Has·tings ['heɪstɪŋz].
Ha·vana [hə'vænə].
Ha·waii [hə'waɪiː].
Heath·row ['hiːθrəʊ].
Heb·ri·des ['hebrɪdiːz] *pl.*
Hel·en ['helɪn] *f.*
Hel·e·na ['helɪnə] *f.*
Hel·i·go·land ['helɪgəʊlænd].
Hel·sin·ki ['helsɪŋkɪ].
Hem·ing·way ['hemɪŋweɪ].
Hen·ley ['henlɪ].
Hen·ry ['henrɪ] *m.*
Her·e·ford and Worces·ter ['herɪfədən 'wʊstə*].
Her·e·ford·shire ['herɪfədʃə*].
Hert·ford(·shire) ['hɑːfəd(ʃə*)].
Hesse ['hesɪ].
High·land ['haɪlənd].
Hi·ma·la·ya [ˌhɪmə'leɪə].
Hi·ro·shi·ma [hɪ'rɒʃɪmə].
Ho·garth ['həʊgɑːθ].
Hol·born ['həʊbən].
Hol·land ['hɒlənd].
Hol·ly·wood ['hɒlɪwʊd].

Holmes [həʊmz].
Ho·mer ['həʊmə*].
Hon·du·ras [hɒn'djʊərəs].
Ho·no·lu·lu [ˌhɒnə'luːluː].
How·ard ['haʊəd] *m.*
Hud·son ['hʌdsn].
Hugh [hjuː] *m.*
Hull [hʌl].
Hum·ber ['hʌmbə*]; **Hum·ber·side** ['hʌmbəsaɪd].
Hume [hjuːm].
Hun·ga·ry ['hʌŋgərɪ].
Hun·ting·don(·shire) ['hʌntɪŋdən (-ʃə*)].
Hux·ley ['hʌkslɪ].
Hyde Park [ˌhaɪd'pɑːk].

I

Ibe·ri·an Pen·in·su·la [aɪ'bɪərɪən pɪ'nɪnsjʊlə].
Ice·land ['aɪslənd].
Ida·ho ['aɪdəhəʊ].
Il·li·nois [ˌɪlɪ'nɔɪ].
In·dia ['ɪndjə].
In·di·ana [ˌɪndɪ'ænə].
In·di·a·nap·o·lis [ˌɪndɪə'næpəlɪs].
In·do·ne·sia [ˌɪndəʊ'niːzjə].
In·dus ['ɪndəs].
In·ver·ness(·shire) [ˌɪnvə'nes(ʃə*)].
Io·wa ['aɪəʊə].
Iran [ɪ'rɑːn].
Iraq [ɪ'rɑːk].
Ire·land ['aɪələnd].
Irene [aɪ'riːnɪ] *f.*
Ir·ving ['ɜːvɪŋ].
Isaac ['aɪzək] *m.*
Is·a·bel ['ɪzəbel] *f.*
Is·lam·abad [ɪz'lɑːməbɑːd].
Isle of Wight ['aɪləv 'waɪt].
Is·ling·ton ['ɪzlɪŋtən].
Is·ra·el ['ɪzreɪəl].
It·a·ly ['ɪtəlɪ].
Ivo·ry Coast ['aɪvərɪ 'kəʊst].

J

Jack [dʒæk] *m.*
Jack·son ['dʒæksn].
Ja·cob ['dʒeɪkəb] *m.*
Jaf·fa ['dʒæfə].
Ja·mai·ca [dʒə'meɪkə].
James [dʒeɪmz] *m.*
Jane [dʒeɪn] *f.*
Jan·et ['dʒænɪt] *f.*
Ja·pan [dʒə'pæn].
Jas·per ['dʒæspə*] *m.*
Ja·va ['dʒɑːvə].
Jef·fer·son ['dʒefəsn].
Je·ho·vah [dʒɪ'həʊvə].
Jen·ny ['dʒenɪ] *f.*
Jer·e·my ['dʒerɪmɪ] *m.*

Je·rome [dʒəˈrəʊm] m.
Jer·sey [ˈdʒɜːzɪ].
Je·ru·sa·lem [dʒəˈruːsələm].
Je·sus [ˈdʒiːzəs].
Jill [dʒɪl] f.
Jim(·my) [ˈdʒɪm(ɪ)] m.
Joan [dʒəʊn] f.
Job [dʒəʊb].
Joe [dʒəʊ] m.
Jo·han·nes·burg [dʒəʊˈhænɪsbɜːg].
John(·ny) [ˈdʒɒn(ɪ)] m.
John o' Groats [ˌdʒɒnəˈgrəʊts].
John·son [ˈdʒɒnsn].
Jon·a·than [ˈdʒɒnəθən] m.
Jon·son [ˈdʒɒnsn].
Jor·dan [ˈdʒɔːdn].
Jo·seph [ˈdʒəʊzɪf] m.
Jo·se·phine [ˈdʒəʊzɪfiːn] f.
Josh·ua [ˈdʒɒʃwə] m.
Joule [dʒuːl].
Joyce [dʒɔɪs].
Ju·lia [ˈdʒuːljə], **Ju·li·et** [ˈdʒuːljət] f.
Ju·lius [ˈdʒuːljəs] m.
Ju·neau [ˈdʒuːnəʊ].

K

Kan·sas [ˈkænzəs].
Kash·mere [kæʃˈmɪə*].
Kate [keɪt] f.
Kath·a·rine, Kath·er·ine [ˈkæθərɪn] f.
Kath·leen [ˈkæθliːn] f.
Keats [kiːts].
Kel·vin [ˈkelvɪn].
Ken·ne·dy [ˈkenɪdɪ].
Ken·sing·ton [ˈkenzɪŋtən].
Kent [kent].
Ken·tucky [kenˈtʌkɪ].
Ken·ya [ˈkenjə].
Kin·car·dine(·shire) [kɪnˈkɑːdɪn(ʃə*)].
Kin·ross(·shire) [kɪnˈrɒs(ʃə*)].
Kirk·cud·bright(·shire) [kəˈkuːbrɪ(-ʃə*)].
Kit·ty [ˈkɪtɪ] f.
Klon·dyke [ˈklɒndaɪk].
Knox [nɒks].
Ko·rea [kəˈrɪə].
Krem·lin [ˈkremlɪn].
Ku·wait [kʊˈweɪt].

L

Lab·ra·dor [ˈlæbrədɔː*].
Lake Erie [ˈleɪk ˈɪərɪ].
Lake Hu·ron [ˈleɪk ˈhjʊərən].
Lake Mich·i·gan [ˈleɪk ˈmɪʃɪgən].
Lake On·tar·io [ˈleɪk ɒnˈteərɪəʊ].
Lake Su·pe·ri·or [ˈleɪk suːˈpɪərɪə*].
Lam·beth [ˈlæmbəθ].
Lan·ark(·shire) [ˈlænək(ʃə*)].
Lan·ca·shire [ˈlæŋkəʃə*].
Lan·ca·ster [ˈlæŋkəstə*].
Land's End [ˌlændzˈend].

Lan·sing [ˈlænsɪŋ].
Laos [ˈlɑːɒs].
Lat·in Amer·i·ca [ˈlætɪn əˈmerɪkə].
Lat·via [ˈlætvɪə].
Laugh·ton [ˈlɔːtn].
Lau·rence, Law·rence [ˈlɒrəns] m.
Lear [lɪə*].
Leb·a·non [ˈlebənən].
Leeds [liːdz].
Leices·ter [ˈlestə*]; **Leices·ter·shire** [ˈlestəʃə*].
Leigh [liː].
Leon·ard [ˈlenəd] m.
Les·lie [ˈlezlɪ, U.S.A. ˈleslɪ] m., f.
Le·so·tho [ləˈsuːtuː].
Lew·is [ˈluːɪs] m.
Lex·ing·ton [ˈleksɪŋtən].
Li·be·ria [laɪˈbɪərɪə].
Lib·ya [ˈlɪbɪə].
Liech·ten·stein [ˈlɪktənstaɪn].
Lil·ian [ˈlɪlɪən] f.
Lin·coln [ˈlɪŋkən].
Lin·coln·shire [ˈlɪŋkənʃə*].
Lind·bergh [ˈlɪndbɜːg].
Li·o·nel [ˈlaɪənl] m.
Lis·bon [ˈlɪzbən].
Lith·u·a·nia [ˌlɪθjuːˈeɪnjə].
Liv·er·pool [ˈlɪvəpuːl].
Liv·ing·stone [ˈlɪvɪŋstən].
Liz(·zie) [ˈlɪz(ɪ)] f.
Lloyd [lɔɪd] m.
Loch Lo·mond [ˌlɒk ˈləʊmənd].
Loch Ness [ˌlɒk ˈnes].
Locke [lɒk].
Lom·bar·dy [ˈlɒmbədɪ].
Lon·don [ˈlʌndən].
Lon·don·der·ry [ˌlʌndənˈderɪ].
Lor·raine [lɒˈreɪn].
Los Al·a·mos [lɒsˈæləməʊs].
Los An·ge·les [lɒsˈændʒɪliːz].
Lo·thi·an [ˈləʊðjən].
Lou·is [ˈluːɪ(s); lʊɪ(s)] m.
Lou·i·sa [luːˈiːzə] f.
Lou·i·si·ana [luːˌɪziːˈænə].
Lu·cia [ˈluːsjə] f.
Lu·cius [ˈluːsjəs] m.
Lu·cy [ˈluːsɪ] f.
Lux·em·b(o)urg [ˈlʌksəmbɜːg].
Lyd·ia [ˈlɪdɪə] f.
Ly·ons [ˈlaɪənz].

M

Mab [mæb].
Ma·bel [ˈmeɪbl] f.
Ma·cau·lay [məˈkɔːlɪ].
Mac·beth [məkˈbeθ].
Mac·ken·zie [məˈkenzɪ].
Mad·a·gas·car [ˌmædəˈgæskə*].
Ma·dei·ra [məˈdɪərə].
Madge [mædʒ].
Mad·i·son [ˈmædɪsn].

Ma·dras [mə'drɑːs].
Ma·drid [mə'drɪd].
Mag·da·len ['mægdəlɪn, Oxford: 'mɔːdlɪn] f.
Mag·gie ['mægɪ] f.
Ma·hom·et [mæ'hɒmɪt] m.
Maine [meɪn].
Ma·la·wi [mə'lɑːwɪ].
Ma·lay·sia [mə'leɪzɪə].
Mal·dives ['mɔːldɪvz] pl.
Ma·li ['mɑːlɪ].
Mal·ta ['mɔːltə].
Man·ches·ter ['mæntʃɪstə*].
Man·chu·ria [mæn'tʃʊərɪə].
Man·hat·tan [mæn'hætn].
Man·i·to·ba [ˌmænɪ'təʊbə].
Mao Tse-tung [ˌmaʊtse'tʊŋ].
Mar·ga·ret ['mɑːgərɪt] f.
Ma·ria [mə'raɪə, mə'rɪə] f.
Mark [mɑːk] m.
Marl·bor·ough ['mɔːlbərə].
Mar·lowe ['mɑːləʊ].
Mar·tha ['mɑːθə] f.
Mary ['meərɪ] f.
Mary·land ['meərɪlænd].
Mary·le·bone ['mærələbən].
Mas·sa·chu·setts [ˌmæsə'tʃuːsɪts].
Ma(t)·thew ['mæθjuː] m.
Maud [mɔːd] f.
Maugham [mɔːm].
Mau·rice ['mɒrɪs] m.
Mau·ri·ta·nia [ˌmɒrɪ'teɪnjə].
Mau·ri·ti·us [mə'rɪʃəs].
May [meɪ] f.
Mayo ['meɪəʊ].
Med·i·ter·ra·nean (Sea) [ˌmedɪtə'reɪnjən ('siː)].
Mel·bourne ['melbən].
Mel·ville ['melvɪl].
Mer·i·on·eth(·shire) [ˌmerɪ'ɒnɪθ(ʃə*)].
Mer·sey·side ['mɜːzɪsaɪd].
Mex·i·co ['meksɪkəʊ].
Mi·ami [maɪ'æmɪ].
Mi·cha·el ['maɪkl] m.
Mich·i·gan ['mɪʃɪgən].
Mid·dle·sex ['mɪdlseks].
Mid Gla·mor·gan ['mɪd glə'mɔːgən].
Mid·lo·thi·an [mɪd'ləʊðjən].
Mid·west ['mɪd'west].
Mi·lan [mɪ'læn].
Mil·dred ['mɪldrɪd] f.
Mil·li·cent ['mɪlɪsnt] f.
Mil·ton ['mɪltən].
Mil·wau·kee [mɪl'wɔːkiː].
Min·ne·ap·o·lis [ˌmɪnɪ'æpəlɪs].
Min·ne·so·ta [ˌmɪnɪ'səʊtə].
Mis·sis·sip·pi [ˌmɪsɪ'sɪpɪ].
Mis·sou·ri [mɪ'zʊərɪ].
Moll [mɒl] f.
Mo·na·co ['mɒnəkəʊ].
Mon·go·lia [mɒŋ'gəʊljə].
Mon·mouth(·shire) ['mɒnməθ(ʃə*)].

Mon·roe [mən'rəʊ].
Mon·ta·na [mɒn'tænə].
Mont·gom·ery [mənt'gʌmərɪ]; Mont·gom·ery·shire [mənt'gʌm-ərɪʃə*].
Mont·pe·lier [mɒnt'piːljə*].
Mon·tre·al [ˌmɒntrɪ'ɔːl].
Mo·ra·via [mə'reɪvjə].
Mor·ay(·shire) ['mʌrɪ(ʃə*)].
More [mɔː*].
Mo·roc·co [mə'rɒkəʊ].
Mos·cow ['mɒskəʊ].
Mo·selle [mə'zel].
Mount Ev·er·est ['maʊnt 'evərɪst].
Mo·zam·bique [ˌməʊzəm'biːk].
Mu·ham·mad [məʊ'hæməd] m.
Mu·nich ['mjuːnɪk].
Mur·ray ['mʌrɪ].

N

Nairn(·shire) ['neən(ʃə*)].
Nai·ro·bi [naɪ'rəʊbɪ].
Nam·ib·ia [nə'mɪbɪə].
Nan·cy ['nænsɪ] f.
Nan·ga Par·bat ['næŋgə 'pʌbət].
Na·ples ['neɪplz].
Na·po·le·on [nə'pəʊljən].
Nash·ville ['næʃvɪl].
Naz·a·reth ['næzərəθ].
Ne·bras·ka [nɪ'bræskə].
Nell [nel], Nel·ly ['nelɪ] f.
Nel·son ['nelsn].
Ne·pal [nɪ'pɔːl].
Neth·er·lands ['neðələndz] pl.
Ne·vada [ne'vɑːdə].
New Bruns·wick [ˌnjuː'brʌnzwɪk].
New·cas·tle ['njuːkɑːsl].
New Del·hi [ˌnjuː'delɪ].
New Eng·land [ˌnjuː'ɪŋglənd].
New·found·land ['njuːfəndlənd].
New Hamp·shire [ˌnjuː'hæmpʃə*].
New Jer·sey [ˌnjuː'dʒɜːzɪ].
New Mex·i·co [ˌnjuː'meksɪkəʊ].
New Or·leans [ˌnjuː'ɔːlɪənz].
New·ton ['njuːtn].
New York [ˌnjuː'jɔːk].
New Zea·land [ˌnjuː'ziːlənd].
Ni·ag·a·ra [naɪ'ægərə].
Nic·a·ra·gua [ˌnɪkə'rægjʊə].
Nich·o·las ['nɪkələs] m.
Ni·ger ['naɪdʒə*].
Ni·ge·ria [naɪ'dʒɪərɪə].
Nile [naɪl].
Nix·on ['nɪksən].
No·bel [nəʊ'bel].
Nor·folk ['nɔːfək].
Nor·man·dy ['nɔːməndɪ].
North·amp·ton [nɔː'θæmptən]; North·amp·ton·shire [nɔː'θæmptən-ʃə*].
North Cape ['nɔːθkeɪp].

North Car·o·li·na ['nɔːθ kærə'laɪnə].
North Da·ko·ta ['nɔːθ də'kəutə].
North Sea ['nɔːθ 'siː].
North·um·ber·land [nɔː'θʌmbələnd].
North West Ter·ri·to·ries ['nɔːθ'west 'terɪtərɪz] *pl.*
Nor·way ['nɔːweɪ].
Nor·wich [Gt. Brit. 'nɒrɪdʒ, U.S.A. 'nɔːwɪtʃ].
Not·ting·ham ['nɒtɪŋəm]; **Not·ting·ham·shire** ['nɒtɪŋəmʃə*].
No·va Sco·tia [ˌnəuvə'skəuʃə].
Nu·rem·berg ['njuərəmbɜːg].

O

Oak Ridge ['əuk'rɪdʒ].
Oce·a·nia [ˌəuʃɪ'eɪnjə].
Ohio [əu'haɪəu].
Okla·ho·ma [ˌəuklə'həumə].
Ol·i·ver ['ɒlɪvə*] *m.*
Oliv·ia [ɒ'lɪvɪə] *f.*
Olym·pia [əu'lɪmpɪə].
Oma·ha ['əuməhaː].
Oman [əu'maːn].
O'Neill [əu'niːl].
On·tar·io [ɒn'teərɪəu].
Or·e·gon ['ɒrɪgən].
Ork·ney ['ɔːknɪ]: ~ *Islands.*
Or·well ['ɔːwəl].
Os·borne ['ɒzbən].
Ost·end [ɒ'stend].
Ot·ta·wa ['ɒtəwə].
Ouse [uːz].
Ox·ford ['ɒksfəd]; **Ox·ford·shire** ['ɒksfədʃə*].
Ozark Pla·teau ['əuzaːk 'plætəu].

P

Pa·cif·ic (Ocean) [pə'sɪfɪk ('əuʃn)].
Pad·ding·ton ['pædɪŋtən].
Pad·dy ['pædɪ] *m.*
Pak·i·stan [ˌpaːkɪ'staːn].
Pal·es·tine ['pæləstaɪn].
Pall Mall [ˌpæl'mæl].
Palm Beach ['paːm 'biːtʃ].
Pal·mer·ston ['paːməstən].
Pan·a·ma [ˌpænə'maː].
Pa·pua-New Guin·ea ['paːpuə ˌnjuː-'gɪnɪ].
Par·a·guay ['pærəgwaɪ].
Par·is ['pærɪs].
Pa·tri·cia [pə'trɪʃə] *f.*
Pat·rick ['pætrɪk] *m.*
Paul [pɔːl] *m.*
Pau·line [pɔː'liːn] *f.*
Pearl Har·bor ['pɜːl 'haːbə*].
Pee·bles(·shire) ['piːblz(ʃə*)].
Peg(·gy) ['peg(ɪ)] *f.*
Pe·king [piː'kɪŋ].
Pem·broke(·shire) ['pembruk(ʃə*)].

Penn·syl·va·nia [ˌpensɪl'veɪnjə].
Per·cy ['pɜːsɪ] *m.*
Per·sia ['pɜːʃə].
Perth(·shire) ['pɜːθ(ʃə*)].
Pe·ru [pə'ruː].
Pe·ter ['piːtə*].
Phil·a·del·phia [ˌfɪlə'delfjə].
Phil·ip ['fɪlɪp] *m.*
Phil·ip·pines ['fɪlɪpiːnz].
Phoe·nix ['fiːnɪks].
Pic·ca·dil·ly [ˌpɪkə'dɪlɪ].
Pied·mont ['piːdmənt].
Pierre ['pɪə*].
Pin·ter ['pɪntə*].
Pitts·burgh ['pɪtsbɜːg].
Plan·tag·e·net [plæn'tædʒənɪt].
Pla·to ['pleɪtəu].
Plym·outh ['plɪməθ].
Poe [pəu].
Po·land ['pəulənd].
Pol·ly ['pɒlɪ] *f.*
Pol·y·ne·sia [ˌpɒlɪ'niːzjə].
Pope [pəup].
Port·land ['pɔːtlənd].
Ports·mouth ['pɔːtsməθ].
Por·tu·gal ['pɔːtjugl].
Po·to·mac [pə'təumək].
Pound [paund].
Pow·ys ['pəuɪs].
Prague [praːg].
Pre·to·ria [prɪ'tɔːrɪə].
Prince Ed·ward Is·land [ˌprɪns'ed-wəd 'aɪlənd].
Prince·ton ['prɪnstən].
Prov·i·dence ['prɒvɪdəns].
Prus·sia ['prʌʃə].
Puer·to Ri·co [ˌpwɜːtəu'riːkəu].
Pul·itz·er ['pulɪtsə*].
Pun·jab [pʌn'dʒɑːb].
Pyr·e·nees [ˌpɪrə'niːz].

Q

Que·bec [kwɪ'bek].
Queens [kwiːnz].

R

Ra·chel ['reɪtʃl] *f.*
Rad·nor(·shire) ['rædnə*(ʃə*)].
Ra·leigh ['rɔːlɪ, 'raːlɪ, 'rælɪ].
Ralph [reɪf, rælf] *m.*
Ray·mond ['reɪmənd] *m.*
Rea·gan ['reɪgən].
Reg·i·nald ['redʒɪnld] *m.*
Ren·frew(·shire) ['renfruː(ʃə*)].
Rhine [raɪn].
Rhode Is·land [ˌrəud 'aɪlənd].
Rhodes [rəudz].
Rho·de·sia [rəu'diːzjə].
Rich·ard ['rɪtʃəd] *m.*
Rich·ard·son ['rɪtʃədsn].
Rich·mond ['rɪtʃmənd].

Rob·ert ['rɒbət] *m.*
Rob·in ['rɒbɪn] *m.*
Rocke·fel·ler ['rɒkɪfelə*].
Rocky Moun·tains ['rɒkɪ 'maʊntɪnz] *pl.*
Rog·er ['rɒdʒə*] *m.*
Ro·ma·nia [ruːˈmeɪnjə].
Rome [rəʊm].
Ro·meo ['rəʊmɪəʊ].
Roo·se·velt ['rəʊzəvelt].
Ross and Crom·ar·ty ['rɒsən 'krɒmətɪ].
Rox·burgh(·shire) ['rɒksbərə(ʃə*)].
Rud·yard ['rʌdjəd] *m.*
Rug·by ['rʌɡbɪ].
Rus·sell ['rʌsl].
Rus·sia ['rʌʃə].
Rut·land(·shire) ['rʌtlənd(ʃə*)].
Rwan·da [rʊˈændə].

S

Sac·ra·men·to [ˌsækrəˈmentəʊ].
Sa·ha·ra [səˈhɑːrə].
Sa·lem ['seɪlem].
Salis·bury ['sɔːlzbərɪ].
Sal·ly ['sælɪ] *f.*
Salt Lake City ['sɔːlt'leɪk 'sɪtɪ].
Sam [sæm] *m.*
Sam·son ['sæmsn].
Sam·u·el ['sæmjʊəl] *m.*
San Fran·cis·co [ˌsænfrənˈsɪskəʊ].
San Ma·ri·no [ˌsænməˈriːnəʊ].
San·ta Fe [ˌsæntəˈfeɪ].
Sar·a(h) ['seərə] *f.*
Sar·din·ia [sɑːˈdɪnjə].
Sas·katch·e·wan [səsˈkætʃɪwən].
Sau·di Ara·bia [ˌsaʊdɪəˈreɪbɪə].
Sa·voy [səˈvɔɪ].
Sax·o·ny ['sæksənɪ].
Scan·di·na·via [ˌskændɪˈneɪvjə].
Scot·land ['skɒtlənd].
Scott [skɒt].
Se·at·tle [sɪˈætl].
Sel·kirk(·shire) ['selkɜːk(ʃə*)].
Sen·e·gal [ˌsenɪˈɡɔːl].
Seoul [səʊl].
Sev·ern ['sevən].
Sey·chelles [seɪˈʃelz] *pl.*
Shake·speare ['ʃeɪkˌspɪə*].
Shaw [ʃɔː].
Shef·field ['ʃefiːld].
Shel·ley ['ʃelɪ].
Sher·lock ['ʃɜːlɒk] *m.*
Shet·land ['ʃetlənd]: ~ *Islands.*
Shrop·shire ['ʃrɒpʃə*].
Shy·lock ['ʃaɪlɒk].
Si·be·ria [saɪˈbɪərɪə].
Si·byl ['sɪbɪl] *f.*
Sic·i·ly ['sɪsɪlɪ].
Sid·ney ['sɪdnɪ] *m.*
Si·er·ra Le·one [sɪˌerəlɪˈəʊn].

Sik·kim ['sɪkɪm].
Si·nai ['saɪnɪaɪ]: ~ *Peninsula.*
Sin·clair ['sɪŋkleə*] *m.*
Sin·ga·pore ['sɪŋɡəpɔː*].
Sing Sing ['sɪŋsɪŋ].
Si·oux [suː].
Snow·don ['snəʊdn].
Soc·ra·tes ['sɒkrətiːz].
So·fia ['səʊfjə].
So·ho ['səʊhəʊ].
Sol·o·mon ['sɒləmən].
So·ma·lia [səʊˈmɑːlɪə].
Som·er·set(·shire) ['sʌməsɪt(ʃə*)].
So·phia [səʊˈfaɪə] *f.*
Soph·o·cles ['sɒfəkliːz].
So·phy ['səʊfɪ] *f.*
South Af·ri·ca [saʊθˈæfrɪkə].
South·amp·ton [saʊθˈæmptən].
South Car·o·li·na ['saʊθ kærəˈlaɪnə].
South Da·ko·ta ['saʊθ dəˈkəʊtə].
South Gla·mor·gan ['saʊθ ɡləˈmɔːɡən].
South·wark ['sʌðək, 'saʊθwək].
So·vi·et Union ['səʊvɪet 'juːnjən].
Spain [speɪn].
Spring·field ['sprɪŋfiːld].
Sri Lan·ka [ˌsriːˈlæŋkə].
Staf·ford(·shire) ['stæfəd(ʃə*)].
Stein·beck ['staɪnbek].
Ste·phen·son ['stiːvnsn].
Ste·ven·son ['stiːvnsn].
Stir·ling(·shire) ['stɜːlɪŋ(ʃə*)].
St. Law·rence [snt'lɒrəns].
St. Lou·is [snt'lʊɪs].
Stone·henge [ˌstəʊn'hendʒ].
St. Pan·cras [snt'pæŋkrəs].
St. Paul [snt'pɔːl].
Stra·chey ['streɪtʃɪ].   ['eɪvn].
Strat·ford-on-Avon [ˌstrætfədɒn-
Strath·clyde [stræθ'klaɪd].
Stu·art [stjʊət].
Su·dan [suːˈdɑːn].
Su·ez ['suːɪz].
Suf·folk ['sʌfək].
Su·ri·nam [ˌsʊərɪˈnæm].
Sur·rey ['sʌrɪ].
Su·san ['suːzn] *f.*
Sus·que·han·na [ˌsʌskwɪˈhænə].
Sus·sex ['sʌsɪks].
Suth·er·land ['sʌðələnd].
Swan·sea ['swɒnzɪ].
Swa·zi·land ['swɑːzɪlænd].
Swe·den ['swiːdn].
Swift [swɪft].
Swit·zer·land ['swɪtsələnd].
Syd·ney ['sɪdnɪ].
Syr·ia ['sɪrɪə].

T

Tai·wan [taɪˈwɑːn].
Tal·la·has·see [ˌtæləˈhæsɪ].

Tan·gier [tæn'dʒɪə*].
Tan·sa·nia [ˌtænzə'nɪə].
Tas·ma·nia [tæz'meɪnjə].
Tay·lor ['teɪlə*].
Tay·side ['teɪsaɪd].
Ted(·dy) ['ted(ɪ)] m.
Teign·mouth ['tɪnməθ].
Ten·nes·see [ˌtenə'siː].
Ten·ny·son ['tenɪsn].
Tex·as ['teksəs].
Thack·er·ay ['θækərɪ].
Thai·land ['taɪlænd].
Thames [temz].
The·o·bald ['θɪəbɔːld] m.
The·o·dore ['θɪədɔː*] m.
The·re·sa [tɪ'riːzə] f.
Thom·as ['tɒməs] m.
Tho·reau ['θɔːrəʊ].
Ti·bet [tɪ'bet].
Ti·gris ['taɪgrɪs].
Tim [tɪm] m.
Ti·mor ['tiːmɔː*].
Tim·o·thy ['tɪməθɪ] m.
To·bi·as [tə'baɪəs] m.
To·by ['təʊbɪ] m.
To·go ['təʊgəʊ].
Tom(·my) ['tɒm(ɪ)] m.
Ton·ga ['tɒŋgə].
To·pe·ka [təʊ'piːkə].
To·ron·to [tə'rɒntəʊ].
Tor·quay [tɔː'kiː].
Toyn·bee ['tɔɪnbɪ].
Tra·fal·gar [trə'fælgə*].
Trans·vaal ['trænzvɑːl].
Trent [trent].
Tren·ton ['trentn].
Tri·este [triː'est].
Trin·i·dad and To·ba·go ['trɪnɪdæd-ən təʊ'beɪgəʊ].
Trol·lope ['trɒləp].
Tru·man ['truːmən].
Tu·dor ['tjuːdə*].
Tu·ni·sia [tjuː'nɪzɪə].
Tur·key ['tɜːkɪ].
Tur·ner ['tɜːnə*].
Twain [tweɪn].
Tyne and Wear ['taɪnənd 'wɪə*].
Ty·rol ['tɪrəl].
Ty·rone [tɪ'rəʊn].

U

Ugan·da [juː'gændə].
Ukraine [juː'kreɪn].
Ul·ster ['ʌlstə*].
Union of So·vi·et So·cial·ist Re·pub·lics ['juːnjənəv 'səʊvɪet 'səʊʃəlɪst rɪ'pʌblɪks].
Unit·ed King·dom [juː'naɪtɪd 'kɪŋdəm].
Unit·ed States of Amer·i·ca [juː'naɪtɪd 'steɪtsəv ə'merɪkə].

Up·per Vol·ta ['ʌpə 'vɒltə].
Uru·guay ['jʊərʊgwaɪ].
Utah ['juːtɑː].

V

Val·en·tine ['væləntaɪn] m., f.
Van·cou·ver [væn'kuːvə*].
Vat·i·can ['vætɪkən].
Vaughan [vɔːn].
Vaux·hall [ˌvɒks'hɔːl].
Ven·e·zu·e·la [ˌvene'zweɪlə].
Ven·ice ['venɪs].
Ver·mont [vɜː'mɒnt].
Vic·to·ria [vɪk'tɔːrɪə] f.
Vi·en·na [vɪ'enə].
Viet·nam, Viet Nam [ˌvjet'næm].
Vir·gin·ia [və'dʒɪnjə].
Viv·i·an ['vɪvɪən] m., f.
Vol·ga ['vɒlgə].

W

Wales [weɪlz].
Wal·lace ['wɒlɪs].
Wal·ter ['wɔːltə*] m.
War·saw ['wɔːsɔː].
War·wick(·shire) ['wɒrɪk(ʃə*)].
Wash·ing·ton ['wɒʃɪŋtən].
Wa·ter·loo [ˌwɔːtə'luː].
Watt [wɒt].
Waugh [wɔː].
Web·ster ['webstə*].
Wedg·wood ['wedʒwʊd].
Wel·ling·ton ['welɪŋtən].
Wem·bley ['wemblɪ].
West·ern Sa·moa ['westən sə'məʊə].
West Gla·mor·gan ['west glə'mɔːgən].
West In·dies ['west 'ɪndɪz].
West Lo·thi·an ['west 'ləʊðjən].
West Mid·lands ['west 'mɪdləndz].
West·min·ster ['westmɪnstə*].
West·mor·land ['westmələnd].
West·pha·lia [west'feɪljə].
West Vir·gin·ia ['west və'dʒɪnjə].
Wey·mouth ['weɪməθ].
White·hall [ˌwaɪt'hɔːl].
Whit·man ['wɪtmən].
Wig·town(·shire) ['wɪgtən(ʃə*)].
Wilde [waɪld].
Wil·der ['waɪldə*].
Will [wɪl], **Wil·liam** ['wɪljəm] m.
Wil·son ['wɪlsn].
Wilt·shire ['wɪltʃə*].
Wim·ble·don ['wɪmbldən].
Win·ches·ter ['wɪntʃɪstə*].
Win·ni·peg ['wɪnɪpeg].
Win·ston ['wɪnstən] m.
Wis·con·sin [wɪs'kɒnsɪn].
Wolfe [wʊlf].
Wol·sey ['wʊlzɪ].
Woolf [wʊlf].

Worces·ter ['wʊstə*]; **Worces·ter-shire** ['wʊstəʃə*].
Words·worth ['wɜːdzwəθ].
Wren [ren].
Wyc·liffe ['wɪklɪf].
Wy·o·ming [waɪ'əʊmɪŋ].

X

Xan·thip·pe [zæn'θɪpɪ] *f.*

Y

Yale [jeɪl].
Yeats [jeɪts].

Yel·low·stone ['jeləʊstəʊn].
Ye·men ['jemən].
York [jɔːk]; **York·shire** ['jɔːkʃə*].
Yo·sem·i·te [jəʊ'semɪtɪ].
Yu·go·sla·via [ˌjuːgəʊ'slɑːvjə].
Yu·kon Ter·ri·to·ry ['juːkɒn 'terɪtərɪ].

Z

Zach·a·ri·ah [ˌzækə'raɪə], **Zach·a·ry** ['zækərɪ] *m.*
Zaire [zɑː'ɪə*].
Zam·bia ['zæmbɪə].
Zet·land ['zetlənd].
Zu·rich ['zjʊərɪk].

Irregular Verbs

abide - abode, abided - abode, abided
arise - arose - arisen
awake - awoke - awoke, awaked
backslide - backslid - backslid
be - was, were - been
bear - bore - borne; born
beat - beat - beaten
become - became - become
befall - befell - befallen
beget - begot - begotten
begin - began - begun
behold - beheld - beheld
bend - bent - bent
bereave - bereft; bereaved - bereft; bereaved
beseech - besought, beseeched - besought, beseeched
beset - beset - beset
bestride - bestrode - bestridden
bet - bet, betted - bet, betted
betake - betook - betaken
bid - bid; bade - bid; bidden
bind - bound - bound
bite - bit - bitten
bleed - bled - bled
bless - blessed, blest - blessed, blest
blow - blew - blown
break - broke - broken
breed - bred - bred
bring - brought - brought
broadcast - broadcast, broadcasted - broadcast, broadcasted
browbeat - browbeat - browbeaten
build - built - built
burn - burnt, burned - burnt, burned
burst - burst - burst
buy - bought - bought
cast - cast - cast
catch - caught - caught
chide - chided, chid - chided, chid, chidden
choose - chose - chosen
cleave - clove, cleft - cloven, cleft
cling - clung - clung
clothe - clothed, (old form) clad - clothed, (old form) clad
come - came - come
cost - cost - cost
creep - crept - crept
crow - crowed; crew - crowed
cut - cut - cut
dare - dared, durst - dared

deal - dealt - dealt
dig - dug - dug
do - did - done
draw - drew - drawn
dream - dreamed, dreamt - dreamed, dreamt
drink - drank - drunk
drive - drove - driven
dwell - dwelt - dwelt
eat - ate - eaten
fall - fell - fallen
feed - fed - fed
feel - felt - felt
fight - fought - fought
find - found - found
flee - fled - fled
fling - flung - flung
fly - flew - flown
forbear - forbore - forborne
forbid - forbade - forbidden
forecast - forecast, forecasted - forecast, forecasted
forego - forewent - foregone
foresee - foresaw - foreseen
foretell - foretold - foretold
forget - forgot - forgotten
forgive - forgave - forgiven
forgo - forwent - forgone
forsake - forsook - forsaken
forswear - forswore - forsworn
freeze - froze - frozen
gainsay - gainsaid - gainsaid
get - got - got, (U.S.A.) gotten
gild - gilded - gilded, gilt
gird - girded, girt - girded, girt
give - gave - given
go - went - gone
grind - ground - ground
grow - grew - grown
hamstring - hamstrung, hamstringed - hamstrung, hamstringed
hang - hung; hanged - hung; hanged
have - had - had
hear - heard - heard
heave - heaved, hove - heaved, hove
hew - hewed - hewn, hewed
hide - hid - hidden
hit - hit - hit
hold - held - held
hurt - hurt - hurt
inlay - inlaid - inlaid
keep - kept - kept

kneel - knelt, kneeled - knelt, kneeled
knit - knitted, knit - knitted, knit
know - knew - known
lay - laid - laid
lead - led - led
lean - leaned, leant - leaned, leant
leap - leaped, leapt - leaped, leapt
learn - learned, learnt - learned, learnt
leave - left - left
lend - lent - lent
let - let - let
lie - lay - lain
light - lit, lighted - lit, lighted
lose - lost - lost
make - made - made
mean - meant - meant
meet - met - met
melt - melted - melted, (old form) molten
misdeal - misdealt - misdealt
misgive - misgave - misgiven
mislay - mislaid - mislaid
mislead - misled - misled
misspell - misspelled, misspelt - misspelled, misspelt
misspend - misspent - misspent
mistake - mistook - mistaken
misunderstand - misunderstood - misunderstood
mow - mowed - mowed, mown
offset - offset - offset
outbid - outbid - outbid
outdo - outdid - outdone
outgo - outwent - outgone
outgrow - outgrew - outgrown
outrun - outran - outrun
overbear - overbore - overborne
overcast - overcast - overcast
overcome - overcame - overcome
overdo - overdid - overdone
overdraw - overdrew - overdrawn
overgrow - overgrew - overgrown
overhang - overhung - overhung
overhear - overheard - overheard
overlay - overlaid - overlaid
override - overrode - overridden
overrun - overran - overrun
oversee - oversaw - overseen
oversleep - overslept - overslept
overtake - overtook - overtaken
overthrow - overthrew - overthrown
partake - partook - partaken
pay - paid - paid
put - put - put
read - read - read
recast - recast - recast
redo - redid - redone
rend - rent - rent
repay - repaid - repaid
rid - rid, ridded - rid
ride - rode - ridden
ring - rang - rung

rise - rose - risen
run - ran - run
saw - sawed - sawn, sawed
say - said - said
see - saw - seen
seek - sought - sought
sell - sold - sold
send - sent - sent
set - set - set
sew - sewed - sewed, sewn
shake - shook - shaken
shear - sheared - shorn, sheared
shed - shed - shed
shine - shone - shone
shoe - shod - shod
shoot - shot - shot
show - showed - shown, showed
shrink - shrank - shrunk
shut - shut - shut
sing - sang - sung
sink - sank - sunk
sit - sat - sat
slay - slew - slain
sleep - slept - slept
slide - slid - slid
sling - slung - slung
slink - slunk - slunk
slit - slit - slit
smell - smelt - smelt
smite - smote - smitten
sow - sowed - sown, sowed
speak - spoke - spoken
speed - sped; speeded - sped; speeded
spell - spelt, spelled - spelt, spelled
spend - spent - spent
spill - spilt, spilled - spilt, spilled
spin - spun, span - spun
spit - spat - spat
split - split - split
spoil - spoilt, spoiled - spoilt, spoiled
spread - spread - spread
spring - sprang - sprung
stand - stood - stood
stave - staved, stove - staved, stove
steal - stole - stolen
stick - stuck - stuck
sting - stung - stung
stink - stank, stunk - stunk
strew - strewed - strewed, strewn
stride - strode - stridden
strike - struck - struck, (old form) stricken
string - strung - strung
strive - strove - striven
swear - swore - sworn
sweat - sweated, (U.S.A.) sweat - sweated, (U.S.A.) sweat
sweep - swept - swept
swell - swelled - swollen, swelled
swim - swam - swum
swing - swung - swung
take - took - taken

teach - taught - taught	**undo** - undid - undone
tear - tore - torn	**unstring** - unstrung - unstrung
telecast - telecast, telecasted - telecast, telecasted	**uphold** - upheld - upheld
tell - told - told	**upset** - upset - upset
think - thought - thought	**wake** - woke, waked - waked, woke(n)
thrive - throve, thrived - thriven, thrived	**waylay** - waylaid - waylaid
throw - threw - thrown	**wear** - wore - worn
thrust - thrust - thrust	**weave** - wove - woven
tread - trod - trodden, trod	**weep** - wept - wept
unbend - unbent - unbent	**wet** - wet, wetted - wet, wetted
undercut - undercut - undercut	**win** - won - won
undergo - underwent - undergone	**wind** - wound - wound
underlie - underlay - underlain	**withdraw** - withdrew - withdrawn
undersell - undersold - undersold	**withhold** - withheld - withheld
understand - understood - understood	**withstand** - withstood - withstood
undertake - undertook - undertaken	**work** - worked, (old form) wrought - worked, (old form) wrought
underwrite - underwrote - underwritten	**wring** - wrung - wrung
	write - wrote - written

British Decimal Coinage (£.p.)

£1 = 100 pence

Coins	½ p	a halfpenny		5 p	a fivepenny piece
	1 p	a penny		10 p	a tenpenny piece
	2 p	a twopenny piece		50 p	a fifty pence piece
Notes	£1, £5, £10, £20				

Former British Coinage (£.s.d.)

(until 14 February 1971)
£1 = 20 shillings = 240 pence.

Coins	halfpenny	½d.	shilling	1/-, 1s.
	penny	1d.	two shillings (florin)	2/-, 2s.
	threepence	3d.	half-crown, half a crown	2/6, 2s. 6d.
	sixpence	6d.		
Notes	ten shillings	10/-, 10s.	five pounds	£5
	one pound	£1	ten pounds	£10

British and American
Weights and Measures

Linear Measure

1 line	= 2.12 mm	
1 inch	= 12 lines	= 2.54 cm
1 foot	= 12 inches	= 30.48 cm
1 yard	= 3 feet	= 91.44 cm
1 (statute) mile		
	= 1760 yards	= 1.609 km
1 hand	= 4 inches	= 10.16 cm
1 rod (perch, pole)		
	= 5½ yards	= 5.029 m
1 chain	= 4 rods	= 20.117 m
1 furlong	= 10 chains	= 201.168 m

Nautical Measure

1 fathom = 6 feet = 1.829 m
1 cable's length
    = 100 fathoms = 182.9 m
    (Gt. Brit., mil.)
    = 608 feet = 185.3 m
    (U.S.A., mil.)
    = 720 feet = 219.5 m
1 nautical mile
    = 10 cables' length
    = 1.852 km

Square Measure

1 square inch = 6.452 cm²
1 square foot = 144 square inches
    = 929.029 cm²
1 square yard = 9 square feet
    = 8361.26 cm²
1 acre   = 4840 square yards
    = 4046.8 m²
1 square mile = 640 acres
    = 259 ha = 2.59 km²
**1 square rod (square pole, square
perch)** = 30¼ square yards
    = 25.293 m²
1 rood   = 40 square rods
    = 1011.72 m²
1 acre   = 4 roods = 4046.8 m²

Cubic Measure

1 cubic inch	= 16.387 cm³	
1 cubic foot	= 1728 cubic inches	
	= 0.02832 m³	
1 cubic yard		
	= 27 cubic feet	
	= 0.7646 m³	

British Measure of Capacity

Dry and Liquid Measure

1 gill	= 0.142 l	
1 pint	= 4 gills	= 0.568 l
1 quart	= 2 pints	= 1.136 l
1 gallon	= 4 quarts	= 4.5459 l
1 quarter	= 64 gallons	= 290.935 l

Dry Measure

1 peck	= 2 gallons	= 9.092 l
1 bushel	= 4 pecks	= 36.368 l

Liquid Measure

1 barrel	= 36 gallons	= 163.656 l

American Measure of Capacity

Dry Measure

1 pint	= 0.5506 l	
1 quart	= 2 pints	= 1.1012 l
1 gallon	= 4 quarts	= 4.405 l
1 peck	= 2 gallons	= 8.8096 l
1 bushel	= 4 pecks	= 35.2383 l

Liquid Measure

1 gill	= 0.1183 l	
1 pint	= 4 gills	= 0.4732 l
1 quart	= 2 pints	= 0.9464 l
1 gallon	= 4 quarts	= 3.7853 l
1 barrel	= 31½ gallons	
	= 119.228 l	
1 barrel petroleum		
	= 42 gallons	= 158.97 l

Apothecaries' Fluid Measure

1 minim
 (Gt. Brit.) = 0.0592 ml
 (U.S.A.) = 0.0616 ml

1 fluid dram = 60 minims
 (Gt. Brit.) = 3.5515 ml
 (U.S.A.) = 3.6966 ml

1 fluid ounce = 8 drams
 (Gt. Brit.) = 0.0284 l
 (U.S.A.) = 0.0296 l

1 pint
 (Gt. Brit.) = 20 fluid ounces
    = 0.5683 l
 (U.S.A.) = 16 fluid ounces
    = 0.4732 l

 (Gt. Brit.) = 112 pounds
    = 50.802 kg
 (U.S.A.) = 100 pounds
    = 45.359 kg

1 long ton
 (Gt. Brit.) = 20 hundredweights
    = 1016.05 kg

1 short ton
 (U.S.A.) = 20 hundredweights
    = 907.185 kg

1 stone = 14 pounds = 6.35 kg

1 quarter (Gt. Brit.) = 28 pounds
    = 12.701 kg
 (U.S.A.) = 25 pounds
    = 11.339 kg

Avoirdupois Weight

1 grain = 0.0648 g
1 dram = 27,3438 grains
   = 1.772 g
1 ounce = 16 drams = 28.35 g
1 pound = 16 ounces = 453.59 g
1 hundredweight = 1 quintal

Troy Weight

1 grain = 0.0648 g
1 pennyweight
   = 24 grains = 1.5552 g
1 ounce = 20 pennyweights
   = 31.1035 g
1 pound = 12 ounces
   = 373.2418 g

Numerals

CARDINAL NUMBERS		ORDINAL NUMBERS	
0	nought, zero, cipher	1st	first
1	one	2nd	second
2	two	3rd	third
3	three	4th	fourth
4	four	5th	fifth
5	five	6th	sixth
6	six	7th	seventh
7	seven	8th	eighth
8	eight	9th	ninth
9	nine	10th	tenth
10	ten	11th	eleventh
11	eleven	12th	twelfth
12	twelve	13th	thirteenth
13	thirteen	14th	fourteenth
14	fourteen	15th	fifteenth
15	fifteen	16th	sixteenth
16	sixteen	17th	seventeenth
17	seventeen	18th	eighteenth
18	eighteen	19th	nineteenth
19	nineteen	20th	twentieth
20	twenty	21st	twenty-first
21	twenty-one	22nd	twenty-second
22	twenty-two	23rd	twenty-third
30	thirty	30th	thirtieth
31	thirty-one	31th	thirty-first
40	forty	40th	fortieth
41	forty-one	41st	forty-first
50	fifty	50th	fiftieth
51	fifty-one	51st	fifty-first
60	sixty	60th	sixtieth
61	sixty-one	61st	sixty-first
70	seventy	70th	seventieth
71	seventy-one	71st	seventy-first
80	eighty	80th	eightieth
81	eighty-one	81st	eighty-first
90	ninety	90th	ninetieth
100	a (or one) hundred	100th	(one) hundredth
101	hundred and one	101st	hundred and first
200	two hundred	200th	two hundredth
572	five hundred and seventy-two	300th	three hundredth
1,000	a (or one) thousand	572nd	five hundred and seventy-second
2,000	two thousand	1,000th	(one) thousandth
1,000,000	a (or one) million	2,000th	two thousandth
2,000,000	two million	1,000,000th	(one) millionth
1,000,000,000	a (or one) milliard, (U.S.A.) billion	2,000,000th	two millionth
1,000,000,000,000	a (or one) billion, (U.S.A.) trillion		

FRACTIONAL NUMBERS

$\frac{1}{2}$	one (*or* a) half
$1\frac{1}{2}$	one and a half
$\frac{1}{2}$ m.	half a mile
$\frac{1}{3}$	one (*or* a) third
$\frac{2}{3}$	two thirds
$\frac{1}{4}$	one (*or* a) fourth
	one (*or* a) quarter
$\frac{3}{4}$	three fourths, three quarters
$2\frac{1}{4}$ h.	two hours and a quarter
$\frac{1}{5}$	one (*or* a) fifth
$\frac{1}{6}$	one (*or* a) sixth
$3\frac{4}{5}$	three and four fifths
.4	point four
2.5	two point five

OTHER NUMERICAL VALUES

Single
double
threefold, treble, triple
fourfold, quadruple
fivefold, etc.

Once
twice
three times
four times
five times, etc.
twice as much (*or* many)
once more

Firstly *or* in the first place
secondly *or* in the second place
thirdly *or* in the third place, etc.

Abkürzungen und Symbole

&, &	and	*engin.*	engineering
abbr.	abbreviation	*esp.*	especial(ly)
adj., adjs.	adjective(s)	*etc.*	et cetera, and others
adv., advs.	adverb(s)		
aer.	aeronautics		
agr.	agriculture	*f.*	feminine
anat.	anatomy	*fig.*	figurative(ly)
arch.	architecture	*Fr.*	French
attrib.	attributive(ly)		
		geogr.	geography
bibl.	biblical	*geol.*	geology
biol.	biology	*geom.*	geometry
bot.	botany	*gram.*	grammar
		Gt. Brit.	Great Britain
cf.	compare		
chem.	chemistry	*hist.*	historical; history
colloq.	colloquial	*humor.*	humorous(ly)
comm.	commerce		
comp.	comparative		
conj.	conjunction	*i.e.*	that is
contp.	contemptuously	*imper.*	imperative
		impers.	impersonal
		indef. art.	indefinite article
def. art.	definite article	*inf.*	infinitive
dem.	demonstrative	*int.*	interjection
derog.	derogatory	*interr.*	interrogative
eccl.	ecclesiastical	*lb.*	pound(s) weight
econ.	economics	*ling.*	linguistics
e.g.	for example	*lit.*	literal(ly)
electr.	electricity	*liter.*	literary style